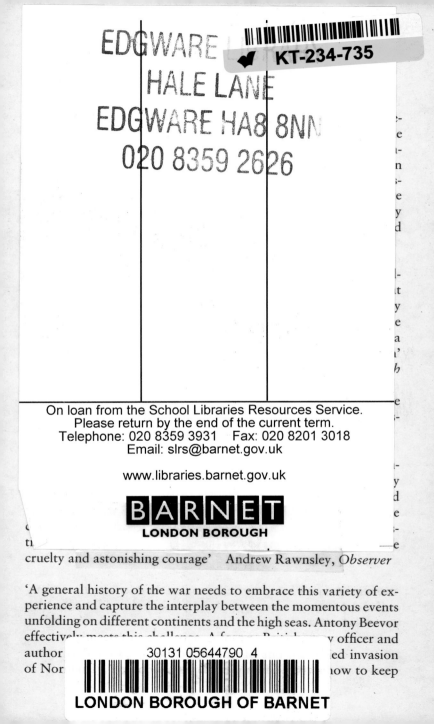

cruelty and astonishing courage'   Andrew Rawnsley, *Observer*

'A general history of the war needs to embrace this variety of experience and capture the interplay between the momentous events unfolding on different continents and the high seas. Antony Beevor effectively meets this challenge. A former British army officer and author ... ed invasion of Nor ... now to keep a good story rolling . . . The brutality and courage of individual soldiers and civilians emerge in Beevor's powerful accounts . . . Beevor's book is a pleasure to read and an example of intelligent, lively historical writing at its best'

Tony Barber, *Financial Times*

'The narrative never flags and the myriad pieces of this intricate kaleidoscope are pieced together with exemplary skill . . . This is a splendid book, erudite, with admirable clarity of thought and expression' Roger Moorhouse, *Independent on Sunday*

'The level of operational command, rather than grand strategy or the horrors of frontline experience, shapes the magisterial narrative of the Second World War. Its military history is presented chronologically, with chapter titles which convey the simultaneity and interconnectedness of events in very different theatres. This is the place to begin if you need to get your knowledge of the war in order. Beevor is not afraid to quote the familiar when it is important or to let his favourite voices have their say, but he also provides plenty of fresh insights for those who kid themselves that they know the story already' Hew Strachan, *Evening Standard*

'Mr Beevor is full of insight about the connection between things – he sets out "to understand how the whole complex jigsaw fits together"' *Economist*

'Utterly absorbing . . . Justly celebrated for recounting the human realities of war . . . Beevor is committed to telling the truth about war, with all its painful contradictions . . . This is as comprehensive and objective an account of the course of the war as we are likely to get, and the most humanly moving to date'

John Gray, *New Statesman*

'You feel yourself being carried along on the narrative flow, channelled this way and that through the pools and rapids by Beevor's expert helmsmanship. As we have come to expect from the author, great events are leavened by telling vignettes and anecdotes'

Patrick Bishop, *Standpoint*

'Brocaded with details of the great campaigns and thoughtful explanations of Hitler's murderous belligerency, *The Second World War* is an absorbing, unsparingly lucid work of military history . . . exceptionally powerful'   Ian Thomson, *The Spectator*

'Readers who may instinctively recoil from another book about the worldwide turmoil of 1939–1945 would be unwise to ignore this one . . . Always at ease with the conduct of battle, Beevor displays his grasp of the German Army's professionalism and tactical skill at all levels of command, as well as Stalin's metamorphosis from paranoid political tyrant to master of history's most enormous battlefield . . . Once action is joined and false assumptions are exposed, Beevor is ruthless in dissecting them, whether featured in the fortunes of friend, foe or – despite their grit and resolve – in our own armed forces'   Michael Tillotson, *The Times*

'A war epic close to perfection'   Keith Lowe, *Mail on Sunday*

'Monumental and magisterial . . . Beevor is excellent at catching the individual in the flood tide of events . . . Few can match his superbly controlled narrative'
John Lewis-Stempel, *Sunday Express*

'This is history writ large . . . unexpected vignettes linger in the memory'   James Owen, *Seven* magazine (*Sunday Telegraph*)

'Remarkably informative and well-written . . . Beevor's enormous strength is that he can sketch out complicated campaigns clearly'
Norman Stone, *Literary Review*

'Everything is pared down to serve the relentless thrust of his storytelling. The result is a magnificent performance – true excitement from one page to the next delivered in faultless prose . . . Beevor offers superbly vivid accounts, often with tiny details that will surprise even those who gorge themselves on shot and ball histories'   Christopher Silvester, *Daily Express*

'The chapters on the Nazi-Soviet war find Beevor at the top of his game, in command of a huge range of sources, with a fine eye for place and detail, deftly manipulating incident and character, and making effective use of soldiers' diaries and letters to create a vast human tapestry of war. The prose is relaxed and contains a spring in every paragraph. He excels too at grand strategy – as a diplomatic historian, he is a match for A. J. P. Taylor. The conferences at Casablanca, Tehran, Yalta and so on, which can have their longueurs, here sparkle with wit and insight, especially into the behaviour of Stalin. There are revelations too'

Ben Shephard, *Observer*

'Beevor is especially good at sweeping summary and lucid explanation'   David Sexton, *Evening Standard*

'This book is a perfect mixture of world history and human experience, unbiased and highly readable'   *The Journal*

'Judged against his own high standards of readability there is no doubt that *The Second World War* succeeds very well indeed . . . This is an immensely readable book, not least for the manner in which it blends together high strategy with the view from below . . . A masterful narrative history'   *History Today*

'An outstanding example of narrative history at its best, at once scholarly, enlightening, entertaining and thought-provoking'

The Tablet

'British military historians are in the vanguard of a genre that has been given new life . . . Beevor has set a new benchmark'

David Cesarini, *Jewish Chronicle*

'Beevor has demonstrated that he understands precisely how to balance meticulous research with captivating prose . . . His book is the definitive history. This is World War II as Tolstoy would have described it – the great and the small'

Gerard DeGroot, *Washington Post*

'A gruelling but gripping account . . . Beevor's trademark – which he has deployed in previous books like *Stalingrad* and *D-Day* – is the use of eyewitness testimony to deliver haunting particulars . . .

another of the book's virtues is its clear-sightedness on military issues' *New York Times*

'Antony Beevor makes the reader believe in the impossible: that he could write a history of magisterial authority about the greatest war of modern times and do justice to the global reach of that war' *Washington Times*

'Narratives of the war have more and more revealed its political ambiguities and moral complexities. Few authors have contributed more to this process of rethinking than the British military historian Antony Beevor . . . anecdotes and quotations make Beevor's account incomparably vivid . . . magnificently readable'
Richard Evans, *New York Review of Books*

'Beevor's forte as a military historian is that he manifests such a wide range of historical sympathy and historical imagination. But none of it comes at the expense of his special expertise in tools of the trade in which he briefly served as a young man. Instead, every page is imbued with the sense that this man really knows what he is talking about – that he knows war is a brutal and degrading experience, albeit with comradeship as a compensating human value and with some potential for military prowess to alleviate the scale of suffering . . . Beevor's human and logistical capacities, in combination, inform the gripping accounts of some of the great set-piece confrontations that determined the outcome of the war . . . All these engagements show Beevor in his mastery'
New Republic

'Beevor has delivered an epic, brilliantly researched work on the defining event of the twentieth century . . . his new research and his pitch-perfect narrative represent a truly astonishing display of art and craft . . . This book, which crowns Beevor's distinguished and bestselling career, is one of the nonfiction events of the decade and for this reader is by far the best nonfiction of 2012 to date'
Sarasota Herald-Tribune

Antony Beevor is the author of *Crete – The Battle and the Resistance*, which won a Runciman Prize; *Paris After the Liberation, 1944–1949* (written with his wife, Artemis Cooper); *Stalingrad*, which won the Samuel Johnson Prize, the Wolfson Prize for History and the Hawthornden Prize for Literature; *Berlin – The Downfall, 1945*, which received the first Longman-*History Today* Award; *The Battle for Spain*; and *D-Day – The Battle for Normandy*, which received the RUSI Duke of Westminster Medal. His books have appeared in thirty languages and sold more than six million copies.

www.antonybeevor.com

By Antony Beevor

Inside the British Army
Crete – The Battle and the Resistance
Paris After the Liberation (with Artemis Cooper)
Stalingrad
Berlin – The Downfall
The Mystery of Olga Chekhova
The Battle for Spain
D-Day – The Battle for Normandy
The Second World War

THE SECOND
WORLD WAR

ANTONY BEEVOR

WEIDENFELD & NICOLSON

A W&N PAPERBACK

First published in Great Britain in 2012
by Weidenfeld & Nicolson
This paperback edition published in 2014
by Weidenfeld & Nicolson,
an imprint of Orion Books Ltd,
Carmelite House, 50 Victoria Embankment,
London EC4 0DZ

An Hachette UK company

9 10 8

A CIP catalogue record for this book
is available from the British Library.

ISBN 978-1-7802-2564-7

Typeset by Input Data Services Ltd, Bridgwater, Somerset

Printed and bound by CPI Group (UK) Ltd, Croydon, CR0 4YY

The Orion Publishing Group's policy is to use papers that
are natural, renewable and recyclable products and
made from wood grown in sustainable forests. The logging
and manufacturing processes are expected to conform to
the environmental regulations of the country of origin.

www.orionbooks.co.uk

To Michael Howard

CONTENTS

ILLUSTRATIONS

MacArthur, Roosevelt and Nimitz at Pearl Harbor, 26 July 1944
  (US National Archives and Record Administration)
US troops land on Bougainville, Solomon Islands, 6 April 1944.
  (Time & Life / Getty)
A Hellcat crash-landed on a carrier. (Getty)
German prisoner in Paris, 26 August 1944. (Bibliothèque
  historique de la Ville de Paris)
Stretcher-bearers in the Warsaw Uprising, September 1944.
  (Warsaw Uprising Museum)
Medical services during the bombing of Berlin. (Bundesarchiv,
  Bild 183–2003–0715–501, photographer unknown)
Churchill in Athens. (Dmitri Kessel)
British troops occupy Athens, December 1944. (Dmitri Kessel)
Red Beach on Iwo Jima, February 1945. (Getty)
Filipina women rescued during the battle for Intramuros in
  Manila. (Time & Life / Getty)

SECTION FOUR
Soviet infantry on a SU-76 self-propelled gun in a burning
  German town. (Planeta, Moscow)
Civilians wait to enter a flak tower bunker in Berlin. (Bildarchiv)
'To Berlin', Soviet traffic controller. (Russian State Documentary
  Film and Photo Archive)
Civilians clearing rubble in Dresden after the bombing, February
  1945. (Bildarchiv)
C-46 transport plane landing at Kunming (William Vandivert for
  Life / Getty)
Japanese kamikaze pilots pose for a memorial picture. (Keystone
  / Getty)
Marble Gallery in the battered Reichschancellery. (Museum
  Berlin-Karlshorst)
German wounded in Berlin, 2 May 1945. (Museum
  Berlin-Karlshorst)
The Japanese surrender on the USS *Missouri*, 2 September 1945.
  (Corbis)
Homeless civilians on Okinawa. (US National Archives and
  Record Administration)

MAPS

Europe, the Mediterranean and the western Soviet Union
August 1942

0	100	200	300	400	500 miles
0	200	400	600	800 km	

Barents Sea

Petsamo

Murmansk

Arkhangelsk

Suomussalmi

FINLAND

Helsinki

Leningrad

Tallinn

Volga

Gorki

Kuibyshev

Riga

Reichskommissariat Ostland

Moscow

U S S R

Königsberg

Vilnius

Smolensk

Tula

Minsk

Briansk

Orel

Voronezh

Warsaw

Kursk

**General-
ouvernement**

Reichskommissariat Ukraine

Kharkov

Stalingrad

Volga

Kraków

Lwów

Kiev

Don

Astrakhan

Dniepropetrovsk

Rostov

Caspian Sea

Odessa

Sea of Azov

Maikop

ROMANIA

Sebastopol

Tbilisi

Bucharest

Black Sea

Batum

Varna

BULGARIA

PERSIA

Sofia

Skopje

Istanbul

Salonika

Ankara

GREECE

TURKEY

İzmir

Athens

SYRIA

CYPRUS

IRAQ

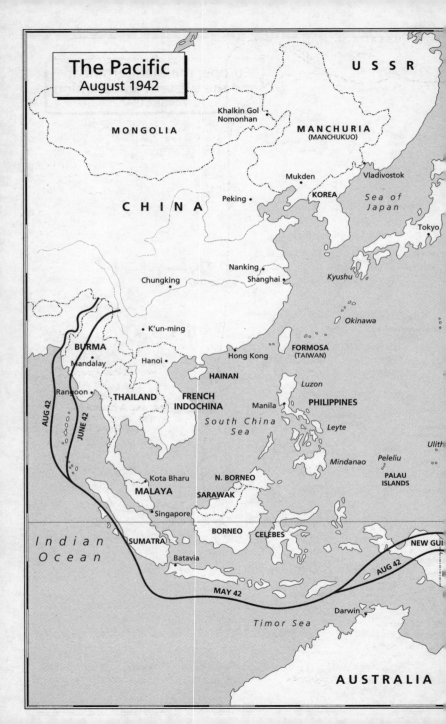

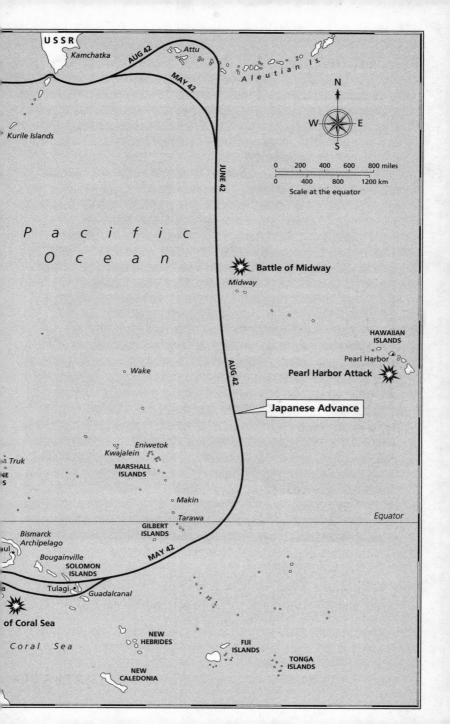

The Korean Yang Kyoungjong who had been forcibly conscripted in turn by the Imperial Japanese Army, the Red Army and the Wehrmacht, is taken prisoner by the Americans in Normandy in June 1944.

INTRODUCTION

In June 1944, a young soldier surrendered to American paratroopers in the Allied invasion of Normandy. At first his captors
thought that he was Japanese, but he was in fact Korean. His
name was Yang Kyoungjong.

In 1938, at the age of eighteen, Yang had been forcibly
conscripted by the Japanese into their Kwantung Army in Manchuria. A year later, he was captured by the Red Army after the
Battle of Khalkhin Gol and sent to a labour camp. The Soviet military authorities, at a moment of crisis in 1942, drafted him along
with thousands of other prisoners into their forces. Then, early
in 1943 he was taken prisoner by the German army at the Battle
of Kharkov in Ukraine. In 1944, now in German uniform, he was
sent to France to serve with an *Ostbataillon* supposedly boosting
the strength of the Atlantic Wall at the base of the Cotentin Peninsula inland from Utah Beach. After time in a prison camp in
Britain, he went to the United States where he said nothing of his
past. He settled there and finally died in Illinois in 1992.

In a war which killed over sixty million people and had
stretched around the globe, this reluctant veteran of the Japanese,
Soviet and German armies had been comparatively fortunate. Yet
Yang remains perhaps the most striking illustration of the helplessness of most ordinary mortals in the face of what appeared to
be overwhelming historical forces.

Europe did not stumble into war on 1 September 1939. Some historians talk of a 'thirty years' war' from 1914 to 1945, with the
First World War as 'the original catastrophe'. Others maintain
that the 'long war', which began with the Bolshevik coup d'état
of 1917, continued as a 'European Civil War' until 1945, or even
lasted until the fall of Communism in 1989.

History, however, is never tidy. Sir Michael Howard argues

persuasively that Hitler's onslaught in the west against France and Britain in 1940 was in many ways an extension of the First World War. Gerhard Weinberg also insists that the war which began with the invasion of Poland in 1939 was the start of Hitler's drive for *Lebensraum* (living space) in the east, his key objective. This is indeed true, yet the revolutions and civil wars between 1917 and 1939 are bound to complicate the pattern. For example, the left has always believed passionately that the Spanish Civil War marked the beginning of the Second World War, while the right claims that it represented the opening round of a Third World War between Communism and 'western civilization'. At the same time, western historians have usually overlooked the Sino-Japanese War from 1937 to 1945, and the way that it merged into the world war. Some Asian historians, on the other hand, argue that the Second World War began in 1931 with the Japanese invasion of Manchuria.

Arguments on the subject can go round and round, but the Second World War was clearly an amalgamation of conflicts. Most consisted of nation against nation, yet the international civil war between left and right permeated and even dominated many of them. It is therefore important to look back at some of the circumstances which led to this, the cruellest and most destructive conflict which the world has ever known.

The terrible effects of the First World War had left France and Britain, the principal European victors, exhausted and determined at any price not to repeat the experience. Americans, after their vital contribution to the defeat of Imperial Germany, wanted to wash their hands of what they saw as a corrupt and vicious Old World. Central Europe, fragmented by new frontiers drawn at Versailles, faced the humiliation and penury of defeat. Their pride shattered, officers of the *Kaiserlich und Königlich* Austro-Hungarian army experienced a reversal of the Cinderella story, with their fairytale uniforms replaced by the threadbare clothes of the unemployed. The bitterness of most German officers and soldiers at their defeat was intensified by the fact that until July 1918 their armies had been unbeaten, and that made the sudden collapse at home appear all the more inexplicable and sinister. In their view, the mutinies and revolts within Germany during the autumn of 1918 which precipitated the abdication of the Kaiser had been caused entirely by Jewish Bolsheviks. Left-wing agitators had indeed played a part and the most prominent German revolutionary leaders in 1918–19 had been Jewish, but the main causes behind the unrest had been war-weariness and hunger. The German right's pernicious conspiracy theory – the stab-in-the-back legend – was part of its inherent compulsion to confuse cause and effect.

The hyper-inflation of 1922–3 undermined both the certainties and the rectitude of the Germanic bourgeoisie. The bitterness of national and personal shame produced an incoherent anger. German nationalists dreamed of the day when the humiliation of the Versailles *Diktat* could be reversed. Life improved in Germany during the second half of the 1920s, mainly due to massive American loans. But the world depression, which began after the Wall Street Crash of 1929, hit Germany even harder once Britain and other countries left the gold standard in September 1931. Fear of another round of hyper-inflation persuaded Chancellor Brüning's government to maintain the Reichsmark's link to the price of gold, making it over-valued. American loans had ceased, and protectionism cut off German export markets. This led to mass unemployment, which dramatically increased the opportunity for demagogues promising radical solutions.

The crisis of capitalism had accelerated the crisis of liberal democracy, which was rendered ineffective in many European countries by the fragmentary effect of voting by proportional representation. Most of the parliamentary systems which had sprung up following the collapse of three continental empires in 1918 were swept away, unable to cope with civil strife. And ethnic minorities, which had existed in comparative peace under the old imperial regimes, were now threatened by doctrines of national purity.

Recent memories of the Russian Revolution and the violent destruction of other civil wars in Hungary, Finland, the Baltic states and indeed Germany itself, greatly increased the process of political polarization. The cycle of fear and hatred risked turning inflammatory rhetoric into a self-fulfilling prophecy, as events in Spain soon showed. Manichaean alternatives are bound to break up a democratic centrism based on compromise. In this new collectivist age, violent solutions appeared supremely heroic

to intellectuals of both left and right, as well as to embittered
ex-soldiers from the First World War. In the face of financial disaster, the authoritarian state suddenly seemed to be the natural
modern order throughout most of Europe, and an answer to the
chaos of factional strife.

In September 1930, the National Socialist Party's share of the
vote jumped from 2.5 per cent to 18.3. The conservative right in
Germany, which had little respect for democracy, effectively destroyed the Weimar Republic, and thus opened the door for Hitler.
Gravely underestimating Hitler's ruthlessness, they thought that
they could use him as a populist puppet to defend their idea of
Germany. But he knew exactly what he wanted, while they did
not. On 30 January 1933, Hitler became chancellor and moved
rapidly to eliminate all potential opposition.

The tragedy for Germany's subsequent victims was that a critical mass of the population, desperate for order and respect, was
eager to follow the most reckless criminal in history. Hitler managed to appeal to their worst instincts: resentment, intolerance,
arrogance and, most dangerous of all, a sense of racial superiority.
Any remaining belief in a *Rechtsstaat*, a nation based on respect
for the rule of law, crumpled in the face of Hitler's insistence that
the judicial system must be the servant of the new order. Public
institutions – the courts, the universities, the general staff and the
press – kowtowed to the new regime. Opponents found themselves
helplessly isolated and insulted as traitors to the new definition of
the Fatherland, not only by the regime itself, but also by all those
who supported it. The Gestapo, unlike Stalin's own secret police,
the NKVD, was surprisingly idle. Most of its arrests were purely
in response to denunciations of people by their fellow Germans.

The officer corps, which had prided itself on an apolitical
tradition, also allowed itself to be wooed by the promise of increased forces and massive rearmament, even though it despised
such a vulgar, ill-dressed suitor. Opportunism went hand in hand
with cowardice in the face of authority. The nineteenth-century
chancellor Otto von Bismarck himself once remarked that moral
courage was a rare virtue in Germany, but it deserted a German
completely the moment he put on a uniform. The Nazis, not surprisingly, wanted to get almost everyone into uniform, not least
the children.

Hitler's greatest talent lay in spotting and exploiting the weakness of his opponents. The left in Germany, bitterly divided between the German Communist Party and the Social Democrats, had presented no real threat. Hitler easily out-manoeuvred the conservatives who thought, with naive arrogance, that they could control him. As soon as he had consolidated his power at home with sweeping decrees and mass imprisonment, he turned his attention to breaking the Treaty of Versailles. Conscription was reintroduced in 1935, the British agreed to an increase in the German navy and the Luftwaffe was openly constituted. Britain and France made no serious protest at the accelerated programme of rearmament.

In March 1936, German troops reoccupied the Rhineland in the first overt breach of the Versailles and Locarno treaties. This slap in the face to the French, who had occupied the region over a decade earlier, ensured widespread adulation of the Führer in Germany, even among many who had not voted for him. Their support and the supine Anglo-French reaction gave Hitler the nerve to continue on his course. Single-handed, he had restored German pride, while rearmament, far more than his vaunted public works programme, halted the rise in unemployment. The brutality of the Nazis and the loss of freedom seemed to most Germans a small price to pay.

Hitler's forceful seduction of the German people began to strip the country of human values, step by step. Nowhere was the effect more evident than in the persecution of the Jews, which progressed in fits and starts. Yet contrary to general belief, this was often driven more from within the Nazi Party than from above. Hitler's apocalyptic rants against Jews did not necessarily mean that he had already decided on a 'Final Solution' of physical annihilation. He was content to allow SA (Sturmabteilung) stormtroopers to attack Jews and their businesses and steal their possessions to satisfy an incoherent mixture of greed, envy and imagined resentment. At that stage Nazi policy aimed at stripping Jews of civil rights and everything they owned, and then through humiliation and harassment to force them to leave Germany. 'The Jews must get out of Germany, yes out of the whole of Europe,' Hitler told his propaganda minister Joseph Goebbels on 30 November 1937. 'That will take some time yet, but will and must happen.'

Hitler's programme to make Germany the dominant power in Europe had been made quite clear in *Mein Kampf*, a combination of autobiography and political manifesto first published in 1925. First he would unite Germany and Austria, then he would bring Germans outside the borders of the Reich back under its control. 'People of the same blood should be in the same Reich', he declared. Only when this had been achieved would the German people have the 'moral right' to 'acquire foreign territory. The plough is then the sword; and the tears of war will produce the daily bread for the generations to come.'

His policy of aggression was stated clearly on the very first page. Yet even though every German couple had to purchase a copy on marriage, few seem to have taken his bellicose predictions seriously. They preferred to believe his more recent and oft-repeated assertions that he did not desire war. And Hitler's daring coups in the face of British and French weakness confirmed them in their hopes that he could achieve all he wanted without a major conflict. They did not see that the over-heated German economy and Hitler's determination to make use of the country's head-start in armaments made the invasion of neighbouring countries a virtual certainty.

Hitler was not interested merely in reoccupying the territory lost by Germany after the Versailles Treaty. He despised such a half-hearted step. He seethed with impatience, convinced that he would not live long enough to achieve his dream of Germanic supremacy. He wanted the whole of central Europe and all of Russia up to the Volga for German *Lebensraum* to secure Germany's self-sufficiency and status as a great power. His dream of subjugated eastern territories had been greatly encouraged by the brief German occupation in 1918 of the Baltic states, part of Belorussia, Ukraine and southern Russia as far as Rostov on the Don. This followed the 1918 Treaty of Brest-Litovsk, Germany's own *Diktat* to the nascent Soviet regime. The 'bread-basket' of Ukraine especially attracted German interest, after the near starvation caused largely by the British blockade during the First World War. Hitler was determined to avoid the demoralization suffered by Germans in 1918, which had led to revolution and collapse. This time others would be made to starve. But one of the main purposes of his *Lebensraum* plan was to seize oil production in the east. Some 85 per cent of the Reich's oil supplies, even in peacetime, had to be imported, and that would be Germany's Achilles heel in war.

Eastern colonies appeared the best means to establish self-sufficiency, yet Hitler's ambition was far greater than that of other nationalists. In line with his social-Darwinist belief that the life of nations was a struggle for racial mastery, he wanted to reduce the Slav population dramatically in numbers through deliberate starvation and to enslave the survivors as a helot class.

His decision to intervene in the Spanish Civil War in the summer of 1936 was not as opportunistic as has often been portrayed. He was convinced that a Bolshevik Spain, combined with a left-wing government in France, presented a strategic threat to Germany from the west, at a time when he faced Stalin's Soviet Union in the east. Once again he was able to exploit the democracies' abhorrence of war. The British feared that the conflict in Spain might provoke another European conflict, while the new Popular Front government in France was afraid to act alone. This allowed Germany's flagrant military support of Generalissimo Francisco Franco's Nationalists to ensure their ultimate victory while Hermann Göring's Luftwaffe experimented with new aircraft and tactics. The Spanish Civil War also brought Hitler and Benito Mussolini closer together, with the Italian Fascist government sending a corps of 'volunteers' to fight alongside the Nationalists. But Mussolini, for all his bombast and ambitions in the Mediterranean, was nervous about Hitler's determination to overturn the status quo. The Italian people were not ready, either militarily or psychologically, for a European war.

Eager to obtain another ally in the coming war with the Soviet Union, Hitler established the Anti-Comintern Pact with Japan in November 1936. Japan had begun its colonial expansion in the Far East during the last decade of the nineteenth century. Profiting from the decay of the Chinese imperial regime, Japan established a presence in Manchuria, seized Formosa (Taiwan) and occupied Korea. Its defeat of Tsarist Russia in the war of 1904–5 made it the major military power in the region. Anti-western feeling grew in Japan with the effects of the Wall Street Crash and the worldwide depression. And an increasingly nationalistic officer class viewed Manchuria and China in a similar way to the Nazis' designs on the Soviet Union: as a landmass and a population to be subjugated to feed the home islands of Japan.

The Sino-Japanese conflict has long been like a missing section in the jigsaw of the Second World War. Having begun well before the outbreak of fighting in Europe, the conflict in China has often been treated as a completely separate affair, even though it saw the largest deployment of Japanese ground forces in the Far East, as well as the involvement of both the Americans and the Soviet Union.

In September 1931, the Japanese military created the Mukden Incident, in which they blew up a railway to justify their seizure of the whole of Manchuria. They hoped to turn the region into a major food-producing region as their own domestic agriculture had declined disastrously. They called it Manchukuo and set up a puppet regime, with the deposed emperor Henry Pu Yi as figurehead. The civilian government in Tokyo, although despised by officers, felt obliged to support the army. And the League of Nations in Geneva refused Chinese calls for sanctions against Japan. Japanese colonists, mainly peasants, poured in to seize land for themselves with the government's encouragement. It wanted 'one million households' established as colonial farmers over the next twenty years. Japan's actions left it isolated diplomatically, but the country exulted in its triumph. This marked the start of a fateful progression, both in foreign expansion and in military influence over the government in Tokyo.

A more hawkish administration took over and the Kwantung Army in Manchuria extended its control almost to the gates of Peking. Chiang Kai-shek's Kuomintang government in Nanking was forced to withdraw its forces. Chiang claimed to be the heir of Sun Yat-sen, who had wanted to introduce a western-style democracy, but he was really a generalissimo of warlords.

The Japanese military began to eye their Soviet neighbour to the north and cast glances south into the Pacific. Their targets were the Far Eastern colonies of Britain, France and the Netherlands, with the oilfields of the Dutch East Indies. The uneasy stand-off in China was then suddenly broken on 7 July 1937 by a Japanese provocation at the Marco Polo Bridge outside the former capital of Peking. The Imperial Army in Tokyo assured Emperor Hirohito that China could be defeated in a few months. Reinforcements were sent across to the mainland and a horrific campaign ensued, fired partly by a Chinese massacre of Japanese civilians. The Imperial Army was unleashed. But the Sino-Japanese War did not end in a rapid triumph as the generals in Tokyo had predicted. The appalling violence of the attacker stimulated a bitter resistance. Hitler failed to recognise the lesson for his own onslaught against the Soviet Union four years later.

Some westerners began to see the Sino-Japanese War as a counterpart to the Spanish Civil War. Robert Capa, Ernest Hemingway, W. H. Auden and Christopher Isherwood, the film-maker Joris Ivens and many journalists all visited and expressed their sympathy and support for the Chinese in general. Left-wingers, a few of whom visited the Chinese Communist headquarters in Yenan, supported Mao Tse-tung, even though Stalin backed Chiang Kai-shek and his party, the Kuomintang. But neither the British nor the American government was prepared to take any practical steps.

Neville Chamberlain's government, like most of the British population, was still prepared to live with a rearmed and revived Germany. Many conservatives saw the Nazis as a bulwark against Bolshevism. Chamberlain, a former lord mayor of Birmingham of old-fashioned rectitude, made the great mistake of expecting other statesmen to share similar values and a horror of war. He had been a highly skilled minister and a very effective chancellor of the Exchequer, but he knew nothing of foreign policy or defence matters. With his wing-collar, Edwardian moustache and rolled umbrella, he proved to be totally out of his depth when confronted by the gleaming ruthlessness of the Nazi regime.

Others, even those of left-wing sympathies, were also reluctant to confront Hitler's regime, for they were still convinced that Germany had been treated most unfairly at the Versailles conference. They also found it hard to object to Hitler's professed desire to bring adjacent German minorities, such as those in Czechoslovakia's Sudetenland, within the Reich. Above all, the British and French were horrified by the idea of another European war. To allow Nazi Germany to annex Austria in March 1938 appeared a small price to pay for world peace, especially when the majority of Austrians had voted in 1918 for *Anschluss*, or union, with Germany and twenty years later welcomed the Nazi takeover. Austrian claims at the end of the war to have been Hitler's first victim were completely bogus.

Hitler then decided that he wanted to invade Czechoslovakia in October. This was timed to be well after German farmers had brought in the harvest because Nazi ministers were afraid of a crisis in the national food supply. But to Hitler's exasperation Chamberlain and his French counterpart Édouard Daladier, during the Munich negotiations in September, offered him the Sudetenland in the hope of preserving peace. This deprived Hitler of his war, but allowed him eventually to take over the whole country without a fight. Chamberlain also made a fundamental error in refusing to consult Stalin. This influenced the Soviet dictator's decision the following August to agree to a pact with Nazi Germany. Chamberlain, rather like Franklin D. Roosevelt later with Stalin, believed with misplaced complacency that he alone could convince Hitler that good relations with the western Allies were in his own interest.

Some historians have argued that, if Britain and France had been prepared to fight in the autumn of 1938, events might have turned out very differently. That is certainly possible from a German point of view. The fact remains that neither the British nor the French people were psychologically prepared for war, mainly because they had been misinformed by politicians, diplomats and the press. Anyone who had tried to warn of Hitler's plans, such as Winston Churchill, was simply regarded as a warmonger.

Only in November were eyes opened to the real nature of Hitler's regime. Following the assassination of a German embassy official in Paris by a young Polish Jew, Nazi stormtroopers unleashed the German pogrom known as *Kristallnacht* from all the broken shop windows. With the warclouds over Czechoslovakia that autumn, a 'violent energy' had brewed up within the Nazi Party. The SA stormtroopers burned synagogues, attacked and murdered Jews, and smashed their shop windows, prompting Göring to complain about the cost in foreign exchange of replacing all the plate glass which came from Belgium. Many ordinary Germans were shocked, but the Nazis' policy of isolating the Jews soon succeeded in persuading the vast majority of their fellow citizens to be indifferent to their fate. And all too many were later tempted by the easy pickings of looted possessions, expropriated apartments and the 'Aryanization' of Jewish businesses. The Nazis were exceptionally clever in the way they drew more and more fellow citizens into their circle of crime.

Hitler's seizure of the rest of Czechoslovakia in March 1939 – a flagrant contravention of the Munich Agreement – finally proved that his claim of bringing ethnic Germans back into the Reich was little more than a pretext to increase his territory. British outrage forced Chamberlain to offer guarantees to Poland as a warning to Hitler against further expansion.

Hitler complained later that he had been thwarted from having a war in 1938 because 'the British and French accepted all my demands at Munich'. In the spring of 1939 he explained his impatience to the Romanian foreign minister: 'I am now fifty,' he said. 'I would rather have the war now than when I am fifty-five or sixty.'

Hitler thus revealed that he intended to achieve his goal of European domination during a single lifetime, which he expected to be short. With his manic vanity, he could not trust anyone else to carry on his mission. He regarded himself as literally irreplaceable and told his generals that the fate of the Reich depended on him alone. The Nazi Party and his whole chaotic form of governance were never designed to produce stability and continuity. And Hitler's rhetoric of the 'Thousand Year Reich' revealed a significant psychological contradiction, coming as it did from a determined bachelor who took a perverse pride in being a genetic dead-end while harbouring an unhealthy fascination with suicide.

On 30 January 1939, the sixth anniversary of his taking power, Hitler made an important speech to the parliamentary deputies of the Reichstag. In it he included his fatal 'prophecy', one to which he and his followers in the Final Solution would compulsively hark back. He claimed that the Jews had laughed at his predictions that he would lead Germany and 'also bring the Jewish problem to its solution'. He then declaimed: 'I want today to be a prophet again: if international Jewry inside and outside Europe should succeed in plunging the nations once more into a world war, the result will be not the Bolshevization of the earth and therefore the victory of

Jewry, but the annihilation of the Jewish race in Europe.' This breathtaking confusion of cause and effect lay at the heart of Hitler's obsessive network of lies and self-deception.

Although Hitler had prepared for war and had wanted war with Czechoslovakia, he still could not understand why the British attitude should now switch so suddenly from appeasement to resistance. He still intended to attack France and Britain later, but that was to be at a time of his own choosing. The Nazi plan, following the bitter lesson of the First World War, was designed to compartmentalize conflicts to avoid fighting on more than one front at the same moment.

Hitler's surprise at the British reaction revealed this autodidact's very imperfect grasp of world history. The pattern of Britain's involvement in almost every European crisis since the eighteenth century should have explained the Chamberlain government's new policy. The change had nothing to do with ideology or idealism. Britain was not setting out to make a stand against fascism or anti-semitism, even if the moral aspect later became useful for national propaganda. Its motives lay in a traditional strategy. Germany's hostile occupation of Czechoslovakia clearly revealed Hitler's determination to dominate Europe. That was a threat to the status quo, which even a weakened and unbellicose Britain could never countenance. Hitler also underestimated Chamberlain's anger at having been so comprehensively deceived at Munich. Duff Cooper, who had resigned as First Lord of the Admiralty over the betrayal of the Czechs, wrote that Chamberlain 'had never met anyone in Birmingham who in the least resembled Adolf Hitler . . . Nobody in Birmingham had ever broken his promise to the mayor.'

Hitler's intentions were now chillingly clear. And the shock of his pact with Stalin in August 1939 confirmed that Poland would be his next victim. 'State boundaries', he had written in *Mein Kampf*, 'are made by man and are changed by man.' In retrospect, the cycle of resentment since the Treaty of Versailles may appear to have made the outbreak of another world war inevitable, but nothing in history is predestined. The aftermath of the First World War had certainly created unstable frontiers and tensions across much of Europe. But there can be no doubt that Adolf Hitler was the chief architect of this new and far more terrible conflagration, which spread across the world to consume millions, including eventually himself. And yet, in an intriguing paradox, the first clash of the Second World War – the one in which Yang Kyoung-jong was first captured – began in the Far East.

I

The Outbreak of War

JUNE–AUGUST 1939

On 1 June 1939, Georgii Zhukov, a short and sturdy cavalry commander, received an urgent summons to Moscow. Stalin's purge of the Red Army, begun in 1937, still continued, so Zhukov, who had been accused once already, presumed that he had been denounced as an 'enemy of the people'. The next stage would see him fed into Lavrenti Beria's 'meatgrinder', as the NKVD's interrogation system was known.

In the paranoia of the 'Great Terror', senior officers had been among the first to be shot as Trotskyite-fascist spies. Around 30,000 were arrested. Many of the most senior had been executed and the majority tortured into making ludicrous confessions. Zhukov, who had been close to a number of the victims, had kept a bag packed ready for prison since the purge began two years before. Having long expected this moment, he wrote a farewell letter to his wife. 'For you I have this request,' it began. 'Do not give in to snivelling, keep steady, and try with dignity to endure the unpleasant separation honestly.'

But when Zhukov reached Moscow by train the next day, he was not arrested or taken to the Lubyanka Prison. He was told to report to the Kremlin to see Stalin's old crony from the 1st Cavalry Army in the civil war, Marshal Kliment Voroshilov, now the people's commissar of defence. During the purge, this 'mediocre, faceless, intellectually dim' soldier had strengthened his position by zealously eliminating talented commanders. Nikita Khrushchev, with earthy directness, later called him 'the biggest bag of shit in the army'.

Zhukov heard that he was to fly out to the Soviet satellite state of Outer Mongolia. There he was to take command of the 57th Special Corps, including both Red Army and Mongolian forces, to inflict a decisive reverse on the Imperial Japanese Army. Stalin was angry that the local commander seemed to have achieved

little. With the threat of war from Hitler in the west, he wanted
to put an end to Japanese provocations from the puppet state of
Manchukuo. Rivalry between Russia and Japan dated from Tsarist times and Russia's humiliating defeat in 1905 had certainly not
been forgotten by the Soviet regime. Under Stalin its forces in the
Far East had been greatly strengthened.

The Japanese military were obsessed by the threat of Bolshevism. And ever since the signature in November 1936 of the
Anti-Comintern Pact between Germany and Japan, tensions on
the Mongolian frontier had increased between Red Army frontier units and the Japanese Kwantung Army. The temperature
had been raised considerably by a succession of border clashes
in 1937, and the major one in 1938, the Changkufeng Incident at
Lake Khasan, 110 kilometres south-west of Vladivostok.

The Japanese were also angry that the Soviet Union was supporting their Chinese enemy not just economically but also with
T-26 tanks, a large staff of military advisers and 'volunteer' air
squadrons. The leaders of the Kwantung Army became increasingly frustrated with Emperor Hirohito's reluctance in August
1938 to allow them to respond to the Soviets in massive force.
Their arrogance was based on the mistaken assumption that
the Soviet Union would not strike back. They demanded carte
blanche to act as they saw fit in any future border incidents. Their
motives were self-interested. A low-level conflict with the Soviet
Union would force Tokyo to increase the Kwantung Army, not
reduce it. They feared that some of their formations might otherwise be diverted south to the war against the Chinese Nationalist
armies of Chiang Kai-shek.

There was some support for the aggressive views of the Kwantung leadership within the imperial general staff in Tokyo. But
the navy and the civilian politicians were deeply concerned. Pressure from Nazi Germany on Japan to regard the Soviet Union
as the main enemy made them most uneasy. They did not want
to become involved in a northern war along the Mongolian
and Siberian borders. This split brought down the government
of Prince Konoe Fumimaro. But the argument in senior government and military circles did not abate as the approach of war
in Europe became self-evident. The army and extreme right-wing
groups publicized and often exaggerated the growing number of

clashes on the northern frontiers. And the Kwantung Army, without informing Tokyo, issued an order allowing the commander on the spot to act as he thought fit to punish the perpetrators. This was passed off under the so-called prerogative of 'field initiative', which allowed armies to move troops for reasons of security within their own theatre without consulting the imperial general staff.

The Nomonhan Incident, which the Soviet Union later referred to as the Battle of Khalkhin Gol after the river, began on 11 May 1939. A Mongolian cavalry regiment crossed the Khalkhin Gol to graze their shaggy little mounts on the wide, undulating steppe. They then advanced some twenty kilometres from the river, which the Japanese regarded as the border, to the large village of Nomonhan, which the Mongolian People's Republic claimed lay on the frontier line. Manchurian forces from the Kwantung Army pushed them back to the Khalkhin Gol, then the Mongolians counter-attacked. Skirmishing back and forth continued for about two weeks. The Red Army brought up reinforcements. On 28 May, the Soviet and Mongolian forces destroyed a Japanese force of 200 men and some antiquated armoured cars. In mid-June, Red Army aviation bombers raided a number of targets while their ground forces pushed forward into Nomonhan.

Escalation rapidly followed. Red Army units in the area were reinforced by troops from the Trans-Baikal military district, as Zhukov had demanded after his arrival on 5 June. The main problem facing the Soviet forces was that they were operating over 650 kilometres from the nearest railhead, which meant a huge logistic effort with trucks over dirt roads that were so bad that the round trip took five days. This formidable difficulty at least lulled the Japanese into underestimating the fighting power of the forces Zhukov was assembling.

They sent forward to Nomonhan the 23rd Division of Lieutenant General Komatsubara Michitaro and part of the 7th Division. The Kwantung Army demanded a greatly increased air presence to support its troops. This caused concern in Tokyo. The imperial general staff sent an order forbidding retaliatory strikes and announced that one of their officers was coming over to report back on the situation. This news prompted the Kwantung commanders to complete the operation before they were restrained.

On the morning of 27 June, they sent their air squadrons in a strike against Soviet bases in Outer Mongolia. The general staff in Tokyo were furious and despatched a series of orders forbidding any further air activity.

On the night of 1 July, the Japanese stormed across the Khalkhin Gol and seized a strategic hill threatening the Soviet flank. In three days of heavy fighting, however, Zhukov eventually forced them back across the river in a counter-attack with his tanks. He then occupied part of the east bank and began his great deception – what the Red Army termed *maskirovka*. While Zhukov was secretly preparing a major offensive, his troops gave the impression of creating a static defensive line. Badly encoded messages were sent demanding more and more materials for bunkers, loudspeakers broadcast the noise of pile-drivers, pamphlets entitled *What the Soviet Soldier Must Know in Defence* were distributed in prodigal quantities so that some fell into enemy hands. Zhukov, meanwhile, was bringing in tank reinforcements under cover of darkness and concealing them. His truck drivers became exhausted from ferrying up sufficient reserves of ammunition for the offensive over the terrible roads from the railhead.

On 23 July, the Japanese attacked again head-on, but they failed to break the Soviet line. Their own supply problems meant that they again had to wait some time before they were ready to launch a third assault. But they were unaware that Zhukov's force had by now increased to 58,000 men, with nearly 500 tanks and 250 aircraft.

At 05.45 hours on Sunday, 20 August, Zhukov launched his surprise attack, first with a three-hour artillery bombardment, then with tanks and aircraft, as well as infantry and cavalry. The heat was terrible. With temperatures over 40 degrees Centigrade, machine guns and cannon are said to have jammed and the dust and smoke from explosions obscured the battlefield.

While the Soviet infantry, which included three rifle divisions and a paratroop brigade, held hard in the centre tying down the bulk of the Japanese forces, Zhukov sent his three armoured brigades and a Mongolian cavalry division from behind in encircling movements. His tanks, which forded a tributary of the Khalkhin Gol at speed, included T-26s, which had been used in the Spanish Civil War to support the Republicans, and much faster prototypes of what later became the T-34, the most effective medium tank of the Second World War. The obsolete Japanese tanks did not stand a chance. Their guns lacked armour-piercing shells.

Japanese infantry, despite having no effective anti-tank guns, fought desperately. Lieutenant Sadakaji was seen to charge a tank wielding his samurai sword until he was cut down. Japanese soldiers fought on from their earth bunkers, inflicting heavy casualties on their attackers, who in some cases brought up flamethrowing tanks to deal with them. Zhukov was undismayed by his own losses. When the commander-in-chief of the Trans-Baikal Front, who had come to observe the battle, suggested that he should halt the offensive for the moment, Zhukov gave his superior short shrift. If he stopped the attack and started it again, he argued, Soviet losses would be ten times greater 'because of our indecisiveness'.

Despite the Japanese determination never to surrender, the Kwantung Army's antiquated tactics and armament produced a humiliating defeat. Komatsubara's forces were surrounded and almost completely destroyed in a protracted massacre inflicting 61,000 casualties. The Red Army lost 7,974 killed and 15,251 wounded. By the morning of 31 August, the battle was over. During its course, the Nazi–Soviet pact had been signed in Moscow, and, as it ended, German troops massed on the Polish frontiers ready to begin the war in Europe. Isolated clashes continued until the middle of September, but Stalin decided in the light of the world situation that it would be prudent to agree to Japanese requests for a ceasefire.

Zhukov, who had come to Moscow fearing arrest, now returned there to receive from Stalin's hands the gold star of Hero of the Soviet Union. His first victory, a bright moment in a terrible period for the Red Army, had far-reaching results. The Japanese had been shaken to the core by this unexpected defeat, while their Chinese enemies, both Nationalist and Communist, were encouraged. In Tokyo, the 'strike north' faction, which wanted war against the Soviet Union, received a major setback. The 'strike south' party, led by the navy, was henceforth in the ascendant. In April 1941, to Berlin's dismay, a Soviet–Japanese non-aggression pact would be signed just a few weeks before Operation Barbarossa, Germany's invasion of the Soviet Union. The battle of

Khalkhin Gol thus represented a major influence on the subsequent Japanese decision to move against the colonies of France, the Netherlands and Britain in south-east Asia, and even take on the United States Navy in the Pacific. The consequent refusal by Tokyo to attack the Soviet Union in the winter of 1941 would thus play a critical role in the geo-political turning point of the war, both in the Far East and in Hitler's life-and-death struggle with the Soviet Union.

Hitler's strategy in the pre-war period had not been consistent. At times he had hoped to make an alliance with Britain in advance of his eventual intention to attack the Soviet Union, but then planned to knock it out of a continental role by a pre-emptive strike against France. To protect his eastern flank in case he did strike west first, Hitler had pushed his foreign minister Joachim von Ribbentrop into making overtures to Poland, offering an alliance. The Poles, well aware of the dangers of provoking Stalin, and rightly suspecting that Hitler wanted their country as a satellite, proved exceedingly cautious. Yet the Polish government had made a serious mistake out of sheer opportunism. When Germany moved into the Sudetenland in 1938, Polish forces occupied the Czechoslovak province of Teschen, which Warsaw had claimed since 1920 to be ethnically Polish, and also pushed forward the frontier in the Carpathian Mountains. This move antagonized the Soviets and dismayed the British and French governments. Polish over-confidence played into Hitler's hands. The Poles' idea of creating a central European bloc against German expansion – a 'Third Europe' as they called it – proved to be a delusion.

On 8 March 1939, shortly before his troops occupied Prague and the rest of Czechoslovakia, Hitler told his generals that he intended to crush Poland. He argued that Germany would then be able to profit from Polish resources and dominate central Europe to the south. He had decided to secure Poland's quiescence by conquest, not by diplomacy, before attacking westwards. He also told them that he intended to destroy the 'Jewish democracy' of the United States.

On 23 March, Hitler seized the district of Memel from Lithuania to add to East Prussia. His programme for war was accelerated because he feared that British and French rearmament would soon catch up. Yet he still did not take seriously Chamberlain's guarantee to Poland, announced in the House of Commons on 31 March. On 3 April, he ordered his generals to prepare plans for Operation White, an invasion of Poland which was to be ready by the end of August.

Chamberlain, reluctant to deal with Stalin out of a visceral anti-Communism, and overestimating the strength of the Poles, was slow to create a defensive bloc against Hitler across central Europe and the Balkans. In fact the British guarantee to Poland implicitly excluded the Soviet Union. Chamberlain's government began to react to this glaring omission only when reports came of German–Soviet trade talks. Stalin, who loathed the Poles, was deeply alarmed by the failure of the British and French governments to stand up to Hitler. Their omission the previous year to include him in the discussions over the fate of Czechoslovakia had only increased his resentment. He also suspected that the British and French wanted to manoeuvre him into a conflict with Germany to avoid fighting themselves. He naturally preferred to see the capitalist states engage in their own war of attrition.

On 18 April, Stalin put the British and French governments to the test by offering an alliance with a pact promising assistance to any central European country threatened by an aggressor. The British were uncertain how to react. The first instinct of both Lord Halifax, the foreign secretary, and Sir Alexander Cadogan, his permanent under-secretary, was to consider the Soviet démarche to be 'mischievous' in intent. Chamberlain feared that to agree to such a move would simply provoke Hitler. In fact it spurred the Führer to seek his own accord with the Soviet dictator. In any case, the Poles and the Romanians were suspicious. They rightly feared that the Soviet Union would demand access for Red Army troops across their territory. The French, on the other hand, having seen Russia as their natural ally against Germany since before the First World War, were much keener on the idea of a Soviet alliance. They felt that they could not move without Britain, and so applied pressure on London to agree to joint military talks with the Soviet regime. Stalin was unimpressed by the hesitant British reaction, but he also had his own secret agenda of pushing the Soviet frontiers further west. He already had his eye on Romanian Bessarabia, Finland, the Baltic states and eastern

Poland, especially the parts of Belorussia and Ukraine ceded to Poland after its victory in 1920. The British, finally accepting the necessity of a pact with the Soviet Union, only began to negotiate towards the end of May. But Stalin suspected, with a good deal of justification, that the British government was playing for time.

He was even less impressed by the Franco-British military delegation which departed on 5 August aboard a slow steamer to Leningrad. General Aimé Doumenc and Admiral Sir Reginald Plunkett-Ernle-Erle-Drax lacked any power of decision. They could only report back to Paris and London. Their mission was in any case doomed to failure for other reasons. Doumenc and Drax faced an insuperable problem with Stalin's insistence on the right of transit for Red Army troops across Polish and Romanian territory. It was a demand which neither country would countenance. Both were viscerally suspicious of Communists in general and of Stalin above all. Time was slipping away as the fruitless talks continued into the second half of August, yet even the French, who were desperate for a deal, could not persuade the government in Warsaw to concede on this point. The Polish commander-in-chief, Marshal Edward Śmigły-Rydz, said that 'with the Germans we risk the loss of our liberty, but with the Russians we lose our soul'.

Hitler, provoked by the British and French attempts to include Romania in a defensive pact against further German aggression, decided that it was time to consider the ideologically unthinkable step of a Nazi–Soviet pact. On 2 August, Ribbentrop first broached the idea of a new relationship with the Soviet chargé d'affaires in Berlin. 'There is no problem from the Baltic to the Black Sea', Ribbentrop said to him, 'that could not be solved between the two of us.'

Ribbentrop did not hide Germany's aggressive intentions towards Poland and hinted at a division of the spoils. Two days later, the German ambassador in Moscow indicated that Germany would consider the Baltic states as part of the Soviet sphere of influence. On 14 August, Ribbentrop suggested that he should visit Moscow for talks. Vyacheslav Molotov, the new Soviet foreign minister, expressed concern at German support for the Japanese, whose forces were still locked in combat with the Red Army either side of the Khalkhin Gol, but he nevertheless indicated a Soviet willingness to continue discussions, especially about the Baltic states.

For Stalin, the benefits became increasingly obvious. In fact he had been considering an accommodation with Hitler ever since the Munich Agreement. Preparations were taken a step further in the spring of 1939. On 3 May, NKVD troops surrounded the commissariat of foreign affairs. 'Purge the ministry of Jews,' Stalin had ordered. 'Clean out the "synagogue".' The veteran Soviet diplomat Maxim Litvinov was replaced as foreign minister by Molotov and a number of other Jews were arrested.

An agreement with Hitler would allow Stalin to seize the Baltic states and Bessarabia, to say nothing of eastern Poland, in the event of a German invasion from the west. And knowing that Hitler's next step would be against France and Britain, he hoped to see German power weakened in what he expected would be a bloody war with the capitalist west. This would give him time to build up the Red Army, weakened and demoralized by his purge.

For Hitler, an agreement with Stalin would enable him to launch his war, first against Poland and then against France and Britain, even without allies of his own. The so-called Pact of Steel with Italy, signed on 22 May, amounted to very little, since Mussolini did not believe his country would be ready for war until 1943. Hitler, however, still gambled on his hunch that Britain and France would shrink from war when he invaded Poland, despite their guarantees.

Nazi Germany's propaganda war against Poland intensified. The Poles were to be blamed for the invasion being prepared against them. And Hitler took every precaution to avoid negotiations because he did not want to be deprived of a war this time by last-minute concessions.

To carry the German people with him, he exploited their deep resentment against Poland because it had received West Prussia and part of Silesia in the hated Versailles settlement. The Free City of Danzig and the Polish Corridor which, created to give Poland access to the Baltic, separated East Prussia from the rest of the Reich were brandished as two of the Versailles Treaty's greatest injustices. Yet on 23 May the Führer had declared that the coming war was not about the Free City of Danzig, but about a war for

Lebensraum in the east. Reports of the oppression against the 800,000 ethnic Germans in Poland were grossly manipulated. Not surprisingly, Hitler's threats to Poland had provoked discriminatory measures against them and some 70,000 fled to the Reich in late August. Polish claims that ethnic Germans were involved in acts of subversion before the conflict began were almost certainly false. In any case, allegations in the Nazi press of persecution of ethnic Germans in Poland were portrayed in dramatic terms.

On 17 August, when the German army was carrying out manoeuvres on the River Elbe, two British captains from the embassy who had been invited as observers found that the younger German officers were 'very self-confident and sure that the German Army could take on everyone'. Their generals and senior foreign ministry officials, however, were nervous that the invasion of Poland would bring about a European war. Hitler remained convinced that the British would not fight. In any case, he reasoned, his forthcoming pact with the Soviet Union would reassure those generals who feared a war on two fronts. But on 19 August, just in case the British and French declared war, Grossadmiral Erich Raeder ordered the pocket battleships *Deutschland* and *Graf Spee*, as well as sixteen U-boats, to put to sea and head for the Atlantic.

On 21 August at 11.30 hours, the German foreign ministry on the Wilhelmstrasse announced that a Soviet–German non-aggression pact was being proposed. When news of Stalin's agreement to talks reached Hitler at the Berghof, his Alpine retreat at Berchtesgaden, he is supposed to have clenched his fists in victory and banged the table, declaring to his entourage: 'I've got them! I've got them!' 'Germans in cafés were thrilled as they thought it would mean peace,' observed a member of the British embassy staff. And the ambassador, Sir Nevile Henderson, reported to London soon afterwards that 'the first impression in Berlin was one of immense relief . . . Once more the faith of the German people in the ability of Herr Hitler to obtain his objective without war was reaffirmed.'

The British were shaken by the news, but for the French, who had counted far more on a pact with their traditional ally Russia, it was a bombshell. Ironically, Franco in Spain and the Japanese leadership were the most appalled. They felt betrayed, having received no warning that the instigator of the Anti-Comintern Pact was now seeking an alliance with Moscow. The government in Tokyo collapsed under the shock, but the news also represented a grave blow to Chiang Kai-shek and the Chinese Nationalists.

On 23 August, Ribbentrop made his historic flight to the Soviet capital. There were few sticking points in the negotiations as the two totalitarian regimes divided central Europe between them in a secret protocol. Stalin demanded all of Latvia, which Ribbentrop conceded after receiving Hitler's prompt approval by telephone. Once both the public non-aggression pact and the secret protocols had been signed, Stalin proposed a toast to Hitler. He said to Ribbentrop that he knew 'how much the German nation loves its Führer'.

That same day, Sir Nevile Henderson had flown down to Berchtesgaden with a letter from Chamberlain in a last-ditch attempt to avoid war. But Hitler simply blamed the British for having encouraged the Poles to adopt an anti-German stance. Henderson, although an arch-appeaser, was finally convinced that 'the corporal of the last war was even more anxious to prove what he could do as a conquering Generalissimo in the next'. That same night, Hitler issued orders for the army to prepare to invade Poland three days later.

At 03.00 hours on 24 August, the British embassy in Berlin received a telegram from London with the codeword Rajah. Diplomats, some of them still in their pyjamas, began to burn secret papers. At midday a warning was issued to all British subjects to leave the country. The ambassador, although short of sleep from his journey to Berchtesgaden, still played bridge that evening with members of his staff.

The following day, Henderson again saw Hitler, who had come up to Berlin. The Führer offered a pact with Britain once he had occupied Poland, but he was exasperated when Henderson said that to reach any agreement he would have to desist in his aggression and evacuate Czechoslovakia as well. Once again, Hitler made his declaration that, if there was to be war, it should come now and not when he was fifty-five or sixty. That evening, to Hitler's genuine surprise and shock, the Anglo-Polish pact was formally signed.

In Berlin, British diplomats assumed the worst. 'We had moved all our personal luggage into the Embassy ballroom,' one of them wrote, 'which was now beginning to look like Victoria station after the arrival of a boat-train.' German embassies and consulates in Britain, France and Poland were told to order German nationals to return to the Reich or move to a neutral country.

On Saturday, 26 August, the German government cancelled the commemoration of the twenty-fifth anniversary of the Battle of Tannenberg. But in fact this ceremony had been used to camouflage a massive concentration of troops in East Prussia. The old battleship *Schleswig-Holstein* had arrived off Danzig the day before, supposedly on a goodwill visit, but without any notification to the Polish government. Its magazines were filled with shells ready to bombard the Polish positions on the Westerplatte Peninsula near the estuary of the Vistula.

In Berlin that weekend, the population revelled in the glorious weather. The beaches along the Grunewald shore of the Wannsee were packed with sunbathers and swimmers. They seemed oblivious to the threat of war, despite the announcement that rationing would be introduced. At the British embassy, the staff began drinking up the stocks of champagne in the cellar. They had noted the greatly increased number of troops on the streets, many of them wearing newly issued yellow jackboots, whose leather had not yet been blackened with polish.

The start of the invasion had been planned for that day, but Hitler, taken off balance by Britain and France's resolution to support Poland, had postponed it the evening before. He was still hoping for signs of British vacillation. Embarrassingly, a unit of Brandenburger commandos, who did not receive the cancellation order in time, had advanced into Poland to seize a key bridge.

Hitler, still hoping to put the blame on Poland for the invasion, pretended to agree to negotiations, with Britain and France and also with Poland. But a black farce ensued. He refused to present any terms for the Polish government to discuss, he would not invite an emissary from Warsaw and he set a time limit of midnight on 30 August. He also rejected an offer from Mussolini's government to mediate. On 28 August, he again ordered the army to be ready to invade on the morning of 1 September.

Ribbentrop, meanwhile, made himself unavailable to both the Polish and British ambassadors. It accorded with his habitual posture of gazing in an aloof manner into the middle distance, ignoring those around him as if they were not worthy to share his thoughts. He finally agreed to see Henderson at midnight on 30 August, just as the uncommunicated peace terms expired. Henderson demanded to know what these terms were. Ribbentrop 'produced a lengthy document', Henderson reported, 'which he read out to me in German, or rather gabbled through to me as fast as he could, in a tone of the utmost annoyance ... When he had finished, I accordingly asked him to let me see it. Herr von Ribbentrop refused categorically, threw the document with a contemptuous gesture on the table and said that it was now out of date since no Polish Emissary had arrived at Berlin by midnight.' The next day, Hitler issued Directive No. 1 for Operation White, the invasion of Poland, which had been prepared over the previous five months.

In Paris, there was a grim resignation, with the memory of more than a million dead in the previous conflict. In Britain, the mass evacuation of children from London had been announced for 1 September, but the majority of the population still believed that the Nazi leader was bluffing. The Poles had no such illusions; yet there were no signs of panic in Warsaw, only determination.

The Nazis' final attempt to manufacture a *casus belli* was truly representative of their methods. This act of black propaganda had been planned and organized by Reinhard Heydrich, deputy to Reichsführer-SS Heinrich Himmler. Heydrich had carefully selected a group of his most trusted SS men. They would fake an attack both on a German customs post and on the radio station near the border town of Gleiwitz, then put out a message in Polish. The SS would shoot some drugged prisoners from Sachsenhausen concentration camp dressed in Polish uniforms, and leave their bodies as evidence. On the afternoon of 31 August, Heydrich telephoned the officer he had put in charge of the project to give the coded phrase to launch the operation: 'Grandmother dead!' It was chillingly symbolic that the first victims of the Second World War in Europe should have been concentration camp prisoners murdered for a lie.

2

'The Wholesale Destruction of Poland'

SEPTEMBER–DECEMBER 1939

In the early hours of 1 September 1939, German forces stood ready to cross the Polish frontier. For all except veterans of the First World War, it would be their first experience of battle. Like most soldiers, they pondered in the isolation of darkness on their chances of survival and whether they would disgrace themselves. As they waited to start their engines, a panzer commander on the border of Silesia described his ghostly surroundings: 'The dark forest, full moon and a light ground mist provide a fantastical scene.'

At 04.48 hours, the first shells fired came from the sea near Danzig. The *Schleswig-Holstein*, a veteran of the 1916 Battle of Jutland, had moved during the pre-dawn darkness into position off the Westerplatte Peninsula. It opened fire on the Polish fortress with its 280mm main armament. A company of Kriegsmarine assault troops, who had been hidden aboard the *Schleswig-Holstein*, later stormed ashore but were bloodily repelled. In Danzig itself, Polish volunteers rushed to defend the central post office on the Heveliusplatz, but they stood little chance against the Nazi stormtroopers, SS and regular forces smuggled into the city. Almost all the Polish survivors were executed after the battle.

Nazi banners appeared on public buildings, and church bells rang while priests, teachers and other prominent Poles in the city were rounded up as well as Jews. Work on the nearby Stutthof concentration camp was to be speeded up to accommodate the influx of new prisoners. Later in the war, Stutthof would supply the bodies for the experiments in the Danzig Anatomical Medical Institute to process human corpses for leather and soap.

Hitler's postponement of the invasion by six days had given the Wehrmacht the opportunity to mobilize and deploy twenty-one more infantry divisions and two extra motorized divisions. Altogether the German army now mustered almost three million men,

Invasion and partition of Poland
September–November 1939

→ German Army
⇨ Red Army

400,000 horses and 200,000 vehicles. One and a half million troops had moved to the Polish frontier, many with blank cartridges on the pretext that they were on manoeuvres. There was no further uncertainty about their mission once they were instructed to load ball ammunition instead.

Poland's forces, in stark contrast, were not fully deployed because the British and French governments had warned Warsaw that a premature call-up might give Hitler the excuse to attack. The Poles had delayed the order for general mobilization until 28 August, but then cancelled it again the next day when the British and French ambassadors urged them to hold back in the last-minute hope of negotiations. It was finally issued once more on 30 August. These changes caused chaos. Only about a third of Poland's front-line troops were in position on 1 September.

Their only hope was to resist until the French could launch their promised offensive in the west. General Maurice Gamelin, the commander-in-chief, had guaranteed on 19 May that the French army would come with 'the bulk of its forces' no later than the fifteenth day after his government ordered mobilization. But time as well as geography was against the Poles. It would not take the Germans long to reach their heartland from East Prussia in the north, Pomerania and Silesia in the west and German-dominated Slovakia in the south. Having no knowledge of the secret protocol to the Molotov–Ribbentrop Pact, the Polish government did not attempt to defend its eastern frontier in strength. The idea of a double invasion coordinated between the Nazi and Soviet governments still seemed to represent a political paradox too far.

At 04.50 hours on 1 September, as German troops waited for the moment of attack they heard the roar of aircraft coming from behind. And as the waves of Stukas, Messerschmitts and Heinkels passed over their heads, they cheered in the knowledge that the Luftwaffe was about to hit Polish airfields in a pre-emptive strike. German soldiers had been told by their officers that the Poles would fight back with underhand tactics, using civilian *francs-tireurs* and sabotage. Polish Jews were said to be 'friendly to the Bolsheviks and German-haters'.

The Wehrmacht's plan was to invade Poland simultaneously from the north, west and east. Its advance was to be 'swift and ruthless', using both armoured columns and the Luftwaffe to catch the Poles before they could establish proper lines of defence. Army Group North's formations attacked from Pomerania and East Prussia. Its priorities were to link up across the Danzig Corridor and advance south-eastwards on Warsaw. Army Group South commanded by Generaloberst Gerd von Rundstedt was to advance rapidly from southern Silesia towards Warsaw on a broader front. The intention was for the two army groups to cut off the bulk of the Polish army west of the Vistula. The Tenth Army, forming the centre of the southern sickle, had the greatest number of motorized formations. To its right, the Fourteenth Army would advance towards Kraków, while three mountain divisions, a panzer division, a motorized division and three Slovak divisions attacked north from the German puppet-state of Slovakia.

In central Berlin on the morning of the invasion, SS guards lined the Wilhelmstrasse and the Pariser Platz as Hitler made his way from the Reichschancellery to the Kroll Opera House. This is where the Reichstag sat after the notorious fire which had burned out the parliament building less than a month after the Nazis came to power in 1933. He claimed that his reasonable demands on Poland, those which he had been careful never to present to Warsaw, had been rejected. This 'sixteen-point peace plan' was published that day in a cynical attempt to demonstrate that the Warsaw government was responsible for the conflict. To great cheers, he announced the return of Danzig to the Reich. Dr Carl Jakob Burckhardt, the League of Nations high commissioner in the Free City, was forced to leave.

In London, once certain clarifications had been obtained on the facts of the invasion, Chamberlain issued the order for general mobilization. In the course of the previous ten days, Britain had been taking initial steps to prepare for war. Chamberlain had not wanted full mobilization because that might provoke a chain reaction in Europe, as had happened in 1914. Anti-aircraft and coastal defences had been the first priority. Attitudes had changed dramatically as soon as news of the German invasion arrived. Nobody now could believe that Hitler was bluffing. The mood in the country and in the House of Commons was much more determined than before the Munich crisis of the previous year. The Cabinet and the foreign office nevertheless took most of the day to draft an ultimatum to Hitler demanding that he withdraw his troops from Poland. Yet even when finished, it did not read like a full ultimatum because it lacked a cut-off point.

After the French council of ministers had received a report from their ambassador Robert Coulondre in Berlin, Daladier gave the order for full mobilization the next day. 'The actual word for "war" is not uttered in the course of the meeting,' one of those present noted. It was referred to only by euphemisms. Instructions for the evacuation of children from both capitals were also issued. There was a widespread expectation that hostilities would commence with massive bombing raids. A blackout was imposed from that evening in both capitals.

In Paris, news of the invasion had come as a shock, since hopes had risen over previous days that a European conflict could be avoided. Georges Bonnet, the foreign minister and most extreme appeaser of all, blamed the Poles for their 'stupid and obstinate attitude'. He still wanted to bring in Mussolini as mediator for another Munich-style agreement. But the 'mobilisation générale' continued, with trains full of reservists pulling out of the Gare de l'Est in Paris towards Metz and Strasbourg.

Not surprisingly, the Polish government in Warsaw began to fear that the Allies had once again lost their nerve. Even politicians in London suspected from the imprecise note and the lack of time limit that Chamberlain might yet try to evade the commitment to Poland. But Britain and France were following the conventional diplomatic route, almost as if to emphasize their difference to the proponent of undeclared Blitzkrieg.

In Berlin, the night of 1 September remained unusually hot. Moonlight illuminated the darkened streets of the Reich capital now under blackout in case of Polish air raids. Another form of blackout was also imposed: Goebbels introduced a law making it a serious crime to listen to a foreign radio station. Ribbentrop refused to see the British and French ambassadors together, so at 21.20 hours Henderson delivered his note demanding an immediate withdrawal of German forces from Poland. Coulondre delivered the French version half an hour later. Hitler, perhaps encouraged by the unrobust phrasing of the notes, remained convinced that both their governments would still back off at the last moment.

The next day, staff at the British embassy bade farewell to their German servants, before moving into the Adlon Hotel just round the corner. A certain diplomatic limbo seemed to ensue in all three capitals. Suspicions of renewed appeasement resurfaced again in London, but the delay was due to a request from the French who said they needed more time to mobilize their reservists and evacuate civilians. Both governments were convinced of the need to act together, but Georges Bonnet and his allies still struggled to put off the fateful moment. Unfortunately, the famously indecisive Daladier allowed Bonnet to continue to foster notions of an international conference with the Fascist government in Rome. Bonnet rang London to urge British support, but both Lord Halifax, the foreign secretary, and Chamberlain insisted that no discussions could take place while German troops remained on Polish territory. Halifax also rang the Italian foreign minister, Count Ciano, to remove any doubt on the matter.

The failure to impose a time limit on the vague ultimatum had brought on a Cabinet crisis in London towards the end of that afternoon. Chamberlain and Halifax explained the need to stay alongside the French, which meant that the final decision lay with them. But the sceptics, backed up by the chiefs of staff who were present, rejected this logic. They feared that, without a firm British initiative, the French would not move. A time limit had to be imposed. Chamberlain was even more shaken by his reception in the House of Commons less than three hours later. His explanation for the delay in declaring war was heard in a hostile silence. Then, when Arthur Greenwood, acting as the Labour Party's leader, rose to reply, even staunch Conservatives were heard to call out: 'Speak for England!' Greenwood made it quite clear that Chamberlain should answer to the House the very next morning.

That night, as a thunderstorm raged outside, Chamberlain and Halifax summoned the French ambassador, Charles Corbin, to Downing Street. They rang Paris to speak to Daladier and Bonnet. The French government still did not wish to be hurried, even though Daladier had received full support for war credits in the Chambre des Députés a few hours earlier. (The very word 'war' was still superstitiously avoided in French official circles. Instead, euphemisms such as the 'obligations de la situation internationale' had been used throughout the debate in the Palais Bourbon.) Since Chamberlain was now convinced that his government would be brought down the next morning if a precise ultimatum was not presented, Daladier finally accepted that France could not delay any longer. He promised that his country's ultimatum would also be delivered the following day. Chamberlain then summoned the British Cabinet. Shortly before midnight a final ultimatum was drafted and agreed. It would be delivered at 09.00 hours the next day by Sir Nevile Henderson in Berlin and would expire two hours later.

On the morning of Sunday, 3 September, Sir Nevile Henderson carried out his instructions to the letter. Hitler, who had been reassured constantly by Ribbentrop that the British would back down, was clearly stunned. After the text had been read out to him, there was a long silence. Finally, he turned angrily to Ribbentrop and demanded: 'What now?' Ribbentrop, an arrogant poseur whose own mother-in-law had described him as 'an extremely dangerous fool', had long assured Hitler that he knew exactly how the British would react. Now he was left without an answer. After Coulondre had delivered France's ultimatum later, Göring said to Hitler's interpreter, 'If we lose this war, may heaven have mercy on us.'

After the thunderstorm of the night before, the morning in London was clear and sunny. There was no reply from Berlin to the ultimatum by the time Big Ben rang eleven times. Henderson in Berlin confirmed in a telephone call that he had also heard nothing. In the Chancery, a third secretary on his staff stopped the clock at eleven and pasted a note to its glass front saying that it would not be restarted until Hitler had been defeated.

At 11.15 hours, Chamberlain made his broadcast to the nation from the Cabinet Room in 10 Downing Street. All over the country, people stood up when the national anthem was played at the end. A number were in tears. The prime minister had spoken both simply and eloquently, but many remarked on how sad and tired he sounded. Just after his brief talk had finished, air-raid sirens began their howling. People trooped down into cellars and shelters expecting waves of black aircraft overhead. But it was a false alarm and the all-clear soon sounded. A widespread and very British reaction was to put on the kettle for a cup of tea. And yet the reaction was far from universally phlegmatic, as a report by the research organization Mass Observation showed. 'Nearly every town of any importance was rumoured to have been bombed to ruins during the early days of the war,' it stated. 'Planes had been *seen* by hundreds of eye-witnesses falling in flames.'

Troops in three-ton army trucks crossing the city were heard to be singing 'It's a Long Way to Tipperary', which despite its jolly tune reminded people of the horrors of the First World War. London was putting on its war apparel. In Hyde Park opposite Knightsbridge barracks, steam shovels began digging truckloads of earth to be poured into the sandbags which would shield government buildings. The King's Guard at Buckingham Palace had changed from bearskins and scarlet tunics. They now wore steel helmets and battledress with knife-edge creases. Silver barrage balloons floated over the city, completely changing the skyline. Red pillar boxes had yellow patches of detector paint sensitive to poison gas. Windows were criss-crossed with strips of sticky paper to reduce the threat of flying glass. The crowds changed too, with many more uniforms and civilians carrying their gas-masks in cardboard cartons. Railway stations were packed with evacuee children, a luggage label tied to their clothes indicating their names and addresses, clutching rag dolls and teddy bears. At night, with the blackout imposed, nothing was recognizable. Only a few drivers ventured forth very cautiously with their car headlights semi-masked. Many simply sat at home listening to the BBC on the wireless behind blackout blinds.

Australia and New Zealand also declared war on Germany in the course of the day. The British-controlled government of India did likewise, but without consulting any Indian political leaders. South Africa declared war three days later after a change of government, and Canada officially entered the war the following week. That night the British liner *Athenia* was sunk by the German submarine *U-30*. Out of the 112 lives lost, 28 were North Americans. Overlooked that day was Chamberlain's less than enthusiastic decision to bring his greatest critic into the government. Churchill's return to the Admiralty, over which he had presided at the start of the last war, prompted the First Sea Lord to signal all ships in the Royal Navy: 'Winston is back!'

There was little celebration in Berlin when the news of Britain's declaration of war was announced. Most Germans were dazed and dejected by the news. They had counted on Hitler's run of brazen luck, believing that it would give him victory over Poland without a European conflict. Then, despite all of Bonnet's attempts to prevaricate, the French ultimatum (whose text still avoided the dreaded word 'war') expired at 17.00 hours. Although the prevailing attitude in France was the resigned shrug of *il faut en finir* – 'it must be got over with' – the anti-militarist left seemed to agree with defeatists on the right that they did not want 'to die for Danzig'. Even more alarmingly, some senior French officers began to convince themselves that the British had pushed them into the war. 'It's to present us with a fait accompli,' wrote General Paul de Villelume, the chief liaison officer with the government, 'because the English fear we might go soft.' Nine months later he was to bring a strongly defeatist influence to bear on the next prime minister, Paul Reynaud.

News of the double declaration of war nevertheless produced scenes of fierce joy in Warsaw. Unaware of French doubts, cheering Poles gathered in front of the two embassies. The national anthems of the three Allies were played on the wireless. A wild optimism convinced many Poles that the promised French offensive would rapidly turn the course of the war in their favour.

There were, however, uglier scenes in other areas. Some Poles turned on ethnic German neighbours to exact revenge for the invasion. In the fear, anger and chaos caused by the sudden war, ethnic Germans were attacked in a number of places. On 3 September at Bydgoszcz (Bromberg), random firing against Poles in the streets led to a massacre in which 223 ethnic Germans died, although the official German history puts the figure at 1,000. Estimates of the total number of ethnic Germans killed throughout Poland vary from 2,000 to 13,000, but the most likely figure is around 6,000. Goebbels later inflated the total to 58,000 in an attempt to justify the German programme of ethnic cleansing against the Poles.

On that first day of European war, the German Fourth Army attacking from Pomerania finally secured the Danzig Corridor at its broadest point. East Prussia was physically rejoined with the rest of the Reich. Leading elements of the Fourth Army also seized a bridgehead across the lower Vistula.

The Third Army attacking from East Prussia pushed southeast towards the River Narew in its move to outflank Modlin and Warsaw. Army Group South, meanwhile, forced back the Łódź and Kraków armies, inflicting heavy casualties. The

Luftwaffe, having eliminated the bulk of the Polish air force, now concentrated on flying in close support to the Wehrmacht ground forces and smashing cities behind the Polish lines to block communications.

German soldiers soon expressed a horror and contempt for the state of the poor Polish villages they passed through. Many seemed empty of Poles, but full of Jews. Soldiers described the villages as 'appallingly dirty and very backward'. The reactions of German soldiers were even more intense when they saw 'eastern Jews' with beards and kaftans. Their physical appearance, their 'evasive eyes' and their 'ingratiatingly friendly' manner as they 'respectfully took off their hats' seemed to correspond much more closely to the caricatures of Nazi propaganda in the viciously anti-semitic newspaper *Der Stürmer* than the integrated Jewish neighbours they had come across back in the Reich. 'Every person', wrote a Gefreiter (lance corporal), 'who was not already a ruthless enemy of the Jews, must become one here.' Ordinary German soldiers, not just members of the SS, took to maltreating Jews with gusto by beatings, cutting off the beards of elders, humiliating and even raping young women (despite the Nuremberg Laws against miscegenation) and setting fire to synagogues.

Above all, soldiers remembered the warnings they had received about the dangers of sabotage and being shot in the back by *francs-tireurs*. If an isolated shot was heard, suspicion often fell on any Jews around, even though partisan attacks were far more likely to have come from Poles. A number of massacres appear to have been carried out after a nervous sentry opened fire, and everyone else joined in, with German troops sometimes shooting at each other. Officers were appalled by the lack of fire discipline, but seemed powerless to stop what they called this *Freischärlerpsychose*, an obsessive fear of being shot at by armed civilians. (They sometimes called it a *Heckenschützenpsychose* – literally an obsession with being shot at from hedgerows.) But few officers did much to stop the blind revenge exacted afterwards. Grenades would be lobbed into cellars, which was where families, rather than partisans, sheltered. Soldiers regarded this as legitimate self-defence, not a war crime.

The German army's long-standing obsession with *francs-tireurs* produced a pattern of summary executions and burned-down villages. Very few units bothered to waste time with legal procedures. In their view, Poles and Jews simply did not deserve such niceties. Some formations murdered civilians more than others. Hitler's bodyguard, the SS *Leibstandarte Adolf Hitler*, appears to have been the worst. Much of the killing, however, was carried out behind the lines by the SS *Einsatzgruppen*, the Security Police and the *Volksdeutscher Selbstschutz* militia (Ethnic German Self-Defence), who longed for revenge.

German sources state that more than 16,000 civilians were executed during the five-week campaign. The true figure may be much higher, as it came close to 65,000 by the end of the year. Some 10,000 Poles and Jews were massacred in gravel pits near Mniszek by ethnic German militia, and another 8,000 in a wood near Karlshof. Houses and occasionally entire villages would also be torched as collective reprisals. Altogether over 500 villages and towns were burned to the ground. In some places, the line of German advance was marked at night by the red glow on the horizon from blazing villages and farms.

Soon Jews as well as Poles hid themselves when German troops arrived. This made the soldiers even more nervous, since they became convinced not only that they were being watched from cellar windows and skylights, but that unseen weapons were pointed at them. At times it almost seems as if many soldiers longed to destroy what they saw as these insalubrious and hostile villages so that the infection they represented in their minds could not spread to neighbouring Germany. This did not, however, stop them from looting at every opportunity – money, clothes, jewellery, food and bedding. In yet another confusion of cause and effect, the hatred they encountered during their invasion somehow seemed to justify the invasion itself.

The Polish army, although fighting often with desperate bravery, was severely handicapped not just by its obsolete weaponry, but above all by its lack of radios. The withdrawal of one formation could not be communicated to those on its flanks, with disastrous results. Marshal Śmigły-Rydz, the commander-in-chief, was already convinced that the war was lost. Even if the French were to launch their promised offensive, it would come too late. On

4 September, an increasingly confident Hitler told Goebbels that he did not fear an attack from the west. He foresaw a *Kartof-felkrieg* there – a stationary 'potato war'.

The ancient university city of Kraków was taken on 6 September by the Fourteenth Army, and the advance of Rundstedt's Army Group South continued apace as the Polish defenders stumbled in retreat. But three days later the army high command – the OKH or Oberkommando des Heeres – became concerned that the Polish armies might be evading the planned encirclement west of the Vistula. Two corps from Army Group North were therefore ordered to push further east, if necessary to the line of the River Bug and beyond to trap them on a second line.

Near Danzig, the heroic Polish defenders of the Westerplatte positions, having run out of ammunition, were finally battered into submission on 7 September by the heavy guns of the *Schleswig-Holstein*. The old battleship then turned north to help in the attack on the port of Gdynia, which held out until 14 September.

In central Poland resistance had hardened as the Germans came closer to the capital. A column from the 4th Panzer Division reached the edges of the city on 10 September, but was forced to make a rapid retreat. The Poles' determination to fight for Warsaw was shown by the concentration of their artillery on the east bank of the Vistula ready to fire into their own city. On 11 September, the Soviet Union withdrew its ambassador and diplomatic personnel from Warsaw, but the Poles still had little idea of the stab-in-the-back being prepared from the east.

Elsewhere, German encirclements of Polish troops using their mechanized forces had already started to produce large numbers of prisoners. On 16 September, the Germans began a massive encirclement battle eighty kilometres west of Warsaw, having trapped two Polish armies in the fork of the Rivers Bzura and Vistula. Polish resistance was finally broken by massive Luftwaffe strikes on troop concentrations. Altogether around 120,000 prisoners were taken. The brave Polish air force, with just 159 old-fashioned fighters – the P-11 which looked rather like a Lysander – did not stand a chance against the sleek Messerschmitts.

*

Any remaining Polish illusions of being saved by an Allied offensive in the west were soon dashed. General Gamelin, with the support of the French prime minister Daladier, refused to consider any move until the British Expeditionary Force had deployed and all his reservists were mobilized. He also argued that France needed to purchase military equipment from the United States. In any case French army doctrine was fundamentally defensive. Gamelin, despite his promise to Poland, shied away from any idea of a major offensive, believing that the Rhine Valley and the Germans' Westwall line of defence could not be breached. The British were scarcely more aggressive. They called the Westwall 'the Siegfried Line': the one on which, according to their cheerful Phoney War song, they wanted to hang out their washing. The British felt that time was on their side, with the curious logic that a blockade of Germany was their best strategy, despite the obvious flaw that the Soviet Union could help Hitler procure whatever his war industries needed.

Many British people felt ashamed at the lack of aggression shown to help the Poles. The RAF began flying over Germany, dropping propaganda leaflets, which led to jokes about 'Mein Pamph' and the 'confetti war'. A bombing raid on the German naval base at Wilhelmshaven on 4 September had proved humiliatingly ineffective. Advance parties of the British Expeditionary Force landed in France the same day, and over the next five weeks a total of 158,000 men crossed the Channel. But there were no clashes with German forces until December.

The French did little more than advance a few kilometres on to German territory near Saarbrücken. At first the Germans feared a major attack. Hitler was particularly concerned, with the bulk of his army in Poland, but the very limited nature of the offensive showed that this was no more than a token gesture. The armed forces high command – the OKW or Oberkommando der Wehrmacht – soon relaxed again. No troops had to be transferred. The French and British had failed in their obligations shamefully, especially since the Poles in July had already handed over to Britain and France their reconstructions of the German Enigma enciphering machine.

On 17 September, Poland's martyrdom was sealed when Soviet forces crossed its long eastern frontier in line with the secret protocol signed in Moscow less than a month before. The Germans were surprised that they had not moved before, but Stalin had calculated that if he attacked too soon the western Allies might feel obliged to declare war on the Soviet Union as well. The Soviets claimed, with perhaps predictable cynicism, that Polish provocations had forced them to intervene to protect ethnic Belorussians and Ukrainians. In addition, the Kremlin argued that the Soviet Union was no longer bound by its non-aggression treaty with Poland because the Warsaw government had ceased to exist. The Polish government had indeed left Warsaw that very morning, but purely to escape before it was trapped by Soviet forces. Its ministers had to race for the Romanian frontier before their route was cut by Red Army units advancing from Kamenets-Podolsk in south-western Ukraine.

The traffic jams of military vehicles and civilian motorcars backed up from the border posts were immense, but eventually the defeated Poles were allowed through that night. Almost all had taken a handful of earth or a stone from the Polish side before they left. Many were in tears. Several committed suicide. The ordinary Romanian people were kind to the exiles, but the government was under pressure from Germany to hand the Poles back. Bribery saved the majority from arrest and internment, unless the officer in charge was a supporter of the fascist Iron Guard. Some Poles escaped in small groups. Larger parties organized by the Polish authorities in Bucharest shipped out of Constanza and other Black Sea ports to make their way to France. Others escaped through Hungary, Yugoslavia and Greece, while a smaller number, who faced greater problems, made their way north into the Baltic states and then across to Sweden.

On Hitler's instruction, the OKW rapidly issued orders to German formations beyond the Bug to prepare to pull back. Close cooperation between Berlin and Moscow ensured that German withdrawals from the areas allocated to the Soviet Union under the secret protocol were coordinated with the advancing Red Army formations.

The first contact between the unlikely allies took place north of Brest-Litovsk (Brześć). And on 22 September the great fortress of Brest-Litovsk was handed over to the Red Army during a ceremonial parade. Unfortunately for the Soviet officers involved, this contact with German officers later made them prime targets for arrest by Beria's NKVD.

Polish resistance continued as surrounded formations still tried to break out, and isolated soldiers formed irregular groups to fight on in the less accessible areas of forest, marsh and mountain. Roads to the east were choked with refugees, using farm-carts, dilapidated vehicles and even bicycles in their attempt to escape the fighting. 'The enemy always came from the air,' wrote a young Polish soldier, 'and even when they flew very low, they were still beyond the range of our old Mausers. The spectacle of the war rapidly became monotonous; day after day we saw the same scenes: civilians running to save themselves from air raids, convoys dispersing, trucks or carts on fire. The smell along the road was unchanging too. It was the smell of dead horses that no one had bothered to bury and that stank to high heaven. We moved only at night and we learned to sleep while marching. Smoking was forbidden out of fear that the glow of a cigarette could bring down on us the all-powerful Luftwaffe.'

Warsaw meanwhile remained the chief bastion of Polish defiance. Hitler was impatient for the subjugation of the Polish capital, so the Luftwaffe began intensive bombing raids. It faced little opposition in the air and the city lacked effective anti-aircraft defences. On 20 September, the Luftwaffe attacked Warsaw and Modlin with 620 aircraft. And the next day, Göring ordered both the First Luftflotte and the Fourth Luftflotte to mount massive attacks. The bombing continued at maximum strength – the Luftwaffe even brought in Junkers 52 transport planes to drop incendiaries – until Warsaw surrendered on 1 October. The stench from corpses buried by rubble and the bloated bodies of horses in the streets became overwhelming. Some 25,000 civilians and 6,000 soldiers had been killed in these raids.

On 28 September, while Warsaw was under attack, Ribbentrop flew to Moscow again and signed an additional 'boundary and friendship treaty' with Stalin making various alterations to the demarcation line. This allowed the Soviet Union almost all of Lithuania in return for a slight increase in German-occupied Polish territory. Ethnic Germans in Soviet-occupied territories would be transferred to Nazi areas. Stalin's regime also handed over many German Communists and other political opponents. Both governments then issued a call for an end to the European war now that the 'Polish question' had been resolved.

There can be little doubt about who gained most from the two agreements which formed the Nazi–Soviet pact. Germany, threatened with a naval blockade by Britain, was now able to obtain all it needed to prosecute the war. Apart from everything supplied by the Soviet Union, including grain, oil and manganese, Stalin's government also acted as a conduit for other materials, especially rubber, which Germany could not purchase abroad.

At the same time as the talks in Moscow, the Soviets began to apply pressure to the Baltic states. On 28 September, a treaty of 'mutual assistance' was imposed on Estonia. Then, over the next two weeks Latvia and Lithuania were forced to sign similar treaties. Despite Stalin's personal assurance that their sovereignty would be respected, all three states were incorporated into the Soviet Union early the following summer, and the NKVD proceeded to deport some 25,000 'undesirables'.

While the Nazis accepted Stalin's takeover of the Baltic states and even his seizure of Bessarabia from Romania, they found his ambitions to control the Black Sea coast and the mouth of the Danube close to the Ploesti oilfields not merely provocative but threatening.

Isolated Polish resistance continued well into October, but the scale of the defeat was savage. The Polish armed forces fighting the Germans are estimated to have lost 70,000 killed, 133,000 wounded and 700,000 captured. Total German casualties ran to 44,400, of whom 11,000 were fatal. The small Polish air force had been annihilated, but the Luftwaffe's losses of 560 aircraft during the campaign, mainly from crashes and ground-fire, were surprisingly heavy. The available casualty estimates from the Soviet invasion are chilling. The Red Army is said to have lost 996 men killed and 2,002 wounded, while the Poles are said to have suffered 50,000 fatal casualties, without any figure for wounded. Such a disparity can perhaps only be explained by executions, and may well include the massacres perpetrated the following spring, including that of the Katyń Forest.

Hitler did not declare the death of the Polish state immediately.

He hoped that October to encourage the British and the French to come to an agreement. The lack of an Allied offensive in the west to help the Poles made him think that the British and especially the French did not really want to continue the war. On 5 October, after taking the salute at a victory parade in Warsaw with Generalmajor Erwin Rommel beside him, he spoke to foreign journalists. 'Gentlemen,' he said. 'You have seen the ruins of Warsaw. Let that be a warning to those statesmen in London and Paris who still think of continuing the war.' The next day, he announced a 'peace offer' in the Reichstag. But when this was rejected by both Allied governments, and once it became clear that the Soviet Union was determined to eradicate any Polish identity in its zone, Hitler finally resolved to destroy Poland completely.

Poland under German occupation was divided between its Generalgouvernement in the centre and south-west and those areas which were to be incorporated into the Reich (Danzig-West Prussia and East Prussia in the north, the Wartheland in the west and Upper Silesia in the south). A massive programme of ethnic cleansing began to empty the latter 'Germanized' areas. They were to be colonized by *Volksdeutsche* from the Baltic states, Romania and elsewhere in the Balkans. Polish cities were renamed. Łódź was called Litzmannstadt after a German general who fought near there in the First World War. Poznań returned to its Prussian name of Posen, and became the capital of the Warthegau.

The Catholic Church in Poland, a symbol of the country's patriotism, was relentlessly persecuted through the arrest and deportation of priests. In an attempt to eliminate Polish culture and destroy a future leadership, schools and universities were closed. Only the most basic education would be permitted, sufficient only for a helot class. The professors and staff at Kraków University were deported in November to Sachsenhausen concentration camp. Polish political prisoners were sent to a former cavalry barracks at Oświęcim, which was renamed Auschwitz.

Nazi Party officials began selecting large numbers of Poles for labour in Germany as well as young women to work as domestic servants. Hitler told the army commander-in-chief General Walther von Brauchitsch they wanted 'cheap slaves' and to clear the 'rabble' out of the newly acquired German territory. Blond children who corresponded to Aryan ideals were seized and sent back to Germany for adoption. Albert Förster, the Gauleiter of Danzig-West Prussia, however, outraged Nazi purists when he permitted a massive reclassification of Poles as ethnic Germans. For the Poles concerned, however humiliating and distasteful, this redesignation of their origins offered the only way to avoid deportation and the loss of their homes. The men, however, soon found themselves conscripted into the Wehrmacht.

Hitler issued an amnesty order on 4 October to troops who had killed prisoners and civilians. They were presumed to have acted 'from bitterness over atrocities committed by Poles'. Many officers were uneasy at what they saw as a loosening of military discipline. 'We have seen and witnessed wretched scenes in which German soldiers burn and plunder, murder, and loot without thinking about it,' an artillery battalion commander wrote. 'Grown men, who without being conscious of what they were doing – and without any scruples – contravene laws and instructions and the honour of the German soldier.'

Generalleutnant Johannes Blaskowitz, the commander-in-chief of the Eighth Army, protested vehemently at the killing of civilians by the SS and their auxiliaries – the Sicherheitspolizei (Security Police) and the *Volksdeutscher Selbstschutz*. Hitler, on hearing of his memorandum, said in a fury that 'you can't run a war on Salvation Army lines'. Any other objections from the army were also dealt with in scathing terms. Yet many German officers still believed that Poland did not deserve to exist. Hardly any had objected to the invasion on moral grounds. As former members of the Freikorps in the violent chaos which followed the First World War, some of the older officers had been involved in bitter fighting against the Poles in frontier battles, especially in Silesia.

In a number of ways the Polish campaign and its aftermath became a trial run for Hitler's subsequent *Rassenkrieg*, or race war against the Soviet Union. Some 45,000 Polish and Jewish civilians were shot, mainly by ordinary German soldiers. The SS *Einsatzgruppen* machine-gunned the inmates of mental asylums. An *Einsatzgruppe* had been allocated to the rear area of each army, under the codename Operation Tannenberg, to capture and even kill aristocrats, judges, prominent journalists, professors and any other person who might provide some form of leadership for a Polish resistance movement in the future. On 19 September,

SS Obergruppenführer Heydrich told General der Artillerie Franz Halder, the army chief of staff, quite openly that there would be 'a clear-out: Jews, intelligentsia, priesthood, aristocracy'. At first the terror was chaotic, especially that carried out by the ethnic German militia, but towards the end of the year it became more coherent and directed.

Although Hitler never wavered in his hatred of the Jews, the industrial genocide which began in 1942 had not always been part of his plan. He exulted in his obsessive anti-semitism and established the Nazi mindset that Europe had to be 'cleansed' of all Jewish influence. But his plans before the war had not included a murderous annihilation. They had concentrated on creating an unbearable oppression which would force Jews to emigrate.

Nazi policy on the 'Jewish question' had fluctuated. In fact the very term 'policy' is misleading when one considers the institutional disorder of the Third Reich. Hitler's dismissive attitude towards administration permitted an extraordinary proliferation of competing departments and ministries. Their rivalries, especially those between the Gauleiters and other Nazi Party officials, the SS, and the army, produced an astonishingly wasteful lack of cohesion which was totally at variance with the regime's image of ruthless efficiency. Seizing on a random comment from the Führer, or trying to second-guess his wishes, competitors for his favour would initiate programmes without consulting other interested organizations.

On 21 September 1939, Heydrich issued an order laying down 'preliminary measures' for dealing with Poland's Jewish population, which, at about three and a half million before the invasion, had represented 10 per cent of the population, the highest proportion in Europe. The Soviet zone held about one and a half million, a figure which was increased by the 350,000 Jews who had fled eastwards in front of the German armies. Heydrich ordered that those who still remained on German territory were to be concentrated in larger cities with good rail links. A massive movement of population was envisaged. On 30 October, Himmler gave instructions that all Jews in the Warthegau were to be forcibly transported to the Generalgouvernement. Their houses would then be given to *Volksdeutsche* settlers, who had never lived within the borders of the Reich and whose spoken German was often said to be incomprehensible.

Hans Frank, the overbearing and corrupt Nazi bully who ran the Generalgouvernement for his own profit from the royal castle in Kraków, was angry when told to prepare for the reception of several hundred thousand Jews as well as displaced Poles. No plan had been made to house or feed the victims of this forced migration, and nobody had thought what to do with them. In theory, those Jews fit enough would be used for forced labour. The rest would be confined in temporary ghettos in the larger cities until they could be resettled. Jews trapped in the ghettos, deprived of money and with little food, were in many cases left to die of starvation and disease. Although not yet a programme of outright annihilation, it represented an important step in that direction. And as the difficulties of resettling Jews in an as yet undesignated 'colony' proved greater than imagined, the idea soon began to grow that killing them might be easier than moving them around.

While the looting, killing and chaotic conditions in Nazi-occupied areas made life appalling, it was scarcely better for Poles on the Soviet side of the new internal frontier.

Stalin's hatred of Poland went back to the Soviet–Polish War and the defeat of the Red Army at the Battle of Warsaw in 1920, which the Poles referred to as the Miracle on the Vistula. Stalin had been strongly criticized for his part in the failure of the 1st Cavalry Army to support the forces of M. N. Tukhachevsky, whom he had executed on false charges in 1937 at the start of his purge of the Red Army. During the 1930s, the NKVD targeted as spies the large number of Poles in the Soviet Union.

Nikolai Yezhov, the head of the NKVD during the Great Terror, became obsessed with imagined Polish conspiracies. Poles in the NKVD were purged, and in Order 00485 of 11 August 1937 Poles were implicitly defined as enemies of the state. When Yezhov reported after the first twenty days of arrests, torture and executions, Stalin praised his work: 'Very good! Keep on digging up and cleaning out this Polish filth. Eliminate it in the interests of the Soviet Union.' In the anti-Polish drive during the Great Terror, 143,810 people were arrested for espionage and 111,091 executed. Poles were about forty times more likely to be executed during this period than other Soviet citizens.

Under the Treaty of Riga in 1921, which had ended the Soviet–Polish War, victorious Poland had incorporated western parts of Belorussia and Ukraine. It then settled them with many of Marshal Józef Piłsudski's legionaries. But following the Red Army's invasion in the autumn of 1939, more than five million Poles found themselves under Soviet rule, which treated Polish patriotism as counter-revolutionary by definition. The NKVD arrested 109,400 people, most of whom were sent to the labour camps of the Gulag, while 8,513 of them were executed. The Soviet authorities targeted all those who might play a role in keeping Polish nationalism alive, including landowners, lawyers, teachers, priests, journalists and officers. It was a deliberate policy of class warfare and national decapitation. Eastern Poland, occupied by the Red Army, was to be split and incorporated into the Soviet Union, the northern region becoming part of Belorussia and the southern joined to Ukraine.

Mass deportations to Siberia or central Asia began on 10 February 1940. The NKVD rifle regiments rounded up 139,794 Polish civilians in temperatures below 30 degrees Centigrade. The first wave of families selected were roused by shouts and the banging of rifle butts on their door. Red Army soldiers or Ukrainian militia, under the command of an NKVD officer, would barge in and point their guns, yelling threats. Beds were overturned and cupboards searched, allegedly for hidden weapons. 'You are Polish elite,' the NKVD man told the Adamczyk family. 'You are Polish lords and masters. You are enemies of the people.' A more frequent formula of the NKVD was 'Once a Pole, always a kulak' – the Soviet term of abuse for a rich and reactionary peasant.

Families were given little time to prepare for the terrible journey, abandoning their homes and farms for good. Most felt paralysed by the prospect. Fathers and sons were forced to kneel facing the wall, while the womenfolk were allowed to gather possessions, such as a sewing machine to earn money wherever they were taken, cooking utensils, bedding, family photographs, a child's rag doll and school books. Some Soviet soldiers were clearly embarrassed by their task and murmured apologies. A few families were allowed to milk their cow before they left or to kill some chickens or a piglet as food for the three-week journey in cattle wagons. Everything else had to be left behind. The Polish diaspora had begun.

3

From Phoney War to Blitzkrieg

Once it became evident that massed enemy bombers were not going to flatten London and Paris immediately, life returned almost to normal. The war had 'a strange, somnambulistic quality', wrote a commentator on daily life in London. Apart from the risk in the blackout of walking into a lamp-post, the greatest danger was being run down by a motorcar. In London, over 2,000 pedestrians were killed in the last four months of 1939. The absolute darkness encouraged some young couples to have sexual intercourse standing up in shop doorways, a sport which soon became a subject for music-hall jokes. Cinemas and theatres gradually reopened. In London, pubs were packed. In Paris, cafés and restaurants were full as Maurice Chevalier sang the hit of the moment, 'Paris sera toujours Paris'. The fate of Poland had almost been forgotten.

While the war on land and in the air languished, the war at sea intensified. For the British, it had begun with a tragedy. On 10 September 1939, the submarine HMS *Triton* sank another submarine, HMS *Oxley*, in the belief that it was a U-boat. The first German U-boat was sunk on 14 September by the escort destroyers to the carrier HMS *Ark Royal*. But on 17 September the *U-29* managed to sink the obsolete carrier HMS *Courageous*. Nearly a month later, the Royal Navy suffered a far greater blow when *U-47* penetrated the defences of Scapa Flow in the Orkneys and sank the battleship HMS *Royal Oak*. Britain's confidence in the strength of its navy was deeply shaken.

The two pocket battleships loose in the Atlantic, the *Deutschland* and the *Admiral Graf Spee*, had meanwhile been given permission to start the war in earnest. But the Kriegsmarine made a grave mistake on 3 October, when the *Deutschland* seized an American freighter as a prize of war. Following the brutal invasion of Poland, this helped to swing public opinion in the United

States against the Neutrality Act, which forbade the sale of arms to a belligerent, and in favour of the Allies who needed to purchase them.

On 6 October, Hitler announced in the Reichstag his offer of peace to Britain and France, assuming that they would accede to his occupation of both Poland and Czechoslovakia. The very next day, without even waiting to hear their reply, Hitler began discussions with commanders-in-chief and General der Artillerie Halder on an offensive in the west. The army high command, the OKH, was instructed to draw up a plan, Case Yellow, for an attack in five weeks' time. But the arguments of his senior commanders about the difficulties of redeployment, provisioning and the lateness of the season for such an operation exasperated him. He must also have been put out when, on 10 October, a wild rumour swept Berlin that the British were agreeing to peace terms. The spontaneous celebrations in street market and *Gasthaus* alike turned to dejection when Hitler's eagerly awaited speech on the radio showed that this was a wishful fantasy. Goebbels was furious, above all at the lack of enthusiasm for the war which had been revealed.

On 5 November, Hitler agreed to see Generaloberst von Brauchitsch, the army commander-in-chief. Brauchitsch, who had been urged by other senior officers to stand firm against an early invasion, warned Hitler not to underestimate the French. Because of ammunition and equipment shortages the army needed more time. Hitler interrupted him to express his contempt for the French. Brauchitsch then tried to argue that the German army in the Polish campaign had shown itself to be ill disciplined and badly trained. Hitler exploded, demanding examples. A very rattled Brauchitsch was unable to cite any off the top of his head. Hitler sent his commander-in-chief away shaking and thoroughly humiliated, with the threatening remark that he knew 'the spirit of Zossen [OKH headquarters] and was determined to crush it'.

Halder, the army chief of staff, who had toyed with the idea of a military coup to remove Hitler, now feared that this remark of the Führer's indicated that the Gestapo knew of his plans. He destroyed anything which might be incriminating. Halder, who looked more like a nineteenth-century German professor

The Winter War
November 1939–March 1940

North Cape

Arctic Ocean

Rybachy

Tromsø
NORWAY
Petsamo
Murmansk

14

KOLA PENINSULA

LAPPLAND

Kandalaksha

SWEDEN
Kemijärvi

White Sea

Oulu
Suomussalmi

Kuhmo

KARELIA

Gulf of Bothnia

FINLAND

8

Lake Ladoga

Vyborg

Turku
Helsinki

10

Hanko
Leningrad

Gulf of Finland

7

Tallinn

Estonia

- - - - Mannerheim Line
☐ Soviet Army
⟵ Soviet attack

0   50   100 miles
0   50   100   150 km

with his hair *en brosse* and his pince-nez, would bear the brunt of Hitler's impatience with the conservatism of the general staff.

Stalin, during this period, had wasted little time in seizing the gains offered by the Molotov–Ribbentrop agreements. Immediately after the Soviet occupation of eastern Poland had been completed, the Kremlin had imposed its so-called 'treaties of mutual assistance' on the Baltic states. And on 5 October, the Finnish government was asked to send envoys to Moscow. A week later Stalin presented them with a list of demands in another draft treaty. These included the leasing to the Soviet Union of the Hanko Peninsula and the transfer to the Soviet Union of several islands in the Gulf of Finland, as well as part of the Rybachy Peninsula near Murmansk and the port of Petsamo. Another demand insisted that the border on the Karelian Isthmus above Leningrad should be moved thirty-five kilometres to the north. In exchange the Finns were offered a largely uninhabited part of Soviet northern Karelia.

The negotiations in Moscow continued until 13 November without a final agreement. Stalin, convinced that the Finns lacked international support and the will to fight, decided to invade. His unconvincing pretext was a puppet 'government-in-exile' composed of a handful of Finnish Communists calling for fraternal aid from the Soviet Union. Soviet forces provoked a frontier incident near Mainila in Karelia. The Finns turned to Germany for help, but the Nazi government refused any support and advised them to concede.

On 29 November, the Soviet Union broke off diplomatic relations. The next day, troops of the Leningrad military district attacked Finnish positions and Red Army aviation bombers raided Helsinki. The Winter War had begun. Soviet leaders assumed that the campaign would be a walkover, like their occupation of eastern Poland. Voroshilov, the commissar of defence, wanted it to be finished in time for Stalin's sixtieth birthday on 21 December. Dmitri Shostakovich was ordered to compose a piece to celebrate the event.

In Finland, Marshal Carl Gustav Mannerheim, a former officer of the Tsar's Chevalier Gardes and the hero of the war of independence against the Bolsheviks, was called out of retirement as commander-in-chief. The Finns, with fewer than 150,000 men, many of whom were reservists and teenagers, faced Red Army forces over a million strong. Their defences across the Karelian Isthmus south-west of Lake Ladoga, known as the Mannerheim Line, consisted mainly of trenches, log-lined bunkers and some concrete strongpoints. The Finns were also aided by the forests and small lakes which funnelled any lines of advance towards their carefully laid minefields.

Despite heavy artillery support, the Soviet 7th Army received a nasty shock. Its infantry divisions were at first delayed by screening forces and snipers close to the border. Lacking mine-detectors and under orders to push forward without delay, Soviet commanders simply marched their men forward through the snow-covered minefields in front of the Mannerheim Line. For Red Army soldiers, who had been told that the Finns would welcome them as brothers and liberators from their capitalist oppressors, the reality of the fighting sapped their morale as they struggled through the snowfields towards the birchwoods which concealed parts of the Mannerheim Line. The Finns, masters of winter camouflage, mowed them down with machine guns.

In the far north of Finland, Soviet troops from Murmansk attacked the mining area and the port of Petsamo, but their attempts further south to slice through the middle of Finland from the east to the Gulf of Bothnia proved the most spectacularly disastrous. Stalin, astonished that the Finns had not immediately given in, ordered Voroshilov to crush them with the Red Army's numerically superior forces. Red Army commanders, terrified by the purges and hamstrung by the stifling military orthodoxy which ensued, could only send more and more men to their deaths. In temperatures of minus 40 degrees Centigrade, Soviet soldiers, ill equipped and untrained for this sort of winter warfare, stood out in their brown greatcoats as they stumbled through the deep snow. Amid the frozen lakes and forests of central and northern Finland, the Soviet columns could only follow the few roads through the woods. There, they were ambushed in lightning attacks by Finnish ski-troops armed with Suomi sub-machine guns, grenades and hunting knives to finish off their victims.

The Finns adopted what they called 'log-cutting' tactics, slicing enemy columns into sections and cutting off their supply routes so that they starved. Appearing silently out of a freezing fog, their ski-troops would hurl grenades or Molotov cocktails at the Soviet tanks and artillery, then disappear just as swiftly. It was a form of semi-guerrilla warfare for which the Red Army was totally unprepared. Farms, byres and barns were burned down by the Finns to deny the Red Army columns any shelter as they advanced. Roads were mined and booby-traps prepared. Anyone wounded in these attacks froze to death rapidly. Soviet soldiers had started to refer to the camouflaged Finnish ski-troops as *belya smert* – or 'white death'. The 163rd Rifle Division was surrounded near Suomussalmi, then the 44th Rifle Division, advancing to its relief, was split up in a series of attacks and also fell victim to the white ghosts flitting between the trees.

'For four miles,' wrote the American journalist Virginia Cowles when visiting the battlefield later, 'the road and forests were strewn with the bodies of men and horses; with wrecked tanks, field kitchens, trucks, gun carriages, maps, books and articles of clothing. The corpses were frozen as hard as petrified wood, and the colour of the skin was mahogany. Some of the bodies were piled on top of each other like a heap of rubbish, covered only by a merciful blanket of snow; others were sprawled against the trees in grotesque attitudes. All were frozen in the positions in which they huddled. I saw one with his hands clasped to a wound in his stomach; another struggling to open the collar of his coat.'

A similar fate had met the 122nd Rifle Division advancing south-westwards from the Kola Peninsula towards Kemijärvi, where they were surprised and massacred by the forces of General K. M. Wallenius. 'How strange were these bodies on this road,' wrote the first foreign journalist to see the effectiveness of the Finns' brave resistance. 'The cold had frozen them into the positions in which they fell. It had, too, slightly shrunken their bodies and features, giving them an artificial, waxen appearance. The whole road was like some huge waxwork representation of a battle scene, carefully staged . . . one man leant against a wagon wheel with a length of wire in his hands; another was fitting a clip of cartridges into his rifle.'

International condemnation of the invasion led to the Soviet Union's expulsion from the League of Nations, its final act. Popular feeling in London and Paris was almost more outraged by this incursion than by the attack on Poland. Stalin's German ally also found itself in a difficult position. While receiving an increased volume of supplies from the Soviet Union, it now feared damaging its relations and trade with Scandinavian countries, especially Sweden. Above all, the Nazi leadership was disturbed by the calls in Britain and France for military aid to be sent to Finland. An Allied presence in Scandinavia risked disrupting Swedish iron-ore deliveries to Germany, whose high quality was vital for its war industries.

Hitler, however, was serenely confident at this time. He had been confirmed in his belief that providence was on his side, preserving him for the accomplishment of his great task. On 8 November, he had made his annual speech in the Bürgerbräukeller in Munich from where the Nazis' failed 1923 Putsch had been launched. Georg Elser, a cabinet-maker, had secretly filled a pillar with explosives close to the platform. But for once Hitler had cut his visit short to return to Berlin, and twelve minutes after his departure a huge explosion had wrecked the place, killing a number of his Nazi 'Old Fighters'. According to one commentator, the reaction in London to the news was 'summed up in a calm British "Bad luck", as though someone had missed a pheasant'. With misplaced optimism, the British comforted themselves with the idea that it was simply a matter of time before the Germans would get rid of their own ghastly regime.

Elser was arrested that evening trying to cross into Switzerland. Even though he had clearly worked entirely alone, Nazi propaganda immediately blamed the British Secret Intelligence Service for the attempt on the Führer's life. Himmler had the perfect opportunity to exploit this fictitious link. Walter Schellenberg, an SS intelligence expert, was already in contact with two British SIS officers, having convinced them that he was part of an anti-Hitler conspiracy in the Wehrmacht. The next day, he persuaded them to meet him again at Venlo on the Dutch frontier. He promised to bring an anti-Nazi German general with him. But the two British officers instead found themselves surrounded and seized by an SS snatch party. It was led by Sturmbannführer Alfred Naujocks, who had commanded the fake attack on the Gleiwitz transmitter at the end of August. It would not be the only British secret operation to go horribly wrong in the Netherlands.

This debacle was concealed from the British public, who at least had their pride restored in the Royal Navy later that month. On 23 November, the armed merchant cruiser HMS *Rawalpindi* fought back against the German battle-cruisers *Gneisenau* and *Scharnhorst*. In a hopeless engagement of great bravery, which was inevitably compared to Sir Richard Grenville in the *Revenge* taking on vast Spanish galleons, guncrews fought on until they were killed. The *Rawalpindi*, blazing from bow to stern, went down with her battle ensign still flying.

Then, on 13 December off the coast of Uruguay, Commodore Henry Harwood's squadron, with the cruisers HMS *Ajax*, *Achilles* and *Exeter*, sighted the pocket battleship *Admiral Graf Spee*, which had already sunk nine ships. Kapitan Hans Langsdorff, her commander, was highly respected because of his good treatment of the crews of his victims. But Langsdorff mistakenly thought that the British ships were only destroyers and so did not avoid battle as he should have done, even though he outgunned his adversaries with his 11-inch main armament. The *Exeter*, drawing the *Graf Spee*'s fire, suffered heavy damage, while the *Ajax* and the New Zealand-crewed *Achilles* attempted to close within range to fire torpedoes. Although the British squadron was badly battered, the *Graf Spee*, which had also been hit, broke off the action under a smokescreen and headed for Montevideo harbour.

Over the following days, the British bluffed Langsdorff into believing that their squadron had been heavily reinforced. And on 17 December, having first disembarked his prisoners and most of the crew, Langsdorff took the *Graf Spee* out into the estuary of the River Plate and scuttled her. He committed suicide soon afterwards. The British celebrated this victory at a time when morale needed a boost. Hitler, afraid that the *Deutschland* might suffer the same fate, ordered that her name should be changed to *Lützow*. He did not want headlines round the world proclaiming that a ship called 'Germany' had been sunk. Symbols were of paramount importance to him, as would become even more evident when the war turned against him.

Having been told by Goebbels's propaganda ministry that the Battle of the River Plate had been a victory, Germans were then shaken to hear that the *Graf Spee* had been scuttled. The Nazi authorities tried to make sure that the news did not spoil their 'war Christmas'. Rationing was eased for the festivities and the population was encouraged to contemplate the devastating victory over Poland. Most convinced themselves that peace would soon come since both the Soviet Union and Germany had called on the Allies to accept the reality of Poland's destruction.

With newsreel film showing children round Christmas trees, the propaganda ministry produced a sickly feast of German sentimentality. But many families were haunted by a terrible disquiet. Although officially informed that a disabled child or elderly relative had died from 'pneumonia' in some institution, suspicions had started to grow that they were in fact being gassed in a programme run by the SS and members of the medical profession. Hitler's order on euthanasia had been signed in October, but was backdated to the outbreak of war on 1 September to cover the first SS massacres of around 2,000 Polish asylum inmates, some of them shot in their straitjackets. The Nazis' covert assault on 'degenerates', 'useless mouths' and 'lives unworthy of life' represented their first step in the deliberate annihilation of those they categorized as 'sub-human'. Hitler had waited for the start of the war to cover this extreme programme of eugenics. More than 100,000 mentally and physically disabled Germans would be killed in this way by August 1941. In Poland, the killings continued, mainly by shooting in the back of the head, but sometimes in sealed trucks with the exhaust fumes piped in, and also, for the first time, in an improvised gas chamber in Posen: a process which Himmler himself came to observe. As well as the disabled, a number of prostitutes and Gypsies were also murdered.

Hitler, who had forsworn his passion for the cinema for the duration of the war, also gave up Christmas. Over the holiday period, he paid a number of highly publicized surprise visits to Wehrmacht and SS units, including the *Grossdeutschland* Regiment, Luftwaffe airfields and flak batteries, and also the SS *Leibstandarte Adolf Hitler*, now relaxing after its murderous campaign in Poland. On New Year's Eve he addressed the nation over the radio. Proclaiming a 'New Order in Europe', he said: 'We shall only talk of peace when we have won the war. The Jewish capitalistic world will not survive the twentieth century.' He made no reference to 'Jewish Bolshevism', having so recently sent sixtieth-birthday greetings to Stalin, a message which also offered best wishes 'for the prosperous future of the peoples of the friendly Soviet Union'. Stalin replied that 'The friendship of the peoples of Germany and the Soviet Union, cemented by blood, has every reason to be lasting and firm.' Even under the hypocritical requirements of their unnatural relationship, the phrase 'cemented by blood' in reference to their dual attack on Poland constituted a pinnacle of shamelessness as well as an ill omen for the future.

Stalin can hardly have been in a good mood as the year came to an end. Finnish forces had now advanced on to Soviet territory. He was forced to accept that the disastrous performance of the Red Army in the Winter War had been partly the fault of his incompetent crony Marshal Voroshilov. The humiliation of the Red Army in the eyes of the world had to be stopped, especially since he had been alarmed by the devastating effectiveness of German Blitzkrieg tactics in the Polish campaign.

He therefore decided to bring in Army Commander S. K. Timoshenko to head up a North-Western Front. Like Voroshilov, Timoshenko was another veteran of the 1st Cavalry Army in which Stalin had served as commissar in the Russian Civil War, but he was at least slightly more imaginative. New weapons and equipment were issued, including the latest rifles, motorized sledges and heavy KV tanks. Instead of massed infantry attacks, the Soviet forces would rely on smashing Finnish defences with artillery.

A new Soviet offensive began against the Mannerheim Line on 1 February 1940. The Finnish forces buckled under the onslaught. Four days later, their foreign minister made an initial contact with Mme Aleksandra Kollontay, the Soviet ambassador in Stockholm. The British and especially the French hoped to maintain Finland's resistance. They accordingly made approaches to the Norwegian and Swedish governments to obtain transit rights for an expeditionary force to help the Finns. The Germans were alarmed and began to study the possibility of sending troops to Scandinavia to pre-empt an Allied landing.

Both the British and French governments also considered the possibility of occupying Narvik in Norway and the mining areas of northern Sweden to cut off iron-ore supplies to Germany. But the Swedish and Norwegian governments were afraid of being drawn into the war. They refused the British and French requests to cross their territory to aid the Finns.

On 29 February the Finns, with no hope of foreign help, decided to seek terms on the basis of the Soviet Union's original demands, and on 13 March a treaty was signed in Moscow. The terms were harsh, but they could have been far worse. The Finns had shown how resolutely they were prepared to defend their independence, but most importantly Stalin did not want to continue a war which might yet drag in the western Allies. He was also forced to accept that Comintern propaganda had been ludicrously self-deluding, so he dropped his puppet government of Finnish Communists. The Red Army had suffered 84,994 killed and missing, with 248,090 wounded and sick. The Finns had lost 25,000 killed.

Stalin, however, continued to take his revenge upon Poland. On 5 March 1940, he and the Politburo approved Beria's plan to murder Polish officers and other potential leaders who had refused all attempts at Communist 're-education'. This was part of Stalin's policy to destroy an independent Poland in the future. The 21,892 victims were taken in trucks from prisons for execution at five sites. The most notorious was in the forest of Katyń near Smolensk in Belorussia. The NKVD had noted the addresses of its victims' families when they had been allowed to write home. They too were rounded up and 60,667 were deported to Kazakhstan. Soon afterwards, more than 65,000 Polish Jews, who had fled the SS but refused to accept Soviet passports, were also deported to Kazakhstan and Siberia.

The French government, meanwhile, wanted to pursue the war as far from its own territory as possible. Daladier, exasperated by French Communist support for the Nazi–Soviet pact, thought that the Allies could weaken Germany by attacking Hitler's ally. He advocated a bombing raid on Soviet oil installations at Baku and in the Caucasus, but the British persuaded the French to abandon the idea because it risked bringing the Soviet Union into the war on the German side. Daladier later resigned and was replaced by Paul Reynaud on 20 March.

The French army, which had borne the brunt of the Allied effort in the First World War, was widely considered to be the strongest in Europe and certainly capable of defending its own territory. More perceptive observers were less convinced. As early as March 1935, Marshal Tukhachevsky had predicted that it would not be able to stand up to a German onslaught. Its fatal flaw, in his view, was that it was too slow to react to an attack. This came not just from a rigidly defensive mentality, but also from an almost complete lack of radio communications. In any case, the Germans had broken the antiquated French codes in 1938.

President Roosevelt, who had paid close attention to despatches from his embassy in Paris, was also well aware of French weaknesses. The air force was only starting to replace its obsolete aircraft. The army, although one of the largest in the world, was cumbersome, old-fashioned and excessively reliant on its Maginot Line of defence along the German border, which imbued it with an immobile frame of mind. Its huge losses in the First World War, with 400,000 casualties in the Battle for Verdun alone, lay at the root of this bunker mentality. And as many journalists, military attachés and commentators observed, the country's political and social malaise after so many scandals and fallen governments had sapped any hope for unity and determination in a crisis.

Roosevelt, with admirable far-sightedness, saw that the only hope for democracy and the long-term interests of the United States was to support Britain and France against Nazi Germany. Finally, on 4 November 1939, the 'cash and carry' bill passed by Congress was ratified. This first defeat for the isolationists allowed the two Allied powers to purchase arms.

In France, the air of unreality persisted. A Reuters correspondent visiting the inert front asked French soldiers why they did not shoot at the German troops wandering about in clear view. They looked shocked. 'Ils ne sont pas méchants,' replied one. 'And if we fire, they will fire back.' German patrols probing along the line soon discovered the ineptitude and lack of aggressive instinct of most French formations. And German propaganda continued to encourage the idea that the British were getting the French to bear the brunt of the war.

Apart from some work on defensive positions, the French army undertook little training. Their troops just waited. Inactivity led to bad morale and depression – *le cafard*. Politicians started to hear of drunkenness, absence without leave and the slovenly appearance of troops in public. 'One can't spend one's whole time playing cards, drinking and writing home to one's wife,' wrote one soldier. 'We lie stretched out on the straw yawning, and even get a taste for doing nothing. We wash less and less, we don't bother to shave any more, we can't raise the effort to sweep the place or clear the table after eating. Along with boredom, filth dominates in the base.'

Jean-Paul Sartre in his army meteorological station found the time to write the first volume of *Chemins de la liberté* and part of *L'Être et le néant*. That winter, he wrote, it was 'a question only of sleeping, eating and not being cold. That was all.' General Édouard Ruby observed: 'Every exercise was considered a vexation, all work a fatigue. After several months of stagnation, nobody believed any more in the war.' Not every officer was complacent. The outspoken Colonel Charles de Gaulle, a fervent advocate of creating armoured divisions as in the German army, warned that 'to be inert is to be beaten'. But his calls were dismissed by irritated generals.

All the French high command did to maintain morale was to organize front-line entertainment with visits from famous actors and singers such as Édith Piaf, Joséphine Baker, Maurice Chevalier and Charles Trenet. Back in Paris, where the restaurants and cabarets were full, the favourite song was 'J'attendrai' – 'I'll wait'. But more alarming for the Allied cause were those right-wingers in influential positions who said 'Better Hitler than Blum', a reference to the socialist leader of the 1936 Popular Front, Leon Blum, who was also Jewish.

Georges Bonnet, the arch-appeaser of the Quai d'Orsay, had a nephew who before the war had served as a conduit for Nazi money to subsidize anti-British and anti-semitic propaganda in France. The foreign minister's friend Otto Abetz, later the Nazi ambassador in Paris during the occupation, had been deeply implicated and expelled from the country. Even the new prime minister Paul Reynaud, a stalwart believer in the war against Nazism, had a dangerous weakness. His mistress, Comtesse Hélène de Portes, 'a woman whose somewhat coarsened features exuded an extraordinary vitality and confidence', believed that France should never have honoured its guarantee to Poland.

Poland, in the form of a government-in-exile, had arrived in France, with General Władysław Sikorski as prime minister and commander-in-chief. Based in Angers, Sikorski set about reorganizing the Polish armed forces from the 84,000 who had escaped mainly through Romania after the fall of their country. A Polish resistance movement had meanwhile begun to develop back in the homeland; in fact it was the most rapidly organized of any occupied country. By the middle of 1940, the Polish underground army numbered some 100,000 members in the Generalgouvernement alone. Poland was one of the very few countries in the Nazi empire where collaboration with the conqueror was virtually unknown.

The French were determined not to share the fate of Poland. Yet most of their leaders and the bulk of the population had totally failed to recognize that this war would not be like earlier conflicts. The Nazis would never be satisfied with reparations and the surrender of a province or two. They intended to reorder Europe in their own brutal image.

4

The Dragon and the Rising Sun

1937–1940

Suffering was not a new experience for the impoverished mass of Chinese peasantry. They knew all too well the starvation which followed flood, drought, deforestation, soil erosion and the depredations of warlord armies. They lived in crumbling mud houses and their lives were handicapped by disease, ignorance, superstition and the exploitation of landowners who exacted between a half and two-thirds of their crop in rent.

City dwellers, including even many left-wing intellectuals, tended to see the rural masses as little more than faceless beasts of burden. 'Sympathy with the people is utterly useless,' a Communist interpreter said to the intrepid American journalist and activist Agnes Smedley. 'There are too many of them.' Smedley herself compared their lives to those of 'peasant serfs of the Middle Ages'. They existed off tiny portions of rice, millet or squash, cooked in an iron cauldron, their most valuable possession. Many went barefoot even in winter and wore reed hats when working in the summer, bent over in the fields. Life was short, so old peasant women, wrinkled with age and hobbling still on bound feet, were comparatively rare. Many had never seen a motorcar or an aeroplane or even electric lighting. In much of the countryside warlords and landlords still ruled with feudal powers.

Life in the cities was no better for the poor, even for those with jobs. 'In Shanghai,' wrote an American journalist out there, 'collecting the lifeless bodies of child labourers at factory gates in the morning is a routine affair.' The poor were also oppressed by greedy tax-collectors and bureaucrats. In Harbin, the traditional beggar cry was 'Give! Give! May you become rich! May you become an official!' Sometimes the cry changed to: 'May you become rich! May you become a general!' Their fatalism was so inherent that real social change was beyond imagination. The revolution of 1911 which had marked the collapse of the Qing dynasty and brought in Dr Sun Yat-sen's republic was middle class and urban. So at first was Chinese nationalism, aroused by the flagrant designs of Japan to exploit the country's weakness.

Wang Ching-wei, who briefly became leader of the Kuomintang after the death of Sun Yat-sen in 1924, was the chief rival of the rising general Chiang Kai-shek. Chiang, proud and slightly paranoid, was deeply ambitious and determined to become the great Chinese leader. A slim, bald man with a neat little military moustache, he was a highly skilled political operator, but he was not always a good commander-in-chief. He had been commandant of the Whampoa Military Academy and his favoured students were appointed to key commands. Yet because of rivalries and factional infighting within the National Revolutionary Army and between allied warlords, Chiang tried to control his formations from afar, often provoking confusion and delay as a result.

In 1932, the year after the Mukden Incident and the Japanese seizure of Manchuria, the Japanese moved marine detachments into their concession in Shanghai with conspicuous belligerence. Chiang foresaw a far worse onslaught to come and began to prepare. General Hans von Seeckt, the former commander-in-chief of the Reichswehr during the Weimar Republic, who arrived in May 1933, advised on how to modernize and professionalize the Nationalist armies. Seeckt and his successor, General Alexander von Falkenhausen, advocated a drawn-out war of attrition as the only hope against the better-trained Imperial Japanese Army. With little foreign exchange available, Chiang decided to trade Chinese tungsten for German weapons.

Chiang Kai-shek was a tireless modernizer and at this time inspired by genuine idealism. During what was known as the Nanking decade (1928–37), he presided over a rapid programme of industrialization, roadbuilding, military modernization and improvements to agriculture. He also sought to end the psychological and diplomatic isolation of China. Yet, being well aware of China's military weakness, he was determined to avoid a war with Japan for as long as possible.

In 1935, Stalin, through the Comintern, instructed the Chinese Communists to create a common front with the Nationalists against the Japanese threat. It was a policy which Mao Tsetung in particular hardly welcomed after Chiang's attacks on

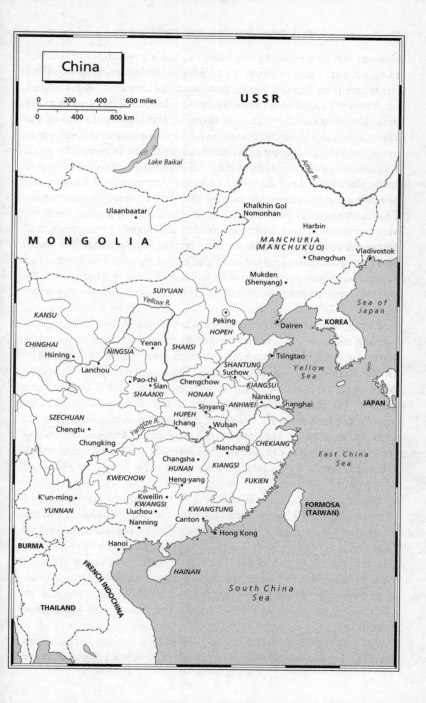

Communist forces which had forced him to embark in October 1934 on the Long March to avoid the destruction of his Red Army. In fact Mao, a large man with a curiously high-pitched voice, was viewed as a dissident by the Kremlin, because he saw that the interests of Stalin and those of the Chinese Communist Party were not the same. He believed along Leninist lines that war prepared the ground for a revolutionary seizure of power.

Moscow, on the other hand, did not want a war in the Far East. The interests of the Soviet Union were seen as far more important than a long-term victory for the Chinese Communists. The Comintern therefore accused Mao of lacking an 'internationalist perspective'. And Mao came close to heresy by arguing that Marxist-Leninist principles of the primacy of the urban proletariat were unsuitable in China, where the peasantry must form the vanguard of the revolution. He advocated independent guerrilla warfare, and the development of networks behind the Japanese lines.

Chiang sent representatives to meet the Communists. He wanted them to incorporate their forces within the Kuomintang army. In return they would have their own region in the north and he would cease attacking them. Mao suspected that Chiang's policy was to push them into an area where they would be destroyed by the Japanese attacking from Manchuria. Chiang, however, knew that the Communists would never compromise or work with any other party in the long term. Their only interest was in achieving total power for themselves. 'The Communists are a disease of the heart,' he once said. 'The Japanese a disease of the skin.'

While trying to deal with the Communists in southern and central China, Chiang could do little to stem Japanese incursions and provocations in the north-east. The Kwantung Army of Manchukuo argued with Tokyo, claiming that this was no time to compromise with China. Its chief of staff, Lieutenant General Tōjō Hideki, the future prime minister, stated that preparing for war with the Soviet Union without destroying the 'menace to our rear' in the form of the Nanking government was 'asking for trouble'.

At the same time, Chiang Kai-shek's policy of caution towards Japanese aggression produced widespread popular anger and student demonstrations in the capital. In late 1936, Japanese forces advanced into Suiyuan province on the Mongolian border, intent on seizing the coal mines and iron-ore deposits in the region. Nationalist forces counter-attacked and forced them out. This strengthened Chiang's position, and his conditions for a united front with the Communists became tougher. The Communists, with the North-Western Alliance of warlords, attacked Nationalist units in the rear. Chiang wanted to suppress the Communists completely while negotiations with them still continued. But at the beginning of December he flew to Sian for discussions with two Nationalist army commanders who wanted a strong line against Japan and an end to the civil war with the Communists. They seized him and detained him for two weeks until he agreed to their terms. The Communists demanded that Chiang Kai-shek should be arraigned before a people's tribunal.

Chiang was released and returned to Nanking, having been forced to change his policy. There was genuine national rejoicing at the prospect of anti-Japanese unity. And on 16 December, Stalin, deeply alarmed by the Anti-Comintern Pact between Nazi Germany and Japan, put pressure on Mao and Chou En-lai, his subtle and more diplomatic colleague, to join a united front with the Nationalists. The Soviet leader feared that if the Chinese Communists made trouble in the north, then Chiang Kai-shek might form an alliance with the Japanese against them. And if Chiang was removed, then Wang Ching-wei, who did not want to fight the Japanese, might take over leadership of the Kuomintang. Stalin encouraged the Nationalists to believe that he might well side with them in a war against Japan, purely to make sure that they resisted. And he continued to dangle that carrot without any intention of committing the Soviet Union to war.

An agreement between the Kuomintang and the Communists had still not been signed when the clash between Chinese and Japanese troops took place at the Marco Polo Bridge south-west of Peking on 7 July 1937. This incident marked the start of the main phase of the Sino-Japanese War. The whole incident was a black farce which demonstrates the terrifying unpredictability of events at a time of tension. A single Japanese soldier had become lost during a night exercise. His company commander demanded entry to the town of Wanping to search for him. When this was refused, he attacked it and the Chinese troops fought back, while the lost soldier found his own way back to barracks. An added irony was that the general staff in Tokyo were at last attempting to control their fanatical officers in China who were responsible for the provocations, while Chiang was now under strong pressure from his side not to compromise any more.

The generalissimo was uncertain about Japanese intentions and called a conference of Chinese leaders. At first, the Japanese military were themselves divided. Their Kwantung Army in Manchuria wanted to widen the conflict, while the general staff in Tokyo feared a reaction by the Red Army along the northern frontiers. There had been a clash on the Amur River just over a week before. Soon afterwards, however, the Japanese chiefs of staff decided on an all-out war. They believed that China could be knocked out rapidly before a wider conflict developed, either with the Soviet Union or with the western powers. Like Hitler with the Soviet Union later, Japanese generals made a grave error in grossly underestimating outrage among Chinese and their determination to resist. And it did not occur to them that China's answering strategy would be to wage a drawn-out war of attrition.

Chiang Kai-shek, well aware of his own army's deficiencies and the unpredictability of his allies in the north, knew the immense risks that war with Japan entailed. But he had little choice. The Japanese issued and repeated an ultimatum, which the Nanking government rejected, and on 26 July their army attacked. Peking fell three days later. Nationalist forces and their allies fell back, offering only sporadic resistance as the Japanese advanced southwards.

'Suddenly, the war was upon us,' wrote Agnes Smedley, who landed by junk on the north bank of the Yellow River at the 'rambling mud town of Fenglingtohkow. This little town, in which we hoped to find lodgings for the night, was a mass of soldiers, civilians, carts, mules, horses and street vendors. As we walked up the mud paths towards the town, we saw on either side long rows of wounded soldiers lying on the earth. There were hundreds of them swathed in dirty, bloody bandages, and some were unconscious . . . There were no doctors, nurses or attendants with them.'

Despite all of Chiang's efforts to modernize Nationalist forces, they, like those of his warlord allies, were not nearly as well trained or as well equipped as the Japanese divisions they faced. The infantry wore blue-grey cotton uniforms in summer, and in winter the luckier ones had padded quilt cotton jackets or the sheepskin coats of Mongolian troops. Their footwear consisted of cloth shoes or straw sandals. Although silent in their shuffling run, they provided no protection against the sharp bamboo pungi stakes, tipped with excrement to cause blood poisoning, which the Japanese used to defend their positions.

Chinese soldiers wore rounded peaked caps with ear flaps tied over the top. They had no steel helmets, except those they took from dead Japanese soldiers and wore with pride. Many also wore tunics taken from enemy soldiers, which became confusing at times of crisis. The most prized trophy was a Japanese pistol. In fact it was often easier for Chinese soldiers to get more ammunition for captured Japanese weapons than for their issued rifles, which came from a wide variety of countries and manufacturers. Their greatest deficiencies were in medical services, artillery and aircraft.

In and out of battle, Chinese troops were directed by bugle calls. Wireless communications existed only between major headquarters, and even they were unreliable. The Japanese were also able to break their codes with ease and thus knew their dispositions and intentions. Chinese military transport consisted of some trucks, but most units in the field relied on mules beaten on with traditional curses, Mongolian ponies and bullock-drawn carts with solid wooden wheels. There were never enough and this meant that soldiers often received no food. And since their pay was almost always months in arrears, and sometimes embezzled by their officers, morale suffered badly. But there can be no doubt about the bravery and determination of Chinese troops in the Battle of Shanghai that summer.

The origins and motives which led to this great clash are still debated. The classic explanation is that Chiang, by opening up a new front at Shanghai while continuing to fight in the north and centre, wanted to split Japanese forces to prevent their concentration for a quick victory. This would be his war of attrition, as advised by General von Falkenhausen. An attack on Shanghai would also force the Communists and other allied armies to commit themselves to the War of Resistance, even if there was always the danger that they would withdraw rather than risk their forces and power base. It also ensured a declaration of Soviet support, with the despatch of military advisers, and the supply of fighters, tanks, artillery, machine guns and vehicles. This would be paid for with raw materials exported to the Soviet Union.

The other explanation is certainly compelling. Stalin, deeply alarmed by Japanese successes in northern China, was the one who really wanted to move the fighting down to the south and away from his far eastern borders. This he was able to do through the regional Nationalist commander General Chang Ching-chong, who was secretly a Soviet 'sleeper'. On several occasions Chang tried to persuade the generalissimo to launch a pre-emptive strike on the Japanese garrison of 3,000 marines in Shanghai. Chiang told him to make no move without specific orders. An attack on Shanghai also carried huge risks. It was only 290 kilometres from Nanking, and defeat there close to the mouth of the Yangtze might lead to a rapid Japanese advance on the capital and into the centre of China. On 9 August, Chang sent a picked group of soldiers to Shanghai airfield, where they shot down a Japanese marine lieutenant and a soldier with him. On Chang's own account, they then shot a Chinese prisoner condemned to death to pretend that the Japanese had fired first. The Japanese, also reluctant to start a battle round Shanghai, did not at first react, except to call for reinforcements. Chiang again told Chang not to attack. On 13 August, Japanese warships began to bombard the Chinese quarters of Shanghai. Next morning, two Nationalist divisions began their assault on the city. An air attack was also launched against the flagship of the Japanese Third Fleet, the old cruiser *Izumo* anchored off the Bund in the centre of the city. It was an inauspicious start. The warship's fire drove off the obsolete aircraft. Some rounds hit the bomb racks of one of them, and as it flew over the international settlement its load dropped on the Palace Hotel, on Nanking Road and on other places crowded with refugees. Some 1,300 civilians were thus killed or injured by their own plane.

Forces on both sides began to build up in a rapid escalation which turned the battle into the largest engagement of the Sino-Japanese War. On 23 August the Japanese, having reinforced their troops in Shanghai, made landings on the coast to the north to outflank Nationalist positions. Their armoured landing craft put tanks ashore, and Japanese naval gunfire was all the more effective when Nationalist divisions had almost no artillery. Nationalist attempts to blockade the Yangtze also failed and their tiny air force stood little chance against Japanese air supremacy.

From 11 September, Nationalist forces directed by Falkenhausen fought with great bravery despite terrible losses. Most divisions, especially Chiang's elite formations, lost more than half their strength, including 10,000 junior officers. Chiang, unable to make up his mind whether to fight on or withdraw, then sent in even more divisions. He hoped to draw international attention to China's fight, just before a meeting of the League of Nations.

Altogether, the Japanese fielded nearly 200,000 men on the Shanghai front, more than they deployed in northern China. In the third week of September they began to achieve breaches in the Nationalist defences, forcing them in October to retreat to the line of the Soochow Creek, an effective water obstacle despite its name. One battalion was left behind to defend a godown or warehouse, to give the impression that the Nationalists still had a foothold in Shanghai. This 'lone battalion' became a great propaganda myth for the Chinese cause.

At the beginning of November, after more desperate fighting, the Japanese crossed the Soochow Creek using small metal assault boats and established bridgeheads in several places. Then, with another amphibious landing on the coast to the south, they forced the Nationalists to retreat. Discipline and morale, which had held up well during the savage fighting and heavy losses, now collapsed. Soldiers threw away their rifles, and refugees were trampled underfoot in the panic caused by Japanese bombers and fighters. During the three months of fighting round Shanghai, the Japanese had suffered more than 40,000 casualties. The Chinese figure was just over 187,000, at least four and a half times more.

In a headlong advance, torching villages along the way, Japanese divisions raced each other towards Nanking. The Imperial

Japanese Navy sent minesweepers and gunboats up the Yangtze
to bombard the city. The Nationalist government began to depart
up the Yangtze mainly by river steamer and junk for Hankow,
which was to be the temporary capital. Chungking on the upper
Yangtze in Szechuan would take over the role later.

Chiang Kai-shek could not decide whether to defend Nanking
or abandon it without a fight. The city was indefensible, and yet
to abandon such an important symbol would be a humiliation.
His generals could not agree. In the event the worst of both worlds
was achieved, with an incomplete defence which simply angered
the attackers. Japanese commanders were in fact planning to use
mustard gas and incendiaries on the capital if the fighting was
likely to approach the intensity of what they had experienced at
Shanghai.

The Chinese certainly had an idea of their enemy's ruthlessness, but even they could not imagine the degree of cruelty to
come. On 13 December, Chinese forces evacuated Nanking, only
to be trapped outside in a sudden encirclement. Japanese troops
entered the city with orders to kill all prisoners. A single unit in
the 16th Division killed 15,000 Chinese prisoners, and just one
company slaughtered 1,300. A German diplomat reported to
Berlin that 'besides mass executions by machinegun fire, other
more individual methods of killing were employed as well, such
as pouring gasoline over a victim and setting him afire'. Buildings
in the city were looted and set alight. To escape the murder, rape
and destruction civilians tried to shelter in the designated 'international safety zone'.

The *furia japonica* shocked the world with its appalling massacres and mass rapes in revenge for the bitter fighting at Shanghai,
which the Japanese army had never expected from the Chinese
they despised. Accounts of civilian casualties vary widely. Some
Chinese sources put them as high as 300,000, but a more likely
figure is closer to 200,000. The Japanese military authorities, in a
series of inept lies, claimed that they were killing only Chinese soldiers who had put on civilian clothes and that the death toll was
little more than a thousand. The scenes of massacre were hellish,
with corpses rotting on every street and in every open space, many
of them chewed by semi-feral dogs. Every pond, stream and river
was polluted with decomposing bodies.

Japanese soldiers had been brought up in a militaristic society. The whole village or neighbourhood, paying homage to these martial values, would usually turn out to bid farewell to a conscript departing to join the army. Soldiers thus tended to fight for the honour of their family and local community, not for the emperor as westerners tended to believe. Basic training was designed to destroy their individuality. Recruits were constantly insulted and beaten by their NCOs to toughen them up and to provoke them, in what might be called the knock-on theory of oppression, to take their anger out in turn on the soldiers and civilians of a defeated enemy. All of them had also been indoctrinated since elementary school to believe that the Chinese were totally inferior to the 'divine race' of Japanese and were 'below pigs'. In a typical case-history of post-war confessions, one soldier admitted that although he had been horrified by the gratuitous torture of a Chinese prisoner, he had asked to be allowed to take over to make up for a perceived insult.

At Nanking, wounded Chinese soldiers were bayoneted where they lay. Officers made prisoners kneel in rows, then practised beheading them one by one with their samurai swords. Their soldiers were also ordered to carry out bayonet practice on thousands of Chinese prisoners bound or tied to trees. Any who refused were beaten severely by their NCOs. The Imperial Japanese Army's process of dehumanizing its troops was stepped up as soon as they arrived in China from the home islands. A Corporal Nakamura, who had himself been conscripted as a soldier against his will, described in his diary how he and his comrades made some new Japanese recruits watch as they tortured five Chinese civilians to death. The newcomers were horrified, but Nakamura wrote: 'All new recruits are like this, but soon they will be doing the same things themselves.' Shimada Toshio, a private second class, recounted his 'baptism of blood' on reaching the 226th Regiment in China later. A Chinese prisoner had been tied by his hands and ankles to a pole on each side of him. Nearly fifty new recruits were lined up to bayonet him. 'My emotion must have been paralyzed. I felt no mercy on him. He eventually started asking us, "Come on. Hurry up!" We couldn't stick the right spot. So he said "Hurry up!" which meant that he wanted to die quickly.' Shimada claimed that it was difficult because the bayonet stuck in him 'like [in] tofu'.

John Rabe, a German businessman from Siemens, who organized the international safety zone in Nanking and showed both courage and humanity, wrote in his diary: 'I am totally puzzled by the conduct of the Japanese. On the one hand, they want to be recognized and treated as a great power on a par with European powers, on the other, they are currently displaying a crudity, brutality and bestiality that bears no comparison except with the hordes of Genghis Khan.' Twelve days later he wrote: 'You can't breathe for sheer revulsion when you keep finding the bodies of women with bamboo poles thrust up their vaginas. Even old women over 70 are constantly being raped.'

The group ethos of the Imperial Japanese Army, instilled by collective punishment in training, also produced a pecking order between experienced troops and newcomers. Senior soldiers organized the gang-rapes, with up to thirty men per woman, whom they usually killed when they had finished with her. Recently arrived soldiers were not permitted to take part. Only when they had been accepted as part of the group would they be 'invited' to join in.

New soldiers were also not permitted to visit 'comfort women' in the military brothels. These were girls and young married women, seized off the street or designated by village headmen under orders from the feared Kempeitai military police to provide a fixed quota. Following the Nanking massacre and rape, the Japanese military authorities demanded another 3,000 women 'for the use of the army'. More than 2,000 had already been seized from the city of Soochow alone after its capture in November. As well as local women carried off against their will, the Japanese imported large numbers of young women from their colony of Korea. A battalion commander in the 37th Division even took three Chinese women slaves along with his headquarters for his personal use. To make them look like men, their heads were shaved in an attempt to disguise their role.

The idea of the military authorities was to reduce cases of venereal disease and to restrict the number of rapes publicly carried out by their own men which might provoke the population into resistance. They preferred that women slaves should be raped perpetually in the secrecy of 'comfort houses'. But the notion that the provision of comfort women would somehow stop Japanese soldiers from raping at will proved to be utterly false. Soldiers clearly preferred random acts of rape to queueing up at the comfort house, and their officers felt that rape contributed to their martial spirit.

On the rare occasions that the Japanese were forced to abandon a town, they would slaughter the comfort women out of anti-Chinese vengeance. For example, when the town of Suencheng not far from Nanking was temporarily retaken, Chinese troops entered 'a building in which the nude bodies of a dozen Chinese civilian women had been found after the Japanese were driven out. The sign on the door-frame facing the street still read: "Consolation [Comfort] House of the Great Imperial Army".'

In northern China, the Japanese experienced some setbacks almost entirely at the hands of Nationalist troops. Communist forces from the Eighth Route Army, who claimed to be able to march more than a hundred kilometres in a day, were kept out of the worst of the fighting on Mao's strict orders. But by the end of the year the Kwantung Army controlled the towns of Chahar and Suiyuan provinces and the northern part of Shansi. South of Peking they seized the province of Shantung and its capital with ease, largely due to the cowardice of the regional commander, General Han Fu-chu.

General Han, who had fled in an aeroplane, taking with him the contents of the local treasury and a silver coffin, was arrested by the Nationalists and sentenced to death. He was made to kneel and then a fellow general shot him through the head. This warning to commanders was widely acclaimed by all parties and contributed greatly to Chinese unity. The Japanese were increasingly dismayed to find how determined the Chinese were to fight on, even after losing their capital and almost all their air force. And they were exasperated by the way the Chinese managed, after the Battle of Shanghai, to avoid the sort of decisive engagement which would destroy them.

In January 1938, the Japanese began to advance north up the railway line from Nanking towards Suchow, a major communications centre and of great strategic value since it was linked to a port on the east coast and lay astride the railway line to the west. If Suchow fell, then the great industrial agglomeration of Wuchang and Hankow (today's Wuhan) would be vulnerable. As in the Russian Civil War, railway lines in China were of immense importance for the movement and supply of armies. Chiang Kai-shek, who had long known that Suchow would represent a key objective in a Japanese invasion, assembled some 400,000 troops in the region, a mixture of Nationalist divisions and those of war-lord allies.

The generalissimo was well aware of the importance of the coming battles. The conflict in China had attracted many foreign journalists and was seen as a counterpart to the Spanish Civil War. Some of the same writers, photographers and film-makers who had been in Spain – Robert Capa, Joris Ivens, W. H. Auden and Christopher Isherwood – arrived to witness and record Chinese resistance to the Japanese onslaught. The forthcoming defence of Wuchang was compared to the Republican defence of Madrid against Franco's Army of Africa in the autumn of 1936. Doctors who had treated Spanish Republican wounded soon began to arrive to help Nationalist and Communist forces in China. The most notable was the Canadian surgeon Dr Norman Bethune, who died in China from blood poisoning.

Stalin also saw certain parallels with the Spanish Civil War, but Chiang was misled by his representative in Moscow, who was far too optimistic in his belief that the Soviet Union would enter the war against Japan. While the fighting continued, Chiang opened indirect negotiations with the Japanese through the German ambassador partly in a bid to force Stalin's hand, but their terms were too harsh. Stalin, presumably well briefed by one of his agents, knew that the Nationalists could not possibly accept them.

In February, Japanese divisions of the 2nd Army coming from the north crossed the Yellow River to encircle the Chinese formations. By the end of March, the Japanese had entered the city of Suchow, where furious fighting continued for several days. The Chinese had few weapons to deal with Japanese tanks, but Soviet armament had begun to arrive, and counter-attacks were made sixty kilometres to the east at Taierchuang, where the Nationalists claimed a great victory. The Japanese rushed in reinforcements from Japan and Manchuria. On 17 May, they believed that they had trapped the bulk of the Chinese divisions, but, splitting into small groups, 200,000 Nationalist troops escaped the encirclement. Suchow was finally lost on 21 May and 30,000 prisoners taken.

In July, the first major border clash between the Japanese and the Red Army took place at Lake Khasan. Again the Nationalists hoped that the Soviet Union would enter the war, but their expectations were dashed. Stalin even tacitly recognized Japanese control of Manchuria. With Hitler's designs on Czechoslovakia, he was deeply concerned about the German threat in the west. But Stalin did begin to send military advisers to the Nationalists. The first had arrived in June, just before the departure of General von Falkenhausen and his team, who had been ordered back to Germany by Göring.

The Japanese then planned to attack Wuchang and Hankow, as Chiang had feared. They also decided to set up their own Chinese puppet government. To slow the enemy advance, Chiang Kai-shek gave orders for the Yellow River dikes to be breached, or, in the words of the high command decision, to 'use water as a substitute for soldiers'. This drowned-earth policy delayed the Japanese by about five months, but the destruction and civilian deaths that it caused over 70,000 square kilometres were horrific. There was no high ground on which people could seek shelter. The official death toll from drowning, starvation and illness reached 800,000, while more than six million people became refugees.

Once the ground was finally dry enough to take their vehicles the Japanese resumed their advance on Wuchang and Hankow, with Imperial Navy forces operating on the Yangtze, and the 11th Army either side following both the north and the south bank. The Yangtze became a vital supply line for their forces, immune to guerrilla attack.

The Nationalists had by then received some 500 Soviet aircraft and 150 'volunteer' Red Army pilots, but since they served for only a three-month tour they were gone as soon as they had gained vital experience. Between 150 and 200 served at a time, and altogether 2,000 of them flew in China. They had mounted a successful ambush on 29 April 1938, when they correctly guessed that the Japanese would launch a large raid on Wuchang for Emperor Hirohito's birthday, but overall the Imperial Japanese Navy pilots imposed their superiority in central and southern

China. Chinese pilots, despite flying unsuitable aircraft, tended to go for spectacular attacks on warships which led to their own destruction.

In July, the Japanese bombed the river port of Kiukiang, almost certainly using chemical weapons which they euphemistically called 'special smoke'. On 26 July, when the town fell, the Namita Detachment carried out another terrible massacre of civilians. But in the intense heat the 11th Army advance slowed, due to the bitter resistance of Chinese forces and large numbers of Japanese soldiers succumbing to malaria and cholera. This gave the Chinese time to dismantle factories and ship them up the Yangtze towards Chungking. On 21 October, the Japanese 21st Army captured the great port of Canton on the south coast in an amphibious operation. Four days later the 6th Division of the 11th Army entered Wuchang as the Chinese forces withdrew.

Chiang Kai-shek railed at the deficiencies in staff work, liaison, intelligence and communications. Divisional headquarters tried to avoid orders from higher command to attack. There was never any defence in depth, just a single line of trenches which could easily be broken, and reserves were seldom deployed in the right place. But the next disaster was largely the fault of Chiang himself.

After the fall of Wuchang, the city of Changsha appeared vulnerable. Japanese aircraft bombed it on 8 November. The next day, Chiang ordered that the town should be prepared for demolition by fire in case the Japanese broke through. He gave the example of the Russians destroying Moscow in 1812. Three days later completely mistaken rumours spread that the Japanese were about to arrive, and in the early hours of 13 November the city was set ablaze. Changsha burned for three days. Two-thirds of the city including the warehouses filled with rice and grain were utterly destroyed. Twenty thousand people died, including all the wounded soldiers, and 200,000 were made homeless.

In spite of its victories, the Imperial Japanese Army was far from complacent. Its commanders knew that they had failed to deliver a knock-out blow. Their supply lines were overextended and vulnerable. And they were only too conscious of Soviet military support for the Nationalists, with Red Army pilots now shooting down many of their planes. The Japanese wondered uneasily what Stalin might be planning. These concerns prompted them in November to propose a general withdrawal of their forces to behind the Great Wall in the north, providing that the Nationalists changed their government, conceded Japan's right to Manchuria, allowed the Japanese exploitation of their resources and agreed to form a joint front against the Communists. Chiang's rival, Wang Ching-wei, left for Indochina in December and made contact with the Japanese authorities in Shanghai. He felt that, as the leader of the peace faction within the Kuomintang, he was their obvious candidate to replace Chiang. But few politicians followed him when he left to join the enemy. Chiang's powerful appeal to national redemption won out.

The Japanese, having abandoned a strategy of shock attack to obtain a rapid victory, now followed a more cautious path. With war in Europe approaching, they suspected that they would soon have to redeploy part of their vast forces in China on other fronts. They also believed, rather obtusely after the atrocities their troops had committed, that they could win over the Chinese population. So although the Nationalist forces and Chinese civilians continued to suffer huge casualties – some twenty million Chinese would die before the war ended in 1945 – the Japanese turned to smaller-scale operations, mainly suppressing guerrilla groups in their rear.

The Communists recruited large numbers of local civilians into their guerrilla militias, such as the New Fourth Army along the valley of the central Yangtze. Many of these peasant partisans were armed with little more than farm implements or bamboo spears. But following the Central Committee plenum in October 1938, Mao's policy was strict. Communist forces were not to fight the Japanese, unless attacked. They were to conserve their strength for seizing territory from the Nationalists. Mao made clear that Chiang Kai-shek was their ultimate opponent, their 'enemy No.1'.

Japanese raids into the countryside used massacre and mass rape as a weapon of terror. Japanese soldiers began by killing any young men in a village. 'They roped them together and then split their heads open with swords.' Then they turned their attention to the women. Corporal Nakamura wrote in his diary in

September 1938 of a raid on Lukuochen, south of Nanking: 'We seized the village and searched every house. We tried to capture the most interesting girls. The chase lasted for two hours. Niura shot one to death because it was her first time and she was ugly and was despised by the rest of us.' Both the rape of Nanking and countless local atrocities provoked a patriotic anger among the peasantry unimaginable before the war when they had had little idea of Japan or even China as a nation.

The next major battle did not take place until March 1939, when the Japanese moved large forces into Kiangsi province to attack its capital of Nanchang. Chinese resistance was fierce, despite the Japanese using poison gas again. On 27 March the city fell after house-to-house fighting. Hundreds of thousands more refugees moved westwards, bent under the heavy bundles on their backs, or pushing wooden wheelbarrows with their worldly possessions – quilts, tools and rice bowls. The hair of their womenfolk was matted with dust, and the old ones had to hobble painfully on their bound feet.

The generalissimo ordered a counter-attack to recapture Nanchang. This took the Japanese by surprise and the Nationalists fought their way into the town in late April, but the effort was too much. Chiang Kai-shek, having threatened commanders with death if the city was not taken, then had to agree to a withdrawal.

Soon after the Soviet–Japanese clashes in May on the Khalkhin Gol, which prompted Stalin to send Zhukov there as commander, the chief Soviet military adviser with Chiang Kai-shek urged him to launch a major counter-offensive to retake the city of Wuchang. Stalin misled Chiang with the idea that he was about to conclude an agreement with the British, when in fact he was already moving towards an arrangement with Nazi Germany. But Chiang stalled, suspecting rightly that Stalin simply wanted pressure to be taken off the Soviet border regions. The Nationalists were alarmed by Communist expansion and by Stalin's increasing support for Mao. Yet Chiang calculated that Stalin's main aim was to keep the Kuomintang in the war against Japan, so he felt he could resist the encroachment of Communist forces. This led to many murderous engagements, in which according to Chinese Communist figures over 11,000 people were killed.

Although Changsha had been half destroyed by the tragic fire, the Japanese were still determined to capture the town because of its strategic position. Changsha was an obvious target as it lay on the railway line between Canton and Wuchang, both of which were now occupied by strong Japanese forces. Its capture would seal off the Nationalists in their western stronghold of Szechuan. The Japanese launched their attack in August, at the same time as their comrades in the Kwantung Army were fighting General Zhukov's forces far to the north.

On 13 September, while German forces advanced deep into Poland, the Japanese advanced on Changsha with 120,000 men in six divisions. The Nationalist plan was to withdraw slowly at first in a fighting retreat, then to allow the Japanese to advance rapidly to the city, before striking with an unexpected counter-attack on their flanks. Chiang Kai-shek had already noted the Japanese tendency to over-extend themselves. Rival generals, keen to gain glory, pushed on without taking account of neighbouring formations. His programme of training since the loss of Wuchang had had an effect, and the ambush worked. The Chinese claimed to have inflicted 40,000 casualties on the Japanese.

Stalin's main priority that August while Zhukov was winning the Battle of Khalkhin Gol was to avoid broadening the conflict with Japan while he began secret negotiations with Germany. Yet the announcement of the Nazi–Soviet pact shook the Japanese leadership to the core. They found it almost impossible to believe that their German ally could come to an agreement with the Communist devil. At the same time, Stalin's refusal to fight the Japanese after Zhukov's victory was naturally a major blow to the Nationalists. The ceasefire agreement on the Mongolian and Siberian borders allowed the Japanese to concentrate on fighting the Chinese without having to look over their shoulder to the Soviet north.

Chiang Kai-shek feared that the Soviet Union and Japan might come to a secret agreement to carve up China, like the Nazi–Soviet partition of Poland in September. Mao, on the other hand, welcomed the possibility as it would greatly increase his power at the expense of the Nationalists. Chiang was also alarmed when Stalin reduced the amount of military aid he supplied to the Nationalists. And the start of the war in Europe in September meant that there was even less chance of assistance from the British and French.

For the Nationalists, the lack of outside help became increasingly grave, especially as they had lost their major industrial bases and tax revenues. The Japanese invasion had not just created a military threat. Harvests and food supplies had been destroyed. Banditry became even more widespread, with deserters and stragglers roaming as gangs. Tens of millions of refugees were trying to escape westwards, if only to save wives and daughters from the cruelty of Japanese troops. Unsanitary overcrowding in cities led to outbreaks of cholera. Malaria had spread to new regions with the mass movement of population. And typhus, the lice-borne curse of fleeing troops and refugees, became endemic. Although great efforts were made to improve Chinese medical services, both military and civilian, the few doctors could do little to help refugees, who suffered from ringworm, scabies, trachoma and all the other burdens of poverty exacerbated by severe malnutrition.

Yet, greatly encouraged by their success at Changsha, the Nationalists launched a series of counter-attacks in a 'winter offensive' right down the length of central China. They intended to cut the supply lines of exposed Japanese garrisons by impeding river traffic on the Yangtze and severing railway communications. But as soon as the Nationalist attacks began in November, the Japanese invaded the south-western province of Kwangsi with an amphibious landing. On 24 November, they took the city of Nanning and threatened the railway line to French Indochina. The few Nationalist troops in the area were taken by surprise and retreated quickly. Chiang Kai-shek rushed in reinforcements, and the fighting which lasted for two months was savage. The Japanese claimed to have killed 25,000 Chinese in one battle alone. Other Japanese offensives further north seized regions important to the Nationalists for grain supplies and recruitment. They also built up their bomber force in China to raid deep into the Nationalists' rear areas and batter their new capital of Chungking. The Communists, meanwhile, secretly negotiated a deal with the Japanese in central China under which they would not attack the railways providing the Japanese would leave alone their New Fourth Army in the countryside.

The world situation was very unfavourable to the Nationalists, since Stalin was in an alliance with Germany and warned
Chiang Kai-shek off any dealings with Britain and France. The
Soviet leader feared that the British as well as the Chinese wanted
to manoeuvre him into a war with Japan. In December 1939,
during the Winter War against Finland, the Nationalists faced a
terrible dilemma when the Soviet Union was faced with expulsion
from the League of Nations for its invasion. They did not want
to provoke Stalin, yet could not use their veto to save him as that
would anger the western powers. In the end, their representative
abstained. This angered Moscow without satisfying the British
and French. Soviet deliveries of military material dropped significantly and were not restored to their previous level for a year.
To put pressure on Stalin to relent, Chiang Kai-shek made noises
about pursuing peace talks with the Japanese.

Even so, the Nationalists' main hope for the future now lay
increasingly with the United States, which had started to condemn Japanese aggression and to reinforce its own bases in the
Pacific. But Chiang Kai-shek also faced two internal challenges.
The Chinese Communist Party under Mao was becoming much
more assertive, increasing its hold on territory behind Japanese
lines, and claiming that it would defeat the Kuomintang at the
end of the Sino-Japanese War. And on 30 March 1940, the Japanese established Wang Ching-wei's 'National Government' of
what was called the Reformed Kuomintang in Nanking. The real
Nationalists referred to him simply as 'the criminal traitor'. They
were concerned that his regime might be recognized not only by
Germany and Italy, Japan's only European allies, but by other
foreign powers as well.

5

Norway and Denmark

Hitler had originally wanted his attack on the Low Countries and France to begin in November 1939, as soon as German divisions could be transferred from Poland. Above all he wanted to seize Channel ports and airfields to strike against Britain, which he regarded as his most dangerous enemy. He was in a desperate hurry to achieve a decisive victory in the west before the United States was in a position to intervene.

German generals were uneasy. They believed that the size of the French army might lead to another stalemate as in the First World War. Germany possessed neither the fuel nor the raw materials for an extended campaign. Some were also reluctant to attack neutral Holland and Belgium, but such moralistic qualms – like the few protests over the killing of Polish civilians by the SS – were furiously dismissed by Hitler. He was even angrier when told that the Wehrmacht was dangerously short of munitions, especially bombs, and of tanks. Even the brief Polish campaign had exhausted their stocks and emphasized the inadequacy of the Mark I and Mark II tanks.

Hitler blamed the army's procurement system for the failure and soon brought in Dr Fritz Todt, his construction chief, to run it. And in a characteristic decision, Hitler decided to use up all raw-material reserves 'without regard to the future and at the expense of later war years'. They could be replenished, he argued, as soon as the Wehrmacht captured the coal and steel areas of the Netherlands, Belgium, France and Luxembourg.

Mists and fogs in the late autumn of 1939 had in any case forced Hitler to accept that the Luftwaffe could not provide the vital support needed for his November target date. (It is tantalizing to speculate how differently things might have turned out if Hitler had launched his attack then rather than six months later.) Hitler then ordered plans to be drawn up for an assault on neutral

Holland in mid-January 1940. Astonishingly, both the Dutch and Belgians received warnings of this from the ministry of foreign affairs in Rome. This was because many Italians, especially Mussolini's foreign minister Count Ciano, had been made both nervous and angry by Germany's rush to war in September. They feared that they would be attacked first in the Mediterranean by the British. In addition, Oberst Hans Oster, an anti-Nazi in the Abwehr (German military intelligence), tipped off the Dutch military attaché in Berlin. Then, on 10 January 1940, a German liaison plane, which had become lost in thick cloud, crash-landed on Belgian territory. The Luftwaffe staff officer on board, who had a copy of the plans to attack Holland, tried to burn the papers, but Belgian soldiers arrived before they were all destroyed.

Paradoxically, this turn of events would prove to be most unfortunate for the Allies. Assuming that a German invasion was imminent, their formations in north-eastern France destined to defend Belgium were immediately moved to the frontier, thus giving away their own plan. Hitler and the OKW felt obliged to rethink their strategy. The replacement plan would be Generalleutnant Erich von Manstein's brilliant project of attacking with panzer divisions through the Ardennes, then striking for the Channel behind the backs of the British and French armies due to advance into Belgium. All the postponements lulled the Allied forces languishing on the French frontiers into a false sense of security. Many soldiers, and even planners in the War Office, began to believe that Hitler would never summon up the courage to invade France.

Grossadmiral Raeder, unlike the senior army commanders, was in complete agreement with Hitler's aggressive strategy. He went even further and urged the Führer to include the invasion of Norway in his plans to give the German navy a flank from which to operate against British shipping. He also used the argument that the northern Norwegian port of Narvik should be seized to secure the supply of Swedish iron ore, so vital for Germany's war industries. He had brought Vidkun Quisling, the pro-Nazi leader in Norway, to meet Hitler, and Quisling helped persuade the Führer that a German occupation of Norway was essential. The threat of British and French intervention in Norway, as part of a plan to support the Finns, had disturbed

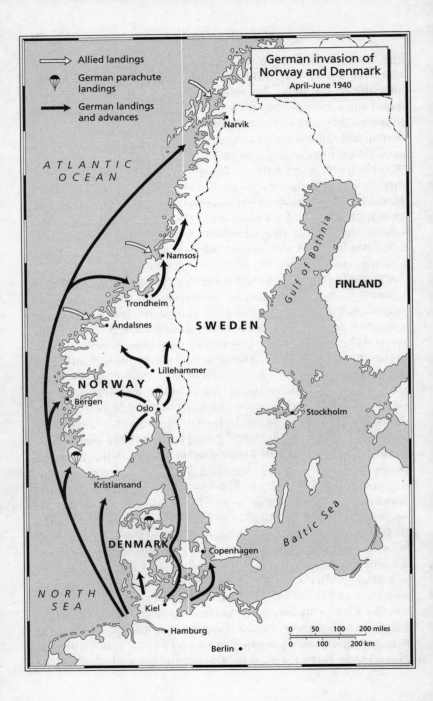

him. And if the British established a naval presence in southern Norway, they might cut off the Baltic. Himmler also had his eye on Scandinavia, but as a recruiting ground for his Waffen-SS military formations. Yet Nazi attempts to infiltrate the Scandinavian countries had not been as successful as they had hoped.

The Nazis did not know that Churchill had originally wanted to go much further than just seal off the Baltic. The pugnacious First Lord of the Admiralty had originally wanted to take the war right into the Baltic by sending a surface fleet there, but, fortunately for the Royal Navy, Operation Catherine was thwarted. Churchill also wanted to halt the supply of Swedish ore transported to Germany from the port of Narvik, but Chamberlain and the War Cabinet were firmly against the violation of Norwegian neutrality.

Churchill then took a calculated risk. On 16 February, HMS *Cossack*, a British tribal-class destroyer, intercepted the *Graf Spee*'s supply ship, the *Altmark*, in Norwegian waters to release some British merchant navy prisoners held on board. The famous cry of the bluejacket boarding party to the prisoners below – 'The Navy's here!' – thrilled a British public who had been suffering the inconveniences of war with little of its drama. In response, the Kriegsmarine increased its presence at sea. But on 22 February two German destroyers were attacked by Heinkel 111s because the Luftwaffe had not been informed in time that they were in the area. The destroyers were hit and struck mines. Both sank.

German warships were then called back to harbour, although for another reason. Hitler issued orders on 1 March to prepare for the invasion of Denmark and Norway, an operation which would require all available surface ships. His decision to attack the two countries alarmed both the German army and the Luftwaffe. They believed that they faced a hard enough problem already with the invasion of France. A diversion in Norway just beforehand might prove disastrous. Göring especially was furious, but mainly out of pique. He felt that he had not been properly consulted first.

On 7 March, Hitler signed the directive. It then seemed to take on a greater urgency, because air reconnaissance reported that the Royal Navy was concentrating its forces at Scapa Flow. This was presumed to be in preparation for a landing on the Norwegian coast. Yet the news a few days later of the Soviet–Finnish accord to end their conflict produced mixed feelings in the German high command. Even Kriegsmarine planners, who had been pressing all along for intervention in Norway, now thought that the pressure was off, since the British and French had no further excuse to land in Scandinavia. But Hitler and others, including Grossadmiral Raeder, felt that preparations were so far advanced that the invasion had to go ahead. A German occupation would also be a very effective way of maintaining pressure on Sweden to continue with its deliveries of iron ore. And Hitler liked the idea of Germany having bases which faced the eastern coastline of Britain and offered access to the northern Atlantic.

The simultaneous invasion of Norway (Weserübung North), with six divisions, and Denmark (Weserübung South), with two divisions and a motorized rifle brigade, was fixed for 9 April. Transport ships escorted by the Kriegsmarine would land their forces at several points, including Narvik, Trondheim and Bergen. The Luftwaffe's X Fliegerkorps would fly paratroopers and airlanding units to other places, especially Oslo. Copenhagen and seven other key towns in Denmark would be attacked by land and from the sea. The OKW suspected that they were in a race for Norway against the British, but they were in fact comfortably ahead.

Chamberlain, unaware of German plans, had stood down the Anglo-French expeditionary force for Norway and Finland after the Soviet–Finnish pact was signed. This was against the advice of the chief of the imperial general staff, General Sir Edmund Ironside. Chamberlain, who dreaded extending the war to neutral Scandinavia, just hoped that Germany and the Soviet Union would now drift apart. But Allied inaction and pious hopes that they could conduct the war according to League of Nations rules were unlikely to impress anyone.

Daladier, when still French prime minister, advocated a much more forceful strategy, providing it kept any fighting away from France. As well as bombing the Baku and mid-Caucasian oilfields, an idea which horrified Chamberlain, Daladier also wanted to occupy the mining area of Petsamo in northern Finland near the Soviet naval base of Murmansk. In addition, he argued strongly for landings on the Norwegian coast and complete control of the North Sea to prevent Swedish iron ore from reaching Germany. The British, however, suspected that he wanted to divert the war to Scandinavia to reduce the chances of a German attack on France. They believed this partly because Daladier obstinately opposed the British plan to block shipping on the Rhine by dropping mines. In any case, Daladier was forced to resign as prime minister on 20 March. When Paul Reynaud took over, Daladier became minister for war in the reshuffle.

Haggling between the Allies over their rival operations wasted precious time. Daladier forced Reynaud to continue to oppose the mining of the Rhine. The British agreed to the French plan to mine the waters off Narvik, which was carried out on 8 April. Churchill wanted to have a landing force ready, as he was certain that the Germans would react, but Chamberlain remained too cautious.

Unknown to the British, a large German naval force with infantry on board had already set sail from Wilhelmshaven on 7 April for Trondheim and Narvik in northern Norway. The battle-cruisers *Gneisenau* and *Scharnhorst* were accompanied by the heavy cruiser *Admiral Hipper* and fourteen destroyers. Another four groups headed for ports in southern Norway.

A British aircraft sighted the main task force under Vice Admiral Günther Lütjens. RAF bombers launched an attack, but failed to score a single hit. The British Home Fleet under Admiral of the Fleet Sir Charles Forbes put to sea from Scapa Flow, but it was well behind. The only naval force in a position to intercept was the battle-cruiser HMS *Renown* and its escorting destroyers acting in support of the mining operation off Narvik. One of these destroyers, HMS *Glowworm*, sighted a German destroyer and gave chase, but Lütjens sent in the *Hipper*, which sank the *Glowworm* as she attempted to ram her.

The Royal Navy, determined to concentrate its forces for a major naval battle, ordered the disembarkation of troops on other warships ready to sail to Narvik and Trondheim. Yet the Home Fleet was having little success in intercepting the main German task force. This gave Lütjens time to send his destroyers into Narvik, but his battle squadron then sighted the *Renown* at dawn on 9 April. The *Renown*, with impressively accurate fire in the heavy seas, battered the *Gneisenau* and damaged the

Scharnhorst, forcing Lütjens to withdraw while his ships carried out emergency repairs.

The German destroyers, having sunk two small Norwegian warships, landed their troops and seized Narvik. Also on 9 April, the *Hipper* and her destroyers landed troops in Trondheim, and another force entered Bergen. Stavanger was also taken by paratroops and two airlanded infantry battalions. Oslo proved a much harder task, even though the Kriegsmarine had sent the new heavy cruiser *Blücher* and the pocket battleship *Lützow* (the former *Deutschland*). Norwegian shore batteries and torpedoes sank the *Blücher*; the *Lützow* had to withdraw after also suffering damage.

At Narvik the following morning, five British destroyers managed to enter the fjords unseen. A heavy snowfall had hidden them from the offshore screen of U-boats. As a result they surprised five German destroyers in the process of refuelling. They sank two of them, but were then attacked by other German destroyers from side-fjords. Two Royal Navy destroyers were sunk and a third badly damaged. Unable to break out, the surviving ships had to wait until 13 April, when the battleship HMS *Warspite* and nine destroyers came to their rescue and finished off every German warship remaining.

In other actions down the coast, two German cruisers, the *Königsberg* and the *Karlsruhe*, were sunk, the former by bombs from carrier-launched Skuas and the latter torpedoed by a submarine. The *Lützow* was so badly damaged that it had to be towed back to Kiel. But the Royal Navy's partial successes did nothing to stop the transport of over 100,000 German troops to Norway in the course of the month.

The occupation of Denmark proved even easier for the Germans. They managed to land troops in Copenhagen before the shore batteries could be alerted. Denmark's government felt obliged to accept the terms dictated by Berlin. The Norwegians, however, rejected any notion of a 'peaceful occupation'. The King, withdrawing with the government from Oslo on 9 April, ordered mobilization. Although German forces seized many bases in their coups de main, they found themselves isolated until reinforcements arrived in strength.

Because of the Royal Navy's decision to disembark troops on 9 April, the first Allied troops did not put to sea until two days later. The situation was not helped by an impatient Churchill changing his mind and interfering constantly in operational decisions, to the exasperation of General Ironside and the Royal Navy. Norwegian troops meanwhile attacked the German 3rd Mountain Division with great bravery. But with German forces already established in Narvik and Trondheim, the Anglo-French landings had to be made on their flanks. A direct assault on the harbours was considered too dangerous. Only on 28 April did British troops and two battalions of the French Foreign Legion begin to land, reinforced by a Polish brigade. They captured Narvik and were able to destroy the port, but the Luftwaffe's air supremacy ensured that the Allied operation was doomed. In the course of the next month the German onslaught on the Low Countries and France would force an evacuation of Allied troops from the northern flank and thus the surrender of Norwegian troops.

The Norwegian royal family and the government sailed to England to continue the war. Raeder's obsession with Norway, with which he had infected Hitler, was however to prove a very mixed blessing for Nazi Germany. The army continued to complain throughout the war that the occupation of Norway tied down far too many troops, who would be of much greater use on other fronts. From an Allied point of view, the Norway campaign was far more disastrous. Although the Royal Navy managed to sink half the Kriegsmarine's destroyers, the combined operation was the worst example of inter-service cooperation. Many senior officers also suspected that Churchill's misdirected enthusiasm had been influenced by a secret desire to blot out the memory of his ill-fated Dardanelles expedition in the First World War. Responsibility for the Norway debacle, as Churchill privately acknowledged later, rested much more with him than with Neville Chamberlain. Yet, with the cruel irony of politics, the reverse would bring him to replace Chamberlain as prime minister.

Along the French frontier, the Phoney War, or *drôle de guerre*, or *Sitzkrieg* as the Germans called it, lasted far longer than Hitler had planned. He despised the French army and he was certain that Dutch resistance would collapse immediately. All he needed was the right plan to replace the one passed to the Allies by the Belgians.

The most senior army officers did not like General von Manstein's daring project and tried to suppress it. But Manstein, when finally given access to Hitler, argued that a German invasion of Holland and Belgium would draw the British and French forces forward from the Franco-Belgian frontier. They could then be cut off by a thrust through the Ardennes and across the River Meuse towards the Somme estuary and Boulogne. Hitler grabbed at the plan, because he needed a knock-out blow. Characteristically, he later claimed that it had been his idea all along.

The British Expeditionary Force with four divisions had taken up positions along the Belgian frontier the previous October. By May 1940, it had been increased to one armoured and ten infantry divisions under General Lord Gort VC. Gort, despite the considerable size of his command, had to take orders from the French commander in the north-east, General Alphonse Georges, and the strangely diffident French commander-in-chief, General Maurice Gamelin. There was no joint Allied command as in the First World War.

The greatest problem both Gort and Georges faced was the obstinate refusal of the Brussels government to compromise Belgium's neutrality, even though it knew that the Germans planned to attack. Gort and his neighbouring French formations would thus have to wait for the German invasion before they could move forward. The Dutch, who had managed to stay neutral in the First World War, were even more determined not to provoke the Germans by making joint plans with the French or the Belgians. Yet they still hoped that Allied forces would come to support their small and under-equipped army when the fighting started. The Grand Duchy of Luxembourg, although sympathetic to the Allies, knew that it could do no more than close its border and point out to the German invaders that they were violating its neutrality.

There was another fatal flaw in French planning. The Maginot Line stretched only from the Swiss border to the southernmost point of the Belgian frontier opposite the Ardennes. Neither the French nor British staffs imagined the Germans attempting a thrust through this heavily wooded region. The Belgians warned the French that this was a danger, but the supercilious Gamelin dismissed the possibility. Reynaud, who called Gamelin 'the nerveless philosopher', wanted to sack him, but Daladier, as minister of war, insisted on keeping him. The paralysis of decision extended right to the top.

The lack of support in France for the war was barely concealed. German claims that Britain had forced the French into the war, and then would leave them to face the bulk of the fighting, were effectively corrosive. Even the French general staff led by General Gamelin showed little enthusiasm. The utterly inadequate gesture of a limited advance near Saarbrücken in September had represented almost an insult to the Poles.

France's defensive mentality affected its military organization. The majority of its tank units, although not technically inferior to the German panzers, were insufficiently trained. Apart from three mechanized divisions – a fourth was hurriedly put together under the command of Colonel Charles de Gaulle – French tanks were split up among its infantry formations. Both French and British forces were short of effective anti-tank guns – the British two-pounder was generally referred to as a 'pea-shooter' – and their radio communications were primitive to say the least. In a war of movement, field telephones and landlines would prove to be of little use.

The French air force was still in a lamentable state. General Vuillemin had written to Daladier during the Czechoslovak crisis in 1938 to warn him that the Luftwaffe would rapidly destroy their squadrons. Only marginal improvements had been made since then. The French therefore expected the RAF to take on most of the burden, but Air Chief Marshal Sir Hugh Dowding, the head of Fighter Command, was deeply opposed to deploying aircraft to France. Fighter Command's primary role was the defence of the United Kingdom, and in any case French airfields lacked effective anti-aircraft protection. In addition, neither the RAF nor the French air force had trained to act in close support for their own ground forces. The Allies had failed to learn this lesson of the Polish campaign, as well as others, such as the Luftwaffe's skill at ruthless pre-emptive strikes against airfields, and the German army's ability with sudden armoured thrusts to disorientate the defenders.

After several more postponements, partly due to the Norwegian campaign and partly, in the last few days, to unfavourable weather forecasts, the German invasion in the west was finally set. Friday, 10 May was to be 'X-Day'. Hitler, with his customary lack of modesty, predicted the 'greatest victory in world history'.

6

Onslaught in the West

MAY 1940

Thursday, 9 May 1940 was a beautiful spring day in most of northern Europe. A war correspondent observed Belgian soldiers planting pansies round their barracks. There had been rumours of a German attack, with reports of pontoon bridges being assembled close to the border, but these were discounted in Brussels. Many seemed to think that Hitler was about to attack south into the Balkans, not westwards. In any case, few imagined that he would invade four countries – Holland, Belgium, Luxembourg and France – all in one go.

In Paris, life continued as usual. The capital had seldom looked so beautiful. Chestnut trees had burst into leaf. Cafés were full. Without any apparent irony, 'J'attendrai' continued as the hit song. Race meetings went on at Auteuil, and smart women thronged the Ritz. Most striking of all were the many officers and soldiers in the streets. General Gamelin had just reinstated permission to go on leave. By a curious coincidence, Paul Reynaud, the prime minister, had offered his resignation that morning to President Albert Lebrun, because Daladier had again refused to sack the commander-in-chief.

In Britain, the BBC news announced that the night before, thirty-three Conservatives had voted against Chamberlain's government in the House of Commons following a debate on the Norway fiasco. Leo Amery's speech attacking Chamberlain would prove fatal for the prime minister. He ended it with Cromwell's dismissal of the Long Parliament in 1653: 'Depart, I say, and let us have done with you. In the name of God, go!' Amid tumultuous scenes, with chants of 'Go! go! go!', a shaken Chamberlain left the chamber, trying to conceal his emotions.

Throughout that sunny day, politicians in Westminster and the clubs of St James's discussed the next step in either hushed or heated tones. Who would succeed Chamberlain: Churchill or Lord

Halifax, the foreign secretary? For most Conservatives, Edward Halifax was the natural choice. Many still distrusted Churchill as a dangerous, even unscrupulous maverick. Yet Chamberlain still tried to hold on. He approached the Labour Party, suggesting a coalition, but was told brusquely that they were not prepared to serve under him as leader. That evening he was forced to face the fact that he had to resign. Thus Britain found itself in a political limbo on the very eve of the great German offensive in the west.

In Berlin, Hitler dictated his proclamation for the morrow to the armies of the western front. 'The battle beginning today will decide the fate of the German nation for the next thousand years,' it concluded. As the moment approached, the Führer was increasingly optimistic, especially after the success of the Norwegian campaign. He predicted that France would surrender within six weeks. The audacious glider assault on the principal Belgian fortress of Eben-Emael near the Dutch border excited him the most. His special train, the *Amerika*, steamed off that afternoon to take him to a new Führer headquarters, designated the Felsennest (or Cliff Nest), in the forested hills of the Eifel close to the Ardennes. At 21.00 hours, the codeword Danzig was sent to all army groups. Meteorological reports had confirmed that the next day would provide perfect visibility for the Luftwaffe. Secrecy had been maintained so carefully that, after all the postponements of the attack date, some officers had been away from their regiments when the order to move out came through.

In the north, astride the Rhine, the German Eighteenth Army was ready to strike into Holland towards Amsterdam and Rotterdam. A third force would head north of Tilburg and Breda towards the sea. Just to their south was Generaloberst Walther von Reichenau's Sixth Army. Its objectives were Antwerp and Brussels. Generaloberst von Rundstedt's Army Group A, with forty-four divisions in all, contained the main panzer forces. Generaloberst Günther von Kluge's Fourth Army would strike into Belgium towards Charleroi and Dinant. The thrust by all these armies into the Low Countries from the east would bring the British and French forces racing northwards to join up with the Belgians and Dutch. At this point, Manstein's *Sichelschnitt*, or sickle-cut, plan would come into play. Generaloberst Wilhelm List's Twelfth Army would advance across northern Luxembourg and the Belgian Ardennes to cross the River Meuse south of Givet and near Sedan, the scene of France's great disaster in 1870.

Once over the Meuse, the panzer group commanded by General der Kavallerie Ewald von Kleist would head towards Amiens, Abbeville and the Somme estuary on the Channel. This would cut off the BEF, the British Expeditionary Force, and the French Seventh, First and Ninth Armies. The German Sixteenth Army would meanwhile advance through southern Luxembourg to protect Kleist's exposed left flank. Generaloberst Ritter von Leeb's Army Group C, with two more armies, would maintain pressure on the Maginot Line to the south so that the French would feel unable to send forces north to rescue their forces trapped in Flanders.

Manstein's left-hook *Sichelschnitt* was thus a reversal of the version of the right-hook Schlieffen plan attempted in 1914, which the French now expected them to try a second time. Admiral Wilhelm Canaris of the Abwehr mounted a very effective disinformation campaign, spreading rumours in Belgium and elsewhere that this was precisely what the Germans were planning. Manstein was confident that Gamelin would send the bulk of his mobile forces into Belgium, because they had promptly moved towards the border following the capture of the documents after the plane crash. (Many senior Allied officers subsequently believed that the plane crash had been a clever plant by the Germans, when it had really been a genuine accident, as Hitler's fury at the time confirmed.) In any case, Manstein's plan to draw the Allies into Belgium played to another French preoccupation. General Gamelin, like most of his countrymen, preferred to fight on Belgian territory rather than in French Flanders, which had suffered such destruction in the First World War.

Hitler was also keen that airborne troops and special forces should play a part. He had summoned Generalleutnant Kurt Student to the Reichschancellery the previous October and ordered him to prepare groups to seize the fortress of Eben-Emael and key bridges on the Albert Canal, using assault groups in gliders. Brandenburger commandos in Dutch uniforms were to secure bridges while others disguised as tourists would infiltrate Luxembourg just before the offensive began. But the main airborne coup de main would consist of an assault on three airfields round The Hague, with units from the 7th Fallschirmjäger Division and the 22nd Luftlande Division under Generalmajor Hans Graf von Sponeck. Their objective was to seize the city and take prisoner the government and members of the royal family.

The Germans had produced a lot of diversionary 'noise': circulating rumours of a concentration on Holland and Belgium, attacks on the Maginot Line and even the suggestion that they might circumvent its southern end by violating Swiss neutrality. Gamelin was certain that the Germans' onslaught on Holland and Belgium would be their main attack. He paid little attention to the sector facing the Ardennes, convinced that its thickly wooded hills were 'impenetrable'. The roads and forest tracks were large enough for the German tanks while the canopy of beech, fir and oak provided perfect concealment for Kleist's panzer group.

Generaloberst von Rundstedt had been reassured by the photo-reconnaissance expert attached to his headquarters that the French defensive positions covering the Meuse were far from finished. Unlike the Luftwaffe, which mounted constant photo-reconnaissance flights over the Allied lines, the French air force refused to send aircraft over German territory. Yet Gamelin's own military intelligence – the Deuxième Bureau – possessed a remarkably accurate picture of the German order of battle. They had located the bulk of the panzer divisions in the Eifel just beyond the Ardennes and had also discovered that the Germans were interested in the routes from Sedan towards Abbeville. The French military attaché in Berne, tipped off by the very effective Swiss intelligence service, warned Gamelin's headquarters on 30 April that the Germans would attack between 8 and 10 May, with Sedan lying on the 'principal axis' of advance.

Gamelin and other senior French commanders nevertheless remained in a state of denial about the threat. 'France is not Poland' was their attitude. General Charles Huntziger, whose Second Army was responsible for the Sedan sector, had only three third-rate divisions on that part of the front. He knew how unprepared and unenthusiastic his reservists were for the fight. Huntziger begged Gamelin for four more divisions because his defences were not ready, but Gamelin refused. Some accounts, however, accuse Huntziger of complacency and say that General André Corap, commanding the neighbouring

German invasion of the
Low Countries and France
May 1940

German Army
Allied Army

North Sea

ENGLAND

HOLLAND
The Hague
Rotterdam
Breda
NL
Antwerp
Belg
Albert Canal
GERMANY
Cologne
18
6
Eben-Emael
Rhine
BELGIUM
Dunkirk
Calais
FR 7
Brussels
Dyle
Scheldt
Wavre
Meuse
Boulogne
BEF
Lille
FR 1
Namur
Malmedy
4
Ardennes
12
Arras
FR 9
Dinant
Bastogne
16
Abbeville
Amiens
Somme
FR 2
Sedan
LUX.
Luxembourg
Moselle
Laon
FRANCE
Seine
Aisne
FR 3
Metz
Maginot Line
1
Seine

0   20   40   60   80 miles
0   50   100 km

Ninth Army, was more aware of the threat. In any case, the concrete positions overlooking the River Meuse built by civilian contractors did not even have embrasures facing in the right direction. Minefields and barbed-wire entanglements were totally inadequate, and suggestions that trees should be felled across the forest tracks on the east bank of the river were rejected because the French cavalry might want to advance.

In the early hours of Friday, 10 May, word of the impending attack reached Brussels. Telephones began ringing all over the city. Police rushed from hotel to hotel to tell night porters to wake any military personnel they had staying there. Officers, still struggling into their uniforms, ran to find taxis to rejoin their regiments or headquarters. As dawn broke, the Luftwaffe appeared. Belgian biplane fighters took off to intercept, but their antiquated machines stood no chance. Civilians in Brussels awoke to the sound of anti-aircraft fire.

Reports of enemy movement had also reached Gamelin's headquarters in the very early hours, but they were dismissed as an overreaction after so many false alarms. The commander-in-chief was not woken until 06.30 hours. His Grand Quartier Général in the medieval fortress of Vincennes on the eastern edge of Paris was far from the battlefield but close to the centre of power. Gamelin was a politician's soldier, adept at maintaining his position in the byzantine world of the Third Republic. Unlike the ferociously right-wing General Maxime Weygand, whom he had replaced in 1935, the Delphic Gamelin had avoided an antirepublican reputation.

Gamelin, credited with planning the Battle of the Marne in 1914 as a brilliant young staff officer, was now a small, fastidious man of sixty-eight in immaculately cut breeches. Many remarked on his surprisingly limp handshake. He enjoyed a rarefied atmosphere with his favourite staff officers who, sharing his intellectual interests, discussed art, philosophy and literature as if they were acting in a high-brow French play cut off from the real world. Since Gamelin did not believe in radio communications and possessed none, the orders to prepare to advance into Belgium were passed by telephone. The French commander-in-chief that morning exuded confidence that the Germans were playing into his hands. One staff officer watched him humming a martial tune as he strode up and down the corridors.

Word of the attack had also reached London. A Cabinet minister went to see Winston Churchill in the Admiralty at 06.00 hours only to find him smoking a cigar while eating eggs and bacon. Churchill was waiting to hear the outcome of Chamberlain's deliberations. Chamberlain, like the King and many Conservative grandees, wanted Lord Halifax to succeed him if he had to go. But Halifax, who had a profound sense of public service, guessed that Churchill would make a better war leader and refused the premiership. Churchill had also emphasized the point that Halifax, as a member of the House of Lords, could not effectively run the government from outside the Commons. In Britain that day, the drama of political change overshadowed the far more serious events across the Channel.

Gamelin's plan was for General Henri Giraud's Seventh Army on the extreme left to advance rapidly up the coast past Antwerp and join up with the Dutch army round Breda. This addition to his advance into the Low Countries would prove a major element in the disaster to follow, because the Seventh Army was his only reserve in north-eastern France. The Dutch had hoped for more assistance, but this was wildly over-optimistic after their refusal to coordinate plans and given the distance to be covered from the French frontier.

According to Gamelin's so-called Plan D, a Belgian force of twenty-two divisions would defend the River Dyle from Antwerp to Louvain. Gort's BEF with nine infantry divisions and one armoured division would join their right and defend the Dyle east of Brussels from Louvain to Wavre. On the BEF's southern flank, General Georges Blanchard's First French Army would hold the gap between Wavre and Namur, while General Corap's Ninth Army would line the River Meuse south from Namur to west of Sedan. The Germans were aware of every detail, having broken the French codes with great ease.

Gamelin had assumed that the Belgian troops defending the Albert Canal from Antwerp to Maastricht would be able to hold off the Germans long enough for the Allies to advance to what they imagined would be previously prepared positions. On paper, the Dyle plan appeared to be a satisfactory compromise, but it utterly failed to predict the speed, ruthlessness and deception of the Wehrmacht's combined operations. The lessons of the Polish campaign had simply not been absorbed.

Once again, the Luftwaffe sent in pre-emptive dawn attacks against airfields in Holland, Belgium and France. Messerschmitts managed to shoot up French aircraft lined up at dispersal. Polish pilots were horrified by 'the French insouciance' and lack of enthusiasm to engage the enemy. RAF squadrons scrambled when ordered up, but once in the air they had little idea where to go. With no effective radar, ground control was of little help. Even so, on that first day the RAF Hurricanes still managed to bring down over thirty German bombers, but they had not had to contend with German fighter escorts, and the Luftwaffe did not make that mistake again.

The bravest pilots were those flying the obsolete Fairey Battle light bombers sent to attack a German column advancing through Luxembourg. Slow and inadequately armed, they were dangerously vulnerable to both enemy fighters and ground fire. Thirteen out of thirty-two were shot down and all the others damaged. The French lost fifty-six aircraft destroyed on that day out of 879 and the RAF forty-nine out of 384. The Dutch air force lost half its strength in a morning. But the battle was far from one-sided. The Luftwaffe lost 126 machines destroyed, of which most were Junkers 52 transports.

The bulk of the Luftwaffe effort was concentrated against Holland in the hope of knocking the country out of the fight rapidly, but also to reinforce the impression that the main attack was coming in the north. This was all part of what the military analyst Basil Liddell Hart later called the 'matador's cloak' tactic to draw Gamelin's mobile forces into the trap.

In a new development in warfare, Junkers 52 transport planes, escorted by Messerschmitts, began dropping the airborne assault troops. The main objective, to seize The Hague with units of the 7th Fallschirmjäger and the 22nd Luftlande Divisions, was however a costly failure. Many of the slow transport planes were shot down en route to the target and less than half the force reached the three airfields around the Dutch capital. Dutch units fought back, inflicting many casualties on the paratroopers, while both the royal family and the government made their escape. Other detachments from the same two divisions managed to seize the Waalhaven airfield near Rotterdam as well as key bridges. But to the east Dutch troops had reacted very quickly and blown the bridges round Maastricht before German commandos, dressed in Dutch uniforms, could seize them.

Hitler at the Felsennest is said to have wept with joy when he heard that the Allies were starting to march into the Belgian trap. He was also thrilled that the assault group of paratroopers in gliders had managed to drop exactly on to the glacis of the Eban-Emael fortress at the confluence of the Meuse and the Albert Canal. They trapped the large Belgian garrison beneath them until the Sixth Army arrived the following evening. Other paratroop detachments seized bridges over the Albert Canal, and the Germans rapidly breached the first main lines of defence. Even if the principal airborne operation against The Hague had failed, the landing of paratroopers deep inside Holland created fearful panic and confusion. It started the wild rumours of paratroops coming down dressed as nuns, of poisoned sweets dropped for children and of fifth columnists signalling from attic windows: a phenomenon which infected Belgium, France and later Britain.

In London, the War Cabinet met no fewer than three times during that day, 10 May. Chamberlain had at first wanted to stay on as prime minister, insisting that there should be no change of government while the battle across the Channel continued, but when confirmation came through that the Labour Party refused to support him, he knew that he had to resign. Halifax again rejected the premiership, so Chamberlain was driven to Buckingham Palace to advise King George VI to send for Churchill. The King, depressed that his friend Halifax had turned down the post, had no alternative.

Now that Churchill's position was confirmed, he wasted no time in turning his attention back to the war and the advance of the BEF into Belgium. The 12th Royal Lancers in their armoured cars had moved out first as a reconnaissance screen at 10.20 hours. Most other British units followed during the day. The 3rd Division's leading column was halted at the border by an uninformed Belgian official demanding a 'permit to enter Belgium'. A truck simply smashed open the barrier. Almost every road into Belgium was filled with columns of military vehicles heading north to the line of the River Dyle, which the 12th Lancers reached at 18.00 hours.

The Luftwaffe's concentration first on airfields and then on Holland had at least meant that the Allied armies advancing into Belgium were spared from air attack. The French appear to have been slower off the mark. Many French formations did not start moving until the evening. This was a grave mistake as the roads rapidly became clogged with refugees coming in the other direction. Their Seventh Army, on the other hand, hurried forward along the Channel coast towards Antwerp, but soon suffered from concentrated Luftwaffe attacks when they reached southern Holland.

Along the route on that hot day, Belgians emerged from cafés to offer mugs of beer to the red-faced marching soldiers, a generous gesture which was not universally welcomed by officers and NCOs. Other British units crossed through Brussels at dusk. 'The Belgians stood cheering,' wrote an observer, 'and the men in the trucks and Bren carriers waved back. Every man was wearing lilac, purple on his steel helmet, in the barrel of his rifle, stuck in his web equipment. They smiled and saluted with thumbs up – a gesture which at first shocked the Belgians, to whom it had a very rude significance, but which they soon recognised as a sign of cheerful confidence. It was a great sight, one to bring tears to the eyes, as this military machine moved forward in all its strength, efficiently, quietly, with the British military police guiding it on at every crossroads as if they were dealing with rush-hour London.'

The great battle, however, was about to be decided well to the south-east in the Ardennes, with Rundstedt's Army Group A. His huge columns of vehicles snaked through the forests which hid them from Allied aircraft. Overhead, a screen of Messerschmitt fighters flew ready to attack enemy bombers or reconnaissance aircraft. Any vehicle or tank which broke down was pushed off the road. The march-table was rigidly adhered to, and despite the fears of many staff officers the system worked far better than expected. All the vehicles in Panzer Group Kleist had a small white 'K' stencilled back and front to give them absolute priority.

Marching infantry and all other transport had to get off the road as soon as they appeared.

At 04.30 hours, General der Panzertruppen Heinz Guderian, the commander of XIX Corps, had accompanied the 1st Panzer Division as it crossed the Luxembourg border. Brandenburger commandos had already seized some important crossroads and bridges. Luxembourg gendarmes could do little more than point out that the Wehrmacht was violating the country's neutrality before they were taken prisoner. The Grand Duke and his family just managed to escape in time, unrecognized by the Brandenburgers.

To the north, XLI Panzer Corps advanced in the direction of the Meuse at Monthermé, and even further north on their right General der Panzertruppen Hermann Hoth's XV Corps, led by Generalmajor Erwin Rommel's 7th Panzer Division, headed for Dinant. But several of the panzer divisions, to their dismay – and Kleist's alarm – found themselves delayed by bridges blown by Belgian sappers attached to the Chasseurs d'Ardennes.

At first light on 11 May, Rommel's 7th Panzer Division, with the 5th Panzer Division behind and to his right, pushed forward again and reached the River Ourthe. The French cavalry screen managed to blow the bridge just in time, but then retreated after a brisk exchange of fire. Divisional pioneers soon constructed a pontoon bridge, and the advance continued towards the Meuse. Rommel noted that, in his division's clashes with the French, the Germans came off best if they immediately opened fire with everything they had.

To the south, Generalleutnant Georg-Hans Reinhardt's XLI Panzer Corps, heading for Bastogne and then Monthermé, had been held up by part of Guderian's force crossing their front. Guderian's XIX Corps itself suffered confusion partly due to a change in orders. But the French cavalry screen, consisting of mounted units and light tanks, was also in disarray. Although the strength of the German drive towards the Meuse was increasingly evident, the French air force mounted no sorties. The RAF sent in eight more Fairey Battles. Seven were destroyed, mostly by ground fire.

Allied aircraft attacking the Maastricht and Albert Canal bridges to the north-west also suffered heavily, but these attempts were too little and too late. The German Eighteenth Army was by now deep into Dutch territory, where resistance was crumbling. Reichenau's Sixth Army was across the Albert Canal, bypassing Liège, while another corps advanced on Antwerp.

The BEF, now established along the pitifully narrow River Dyle, and the French formations advancing to their positions received little attention from the Luftwaffe. This worried some of the more perceptive officers who wondered whether they were being drawn into a trap. The most immediate concern, however, was the French First Army's slow progress, now made infinitely worse by the growing volume of Belgian refugees. There were many more waves to come as scenes observed in Brussels indicated. 'They walked, they rode in cars and carts or on donkeys, were pushed in bathchairs, even in wheelbarrows. There were youths on bicycles, old men, old women, babies, peasant women, kerchiefs covering their heads, riding on farm carts piled with mattresses, furniture, pots. A long line of nuns, their faces red with perspiration under their coifs, stirred the dust with their long grey robes . . . The stations were like drawings from those of Russia during the revolution, with people sleeping on the floor, huddled against the walls, women with weeping babies, men pale and exhausted.'

On 12 May, both in Paris and in London, newspapers gave the impression that the German onslaught had been halted. The *Sunday Chronicle* announced 'Despair in Berlin'. But German forces had crossed Holland to the sea, and the remnants of the Dutch army had pulled back into the triangle of Amsterdam, Utrecht and Rotterdam. General Giraud's Seventh Army, having now reached southern Holland, continued to suffer heavy attacks by the Luftwaffe.

In Belgium, General René Prioux's Cavalry Corps, the advance guard of the delayed First Army, managed to beat back the over-extended German panzer units advancing on the Dyle line. But again Allied squadrons attempting to bomb bridges and columns were massacred by German light flak units with their quadruple 20mm guns.

To the slight resentment of the German forces fighting to cross the Meuse, German news broadcasts emphasized only the battles in Holland and northern Belgium. Little was said about the main attack in the south. This was a deliberate part of the deception plan to distract the Allies' attention from the Sedan and Dinant sectors. Gamelin still refused to acknowledge the threat to the upper Meuse despite several warnings, but General Alphonse Georges, the commander-in-chief of the north-eastern front, a sad-faced old general much admired by Churchill, intervened to give air priority to Huntziger's sector around Sedan. Georges, who was detested by Gamelin, had never quite recovered from serious wounds to the chest in 1934 inflicted by the assassin of King Alexander of Yugoslavia.

Matters were not helped by the confusing chain of command in the French army, largely designed by Gamelin in his determination to undermine the position of his deputy. But even Georges had reacted to the threat too late. French units north-east of the Meuse were pulled back across the river, some in complete disorder. Guderian's 1st Panzer Division entered the town of Sedan against little opposition. The withdrawing French troops at least managed to blow the bridges at Sedan, but already German pioneer bridging companies had demonstrated their speed and skill.

That afternoon, Rommel's 7th Panzer Division also reached the Meuse downstream near Dinant. Although the Belgian rearguard blew up the main bridge, grenadiers from the 5th Panzer Division had discovered an old weir at Houx. Concealed by a heavy river mist that night, several companies managed to cross and establish a bridgehead. Corap's Ninth Army had failed to get troops forward in time to defend the sector.

On 13 May, Rommel's troops began to force a crossing of the Meuse at two other points, but came under heavy fire from well-positioned French regulars. Rommel came to the crossings near Dinant in his eight-wheeled armoured car to assess the situation. Finding that his armoured vehicles had no smoke shells with them, he ordered his men to set some houses on fire upwind of the crossing point. Then, bringing in some heavier Mark IV Panzers, he had them firing across the river at the French positions to cover the infantry in their heavy rubber assault boats. 'Hardly had the first boats been lowered into the water than all hell broke loose,' wrote an officer with the 7th Panzer's reconnaissance battalion.

'Snipers and heavy artillery straddled the defenceless men in the boats. With our tanks and our own artillery we tried to neutralize the enemy, but he was too well screened. The infantry attack came to a standstill.'

This day marked the start of the Rommel legend. To his officers it appeared as if he was almost everywhere: climbing on to tanks to direct the fire, accompanying the combat pioneers, and crossing the river himself. His energy and bravery kept his men going, when the attack might have flagged. At one stage he took command of an infantry battalion across the Meuse when French tanks appeared. Perhaps it is part of the myth, but Rommel is supposed to have ordered his men, who had no anti-tank weapons, to fire signal flares at them. The French tank crews, thinking they were armour-piercing shells, promptly withdrew. German losses were heavy, but by the evening Rommel had two bridgeheads established, the one at Houx and the other at the heavily contested crossing at Dinant. That night his pioneers built pontoon bridges to take the tanks across.

Guderian, preparing his own crossings either side of Sedan, had been involved in a furious row with his superior, Generaloberst von Kleist. Guderian took the risk of ignoring him and persuaded the Luftwaffe to support his plan with a massive concentration of aircraft from II and VIII Fliegerkorps. The latter was commanded by Generalmajor Wolfram Freiherr von Richthofen, a younger cousin of the First World War air ace the 'Red Baron' and the former commander of the Condor Legion responsible for the destruction of Guernica. Richthofen's Stukas, screaming down with their 'Jericho trumpets', would shake the morale of the French troops defending the Sedan sector.

Astonishingly, the French artillery, which had a great concentration of German vehicles and men to aim at, had been ordered to limit their fire, to save ammunition. The divisional commander had expected the Germans to take another two days to bring up their own field guns before crossing the river. He still had not realized that the Stukas were now the flying artillery of the panzer spearheads, and the Stukas attacked his gun positions with remarkable accuracy. As the town of Sedan burned furiously from heavy shelling and bombing, the Germans rushed the river in their heavy rubber assault boats, paddling furiously. They suffered many casualties, but eventually assault pioneers were across and attacking the concrete bunkers with flamethrowers and satchel charges.

As dusk was falling, a wild rumour spread among the terrorized French reservists that enemy tanks were already across the river and that they were about to be cut off. Communications between units and commanders had virtually collapsed as a result of the bombs severing field telephone lines. First the French artillery, then the divisional commander himself, began to retreat. A spirit of *sauve qui peut* took hold. The ammunition stockpiles which had been hoarded for another day fell to the enemy without a fight. The older reservists, nicknamed 'crocodiles', had survived the First World War and did not wish to perish now in what they saw as an unfair fight. The anti-war tracts of the French Communist Party had influenced many, but German propaganda claiming that the British had got them into this war was the most effective. Reynaud's pledge in March to the government in London that France would never seek a separate peace with Germany had only increased their suspicions.

French generals, with their mindset from the great victory of 1918, were completely overtaken by events. General Gamelin, during his visit that day to the headquarters of General Georges, still expected the main thrust to come through Belgium. Only in the evening did he discover that the Germans were across the Meuse. He ordered Huntziger's Second Army to mount a counter-offensive, but by the time the general had redeployed his formations it was too late to launch anything more than local attacks.

In any case, Huntziger had completely misunderstood Guderian's intentions. He assumed that the breakthrough was intended to strike south and roll up the Maginot Line from behind. As a result he strengthened his forces on the right when Guderian was advancing through his far weaker left. The fall of Sedan, with all its echoes of Napoleon III's surrender in 1870, struck horror into the hearts of French commanders. In the early hours of the next morning, 14 May, Captain André Beaufre, accompanying General Doumenc, entered the headquarters of General Georges. 'The atmosphere was that of a family in which there had been a death,' Beaufre wrote later. 'Our front has broken at Sedan!'

Georges told the new arrivals. 'There has been a collapse.' The exhausted general flung himself into a chair and burst into tears.

With three German bridgeheads established round Sedan, Dinant and a smaller one in between near Monthermé, where Reinhardt's XLI Panzer Corps was starting to catch up after a tough fight, a breach nearly eighty kilometres across was about to open in the French front. There would have been a good chance of crushing the German spearheads if French commanders had reacted more rapidly. On the Sedan sector, General Pierre Lafontaine of the 55th Division had already been given two extra infantry regiments and two battalions of light tanks, but he did not issue his orders for the counter-attack for nine hours. The tank battalions were also slowed by fleeing soldiers from the 51st Division blocking the roads and by poor communications. During the night, the Germans had wasted no time in getting more of their panzers across the Meuse. The French tanks finally went into action in the early morning, but the vast majority were knocked out. The collapse of the 51st Division had meanwhile triggered panic in neighbouring formations.

The Allied air forces sent in 152 bombers and 250 fighters that morning to attack the pontoon bridges over the Meuse. But the targets proved too small to hit, Luftwaffe Messerschmitt squadrons were out in force and the German flak detachments put up a murderous fire. The RAF suffered its worst casualty rate ever, with forty bombers out of seventy-one shot down. The French, in desperation, then sent in some of their most obsolete bombers which were massacred. Georges ordered forward an untested armoured division and a motorized infantry division under General Jean Flavigny, but they were delayed by lack of fuel. Flavigny was directed to attack the Sedan bridgehead from the south because, like Huntziger, Georges thought that the main threat was on the right.

Another counter-attack was attempted to the north by the 1st Armoured Division against Rommel's bridgehead. But again delays proved fatal due to Belgian refugees blocking roads and petrol bowsers unable to get through. The next morning, 15 May, Rommel's spearhead surprised the division's heavy B1 tanks as they were refuelling. A confused battle began, with the French tank crews at a severe disadvantage. Rommel left the 5th Panzer

Division to continue the battle while he surged on ahead. If they had been ready, the French tanks could have scored a significant victory. In the event, although the French 1st Armoured Division managed to destroy nearly a hundred German tanks, it was virtually annihilated by the end of the day, mainly by German anti-tank guns.

The Allied forces in the Low Countries still had little idea of the threat to their rear. On 13 May, General Prioux's Cavalry Corps fought a determined withdrawal to the line of the Dyle, where the rest of Blanchard's First Army was getting into position. Although Prioux's Somua tanks were well armoured, German gunnery and manoeuvre were far better, and the lack of radios in the French tanks proved a major handicap. Having lost nearly half its strength after a valiant battle, Prioux's corps was withdrawn. It was in no state to attack south-east against the Ardennes breakthrough as Gamelin wanted.

The French Seventh Army began to withdraw towards Antwerp after its fruitless advance to Breda to link up with the isolated Dutch forces. Although ill trained and badly armed, the Dutch troops fought bravely against the 9th Panzer Division fighting its way towards Rotterdam. The German Eighteenth Army commander was frustrated by their resistance, but finally that evening the panzers broke through.

The next day, the Dutch negotiated the surrender of Rotterdam, but the German commander had failed to inform the Luftwaffe. A major bombing raid was mounted on the city. Over 800 civilians were killed. The Dutch foreign minister claimed that evening that 30,000 had been killed, an announcement which caused horror in Paris and London. In any case, General Henri Winkelman, the Dutch commander-in-chief, decided on a general surrender to avoid further loss of life. Hitler, on hearing the news, promptly ordered a triumphal march through Amsterdam with units from the SS *Leibstandarte Adolf Hitler* and the 9th Panzer Division.

Hitler was both amused and exasperated when he received a telegram from the former Kaiser Wilhelm II, still in his Dutch exile at Doorn. 'My Führer,' it read, 'I congratulate you and hope that under your marvellous leadership the German monarchy will be restored completely.' Hitler was amazed that the old Kaiser expected him to play Bismarck. 'What an idiot!' he said to his valet, Linge.

The French counter-attack planned against the eastern part of the Sedan salient for 14 May was first delayed and then called off by General Flavigny, the commander of XXI Corps. He made the disastrous decision to split up the 3rd Armoured Division simply to create a defensive line between Chémery and Stonne. Huntziger was still convinced that the Germans were heading south behind the Maginot Line. He accordingly pivoted his army round to bar the route to the south. This succeeded only in opening up the route to the west.

General von Kleist, when informed of the arrival of French re-inforcements, ordered Guderian to halt until more forces came up to protect that flank. After another fierce row, Guderian man-aged to convince him that he could continue his advance with the 1st and 2nd Panzer Divisions, providing he sent the 10th Panzer Division and the *Grossdeutschland* Infantry Regiment under Graf von Schwerin against the village of Stonne, high on a command-ing hill. Early on 15 May, the *Grossdeutschland* went straight into the attack without waiting for the 10th Panzer. Flavigny's tank crews fought back, and the village changed hands several times in the course of the day with heavy casualties on both sides. In the narrow streets of the village, the *Grossdeutschland* anti-tank guns finally knocked out the heavy B1 tanks, and the exhausted German infantrymen were reinforced by panzergrenadiers from the 10th Panzer. The *Grossdeutschland* had lost 103 men killed and 459 wounded. It was the heaviest German loss in the whole campaign.

General Corap began to withdraw his Ninth Army, but that sparked a rapid disintegration and further widened the gap. Rein-hardt's Panzer Corps in the middle had not only caught up with the other two on 15 May, its 6th Panzer Division outpaced them dramatically, with an advance of sixty kilometres to Montcornet which split the hapless French 2nd Armoured Division in two. It was this deep strike into the French rear which convinced General Robert Touchon, who was trying to assemble a new Sixth Army to plug the gap, that they were too late. He ordered his formations to fall back to south of the River Aisne. There were now very few

French forces left between the German panzers and the Channel coast.

Guderian had been instructed not to advance until sufficient infantry divisions had been brought across the Meuse. All his superiors, Kleist, Rundstedt and Halder, were deeply nervous about an over-extended panzer spearhead exposed to a major French counter-attack from the south. Even Hitler was fearful of the risks. But Guderian sensed that the French were in chaos. The opportunity was too good to miss. Thus what has erroneously been described as a Blitzkrieg strategy was to a large degree improvised on the ground.

The German spearheads raced on, with their reconnaissance battalions out ahead in eight-wheeled armoured cars and motorcycles with sidecars. They seized bridges which the French had not had time to prepare for demolition. The black-uniformed panzer crews were filthy, unshaven and exhausted. Rommel allowed the 7th and 5th Panzer Divisions little time to rest or even to service their vehicles. Most men kept going on Pervitin tablets (a metamphetamine) and the intoxication of overwhelming victory. Any French troops they encountered were so stunned that they surrendered immediately. They were simply told to throw down their arms and keep marching ahead so that the German infantry coming along behind could deal with them.

The second wave closely following the panzer divisions consisted of motorized infantry. Alexander Stahlberg, then a lieutenant with the 2nd Infantry Division (Motorized) but later Manstein's aide-de-camp, gazed at 'the ruins of a defeated French army: bullet-ridden vehicles, battered and burned-out tanks, abandoned guns, an unending chain of destruction'. They passed through empty villages, advancing with as little fear of a real enemy as they had on manoeuvres. Way behind came the infantry on foot, their jackboots burning, forced on by their officers to catch up. 'Marching, marching. Always further, always towards the west,' wrote one in his diary. Even their horses were 'dead tired'.

If Hitler had had his way the previous autumn the invasion of France would almost certainly have been a disaster. The success at Sedan was truly a miracle for the German army, which was short of ammunition. The Luftwaffe had enough bombs for only fourteen days of combat. In addition, the motorized and panzer formations would have been in a very vulnerable position. The heavier tanks – the Mark IIIs and Mark IVs – which were capable of taking on the French and British tanks had simply not been available then. And the need for training, especially of officers in an army which had expanded from 100,000 to 5.5 million, had also required those extra months. The twenty-nine postponements of Operation Yellow had allowed the Wehrmacht to replenish its reserves sufficiently and prepare properly.

In London on 14 May, even the War Cabinet had little idea of the situation west of the Meuse. Purely by coincidence Anthony Eden, the secretary of state for war, announced that day the creation of the Local Defence Volunteer Corps (soon renamed the Home Guard). Some 250,000 men put down their names in under a week. Yet Churchill's government started to appreciate the scale of the crisis only when Reynaud sent a signal from Paris late on that afternoon of the 14th. He requested ten more fighter squadrons from Britain to protect his troops from Stuka attacks. He admitted that the Germans had broken through south of Sedan, and said he believed that they were heading for Paris.

General Ironside, the chief of the imperial general staff, gave orders to send a liaison officer to the headquarters of either Gamelin or Georges. Little information was forthcoming, so Ironside concluded that Reynaud was being a 'little hysterical'. But Reynaud soon found that the situation was even more catastrophic than he had feared. Daladier, the minister of war, had just heard from Gamelin, who had been shaken out of his complacency by a report on the disintegration of the Ninth Army. Information also came in that Reinhardt's panzer corps had reached Montcornet. Late that night, Reynaud called a meeting at the ministry of the interior with Daladier and the military governor of Paris. If the Germans were heading for Paris, they had to discuss how to avoid panic and maintain law and order.

At 07.30 hours the next morning, Churchill was woken by a telephone call from Reynaud. 'We have been defeated,' Reynaud blurted out. Churchill, still half asleep, did not immediately respond. 'We are beaten; we have lost the battle,' Reynaud emphasized.

'Surely it can't have happened so soon?' Churchill said.

'The front is broken near Sedan; they are pouring through in great numbers with tanks and armoured cars.' According to Roland de Margerie, Reynaud's foreign affairs adviser, he added: 'The road to Paris is open. Send us all the planes and all the troops you can.'

Churchill decided to fly to Paris to stiffen Reynaud's resolve, but first he called a War Cabinet meeting to discuss the request for ten more fighter squadrons. He was determined to do all in his power to help the French. But Air Chief Marshal Dowding, the head of Fighter Command, resolutely opposed the despatch of any more aircraft. After a heated argument, he walked round the table and placed a paper in front of Churchill showing the likely rate of loss based on current casualties. Within ten days, there would be no Hurricanes left either in France or in Britain. The War Cabinet was impressed by his arguments, but still felt that another four squadrons should be sent to France.

The War Cabinet came to another decision that day. Bomber Command should at last go on the offensive against German territory. It should mount a raid on the Ruhr in retaliation for the Luftwaffe attack on Rotterdam. Few of the aircraft found their targets, but this still marked the first step towards the strategic bombing campaign.

Deeply disturbed by the possibility that France might collapse, Churchill sent a telegram to President Roosevelt in the hope of shocking him into action on behalf of the Allies. 'As you are no doubt aware, the scene has darkened swiftly. If necessary, we shall continue the war alone and we are not afraid of that. But I trust you realise, Mr President, that the voice and the force of the United States may count for nothing if they are withheld too long. You may have a completely subjugated, Nazified Europe established with astonishing swiftness, and the weight may be more than we can bear.' Roosevelt's reply was friendly, but he offered no commitment to intervene. Churchill composed another letter emphasizing Britain's determination 'to persevere to the very end whatever the result of the great battle raging in France may be', and again urged the need for rapid American help.

Still feeling that Roosevelt did not appreciate the urgency, he wrote yet another message on 21 May, which he hesitated to send.

Although he insisted that his government would never consent to surrender, he raised another danger. 'If members of the present administration were finished and others came to parley amid the ruins, you must not be blind to the fact that the sole remaining bargaining counter with Germany would be the fleet, and if this country was left by the United States to its fate no one would have the right to blame those then responsible if they made the best terms they could for the surviving inhabitants. Excuse me, Mr President, putting this nightmare bluntly. Evidently I could not answer for my successors who in utter despair and helplessness might well have to accommodate themselves to the German will.'

Churchill did send this signal, but, as he later realized, his shock tactics, implying that the Germans might even obtain the Royal Navy's warships to challenge the United States, proved counter-productive. They were bound to weaken Roosevelt's confidence in Britain's determination to fight alone, and the President raised with his own advisers the possibility of the British fleet being moved to Canada. He even contacted William Mackenzie King, the Canadian prime minister, to discuss the matter. Churchill's mistake was to have a tragic influence some weeks later.

On 16 May in the afternoon, Churchill flew to Paris. He was unaware that Gamelin had rung Reynaud to tell him that the Germans might reach the capital that night. They were already approaching Laon, less than 120 kilometres away. The military governor advised that the whole administration should leave as soon as possible. Ministries began to burn bonfires of files in their courtyards, with civil servants throwing armful of papers out of the windows.

'The wind in eddies', wrote Roland de Margerie, 'blew away sparks and fragments of paper which soon covered the whole district.' He noted that Reynaud's defeatist mistress, the Comtesse de Portes, made a caustic comment about 'the idiot who gave this order'. The *chef de service* replied that it was Reynaud himself: 'C'est le Président du Conseil, Madame.' But at the last moment Reynaud decided that the government should remain. This did little good, since word had spread. The population of Paris, kept in total ignorance of the disaster by strict press censorship, was soon seized by panic. *La grande fuite* had started. Motorcars with cases piled on the roof began to cross to the Porte d'Orléans and the Porte d'Italie.

Churchill, accompanied by General Sir John Dill, the new chief of the imperial general staff, and Major General Hastings Ismay, secretary of the War Cabinet, landed in his Flamingo aircraft to find that 'the situation was incomparably worse than we had imagined'. At the Quai d'Orsay, they had a meeting with Reynaud, Daladier and Gamelin. The atmosphere was such that they did not even sit down. 'Utter dejection was written on every face,' Churchill wrote later. Gamelin stood by a map on an easel on which a bulge at Sedan was shown and tried to explain the position.

'Where is the strategic reserve?' Churchill asked, and then repeated in his idiosyncratic French: 'Où est la masse de manoeuvre?'

Gamelin turned to him and, 'with a shake of the head and a shrug', replied: 'Aucune.' Churchill then noticed smoke drifting up outside the building. From the window he saw foreign ministry officials carting piles of dossiers in wheelbarrows to dump them on the large bonfires. He was dumbfounded that Gamelin's plan had not allowed for a large reserve to counter-attack a breakthrough. He was also shocked by his own ignorance of the danger and the lamentable state of inter-Allied liaison.

When he asked Gamelin about preparations for counterattacks, the commander-in-chief could only shrug hopelessly. The French army was bankrupt. They now expected the British to bail them out. Roland de Margerie quietly warned Churchill that the situation was even worse than Daladier or Gamelin had said. And when he added that they might have to withdraw to the River Loire or even continue the war from Casablanca, Churchill looked at him 'avec stupeur'.

Reynaud asked about the ten fighter squadrons he had requested. Churchill, with Dowding's warning fresh in his ears, explained that to strip Britain of its defences would be disastrous. He reminded them of the terrible losses the RAF had suffered trying to bomb the Meuse crossings and said that another four squadrons were coming and that others based in Britain were in action over France, but his audience was far from satisfied. That evening, Churchill sent a message from the British embassy to the War Cabinet asking for the other six squadrons. (For security purposes on an open line, it was dictated in Hindustani by General Ismay and taken down by a fellow Indian Army officer in London.) When their agreement was obtained shortly before midnight, Churchill went round to see Reynaud and Daladier to restore their courage. Reynaud received him wearing a dressing gown and slippers.

In the event, the extra squadrons had to be based back in Britain and fly across to fight on a daily basis. With the German advance there were insufficient airfields, and they all lacked repair facilities. Altogether, 120 Hurricanes based across the Channel which had been damaged in combat had to be abandoned in the headlong retreat. The pilots were totally exhausted. Most were flying up to five sorties a day, and because the French fighters stood little chance against the Messerschmitt 109, the Hurricane squadrons had to shoulder the brunt of a very unequal battle.

More and more reports came in of disintegration in the French army and bad discipline. Attempts were made to force units to stand and fight by executing some officers accused of abandoning their commands. Spy-mania took over. Numerous officers and soldiers were shot at random by frightened troops convinced that they were Germans in Allied uniforms. Panics were set off by wild rumours of German secret weapons and invented fears of a fifth column. Treachery seemed the only way to explain such a bewildering defeat, with the angry cry: 'Nous sommes trahis!'

Chaos mounted with the growing volumes of refugees in northeast France. Including Dutch and Belgians, some eight million refugees are said to have taken to the roads that summer, hungry, thirsty and exhausted, the rich in cars, the rest in farm-carts or pushing loaded bicycles, prams or hand-carts with their pitiful possessions. 'They are the most pathetic sight,' wrote Lieutenant General Sir Alan Brooke, commander of the BEF's II Corps, in his diary, 'with lame women suffering from sore feet, small children worn out with travelling but hugging their dolls, and all the old and maimed struggling along.' The fate of Rotterdam had struck fear into many. The vast majority of the population of Lille abandoned the city as the Germans advanced. Although there is

no evidence that the Luftwaffe issued orders to its fighter pilots
to strafe refugee columns, members of the Allied forces witnessed
such incidents. The French army, which had relied on a static defence, was even less able to react to the unexpected with the roads
jammed by terrified civilians.

The Fall of France

MAY–JUNE 1940

German morale could hardly have been higher. Tank crews in their black panzer uniforms cheered their commanders whenever they saw them as they charged on towards the Channel through deserted countryside, refuelling their tanks at abandoned petrol stations and from French army fuel dumps. Their own supply lines were completely unprotected. Delays to their headlong advance came mainly from roads blocked by broken-down French vehicles and refugee columns.

As Kleist's panzers raced towards the Channel coast, Hitler became increasingly alarmed that the French might attack their flank from the south. Usually the great gambler, he could not believe his luck. Memories of 1914, when the invasion of France had been thwarted by a counter-attack in their flank, also haunted the older generals. Generaloberst von Rundstedt agreed with Hitler, and on 16 May he ordered Kleist to halt his panzer divisions to allow the infantry to catch up. But General Halder, a late convert to the audacity of Manstein's plan, urged him to keep going. Kleist and Guderian had another row the next day, with Kleist quoting Hitler's order. But a compromise was reached, allowing 'battle-worthy reconnaissance formations' to probe towards the coast while XIX Corps headquarters stayed where it was. This gave Guderian the chance he wanted. Unlike Hitler in his Felsennest, he knew that the French were paralysed by the audacity of the German strike. Only isolated pockets of resistance remained, with the remnants of some French divisions fighting on in the face of disaster.

By coincidence, on the same day that the panzer divisions were halted (and took a much needed opportunity to rest and service their vehicles), a French counter-attack took place from the south. Colonel Charles de Gaulle, the foremost proponent of armoured warfare in the French army (who had thus made himself very unpopular with the elderly, fixed-line generals), had just been given command of the so-called 4th Armoured Division. De Gaulle's passionate advocacy of mechanized warfare had led to his nickname of 'Colonel Motors'. But the 4th Armoured was an ill-assorted collection of tank battalions, with little infantry support and almost no artillery.

General Georges briefed him and sent him on his way with the words: 'Go on, de Gaulle! For you who have so long held the ideas which the enemy is putting into practice, here is the chance to act.' De Gaulle was longing to attack, having heard of the insolence of German panzer crews. As they charged past French troops on the road, they simply told them to throw down their weapons and march eastward. Their casual parting cry, 'We haven't got time to take you prisoner,' outraged his patriotism.

From Laon, de Gaulle decided to strike north-east towards Montcornet, an important road junction on Guderian's supply route. The 4th Armoured Division's sudden advance took the Germans by surprise and nearly overran the headquarters of the 1st Panzer Division. But the Germans reacted with great speed, using a few tanks which had just been repaired and some self-propelled guns. Air support from the Luftwaffe was called in, and de Gaulle's battered force, lacking any anti-aircraft guns and fighter cover, was obliged to withdraw. Guderian, needless to say, did not inform Rundstedt's army group headquarters about the action that day.

The BEF, which had fought off German attacks on its sector of the Dyle, was astonished on the evening of 15 May when it heard by chance that General Gaston Billotte, the First Army Group commander, was preparing to withdraw to the line of the River Escaut. This meant abandoning Brussels and Antwerp. Belgian generals only discovered the decision the following morning and were furious at the lack of warning.

Billotte's headquarters were in a state of psychological collapse, with many officers in tears. Gort's chief of staff was so horrified by what he had heard from the British liaison officer that he rang the War Office in London to warn them that the BEF might have to be evacuated at some point. For the British, 16 May marked the start of a fighting retreat. Just south of Brussels, on a ridge near

Waterloo, Royal Artillery batteries with 25-pounders took up position. This time their guns were aimed towards Wavre from where the Prussians had come to help their forebears in 1815. But by the following night German troops were entering the Belgian capital.

That day, Reynaud sent a signal to General Maxime Weygand in Syria, asking him to fly back to France to take over the supreme command. He had decided to get rid of Gamelin, whatever Daladier said. He also intended to change his ministers. Georges Mandel, who had been the former prime minister Georges Clemenceau's right-hand man and was determined to fight on to the end, would become minister of the interior. Reynaud himself took on the ministry of war, and planned to bring in Charles de Gaulle, now with the temporary rank of a junior general, as under-secretary of state. Reynaud was confirmed in his decision when he heard next day from the writer André Maurois working as a liaison officer that, although the British were fighting well, they had lost all confidence in the French army and especially its senior commanders.

Yet Reynaud made a fatal mistake at the same time, probably influenced by his *capitulard* mistress, Hélène de Portes. He sent a representative to Madrid to persuade Marshal Philippe Pétain, then France's ambassador to Franco, to become his deputy prime minister. Pétain's prestige, as the victor of Verdun, had given him heroic status. But the eighty-four-year-old marshal, like Weygand, was more preoccupied by a fear of revolution and of the disintegration of the French army than by the prospect of defeat. He, like many on the right, believed that France had been unfairly pushed into this war by the British.

On the morning of 18 May 1940, just eight days after Churchill had become prime minister and while the Germans were threatening to encircle the BEF in northern France, Randolph Churchill visited his father. The prime minister, who was shaving, told him to read the paper until he had finished. But then he suddenly said, 'I think I see my way through,' and returned to scraping away. His astounded son replied: 'Do you mean that we can avoid defeat? . . . or beat the bastards?'

Churchill put down his razor and turned round. 'Of course I mean we can beat them.'

'Well, I'm all for it, but I don't see how you can do it.'

His father dried his face before saying with great intensity: 'I shall drag the United States in.'

By chance, it was also the day on which the government, at Halifax's urging, sent the austere socialist Sir Stafford Cripps to Moscow to seek better relations with the Soviet Union. Churchill felt that Cripps was a bad choice, on the grounds that Stalin hated socialists almost more than he hated conservatives. He also thought that the high-minded Cripps was hardly the person to deal with a rough, suspicious and calculating cynic like Stalin. Yet Cripps was a good deal more far-sighted than the prime minister in some directions. He had already predicted that the war would bring an end to the British Empire and introduce fundamental social change afterwards.

On 19 May, the Panzer Corridor, as the German salient became known, now extended across the Canal du Nord. Both Guderian and Rommel needed to rest their crews, but Rommel persuaded his corps commander that he should push on that night towards Arras.

The RAF contingent in France was now completely cut off from British forces on the ground, so the decision was taken to return the sixty-six remaining Hurricanes in France back to Britain. The French, of course, felt betrayed by this move, but the loss of airfields and the exhaustion of the pilots made it unavoidable. The RAF had already lost a quarter of its total fighter force in the Battle of France.

Far to the south that day, General Erwin von Witzleben's First Army made the first breach in the Maginot Line. This was designed to prevent the French from sending troops up against the southern flank of the Panzer Corridor, even though that flank had begun to be protected by German infantry divisions, arriving exhausted from forced marches.

Colonel de Gaulle launched another attack that day northwards with 150 tanks towards Crécy-sur-Serre. He had been promised fighter cover by the French air force to ward off Stuka attacks, but bad communications meant that they arrived too late. De Gaulle had to pull his battered remnants back across the River Aisne.

Bad liaison between the Allied armies continued, and this led to suspicions that the BEF was already preparing to evacuate. General Lord Gort was not ruling out the possibility, but no plans had been made at this stage. He could not obtain a straight answer from General Billotte on the true situation to their south and what reserves the French had at their disposal. Back in London, General Ironside spoke to the Admiralty to see what small ships they had available.

Even though the British people had little idea of the true gravity of the situation, nervous rumours suddenly increased: that the King and Queen were sending Princess Elizabeth and Princess Margaret Rose to Canada; that Italy had entered the war already and its army was marching into Switzerland; that German paratroopers had landed; and that Lord Haw-Haw (the pro-Nazi William Joyce) was sending secret messages to German agents in Britain through his broadcasts from Berlin.

That Sunday, the last day of General Gamelin's command, the French government attended a service in Notre Dame to pray for divine intervention. The francophile American ambassador, William Bullitt, was in tears during the ceremony.

General Weygand, small, energetic and with a wizened foxy face, insisted on a good sleep after his long flight from Syria. In many ways this monarchist was a surprising choice since he loathed Reynaud, who had appointed him. But Reynaud, in desperation, was reaching for victorious symbols in the form of Pétain and Weygand, who as Marshal Ferdinand Foch's deputy was associated with the final triumph of 1918.

On Monday, 20 May, the first day of Weygand's command, the 1st Panzer Division reached Amiens, which had been heavily bombed the day before. A battalion of the Royal Sussex Regiment, the only Allied force in the city, was annihilated in a doomed defence. Guderian's force also seized a bridgehead over the River Somme, ready for a subsequent phase of the battle. Guderian then sent the Austrian 2nd Panzer Division on to Abbeville, which it reached that evening. And a few hours later, one of its panzer battalions reached the coast. Manstein's *Sichelschnitt* had been achieved. Hitler, beside himself with joy, could hardly believe the news. The surprise was so great that the army high command could not make up its mind what to do next.

On the northern side of the corridor, Rommel's 7th Panzer Division had pushed forward to Arras, but was halted there by a battalion of the Welsh Guards. That evening, General Ironside reached Gort's headquarters with an order from Churchill to force his way through the corridor to join up with the French on the south side. But Gort pointed out that the bulk of his divisions were defending the line of the Scheldt and could not be withdrawn at this stage. He was, however, organizing a two-division attack on Arras, but he had no idea what French plans were.

Ironside then went to Billotte's headquarters. The huge Ironside, finding the French general in a state of total dejection, grabbed him by the tunic and shook him. Billotte finally agreed to launch a simultaneous counter-attack with another two divisions. Gort was deeply sceptical that anything would happen. He was right. General René Altmayer, who commanded the French V Corps ordered to support the British, was simply weeping on his bed, according to a French liaison officer. Only a small force from General Prioux's fine cavalry corps came to assist.

The British counter-attack round Arras was designed to seize ground south of the city to cut off Rommel's panzer spearhead. The force consisted principally of seventy-four Matilda tanks from the 4th and 7th Royal Tank Regiment, two battalions of the Durham Light Infantry, part of the Northumberland Fusiliers and the armoured cars of the 12th Lancers. Once again the artillery support and air cover promised for the operation failed to materialize. Rommel himself witnessed his infantry and gunners run for their lives, and the newly arrived SS *Totenkopf* mechanized infantry division was panic-stricken, but he rapidly brought some anti-tank and anti-aircraft guns into action against the lumbering Matilda tanks. He was nearly killed in the firefight, yet the risks he took intervening like a junior officer almost certainly saved the Germans from a setback.

The other British column was more successful, even though most of their tanks broke down. The German anti-tank shells bounced off the heavy armour of the remaining Matildas, but many of them eventually succumbed to mechanical failure after inflicting considerable damage on German armoured and soft-skinned vehicles. The counter-attack, although courageously carried out, simply did not have the strength or the support to achieve its goal. The failure of the French (with the honourable exception of Prioux's cavalry) to join the battle convinced British commanders that their army had lost the will to fight. The alliance, to Churchill's great distress, was now doomed to deteriorate into mutual suspicion and recrimination. In fact the French launched another counter-attack towards Cambrai, but this too had little lasting success.

That morning, the main force of the BEF had been heavily attacked along the Escaut line and fought off the Germans with great determination. Two Victoria Crosses were won during the action. The Germans, unprepared to lose so many men on another attempt, resorted to bombarding the British with artillery and mortars. The whole Allied position was about to collapse due to bad liaison and misunderstandings among the most senior commanders when Weygand called a conference in Ypres in the afternoon. He wanted the British to withdraw so as to launch a stronger attack across the German corridor towards the Somme. But Gort was out of touch and arrived far too late. And Weygand's agreement with King Leopold III of the Belgians to keep his troops on Belgian territory led to disaster. This was compounded by General Billotte's death when his staff car ran into the back of a truck packed with refugees. General Weygand and some French commentators later suggested that Gort had deliberately avoided the meeting at Ypres as he was already planning secretly to evacuate the BEF, but there is no evidence of this.

'The face of war is dreadful,' a German soldier from the 269th Infantry Division wrote home on 20 May. 'Towns and villages shot to pieces, plundered shops everywhere, values are trodden on with jackboots, cattle are drifting, abandoned, and dogs are slinking despondently along the houses . . . We live like gods in France. If we need meat, a cow is slaughtered and only the best cuts are taken and the rest is discarded. Asparagus, oranges, lettuces, nuts, cocoa, coffee, butter, ham, chocolate, sparkling wine, wine, spirits, beer, tobacco, cigars and cigarettes, as well as complete sets of laundry are there in abundance. Due to the long stretches that we have to march we lose contact with our units. With our rifles in our hand we then break open a house and our hunger is sated. Terrible, isn't it? But one gets used to anything. Thank God that these conditions don't prevail at home.'

'By the roads, shattered and burned-out French tanks and vehicles lie in immeasurable rows,' an artillery corporal wrote to his wife. 'Of course there are a few German ones among them, but amazingly few.' Some soldiers complained how little there was to do. 'There are many, many divisions here who haven't fired a shot,' a corporal in the 1st Infantry Division wrote. 'And at the front the enemy are running away. French and English, equal adversaries in the world war, refuse to take us on now. In truth, our aircraft are in command of the skies. We haven't seen one enemy aircraft, only our own. Just imagine. Positions like Amiens, Laon, Chemin des Dames are falling within hours. In 14–18 they were fought over for years.'

The triumphant letters home did not mention the occasional massacres of British or French prisoners and even civilians. Nor did they relate the more frequent massacres of captured French colonial troops, especially Senegalese *tirailleurs*, who fought bravely to the racist fury of German troops. They were shot, sometimes fifty or a hundred at a time, by German formations which included the SS *Totenkopf*, the 10th Panzer Division and the *Grossdeutschland* Regiment. Altogether it is estimated that up to 3,000 colonial soldiers were shot out of hand after capture during the Battle of France.

In the rear of the British and French forces, Boulogne was in chaos, with some of the French naval garrison dead drunk, and others destroying the coastal batteries. A battalion of Irish Guards and another of Welsh Guards were landed to defend the town. As the 2nd Panzer Division advanced north towards the port on 22 May, it was ambushed by a detachment of the French 48th Regiment, mainly headquarters personnel manning unfamiliar anti-tank guns. It was a courageous defence in stark contrast to the disgraceful scenes in Boulogne, but they were overwhelmed and the 2nd Panzer Division continued on to attack the port.

The two Guards battalions there had few anti-tank guns, and were soon forced to withdraw into the town and then to an inner perimeter round the port. As it became clear that they could not hold Boulogne, British rear-echelon personnel began to be evacuated by Royal Navy destroyers on 23 May. An extraordinary battle developed with British warships entering the port and taking on German panzers with their main armament. But the French commander, who had been ordered to fight to the last man, was outraged. He accused the British of desertion, and this did much to embitter relations further between the Allies. It also made Churchill determined to defend Calais, come what may.

Calais, although reinforced with four battalions and some tanks, stood little chance of holding out despite the order that there would be no evacuation 'for [the] sake of Allied solidarity'. The 10th Panzer Division called in Stukas and Guderian's heavy artillery on 25 May and began to bombard the old town where the remnants of the defenders had withdrawn. The defence of Calais continued throughout the next day. The flames of the burning town could be seen from Dover. French troops fought until they ran out of ammunition. The French naval commander decided to surrender, and the British, who had suffered massive casualties, had no option but to do the same. The defence of Calais, although doomed, had at least slowed the 10th Panzer Division's advance along the coast towards Dunkirk.

In Britain civilian morale was steady, largely through ignorance of the true state of affairs across the Channel. But Reynaud's reported remark that 'only a miracle can save France' caused great alarm on 22 May. The country had suddenly started to wake up. The Emergency Powers Act was widely welcomed, along with the arrest of Sir Oswald Mosley, the leader of the British Union of Fascists. Mass Observation noted that in general the mood was more determined in villages and rural areas than in large towns, and that women were much less confident than men. The middle classes were also more nervous than the working class: 'The whiter the collar, the less the assurance,' it was said. In fact, the greatest proportion of defeatists was among the rich and the upper classes.

Many people became convinced that wild rumours, such as the notion that General Gamelin had been shot as a traitor or had committed suicide, were being spread deliberately by some fifth column. But Mass Observation reported to the ministry of information that the 'evidence before us at the moment suggests that most rumours are passed on by idle, frightened, suspicious people'.

On 23 May, General Brooke, commander of II Corps, wrote in his diary: 'Nothing but a miracle can save the BEF now and the end cannot be very far off!' But, fortunately for the British Expeditionary Force, the failed counter-attack at Arras had at least made the Germans rather more cautious. Rundstedt and Hitler insisted that the area had to be secured before the advance began again. And the delay to the 10th Panzer Division at Boulogne and Calais meant that Dunkirk had not been captured behind the backs of the BEF.

On the evening of 23 May, Generaloberst von Kluge halted the thirteen German divisions along what the British called the Canal Line on the western side of what was becoming the Dunkirk pocket. This ran for just over fifty kilometres from the Channel along the River Aa and its canal via Saint-Omer, Béthune and La Bassée. Kleist's two panzer corps urgently needed maintenance work on their vehicles. His panzer group had already lost half its armoured strength. In three weeks, 600 tanks had been destroyed by enemy action or had suffered serious mechanical trouble, which represented just over a sixth of the entire German force on all fronts.

Hitler approved this order the following day, but it was not his personal intervention, as has so often been believed. Generaloberst von Brauchitsch, the commander-in-chief of the German army, backed by Halder, gave the order on the night of 24 May to continue the advance, but Rundstedt, with Hitler's support, insisted that the infantry should catch up first. They wanted to preserve their panzer forces for an offensive across the Somme and the Aisne before the main bulk of the French army had a chance to reorganize itself. An advance across the canals and the wetlands of Flanders seemed to them an unnecessary risk when Göring claimed that his Luftwaffe could deal with any British attempt at evacuation. Although they marched at a rapid tempo, the German infantry divisions had struggled to catch up with the panzer formations. It is a striking fact that the BEF and most of the French formations possessed far more motor transport than the German army, in which only sixteen divisions out of 157 were fully motorized. All the rest had to rely on horses to pull their artillery and baggage.

The British had another stroke of luck. A German staff car was captured, containing documents which showed that the next attack would come in the east near Ypres, between the Belgian forces and the British left flank. Lord Gort was persuaded by General Brooke that he should move one of his divisions, which had been allocated for another counter-attack, round to plug this gap.

On hearing that the French could not mount an attack across the Somme, Anthony Eden, as secretary of state for war, instructed Gort on the night of 25 May that the safety of the BEF must be the 'predominant consideration'. He should therefore withdraw towards the Channel coast for evacuation. The War Cabinet, now forced to face the fact that the French army could not recover from its collapse, had to consider the implications of Britain fighting on alone. Gort had already warned London that the BEF was likely to lose all of its equipment and he doubted that more than a small proportion of its forces could be evacuated.

Eden did not know that an increasingly harassed Reynaud had been ambushed by Marshal Pétain and General Weygand. Pétain had been in touch with Pierre Laval, a politician who loathed the British and was awaiting his chance to replace Reynaud. Laval had made contact with an Italian diplomat to sound out the possibility of negotiating with Hitler through Mussolini. Weygand, the commander-in-chief, blamed the politicians for a 'criminal lack of prudence' in going to war in the first place. Supported by Pétain, he demanded that France's guarantee not to seek a separate peace should be withdrawn. Their priority was to preserve the army to maintain order. Reynaud agreed to fly to London the next day to consult with the British government.

Weygand's hope that Mussolini could be persuaded to stay out of the war through the promise of more colonies, and that he might negotiate a peace, was completely misplaced. Hitler's claim that he had achieved victory provoked a hesitant Mussolini into telling the Germans and his own general staff that Italy would enter the war soon after 5 June. Both he and his generals knew that Italy was incapable of any effective offensive action. They did, however, consider an attack on Malta, but then decided that it was unnecessary since they could take over the island as soon as Britain collapsed. During the following days, Mussolini is supposed to have said: 'This time I'll declare war, but I won't wage it.' The chief victims of this disastrous attempt at sleight of hand were to be his woefully under-equipped stage armies. Bismarck had once remarked, with one of his pithy comments, that Italy had a large appetite but poor teeth. It would prove disastrously true in the Second World War.

On the morning of Sunday, 26 May, as British troops pulled back towards Dunkirk under a heavy storm – 'thunderclaps mingled with the booming of the artillery' – the War Cabinet met in London unaware of Mussolini's intentions. Lord Halifax raised the possibility that the government should consider approaching the Duce to find out what terms Hitler might be prepared to accept for peace. He had even met the Italian ambassador privately the previous afternoon to sound him out. Halifax was convinced that, with no prospect of assistance from the United States in the near future, Britain was not strong enough to resist Hitler alone.

Churchill replied that British liberty and independence were paramount. He had used a paper prepared by the chiefs of staff entitled 'British Strategy in a Certain Eventuality' – a euphemism for French surrender. This discussion paper envisaged British options for fighting on alone. Some aspects were unduly pessimistic as things turned out. The report assumed that most of the BEF would be lost in France. The Admiralty did not expect to get off more than 45,000 men, and the chiefs of staff feared that the Luftwaffe would destroy the aircraft factories in the Midlands. Other assumptions were over-optimistic: for example, the chiefs of staff predicted that Germany's war economy would be weakened by a shortage of raw materials – a strange assumption if Germany were to control most of western and central Europe. But the main conclusion was that Britain could probably hold out against invasion, providing the RAF and the Royal Navy remained intact. This was the vital point to support Churchill's argument against Halifax.

Churchill went off to Admiralty House to have lunch with Reynaud, who had just flown over to London. It was clear from what

Reynaud said that General Weygand's wildly favourable view of the situation just a couple of days previously had now swung to outright defeatism. The French were already contemplating the loss of Paris. Reynaud even said that, although he would never sign a separate peace, he might be replaced by somebody who would. He was already under pressure to persuade the British – 'in order to reduce proportionately our own contribution' – to hand over Gibraltar and Suez to the Italians.

When Churchill returned to the War Cabinet and reported this conversation, Halifax revived his suggestion of approaching the Italian government. Churchill had to play his cards carefully. He could not risk an open breach with Halifax, who commanded the loyalty of too many Conservatives, while his own position was unsecured. Fortunately, Chamberlain started to come round to support Churchill, who had treated him with great respect and magnanimity despite their previous antagonism.

Churchill argued that Britain should not be linked to France if it sought terms. 'We must not get entangled in a position of that kind before we had been involved in any serious fighting.' No decision should be taken until it was clear how much of the BEF could be saved. In any case, Hitler's terms would certainly prevent Britain from 'completing our re-armament'. Churchill rightly assumed that Hitler would offer far more lenient terms to France than he would to Britain. But the foreign secretary was determined not to give up the idea of negotiations. 'If we got to the point of discussing the terms which did not postulate the destruction of our independence, we should be foolish if we did not accept them.' Again Churchill had to imply that he acceded to the idea of an approach to Italy, but in fact he was playing for time. If the bulk of the BEF were saved, his own position as well as the country's would be immeasurably strengthened.

That evening, Anthony Eden sent a signal to Gort confirming that he should 'fall back upon the coast . . . in conjunction with French and Belgian armies'. That same evening, Vice Admiral Bertram Ramsay in Dover was ordered to launch Operation Dynamo, the evacuation by sea of the BEF. Unfortunately, Churchill's message to Weygand confirming the retreat to the Channel ports did not spell out the evacuation plan. It was unwisely assumed that this was self-evident in the circumstances.

The consequences for Britain's deteriorating relationship with the French would be grave.

The halting of the panzer divisions had given Gort's staff the chance to prepare a new defensive perimeter based on a line of fortified villages while the bulk of the BEF retired. But the French commanders in Flanders were incensed when they discovered that the British were planning to evacuate. Gort had assumed that London had informed General Weygand at the same time as he had received his instructions to pull back to the coast. He also believed that the French had received instructions to embark too and was horrified to find that this was not the case.

From 27 May, the 2nd Battalion of the Gloucestershire Regiment and a battalion of the Oxford and Buckinghamshire Light Infantry defended Cassel to the south of Dunkirk. Platoons occupied outlying farms, in some cases for three days against vastly superior forces. To their south, the British 2nd Division, which had been moved to defend the Canal Line from La Bassée up to Aire, suffered very heavy attacks. Having run out of anti-tank ammunition, soldiers of the exhausted and badly depleted 2nd Royal Norfolk Regiment were reduced to dashing out with hand-grenades to drop them into the tracks of the panzers. The remnants of the battalion were surrounded by the SS *Totenkopf* and taken prisoner. That night, the SS massacred ninety-seven of them. On the Belgian sector that day, the German 255th Division avenged their losses near the village of Vinkt by executing seventy-eight civilians, falsely claiming that some of them had been armed. The next day, a group of the SS *Leibstandarte* commanded by Hauptsturmführer Wilhelm Mohnke at Wormhout killed nearly ninety British prisoners, mainly from the Royal Warwicks who were also acting as rearguard. Thus the murderous war against Poland produced a few echoes on the supposedly civilized western front.

South of the Somme, the British 1st Armoured Division mounted a counter-attack against a German bridgehead. Once again French artillery and air support did not materialize, and the 10th Hussars and the Queen's Bays lost sixty-five tanks, mainly to German anti-tank guns. A more effective counter-attack was launched by de Gaulle's 4th Armoured Division against the German bridgehead near Abbeville, but this too was repulsed.

In London, on 27 May, the War Cabinet met again three times. The second meeting, in the afternoon, perhaps encapsulated the most critical moment of the war, when Nazi Germany might have won. This was when the developing clash between Halifax and Churchill came out into the open. Halifax was even more determined to use Mussolini as a mediator to discover what terms Hitler might offer to France and Britain. He believed that, if they delayed, the terms offered would be even worse.

Churchill argued strongly against such weakening, and insisted that they should fight on. 'Even if we were beaten,' he said, 'we should be no worse off than we should be if we were now to abandon the struggle. Let us therefore avoid being dragged down the slippery slope with France.' He understood that once they started to negotiate, they would be 'unable to turn back' and revive a spirit of defiance in the population. Churchill at least had the implicit support of Clement Attlee and Arthur Greenwood, the two Labour leaders, and also of Sir Archibald Sinclair, the Liberal leader. Chamberlain too was convinced by Churchill's key argument. During this stormy meeting, Halifax made it clear to Churchill that he would resign if his views were ignored, but Churchill afterwards managed to calm him.

Another blow fell that evening. After the Belgian line on the River Lys had been breached, King Leopold decided to capitulate. The following day, he surrendered unconditionally to the Sixth Army. Generaloberst von Reichenau and his chief of staff Generalleutnant Friedrich Paulus dictated the terms at their headquarters. The next surrender which Paulus would conduct would be his own at Stalingrad two years and eight months later.

The French government was outwardly scathing about the 'betrayal' of King Leopold, yet in private rejoiced. One of the *capitulards* expressed the mood when he said: 'Finally, we have a scapegoat!' The British, however, were hardly surprised by the Belgian collapse. Gort, on General Brooke's advice, had wisely taken precautions by moving his own troops in behind the Belgian lines to prevent a German breakthrough between Ypres and Comines on the eastern flank.

General Weygand, now officially informed that the British had decided to pull out, was furious at the lack of frankness. Unfortunately, he did not give the order to his own units to evacuate until the following day, and as a result French troops reached the beaches well after the British. Marshal Pétain argued that the lack of British support should lead to the revision of Reynaud's agreement signed in March not to seek a separate peace.

On the afternoon of 28 May, the War Cabinet met again, but this time at the House of Commons at the prime minister's request. The battle between Halifax and Churchill broke out anew, with Churchill taking an even more resolute line against any form of negotiation. Even if the British were to get up and leave the conference table, he argued, 'we should find that all the forces of resolution which were now at our disposal would have vanished'.

As soon as the War Cabinet meeting ended, Churchill called a meeting of the whole Cabinet. He told them that he had considered negotiations with Hitler, but he was convinced that Hitler's terms would reduce Britain to a 'slave-state' ruled by a puppet government. Their support could hardly have been more emphatic. Halifax had been decisively outmanoeuvred. Britain would fight on to the end.

Hitler, not wanting to use up his depleted panzer forces, limited them in their new advance towards Dunkirk. They were to halt as soon as their artillery regiments were within range of the port. The shelling and bombing of the town began in earnest, but it was insufficient to prevent Operation Dynamo, the evacuation. Luftwaffe bombers, often still flying from bases back in Germany, lacked effective fighter support and were frequently intercepted by Spitfire squadrons taking off from much closer airfields in Kent.

The hapless British troops crowding the sand dunes and town as they waited their turn for embarkation cursed the RAF, not realizing that its fighters were engaging the German bombers inland. The Luftwaffe, despite Göring's boast that he would eliminate the British, inflicted comparatively few casualties. The lethal effect of the bombs and shells was reduced greatly by the soft sand dunes. More Allied soldiers were killed on the beaches by strafing attacks than by bombs.

By the time the German advance had resumed with infantry, the strong defence by both British and French troops had prevented a German breakthrough. The few who escaped from the defended villages were exhausted, hungry, thirsty and in many cases injured. The more severely wounded had had to be left behind. With Germans all around them, it was a nerve-racking retreat, never knowing when they were going to bump into an enemy force.

The evacuation had started on 19 May, when wounded and rear troops were taken off, but the main effort began only on the night of 26 May. Following an appeal over the BBC, the Admiralty contacted the volunteer owners of small vessels, such as yachts, river launches and cabin cruisers. They were told to rendezvous, first off Sheerness, then off Ramsgate. Some 600 were used in the course of Operation Dynamo, almost all crewed by 'weekend sailors', to augment the force of over 200 Royal Navy vessels.

Dunkirk was easy to identify at a great distance, both from the sea and from the landward side. Columns of smoke rose into the sky from the burning town attacked by German bombers. Oil tanks blazed fiercely with thick, black billowing clouds. Every road leading into the town was jammed with abandoned and destroyed army vehicles.

Relations between senior British and French officers, especially the staff of Admiral Jean Abrial, commander of northern naval forces, became increasingly acrimonious. The situation was not helped by both British and French troops looting in Dunkirk, with each side blaming the other. Many were drunk, having tried to quench their thirst with wine, beer and spirits as the mains water was no longer working.

The beaches and the port were packed with troops queueing for embarkation. Each time a Luftwaffe attack came in, with Stuka sirens screaming as they dived 'like a flock of huge infernal seagulls', men scattered for their lives. The noise was deafening, with all the anti-aircraft pom-poms of the destroyers off the mole firing flat out. Then, once it was over, the soldiers dashed back, afraid to lose their place in the queue. Some cracked up under the strain. There was little that could be done for casualties of combat fatigue.

At night, soldiers waited in the sea with water up to their shoulders, as lifeboats and small boats edged in to pick them up. Most were so tired and helpless in their sodden battledress and boots that the cursing sailors had to haul them up over the gunwhales, grasping them by their webbing equipment.

The Royal Navy suffered just as much as the troops they were rescuing. On 29 May, when Göring, under pressure from Hitler, launched a major effort against the evacuation, ten destroyers were sunk or seriously damaged, as well as many other vessels. This prompted the Admiralty to withdraw the larger fleet destroyers which would be vital for the defence of southern England. But they were brought back a day later as the evacuation flagged, for each destroyer could take off up to a thousand soldiers at a time.

That day also saw a furious defence of the inner perimeter by the Grenadier Guards, the Coldstream Guards and the Royal Berkshires from the 3rd Infantry Division. They just managed to hold off the German attacks which, if successful, would have put paid to any further evacuation. French troops from the 68th Division continued to hold the western and south-western part of the Dunkirk perimeter, but the strains in the Franco-British alliance became acute.

The French were certain that the British would give priority to their own men, and in fact contradictory instructions were sent from London on this point. French troops often turned up at British embarkation points and were refused permission to pass, which naturally led to furious scenes. British soldiers, irritated that the French were bringing packs, when they had been told to abandon their own possessions, pushed them off the harbour wall into the sea. In another case, British troops rushed a ship which had been allocated for the French, while a number of French soldiers trying to climb aboard a British ship were thrown back into the sea.

Even the famous charm of Major General Harold Alexander, commander of the 1st Division, was unable to deflect the anger of General Robert Fagalde, commanding XVI Corps, and Admiral Abrial, when he told them that his orders were to embark as many British troops as possible. They produced a letter from Lord Gort assuring them that three British divisions would be left behind to hold the perimeter. Admiral Abrial even threatened to close the port of Dunkirk to British troops.

The dispute was referred to London and to Paris, where Churchill was meeting Reynaud, Weygand and Admiral François Darlan, the head of the French navy. Weygand accepted that

Dunkirk could not expect to hold out indefinitely. Churchill insisted that the evacuation should continue on equal terms, but his hope of maintaining the spirit of the alliance was not shared in London. There, the unspoken assumption was that, since France was likely to give up the battle, the British had better look out for themselves. Alliances are complicated enough in victory, but in defeat they are bound to produce the worst recriminations imaginable.

On 30 May, it looked as if half of the BEF would be left behind. But the following day the Royal Navy and the 'little ships' arrived in strength: destroyers, minelayers, yachts, paddle-steamers, tugs, lifeboats, fishing boats and pleasure craft. Many of the smaller vessels ferried soldiers out from the beaches to the larger ships. One of the yachts, the *Sundowner*, was owned by Commander C. H. Lightoller, who had been the senior surviving officer of the *Titanic*. The miracle of Dunkirk lay in the generally calm sea during the vital days and nights.

On board the destroyers, Royal Navy ratings handed out mugs of cocoa, tins of bully beef and bread to the exhausted and famished soldiers. But, with the Luftwaffe stepping up their attacks whenever there were breaks in the RAF's fighter cover, reaching a ship did not guarantee a safe haven. The description of the terrible injuries inflicted by air attack, of those drowning as ships sank and of the unanswered cries for help are hard to forget. Conditions for the wounded left behind within the Dunkirk perimeter were far worse, with medical orderlies and doctors able to do little to comfort the dying.

Even those evacuated found little relief to their suffering on reaching Dover. The mass evacuation had overwhelmed the system. Hospital trains distributed them far and wide. One wounded soldier, back from the horror of Dunkirk, could hardly believe his eyes when he saw out of the train window white-flannelled teams playing cricket as if Britain were still at peace. Many men, when eventually treated, were found to have maggots in their wounds under field dressings or were suffering from gangrene and had to have a limb amputated.

On the morning of 1 June, the rearguard at Dunkirk, which included the 1st Guards Brigade, was overwhelmed by a determined German offensive across the Bergues–Furnes Canal. Some men and even platoons collapsed, but the bravery shown that day led to the award of a Victoria Cross and several other medals. Evacuation in daylight now had to be cancelled because of the Royal Navy's heavy losses and that of two hospital ships, one sunk and the other damaged. The last ships arrived off Dunkirk during the night of 3 June. Major General Alexander in a motorboat made a final tour up and down the beaches and harbour calling for any soldiers left to show themselves. Shortly before midnight, Captain Bill Tennant, the naval officer with him, felt able to signal to Admiral Ramsay in Dover that their mission had been completed.

Instead of the 45,000 troops, which the Admiralty had hoped to save, the warships of the Royal Navy and the assorted civilian craft had taken off some 338,000 Allied troops, of whom 193,000 were British and the rest French. Some 80,000 soldiers, mostly French, were left behind due to confusion and the slowness of their commanders to withdraw them. During the campaign in Belgium and north-eastern France, the British had lost 68,000 men. Almost all their remaining tanks and motor transport, most of their artillery and the vast majority of their stores had to be destroyed. The Polish forces in France also made their way to Britain, prompting Goebbels to refer to them contemptuously as 'the Sikorski tourists'.

The reaction in Britain was strangely mixed, with some exaggerated fears but also emotional relief that the BEF had been saved. The ministry of information was concerned that popular morale was 'almost too good'. And yet the possibility of invasion had really begun to sink in. Rumours of German parachutists dressed as nuns circulated. Some people apparently even believed that in Germany 'mentally defective patients [were] being recruited for a suicide corps', and that 'the Germans dug through under Switzerland and came up in Toulouse'. The threat of invasion inevitably produced an incoherent fear of aliens in their midst. Mass Observation also noted in the wake of the evacuation from Dunkirk that French troops were warmly welcomed, while Dutch and Belgian refugees were shunned.

The Germans wasted little time in launching the next phase of their campaign. On 6 June, they attacked the line of the River Somme and the Aisne, enjoying a considerable superiority in numbers and air supremacy. French divisions, having got over the initial shock of the disaster, now fought with great bravery, but it was too late. Churchill, warned by Dowding that he did not have sufficient fighters to defend Britain, refused French requests to send more squadrons across the Channel. There were still over 100,000 British troops south of the Somme, including the 51st Highland Division which was soon cut off at Saint-Valéry with the French 41st Division.

In an attempt to keep France in the war, Churchill sent another expeditionary force under General Sir Alan Brooke across the Channel. Before leaving, Brooke warned Eden that, while he understood the diplomatic requirement of his mission, the government must recognize that it offered no chance of military success. Although some French troops were fighting well, many others had started to slink away and join the columns of refugees fleeing towards the south-west of France. Panic spread with rumours of poison gas and German atrocities.

Motorcars streamed forth, led by the rich who seemed well prepared. Their head-start enabled them to corner the diminishing petrol supplies along the way. The middle class followed in their more modest vehicles, with mattresses strapped to the roof, the inside filled with their most prized possessions, including a dog or a cat, or a canary in a cage. Poorer families set out on foot, using bicycles, hand-carts, horses and perambulators to carry their effects. With the jams extending for hundreds of kilometres, they were often no slower than those in motorcars, whose engines boiled over in the heat, advancing just a few paces at a time.

As these rivers of frightened humanity, some eight million strong, poured towards the south-west, they soon found that not only petrol was unobtainable, but also food. The sheer numbers of city-dwellers, buying every baguette and grocery available, soon produced a growing resistance to compassion and a resentment of what came to be seen as a plague of locusts. And this was in spite of the numbers who had been wounded by German aircraft strafing and bombing the packed roads. Once again it was the women who bore the brunt of the disaster and who rose to the occasion with self-sacrifice and calm. The men were the ones in tears of despair.

On 10 June, Mussolini declared war on France and Britain,

although well aware of his country's military and material weakness. He was determined not to miss his chance to profit territorially before peace came. But the Italian offensive in the Alps, of which the Germans had not been informed, proved disastrous. The French lost just over 200 men. The Italians suffered 6,000 casualties, including more than 2,000 cases of severe frostbite.

In a decision which only increased the confusion, the French government had moved to the Loire Valley, with different ministries and headquarters established in various chateaux. On 11 June, Churchill flew to Briare on the Loire for a meeting with the French leaders. Escorted by a squadron of Hurricanes, he and his team landed at a deserted airfield near by. Churchill was accompanied by General Sir John Dill, now chief of the general staff, Major General Hastings Ismay, the secretary of the War Cabinet, and Major General Edward Spears, his personal representative to the French government. They were driven to the Château du Muguet, which was the temporary headquarters of General Weygand.

In the gloomy dining room, they were awaited by Paul Reynaud, a small man, with high arching eyebrows and a face which was 'puffy with fatigue'. Reynaud was close to a state of nervous exhaustion. He was accompanied by an ill-tempered Weygand and Marshal Pétain. In the background stood Brigadier General Charles de Gaulle, now Reynaud's under-secretary of war, who had been Pétain's protégé until they fell out before the war. Spears noted that, in spite of Reynaud's polite welcome, the British delegation were made to feel like 'poor relations at a funeral reception'.

Weygand described the catastrophe in the bleakest terms. Churchill, although wearing a heavy black suit on this hot day, did his best to sound genial and enthusiastic in his inimitable mixture of English and French. Not knowing that Weygand had already given orders to abandon Paris to the Germans, he advocated a house-by-house defence of the city and guerrilla warfare. Such ideas horrified Weygand and also Pétain who, emerging from his silence, said: 'That would be the destruction of the country!' Their main concern was to preserve enough troops to crush revolutionary disorder. They were obsessed with the idea that the Communists might seize power in an abandoned Paris.

Weygand, trying to shift responsibility for the collapse of French resistance, demanded more RAF fighter squadrons, knowing that the British must refuse. Just a few days before he had blamed France's defeat not on the generals, but on the Popular Front and schoolteachers 'who have refused to develop in the children a sense of patriotism and sacrifice'. Pétain's attitude was similar. 'This country', he said to Spears, 'has been rotted by politics.' Perhaps more to the point, France had become so bitterly divided that accusations of treason were bound to fly.

Churchill and his companions flew back to London with no illusions left, although they had extracted a promise that they would be consulted before an armistice. The key issues from a British point of view were the future of the French fleet and whether Reynaud's government would continue the war from French North Africa. But Weygand and Pétain were resolutely opposed to the idea, since they were convinced that in the absence of government France would descend into chaos. The following evening, 12 June, Weygand openly demanded an armistice at a meeting of the council of ministers, of which he was not a member. Reynaud tried to remind him that Hitler was not an old gentleman like Wilhelm I in 1871, but a new Genghis Khan. This, however, was Reynaud's last attempt to control his commander-in-chief.

Paris was an almost deserted city. A huge column of black smoke arose from the Standard Oil refinery, which had been set on fire at the request of the French general staff and the American embassy to deny petrol to the Germans. Franco-American relations were extremely cordial in 1940. The United States ambassador, William Bullitt, was so trusted by the French administration that he was temporarily made mayor and asked to negotiate the surrender of the capital to the Germans. After German officers under a flag of truce had been shot at near the Porte Saint-Denis on the northern edge of Paris, Generaloberst Georg von Küchler, the commander-in-chief of the German Tenth Army, ordered that Paris should be bombarded. Bullitt intervened and managed to save the city from destruction.

On 13 June, as the Germans were poised to enter Paris, Churchill flew to Tours for another meeting. His worst fears were confirmed. At Weygand's prompting, Reynaud asked whether Britain would release France from its engagement not to ask for a separate peace. Only a handful, including Georges Mandel, the minister of the interior, and the very junior General de Gaulle, were resolved to fight on whatever the cost. Reynaud, although in agreement with them, appeared, in Spears's words, to have been wrapped up in bandages by the defeatists and become a paralysed mummy.

When faced with the French demand for a separate peace, Churchill indicated that he understood their position. The defeatists twisted his words to imply assent, which he hotly denied. He was not prepared to release the French from their commitment until the British were certain that the Germans could never get hold of the French fleet. In enemy hands, it would make an invasion of Britain much more likely to succeed. He demanded that Reynaud should approach President Roosevelt to see whether the United States might be prepared to assist France *in extremis*. Every day that France continued to resist would give Britain a better chance to prepare for a German onslaught.

That evening a council of ministers was held at the Château de Cangé. Weygand, insisting on an armistice, claimed that the Communists had seized power in Paris, and that their leader, Maurice Thorez, had taken over the Palais de l'Élysée. This was a grotesque delusion. Mandel promptly rang the prefect of police in the capital, who confirmed that it was totally untrue. Although Weygand was silenced, Marshal Pétain brought out a paper from his pocket and began to read. Not only did he insist on an armistice, he rejected any idea of the government leaving the country. 'I will remain with the French people to share their pain and suffering.' Pétain, now emerging from his silence, had revealed his intention to lead France in its servitude. Reynaud, although he had the support of sufficient ministers, as well as the presidents of the Chambre des Députés and the Sénat, lacked the courage to sack him. A fatal compromise was agreed. They would await the reply of President Roosevelt before making a final decision on an armistice. Next day, the government left for Bordeaux in the last act of the tragedy.

General Brooke's worst fears had been confirmed soon after he landed at Cherbourg. He reached Weygand's headquarters near Briare on the evening of 13 June, but Weygand had been at the

Château de Cangé for the council of ministers. Brooke saw him next day. Weygand was less concerned by the collapse of the army than by the fact that his military career had not ended on a high note.

Brooke rang London to say that he did not agree with his orders for the second BEF to defend a redoubt in Brittany, a project close to the heart of de Gaulle and Churchill. General Dill understood immediately. He would stop any further reinforcements from being sent to France. They agreed that all British troops remaining in north-west France should pull back to ports in Normandy and Brittany for evacuation.

Churchill, having returned to London, was horrified. An exasperated Brooke had to spend half an hour on the telephone to him, spelling out the situation. The prime minister insisted that Brooke had been sent to France to make the French feel that the British were supporting them. Brooke replied that 'it was impossible to make a corpse feel, and that the French army was, to all intents and purposes, dead'. To carry on 'would only result in throwing away good troops to no avail'. Brooke was riled by the implication that he had 'cold feet', and he refused to back down. Eventually, Churchill accepted that it was the only course.

German troops were still bemused by the readiness of most French troops to surrender. 'We were the first to enter one particular town,' wrote a soldier with the 62nd Infantry Division, 'and the French soldiers had been sitting in the bars for two days, waiting to be taken prisoner. So that's how it was in France, that was the celebrated "Grande Nation".'

On 16 June, Marshal Pétain declared that he would resign unless the government sought an immediate armistice. He was persuaded to wait until a reply had been received from London. President Roosevelt's answer to Reynaud's earlier appeal was full of sympathy but promised nothing. From London, General de Gaulle read out a proposal by telephone apparently first suggested by Jean Monnet, later regarded as the founding father of the European ideal, but then in charge of arms purchases. Britain and France should form a united state with a single war cabinet. Churchill was enthusiastic about this plan to keep France in the war, and Reynaud too was filled with hope. But the moment he put it to the council of ministers, most reacted with savage disdain.

Pétain described it as 'marriage with a corpse', while others feared that 'perfidious Albion' was attempting a takeover of their country and colonies at their moment of greatest weakness.

A totally dejected Reynaud saw President Lebrun and tendered his resignation. He was on the edge of a nervous breakdown. Lebrun tried to persuade him to stay on, but Reynaud had lost all hope of resisting the demands for an armistice. He even recommended that Marshal Pétain should be called on to form a government to arrange an armistice. Lebrun, although basically on Reynaud's side, felt obliged to do as he suggested. At 23.00 hours Pétain presided over a new council of ministers. The Third Republic was effectively dead. Some historians have argued with a degree of justification that the Third Republic had already been killed off by an internal military coup mounted by Pétain, Weygand and Admiral Darlan, who had been won over on 11 June at Briare. Darlan's role was to ensure that the French fleet could not be used to evacuate the government and troops to North Africa to continue the fight.

That night de Gaulle had flown back to Bordeaux in an aircraft provided on Churchill's orders. On arrival, he found that his patron had resigned and that he himself was no longer part of the government. At any moment he might receive orders from Weygand, which as a serving soldier he would find hard to refuse. Keeping a low profile, which was not easy with his height and memorable face, he went to see Reynaud and told him that he intended to return to England to resume the struggle. Reynaud provided him with 100,000 francs from secret funds. Spears tried to persuade Georges Mandel to leave with them, but he refused. As a Jew, he did not want to be seen as a deserter, but he underestimated the anti-semitism which was resurgent in his country. It would eventually cost him his life.

De Gaulle, his aide-de-camp and Spears took off from the aerodrome amid wrecked aircraft. As they flew to London via the Channel Islands, Pétain broadcast to France the news that he was seeking an armistice. The French had suffered 92,000 killed and 200,000 wounded. Nearly two million men were rounded up as prisoners of war. The French army, divided against itself, partly through Communist and extreme right-wing propaganda, had handed Germany an easy victory, to say nothing of large quantities of motor transport, which would be used the following year in the invasion of the Soviet Union.

In Britain, people were shocked into silence by the news of France's surrender. The implications were underlined by the government announcement that henceforth church bells should not be rung except to warn of invasion. Official pamphlets distributed by postmen to every house warned that, in the event of a German landing, people should stay at home. If they fled, packing the roads, they would be machine-gunned by the Luftwaffe.

General Brooke had wasted no time in organizing the evacuation of the remaining British troops from France. This was fortunate, since Pétain's announcement placed his men in an invidious position. By the morning of 17 June, 57,000 of the 124,000 army and RAF personnel still in France had got away. A massive seaborne effort was mounted to take as many of the rest as possible from Saint-Nazaire in Brittany. It is thought that over 6,000 servicemen and British civilians boarded the Cunard liner *Lancastria* that day. German aircraft bombed the ship and probably over 3,500 drowned, including many trapped below. It was the worst maritime disaster in British history. In spite of this appalling tragedy, another 191,000 Allied troops returned to England in this second evacuation.

Churchill welcomed de Gaulle to London, hiding his disappointment that neither Reynaud nor Mandel had come. On 18 June, the day after his arrival, de Gaulle made his broadcast to France from the BBC, a date which would be celebrated for years to come. (He appears to have been unaware that that day also happened to be the 125th anniversary of the Battle of Waterloo.) Duff Cooper, the francophile minister of information, found that the foreign office was firmly opposed to de Gaulle speaking. It was afraid of provoking Pétain's administration at this moment when the future of the French fleet was unclear. But Cooper, backed by Churchill and the Cabinet, told the BBC to go ahead.

In this famous address, admittedly heard by very few people at the time, de Gaulle used the wireless to 'hoist the colours' of the Free French, or *la France combattante*. Although unable to attack the Pétain administration directly, it was a stirring call to arms, albeit improved in the rewriting later: 'La France a perdu une bataille! Mais la France n'a pas perdu la guerre!' In any case, he revealed a remarkable perception of the future development of the war. While acknowledging that France had been defeated by a new form of modern and mechanized warfare, he predicted that the industrial power of the United States would turn the tide of what was becoming a world war. He thus implicitly rejected the belief of the *capitulards* that Britain would be defeated in three weeks and that Hitler would dictate a European peace.

Churchill in his 'finest hour' speech, delivered the same day in the House of Commons, also made reference to the need of the United States to enter the war on the side of freedom. The Battle of France was indeed over, and the Battle of Britain was about to begin.

8

Operation Sealion and the Battle of Britain

JUNE–NOVEMBER 1940

On 18 June 1940, Hitler met Mussolini in Munich to inform him of the armistice terms with France. He did not want to impose punitive conditions, so he would not allow Italy to take over the French fleet or any of the French colonies, as Mussolini had hoped. There would not even be an Italian presence at the armistice ceremony. Japan, meanwhile, wasted little time in exploiting the defeat of France. The government in Tokyo warned Pétain's administration that supplies to Chinese Nationalist forces through Indochina must be halted immediately. An invasion of the French colony was expected at any moment. The French governor-general buckled under pressure from the Japanese, and allowed them to station troops and aircraft in Tongking.

On 21 June, preparations for the armistice were complete. Hitler, who had long dreamed of this moment, had ordered that Marshal Foch's railway carriage in which German representatives had signed the surrender in 1918 should be brought back from its museum to the Forest of Compiègne. The humiliation which had haunted his life was about to be reversed. Hitler seated himself in the carriage as he, Ribbentrop, the deputy Führer Rudolf Hess, Göring, Raeder, Brauchitsch and Generaloberst Wilhelm Keitel, chief of the OKW, awaited General Huntziger's delegation. Hitler's SS orderly Otto Günsche had brought a pistol with him in case any of the French delegates tried to harm the Führer. While Keitel read out the armistice terms Hitler remained silent. He then left and later rang Goebbels. 'The disgrace is now extinguished,' Goebbels noted in his diary. 'It is a feeling of being born again.'

Huntziger was informed that the Wehrmacht would occupy the northern half of France and the Atlantic coast. Marshal Pétain's administration would be left with the remaining two-fifths of the country and be allowed an army of 100,000 men. France would have to pay the costs of the German occupation and the Reichsmark was fixed at a grotesquely advantageous rate against the French franc. On the other hand, Germany would not touch France's fleet or its colonies. As Hitler had guessed, these were the two points which even Pétain and Weygand would not concede. He wanted to divide the French from the British and simply ensure that they would not hand over their fleet to their former ally. The Kriegsmarine, which had longed to get its hands on the French navy 'for continuing the war against Britain', was sorely disappointed.

After signing the terms on Weygand's instruction, General Huntziger was deeply uneasy. 'If Great Britain is not forced to its knees in three months,' he is supposed to have said, 'then we are the greatest criminals in history.' The armistice officially came into effect in the early hours of 25 June. Hitler issued a proclamation hailing the 'most glorious victory of all time'. Bells were to be rung in Germany for a week in celebration and flags flown for ten days. Hitler then toured Paris in the early morning of 28 June accompanied by the sculptor Arno Breker, and the architects Albert Speer and Hermann Giesler. Ironically, they were escorted by Generalmajor Hans Speidel, who was to be the chief conspirator against him in France four years later. Hitler was not impressed by Paris. He felt that his planned new capital of Germania would be infinitely more grand. He went back to Germany where he planned his triumphal return to Berlin and considered an appeal to Britain to come to terms, which would be delivered to the Reichstag.

Hitler was, however, disturbed by the Soviet Union's seizure of Bessarabia and the northern Bukovina from Romania on 28 June. Stalin's ambitions in the region might threaten the Danube delta and the oilfields of Ploesti, which were vital to German interests. Three days later, the Romanian government renounced the Anglo-French guarantee of its frontiers and sent emissaries to Berlin. The Axis was about to gain another ally.

Churchill, as determined as ever to fight on, had meanwhile come to a harsh decision. He evidently regretted his telegram to Roosevelt of 21 May, in which he had raised the prospect of British defeat and the loss of the Royal Navy. Now he needed a gesture to the United States and the world at large which demonstrated a ruthless intention to resist. And since the risk of the French fleet falling into German hands still preoccupied him greatly, he decided to force the issue. His messages to the new French administration urging it to send its warships to British ports had not been answered. Admiral Darlan's previous assurances no longer convinced him after he had secretly joined the *capitulards*. And Hitler's guarantee in the armistice conditions could easily be discarded like all his previous promises. The French fleet would be of inestimable value to the Germans in an invasion of Britain, especially after the Kriegsmarine's losses off Norway. And with Italy's entry into the war, the Royal Navy's mastery of the Mediterranean could be challenged.

The neutralizing of the most powerful French naval force was bound to be an almost impossible mission. 'You are charged with one of the most disagreeable and difficult tasks that a British Admiral has ever been faced with,' Churchill had signalled to Admiral Sir James Somerville as his Force H left Gibraltar the night before. Somerville, like most Royal Navy officers, was deeply opposed to the use of force against an allied navy with which he had worked closely and amicably. He questioned his orders for Operation Catapult in a signal to the Admiralty, only to receive in return very specific instructions. The French could either join the British to continue the war against Germany and Italy; sail to a British port; sail to a French port in the West Indies, such as Martinique, or to the United States; or scuttle their ships themselves within six hours. If they refused all of these options, then he had 'the orders of His Majesty's Government to use whatever force may be necessary to prevent [their] ships falling into German or Italian hands'.

Shortly before dawn on Wednesday, 3 July, the British made their move. French warships concentrated in southern British ports were taken over by armed boarding parties, with only a few casualties. In Alexandria, a more gentlemanly system, blockading the French squadron in the harbour, was arranged by Admiral Sir Andrew Cunningham. The great tragedy was to take place at the French North African port of Mers-el-Kébir near Oran, the old base of the Barbary Coast pirates. The destroyer HMS *Foxhound* appeared off the harbour at dawn and, once the morning mist had risen, Captain Cedric Holland, Somerville's emissary, signalled that he wished to confer. Admiral Marcel Gensoul, in his flagship *Dunkerque*, also commanded the battle-cruisers *Strasbourg*, *Bretagne* and *Provence*, as well as a small flotilla of fast fleet destroyers. Gensoul refused to receive him, so Holland had to carry out a very unsatisfactory attempt at negotiations through the gunnery officer of the *Dunkerque* whom he knew well.

Gensoul insisted that the French navy would never allow its ships to be taken by the Germans or the Italians. If the British persisted in their threat, his squadron would meet force with force. Since Gensoul still refused to receive Holland, he passed on the written ultimatum with the different options available. The possibility of sailing to Martinique or the United States, which even Admiral Darlan had considered an option, has seldom been mentioned in French accounts of this incident. Perhaps this is because Gensoul never mentioned it in his signal to Darlan.

As the day became hotter and hotter, Holland kept trying, but Gensoul refused to change his original reply. As the deadline of 15.00 hours approached, Somerville ordered Swordfish aircraft from the *Ark Royal* to drop magnetic mines across the harbour entrance. He hoped that this would convince Gensoul that he was not bluffing. Gensoul finally agreed to meet Holland face to face, and the deadline was extended to 17.30 hours. The French were playing for time, but Somerville, revolted by his task, was prepared to take that risk. As Holland climbed aboard the *Dunkerque*, no doubt reflecting on the unfortunate coincidence of its name, he noted that the French ships were now at battle stations, with tugs ready to pull the four battleships clear from the jetty.

Gensoul warned Holland that it would be 'tantamount to a declaration of war' if the British opened fire. He would scuttle his ships only if the Germans tried to take them over. But Somerville had come under pressure from the Admiralty to settle matters quickly, because wireless intercepts indicated that a French cruiser squadron was on its way from Algiers. He sent a signal to Gensoul insisting that if he did not agree to one of the options immediately, he would have to open fire at 17.30 hours as stipulated. Holland had to leave rapidly. Somerville waited nearly another half an hour beyond even the delayed deadline in the hope of a change of heart.

At 17.54 hours, the battle-cruiser HMS *Hood* and the battleships *Valiant* and *Resolution* opened fire with their 15-inch main armament. They soon found their range. The *Dunkerque* and the *Provence* were badly damaged while the *Bretagne* blew up and capsized. Other ships remained miraculously untouched, but Somerville ceased fire to give Gensoul another chance. He did not see that the *Strasbourg* and two of the three fleet destroyers, hidden by the thick smoke, had managed to reach the open sea. When a spotter plane warned the flagship of their escape, Somerville did not believe it because he had assumed that the mines would have prevented it. Eventually, the *Hood* gave chase and Swordfish and Skuas were launched from the *Ark Royal*, but their attacks failed when intercepted by French fighters scrambled from Oran airfield. By then, night was falling swiftly over the North African coast.

The carnage aboard the stricken ships in Mers-el-Kébir was appalling, especially for those trapped below in engine rooms. Many suffocated from the smoke. Altogether 1,297 French sailors were killed and another 350 wounded. Most of the dead were from the *Bretagne*. The Royal Navy quite rightly regarded Operation Catapult as the most shameful task it had ever been called upon to perform. And yet this one-sided battle had an extraordinary effect around the world in its demonstration that Britain was prepared to fight on as ruthlessly as it needed. Roosevelt in particular was convinced that the British would not now surrender. And in the House of Commons, Churchill was cheered for similar reasons, and not because of any hatred of the French for seeking an armistice.

The rampant anglophobia of Pétain's administration, which had shaken American diplomats, turned to a visceral loathing after Mers-el-Kébir. But even Pétain and Weygand realized that a declaration of war would achieve no benefit. They simply broke off diplomatic relations. For Charles de Gaulle, it was naturally a terrible period. Very few French sailors and soldiers in Britain were prepared to join his nascent forces, which at first numbered just a few hundred men. The homesick majority asked for repatriation instead.

Hitler too was forced to reflect on these events as his great triumphal entry into Berlin was prepared. He had been about to make a 'peace offer' to Britain just after his return, but now he felt less certain.

Most Germans, having feared another bloodbath in Flanders and Champagne, were overjoyed by the astonishing victory. This time, they were certain that the war would come to an end. Like the French *capitulards*, they were convinced that Britain could never hold out alone. Churchill would be deposed by a peace party. On Saturday, 6 July, girls in the uniform of the Bund Deutscher Mädel, the female equivalent of the Hitler Youth, strewed flowers along the road from the Anhalter Bahnhof, the station where the Führer's train would arrive, all the way to the Reichschancellery. Vast crowds had begun to gather six hours before his appearance. The fever of excitement was extraordinary, especially after the strikingly muted reaction in Berlin to the news of German forces occupying Paris. It far surpassed the fervour following the Anschluss, the annexation of Austria. Even opponents of the regime were caught up in the frenzied rejoicing of victory. This time it was galvanized by a hatred of Britain, the only remaining obstacle to a *Pax Germanica* across Europe.

Hitler's Roman triumph lacked only the captives in chains and the slave murmuring in his ear that he was still a mortal. The afternoon was sunny for his arrival, which again seemed to confirm the miracle of 'Führer weather' for the great occasions of the Third Reich. The route was packed with 'cheering thousands who shouted and wept themselves into a frantic hysteria'. After Hitler's convoy of six-wheeled Mercedes reached the Reichschancellery, the ear-piercing cries of adulation from the girls of the BDM mixed with the roar of the crowds as they called for their Führer to appear on the balcony.

A few days later, Hitler came to a decision. Having mulled over possible strategies against Britain and discussed an invasion with his commanders-in-chief, he issued 'Directive No. 16 for Preparations of a Landing Operation against England'. The first contingency plans for an invasion of Britain, 'Studie Nordwest', had been finalized the previous December. Yet even before the Kriegsmarine's losses during the Norwegian campaign, Grossadmiral Raeder had insisted that an invasion could be attempted only after the Luftwaffe had achieved air superiority. Halder, for the army, urged that an invasion should be a last resort.

The Kriegsmarine faced the almost impossible task of assembling enough ships and craft to transport the first wave of

100,000 men with tanks, motor transport and equipment across the Channel. It also had to consider its decided inferiority in warships against the Royal Navy. The OKH initially allocated the Sixth, Ninth and Sixteenth Armies, positioned along the Channel coast between the Cherbourg Peninsula and Ostend, to the invasion force. Later, this was reduced to just the Ninth and Sixteenth Armies landing between Worthing and Folkestone.

Wrangling between the armed forces over the insuperable problems made any operation look increasingly unlikely before the unsettled weather of the autumn. The only part of the Nazi administration which seemed to take the invasion of Britain seriously was Reinhard Heydrich's RSHA (Reichssicherheitshauptamt, the Reich Security Head Administration) which included the Gestapo and the SD (Sicherheitsdienst). Its counterespionage department, led by Walter Schellenberg, produced an extraordinarily detailed (and at times amusingly inaccurate) briefing on Great Britain, with a 'Special Search List' of 2,820 people whom the Gestapo intended to arrest after the invasion.

Hitler was cautious on other grounds. He was concerned that the disintegration of the British Empire might lead to the United States, Japan and the Soviet Union grabbing its colonies. He decided that Operation Sealion should go ahead only if Göring, now promoted to the new rank of Reichsmarschall, could bring Britain to its knees with his Luftwaffe. As a result the invasion of Britain was never treated with urgency at the highest levels.

The Luftwaffe was not ready. Göring had assumed that the British were bound to sue for peace after the defeat of France and his *Luftflotten* needed time re-equip their squadrons. German losses in the Low Countries and France had been far higher than expected. Altogether 1,284 of its aircraft had been destroyed, while the RAF had lost 931. Also redeploying fighter and bomber units to airfields in northern France took longer than expected. During the first part of July, the Luftwaffe simply concentrated on shipping in the Channel, the Thames estuary and the North Sea. This they called the *Kanalkampf*. Attacks mainly by Stuka dive-bombers and by fast S-Boote (motor torpedo boats which the British called E-boats) virtually closed the Channel to British convoys.

On 19 July, Hitler made a lengthy speech to members of the

Reichstag and his generals assembled with great pomp in the Kroll Opera House. After hailing his commanders and exulting in Germany's military achievements, he turned to England, attacking Churchill as a warmonger and making an 'appeal to reason', which was immediately rejected by the British government. He had completely failed to understand that Churchill's position had now become unassailable as the epitome of dogged determination.

Hitler's frustration was all the greater after his triumph in the railway carriage in the Forêt de Compiègne and the huge increase in German power. The Wehrmacht's occupation of northern and western France provided overland access to the raw materials of Spain and naval bases along the Atlantic coast. Alsace, Lorraine, the Grand Duchy of Luxembourg and Eupen-Malmedy in eastern Belgium were all incorporated in the Reich. The Italians controlled part of south-eastern France while the rest of south-central France, the unoccupied zone, was left to Marshal Pétain's 'French State' based in the spa-town of Vichy.

On 10 July, a week after Mers-el-Kébir, the Assemblée Nationale gathered in Vichy's Grand Casino. They voted full powers to Marshal Pétain, with only eighty members out of 649 opposing. The Third Republic had ceased to exist. The État Français, supposedly incarnating the traditional values of *Travail, Famille, Patrie*, created a moral and political asphyxiation which was xenophobic and repressive. It never acknowledged that it was assisting Nazi Germany by policing unoccupied France in the German interest.

France had to pay not only for the costs of its own occupation, but also a fifth of the costs of Germany's war so far. The inflated calculations and the exchange rate for the Reichsmark fixed by Berlin could not be questioned. This was an enormous bonus for the army of occupation. 'Now there's a lot to be bought for our money,' wrote one soldier, 'and many a *pfennig* is being spent. We are stationed in a large village and the shops are almost empty now.' Those in Paris were stripped bare, especially by officers on leave. In addition, the Nazi government was able to seize what raw-material stocks it needed for its own war industries. And the military booty taken, in weapons, vehicles and horses, would furnish a considerable part of the Wehrmacht's needs for the invasion of the Soviet Union a year later.

French industry, meanwhile, reorganized itself to serve the

needs of the conqueror, and French agriculture helped the Germans live better than they had since before the First World War. The French daily ration of meat, fats and sugar had to be reduced to around half that of the German. Germans regarded this as a just revenge for the hunger years they had endured after the First World War. The French, on the other hand, were encouraged to console themselves with the idea that as soon as Britain came to terms a general peace settlement would improve conditions for everyone.

After Dunkirk and the French capitulation, the British were in a state of shock similar to a wounded soldier who feels no pain. They knew that the situation was desperate, if not catastrophic, with almost all the army's weapons and vehicles abandoned on the other side of the Channel. And yet, helped by Churchill's words, they almost welcomed the stark clarity of their fate. A self-comforting belief developed that, although the British always did badly at the beginning of a war, they would 'win the last battle', even if nobody had the remotest idea how. Many, including the King, professed a relief that the French were no longer their allies. Air Chief Marshal Dowding later claimed that, on hearing of the French surrender, he had gone down on his knees and thanked God that no more fighters needed to be risked across the Channel.

The British expected the Germans to follow up their conquest of France with a rapid invasion. General Sir Alan Brooke, now responsible for the defence of the south coast, was most concerned about the lack of weapons, armoured vehicles and trained units. The chiefs of staff were still deeply worried by the threat to aircraft factories, on which the RAF would depend for replacements for the aircraft lost in France. But the time the Luftwaffe took to get ready for its onslaught on Britain provided a vital period of preparation.

The British may have had only 700 fighters at the time, but the Germans failed to appreciate that their enemy was capable of producing 470 a month, double the rate of their own armaments industry. The Luftwaffe was also confident that its pilots and aircraft were manifestly superior. The RAF had lost 136 pilots, killed or captured in France. Even when reinforced by other nationalities, they were still short. Flight training schools were pushing through as many as they could, but freshly qualified pilots were almost always the first to be shot down.

The Poles formed the largest foreign contingent, with over 8,000 air force personnel. They were the only ones with combat experience, but their integration into the RAF was slow. Negotiations with General Sikorski, who wanted an independent Polish air force, had been complicated. But, once the first groups of pilots were brought into the RAF Volunteer Reserve, they rapidly proved their skill. British pilots often referred to the 'crazy Poles' because of their bravery and disdain for authority. Their new comrades soon showed their exasperation with the bureaucracy of the RAF, and yet they acknowledged that it was far better run than the French air force.

Discipline was often a problem, partly because the Polish pilots were still angry with their own commanders for the state of their air force at the time of the German invasion the previous September. They had faced the prospect of fighting the Luftwaffe with fierce joy, convinced that although their P-11 machines were slow and badly armed they would win by skill and courage. Instead, they had been overwhelmed by the numerical and technical superiority of the German air fleets. That bitter experience, to say nothing of the dreadful treatment of their country by Hitler and Stalin, had created a burning desire for revenge now that they had modern fighters. Senior RAF officers could not have been more wrong when they arrogantly assumed that the Poles had been 'demoralized' by their defeat, and wanted to train them for bomber squadrons.

The difference in British attitudes, manners and food had been a shock to the Poles. Few got over the memory of the fish-paste sandwiches offered them on arrival in England, and they were made even more homesick by the horrors of British cuisine, from over-cooked mutton and cabbage to the ubiquitous custard (which also appalled the Free French). But the warmth of their reception by most Britons, greeting them with cries of 'Long live Poland!', astonished them. Polish pilots, seen as dashing and heroic, found themselves mobbed and propositioned to an extraordinary degree by young British women achieving a degree of freedom for the first time. Language proved less of a problem on the dance-floor than in the air.

The Polish pilots' reputation for reckless bravery was misleading. In fact their casualty rates were lower than those of RAF pilots, partly because of their experience, but also because they were better at constantly searching the sky for ambushes by German fighters. They were certainly individualistic and showed contempt for the RAF's outdated tactics of flying in tight formations of V-shaped 'vics' of three. It took time, and many unnecessary casualties, before the RAF began to copy the German system learned in the Spanish Civil War of flying in double pairs, known as 'finger four'.

By 10 July, there were forty Polish pilots in RAF Fighter Command squadrons, and the number mounted steadily as more and more of their men from France became qualified. By the time the Battle of Britain reached its climax, over 10 per cent of the fighter pilots in the south-east were Polish. On 13 July, the first Polish squadron was formed. Within a month, the British government relented, and agreed to Sikorski's request for a Polish air force, with its own fighter and bomber squadrons, but under RAF command.

On 31 July, Hitler summoned his generals to the Berghof above Berchtesgaden. He was still perplexed by Britain's refusal to come to terms. Since there was little prospect of the United States entering the war for the foreseeable future, he sensed that Churchill was counting on the Soviet Union. This played a major part in his decision to go ahead with his greatest project of all, the destruction of 'Jewish Bolshevism' in the east. Only the defeat of Soviet power by a massive invasion would force Britain to concede, he reasoned. Thus Churchill's determination in late May to fight on alone had far wider consequences than just deciding the fate of the British Isles.

'With Russia smashed,' Hitler told his commanders-in-chief, 'Britain's last hope would be shattered. Germany will then be master of Europe and the Balkans.' This time, unlike the nervousness shown before the invasion of France, his generals showed remarkable resolution when faced with the prospect of attacking the Soviet Union. Without even a direct order from Hitler, Halder had ordered staff officers to examine outline plans.

In the euphoria of victory over France and the total reversal of the humiliation of Versailles, the Wehrmacht commanders-in-chief hailed the Führer as 'the first soldier of the Reich', who would secure Germany's future for all time. Two weeks later Hitler, privately cynical about the ease with which he could bribe his leading commanders with honours, medals and money, made a presentation of twelve field marshals' batons to the conquerors of France. But before turning against the Soviet Union, which Hitler had said would be 'child's play' after the defeat of France, he still felt obliged to deal with Britain to avoid war on two fronts. The OKW directive had instructed the Luftwaffe to concentrate on the destruction of the RAF, 'its ground-support organization, and the British armaments industry', as well as ports and warships. Göring predicted that it would take less than a month. His pilots' morale was high due to the victory over France and their numerical superiority. The Luftwaffe in France had 656 Messerschmitt 109 fighters, 168 Me 110 twin-engined fighters, 769 Dornier, Heinkel and Junkers 88 bombers, and 316 Ju 87 Stuka dive-bombers. Dowding had only 504 Hurricanes and Spitfires.

Before the main onslaught took place in early August, the two Fliegerkorps in northern France concentrated on reconnaissance of RAF airfields. They mounted probing raids to provoke the British fighters into the sky and wear them down before the battle started, and attacked the coastal radar stations. The radar stations, combined with the Observer Corps and good communications from command centres, meant that the RAF did not have to waste flying time on air patrols over the Channel. At least in theory, squadrons could be scrambled with enough time to achieve altitude, yet late enough to save fuel and keep them in the air for the maximum amount of time. Fortunately for the British, the radar towers proved hard to hit, and even when damaged they were soon back in service.

Dowding had held back the Spitfire squadrons during the fighting over France, except during the evacuation from Dunkirk. He now husbanded his forces, guessing what the German tactics signified. Dowding may have appeared aloof and sad after the death of his wife in 1920, but he was quietly passionate about his 'dear fighter boys' and inspired great loyalty in return. He had a good idea of what they were about to face. He also made sure that he had the right man commanding 11 Group, which defended London and the south-east of England. Air Vice Marshal Keith

Park was a New Zealander who had shot down twenty German aeroplanes in the previous war. Like Dowding, he was prepared to listen to his pilots and allow them to ignore the hide-bound tactics of pre-war doctrine and develop their own.

In that momentous summer, Fighter Command took on the character of an international air force. Out of some 2,940 aircrew who served during the Battle of Britain, just 2,334 were British. The rest included 145 Poles, 126 New Zealanders, 98 Canadians, 88 Czechs, 33 Australians, 29 Belgians, 25 South Africans, 13 Frenchmen, 11 Americans, 10 Irishmen and several other nationalities.

The first major clash took place before the official start of the German air offensive. On 24 July, Adolf Galland led a force of forty Me 109s and eighteen Dornier 17 bombers to attack a convoy in the Thames estuary. Spitfires from three squadrons rose to attack them. And although they shot down only two German aircraft, instead of the sixteen claimed, Galland was shaken by the determination of the outnumbered British pilots. He berated his own pilots after they returned for their reluctance to attack the Spitfires, and began to suspect that the battle ahead would not be as easy as the Reichsmarschall had supposed.

With typical Nazi bombast, the German offensive was code-named Adlerangriff (Eagle Attack), and Adlertag (Eagle Day) was set, after several postponements, for 13 August. After some confusion over weather forecasts, formations of German bombers and fighters took off. The largest group was to attack the naval base of Portsmouth, while others raided RAF airfields. Despite all their reconnaissance, Luftwaffe intelligence was faulty. They mostly attacked satellite fields or bases which did not belong to Fighter Command. As the sky cleared in the afternoon, radar posts on the south coast picked out a force of some 300 aircraft heading towards Southampton. Eighty fighters were scrambled, an unimaginable number in previous weeks. 609 Squadron managed to get in among a group of Stukas and shot down six of them.

In total, the RAF fighters had shot down forty-seven aircraft, losing thirteen themselves and three pilots killed. But the German loss of aircrew was far greater, with eighty-nine killed or taken prisoner. The Channel now worked in the RAF's favour. During the Battle for France, the pilots of damaged aircraft returning home had dreaded having to ditch, or crash-land, in the sea. Now the Germans faced this greater danger, as well as the certainty of being taken prisoner if they had to bale out over England.

Göring, smarting from the disappointing result of Adlertag, launched an even bigger onslaught on 15 August, with 1,790 fighters and bombers attacking from Norway and Denmark as well as from northern France. The formations from the Fifth Luftflotte in Scandinavia lost nearly 20 per cent of their number, and they were not brought back into the battle. The Luftwaffe referred to that day as 'Black Thursday', but the RAF could hardly afford to be jubilant. Its own losses had not been light, and through sheer numerical superiority the Luftwaffe would continue to smash through. The constant attacks on airfields also killed and wounded fitters, riggers, batmen and even the drivers and plotters of the Women's Auxiliary Air Force. On 18 August, 43 Squadron achieved a satisfactory revenge when its fighters swooped on to a force of Stukas dive-bombing a radar station. They accounted for eighteen of these vulnerable predators before their escorting Me 109s joined the fray.

Fresh pilot officers arriving as reinforcements eagerly questioned those who had been in action. They were thrown into the routine. Woken before dawn with a cup of tea by their batman, they were driven out to dispersal where they had breakfast, and then they waited around as the sun came up. Unfortunately for Fighter Command, the weather during most of that August and September was perfect for the Luftwaffe, with clear blue skies.

The waiting was the worst part. That was when pilots suffered from dry mouths and the metallic taste of fear. Then they would hear the dreaded sound of the field telephone's cranking ring, and the cry of 'Squadron scramble!' They would run out to their aircraft, their parachutes thumping against their back. The ground crew would help them clamber into the cockpit, where they ran through the safety checks. When their Merlin engines had roared into life, chocks were hauled away and the pilots taxied their fighters into position for take-off; they had too much to think about to be scared, at least for the moment.

Once airborne, with the engines straining as they gained altitude, the newcomers had to remember to keep looking all around.

They soon realized that the more experienced pilots did not wear silk scarves just for affectation. With a constantly swivelling head, necks were rubbed raw by regulation collars and ties. It had been drummed into them to keep their 'eyes skinned at all times'. Assuming they survived their first action, and a number did not, they returned to base to wait once more, eating bully-beef sandwiches washed down with mugs of tea while their planes were refuelled and rearmed. Most fell asleep immediately from exhaustion on the ground or in deckchairs.

When back in the air again, the sector controllers would direct them towards a formation of 'bandits'. A cry of 'Tally ho!' over the radio signified that a formation of black dots had been spotted. The pilot would switch on the reflector sight, and the tension mounted. The vital discipline was to keep fear under control, otherwise it would lead rapidly to your death.

The priority was to break up the bombers before the umbrella of Me 109s could intervene. If several squadrons had been 'vectored' on to the enemy force, the faster Spitfires would take on the enemy fighters, while the Hurricanes tried to deal with the bombers. Within seconds the sky was a scene of chaos, with twisting, diving aircraft jockeying for position to 'squeeze off' a rapid burst of gunfire, while trying to remember to watch out behind. Obsessive concentration on your target gave an enemy fighter the chance to come in behind you without being spotted. Some new pilots, when fired on for the first time, felt paralysed. If they did not break out of their frozen state, they were done for.

If the engine was hit, glycol or oil streamed back and covered the windscreen. The greatest fear was of fire spreading back. The heat might make the cockpit hood jam, but once the pilot had forced it open and released his harness straps, he needed to roll his machine upside down so that he fell clear. Many were so dazed by the disorientating experience that they had to make a conscious effort to remember to pull the ripcord. If they had a chance to look around on the way down, they often found that the sky, which had been so full of aircraft, was now suddenly deserted and they were all alone.

Providing that they were not out over the Channel, RAF pilots at least knew that they were dropping on to home territory. The Poles and Czechs understood that, despite their uniforms, they might be mistaken for Germans by over-enthusiastic locals or members of the Home Guard. The parachute of one Polish pilot, Czesław Tarkowski, caught in an oak tree. 'People with pitch-forks and staves ran up,' he recorded. 'One of them, armed with a shotgun, was screaming "Hände hoch!" "Fuck off," I answered in my very best English. The lowering faces immediately bright-ened up. "He's one of ours!" they shouted in unison.' Another Pole landed one afternoon in the grounds of a very respectable lawn tennis club. He was signed in as a guest, given a racket, lent some white flannels and invited to take part in a match. His oppo-nents were thrashed and left totally exhausted by the time an RAF vehicle came to collect him.

The honest pilot would admit to 'a savage, primitive exalt-ation' when he saw the enemy plane he had hit going down. Polish pilots, told by the British that it was not done to shoot German pilots who baled out, resorted in some cases to flying over their parachute canopy instead so that it collapsed in the slipstream and their enemy plummeted to his death. Others felt a moment of compassion when reminded that they were killing or maiming a human being, rather than just destroying an aeroplane.

The combination of exhaustion and fear built up dangerous levels of stress. Many suffered from terrible dreams each night. Inevitably some cracked under the strain. Almost everyone had 'an attack of the jitters' at some stage, but pushed themselves to continue. A number, however, turned away from combat, pre-tending they had engine trouble. After a couple of occurrences, this was noted. In official RAF parlance it was attributed to 'lack of moral fibre', and the pilot concerned transferred to menial duties.

The vast majority of British fighter pilots were aged under twenty-two. They had no option but to grow up rapidly, even while the nicknames and public school boisterousness in the mess continued, to the astonishment of fellow pilots from other coun-tries. But as Luftwaffe attacks on Britain mounted, with increasing civilian casualties, a mood of angry indignation developed.

German fighter pilots were also suffering from stress and ex-haustion. Operating from improvised and uneven airfields in the Pas de Calais, they suffered many accidents. The Me 109 was an excellent aircraft for experienced pilots, but for those rushed forward from flying school, it proved a tough beast to master. Unlike Dowding, who circulated his squadrons to make sure that they had a rest in a quiet area, Göring was pitiless towards his aircrews, whose morale began to suffer from mounting losses. The bomber squadrons complained that the Me 109s were turning back, leaving them exposed, but this was because the fighters simply did not have the fuel reserves to remain over England for more than thirty minutes, and even less if involved in heavy dogfights.

Pilots of the Me 110 twin-engined fighters were meanwhile depressed by their losses and wanted Me 109s to escort them. British pilots with steel nerves had discovered that a head-on attack was the best way to deal with them. And even a furious Göring was forced to withdraw the Stuka dive-bombers from major operations after the massacre on 18 August. Yet the Reichsmarschall, spurred on by hopelessly optimistic assessments from his chief intelligence officer, was certain that the RAF was about to collapse. He ordered an intensification of attacks on airfields. His own pilots, however, became dejected at being told constantly that the RAF was at its last gasp when they met as furious a response on every sortie.

Dowding had foreseen this battle of attrition, and the mounting damage to airfields was a major concern. Although the RAF downed more German planes than it lost on almost every single day, it was operating from a much smaller base. An impressive increase in fighter production had removed one worry, but pilot losses remained Dowding's greatest anxiety. His men were so tired that they were falling asleep at meals and even in the middle of a conversation. To reduce casualties, fighter squadrons were ordered not to pursue German raiders over the Channel and not to react to strafing attacks by small groups of Messerschmitts.

Fighter Command was also affected by a dispute over tactics. Air Marshal Trafford Leigh-Mallory, the commander of 10 Group, north of London, favoured the 'big wing' approach, concentrating numerous squadrons. This had first been advocated by Squadron Leader Douglas Bader, a courageous but obstinate officer, famous for having made his way back as a fighter pilot after losing both his legs in a pre-war crash. But both Keith Park and Dowding were deeply unhappy about the 'big wing' innovation.

By the time 10 Group had assembled one of these formations in the air, the German raiders had usually left.

On the night of 24 August, a force of more than a hundred German bombers overflew their targets and bombed eastern and central London by mistake. This provoked Churchill into ordering a string of retaliatory bombing raids on Germany. The consequences were to be grave for Londoners, but they also contributed to Göring's fatal decision later to switch targets away from airfields. This saved RAF Fighter Command at a crucial stage of the battle.

Under pressure from Göring, German attacks intensified even more at the end of August and during the first week of September. On one day alone, Fighter Command lost forty aircraft, with nine pilots dead and eighteen seriously wounded. Everyone was under intense strain, but the knowledge that the battle was literally a fight to the finish and that Fighter Command was inflicting heavier losses on the Luftwaffe steeled the pilots' resolve.

On the afternoon of 7 September, with Göring watching from the cliffs of the Pas de Calais, the Luftwaffe sent over a thousand aircraft in a massive attack. Fighter Command scrambled eleven squadrons of fighters. All over Kent, farmworkers, Land Girls and villagers strained their eyes watching the vapour trails as the battle developed. It was impossible to distinguish which side fighters belonged to, but every time a bomber came down belching smoke, there was a cheer. Most of the bomber squadrons were headed for the docks in London. This was Hitler's retaliation for Bomber Command's attacks on Germany. The smoke from the fierce fires caused by incendiaries guided the following waves of bombers to the target area. London, with over 300 civilians dead and 1,300 injured, suffered the first of many heavy blows. But Göring's belief that Fighter Command was spent, and the decision to attack cities instead, mostly at night, meant that the Luftwaffe had failed to win the battle.

The British, however, still expected at any moment the ringing of church bells to announce the invasion. Bomber Command continued to attack the barges assembled in Channel ports. Nobody knew Hitler's own doubts. If the RAF were not destroyed by mid-September, then Operation Sealion would be postponed. Göring, well aware that he would be blamed for the failure to crush the RAF, as he had boasted he would do, ordered another major assault on Sunday, 15 September.

That day, Churchill had decided to visit the headquarters of 11 Group at Uxbridge, where he stood in the control room alongside Park. He watched avidly as the information from the radar stations and the Observer Corps was converted into German raiders on the plotting board below. By midday, Park, following his instinct that this was an all-out effort, had scrambled twenty-three squadrons of fighters. This time, the Spitfire and Hurricane squadrons had received plenty of warning to gain altitude. And once the escorting Me 109s had to turn back when short of fuel, the bombers found themselves overwhelmed by the fighters of an air force they had been told was finished.

The pattern repeated itself during the afternoon, with Park calling in more reinforcements from 10 Group and 12 Group in the west of England. By the end of the day, the RAF had destroyed fifty-six aircraft for the loss of twenty-nine fighters and twelve pilots killed. There were more attacks a few days later, but nothing on the same scale. And yet, on 16 September, Göring was convinced by his ever optimistic chief intelligence officer that Fighter Command was down to 177 aircraft.

A fear of invasion remained, but Hitler decided on 19 September to postpone Sealion until further notice. The Kriegsmarine and the OKH were even less keen to invade now that the Luftwaffe's failure to crush Fighter Command had become clear. With the war in the west approaching a stalemate, indications of it turning into a global conflict began to appear. The Japanese had recently been taken aback by Communist forces in northern China launching a series of attacks. The Sino-Japanese War was flaring up again in another round of brutal fighting. On 27 September, the Japanese signed a tripartite pact in Berlin. This was clearly aimed at the United States. President Roosevelt promptly summoned his military advisers to discuss the implications, and two days later Britain reopened the Burma Road for the transport of war materials to the Chinese Nationalists.

The Battle of Britain was deemed to have ended at the end of October, when the Luftwaffe concentrated on the night bombing of London and of industrial targets in the Midlands. If one takes the figures for August and September, the core of the battle, the RAF lost 723 aircraft, while the Luftwaffe lost over 2,000. A strikingly high proportion came not from 'enemy action' but from 'special circumstances', which mainly meant accidents. In October the RAF shot down 206 German fighters and bombers, yet the total Luftwaffe loss for that month was 375.

The so-called Blitz on London and other cities continued throughout the winter. On 13 November, RAF Bomber Command hit back at Berlin on Churchill's orders. This was because the Soviet foreign minister, Molotov, had arrived the day before for talks. Stalin was uneasy about the presence of German troops in Finland and about Nazi influence in the Balkans. He also wanted a German guarantee of Soviet shipping rights from the Black Sea through the Dardanelles to the Mediterranean. Many found it strange to hear a Wehrmacht band playing the 'Internationale' on Molotov's arrival at the Anhalter Bahnhof, which was festooned with red Soviet banners.

The meetings were not a success, producing only mutual irritation. Molotov demanded answers to specific questions. He asked whether the Nazi–Soviet pact of the year before was still valid. When Hitler replied that of course it was, Molotov pointed out that the Germans were establishing close relations with their enemies, the Finns. Ribbentrop urged the Soviets to attack south towards India and the Persian Gulf, and share in the spoils of the British Empire. The suggestion that the Soviet Union should join the Tripartite Pact with Italy and Japan for this purpose was not one that Molotov took seriously. Nor was he inclined to agree when Hitler, in a characteristic monologue, lectured him on how the British were as good as beaten, as did Ribbentrop. So when the air-raid sirens sounded, and Molotov was led downstairs into the Wilhelmstrasse bunker, he could not resist remarking to the Nazi foreign minister: 'You say that England is defeated. So why are we sitting here now in this air-raid shelter?'

The Luftwaffe attacked Coventry the next night, but this had been planned in advance and was not a reprisal. The heavy raid hit twelve armaments factories and destroyed the ancient cathedral, as well as killing 380 civilians. But the night-bombing campaign failed to break the will of the British people, even though 23,000 civilians were killed and 32,000 seriously injured by the end of the year. Many complained of the sirens, whose 'prolonged ban-shee howlings', as Churchill called them, were soon reduced to give people a chance to sleep. 'The sirens go off at approximately the same time every evening and in the poorer districts queues of people carrying blankets, thermos flasks, and babies begin to form quite early outside the air-raid shelters.' Boarded-up shop windows smashed by bomb blast carried stickers announcing 'Business as usual' and the inhabitants of houses destroyed in the east end of London placed paper Union Jacks on the piles of rubble which had been their homes.

'Worse than the tedium of our days', wrote Peter Quennell working in the ministry of information, 'was the squalor of our restless nights. Very often we were required to work in shifts – so many hours in a stifling subterranean dormitory under hairy much-used blankets; so many above ground crouched at our usual desks or, during a lull, asleep upon the floor, ready to be woken up by an elderly office messenger, who brought some hid-eous piece of news – say, a direct hit on a crowded bomb-shelter – from which we had to draw the sting. Yet it is odd how quickly a habit forms, how easily we adapt ourselves to an unfamiliar way of life, and how often supposed necessities are revealed as superfluities.'

Although Londoners faced up far better than expected to the hardships, displaying the 'spirit of the Blitz' in Underground sta-tions, a fear of German paratroopers continued, especially among women outside London. Rumours of an invasion spread from week to week. Yet on 2 October Operation Sealion had been effectively postponed until the next spring. Sealion had played a double role. The menace of a German invasion had helped Churchill unify the country and steel it for a long war. But Hitler was canny in the way he maintained the psychological threat for long after he had discarded the idea. This persuaded the British to maintain far larger defence forces in the United Kingdom than were necessary.

In Berlin, Nazi leaders were resigned to the fact that even the bombing campaign was unlikely to bring Britain to its knees. 'The view now prevails', wrote Ernst von Weizsäcker, the state secretary of the German foreign office, in his diary on 17 Novem-ber, 'that starvation caused by a blockade is the most important weapon against Britain, and not smoking the British out.' The very word 'blockade' carried an emotional note of revenge in Germany, obsessed with memories of the First World War and the Royal Navy's blockade. This strategy would now be turned against the British Isles by submarine warfare.

9

Reverberations

JUNE 1940–FEBRUARY 1941

The Fall of France in the summer of 1940 created reverbera-
tions, both direct and indirect, all around the world. Stalin
was deeply disturbed. His hopes that Hitler's power would be
greatly weakened in a war of attrition against France and Britain
had proved utterly wrong. Germany was now far more powerful
with a large part of the French army's vehicles and weaponry captured intact.

Further east, it represented a doubly serious blow to Chiang
Kai-shek and the Chinese Nationalists. After the loss of Nanking,
they had relocated their industrial base to the south-western
provinces of Yunnan and Kwangsi, close to the frontier of French
Indochina, believing that to be their most secure area with access
to the outside world. But the new Vichy regime of Marshal Pétain
began to bow to Japanese demands in July, and agreed to accept a
Japanese military mission in Hanoi. The Nationalist supply route
through Indochina was cut.

The advance of the Japanese 11th Army in that summer of
1940 up the Yangtze valley split the Nationalist armies and caused
huge losses. On 12 June, the fall of the major river port of Ichang
represented a terrible blow. It also isolated the Nationalist capital of Chungking and allowed Japanese naval aircraft to attack
it with continual raids. There were no river mists at that time of
year to impede visibility. As well as bombing towns and villages
along the river, Japanese aircraft attacked steamers and junks
overcrowded with wounded and refugees as they escaped upriver
through the great Yangtze gorges.

Agnes Smedley asked a Red Cross doctor about the situation.
He admitted that of the 150 military hospitals on the central
front, only five had survived. 'What about the wounded?' Smedley asked. 'He said nothing, and I knew the answer.' Death was
all around. 'Each day,' she added, 'we saw the bloated corpses

of human beings slowly floating down the river, drifting against junks, and being shoved away by boatmen with long, spiked poles.'

When Smedley reached Chungking on its cliffs high above the confluence of the Yangtze and Chialing rivers, she was startled by explosions, but these were not bombs. Chinese engineers were blasting tunnels in the cliffs to make air-raid shelters. She found that during her absence much had changed, both good and bad. A provincial city of 200,000 inhabitants was swelling towards a population of a million. The growth of industrial cooperatives was very encouraging, but increasingly powerful right-wing elements in the Kuomintang saw them as crypto-Communist. Improvements had been made in the army medical services, with free clinics set up in Nationalist areas, but again Kuomintang bosses wanted to control the health services, most likely for their own enrichment.

Most sinister of all was the rise in power of the security chief General Tai Li, who was said now to have a force of 300,000 men, both uniformed and plain clothes. His power was so great that some even suspected that he controlled Generalissimo Chiang Kai-shek himself. General Tai was stamping down not just on dissent but on free speech in any form. Chinese intellectuals began to flee to Hong Kong. Even the most innocuous organizations, such as the Young Women's Christian Association, were closed down in the atmosphere of crisis.

Foreigners in Chungking, according to Smedley, regarded the Chinese armies with contempt. 'China, they said, couldn't fight; its generals were rotten; its soldiers illiterate coolies or mere boys; its people ignorant; the care of the wounded an abomination. Some charges were true, some untrue, but almost all were based on a lack of appreciation of the fearful burdens under which China staggered.' Europeans and Americans failed completely to understand what was at stake and did little to help. The only substantial aid for medical services came from expatriate Chinese, whether in Malaya, Java, the United States or elsewhere. Their generosity was considerable, and in 1941 the Japanese conquerors would make them suffer for it.

Chiang Kai-shek had continued with meaningless peace negotiations in the hope of putting pressure on Stalin to bring his military support back to earlier levels. But in July 1940 a change of government in Tokyo brought General Tōjō Hideki into the Cabinet as minister of war. These shadow negotiations were broken off. Tōjō wanted to starve the Nationalists of supplies by making a stronger agreement with the Soviet Union and cutting off their other supply routes. In Tokyo, military leaders were turning their gaze south to the Pacific and south-west to the British, French and Dutch possessions around the South China Sea. This would give them rice and deprive the Nationalist Chinese of imports, but above all Japan wanted the oilfields of the Dutch East Indies. Any idea of compromise with the United States which involved a retreat from China was unthinkable to the regime in Tokyo after the deaths so far of 62,000 Japanese soldiers in the 'China Incident'.

In the second half of 1940 the Chinese Communist Party, under instructions from Moscow, launched its Hundred Regiments campaign in the north with almost 400,000 men. The intention was to undermine Chiang Kai-shek's negotiations with the Japanese: they did not know that these had been broken off and had never been serious in the first place. The Communists managed to push back the Japanese in many places, cut the Peking–Hankow railway, destroy coal mines and even carry out attacks into Manchuria. This major effort, using their forces in more conventional tactics, cost them 22,000 casualties which they could ill afford.

In Europe, Hitler demonstrated an astonishing degree of loyalty to Mussolini, often to the despair of his generals. But the Duce, his former mentor, tried every trick to avoid becoming his subordinate. The Fascist leader wanted to conduct a 'parallel war' separate from that of Nazi Germany. He failed to tell Hitler in advance of his plan to occupy Albania in April 1939, and pretended it was a companion piece to the German takeover of Czechoslovakia. Nazi leaders, on the other hand, were reluctant to share secrets with the Italians. Yet the Germans had still wanted to sign the Pact of Steel just over a month later.

Like imprudent lovers hoping to profit from a relationship, both men misled each other, and both felt misled. Hitler had never warned Mussolini of his intention to crush Poland, but still expected his backing against France and Britain, while the Italian leader believed that there would be no general conflict in Europe for at least another two years. Mussolini's subsequent refusal to enter the war in September 1939 at Germany's side disappointed Hitler greatly. The Duce knew that his country was simply not ready, and his excessive demands for military equipment as a condition for support constituted his only excuse.

Mussolini was, however, determined to come into the war at some point to gain more colonies and make Italy appear a great power. As a result he did not want to miss the opportunity when the two great colonial powers, Britain and France, suffered a major defeat in the early summer of 1940. The astonishing rapidity of Germany's campaign against France and the widespread belief that Britain would have to come to terms sent him into a fever of uncertainty. Germany would dictate the shape of Europe, almost certainly becoming the dominant power in the Balkans, while Italy risked being sidelined. For that reason alone, Mussolini was desperate to obtain the right to involvement in peace negotiations. He calculated that a few thousand Italian casualties would buy him that seat at the table.

The Nazi regime certainly did not oppose Italy's entry into the war, even beyond the eleventh hour. Yet Hitler greatly overestimated Italy's fighting strength. Mussolini had famously boasted of 'eight million bayonets' when he had fewer than 1.7 million soldiers, and many of them lacked the rifles on which to place a bayonet. The country was desperately short of money, raw materials and motor transport. To increase the number of divisions, Mussolini reduced them from three regiments to two. Out of seventy-three divisions, only nineteen were fully equipped. In fact Italy's forces were smaller and less well armed than they had been on entering the First World War in 1915.

Hitler unwisely took Mussolini's estimates of Italian strength at face value. In his very limited military vision, conditioned by marked-up maps at Führer headquarters, a division of troops was a division, however under-strength, ill equipped or badly trained. Mussolini's fatal miscalculation was to believe, in the summer of 1940, that the war was as good as over when it had hardly started. He did not appreciate that Hitler's former rhetoric of *Lebensraum* in the east would become a concrete plan. On 10 June, the Duce had declared war on Britain and France. In his bombastic speech from the balcony of the Palazzo Venezia in Rome he puffed out his chest and claimed that the 'young and fertile nations' would crush the tired democracies. This was hailed by the crowd of loyal Blackshirts, but most Italians were far from happy.

The Germans were unimpressed by Mussolini's attempt to bask in the Wehrmacht's reflected glory. The state secretary at the Wilhelmstrasse saw their Axis partner 'as a circus clown rolling up the carpet after the acrobat's performance and claiming the applause for himself'. Many more compared the Fascist leader's declaration of war on a defeated France as the action of a 'jackal' trying to snatch part of the prey killed by a lion. The opportunism was indeed shameless, but it hid something worse. Mussolini had made his country the captive and the victim of his own ambitions. He realized that he could not avoid an alliance with the dominant Hitler, yet he persisted in his wishful thinking that Italy could pursue a separate policy of colonial expansion while the rest of Europe was involved in a far more deadly conflict. Italy's weakness was to prove an utter disaster for itself and a grave vulnerability for Germany.

On 27 September 1940, Germany signed the Tripartite Pact with Italy and Japan. Part of the idea was to deter the United States from intervening in the war, which was in a state of limbo after the failure to bring Britain to its knees. When Hitler met Mussolini at the Brenner Pass on 4 October, he reassured him that neither Moscow nor Washington had reacted dangerously to the announcement of the pact. What he wanted was a continental alliance against Britain.

Hitler had intended to leave the Mediterranean region as an Italian sphere of interest, but he soon found after the fall of France that the issues were far more complicated. He had to try to balance the conflicting expectations of Italy, Vichy France and Franco's Spain. Franco wanted Gibraltar, yet he also sought French Morocco and other African territories. But Hitler did not want to provoke Pétain's French State and its loyal forces in the country's colonial possessions. It was far better from his point of view for Vichy France to police itself and the North African colonies in Germany's interest as long as the war lasted. Once it was won, then he could give away France's colonies either to Italy or to Spain. But Hitler, despite his apparently limitless power after the defeat of France in 1940, proved incapable that October of persuading his debtor Franco, his vassal Pétain or his ally Mussolini to support his strategy of a continental bloc against Britain.

On 22 October, Hitler's armoured train, the *Führersonderzug Amerika*, with its pair of engines in tandem and two flak wagons, halted at the station of Montoire-sur-le-Loir. There, he met Pétain's deputy, Pierre Laval, who tried to obtain guarantees on the status of the Vichy regime. Hitler avoided giving any, while trying to recruit Vichy to a coalition against Britain.

The gleaming carriages of the *Amerika* carried on towards the Spanish frontier at Hendaye, where he met Franco the next day. The Caudillo's train had been delayed due to the dilapidated state of the Spanish railways, and the long wait had not put Hitler in a good mood. The two dictators inspected a guard of honour from his personal escort, the Führer-Begleit-Kommando, drawn up on the platform. The black-uniformed troopers towered over the pot-bellied Spanish dictator, whose smile, both complacent and ingratiating, seldom left his face.

When Hitler and Franco began their discussions, the Caudillo's torrent of words prevented his visitor from speaking, a state of affairs to which the Führer was not accustomed. Franco spoke of their comradeship in arms during the Spanish Civil War and his gratitude for all that Hitler had done, and evoked the 'alianza espiritual' which existed between their countries. He then expressed his deep regret for not being able to enter the war immediately on Germany's side as a result of Spain's impoverished condition. For much of the three hours, Franco rambled on about his life and experiences, prompting Hitler to say later that he would prefer to have three or four teeth pulled than go through another conversation with the Spanish dictator.

Hitler finally intervened to say that Germany had won the war. Britain only hung on in the hope of being saved by the Soviet Union or the United States and the Americans would need a year and a half or two years to prepare for war. The only threat from the British was that they might occupy islands in the Atlantic or, with the help of de Gaulle, stir up trouble in the French colonies. This was why he wanted a 'broad front' against Britain.

Hitler wanted Gibraltar and so did Franco and his generals, but they were not happy with the idea of Germans commanding the operation. Franco also feared that the British would seize the Canary Isles as a reprisal. He had, however, been taken aback by the overbearing German demands to be given one of the Canary Islands as well as bases in Spanish Morocco. Hitler was also interested in the Portuguese Azores and Cape Verde Islands. The Azores did not just offer an Atlantic naval base for the Kriegsmarine. The OKW war diary later noted: 'The Führer sees the value of the Azores in two ways. He wants to have them in case of America's intervention and for after the war.' Hitler was already dreaming of a new generation of 'bombers with a range of 6,000 kilometres' to attack the eastern seaboard of the United States.

Franco's expectation that French Morocco and Oran would be promised to him before even entering the war struck the Führer as presumptuous to say the least. Hitler is also supposed to have expostulated on another occasion that Franco's attitude almost made him feel 'like a Jew who wants to bargain with the most sacred possessions'. Then, in another outburst to his entourage after his return to Germany, he described Franco as a 'Jesuit swine'. Although ideologically closer to Germany, and with a new pro-Nazi foreign minister Ramón Serrano Suñer who wanted to enter the war, Franco's government was worried about provoking Britain. Spain's survival depended on imports, partly from Britain, but above all on grain and oil from the United States. Spain was in a terrible state after the ravages of its civil war. It was not uncommon to see people fainting in the streets from malnutrition. The British and then the Americans applied economic leverage most skilfully, knowing that Germany was in no position to make up the difference in imports. So when it became increasingly clear that Britain had no intention of coming to terms with Germany, Franco's government, by then critically short of foodstuffs and fuel, could do little more than profess its support for the Axis and promise to enter the war at a later, unspecified date. That still did not stop Franco from considering his own 'parallel war', which consisted of invading Britain's traditional ally, Portugal. Fortunately, it was a project which never came close to fruition.

*

After the meeting in Hendaye, the *Sonderzug* turned round and headed back towards Montoire, where Pétain himself awaited Hitler. Pétain greeted Hitler as though they were equals, which did not endear him to the Führer. The old marshal expressed the hope that relations with Berlin would be marked by cooperation, but his demand that France's colonial possessions should be guaranteed was brusquely rejected. France had started the war against Germany, Hitler retorted, and now it would have to pay for it 'territorially and materially'. Hitler, far less exasperated with Pétain than he had been with Franco, left things open. He still wanted Vichy to join in an anti-British alliance, but eventually came to realize that he could not count on the 'Latin' countries when it came to forming a continental bloc.

Hitler had mixed feelings about a peripheral strategy of continuing the war against Britain in the Mediterranean, now that an invasion of southern England was considered unlikely to succeed. His thoughts were mostly fixed on the invasion of the Soviet Union, although he vacillated, and considered its postponement. In early November, the OKW nevertheless prepared contingency plans codenamed Operation Felix, for the seizure of Gibraltar and the Atlantic islands.

In the autumn of 1940, Hitler had hoped to seal off Britain and drive the Royal Navy from the Mediterranean before embarking on his overriding scheme, the invasion of the Soviet Union. He then convinced himself that the easiest way to force Britain to terms was to defeat the Soviet Union. For the Kriegsmarine this was frustrating, as armament priority passed to the army and Luftwaffe.

Hitler was certainly prepared to assist the Italians in their plan to launch an attack from their colony of Libya on British forces in Egypt and the Suez Canal, as that would tie down the British and threaten their communications with India and Australasia. The Italians, however, while happy to receive Luftwaffe support, were unwilling to have the Wehrmacht's ground forces in their area of operations. They knew that the Germans would want to run everything.

Hitler was particularly interested in the Balkans, since they represented the base of his southern flank for the invasion of Russia.

After the Soviet occupation of Bessarabia and northern Bukovina, Hitler, unwilling to disturb the Nazi–Soviet pact for the moment, had advised the Romanian government to 'accept everything for the time being'. He decided to send a military mission and troops to Romania to secure the oilfields of Ploesti. The one thing Hitler did not want was Mussolini stirring up the Balkans with an attack on Yugoslavia or Greece from Italian-occupied Albania. Unwisely, he counted on Italian inertia.

At first, it looked as if Mussolini would do little. The Italian navy, despite its earlier claims of aggressive action, had failed to put to sea, except to escort convoys to Libya. Not wanting to take on the Royal Navy, it left the air force to bomb Malta. And in Libya, the governor-general Marshal Italo Balbo held back, insisting that he would advance against the British in Egypt only when the Germans invaded England.

The British in Egypt wasted little time in getting the measure of their opponent. On the evening of 11 June, just after Mussolini's declaration of war, the 11th Hussars in their elderly Rolls-Royce armoured cars moved off towards the setting sun and crossed the Libyan frontier just after dark. They headed for Fort Maddalena and Fort Capuzzo, the two main Italian defensive positions on the border. Laying ambushes, they took seventy prisoners.

The Italians were most upset. Nobody had bothered to tell them that their government had declared war. On 13 June, both forts were captured and destroyed. In another raid two days later on the road between Bardia and Tobruk, the 11th Hussars captured another hundred soldiers. Their haul included a fat Italian general in a Lancia staff car accompanied by a 'lady friend', who was heavily pregnant and not his wife. This caused a scandal in Italy. More importantly for the British, the general had with him all the plans showing the defences of Bardia.

Marshal Balbo's command in Libya was short-lived. On 28 June, over-enthusiastic Italian anti-aircraft batteries in Tobruk shot down his plane by mistake. Less than a week later, his replacement Marshal Rodolfo Graziani was horrified when he received Mussolini's order to advance into Egypt on 15 July. The Duce regarded the march on Alexandria as a 'foregone conclusion'. Predictably, Graziani did everything he could to postpone operations, arguing first that he could not attack in high summer, and then that he lacked equipment.

In August the Duke of Aosta, the viceroy of Italian East Africa, had achieved an easy victory by advancing from Abyssinia into British Somaliland, forcing its few defenders to withdraw across the gulf to Aden. But Aosta knew that his situation was hopeless unless Marshal Graziani conquered Egypt. Hemmed in on the western side by the Anglo-Egyptian Sudan and British Kenya, and with the Royal Navy controlling the Red Sea and the Indian Ocean, he could expect no supplies until Egypt was taken.

Mussolini lost patience as Graziani continued to procrastinate. Finally on 13 September the Italians began to advance. They enjoyed a marked superiority with five divisions against three under-strength British and Commonwealth divisions. The 7th Armoured Division, the Desert Rats, had just seventy serviceable tanks.

The Italians managed to get lost even before reaching the Egyptian frontier. As planned, British troops conducted a fighting retreat and even gave up Sidi Barrani, where Graziani halted his advance. Mussolini insisted that he should push on along the coast road to Mersa Matruh. But with the imminent Italian attack on Greece, Graziani's forces did not receive the supplies they needed to continue.

The Germans had warned Mussolini on several occasions against an attack on Greece. On 19 September, Mussolini had assured Ribbentrop that he would conquer Egypt before attacking Greece or Yugoslavia. The Italians appeared to agree that the British should be the first target. But then on 8 October Mussolini felt slighted when he heard that the Germans were sending troops to Romania. His foreign secretary, Count Ciano, had forgotten to tell him that Ribbentrop had mentioned it earlier. 'Hitler keeps confronting me with *faits accomplis*,' the Duce said to Ciano on 12 October. 'This time I shall pay him back in his own coin.'

The next day, Mussolini ordered the Comando Supremo of the armed forces to plan for the immediate invasion of Greece from Italian-occupied Albania. None of his most senior officers, particularly the commander in Albania General Sebastiano Visconti Prasca, had the courage to warn the Duce of the huge problems of transport and supply for a winter campaign in the mountains of Epirus. The preparations were chaotic. For mainly economic reasons, a large part of the Italian armed forces were being demobilized. Units short of men had to be re-formed. The plan required twenty divisions, but three months would be needed to transport most of them across the Adriatic. Mussolini wanted to attack on 26 October, less than two weeks away.

The Germans knew of the preparations, but they assumed that no attack on Greece would be mounted before the Italians had advanced into Egypt and captured Mersa Matruh. Hitler was in his armoured train on the way back from his meetings with Franco and Pétain when he heard that the invasion of Greece was going ahead. Instead of continuing on to Berlin, the *Sonderzug* was turned round. Hitler headed south to Florence where the German foreign ministry had urgently requested that Mussolini should meet the Führer.

Early on the morning of 28 October, shortly before the meeting with Mussolini, Hitler was told that the Italian invasion of Greece had already begun. He was furious. He guessed that Mussolini was jealous of German influence in the Balkans and foresaw that the Italians might have a nasty surprise. Above all he feared that this move would draw British forces to Greece and provide them with a bombing base against the Ploesti oilfields in Romania. Mussolini's irresponsibility might even put Operation Barbarossa at risk. But Hitler had mastered his anger by the time the *Sonderzug* halted alongside the platform in Florence where Mussolini awaited him. In the event, the two leaders' discussion in the Palazzo Vecchio barely touched on the invasion of Greece, except for Hitler's offer of an airlanding division and a parachute division to secure the island of Crete against a British occupation.

At 03.00 hours that day, the Italian ambassador in Athens had presented an ultimatum to the Greek dictator, General Ioannis Metaxas, which was due to expire in three hours. Metaxas replied with a single 'No', but the Fascist regime was not interested in his refusal or compliance. The invasion, with 140,000 men, began two and a half hours later.

Italian troops advanced in a heavy downpour. They did not get far. It had already rained solidly for two days. Torrential streams and rivers washed away bridges and the Greeks, well aware of the attack which had been an open secret in Rome, blew up others. Unpaved roads became virtually impassable in the thick mud.

The Greeks, uncertain whether the Bulgarians would also attack in the north-east, had to leave four divisions in eastern Macedonia and Thrace. Against the Italian attack from Albania, their line of defence ran from Lake Prespa on the Yugoslav border via the Grammos Mountains and then along the fast-flowing River Thyamis to the coast opposite the southern tip of Corfu. The Greeks lacked tanks and anti-tank guns. They had few modern aircraft. But their greatest strength lay in the universal outrage of their soldiers, determined to repel this attack by the despised *macaronides*, as they called them. Even the Greek community in Alexandria was caught up in the patriotic fervour. Some 14,000 sailed to Greece to fight, and the funds raised there for the war effort were greater than the whole of the Egyptian defence budget.

The Italians relaunched their offensive on 5 November, but they broke through only on the coast and north of Konitsa, where the Julia Division of the Alpini advanced over twenty kilometres. But the Julia, one of the finest Italian formations, was unsupported and soon found itself virtually surrounded. Only part of it escaped and General Prasca ordered his troops on to the defensive, along the 140-kilometre front. The Comando Supremo in Rome had to postpone the offensive in Egypt and divert troops to reinforce the army in Albania. Mussolini's boast that he would occupy Greece in fifteen days was revealed as empty bombast, yet he still convinced himself that his forces would win. Hitler was unsurprised by this humiliation of his ally, having already predicted that the Greeks would prove better soldiers than the Italians. General Alexandros Papagos, the chief of the Greek general staff, was already bringing up his own reserves in preparation for a counter-attack.

Another blow to Italian pride took place on the night of 11 November, when the Royal Navy attacked the naval base of Taranto with Fairey Swordfish aircraft from the carrier HMS *Illustrious* and a squadron of four cruisers and four destroyers. Three Italian battleships, the *Littorio*, the *Cavour* and the *Duilio*, were hit with torpedoes for the loss of two Swordfish. The *Cavour* sank. Admiral Sir Andrew Cunningham, the commander-in-chief in the Mediterranean, could reassure himself that he had little to fear from the Italian navy.

On 14 November, General Papagos launched his counter-offensive, secure in the knowledge that he had numerical superiority on the Albanian front until Italian reinforcements arrived. His men, with great bravery and stamina, began to advance. By the end of the year, the Greeks had forced their attackers back into Albania between fifty and seventy kilometres from the frontier. Italian reinforcements, which brought their army in Albania up to 490,000 strong, made little difference. By the time of Hitler's invasion of Greece the following April, the Italians had lost nearly 40,000 dead, and 114,000 casualties from wounds, sickness and frostbite. Italian claims to great-power status had been utterly destroyed. Any idea of a 'parallel war' was at an end. Mussolini was no longer Hitler's ally, but his subordinate.

Italy's chronic military weakness was soon evident in Egypt too. General Sir Archibald Wavell, the commander-in-chief Middle East, had a daunting array of responsibilities covering North Africa, East Africa and the Middle East as a whole. He had begun with only 36,000 men in Egypt facing 215,000 Italians in their Libyan army. To his south, the Duke of Aosta commanded a quarter of a million men, of whom many were locally raised troops. But British and Commonwealth forces soon began to arrive in Egypt to reinforce Wavell's command.

Wavell, a taciturn and intelligent man who loved poetry, did not inspire Churchill's confidence. The pugnacious prime minister wanted fire-eaters, especially in the Middle East where the Italians were vulnerable. Churchill was also impatient. He underestimated the 'quartermaster's nightmare' of desert warfare. Wavell, who feared the prime minister's interference in his planning, did not tell him that he was preparing a counter-attack, codenamed Operation Compass. He told Anthony Eden, then on a visit to Egypt, only when asked to send badly needed weapons to help the Greeks. Churchill, when he heard of Wavell's plan on Eden's return to London, claimed to have 'purred like six cats'. He immediately urged Wavell to launch his attack as soon as possible, and certainly within the month.

The field commander of the Western Desert Force was

Lieutenant General Richard O'Connor. A wiry and decisive little man, O'Connor had the 7th Armoured Division and the 4th Indian Division, which he deployed some forty kilometres south of the main Italian position at Sidi Barrani. A smaller detachment, Selby Force, took the coast road from Mersa Matruh to advance on Sidi Barrani from the west. Ships of the Royal Navy steamed along close to the coast ready to provide gunnery support. O'Connor had already concealed forward supply dumps.

Since the Italians were known to have many agents in Cairo, including in King Farouk's entourage, secrecy was hard to maintain. So, to give the impression of having nothing on his mind, General Wavell, accompanied by his wife and daughters, went to the races at Gezira just before the battle. That evening he gave a party at the Turf Club.

When Operation Compass began early on 9 December, the British found that they had achieved complete surprise. The Indian Division, spearheaded by the Matilda tanks of the 7th

Royal Tank Regiment, took the main Italian positions right up to the edge of Sidi Barrani in less than thirty-six hours. A detachment from the 7th Armoured Division, striking north-west, cut the coast road between Sidi Barrani and Buqbuq, while its main force attacked the Catanzaro Division in front of Buqbuq. The 4th Indian Division took Sidi Barrani by the end of 10 December, and four divisions of Italians in the area surrendered the next day. Buqbuq was also captured and the Catanzaro Division destroyed. Only the Cirene Division, forty kilometres to the south, managed to escape by pulling back rapidly towards the Halfaya Pass.

O'Connor's troops had won a stunning victory. At a cost of 624 casualties, they had captured 38,300 prisoners, 237 guns and seventy-three tanks. O'Connor wanted to push on with the next phase, but he had to wait. Most of the 4th Indian Division was transferred to the Sudan to face the Duke of Aosta's forces in Abyssinia. As a replacement, he received the 16th Australian Infantry Brigade, the advance formation of the 6th Australian Division.

Bardia, a port just inside Libya, was the main objective. On Mussolini's orders, Marshal Graziani concentrated six divisions around it. O'Connor's infantry attacked on 3 January 1941, supported by their remaining Matildas. After three days, the Italians surrendered to the Australian 6th Division, and 45,000 men, 462 field guns and 129 tanks were captured. Their commander General Annibale Bergonzoli, known as 'Electric Whiskers' because of his startling facial hair, managed to escape westwards. The attackers had lost only 130 dead and 326 wounded.

Meanwhile the 7th Armoured Division had charged ahead to cut off Tobruk. Two Australian brigades hurried on from Bardia to complete the siege. Tobruk also surrendered, offering up another 25,000 prisoners, 208 guns, eighty-seven armoured vehicles and fourteen Italian army prostitutes who were sent back to a convent in Alexandria where they languished miserably for the rest of the war. O'Connor was horrified to hear that Churchill's offer to Greece of ground forces as well as aircraft put the rest of his offensive at risk. Fortunately, Metaxas refused. He felt that anything less than nine divisions risked provoking the Germans without offering any hope of holding them off.

*

The collapse of the Italian Empire meanwhile continued in East Africa. On 19 January, with the 4th Indian Division ready in the Sudan, Major General William Platt's force advanced against the isolated and unwieldy army of the Duke of Aosta in Abyssinia. Two days later the emperor Haile Selassie returned to join in the liberation of his country, accompanied by Major Orde Wingate. And in the south, a force under Major General Alan Cunningham, the younger brother of the admiral, attacked from Kenya. Aosta's army, crippled by a lack of supplies, could not resist for very long.

In Libya, O'Connor decided to go all out to trap the bulk of the Italian armies in the coastal bulge of Cyrenaica by sending the 7th Armoured Division straight across it to the Gulf of Sirte south of Benghazi. But many of its tanks were unserviceable, and the supply situation was desperate, with lines of communication stretching over 1,300 kilometres back to Cairo. O'Connor ordered the division to halt for the moment in front of a strong Italian position at Mechili, south of the Jebel Akhdar massif. But then armoured car patrols and RAF aircraft spotted signs of a major retreat. Marshal Graziani was starting to evacuate the whole of Cyrenaica.

On 4 February, the race which cavalry regiments called the 'Benghazi Handicap' began in earnest. Led by the 11th Hussars, the 7th Armoured Division pushed across the inhospitable terrain to cut off the remains of the Italian Tenth Army before they could escape. The 6th Australian Division pursued the retreating forces round the coast, and entered Benghazi on 6 February.

On hearing that the Italians were evacuating Benghazi, Major General Michael Creagh of the 7th Armoured Division sent a flying column on ahead to cut them off at Beda Fomm. This force, the 11th Hussars, 2nd Battalion of the Rifle Brigade and three batteries of the Royal Horse Artillery, reached the road just in time. Facing 20,000 Italians desperate to escape, they feared that they would be overwhelmed by weight of numbers. But just as it looked as if they would be engulfed on the landward side, the light tanks of the 7th Hussars appeared. They charged the left flank of the Italian mass in line abreast, causing alarm and confusion. Fighting died down only as the sun set.

The battle recommenced after dawn as more Italian tanks

arrived. But the British flying column also began to receive support as more squadrons caught up from the 7th Armoured Division. Over eighty Italian tanks were destroyed as they tried to break through. Meanwhile, the Australians advancing from Benghazi increased the pressure from behind. After a last attempt to escape had failed on the morning of 7 February, General Bergonzoli surrendered to Lieutenant Colonel John Combe of the 11th Hussars. 'Electric Whiskers' was the surviving senior officer of the Tenth Army.

Exhausted and miserable Italian soldiers sat en masse, huddled under the rain, as far as the eye could see. One of Combe's subalterns, when asked over the radio how many prisoners the 11th Hussars had taken, is reputed to have answered with true cavalry insouciance: 'Oh, several acres, I would think.' Five days later, Generalleutnant Erwin Rommel landed in Tripoli, followed by the advance elements of what was to be known as the Afrika Korps.

Hitler's Balkan War

MARCH–MAY 1941

Once Hitler saw that his attempts to defeat Britain had failed, he concentrated on the main objective of his lifetime. But before invading the Soviet Union he was determined to secure both his flanks. He began negotiations with Finland, but the Balkans in the south were more important. The oilfields of Ploesti would provide the fuel for his panzer divisions, while the Romanian army of Marshal Ion Antonescu would be a source of manpower. Since the Soviet Union also regarded south-eastern Europe as belonging to its sphere of influence, Hitler knew that he needed to act carefully to avoid provoking Stalin before he was ready.

Mussolini's disastrous attack on Greece had achieved precisely what Hitler feared, a British military presence in south-eastern Europe. In April 1939, Britain had given Greece a guarantee of support, and General Metaxas had called for help accordingly. The British offered fighters – the first squadrons of the Royal Air Force crossed to Greece in the second week of November 1940 – and British troops landed on Crete to free the Greek troops there for service on the Albanian front. Hitler, increasingly afraid that the British would use Greek airfields to attack the Ploesti oilfields, asked the Bulgarian government to set up early-warning observation posts along their border. But Metaxas insisted that the British should not attack the Ploesti oilwells, which would provoke Nazi Germany. His country could deal with the Italians, but not with the Wehrmacht.

Hitler, however, had now begun to consider his own invasion of Greece, partly to end the Italian humiliation, which reflected badly on the Axis as a whole, but above all to protect Romania. On 12 November, he ordered the OKW to plan for an invasion through Bulgaria to secure the northern Aegean coastline. This was given the codename Operation Marita. The Luftwaffe and

Kriegsmarine soon persuaded him to include the whole of mainland Greece in the plan.

Marita would follow the completion of Operation Felix, the
attack on Gibraltar in the spring of 1941, and the occupation of
north-west Africa with two divisions. Fearing that the French
colonies might defect from Vichy, Hitler ordered contingency
planning for Operation Attila, the seizure of French possessions
and the French fleet. These actions were to be carried out with
great ruthlessness if opposed.

With Gibraltar as the key to the British presence in the Mediterranean, Hitler decided that he would send Admiral Canaris, the
head of the Abwehr, to see Franco. He was to obtain agreement
for the transit of German troops down Spain's Mediterranean
coastal road in February. But Hitler's confidence that Franco
would finally agree to enter the war on the Axis side proved
over-optimistic. The Caudillo made it 'clearly understood that he
could enter the war only when Britain was facing immediate collapse'. Hitler was determined not to give up on this project, but,
temporarily thwarted in the western Mediterranean, he focused
his attention on Barbarossa's southern flank.

On 5 December 1940, Hitler asserted that he intended to send
only two Luftwaffe *Gruppen* to Sicily and southern Italy to attack
British naval forces in the eastern Mediterranean. At that stage,
he was against the idea of sending ground troops to support the
Italians in Libya. But in the second week of January 1941 the
devastating success of O'Connor's advance prompted second
thoughts. He cared little for Libya, but if Mussolini were overthrown as a consequence, it would represent a major blow to the
Axis and give heart to his enemies.

The Luftwaffe's presence in Sicily was increased to include the
whole of X Fliegerkorps, and the 5th Light Division was ordered
to prepare for North Africa. But by 3 February it became clear
with O'Connor's dramatic victory that Tripolitania was also at
risk. Hitler ordered the despatch of a corps to be commanded by
Generalleutnant Rommel, whom he knew well from the Poland
campaign and France. The force was to be called the Deutsches
Afrika Korps and the project given the codename Operation
Sunflower.

Mussolini had no choice but to agree to Rommel being given effective command over Italian forces. After meetings in Rome on 10 February, Rommel flew to Tripoli two days later. He wasted no time in tearing up Italian plans for the defence of the city. The front would be held much further forward at Sirte until his troops had unloaded, but that, he soon discovered, would take time. The 5th Light Division would not be ready for action until early April.

In the meantime, X Fliegerkorps on Sicily pounded the island of Malta, especially airfields and the naval base of Valletta, and attacked British convoys running the Mediterranean gauntlet. The Kriegsmarine also tried to persuade the Italian navy to attack the British Mediterranean Fleet, but their arguments had little effect until the end of March.

Preparations for Operation Marita, the invasion of Greece, continued through the first three months of 1941. Formations of the Twelfth Army under Generalfeldmarschall Wilhelm List moved through Hungary into Romania. Both countries had anti-Communist regimes and had become Axis allies as a result of energetic diplomacy. Bulgaria also had to be won over so that German forces could cross its territory. Stalin watched these developments with deep suspicion. He was not convinced by the Germans' assurances that their presence was aimed only against the British, but he could do little.

The British, all too aware of the German military build-up on the lower Danube, decided to act. Churchill, for reasons of British credibility and in the hope of impressing the Americans, ordered Wavell to abandon any thoughts of advancing into Tripolitania and to send three divisions to Greece instead. Metaxas had just died, and the new prime minister Alexandros Koryzis, faced with the reality of the German threat, was now ready to accept any help, however small. Neither a lugubrious Wavell nor Admiral Cunningham felt that this expeditionary force could hope to hold off the Germans, but since Churchill believed that British honour was at stake and Eden was utterly convinced that it was the right course, on 8 March they had to concede. In fact over half the 58,000-strong force sent to fulfil the British guarantee to Greece consisted of Australians

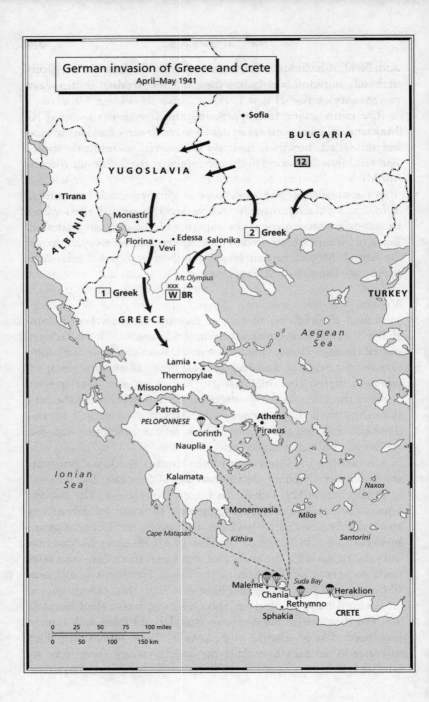

German invasion of Greece and Crete
April–May 1941

and New Zealanders. They were the formations most readily at hand, but this was to produce a good deal of Antipodean resentment later.

The commander of the expeditionary force was General Sir Maitland Wilson, known as 'Jumbo' because of his enormous height and girth. Wilson had no illusions about the battle ahead. After an over-optimistic briefing by the British minister in Athens, Sir Michael Palairet, he was heard to say: 'Well, I don't know about that. I've already ordered my maps of the Peloponnese.' This, the southernmost part of the Greek mainland, was where his troops would have to be taken off in the event of defeat. The Greek adventure was seen by senior officers as likely to be 'another Norway'. More junior Australian and New Zealand officers, on the other hand, enthusiastically spread out maps of the Balkans to study invasion routes up through Yugoslavia towards Vienna.

Wilson's W Force prepared to face a German invasion from Bulgaria. It took up positions along the Aliakmon Line which ran partly along the river of that name and diagonally from the Yugoslav border down to the Aegean coast north of Mount Olympus. Major General Bernard Freyberg's 2nd New Zealand Division was on the right and the 6th Australian Division on the left, with the British 1st Armoured Brigade out in front as a screen. The Allied troops remembered those days of waiting as idyllic. Although the nights were cold, the weather was glorious, wild flowers covered the mountains in profusion and Greek villagers could not have been more generous and welcoming.

While British and Dominion troops in Greece waited for the German attack, the Kriegsmarine put pressure on the Italian navy to attack the British fleet to divert attention away from the transports carrying Rommel's troops to North Africa. The Italians would be supported by X Fliegerkorps in southern Italy and were encouraged to take revenge for the Royal Navy's bombardment of Genoa.

On 26 March, the Italian navy put to sea with the battleship *Vittorio Veneto*, six heavy cruisers, two light cruisers and thirteen destroyers. Cunningham, warned of this threat through an Ultra intercept of Luftwaffe traffic, deployed available warships accordingly: his own Force A, with the battleships HMS *Warspite*,

Valiant and *Barham*, the aircraft carrier HMS *Formidable* and nine destroyers; and Force B, with four light cruisers and four destroyers.

On 28 March, an Italian seaplane from the *Vittorio Veneto* sighted the cruisers of Force B. Admiral Angelo Iachino's squadron set off in pursuit. He had no idea of Cunningham's presence east of Crete and south of Cape Matapan. Torpedo aircraft from HMS *Formidable* hit the *Vittorio Veneto*, yet it managed to escape. A second wave damaged the heavy cruiser *Pola*, bringing it to a halt. Other Italian ships were ordered to help and this gave the British their chance. Devastating gunnery sank three heavy cruisers, including the *Pola*, and two destroyers. Although Cunningham was deeply frustrated by the escape of the *Vittorio Veneto*, the Battle of Cape Matapan represented a great psychological victory for the Royal Navy.

The German attack on Greece was planned to begin early in April, but an unexpected crisis exploded in Yugoslavia. Hitler had been trying to win over the country, and especially its regent, Prince Paul, as part of his diplomatic offensive to secure the Balkans before Operation Barbarossa. Yet resentment had been growing among the Yugoslavs, largely due to heavy-handed German attempts to obtain all their raw materials. Hitler urged the Belgrade government to join the Tripartite Pact, and on 4 March he and Ribbentrop put heavy pressure on Prince Paul.

The Yugoslav government delayed, well aware of growing opposition within the country, but the demands from Berlin became too insistent. Finally, Prince Paul and representatives of the government signed the pact on 25 March in Vienna. Two days later, Serbian officers seized power in Belgrade. Prince Paul was removed as regent and the young King Peter II placed on the throne. Anti-German demonstrations in Belgrade included an attack on the car of the German minister. Hitler, according to his interpreter, was left 'gasping for revenge'. He became convinced that the British had a hand in the coup. Ribbentrop was immediately called out of a meeting with the Japanese foreign minister, to whom he had just suggested that Japanese forces should seize Singapore. Hitler then ordered the OKH to prepare an invasion. There would be no ultimatum or declaration of war. The Luftwaffe was to attack Belgrade as soon as possible. The operation would be called Strafgericht – Retribution.

Hitler came to see the coup in Belgrade of 27 March as 'final proof' of the 'conspiracy of the Jewish Anglo-Saxon warmongers and the Jewish men in power in the Moscow Bolshevik head-quarters'. He even managed to convince himself that it was a vile betrayal of the German–Soviet friendship pact, which he had already planned to break.

Although the Yugoslav government had declared Belgrade an open city, Strafgericht went ahead on Palm Sunday, 6 April. Over two days, the Fourth Luftflotte destroyed most of the city. Civilian casualties are impossible to assess. Estimates vary between 1,500 dead and 30,000, with the probable figure roughly halfway between. The Yugoslav government hurriedly signed a pact with the Soviet Union, but Stalin did nothing because he was afraid of provoking Hitler.

While the bombing of Belgrade went ahead that Sunday morning with 500 aircraft, the German minister in Athens informed the Greek prime minister that Wehrmacht forces would invade Greece because of the presence of British troops on its soil. Koryzis answered that Greece would defend itself. Just before dawn on 6 April, List's Twelfth Army began simultaneous offensives south into Greece and west into Yugoslavia. 'At 05.30 hours the attack on Yugoslavia began,' a Gefreiter in the 11th Panzer Division recorded in his diary. 'The panzers started up. Light artillery opened fire, heavy artillery came into action. Reconnaissance aircraft appeared, then 40 Stukas bombed the positions, the barracks caught fire . . . a magnificent sight at daybreak.'

Early the same morning, the famously arrogant General der Flieger Wolfram von Richthofen, the commander of VIII Fliegerkorps, went to watch the attack of the 5th Mountain Division by the Rupel Pass near the Yugoslav border and see his Stukas in action. 'At the command post at 04.00 hours,' he wrote in his diary. 'As it became light, the artillery began. Powerful fireworks. Then the bombs. The thought arises whether we are not paying the Greeks too much of a compliment.' But the 5th Mountain Division received a nasty surprise and Richthofen's aircraft bombed their own troops by mistake. The Greeks proved much more tenacious than he had expected.

The hastily mobilized Yugoslav army, lacking both anti-aircraft and anti-tank guns, did not stand a chance against the might of the Luftwaffe and German panzer divisions. The Germans noted that Serbian units resisted with rather more determination than Croats or Macedonians, who often surrendered at the first opportunity. One column of 1,500 prisoners was attacked in error by Stukas, killing a 'horrifying number' of them. 'That's war!' was Richthofen's reaction.

The invasion of Yugoslavia created an unexpected danger to the Aliakmon Line. If the Germans came south through the Monastir Gap near Florina, as surely they would, then the Allied positions would be outflanked immediately. The troops on the Aliakmon Line had to be pulled back to meet this threat.

Hitler wanted to cut off the Allied expeditionary force in Greece and destroy it. He did not know that General Wilson had a secret advantage. For the first time, Ultra intercepts decoded at Bletchley Park were able to provide a commander in the field with warnings of Wehrmacht moves. But both the British and Greek commands were dismayed by the rapid collapse of the Yugoslav army, which killed only 151 Germans in the whole campaign.

Greek forces defending the Metaxas Line up near the Bulgarian border fought with great bravery, but eventually part of the German XVIII Mountain Corps broke through via the southeastern extremity of Yugoslavia and opened the route to Salonika. On the morning of 9 April, Richthofen heard the 'astonishing news' that the 2nd Panzer Division had entered its suburbs. Yet the Greeks continued to mount counter-attacks near the Rupel Pass, which forced a now more respectful Richthofen to divert bombers to break them up.

On 11 April, the British 1st Armoured Brigade south of Vevi found itself facing part of the SS *Leibstandarte Adolf Hitler*. Major Gerry de Winton, the commander of the signal squadron, remembered the valley scene in the evening light as 'just like a picture by Lady Butler, with the sun going down on the left, the Germans attacking from the front, and on the right the gunners drawn up in position with their limbers'. An Ultra intercept indicated that this stand was effective: 'Near Vevi Schutzstaffel Adolf Hitler meeting violent resistance.' But such actions were few. A withdrawal from mountain pass to mountain pass began, with the Allied units managing to stay just one jump ahead of the Germans. Greek units lacking motor transport could not keep up, so a great hole in the line opened between W Force and the Greek Army of Epirus on the Albanian front.

Tanks and vehicles, unable to cope with the stony tracks, had to be abandoned and destroyed as withdrawing columns were harassed by relentless air attacks. The few Hurricane squadrons of the RAF, completely outnumbered by Richthofen's Messerschmitts, could do little to help. And during the retreat, pulling back from one improvised airfield to another, their men were uncomfortably reminded of the Fall of France. Any German pilots shot down, however, faced rough handling from Greek villagers longing for revenge.

On 17 April, the Yugoslavs surrendered. Invaded from Austrian territory in the north, from Hungary, from Romania, as well as from Bulgaria by List's army, their scattered forces had stood little chance. The 11th Panzer Division felt very satisfied with itself. 'In just under five days seven enemy divisions destroyed,' a Gefreiter noted in his diary, 'a huge amount of war materiel taken, 30,000 prisoners captured, Belgrade forced to surrender. Own losses very small.' A member of the 2nd SS Division *Das Reich* wondered: 'Did [the Serbs] perhaps believe that with their incomplete, old-fashioned and badly trained army they could form up against the German Wehrmacht? That's just like an earthworm wanting to swallow a boa constrictor!'

Despite the easy victory, Hitler the Austrian was bent on vengeance against the Serbian population, whom he still regarded as the terrorists responsible for the First World War and all its ills. Yugoslavia was to be broken up, with morsels of territory given to his Hungarian, Bulgarian and Italian allies. Croatia, under a fascist government, became an Italian protectorate, while Germany occupied Serbia. The Nazis' harsh treatment of the Serbs was to prove dangerously counter-productive, since it led to the most savage guerrilla war and interfered with their exploitation of the country's raw materials.

The retreat in Greece, with Yugoslavs mixed in among Allied forces and Greeks, produced hallucinatory images. In the middle of one military traffic jam, a Belgrade playboy wearing co-respondent shoes was spotted in an open Buick two-seater accompanied by his mistress. And a British officer thought he was dreaming when he saw 'by moonlight a squadron of Serbian lancers in long cloaks pass like ghosts of the defeated in wars long past'.

With all contact lost between the Greek army on the left and W Force, General Wilson ordered a retreat to the Thermopylae Line. This was made possible only by the brave defence of the Vale of Tempe, in which the 5th New Zealand Brigade managed to hold off the 2nd Panzer Division and the 6th Mountain Division for three days. But an Ultra intercept warned that the Germans were breaking through on the Adriatic coast towards the Gulf of Corinth.

Allied troops in Greece felt deeply embarrassed to be destroying bridges and railways as they withdrew, yet the locals continued to treat them with the greatest friendship and forgiveness. Orthodox priests would bless their vehicles and village women gave them flowers and bread as they departed, even though their own prospects under enemy occupation were extremely bleak. They did not know how terrible their fate would be. Within a few months, a loaf of bread would cost two million drachmas, and in the first year of occupation over 40,000 Greeks starved to death.

On 19 April, the day after the Greek prime minister had committed suicide, General Wavell flew into Athens for consultations. Because of the uncertain situation, his staff officers carried service revolvers. The decision to evacuate all of Wilson's troops was taken the following morning. Over Athens that day, the last fifteen Hurricanes took on 120 German aircraft. The British legation and the Military Mission headquarters in the Hotel Grande Bretagne began to burn papers, of which the most important were the Ultra decrypts.

When news of the evacuation order spread, the Allied troops were still cheered on their way. 'Come back with good fortune!' the Greeks called. 'Return with victory!' Many officers and soldiers were close to tears at the idea of leaving them to their fate. Only the need for speed amid the chaos of departure concentrated their minds. With a strong rearguard of Australians and New Zealanders to hold back the Germans, the remnants of W Force made their way to the embarkation points either south of

Athens at Rafina and Porto Rafti or on the southern coast of the Peloponnese. The Germans were determined not to allow another *Dünkirchen-Wunder* – or Dunkirk miracle – to take place.

Although General Papagos and King George II of Greece wanted to fight on while the Allied expeditionary force remained on the mainland, the commanders of the Army of Epirus, facing the Italians, decided to surrender to the Germans. On 20 April, General Georgios Tsolakoglou began negotiations with Generalfeldmarschall List on condition that the Greek army should not have to deal with the Italians. List agreed. On hearing of this, an outraged Mussolini complained to Hitler, who once again did not want his ally to be humiliated. He sent Generalleutnant Alfred Jodl of the OKW to take the surrender ceremony, with Italian officers present, instead of a furious List.

The thrill of easy victory was expressed by a German artillery officer in the 11th Panzer Division, who wrote to his wife on 22 April: 'If I saw the enemy, I would fire at them and always experienced a wild, genuine pleasure in fighting. It was a joyous war . . . We are suntanned and certain of victory. It's a wonderful thing to belong to such a division.' A Hauptmann with the 73rd Infantry Division reflected that peace would come even to the Balkans with a New European Order 'so that our children would experience no more war'. Immediately after the first German units had driven into Athens on 26 April, a huge red swastika flag was raised over the Acropolis.

That same day at dawn, German paratroop units landed on the south side of the Corinth Canal in an attempt to cut off the Allied retreat. In chaotic fighting, they suffered heavy casualties at the hands of some New Zealanders manning Bofors guns and a few light tanks of the 4th Hussars. The paratroopers also failed in their main mission to seize the bridge. The two sapper officers who had prepared its demolition managed to creep back and blow it.

While the Germans celebrated their victory in Attica, the evacuation of Wilson's forces continued at a desperate pace. Every means available was used. Blenheim light bombers and Sunderland flying-boats just managed to take off with men uncomfortably crammed into bomb-bays and gun turrets. Caiques, tramp-steamers and any other ship available steamed south towards Crete. The Royal Navy sent in six cruisers and nineteen destroyers to take off a beaten army once again. The roads into the embarkation ports of the southern Peloponnese were blocked with hastily sabotaged military transport. In the end, only 14,000 men were made prisoner out of the 58,000 sent to Greece. Another 2,000 had been killed or wounded during the fighting. In terms of manpower, the defeat could have been much worse, but the loss of armoured vehicles, transport and weapons was disastrous at a time when Rommel was advancing on Egypt.

Hitler was relieved to have secured his southern flank, but just before the end of the war he attributed the delay in launching Barbarossa to this campaign. In more recent years, historians have argued over the effect Operation Marita had on the invasion of the Soviet Union. Most accept that it made little difference. The postponement of Barbarossa from May to June is usually attributed to other factors, such as the delay in distributing motor transport, principally vehicles captured from the French army in 1940; or problems of fuel distribution; or the difficulty of establishing forward airfields for the Luftwaffe due to the heavy rains late in the spring. But one consequence of which there is little doubt was the way that Operation Marita helped convince Stalin that the Germans' thrust south meant that they were focusing on the capture of the Suez Canal, not on an invasion of the Soviet Union.

Crossing the Aegean, the overloaded vessels carrying the remnants of W Force tried with limited success to avoid Richthofen's Stukas, Junkers 88s and Messerschmitts. Twenty-six were sunk, including two hospital ships, and over 2,000 men were killed. Over a third of the casualties were inflicted when two Royal Navy destroyers, HMS *Diamond* and HMS *Wryneck*, tried to save the survivors from a sinking Dutch merchantman. Both were sunk in turn by succeeding waves of German aircraft.

Most of the evacuated troops, some 27,000, were landed in the great natural harbour of Suda Bay on the north coast of Crete during the last days of April. Exhausted men trudged out to shelter in olive groves, where they received hard tack biscuits and tins of bully beef. Stragglers, fitters, base units without officers and British civilians mingled in chaos, not knowing where to go. Freyberg's New Zealand Division disembarked in good order, along with several Australian battalions. They all expected to be taken back to Egypt to continue the battle against Rommel.

An invasion of Malta had been studied by the OKW early in February. Both the German army and the Kriegsmarine supported the plan to secure the convoy route to Libya. But Hitler decided that it should wait until later in the year, after the defeat of the Soviet Union. The British on Malta would prove a nuisance to the resupply of Axis forces in Libya, but Allied bases on Crete posed a greater danger in his view since the island could be used for bombing raids against the Ploesti oilfields. For similar reasons, Hitler urged the Italians to hold on to their islands in the Dodecanese at all costs. A German occupation of Crete would also have a positive advantage. The island could be used as a Luftwaffe base for bombing the port of Alexandria and the Suez Canal.

Even before the fall of Athens, Luftwaffe officers began studying the possibility of an airborne assault on the island. General der Flieger Kurt Student, the founder of German airborne forces, was especially keen. The Luftwaffe felt that it would restore its prestige after the failure to defeat the Royal Air Force in the Battle of Britain. Göring gave the project his blessing and took Student to see Hitler on 21 April. Student outlined a plan to use his XI Fliegerkorps to take Crete, and then later make a drop in Egypt when Rommel's Afrika Korps approached. Hitler was slightly sceptical and predicted heavy casualties. He rejected the second part of Student's project outright, but gave his approval to the invasion of Crete on condition that it did not delay the start of Barbarossa. The operation was given the codename Merkur (Mercury).

Crete, as both Wavell and Admiral Cunningham knew only too well, was a difficult island to defend. The harbours and existing airfields were almost all on the north coast. They were extremely vulnerable to attack from Axis airfields in the Dodecanese, as were ships resupplying the island. At the end of March, Ultra intercepts had identified the presence in Bulgaria of part of General Student's XI Fliegerkorps, which included the 7th Fallschirmjäger (Paratroop) Division. In mid-April, another signal revealed that 250 transport aircraft had been transferred there too. Evidently a major airborne operation was being planned, with Crete a likely target, especially if the Germans wanted to use it as a stepping stone to the Suez Canal. A flurry of Ultra intercepts in the first week of May confirmed that Crete was indeed the target.

Ever since the British occupation of the island in November 1940, it had been clear to British planners that the Germans could capture Crete only by airborne assault. The strength of the Royal Navy in the eastern Mediterranean and the lack of Axis warships ruled out an amphibious attack. Brigadier O. H. Tidbury, the first commander on the island, made a careful reconnaissance and identified all the likely German drop zones: the airfields of Heraklion, Rethymno and Maleme, as well as a valley south-west of Chania. On 6 May, an Ultra intercept confirmed that Maleme and Heraklion would be used for the 'air landing of remainder XI Fliegerkorps including headquarters and subordinated army units', as well as forward bases for dive-bombers and fighters.

British forces had been on Crete for nearly six months but little had been done to turn the island into a fortress as Churchill had demanded. This was partly due to inertia, confused thinking and the island being low on Wavell's list of priorities. The road from the less exposed south coast had barely been started and airfield construction had languished. Even Suda Bay, which Churchill had seen as a second Scapa Flow for the navy, lacked facilities.

Major General Bernard Freyberg VC, the commander of the New Zealand Division, reached Crete aboard HMS *Ajax* only on 29 April. Characteristically, he had waited until almost the last moment in Greece to make sure that his men got away. Freyberg, a great bear of a man, had long been a hero to Churchill for his bravery during the ill-fated Gallipoli campaign. Churchill called him the 'great St Bernard'. The day after his arrival, Freyberg was summoned to a conference by Wavell, who flew into Crete that morning in a Blenheim bomber. They met in a seaside villa. To Freyberg's dismay, Wavell asked him to stay on Crete with his New Zealanders and command the defence of the island. Wavell briefed him on their intelligence about the German attack, which was then estimated to consist of 'five to six thousand airborne troops plus a possible sea attack'.

Freyberg was even more dejected when he discovered the lack

of air cover available, and he feared that the Royal Navy would not be able to provide protection against a 'seaborne invasion'. He appears to have seized the wrong end of the stick right from the start. He could not imagine Crete being taken in an airborne attack, so he put increasing emphasis on a seaborne threat. Wavell, however, was perfectly clear in his own mind, as his signals to London showed, that the Axis simply did not have the naval strength to come by sea. This fundamental misunderstanding on Freyberg's part influenced both the original disposition of his forces and his conduct of the battle at the critical moment.

The Allied troops on the island under Freyberg's command became known as Creforce. Heraklion airfield to the east was defended by the British 14th Infantry Brigade and an Australian battalion. Rethymno airfield was covered by two battalions of Australians and two Greek regiments. But Maleme airfield in the west, the Germans' main objective, had only a single New Zealand battalion to defend it. This was because Freyberg believed that an amphibious assault would come on the coast just west of Chania. As a result he concentrated the bulk of his division along that stretch, with the Welch Regiment and another New Zealand battalion as reserve. No forces at all were positioned on the far side of Maleme.

On 6 May, an Ultra decrypt showed that the Germans were planning to land two divisions by air, more than double the number of men that Wavell had first indicated. Further confirmation and details of the German plan arrived, making it absolutely clear that the main effort was an airborne assault. Unfortunately, the Directorate of Military Intelligence in London had mistakenly increased the number of reserves being transported by sea on the second day. Yet Freyberg went much further, imagining the possibility of 'a beach landing with tanks', which had never been mentioned. After the battle, he admitted: 'We for our part were mostly preoccupied by seaborne landings, not by the threat of air landings.' Churchill, on the other hand, was exultant at the detail offered in the Ultra decrypts about the airborne invasion. It was a rare chance in war to know the exact timing and the primary objectives of an enemy attack. 'It ought to be a fine opportunity for killing the parachute troops,' he had signalled to Wavell.

While the Allied defenders had a huge advantage in their

information, German military intelligence was extraordinarily inept, perhaps due to over-confidence after all Germany's easy victories. A summary on 19 May, the eve of the attack, estimated that there were only 5,000 Allied troops on the island, with just 400 at Heraklion. Photo-reconnaissance flights by Dornier aircraft had failed to spot the well-camouflaged British and Dominion positions. Most astonishing of all, the briefing claimed that the Cretans would welcome the German invaders.

Because of delays in the delivery of aviation fuel, the operation was postponed from 17 May until the 20th. And during the last days before the attack, the onslaught from Richthofen's Stukas and Messerschmitts increased dramatically. Their main target was anti-aircraft gun positions. The Bofors gunners had a terrible time, except at Heraklion airfield, where they were told to abandon their guns and make them appear to have been destroyed. Very wisely, 14th Infantry Brigade wanted to hold them in readiness for when the transports arrived with the paratroopers. But in an another example of confused thinking, Freyberg, although warned by Ultra intercepts that the Germans did not want to damage the airfields as they intended to use them immediately, failed to sabotage the runways with craters.

At dawn stand-to on 20 May, the sky was clear. It was to be another beautiful and hot Mediterranean day. The usual air attacks began at 06.00 hours and lasted an hour and a half. Once they were over, soldiers climbed out of their slit-trenches and brewed up for breakfast. Many thought that the airborne invasion, which they had been warned would come on 17 May, might never come at all. Freyberg, even though he knew it was now scheduled for that morning, had decided not to pass on the information.

Just before 08.00 hours, the sound of a different sort of aero-engine could be heard as Junkers 52 transports approached the island. Men grabbed their rifles and ran back to their positions. At Maleme and on the Akrotiri Peninsula near Freyberg's headquarters, strangely shaped aircraft with long, tapering wings swished low overhead. The shout of 'Gliders!' went up. Rifles, Bren guns and machine guns opened fire. At Maleme forty gliders were seen to sweep over the airfield and land beyond the western perimeter in the dead ground of the Tavronitis riverbed and on the far side.

A number of the gliders crashed, several were hit by ground-fire. Freyberg's failure to position troops west of Maleme became immediately apparent. The gliders carried I Battalion of the Fallschirmjäger Storm Regiment, commanded by Major Koch, who had led the assault on the Belgian fortress of Eben-Emael the year before. Very soon afterwards an even greater sound of aero-engines heralded the arrival of the main force of paratroopers.

To the surprise of more junior officers at Creforce headquarters, General Freyberg, on hearing the sound, carried on with his breakfast. He glanced up, simply remarking: 'They're dead on time.' His imperturbable attitude was both impressive and worrying to some of those present. His staff watched through binoculars as the waves of Junkers transports dropped paratroopers and the battle erupted up and down the coastal strip. Several of the younger officers joined the hunt for glider crews which had crashed just to the north of the quarry in which Creforce headquarters was established.

The New Zealanders set to killing the paratroopers with gusto as they descended. Officers told their men to aim at their boots as they came down to allow for the speed of descent. At Maleme, two more German battalions dropped beyond the Tavronitis. The New Zealand 22nd Battalion responsible for the airfield had positioned only a company around the airfield, with a single platoon on the vulnerable western side. Just south of the airfield was a rocky feature known as Hill 107 where Lieutenant Colonel L. W. Andrew VC had sited his command post. The company commander on the west side of the hill directed his men's fire to great effect, but when he suggested that the two coastal guns should also be brought into action, he received the reply that they were for use only against targets at sea. Freyberg's obsession with a 'seaborne invasion' made him refuse to use his artillery and deploy his reserves, a profound error since the wisest tactical response was to launch an immediate counter-attack before enemy paratroopers had a chance to organize.

Many of the Germans dropping south-west of Chania into what was known as Prison Valley faced a massacre as they fell right on to well-camouflaged positions. One group dropped on to the 23rd Battalion's headquarters. The commanding officer shot five and his adjutant shot two from where he was sitting. Cries of

'Got the bastard!' could be heard in all directions. Very few prisoners were taken in the heat of the fighting.

None were more merciless in their determination to defend the island than the Cretans themselves. Old men, women and boys, using shotguns, old rifles, spades and kitchen knives, went into action against German paratroopers in the open and those caught in olive trees by their chutes. Father Stylianos Frantzeskakis, hearing of the invasion, ran to the church and sounded the bell. Taking a rifle himself, he led his parishioners north from Paleochora to fight the enemy. The Germans, who had a Prussian hatred of *francs-tireurs*, ripped shirts or dresses from the shoulders of civilians. If any showed marks from the recoil of a gun or were found with a knife, they were executed on the spot, whatever their age or sex.

Creforce was hampered by bad communications due to a shortage of wireless sets, since none had been shipped out from Egypt in the three weeks before the attack. As a result, the Australians at Rethymno and the British 14th Infantry Brigade at Heraklion had no idea until 14.30 hours that the invasion had begun in the west of the island.

Fortunately for the British, problems in refuelling on the airfields in Greece had delayed the departure of Oberst Bruno Bräuer's 1st Fallschirmjäger Regiment. This meant that the preliminary attack by Stukas and Messerschmitts was well over before the wave of Junkers 52 transports began to arrive. Buglers sounded the General Alarm just before 17.30 hours. Soldiers threw themselves into their well-camouflaged positions. The Bofors gun crews, which had again avoided reacting during the air raid, now traversed their barrels, ready to take on the lumbering transport planes. They were able to shoot down fifteen of them in the next two hours.

Bräuer, misled by the bad intelligence, had decided to spread his drops, with the III Battalion dropping south-west of Heraklion, the II Battalion landing on the airfield to the east of the city, and the I Battalion around the village of Gournes even further to the east. Hauptmann Burckhardt's II Battalion faced a massacre. The highlanders of the Black Watch opened a murderous fire. The few survivors were then crushed in a counter-attack with a troop of the 3rd Hussars in Whippet tanks running over and gunning down any who tried to flee.

Major Schulz's III Battalion, having dropped into maize fields and vineyards, fought its way into Heraklion despite a fierce defence of the old Venetian city walls by Greek troops and Cretan irregulars. The mayor surrendered the city, but then the York and Lancaster Regiment and the Leicestershire Regiment counter-attacked, and forced the German paratroopers back out. By nightfall, Oberst Bräuer realized that his operation had gone drastically wrong.

At Rethymno, between Heraklion and Chania, part of Oberst Alfred Sturm's 2nd Fallschirmjäger Regiment also dropped into a trap. Lieutenant Colonel Ian Campbell had spread his two Australian battalions on the high ground overlooking the coast road and the airfield, with the ill-armed Greek troops in between. As the Junkers flew along parallel to the sea, the defenders opened a withering fire. Seven aircraft were shot down. Others, trying to escape, dropped their paratroopers into the sea where a number drowned, smothered by their chutes. Some paratroopers dropped on rocky ground and were injured, and several suffered a terrible death by dropping into cane breaks where they were impaled on the bamboo. Both Australian battalions launched counter-attacks. The German survivors had to escape eastwards where they took up position in an olive-oil factory. And another group which had dropped closer to Rethymno withdrew into the village of Perivolia to defend itself when attacked by Cretan gendarmerie and irregulars from the town.

As night fell rapidly on Crete, troops on both sides collapsed in exhaustion. Firing died away. German paratroopers suffered agonies of thirst. Their uniforms were designed for northern climates and many experienced severe dehydration. Cretan irregulars laid ambushes for them near wells and continued to stalk them all night. A large number of German officers, including the commander of the 7th Fallschirmjäger Division, had been killed.

In Athens, news of the disaster spread. General Student stared at the giant map of the island on the wall of the ballroom in the Hotel Grande Bretagne. Although his headquarters lacked detailed figures, they knew that casualties had been very heavy and that none of the three airfields had been secured. Only Maleme still seemed possible, but the Storm Regiment in the Tavronitis Valley was almost out of ammunition. Generalfeld-marschall List's Twelfth Army headquarters and Richthofen's VIII Fliegerkorps were convinced that Operation Mercury had to be aborted, even if that meant abandoning the paratroop-ers on the island. One captured officer had even acknowledged to an Australian battalion commander: 'We do not reinforce failure.'

General Freyberg, meanwhile, signalled to Cairo at 22.00 hours to say that as far as he knew his troops still held the three airfields and the two harbours. He was woefully misinformed, however, about the situation at Maleme. Colonel Andrew's battered battal-ion had fought as well as it possibly could, but his requests for a counter-attack on the airfield were effectively ignored. Andrew's superior Brigadier James Hargest, presumably influenced by Frey-berg's emphasis on a threat from the sea, did not send help. When Andrew warned him that he would have to withdraw if he did not receive support, Hargest replied: 'If you must, you must.' Maleme and Hill 107 were thus abandoned during the night.

General Student, determined not to give up, came to a deci-sion without warning Generalfeldmarschall List. He sent for Hauptmann Kleye, the most experienced pilot in his command, and asked him to make a test landing on the airfield at first light. Kleye returned to report that he had not come under direct fire. Another Junkers was also despatched to take ammunition to the Storm Regiment and evacuate some of its wounded. Student immediately ordered Generalmajor Julius Ringel's 5th Moun-tain Division to prepare to be flown out, but first he sent every available reserve from the 7th Fallschirmjäger Division under the command of Oberst Hermann-Bernhard Ramcke to be dropped near Maleme. With the airfield secured, the first troop carriers began landing at 17.00 hours with part of the 100th Mountain Regiment.

Freyberg, still expecting an invasion fleet, refused to allow any of his other reserves to be used in a counter-attack apart from the 20th New Zealand Battalion. The Welch Regiment, his largest and best-equipped unit, was to be held back because he still feared a 'seaborne attack in area Canea [Chania]'. Yet one of his own staff officers had told him from captured German plans that the Light Ships Group, bringing reinforcements and supplies, was heading for a point west of Maleme, some twenty kilometres from Chania. Freyberg had also refused to listen to the assurance of the senior naval officer on the island that the Royal Navy was perfectly capable of dealing with the small boats coming by sea.

At dusk, once the Luftwaffe had disappeared from the Aegean, three Royal Navy task forces returned at full steam round both ends of the island. Thanks to Ultra intercepts, they knew the course of their prey. Force D, with three cruisers and four destroyers using radar, ambushed the flotilla of caiques escorted by an Italian light destroyer. The searchlights flashed on and the massacre began. Only one caique escaped their net and made it to shore.

Watching this naval action on the northern horizon, Freyberg became carried away with excitement. One of his staff officers remembered him jumping up and down with schoolboy enthusiasm. When it was over, Freyberg's remarks indicated that he thought that the island was now safe. He went to bed relieved, having not even asked about progress on the counter-attack against Maleme.

The attack was due to start at 01.00 hours on 22 May, but Freyberg had insisted that the 20th Battalion should not move until it had been replaced by an Australian battalion from Georgioupolis. Lacking sufficient transport, the Australians were delayed, and as a result the 20th Battalion was not ready to join the 28th (Maori) Battalion in the advance until 03.30 hours. The precious hours of darkness had been wasted. Despite the great bravery of the attackers – Lieutenant Charles Upham won the first of his two VCs during the battle – they stood little chance against the reinforced paratroopers and mountain battalions, to say nothing of the constant strafing from Messerschmitts once the sun rose. The exhausted New Zealanders had to pull back in the afternoon. They could only watch in fury as the Junkers 52 troop carriers carried on landing at a terrifyingly impressive rhythm of twenty planes an hour. The island was now doomed.

Disaster also extended to the war at sea that day. Cunningham, determined to hunt down the second Light Ships Group which had

been delayed, sent Force C and Force A1 into the Aegean in daylight. Finally, they sighted the group and inflicted some damage,
but the intensity of German air attack led to greater and greater
losses. The Mediterranean Fleet lost two cruisers and a destroyer
sunk. Two battleships, two cruisers and several destroyers suffered heavy damage. The navy had not yet learned the lesson that
the age of the battleship was over. Another two destroyers, Lord
Louis Mountbatten's HMS *Kelly* and HMS *Kashmir*, were sunk
the following day.

On the evening of 22 May, Freyberg decided not to risk a last
all-out counter-attack with his three uncommitted battalions.
He clearly did not want to be remembered as the man who lost
the New Zealand Division. The anger among the Australians at
Rethymno and the British 14th Infantry Brigade at Heraklion can
be imagined as they thought that they had won their battles. A
terrible withdrawal began over the rocky paths of the White Mountains as the footsore, thirsty and exhausted members of Creforce
made their way to the port of Sphakia, where the Royal Navy was
preparing yet again to take off a defeated army. Brigadier Robert
Laycock's commando brigade, arriving as reinforcements, landed
at Suda Bay only to hear that the island was being abandoned.
They watched in disbelief as stores were burned on the quayside.
An unamused Laycock found that his men were to form the rearguard against Ringel's mountain troops.

The Royal Navy never flinched despite its heavy losses around
Crete. The 14th Infantry Brigade was evacuated on two cruisers and six destroyers after a brilliantly concealed withdrawal
to Heraklion harbour on the night of 28 May. Officers thought
of the burial of Sir John Moore at Corunna, a poem about the
most famous evacuation in the Napoleonic Wars which they had
almost all learned to recite at school. But everything had gone too
well. Slowed by a damaged destroyer, the ships had not cleared
the channel round the eastern end of the island as the sun began to
rise. Stukas attacked after dawn. Two of the destroyers were lost
and two cruisers badly damaged. The squadron limped into Alexandria harbour piled with dead. A fifth of 14th Brigade had been
killed at sea, a far higher proportion than in the fight against the
paratroopers. A Black Watch piper, lit by a searchlight, played a
lament. Many of the soldiers wept unashamedly. The Germans

saw the losses inflicted on the Royal Navy during the Crete campaign as revenge for the sinking of the *Bismarck* (see next chapter). Richthofen and his guest General Ferdinand Schörner toasted the victory with champagne in Athens.

The evacuation from the south coast also began on the night of 28 May, but the Australians at Rethymno never received the order to withdraw. 'Enemy still shooting,' the German paratroopers reported back to Greece. In the end, just fifty of the Australians got away by crossing the mountains, and they were not taken off by submarine until some months later.

At Sphakia there was chaos and disorder caused mainly by the mass of leaderless base troops who had swarmed ahead. The New Zealanders, Australians and Royal Marines who had retreated in good order set up a cordon to prevent the boats being rushed. The last ships left in the early hours of 1 June as the German mountain troops closed in. The Royal Navy had managed to take off 18,000 men, including almost all the New Zealand Division. Another 9,000 men had to be left behind and became prisoners.

Their bitterness is easy to imagine. On the first day alone, Allied troops had killed 1,856 paratroopers. Altogether, Student's forces suffered some 6,000 casualties, with 146 aircraft destroyed and 165 badly damaged. These Junkers 52 transports would be sorely missed by the Wehrmacht later in the summer during the invasion of the Soviet Union. Richthofen's VIII Fliegerkorps lost another sixty aircraft. The Battle of Crete represented the greatest blow which the Wehrmacht had suffered since the start of the war. But, despite the Allies' furious defence, the battle had then turned into a needless and poignant defeat. Bizarrely, both sides drew very different lessons from the outcome of the airborne operation. Hitler was determined never to attempt a major drop again, while the Allies were encouraged to develop their own paratroop formations, with very mixed results later in the war.

II

Africa and the Atlantic

FEBRUARY–JUNE 1941

The diversion of Wavell's forces to Greece in the spring of 1941 could not have come at a worse time. It was another classic British example of stretching insufficient resources in too many different directions. The British, and above all Churchill, appeared to be incapable by character of matching the German army's talent for ruthless prioritization.

The opportunity for the British to win the war in North Africa in 1941 was lost as soon as forces were withdrawn for Greece and Rommel landed in Tripoli with leading elements of the Afrika Korps. Hitler's selection of Rommel was not welcomed by senior officers in the OKH. They would have far preferred Generalmajor Hans Freiherr von Funck, who had been sent out to report on the situation in Libya. But Hitler detested Funck, mainly because he had been close to Generaloberst Werner Freiherr von Fritsch, whom Hitler had dismissed as head of the army in 1938.

Hitler liked the fact that Rommel was no aristocrat. He spoke with a marked Swabian accent, and was something of an adventurer. His superiors in the army and many contemporaries considered him an arrogant publicity seeker. They also distrusted the way he exploited the admiration of Hitler and Goebbels to bypass the chain of command. The isolated campaign in Africa, as Rommel quickly sensed, presented the perfect opportunity to ignore instructions from the OKH. In addition, Rommel did not make himself popular by arguing that, instead of invading Greece, Germany should have diverted those forces to North Africa in order to seize the Middle East and its oil.

Hitler, having changed his mind several times about the importance of Libya and the need to send troops to North Africa, now felt it essential to prevent the collapse of Mussolini's regime. He also feared that the British might link up with French North Africa and that the Vichy army, influenced by General Maxime

Weygand, might rejoin the British. Even after the disastrous Dakar expedition the previous September, when the Free French and a British naval squadron were repulsed by Vichy loyalists, Hitler greatly overestimated the influence of General Charles de Gaulle at this stage.

When Rommel landed in Tripoli on 12 February 1941, he was accompanied by Oberst Rudolf Schmundt, Hitler's chief military adjutant. This greatly increased his authority both with the Italians and with senior German officers. The day before, the two men had been amazed when the commander of X Fliegerkorps on Sicily told them that Italian generals had beseeched him not to bomb Benghazi, as many of them owned property there. Rommel asked Schmundt to telephone Hitler immediately. A few hours later, German bombers were on their way.

Rommel was briefed on the situation in Tripolitania by a German liaison officer. Most of the retreating Italians had thrown away their weapons and seized trucks to escape. General Italo Gariboldi, Graziani's replacement, refused to hold a forward line against the British, by then at El Agheila. Rommel took matters in hand. Two Italian divisions were sent forward, and on 15 February he ordered the first German detachments to land, a reconnaissance unit and a battalion of assault guns, to follow. Kübelwagen cross-country vehicles were disguised as tanks in an attempt to deter the British from advancing further.

By the end of the month, the arrival of more units from the 5th Light Division encouraged Rommel to start engaging the British in skirmishes. Only at the end of March, when Rommel had 25,000 German troops on African soil, did he feel ready to advance. Over the next six weeks, he would receive the rest of the 5th Light and also the 15th Panzer Division, but the front was 700 kilometres east of Tripoli. Rommel was faced with a huge logistical problem, which he tried to ignore. When things became difficult, he instinctively blamed jealousy within the Wehrmacht for depriving him of supplies. In fact, the crises usually came when transports were sunk in the Libyan Sea by the RAF and Royal Navy.

Rommel also failed to realize that preparations for Barbarossa made the North African campaign even more of a sideshow. Other problems arose due to reliance on the Italians. The Italian army was chronically short of motor transport. Its fuel was of such low quality that it often proved unsuitable for German engines, and Italian army rations were notoriously bad. They usually consisted of tins of meat, stamped AM for Administrazione Militar. Italian soldiers said the initials stood for 'Arabo Morte' or 'Dead Arab', while their German counterparts nicknamed it 'Alter Mann' ('Old Man') or 'Mussolini's ass'.

Rommel was lucky that the Allies' Western Desert Force was so weak at this point. The 7th Armoured Division had been withdrawn to Cairo for refitting and was replaced by a very reduced and unprepared 2nd Armoured Division, while the newly arrived 9th Australian Division had taken the place of the 6th Australian Division sent to Greece. Yet Rommel's demands for reinforcements to advance into Egypt were rejected. He was told that a panzer corps would be sent that winter as soon as the Soviet Union had been defeated. He should not attempt a full-scale offensive until then.

Rommel soon ignored his orders. To the horror of General Gariboldi, he began to push the 5th Light Division into Cyrenaica, exploiting the weakness of the Allied forces. One of Wavell's greatest mistakes was to replace O'Connor with the inexperienced Lieutenant General Philip Neame. Wavell also underestimated Rommel's determination to advance straight away. He assumed he would not attack until the beginning of May. The midday temperature out in the desert had already reached 50 degrees Centigrade. Soldiers in steel helmets suffered from splitting headaches, largely brought on through dehydration.

On 3 April, Rommel decided to push the Allied forces from the bulge of Cyrenaica. While the Italian Brescia Division was sent on to take Benghazi, which Neame evacuated in a hurry, Rommel ordered the 5th Light Division to cut the coastal road short of Tobruk. Disaster rapidly overtook the Allied force, and Tobruk itself was cut off. The weak 2nd Armoured Division lost all its tanks in the withdrawal because of breakdowns and lack of fuel. On 8 April, its commander, Major General Gambier Parry, and his headquarters staff were taken prisoner at Mechili along with most of the 3rd Indian Motorized Brigade. The same day, General Neame, accompanied by General O'Connor who had come forward to advise him, were both captured when their driver took the wrong road.

The Germans rejoiced at the quantity of stores they found at Mechili. Rommel selected a pair of British tank goggles, which he wore up on his cap as a sort of trademark. He decided to seize Tobruk, having convinced himself that the British were preparing to abandon it, but he soon discovered that the 9th Australian Division was not about to give up the fight. Tobruk was reinforced by sea, giving its commander, Major General Leslie Morshead, a total of four brigades, with strong artillery and anti-tank gun units. Morshead, a forceful character, known to his men as 'Ming the Merciless', hastily strengthened Tobruk's defences. The 9th Australian, although inexperienced and ill disciplined to a point which left British officers almost speechless with rage, proved to be a collection of formidable fighters.

On the night of 13 April, Rommel began his main assault on Tobruk. He had no idea quite how strongly it was defended. Despite heavy losses and a repulse, he tried again several times to the dismay of his officers, who soon came to regard him as a brutal commander. This was the perfect moment for an Allied counter-attack, but the British and Australians were persuaded by clever deception that Rommel's forces were far larger than they really were.

Rommel's calls for reinforcements and increased air support exasperated General Halder and the OKH, especially since he had ignored their warnings not to overreach himself. Even now, Rommel sent ahead some of his exhausted units to the Egyptian frontier, which Wavell defended with the 22nd Guards Brigade until other units arrived from Cairo. Rommel sacked Generalmajor Johannes Streich, the commander of the 5th Light Division, for being too concerned with preserving the lives of his troops. Generalmajor Heinrich Kirchheim who replaced him was equally disenchanted with Rommel's style of command. He wrote to General Halder later in the month: 'All day long he races about between his widely scattered forces, ordering raids and dissipating his troops.'

General Halder, having heard such conflicting reports on what was going on in North Africa, decided to send out Generalleutnant Friedrich Paulus, who had served in the same infantry regiment as Rommel in the First World War. Halder felt that Paulus was 'perhaps the only man with enough personal influence to head off this soldier gone stark mad'. Paulus, a punctilious staff officer, could hardly have been more different from Rommel, the aggressive field commander. Their sole similarity lay in their comparatively humble birth. Paulus's task was to convince Rommel that he could not count on massive reinforcements and to find out what he intended to do.

The answer was that Rommel refused to pull back his forward units on the Egyptian frontier, and with the newly arrived 15th Panzer Division he intended to attack Tobruk again. This took place on 30 April and was again repulsed with heavy losses, especially in tanks. Rommel's forces were also very low on ammunition. Paulus, using his authority from the OKH, gave Rommel a written order on 2 May that the attacks could not be renewed unless the enemy was seen to withdraw. On his return, he reported to Halder that 'the crux of the problem in North Africa' was not Tobruk, but resupplying the Afrika Korps and Rommel's character. Rommel simply refused to acknowledge the immense problem of transporting his supplies across the Mediterranean and unloading them in Tripoli.

Wavell was concerned after the losses in Greece and Cyrenaica about his lack of tanks to face the 15th Panzer Division. Churchill mounted Operation Tiger, the transport in early May of nearly 300 Crusader tanks and over fifty Hurricanes by convoy through the Mediterranean. With part of X Fliegerkorps still on Sicily it represented a serious risk, but thanks to bad visibility only one transport was sunk on the way.

An impatient Churchill pushed Wavell into an offensive on the frontier even before the new tanks arrived. But although Operation Brevity commanded by Brigadier 'Strafer' Gott began well on 15 May, it provoked a rapid flanking counter-attack by Rommel. The Indian and British troops were forced back and the Germans eventually recaptured the Halfaya Pass. Once the new Crusader tanks arrived, Churchill again demanded action, in this case another offensive codenamed Operation Battleaxe. He did not want to hear that many of the unloaded tanks required work on them, nor that the 7th Armoured Division needed time for crews to familiarize themselves with the new equipment.

Wavell again found himself weighed down by conflicting demands from London. At the beginning of April, a pro-German faction, encouraged by British weakness in the Middle East, had taken power in Iraq. The chiefs of staff in London recommended that Britain should intervene. Churchill immediately agreed and troops from India landed at Basra. Rashid Ali al-Gailani, the leader of the new Iraqi government, sought help from Germany, but received no reply because of confusion in Berlin. On 2 May, fighting broke out after the Iraqi army besieged the British air base at Habbaniyah near Fallujah. Four days later the OKW decided to send Messerschmitt 110s and Heinkel 111 bombers via Syria to Mosul and Kirkuk in northern Iraq, but they were soon unserviceable. Meanwhile, British imperial troops from India and Jordan advanced on Baghdad. Gailani's government had no option but to accept the British demand on 31 May for the continued passage of troops across Iraqi territory.

Although the Iraq crisis did not deplete Wavell's forces, he was ordered by Churchill to invade Lebanon and Syria, where the French Vichy forces had aided the Germans in the Luftwaffe's ill-fated deployment to Mosul and Kirkuk. Churchill wrongly feared that the Germans would use Syria as a base for attacks on Palestine and Egypt. Admiral Darlan, Pétain's deputy and Vichy's minister of defence, asked the Germans to desist from provocative operations in the region while he sent French reinforcements to their colony to resist the British. On 21 May, the day after the invasion of Crete, a Vichy French fighter group landed in Greece on its way to Syria. 'The war is becoming ever more bizarre,' Richthofen noted in his diary. 'We are supposed to supply them and *entertain* them.'

Operation Exporter, the Allied invasion of Vichy Lebanon and Syria, which included Free French troops, began on 8 June with an advance north from Palestine across the Litani River. The Vichy commander, General Henri Dentz, asked for Luftwaffe assistance as well as for reinforcements from other Vichy forces in North Africa and France. The Germans decided that they could not offer air cover, but allowed French troops with anti-tank guns to travel by train through the occupied Balkans to Salonika, and then by ship to Syria. But the British naval presence was too strong, and Turkey, not wanting to get involved, refused transit rights. The French Army of the Levant soon knew that it was doomed, but remained determined to put up a strong resistance. Fighting continued until 12 July. After an armistice was signed at Acre, Syria was declared to be under the control of the Free French.

Wavell's lack of enthusiasm for the Syrian campaign and his pessimism over the prospects of Operation Battleaxe put him on a collision course with the prime minister. Churchill's impatience and his complete lack of appreciation of the problems in mounting two offensives at the same time brought Wavell close to despair. The prime minister, over-confident after the delivery of tanks in Operation Tiger, brushed aside Wavell's warning about the effectiveness of German anti-tank guns. They, rather than the German panzers, were destroying the bulk of his armoured vehicles. The British army was unforgivably slow in developing a weapon comparable to the feared German 88mm gun. Its own two-pounder 'pea-shooter' was useless. And the conservatism of the British army prevented the adaptation of the 3.7 inch anti-aircraft gun as an anti-tank weapon.

On 15 June, Battleaxe began in a similar way to Brevity. Although the British retook the Halfaya Pass and had some other local successes, they were soon pushed back when Rommel brought forward all his panzers from the Tobruk encirclement. In three days of heavy fighting, the British were outflanked once more and again had to withdraw to the coastal plain, just managing to avoid encirclement. The Afrika Korps suffered higher casualties, but the British lost ninety-one tanks, mainly to anti-tank gunfire, while the Germans lost only a dozen. The RAF also lost many more aircraft than the Luftwaffe during the battle. German soldiers, with considerable exaggeration, claimed that they had destroyed 200 British tanks and won the 'greatest tank battle of all time'.

On 21 June, Churchill replaced Wavell with General Sir Claude Auchinleck, universally known as 'the Auk'. Wavell took over Auchinleck's position of commander-in-chief India. Soon afterwards Hitler promoted Rommel to General der Panzertruppe, and to Halder's dismay and disgust ensured that he would have even greater independence.

Churchill's irritation with Wavell and the dejected leadership of the British army was fired by two imperatives. One was the need

(*Above*) Japanese bayonet Chinese prisoners in Nanking
(*Below*) Japanese horse artillery in southern China

(*Left*) Goebbels and Göring

(*Below*) Warsaw,
August 1939

(*Right*) Narvik, April 1940

(*Above*) The crew of a French B1 tank surrender
(*Right*) Dunkirk, rescue of survivors from the destroyer *Bourrasque*

(*Above left*) German aircrew taken prisoner, September 1940
(*Below left*) Hans Frank of the Generalgouvernement and Polish clergy
(*Above*) German paratroopers, Crete
(*Below*) The crew of a British Bren gun carrier in Syria, June 1941

(*Above*) A Ukrainian village ablaze in July 1941
(*Below*) Soviet troops counter-attack near Moscow, December 1941

for aggressive action to keep up morale at home and prevent the country from slipping into a gloomy inertia. The other was to impress the United States and President Roosevelt. Above all, he needed to counter the partly justified impression that the British were waiting for the United States to enter the war and save the situation.

Roosevelt, to Churchill's great relief, had been re-elected president in November 1940. The British prime minister was further encouraged when he heard of the strategic review prepared that month by the US Navy's chief of operations. 'Plan Dog', as it was known, led to American–British staff talks at the end of January 1941. These discussions which took place in Washington under the codeword ABC-1 carried on until March. They formed the basis of Allied strategy when the United States entered the war. The policy of 'Germany first' was agreed as the basic principle. This accepted that, even with a war in the Pacific against Japan, the United States would first concentrate on the defeat of Nazi Germany, because without a major commitment of American forces to the European theatre the British were clearly incapable of winning on their own. If they lost, then the United States and its world trade would be in danger.

Roosevelt had recognized the threat posed by Nazi Germany even before the Munich agreement of 1938. Foreseeing the importance of air power in the coming war, he had rapidly inaugurated a programme to build 15,000 aircraft a year for the United States Army Air Corps. The assistant chief of staff of the US Army, General George C. Marshall, was present at the meeting to discuss this. Marshall, while agreeing with the plan, took the President to task for overlooking the need to increase their pitifully small ground forces. With little more than 200,000 men, the United States Army had only nine under-strength divisions, a mere tenth of the German army's order of battle. Roosevelt was impressed. Less than a year later, he backed Marshall's appointment as chief of staff, which took place on the day Germany invaded Poland.

Marshall was a formal man of great integrity and a superb organizer. Under his direction, the US Army was to grow from 200,000 men to eight million in the course of the war. He always told Roosevelt exactly what he thought and remained impervious to the President's charm. His greatest problem was Roosevelt's frequent failure to keep him informed of discussions and decisions made with others, particularly those with Winston Churchill.

For Churchill, his relationship with Roosevelt was by far the most important element in British foreign policy. He devoted enormous energy, imagination and sometimes shameless flattery to win over Roosevelt and obtain what his virtually bankrupt country needed to survive. In a very long and detailed letter dated 8 December 1940, Churchill called for 'a decisive act of constructive non-belligerency' to prolong British resistance. This would include the use of US Navy warships to protect against the U-boat threat and three million tons of merchant shipping to maintain Britain's Atlantic lifeline after the devastating losses – over two million gross tons – suffered so far. He also asked for 2,000 aircraft a month. 'Last of all I come to the question of Finance,' Churchill wrote. Britain's dollar credits would soon be exhausted; in fact the orders already placed or under negotiation 'many times exceed the total exchange resources remaining at the disposal of Great Britain'. Never had such an important or dignified begging letter been written. It was almost exactly a year from the day when the United States would find itself at war.

Roosevelt received the letter when aboard the USS *Tuscaloosa* in the Caribbean. He pondered over the contents and the day after he returned he called a press conference. On 17 December, he made his famous but simplistic parable of a man whose house is on fire asking his neighbour for the loan of his hose. This was Roosevelt's preparation of public opinion before the Lend–Lease Bill was presented to Congress. In the House of Commons, Churchill hailed it as 'the most unsordid act in the history of any nation'. But privately the British government was shaken by the harsh conditions attached to Lend–Lease. The Americans had demanded an audit of all British assets, and insisted that there could be no subsidy until all foreign exchange and gold reserves had been used up. A US Navy warship was sent to Cape Town to take the last British gold stockpiled there. British-owned companies in the United States, most notably Courtaulds, Shell and Lever, had to be sold off at knock-down prices, and were then resold at a large profit. Churchill magnanimously attributed all this to Roosevelt's need to wrongfoot the anti-British critics of Lend–Lease, many of whom harked back to the British and French default on debts from the First World War. The British as a whole underestimated how many Americans disliked them as imperialists, snobs and experts in the art of getting others to fight their wars for them.

But Britain was over a barrel and in no position to protest. Resentment at the terms would linger into the post-war years, if only because it had been the British cash payments of $4.5 billion for arms orders in 1940 which rescued the United States from the depression era and primed its wartime boom economy. Unlike the high-quality materiel which came later, the equipment bought in the desperate days of 1940 had not been impressive, nor did it make a great deal of difference. The fifty First World War destroyers provided in exchange for the British Virgin Islands in September 1940 had required a huge amount of work to make them seaworthy.

On 30 December, Roosevelt addressed the American people on the radio in a 'fireside chat' to defend the agreement. 'We must be the great arsenal of Democracy,' he declared. And so it came to be. On the night of 8 March 1941, the Lend–Lease Bill was passed by the Senate. Roosevelt's assertive new policy included the declaration of a Pan-American security zone in the western Atlantic; the establishment of bases on Greenland; and the plan to replace British troops on Iceland, which finally took place in early July. British warships, beginning with the damaged aircraft carrier HMS *Illustrious*, could now be repaired in American ports, and RAF pilots started training at US Army Air Force bases. One of the most important developments was that the US Navy began to take on escort duties for British convoys as far as Iceland.

The German foreign office reacted to these developments by expressing the hope that Britain would be defeated before American armaments began to play a significant role, which it estimated would be in 1942. But Hitler was too preoccupied with Barbarossa to pay much attention. His main concern at this stage was that America should not be provoked into entering the war before he defeated the Soviet Union. He refused Grossadmiral Raeder's request that his U-boats should operate in the western Atlantic right up to the three-mile zone of American coastal waters.

Churchill later said that the U-boat threat was the only thing that ever really frightened him during the war. At one stage he even considered seizing back the southern ports of neutral Ireland by force if necessary. The Royal Navy was desperately short of escort vessels for convoys. It had suffered heavy losses during the ill-fated intervention in Norway, and then destroyers had to be held back ready for a German invasion. During the 'east coast rampage', U-boats attacked coastal shipping in the North Sea and laid mines so that any neutral ships which were torpedoed could be said to have struck a mine.

From the autumn of 1940, the German U-boat fleet had finally begun to inflict grave damage on Allied shipping. It possessed bases on France's Atlantic coast and the torpedo detonator problem, which had bedevilled U-boat operations early in the war, had been sorted out. In a single week in September, U-boats sank twenty-seven British ships amounting to more than 160,000 tons. Such losses were even more striking considering how few submarines the Germans had at sea. Grossadmiral Raeder still had no more than twenty-two ocean-going U-boats operational in February 1941. Despite all his pleas to Hitler, the submarine-construction programme became a lower priority with the preparations for the invasion of the Soviet Union.

The German navy had initially expected much from its pocket battleships and armed merchant raiders. The *Graf Spee* may have been scuttled to British jubilation off Montevideo, but the most successful sortie had been that of the pocket battleship *Admiral Scheer*. During a voyage lasting 161 days in the Atlantic and Indian Oceans, she accounted for seventeen ships. It soon became clear, however, that U-boats were far more cost effective than pocket battleships and other surface raiders, which sank only 57,000 tons of shipping. The most successful U-boat commander, Otto Kretschmer, sank thirty-seven ships totalling over twice the tonnage sunk by the *Admiral Scheer*. The Royal Navy's forces of escort vessels began to increase only after the fifty ancient American destroyers had been refitted, and corvettes began to be launched from British shipyards.

Admiral Karl Dönitz, the head of the Kriegsmarine's U-boat command, saw his mission as a 'tonnage war': his submarines had to sink ships faster than the British could build them. In mid-October 1940, Dönitz began 'wolfpack' tactics in which up to a dozen U-boats would congregate once a convoy was sighted, and then start sinking them at night. The blaze of one ship would illuminate or silhouette the others. The first wolfpack struck against Convoy SC-7 and sank seventeen ships. Immediately afterwards, Günther Prien, the U-boat commander who had sunk HMS *Royal Oak* in Scapa Flow, led a wolfpack attack against Convoy HX-79 from Halifax. With just four submarines, they sank twelve ships out of forty-nine. In February 1941, Allied losses soared again. Only in March did the Royal Navy escort vessels achieve a measure of revenge through the sinking of three U-boats, including the *U-47* commanded by Prien, and the capture of *U-99* and its commander Otto Kretschmer.

The introduction of the long-range Type IX submarine soon caused losses to mount again until the summer, when Ultra intercepts made a difference and assistance came with the US Navy in September escorting ships in the western Atlantic. Bletchley Park's output of intercepted signals did not often lead directly to the sinking of U-boats at this stage, but it greatly helped convoy planners with 'evasive routing', which meant diverting them away from gathering wolfpacks. It also provided Naval Intelligence and Coastal Command with a much clearer idea of the Kriegsmarine's resupply and operational procedures.

The Battle of the Atlantic was a life of maritime monotony against a constant background of fear. The bravest of the brave were the crews of oil tankers, knowing they were sailing on a giant incendiary bomb. Everyone from captain to deckhand could not help wondering whether they were already being stalked by U-boats and whether they would be hurled from their bunks by the juddering shock of a torpedo explosion. Only appalling weather and heavy seas appeared to reduce the danger.

Theirs was a perpetually damp and cold existence spent in duffel-coats or sou'westers, with few chances to dry their clothes. The eyes of lookouts ached from scanning the grey seas in the hopeless search for a periscope. Mugs of hot cocoa and corned-beef sandwiches offered their only break and comfort. On the escort vessels, mainly destroyers and corvettes, the sweep of radar screens and the ping of Asdic or sonar echoes provided a hypnotizing yet fearful fascination. The psychological strain was even greater for merchant navy sailors because of their inability to hit back. Everyone knew that if the convoy was attacked by a wolfpack, and they had to leap into the oily water after being torpedoed, their chances of being pulled out of the sea were very small. A ship stopping to rescue survivors provided an easy target for another U-boat. The relief of reaching the Mersey or the Clyde on the return journey transformed the atmosphere on board.

German U-boat crews lived in even greater discomfort. The bulkheads streamed with condensation and the air was foul with the stench of wet clothing and unwashed bodies. But morale was generally high at that stage of the war, when they were achieving such successes and British counter-measures were still evolving. Much of the time was spent on the surface, which improved speed and fuel consumption. The greatest danger came from Allied flying-boats. As soon as one of these aircraft was sighted, the klaxon sounded a warning and the U-boat went into a well-practised crash-dive. But until radar was mounted in the aircraft, the chances of the U-boats being found remained fairly remote.

In April 1941, Allied shipping losses reached 688,000 tons, but there were encouraging developments. Air cover to convoys was extended, although the 'Greenland gap', the large central area of the north Atlantic beyond the range of the Royal Canadian Air Force and RAF Coastal Command, still remained. A German armed trawler was seized off Norway, with two Enigma coding machines on board with the settings for the previous month. And on 9 May, HMS *Bulldog* succeeded in forcing *U-110* to the surface. An armed boarding party managed to seize her codebooks and Enigma cipher machine before they could be destroyed. Other captured vessels, a weather ship and a transport, also provided valuable pickings. But as Allied convoys began to escape the U-boat screens, and then when three submarines were ambushed off Cape Verde, Dönitz began to suspect that their codes might have been compromised. Enigma security was tightened.

The year as a whole had been a very hard one for the Royal Navy. While losses mounted in the Mediterranean during the Battle of Crete, the great battle-cruiser HMS *Hood* exploded when hit by a single shell from the *Bismarck* on 23 May in the Denmark Strait between Greenland and Iceland. Admiral Günther Lütjens in the *Bismarck* had sailed from the Baltic accompanied by the heavy cruiser *Prinz Eugen*. The shock in London was considerable. So was the desire for revenge. More than a hundred warships were involved in the hunt for the *Bismarck*, including the battleships HMS *King George V* and *Rodney* and the aircraft carrier *Ark Royal*.

Contact was lost by the shadowing cruiser HMS *Suffolk*, but on 26 May, when the British battle squadron was running short of fuel, a Catalina flying-boat sighted the *Bismarck*. The next day Swordfish torpedo bombers took off from the *Ark Royal* in bad weather. Two torpedoes wrecked the *Bismarck*'s steering gear as she headed for the safety of Brest. The great German warship could only go round and round in a circle. This gave the *King George V* and *Rodney*, escorted by the 4th Destroyer Flotilla, time to close in for the kill with massive broadsides from their main armament. Admiral Lütjens sent a final signal: 'Ship incapable of manoeuvring. Will fight to the last shell. Long live the Führer.' The cruiser HMS *Dorsetshire* was sent in to finish her off with torpedoes. Lütjens, who ordered the ship to be scuttled, died along with 2,200 of his sailors. Only 115 men were saved from the sea.

12

Barbarossa

In the spring of 1941, while Hitler's invasion of Yugoslavia achieved a rapid success, Stalin decided on a policy of caution. On 13 April, the Soviet Union signed a five-year 'neutrality agreement' with Japan, recognizing its puppet regime of Manchukuo. This was the culmination of what Chiang Kai-shek had feared ever since the signing of the Molotov–Ribbentrop Pact. Chiang had been trying to play a double game in 1940, through offering peace feelers to Japan. He had hoped to force the Soviet Union to increase its greatly diminished level of support and thus sabotage its rapprochement with Tokyo. But Chiang also knew that an actual agreement with the Japanese would hand leadership of the Chinese masses to Mao and the Communists because it would be seen as a terrible and cowardly betrayal.

After Japan's signature of the Tripartite Pact in September 1940, Chiang, like Stalin, had seen that the chances of Japan fighting America were increased and he was greatly encouraged by the prospect. China's survival now lay in the hands of the United States, even though Chiang sensed that the Soviet Union would also end up as part of an anti-fascist alliance. The world, he foresaw, was about to polarize in a more coherent way. The three-dimensional game of chess would finally become two-dimensional.

Both the Soviet and Japanese regimes, which loathed each other, wanted to secure their own back door. In April 1941, after signing the Soviet–Japanese neutrality pact, Stalin turned up in person at the Yaroslavsky railway station in Moscow to bid farewell to the Japanese foreign minister Yōsuke Matsuoka, who was still drunk from the Soviet leader's heavy-handed hospitality. Among the crowd on the platform, Stalin suddenly spied Oberst Hans Krebs, the German military attaché (who would become the last chief of the general staff in 1945). To the German's astonishment, Stalin slapped him on the back and said: 'We must always stay friends, whatever happens.' The dictator's bonhomie was belied by his strained and sickly appearance. 'I'm convinced of it,' Krebs had replied, recovering from his surprise. He clearly found it hard to believe that Stalin had not yet guessed that Germany was preparing to invade.

Hitler was supremely confident. He had decided to ignore both Bismarck's warning against invading Russia and the recognized dangers of a war on two fronts. He justified his long-held ambition of smashing 'Jewish Bolshevism' as the surest way to force Britain to come to terms. Once the Soviet Union was defeated, then Japan would be in a position to divert American attention to the Pacific and away from Europe. Yet the Nazi leadership's primary objective was to secure the Soviet Union's oil and food, which they believed would make them invincible. Under the 'Hunger Plan' devised by Staatssekretär Herbert Backe, the Wehrmacht's seizure of Soviet food production was intended to lead to the deaths of thirty million people, mainly in the cities.

Hitler, Göring and Himmler had seized on Backe's radical plan with enthusiasm. It seemed to promise both a dramatic solution to Germany's growing food problem and a major weapon in its ideological war against Slavdom and 'Jewish Bolshevism'. The Wehrmacht also approved. By feeding its three million men and 600,000 horses from local sources, the difficulties of supply over huge distances with insufficient rail transport would be greatly eased. Clearly, Soviet prisoners of war would also be systematically starved under the guidelines. Thus the Wehrmacht became an active participant, even before the first shots had been fired, in a genocidal war of annihilation.

On 4 May 1941, flanked by his deputy Rudolf Hess and Reichsmarschall Göring, Hitler addressed the Reichstag. He proclaimed that the National Socialist state would 'last for a thousand years'. Six nights later, Hess took off in a Messerschmitt 110 without warning anyone in Berlin. He flew to Scotland by the light of a full moon and baled out, but broke his ankle on landing. Astrologers had convinced him that he could arrange peace with Britain. Although slightly deranged, Hess clearly sensed like Ribbentrop that the invasion of the Soviet Union might prove disastrous. But his self-appointed peace mission was doomed to ignominious failure.

His arrival coincided with one of the heaviest raids of the Blitz. The Luftwaffe, also making use of the 'bomber's moon' that night, attacked Hull and London, damaging Westminster Abbey, the House of Commons, the British Museum, numerous hospitals, the City, the Tower of London and the docks. Incendiary bombs started 2,200 major fires. The raids brought the total of civilian casualties up to 40,000 killed and 46,000 badly injured.

Hess's bizarre mission caused embarrassment in London, consternation in Germany and deep distrust in Moscow. The British government mishandled the whole episode. It should have announced straight away that Hitler had tried to make a peace overture, and it had rejected it outright. Instead, Stalin was convinced that Hess's aircraft had been guided in by the British Secret Intelligence Service. He had long suspected Churchill of trying to provoke Hitler into attacking the Soviet Union. He now wondered whether that arch anti-Bolshevik Churchill was plotting with Germany. Stalin had already dismissed all warnings from Britain about German preparations to invade the Soviet Union as 'angliiskaya provokatsiya'. Even detailed information from his own intelligence services was angrily rejected, often on the grounds that officers abroad had become corrupted by foreign influences.

Stalin still accepted Hitler's assurance, given in a letter at the beginning of the year, that German troops were being moved eastwards purely to put them out of range of British bombing. Lieutenant General Filipp Ivanovich Golikov, the inexperienced director of GRU military intelligence, was also convinced that Hitler would not attack the Soviet Union until he had conquered Britain. Golikov refused to pass on any of his department's intelligence on German intentions to Zhukov, the chief of the general staff, or to Timoshenko, who had replaced Voroshilov as the commissar of defence. Yet they were well aware of the Wehrmacht build-up and had produced a contingency planning document dated 15 May, discussing a pre-emptive strike to upset German preparations. In addition, Stalin had agreed to a general build-up of forces as a precaution, with 800,000 reservists called up and almost thirty divisions deployed along the western borders of the Soviet Union.

Some revisionist historians have tried to suggest that all this constituted a real plan to attack Germany, thus somehow attempting to justify Hitler's subsequent invasion. But the Red Army was simply not in a state to launch a major offensive in the summer of 1941, and in any case Hitler's decision to invade had been made considerably earlier. On the other hand, it cannot be excluded that Stalin, alarmed by the rapid defeat of France, may have been considering a preventive attack in the winter of 1941 or more probably in 1942, when the Red Army would be better trained and equipped.

More and more intelligence arrived confirming the danger of a German invasion. Stalin rejected the reports from Richard Sorge in the German embassy in Tokyo, his most effective agent. In Berlin, the Soviet military attaché had discovered that 140 German divisions were now deployed along the USSR's frontier. The Soviet embassy in Berlin had even obtained the proofs of a Russian phrase-book to be issued to troops so that they could say 'Hands up', 'Are you a Communist?', 'I'll shoot!' and 'Where is the collective farm chairman?'

The most astonishing warning of all came from the German ambassador in Moscow, Graf Friedrich von der Schulenburg, an anti-Nazi who was later executed for his part in the 20 July 1944 plot to assassinate Hitler. Stalin, when told of the warning, exploded in disbelief. 'Disinformation has now reached ambassadorial level!' he exclaimed. In a state of denial, the Soviet leader convinced himself that the Germans were simply trying to put pressure on him to concede more in a new pact.

Ironically, Schulenburg's frankness was the one exception in the skilful game of deception played by German diplomacy. Even the despised Ribbentrop played cleverly to Stalin's suspicions of Churchill so that British warnings about Barbarossa produced a contrary reaction in the Soviet dictator. Stalin had also been told of the Allied plans to bomb the Baku oilfields during the war with Finland. And the Soviet occupation of Bessarabia in June 1940, which Ribbentrop had persuaded King Carol to accept, had in fact pushed Romania straight into Hitler's cynical embrace.

Stalin's appeasement of Hitler had continued with a large increase in deliveries to Germany of grain, fuel, cotton, metals and rubber purchased in south-east Asia, circumventing the British blockade. During the period of the Molotov–Ribbentrop Pact, the Soviet Union had provided 26,000 tons of chromium, 140,000 tons of manganese and more than two million tons of oil to the Reich. Despite having received well over eighty clear indications of a German invasion – indeed probably more than a hundred – Stalin seemed more concerned with 'the security problem along our north-west frontier', which meant the Baltic states. On the night of 14 June, a week before the German invasion, 60,000 Estonians, 34,000 Latvians and 38,000 Lithuanians were forced on to cattle trucks for deportation to camps in the distant interior of the Soviet Union. Stalin remained unconvinced even when, during the last week before the invasion, German ships rapidly left Soviet ports and embassy staff were evacuated.

'This is a war of extermination,' Hitler had told his generals on 30 March. 'Commanders must be prepared to sacrifice their personal scruples.' The only concern of senior officers was the effect on discipline. Their visceral instincts – anti-Slav, anti-Communist and anti-semitic – were in line with Nazi ideology, even if many of them disliked the Party and its functionaries. Famine, they were told, would be a weapon of war, with an estimated thirty million Soviet citizens starving to death. This would clear out part of the population, leaving just enough to be slaves in a German-colonized 'Garden of Eden'. Hitler's dream of *Lebensraum* at last seemed within his grasp.

On 6 June, the Wehrmacht's notorious 'Commissar Order' was issued, specifically rejecting any observance of international law. This and other instructions required that Soviet *politruks* or political officers, card-carrying Communists, saboteurs and male Jews were to be shot as partisans.

During the night of 20 June, the OKW issued the codeword Dortmund. Its war diary noted: 'Thus the start of the attack is once and for all ordered for 22 June. The order is to be transmitted to the Army Groups.' Hitler, keyed up for the great moment, prepared to leave for his new Führer headquarters near Rastenburg, codenamed the Wolfsschanze, or Wolf's Lair. He remained convinced that the Red Army and the whole Soviet system would collapse. 'We have only to kick in the door and the whole rotten edifice will come crashing down,' he had told his commanders.

More thoughtful officers on the eastern borders had private

doubts. Some had re-read General Armand de Caulaincourt's account of Napoleon's march on Moscow and the dreadful retreat. Older officers and soldiers who had fought in Russia during the First World War also were uneasy. Yet the Wehrmacht's series of triumphant conquests – in Poland, Scandinavia, the Low Countries, France and the Balkans – reassured most Germans that their forces were invincible. Officers told their men they were 'on the eve of the greatest offensive ever'. There were almost three million German troops, soon to be supported by armies from Finland, Romania, Hungary and eventually Italy, in the crusade against Bolshevism.

In the forests of birch and fir which concealed vehicle parks, tented headquarters and signal regiments as well as fighting units, officers briefed their men. Many reassured them that it would take only three or four weeks to crush the Red Army. 'Early tomorrow morning,' wrote a soldier in a mountain division, 'we are off, thanks be to God, against our mortal enemy Bolshevism. For me, a real stone has fallen from my heart. Finally this uncertainty is over, and one knows where one is. I am very optimistic ... And I believe that if we can take all the land and raw materials up to the Urals, then Europe will be able to feed itself and the war at sea can last as long as it will.' A signals NCO in the SS Division *Das Reich* was even more confident. 'My conviction is that the destruction of Russia will take no longer than that of France, and then my assumption of getting leave in August will still be correct.'

Around midnight on this midsummer's eve, the first units moved forward to their attack positions as the last goods train with Soviet deliveries continued past them on its way to Germany. The dark silhouettes of panzers in formation emitted clouds of exhaust as they started their engines. Artillery regiments removed the camouflage netting from their guns to tow them into position close to the concealed piles of shells at their firing positions. Along the west bank of the River Bug, heavy rubber assault boats were dragged to the marshy edge, men whispering in case their voices carried across the water to the NKVD border guards. Opposite the great fortress of Brest-Litovsk, sand had been spread on the roads so that their jackboots made no noise. It was a cool, clear morning, with dew on the meadows. Men's thoughts turned instinctively to their wives and children or sweethearts and parents, all asleep at home in Germany and blissfully unaware of this mighty undertaking.

During the evening of 21 June, Stalin in the Kremlin became increasingly nervous. The deputy head of the NKVD had just reported that there had been no fewer than 'thirty-nine aircraft incursions over the state border of the USSR' the previous day. When told of a German deserter, a former Communist who had crossed the lines to warn of the attack, Stalin promptly ordered that he should be shot for disinformation. All he conceded to his increasingly desperate generals was to put the anti-aircraft batteries round Moscow on standby and issue a warning order to commanders along the frontier districts to be prepared, but not to fire back. Stalin clung to the notion that any attack was not Hitler's doing. It would be a *provokatsiya* by German generals.

Stalin retired to bed unusually early in his dacha just outside Moscow. Zhukov rang at 04.45 hours and insisted that he be woken. There had been reports of a German bombing raid on the Soviet naval base of Sebastopol and other attacks. Stalin was silent for a long time, just breathing heavily, then he told Zhukov that the troops were not to reply with artillery. He was to summon a meeting of the Politburo.

When they were assembled in the Kremlin at 05.45 hours, Stalin still refused to believe that Hitler knew anything about this attack. Molotov was told to summon Schulenburg, who informed him that a state of war existed between Germany and the Soviet Union. After his earlier warning, Schulenburg was amazed at the astonishment this announcement produced. A shaken Molotov returned to the meeting to tell Stalin. An oppressive silence followed.

In the early hours of 22 June, right down the belt of eastern Europe from the Baltic to the Black Sea, tens of thousands of German officers began glancing at their synchronized watches with the light of a shaded torch. Right on time, they heard aero-engines to their rear. The waiting troops looked up into the night sky as massed squadrons of the Luftwaffe streamed overhead, flying towards the gleam of dawn along the vast eastern horizon.

At 03.15 hours German time (one hour behind Moscow), a heavy artillery bombardment opened. On this, the very first day of the Soviet–German war, the Wehrmacht smashed through the frontier defence line with ease along an 1,800-kilometre front. Border guards were shot down still in their underwear, and their families were killed in their barracks by the artillery fire. 'In the course of the morning,' the OKW war diary noted, 'the impression is strengthening that surprise has been accomplished on all sectors.' One army headquarters after another reported that all the bridges on its front had been seized intact. In a matter of hours, the leading panzer formations were overrunning Soviet supply dumps.

The Red Army had been caught almost completely unprepared. In the months before the invasion, the Soviet leader had forced it to advance from the Stalin Line inside the old frontier and establish a forward defence along the Molotov–Ribbentrop border. Not enough had been done to prepare the new positions, despite Zhukov's energetic attempts. Less than half of the strongpoints had any heavy weapons. Artillery regiments lacked their tractors, which had been sent to help with the harvest. And Soviet aviation was caught on the ground, its aircraft lined up in rows, presenting easy targets for the Luftwaffe's pre-emptive strikes on sixty-six airfields. Some 1,800 fighters and bombers were said to have been destroyed on the first day of the attack, the majority on the ground. The Luftwaffe lost just thirty-five aircraft.

Even after Hitler's lightning campaigns against Poland and France, the Soviets' plan of defence assumed that they would have ten to fifteen days before the main forces engaged. Stalin's refusal to react, and the Wehrmacht's ruthlessness, gave them no time at all. Brandenburger commandos from Regiment 800 had infiltrated before the attack or parachuted in to secure bridges and cut telephone lines. In the south, Ukrainian nationalists had also been sent in to cause chaos and urge an uprising against their Soviet masters. As a result, Soviet commanders had no idea what was happening and found themselves incapable of issuing orders or communicating with superiors.

From the East Prussian border, Generalfeldmarschall Wilhelm Ritter von Leeb's Army Group North attacked into the Baltic states and headed for Leningrad. Its advance was greatly

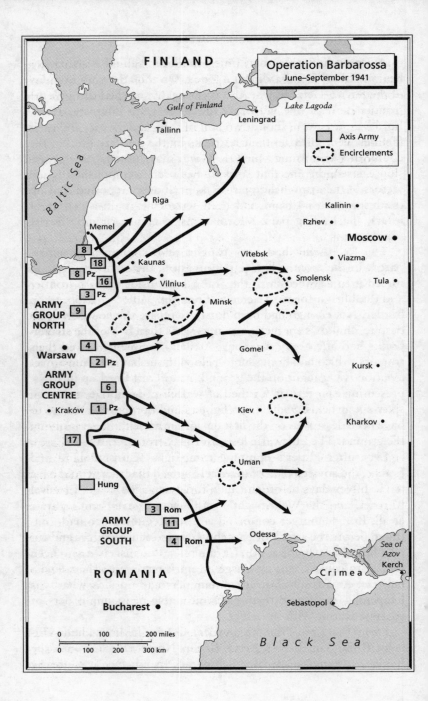

aided by Brandenburgers in brown Soviet uniforms seizing twin rail and road bridges over the River Dvina on 26 June. General-leutnant von Manstein's LVI Panzer Corps, advancing nearly eighty kilometres a day, would be halfway to their objective in just five days. This 'impetuous dash', he wrote later, 'was the fulfilment of a tank commander's dream'.

North of the Pripet Marshes, Army Group Centre, commanded by Generalfeldmarschall Fedor von Bock, advanced rapidly into Belorussia, soon fighting a great encirclement battle round Minsk with the panzer groups of Guderian and Generaloberst Hermann Hoth. The only fierce resistance encountered was from the massive fortress of Brest-Litovsk on the border. The Austrian 45th Infantry Division suffered heavy casualties, far more than in the whole campaign for France, as its storm groups tried to winkle out the tenacious defenders with flamethrowers, tear gas and grenades. The survivors, suffering terribly from thirst and without medical supplies, fought on for three weeks until wounded or out of ammunition. But on their return in 1945 from German imprisonment their incredible courage did not save them from being sent to the Gulag. Stalin had ordered that surrender constituted treason to the Motherland.

Frontier guards from the NKVD forces also fought back desperately, when not taken by surprise. But all too often Red Army officers deserted their men, fleeing in panic. With their communications in chaos, commanders were paralysed either by a lack of instructions or by orders to counter-attack which bore no relation to the situation on the ground. The purge of the Red Army had left officers with no experience of command in charge of whole divisions and army corps, while fear of denunciation and arrest by the NKVD had destroyed any initiative. Even the bravest commander was likely to tremble and sweat with fear if officers with the green tabs and cap band of the NKVD suddenly appeared in his headquarters. The contrast with the German army's system of *Auftragstaktik*, in which junior commanders were set a task and then relied on to carry it out as best they thought, could not have been greater.

Army Group South, commanded by Generalfeldmarschall von Rundstedt, advanced into Ukraine. Rundstedt was soon supported by two Romanian armies eager to take back Bessarabia from the Soviets. Their dictator and commander-in-chief, Marshal Ion Antonescu, had assured Hitler ten days before: 'Of course I'll be there from the start. When it's a question of action against the Slavs, you can always count on Romania.'

Stalin, having drafted a speech announcing the invasion, told Molotov to read it on Soviet radio at noon. It was broadcast over loudspeakers to the crowds in the streets. The foreign minister's wooden delivery ended with the declaration: 'Our cause is just, the enemy will be smashed, victory will be ours.' Despite his uninspiring tone, the people as a whole were outraged by this violation of the Motherland. Vast queues of volunteers immediately formed at recruiting centres. But other, less orderly queues also developed, with the panic-buying of tinned or dried foods and the withdrawal of money from banks.

There was also a strange sense of relief that the treacherous attack had released the Soviet Union from the unnatural alliance with Nazi Germany. The young physicist Andrei Sakharov was later greeted by an aunt in a bomb shelter during a Luftwaffe raid on Moscow. 'For the first time in years,' she said, 'I feel like a Russian again!' Similar emotions of relief were also expressed in Berlin that at last they were fighting 'the real enemy'.

Fighter regiments of Red Army aviation, with inexperienced pilots in obsolete machines, stood little chance against the Luftwaffe. German fighter aces soon began to clock up huge scores, and referred to their easy kills as 'infanticide'. Their Soviet opponents felt psychologically defeated even before encountering their enemy. But, although many pilots avoided battle, a longing for vengeance began to grow. A handful of the bravest simply rammed a German aircraft if they got a chance, knowing that there was little hope of fastening on to its tail to shoot it down.

The novelist and war correspondent Vasily Grossman described waiting for the aircraft of a fighter regiment to return to an airfield near Gomel in Belorussia. 'Finally, after a successful attack on a German column, the fighters returned and landed. The commander's aircraft had human flesh stuck in the radiator. That's because the supporting aircraft had hit a truck with ammunition that blew up at the very moment when the leader was flying over it. Poppe, the commander, is picking the mess out with a file. They summon a doctor who examines the bloody mass attentively and pronounces it "Aryan meat!" Everyone laughs. Yes, a pitiless time – a time of iron – has come!'

'The Russian is a tough opponent,' wrote a German soldier. 'We take hardly any prisoners, and shoot them all instead.' When marching forward, some took pot-shots for fun at crowds of Red Army prisoners being herded back to makeshift camps, where they were left to starve in the open. A number of German officers were appalled, but most were more concerned about the lack of discipline.

On the Soviet side, Beria's NKVD massacred the inmates of its prisons near the front so that they would not be saved by the German advance. Nearly 10,000 Polish prisoners were murdered. In the city of Lwów alone, the NKVD killed around 4,000 people. The stench of decomposing bodies in the heat of late June permeated the whole town. The NKVD slaughter prompted Ukrainian nationalists to begin a guerrilla war against the Soviet occupiers. In a frenzy of fear and hatred, the NKVD massacred another 10,000 prisoners in the areas of Bessarabia and the Baltic states, seized the year before. Other prisoners were forced to march eastwards, with NKVD guards shooting any who collapsed.

On 23 June, Stalin set up a supreme command headquarters, giving it the old Tsarist name of the Stavka. A few days later, he entered the commissariat of defence, accompanied by Beria and Molotov. There they found Timoshenko and Zhukov attempting in vain to establish some sort of order along the enormous front. Minsk had just fallen. Stalin peered at the situation maps and read some of the reports. He was clearly shaken to find that the situation was even more disastrous than he had feared. He cursed Timoshenko and Zhukov, who did not hold back in their replies. 'Lenin founded our state,' he was heard to say, 'and we've fucked it up.'

The Soviet leader disappeared to his dacha at Kuntsevo, leaving the other members of the Politburo bewildered. There were mutterings that Molotov should take over, but they were far too frightened to move against the dictator. On 30 June, they decided that a State Committee for Defence with absolute power had to be set up. They drove out to Kuntsevo to see Stalin. He looked haggard and wary when they entered, clearly believing that they had come to arrest him. He asked why they had come. When they explained that he had to lead this emergency war cabinet, he betrayed his surprise, but agreed to take on the role. There have been suggestions that Stalin's departure from the Kremlin was a ploy in the tradition of Ivan the Terrible to encourage any opponents within the Politburo to reveal themselves, enabling them to be crushed, but this is pure speculation.

Stalin returned to the Kremlin the next day, 1 July. Two days later he made his own broadcast to the Soviet peoples. His instincts served him well. He surprised his listeners by addressing them as 'Comrades, citizens, brothers and sisters'. No master of the Kremlin had ever addressed his people in such familial terms. He called upon them to defend the Motherland in a scorched-earth policy of total warfare, evoking the Patriotic War against Napoleon. Stalin understood that the Soviet peoples were far more likely to lay down their lives for their country than for any Communist ideology. Knowing that patriotism is shaped by war, Stalin perceived that this invasion would revive it. Nor did he conceal the gravity of the situation, even if he did nothing to acknowledge his part in the catastrophe. He also ordered a people's levy – *narodnoe opolchenie* – to be set up. These militia battalions of ill-armed cannon-fodder were expected to slow the German panzer divisions, with little more than their bodies.

The terrible suffering of civilians caught up in the fighting did not enter Stalin's calculations. Refugees, driving the cattle from collective farms in front of them, tried in vain to stay ahead of the panzer divisions. On 26 June, the writer Aleksandr Tvardovsky saw an extraordinary sight from his carriage window when the train halted at a wayside stop in Ukraine. 'The whole field was covered with people who were lying, sitting, swarming,' he wrote in his diary. 'They had bundles, knapsacks, suitcases, children and handcarts. I had never seen such huge quantities of household things that people took with them when leaving home in haste. There were probably tens of thousands of people in this field . . . The field got up, started moving, advanced towards the railway, towards the train, started knocking on the walls and windows of carriages. It seemed capable of tipping the train off the rails. The train began to move . . .'

Hundreds if not thousands died in the bombing of the cities of Belorussia. Survivors fared little better in their attempts to escape eastwards. 'After Minsk began to burn,' a journalist noted, 'blind men from the home for invalids walked along the highway in a long file, tied to one another with towels.' Already there were large numbers of war orphans, children whose parents had been killed or lost in the confusion. Suspecting that some of them were used for spying by the Germans, the NKVD treated them with little compassion.

Following their astonishing success in France, the panzer formations dashed ahead in the perfect summer conditions, leaving the infantry divisions to catch up as best they could. Sometimes, when the tank spearhead ran out of ammunition, Heinkel 111s had to be diverted to drop supplies by parachute. The lines of advance in the heat could be seen by burning villages, the dustclouds churned up by tracked vehicles, and the steady tramp of marching infantry and their horse-drawn artillery. Gunners riding on limbers were coated in a pale dust which made them look like terracotta figures, and their plodding draught animals coughed with a resigned regularity. More than 600,000 horses, assembled from all over Europe, just like for Napoleon's Grande Armée, formed the basis of transport for the bulk of the Wehrmacht in the campaign. Ration supplies, ammunition and even field ambulances depended on horse-power. Had it not been for the vast quantities of motor-transport which the French army had failed to destroy before the armistice – a subject which provoked Stalin's bitter anger – the German army's mechanization would have been limited almost entirely to the four panzer groups.

Already the two large panzer formations of Army Group Centre had achieved their first major encirclement, trapping four Soviet armies with 417,000 men in the Białystok pocket west of Minsk. Hoth's Third Panzer Group on the north side of the pincer and Guderian's Second Panzer Group on the south met on 28 June. The bombers and Stukas of the Second Luftflotte then pounded the trapped Red Army forces. This advance meant that Army Group Centre was well on its way to the 'land bridge' between the rivers Dvina, which flowed into the Baltic, and the Dnepr, which ran down to the Black Sea.

General Dmitri Pavlov, a Soviet tank commander in the Spanish Civil War and now the hapless chief of the Western Front, was replaced by Marshal Timoshenko. (In the Red Army a front was a military formation similar to an army group.) Pavlov was soon arrested along with other senior officers from his command, then summarily tried and executed by the NKVD. Several desperate senior officers committed suicide, one of them blowing his brains out in the presence of Nikita Khrushchev, the commissar responsible for Ukraine.

In the north, Leeb's army group was widely welcomed in the Baltic states after the waves of Soviet oppression and the deportations of the week before. Groups of nationalists attacked the retreating Soviets, and seized towns. The NKVD 5th Motorized Rifle Regiment was sent in to Riga to restore order, which meant immediate reprisals against the Latvian population. 'Before the corpses of our fallen comrades, the personnel of the regiment swore an oath to smash the fascist reptiles mercilessly, and on the same day the bourgeoisie of Riga felt our revenge on its hide.' But they too were soon forced to pull back up the Baltic coast.

North of Kaunas in Lithuania, a Soviet mechanized corps surprised the advancing Germans with a counter-attack, using heavy KV tanks. Panzer shells just bounced off them and they could be dealt with only when 88mm guns were brought up. The Soviet North-Western Front withdrew into Estonia, harried by improvised nationalist forces, which neither the Red Army nor the Germans had expected. Almost before the Germans marched in, murderous pogroms began against the Jews, who were accused of siding with the Bolsheviks.

Rundstedt's Army Group South was less fortunate. Colonel General Mikhail Kirponos, who commanded the South-Western Front, had been forewarned by NKVD border guards of the attack. He also had stronger forces, for this is where Timoshenko and Zhukov had expected the main thrust to come. Kirponos was ordered to launch a massive counter-attack with five mechanized corps. The most powerful, with heavy KV tanks and the new T-34s, was commanded by Major General Andrei Vlasov. Kirponos, however, was unable to deploy his forces effectively because the landlines had been cut and his formations were widely spread.

On 26 June, General der Kavallerie von Kleist's First Panzer Group advanced towards Rovno with Kiev, the capital of Ukraine, as his ultimate objective. Kirponos ordered in five of his mechanized corps with very mixed results. The Germans were shaken to find that the T-34s and heavy KV tanks were superior to anything they had, but even the People's Commissar for Defence had found Soviet tank gunnery 'inadequate on the eve of war', and out of 14,000 Soviet tanks, 'only 3,800 were ready to fight' on 22 June. German army training, tactics, radio communications and speed of reaction in their panzer crews generally proved far superior. In addition, they had strong support from Stuka squadrons. Their main danger was over-confidence. Major General Konstantin Rokossovsky, a former cavalry officer of Polish origin who later became one of the outstanding commanders of the war, managed to draw the 13th Panzer Division into an artillery ambush after his own obsolete tanks had been mauled the day before.

Faced with continuing panic and mass desertions, Kirponos introduced 'blocking detachments' to force men back to fight. Wild rumours caused chaos, as they had in France. But the Soviet counter-attacks, although costly and unsuccessful, at least managed to delay the German advance. Nikita Khrushchev had already, on Stalin's order, begun a massive effort to evacuate the machinery from Ukrainian factories and workshops. Ruthlessly carried out, this process succeeded in transporting by train the bulk of the republic's industry back towards the Urals and beyond. Similar operations were carried out on a smaller scale in Belorussia and elsewhere. In all, 2,593 industrial units were removed in the course of the year. This would eventually allow the Soviet Union to recommence armaments production well out of the range of German bombers.

The Politburo had also decided to send Lenin's mummified body, as well as the gold reserves and Tsarist treasures, in great secrecy from Moscow to Tyumen in western Siberia. A special train, with the necessary chemicals and attendant scientists to maintain the corpse's preservation, departed in early July, guarded by NKVD troops.

On 3 July, General Halder noted in his diary that it was 'probably no overstatement to say that the Russian campaign has been won in the space of two weeks'. He did, however, acknowledge that the sheer vastness of the country and continued resistance would keep the invasion forces occupied 'for many more weeks to come'. Back in Germany, the SS survey on attitudes reported that people were betting on how quickly the war would be over. Some convinced themselves that their armies were already within a hundred kilometres of Moscow, but Goebbels tried to damp down such speculation. He did not want their victory to be undermined by an impression that it had taken longer than expected.

The overwhelming immensity of the landmass which the Wehrmacht had invaded, with its endless horizons, began to have its effect on the German *Landser*, as the ordinary infantryman was known. Those from Alpine regions were the most depressed by the flatness of what seemed like an infinite ocean of land. Front formations soon found that, unlike in France, pockets of Soviet soldiers fought on even after they had been bypassed. They would suddenly open fire from hiding places in the enormous cornfields and attack reinforcements or headquarters moving up. Any of them taken alive were shot out of hand as partisans.

Many Soviet citizens also suffered from over-optimism. Some told themselves that the German proletariat would rise up against their Nazi masters, now that they were attacking the 'Motherland of the oppressed'. And those who pinned up maps to mark the successes of the Red Army soon had to take them down as it became clear how deeply the Wehrmacht had advanced into Soviet territory.

The triumphalism of the German armies, however, soon began to wane. The great encirclement battles, especially Smolensk, became increasingly arduous. The panzer formations achieved their sweeping manoeuvres with little difficulty, but they had insufficient panzergrenadiers with them to hold the immense circle against attacks both from within and without. Many Soviet troops slipped through before the hard-driven German infantry caught up, stiff and footsore from the forced marches of up to fifty kilometres a day in full kit. And those Red Army soldiers who were trapped did not surrender. They fought on with a desperate courage, even if it was often enforced by commissars and officers at the point of a gun. Out of ammunition, great waves of men surged forward, bellowing, in an attempt to break the cordon.

Some charged with linked arms, as the German machine-gunners scythed them down, their weapons over-heating from constant use. The screams of the wounded continued for hours afterwards, grating on the nerves of the exhausted German soldiers.

On 9 July, Vitebsk fell. Like Minsk, Smolensk and later Gomel and Chernigov, it was an inferno of blazing wooden houses from Luftwaffe raids with incendiaries. The fires were so intense that many German troops in their vehicles felt obliged to turn back. It took a total of thirty-two German divisions to reduce the Smolensk *Kessel*, or cauldron, as they called an encirclement. The *Kesselschlacht*, or cauldron battle, did not cease until 11 August. The Soviet forces suffered 300,000 'irrecoverable losses', of men killed or taken prisoner, along with 3,200 tanks and 3,100 guns. But Soviet counter-attacks from the east helped more than 100,000 men escape, and the delay to the German advance proved critical.

Vasily Grossman visited a field hospital. 'There were about nine hundred wounded men in a little clearing among young aspens. There were bloodstained rags, scraps of flesh, moans, subdued howling, hundreds of dismal, suffering eyes. The young red-haired "doctoress" had lost her voice – she had been operating all night. Her face was white, as if she might faint at any minute.' She told him with a smile how she had operated on his friend, the poet Iosef Utkin. '"While I was making incisions, he recited poetry for me." One could barely hear her voice, she was helping herself speak with gestures. Wounded men kept arriving. They were all wet with blood and rain.'

Despite their formidable advances and the erection of signposts pointing to Moscow, the German army on the *Ostfront* had suddenly begun to fear that victory might not be achieved that year after all. The three army groups had suffered 213,000 casualties. The figure may have represented only a tenth of Soviet losses, but if the battle of attrition continued much longer, the Wehrmacht would find it hard to defend its over-extended supply lines and defeat the remaining Soviet forces. The prospect of fighting on through a Russian winter was deeply troubling. The Germans had not managed to destroy the Red Army in the western Soviet Union, and now the Eurasian landmass broadened out ahead of them. A front of 1,500 kilometres was increasing to 2,500 kilometres.

Estimates of Soviet strength by the army intelligence department soon appeared to be woefully short. 'At the outset of the
war,' General Halder wrote on 11 August, 'we reckoned on about
200 enemy divisions. Now we have already counted 360.' The
fact that a Soviet division might be manifestly inferior in fighting
power to a German one was insufficiently reassuring. 'If we smash
a dozen of them, the Russians simply put up another dozen.'

For Russians, the idea that the Germans were on Napoleon's
route to Moscow was traumatic. Yet Stalin's order to mount massive counter-attacks west towards Smolensk had an effect, even
though the cost in men and equipment was terrifying. It contributed to Hitler's decision to direct Army Group Centre to go on to
the defensive, while Army Group North advanced on Leningrad
and Army Group South on Kiev. Third Panzer Group was diverted
towards Leningrad. Hitler, according to Generalleutnant Alfred
Jodl of the OKW staff, wanted to avoid Napoleon's mistakes.

Generalfeldmarschall von Bock was horrified by this change
of emphasis, as were other senior commanders who had assumed
that Moscow, the centre of Soviet communications, would remain
the principal objective. But a number of generals believed that,
before advancing on Moscow, the huge Soviet forces defending
Kiev should be eliminated in case they attacked their southern
flank.

On 29 July, Zhukov warned Stalin that Kiev could be encircled
and urged that the Ukrainian capital should be abandoned. The
Vozhd (or boss), as he was known, told Zhukov he was talking
rubbish. Zhukov demanded to be relieved of his position as chief
of staff. Stalin put him in command of the Reserve Front, but kept
him on as a member of the Stavka.

Guderian's Second Panzer Group was given the task of making
a surprise right turn from the Roslavl salient and advancing 400
kilometres south to Lokhvitsa. There, 200 kilometres east of Kiev,
he was to meet up with Kleist's First Panzer Group, which had
begun to encircle the Ukrainian capital from below. Guderian's
dash caused chaos on the Soviet side. Gomel, the last major city
in Belorussia, had to be abandoned hurriedly. But Kirponos's
South-Western Front, reinforced on Stalin's orders, was still not
permitted to abandon Kiev.

Vasily Grossman, escaping into Ukraine, only just managed to avoid being caught by Guderian's panzer divisions during their drive south. In the confusion of the invasion, some Russians at first thought that Guderian must be on their side because his name sounded Armenian. Grossman, unlike most Soviet war correspondents, was deeply moved by the suffering of civilians. 'Whether they are riding somewhere, or standing by their fences, they begin to cry as soon as they begin to speak, and one feels an involuntary desire to cry too. There's so much grief!' He was scornful of the propaganda clichés of fellow journalists who never went nearer the front than an army headquarters and resorted to dishonest formulae such as 'the much battered enemy continued his cowardly advance'.

Rundstedt's Army Group South had already captured 107,000 prisoners near Uman in Ukraine on 10 August. Stalin issued an order condemning to death the Red Army generals who had surrendered there. Underestimating the threat of Guderian's strike south, Stalin still refused to allow Kirponos to withdraw from the line of the Dnepr. The vast dam and hydroelectric plant at Zaporozhye, the great symbol of Soviet progress, was blown up as part of the scorched-earth strategy.

Evacuation of civilians, livestock and equipment continued with an even greater urgency, as Grossman described. 'At night, the sky became red from dozens of distant fires, and a grey screen of smoke hung all along the horizon during the day. Women with children in their arms, old men, herds of sheep, cows and collective farm horses sinking in the dust were moving east on the country roads, by cart and on foot. Tractor drivers drove their machines which rattled deafeningly. Trains with factory equipment, engines and boilers went east every day and night.'

On 16 September, Guderian's and Kleist's panzer groups met at Lokhvitsa, trapping more than 700,000 men in the encirclement. Kirponos along with many staff officers and some 2,000 men were wiped out by the 3rd Panzer Division near by. Generalfeldmarschall von Reichenau's Sixth Army advanced into the heavily bombed ruins of Kiev. The civilian population left behind was condemned to starvation. The Jews faced a quicker death by firing squad. Further to the south, the Eleventh Army and the Fourth Romanian Army moved on Odessa. Army Group South's next objectives would be the Crimea, with the great naval base of Sebastopol, and Rostov-on-Don, the gateway to the Caucasus.

The Kiev *Kesselschlacht* was the largest in military history. German morale soared again. The conquest of Moscow again seemed possible. To Halder's relief, Hitler had already come round to the idea. On 6 September, he issued Führer Directive No. 35, authorizing the advance on Moscow. And on 16 September, the day that the two panzer groups had met at Lokhvitsa, Generalfeldmarschall von Bock issued preliminary orders for Operation Typhoon.

Leeb's army group, after its rapid advance through the Baltic states, had found resistance increasing the closer it came to Leningrad. In mid-July, a counter-attack by Lieutenant General Nikolai Vatutin caught the Germans by surprise near Lake Ilmen. Even with the support of Hoth's Third Panzer Group, Leeb's advance had slowed in the difficult terrain of birchwoods, lakes and mosquito-ridden marshes. Half a million men and women from the threatened city were mobilized to dig a thousand kilometres of earthworks and 645 kilometres of anti-tank ditches. On 8 August, Hitler ordered Leeb to encircle Leningrad, while the Finns retook their lost territory either side of Lake Ladoga. The untrained and scarcely armed People's Levy, the *narodnoe opolchenie*, was thrown into futile and murderous attacks, literally acting in the Russian phrase as 'meat for the cannon'. Altogether over 135,000 Leningraders, factory workers as well as professors, had volunteered, or been forced to volunteer. They had no training, no medical assistance, no uniforms, no transport and no supply system. More than half lacked rifles, and yet they were still ordered into counter-attacks against panzer divisions. Most fled in terror of the tanks, against which they had no defence at all. This massive loss of life – perhaps some 70,000 – was tragically futile, and it is far from certain that their sacrifice even delayed the Germans at all on the line of the River Luga. The Soviet 34th Army was shattered. As men fled, 4,000 were arrested as deserters and nearly half of the wounded were suspected of self-inflicted wounds. In one hospital alone 460 men out of a thousand had gunshot injuries in the left hand or left forearm.

The Estonian capital of Tallinn had been cut off by the German advance, but Stalin refused to allow its Soviet defenders to evacuate by sea up the Gulf of Finland to Kronstadt. By the time he had changed his mind, it was too late for an orderly withdrawal. On 28 August, the ships of the Red Banner Baltic Fleet in Tallinn embarked 23,000 Soviet citizens as German troops fought their way into the city. Lacking air cover, the improvised fleet set sail. Altogether German mines, Finnish motor torpedo boats and the Luftwaffe sank sixty-five ships, with up to 14,000 killed. It was the greatest Russian naval disaster in history, even worse than the defeat in 1905 at Tsushima.

To the south of Leningrad, the Germans pushed across the main railway line to Moscow. On 1 September, their heavy artillery was within range and began bombarding. Soviet army trucks full of wounded and a last rush of refugees pulled back into Leningrad, with peasants driving overloaded carts, others carrying bundles and a boy dragging a reluctant goat on a piece of rope, as their villages burned behind them.

Stalin raged against Andrei Zhdanov, the Communist Party boss in Leningrad, and Voroshilov, the local defence supremo, when he heard of one town after another falling to the Germans as they encircled the city from the south. He insinuated that traitors must be at work. 'Doesn't it seem to you that someone is deliberately opening the road to the Germans?' he signalled to Molotov, who was on a fact-finding visit to the city. 'The uselessness of the Leningrad command is so absolutely incomprehensible.' But instead of Voroshilov or Zhdanov 'being put in front of a tribunal', a small wave of terror swept the city as the NKVD rounded up the usual suspects, often because they had a foreign-sounding family name.

On 7 September, the German 20th Motorized Division advanced north from Mga to take the Sinyavino Heights. And the next day, reinforced with part of the 12th Panzer Division, it reached the town of Shlisselburg, with its Tsarist fortress at the south-western point of Lake Ladoga where the Neva flowed into it. Leningrad was now entirely cut off by land. The only route left was across the huge lake. Voroshilov and Zhdanov took a whole day before they summoned up the courage to tell Stalin that the Germans had seized Shlisselburg. The siege of Leningrad, the longest and most pitiless in modern history, had begun.

As well as half a million troops, the civilian population of

Leningrad stood at more than two and a half million people, including 400,000 children. Führer headquarters decided that it did
not want to occupy the city. Instead the Germans would bombard
it and seal it off to let the population starve and die of disease.
Once reduced, the city itself would be demolished and the area
handed over to Finland.

Stalin had already decided that he needed a change of command in Leningrad. He ordered Zhukov to take over, trusting in
his ruthlessness. Zhukov flew from Moscow as soon as he had
received his orders. On arrival, he drove straight to the military
council in the Smolny Institute where he claimed to have encountered defeatism and drunkenness. He soon went even further than
Stalin in his readiness to threaten the families of soldiers who surrendered. He ordered commanders of the Leningrad front: 'Make
it clear to all troops that all the families of those who surrender
to the enemy will be shot, and they themselves will be shot upon
return from prison.'

Clearly Zhukov did not realize that his order, if carried out to
the letter, would have meant the execution of Stalin himself. The
Soviet dictator's own son, Lieutenant Yakov Djugashvili, had
been captured in an encirclement. Stalin declared in private that it
would be better if he had never been born. Nazi propaganda services soon made use of their trophy prisoner. 'A German aircraft
appeared,' a soldier called Vasily Churkin wrote in his diary. 'It
was a sunny day and we saw a large heap of leaflets fall out of
the aircraft. On them was a photograph of Stalin's son supported
on two sides by smiling German officers. But it was cooked up
by Goebbels and had no success.' Stalin's pitilessness towards his
son only eased in 1945 when it appeared that Yakov had thrown
himself at the barbed wire in his camp, forcing the guards to shoot
him.

Stalin had no feelings for civilians. On hearing that the Germans had forced 'old men and women, mothers and children'
forward as human shields or as emissaries to demand surrender, he sent orders that they were to be shot down. 'My answer
is – No sentimentality. Instead smash the enemy and his accomplices, sick or healthy, in the teeth. War is inexorable, and those
who show weakness and permit wavering are the first to suffer
defeat.' A Gefreiter with the 269th Infantry Division wrote on

21 September: 'Crowds of civilians are escaping from the siege, and one has to shut one's eyes to avoid seeing the misery. Even at the front, where at the moment there are some sharp exchanges of fire, there are many children and women. As soon as a shell screams ominously near, they run for cover. It seems so comical and we laugh at it; but it is in fact sad.'

As the last wounded and defeated stragglers limped back into the city, the authorities tried to exert an iron rule, enforced by NKVD troops ready to shoot any deserter or 'defeatist' on the spot. Stalinist paranoia surged, with orders to the NKVD to arrest twenty-nine categories of potential enemy. Spy-mania in the city became feverish, spurred on by fantastical rumours, largely because the Soviet authorities revealed so little information. But while a minority of Leningraders secretly hoped that the Stalinist regime might fall, there is no evidence of organized German or Finnish intelligence agents at work.

Zhukov gave orders for the guns of the Baltic Fleet at Kronstadt to be deployed, either as floating batteries or to be dismounted and taken up to the Pulkovo Heights outside Leningrad to shoot back at enemy artillery positions. Their fire was directed by General of Artillery Nikolai Voronov from the cupola of St Isaac's Cathedral. Its great gilded dome, visible from Finland, was soon camouflaged with grey paint.

On 8 September, the day that the Germans took Shlisselburg, Luftwaffe bombers targeted the food depots in the south of the city. 'Columns of thick smoke are rising high,' Churkin wrote in his diary, appalled by the implications. 'It's the Badaevskiye food depots burning. Fire is devouring the six-months' food supplies for the whole population of Leningrad.' The failure to disperse the stores had been a major error. Rations would have to be dramatically reduced. In addition, little had been done to bring in firewood for the winter. But the greatest mistake was the failure to evacuate more civilians. Apart from refugees, fewer than half a million Leningraders had been sent east before the Moscow line had been cut by the German advance.

In the second half of September, the Germans launched furious attacks with heavy air raids. Soviet pilots in their obsolete aircraft were again reduced to ramming German bombers. But the defenders, largely thanks to their artillery support, managed to beat off the ground attacks. Marine infantry from the Red Banner Baltic Fleet played a key role. They wore their midnight-blue sailor hats at a rakish angle, with a forelock emerging at the front as a proud trademark.

On 24 September, Generalfeldmarschall von Leeb acknowledged that he lacked the strength to break through. This coincided with further pressure from other German commanders to relaunch the advance on Moscow. Hoth's panzer group was ordered back to Army Group Centre. With both sides on the defensive as winter approached, bringing stronger frosts at night, the fighting had turned to trench warfare. At the end of the month, the bitterly contested front lapsed into sporadic artillery duels.

Soviet casualties in the north had been dreadful, with 214,078 'irrecoverable losses'. This represented between a third and a half of all troops deployed. But they would be small in comparison to the mass deaths from starvation to come. Even if Leningrad surrendered, Hitler had no intention of occupying the city and even less of feeding its inhabitants. He wanted both of them completely erased from the earth.

13

Rassenkrieg

JUNE–SEPTEMBER 1941

German soldiers, who had been horrified by the misery of Polish villages in 1939, expressed even greater disgust on Soviet territory. From the massacres of prisoners by the NKVD to the primitive conditions of collective farms, the 'Soviet paradise' as Goebbels referred to it with cutting sarcasm entrenched their prejudices. The Nazi propaganda minister, with his diabolic genius, had perceived that contempt and hatred alone were not enough. The combination of hatred and fear provided the most effective way to inspire a mentality of annihilation. All his epithets, 'asiatic', 'treacherous', 'Jewish Bolshevik', 'bestial', 'sub-human', combined towards this end. Most soldiers were convinced by Hitler's claim that the Jews had started the war.

The atavistic and fearful fascination which many, if not most, Germans felt towards the eastern Slavs had of course been heightened by reports of unbelievable cruelties in the Russian Revolution and civil war. Nazi propaganda sought to exploit a notion of culture clash between German order on the one hand and Bolshevik chaos, squalor and atheism on the other. Yet, despite superficial similarities in the Nazi and Soviet regimes, the ideological and cultural divide between the two countries was profound, from the significant to the trivial.

During the heat of the summer, German motorcyclists often drove around wearing little more than shorts and goggles. In Belorussia and Ukraine, old women were shocked by their flaunted torsos. They were even more shocked when German soldiers walked around naked in their *izbas*, or peasant houses, and harassed young women. Although there appear to have been comparatively few cases of outright rape by German soldiers quartered in villages close to the front, many more occurred well behind the lines, especially against young Jewish women.

The worst crime was carried out with official approval. Young

Ukrainian, Belorussian and Russian women were rounded up and forced into army brothels. This slavery subjected them to continual rape by off-duty soldiers. If they resisted, they were brutally punished and even shot. Despite the fact that sexual relations with *Untermenschen* (sub-humans) was an offence under Nazi law, the military authorities regarded this system as a pragmatic solution both for reasons of discipline and for the physical health of their soldiers. The young women could at least be inspected for infectious diseases on a regular basis by Wehrmacht doctors.

Yet German soldiers could also feel pity for Soviet women who had been left behind in the retreat and had to cope without men, animals or machines. 'One even sees a couple of women pulling a home-made plough, while another guides it,' wrote a signals corporal in a letter home. 'A whole crowd of women are repairing the road under the eyes of an Organisation Todt man. It's obligatory to use the knout to instil obedience! There's scarcely a family in which the man is still alive. In 90% of cases the answer to the question is always: "Husband dead in war!" It is frightful. The Russian loss of men is completely terrible.'

Many Soviet, especially Ukrainian, citizens had not expected the horrors of a German occupation. In Ukraine, numerous villagers at first welcomed German troops with the traditional gift of bread and salt. After Stalin's enforced collectivization of farms and the terrible famine of 1932–3, which had killed an estimated 3.3 million people, hatred for the Communists was widespread. Older, more religious Ukrainians had been encouraged by the black crosses on the German armoured vehicles, thinking that they represented a crusade against Godless Bolshevism.

Officers from the Abwehr sensed that, with the vast areas to be conquered, the Wehrmacht's best strategy would be to recruit a Ukrainian army of a million men. Their suggestion was rejected by Hitler, who did not want weapons given to Slav *Untermenschen*, but his wishes were soon quietly ignored, both by the army and by the SS, both of whom began to recruit. The Organization of Ukrainian Nationalists, on the other hand, whose members had been helping the Germans just before the invasion, were suppressed. Berlin wanted to crush their hopes for an independent Ukraine.

After all the Soviet propaganda claims about its industrial

triumphs, Ukrainians and others were bewildered by the quality and variety of German equipment. Vasily Grossman described villagers crowding round a captured Austrian motorcyclist. 'Everyone admires his long, soft, steel-coloured leather coat. Everyone is touching it, shaking their heads. This means: how on earth can we fight people who wear such a coat? Their aircraft must be as good as their leather coats.'

In letters home, German soldiers complained that there was little worth looting in the Soviet Union, except for food. Ignoring the early gifts, they seized geese and chickens and livestock. They smashed hives to get the honey and paid no heed to the pleas of their victims that they would have nothing left to survive the winter. The *Landser* thought wistfully of the campaign in France, with its rich pickings. And unlike the French, Red Army soldiers fought on, refusing to acknowledge that they had been defeated.

Any German soldier who showed compassion for the suffering of Soviet prisoners was jeered at by his comrades. The vast majority regarded the hundreds of thousands of prisoners as little more than human vermin. Their pitiful condition, filthy as a result of the treatment they received, served only to reinforce the prejudices influenced by the propaganda of the previous eight years. Victims were thus dehumanized in a form of self-fulfilling prophecy. A soldier guarding a column of Soviet prisoners wrote home that they were eating 'grass like cattle'. And when they passed a field of potatoes, 'they fell on the ground, digging with their fingers and eating them raw'. Despite the fact that the key element in the plan for Barbarossa had been battles of encirclement, German military authorities had deliberately done little to prepare for the mass of prisoners. The more that died from neglect the fewer there would be to feed.

A French prisoner of war described the arrival of a group of Soviet prisoners at a Wehrmacht camp in the Generalgouvernement: 'The Russians arrived in rows, five by five, holding each other by the arms, as none of them could walk by themselves – "walking skeletons" was really the only fitting description. The colour of their faces was not even yellow, it was green. Almost all squinted as if they had not strength enough to focus their sight. They fell by rows, five men at a time. The Germans rushed on them and beat them with rifle butts and whips.'

German officers subsequently tried to attribute the treatment of the three million prisoners of war they captured by October to the lack of troops to guard them and the shortage of transport to feed them. Yet thousands of Red Army prisoners died on forced marches simply because the Wehrmacht did not want their vehicles or trains to be 'infected' by the 'foul-smelling' mass. No camps had been prepared, so they were herded in their scores of thousands into barbed-wire encirclements under open skies. Little food or water was provided. This formed part of the Nazis' Hunger Plan designed to kill thirty million Soviet citizens to cure the problem of 'over-population' in the occupied territories. Any wounded were left to the care of Red Army doctors but deprived of medical supplies. When German guards threw totally insufficient quantities of bread over the wire, they amused themselves watching men fight over it. In 1941 alone, more than two million Soviet prisoners died from starvation, disease and exposure.

Soviet troops responded in kind, shooting and bayoneting prisoners out of anger, which came from the shock of the invasion and the ruthlessness of German warfare. In any case, the impossibility of feeding and guarding captives in the chaos of retreat meant that few were likely to be spared. Senior commanders were exasperated at the loss of 'tongues' to be interrogated for intelligence purposes.

The combination of fear and hatred also played a large part in the cruelty of the war against partisans. Traditional German military doctrine had long fostered a sense of outrage against guerrilla warfare in any form, well before the OKW's instructions to shoot commissars and partisans. Even before Stalin called for insurrection behind German lines in his speech on 3 July 1941, Soviet resistance had begun spontaneously with bypassed groups of Red Army soldiers. Bands began to form in forests and marshes, swelled by civilians fleeing persecution and the destruction of their villages.

Using the fieldcraft and camouflage which came naturally to those who had lived their lives in the countryside and forests, Soviet partisans soon became a far greater threat than the planners of Barbarossa had ever imagined. By the beginning of September 1941, sixty-three partisan detachments with a total of nearly 5,000 men and women were operating behind German lines in Ukraine alone. The NKVD was also planning to insert another eighty groups, while a further 434 detachments were being trained as stay-behind groups. Altogether over 20,000 partisans were already in place or being prepared. A number included specially trained assassins who could pass themselves off as German officers. Railway lines, rolling stock and locomotives, troop trains, supply trucks, motorcycle couriers, bridges, fuel, ammunition and food depots, landlines, telegraph and airfields, all were targeted. Using parachuted radios, partisan detachments led by officers mainly from NKVD frontier forces transmitted intelligence back to Moscow and received instructions.

Not surprisingly, the partisan campaign made the idea of colonizing Hitler's 'Garden of Eden' rather less appealing to potential Germans and *Volksdeutsche* settlers who had been promised farms there. The whole *Lebensraum* plan in the east required 'cleansed' areas and a completely subservient peasantry. Predictably, Nazi reprisals became increasingly savage. Villages near partisan attacks were burned to the ground. Hostages were executed. Conspicuous punishments included the public hanging of young women and girls accused of aiding the partisans. But the harsher the reaction, the greater the determination to resist. In many cases, Soviet partisan leaders deliberately provoked German reprisals to increase hatred for the invader. It was indeed a 'time of iron'. The life of an individual seemed to have lost all value on both sides, especially in German eyes if the individual was Jewish.

There were essentially two parts to the Holocaust – what Vasily Grossman later called 'the Shoah by bullets and the Shoah by gas' – and the process which eventually led to the industrialized murder of the death camps was uneven, to say the least. Until September 1939, the Nazis had hoped to force German, Austrian and Czech Jews to emigrate through maltreatment, humiliation and the expropriation of their property. Once war began, that became increasingly difficult. And the conquest of Poland brought a further 1.7 million Jews under their jurisdiction.

In May 1940, during the invasion of France, Himmler had written a paper for Hitler entitled 'Some Thoughts on the Treatment of Alien Populations in the East'. He suggested screening the Polish population so that the 'racially valuable' could be Germanized, while the rest were turned into slave labour. As for the Jews, he wrote: 'I hope completely to erase the concept of Jews through the possibility of a great emigration to a colony in Africa or elsewhere.' At that stage, Himmler considered genocide – 'the Bolshevik method of physical extermination' – to be 'un-German and impossible'.

Himmler's idea of shipping European Jews abroad focused on the French island of Madagascar. (Adolf Eichmann, still a junior functionary, was thinking of Palestine, a British mandate.) Reinhard Heydrich, Himmler's deputy, also argued that the problem of 3.75 million Jews then on German-occupied territory could not be resolved through emigration, so a 'territorial solution' was needed. The problem was that, even if Vichy France agreed, the 'Madagaskar Projekt' could not work in the face of British naval superiority. Yet the idea of deporting Jews to a reservation somewhere still remained the preferred option.

In March 1941, with the ghettos in Poland overflowing, mass sterilization was considered. Then, with Hitler's plans for Operation Barbarossa, senior Nazis embraced the idea of removing Europe's Jews, as well as thirty-one million Slavs, to some area deep in the Soviet Union once victory was achieved. This would be when German armies reached the Arkhangelsk–Astrakhan line, and the Luftwaffe could switch to the long-range bombing of any remaining Soviet arms factories and communication centres in the Urals and beyond. For Hans Frank, the regent of the Generalgouvernement, the invasion promised the opportunity to deport all Jews who had been dumped in his territory.

Others, including Heydrich, concentrated on more immediate concerns, particularly the 'pacification' of the conquered territories. Hitler's notion of 'pacification' was quite clear. 'This will happen best', he told Alfred Rosenberg, the minister for the eastern territories, 'by shooting dead anyone who even looks sideways at us.' Soldiers should not be prosecuted for crimes against civilians, unless the needs of discipline absolutely required it.

Army commanders, now in Hitler's thrall after the triumph over France which they had openly doubted, failed to raise any objections. Some of them embraced with enthusiasm the idea of a war of annihilation – *Vernichtungskrieg*. Any lingering outrage about the murderous actions of the SS in Poland had dissipated. Generalfeldmarschall von Brauchitsch, the commander-in-chief, worked closely with Heydrich on liaison between the army and the SS during Barbarossa. The German army would provision the Einsatzgruppen, and would liaise with them through the senior intelligence officer at each army headquarters. Thus at army command and senior staff level nobody could plead ignorance about their activities.

The 'Shoah by bullets' is usually remembered by the activities of the 3,000 men in the SS Einsatzgruppen. As a result, the massacres carried out by the 11,000 men in twenty-one battalions of Ordnungspolizei, acting as a second wave well to the rear of the advancing armies, have often been overlooked. Himmler also assembled an SS cavalry brigade and two other Waffen-SS brigades to be ready to assist. The commander of the 1st SS Cavalry Regiment was Hermann Fegelein, who in 1944 married Eva Braun's sister and thus became part of the Führer's entourage. Himmler ordered his SS cavalry to execute all male Jews and drive their women into the swamps of the Pripet Marshes. By mid-August 1941, the cavalry brigade claimed to have killed 200 Russians in combat and to have shot 13,788 civilians, most of whom were Jews described as 'plunderers'.

Each of the three army groups in the invasion was to be closely followed by an Einsatzgruppe. A fourth would be added later down in the south on the Black Sea coast, following the Romanians and the Eleventh Army. The *Einsatzgruppen* personnel were recruited from all sections of Himmler's empire, including the Waffen-SS, the Sicherheitsdienst (SD), the Sicherheitspolizei (Sipo), the Kriminalpolizei (Kripo) and the Ordnungspolizei. Each Einsatzgruppe of around 800 men would consist of two Sonderkommandos operating closely behind the troops and two Einsatzkommandos a little further back.

Heydrich instructed the Einsatzgruppen commanders who came from the intellectual elite of the SS – the majority had doctorates – to encourage local anti-semitic groups to kill Jews and Communists. These activities were described as 'self-cleansing efforts'. But they were not to indicate official German approval, or allow these groups to believe that their actions might gain them any form of political independence. The Einsatzgruppen themselves were to execute Communist Party officials, commissars, partisans and saboteurs and 'Jews in party and state positions'. Presumably, Heydrich had also suggested that they could and should go beyond these categories as they saw fit when fulfilling their duties with 'unprecedented harshness', such as shooting male Jews of military age. But there seems to have been no official indication at this stage of encouraging the murder of Jewish women and children.

The killing of Jewish males began as soon as the German armies crossed the Soviet frontier on 22 June. Many of the early massacres were carried out by Lithuanian and Ukrainian anti-semites, as Heydrich had predicted. In western Ukraine, they killed 24,000 Jews. In Kaunas, 3,800 were slaughtered. Sometimes watched by German soldiers, Jews were rounded up and tormented, with rabbis having their beards pulled or set on fire. Then they were beaten to death to the cheers of the crowd. The Germans fostered the idea that these killings were revenge for the massacres carried out by the NKVD before it retreated. Einsatzgruppen and police battalions also began to round up and shoot Jews in hundreds and even thousands.

Their victims had to prepare their own mass graves. Any who did not dig fast enough were shot. They were then forced to undress, partly so that their clothes could be redistributed later, but also in case they had concealed valuable items or money in them. Forced to kneel on the edge of the pit, they were shot in the back of the head so that the body would roll forwards and drop. Other SS and police units considered it tidier to make their first victims lie in a row along the bottom of the great trench, and shoot them *in situ* with sub-machine guns. Then the next batch would be made to lie down on the bodies, head to toe, and they too would be shot. This was known as the 'sardine' method. In a few cases, Jews were driven into a synagogue, which would be set on fire. Any who tried to escape were shot down.

With Himmler's constant visits to provide unspecified encouragement to his men, the process became self-escalating. The original target group of 'Jews in party and state positions' immediately expanded to include all male Jews of military age, then to all male Jews regardless of age. In late June and early July, it was mainly local anti-semitic groups who killed Jewish women and children. But by the end of July SS Einsatzgruppen, Himmler's Waffen-SS brigades and the police battalions were regularly killing women and children too. They were assisted, despite Hitler's instruction against arming Slavs, by some twenty-six battalions of locally recruited police, most of whom were attracted by the chance of robbing their victims.

Ordinary German soldiers and even Luftwaffe personnel also took part in killings, as interrogators from the NKVD 7th Department later found out from German prisoners. 'A pilot from the third air squadron said that he participated in the execution of a group of Jews in one of the villages near Berdichev at the beginning of the war. They were executed as a punishment for handing over a German pilot to the Red Army. A Gefreiter from the 765th Pioneer Battalion named Traxler witnessed executions by SS soldiers of Jews near Rovno and Dubno. When one of the soldiers remarked that it was a terrible sight, an Unteroffizier from the same unit, Graff, said "the Jews are swine and eliminating them is to show that you are a civilized person".'

One day, a German transport Gefreiter accompanied by his company clerk happened to see 'men, women and children with their hands bound together with wire being driven along the road by SS people'. They went to see what was happening. Outside the village, they saw a 150-metre trench about three metres deep. Hundreds of Jews had been rounded up. The victims were forced to lie in the trench in rows so that an SS man on each side could walk along shooting them with captured Soviet sub-machine guns. 'Then people were again driven forward and they had to get in and lie on top of the dead. At that moment a young girl – she must have been about 12 years old – cried out in a clear, piteous shrill voice. "Let me live, I'm still only a child!" The child was grabbed, thrown into the ditch, and shot.'

A few managed to slip away from these massacres. Not surprisingly, they were completely traumatized by what they had experienced. On the north-eastern edge of Ukraine, Vasily Grossman encountered one of them. 'A girl – a Jewish beauty who has managed to escape from the Germans – has bright, absolutely insane eyes,' he wrote in his notebook.

Younger officers in the Wehrmacht seem to have assented to the killing of Jewish children more than the older generation, mainly because they believed that otherwise those spared would return to take revenge in the future. In September 1944, a conversation between General der Panzertruppe Heinrich Eberbach and his son in the Kriegsmarine was secretly taped while they were in British captivity. 'In my opinion,' said General Eberbach, 'one can even go as far as to say that the killing of those million Jews, or however many it was, was necessary in the interests of our people. But to kill the women and children wasn't necessary. That is going too far.' His son replied: 'Well, if you are going to kill off the Jews, then kill the women and children too, or the children at least. There is no need to do it publicly, but what good does it do me to kill off the old people?'

In general, front-line formations did not participate in the massacres but there were notable exceptions, especially the SS *Wiking* Division in Ukraine, and some infantry divisions, which took part in killings such as those in Brest-Litovsk. While there can be no doubt of the close cooperation between SS and army group headquarters, at the same time senior army officers tried to distance themselves from what was happening. Orders were issued against members of the Wehrmacht taking part in or witnessing mass killings, yet increasing numbers of off-duty soldiers turned up to watch and photograph the atrocities. Some even volunteered to take over when the executioners wanted a rest.

As well as in Lithuania, Latvia and Belorussia, the mass killings spread across Ukraine, often assisted by local men recruited as auxiliaries. Anti-semitism had greatly increased during the great Ukrainian famine because Soviet agents had started rumours suggesting that Jews were primarily responsible for the starvation, so as to deflect responsibility away from Stalin's own policies of collectivization and dekulakization. Ukrainian volunteers were also used for guarding Red Army prisoners. 'They're willing and comradely,' a Gefreiter wrote. 'They represent a considerable relief for us.'

After the massacres in Lwów and other cities, Ukrainians helped by denouncing and rounding up Einsatzgruppe C's victims in Berdichev, which had one of the highest concentrations of Jews. When German forces entered the city, 'the soldiers were shouting "Jude kaputt!" from their trucks and waved their arms', Vasily Grossman discovered much later in the war. More than 20,000

Jews were killed in batches out by the airstrip. They included Grossman's mother, and for the rest of his life he was tormented by guilt that he had not brought her back to Moscow the moment the German invasion began.

A Jewish woman called Ida Belozovskaya described the scene when the Germans entered her town near Kiev on 19 September. 'People with fawning, happy, servile faces were standing along both sides of the road greeting their "liberators". On that day I knew already that our life was coming to an end, that our ordeal was beginning. We were all in a mouse-trap. Where could one go? There was nowhere to escape.' Jews were not just denounced to the German authorities out of anti-semitism, but also out of fear, as Belozovskaya testified. The Germans would kill any family found sheltering Jews, so even those who were sympathetic and prepared to give food did not dare to take them in.

Although the Hungarian army attached to Rundstedt's Army Group South did not take part in mass killings, the Romanians attacking Odessa, a city with a large Jewish population, committed appalling atrocities. Already in the summer of 1941 Romanian troops were said to have killed about 10,000 Jews when seizing back the Soviet-occupied areas of Bessarabia and the Bukovina. Even German officers regarded the conduct of their ally as chaotic and unnecessarily sadistic. In Odessa, the Romanians killed 35,000.

The German Sixth Army, commanded by Generalfeldmarschall von Reichenau, the most convinced Nazi among all senior commanders, had the 1st SS Brigade attached to it. An army security division, the Feldgendarmerie, and other military units were also involved in mass killings along the way. On 27 September, shortly after the capture of Kiev, Reichenau attended a meeting with the town commandant and SS officers from Sonderkommando 4a. It was agreed that the town commandant should put up posters instructing the Jews to muster for 'evacuation', bringing with them identity papers, money, valuables and warm clothing.

The Nazis' murderous intentions were unexpectedly helped by a curious by-product of the Molotov–Ribbentrop Pact. Stalinist censorship had stifled any hint of Hitler's virulent anti-semitism. As a result, when the Jews in Kiev were ordered to report for 'resettlement', no fewer than 33,771 turned up as instructed. The

Sixth Army, which was assisting with transport, had expected no more than 7,000 to appear. It took the SS Sonderkommando three days to murder them all in the ravine of Babi Yar outside the city.

Ida Belozovskaya, who was married to a Gentile, described the assembly of Jews in Kiev, including members of her own family. 'On 28 September, my husband and his Russian sister went to see my unfortunate ones off on their last journey. It seemed to them, and we all wanted to believe this, that the German barbarians would just send them away somewhere, and for several days people kept moving in big groups to their "salvation". There was no time to receive everyone, people were ordered to come back on the following day (the Germans didn't overload themselves with work). And the people kept turning up day after day, until their turn to leave this world finally came.'

Her Russian husband followed one of the transports to Babi Yar to find out what was happening. 'That's what he saw through a little crack in the high fence. The people were being separated, men were told to go to one side, and women and children to the other side. They were naked (they had to leave their things in another place), and then they were mowed down by sub-machine guns and machine guns, the sound of firing drowning their screams and howling.'

It has been estimated that more than one and a half million Soviet Jews escaped the killing squads. But the concentration of most of the Soviet Union's Jews in the western parts, especially in cities and large towns, made the work of the *Einsatzgruppen* much easier. The *Einsatzgruppen* commanders were also pleasantly surprised by how cooperative and often eager to help their army counterparts proved to be. By the end of 1942, the total number of Jews killed by SS *Einsatzgruppen*, Ordnungspolizei, anti-partisan units and the German army itself is estimated to have exceeded 1.35 million people.

The 'Shoah by gas' also had a haphazard development. As early as 1935, Hitler had indicated that once war came he would introduce a programme of euthanasia. The criminally insane, the 'feeble-minded', the incapacitated and children with birth defects, all were included in the Nazi category of 'life unworthy of life'. The first case of euthanasia was carried out on 25 July 1939 by

Hitler's personal physician, Dr Karl Brandt, whom the Führer had asked to set up an advisory committee. Less than two weeks before the invasion of Poland, the ministry of the interior ordered hospitals to report back on every case of 'deformed newborns'. The reporting process was extended to adults at about the same time.

The first mental patients to be killed, however, were in Poland three weeks after the invasion. They were shot in a nearby forest. Massacres of other asylum inmates rapidly followed. Over 20,000 were killed in this way. German patients from Pomerania were then shot. Two of the hospitals thus emptied were turned into barracks for the Waffen-SS. By late November, gas chambers using carbon monoxide were in operation, and Himmler observed one of these killings in December. Early in 1940, experiments had been tried using sealed trucks as mobile gas chambers. This was regarded as a success because it reduced the complications of transporting patients. The organizer was promised ten Reichsmark a head.

Directed from Berlin, the system was extended within the Reich under the name T4. Parents were persuaded that their handicapped children, some of whom simply had learning difficulties, could be better cared for at another institution. They were then told that the child had died of pneumonia. Some 70,000 German adults and children were murdered in gas chambers by August 1941. This figure also included German Jews who had been hospitalized for a significant time.

The vast numbers of victims and the unconvincing death certificates had failed to keep the euthanasia programme secret. Hitler ordered it to be halted that August after churchmen, led by Bishop Clemens August Graf von Galen, had denounced it. But a covert version continued afterwards, killing another 20,000 by the end of the war. Personnel involved in the euthanasia programme were recruited for the death camps of eastern Poland in 1942. As several historians have emphasized, the Nazis' euthanasia programme provided not just the blueprint for the Final Solution, but also the foundation for their ideal of a racially and genetically pure society.

Because of Hitler's avoidance of confiding controversial decisions to paper, historians have interpreted the evasive and often euphemistic language of subsidiary documents in different ways when trying to assess the exact moment at which the decision was made to launch the Final Solution. This has proved an impossible task, especially since the movement towards genocide consisted of unrecorded encouragement from the top, as well as an unco-ordinated series of steps and experiments carried out on the spot by the different killing groups. In a curious way, it happened to mirror the *Auftragstaktik* of the army, whereby a general instruc-tion was translated into action by the commander on the ground.

Some historians argue plausibly that the basic decision to go for outright genocide took place in July or August 1941, when a quick victory still seemed to be within the Wehrmacht's grasp. Others think that it did not take place until the autumn, when the German advance in the Soviet Union slowed perceptibly and a 'territorial solution' looked increasingly impracticable. Some put it even later, suggesting the second week of December when the German army was halted outside Moscow, and Hitler declared war on the United States.

The fact that each different *Einsatzgruppe* interpreted its mis-sion slightly differently suggests that there was no centrally issued instruction. Only from the month of August did total genocide become standard, with Jewish women and children also killed en masse. Also on 15 August, Himmler witnessed for the first time an execution of a hundred Jews near Minsk, a spectacle organized at his request by Einsatzgruppe B. Himmler could not bear to look. Afterwards, Obergruppenführer Erich von dem Bach underlined the point that on that occasion only a hundred had been shot. 'Look at the eyes of the men in this *Kommando*,' Bach said to him, 'how deeply shaken they are! These men are finished for the rest of their lives. What kind of followers are we training here? Either neurotics or savages!' Bach himself, suffering from nightmares and stomach pains, was later taken to hospital to be treated on Himmler's orders by the head physician of the SS.

Himmler made a speech afterwards to the men justifying their action and indicated that Hitler had issued an order for the li-quidation of all Jews in the eastern territories. He compared their work to the elimination of bedbugs and rats. That afternoon, he discussed with Arthur Nebe, the *Einsatzgruppe* commander, and Bach alternatives to shooting. Nebe suggested an experiment with explosives, which Himmler approved. This proved a crude, messy and embarrassing failure. The next stage was the gas van, using carbon monoxide from the exhaust. Himmler wanted to find a method which was more 'humane' for the executioners. Concerned for their spiritual welfare, he urged commanders to organize social events in the evenings with sing-songs. Most of the killers, however, preferred to seek oblivion in the bottle.

An intensification of the slaughter of Jews also coincided with the Wehrmacht's increasingly brutal treatment and outright killing of Soviet prisoners of war. On 3 September, the insecticide Zyklon B, developed by the chemical conglomerate IG Farben, was used at Auschwitz for the first time in a test on Soviet and Polish prisoners. At the same time, Jews from Germany and western Europe transported to the eastern territories were being murdered on arrival by police officials, who claimed that this was the only way to cope with the numbers foisted on them. Senior officials in the German-occupied eastern territories, the Reichskommissariat Ostland (the Baltic states and part of Belorussia) and the Reichskommissariat Ukraine, had no idea what the policy was. This would only be made clear after the Wannsee conference the following January.

14

The 'Grand Alliance'

JUNE–DECEMBER 1941

Churchill was notorious for his incontinent rush of ideas on prosecuting the war. One of his colleagues remarked that the trouble was that he did not know which of them were any good. Yet Churchill was not just a fox, in Isaiah Berlin's definition. He was also a hedgehog, with one big idea right from the start. Britain alone did not stand a chance against Nazi Germany. He knew that he needed to bring the Americans in to the war, just as he had predicted to his son Randolph in May 1940.

While never wavering over this objective, Churchill wasted no time in forming an alliance with the Bolshevik regime he had always loathed. 'I will unsay no word that I have spoken about it,' he declared in a broadcast on 22 June 1941, following news of the German invasion of the Soviet Union. 'But all this fades away before the spectacle which is now unfolding.' And he remarked later to his private secretary, John Colville, that 'if Hitler invaded Hell, I would at least make a favourable reference to the Devil in the House of Commons'. His speech that evening, prepared with the American ambassador John G. Winant, promised the Soviet Union 'any technical or economic assistance in our power'. It made a fine impression in Britain, in the United States and in Moscow, even though Stalin and Molotov remained convinced that the British were still hiding the true nature of Rudolf Hess's mission.

Two days later, Churchill instructed Stewart Menzies, the head of the Secret Intelligence Service, to send Ultra decrypts to the Kremlin. Menzies warned that 'it would be fatal'. The Red Army did not possess effective cyphers, and the Germans would trace the source of the intelligence very quickly. Churchill agreed, but Ultra-sourced intelligence was passed on later, suitably disguised. An agreement on military cooperation between the two countries was negotiated soon afterwards, although at this stage the British government did not expect the Red Army to survive the Nazi onslaught.

Churchill was encouraged by developments across the Atlantic. On 7 July, Roosevelt informed Congress that US forces had landed in Iceland to replace British and Canadian troops. On 26 July, the United States and Britain acted together to freeze Japanese assets in retaliation for their occupation of French Indochina. The Japanese wanted air bases from which to attack the Burma Road, along which arms and supplies reached the Nationalist Chinese forces. Roosevelt was keen to support Chiang Kai-shek's Nationalists, and a force of mercenary American pilots, known as the Flying Tigers, was recruited in the United States to defend the Burma Road from Mandalay along which their supplies came. But when the United States and Britain placed an embargo on the sale of oil and other materials to Japan, the stakes were raised much further. The Japanese were now within easy striking distance of Malaya, Thailand and the oilfields of the Dutch East Indies, which looked increasingly like their next objective. Not surprisingly, Australia also saw itself at risk.

No suitor prepared as carefully as Churchill for his first wartime meeting with the American President in early August. Secrecy on both sides was effectively maintained. Churchill and his party, many of whom had no idea where they were headed, embarked on the battleship HMS *Prince of Wales*. The prime minister took with him some grouse shot before the season opened to entertain the President, as well as some 'golden eggs' of Ultra decrypts to impress him. He grilled Harry Hopkins, Roosevelt's close friend and adviser who accompanied them, on everything he could tell him about the American leader. Churchill had no recollection of his first meeting with Roosevelt in 1918, when he had failed to make a good impression on the future President.

Roosevelt, with his chiefs of staff, had also gone to some trouble for this meeting. Outwitting the press, he had transferred from the presidential yacht *Potomac* to the heavy cruiser USS *Augusta*. Then, with a strong escort of destroyers, they had sailed on 6 August to the rendezvous of Placentia Bay off Newfoundland. Warm relations rapidly developed between the two leaders, and a combined church service on the after-deck of the *Prince of Wales*, carefully stage-managed by Churchill, produced a deep emotional effect. Yet Roosevelt, although charmed and impressed by the British prime minister, remained detached. He had, as one biographer noted, 'a gift for treating every new acquaintance as if the two had known each other all their lives, a capacity for forging a semblance of intimacy which he exploited ruthlessly'. In the interests of amity divisive questions were avoided, particularly Britain's empire of which Roosevelt so disapproved. The joint document known as the Atlantic Charter, which they signed on 12 August, promised self-determination to a liberated world, with the implicit exception of the British Empire, and no doubt the Soviet Union.

The discussions over several days had ranged far and wide, from the danger of Spain joining the Axis camp to the threat from Japan in the Pacific. For Churchill, the most important results included an American agreement to provide convoy escorts west of Iceland, bombers for Britain and an undertaking to give the Soviet Union massive aid to stay in the war. Yet Roosevelt faced a widespread reluctance within the United States to move towards war with Nazi Germany. During his return from Newfoundland, he heard that the House of Representatives had passed the Selective Service Bill, inaugurating the very first peacetime draft, by no more than a single vote.

American isolationists refused to acknowledge that the Nazi invasion of the Soviet Union was bound to widen the scope of the war far beyond Europe. On 25 August, Red Army troops and British forces from Iraq invaded neutral Iran, to secure its oil and ensure a supply route from the Persian Gulf to the Caucasus and Kazakhstan. During the summer of 1941, Britain's fears of a Japanese attack on its colonies increased. On Roosevelt's advice, Churchill cancelled an attack planned by the Special Operations Executive (SOE) on a Japanese freighter, the *Asaka Maru*, loading up in Europe with vital supplies for the Japanese war machine. Britain could not risk a war in the Pacific alone against Japan. Its first priority was to secure its position in North Africa and the Mediterranean. Until the United States entered the war, Churchill and his chiefs of staff could look no further than ensuring their country's survival, creating a bomber force to attack Germany and helping to keep the Soviet Union fighting the Germans.

*

A bombing offensive against Germany represented one of Stalin's chief expectations of Allied assistance, as the Wehrmacht inflicted such devastating losses on the Red Army in the summer of 1941. He also demanded an invasion of northern France at the earliest possible moment to take pressure off the eastern front. In a meeting with Sir Stafford Cripps five days after the invasion, Molotov tried to force the British ambassador to specify the scale of the aid which Churchill appeared to be offering. But Cripps was in no position to do so. The Soviet foreign minister pressed him further two days later, after meetings in London between Lord Beaverbrook, Churchill's minister of supply, and the Soviet ambassador, Ivan Maisky. It appears that Beaverbrook had discussed the possibility of an invasion of France with Maisky, without having consulted the British chiefs of staff. From then on, one of the key objectives of Soviet foreign policy was to pin down the British to a firm promise. The Russians suspected, with justification, that British reticence came from a belief that the Soviet Union could not hold out 'for much longer than five or six weeks'.

A more serious failure of imagination on the Soviet side poisoned relations right up until early 1944. Stalin, judging the Allies by himself, expected them to launch a cross-Channel operation, whatever the losses and difficulties. Churchill's reluctance to commit to an invasion of north-west Europe aroused his suspicion that Britain wanted the Red Army to suffer the brunt of the war. There was, of course, a strong element of truth in this, as well as a strong streak of hypocrisy on the Soviet side since Stalin himself had hoped that the western capitalists and the Germans would bleed each other to death in 1940. But the Soviet dictator totally failed to understand the pressures under which democratic governments worked. He wrongly assumed that Churchill and Roosevelt enjoyed absolute power in their own countries. The fact that they had to answer to the House of Commons or Congress, or take account of the press, was in his view a pathetic excuse. He could never accept the idea that Churchill really might be forced to resign if he launched an operation which resulted in disastrous casualties.

Even after decades of obsessive reading, Stalin had also failed to understand the basis of Britain's traditional strategy of peripheral warfare, mentioned earlier. Britain was not a continental power.

It still relied on its maritime strength and on coalitions to maintain a balance of power in Europe. With the notable exception of the First World War, it avoided involvement in a major confrontation on land until the end of a war was in sight. Churchill was determined to follow this pattern, even though both his American and Soviet allies were wedded to the diametrically opposed military doctrine of a massive clash as soon as possible.

On 28 July, just over two weeks after the signature of the Anglo-Soviet agreement, Harry Hopkins reached Moscow on a fact-finding mission at Roosevelt's request. Hopkins had to find out what the Soviet Union needed to continue the war, both immediately and in the longer term. The Soviet leadership took to him immediately. Hopkins questioned the relentlessly pessimistic reports from the US military attaché in Moscow who believed the Red Army would collapse. He was soon convinced that the Soviet Union would hold out.

Roosevelt's decision to aid the Soviet Union was genuinely altruistic as well as munificent. Soviet Lend–Lease took time to get under way, much to the President's exasperation, but its scale and scope would play a major part in the eventual Soviet victory (a fact which most Russian historians are still loath to acknowledge). Apart from high-quality steel, anti-aircraft guns, aircraft and huge consignments of food which saved the Soviet Union from famine in the winter of 1942–3, the greatest contribution was to the mobility of the Red Army. Its dramatic advances later in the war were possible thanks only to American Jeeps and trucks.

In contrast, Churchill's rhetoric of assistance was never matched by results, largely because of Britain's poverty and the urgency of its own immediate needs. Much of the material provided was obsolete or unsuitable. British army greatcoats were useless in the Russian winter, steel-studded ammunition boots accelerated frostbite, the Matilda tanks were distinctly inferior to the Soviet T-34, and Red Army aviation criticized the second-hand Hurricanes, asking why they had not been sent Spitfires instead.

The first important conference between the western Allies and the Soviet Union began in Moscow at the end of September after Lord Beaverbrook and Roosevelt's representative Averell Harriman reached Arkhangelsk aboard the cruiser HMS *London*.

Stalin received them in the Kremlin, and began to list all the military equipment and vehicles the Soviet Union needed. 'The country that could produce the most engines would ultimately be the victor,' he said. He then suggested to Beaverbrook that Britain should also send troops to help defend Ukraine, an idea which clearly took Churchill's crony aback.

Stalin, unable to drop the matter of Hess, proceeded to quiz Beaverbrook about Hitler's deputy and about what he had said when he reached England. The Soviet leader again caused surprise when he suggested that they should discuss the post-war settlement. Stalin wanted recognition of the 1941 Soviet frontier which encompassed the Baltic states, eastern Poland and Bessarabia. Beaverbrook declined to become involved in a subject which struck him as decidedly premature, with German armies less than a hundred kilometres from where they were sitting in the Kremlin. Although he did not know it, Guderian's Second Panzer Army had begun the first phase of Operation Typhoon against Moscow the day before.

British diplomats were irritated by Stalin's jibes that their country 'refused to undertake active military operations against Hitlerite Germany', while British and Commonwealth troops were fighting in North Africa. But in the Soviets' eyes, when faced with three German army groups deep in their country, the fighting around Tobruk and the Libyan frontier hardly even qualified as a sideshow.

Soon after the German invasion of the Soviet Union, Rommel had begun to plan a new attack on the besieged port of Tobruk, which had become the key to the war in North Africa. He needed it to supply his troops and to eliminate the threat to his rear. Tobruk was now held by the British 70th Division, reinforced with a Polish brigade and a Czech battalion.

During the desert summer, with its mirage shimmer of the desert under a blazing sky, a sort of phoney war had developed, with little more than the odd skirmish along the wire of the Libyan frontier. British and German reconnaissance patrols chatted to each other by radio, on one occasion complaining when a newly arrived German officer forced his men to open fire after a tacit ceasefire had been arranged. For the infantry on both sides, life was less amusing under such conditions, with just a litre of water a day for drinking and washing. In their trenches, they had to cope with scorpions, sand-fleas and the aggressive desert flies which swarmed over every piece of food and every inch of exposed flesh. Dysentery became a major problem, especially for the Germans. Even the defenders of Tobruk were short of water, as a Stuka attack had wrecked the desalination plant. The town itself was badly battered by shellfire and bombing, and the harbour half full of sunken ships. Only the determination of the Royal Navy kept them supplied. Members of the remaining Australian brigade began bartering war loot for beer as soon as a ship arrived.

Rommel had a much greater problem of resupply across the Mediterranean. Between January and late August 1941, the British had managed to sink fifty-two Axis ships and damage another thirty-eight. In September the submarine HMS *Upholder* sank two large passenger ships carrying reinforcements. (Afrika Korps veterans began to call the Mediterranean the 'German swimming pool'.) The Axis failure to invade Malta in 1940 was now shown to have been a major mistake. The Kriegsmarine especially had been dismayed earlier in the year when Hitler insisted that the airborne forces should be used against Crete rather than Malta, because he feared Allied raids against the Ploesti oilfields. Since then, the constant bombing of airfields on Malta and the Grand Harbour of Valletta had not proved an effective substitute for outright capture.

British intercepts of Italian naval codes provided rich rewards. On 9 November, K Force sailing from Malta, with the light cruisers HMS *Aurora* and *Penelope* and two destroyers, struck a Tripoli-bound convoy. Although the convoy was escorted by two heavy cruisers and ten destroyers, the British force dashed in at night using radar. In less than thirty minutes the three Royal Navy warships sank all seven freighters and a destroyer without suffering any damage. The German Kriegsmarine was livid, and threatened to take over control of Italian naval operations. The Afrika Korps adopted a similarly patronizing view of its allies. 'One has to treat the Italians like children,' a Leutnant in the 15th Panzer Division wrote home. 'They are no good as soldiers, but they are the best of comrades. You can get anything from them.'

After all the delays and waiting for supplies which never came,

Rommel planned his strike against Tobruk for 21 November. He disbelieved Italian warnings that the British were about to launch a major offensive, yet he felt compelled to leave the 21st Panzer Division between Tobruk and Bardia just in case. This would probably have left him with insufficient forces for a successful attack on Tobruk. In any case, on 18 November, three days before his planned assault on the port, the newly named British Eighth Army, commanded by Lieutenant General Sir Alan Cunningham, crossed the Libyan frontier in Operation Crusader. Having made approach marches at night under strict radio silence, and concealed by day with sandstorms and then thunderstorms, the Eighth Army achieved total surprise.

The Afrika Korps now consisted of the 15th and 21st Panzer Divisions, and a mixed division which was later renamed the 90th Light Division. This formation included an infantry regiment, largely made up of Germans who had been serving in the French Foreign Legion. Yet due to malnutrition and sickness the 45,000-strong Afrika Korps lacked 11,000 men in its front-line units. The disastrous supply situation also meant that its panzer divisions, with 249 tanks, badly needed replacements. The Italians fielded the Ariete Armoured Division and three semi-motorized divisions.

The British, on the other hand, were for once plentifully supplied, with 300 Cruiser tanks and 300 American Stuart light tanks, which they called 'Honeys', together with more than a hundred Matildas and Valentines. The Western Desert Air Force possessed 550 serviceable aircraft against only seventy-six for the Luftwaffe. With such advantages, Churchill expected a long-awaited victory, especially since he badly needed something to show Stalin. But, although the British were at last fully equipped, their weapons were decidedly inferior to those of the Germans. The new Stuarts and the Cruiser tanks with their two-pounder guns did not stand a chance against the German 88mm gun, 'the long arm' of the Afrika Korps, which could knock them out well before they were in range to fire back. Only the British 25-pounder field gun was impressive, and commanders had finally learned to use it over open sights against German panzer attacks. The Germans called it the 'Ratsch-bum'.

The British plan was to concentrate XXX Corps, with the bulk of the armour, in an attack north-westwards from the Libyan frontier. These forces were to defeat the German panzer divisions and then advance to Tobruk to break the siege. The 7th Armoured Brigade was to lead the 7th Armoured Division's thrust to Sidi Rezegh, on the escarpment south-east of Tobruk's defensive perimeter. On the right, XIII Corps was to engage the German positions close to the coast at the Halfaya Pass and Sollum. Ideally, the Eighth Army should have waited until Rommel had begun his attack on Tobruk, but Churchill refused to allow General Auchinleck to delay any longer.

The 7th Armoured Brigade reached Sidi Rezegh, occupied the airfield and captured nineteen aircraft on the ground before the Germans had time to react. But the 22nd Armoured Brigade on its left received a surprise battering from the Ariete Division, while the 4th Armoured Brigade on its right found itself up against parts of the 15th and 21st Panzer Divisions attacking south from the Via Balbia coast road. Fortunately for the British, the Germans were short of diesel. Fuel consumption for all vehicles was heavy in such terrain. A New Zealand officer described the Libyan Desert as 'a bare flat plain tufted with camel thorn, with wide acres of barren rock scree, stretches of soft sand, and shallow twisting wadis'. It also increasingly resembled a military rubbish dump, with discarded ration tins, empty oil barrels and burned-out vehicles.

On 21 November, General Cunningham, with excessive optimism, decided to order the breakout to begin from Tobruk, even though the destruction of the German panzer force had not begun. This led to heavy losses, both among the besieged and within 7th Armoured Brigade, one of whose regiments lost three-quarters of its tanks to 88mm guns attached to a German reconnaissance battalion. 7th Armoured soon found its rear threatened by the two panzer divisions, and was reduced to twenty-eight tanks by nightfall.

Unaware of the losses, Cunningham launched the next phase of the operation, with the advance of XIII Corps northwards behind the Italian positions along the frontier. It was led in determined style by General Freyberg's New Zealand Division, supported by a tank brigade with Matildas. Cunningham also ordered the breakout from Tobruk to recommence. But 7th Armoured Brigade, attacked on two sides at Sidi Rezegh, was by now down to just ten tanks. And 22nd Armoured Brigade, which had come to its support, had only thirty-four. They were forced back towards the south to join the 5th South African Brigade's defensive position. Rommel wanted to crush them between his panzer divisions on one side and the Ariete on the other.

On 23 November, which happened to be *Totensonntag*, the German Sunday for remembering the dead, an encirclement battle began south of Sidi Rezegh against 5th South African Brigade and the remnants of the two British armoured brigades. It represented a Pyrrhic victory for the Germans. The South African brigade was virtually wiped out, but it and the 7th Armoured support group exacted a heavy price on their attackers. The Germans lost seventy-two tanks, which were hard to replace, and an extraordinarily high percentage of officers and NCOs. The 7th Indian Division and the New Zealanders to the east also fought some effective engagements, with Freyberg's New Zealanders capturing part of the Afrika Korps staff.

After the terrible British tank losses, Cunningham wanted to withdraw, but Auchinleck overruled him. He told Cunningham to continue the operation whatever the cost. It was a brave decision, and the right one as events turned out. The next morning Rommel, eager to complete the destruction of the 7th Armoured Division and force a general retreat, became carried away by the scent of victory. In person he led the 21st Panzer Division on a race to the frontier, thinking he could encircle most of the Eighth Army. But this led to chaos, with contradictory orders and bad communications. At one point, Rommel's command vehicle broke down, and he found himself out of radio contact and trapped on the Egyptian side of the thick wire fence along the frontier. His insistence on leading from the front once again created major problems in a complex battle.

On 26 November, he heard from the headquarters of the Afrika Korps that the New Zealand Division, supported by another armoured brigade with Valentine tanks, had retaken the airfield at Sidi Rezegh on its route to Tobruk. The 4th New Zealand Brigade had also seized the airfield at Kambut, which meant that the Luftwaffe was left without any forward bases. Later in the day, the Tobruk garrison joined up with Freyberg's forces.

Rommel's dash to the frontier had proved a disastrous mistake.

The 7th Armoured Division was rearming with most of the 200 reserve tanks, while his own men were exhausted. And when they turned back from his futile thrust on 27 November, they were harried on their return by the Hurricanes of the Western Desert Air Force, which now enjoyed air supremacy.

Auchinleck decided to relieve Cunningham, whom he regarded as insufficiently aggressive and who was anyway on the point of a nervous breakdown. He replaced him with Major General Neil Ritchie. Ritchie renewed the attack westward, taking advantage of Rommel's supply crisis. The Italians had warned Rommel yet again that he could expect no more than the most basic levels of ammunition, fuel and rations. And yet the self-confidence of the Italian navy returned as its ships managed to transport more supplies through to Benghazi. Italian submarines were used to bring urgently needed ammunition to Darna, and the light cruiser *Cardona* was turned into a tanker. The Kriegsmarine was suddenly impressed by the efforts of its ally.

On 2 December, Hitler transferred II Fliegerkorps from the eastern front to Sicily and North Africa. Determined to support Rommel, he was horrified to hear of the supply situation due to British attacks on Axis convoys. He ordered Admiral Raeder to transfer twenty-four U-boats to the Mediterranean. Raeder complained that 'the Führer is prepared practically to abandon the U-boat war in the Atlantic to deal with our problems in the Mediterranean'. Hitler ignored Raeder's arguments that most of the Axis transport ships were being sunk by Allied aircraft and submarines, so U-boats were not the right counter-measure to protect Rommel's convoys. But in the event, the German submarines inflicted serious losses on the Royal Navy. In November U-boats in the Mediterranean sank both the aircraft carrier HMS *Ark Royal* and then the battleship HMS *Barham*. Further losses followed, and on the night of 18 December an Italian human-torpedo group led by Prince Borghese penetrated Alexandria harbour to sink the battleships HMS *Queen Elizabeth* and *Valiant* as well as a Norwegian tanker. Admiral Cunningham was left without any capital ships in the Mediterranean. The timing could hardly have been worse coming just eight days after Japanese aircraft sank both the battleship HMS *Prince of Wales* and the battle-cruiser *Repulse* off the coast of Malaya.

Despite the improvement for the Axis in the Mediterranean, Rommel's appeal on 6 December to the OKW and OKH for replacement vehicles and weapons, as well as reinforcements, was bound to be rejected at this critical moment for the eastern front. On 8 December, Rommel lifted the siege of Tobruk and began to withdraw to the Gazala Line over sixty kilometres to the west. Then, during the rest of December and early January 1942, he abandoned the whole of Cyrenaica and drew back to the line where he had started the year before.

The British celebrated the victory of Operation Crusader, but it was a temporary success achieved mainly through superior force, and certainly not by better tactics. The failure to keep the armoured brigades together had been the greatest mistake. Over 800 tanks and 300 aircraft had been lost. And by the time the Eighth Army reached the frontier of Tripolitania, a year after its victory over the Italians, it found itself severely weakened, with excessively long supply lines. In the see-saw of the North African campaign, and now with urgent demands from the Far East, the British and Dominion forces were vulnerable to yet another defeat in 1942.

Even before the war in the Far East began, the British government felt that it had more than enough to cope with. Then, on 9 December, Stalin put pressure on Britain to declare war on Finland, Hungary and Romania as they were Germany's allies on the eastern front. Yet Stalin's desire to get his new western Allies to agree to post-war frontiers even before the Battle for Moscow had begun was partly an attempt to overcome an embarrassing contradiction. Soviet prisons and labour camps still contained over 200,000 Polish troops taken in 1939 during his joint operation with Nazi Germany. Now the Poles were allies, with their government-in-exile recognized by both Washington and London. Energetic representations by General Sikorski, backed by Churchill's government, persuaded a very reluctant Soviet regime that the NKVD should release its Polish prisoners of war to form a new army.

Despite constant obstruction by Soviet officials, newly released Poles began to assemble and form units under General Władysław Anders, who had been held in the Lubyanka for the previous twenty months. In early December, a review of the Anders army was organized near Saratov on the Volga. It was an occasion full of bitter irony, as the writer Ilya Ehrenburg witnessed. General Sikorski arrived accompanied by Andrei Vyshinsky. The notorious prosecutor from the show trials of the Great Terror had apparently been chosen because of his Polish origins. 'He clinked glasses with Sikorski, smiling very sweetly,' observed Ehrenburg. 'Among the Poles there were many grim-looking men, full of resentment at what they had been through; some of them could not refrain from admitting that they hated us . . . Sikorski and Vyshinsky called each other "allies" but hostility made itself felt behind the cordial words.' Stalin's hatred and distrust of the Poles had only changed on the surface, as subsequent events would show.

15

The Battle for Moscow

SEPTEMBER–DECEMBER 1941

On 21 July 1941, the Luftwaffe bombed the Soviet capital for the first time. Andrei Sakharov, a fire-sentry at the university, spent most nights 'on the roof watching as searchlights, tracer bullets, criss-crossed the uneasy skies over Moscow'. But, following their losses in the Battle of Britain, German bomber formations were still reduced severely. Unable to inflict serious damage on the city, they returned to operations in support of ground forces.

After the halt of Army Group Centre to concentrate on Leningrad and Kiev, Hitler had finally come round to a major offensive against Moscow. His generals had mixed feelings. The huge encirclement east of Kiev had restored a sense of triumph, yet the vastness of the landmass, the length of their lines of communication and the unexpected size of the Red Army made them uneasy. Few now believed that victory would be achieved that year. They feared the Russian winter ahead for which they were sorely ill equipped. Their infantry divisions were short of boots after the hundreds of kilometres they had marched, and little had been done to provide warm clothing because Hitler had forbidden any discussion of the subject. Panzer units suffered from a shortage of replacement tanks and engines, which had been damaged by the thick dust. Yet, to the dismay of their commanders, Hitler was reluctant to release reserves. The great offensive against Moscow, Operation Typhoon, was not ready until the end of September. It had been delayed because Generaloberst Erich Hoepner's Fourth Panzer Group had been tied down in the stalemate round Leningrad. Generalfeldmarschall von Bock's Army Group Centre mustered one and a half million men, including three rather weakened panzer groups. They faced Marshal Semyon Budenny's Reserve Front and Colonel General Andrei Yeremenko's Briansk Front. Colonel General Ivan Konev's Western Front formed a second line behind Budenny's armies. Twelve of the divisions consisted of pathetically armed and untrained militia, including students and professors from Moscow University. 'Most of the militia soldiers were wearing civilian overcoats and hats,' wrote one of them. As they were marched through the streets, onlookers thought they were partisans to be sent against the German rear.

On 30 September, in an early-morning autumn mist, the preliminary phase of Operation Typhoon began as Guderian's Second Panzer Army attacked north-east towards the city of Orel, which lay more than 300 kilometres south of Moscow. The sky soon cleared, allowing the Luftwaffe to fly in close support to the panzer spearheads. The sudden attack created panic in the countryside.

'I thought I'd seen retreat,' Vasily Grossman wrote in his notebook, 'but I've never seen anything like what I am seeing now . . . Exodus! Biblical Exodus! Vehicles are moving eight abreast, there's the violent roaring of dozens of trucks trying simultaneously to tear their wheels out of the mud. Huge herds of sheep and cows are driven through the fields. They are followed by trains of horse-drawn carts, there are thousands of wagons covered with coloured sackcloth. There are also crowds of pedestrians with sacks, bundles, suitcases . . . Children's heads, fair and dark, are looking out from under the improvised tents covering the carts, as well as the beards of Jewish elders, and the black-haired heads of Jewish girls and women. What silence in their eyes, what wise sorrow, what a sensation of fate, of a universal catastrophe! In the evening, the sun comes out from the multi-layered blue, black and grey clouds. Its rays are wide, stretching from the sky down to the ground, as in Doré's paintings depicting those frightening biblical scenes when celestial forces strike the Earth.'

On 3 October rumours of the rapid advance reached Orel, but the senior officers in the city refused to believe the reports and carried on drinking. Dismayed by this fatal complacency, Grossman and his companions set off on the road to Briansk, expecting to see German tanks at any moment. But they were just ahead. Guderian's spearhead entered Orel at 18.00 hours, the leading panzers passing tramcars in the street.

The day before, 2 October, the main phase of Typhoon had begun further north. After a short bombardment and the laying of a smokescreen, Third Panzer Group and Fourth Panzer Group smashed through on either side of the Reserve Front commanded by Marshal Budenny. Budenny, another cavalry crony of Stalin's from the civil war, was a moustachioed buffoon and drunkard who could not find his own headquarters. Konev's chief of staff was put in charge of launching the Western Front's counter-attack with three divisions and two tank brigades, but they were brushed aside. Communications collapsed, and within six days the two panzer groups had surrounded five of Budenny's armies, linking up at Viazma. German tanks chased Red Army soldiers, trying to crush them under their tracks. It became a form of sport.

The Kremlin had little information about the chaotic disaster taking place to the west. Only on 5 October did the Stavka receive a report from a fighter pilot who had sighted a twenty-kilometre column of German armoured vehicles advancing on Yukhnov. No one dared believe it. Another two reconnaissance flights were sent out, both of which confirmed the sighting, yet Beria still threatened to put their commander in front of an NKVD tribunal as a 'panic-monger'. Stalin, nevertheless, recognized the danger. He summoned a meeting of the State Defence Committee and sent Zhukov in Leningrad a signal telling him to return to Moscow.

Zhukov arrived on 7 October. He claimed later that when he entered Stalin's room he overheard him telling Beria to use his agents to make contact with the Germans about the possibility of making peace. Stalin ordered Zhukov to go straight to Western Front headquarters and report back on the exact situation. He arrived after nightfall to find Konev and his staff officers bent over a map by candlelight. Zhukov had to telephone Stalin to tell him that the Germans had encircled five of Budenny's armies west of Viazma. In the early hours of 8 October, he discovered at Reserve Front headquarters that Budenny had not been seen for two days.

The conditions within the encirclements at Viazma and Briansk were indescribable. Stukas, fighters and bombers attacked any groups large enough to merit their attention, while the surrounding panzers and artillery fired constantly at the trapped forces. Rotting bodies piled up, filthy and starving Red Army soldiers slaughtered horses to eat, while the wounded died untended in the chaos. Altogether, nearly three-quarters of a million men had been cut off. Those who surrendered were ordered to throw away their weapons and march westwards without food. 'The Russians are beasts,' wrote a German major. 'They are reminiscent of the brutalized expressions of the Negroes in the French campaign. What a rabble.'

When Grossman escaped from Orel on 3 October just ahead of the Germans, he had been heading for Yeremenko's headquarters in the forest of Briansk. Throughout the night of 5 October, Yeremenko waited for an answer to his request to withdraw, but no authorization came from Stalin. In the early hours of 6 October, Grossman and the correspondents with him were told that even front headquarters was now threatened. They had to drive as fast as possible towards Tula before the Germans cut the road. Yeremenko was wounded in the leg and nearly captured during the encirclement of the Briansk Front. Evacuated by aeroplane, he was more fortunate than Major General Mikhail Petrov, the commander of the 50th Army, who died of gangrene in a woodcutter's hut deep in the forest.

Grossman was dismayed by the chaos and fear behind the lines. In Belev on the road to Tula, he noted: 'Lots of mad rumours are circulating, ridiculous and utterly panic-stricken. Suddenly, there is a mad storm of firing. It turns out that someone has switched on the street lights, and soldiers and officers opened rifle and pistol fire at the lamps to put them out. If only they had fired like this at the Germans.'

Not all Soviet formations were fighting badly, however. On 6 October the 1st Guards Rifle Corps, commanded by Major General D. D. Lelyushenko, supported by two airborne brigades and Colonel M. I. Katukov's 4th Tank Brigade, counter-attacked Guderian's 4th Panzer Division near Mtsensk in a clever ambush. Katukov concealed his T-34s in the forest, allowing the leading panzer regiment to pass by. Then, when they were halted by Lelyushenko's infantry, his tanks emerged from the trees and attacked. Handled well, the T-34 was superior to the Mark IV panzer, and the 4th Panzer Division suffered heavy losses. Guderian was clearly shaken to discover that the Red Army was starting to learn from its mistakes and from German tactics.

That night it snowed, then thawed rapidly. The *rasputitsa*, the season of rain and mud, had arrived just in time to slow the

German advance. 'I don't think anyone has seen such terrible mud,' Grossman noted. 'There's rain, snow, hailstones, a liquid, bottomless swamp, black pastry mixed by thousands and thousands of boots, wheels and caterpillar tracks. And everyone is happy once again. The Germans must get stuck in our hellish autumn.' But the advance, although slowed, carried on towards Moscow.

On the Orel–Tula road, Grossman could not resist visiting the Tolstoy estate at Yasnaya Polyana. There he found Tolstoy's granddaughter packing up the house and museum to evacuate it before the Germans arrived. He immediately thought of the passage in *War and Peace* when old Prince Bolkonsky had to leave his house of Lysye Gory as Napoleon's army approached. 'Tolstoy's grave,' he jotted in his notebook. 'Roar of fighters over it, humming of explosions and the majestic autumn calm. It is so hard. I have seldom felt such pain.' The next visitor after their departure was General Guderian, who was to make the place his headquarters for the advance on Moscow.

Only a few Soviet divisions escaped from the Viazma encirclement to the north. The smaller Briansk pocket was proving to be the greatest disaster so far, with more than 700,000 men dead or captured. The Germans scented victory and euphoria spead. The route to Moscow was barely defended. Soon the German press was claiming total victory, but this made even the ambitious Generalfeldmarschall von Bock feel uneasy.

On 10 October, Stalin ordered Zhukov to take over command of the Western Front from Konev and the remnants of the Reserve Front. Zhukov managed to persuade Stalin that Konev (who would later become his great rival) should be retained rather than made a scapegoat. Stalin told Zhukov to hold the line at Mozhaisk, just a hundred kilometres from Moscow on the Smolensk highway. Sensing the scale of the disaster, the Kremlin ordered a new line of defence to be constructed by a quarter of a million civilians, mostly women, conscripted to dig trenches and anti-tank ditches. Numbers of them were killed by strafing German fighters as they worked.

Discipline became even more ferocious, with NKVD blocking groups ready to shoot anyone who retreated without orders.

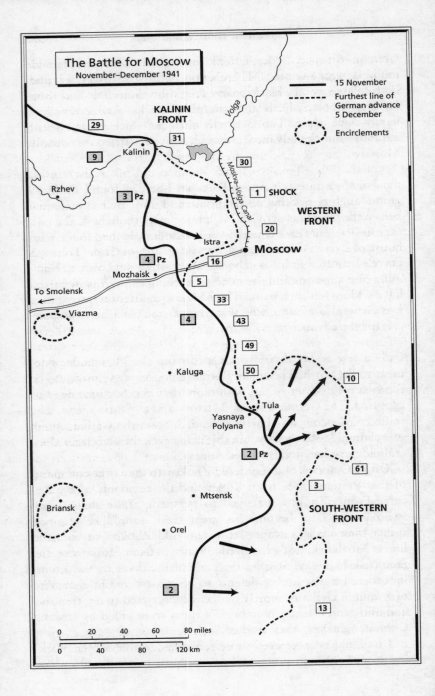

The Battle for Moscow
November–December 1941

— 15 November

- - - Furthest line of
German advance
5 December

- - - Encirclements

KALININ
FRONT

Volga

29

31

9

Kalinin

30

Rzhev

3 Pz

Moskva-Volga Canal

1 SHOCK

WESTERN
FRONT

20

Istra

Moscow

4 Pz

16

Mozhaisk

5

To Smolensk

33

Viazma

4

43

49

50

Kaluga

10

Tula

Yasnaya
Polyana

2 Pz

61

3

Mtsensk

SOUTH-WESTERN
FRONT

Briansk

Orel

2

13

0   20   40   60   80 miles

0   40   80   120 km

'They used fear to conquer fear,' an NKVD officer explained. The NKVD Special Detachments (which in 1943 became SMERSh) were already interrogating officers and soldiers who had escaped from encirclements. Any classed as cowards or suspected of having had contact with the enemy were shot or sent to *shtrafroty* – punishment companies. There, the most deadly tasks awaited them, such as leading attacks through minefields. Criminals from the Gulag were also conscripted as *shtrafniks*, and criminals they remained. Even the execution of a gang boss by an NKVD man shooting him in the temple had only a temporary effect on his followers.

Other NKVD squads went to field hospitals to investigate possible cases of self-inflicted injuries. They immediately executed so-called 'self-shooters' or 'left-handers' – those who shot themselves through the left hand in a naive attempt to escape fighting. A Polish surgeon with the Red Army later admitted to amputating the hands of boys who tried this, just to save them from a firing squad. Prisoners of the NKVD of course fared even worse. Beria had 157 prominent captives executed, including Trotsky's sister. Others were dealt with by guards throwing hand-grenades into their cells. Only at the end of the month, when Stalin told Beria that his conspiracy theories were 'rubbish', did the 'mincing machine' slacken.

The deportation of 375,000 Volga Germans to Siberia and Kazakhstan, which had begun in September, was accelerated to include all those of German origin in Moscow. Preparations to blow up the metro and key buildings in the capital began. Even Stalin's dacha was mined. NKVD assassination and sabotage squads moved to safe houses in the city, ready to carry out guerrilla warfare against a German occupation. The diplomatic corps received instructions to depart for Kuibyshev on the Volga, a city which had already been earmarked as a reserve capital for the government. The main theatre companies in Moscow, symbols of Soviet culture, were also told to evacuate the capital. Stalin himself could not make up his mind whether to stay or leave the Kremlin.

On 14 October, while part of Guderian's Second Panzer Army in the south circumvented the fiercely defended city of Tula, the 1st Panzer Division captured Kalinin north of Moscow, seizing the bridge over the upper Volga and severing the Moscow–Leningrad railway line. In the centre, the SS *Das Reich* Division and the 10th Panzer Division arrived at the Napoleonic battlefield of Borodino, just 110 kilometres from the capital. Here they faced a hard fight against a force strengthened by the new Katyusha rocket launchers and two Siberian rifle regiments, forerunners of many divisions whose deployment round Moscow would take the Germans by surprise.

Richard Sorge, the key Soviet agent in Tokyo, had discovered that the Japanese were planning to strike south into the Pacific against the Americans. Stalin did not trust Sorge entirely, even though he had been right about Barbarossa, but the information was confirmed by signals intercepts. The reduced threat to the far east of the Soviet Union allowed Stalin to start bringing even more divisions westwards along the Trans-Siberian Railway. Zhukov's victory at Khalkhin Gol had played an important part in this major strategic shift by the Japanese.

The Germans had underestimated the effect on their advance of the rain and snow, turning routes into quagmires of thick, black mud. Supplies of fuel, ammunition and rations could not get through, and the advance slowed. It was also delayed by the resistance of soldiers still trapped in the encirclement, preventing the invaders from releasing troops to continue the advance on Moscow. General der Flieger Wolfram von Richthofen flew at low altitude over the remains of the Viazma pocket, and noted the piles of corpses and the destroyed vehicles and guns.

The Red Army was also helped by interference from Hitler. The 1st Panzer Division at Kalinin, poised to attack south towards Moscow, was suddenly told to move in the opposite direction with the Ninth Army to attempt another encirclement with Army Group North. Hitler and the OKW had no idea of the conditions in which their troops were fighting, but *Siegeseuphorie*, or victory euphoria in Führer headquarters, was dissipating the concentration of forces against Moscow.

Stalin and the State Defence Committee decided on 15 October to evacuate the government to Kuibyshev. Officials were told to leave their desks and climb into lines of trucks outside which would take them to the Kazan railway station. Others had the same idea.

'Bosses from many factories put their families on trucks and got out of the capital and that is when it started. Civilians started looting the shops. Walking along the street, one saw everywhere the red, contented drunken faces of people carrying rings of sausage and rolls of fabric under their arm. Things were happening which would be unthinkable even two days ago. One heard in the street that Stalin and the government had fled Moscow.'

The panic and looting were spurred on by wild rumours that the Germans were already at the gates. Frightened functionaries destroyed their Communist Party cards, an act many of them were to regret later once the NKVD restored order, because they would be accused of criminal defeatism. On the morning of 16 October, Aleksei Kosygin entered the building of Sovnarkom, the Council of People's Commissars, of which he was deputy chairman. He found the place unlocked and abandoned, with secret papers on the floor. Telephones rang in empty offices. Guessing that they were calls from people trying to discover whether the government had left, he answered one. An official asked whether Moscow would be surrendered.

Out in the streets, the police had vanished. As in western Europe the year before, Moscow suffered from enemy-paratrooper psychosis. Natalya Gesse, hobbling on crutches after an operation, found herself 'surrounded by mobs suspicious that I had broken my legs parachuting in from a plane'. Many of the looters were drunk, justifying their actions on the grounds that they had best take what they could before the Germans seized it. Panic-stricken crowds at stations trying to storm departing trains were described as 'human whirlpools' in which children were torn from their mothers' arms. 'What went on at Kazan station defies description,' wrote Ilya Ehrenburg. Things were little better at the western train stations of Moscow, where hundreds of wounded soldiers had been dumped, uncared for, on stretchers along the platforms. Women searching desperately for a son, a husband or a boyfriend moved among them.

Stalin, emerging from the Kremlin fortress, was shocked by the sights he saw. A state of siege was declared and NKVD rifle regiments marched in to clear the streets, shooting looters and deserters on sight. Order was brutally restored. Stalin then decided that he would stay, and this was announced on the radio. It was a critical moment, and the effect was considerable. The mood turned from mass panic to a mass determination to defend the city at all costs. It was a phenomenon similar to the change of heart during the defence of Madrid five years before.

Stressing the need for secrecy, Stalin told the State Defence Committee that the celebrations for the anniversary of the Bolshevik Revolution would still go ahead. Several members were aghast, but they recognized that it was probably worth the risk as a demonstration to the country and the world at large that Moscow would never yield. On the 'eve of Revolution', Stalin gave a speech, which was broadcast from the vast ornate hall of the Mayakovsky metro station. He evoked the great, but scarcely proletarian, heroes of Russian history, Aleksandr Nevsky, Dmitri Donskoy, Suvorov and Kutuzov. 'The German invaders want a war of extermination. Very well then. They shall have one!'

This was Stalin's conspicuous re-emergence into Soviet consciousness, after several months of avoiding association with the disasters of retreat. 'I have looked through the files of old newspapers from July to November 1941,' wrote Ilya Ehrenburg many years later. 'Stalin's name was hardly ever mentioned.'

The leader was now inextricably linked with the courageous defence of the capital. And the following day, 7 November, Stalin took the salute from Lenin's empty mausoleum on Red Square, as rank upon rank of reinforcements marched through the falling snow, ready to turn north-westwards and on to the front. The canny Stalin had foreseen what an effect this coup de théâtre would have, and ensured that it was filmed for foreign and domestic newsreels.

During the following week hard frosts set in, and on 15 November the Germans' advance resumed. It soon became clear to Zhukov that their main line of attack would be on the Volokolamsk sector, where Rokossovsky's 16th Army was forced to conduct a fighting retreat. Zhukov was under great pressure, and lost his temper with Rokossovsky. The contrast between the two could hardly have been greater, even though they were both former cavalrymen. Zhukov was a rather squat fireball of energy and ruthlessness, while the tall and elegant Rokossovsky was calm and pragmatic. Rokossovsky, from a family of minor Polish nobility, had been arrested towards the end of the purge of the Red Army. He had nine steel teeth to replace those knocked out of him during the 'conveyor belt' of interrogation sessions. Stalin had ordered his release, but reminded him from time to time that this was a temporary concession. Any mistakes and he would be returned to Beria's thugs.

On 17 November, Stalin signed an order that all forces and partisans should 'destroy and burn to ashes' all buildings in the combat zone and behind, to deny the Germans shelter in the approaching frosts. The fate of civilians was not considered for a moment. The suffering of soldiers, especially the wounded dumped on railway platforms, was also appalling. 'Stations were covered by human excrement and wounded soldiers with blood-stained bandages,' wrote a Red Army officer.

By the end of November, the German Third Panzer Army was within forty kilometres of Moscow on the north-west side. One of its lead units had even seized a bridgehead across the Moscow–Volga Canal. Fourth Panzer Army had meanwhile reached a point sixteen kilometres from the western edge of Moscow, having pushed back Rokossovsky's 16th Army. It is said that in a heavy fog a motorcyclist from the SS *Deutschland* Regiment drove right into Moscow and was shot down by an NKVD patrol next to the Belorussian Station. Other German units could make out the onion cupolas of the Kremlin through powerful binoculars. The Germans had been fighting desperately in the knowledge that the full force of the Russian winter would soon be upon them. But their troops were exhausted, and already many were suffering from frostbite.

Defence works on the approaches to Moscow had continued at a frenzied rhythm. Steel 'hedgehogs' made of girder lengths welded together like giant caltraps acted as anti-tank barriers. The NKVD had organized 'destroyer battalions' to combat paratroop or sabotage attacks on key factories and as a last line of defence. Each man was issued with a rifle, ten rounds and a few grenades. Stalin, afraid that Moscow might be encircled from the northern side, ordered Zhukov to prepare a series of counter-attacks. But first he needed to reinforce the armies north-west of Moscow, battered by the Third and Fourth Panzer Armies.

*

The situation also appeared critical in the south of the country. Rundstedt's army group had secured the Donbas mining and industrial region in mid-October, just when the Romanians finally took Odessa. Manstein's Eleventh Army in the Crimea was laying siege to the great naval base of Sebastopol. The First Panzer Army advanced rapidly ahead towards the Caucasus, leaving behind the infantry. And on 21 November, the 1st SS Panzer Division *Leibstandarte Adolf Hitler*, commanded by Brigadeführer Sepp Dietrich whom Richthofen called 'the good old war-horse', had entered Rostov at the entrance to the Caucasus and seized a bridgehead across the River Don. Hitler was exultant. The oilfields further south seemed within his grasp. But Kleist's panzer spearhead was over-extended, its left flank guarded only by weakly armed Hungarian troops. Marshal Timoshenko seized the opportunity and counter-attacked across the frozen Don.

Rundstedt, realizing that a full advance into the Caucasus was impossible before the next spring, pulled his forces back to the line of the River Mius which flowed into the Sea of Azov west of Taganrog. Hitler reacted to this first withdrawal by the German army in the war with angry disbelief. He ordered that the retreat be cancelled at once. Rundstedt offered his resignation, which was immediately accepted. On 3 December, Hitler flew down to Army Group South's headquarters at Poltava, where that earlier invader, Charles XII of Sweden, had been decisively defeated. The next day, Hitler appointed Generalfeldmarschall von Reichenau, a convinced Nazi, whom Rundstedt disparagingly described as a roughneck who ran 'around half-naked when taking physical exercise'.

But Hitler was taken aback to find that Sepp Dietrich, the commander of the SS *Leibstandarte*, agreed with Rundstedt's decision. And Reichenau, having assured Hitler that he would not pull back, promptly carried on with the withdrawal, presenting Führer headquarters with a fait accompli. With his hand forced, Hitler then compensated the sacked Rundstedt with a birthday present of 275,000 Reichsmark. He was often cynical about how easy it was to bribe his generals with money, the grant of estates and decorations.

*

Leningrad had been saved from annihilation, partly due to Zhukov's ruthless leadership and the determination of the troops, but mainly because of the German decision to concentrate on Moscow. Army Group North from then on was to be the poor relation on the eastern front, hardly ever receiving reinforcements and constantly afraid of being stripped of units to strengthen formations in the centre and south of the country. This neglect on the German side was exceeded on the Soviet side, with Stalin on several occasions wanting to strip Leningrad of troops to defend Moscow. Stalin had no warm feelings for what he saw as a city of intellectuals, who despised Muscovites and were suspiciously fond of western Europe. How seriously he considered giving up the city is hard to tell, but it is quite clear that during that autumn and winter he was far more concerned about preserving the forces of the Leningrad Front than the city, let alone its citizens.

Soviet attempts to break the encirclement from outside with the 54th Army failed to dislodge the Germans from the southernmost shore of Lake Ladoga. But at least the defenders still held the isthmus between the city and the lake, although this was partly due to the caution of the Finns who hesitated to advance on to pre-1939 Soviet territory.

The siege settled down into a pattern, with regular German bombardments of the city at fixed times. Civilian casualties mounted, but mainly from starvation. Leningrad was effectively an island. The only connection still possible with the 'mainland' was across Lake Ladoga or by air. Some 2.8 million civilians were trapped, and, with half a million troops, the authorities had to cater for 3.3 million people. Food distribution was shockingly uneven in a supposedly egalitarian society. Party officials made sure that their families and close relations did not suffer, and those who controlled the supply of food, right down to individual breadshops and canteens, profited shamelessly. Bribery was often needed to obtain even the basic ration.

Food was indeed power, both for the corrupt individual and for the Soviet state, which had long used it to coerce submission, or to take revenge upon unfavoured categories of people. Industrial workers, children and soldiers received a full ration, but others, such as wives who did not work and teenage children, received only a 'dependant's' ration. Their ration card became known as the 'smertnik' – the death card. With a truly Soviet attitude to hierarchy, they were considered 'useless mouths', while Party bosses received supplementary rations to help their decision-making on behalf of the common good.

'Our situation with food is very bad,' Vasily Churkin noted in late October when defending the line near Shlisselburg on Lake Ladoga. 'We get 300 grams of bread that is as black as earth, and watery soup. We feed our horses with birch twigs with no leaves on them, and they die one after another. Locals from Beryozovka and our soldiers leave just the bones on a horse that's fallen down. They chop off pieces of meat and boil them.'

Soldiers were far better off than civilians, and those who had families in the city waited for winter with mounting anxiety. Frightful stories of cannibalism began to circulate. Churkin recorded how 'Our corporal Andronov, a tall, broad-shouldered fellow, full of energy, made a mistake for which he paid with his life. The chief of supplies sent him in a vehicle to Leningrad under some pretext. At that time in Leningrad they were more starved than we were, and most of us had families there. The vehicle with Andronov was stopped on the way. In the vehicle they found canned food, meat, and cereal, which we had taken from our own meagre rations [to send to our families]. The tribunal sentenced Andronov and his chief to death. His wife with a small child were in Leningrad. People say that their neighbour ate the child, and the wife lost her sanity.'

The starving city needed hard frosts so that the ice on Lake Ladoga was strong enough to support trucks bringing in food supplies across the 'ice road'. Great risks were taken in the first week of December. 'I saw a Polutorka truck,' Churkin wrote. 'Its hind wheels had fallen through the ice. In it were sacks with flour, they were dry . . . Its cabin pointed up, its front wheels stood on the ice. I passed about a dozen Polutorka trucks loaded with flour that froze into the ice. They were the pioneers of the "Road of Life". There was no one by the trucks.' The inhabitants of Leningrad would have to wait a little longer for the stockpiles already assembled. At the lakeside settlement of Kabona, Churkin saw that 'all along the bank, stretching for so many kilometres that one couldn't even see the end, lay an enormous amount of sacks with flour and boxes with foodstuffs prepared to be sent across the ice to starving Leningrad'.

By the beginning of December, many German commanders in Army Group Centre realized that their exhausted and frozen troops could not now take Moscow. They wanted to withdraw their depleted forces to a defensible line until the spring, but such arguments had already been overruled by General Halder on the instructions of Führer headquarters. Some began to think of 1812 and the terrible retreat of Napoleon's army. Even with the mud now frozen hard, the supply situation had failed to improve. With temperatures dropping to below minus 20 degrees Centigrade, and often with zero visibility, the Luftwaffe was grounded most of the time. Like airfield ground crews, motorized troops had to light fires under the engines of their vehicles before they could hope to start them. Machine guns and rifles froze solid because the Wehrmacht did not have the right oil for winter warfare, and radios failed to work in the extreme temperatures.

Artillery and transport draught horses brought from western Europe were unused to the cold and lacked forage. Bread arrived frozen solid. Soldiers had to cut it up with hacksaws and thaw it out in their trouser pockets before they could eat it. The weakened *Landser* could not dig trenches in the iron-hard ground, without having melted it first with large bonfires. Few replacements had arrived for their jackboots, which had fallen to pieces after so much marching. There was also a shortage of proper gloves. Frostbite casualties now exceeded the number of those wounded in battle. Officers complained that their soldiers had started to look like Russian peasants because they had stolen the winter clothing of civilians, sometimes even forcing them at gunpoint to hand over their boots.

Women, children and old men were forced out into the snow from their log cabins, or *izbas*, where the soldiers ripped up the floors to search for their reserves of potatoes. It might have been less cruel to kill their victims than to force them to starve or freeze to death, half stripped of their clothes in what was turning out to be the most savage winter for years. Conditions for Soviet prisoners were worst of all. They died in their thousands from exhaustion on forced marches westwards through the snow, from

starvation and from disease, mainly typhus. Some were reduced
to cannibalism in their dehumanized state of abject suffering.
Each morning, their guards made them run for a few hundred
metres, beating them. Any who collapsed were shot immediately.
Cruelty had become addictive in those who had total control over
beings they had been taught to despise and hate.

By 1 December, German heavy artillery was finally within range
of Moscow. On that day Generalfeldmarschall von Kluge's
Fourth Army began the final assault on the city from the west.
The icy wind created deep snowdrifts, and the soldiers became
exhausted trudging through them. But with a surprise artillery
barrage and some air support from the Luftwaffe, his XX Corps
managed to break through the 33rd Army towards the Minsk–
Moscow highway. The rear of the adjacent Soviet 5th Army was
also threatened. Zhukov reacted immediately, and threw in all the
reinforcements he could put together, including the Siberian 32nd
Rifle Division.

Late on 4 December, the Red Army's position was restored.
The German infantry was collapsing from exhaustion and the
cold. The temperature had dropped below minus 30 degrees Centigrade. 'I cannot describe to you what this means,' a Gefreiter
in the 23rd Infantry Division wrote home that day. 'First the appalling cold, blizzards, feet soaked through and through – our
boots never dry out and we are not allowed to take them off –
and secondly the stress from the Russians.' Kluge and Bock knew
that they had failed. They tried to console themselves with the
idea that the Red Army too must be at its last gasp, as Hitler had
so often insisted. They could not have been more wrong. During
the last six days, Zhukov and the Stavka had been preparing a
counter-attack.

With leaders such as Zhukov, Rokossovsky, Lelyushenko and
Konev, a new professionalism was starting to have an effect. This
was no longer the sclerotic organization of June, in which commanders, terrified of arrest by the NKVD, did not dare show the
slightest initiative. The unwieldy formations of that period had
also been abandoned. A Soviet army now consisted of little more
than four divisions. For the time being, the corps level of command had been stripped out to improve control.

Eleven new armies had been formed behind the lines. Some included ski battalions and the well-trained Siberian divisions, properly equipped for winter warfare, with padded jackets and white camouflage suits. The new T-34 tank, with its broad tracks, could cope with ice and snow far better than the German panzers. And in contrast to German equipment, Soviet weapons and vehicles had the right lubricants to resist the low temperatures. Red Army aviation regiments assembled on airfields round Moscow. With their Yak fighters and Shturmovik ground-attack aircraft, they were to achieve air superiority for the first time while most of the Luftwaffe remained frozen to the ground.

Zhukov's plan, approved by Stalin, was intended to eliminate the two German salients either side of Moscow. The main one to the north-west contained the German Fourth Army and the depleted Third and Fourth Panzer Armies. The southern one, just east of Tula, was held by Guderian's Second Panzer Army. But Guderian, sensing the danger, was starting to pull back some of his forward units.

At 03.00 hours on Friday, 5 December, Konev's newly formed Kalinin Front moved against the north side of the main bulge with the 29th and 31st Armies attacking across the frozen Volga. Next morning, the 1st Shock Army and the 30th Army advanced due west. Then Zhukov sent another three armies, including Rokossovsky's reinforced 16th Army and Vlasov's 20th Army, in against the southern side. He intended to cut off the Third and Fourth Panzer Armies. As soon as a gap opened, Major General Lev Dovator's 2nd Guards Cavalry Corps charged in to create mayhem in the German rear. The hardy Cossack ponies could cope with snow a metre deep and soon caught up with the German infantry struggling to retreat through it.

To the south, the 50th Army attacked the northern flank of Guderian's Second Panzer Army from Tula, while the 10th Army advanced from the north-east. Pavel Belov's 1st Guards Cavalry Corps supported by tanks struck into the German rear. Guderian moved fast, and managed to extricate the majority of his forces. But he was not able to restore the line as he had hoped, because the South-Western Front then sent the 13th Army and an operational group against the Second Army on his southern flank. Guderian had to pull back another eighty kilometres. This left a large gap between him and the Fourth Army on his left.

The Red Army was still short of tanks and artillery, but with the new armies it was now close to German manpower strengths on the Moscow front. Its main advantage was the element of surprise. The Germans had completely discounted reports from Luftwaffe pilots of major military formations moving behind the lines. They also had no reserves. And with heavy fighting south-east of Leningrad and the withdrawal of Army Group South to the Mius, Bock could not obtain reinforcements from the flanks. The sense of precariousness even reached down to a supply Obergefreiter in the 31st Infantry Division. 'I don't know what's wrong,' he wrote home. 'One simply has a bad feeling that this vast Russia is just too much for our strength.'

By 7 December, the battle for the main salient was going well. It looked as if the Soviet objective of trapping the Third Panzer Army and part of the Fourth might succeed. But the advance was slow, to Zhukov's intense frustration. The armies involved were held up by trying to eliminate every enemy strongpoint, defended by improvised German *Kampfgruppen* or combat groups. Two days later Zhukov ordered his commanders to stop frontal attacks, and to bypass centres of resistance so as to get well into the German rear.

On 8 December, a German soldier wrote in his diary: 'Are we going to have to pull out? Then God have pity on us.' They knew what that would mean in the open snowfields. The retreat all along the front was marked by burning villages, set on fire as they struggled to withdraw through deep snow. Their route became littered with vehicles abandoned from lack of fuel, horses dead from exhaustion and even wounded men left behind in the snow. Hungry troops hacked lumps of frozen flesh from the flanks of the horses.

Siberian ski battalions swooped out of the freezing mists to harry and attack. With grim satisfaction, they noted the totally inadequate equipment of the Germans, reduced to wrapping themselves in the mittens and shawls of old women looted from the villages or straight off their backs. 'The frosts were exceptionally severe,' wrote Ehrenburg, 'but the Red Army Siberians grumbled: "Now if a real frost set in, that'd kill them off at once."'

Their revenge was fierce after what they had heard of German treatment of prisoners and civilians. Virtually unhindered by the Luftwaffe, Red Army aviation fighters and Shturmovik regiments harried the long columns of retreating troops, black against the snow. Raiding groups from Belov's and Dovator's Guards Cavalry Corps struck deep in the rear, attacking depots and artillery batteries with drawn sabres. Partisans raided supply lines, sometimes linking up with the cavalry. And Zhukov decided to drop the 4th Airborne Corps by parachute behind the German front lines. Soviet troops felt no pity for the frost-bitten and lice-infested German infantry.

German field hospitals were having to amputate increasing numbers of limbs as untreated frostbite led to gangrene. With temperatures below minus 30, blood froze instantly in wounds, and many soldiers suffered intestinal problems from sleeping on the ice-hard ground. Almost all suffered from diarrhoea, an even worse affliction in such conditions. Those who could not move by themselves were doomed. 'Many of the wounded shoot themselves,' a soldier noted in his diary.

Frozen weapons often failed to work. Tanks had to be abandoned from lack of fuel. A fear of being cut off spread. More and more officers and soldiers began to regret their treatment of Soviet prisoners of war. And yet despite the constant thoughts of 1812 and a sense that the Wehrmacht was now accursed like Napoleon's Grande Armée, the retreat did not quite become a rout. The German army, especially on the edge of disaster, often surprised its enemies by the way it fought back. Improvised *Kampfgruppen*, formed at gunpoint by Feldgendarmerie rounding up stragglers in a retreat and led by determined officers and NCOs, managed to hold firm, with a mixture of infantry, pioneers and assorted weapons such as flak guns and the odd self-propelled gun. On 16 December, one group which had broken through an encirclement finally reached German lines. 'There's an enormous number of men suffering from nervous collapse,' one of them noted in his diary. 'Our officer is in tears.'

Hitler at first reacted in disbelief to the news of the Soviet offensive, having convinced himself that reports of new armies were a bluff. He could not understand where they had come from. Humiliated by this totally unexpected turn in the fortunes of war after all the recent claims of victory over the Slav *Untermensch*, he was angry and baffled. Instinctively, he fell back on his visceral creed that the will would triumph. The fact that his men lacked proper clothing, ammunition, rations and fuel for their armoured vehicles was almost irrelevant to him. Obsessed with Napoleon's retreat of 1812, he was determined to defy a repetition of history. He ordered his troops to stand fast even though they were incapable of digging defensive positions in the rock-hard ground.

With all attention in Moscow fixed on the great struggle to the west of the capital, news of the Japanese attack on Pearl Harbor did not make much impact. But the effect was considerable in the city of Kuibyshev, where all the foreign correspondents were held (still under firm instructions from Soviet censors to put a Moscow dateline on all their articles). Ilya Ehrenburg observed with amusement how 'the Americans in the Grand Hotel came to blows with Japanese journalists'. For the Americans and Japanese, that would truly be the least of it.

16

Pearl Harbor

On 6 December 1941, just as the Soviet counter-attack round Moscow began, US Navy cryptanalysts deciphered a message between Tokyo and the Japanese ambassador in Washington. Although the final section was missing, the import was abundantly clear. 'This means war,' Roosevelt said to Harry Hopkins, who was in the Oval Office that evening when the signal was brought in. The President had only just sent a personal message to Emperor Hirohito urging his country to draw back from the conflict.

Over at the War Department, the head of intelligence passed the intercepts to Brigadier General Leonard Gerow of the War Plans Division, with instructions to warn bases in the Pacific. But Gerow decided to do nothing. 'I think they have had plenty of notification,' he is recorded as saying. This was because both US Navy and US Army headquarters in the Pacific had been told on 27 November that war was imminent. This intelligence had also been based on Magic intercepts of Japanese diplomatic signal traffic.

Curiously, or perhaps significantly, no warning had come from the Kremlin, despite Roosevelt's desire to help the Soviet Union. One can only speculate about Stalin's motives, but he refused to pass on to the Americans Richard Sorge's intelligence before the Battle for Moscow that the Japanese were planning to make a surprise attack on American forces in the Pacific. Yet one of the most striking coincidences of the Second World War was the decision by President Roosevelt on 6 December 1941, the day before the Japanese attack, to go ahead with the project to research an atomic weapon.

In the first week of September, Japan's military leaders had forced Emperor Hirohito to accept their decision to go to war. His only protest had been to read them a poem in favour of peace written by his grandfather. But Hirohito's position as commander of the armed forces was extremely ambivalent. His opposition to the war was not moral, but simply reflected a fear that it might fail. The extreme militarists, mainly junior and middle-ranking officers, believed that the country had a divine mission to forge an empire under the euphemistic title of the Greater East Asia Co-Prosperity Sphere, or what the far-sighted American ambassador in Tokyo had warned in 1934 would be a 'pax japonica'. By November 1941, he feared that the military were prepared to lead their country to 'national hara-kiri'.

The Japanese drive for imperial expansion had produced conflicting priorities: the war in China, fear and hatred of the Soviet Union to the north and the opportunity to seize the French, Dutch and British colonies to the south. The foreign minister Yōsuke Matsuoka had arranged a Japanese–Soviet neutrality pact in April 1941, shortly before Hitler's invasion. Once German armies were advancing rapidly eastwards, Matsuoka did an about-turn and advocated a strike north against the Soviet rear. But senior officers in the Imperial Japanese Army opposed this plan. They remembered their defeat at Zhukov's hands in August 1939, and most preferred to finish the war in China first.

The occupation of French Indochina in 1940 had been undertaken primarily to stop supplies to Chiang Kai-shek's Nationalist armies, but this proved to be the decisive step towards the 'strike south' strategy, advocated mainly by the Imperial Japanese Navy. Indochina provided an ideal base from which to seize the oilfields of the Dutch East Indies. And following the American and British embargo imposed on Japan in retaliation for their occupation of Indochina, the commander of the Imperial Fleet, Admiral Yamamoto Isoroku, had been warned that his ships would run out of fuel within a year. Japanese militarists felt that they had to go forward to seize all they needed. To go back involved an unbearable loss of face.

The minister of war General Tōjō Hideki acknowledged that to take on the United States, with its industrial might, was a terrible gamble. And Yamamoto, who also feared the consequences of a prolonged war with the United States, felt that their only chance of survival was to get in first with a massive attack. 'In the first six to twelve months of a war with the United States and Britain, I will run wild and win victory after victory,' he predicted with considerable accuracy. 'After that . . . I have no expectation of success.'

The military leaders had outwardly accepted the preference of the Emperor and the prime minister Prince Konoe Fumimaro to seek a diplomatic solution with the United States, but they never had any intention of accepting a deal which involved significant concessions. The Imperial Army was resolutely opposed to any withdrawal from China. Although in many cases fatalistic about their prospects, especially if the war dragged on, Japan's military commanders preferred the risk of national suicide to a loss of face.

Roosevelt had been convinced that a firm line was the best policy, even though he did not want war at that stage. Both General Marshall and Admiral Harold R. Stark, the army and navy chiefs of staff, had warned him clearly that the United States was not yet sufficiently prepared. But his secretary of state, Cordell Hull, while negotiating with a Japanese envoy, was outraged when he heard on 25 November of a massive convoy of warships and troop transports heading through the South China Sea. He responded with a series of demands which was seen in Tokyo as tantamount to an ultimatum.

Hull's 'Ten Points' document insisted among other things that the Japanese should withdraw from Indochina and China, as well as renounce the Tripartite Pact with Germany. This stern reaction had been encouraged by the Chinese Nationalists and the British. Only a complete and immediate climbdown by the United States and Britain might have averted conflict at that stage. Yet such a sign of western weakness would probably have encouraged Japanese aggression.

Hull's intransigence convinced the Japanese military leaders that their preparations for war were vindicated. Delay would only weaken them and postponement of the war would reduce Japan, as Tōjō had said at the crucial conference on 5 November, to a 'third-class nation'. In any case, Yamamoto's carrier fleet had just set forth from the Kurile Islands in the northern Pacific with Pearl Harbor as its objective. Zero hour had already been set for 08.00 hours on 8 December (Tokyo time).

The Japanese plan aimed to secure a perimeter around the western Pacific and the South China Sea. Five armies would seize the five main objectives. The 25th Army would attack down the Malay Peninsula to take the British naval base of Singapore. The 23rd Army in southern China would seize Hong Kong. The 14th Army would land in the Philippines, where General Douglas MacArthur, American commander-in-chief and proconsul, had his headquarters. The 15th Army would invade Thailand and southern Burma. The 16th Army would secure the Dutch East Indies (modern Indonesia) with the oilfields so vital to the Japanese war effort. Against the severe doubts of his colleagues in the Imperial Japanese Navy, Admiral Yamamoto had insisted that some of these operations, especially the attack on the Philippines, would be at risk unless he first sent his carrier force to destroy the US fleet.

Yamamoto's navy pilots had been practising torpedo and bombing attacks for several months in preparation. Intelligence on their targets was provided by the Japanese consul-general in Honolulu, who had been watching the movements of the US warships. They were always in harbour at the weekend. The pre-emptive strike was fixed for just after dawn on Monday, 8 December, which would still be 7 December Washington time. At dawn on 26 November, the carrier force, led by the flagship *Akagi*, sailed under strict radio silence from the Kurile Islands in the northern Pacific.

In Hawaii, Admiral Husband E. Kimmel, the commander-in-chief of the Pacific Fleet, had been deeply concerned that his intelligence staff had no knowledge of the position of the carriers from the Japanese First and Second Fleets. 'Do you mean to say', he retorted on 2 December when told of this, 'that they could be rounding Diamond Head [near the entrance to Pearl Harbor] and you wouldn't know it?' Yet even Kimmel could not imagine an attack on Hawaii out in the middle of the Pacific. Like the naval and army staffs in Washington, he believed a Japanese attack was much more likely to take place around the South China Sea, against Malaya, Thailand or the Philippines. So the peacetime routine had continued, with officers in their white tropical uniforms, and sailors looking forward to a weekend of beer and relaxing on Waikiki Beach with local girls. Many ships were manned with little more than skeleton crews at the weekend.

*

At 06.05 hours on Monday, 8 December, a green lamp was waved on the flight deck of the *Akagi*. Pilots adjusted their *hachimaki*, a white headband with a red rising-sun symbol on the forehead, which indicated that they had promised to die for the Emperor. A cheer of 'Banzai!' arose from the ground crews as each aircraft took off. Despite the heavy swell, the six carriers in the task force launched a first wave of 183 aircraft including Zero fighters, Nakajima bombers, torpedo planes and Aichi dive-bombers. The island of Oahu lay 370 kilometres to their south.

The aircraft circled over the carrier fleet, then set off in formation towards their objective. Flying above the cloud as dawn came up it was hard to check their drift, so the bomber leader, Commander Fuchida Mitsuo, tuned into the American radio station on Honolulu. It was playing dance music. He then switched on his direction-finder. He corrected their course by five degrees. The music was interrupted by a weather report. He was relieved to hear that visibility over the islands was improving, with breaks in the cloud.

An hour and a half after take-off the leading pilots spotted the northern tip of the island. The reconnaissance plane which had gone ahead reported that the Americans appeared to be unaware of their presence. Fuchida fired a 'black dragon' flare from his cockpit to signal that they could still follow the plan for a surprise attack. The reconnaissance plane then reported the presence of ten battleships, a heavy cruiser and ten light cruisers. As they came in sight of Pearl Harbor, Fuchida studied the anchorage through binoculars. At 07.49 hours he gave the order to proceed, then passed back to the Japanese carrier fleet the signal 'Tora, tora, tora!' The codeword, meaning Tiger, signified that complete surprise had been achieved.

Two dive-bomber groups with fifty-three aircraft sheered off to attack the three nearby airfields. The torpedo planes went straight into low-level runs against the seven capital ships in 'Battleship Row'. Honolulu radio was still playing music. Fuchida could already see waterspouts exploding alongside the battleships. He ordered his pilot to bank as the signal for his ten squadrons to make their bomb-run in line ahead. 'A gorgeous formation,' he noted. But, as they went in, American anti-aircraft guns opened fire. Dark-grey bursts exploded all around them, making the aircraft shudder. The first torpedoes struck the battleship USS *Oklahoma*, which slowly rolled over. More than 400 men died, trapped beneath the hull.

Fuchida was taken aback by the speed of the American response as his aircraft headed for the USS *Nevada* at 3,000 metres. He now regretted having decided to attack in line ahead. They were buffeted as the USS *Arizona* blew up in a massive explosion, killing more than a thousand men on board. The black smoke from blazing oil was so thick that many aircraft overshot their bombing point and had to return for a second run.

Part of Fuchida's force of dive-bombers and fighters had peeled off to attack the US Army Air Corps bases at Wheeler Field and Hickam Field and the Naval Air Station on Ford Island. Ground crews and pilots were at breakfast when the strike came in. The first man to fight back at Hickam Field was an army chaplain, who had been outside preparing his altar for an open-air mass. He seized a nearby machine gun and, resting it on his altar, began firing at the swooping enemy planes. But at both fields the aircraft lined up neatly beside the runway made an easy target for the Japanese pilots.

Almost exactly an hour after the first aircraft had sighted their targets a second wave of Japanese attackers arrived, but their task was more difficult with the thick smoke and the volume of fire coming up at them. Even five-inch naval guns were firing at the aircraft. Some of their shells are said to have landed in the town of Honolulu, killing civilians.

Suddenly, the sky was empty. The Japanese pilots had turned back to the north to catch up with their carriers, already steaming for home. As well as the battleships *Arizona* and *Oklahoma*, the US Navy at Pearl Harbor had lost two destroyers. Another three battleships were sunk or beached but later refloated and repaired, and three more were damaged. The Army Air Corps and navy lost 188 aircraft destroyed and 159 damaged. Altogether 2,335 American servicemen were killed and 1,143 wounded. Only twenty-nine Japanese aircraft had been destroyed; but the Imperial Navy also lost an ocean-going submarine and five midget submarines, all of which were supposed to have provided a diversion.

Despite the shock of the attack, many sailors and Hawaiian

shipyard workers promptly dived into the water to save those blown off the ships. Most of those struggling in the harbour were covered in oil and had to have their skin cleaned with cotton-waste. Small parties with oxyacetylene cutters started to cut through bulkheads and even hulls to rescue trapped comrades. All around were damaged warships wreathed in black smoke, twisted and tangled dockside cranes, and port buildings riddled with holes. It would take two weeks to put the last of the fires out. Anger drove everyone in their task to restore the fighting power of the US Pacific Fleet. They had at least one important consolation. None of the aircraft carriers had been in port. For they were to provide the only means to hit back in a naval war which had changed for ever.

Pearl Harbor was far from the only target. Bombers of the Imperial Air Fleet had been waiting to take off from the island of Formosa (Taiwan) to attack American airfields on the Philippines – but a thick fog had kept them grounded.

General MacArthur had been woken in his suite at a Manila hotel with news of the attack on Pearl Harbor. He immediately called a staff conference at his headquarters. Major General Lewis Brereton, chief of the Far East Air Force, asked for permission to send his B-17 Flying Fortresses against the airfields on Formosa. But MacArthur hesitated. He had been told that the Japanese bombers based there did not have the range to attack the Philippines. Brereton was unconvinced. He sent his B-17s up, with fighter escorts, so that they would not be caught on the ground. MacArthur finally gave permission for a reconnaissance flight over Formosa, to be followed by a bombing raid the next day. Brereton ordered his bombers to return to Clark Field to refuel, some ninety kilometres from Manila, and the fighters to land at their base near Iba to the north-west.

At 12.20 hours local time, while the crews were having lunch, the Japanese raiders arrived overhead. They could not believe their luck in finding that their targets were all lined up for them. Altogether eighteen B-17 bombers and fifty-three P-40 fighters were destroyed. Half of the Far East Air Force had been destroyed on the first day. The Americans had received no warning because their radar set had not yet been installed.

Other Japanese bombers attacked the capital, Manila. Philippine civilians had no idea what to do. An American marine saw 'Women clustered under the acacia trees in the park. A few of them had opened their umbrellas for additional protection.'

Wake Island, halfway between Hawaii and the Mariana Islands, was also attacked by Japanese aircraft on 8 December, but the Americans were ready. Major James Devereux, the commander of the 427 US marines there, had ordered his bugler to sound 'Call to Arms' as soon as he heard of the attack on Pearl Harbor. Four marine pilots in Grumman Wildcats managed to shoot down six Zero fighters after the other eight Wildcats had been destroyed or damaged on the ground. On 11 December, Japanese warships arrived offshore to land troops, but the marines' five-inch guns sank two destroyers and damaged the cruiser *Yubari*. The Japanese force withdrew without even attempting to land its marines.

Although elated by their extraordinary achievement, the US marines on Wake knew that the Japanese would be back in even greater numbers. On 23 December a much larger task force appeared, this time with two aircraft carriers and six cruisers. The marines fought back courageously against odds of five to one, supported by a massive naval artillery bombardment and air attacks. Although they managed to inflict heavy losses, the Americans were forced to surrender to avoid heavy civilian casualties on the island.

On 10 December, 5,400 Japanese marines landed on Guam, in the Mariana Islands, some 2,500 kilometres east of Manila. The small and lightly armed garrison of US Marines did not stand a chance.

The British in Hong Kong and Malaya had been expecting a Japanese invasion since the end of November. Malaya was a rich prize with its tin mines and vast rubber plantations. The governor, Sir Shenton Thomas, had described the country as the 'dollar arsenal of the Empire'. Malaya thus represented almost as high a priority for the Japanese as the oilfields of the Dutch East Indies. A state of emergency was declared in Singapore on 1 December, but the British were still woefully ill prepared. The colonial authorities feared that an overreaction might unsettle the native population.

The appalling complacency of colonial society had produced a self-deception largely based on arrogance. A fatal underestimation of their attackers included the idea that all Japanese soldiers were very short-sighted and inherently inferior to western troops. In fact they were immeasurably tougher and had been brainwashed into believing that there was no greater glory than to give their lives for their Emperor. Their commanders, imbued with a sense of racial superiority and convinced of Japan's right to rule over East Asia, remained impervious to the fundamental contradiction that their war was supposed to free the region from western tyranny.

The Royal Navy had a vast and modern naval base on the north-east corner of Singapore island. Powerful coastal batteries covered the approaches, ready to destroy an amphibious attack, but this magnificent complex which had cost a large part of the naval budget was almost empty. The original plan had been that a fleet could be sent out there from Britain in the event of war. But because of naval commitments in the Atlantic and the Mediterranean and the need to protect Arctic convoys to Murmansk taking supplies to the Russians, the British had no battle fleet in the Far East. Churchill's promise to aid the Soviet Union also meant that the Far East Command lacked modern aircraft and tanks, as well as a range of other equipment. The only fighter available – the Brewster Buffalo, known as the 'flying beer barrel' because of its tubby shape and sluggish handling – stood no chance against Japanese Zeros.

The British commander in Malaya was Lieutenant General Arthur Percival, a very tall, thin man with a military moustache which failed to divert attention from his buck teeth and weak chin. Although Percival had acquired a perhaps undeserved reputation for ruthlessness with IRA prisoners during the Troubles in Ireland, he had the obstinacy of a faint-hearted man when it came to dealing with subordinate commanders. Lieutenant General Sir Lewis Heath, the commander of III Indian Corps, had no respect for Percival and bitterly resented his promotion over him. And relations between the various army and RAF commanders, as well as between them and the tempestuous and paranoid Australian commander, Major General Henry Gordon Bennett, were far from amicable. In theory, Percival commanded nearly 90,000 men, but fewer than 60,000 were front-line troops. Hardly any had experience of the jungle, and the Indian battalions and local volunteers were virtually untrained. The sorry state of British defences was well known in Tokyo. The 3,000 Japanese civilians then resident in Malaya had been passing back detailed intelligence through their consulate-general in Singapore.

On 2 December, a Royal Navy squadron commanded by the diminutive Admiral Sir Thomas Phillips reached Singapore. It consisted of the modern battleship HMS *Prince of Wales*, the old battle-cruiser HMS *Repulse* and four destroyers. Crucially, it lacked fighter cover, because the aircraft carrier HMS *Indomitable* with forty-five Hurricanes had been halted for repairs. But this did not seem to worry the British in Singapore. They did not think that the Japanese would dare to launch an invasion of Malaya now, with such powerful ships based there. General Percival, meanwhile, was refusing to construct defence lines with the argument that it reduced the offensive spirit of his soldiers.

On Saturday, 6 December, a Royal Australian Air Force bomber, based at Kota Bahru in the far north-east of Malaya, sighted Japanese transports escorted by warships. They had sailed from the island of Hainan off the south China coast and were due to be joined by two convoys from Indochina. This force, which would split again, was headed for the southern Thai ports of Patani and Singora on the Kra Isthmus and the air base of Kota Bahru. From the Kra Isthmus, General Yamashita Tomoyuki's 25th Army would attack both north-westwards towards southern Burma and south into Malaya.

The British had evolved a plan, Operation Matador, to advance into southern Thailand and delay the Japanese there. But the Thai government, bowing to the inevitable and hoping to regain territory in north-west Cambodia, had virtually accepted Japanese overlordship in advance. Air Chief Marshal Sir Robert Brooke-Popham, the elderly commander-in-chief Far East, could not make up his mind whether to launch Operation Matador or not. Brooke-Popham was known as 'Pop-off' because of his tendency to fall asleep during meetings. General Heath was furious about the indecision, since his Indian troops were still on standby to move into Thailand when they should have been moving to Jitra in the far north-west to prepare defensive positions there.

They were becoming increasingly demoralized, soaked to the skin in the monsoon rains.

Finally, in the early hours of 8 December, news reached Singapore that the Japanese were landing to attack Kota Bahru. At 04.30 hours, while the senior commanders and the governor were in conference, Japanese bombers made their first raid on Singapore. The city was still a blaze of lights. Admiral Phillips, although well aware of the lack of fighter cover, decided to take his squadron up the east coast of Malaya to attack the Japanese invasion fleet.

At Kota Bahru, the only explosions which had taken place so far had been caused by mines on the beach being set off by stray dogs or by coconuts dropping on them. A little way inland, the 8th Brigade had concentrated one battalion round the airfield, but the beaches were guarded by only two battalions stretched over fifty kilometres.

The Japanese assault had started around midnight on 7 December, in fact about an hour before the attack on Pearl Harbor even though the two were supposed to have been simultaneous. The seas in this monsoon period were heavy, but that did not stop the Japanese from getting ashore. The Indian infantry platoons managed to kill quite a number of their attackers, but they were too thinly spread and the visibility in the heavy rain was poor.

The Australian pilots at the landing strip scrambled their ten serviceable Hudson bombers and attacked the transports offshore, destroying one, damaging another and sinking a number of landing barges. But after dawn the Kota Bahru airfield and others down the coast began to suffer repeated attacks from Japanese Zeros flying in from French Indochina. By the end of the day, the British and Australian squadrons in Malaya were reduced to just fifty aircraft. Percival's deployment of his troops to guard airfields as a first priority proved a grave mistake. And Brooke-Popham's indecision over Operation Matador meant that the Japanese air force was soon operating from bases in southern Thailand. General Heath, to Percival's anger, began a retreat the next day from the north-east.

*

President Roosevelt, following his celebrated statement that 7 December was 'a date which will live in infamy', cabled Churchill in London to report on the declaration of war passed by the Senate and the House of Representatives. 'Today all of us are in the same boat with you and the people of the Empire, and it is a ship which will not and cannot be sunk.' It was an unfortunate metaphor just as HMS *Prince of Wales* and HMS *Repulse* were steaming out of the naval base escorted by their destroyers. While Admiral Phillips was leaving he was warned that he could expect no fighter protection and that Japanese bombers were now based in southern Thailand. Phillips felt that, in the best traditions of the service, he could not back out.

Phillips's Force Z was not sighted by Japanese seaplanes until the late afternoon of 9 December. Not finding any transports or warships, Phillips decided to turn back that night and return to Singapore. But in the early hours of 10 December his flagship received a report of another landing at Kuantan, which was on his way.

The Royal Navy warships of Force Z were called to action stations after a hurried breakfast of ham and marmalade sandwiches. Guncrews wearing anti-flash protection, steel helmets, goggles and asbestos gloves manned the pom-poms. '*Prince of Wales* looked magnificent,' wrote an observer on board the *Repulse*. 'White-tipped waves rippled over her plunging bows. The waves shrouded them with watery lace, then they rose high again and once again dipped. She rose and fell so methodically that the effect of staring at her was hypnotic. The fresh breeze blew her White Ensign out stiff as a board. I felt a surge of excited anticipation rise within me at the prospect of her and the rest of the force sailing into enemy landing parties and their escorting warships.'

In fact the report of landings at Kuantan proved false. This diversion and delay to their return proved fatal. Later in the morning, a Japanese reconnaissance aircraft was sighted. At 11.15 hours, the *Prince of Wales* opened fire at a small group of enemy aircraft. Another group of torpedo planes appeared a few minutes later. The two ships' multiple pom-pom guns began firing. Their crews called them 'Chicago pianos'. The glowing tracers arced outwards in a mass of shallow curves towards their targets. But while the gunners were concentrating on the torpedo planes, nobody had noticed bombers at a much higher altitude. The *Repulse* was struck by a bomb which went right through the catapult deck. Smoke emerged through the hole, yet attention remained fixed on the attacking aircraft. As the pom-pom gunners knocked one of their low-level attackers out of the sky, everyone cheered: 'Duck down!' But then, reminding them of the more immediate danger, a marine bugler sounded the dreaded warning 'ship on fire'. Fire-hoses played on the hole billowing black smoke but proved of little use.

The next wave of attacking aircraft concentrated on the *Prince of Wales*. A torpedo struck her stern, sending up a 'tree-like column' of water and smoke. The great ship began to list to port. 'It doesn't seem possible that those slight-looking planes could do that to her,' the same observer on *Repulse* noted, still barely able to believe that the age of the battleship was truly over. Even if the carrier HMS *Indomitable* had been with them, it is far from certain that her aircraft would have been sufficient to ward off the determined Japanese attacks.

With her steering gear and engines out of action, HMS *Prince of Wales* was doomed as another wave of torpedo aircraft appeared. *Repulse*'s guncrews did what they could to break up the attack, but three more torpedoes struck home. The battleship's list increased dramatically. It was obvious that she was about to go down. Then the *Repulse* herself was hit by two torpedoes, one after the other. The order came to abandon ship. There was little panic. Some sailors even had time to light a last cigarette as they formed lines. When it was their turn, they took a deep breath and leaped into the black oil-covered sea below.

Churchill, who had exulted in the great ships of the Royal Navy from his times as First Lord of the Admiralty, was stunned by the disaster. The tragedy felt even more personal to him after his voyage in the *Prince of Wales* to Newfoundland in August. The Imperial Japanese Navy was now unchallenged in the Pacific. Hitler rejoiced at the news. It augured well for his declaration of war on the United States, announced on 11 December.

Hitler had always assumed that he would have to fight America at some point and he now calculated that, with its small army and a crisis in the Pacific, it would not be able to play a decisive part in Europe for nearly two years. He was above all encouraged in this decision by Admiral Dönitz, who wanted to send his U-boat wolfpacks against American shipping. All-out submarine warfare might still bring Britain to its knees.

Hitler's announcement to the Reichstag prompted its Nazi representatives to rise cheering to their feet. They saw the United States as the great Jewish power in the west. But German officers, still fighting in the desperate retreat on the eastern front, did not know what to think when they heard the news. The more far-sighted sensed that this world war, with the United States, the British Empire and the Soviet Union aligned against them, would be unwinnable. The repulse before Moscow combined with the American entry into the war made December 1941 the geo-political turning point. From that moment, Germany became incapable of winning the Second World War outright, even though it still retained the power to inflict appalling damage and death.

On 16 December, Generalfeldmarschall von Bock, suffering from some sort of psychosomatic illness, informed Hitler that he must decide whether Army Group Centre should stand and fight, or withdraw. Both courses risked its destruction. He clearly wanted to be relieved of his failed command, and he was replaced a few days later by Kluge, who initially agreed with Hitler's refusal to retreat. Brauchitsch, the army commander-in-chief, was also dismissed for pessimism. Hitler promptly appointed himself commander-in-chief in his stead. Several other senior commanders were also removed, but it was the sacking of Guderian, the symbol of offensive dash, which depressed German officers the most. Guderian had characteristically defied orders to hold positions whatever the cost. The wisdom or folly of Hitler's decision to stand fast has long been debated. Did it prevent an 1812-style debacle, or did it cause huge and unnecessary losses?

On 24 December, German soldiers, so far from home, felt an urge to celebrate Christmas, even in the most abject circumstances. A Christmas tree was easy to come by, which they decorated with stars made from the silver paper from cigarette packets. In some cases, they were even given candles by Russian peasants. Huddled together for warmth in villages which had not yet been burned, they exchanged pathetic little presents and sang 'Stille Nacht, heilige Nacht'. Although they felt lucky to be alive after so many of their comrades had died, they felt an overwhelming loneliness as they thought of their families at home.

Only a few recognized the paradox of German sentimentality amid the vicious war which they had unleashed. On Christmas Day, the prisoner-of-war camp outside Kaluga was evacuated in temperatures below minus 30 degrees. Many of the Soviet prisoners, of whom some had been reduced to cannibalism, collapsed in the snow and were shot. It was perhaps hardly surprising that Soviet soldiers exacted revenge by killing German wounded abandoned in the retreat, in at least one case by pouring captured fuel stocks over them and setting them on fire.

Nobody was more conscious of the dramatic shift in world affairs than Stalin. But his impatience to exact revenge on the Germans and seize the opportunities offered by their retreat led him into demanding a general offensive along the whole front, a series of operations for which the Red Army lacked the necessary vehicles, artillery, supplies and above all training. Zhukov was horrified, even though operations so far had gone better than he had expected. The vastly over-ambitious Stavka plans aimed for the destruction of both Army Group Centre and Army Group North, and a massive strike back into Ukraine.

After so many months of suffering, the mood of the Soviet people also swung wildly towards excessive optimism. 'We'll get it over by spring,' many were saying. But they, like their leader, still had many shocks ahead.

The British colony of Hong Kong, which had maintained a form of neutrality during the last four years of the Sino-Japanese War to the north, represented an obvious target. Apart from its wealth, Hong Kong had been one of the main supply routes to Nationalist forces. As in Singapore, the Japanese community had provided detailed information on its defences and weaknesses to Tokyo. Plans for its capture had been considered for the previous two years. A fifth column, largely based on heavily bribed Triad gangs, had also been prepared.

The British community, after so many years of asphyxiating supremacy, had no idea whether the Hong Kong Chinese, the refugees from Kwangtung province to the north, the Indians or even the Eurasians were likely to stay loyal. As a result they did little to inform them of the situation, and shrank from arming them to resist the Japanese. Instead, they decided to rely on the 12,000 British and Dominion troops and the Hong Kong Volunteer Defence Corps, which was almost entirely European. Chiang Kai-shek's Nationalists offered help in defending Hong Kong, but the British were extremely reluctant to accept it. They knew that Chiang wanted to regain the colony for China. Paradoxically, British officers were to enjoy much closer relations with Chinese Communist partisans, and later provided arms and explosives to them, a move which appalled the Nationalists. Both the Communists and the Nationalists suspected that the British would prefer to lose Hong Kong to the Japanese than to the Chinese.

Churchill had no illusions from a purely military point of view. If the Japanese invaded, he believed, there was 'not the slightest chance of holding Hong Kong or relieving it'. But pressure from the Americans persuaded him to reinforce the colony in a show of solidarity with the equally threatened Philippines. On 15 November, 2,000 Canadian soldiers had arrived to augment the garrison. Although inexperienced, they could foresee the fate in store for them should the Japanese army attack. They were not convinced by the Allied plan that the colony should be defended for up to ninety days to provide time for the US Navy at Pearl Harbor to come to their aid.

On 8 December, just as Japanese forces moved in to occupy Shanghai, Japanese aircraft in a strike on Kai Tak airfield wiped out the colony's five aircraft. A division of Lieutenant General Sakai Takashi's 23rd Army crossed the Sham Chun River which marked the border of the New Territories. The British commander Major General C. M. Maltby and his men were caught off balance. Apart from blowing up a few bridges, his forces withdrew rapidly to what was called the Gin-Drinkers' Line of defence across the isthmus of the New Territories. The lightly equipped and camouflaged Japanese moved silently and rapidly across country on their rubber-soled shoes, while the defenders clumped around in the rocky hills in metal-studded ammunition boots and full battle-order. Triad members and supporters of the Chinese puppet leader on the mainland, Wang Ching-wei, guided Japanese troops round behind the defensive line. Maltby had deployed only a quarter of his force in the New Territories. The majority were held back on Hong Kong Island, ready to face an attack from the sea which never came.

The Chinese population in Hong Kong felt that this was not their war. The food rationing and air-raid shelters organized by the colonial authorities proved totally insufficient for them. Those employed as auxiliary drivers slipped away, abandoning their vehicles. Chinese police and air-raid precaution personnel simply discarded their uniforms and went home. Staff in hotels and servants in private houses also disappeared. Fifth columnists stirred up trouble in the refugee camps filled with those fleeing the war in China, by stealing all the rice. Soon riots and looting began, led by Triad gangs. Somebody raised a large Japanese flag over the tall Peninsula Hotel near the Kowloon waterfront. This caused panic among some Canadian soldiers, who thought they had been outflanked. At midday on 11 December, General Maltby felt that he had no choice but to pull all his troops back across the harbour to Hong Kong Island. This produced chaos as crowds tried to storm the departing boats.

News of the sinking of the *Prince of Wales* and the *Repulse* confirmed that there was no hope of relief from a Royal Navy task force. The island itself was also in a state of ferment after the relentless artillery bombardment and bombing by Japanese aircraft. Sabotage by fifth columnists increased the hysteria. The British police rounded up Japanese on the island and arrested saboteurs, of whom a number were shot out of hand. The crisis forced the British to approach Chiang Kai-shek's representative in Hong Kong, the one-legged Admiral Chan Chak. His Nationalist network of paid vigilantes was called upon to help restore some sort of order and combat the Triads, who were plotting to massacre the Europeans.

The most effective method was bribery. Triad leaders agreed to a meeting in the Cecil Hotel. Their demands were outrageous, but a deal was struck. Admiral Chan Chak's vigilantes, operating under the name of the Loyal and Righteous Charitable Association, soon grew to 15,000 strong, of whom 1,000 were attached to the Special Branch. An underground war was then waged against Wang Ching-wei's partisans. Most of those captured were executed in back alleys. The British became rather fond of the piratical Chinese admiral who had saved the situation, and they finally agreed to seek help from the Nationalist armies.

With rumours of relief and order virtually restored, morale on the besieged island rose. But Maltby, uncertain where to concentrate his troops to repel a landing, failed to strengthen his forces on the north-east corner of the island. A group of four Japanese swam across at night to reconnoitre this stretch; and on the following night of 18 December 7,500 troops crossed, using every small craft they could find. The 38th Division, once established, did not try to push round the coast towards Victoria, as Maltby expected. Instead they forced their way across the hilly interior, pushing back the two Canadian battalions, to split the island in two. Soon both Stanley and Victoria were without electricity or water, and much of the Chinese population was starving.

Already the governor, Sir Mark Young, had been persuaded by General Maltby that there was no hope of holding out. Young sent a signal to London on 21 December, requesting permission to negotiate with the Japanese commander. Churchill replied via the Admiralty that 'There must be no thought of surrender. Every part of the Island must be fought over and the enemy resisted with the utmost stubbornness. Every day that you are able to maintain your resistance you help the Allied cause all over the world.' Young, apparently dismayed to think of himself as 'the first man to surrender a British colony since Cornwallis at Yorktown', agreed to fight on.

Despite some brave stands, the morale of the doomed defenders was collapsing. Indian troops, especially the Rajputs who had suffered heavy casualties, were in a very bad state. Their morale had also been sapped by constant Japanese propaganda urging them to defect, with the implication that the defeat of the British Empire would bring freedom to India. The Sikh police had deserted almost to a man. Their resentment of the British was fuelled by memories of the Amritsar massacre in 1919.

With fires raging and with water supplies cut, which had also created a major sanitation problem, the British community, especially the wives, started to put pressure on Maltby and the governor to end the fighting. Young remained obstinate, but on the afternoon of Christmas Day, after the Japanese had intensified their bombardment, Maltby insisted that resistance was no longer possible. That evening the two men were taken across the harbour in a motorboat by Japanese officers to surrender to General Sakai by candle-light in the Peninsula Hotel. Admiral Chan Chak, with several British officers, escaped in motor torpedo boats that night to join up with Nationalist forces on the mainland.

Over the next twenty-four hours, the Triads looted at will, especially the British houses on the Peak. Despite General Sakai's orders to his troops to treat their prisoners well, the heavy fighting on the island had enraged them. In a number of cases medical staff and wounded were bayoneted, hanged or decapitated. There were, however, relatively few cases of rape of European women, and the offenders were severely punished, which made a surprising contrast to the terrifying performance of the Imperial Japanese Army in the war on the mainland. In fact, Europeans were generally treated with some respect, as if to prove that the Japanese were just as civilized. But then, in a perverse contradiction of Japanese propaganda, which claimed that they were undertaking a war to liberate Asia from the whites, officers made little effort to restrain their men from raping Hong Kong Chinese women. More than 10,000 are estimated to have been gang-raped and several hundred civilians were killed during the 'holiday' after the battle.

General Yamashita's army, successfully established on the Malay Peninsula, although inferior in numbers, enjoyed the support of an armoured division and air superiority. The Indian troops, most of whom had never seen a tank before, were overawed. They were also spooked by the jungle and the eerie gloom of the rubber plantations. But the most effective Japanese tactic was to advance down the eastern and western coast roads, led by their tanks, and on reaching a roadblock to outflank the defenders with infantry skirting round them through paddy fields or jungle. The speed of the Japanese advance was greatly increased by bicycle troops, who often overtook the retreating defenders.

Advancing down both the west and the east coast of the Malay Peninsula, Yamashita's battle-hardened troops pushed back the mixture of British, Indian, Australian and Malay units towards the southern tip of Johore. In a number of actions, certain units fought well and inflicted heavy casualties. But the incessant retreats were both utterly exhausting and demoralizing against Japanese tanks and constant strafing by Zero fighters.

General Percival still refused to establish a defence line in Johore because he thought it would be bad for morale. This lack of prepared positions was disastrous for the defence of Singapore. Even so, the Australian 8th Division in particular managed to hold the Japanese Imperial Guards Division and throw it off balance with ambushes.

A force of Hurricanes had also arrived to strengthen Singapore's defences, but they proved inferior to the Zero. After two weeks of fighting in Johore, the remnants of the Allied forces were pulled back to Singapore island. The causeway across the Johore Strait was then blown up on 31 January 1942, just after the Argyll and Sutherland Highlanders crossed, bagpipes playing. The Japanese are said to have decapitated 200 Australian and Indian soldiers who had been left behind, too badly wounded to move.

Raffles Hotel continued to offer dinner dances on most nights, with the idea that business as usual would keep up morale. But to officers back from fighting down the Malay Peninsula it seemed more like the band playing on board the *Titanic*. Under relentless Japanese bombing, much of the city lay in ruins. Many European families had begun to leave, either by flying-boat to Java, or to Ceylon on the returning troopships which had just delivered reinforcements. Their fathers and husbands had mostly enrolled in volunteer units. Some women bravely stayed on as nurses despite fears for their fate when the Japanese conquered the city.

The inherent weakness of Singapore island along the Johore Strait was made worse by Percival's conviction that the Japanese would attack the north-east of the island. This derived from his strange belief that the naval base, which had already been destroyed, was the key element to be defended. He ignored instructions from General Wavell, now the Allied commander-in-chief in the region, to strengthen the north-west part of the island which, with its mangrove swamps and creeks, was the most difficult sector to defend.

The Australian 8th Division, which was given this sector, immediately saw the danger. It lacked clear fields of fire as well as mines and barbed wire, because the bulk had been allocated for the north-eastern side. Its battalions had been reinforced with fresh troops who had just arrived, but most of them hardly knew how to handle a rifle. General Gordon Bennett, although aware of Percival's fundamental mistake, said little and simply retired to his headquarters.

On 7 February, Japanese artillery opened fire for the first time on Singapore, which lay under a huge pall of black smoke from the naval base's oil dump bombed the night before. The next day, the bombardment intensified dramatically on the north-east flank as a diversion. This convinced Percival even more that this was where the attack would come.

Yamashita observed events from a tower of the palace belonging to the Sultan of Johore overlooking the narrow strait. He had decided to use up the last of his artillery ammunition just before his troops crossed in boats and barges that night to the mangrove swamps on Singapore's north-west shore. Vickers machine guns inflicted heavy casualties on the attackers, but the 3,000 Australians holding the sector were rapidly overrun by Yamashita's sixteen battalions, who surged on inland. The massive Japanese bombardment had cut all the field telephone lines, so the artillery in support took some time to react, and 8th Division headquarters had little idea what was going on. Even the Very lights shot into the sky by the Australian front line remained unseen.

By dawn on 9 February, nearly 20,000 Japanese troops had landed. Yet Percival still did not make any major changes to his deployment, apart from sending two under-strength battalions to form a blocking line. He also allowed the last Hurricane squadron to be withdrawn to Sumatra. Confusion rapidly led to the collapse of his hopes of forming a last-ditch defence line north-west of Singapore city. The Japanese had landed tanks, and they soon smashed through any remaining roadblocks. On the governor's orders, the treasury began to burn all the banknotes in its possession. Motorcars were pushed into the harbour to prevent them falling into the hands of the Japanese, but most were burned-out wrecks on the streets. The bombed and burning city stank from rotting bodies, and the hospitals were submerged in wounded and dead. The evacuation of women, including nurses, had accelerated as the last ships set sail, but a number of these vessels were bombed. Some of the survivors who managed to get ashore were bayoneted or shot down by Japanese patrols. The naval craft trying to escape ran straight into a Japanese flotilla of warships.

Percival, who had been ordered by Churchill and Wavell to fight to the very last, was under pressure from his subordinate commanders to surrender to avoid further loss of life. He signalled Wavell, who was firm in his order to continue fighting, street by street. But the city was running out of water, due to pipes broken by the bombing. Japanese troops charged into the military hospital at Alexandra and bayoneted patients and staff. One man under anaesthetic was stabbed to death on the operating table.

Finally, on Sunday, 15 February, General Percival surrendered to General Yamashita. General Bennett, after ordering his men to unload and stay where they were, slipped away. With a group of other men, he swam out to a sampan and then, after bribing the captain of a Chinese junk, made it to Sumatra. He claimed, on reaching Australia, that he had escaped to pass on his experience of fighting the Japanese, but the soldiers he had left behind were understandably bitter.

The recriminations against Percival, the governor Shenton Thomas, Bennett, Brooke-Popham, Wavell and several others were overwhelming in the aftermath of the humiliating disaster. 'We are paying very heavily now,' General Sir Alan Brooke, who had succeeded Sir John Dill as chief of the imperial general staff, wrote in his diary, 'for failing to pay the insurance premiums essential for security of an Empire.' But even though the preparation and the conduct of the Malayan campaign had been deplorable, Singapore could never have been an impregnable fortress with Japanese control of the surrounding air and seas. As well as the troops, there were over a million civilians on the island, so they would soon have been starved out in any case.

On 19 February, Japanese aircraft attacked the port of Darwin in the north of Australia, sinking eight ships and killing 240 civilians. The Australian government was both angry and alarmed. The country was exposed since its best divisions were still in the Middle East. Australians had only started to wake up to their vulnerability the previous November when the cruiser HMAS *Sydney* was sunk off their coast while intercepting the

German armed raider *Kormoran* flying a Dutch flag. During the long and heated debate that ensued, with two government inquiries carried out since 1998, many suspected that the German raider was not alone. They believed that the *Sydney* was torpedoed by a Japanese submarine operating with the *Kormoran* eighteen days before the attack on Pearl Harbor. Australian anger at the British failure to defend Malaya was justified, but the fact remained that the country had spent little on defence. And ironically it was mainly the ferocity of Australian criticism which had pushed Churchill into sending more reinforcements to Singapore, almost all of whom fell into Japanese hands.

Sumatra in the Dutch East Indies lay just across the Malacca Straits from Singapore, and the Japanese wasted no time in continuing their conquests. On 14 February 1942, the day before Percival's surrender, Japanese paratroops dropped on Palembang to secure the oilfields and Dutch Shell refineries. A Japanese task force, with a carrier, six cruisers and eleven destroyers to escort the troop transports, arrived offshore.

The island of Java was the next objective. The Battle of the Java Sea on 27 February rapidly decided the matter. An Allied force of Dutch, American, Australian and British cruisers and six destroyers attacked two Japanese convoys escorted by three heavy cruisers and fourteen destroyers. During the next thirty-six hours, the Allied ships were outgunned and out-torpedoed. It was a gallant but doomed engagement. By 9 March, Batavia (now Jakarta) and the rest of the Dutch East Indies had surrendered.

Japanese army commanders in China saw Burma as the most important objective for them. This offered the best way of cutting off supplies to Chiang Kai-shek's Nationalist armies as well as defending the whole western flank in south-east Asia. Imperial General Headquarters had originally planned to occupy only southern Burma, but this soon changed with the momentum of their advance.

The battle for Burma had begun on 23 December 1941, when Japanese bombers attacked Rangoon. Further raids caused a stampede of refugees out of the city. The Allies had only an RAF squadron of Brewster Buffaloes and a squadron of

American volunteer pilots known as the Flying Tigers with P-40 Curtiss Warhawks. Three Hurricane squadrons, diverted from Malaya, arrived soon afterwards.

On 18 January 1942, General Iida Shojiro's 15th Army attacked over the border from Thailand. Major General John Smyth VC, who commanded the 17th Indian Division, wanted to form a line along the Sittang River which provided a strong barrier. But Wavell ordered him to advance to the south-east towards the Thai frontier to slow the Japanese advance as far forward as possible, because he needed more time to reinforce Rangoon. This proved to be disastrous, with just one under-strength division trying to defend the whole of southern Burma.

On 9 February, Japanese policy suddenly changed. 'Victory fever' convinced Imperial General Headquarters that they could take most of Burma as well in order to cut off the Chinese supply route at source. Smyth was later forced, as he had foreseen, to retreat to the Sittang, but this now meant pulling his division back across a single-file, planked bridge during the night of 21 February. A truck jammed, and the whole column was halted for three hours. When dawn rose, most of the division was caught in a totally exposed position east of the fast-flowing river. Attempting to cut them off, a Japanese force threatened to capture the bridge. Smyth's second-in-command felt obliged to blow it up. Less than half the division got away. A chaotic retreat to Rangoon ensued.

The Burmese capital had been protected by the Flying Tigers and the RAF, who had forced the Japanese to switch to night-bombing. As a result reinforcements were landed in the port, including the 7th Armoured Brigade with light Stuart tanks. But Rangoon was doomed, and stores were shifted north before the place was finally abandoned. A zoo-keeper let out all the animals, including the dangerous ones, which caused some panic. In the half-deserted city, the governor Sir Reginald Dorman-Smith and his aide had a final game of billiards after finishing the last few bottles in the wine-cellar. Then, to deny the Japanese the stern portraits of former governors, they threw their billiard balls through the canvases.

General Sir Harold Alexander, appointed commander-in-chief Burma, flew in to Rangoon as the Japanese approached. On 7 March, he ordered the destruction of Burmah Oil's storage tanks outside the city, and instructed the remaining British forces to withdraw north. Fortunately for the British, the Japanese failed to carry out a major ambush effectively the following day, and they escaped. The plan was to form a new line of defence in the north along with the 1st Burma Division of Keren hill tribesmen, ferociously opposed to the Japanese, and 50,000 Chinese Nationalist troops led by the American commander in China, Major General Joseph Stilwell. 'Vinegar Joe' was a ferocious anglophobe. He claimed unconvincingly that Alexander was 'astonished to find ME – mere me, a goddam American – in command of Chinese troops. "Extrawdinery!" Looked me over as if I had just crawled from under a rock.'

The Japanese, having occupied Rangoon with its port, were able to reinforce their army rapidly. Their aircraft, now operating from airfields inside Burma, managed to destroy almost all the remaining RAF and Flying Tiger fighters on an airfield further north.

At the end of March, the Chinese forces were beaten back and what now became the Burma Corps, commanded by Lieutenant General William Slim, was forced to retreat rapidly to avoid encirclement. Chiang Kai-shek accused the British of failing to hold the line. Certainly, liaison between the two armies was ineffectual, if not chaotic, partly because the Chinese had no maps, and they could not read the place names on the ones the British provided. Disaster was then made certain by Stilwell insisting on an offensive, which the Chinese armies were incapable of carrying out.

Stilwell rejected Chiang Kai-shek's plan to defend Mandalay as too passive. Without warning the British, he sent two Chinese divisions into an attack south, and refused to allow the 200th Division to retreat from Taunggoo. The Japanese rapidly took advantage of these over-extended formations by advancing past them to Lashio, north-east of Mandalay, and thus outflanking the British as well. Stilwell, refusing to admit responsibility for the disaster, blamed his Chinese forces for a stupid reluctance to attack and losing the chance of a great victory. The British were rather more appreciative of their efforts and as furious with Stilwell as was Chiang Kai-shek.

On 5 April, a powerful Japanese task force entered the Bay of Bengal to attack the British naval base at Colombo. Admiral

Sir James Somerville managed to send most of his ships out of the way in time, but the damage inflicted was still extremely serious. By the beginning of May, the Japanese had seized Mandalay and even crossed into China by the Burma Road, forcing some of the Chinese Nationalist forces back into Yunnan province. But it was Indian civilians from the large community in Burma who suffered most in the retreat north, including small merchants and their families unused to hardship. They were attacked and robbed by the Burmese, who hated them. The remaining Allied troops had to retreat towards the Indian frontier, having suffered some 30,000 casualties. The Japanese occupation of south-east Asia appeared complete.

17

China and the Philippines

The year 1941 had begun more encouragingly for the Chinese Nationalists. The Japanese 11th Army was so spread out that it could not concentrate for an effective offensive. South of the Yangtze, the Nationalists even managed to inflict a severe reverse at the Jin River on the 33rd and 34th Divisions, causing some 15,000 Japanese casualties. And Chiang Kai-shek, in a calculated gamble, had forced the Communist guerrilla New Fourth Army to abandon its areas south of the Yangtze and move north of the Yellow River. It appears that although an agreement was reached on this withdrawal, Mao ensured that it broke down. Bitter fighting broke out when Communist troops, deliberately misdirected by Mao, blundered into Nationalist forces. Inevitably, accounts of what happened differed entirely on both sides. All that is certain is that it made a subsequent civil war even more difficult to avoid. Soviet representatives restricted themselves to expressing concern that Nationalists and Communists were fighting each other when they should be attacking the Japanese. But, in the wider world, foreign Communist parties used the incident as propaganda to claim that the Nationalists were always the aggressors.

The generalissimo, meanwhile, was outraged by the growing Soviet control over the extreme north-western province of Sinkiang which bordered Mongolia, the USSR and India. Working through the local warlord, Sheng Shih-tsai, the Soviet Union had constructed bases and factories, installed a military garrison and started mining for tin and drilling for oil. A secret camp also trained cadres for the Chinese Communist Party as their influence in the province grew. Sheng Shih-tsai had even applied for membership of the Chinese Communist Party. This move was vetoed by Stalin, but he was then accepted into the Communist Party of the Soviet Union instead. As Sinkiang was an essential staging post for supplies and trade with the USSR, the Nationalists' hands were tied. Chiang Kai-shek could only bide his time until a more favourable moment arose to reassert control over what had become a Soviet fiefdom.

In spite of these tensions, Soviet supplies had resumed for the moment at least, mainly because Stalin feared a revived Japanese threat in the Far East. In a battle for southern Hunan province the Nationalists again used their tactics of withdrawal followed by a counter-attack. Only in southern Shensi did the Japanese achieve a significant advance and seize valuable agricultural areas on which the Nationalists depended for food and recruits. This came about with their crushing victory in the Battle of Zhongyuan, which Chiang Kai-shek described as 'the greatest shame in the history of the anti-Japanese War'.

Ernest Hemingway and his new wife Martha Gellhorn were travelling in China at this time, and the misery and squalor around them ground down even the intrepid Gellhorn. 'China has cured me – I never want to travel again,' she wrote to her mother. 'The real life of the East is agony to watch and horror to share.' The dirt, the smells, the rats and the bedbugs had their effect. In the Nationalist capital of Chungking, which Hemingway described as 'grey, shapeless, muddy, a collection of drab cement buildings and poverty shacks', they lunched with Madame Chiang Kai-shek and the generalissimo, and were told afterwards that it was a great honour to be received by him without his dentures.

The generalissimo would not have been pleased to learn that Gellhorn had been bowled over by the Communist representative in Chungking, Chou En-lai. Hemingway, on the other hand, showed that he was not as uncritical of the Communists as he had been in Spain. He was well aware of the effectiveness of their propaganda, and how Communist supporters such as Edgar Snow had managed to persuade readers in the United States that Mao's forces were fighting hard while the corrupt Nationalists were doing little, when in fact the opposite was true.

Corruption there certainly was in Nationalist China, but it varied from army to army and officer to officer. Old-style staff officers in the Fiftieth Army used military trucks to bring opium from Szechuan to sell in the Yangtze valley, but not all Nationalist officers followed traditional warlord behaviour. While some profited shamelessly from the theft and sale of their own soldiers' rations, others, more modern and liberal, dug into their own pockets to buy medical supplies for their men. The Communists soon proved no better. Their production and sale of opium was designed to create a war-chest to fight the Nationalists later. In 1943, the Soviet ambassador estimated Communist opium sales at 44,760 kilos, worth $60 million at the time.

Hitler's invasion of the Soviet Union in June 1941 was a double-edged development from the Nationalists' point of view. On the positive side, it meant that Stalin could not afford to be so assertive in his bid to take over the province of Sinkiang. And above all it clarified the battle-lines of the Second World War, putting Britain, the United States and the Soviet Union on the same side against Germany and Japan. On the other hand, it made Stalin even more determined to avoid a clash with Japan. Stalin feared a build-up of Japanese forces in the north and asked the Chinese Communists to launch major guerrilla attacks, but Mao, while signalling assent, did nothing. The only Communist offensive, Operation a Hundred Regiments, had taken place the summer before. Mao had been furious, since it had helped the Nationalists when they were hard pressed, and although it caused severe damage to railways and mines, Communist casualties had been heavy.

Despite the return of Communist forces to virtual neutrality in the course of 1941, the Japanese commander, General Okamura Yasuji, launched his savage 'Three All' anti-partisan drives – 'kill all, burn all, destroy all' – against Communist base areas. Younger men, if they were not slaughtered, were seized for forced labour. Starvation was also used as a weapon. The Japanese burned all the harvest which they could not take for themselves. It has been estimated that the population of Communist base areas fell from forty-four million to twenty-five million during this period.

To Moscow's fury, Mao withdrew many of his forces, and split up those still behind Japanese lines. In Soviet eyes, this was a betrayal of 'proletarian internationalism' which obliged Communists everywhere to make every sacrifice for the 'Motherland of the oppressed'. Stalin now knew for certain that Mao was more interested in seizing territory from the Nationalists than in fighting the Japanese. Mao was also doing everything he could to reduce Soviet influence within the Chinese Communist Party.

Although Stalin had signed a non-aggression pact with Japan in April and subsequently ceased delivering military supplies to the Nationalists, he still continued to provide them with military advisers. The chief adviser at this time was General Vasily Chuikov, who would later command the 62nd Army in the defence of Stalingrad. Altogether some 1,500 Red Army officers had served in China, obtaining experience and assessing weapons systems there as they had in the Spanish Civil War.

The British also offered arms and training for Chinese guerrilla detachments. This had been organized by the Special Operations Executive office in Hong Kong, but because its officers began to arm Communist groups in the East River area, Chiang demanded that the programme be stopped. The Americans, meanwhile, had begun to provide assistance. This included the formation of the American Volunteer Group, the Flying Tigers, commanded by the retired US Army Air Corps officer Claire Chennault, Chiang Kai-shek's aviation adviser, and equipped with a hundred Curtiss P-40s. They were based in Burma to help protect the road link to south-west China, but the P-40 stood little chance against the Japanese Mitsubishi Zero unless the pilot used special tactics.

Over China itself, and especially the capital of Chungking, pilots in the tiny Nationalist air force did what they could to break up formations of Japanese bombers. Imperial General Headquarters had been forced to accept in December 1938 that Nationalist Chinese tactics had thwarted any hope of a quick victory. So they resorted to strategic bombing in the hope of destroying the Chinese will to resist. All industrial concerns were targeted but the main objective was the Nationalists' capital, which was attacked relentlessly with high explosive and incendiaries. The Japanese adopted a strategy of multiple small raids, to keep the city on constant alert and wear down its air defences. Chinese historians refer to the 'Great Bombing of Chungking', of which the most intense stage continued from January 1939 until December 1941 when Japanese naval aviation units were redeployed to the Pacific. More than 15,000 Chinese civilians were killed and 20,000 badly injured.

On 18 September 1941, the Japanese 11th Army launched a fresh offensive against the strategically important city of

Changsha with four divisions. The fighting was heavy as the Chinese forces withdrew. As always, the wounded suffered the most in a retreat. A Chinese doctor from Trinidad in the West Indies described one scene, which was sadly typical. 'A Red Cross ambulance stood on the road surrounded by hundreds of wounded men standing or lying down. It was loaded and the lightly wounded had clambered onto the roof. Some had even crowded into the chauffeur's seat. The driver was standing in front of them, his arms uplifted, pleading desperately. This was not an uncommon scene. Wounded men would lie down on the highway to prevent the trucks from leaving them behind.'

During this renewed attempt to encircle Changsha, the Japanese for once suffered more casualties than they inflicted. The Nationalists' combination of conventional and semi-guerrilla operations was becoming more effective. The plan had been drawn up by General Chuikov. Yet again the Chinese counter-attacked just as the Japanese entered the city. Japanese sources claimed that they pulled back only because of orders from Imperial General Headquarters, while the Chinese hailed a great victory.

The Chinese, meanwhile, had sent a large force against the important Yangtze river-port of Ichang in an attempt to retake it. On 10 October, they nearly succeeded in crushing the Japanese 13th Division defending the place. 'The division's situation was so desperate that the staff prepared to burn regimental flags, destroy secret papers and commit suicide.' But they were saved just in time by the 39th Division coming to their rescue.

Both the Nationalist armies and their warlord allies, as well as the Chinese Communists, deliberately fought a long and geographically extended campaign, avoiding major offensives themselves. At times both Nationalists and, especially, the Communists sought local truces with the Japanese. The Imperial Japanese Army, on the other hand, used operations in China as a training ground for newly raised formations. And although China's continuing resistance to Japan did not alter the outcome of the war in the Far East, it had considerable indirect effects.

Even by the time the Japanese began the wider Pacific war in December 1941, their China Expeditionary Army was still 680,000 strong. This was four times larger than the total of the Japanese ground forces used to attack the British, Dutch and United States possessions. Also, as several historians have pointed out, the treasury and resources devoted to the Sino-Japanese War since 1937 could have been used to far greater effect in preparation for the Pacific war, particularly the construction of more aircraft carriers. Yet the most important consequence of Chinese resistance, combined with the Soviet victory at Khalkhin Gol, was the Japanese refusal to attack Siberia when the Red Army was at its most vulnerable in the autumn and early winter of 1941. The course of the Second World War might well have been very different had such an attack been launched.

In February 1942, General Marshall selected Major General Joseph Stilwell as the US commander in China and Burma. Stilwell had been the US military attaché in Nanking with the Nationalist government when the War of Resistance against Japan had begun in 1937. He was therefore regarded in Washington as an old China hand. But 'Vinegar Joe' Stilwell regarded Chinese officers as lazy, duplicitous, byzantine, inscrutable, unmilitary, corrupt and even stupid. His view remained largely that nineteenth-century one of seeing China as 'the sick man of Asia'. He seems to have had little understanding of the very real difficulties that Chiang Kai-shek's regime faced, especially in the problems of food supply, which had forced the withdrawal of many troops to richer agricultural areas simply to prevent them from deserting through hunger.

Food, as Stilwell refused to acknowledge, was bound to be the Nationalists' main preoccupation, especially since their areas had been swamped with more than fifty million refugees fleeing Japanese cruelty. After bad harvests and the loss of agricultural areas to the enemy, food prices rose vertiginously. The poor and the refugees starved, and even minor officials struggled to feed their families. The government found it virtually impossible to prevent speculators and officers from holding back grain and rice to make large profits later, even though part of their hoarded stocks rotted. The corruption which Stilwell condemned was very hard to combat.

The Nationalists' solution was to tax the peasantry in kind, but this shifted the burden of feeding the vast armies to their shoulders, when they were also conscripted in huge numbers for military labour. Famine soon followed in many regions.

Conscription also became harder as a result, with recruiters resorting to force, and ignoring all exemptions. Rations were constantly reduced and by the end of the war inflation made a soldier's pay for a whole month less than the cost of two cabbages. An extended and ravaged agrarian society in which communications had broken down was bound to find it almost impossible to wage a modern war. The Communists did better in their less populated areas, mainly by imposing ferocious controls at every level. They were also far-sighted in the way they used labour more effectively, and even brought in their troops to help with the harvest. Communist armies also set up their own farms to make them self-sufficient. They thus attracted far more support among poor peasants than the Nationalists. But their great advantage was to be left comparatively undisturbed while the Japanese concentrated their forces against the Nationalists.

Marshall had also chosen Stilwell because he was utterly committed to the US Army doctrine which emphasized the importance of the offensive. But the Nationalists and their allied armies were simply not in a position to launch effective operations. They lacked the transport to concentrate forces, they lacked air support and they lacked tanks. This was why Chiang Kai-shek had decided even before the war began that their sole chance of survival was a drawn-out war of attrition. Chiang, a realist who knew his country and the limitations of his armies far better than Stilwell, had to put up with constant harangues about his lack of 'offensive spirit'. Stilwell referred to the generalissimo contemptuously as 'Peanut'. Chiang, underestimating the American public's anger with Japan, wrongly feared that the United States might make peace with Tokyo and abandon him. So in his desperate need for its aid he felt that he had to put up with such a disrespectful ally.

Stilwell also shared the general suspicion of Marshall and his followers that the British were interested only in regaining their empire, and were prepared to manipulate American support to achieve this end. But in his belief that the Japanese could most effectively be defeated in China, Stilwell was entirely alone. This view was completely at odds with Washington's strategy of encouraging Chiang Kai-shek to tie down large Japanese forces in China while the United States won mastery of the Pacific.

Marshall firmly refused Stilwell's request for an American army corps to spearhead the fighting in China.

Stilwell's belief in the primacy of the war in China led him, however, to focus on Burma to secure the Nationalists' supply line. The British, on the other hand, regarded Chiang Kai-shek's forces as a means to defend India, and later as an ally to help them recover the lost imperial possessions of Burma and Malaya. Hong Kong would be a much more complex matter, as they knew, because Chiang was set on regaining it for China.

Despite being partly responsible for the disaster in Burma, Stilwell was depicted as a hero in the American press, which remained woefully ignorant about the war in China. The Nationalists had in fact been effective in their management of the war up until 1941, by managing to balance the needs of the rural economy with the conscription of two million men a year and the necessity of feeding them. But the Japanese offensive from southern Shensi, capturing the communications centre of Ichang on the Yangtze, cut most Nationalist armies off from their food supplies in Szechuan.

Chiang Kai-shek was displeased that Stilwell, after the long withdrawal in Burma, had retreated into India in 1942 with two of his best divisions. He rightly suspected that Stilwell was trying to build his own independent command, but tolerated it since he was even more concerned that these formations did not come under the control of the British. These two divisions, the 22nd and 38th, were re-equipped with the backlog of Lend–Lease equipment destined for Chiang's armies in China, and which now could not get through because of the loss of the Burma Road. Only transport planes flying over 'the Hump' of the Himalayas could bring in a small amount of supplies. Even more aid intended for the Nationalists was either stockpiled in the USA or given to the British. Stilwell's control over Lend–Lease supplies was bound to lead to tensions and suspicion in his relations with the generalissimo, whose chief of staff he was supposed to be. Stilwell strongly believed that, as the dispenser of aid, he should use it as a lever to force Chiang to do what he was told.

The Pacific war, with its emphasis on sea and air power in support of amphibious landings, was very different from the continental war on mainland China. In the Philippines, General MacArthur had held back the bulk of his troops when the Japanese, on 10 December 1941, made small landings on the northern end of the main island of Luzon. He rightly guessed that these were diversionary attacks to split his forces. Two days later, another Japanese landing was made on the south-eastern peninsula of Luzon. The main assault did not come until 22 December, when 43,000 men of the 14th Army landed on beaches 200 kilometres north of Manila.

The two principal landings indicated the Imperial Japanese Army's intention to mount a pincer attack on the Philippine capital. In theory, MacArthur commanded a force of 130,000 men, but the vast majority were Philippine reserve units. He had only 31,000 American and Philippine troops on whom he felt able to count. The battle-hardened Japanese troops, with armoured spearheads, were soon pushing his forces back towards Manila Bay. MacArthur put into effect the established contingency plan Orange. This was to withdraw his troops into the Bataan Peninsula on the west side of Manila Bay and hold out there. The island of Corregidor at the mouth of the great inlet could control the entrance with its coastal artillery batteries, and defend the south-eastern end of the fifty-kilometre-long peninsula.

Lacking sufficient military transport to withdraw his southern forces, MacArthur commandeered Manila's gaudily painted buses. On the evening of 24 December, accompanied by President Manuel Quezon and his government, MacArthur left the capital by steamer to set up his headquarters on the island fortress of Corregidor, known as 'the Rock'. Huge oil depots and stores around Manila and in the navy yard were set on fire, sending billowing pillars of black smoke into the sky.

The withdrawal of the 15,000 American and 65,000 Philippine soldiers to Bataan and its first defence line along the Pampanga River was carried out with difficulty. Many of the Filipino reservists had slipped away to return home, but others took to the hills to continue a guerrilla war against the invaders. Across the bay from Bataan, the Japanese entered Manila on 2 January 1942. MacArthur's biggest problem was to feed 80,000 soldiers and 26,000 civilian refugees on the peninsula now that the Japanese navy had set up an effective blockade and enjoyed air supremacy.

The Japanese attacks began on 9 January. MacArthur's forces holding the neck of the Bataan Peninsula were divided by Mount Natib in the middle. The terrain of thick jungle and ravines on the western side and the swamps on the eastern side along Manila Bay both provided a hellish terrain in their different ways. Malaria and dengue fever ravaged MacArthur's troops, who were short of quinine as well as other medical supplies. Most were already weakened by dysentery, which the US Marine Corps called the 'Yangtze rapids'. MacArthur's main mistake was to have dispersed his supplies rather than concentrate them on Bataan and Corregidor.

After two weeks of bitter fighting, the Japanese broke through in the mountainous centre on 22 January and forced MacArthur's troops to pull back to another line halfway down the peninsula. His sick soldiers, their uniforms in tatters, and their skin starting to rot from the jungle and swamps, were already exhausted and severely weakened. A new threat appeared with four Japanese amphibious landings around the south-west tip of the peninsula. These were contained and fought off with the greatest difficulty, causing heavy casualties on both sides.

The resistance of the American and Filipino troops had been so effective, inflicting such heavy losses on the Japanese, that in mid-February Lieutenant General Homma Masaharu pulled back his troops a little way to rest them and await reinforcements. Although the defenders' morale was boosted, and they took the opportunity to improve their defences, the toll of sickness and the realization that no outside help could be expected soon had its effect. Many of the 'Battling Bastards of Bataan', as they called themselves, became embittered by the idea of MacArthur exhorting them to further effort from the safety of the concrete tunnels on Corregidor. He became known as 'Dugout Doug'. MacArthur had wanted to stay in the Philippines, but he received a direct order from Roosevelt to leave for Australia to prepare to fight back. On 12 March, MacArthur, with his family and staff, left on a flotilla of four fast patrol torpedo or PT boats.

Those remaining behind under the command of Major General Jonathan Wainwright knew that the situation was hopeless. Through starvation and sickness, less than a quarter were able to fight. General Homma's forces, on the other hand, had been reinforced with another 21,000 men, bombers and artillery. On 3 April, the Japanese attacked again with overwhelming force. The defence collapsed and on 9 April the troops on Bataan under Major General Edward King Jr surrendered. Wainwright on Corregidor still held out, but the Rock was pulverized by continual bombing, naval gunfire from the sea and artillery from the land. On the night of 5 May, Japanese troops landed on the island, and the following day a devastated Wainwright was forced to surrender his remaining 13,000 men. Yet the agony for the defenders of both Bataan and Corregidor was far from over.

18

War across the World

DECEMBER 1941–JANUARY 1942

Although the war with Germany and the war with Japan were conducted as two separate conflicts, they influenced each other far more than may appear on the surface. The Soviet victory at Khalkhin Gol in August 1939 had not only contributed to the Japanese decision to attack south, and bring the United States into the war, it also meant that Stalin could move his Siberian divisions west to defeat Hitler's attempt to take Moscow.

The Nazi–Soviet pact, which had come as a great shock to Japan, had also affected its strategic thinking. This was not helped by the astonishing lack of liaison between Germany and Japan, which concluded its neutrality pact with Stalin just two months before Hitler launched his invasion of the Soviet Union. The 'strike south' faction in Tokyo prevailed, not just over those who wanted war with the Soviet Union, but also against those in the Imperial Japanese Army who wanted to finish the war in China first. In any case, the Soviet–Japanese neutrality pact meant that the United States now became the chief supplier of the Chinese Nationalists. Chiang Kai-shek still tried to persuade President Roosevelt to exert pressure on Stalin to join the war against Japan, but he refused to bargain over Lend–Lease. Stalin was adamant that the Red Army could deal with only one front at a time.

Roosevelt's greatly increased support in 1941 for Chiang Kai-shek infuriated Tokyo, but it was Washington's decision to impose the oil embargo that the Japanese saw as tantamount to a declaration of war. The fact that it was in response to their occupation of Indochina and a warning not to invade other countries did not penetrate their own version of logic, which was based on national pride.

Because of their supremacist beliefs, Japanese militarists, like the Nazis, were compelled to confuse cause and effect. Perhaps predictably, they were enraged by Roosevelt's and Churchill's

Atlantic Charter, which they saw as an attempt to impose the Anglo-American version of democracy upon the world. They could well have pointed to the paradox of the British Empire promoting self-determination, and yet their own notion of imperial liberation with the Greater East Asia Co-Prosperity Sphere was far more oppressive. In fact, their Asian new order was strikingly similar to the German version, and their treatment of the Chinese ran parallel to the Nazi attitude towards Slav *Untermenschen*.

Japan would never have dared to attack the United States if Hitler had not started the war in Europe and the Atlantic. A two-ocean war offered its only chance against the naval power of the United States and the British Empire. It was for this reason that the Japanese sought assurances from Nazi Germany in November 1941 that it would declare war on the United States as soon as they attacked Pearl Harbor. Ribbentrop, no doubt still piqued that Japan had refused the German request in July to move against Vladivostok and Siberia, was evasive at first. 'Roosevelt is a fanatic,' he said, 'so it is impossible to foresee what he would do.' General Oshima Hiroshi, the Japanese ambassador, asked bluntly what Germany would do.

'Should Japan become engaged in a war against the United States,' Ribbentrop was forced to reply, 'Germany, of course, would join the war immediately. There is absolutely no possibility of Germany's entering into a separate peace with the United States, under such circumstances: the Führer is determined on that point.'

The Japanese had not told Berlin of their plans, so the report of the attack on Pearl Harbor came, according to Goebbels, 'like a bolt from the blue'. Hitler greeted the news with intense joy. The Japanese would keep the Americans occupied, he reasoned, and the war in the Pacific would surely reduce supplies sent to the Soviet Union and Britain. He calculated that the United States was bound to enter the war against him in the near future, yet it would not be in a position to intervene in Europe until 1943 at the earliest. He knew nothing of the 'Germany first' policy agreed between the American and British chiefs of staff.

On 11 December 1941, the American chargé d'affaires in Berlin was summoned to the Wilhelmstrasse where Ribbentrop read out the text of Nazi Germany's declaration of war on the United

States. Later in the afternoon, to acclamations of 'Sieg heil!' from Party members in the Reichstag, Hitler himself declared that Germany and Italy were at war with America, alongside Japan, in accordance with the Tripartite Pact. In fact the Tripartite Pact was an alliance of mutual defence. Germany was not in any way obliged to aid Japan if it were the aggressor.

At a time when German troops were in retreat before Moscow, Hitler's declaration of war on the United States appears rash to say the least. The decision reeked of hubristic pride, especially when Ribbentrop (probably echoing Hitler's own words) stated in grandiose manner, 'A great power doesn't let itself have war declared on it – it declares war itself.' Yet Hitler had not even consulted the OKW and key military officers at Führer headquarters, such as General Alfred Jodl and General Walter Warlimont. They were alarmed by the lack of calculation in the decision, especially since Hitler had maintained the previous summer that he did not want war with America until he had smashed the Red Army.

At a stroke, Hitler's self-justifying strategy that a victory over the Soviet Union would eventually force Britain out of the war was turned on its head. Now Germany really would face a war on two fronts. The generals were dismayed by his apparent ignorance of America's industrial might. And most ordinary Germans started to fear that the conflict would stretch on for years. (It was later striking how many Germans convinced themselves by the end of the war that it had been the United States which declared war on Germany, not the other way round.)

Soldiers on the eastern front listened to the announcement, determined to see it in the best light. 'On 11 December itself we were able to listen to the Führer's speech, an exceptional event,' wrote a Gefreiter in the 2nd Panzer Division, boasting that they had been within twelve kilometres of the Kremlin. 'Now the right world war has begun. It had to come.'

The key element in Hitler's thinking lay in the war at sea. Roosevelt's increasingly aggressive 'shoot on sight' policy, ordering US warships to attack German U-boats wherever they found them, and the decision to provide escorts to convoys west of Iceland had begun to tilt the Battle of the Atlantic in the Allies' favour. Grossadmiral Raeder had been pressing Hitler to allow his wolfpacks to hit back. Hitler had shared his frustration, but until the

Japanese tied down the US Navy in the Pacific and agreed formally not to seek a separate peace with the United States, he had not dared make a move. Now the western Atlantic and the whole North American coastline could become a free-fire zone in the 'torpedo war'. This, in Hitler's view, could finally offer another way of bringing Britain to its knees, even before the conquest of the Soviet Union.

Konteradmiral Karl Dönitz, the commander of the U-boat fleet, had asked Hitler in September 1941 to give him as much warning as possible of a declaration of war on the United States. He wanted time to prepare his wolfpacks so that they could be in position to strike mercilessly at American shipping along the east coast while the United States was still unready. But, as things turned out, Hitler's sudden decision came at a time when there were no U-boats available in the area.

Hitler's anti-semitic obsessions had convinced him that the United States was basically a Nordic country dominated by Jewish warmongers, and this was another reason why a showdown between his New Order in Europe and America was inevitable. Yet he failed to appreciate that the attack on Pearl Harbor had united America far more powerfully than Roosevelt could ever have hoped to do on his own. The isolationist lobby led by the slogan 'America First' was utterly silenced, and now Hitler's declaration of war played straight into Roosevelt's hands. The President could not have counted on Congress to take his 'undeclared war' in the Atlantic any further without it.

That second week of December 1941 was without doubt the turning point of the war. Churchill, in spite of the horrific news from Hong Kong and Malaya, now knew that Britain could never be defeated. After hearing of the news of Pearl Harbor, Churchill said that he 'went to bed and slept the sleep of the saved and thankful'. The repulse of the German armies before Moscow also demonstrated that Hitler was unlikely to achieve victory there, over his most formidable adversary on land. There was in addition a temporary easing in the Battle of the Atlantic, and even in North Africa the news was for once encouraging, with Auchinleck's Crusader offensive pushing Rommel back out of Cyrenaica. It was therefore with great optimism that Churchill sailed again for the New World, this time in the battleship HMS

Duke of York, the sister ship of the *Prince of Wales*. His series of meetings with Roosevelt and the American chiefs of staff was codenamed Arcadia.

As he crossed the Atlantic, Churchill prepared his views on the future conduct of the war in a ferment of ideas. These, debated with his own chiefs of staff, were honed to form British strategic planning. No attempt to land in northern Europe should be made until German industry, especially aircraft production, had been reduced by heavy bombers, a campaign which they wanted the US air force to join. American and British forces should land in North Africa in 1942 to help defeat Rommel and to secure the Mediterranean. Then landings could be made in 1943 in Sicily and Italy, or at places on the northern European coastline. Churchill also recognized that the Americans should fight back against the Japanese with aircraft carriers.

After a rough crossing in heavy seas, the *Duke of York* finally reached the United States on 22 December. Welcomed by Roosevelt, Churchill was installed in the White House, where he proved an exhausting guest over the next three weeks. But he was in his element, and he received a rapturous reception when he addressed Congress. The two leaders could hardly have been more different. Roosevelt was undoubtedly a great man, but while deploying charm and a contrived impression of intimacy to great effect, he was essentially rather vain, cold and calculating.

Churchill, on the other hand, was passionate, expansive, sentimental and mercurial. His well-known 'black dog' depressions almost suggest a form of bipolar disorder. Their greatest difference lay in their attitudes to empire. Churchill was proud of his descent from the great Duke of Marlborough and remained an old-fashioned imperialist. Roosevelt regarded such attitudes as not just outdated but profoundly wrong. Roosevelt also believed that he despised realpolitik, yet showed himself constantly ready to bend smaller countries to his will. Anthony Eden, now foreign secretary again, soon observed drily on the difficulties of the triangular relationship with the Soviet Union that 'United States policy is exaggeratedly moral, at least where non-American interests are concerned.'

The British delegation was reassured by the American chiefs of staff that 'Germany first' was still their policy. This decision was also influenced by the problem of shipping shortages. Because of the huge distances involved, each vessel could make only three round-trips a year to the Pacific theatre. But the lack of shipping also meant that the build-up of American forces in Britain for a cross-Channel invasion would take longer than imagined. This problem would start to be solved only once the 'Liberty ship' building programme got under way, mass-producing transports.

The United States, with its own entry into the war, was about to become much more than 'the great arsenal of democracy'. The Victory Program, originally suggested by Jean Monnet, one of the few Frenchmen whom the American administration truly respected, was already starting. Working on a plan to increase US forces to more than eight million men, and with generous estimates of the armaments, aircraft, tanks, munitions and ships needed to defeat both Germany and Japan, American industry began to convert to all-out war production. The budget ran to £150 billion. The military munificence would become staggering. As one general remarked: 'The American Army does not solve its problems, it overwhelms them.'

Lend–Lease to the Soviet Union had also been approved by Congress in October. In addition, $5 million of medical supplies were provided through the American Red Cross. Roosevelt pushed hard on deliveries to the Soviet Union. Churchill, on the other hand, had fuelled Stalin's suspicions by making extravagant promises of aid and then failing to deliver. On 11 March 1942, Roosevelt said to Henry Morgenthau, his secretary of the Treasury, that 'every promise the English have made to the Russians, they have fallen down on . . . The only reason we stand so well with the Russians is that up to date we have kept our promises.' He wrote to Churchill: 'I know you will not mind my being brutally frank when I tell you that I think that I can personally handle Stalin better than either your Foreign Office or my State Department. Stalin hates the guts of all your top people. He thinks he likes me better, and I hope he will continue to do so.' Roosevelt's rather arrogant and exaggerated confidence in his influence over Stalin was to become a dangerous liability, especially towards the end of the war.

Stalin wanted Britain to recognize the Soviet Union's claim to eastern Poland and the Baltic states occupied after the

Molotov–Ribbentrop Pact, and had put pressure on Anthony Eden to agree. At first the British had refused to discuss this flagrant contradiction of the Atlantic Charter's insistence on self-determination. But Churchill, afraid that Stalin might still seek a separate peace with Hitler, raised the possibility with Roosevelt that they should perhaps agree to this. Roosevelt rejected the suggestion outright. Then, paradoxically, it was Roosevelt who was to create the greatest distrust with Stalin with an unrealizable promise. In April 1942, without having studied the matter, he offered the Soviet leader a Second Front later that year.

General Marshall was horrified by Churchill's access to the President in the White House, knowing Roosevelt's tendency to formulate policy behind the backs of his own chiefs of staff. He was even more appalled when he subsequently discovered in June 1942, on another of Churchill's visits, that Roosevelt had agreed to his plan for landings in North Africa, Operation Gymnast, which many senior American officers saw as a British scheme to save the empire.

Churchill returned triumphant from the United States, yet soon, exhausted and ill, he was weighed down by a fresh series of disasters. On the night of 11 February 1942 and during the following day, the German battle-cruisers *Scharnhorst* and *Gneisenau* along with the heavy crusier *Prinz Eugen* accomplished their 'Channel dash' from Brest back to home waters in bad visibility. Numerous attacks along the way by RAF bombers and Royal Navy motor torpedo boats failed. The country was dismayed and angry. There was even a mood of defeatism in many corners. Then, on 15 February, Singapore surrendered. British humiliation appeared complete. Churchill, the revered war leader, now found himself attacked on all sides, by the press, in Parliament and by the Australian government. To make matters worse, large meetings and demonstrations began to demand 'A Second Front Now' to aid the Soviet Union – the one offensive operation which Churchill could not and did not want to undertake.

Yet the greatest threat at that time had nothing to do with British military failures. The Kriegsmarine had just changed its Enigma settings by adding an extra rotor. Bletchley Park was unable to decipher a single transmission. Dönitz's wolfpacks, now fully deployed in the North Atlantic and along the North

American seaboard, began to inflict a level of losses which answered Hitler's dreams. Altogether 1,769 Allied and 90 neutral ships were sunk in 1942. After Churchill's euphoria at America's entry into the war, Britain faced starvation and collapse if the Battle of the Atlantic were lost. Not surprisingly, with all the problems and humiliations heaped upon him, he greatly envied Stalin's success in repelling the Germans from Moscow.

The Red Army's great achievement in the Battle for Moscow in December was soon undermined by Stalin himself. On the evening of 5 January 1942, he summoned a meeting of the Stavka and the State Defence Committee at the Kremlin. The Soviet leader had become intoxicated with revenge and persuaded himself that the moment had come for a general offensive. The Germans were in disarray. They had not prepared for the winter and would not be ready to repel a major attack until spring came. As he walked up and down his office, puffing on his pipe, he insisted on his plan to launch massive encirclement operations of the central front opposite Moscow, in the north round Leningrad to break the siege, and in the south against Manstein's army in the Crimea, in the Donbass, and to recapture Kharkov.

Zhukov, who had not been told of Stalin's instructions to the Stavka, was horrified. In a conference with Stalin, he argued that the offensive should be concentrated on the 'Western axis' near Moscow. The Red Army lacked sufficient reserves and supplies, especially of ammunition, for a general advance. After the Battle for Moscow, the armies involved had suffered heavy losses and were exhausted. Stalin listened, but ignored all Zhukov's warnings. 'Carry out your orders!' he said. The meeting was over. Only later did Zhukov discover that he had been wasting his breath. Behind his back detailed instructions had already been issued to front commanders.

The German army was indeed battered and suffering badly. Wearing clothes looted from peasants, its frostbitten soldiers, with unkempt beards, noses peeling and cheeks burned by the cold, were unrecognizable from those who had advanced eastwards the previous summer, singing marching songs. German troops followed the local practice of sawing off the legs of the dead to thaw them over a fire in order to pull off the boots. Even wrapping their footwear in cloth could be insufficient to ward off frostbite on sentry duty. Frostbitten limbs, unless treated quickly, soon became gangrenous and had to be amputated. Army surgeons in field hospitals, overwhelmed by the casualty rate, simply threw the sawn-off hands and legs outside into piles in the snow.

Yet opponents always underestimated the German army's ability to recover from disaster. Discipline, which had been on the verge of breakdown, had been rapidly re-established. During the chaotic retreat officers had improvised *Kampfgruppen* of infantry mixed with assault guns, pioneers and a few panzers. And by the first week in January, at Hitler's insistence, villages had been turned into strongpoints. When the ground was frozen too hard to dig trenches, they used explosives or shells to blast craters, or they created mortar pits and firing points behind packed snow and ice reinforced with logs. Sometimes they were reduced to shovelling snow with their rifle butts. German soldiers had still not received any winter clothing. They hoped to strip Soviet casualties of their padded jackets before they froze solid, but in the hard frosts that seldom proved possible. Dysentery, from which almost all soldiers suffered, was a double curse when one was forced to drop one's trousers in such temperatures. And eating snow to rehydrate usually made things worse.

Rokossovsky's 16th Army and General Andrei Vlasov's 20th Army attacked north of Moscow and, when a gap opened, the 2nd Guards Cavalry Corps, supported by tank and ski battalions, forced into it. But, as Zhukov had warned, the Germans were no longer disorganized. Soviet forces soon found that instead of surrounding the Germans, they themselves were cut off. Some German formations were bypassed, but they stood and fought, supplied by air. The largest *Kessel* consisted of six German divisions encircled around Demyansk on the Leningrad highway towards Novgorod.

Even further to the north-west, General Kirill Meretskov's Volkhov Front tried again to break the siege of Leningrad, using the 54th Army and the 2nd Shock Army. Stalin bullied him into a premature attack, with untrained formations and artillery which lacked gunsights, until General Voronov flew up with a consignment. The 2nd Shock Army advanced across the River Volkhov and rapidly penetrated into the German rear, threatening to cut off the German Eighteenth Army. But the advance was slowed by German counter-attacks and the winter conditions. 'In order to beat a path through the deep snow, they had to form columns in ranks of fifteen. The first rank went forward, trampling the snow, which in places came up to their waists. After ten minutes the front rank was withdrawn and took up position at the rear of the column. The difficulty of movement was increased because from time to time they would come across half-frozen patches of bogs and streams covered with a thin layer of ice.' With soaked and frozen feet, they suffered heavy frostbite casualties. Their ill-fed horses were exhausted, so they had to carry the ammunition and supplies themselves.

General Vlasov, who had so recently been lauded for his part in the defence of Moscow, was sent by Stalin to take command. Vlasov was promised reinforcements and supplies but none came until it was too late. Ammunition was dropped by parachute but most fell behind German lines. Vlasov's army was soon cut off entirely in the frozen marshes and birchwoods. Meretskov warned Stalin of the impending disaster. Not long after the spring thaw, the 2nd Shock Army had virtually ceased to exist. Some 60,000 men were lost. Only 13,000 escaped. An embittered Vlasov was eventually captured in July. The Germans soon persuaded him to form a Russian Liberation Army, or ROA. Most of those who volunteered joined purely to avoid starvation in the prisoner-of-war camps. Stalin's reaction to Vlasov's betrayal revealed his misleading obsessions from the Great Terror and purge of the Red Army: 'How did we miss him before the war?' he asked Beria and Molotov.

Stalin's emissaries, including the sinister and incompetent commissar Lev Mekhlis, simply harried front commanders, blaming them for every shortcoming, even though the lack of supplies and vehicles was not their fault. Nobody dared tell Stalin of the chaos caused by his ludicrously ambitious plan, which extended even to recapturing Smolensk. German reinforcements brought in from France were thrown straight into the fighting, still with no winter equipment, while many of the Soviet divisions were reduced to little more than 2,000 men each.

The attempt to create a major encirclement around Vyazma failed. Zhukov even had part of the 4th Airborne Corps dropped behind German lines, but the Luftwaffe struck back at their air-fields round Kaluga, which the Germans knew well, having only just abandoned them. Down the whole of the eastern front, from Leningrad to the Black Sea, the German strongpoints succeeded in preventing any major breakthroughs. In the Crimea, Manstein managed to bottle up a Soviet amphibious invasion of the Kerch Peninsula attempting to break his siege of Sebastopol.

The greatest crisis came at Rzhev where the German Ninth Army was in danger of encirclement. General Walther Model, who became one of Hitler's favourites with his pitiless energy, was sent in to take command. Model demonstrated not only great physical courage, but also on other occasions moral courage in the way he stood up to Hitler. He immediately launched a counter-attack that caught the Soviet forces on the wrong foot. This succeeded in restoring the front line and in trapping the 29th Army. But the encircled Red Army soldiers, told of the fate awaiting them if taken prisoner by Model's troops, fought to the end.

Another favourite of Hitler, Generalfeldmarschall von Reichenau, who had been appointed commander-in-chief of Army Group South after Rundstedt's dismissal, had already become a different sort of casualty. On 12 January, he had gone for his morning run near his headquarters at Poltava. At lunch he felt unwell and collapsed from a heart attack. Hitler immediately ordered that Reichenau should be flown back to Germany for treatment, but the field marshal died on the way. Shortly before his death, Reichenau, whose Sixth Army had assisted the SS Sonderkommando in the massacre of Babi Yar, had persuaded Hitler to appoint his chief of staff Generalleutnant Friedrich Paulus to take over command of the Sixth Army.

The Germans also managed to resupply their encircled troops at Demyansk, Kholm and Belyi. The large Demyansk pocket was kept going by a daily run of over a hundred Junkers 52 transports. This success was to have serious consequences a year later, when Göring assured Hitler that he could maintain Paulus's Sixth Army trapped round Stalingrad. But although the German troops around Demyansk received enough food to fight on, the Russian civilians inside the Kessel were left to starve.

Around Kursk, Timoshenko's forces managed to drive the Germans back in desperate struggles. The battlefields were left in a frozen *tableau mort*. A Red Army officer called Leonid Rabichev came across 'a beautiful girl, a telephone operator who had been hiding in the forest since the Germans came. She wanted to join the army. I told her to get into the cart.' A little further on, 'I saw a horrifying sight. An enormous space stretching to the horizon was filled with our tanks and German tanks. In between them there were thousands of sitting, standing or crawling Russians and Germans frozen solid. Some of them were leaning against each other, others hugging each other. Some propping themselves with a rifle, others holding a submachine gun. Many of them had their legs chopped off. This had been done by our infantry who had been unable to pull off the boots from the Fritzs' frozen legs so they chopped them off in order to be able to warm them up in the bunkers. Grishechkin [his orderly] checked the pockets of the frozen soldiers and found two cigarette lighters and several packs of cigarettes. The girl was looking at all this indifferently. She had seen it many times before, but I was horrified. There were tanks which had tried to ram or run over each other and were standing on their hind legs after colliding with each other. It was terrible to think of the wounded, both ours and Germans, freezing to death. The front had advanced and they had forgotten to bury these men.'

The suffering of civilians was even greater. They were crushed between the cruelty of the Germans and that of their own Red Army and partisans, ordered by Stalin to destroy any buildings which the Germans might use for shelter. In any newly liberated areas, NKVD troops seized peasants who might have collaborated with the Germans. Nearly 1,400 people were arrested during January, even though the dividing line between survival and collaboration was hard to define. Advancing Soviet troops came across gallows and heard from villagers of other examples of German atrocities, but in some cases, German soldiers had been merciful. It was better for villagers to remain silent in this case to avoid accusations of treason to the Motherland.

Stalin's utterly misplaced hopes that the Wehrmacht was about to suffer the fate of Napoleon's Grande Armée were not abandoned until April, by which time Soviet casualties had risen to just over the million mark, of which half were dead or missing.

*

Because the highest priority for transport went to the movement of troops and military supplies, the population of Moscow was close to starvation. A black market developed with clothes and footwear exchanged for potatoes. Older people were reminded of the hunger years during the civil war. Children suffered from rickets. There was no fuel or wood for stoves, so water and sewage pipes froze. A hundred thousand women and children were sent out into the surrounding woods to cut firewood. Electricity was in short supply, with many blackouts. Twice as many people died from tuberculosis as the year before, and overall the mortality rate trebled. A typhus epidemic was feared, but the strenuous efforts of the Moscow medical authorities kept it at bay.

Conditions in besieged Leningrad were immeasurably worse. German artillery shelled the city regularly four times a day. But the defences held, mostly thanks to the naval guns, both dismounted and those still on ships of the Baltic Fleet at the Kronstadt naval base and moored in the Neva. The key to the survival of the city now lay more in its tenuous lifeline.

The Soviet authorities made strenuous but often incompetent efforts to keep the city's fragile link to the east open. With the Germans on the southern shore of Lake Ladoga, the only route was by the 'ice road'. The ice had become thick enough to carry motor and horse-drawn transport only after the third week of November when the city had supplies for just two days left. The great danger was a sudden thaw.

On the eastern side, the Germans had seized Tikhvin on 8 November 1941. This forced the Soviets to build a 'corduroy' road of felled birch trees through the forests to the north. Several thousand of the forced labourers – peasants, Gulag prisoners and rear troops – died in the process, and their bodies were thrown into the mud under the wooden track. Such sacrificial efforts were almost entirely wasted because Meretskov's troops, aided by partisan detachments in the German rear, retook Tikhvin on 9 December, three days after the corduroy road was finished. This reopened the railhead and greatly reduced the journey to the south-eastern point of Lake Ladoga.

The two-way traffic across the frozen lake, with factory machinery from the city going east and supplies going west, constituted an extraordinary achievement. The road over the ice was defended against attack from German ski troops with machine-gun posts and anti-aircraft guns in strongpoints on the ice. These had igloos attached for the Red Army soldiers to shelter in. The Soviets also built armed aerosleighs powered by aircraft engines, with propellers at the back like a winter version of a swamp glider. Medical centres and manned control points to direct the traffic were set up across the ice. But the handling of civilian evacuees from Leningrad was often brutally incompetent and unimaginative. Even the NKVD complained of their 'irresponsible and heartless treatment' and the 'inhuman' conditions on the trains. Nothing was done to help those who reached the 'mainland' alive. Their survival depended on having family or friends to help them with food and shelter.

Even after the recapture of Tikhvin, Leningraders were so weak from starvation that many collapsed on the frozen streets as they searched aimlessly for fuel or food. Their ration books were promptly stolen. Bread was seized from the hands of people returning from a bakery. Nothing destroys basic morality more rapidly than starvation. When a member of a family died, the corpse would often be hidden in the freezing apartment so that their rations could still be claimed.

Yet, despite the fears of the authorities, there were few attempts to storm and loot bread shops. Only the Party bosses and those close to the food chain, the distributors and the counter assistants, were likely to have the strength. Those at the bottom of the heap who did not work in a factory, with its privileged access to a subsidized canteen, were unlikely to survive. They began to look old so swiftly that a close relative might fail to recognize them. Crows, pigeons and seagulls were eaten first, then cats and dogs (even Pavlov's famous experimental dogs were consumed at the Physiological Institute) and finally rats.

Almost everyone trying to walk to work or to queue for food had to stop to rest every few metres, because they were so weak. Children's sleds were used to carry firewood. Soon they were used for carrying corpses, called 'mummies' because they were wrapped in paper or cloth shrouds, to the mass graves. Wood could not be spared for coffins. It was needed for heating to stay alive.

Out of a population of 2,280,000 in December 1941, a total of 514,000 were evacuated to the 'mainland' by the spring, and 620,000 died. For older citizens, the siege was the second major famine they had endured, the first having started in 1918 with the civil war. Many observed that a foreknowledge of death came some forty-eight hours before a person expired. With their last strength, many people reported to their workplace to warn that they would not be coming back and begged their boss to take care of their family.

Leningrad, which prided itself on its intellectual heritage, turned the Astoria Hotel into a hospital for writers and artists. There, they were fed vitamins in the form of fresh pine needles crushed into a bitter drink. Attempts too were made to care for orphans. 'They hardly looked like children any more,' a head-teacher said. 'They were strangely silent, with a kind of concentrated look in their eyes.' But in some institutions the kitchen staff pilfered the food from the kitchens for their own families, and left the children to starve.

The city authorities had failed to stock firewood before the siege began, so most were left trying to keep warm by burning books, as well as smashed-up furniture and doors, in their pot-bellied stoves. Old wooden buildings were dismantled to provide fuel for public buildings. In January 1942, the temperature in Leningrad at times fell below minus 40 degrees. Many people simply retired to bed to keep warm, but then wasted away. Death by starvation came silently and anonymously. A half-life drifted into non-life. 'You don't know what it was like,' a woman told a British journalist soon afterwards. 'You just stepped over corpses in the street, and on stairs! You simply stopped taking any notice.'

Most died from the combination of starvation and cold. Hypothermia and stress, combined with starvation, so upset the metabolism that people could not properly absorb even the few calories they did consume. In theory, soldiers were guaranteed a much better ration than civilians, but in many cases their rations never arrived. Officers stole them for themselves and their families.

'People turn into animals before our eyes,' wrote a diarist. Some were driven insane by starvation. Soviet history has tried to pretend that there was no cannibalism, but both anecdotal and archive sources indicate otherwise. Some 2,000 people were arrested for 'the use of human meat as food' during the siege, 886 of them during the first winter of 1941–2. 'Corpse-eating' was the consumption of meat from somebody already dead. Some people even snatched bodies from the morgue or mass graves. Outside Leningrad, a number of soldiers and officers resorted to eating corpses and even the amputated limbs from field hospitals.

'Person-eating', which was rarer, came from the deliberate murder of an individual for the purpose of cannibalism. Parents, not surprisingly, kept their children in their apartments for fear of what might befall them. It was said that the flesh of children, followed by that of young women, was the tenderest. Although stories abounded of gangs selling human meat ground into *kotleta*, or rissoles, almost all cannibalism took place within the apartment block, with crazed parents eating their own children, or neighbours preying on those of neighbours. Some starving soldiers in the 56th Rifle Division of the 55th Army ambushed ration carriers, killed them, took their supply of food, buried the body in the snow and returned later to eat it bit by bit.

Yet while starvation brought out the worst in people, there were examples of self-sacrificial altruism, to neighbours and even complete strangers. Children appear to have had a better rate of survival than their parents, presumably because the adults gave their offspring part of their own rations. Women usually survived longer than men, but often collapsed later. They also faced the terrible dilemma of whether to give in to the pleading of their children or to eat enough themselves to keep up their strength to look after their family. The birthrate plunged, partly from extreme malnutrition since women stopped menstruating and men became infertile, but also because most males were away at the front.

Red Army soldiers and the marine infantry in Leningrad became confident that the Germans would never break through. They were convinced that the main reason why the Germans persisted in the siege was to keep the Finns in the war. Leningraders were angry that the western Allies were reluctant to regard Finland as an enemy country. They could not accept that Stalin's assault on Finland in 1939 had been entirely unprovoked. Hatred of the enemy was continually fomented by the propaganda services of the Red Army. Posters showed a wild-eyed little boy, with a burning village in the background, crying out: 'Papa, ubei nemtsa!' ('Daddy, kill a German!').

Stalin's general offensive was not the only one in the new year of 1942. On 21 January, Rommel took the British in North Africa by surprise. Ever since his supply situation had begun to improve a little, the ambitious Rommel had been planning another attack. The reinforcement of the Mediterranean theatre had depended on a rapid conquest of the Soviet Union, but the failure of Operation Typhoon against Moscow did not deter him. When a convoy reached Tripoli on 5 January with fifty-five panzers, as well as armoured cars and anti-tank guns, his determination to strike back grew while he had a temporary advantage.

The Eighth Army was in a sorry state. The 7th Armoured Division, then refitting in Cairo, had been replaced by the inexperienced 1st Armoured Division. Other veteran formations, including the Australians, had been transferred to the Far East. The Germans were well aware of the British order of battle thanks to intercepts of reports from the American military attaché in Cairo, whose code they broke easily. But Rommel, who harboured wild notions of sweeping through Egypt and the Middle East, did not inform either the Italian Comando Supremo or the OKW of what he was plotting. Most of his soldiers, however, were thrilled to be on the attack again. A member of the 15th Panzer Division wrote home on 23 January to say: 'once again we are rommeling ahead!'

As Rommel struck back into Cyrenaica on 21 January, he ignored all orders to halt. One column advanced up the coast road to Benghazi, while the two panzer divisions swung inland. The panzers found the going very difficult, yet in five days of fighting the British lost nearly 250 armoured vehicles. Hitler was exultant and promoted Rommel to Generaloberst. The hapless and over-promoted General Ritchie, who had assumed that this was just a raid, soon found that his 1st Armoured Division was at risk of encirclement. Fortunately for the British, Rommel's over-ambition and the slow advance of the two panzer divisions allowed the bulk of their forces to flee in time. Ritchie pulled them all back to the Gazala Line, abandoning most of Cyrenaica.

Rommel's exhausted and fuel-starved troops did not bother to keep up. They knew that they could deal with them later.

German soldiers sent across the Mediterranean as reinforcements were excited and proud to join 'the small Afrika Korps' in the desert. A medical Unteroffizier looked favourably on the 'colonizing work' of the Italians in Tripoli. 'Also the Italian warships escorting our convoy were dashing,' he wrote home. But many initial impressions would not last. Out in the Libyan Desert, they found 'always the same landscape, sand and stone'. The war in North Africa was 'quite, quite different' to that in Russia, he emphasized. Yet they too suffered from homesickness as someone played the harmonica in the evening under the stars and they thought of the spring to come at home in Germany.

19

Wannsee and the SS Archipelago

Heinrich Himmler's energetic deputy was SS Obergruppen-führer Reinhard Heydrich. He led the Reich Security Head Administration (RSHA), which directed the burgeoning SS empire. Heydrich, a tall, immaculate, violin-playing anti-semite, was rumoured to have more than a trace of Jewish blood which seemed only to intensify his hatred.

In the summer of 1941, Heydrich became irritated by the messy, ad-hoc ways of dealing with the 'Jewish question' and the lack of a central programme. As well as the massacres of Jews carried out by local security officials in the eastern territories, some SS satraps began to experiment with more industrial versions of extermination. In the Warthegau, unsatisfactory tests were carried out, pumping exhaust fumes into the interiors of sealed vans. In the Generalgouvernement, SS Polizeiführer Odilo Globocnik began to construct an extermination camp at Bełżec near Lublin. Himmler, meanwhile, was impatient to resolve the problems of psychological stress which the Einsatzgruppen suffered as a result of their work.

Heydrich had instructed Adolf Eichmann to draft an authorization which Göring signed on 31 July. The document instructed Heydrich to 'undertake, by emigration or evacuation, a solution of the Jewish question', and charged him 'with making all necessary organizational, functional, and material preparations for a complete solution of the Jewish question in the German sphere of influence in Europe'. About a month later, Eichmann was summoned to Heydrich's office, where he was told that Himmler had received instructions from Hitler to proceed with 'the physical annihilation of the Jews'. Although senior Nazi officials occasionally liked to take the Führer's name in vain to advance their own policies, it would be unthinkable in this case that Himmler or

Heydrich would have dared to do so on quite so important a matter.

Earlier ideas that the total annihilation of the Jews would take place only after victory had been achieved were forgotten. One senses for the first time an unspoken anxiety that the opportunities presented by the war in the east should not be missed. Pressure also grew in Germany and in occupied countries, including France, that they should send their Jews eastwards. In Paris, the SS ordered the French police to round up French and foreign Jews, an initial operation which on 10 May 1941 sent 4,323 people to two holding camps.

On 18 September, an instruction from Himmler revealed that the ghettos were now to be used as 'storage' camps. More than half a million Jews had died of starvation and disease in the Polish ghettos, but this was seen as far too slow a process. Further discussion showed that the plan was to put all Jews in concentration camps. But even in a totalitarian state there were legalistic problems to overcome, such as how to deal with Jews possessing foreign passports, and what to do with those married to Aryans.

On 29 November 1941, Heydrich issued an invitation to senior officials from the Ostministerium and other ministries and agencies to discuss a common policy with him and representatives of the RSHA. This was due to take place on 9 December. At the last moment, the meeting was postponed. Marshal Zhukov's great counter-attack had been launched on 5 December, and two days later the Japanese attacked Pearl Harbor. Time was needed to assess the implications of these momentous events, and then on 11 December Hitler announced to the Reichstag his declaration of war on the United States. The following day, he summoned Nazi Party leaders to a meeting in the Reich Chancellery. There, he referred to his prophecy of 30 January 1939, that if a world war ensued, 'the instigators of this bloody conflict will thus have to pay for it with their lives'.

With Hitler's declaration of war and the Japanese attacks in the Far East, the conflict had become truly global. In Hitler's distorted logic, the Jews had to suffer for their guilt. 'The Führer is determined to make a clean sweep,' Goebbels wrote in his diary for 12 December. 'He prophesied to the Jews that if they were once again to cause a world war, the result would be their own destruction. That was no figure of speech. The world war is here, the destruction of Jewry must be the inevitable consequence. This question is to be viewed without sentimentality.'

Less than a week later, Hitler had a meeting with Himmler to discuss the 'Jewish question'. Yet despite a heightened, even feverish, atmosphere, when Hitler frequently referred back to his pre-war prediction that the Jews were bringing their own destruction upon themselves, he still does not appear to have made an irrevocable decision on a 'Final Solution'. Despite his apocalyptic diatribes against the Jews, he does seem to have been remarkably reluctant to hear details of mass killings, rather as he shied away from any image of suffering in battle or from bombing. His desire to keep violence abstract was a significant psychological paradox in one who had done more than almost anyone else in history to promote it.

After the delay, Heydrich's conference finally took place on 20 January 1942, in offices of the RSHA in a large villa on the shore of the Wannsee on the south-western edge of Berlin. SS Ober-gruppenführer Heydrich presided, and SS Obersturmbannführer Eichmann took notes. Apart from other members of the RSHA, most of those present were senior representatives from the occupied territories, the Reichschancellery, and four *Staatssekretäre*, the head officials of key ministries. They included Dr Roland Freisler of the justice ministry, who later became notorious as the persecutor of the July plotters. The foreign ministry was represented by Unterstaatssekretär Martin Luther, the namesake of a far more famous and influential anti-semite. He arrived with a carefully prepared memorandum entitled 'Requests and Ideas of the Foreign Ministry in Connection with the Intended Final Solution of the Jewish Question in Europe'. Just over half of those present had doctorates, and a significant minority were lawyers.

Heydrich began by asserting his powers for the preparation of the Final Solution over all territories and official functions. He presented statistics on all Jewish communities throughout Europe, including even British Jews, who would be 'evacuated to the east'. Their numbers – his estimated total was eleven million – would first be whittled down through hard labour, then the survivors would be 'treated accordingly'. Elderly Jews and those who had fought for the Kaiser would be sent to the show camp of Theresienstadt in Bohemia.

Luther, on behalf of the foreign ministry, urged caution and delay in the rounding up of Jews in countries such as Denmark and Norway, where this might provoke an international reaction. Much time was then spent arguing over the complicated question of those of partial Jewish descent – the so-called *Mischlinge* – and those married to Aryans. Perhaps predictably, the representative of the Generalgouvernement urged that its Jews should be dealt with first. Finally, while they drank brandy after lunch, the participants discussed the various methods available of achieving their objective. But the minutes of the meeting retained the usual euphemisms, such as 'evacuation' and 'resettlement'.

One thing, however, was clear to everyone involved. All ideas of a 'territorial solution' had come to nothing. With Stalin's erratic general offensive following the Battle of Moscow, there was no suitable area of the occupied Soviet territories where the Jews could be dumped to starve. The only certain solution now seemed to be industrialized slaughter.

A great impatience to get on with tackling the task permeated the Nazi administration, both in Berlin and, especially, in Hans Frank's fiefdom of the Generalgouvernement. And Gauleiter Arthur Greiser wanted to eliminate 35,000 Poles suffering from tuberculosis in the Warthegau. SS lawyers even discussed the possibility of killing German and other prisoners who had the misfortune to look 'like the miscarriages of hell'. During the 'Shoah by bullets', 'the killers in the occupied USSR moved to [find] the victims', but in the 'Shoah by gas' 'the victims were brought to the killers'. This process began to be put into effect initially in the extermination camps of Chełmno (Kulmhof) where gas vans were used, and continued in Bełżec, Treblinka, Sobibór and then Auschwitz-Birkenau in the summer.

A formidable administrative apparatus was set up to cope with the Jews who had not yet died in the ghettos or been shot. Eichmann, who was responsible for rounding up all the Jewish populations outside Poland, worked closely with Gruppenführer Heinrich Müller, the head of the Gestapo. Eichmann, another who loved the violin, played chess with Müller once a week while they continued to mull over their immense task. The most essential element in the operation was transport.

Planning and timetables were of critical importance. The Reichsbahn, with 1.4 million employees, was the largest organization in Germany after the Wehrmacht, and it made a considerable profit. Jews were transported in freight cars and cattle wagons at the same price as fare-paying passengers, in coaches on a one-way ticket. Journeys for the guards from the Ordnungspolizei were charged on the basis of return fares. The Gestapo took the money to pay for this from Jewish funds. But the ideological obsession of Hitler, Himmler and Heydrich often proved totally at odds with the conduct of the war they were trying to win. The Wehrmacht began to complain about the elimination of skilled Jewish labour in the armaments industry and the huge diversion of rail transport, when it was so badly needed to resupply the eastern front.

Jewish community leaders were told to organize their own policing of the 'relocation', with the threat that if they did not do it, then the SA or the SS would do it instead. They knew what that signified in terms of broken heads. They also had to draw up lists for the 'transports'. Those sent to the Ostland were executed by shooting on arrival mainly in Minsk, Kaunas and Riga. The majority, depending on their point of departure, were soon despatched to the extermination camps. The elderly and 'privileged' Jews sent to Theresienstadt did not know that their death sentence was merely in abeyance.

Ordnungspolizei and Gestapo men employed in clearing the ghettos were allocated a ration of brandy. Ukrainian auxiliaries were not. Those Jews who tried to hide or escape were shot on the spot. So too were the old who could not move to the transports unaided. The vast majority departed in the railway wagons, apparently accepting their fate. But a number managed to escape from the trains into the woods. Some were helped by Poles and others managed to join partisan groups.

Nazi concentration camps had been set up soon after Hitler's seizure of power in 1933. Himmler organized one of the first for political prisoners at Dachau just north of Munich, and soon he took over the administration of all such camps. The guards came from the *Totenkopfverbände* or Death's Head Units and received their name from the skull cap-badge they wore. In 1940, when the scale of the camp network expanded dramatically following the conquest of Poland, Obergruppenführer Oswald Pohl created his own sub-empire within the SS, turning labour camps into a means of raising revenue. He also became a key figure in the development of the camp system.

Although tests had been carried out with Zyklon B at Auschwitz in September 1941, the first extermination camp with proper gas chambers constructed under Pohl's direction was Bełżec. Work began in November 1941, two months before the Wannsee conference. The preparation of others rapidly followed. The work of the extermination camps was greatly assisted by the expertise of those who had been involved in the euthanasia programme under the direction of the Reichschancellery.

Some have argued that the production-line method of the extermination camps was strongly influenced by Henry Ford, who in turn had obtained his ideas from the Chicago slaughterhouses. Ford, who had been a ferocious anti-semite since 1920, was revered by Hitler and other leading Nazis. He may even have helped fund the Nazi Party, but nobody has managed to obtain documentary evidence of this. In any case, his book *The International Jew* had been translated and published in Germany, where it had a great influence in Nazi circles. Hitler kept a portrait of Ford hanging on the wall in his office in Munich, and in 1938 awarded him the Grand Cross of the Supreme Order of the German Eagle. But there is no real evidence that the Ford production-line techniques were copied in the extermination camps.

By the end of 1942, close to four million Jews from western and central Europe as well as the Soviet Union would be killed in the extermination camps, along with 40,000 Roma. The active participation of the Wehrmacht, officials in almost every ministry, a large part of industry and the transport system spread the guilt to a degree which German society took a long time to acknowledge in the post-war years.

The Nazi regime did everything that it could to keep the extermination process secret, but many tens of thousands were involved. Himmler, speaking to senior SS officers in October 1943, described it as 'an unwritten, and never to be written, page of glory in our history'. Rumours spread rapidly, especially after the photographs taken by soldiers of mass executions of Jews in the Soviet Union. At first, most civilians could not believe that Jews were being killed by production-line gassing. But so many Germans were involved in various aspects of the Final Solution, and so many were profiting from the confiscation of Jewish property, both businesses and apartments, that a large minority of Germans soon had a fairly good idea of what was happening.

Although a certain amount of sympathy had been shown to Jews when they were forced to wear the yellow star, once the deportations began Jews became non-persons in the eyes of their fellow citizens. Germans preferred not to dwell on their fate. This, they later persuaded themselves, was due to ignorance when it was in truth much closer to denial. As Ian Kershaw wrote: 'the road to Auschwitz was built by hatred, but paved with indifference'.

German civilians, on the other hand, had little idea of the infamous medical experiments at Auschwitz carried out by Dr Josef Mengele and his colleagues. Even today, those carried out on Russian, Polish, Roma, Czech, Yugoslav, Dutch and German political prisoners at Dachau by SS doctors are comparatively unknown. More than 12,000 died, usually in agony, as a result of tests and practice operations and amputations. The victims included those injected with diseases, but also at the request of the Luftwaffe, those subjected to extremes of high and low pressure, immersed in freezing water as research for aircrew shot down over the sea, force-fed salt water and subjected to liver-puncture experiments. In addition, prisoners in the autopsy room were forced by SS personnel to remove and treat the good-quality skin of corpses (but not those of Germans) 'for use as saddles, riding breeches, gloves, house slippers and ladies' handbags'.

In Danzig at the Anatomical Medical Institute, Professor Rudolf Spanner had 'Poles, Russians and Uzbeks' killed at the nearby concentration camp of Stutthof so that he could carry out experiments on recycling their corpses to make soap and leather. Such a mentality in a doctor may be beyond our comprehension, but as a traumatized Vasily Grossman observed after describing the horrors of Treblinka: 'It is the writer's duty to tell this terrible truth, and it is the civilian duty of the reader to learn it.'

*

Despite the progressive industrialization of the Final Solution, the 'Shoah by bullets' still continued in both the Reichskommissariat Ostland and the Reichskommissariat Ukraine. Even Jews who had been retained as specialist workers were rounded up and shot. Throughout the early spring and summer of 1942, the SS *Einsatzgruppen* and the nine regiments of Ordnungspolizei competed to eliminate all Jews in their respective areas through 'Grossaktionen'. In July, a German paymaster wrote home: 'In Bereza-Kartuska where I took my midday break, 1,300 Jews had been shot the day before. They were taken to a hollow outside the town. Men, women and children were forced to undress completely and were dealt with by a shot through the back of the head. Their clothes were disinfected for reuse. I am convinced that if the war lasts much longer Jews will be processed into sausage and be served up to Russian prisoners of war or to qualified Jewish workers.'

Ghetto after ghetto was surrounded. Some Jewish businessmen tried to buy their survival with bribes. 'Jewish girls who wanted to save their lives offered themselves to policemen. As a rule, the women were used during the night and killed in the morning.' The police and their auxiliaries moved in during the early hours or just before dawn, under the glare of searchlights or flares. Many Jews tried to conceal themselves under floors, but the killers rolled hand-grenades under the shacks. In some cases, the buildings were set on fire.

Those rounded up were taken off to the execution pits, where they too were made to strip before being shot on the edge, or forced to lie down in the 'sardine' method. Once again, the killers were amazed by the submission of the Jews. Many executioners were drunk and failed to finish their victims off. Quite a number of them were buried alive. Some even managed to dig themselves out afterwards.

Not all were submissive. The 'forest Jews' who had escaped the round-ups either joined Soviet partisan groups or formed their own, especially in Belorussia. Anti-partisan sweeps under the command of Bach continued into the spring of 1944. In Lwów and the rest of Galicia, German security police and Ukrainian Hilfspolizei, known as Hipos, continued the killings. Attempts to form resistance groups in ghettos were seldom successful until the desperate rising of the Warsaw ghetto in January 1943. There were attempts at resistance in the ghettos of Lwów and Białystok, but nothing on the scale or determination of Warsaw.

Jews who had initially argued against resistance now knew the truth. The Germans wanted them all dead. After the deportation of more than 300,000 Jews during 1942, only 70,000 were left in the Warsaw ghetto. Most of those remaining were young and comparatively strong. The sick and old had been taken away already. The different Jewish political groups, Bundists, Communists and Zionists, agreed to fight back. They began by killing collaborators, and then prepared defensive positions linked to the sewers. Weapons and explosives were obtained from the Home Army, or Armia Krajowa, which was loyal to the government-in-exile, and also from the Polish Communist resistance, the People's Guard. A few hundred pistols and revolvers were bought from citizens in Warsaw who had kept them hidden despite the risk of execution. In January 1943, the first armed clash occurred when the Germans rounded up 6,500 Jews for deportation.

An enraged Himmler ordered that the whole Warsaw ghetto should be destroyed. But it was not until 19 April that the main attempt to storm the area took place. Waffen-SS troops entered from the north end, where prisoners were loaded on to cattle trucks in the sidings. The attackers soon withdrew with their wounded after coming under heavy fire and losing their only armoured vehicle to a Molotov cocktail. Himmler was appalled when he heard of their repulse and he sacked the commander. From then on, the SS attacked with small raiding groups at different points.

After a doomed defence of the factories which the Germans set on fire with flamethrowers, the Jewish defenders pulled back into the sewers, from where they would emerge to shoot at German troops from behind. The SS pumped in water in attempts to drown them, but the Jewish fighters managed to avoid or divert the flood. Others had seized a large building used by an armaments firm and defended it. Brigadeführer Jürgen Stroop ordered his men to set the building on fire. When Jews threw themselves from the top floors, the SS troopers called them 'parachutists' and tried to shoot them before they hit the ground.

After the war, Stroop still seemed to be excited by the fighting, which he described to his cellmate in prison. 'The uproar was monstrous,' he said, 'burning houses, smoke, flames, flying sparks, whirling bed feathers, the stench of singed bodies, thunder of guns, cracking grenades, the glow of fire, Jews with their wives and children leaping from windows and burning houses.' He admitted, however, that the 'battle-courage' of the Jews had taken him and his men entirely by surprise.

The bitter resistance continued for nearly a month until 16 May. Thousands had died in the battle, and 7,000 of the 56,065 prisoners were executed immediately. The remainder were sent to Treblinka for gassing, or to forced-labour battalions to be worked to death. The ghetto was razed to the ground. Vasily Grossman, who entered Warsaw with the Red Army in January 1945, described the scene: 'Waves of stone, crushed bricks, a sea of brick. There isn't a single wall intact – the beast's anger was terrible.'

20

Japanese Occupation and the
Battle of Midway

FEBRUARY–JUNE 1942

The Japanese occupation of Hong Kong had begun with intentions of moderation, yet rapidly became violent and uncontrolled. While European victims suffered comparatively little, drunken Japanese soldiers continued to rape and kill the local population, underlining the hypocrisy in their slogan 'Asia for the Asians'. The Japanese showed a certain respect for their fellow imperialists, the British, but none for other Asian races, especially the Chinese. A senior officer is said to have ordered the execution of the nine soldiers guilty of the rape of British nurses at the hospital in Happy Valley. Nothing was done to restrict the violent abuse of Chinese women.

There was almost no restriction on looting, either by Japanese soldiers or by the Triads and supporters of the puppet Nanking regime of Wang Ching-wei who were used as irregular police. In return, the military authorities allowed the Triads to set up gambling dens. Smaller-scale criminal gangs also operated with impunity. The Japanese made an attempt to win over the Indian community, encouraging hatred of the British and giving them a privileged status with better rations. Sikhs and Rajputs were recruited for the police and even given guns. A policy of divide and rule between the Indian and Chinese communities continued until the end of 1942, when after a falling out between the Japanese and the Indian Independence League in Singapore, the Japanese suddenly removed the Indians' privileges and they found themselves worse off than they had been under the British. Under the brutal regime of the Kempeitai military security police, the Hong Kong Chinese, even including the Triads, soon began to feel almost a nostalgia for British rule.

The new Japanese governor sought to win over the Eurasians and prominent Chinese merchant families to get the port's economy flourishing again. At the same time senior Japanese officers, excited by the contents of the godowns or warehouses, organized a more systematic form of looting, partly for personal profit, but also as war booty to be sent back to Tokyo. As in many places occupied by Japanese forces, the situation became even more confused by rivalries between the navy and the army. The army wanted Hong Kong as a base for furthering the war against Chiang Kai-shek's Nationalists, while the navy planned to use the port to assist its expansion to the south.

Shanghai, which had been rapidly occupied by the Japanese on 8 December 1941, came nominally under the puppet government in Nanking of Wang Ching-wei. In the city port of big business, glittering corruption, prostitution and dance halls, conditions deteriorated drastically for the remaining Europeans, the White Russian community and especially the Chinese poor. A cholera epidemic killed thousands, food was hard to find and the black market was rampant.

Anything and almost everyone was for sale. Shanghai was the spying capital of the Far East. The Abwehr and the Gestapo spied on the Japanese, who in turn spied on them. Japanese distrust of their ally had increased enormously since their arrest of the German Communist spy Richard Sorge in October 1941. But the Japanese occupation forces suffered from their own intense rivalries. Hell hath no fury like competing intelligence agencies.

In Singapore on 17 February 1942, the Kempeitai military police rounded up the Straits Chinese community. They were to be punished for having supported Nationalist China in its resistance. General Yamashita ordered the whole community to pay $50 million as a 'gift of atonement'. Any male between twelve and fifty was liable to be shot. Many of them were taken bound to Changi Beach where they were machine-gunned. The Kempeitai admitted to having executed no fewer than 6,000 for being 'anti-Japanese', but the true figure was many times that, especially if executions on the mainland are included. Victims under this definition were supposedly Communists or former servants of the British. The Japanese also killed anyone with tattoos on the assumption that they belonged to a criminal society.

Around Changi barracks, the stores of barbed wire which

should have been used by the British to create defences were now used to hold Allied prisoners of war. They were forced out to line the streets for a victory parade to honour General Yamashita, now known as 'the Tiger of Malaya'. Raffles Hotel was turned into a brothel for senior officers. The comfort women there had either been imported forcibly from Korea or were beautiful young Chinese girls seized off the street.

Most of the European women and male civilians were interned separately at Changi Jail. Two thousand people were forced into accommodation designed for 600. Bribery was the only way for prisoners to improve rations or purchase medicines. The polished rice they received had little nutritional value, and soon there were many cases of beriberi among the increasingly emaciated British and Australian prisoners of war. Among their guards were Koreans and anti-British Sikhs who had deserted during the fighting and then volunteered to serve the Japanese. With bitter memories of the Amritsar massacre, they now enjoyed humiliating their former overlords. Some followed the Japanese custom of slapping their faces if they did not bow to their guards, and a few even acted as firing squads for the Japanese. In Singapore city, meanwhile, looters and thieves were beheaded and their heads displayed on poles as in medieval times. To be buried with part of your body missing was considered the worst possible fate in the Far East.

Many Malays had believed Japanese propaganda claims that the Imperial Army would bring their liberation and they welcomed the troops, waving small rising-sun flags. They soon found this to be far from the truth. Japanese carpetbaggers and racketeers arrived to dabble in every form of dubious business, dance-halls, drugs, prostitution and gambling.

In the Dutch East Indies, the Japanese military authorities were furious to find that most of the oil installations had been destroyed before surrender. The Dutch and other Europeans faced a terrible revenge. In Borneo and Java, almost all the white male civilians were shot or decapitated, and many of their wives and daughters gang-raped. Both Dutch and Javanese women were forced into comfort houses and given a daily 'quota of twenty enlisted men in the morning, two NCOs in the afternoon and the senior officers at night'. If these press-ganged young comfort women managed to run away or were uncooperative, they would be brutally punished and their parents or family would suffer. Altogether, it is estimated that the Imperial Japanese Army press-ganged up to 100,000 girls and young women into sexual slavery. A large number were Korean and sent overseas to Japanese garrisons in the Pacific and round the South China Sea, but Malay, Straits Chinese, Filipina and Javanese women as well as those of other nationalities were also seized by the Kempeitai. The policy of using the women of conquered nations as a resource for their soldiers was clearly approved at the most senior levels in the Japanese government.

A young nationalist called Achmed Sukarno served as a propagandist and adviser to the Japanese military authorities, hoping that they would grant the former Dutch colony independence. After the war, instead of being accused of collaboration, he became the first president of Indonesia, despite the fact that tens of thousands of his fellow citizens had suffered from starvation. Some five million people in south-east Asia are thought to have died from the Japanese occupation during the war. At least a million of them were Vietnamese. Rice paddies were forcibly converted to other crops for the Japanese, and rice and grain were seized to make fuel alcohol.

Political parties and a free press were all banned. The Kempeitai, using its cruelly unsophisticated torture techniques, took revenge on any attempt at subversion or even the slightest hint of 'anti-Japanese' attitudes. In a programme of Nipponization, the Japanese language and the Japanese calendar were imposed in some places. Occupied countries were looted of food and raw materials and unemployment rose to such an extent that the Greater East Asia Co-Prosperity Sphere was soon known as the 'Co-Poverty Sphere'. The Japanese occupation currency was regarded as a bad joke when inflation rose uncontrollably.

In Burma, many Burmese initially welcomed the Japanese in the hope of independence, although the ethnically different tribes in the north remained loyal to the British. The Japanese raised a force of nearly 30,000 to serve in their Burmese National Army, but they treated them as inferior. Even Burmese officers were expected to salute Japanese privates. The Japanese also recruited some 7,000 Indians from among those captured in Malaya and Singapore for the Indian National Army, which would supposedly be used to liberate their country from British colonial rule.

British and Australian prisoners of war in Singapore were sent north to work on the infamous Burma Railway, however sick, weak and emaciated they were. They suffered from blackwater fever, beriberi, dysentery, diphtheria, dengue fever, malaria and pellagra. No medical supplies were provided, and wound sepsis rapidly set in when flesh was torn by thorns while clearing jungle. Prisoners had to bow not just to officers, but also to private soldiers. Their faces were slapped or they were beaten with the flat of a sword by an NCO or officer. Insubordination or subversion was punished by a favourite torture. After the prisoner had been force-fed water to bursting point, guards would stake him out, spread-eagled on the ground, then jump on his stomach. Any prisoner recaptured after a failed attempt to escape usually faced a public beheading.

Japanese guards yelled 'Speedo! Speedo!' at their exhausted victims, thrashing them to work harder. Starved, thirsty and bitten by insects, the prisoners of war worked almost naked in the terrible heat. Many collapsed from dehydration. Altogether a third of the 46,000 Allied prisoners of war died, but conditions were even worse for the 150,000 local forced labourers, of whom around half died.

The Japanese occupation of French Indochina did not change greatly after the original agreement with Admiral Darlan signed at Vichy on 29 July 1941. A further agreement on the defence of Indochina was signed by the governor-general Admiral Jean Decoux in December, and the French administration which recognized Vichy continued in place until March 1945. The main difference was that with Indochina effectively cut off from France, the country came into the Japanese economic sphere. Some nationalist groups sided with the Japanese in the hope of obtaining independence from France, but the Japanese commander ensured the continuance of the French colonial regime. Roosevelt, on the other hand, was determined that Indochina should not be handed back to France at the end of the war.

On 9 April 1942, just before Major General Edward King Jr surrendered the American and Filipino forces on the Bataan Peninsula, he asked Colonel Nakayama Motoo whether his men would be well treated. Nakayama retorted that they were not barbarians. Yet Japanese officers had not expected to take so many prisoners on Bataan. Indoctrinated from the day they joined the army to believe in the Bushido code that a soldier never capitulates, they regarded any enemy who surrendered as unworthy of respect. In a flagrant paradox, their anger was even greater towards enemies who had put up a ferocious defence.

Of the 76,000 Americans and Filipinos, at least 6,000 were too sick or wounded to walk. Already filthy, emaciated and exhausted from fighting for so long on starvation rations, some 70,000 men were forced forward on the hundred-kilometre march to Camp O'Donnell. The 'Bataan death march' was a grotesque contradiction of Nakayama's assurance. Beaten and robbed of everything they possessed, tortured by thirst and denied food, forced on by jabs from bayonets, the prisoners were subjected to deliberate cruelty to exact revenge and inflict humiliation. Over the days which followed, few of their guards allowed them to rest in the shade or lie down. More than 7,000 American and Filipino soldiers from Bataan died. Some 400 Filipino officers and NCOs of the 91st Division were killed with swords in a massacre on 12 April at Batanga. Of the 63,000 who made it alive to the camp, hundreds more died each day. Also 2,000 of the survivors of Corregidor died from hunger or disease in their first two months of captivity.

The series of disasters, surrenders and humiliations inflicted on the Allies prompted the disdain of the Chinese Nationalists, who had been resisting far greater Japanese armies for four years. The British had refused to ask for their help in defending Hong Kong, and had failed to arm the Chinese and allow them to defend themselves. This gravely undermined their claim to the colony, in the event of victory over the Japanese. The Chungking government of Chiang Kai-shek was, in any case, resolutely opposed to a foreign presence in the treaty ports. The administration of President Roosevelt sympathized strongly with such anti-colonial attitudes, and American public opinion supported the idea that the United States should not help to restore the British, French and Dutch possessions in the Far East.

British failure to resist the Japanese was largely blamed on their colonialist behaviour. However tempting an explanation at the time, it was far from the whole truth when the major part of the nation's war effort had to be concentrated on the other side of the wall. In the first half of 1942, the British government nearly gave in to pressure from Washington and Chungking to renounce Hong Kong, but later in the year London would agree only to discuss the handover at the end of the war. The Nationalists, convinced that their forces would occupy the city first, did not press the matter.

Chiang Kai-shek believed that, since Britain was no longer a great power in the Far East, Nationalist China should now be recognized as one. Roosevelt was happy to comply, but he knew that Stalin would not accept China joining the 'Big Three'. And Chiang, ever the realist, knew that whatever his feelings about the British he would need Churchill's support, which partly explains his flexibility over the postponement of discussions on Hong Kong. On the other hand, the Nationalists were enraged that Britain's Special Operations Executive was working with Chinese Communist guerrillas in south China on the East River and in the New Territories of Hong Kong. The Communists helped British prisoners of war who escaped from the colony. One party was treated to a feast of goose and rice wine round a fire, during which an officer taught the Communist guerrillas to sing 'The British Grenadiers' and 'The Eton Boating Song'.

In India, relations between the British and the Congress Party, which wanted independence for the country, had deteriorated badly. Lord Linlithgow, the viceroy, proved both arrogant and inept, politically and economically. In 1939, he had made no effort to consult the leaders of the Congress Party and obtain their support for the war. Churchill was no better, with his romantic notions of empire and the Raj. Forced against his will to send a mission to India led by Sir Stafford Cripps, his least favourite politician, Churchill hated the idea of offering Dominion status to India once the war was over. Mahatma Gandhi famously described the proposal as a 'post-dated cheque' and Congress leaders were unimpressed. On 8 August 1942, prompted by Gandhi, Congress issued a call to the British to 'Quit India' at once, but to keep their troops there as defence against the Japanese. Next morning, the British authorities arrested its leaders. Demonstrations and riots followed, with a thousand people killed and a hundred thousand thrown into jail. The disturbances confirmed Churchill in his prejudice that the Indians were ungrateful and treacherous.

The loss of Burma to the Japanese in the spring of 1942 reduced India's supplies of rice by 15 per cent. Prices shot up. Traders and merchants, in the hope of pushing up the price further, hoarded supplies, and an inflationary spiral began. The poor simply could not afford to eat. The government in New Delhi did nothing to control this ferocious black market. It simply passed the responsibility to regional administrations which reacted with 'insane provincial protectionism'. Those with surpluses, such as Madras, refused to sell to those with acute shortages of grain.

Bengal bore the brunt of the gathering disaster. At least 1.5 million died as a direct result of the famine which began at the end of 1942 and lasted all through the following year. A similar number again are estimated to have perished through disease – cholera, malaria and smallpox – because they were so malnourished that they had no resistance. Churchill, already furious with India, refused to interfere with the shipping programme to bring relief. Only when Field Marshal Wavell was made viceroy in September 1943 did the government of India begin to get a firm grip on the problem by using troops to distribute food reserves. Wavell made himself even more unpopular with Churchill by pursuing this policy. The whole episode was probably the most shameful in the history of the British Raj. If nothing else, it completely undermined the imperialist argument that British rule protected the poor of India from the rich.

The Japanese attack on Pearl Harbor had one saving grace for the Americans. It was their battleships, and not their aircraft carriers, that had been in port that fateful weekend. Admiral Yamamoto, the most far-sighted of senior Japanese commanders, had not joined in the jubilation after the attack for this very reason.

In Washington, uncertainty reigned in the offices of the Main Navy Building. The desire to hit back was overwhelming, but the badly battered Pacific Fleet needed to exercise caution. Fleet Admiral Ernest J. King, the new commander-in-chief, was famously irascible. He was furious that the British had persuaded General Marshall and Roosevelt to adopt the 'Germany first' policy, which meant that the Pacific theatre was obliged to go on to the defensive. British officers felt that King was a confirmed anglophobe, but their American counterparts reassured them that Admiral King was not prejudiced. He simply hated everybody.

The naval staff in Washington decided that it was too dangerous to send a carrier task force to relieve Wake Island. The three task force commanders bitterly resented the decision, but it was almost certainly the right one at the time. In late December 1941, Admiral Chester W. Nimitz arrived in Pearl Harbor to take over as the new commander-in-chief Pacific Fleet. The unfortunate Admiral Kimmel was still there, waiting to hear his fate, although he was treated with great sympathy by his colleagues. The most senior levels of the US Navy suffered remarkably little from rivalries and prima-donna ego clashes. Nimitz was an inspired choice for the post. A white-haired Texan descended from impoverished German nobility, he was soft-spoken, decisive and able to get things moving with quiet authority. Not surprisingly, he inspired great loyalty and trust. This was particularly useful at a time when Washington had not yet developed a clear approach to the war in the Pacific.

Washington did, however, insist on launching a raid on Tokyo to raise morale. This was to be led by Lieutenant Colonel James Doolittle of the Army Air Corps, with B-25 medium bombers flown off a carrier for the first time. Vice Admiral William F. Halsey set off on 8 April 1942, with the carriers *Enterprise* and *Hornet*. Halsey welcomed the chance to hit back, but Nimitz was dubious about an operation which sacrificed so many bombers for a gesture that caused little damage to the enemy. He was also concerned about having sufficient forces available to counter the next Japanese offensive, expected somewhere around the Solomon Islands and New Guinea. This was in the south-west Pacific region which was under the command of General MacArthur.

Commander Joseph Rochefort, the chief cryptanalyst at Pearl Harbor, had helped break the Japanese naval code in 1940. An unconventional officer, usually attired in carpet slippers and a red smoking jacket, Rochefort had not been able to warn of the attack on Pearl Harbor due to the strict radio silence imposed on the Japanese carrier fleet. Fortunately for the US Navy, Rochefort had now been able to decode a signal which revealed that the

Japanese were planning to land on the south-eastern edge of New Guinea in May and seize the airfield at Port Moresby. This would give their air force control over the Coral Sea and enable them to attack northern Australia at will.

With the huge distances involved in the Pacific, refuelling at sea presented a critical challenge for both sides. Each US task force of two carriers and escort vessels had to sail with at least one tanker or 'oiler', which Japanese submarines would target first. But, as the war progressed, US Navy submarines proved to be the most cost-efficient way of destroying Japanese freighters and tankers. This effort, in which US submarines accounted for 55 per cent of all Japanese vessels sunk, had a devastating effect on naval and land forces short of fuel and supplies.

Halsey, who had returned from launching the Tokyo raid, was the obvious candidate to lead this first major counter-attack. On 30 April 1942, he sailed with Task Force 16. But, as Nimitz suspected, Task Force 17 commanded by Vice Admiral Frank J. Fletcher, which was already operating in the Coral Sea, would face the bulk of the fighting before Halsey arrived.

On 3 May, a Japanese force landed on Tulagi in the Solomon Islands. The Japanese commanders were supremely confident that they would crush any American naval force in the Coral Sea south of New Guinea and the Solomons. Fletcher, supported by Australian and New Zealand warships, sailed north-westwards on hearing that another Japanese force was heading for Port Moresby in New Guinea. Confusion followed on both sides, but aircraft from the USS *Lexington* sighted the Japanese carrier *Shohu* and sank her. Japanese aircraft thought they had found the American carrier force and sank a destroyer and a tanker.

On 8 May, the American and Japanese carriers launched strikes against each other. The aircraft from *Yorktown* managed to damage the *Shokaku* enough to render her incapable of launching any more planes, while the Japanese hit both the *Lexington* and the *Yorktown*. The Japanese, unable to protect their invasion fleet, decided to withdraw from Port Moresby, much to Admiral Yamamoto's disgust. The *Lexington*, which had appeared to recover, then began to sink after explosions caused by leaking fuel.

The Coral Sea battle was a partial success for the Americans since it prevented a landing, while the Japanese convinced themselves that their enemy had received a 'beating'. In any case, it provoked much thought on the American side about technical defects in their aircraft and armament. Most were unresolved by the time the next engagement took place.

Admiral Yamamoto, well aware of the United States' potential to produce aircraft carriers more rapidly than Japan, wanted to get in a knockout blow before his fleet lost the initiative. An attack on the island base of Midway would force the few American carriers into battle. After the Doolittle Raid on Japan, critics in the naval general staff in Tokyo had now suddenly come round to his point of view. Signals intercepts analysed by Commander Rochefort and his colleagues indicated that the Japanese were about to turn west and north to attack the Midway Islands. This would suggest that they wished to establish a base from which to attack Pearl Harbor itself. The naval staff in Washington rejected this idea, but Nimitz summoned all available warships back to Pearl Harbor at best speed.

By 26 May, when the main Japanese invasion fleet left Saipan in the Marianas, its destination was no longer in any doubt. Rochefort had set a signals trap, sending a message in clear to say that Midway was short of water. This was repeated in a Japanese message on 20 May using the letters 'AF' to identify Midway. Since previous references using this code had signified their principal objective, Nimitz now knew for certain what Yamamoto's overall plan was. This offered the opportunity of evading the massive trap ahead and turning it to his advantage. Halsey was suffering from a stress-related illness and had to go into hospital. So Nimitz chose Rear Admiral Raymond Spruance, a fitness fanatic, to command Task Force 16.

On 28 May, Spruance sailed from Pearl Harbor with the carriers *Enterprise* and *Hornet*, escorted by two cruisers and six destroyers. Fletcher, who was to have overall command, left two days later with two cruisers, six destroyers and the *Yorktown*, which had been repaired with astonishing speed. The American warships had departed just in time. A line of Japanese submarines, hoping to ambush them, took up station between Hawaii and Midway hours after the two task forces had passed by.

Spruance and Fletcher faced a formidable array. The Imperial Japanese Navy had four fleets at sea, with eleven battleships, eight carriers, twenty-three cruisers, sixty-five destroyers and twenty submarines. Three task forces were heading for Midway and one for the Aleutian Islands some 3,200 kilometres to the north round the bottom edge of the Bering Sea. The Japanese believed that the Americans were 'not aware of our plans'.

On 3 June, shore-based aircraft from Midway were the first to sight Japanese ships approaching from the south-west. The next day, the Japanese launched their first air attacks on Midway. US Army Air Force bombers and Marine dive-bombers from Midway responded. They suffered terrible losses and failed to score many hits, which increased Japanese complacency. Admiral Nagumo Chuichi, the commander of the Japanese task force, still had no idea of the presence of American carriers. Yamamoto on the other hand now suspected they might be there after a signal from Tokyo warning of increased signals traffic from Pearl Harbor, but he did not want to break radio silence.

For the young American flyers operating over the seemingly endless blue of the Pacific, the prospect of such a battle was both exhilarating and terrifying. Many of the pilots were barely out of flying school, and lacked the experience of their opponents, but these young, sunburned and enthusiastic aviators demonstrated an astonishing courage. It was bad enough to be shot down over the sea, but to be picked up by a Japanese warship meant almost certain execution by beheading.

The Japanese Zero fighter was superior to the stubby Grumman F4F Wildcat, but the Wildcat could survive a lot of damage, because it had self-sealing petrol tanks when hit. American torpedo bombers and dive-bombers stood little chance against the Zeros unless they had a fighter escort. The obsolete Douglas TBD Devastator torpedo bomber was slow and its torpedo seldom worked, so to attack a Japanese warship was close to a suicide mission for the pilot. The Douglas SBD Dauntless dive-bomber, on the other hand, was far more effective, especially in a near vertical dive, as events were soon to prove.

A Catalina flying-boat sighted the Japanese carrier force and passed back its position. Fletcher ordered Spruance to join his aircraft in an attack. Spruance's task force went to full speed. Their targets were at maximum range for his torpedo bombers, but the risk was worth while if he could catch the Japanese carriers just before they launched their aircraft. Due to confusion, the Devastator torpedo bombers arrived first and without fighter cover. They were massacred by Zero fighters. The Japanese assumed that they had achieved a victory, but their elation was premature.

'Service crews cheered the returning pilots, patted them on the shoulder and shouted words of encouragement,' wrote the naval air commander Fuchida Mitsuo on the *Akagi*. Planes were rearmed and others hoisted from the hangar to the flight deck, to be ready for a counter-strike against the US carriers. Admiral Nagumo now decided to wait until the Nakajima torpedo bombers were rearmed with ground-attack bombs for another strike against Midway. Some historians argue that this caused a critical delay and was unnecessary. Others point out that it was standard practice not to launch until all types of planes were ready to operate together.

'At 10.20, Admiral Nagumo gave the order to launch when ready,' Fuchida continued. 'On *Akagi*'s flight deck all planes were in position with engines warming up. The big ship began turning into the wind. Within five minutes all her planes would be launched . . . At 10.24 the order to start launching came from the bridge by voice-tube. The air officer flapped a white flag and the first Zero fighter gathered speed and whizzed off the deck. At that instant a look-out screamed, "Hell-divers!" I looked up to see three black enemy planes plummeting towards our ship. Some of our machineguns managed to fire a few frantic bursts at them, but it was too late. The plump silhouettes of the American Dauntless dive-bombers quickly grew larger, and then a number of black objects suddenly floated eerily from their wings.'

The Dauntless dive-bombers from the *Enterprise* and from Fletcher's *Yorktown* had managed to conceal themselves in cloud at 3,000 metres, so surprise was complete and the flight deck of the *Akagi* presented the perfect target. Fully fuelled and armed aircraft exploded one after another. One bomb blew a huge hole in the flight deck, and another blasted the elevator for raising aircraft from the hangar below. Neither this hit nor the other on the rear port side of the flight deck would have been enough to sink the ship, but the exploding planes with their bombs and the torpedoes stacked near by reduced the *Akagi* to a blazing hulk. The

Emperor's portrait on board the *Akagi* was hastily transferred to a destroyer.

The *Kaga* near by was also mortally wounded, with black clouds billowing into the air. American dive-bombers then hit the *Soryu*. Gasoline spread, creating an inferno. Ammunition and bombs began to explode. Suddenly, an enormous blast hurled those on deck into the water. 'As soon as the fires broke out aboard ship,' Admiral Nagumo related, 'the captain, Yanagimoto Ryusaku, appeared on the signal tower to the starboard of the bridge. He took command from this post and pleaded that his men seek shelter and safety. He would allow no man to approach him. Flames surrounded him but he refused to give up his post. He was shouting "Banzai" over and over again when heroic death overtook him.'

Soon afterwards, the *Yorktown* was crippled by Japanese torpedo bombers. Her returning aircraft were diverted to Spruance's carriers, replacing some of their earlier losses. And in a later strike, planes from the *Enterprise* hit the *Hiryu*, which also sank. 'At 23.50,' Admiral Nagumo reported, 'Captain Kaki Tomeo and Squadron Commander Rear-Admiral Yamaguchi Tamon delivered messages to the crew. This was followed by expressions of reverence and respect to the Emperor, the shouting of Banzais, the lowering of the battle flag and command flag. At 00.15, all hands were ordered to abandon ship, His Imperial Highness's portrait was removed, and the transfer of personnel to the destroyers *Kazagumo* and *Makigumo* put underway. The transfer of portrait and men was completed at 01.30. After completion of the transfer operations, the Division Commander and Captain remained aboard ship. They waved their caps to their men and with complete composure joined their fate with that of their ship.'

Yamamoto, unaware of the disaster which had overtaken his carriers, ordered further attacks. His reaction can well be imagined when he was informed of the true situation. He ordered his massive fleet of ten battleships, including the *Yamato*, the largest warship afloat, and two escort carriers, with a host of cruiser and destroyer escorts, to engage with all speed. Spruance, aware of Yamamoto's force, changed course in the night back towards Midway to benefit from land-based air cover. The following day, his dive-bombers managed to sink one cruiser and severely damage another. But the damaged *Yorktown*, while salvage operations were proceeding on 6 June, was hit by torpedoes from a Japanese submarine and sank the following morning.

With four Japanese carriers and a cruiser sunk, and a battleship severely damaged, to say nothing of 250 aircraft destroyed, and all for the loss of one American carrier, Midway represented a decisive victory, and a clear turning point in the Pacific war. Yamamoto's hopes of smashing the US Pacific Fleet were completely dashed. But as Nimitz acknowledged in his report: 'Had we lacked early information of the Japanese movement, and had we been caught with Carrier Task Forces dispersed, possibly as far away as the Coral Sea, the Battle of Midway would have ended far differently.'

21

Defeat in the Desert

MARCH–SEPTEMBER 1942

After the humiliating retreat across Cyrenaica in January and February 1942, the Rommel myth, so fervently propagated by Goebbels, was also promoted by the British. The legend of the 'Desert Fox' was a very misguided attempt to explain away their own failures. Hitler was amazed and delighted by such hero-worship. It encouraged his belief that the British, after all their defeats in the Far East, were close to collapse.

He was, however, prepared to rein in his favourite general to appease the Italians. Mussolini's position was threatened by growing opposition within the Comando Supremo, whose members felt that the Duce was too much in Hitler's pocket. And they had been affronted by Rommel's arrogance and peremptory demands, to say nothing of his constant complaints about their failure to provide and protect the supply convoys he needed. In addition, Halder and the OKH were still resolutely opposed to reinforcing Rommel. They argued that the Suez Canal should be taken only after an advance through the Caucasus. The priority of the eastern front remained a powerful argument as they prepared their great offensive in southern Russia. Only the Kriegsmarine, which wanted a policy of defeating Britain first, supported Rommel's ambitions.

The island of Malta was in a desperate position after a renewed Luftwaffe bombing offensive against the airfields and the main harbour of Valletta. All five ships in a convoy in March were sunk and the troops and civilian population faced starvation. But in May a reinforcement of sixty Spitfires flown off the aircraft carrier USS *Wasp* and the arrival of a minelayer with supplies saved the island. Generalfeldmarschall Albert Kesselring, the German commander-in-chief in the Mediterranean, had made plans for an airborne invasion of Malta, Operation Hercules, but these had to be put aside. Not only was Hitler dubious of success, but X

Fliegerkorps was needed further east. Also the Italians demanded excessive support before committing themselves.

Rommel once again ignored both his orders and his supply problems, and began to move the Panzer Army Afrika forward towards the Gazala Line. 'The fighting has none of the horror, that indescribable misery of the Russian campaign,' an Unteroffizier wrote home in April. 'No villages and towns destroyed or laid waste.' In another letter that evening, he wrote to his mother: 'The Tommy out here takes everything in a more sporting way . . . Onwards to a decisive victory.' Although Rommel's soldiers were also afflicted by the mass of flies and the intense heat which baked their bread hard, they soon expected a victory from 'the great offensive in Russia, then the Tommies here will be crushed from both sides'. They looked forward to visiting Cairo.

The OKW then suddenly came round to the idea of Rommel's dream of seizing Egypt and the Suez Canal. Hitler had begun to fear that American military support might arrive earlier than he had originally thought. Even an Allied attack across the Channel could not be ruled out. If Rommel could smash the Eighth Army, he reasoned, British morale would be shattered. Also the Japanese had indicated that they would advance westwards into the Indian Ocean only if the Germans took the Suez Canal.

The first stage of Rommel's invasion of Egypt, codenamed Operation Theseus, was to outflank the British defensive line. This extended in defended boxes from Gazala on the coast, some eighty kilometres west of Tobruk, southwards to Bir Hakeim, an outpost in the desert defended by General Marie-Pierre Koenig's 1st Free French Brigade. There were seven boxes, each defended by an infantry brigade group, with artillery, barbed wire and minefields which extended down to the next box. To the rear, Ritchie had placed his armoured formations ready to make a counter-attack. Rommel then intended to seize Tobruk. The capture of this port was regarded as essential for resupply, otherwise it would take his Opel Blitz trucks fourteen days for each round trip up from Tripoli and back again.

Operation Theseus should not have taken the British unawares since Bletchley had passed the relevant Ultra decrypts to GHQ Middle East. But the chain of command was reluctant to pass the information down, except to say that an attack was probable in

May and that it might well take the form of a right hook from the south. The attack began on 26 May, with Italian infantry divisions advancing against the northern half of the line in a feint. To the south the Trieste Motorized Division and Ariete Armoured Division, together with the three German panzer divisions, moved deep into the desert. A sandstorm concealed their 10,000 vehicles from the eyes of the British. Then, during the night, Rommel's main striking force outflanked the Gazala Line from the south.

Rommel led his divisions rapidly round in a wide sweep, making use of the bright moon once the *khamsin* dropped. They were in position before dawn, ready to attack. Some thirty kilometres north-east of Bir Hakeim, the 15th Panzer Division clashed with the 4th Armoured Brigade, inflicting heavy losses on the 3rd Royal Tank Regiment and the 8th Hussars. Soon afterwards eighty British tanks counter-attacked the 21st Panzer Division. The Eighth Army now had 167 American Grant tanks. These were heavy, unusually tall and not very manoeuvrable when it came to firing, but their 75mm guns were far more effective than the pathetic two-pounders on the Crusaders.

The 3rd Indian Motorized Brigade, to the south-east of Bir Hakeim, had meanwhile been hit at 06.30 hours on 27 May. Their commander radioed back that they were facing 'a whole bloody German armoured division', when in fact it was the Italian Ariete Division. The Indian troops destroyed fifty-two tanks, but they were overwhelmed once all their anti-tank guns had been knocked out.

Koenig's Free French brigade in their equally lonely position at Bir Hakeim knew what awaited them, having heard the sound of tank engines out in the desert during the night. In the morning, a patrol confirmed that the enemy was behind them and had cut them off from their supply depot. Koenig's force of some 4,000 men included a half-brigade of the Foreign Legion, two battalions of colonial troops and marine infantry. They also had their own artillery support, with fifty-four French 75mm field guns and Bofors guns. Like the other boxes, their first line of defence consisted of minefields and barbed wire.

The tanks of the Ariete Division now turned against them and attacked in a mass. French gunners knocked out thirty-two. Only six Italian tanks managed to break through the mines and wire, but French legionnaires destroyed them at close range. Some even climbed on to the Italian tanks and fired through slits and hatches. The attack was unsupported by infantry, and the French bravely fought off every wave, inflicting heavy losses and taking ninety-one prisoners, including a regimental commander. Skirmishes were also fought against the German 90th Light Division. 'For the first time since June 1940,' General de Gaulle later wrote proudly, 'French and Germans were in action against each other.'

To the north-east, the rest of the 90th Light Division attacked the 7th Motorized Brigade and forced the outnumbered British to withdraw. Its units then overran the 7th Armoured Division headquarters and took various supply dumps. Although the 90th Light advanced rapidly, Rommel's two panzer divisions were hampered by counter-attacks and heavy artillery fire on their advance north towards the airfield at El Adem, which had been the scene of such heavy fighting the year before.

Rommel's daring plan had not succeeded as he had hoped. His forces were in a vulnerable position between the Gazala Line boxes and the remainder of the British armour to the west. Rommel had also expected the French at Bir Hakeim to be rapidly crushed, but they still held out. He was deeply worried and many of his officers thought that the offensive had failed. His chief of staff even suggested telling the OKW that the operation had merely been a reconnaissance in strength in an attempt to protect the Panzerarmee Afrika's reputation. But they need not have worried. Once again the British had failed to concentrate their tanks sufficiently to make an impact.

Rommel wanted to forge on north to the coastal road and break the British line there, so as to re-establish his supply line back to Tripoli. But from 28 May fighting became chaotic inside the centre of the Gazala Line. Rommel's divisions were hampered by fuel and ammunition shortages, but again he was saved by the slowness of British commanders to exploit their considerable advantage. Ritchie wanted to send in a major night attack, but his corps and divisional commanders argued that they needed more time. They thought that the Germans were trapped, but Axis troops had been making a gap in the minefield to the west and supplies began to come through. However, this passage was close to the 150th Brigade's box, whose Yorkshire battalions suddenly provided Rommel with a major problem.

At the Wolfsschanze in East Prussia, Hitler's attention was not on North Africa. His Luftwaffe adjutant, Nicolaus von Below, returned from a visit to Rommel to find a 'very unpleasant situation'. On 27 May, Reinhard Heydrich had been attacked in Prague by young Czechs, equipped by the British Special Operations Executive. Heydrich was still just alive, but would succumb to infections from his wounds within a week. And on the night of 30 May the RAF had launched its first thousand-bomber raid against Cologne. Hitler was beside himself with rage, mainly directed against Göring.

From 31 May, during the scrappy battle which the British called the 'Cauldron' and the Germans 'the sausage pot', Rommel then threw his forces against 150th Brigade's position. The onslaught, with tanks, artillery and Stukas, was massive. The brigade fought to the end with great courage, winning the admiration of the Germans. But the continuing failure of British commanders to counter-attack in force from the west was one of the least impressive examples of generalship in the war. Rommel then ordered the 90th Light Division and the Trieste Division to destroy the French at Bir Hakeim, so that he could start to break up the Gazala Line from the south.

On 3 June, Koenig's men fought off the overwhelming force attacking them. The British sent a relief force, but it ran into the 21st Panzer Division and pulled back. No other attempt was made to relieve the French garrison, partly because the counter-attack further north on 5 June collapsed due to the incompetence and timidity of formation commanders reluctant to risk their tanks against the Germans' 88mm guns. Some supplies got through. The RAF provided as much support as possible, helping to break up attacks and fight off the Stukas and Heinkels. French colonial troops made short work of any Stuka pilots who parachuted down. Koenig's men, suffering in the intense heat and dust from thirst and hunger, dug their foxholes deeper, waiting for a greater onslaught. By holding on, they knew that they could greatly aid the withdrawal of the Eighth Army.

Exasperated by the tenacity of the French defence, Rommel took command himself. On 8 June, German artillery and Stukas began to pound the position again. One bomb killed seventeen wounded in the dressing station. The determination of the defenders never slackened. One officer saw the sole survivor of a guncrew, a legionnaire with a hand blown off, reload the 75mm by ramming home the shell with his bloody stump. On 10 June the French defences were breached. The defenders of Bir Hakeim had no more ammunition.

That night the British 7th Armoured Division, the only formation which might have saved them, withdrew. Koenig was ordered to pull back. He led most of his remaining men out through the German encirclement in the dark, at first undetected and then under heavy fire. He was accompanied by his courageous English driver and mistress Susan Travers, who was later made a warrant officer in the French Foreign Legion. Rommel received an order from Hitler to execute any captured legionnaires, whether Frenchmen who should be treated as insurgents, or anti-fascist Germans, or citizens of other Nazi-occupied countries. To his credit, he ensured that they were treated as ordinary prisoners of war.

When General de Gaulle heard from General Sir Alan Brooke, the chief of the imperial general staff, that Koenig and most of his men had escaped back to British lines, his sentiments were so intense that he had to shut himself alone in a room. 'Oh, the heart beating with emotion, sobs of pride, tears of joy,' he wrote later in his memoirs. This moment, he knew, marked 'the start of the resurrection of France'.

Further north, the battle of the Cauldron continued, with the British and Indian brigades fighting stubbornly in defence, but the Eighth Army still remained incapable of launching an effective counter-attack. On 11 June, just after the fall of Bir Hakeim, Rommel ordered his three German divisions to destroy the remaining British positions, including the 'Knightsbridge' box held by the 201st Guards Brigade and 4th Armoured Brigade. They were then to seize the Via Balbia. This prompted a sudden withdrawal on 14 June, when the South Africans and the 50th Division near the coast were ordered to pull back to the Egyptian frontier to avoid being cut off. An undignified general retreat ensued, which became known as the 'Gazala gallop'.

Tobruk was left exposed, and the Italian infantry advanced to encircle it from the east. Rommel brought up his German divisions, although 21st Panzer was severely mauled in the process by RAF Hurricane and P-40 Kittyhawk fighter-bombers. Air Vice Marshal Arthur Coningham's Desert Air Force was improving its techniques all the time, and without its support the fate of the Eighth Army might have been catastrophic.

Churchill sent orders to Auchinleck that Tobruk had to be held at all costs. But Tobruk lacked sufficient troops and guns, and many of the mines from its defences had been taken to strengthen the Gazala Line. On 17 June, Rommel began his assault with a feint against one corner of the perimeter, while secretly preparing to attack elsewhere.

Unlike the Australians who had defended Tobruk so doggedly the year before, the 2nd South African Division commanded by Major General Hendrik Klopper was inexperienced. In any case, Admiral Cunningham was well aware that he did not have the ships to supply Tobruk through another siege. The 33,000-strong garrison included another two infantry brigades and a weak armoured brigade with obsolete tanks.

At dawn on 20 June, Kesselring sent in all the Stuka and bomber groups available in the Mediterranean supported by squadrons of the Italian air force, the Regia Aeronautica. This was accompanied by a concentrated artillery bombardment, while German pioneer battalions cleared a route through the minefields. The 11th Indian Brigade was shocked by the unprecedented onslaught, and by 08.30 hours the first panzers were through the outer defences. In the course of a single day, as columns of smoke rose into the sky from the battered town, the Germans advanced all the way to the port, cutting the twenty-kilometre-long fortress position in two. It was a bewilderingly swift victory.

General Klopper surrendered the following morning, before the port and many of the supply dumps had been destroyed. Four thousand tons of oil fell into Rommel's hands, the best gift he could have hoped for. His hungry soldiers, whose clothes were almost in rags, became ecstatic at the booty. 'We've got chocolate, tinned milk, canned vegetables and biscuits by the crate,' an Unteroffizier wrote home. 'We've got English vehicles and weapons in vast quantities. What a feeling to put on English shirts and stockings!' Italian soldiers did not get to share in the rich pickings. The same Unteroffizier acknowledged that 'they have it harder than us, with less water, less food, less pay and not the same equipment as we have'.

Mussolini tried to pretend that the capture of Tobruk was an Italian victory, so to emphasize the truth Hitler immediately promoted the forty-nine-year-old Rommel to the rank of Generalfeldmarschall. This promotion produced a good deal of jealousy and resentment in the highest levels of the Wehrmacht, which Hitler no doubt enjoyed. On this, the first anniversary of Operation Barbarossa, the German dictator was overjoyed in his certainty that the British Empire had now begun to disintegrate as he had claimed. And in a week's time Operation Blue was to be launched in southern Russia to seize the Caucasus. The Third Reich once more appeared invincible.

On that June day, Churchill was in the White House with Roosevelt when an aide came in and passed a slip of paper to the President. He read it and then passed it to the prime minister. Churchill felt sick with disbelief. He asked General Ismay to check with London whether Tobruk really had fallen. Ismay returned to confirm that it was true. The humiliation at such a moment could not have been greater. Churchill later wrote: 'Defeat is one thing; disgrace is another.'

Roosevelt, showing his most generous instincts, immediately asked what he could do to help. Churchill requested as many of the new Sherman tanks as the Americans could spare. Four days later, the American chiefs of staff agreed to the despatch of 300 Shermans as well as a hundred 105mm self-propelled guns. It was an act of great selflessness, especially since the Shermans had to be snatched back from US Army formations, which had been longing to replace their obsolete vehicles.

Deeply depressed and shocked, Churchill returned to face a motion of no confidence in the House of Commons. He put most of the blame on Auchinleck, which was hardly fair. The Auk's main mistake was to have appointed Ritchie. The acute shortage of competent and decisive commanders at the most senior levels in the British army clearly had a terrible influence on its performance. Brooke ascribed this to the deaths of the best young officers in the First World War.

An equally crippling handicap was the long-standing disaster of the arms procurement system. Unlike the RAF, which had attracted the most talented designers and engineers in an age when aviation was exciting, the army accepted armaments which were already obsolete and then continued to mass-produce them, rather than go back to the drawing-board. This cycle had begun with the loss of so much equipment at Dunkirk and the need to replace weapons rapidly, but had not been broken.

Some of the new six-pounder anti-tank guns had been used with good effect in the Gazala battles, but to send badly designed tanks with two-pounder guns into action against the Panzer IV, and especially the 88mm gun, was like sending up Gloster Gladiator biplanes against Messerschmitt 109s. One can only admire the bravery of crews going into the attack well aware that their own tanks were virtually useless, except against infantry. The British did not produce a truly battleworthy tank, the Comet, until the very last days of the war.

Churchill's only consolation from his visit to the United States was that he had managed to persuade Roosevelt to agree to the invasion of French North Africa. Operation Gymnast, which later became Operation Torch, had been fiercely opposed by General Marshall and the other American chiefs of staff. Marshall's fears of Churchill getting at Roosevelt when none of the President's military advisers were present had been vindicated. They suspected, with a degree of justification, that Britain wanted to preserve its position in the Middle East. But Churchill was afraid that if Britain lost Egypt, and the Germans managed to link up an invasion through the Caucasus with Rommel's advance, then not just the Suez Canal but the oilfields of the region could be lost. It might also encourage the Japanese to extend their operations into the western Indian Ocean.

Churchill had another reason which chimed well with Roosevelt's thinking. Since an early invasion of northern France was out of the question because of a lack of air superiority and a shortage of shipping and landing craft, there was no other area in which American troops could be deployed against Germany. And the prime minister knew that Admiral King, as well as the American public, wanted to drop the 'Germany first' strategy, and concentrate on the Pacific. Even Brooke was highly dubious about the North Africa landings, but Churchill was proved right, albeit for very different reasons to the ones he had put forward. The US Army needed battle experience before it could take on the Wehrmacht in major battles on the mainland of Europe. And the Allies needed to learn the dangers of amphibious operations before they attempted a cross-Channel invasion.

Kesselring still wanted to conquer Malta first, but Rommel was adamant. He had to have the Luftwaffe supporting him so that he could destroy the Eighth Army before it had a chance to recover. Hitler supported Rommel, with the argument that the capture of Egypt would make Malta irrelevant. But they both overlooked the fact that while the Luftwaffe was being diverted to support Rommel during the Gazala battles, Malta had been reinforced. Yet again, supply lines across the Mediterranean were at risk, and the seizure of Tobruk with its port had not solved the logistic conundrum of the desert war as Rommel had hoped. In what was referred to as the 'rubber-band' effect of these campaigns, the over-extended supply line led to disaster, hauling back the attacker.

Even before the fall of Tobruk, Rommel had ordered the 90th Light Division to push on towards Egypt along the coast road. And on 23 June the two panzer divisions were also sent in pursuit of the Eighth Army. Auchinleck meanwhile sacked Ritchie and took command himself. He wisely cancelled orders to make a stand at Mersa Matruh and instructed all formations to withdraw rapidly to El Alamein, a small railway halt near the sea. Between Alamein and the Qattara Depression to the south, with its salt marshes and quicksands, he intended to establish his defensive line, secure in the knowledge that Rommel would not be able to outflank it as easily as he had at Gazala.

Morale in the Eighth Army could not have been worse. Despite Auchinleck's determination to pull back to El Alamein, Ritchie's earlier order had left the 10th Indian Division defending Mersa Matruh. It was caught by the speed of Rommel's advance units, which encircled the town, cutting the coast road. Part of X Corps managed to break out, but lost over 7,000 men taken prisoner in the process. Further south, the New Zealand Division broke through the 21st Panzer Division in a vicious night attack, killing wounded, medics and combatants alike, an action which the Germans considered a war crime.

Rommel was still convinced that he had the Eighth Army on the run and could strike through to the Middle East. Mussolini was so certain of success that he arrived in the port city of Derna followed by a magnificent grey stallion, on which he would take the victory parade in the Egyptian capital. In Cairo itself, panic and confusion reigned in all the offices of GHQ Middle East and the British embassy, to the amusement or alarm of most Egyptians. Long queues formed outside banks. On 1 July, columns of smoke rose into the air from documents burned in the gardens of official buildings. They created a snowstorm of partly charred secret papers around the city. Street vendors snatched them up to make cones for their peanuts, and the day became known as 'Ash Wednesday'. Members of the European community began to leave by car, with mattresses strapped to the roof in scenes reminiscent of Paris two years before.

The 'flap', as it was called, had started in Alexandria, when Vice Admiral Sir Henry Harwood, who had just taken over from Cunningham, ordered the dispersal of the British fleet to other ports in the Levant. Rumours spread that the Germans would arrive in twenty-four hours and that an airborne invasion was expected at any moment. Egyptian shopkeepers prepared portraits of Hitler and Mussolini ready to hang in their establishments. Others went much further. Nationalist officers, hoping that the Germans would give them independence from the British, began to prepare for an uprising. One officer named Anwar Sadat, later president of the country, bought up 10,000 empty bottles for making Molotov cocktails.

For the Jewish community the prospect was terrifying, but although the British authorities in Cairo offered them priority on the trains to Palestine, the Palestine administration refused them visas. Jewish fears were not misplaced. An SS *Einsatzkommando* unit was waiting in Athens to begin work in Egypt, and then in Palestine if Rommel's string of victories continued.

Desertions in the British Army of the Nile, as Churchill called it, rose dramatically, bringing the estimated total in the city and the Delta to 25,000 men. British officers felt a characteristic urge to make jokes in the face of disaster. Having always complained about the slowness of the service in Shepheard's Hotel, they said:

'Just wait till Rommel gets to Shepheard's. That'll slow him up.'
A rumour went round that Rommel had already telephoned to
book a room. Certainly German radio had broadcast a message
to the women of Alexandria: 'Get out your party frocks, we're on
the way!' But Axis triumphalism was premature.

Although the Germans had been intercepting British signals
traffic on a tactical level, Auchinleck was well aware of Rommel's
plans through Ultra. In the early hours of 1 July, the Afrika Korps
with the two panzer divisions set off to make a feint attack towards the south of the Alamein Line. Rommel's real target lay
further north, but in his impatience to catch the Eighth Army off
balance he had dispensed with reconnaissance. This proved a bad
mistake, made worse by a sandstorm. The 90th Light Division
tried to attack the Alamein box but was repulsed by unexpectedly heavy artillery fire. Soon afterwards the 21st Panzer Division
advanced on one of the central boxes held by the 18th Indian Brigade. Although it took the position, it lost a third of its tanks,
many of them to RAF fighter-bombers.

Coningham's Desert Air Force continued its relentless attacks.
His pilots were maintaining an even greater rhythm of sorties
than during the Battle of Britain. With pilots from many nations,
the air force included the Free French Groupe de Chasse Alsace,
armed with a mixed complement of aircraft. Coningham badly
needed Spitfires to take on the Messerschmitts, but the air ministry in London was reluctant to release them from home defence.
His Desert Air Force was now helped by an American bombing
group of B-24 Liberators attacking Axis ships and the ports of
Benghazi, Tobruk and Mersa Matruh. The US Middle East Army
Air Force was assembling under the command of Major General
Lewis H. Brereton, with both fighter and bombardment groups.
British and American forces were for the first time in action along-
side each other.

German expectations of an easy victory began to falter.
Auchinleck counter-attacked with mobile groups and concentrated his artillery to great effect. And the New Zealand Division
again excelled itself by seizing the perfect moment for a sudden
counter-attack on the Ariete Division, sending it back in disorder.
On the night of 3 July, Rommel ordered the Panzerarmee Afrika
on to the defensive. It had less than fifty tanks in a battleworthy

state. His men were totally exhausted and short of ammunition and fuel. He simply could not afford a battle of unremittant hard pounding.

The rock, scree and sand of the Alamein Line did not offer a hospitable environment for the men of the Eighth Army either. They were tormented by ubiquitous swarms of aggressive flies and by sandstorms whipped up by the winds, as well as by the enervating heat of the desert. Tanks were literally like ovens under the blazing sun. At night, soldiers wrapped themselves tightly in a groundsheet to keep out scorpions. They suffered from dysentery spread by the flies, as well as from desert sores which also attracted these voracious insects. And whenever they tried to eat their corned-beef hash or hardtack biscuits ground up to make a porridge with the consistency of plaster of Paris, it was hard not to swallow a few flies in the process. A brew-up of tea was the only consolation, even if the water used to make it tasted pretty foul. Not surprisingly, the soldiers' thoughts tended to focus on home cooking and home comforts. A rifleman declared to his comrades that 'when he made it home he was going to spend his time eating chocolate ice creams while sitting on the toilet and enjoying the luxury of pulling the chain'.

The Eighth Army was also too exhausted to seize the opportunity to counter-attack. Instead it concentrated on strengthening its position along the line, with a fresh Australian brigade brought up to the Ruweisat Ridge. Rommel attacked again on 10 July. But in the north the 9th Australian Division, supported by an armoured brigade, broke through the Italians near El Alamein and put them to flight. Their most important prize was to capture Rommel's own signals intelligence unit, a coup which made him effectively blind now that the Germans were no longer able to break the American code. The American military attaché, Bonner Fellers, who had unwittingly provided the Germans with their most reliable intelligence source, had left at the end of June.

Throughout most of July, the two sides attacked and counterattacked in a military version of scissors, paper, stone. Rommel was incensed by the performance of most Italian formations, which produced bitter arguments between the Axis allies. He felt forced to split up some of his formations to insert 'corset stiffeners' among some of the Italian divisions. And his outraged protests about the lack of resupply again proved futile, for the RAF and the Royal Navy were once more inflicting heavy losses on Axis convoys and port installations. His dream that the capture of Tobruk and Mersa Matruh would solve his problems at a stroke were rudely shattered. On the night of 26 July, the recently formed Special Air Service in Jeeps attacked an airfield near Fuka and destroyed thirty-seven aircraft on the ground, many of them Junkers 52 transports. It brought their total for the month to eighty-six aircraft destroyed.

Auchinleck's achievement should not be underestimated. He had at the very least saved a heavily battered Eighth Army from disaster and stabilized the line, while inflicting heavy losses on the Germans. Churchill viewed things in a very different light. He saw only missed opportunities, and refused to acknowledge the exhaustion of the troops and the scandalous inferiority of British armoured vehicles.

The prime minister, accompanied by General Sir Alan Brooke, arrived in Cairo on 3 August on his way to Moscow to warn Stalin about the postponement of the Second Front. The British thought that they had finally stonewalled the Americans into abandoning Operation Sledgehammer, the cross-Channel attack to invade the Cotentin Peninsula so rashly promised to Molotov. But in the second week of July, there were signs of rebellion among the American chiefs of staff and the secretary of war Henry L. Stimson. In the belief that the British were secretly against any invasion of northern France, they argued for an abandonment of the 'Germany first' policy and a switch of focus to the Pacific.

Roosevelt, invoking his role as commander-in-chief, stopped them in their tracks on 14 July. Sending troops to capture odd islands in the Pacific was just what Germany hoped they would do, he wrote to Marshall, and would 'not affect the world situation this year or next'. And it certainly would not help Russia or the Middle East. Whether or not this was largely a bluff on Marshall's part aimed at forcing the British to commit themselves to a cross-Channel invasion is still unclear. But Marshall and Admiral King returned to the charge later in the month when they visited Churchill at Chequers and tried to revive Sledgehammer. The British remained resolutely opposed. It would be a disaster, and could do nothing to help the Red Army.

Harry Hopkins, who was also in London, privately encouraged the British in the knowledge that Roosevelt wanted to see American troops in action in North Africa. Marshall, finally obliged to make the best of what he considered a bad job of fighting Britain's war, sent one of his best staff officers, Major General Dwight D. Eisenhower, to begin planning the North African landings in London, with a view to taking overall command.

Before continuing his journey on to the Soviet Union, Churchill was determined to sort out the command structure in the Middle East. Auchinleck told him that it would not be wise to launch another attack before mid-September, so Churchill decided to replace him with General Sir Harold Alexander as commander-in-chief. He also chose Lieutenant General 'Strafer' Gott, the commander of XIII Corps, to take over the Eighth Army. Gott, although he had been one of the better desert commanders, was tired out and demoralized by this stage. Brooke wanted Lieutenant General Bernard Montgomery instead, but Churchill was adamant. The situation was resolved when Gott was killed, after his plane was shot down by a Messerschmitt. Montgomery would take command after all.

Montgomery took a pride in being different from the usual senior officer of the British army. And the short, wiry little general with a beaky nose could hardly have been more of a contrast to the unassuming, aristocratic and immaculate Alexander. Monty dressed differently too, preferring a shapeless pullover and corduroys, topped later by a black Royal Tank Regiment beret as his hallmark. Yet he was a military conservative, believing in detailed staffwork and the deployment of divisions, not the informal battle-groups which had evolved in the desert campaign. He played shamelessly to the crowd, whether soldiers or journalists, despite his rather shrill voice and inability to pronounce his Rs. A non-smoker and teetotaller, he was egotistic, ambitious and ruthless, possessing a boundless self-confidence which occasionally bordered on the fatuous. But this self-belief, which he was able to convey to all he met, lay at the heart of his mission to turn the badly bruised Eighth Army into one confident of victory. Commanders had to 'get a grip' and there was to be no more 'bellyaching' or querying of orders.

The situation that Montgomery inherited in August 1942 was by no means as dire as his own myth-making later pretended. Rommel's German and Italian divisions had suffered a considerable battering during the July battles. But Montgomery was rightly appalled by the defeatist attitude of many senior officers on the staff, although he was wrong to imply that Auchinleck shared their views. Auchinleck's failing had been his ignorance of this mood among the 'Gaberdine Swine', as fighting officers called the inhabitants of Headquarters Middle East in Cairo. Montgomery announced to the Eighth Army that he had ordered the burning of all contingency plans for withdrawal. And with considerable theatrical effect, he managed to rebuild its morale and confidence through visits and training programmes. An impression of dramatic change worked wonders, even if Montgomery was claiming for himself a number of innovations which had begun under Auchinleck.

Montgomery had no intention of launching a premature offensive, even though such caution had been the main reason behind Auchinleck's dismissal. But he was much cleverer in the way he handled the prime minister. In fact, Montgomery planned to take longer than Auchinleck's date of mid-September. He was determined to build up his army to such an overwhelming strength that victory could be virtually guaranteed. In this he was almost certainly correct, because Britain could not have faced another fiasco.

Rommel had been reinforced with the 164th Division and a brigade of paratroopers, but he knew his position was now worse than precarious. His forces were too weak to continue a battle of attrition against the Alamein Line. Instead, he wanted to withdraw so as to bring the British out of their positions, and to impose on them a battle of movement in which his panzer troops would have the advantage. He was still short of transport and fuel as the RAF and Royal Navy sank one supply ship after another. Suffering from stress and furious frustration, he criticized in bitter and sweeping terms the performance of Italian troops, even though some formations, especially the Folgore Division, were fighting well.

In the second half of August roles were reversed, with

Mussolini and Kesselring urging Rommel to launch an offensive as soon as possible, while he had become reluctant and pessimistic. On 30 August, sensing that he was damned if he did and damned if he didn't, Rommel launched his right hook against the southern part of the Eighth Army line, to swing round behind and attack the Alam Halfa Ridge. He knew that the greatest risk lay in running out of fuel, but Kesselring had promised that tankers were due to dock and that the supplies would be rushed forward.

Montgomery, aware of Rommel's plan through Ultra decrypts, placed his armoured formations ready to parry the thrust, more or less as Auchinleck had planned. Rommel's reconnaissance and intelligence was poor. His staff had underestimated the extent of the minefields they had to cross in the south, and failed to appreciate the effect of the Desert Air Force in the coming battle. As his two panzer divisions struggled in the minefields, Coningham's squadrons of bombers and fighter-bombers attacked them relentlessly through a night illuminated by flares. The panzers, bunched together in the narrow corridors, made comparatively easy targets. The Afrika Korps and the Littorio Armoured Division did not get through until the following morning, and only then did the advance north towards the Alam Halfa Ridge accelerate. Rommel was encouraged to continue, and Kesselring sent in his Stukas to batter the defensive positions ahead. But the slow and vulnerable Stukas were badly mauled by the squadrons of the Desert Air Force.

The ridge was well defended, forcing the panzer divisions to a halt. Rommel expected a massive counter-attack on 1 September, but Montgomery did not want to risk his armoured formations in any more cavalry charges and held most of them in their positions, hull down. Only one armoured counter-attack was launched. Then Rommel received the worst possible news. The tankers on which he had counted had been attacked, with devastating results. Ultra had once again enabled the British to find them.

Rommel was in an unenviable position, with his panzer divisions stuck in the open between the Alamein Line to the west and the British armour to the east and south, and continually attacked by the Desert Air Force. On 5 September, he ordered a withdrawal. Apart from an inept counter-attack by XXX Corps in the south, Montgomery failed to seize the opportunity offered to mount a devastating blow. But the repulse of the Afrika Korps, and the damage inflicted by the Desert Air Force, did much to boost Eighth Army morale.

Rommel had extricated the bulk of his forces, but he knew that the tide of war in North Africa had turned irrevocably against him, even though he still had no idea of the threat to his rear being planned by Eisenhower.

22

Operation Blau – Barbarossa Relaunched

MAY–AUGUST 1942

Once the snows began to melt in the spring of 1942, the hidden horrors of the winter fighting emerged. Soviet prisoners were put to work burying the corpses of their comrades killed during the January offensive. 'Now that it's fairly warm during the day,' a German soldier wrote home on paper taken from the pocket of a dead commissar, 'the corpses are beginning to stink and it's time to bury them.' A soldier with the 88th Infantry Division wrote that, after capturing a village during a rapid thaw, the bodies of 'around eighty German soldiers from a reconnaissance battalion appeared from under the snow with chopped off limbs and smashed in skulls. Most had then been burned.'

Yet once the birch trees came into leaf and the sun began to dry out the waterlogged land, the morale of German officers experienced an extraordinary revival. It was as if the terrible winter had been little more than a bad dream, and now their run of victories would recommence. Panzer divisions were re-equipped, reinforcements absorbed into units, and ammunition dumps prepared for a summer offensive. The *Grossdeutschland* Infantry Regiment which had been reduced to a rump in the winter disaster was now expanded into a motorized division, with two panzer battalions and assault guns. Waffen-SS divisions were upgraded into panzer formations, but many ordinary divisions received little more than replacements. Tensions between the SS and the army increased. A battalion commander in the 294th Infantry Division wrote in his diary of 'the great alarm which we all feel about the power and the importance of the SS . . . They already say in Germany that as soon as the Army returns home with victory, the SS will disarm it on the frontier.'

Many soldiers who had been awarded the winter campaign medal were unimpressed. They referred to it as the 'Order of the

Frozen Flesh'. At the end of January, new instructions had been issued to those allowed home on leave. 'You are under military law,' it reminded them, 'and you are still subject to punishment. Don't speak about weapons, tactics or losses. Don't speak about bad rations or injustice. The intelligence service of the enemy is ready to exploit it.'

The troops' cynicism increased with the belated arrival of civilian winter clothing, skiing outfits and women's fur coats, which had been donated as a result of the appeal by Goebbels to provide warm clothes for the soldiers of the *Ostfront*. The smell of mothballs and images of the homes from which they had come only deepened the feeling that they were marooned on another planet in which filth and lice reigned. The sheer vastness of the Soviet Union was deeply unsettling and depressing. The same captain in the 294th Division wrote of the 'endless uncultivated fields, no woods, only a few trees from time to time. Sad collective farms with destroyed houses. A few people, dirty, wearing rags, were standing by the railway track with indifferent faces.'

While Stalin still expected that the Wehrmacht would make another thrust towards Moscow, Hitler had very different ideas. Knowing that Germany's survival in the war depended on food and especially fuel, he intended to consolidate his hold on Ukraine and seize the oilfields of the Caucasus. It would be Stalin who stumbled first in this military *danse macabre*, and Hitler who would overreach himself eventually with catastrophic consequences. For the moment, however, everything seemed to go the Führer's way.

On 7 May, Manstein's Eleventh Army in the Crimea counterattacked the Soviet forces attempting to advance out of the Kerch Peninsula. Sending in his panzers on the flank, he surrounded them. Many fought bravely and were buried in their trenches by German tanks, twisting and turning on their tracks to force the earth in. The disaster which ensued over the next ten days – almost entirely the making of Stalin's favourite commissar, Lev Mekhlis – led to the loss of 176,000 men, 400 aircraft, 347 tanks and 4,000 guns. Mekhlis tried to put the blame on the troops, especially the Azeris, but the terrible losses created a great hatred in the Caucasus. Mekhlis was demoted, but Stalin soon found him another post.

According to German accounts, soldiers from central Asia were the ones most likely to desert. 'They have been hurriedly and badly trained, and sent to the front line. They say that the Russians stay behind them and force them forwards. They crossed the river during the night. They were walking in the mud and water up to their knees and looked at us with shining eyes. Only in our prison could they feel free. The Russians are undertaking more and more measures on preventing desertion and absconding from the battlefield. Now there are so-called guard companies, which have only one task: to prevent their own units from retreating. If it really is this bad, then all the conclusions about the demoralization of the Red Army are true.'

An even greater disaster than Kerch soon followed. Marshal Timoshenko, supported by Nikita Khrushchev, had proposed in March that the armies of the South-Western and Southern Fronts should disrupt any offensive against Moscow, by mounting a pincer attack on Kharkov. This was supposed to coincide with the break-out from the Kerch Peninsula to relieve the embattled garrison of Sebastopol.

The Stavka had little idea of German strength, having assumed that their forces were still facing the battered units of the winter. Soviet military intelligence had failed to spot the great increase in the strength of Army Group South, even if many of the forces diverted there consisted of Romanian, Hungarian and Italian formations, all of which were under armed and ill equipped. Hitler's relaunch of Barbarossa was to be named Fall Blau (Operation Blue). The Germans were aware of Timoshenko's preparations for an offensive, although it came earlier than they had expected. They were planning their own attack south of Kharkov to cut off the Barvenkovo Salient, which the Red Army had carved out in the January offensive. This plan was codenamed Operation Fridericus and was the preparatory phase to Blau.

On 12 May, five days after the failed attack from the Kerch Peninsula, Timoshenko's offensive began. The southern pincer of his attack broke through a weak security division and advanced fifteen kilometres on the first day. Soviet soldiers were amazed by the evidence of German plenty in the positions they captured, with luxuries such as chocolate, tins of sardines and meat, white bread, cognac and cigarettes. But their own casualties were heavy. 'It was terrible', wrote Yuri Vladimirov from an anti-aircraft battery, 'to pass the heavily injured men who were dying from loss of blood and who were begging for help loudly or quietly and we were unable to do anything.'

The northern part of the offensive was ill coordinated and attracted constant attacks by the Luftwaffe. 'We advanced from Volchansk towards Kharkov and could see the chimneys of the famous tractor plant,' wrote a soldier with the 28th Army. 'The German aviation would not leave us in peace, they bombed us incessantly from three in the morning until nightfall with a lunch-break of two hours. Everything was destroyed by the bombs.' There was confusion among the commanders and a lack of ammunition. 'Even the military tribunal had to fight,' the soldier added.

Timoshenko realized that he had hit the Germans while they were preparing their own offensive. But he did not suspect that he might be heading into a trap. General der Panzertruppe Paulus, a talented staff officer who had never commanded a formation, was taken aback by the severity of Timoshenko's attack on his Sixth Army. Sixteen of his battalions were badly mauled in the fighting, under heavy spring rains. But Generalfeldmarschall von Bock saw the opportunity for a major victory. He persuaded Hitler that Kleist's First Panzer Army could move to cut off Timoshenko's forces in the Barvenkovo Salient from the south. Hitler leaped at the idea and claimed it for his own. On 17 May, Kleist struck just before dawn.

Timoshenko rang Moscow to ask for reinforcements, but had not yet grasped the danger of his position. Finally, on the night of 20 May, he persuaded Khrushchev to telephone Stalin to request that the offensive be cancelled. Khrushchev was put through to the dacha at Kuntsevo. Stalin told Georgii Malenkov, the secretary of the Central Committee, to speak to him. Khrushchev demanded to speak to Stalin himself. Stalin refused and told Malenkov to find out what he wanted. When Stalin heard the reason he shouted that 'Military orders must be obeyed,' and instructed Malenkov to end the call. Khrushchev's hatred for Stalin is said to have dated from this point, and led to his passionate denunciation of the dictator at the XX Party Conference in 1956.

It took another two days before Stalin allowed the offensive to be called off, but by then the bulk of the 6th and 57th Soviet Armies had been surrounded. The encircled troops made desperate attempts to break out, even charging with linked arms, and the massacre was terrible. Corpses piled up in waves in front of the German positions. The skies had cleared, allowing the Luftwaffe perfect visibility. 'Our pilots work night and day in their hundreds,' wrote a soldier in the 389th Infantry Division. 'The whole horizon is shrouded in smoke.' Despite the battle, Yuri Vladimirov was able to listen to a lark singing on a hot, cloudless day. But then he heard the cry of 'Tanks! Tanks coming!' and he ran to hide in a trench.

The end was close. To avoid immediate execution, commissars stripped off their own distinctive uniforms and took those of dead Red Army men. They also shaved their heads to look more like an ordinary soldier. On surrendering, the troops stuck their rifles with bayonets fixed into the ground. 'It looked like a magical forest after a big fire in which all the trees had lost their leaves,' wrote Vladimirov. He considered suicide, in his filthy, lice-ridden state, knowing what lay ahead, but allowed himself to be rounded up. Among the abandoned helmets and gas-masks, they gathered up the wounded and carried them on improvised stretchers made out of rain capes. The German soldiers then marched the hungry and exhausted men off in columns, five men wide.

Some 240,000 men were taken prisoner, along with 2,000 field guns and the bulk of the tank forces deployed. One army commander and many other officers committed suicide. Kleist observed after the battle that the area was so clogged up by the corpses of men and horses that his command vehicle had trouble getting through.

This second Battle of Kharkov represented a terrible blow to the Soviet Union's morale. Khrushchev and Timoshenko were sure that they would be executed. Even though they had been friends they started to accuse each other, and Khrushchev had what appeared to be a nervous breakdown. Stalin, in characteristic fashion, simply humiliated Khrushchev by tapping out the ash from his pipe on Khrushchev's bald crown, saying that it was a Roman tradition for a commander who had lost a battle to pour ashes on his head in penance.

The Germans were jubilant, but the victory produced one

dangerous effect. Paulus, who had wanted to withdraw during
the early stages of the battle, was awed by what he assumed to
have been Hitler's perspicacity in ordering him to stand fast while
Kleist prepared the fatal blow. He had a passion for order and
was imbued with respect for the chain of command. These qualities, combined with his renewed admiration for Hitler, were to
exert a major influence at the critical moment six months later at
Stalingrad.

Despite the danger threatening the Soviet Union's very survival
that year, Stalin remained preoccupied with post-war frontiers.
The Americans and British rejected his demands that they should
recognize the Soviet border of June 1941, which included the
Baltic states and eastern Poland. But in the spring of 1942 Churchill had second thoughts. He considered agreeing to his claim as an
inducement to keep him in the war, despite its flagrant contravention of the Atlantic Charter which guaranteed self-determination.
Both Roosevelt and his secretary of state, Sumner Welles, indig-
nantly refused to support Churchill's proposal. Yet later in the
war it would be Churchill who would oppose Stalin's imperial
project, and Roosevelt who would accept it.

Relations between the western Allies and Stalin were bound
to be fraught with suspicion. Churchill especially had promised
far more military supplies than Britain was able to deliver. And
the American President's disastrous assurance to Molotov in May
that they would launch a Second Front before the end of the year
did more to poison the Grand Alliance than anything else. Stalin's
paranoid tendencies persuaded him that the capitalist countries
simply wanted the Soviet Union to be weakened while they waited.

The manipulative Roosevelt had told Molotov, via Harry Hopkins, that he was in favour of opening a Second Front in 1942,
but that his generals were against the idea. Roosevelt, it seems,
was prepared to say anything to keep the Soviet Union in the
war, whatever the consequences. And when it became clear that
the Allies had no intention of launching an invasion of northern
France that year, Stalin felt that he had been tricked.

Churchill found himself bearing the brunt of Stalin's resentment over unfulfilled promises. Although both he and Roosevelt
had been wildly imprudent, Stalin refused to acknowledge any

genuine difficulties. The losses suffered by the Arctic convoys to Murmansk never entered his calculations. The PQ convoys, which had started to sail from Iceland to Murmansk in September 1941, faced appalling dangers. In winter, the ships were coated in ice, and the seas treacherous, but in summer, with the short nights, they were vulnerable to German air attack from bases in northern Norway as well as from the constant U-boat menace. A quarter of the ships in PQ-13 in March were sunk. Churchill forced the Admiralty to send PQ-16 in May, even if it meant that only half the ships got through. He was under no illusions about the political consequences of cancelling it. In the event, only six out of thirty-six ships went down.

The next convoy, PQ-17, the largest yet sent to the Soviet Union, turned into one of the greatest naval disasters of the war. Faulty intelligence had suggested that the German battleship *Tirpitz*, together with the *Admiral Hipper* and *Admiral Scheer*, had left Trondheim to engage the convoy. This prompted the First Sea Lord, Admiral Sir Dudley Pound, to order the convoy to scatter on 4 July. It was a catastrophic decision. Altogether twenty-four ships out of thirty-nine were sunk by aircraft and U-boats, with the loss of nearly 100,000 tons of tanks, aircraft and vehicles. Following the loss of Tobruk in North Africa, and combined with the German advance into the Caucasus, the British began to think that they might lose the war after all. All further summer convoys were suspended, to Stalin's great displeasure.

Once the Soviet forces on the Kerch Peninsula had been destroyed, Manstein turned his Eleventh Army against the port and fortress of Sebastopol. Massive artillery and air bombardment with Stukas failed to dislodge the defenders, who fought on from caves and tunnels deep in the rock. At one stage, the Germans are said to have used chemical weapons to dislodge them, but this is far from certain. The Luftwaffe was determined to deal with harassing attacks from Red Army bombers. 'We are really going to show the Russians', wrote an Obergefreiter, 'what it means to play with Germany.'

Soviet partisans harried the German rear, and one group blew up the single railway track across the Perekop Isthmus. Anti-Soviet Crimean Tatars were recruited to help hunt them down.

Manstein brought up an 800mm monster of a siege gun mounted on railway wagons to pound the ruins of the great fortress. 'I can only say that this is no longer a war,' wrote a motorcycle reconnaissance soldier, 'but just the destruction of two world views.'

Manstein's most effective tactic was to launch a surprise attack in assault boats across Severnaya Bay, outflanking the first line of defence. The soldiers and the sailors of the Black Sea Fleet fought on. Political officers summoned meetings to tell them that they had been ordered to stand and die. Anti-aircraft batteries were switched to an anti-tank role, but gun after gun was blown out of action. 'The explosions blended into a huge continuous one,' recorded a member of the marine infantry. 'You could no longer distinguish individual blasts. Bombing would begin early in the morning and finish late at night. Bomb and shellbursts buried men and we had to dig them out again to continue fighting. Our telephone linesmen were all killed. Soon our last anti-aircraft gun was hit. We took up "infantry defence" in bomb craters.

'The Germans pushed us back to the sea and we had to use a rope to get down to the bottom of the cliffs. Knowing we were there, the Germans threw over the corpses of our comrades killed in the battle, as well as burning barrels of tar, and grenades. The situation was hopeless. I decided to push along the shore to Balaklava and swim across the bay during the night and escape to the hills. I organized a group of marine infantry. But we did not manage to make it for more than a kilometre.' They were captured.

The Battle for Sebastopol lasted from 2 June until 9 July, and German losses were also heavy. 'I lost many comrades at my side,' wrote an Unteroffizier as it ended. 'Once in the middle of a battle I began to cry for one like a child.' When it was finally over, an exultant Hitler promoted Manstein to field marshal. He wanted Sebastopol to become the major German naval base in the Black Sea and the capital of a completely Germanized Crimea. But the vast effort to take Sebastopol, as Manstein himself observed, reduced the forces available to Operation Blau at a critical time.

Stalin received detailed warning of the coming German offensive in southern Russia by a stroke of luck, yet he rejected it as disinformation, just as he had dismissed intelligence on Barbarossa

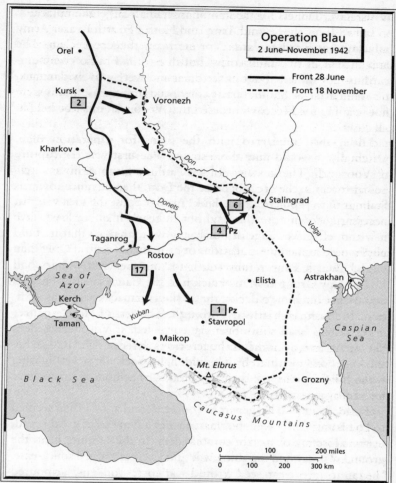

Operation Blau
2 June–November 1942

Front 28 June
Front 18 November

Orel

Kursk

2

Voronezh

Kharkov

Don

Donets

6

Stalingrad

4 Pz

Taganrog

Rostov

17

Sea of Azov

Kerch

Elista

Astrakhan

Volga

Kuban

1 Pz

Stavropol

Taman

Maikop

Caspian Sea

Black Sea

Mt. Elbrus

Grozny

Caucasus Mountains

0   100   200 miles
0   100   200   300 km

the year before. On 19 June, Major Joachim Reichel, a German staff officer carrying the plans for Fall Blau, was shot down in a Fieseler Storch plane behind Soviet lines. Yet Stalin, certain that the main German attack was aimed at Moscow, decided that the documents were fakes. Hitler was furious when told of this intelligence disaster and dismissed both Reichel's corps and divisional commanders. But preliminary attacks to secure the start-line east of the River Donets for the first phase had already taken place.

On 28 June, the Second Army and Hoth's Fourth Panzer Army attacked eastward towards Voronezh on the upper Don. The Stavka sent in two tank corps, but due to bad radio communications they milled about in the open and were gravely damaged by Stuka attacks. Stalin, finally convinced that the Germans were not heading for Moscow, ordered that Voronezh must be held at all costs.

Hitler then interfered with the plans for Operation Blau. Originally it would take three stages. The first was the capture of Voronezh. The next would see Paulus's Sixth Army encircle Soviet forces in the great bend of the Don, then advance towards Stalingrad to protect the left flank. At that point the idea was not necessarily to capture the city, but to reach it or 'at least have it within effective range of our heavy weapons', so that it could not be used as a communications or armaments centre. Only then would Fourth Panzer turn south to join Generalfeldmarschall List's Army Group A in its attack into the Caucasus. But Hitler's impatience led him to decide that a single panzer corps was sufficient to finish the battle at Voronezh. The rest of Hoth's panzer army should head south. Yet the corps left at Voronezh lacked the strength to overwhelm the ferocious defence. The Red Army showed how obstinately it could fight back in street-fighting when the Germans lost their advantages of armoured manoeuvre backed by air superiority.

Hitler dismissed his generals' concerns, and at first Blau seemed to go triumphantly well. German armies advanced at great speed, to the fierce joy of panzer commanders. In the summer heat, the ground was dry and the going was good as they surged south-east. 'As far as the eye can see,' wrote a war correspondent, 'armoured vehicles and half-tracks are rolling forward over the steppe. Pennants float in the shimmering afternoon air.' On one day, a temperature of '53 degrees in the sun' was recorded. Their only frustrations were that they were short of vehicles and frequently had to halt through lack of fuel.

Attempting to slow the German advance, Soviet aircraft dropped incendiaries at night to set the steppe on fire. The Germans pressed on. Dug-in Red Army tanks camouflaged themselves, but were rapidly outflanked and destroyed. Soviet infantrymen hidden in stooks of corn tried to fight back, but the panzers simply crushed them under their tracks. Panzer troops stopped in villages of thatched and whitewashed little houses, which they raided for eggs, milk, honey and fowl. Anti-Bolshevik Cossacks who had welcomed the Germans found their hospitality shamelessly abused. 'For the local people, we come as liberators,' wrote an Obergefreiter bitterly, 'as liberators of their last seed corn, vegetables, cooking oil and so forth.'

On 14 July, forces from Army Groups A and B met up at Millerovo, but the huge encirclements which Hitler expected were not taking place. A certain realism had crept into Stavka thinking after the Barvenkovo pocket. Soviet commanders pulled their armies back before they were surrounded. As a result, Hitler's plan to encircle and destroy the Soviet armies west of the River Don could not be fulfilled.

Rostov-on-Don, the gateway to the Caucasus, fell on 23 July. Hitler promptly ordered that the Seventeenth Army should capture Batum, while the First and Fourth Panzer Armies were to head for the oilfields of Maikop and to Grozny, the capital of Chechnya. 'If we don't take Maikop and Grozny,' Hitler had told his generals, 'then I must put an end to the war.' Stalin, shaken to find that his predictions of another offensive against Moscow had been so wrong, and realizing that the Red Army lacked sufficient troops in the Caucasus, sent Lavrenti Beria down to put fear into his generals.

Paulus was now ordered to capture Stalingrad with the Sixth Army, while his left flank along the Don would be protected by the Fourth Romanian Army. His infantry divisions had been marching for sixteen days without a rest. And Hoth's XXIV Panzer Corps, which had raced south towards the Caucasus, was now turned round to assist the attack on Stalingrad. Manstein was amazed to hear that his Eleventh Army, having secured the Crimea, was to be sent north for a new offensive on the Leningrad front. Once again Hitler was failing to concentrate his forces, at the very moment when he was trying to seize a huge new expanse of territory.

On 28 July, Stalin issued his Order No. 227 entitled 'Ni shagu nazad' – 'Not one step back' – drafted by Colonel General Aleksandr Vasilevsky. 'Panic-mongers and cowards must be destroyed on the spot. The retreat mentality must be decisively eliminated. Army commanders who have allowed the voluntary abandonment of positions must be removed and sent for immediate trial by military tribunal.' Blocking groups were to be set up in each army to gun down those who retreated. Punishment battalions were strengthened that month with 30,000 Gulag prisoners up to the age of forty, however weak and under-nourished. In that year, 352,560 prisoners of the Gulag, a quarter of its whole population, died.

The brutality of Order No. 227 led to scandalous injustices when impatient generals demanded scapegoats. One divisional commander ordered a colonel whose regiment had been slow in the advance to shoot somebody. 'This is not a trade union meeting,' the general said. 'This is war.' The colonel selected Lieutenant Aleksandr Obodov, the much admired commander of their mortar company. The regimental commissar and a captain from the NKVD Special Detachment arrested Obodov. 'Comrade commissar I've always been a good man,' said Obodov, unable to believe his fate. 'The two arresting officers wound themselves up into an anger, and began to shoot him,' a friend of his recorded. 'Sasha was trying to brush the bullets off with his arms as if they were flies. After the third volley, he collapsed on the ground.'

Even before Paulus's Sixth Army reached the great bend in the River Don, Stalin had set up a Stalingrad Front and put the city on a war footing. If the Germans crossed the Volga, the country would be split in two. The Anglo-American supply line across Iran was now threatened, just after the British had cancelled further convoys to northern Russia. Women and even schoolgirls were marched out to dig anti-tank ditches and berms to protect the oil-storage tanks beside the Volga. The 10th NKVD Rifle Division had arrived to control the Volga crossing points and bring discipline to a city increasingly seized by panic. Stalingrad was now threatened by Paulus's Sixth Army in the Don bend, and by Hoth's Fourth Panzer Army, suddenly sent back north by Hitler to accelerate the capture of the city.

At dawn on 21 August, infantry from the LI Corps crossed the Don in assault boats. A bridgehead was secured, pontoon bridges built across the river, and the following afternoon Generalleutnant Hans Hube's 16th Panzer Division began to rattle over. Just before first light on 23 August, Hube's leading panzer battalion, commanded by Oberst Hyazinth Graf Strachwitz, advanced towards the rising sun and Stalingrad, which lay just sixty-five kilometres to the east. The Don steppe, an expanse of scorched grass, was rock hard. Only *balkas* or gullies slowed their headlong advance. But Hube's headquarters suddenly halted, having received a radio message. They waited with their engines switched off, then a Fieseler Storch appeared, circled and landed beside Hube's command vehicle. General Wolfram Freiherr von Richthofen, the brutal and shaven-headed commander of the Fourth Luftflotte, strode over. He told Hube that on orders from Führer headquarters the whole of his air fleet was to attack Stalingrad. 'Make use of us today!' he told Hube. 'You'll be supported by 1,200 aircraft. Tomorrow I cannot promise you any more.' A few hours later, German tank crews waved enthusiastically as they saw the massed squadrons of Heinkel 111s, Junkers 88s and Stukas flying over their heads towards Stalingrad.

That Sunday, 23 August 1942, was a day Stalingraders would never forget. Unaware of the proximity of German forces, civilians were picnicking in the sun on the Mamaev Kurgan, the great Tatar burial mound which dominated the centre of a city which stretched for over thirty kilometres along the curve of the Volga's west bank. Loudspeakers in the streets broadcast air-raid warnings, but only when anti-aircraft batteries began firing did people begin to run for cover.

Richthofen's aircraft started to carpet-bomb the city in relays. 'In the late afternoon', he wrote in his diary, 'began my two-day major assault on Stalingrad with good incendiary effects right from the start.' Petroleum-storage tanks were hit, creating fireballs and then huge columns of black smoke which became visible from more than 150 kilometres away. A thousand tons of bombs and incendiaries turned the city into an inferno. The tall apartment buildings, the pride of the city, were smashed and gutted. It was the most concentrated air assault during the whole war in the east. With refugees swelling the population to around 600,000, some 40,000 are estimated to have been killed in the first two days by air attack.

Hube's 16th Panzer Division waved and cheered the aircraft on their return, and the Stukas sounded their sirens in reply.

By late afternoon, Strachwitz's panzer battalion was approaching the Volga just north of the city. But then it came under fire from anti-aircraft batteries with their 37mm guns depressed in the ground role. The young women operating the guns, many of them students, fought on until they were all killed. Panzer commanders were shaken and uneasy when they discovered the sex of the defenders.

The Germans had gone all the way from the Don to the Volga in a single day, and it seemed a great achievement. They had now reached what they considered to be the border of Asia as well as Hitler's ultimate objective, the Arkhangelsk–Astrakhan line. Many felt that the war was as good as over. They took triumphant photographs of each other posing on their tanks, and also snaps of the smoke clouds rising from Stalingrad. A Luftwaffe fighter ace and his wingman, spotting the panzers below, performed victory rolls.

One commander, standing on the top of his panzer on the high western bank of the Volga, gazed across the river through his binoculars. 'We looked at the immense steppe towards Asia, and I was overwhelmed,' he remembered. 'But then I could not think about it for very long because we had to make an attack against another anti-aircraft battery that had started firing at us.' The bravery of the young women became a legend. 'This was the first page of the Stalingrad defence,' wrote Vasily Grossman, who heard first-hand accounts very soon afterwards.

In that summer of crisis for the Grand Alliance, Churchill decided that he had to visit Stalin to explain, face to face, the reasons for the suspension of convoys and why a Second Front was impossible for the moment. He was also enduring strong criticism at home, after the fall of Tobruk and heavy losses in the Battle of the Atlantic. Churchill was not therefore in the best frame of mind for a series of gruelling meetings with Stalin.

He flew from Cairo via Teheran to Moscow, where he arrived on 12 August. Stalin's interpreter watched Churchill inspecting the guard of honour with his chin thrust forward, looking 'intently at each soldier as if gauging the mettle of the Soviet fighting men'. It was the first time that this staunch anti-Bolshevik had set foot on their territory. He was accompanied

(*Above*) Pearl Harbor, 7 December 1941
(*Below*) Hitler declares war on the United States, 11 December 1941

(*Left*) The Soviet counter-offensive near Moscow

(*Below left*) German supply services December 1941

(*Right*) A Soviet medical orderly

(*Below*) The effects of starvation: three identity photos of Nina Petrova in Leningrad, May 1941, May 1942, October 1942

(*Bottom*) Evacuees from Leningrad on the 'Ice Road' across Lake Ladoga

(*Left*) Rommel in North Africa

(*Below*) The Japanese advance in Burma, with soldiers acting as bridge supports

(*Right*) Japanese victory on Corregidor, 6 May 1942

(*Below right*) German officers relax in Paris

(*Above*) German infantry in Stalingrad
(*Below*) US Marines storm Tarawa atoll, 19 November 1943

(*Above*) Camp prisoner about
to be executed
(*Right*) HMS *Belfast* on an
Arctic convoy, November 1943
(*Below*) Soviet war industry
mobilization

(*Above*) Japanese cavalry detachment in China
(*Below*) Hamburg after the firestorm raids of July 1943

by Averell Harriman, who represented Roosevelt at the talks, but had to get into the first car alone with the dour Molotov.

Churchill and Harriman were taken that evening to Stalin's gloomy and austere apartment in the Kremlin. The British prime minister asked about the military situation. This played into Stalin's hands. He accurately described the very dangerous developments in the south just before Churchill had to explain why the Second Front was to be postponed.

Churchill began by describing the great build-up of forces in the United Kingdom. He then spoke of the strategic bombing offensive with the massive raids on Lübeck and Cologne, knowing that they would appeal to Stalin's thirst for revenge. Churchill tried to convince him that German forces in France were too strong to launch a cross-Channel operation before 1943. Stalin protested vigorously, and 'disputed the figures Churchill had cited concerning the size of the German forces in Western Europe'. He said contemptuously that 'someone who was unwilling to take risks could never win a war'.

Hoping to deflect Stalin's anger, Churchill then outlined plans for landings in North Africa, which he was persuading Roosevelt to accept over General Marshall's head. He seized a piece of paper and drew a crocodile, to illustrate his idea that they would be attacking the 'soft underbelly' of the beast. But Stalin was not satisfied with his substitute for a Second Front. And when Churchill mentioned the possibility of an invasion of the Balkans, Stalin immediately sensed that his real purpose was to pre-empt their occupation by the Red Army. Yet the meeting ended in a better atmosphere than Churchill had expected.

But the next day the Soviet dictator's bitter condemnation of Allied perfidy, and Molotov's bullet-headed repetition of all his accusations, angered and depressed Churchill so much that Harriman had to spend several hours trying to restore his spirits. On 14 August, Churchill wanted to break off talks and avoid the banquet prepared in his honour that evening. The British ambassador, Sir Archibald Clark Kerr, a genial eccentric, just managed to change his mind. But Churchill insisted on attending dressed in his 'siren suit', an overall which Clark Kerr compared to a child's rompers, when all the Soviet functionaries and generals would be wearing their dress uniforms.

The dinner in the magnificent Catherine Hall lasted until after midnight, with nineteen courses and constant toasts, mostly initiated by Stalin who came round to clink glasses. 'He has got an unpleasantly cold, crafty, dead face,' General Sir Alan Brooke wrote in his diary, 'and whenever I look at him I can imagine him sending off people to their doom without ever turning a hair. On the other hand there is no doubt that he has a quick brain and a real grasp of the essentials of war.'

Clark Kerr had to use all his charm and persuasion again the next day. Churchill was infuriated by Soviet accusations of British cowardice. But after the meeting was over Stalin invited him back to his office for supper. The atmosphere soon changed, loosened by alcohol and a visit by Stalin's daughter Svetlana. Stalin became friendly, with jokes on both sides, and Churchill suddenly viewed the Soviet tyrant in a completely new light. He convinced himself that he had turned Stalin into a friend, and left Moscow the next day full of glee at his success. Churchill, for whom emotions were often more real than facts, had failed to see that Stalin was even more successful than Roosevelt when it came to manipulating people.

At home there was more bad news awaiting him. On 19 August, Combined Operations commanded by Lord Louis Mountbatten had mounted a major raid on Dieppe on the northern coast of France. Operation Jubilee was launched with just over 6,000 men, most of whom were Canadian troops. They also included some Free French forces and a US Ranger battalion. In the early hours, the eastern assault force ran into a German convoy, and this gave the Wehrmacht warning of the attack. A destroyer and thirty-three landing craft were sunk. All the tanks put ashore were destroyed, and the Canadian infantry were trapped on the beach by the heavy defences and barbed wire.

The raid, which cost over 4,000 casualties, produced harsh, even if obvious, lessons. It convinced the Allies that defended ports could not be taken from the sea, that landings had to be preceded by massive aerial and naval bombardment and, most important of all, that an invasion of northern France should not be undertaken before 1944. Once again, Stalin would be furious about the postponement of what he regarded as the only valid Second Front. Yet the disaster did create one major advantage.

Hitler believed that what he would soon call his Atlantic Wall was virtually impregnable, and that his forces in France could easily defeat an invasion.

In the Soviet Union, news of the Dieppe raid prompted hopes that it was the start of the Second Front, but optimism soon turned to bitter disappointment. The operation was seen as just a weak sop to foreign opinion. The Second Front became a double-edged weapon in Soviet propaganda, both a symbol of hope for the population at large and a way to shame the British and Americans. Red Army soldiers were more cynical. When opening tins of American Lend–Lease Spam (which they called *tushonka* – or stewed meat), they would say 'Let's open the Second Front.'

Unlike their comrades in southern Russia, the morale of German forces around Leningrad was not high. Their failure to strangle 'the first city of Bolshevism' rankled deeply. The harshness of the winter had been replaced by the discomforts of the marshes and swarms of mosquitoes.

The Soviet defenders, on the other hand, gave thanks that they had survived the famine of that terrible winter, which had killed nearly a million people. Major efforts were made to clean up the city and remove the accumulated filth which threatened an epidemic. The population was put to work planting cabbages on every spare plot of ground, including the whole of the Champ de Mars. The Leningrad Soviet claimed that 12,500 hectares of vegetables had been planted in and around the city in the spring of 1942. To prevent another famine next winter, the evacuation of civilians restarted across Lake Ladoga, and over half a million left the city, to be replaced by troop reinforcements. Other preparations included a stockpiling of supplies and the laying of a fuel pipeline across the bottom of Lake Ladoga.

On 9 August, in a great coup to build morale, Shostakovich's Seventh (Leningrad) Symphony was played in the city and broadcast around the world. German artillery attempted to disrupt the performance, but Soviet counter-battery fire reduced it to insignificance, to the joy of Leningraders. They also took great comfort from the fact that the relentless Luftwaffe attacks on shipping across Lake Ladoga were weakened by the destruction of 160 German aircraft.

Soviet intelligence knew that the Germans under Generalfeld-marschall von Manstein, with his newly arrived Eleventh Army, were about to launch a major assault. In an operation codenamed Nordlicht, Hitler ordered Manstein to smash the city and link up with the Finns. To disrupt the attack, Stalin ordered the Lenin-grad and Volkhov Fronts to make another attempt to crush the German salient, which reached up to the southern shore of Lake Ladoga, and thus break the siege. This was known as the Sinyav-ino Offensive, which began on 19 August.

A young Red Army soldier described his first dawn attack in a letter home. 'The air filled with a humming, thundering, howling of shrapnel, the ground was shaking, smoke enveloped the battle-field. We crawled on without stopping. Forward, forward only, otherwise death. A piece of shrapnel cut my lip, blood covered my face, endless pieces of shrapnel were falling from above like hail, burning one's hands. Our machine gun was already working, fire increased, one couldn't raise one's head. A shallow trench was our protection from the shrapnel. We tried to go forward as fast as we could in order to leave the zone of fire. Aircraft started droning above. Bombing began. I can't remember for how long this hell went on. A word went round that German armoured vehicles had appeared. We panicked but the vehicles turned out to be our own tanks ironing the barbed-wire fences. We soon reached this wire and were met with a horrendous fire. It was there that I saw a killed soldier for the first time, he was lying headless along the ditch blocking our way. Only then did it occur to me that I could also get killed. We jumped over the dead man.

'We left the inferno of fire behind. In front of us was an anti-tank trench. From the side somewhere, sub-machine guns were clattering. We ran, bent double. There were two or three explosions. "Hurry up, they're throwing grenades," Puchkov shouted. We ran even faster. Two dead machine-gunners were pressing at a log as if trying to crawl over it, they were blocking our way. We left the trench, ran across a flat space and jumped into [another trench]. A dead German officer was lying on the bottom, his face in the mud. It was empty and quiet here. I'll never forget this long earthen corridor with one wall lit by the sun. Bullets were whistling everywhere. We didn't know where the Germans were, they were both behind us and in front of us.

One of the machine-gunners jumped up to see but was immediately killed by a sniper. He sat down as if lost in thought, his head bent to his chest.'

Soviet losses were heavy – 114,000 casualties including 40,000 dead – but to Hitler's fury this pre-emptive strike completely wrecked Manstein's operation.

Still obsessed with the oilfields of the Caucasus and with the city which bore Stalin's name, Hitler felt sure 'that the Russians were finished', even though far fewer prisoners had been taken than expected. Now established in his new Führer headquarters, code-named Werwolf, outside Vinnitsa in Ukraine, he was tormented by flies and mosquitoes and became increasingly restless in the oppressive heat. Hitler began to grasp at symbols of victory, rather than military reality. On 12 August he had told the Italian ambassador that the Battle of Stalingrad would decide the outcome of the war. On 21 August, German mountain troops scaled the 5,600-metre-high Mount Elbrus, the greatest mountain in the Caucasus, to raise the 'Reich's battle flag'. Three days later the news that Paulus's panzer vanguard had reached the Volga raised the Führer's spirits still further. But then on 31 August he was enraged when Generalfeldmarschall List, the commander-in-chief of Army Group A in the Caucasus, told him that his troops were at the end of their strength and facing much greater resistance than expected. Disbelieving List, he ordered an attack on Astrakhan and the seizure of the western coastline of the Caspian Sea. He simply refused to accept that his forces were inadequate for the task and short of fuel, ammunition and supplies.

German soldiers in Stalingrad, on the other hand, remained highly optimistic. They thought that the city would soon be in their hands, and they could then return home. 'Anyway, we will not be taking up winter quarters in Russia,' wrote a soldier in the 389th Infantry Division, 'as our division has rejected any winter clothing. We should, God willing, see you dear ones again this year.' 'Hopefully the operation will not last too long,' a motorcycle reconnaissance Gefreiter with the 16th Panzer Division remarked casually after commenting that the Soviet women soldiers they had captured were so ugly that you could hardly look at their faces.

Sixth Army headquarters became increasingly anxious about their long supply lines which stretched back over the River Don for hundreds of kilometres. The nights, Richthofen noted in his diary, had suddenly become 'very cool'. Winter was not far off. Staff officers were also concerned about the weak Romanian, Italian and Hungarian armies guarding the right bank of the Don to their rear. Red Army counter-attacks had pushed them back in a number of places to seize bridgeheads across the river which would play a vital part later.

Soviet intelligence officers were already collecting all the material they could on these allies of the Nazis. Many Italian soldiers had been forced to the front against their will, some even brought 'in chains'. Romanian soldiers, the Russians discovered, had been promised by their officers that they would be 'given land in Transylvania and in Ukraine after the war'. Yet the soldiers received a pitiful salary of just sixty lei per month, and their rations amounted to half a mess tin of hot food per day and 300–400 grams of bread. They hated the members of the Iron Guard in their ranks, who acted as spies. The demoralization of the Third and Fourth Romanian Armies was carefully noted in Moscow.

The fate of the fronts at Stalingrad, in the Caucasus and in Egypt was closely linked. A grossly over-extended Wehrmacht, relying excessively on weak allies, was now doomed to lose its great advantage of *Bewegungskrieg* – a war of movement. That era was finished, because the Germans had finally lost the initiative. Führer headquarters, like Rommel in North Africa, could no longer expect the impossible from exhausted troops and unsustainable supply lines. Hitler had begun to suspect that the high water mark of the Third Reich's expansion had been reached. He became even more determined not to permit any of his generals to retreat.

23

Fighting Back in the Pacific

JULY 1942–JANUARY 1943

Following the decision in July 1942 to postpone a cross-Channel invasion and land instead in French North Africa, Admiral King had seized the opportunity to reinforce the Pacific. As far as possible, he intended to keep the war against Japan under the control of the US Navy, using the US Marine Corps to spearhead amphibious operations. The US Army, meanwhile, planned to send nearly 300,000 troops to the region, most of whom would come under the command of General Douglas MacArthur with his headquarters for the south-west Pacific in Australia. King did not share the American public's admiration of MacArthur, in fact he hated him. Even MacArthur's former protégé General Eisenhower regretted that MacArthur had been evacuated from the Philippines.

MacArthur set himself up as a military viceroy, with a court of sycophantic staff officers known as 'the Bataan gang'. Unlike the modest Admiral Nimitz, the ruggedly handsome MacArthur was a master of public relations who liked to be photographed smoking his corncob pipe as he gazed out at the Pacific horizon. He paid little attention to the wishes of his political masters, who were Democrats. He despised Roosevelt and in 1944 seriously considered running against him in the presidential elections. Republican leaders wanted the rabidly right-wing MacArthur to be appointed supreme commander over both the army and the navy. The idea of such an autocratic general interfering in naval strategy horrified Admiral King.

The Far East, at Roosevelt's instigation, had been divided into two areas of responsibility. The British would look after China–Burma–India, known as CBI, even though China was essentially an American interest. The Americans would control operations in the Pacific and the South China Sea, and guarantee the defence of Australia and New Zealand. The two Dominion governments were far from content about an arrangement in which they had no say in strategy, because the joint chiefs of staff in Washington had not the slightest intention of complicating operations by having to consult with allies. In April 1942 they had set up a Pacific War Council of representatives from interested countries, but the body was there solely to allow the Chinese, Dutch, Australians and others 'to let off steam' and no more.

Australia had been the first priority for defence since January when the Japanese seized Rabaul on New Britain and turned it into a major naval and air base. This presented a threat to the shipping route from the United States to Australia. Everyone agreed on the need for action, but a futile quarrel developed over whether operations in the region came under the command of MacArthur or Admiral Nimitz, the commander-in-chief Pacific, or CINCPAC. The subsequent Japanese attempt to take Port Moresby on the south coast of Papua New Guinea in May was postponed after the rather chaotic Battle of the Coral Sea. The Japanese did, however, take the port of Tulagi in the Solomon Islands to the east. Rabaul was the main target for the Americans and MacArthur wanted to attack it immediately, but before attempting its recapture the US Navy insisted that the southern Solomon Islands needed to be secured first. The last thing Nimitz wanted was MacArthur throwing the 1st Marine Division against Rabaul and putting at risk their carriers in waters controlled by Japanese aircraft.

Intelligence from the highly effective Australian 'coast-watcher' groups hidden with radios on the islands warned that the Japanese were building an airfield on Guadalcanal near the south-eastern end of the Solomon archipelago. But at dusk on 21 July, while the Americans were preparing an invasion of Tulagi and Guadalcanal with the 1st Marine Division, and MacArthur was transferring his headquarters from Melbourne to Brisbane, news arrived of a Japanese force of 16,000 men landing at Buna on Papua's north coast. They clearly intended to try once more to capture Port Moresby on the southern side, as a base for attacking Australia.

The Japanese quickly established a bridgehead, then began to advance up the Kokoda Trail. This ran through thick jungle, twisting up and over the 4,000-metre-high Owen Stanley

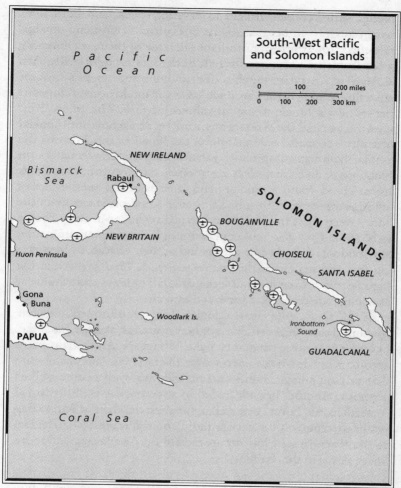

South-West Pacific
and Solomon Islands

Pacific
Ocean

Bismarck
Sea

NEW IRELAND

Rabaul

SOLOMON ISLANDS

BOUGAINVILLE

NEW BRITAIN

CHOISEUL

Huon Peninsula

SANTA ISABEL

Gona
Buna

Woodlark Is.

PAPUA

Ironbottom
Sound

GUADALCANAL

Coral Sea

mountain range. Although heavily outnumbered, the Australian defenders fought a courageous rearguard action, slowing the Japanese down. Both sides suffered in the extreme tropical humidity of the cloudforest from dysentery, typhus, malaria and dengue fever. The slopes of the mountain jungle were so steep that knees and calves managed to ache and feel like jelly at the same time.

Amid the stench of slimy, rotting vegetation, clothes fell to pieces, skin became infected from insect bites, and both sides were half starved because of the difficulties of bringing up supplies. Airdrops for the Australians fell wide of the mark and only a few containers were recovered. Both sides used local Papuans as bearers, carrying supplies and ammunition on poles, or as stretcher-bearers for the wounded. On the muddy, steep slopes of the mountain range, it was an exhausting task. The 10,000 Papuans supporting the Australians were on the whole well looked after, but those coerced to work for the Japanese fared very badly.

The fighting was pitiless. Japanese soldiers, with hooks on their boots, hid themselves in trees to snipe at the Australians from behind. Many would pretend to be dead and hid themselves among corpses until they had a chance to shoot an enemy in the back. Australian soldiers soon learned to bayonet every corpse to be sure. They also took a malicious pleasure in contaminating any food which had to be left behind in their retreat, by bayoneting tins and scattering the rest in the mud. They knew that the Japanese were even more desperate than they were and would eat anything, whatever the gastric consequences.

MacArthur, who was scandalously ill informed, became convinced that the Australian soldiers outnumbered the Japanese, but were just not prepared to fight. In fact the Australians managed to wear down the enemy over the next few months despite the most appalling conditions, and held them well in front of Port Moresby. Another brigade, aided by two squadrons of the Royal Australian Air Force, defeated a Japanese landing at Milne Bay on the extreme south-eastern tip of Papua. The Australian legend of the Kokoda trail has unfortunately put the heroic action by Milne Force in the shade.

On 6 August, shielded by cloud and heavy rain, the eighty-two ships of Task Force 61 approached the islands of Guadalcanal and Tulagi. The 19,000 US marines occupied themselves with checking their weapons, sharpening bayonets and blacking the iron sights of their rifles. There was little of the usual horseplay and friendly insults. At dawn the next morning, as the heavily laden marines clambered down cargo nets into their landing craft, the guns of their escorting warships opened the bombardment. Aircraft from the carriers swept in over their heads to attack

Japanese positions. Soon the landing craft reached the beaches and the marines fanned out under the coconut palms. The American invasion fleet had achieved surprise at both Guadalcanal and Tulagi. The Japanese had not expected the Americans to fight back so soon after all the defeats they had inflicted.

Fighting was fierce on Tulagi, but by nightfall the next day the reinforced 1st Marine Division had secured the two islands. Vice Admiral Fletcher, who commanded the naval task force covering the invasion, was deeply concerned that his three carriers might be attacked by land-based and possibly carrier-launched aircraft. To the fury and disgust of Rear Admiral Richmond K. Turner, the commander of the amphibious force, Fletcher insisted on sailing for home with his carriers and escort vessels within forty-eight hours. Turner considered Fletcher's decision to be tantamount to desertion in the face of the enemy.

In the early hours of 9 August, Turner's covering force was surprised by a strong Japanese cruiser squadron sailing from Rabaul. The Imperial Japanese Navy knew that it enjoyed a decisive advantage in night actions. The Australian cruiser HMAS *Canberra* and three US Navy cruisers and a destroyer were sunk in a little over half an hour. Altogether 1,023 Australian and American sailors were killed. Fortunately for the Allies, Vice Admiral Mikawa Gunichi, fearing an air strike at dawn from the US carriers, which by then were far away, returned towards Rabaul. Turner continued to land more of the marines' equipment on Guadalcanal, then he had to take his ships away after his heavy losses of escort vessels.

The marines, well aware of their dangerous situation, wasted no time in finishing the Japanese aerodrome, which they rechristened Henderson Field. It was on the north coast of Guadalcanal and was surrounded by coconut groves. They were bombed regularly around the middle of every day. The marines called it 'Tojo time'. And Japanese cruisers and destroyers sailing into what was dubbed 'Ironbottom Sound' after the sinkings, shelled the airfield on numerous occasions. On 15 August, US ships slipped in bringing fuel and bombs for the aircraft to be based there. Nineteen Wildcat fighters and twelve dive-bombers, flown off a carrier, arrived five days later. Major General Alexander A. Vandegrift, commander of the 1st Marine Division, admitted that he was close to tears of relief and joy when they landed safely. They were called the Cactus Air Force since Cactus had been the codeword for Guadalcanal.

The nights of waiting for the inevitable Japanese counter-attack were the worst. Sudden noises, whether from large land-crabs, wild pigs in the undergrowth, screeching birds or the dull thud of a coconut dropping on the sand, were enough to spook a sentry to fire into the dark. The days were spent increasing their defences, even though much of the material was still aboard the transports which Admiral Turner had felt obliged to withdraw after Fletcher's departure and the disastrous battle in Ironbottom Sound.

Fortunately for the marines, the Japanese had woefully underestimated their strength. During the night of 18 August, Japanese destroyers from Rabaul landed the 28th Regiment commanded by Colonel Ichiki Kiyono thirty kilometres to the east of Henderson Field. As soon as Vandegrift was informed by patrols of their landing, he ordered the line of the Ilu River to be defended. On the night of 21 August, Colonel Ichiki ordered his men, around a thousand strong, to attack through a mangrove swamp. The marines on the far bank were waiting for them.

Under the deathly green light of illumination flares, they massacred the charging Japanese with machine guns and anti-tank guns firing canister. 'The Fever was on us,' wrote a marine of their bloodlust. Only a few broke through, but they were soon gunned or hacked down. The marines launched a flanking attack with a reserve battalion. 'Some of the Japanese threw themselves into the channel and swam away from the grove of horror,' the same marine continued. 'They were like lemmings. They could not come back. Their heads bobbed like corks on the horizon. The marines lay on their bellies in the sand and shot them through the head.' More than 800 Japanese out of the thousand had been killed. Marine souvenir hunters stripped the fly-infested bodies of anything which might be worth bartering later. One marine nicknamed 'Souvenirs' went from corpse to corpse with a pair of pliers, kicked open the mouth and then removed any gold teeth. Crocodiles soon congregated and had a feast. The marines, huddled in their gunpits, listened to the crunching in the dark with mixed feelings. Colonel Ichiki, who had survived the attack, committed *seppuku*, or ritual disembowelling.

On 23 August, the Japanese sent another landing force, this time with a strong escort from the Combined Fleet. This developed into the Battle of the Eastern Solomons. Admiral Fletcher's carriers were ordered back. His aircraft attacked and sank the small carrier *Ryujo* escorting a squadron of cruisers bombarding Henderson Field, but Fletcher had no idea that the large carriers *Zuikaku* and *Shokaku* were also in the area. The Japanese launched their aircraft against Fletcher's task force and damaged his carrier USS *Enterprise*, but the Japanese lost ninety aircraft while the Americans lost only twenty. The carriers on both sides then withdrew, but marine pilots from Henderson Field and some B-17 Fortresses managed to attack the landing force with unaccustomed success, smashing the main troop transport, sinking a destroyer and severely damaging Rear Admiral Tanaka Raizo's flagship *Jintsu*.

With the Cactus Air Force dominating the sea approaches by day, the Japanese could run in reinforcements only by night. Aircraft losses meant that the Americans too had to land replacements after dark. The marines' obsolete Wildcat fighters were no match for the Zeros, but they still managed to score an impressive number of kills. On the ground, Vandegrift's marines lived rough in their gunpits on the jungle edge or in the coconut groves. Constantly bombed or shelled from the sea, they also fought running battles with small groups of Japanese. And every night a bomber, which they called 'Washing Machine Charlie', droned overhead keeping them awake. The Japanese, short of ammunition, would try to provoke the marines into revealing their positions at night, by cracking together two pieces of bamboo to simulate rifle fire. They would then creep up in the dark and leap into foxholes or gunpits with a machete, hacking in all directions, then leap out again hoping that in the confusion the survivors would kill each other.

Hunger was hardly mitigated by the supplies of worm-infested rice which they had captured from the Japanese. But their worst enemies were tropical fevers, dysentery and rotting flesh from tropical ulcers in the extreme humidity. Courage was an exhaustible currency. A few men broke down under the strain of bombardment, to the intense embarrassment of their comrades. 'Everyone looked the other way,' wrote the same marine, a former sports writer, 'like millionaires confronted by the horrifying sight of a club member borrowing five dollars from the waiter.'

At the end of August, Admiral Tanaka managed to land a force of 6,000 men commanded by Major General Kawaguchi Kiyotake in night runs by destroyers. Their deployment to Guadalcanal instead of to Papua relieved the pressure on the Australians fighting on the Kokoda trail. The main force was brought in where Ichiki's regiment had come ashore, while another landed to the west of Henderson airfield. Kawaguchi was almost as arrogant and unimaginative as Ichiki. Without carrying out any reconnaissance, he decided to launch an attack from the south of Henderson Field.

As soon as he set out, a raiding force attacked his base and destroyed his artillery and radios; the marines then urinated all over the Japanese food supplies. Kawaguchi's force, unaware of this attack, blundered on through the jungle, losing its way frequently. Finally, on the evening of 12 September, Kawaguchi began the attack on the low ridge to the south of Henderson Field. The marines, having heard that they could expect no help from the US Navy after the Japanese force at Rabaul had been reinforced, awaited the worst. If overrun, they would have no option but to break out into the hills and fight a guerrilla war from there. And they were already very short of food.

The Battle of 'Bloody Ridge' cost the marines a fifth of their strength, but the Japanese lost over half their men. Kawaguchi had to admit defeat when his other forces were also beaten off. The survivors had to retreat to the hills, where they and the remnants of Ichiki's failed attack literally starved and their uniforms rotted. Guadalcanal became known in the Japanese forces as 'starvation island'.

Admiral Yamamoto was outraged when he heard of the failure. The insult to Japanese arms had to be avenged, so forces were assembled from all directions to crush the American defenders. Admiral Turner came back with his task force to land reinforcements on 18 September in the shape of the 7th Marine Regiment, but the carrier USS *Wasp* was sunk by a Japanese submarine.

On 9 October, a much larger Japanese force commanded by Lieutenant General Hyakutake Haruyoshi was landed on the island. But two nights later Turner returned again to land the 164th Regiment of the Americal Division. He first had another plan in mind: to ambush what the marines called the 'Tokyo Express', the Japanese warships which brought troops and supplies to Guadalcanal. In this case it consisted of three heavy cruisers and eight destroyers. In the confused night action which followed, known as the Battle of Cape Esperance, the Japanese lost a heavy cruiser and a destroyer, and another heavy cruiser was severely damaged. The Americans suffered serious damage to just one cruiser. American morale soared, and Turner's force landed the 164th Infantry and all the supplies safely. Marines slipped down to the beach to steal some of the 'doggies'' kit and barter with the sailors, using trophies taken from the Japanese dead. A samurai sword went for three dozen large Hershey bars. A 'meatball' flag of the rising sun achieved a dozen.

Over the next two nights, Japanese battleships sailing down Ironbottom Sound bombarded the airfield, destroying nearly half the Cactus Air Force and putting the runway out of commission for a week. But a second runway was under construction, and the reinforcements had made a great difference. The most comforting news for Vandegrift was Vice Admiral Halsey's appointment as commander-in-chief South Pacific. Halsey, well aware that Guadalcanal had turned into a trial of strength between Japan and the United States, was prepared to cancel other operations in order to concentrate maximum force where it was most urgently needed. Roosevelt had exactly the same idea.

The rainy season began and the downpours filled weapon pits and foxholes. Bearded men shivered, soaked to the skin for days on end. The great priority was to keep the ammunition dry. Vandegrift's force managed to repel General Hyakutake's attacks, which were no more subtle than the earlier ones. The marines had cleared scrub and *kunai* grass with machetes to create fields of fire in front of their foxholes and pits. Yet the struggle for Guadalcanal became even more of a battle royal at sea. A series of engagements from the end of October until the end of November turned into a naval war of attrition. American losses were heavier to begin with, and in mid-November clashes over three days ended with the Americans losing two light cruisers and seven destroyers. But they sank two Japanese battleships, a heavy cruiser, three destroyers and seven transports, in which 6,000 reinforcements for General Hyakutake were killed. By the beginning of

December, the US Navy controlled the approaches to the island.

In the second week of December, the exhausted 1st Marine Division was evacuated to rest in Melbourne where it received a riotous welcome from the young women and a Presidential Unit Citation. It was replaced by the 2nd Marine Division, the Americal Division and the 25th Infantry Division commanded as XIV Corps by Major General Alexander M. Patch. Over the next two months, after bitter fighting for Mount Austen south of Henderson Field, Japanese destroyers on the last Tokyo Express evacuated the 13,000 remnants of Hyakutake's 36,000-strong force. Some 15,000 of those who died had succumbed to starvation. The Japanese now referred to Guadalcanal as 'the Island of Death'. For the Americans, Guadalcanal turned out to be the first of the 'stepping stones' which would eventually lead them across the Pacific towards Tokyo.

The events on Guadalcanal had also helped the Australians defending Port Moresby. The Japanese, unable to reinforce or resupply their troops, ordered them to withdraw to Buna on the north coast of Papua where they had landed. The Australians finally enjoyed numerical superiority with their 7th Division returned from the Middle East. For the starved and sick Japanese, their uniforms and boots in tatters, the retreat back through the mountain rainforest was a terrible experience. Many did not survive it. Advancing Australians found that the Japanese had been eating meat from human corpses.

Yet when the Australians and Americans of the 32nd Infantry Division attacked the bridgehead at Gona and Buna, it proved a dangerous undertaking. The Japanese soldiers had constructed brilliantly camouflaged bunkers in the jungle, using the dense trunks of coconut palms which were impervious to machine-gun bullets. On 21 November, after General MacArthur had ordered the 32nd Infantry Division to 'take Buna today at all costs', his soldiers suffered for it. They lacked heavy weapons, were short of food and were also repeatedly bombed by their own air force. Their morale could hardly have been lower.

The 7th Australian Division attacking Gona had an equally bloody experience. On 30 November, part of the 32nd managed to infiltrate the Japanese positions at night by creeping through the tall, sharp *kunai* grass. But the battle for both Buna and Gona continued as a result of the desperate Japanese resistance. Only the arrival of some light tanks and more artillery to deal with the Japanese bunkers allowed the Allies to make headway at last. When the Australians finally took Gona on 9 December, they found that the Japanese had piled their own rotting dead as sandbags round their positions.

Only in January 1943 did the 32nd Division and the Australians finally crush the last resistance in the Buna area. The Japanese defenders had been living on wild grasses and roots. Many had succumbed to amoebic dysentery and malaria as a result of malnutrition, and the few prisoners taken alive were completely emaciated. MacArthur claimed a 'striking victory', and then blamed the 'slowness' of Australian commanders for it having taken so long. But both the Guadalcanal and Papuan battles, which coincided with the Stalingrad campaign in very different climatic conditions, had put an end to the myth of Japanese invincibility. They represented a psychological turning point in the Pacific war, even if the naval battle of Midway was the real one in strategic terms.

In Burma, on the other hand, no turning point was imaginable after the 1,800-kilometre retreat to Assam. For the Allied troops forced back into India, the war in Europe could have been on another planet, even if it affected them directly by reducing their call on reinforcements, air support and supplies. Churchill recognized that the Burma theatre was not central to the war against Japan, except to reopen the road to China. He was interested in recapturing the country only to wipe out the humiliation of defeat and restore Britain's very tarnished prestige.

Field Marshal Wavell, aware that he could not keep troops idle for too long, decided on a limited offensive to recapture the Mayu Peninsula on the Bay of Bengal and the island of Akyab over eighty kilometres down the coast from the frontier. The first offensive in Arakan took place in country consisting of 'steep little hills covered with jungle, of paddy fields and swamps'. The mangrove swamps and little creeks made much of the coastal strip almost impassable.

This operation was seen as a pre-emptive strike to forestall a Japanese invasion of India. The plan was for the 14th Indian

Division to advance from Cox's Bazaar down to the Mayu Peninsula, while the 6th Infantry Brigade was to land at the mouth of the Mayu River to take Akyab with its Japanese airfield. In the event, no landing craft were available as a result of Operation Torch and American needs in the Solomon Islands. General Noel Irwin, the commander of the Eastern Army, had refused to use Slim's XV Corps out of personal antipathy, because Slim had sacked a friend of his in 1940 in the Sudan. He was unbelievably rude to Slim, and when the latter complained, Irwin retorted: 'I can't be rude. I'm senior.'

The advance down the coast was blocked by the Japanese between Maungdaw and Buthidaung, and exceptionally heavy rain made movement extremely hard. The smaller Japanese force then withdrew in December. The 14th Indian Division pushed on, both down the Mayu Peninsula and on the east side of the Mayu River to Rathedaung. But the Japanese had brought in reinforcements, who blocked the peninsula at Donbaik and counter-attacked near Rathedaung.

Like the Americans and Australians elsewhere, the Indian battalions on the peninsula, now reinforced with the British 6th Brigade, suffered heavy casualties from Japanese in well-camouflaged bunkers round Donbaik. In March 1943, a Japanese thrust across the Mayu River threatened the rear of their position, and forced the British to withdraw. One force from the Japanese 55th Division even managed to capture the headquarters of the 6th Brigade and its commander. Eventually the exhausted British and Indian troops, riddled with malaria, retreated back into India. Their 3,000 casualties were twice those of the Japanese. A contemptuous General Stilwell decided that the British were as reluctant as Chiang Kai-shek's Nationalists to fight the Japanese.

On 17 January 1943, Britain and the United States officially gave up any rights to the international settlements, which had been forced upon China in the 'unequal treaties' signed after the Opium Wars and the Boxer Rebellion. This agreement, reluctantly conceded by the British, was an attempt to keep China in the war while the main offensive against Japan was fought in the Pacific. The Doolittle Raid on Tokyo in April 1942 from the carrier USS *Hornet*, with the surviving aircraft landing on the Chinese coast, had provoked a Japanese offensive which destroyed one town and wrecked a Nationalist air base.

Stilwell, perhaps influenced by his responsibility for the disaster which had led to the loss of Mandalay, became obsessed with recapturing Burma. His long-term plan, once the Burma Road was reopened, was to rearm and retrain Chiang Kai-shek's forces to defeat the Japanese in China. On 7 December 1942, General Marshall in Washington decided that America's only interest in retaking northern Burma was to reopen the supply route, not to reinforce Chiang Kai-shek's armies. He wanted only 'the rapid build-up of air operations out of China'.

Marshall was impressed by the reports of Chennault's former Flying Tigers, which became the US Fourteenth Air Force after Pearl Harbor. 'Already the bombing attacks, with very light US casualties,' he added, 'have done damage out of all proportion to the number of planes involved.' Chennault, writing directly to Roosevelt, had claimed that he could destroy the Japanese air force in China, attack Japan's supply lines in the South China Sea and even launch raids on Tokyo itself. Chennault was convinced that he could 'accomplish the downfall of Japan', rather as Air Chief Marshal Sir Arthur Harris in Britain believed that Bomber Command on its own could defeat Germany. Although Washington did not swallow such excessive optimism, a China-based air campaign seemed a much more encouraging proposition than Stilwell's hopes of building up Chinese armies later. Stilwell was outraged at being sidelined and began a feud against Chennault. Marshall had to write him a stiff letter in January 1943, urging him to assist Chennault, but it did little good.

A clash of personalities also contributed to the lack of a coherent strategy in the Pacific, almost entirely due to General MacArthur's personal fixation with the Philippines and his determination to honour his promise 'I will return.' He insisted on a drive through New Guinea to clear the remaining Japanese forces, then he intended to prepare for the invasion of the Philippines. With his brilliant manipulation of the press, MacArthur managed to convince American public opinion that their great moral duty was to liberate their semi-colonial ally from the horrors of Japanese occupation.

The US Navy, with a much more practical plan, wanted to

advance, island group by island group, towards Japan, cutting off supplies from all its far-flung garrisons and forces of occupation. Unable to resolve the impasse with MacArthur, the joint chiefs of staff compromised with a so-called Twin Axis policy which would follow both courses of action at once. Only the United States, with its astonishing output of ships and aircraft, was capable of achieving anything with such a prodigal dispersal of forces.

The fast-growing might of the United States in the Pacific did little to help the Chinese Nationalists, and the Twin Axis policy made them an even lower priority for resources. On the other hand, the marked turn in the fortunes of war by the end of 1942, especially at Guadalcanal, forced Tokyo to cancel plans for the Gogō Offensive, in which the China Expeditionary Army would advance into Szechuan and destroy the Nationalist government in Chungking.

Stalingrad

AUGUST–SEPTEMBER 1942

Stalin was furious when he heard that Soviet forces had been pushed back to the outskirts of Stalingrad. 'What's the matter with them?' he exploded on the telephone to General Aleksandr Vasilevsky, whom he had sent down to report back to the Stavka. 'Don't they realise that this is not only a catastrophe for Stalingrad? We would lose our main waterway and oil too!' As well as Paulus's forces threatening the north of the city, Hoth's two panzer corps were advancing rapidly from the south.

Vasily Grossman, the first correspondent to reach the city smashed by the Luftwaffe, was as alarmed as everyone else. 'This war on the border of Kazakhstan, on the lower reaches of the Volga, gives one the terrifying feeling of a knife driven deep.' As he surveyed the bombed buildings with empty windows and burned-out trams in the street, he compared the ruins of the city to 'Pompeii, seized by disaster on a day when everything was flourishing'.

On 25 August 1942, a state of siege was proclaimed in Stalingrad. The 10th NKVD Rifle Division organized 'destroyer battalions' of male and female workers from the Barrikady Ordnance Factory, the Red October Steel Works and the Dzerzhinsky Tractor Factory. Barely armed, they were sent into action against the 16th Panzer Division with predictable results. Blocking groups of Komsomol (Communist Youth) members with automatic weapons were positioned behind them to stop any retreat. Northwest of the city, the 1st Guards Army was ordered to attack the flank of General Gustav von Wietersheim's XIV Panzer Corps, which was awaiting reinforcements and supplies. The plan was to link up with the 62nd Army which was being forced back into the city, but the panzers, supported by Richthofen's aircraft, pushed the 1st Guards back during the first week of September.

The Luftwaffe continued to smash the ruined city. It also

bombed and strafed river ferries, paddle-steamers and small craft trying to evacuate civilians from the west bank across the Volga. Hitler, bent on the annihilation of the Bolshevik enemy, issued a new instruction on 2 September. 'The Führer commands that on entering the city the entire male population should be eliminated since Stalingrad, with its convinced Communist population of one million, is particularly dangerous.'

The feelings of German soldiers were very mixed, as letters home indicated. Some were exultant at the approaching victory, some grumbled that, unlike in France, there was nothing to buy to send home. Their wives were asking for fur, especially Astra-khan. 'Please send me a present from Russia, no matter what it is,' pleaded one wife. With the RAF raids, news from home was not encouraging. Relatives complained at the increasing call-up. 'When is all this *Schweinerei* going to end?' Soldat Müller read in a letter. 'Soon sixteen-year-olds will be sent into battle.' And his girlfriend told him that she did not go to the *Kino* any more, as she found it 'too sad to watch the newsreels with news of the Front'.

On the evening of 7 September, even though the advance into Stalingrad appeared successful, Hitler went into an unprecedented rage. General Alfred Jodl had just come back to the Führer head-quarters at Vinnitsa from a visit to Generalfeldmarschall List, the commander-in-chief of Army Group A in the Caucasus. When Hitler complained about List's failure to achieve what he had ordered, Jodl replied that List had done what he had been told. Hitler screamed: 'That is a lie!' and stormed out of the room. He then gave orders that stenographers should take down every word said at the daily situation conference.

General Warlimont of the OKW staff, who returned after a short absence, was struck by the dramatic change in atmosphere. Hitler greeted him with a 'long stare of burning hate'. Warlimont later claimed to have thought: 'This man has lost face; he has realized that his fatal gamble is over.' Other members of Hitler's staff also found that he had become completely withdrawn. He no longer ate with his staff or shook their hands. He seemed to distrust everyone. Just over two weeks later Hitler dismissed Gen-eral Halder as chief of the general staff.

The Third Reich had achieved its greatest occupation of

territory. Its forces spread from the Volga to France's Atlantic coast, and from the North Cape to the Sahara. But now Hitler became obsessed with the capture of Stalingrad, mainly because it bore Stalin's name. Beria referred to the battle there as 'a confrontation between two rams' since it had become a matter of prestige for both leaders. Hitler above all grasped at the idea of a symbolic victory at Stalingrad, to replace the looming failure to seize the Caucasian oilfields. The Wehrmacht had indeed reached the 'culminating point', where its offensive had run out of steam and it was no longer able to defeat subsequent attacks.

Yet in the anxious eyes of the outside world, nothing appeared capable of stopping a German advance into the Middle East from both the Caucasus and North Africa. The American embassy in Moscow expected a Soviet collapse at any moment. In that year of disasters for the Allies, most people failed to recognize that the Wehrmacht had become dangerously over-extended. Nor did they appreciate the resolve of the battered Red Army to fight back.

As the 62nd Army pulled back to the edge of the city, General Yeremenko, the commander of the Stalingrad Front, and Khrushchev its chief political officer, summoned Major General Vasily Chuikov to their new headquarters on the east bank of the Volga. He was to take over command of the 62nd Army in Stalingrad.

'Comrade Chuikov,' said Khrushchev, 'how do you interpret your task?'

'We will defend the city or die in the attempt,' Chuikov replied. Yeremenko and Khrushchev said that he had understood correctly.

Chuikov, with a strong Russian face and a shock of crinkly hair, proved to be a ruthless leader, ready to hit or shoot any officer who failed in his duty. In the mood of panic and chaos, he was almost certainly the best man for the task. Strategic genius was not needed in Stalingrad: just peasant cunning and pitiless determination. The German 29th Motorized Division had reached the Volga on the southern edge of the city, cutting the 62nd Army off from its neighbour, the 64th Army commanded by Major General Mikhail Shumilov. Chuikov knew that he had to hang on, wearing the Germans down, whatever the casualties. 'Time is blood,' as he put it later, with brutal clarity.

To block the increasing attempts by troops to escape back across the Volga, Chuikov ordered Colonel Saraev, commander of the 10th NKVD Rifle Division, to place pickets on every crossing point to shoot deserters. He knew that morale was collapsing. Even an assistant political officer had unwisely written in his diary: 'Nobody believes that Stalingrad is going to hold out. I don't think that we will ever win.' Saraev, however, was outraged when Chuikov then told him to deploy the rest of his troops for combat duty, under his orders. The NKVD did not take kindly to any army officer assuming control over its men, but Chuikov knew that he could withstand any threats. He had nothing to lose. His army was down to 20,000 men, with fewer than sixty tanks, many of which were immobile, so they were towed to fire positions to be dug in.

Chuikov had already sensed that German troops did not like close-quarter fighting, so he intended to keep his lines as near to the enemy as possible. This proximity would also hinder the Luftwaffe bombers, afraid of hitting their own men. But perhaps the greatest advantage was the damage they had already done to the city. The landscape of ruins which Richthofen's bombers had created would provide the killing ground for their own men. Chuikov also made the right decision in keeping his heavy and medium artillery on the east bank of the Volga, to fire across at German troop concentrations as they formed up for attacks.

The first major German assault began on 13 September, the day after Hitler had forced Paulus to name a date for the capture of the city. Paulus, suffering from a nervous tic as well as from chronic dysentery, estimated that his forces would take it in twenty-four days. German officers had encouraged their men with the idea that they could sweep through to the bank of the Volga in a great charge. Richthofen's Luftwaffe squadrons had already begun their bombardment, mainly with Stukas screaming down. 'A mass of Stukas came over us,' a Gefreiter in the 389th Infantry Division wrote, 'and after their attack, one could not believe that even a mouse was left alive.' Clouds of pale dust from smashed masonry mingled with the smoke from buildings and the burning oil tanks.

Exposed in his headquarters on the Mamaev Kurgan, Chuikov was out of contact with his divisional commanders because of telephone lines cut by the bombing. He was forced to take his staff in a crouching run to a bunker cut deep into the bank of the Tsaritsa River. Although most German attacks had been slowed by fierce resistance, the 71st Infantry Division broke through into the centre of the city. Yeremenko had the unenviable task of informing Stalin by telephone, when he was in the middle of a conference with Zhukov and Vasilevsky. Stalin immediately gave orders that the 13th Guards Division commanded by Major General Aleksandr Rodimtsev, a hero of the Spanish Civil War, should cross the Volga to join the fighting in the city.

Two of Saraev's NKVD rifle regiments managed to hold the 71st Infantry Division during 14 September, and even retook the central railway station. This gave just enough time for Rodimtsev's guardsmen to start their crossing that night, in a mixture of rowing boats, pinnaces, gunboats and lighters. It was a long and terrifying journey under fire, for the Volga at Stalingrad was 1,300 metres wide. As men in the first boats neared the western side, they could see German infantrymen silhouetted against the flames of blazing buildings on the high bank above them. The first Soviet soldiers ashore charged straight up the steep slope into the attack, lacking even the time to fix bayonets. Joining up with the NKVD riflemen on their left, they pushed the Germans back. As more battalions landed, they fought forward to the railway line at the base of the Mamaev Kurgan, where a bitter battle continued for its 102-metre summit. If the Germans took it, they could control the river crossings with their artillery. The hill was to be churned by shellfire for three months, with corpses buried and disinterred again and again.

Clearly a number of the NKVD riflemen thrown into the front line cracked under the strain. The Special Detachment reported that 'the blocking unit of the 62nd Army arrested 1,218 soldiers and officers between 13 and 15 September, of whom 21 were executed, ten imprisoned and others sent back to their units. Most of the troops arrested are from the 10th NKVD Division.'

'Stalingrad looks like a cemetery or a heap of garbage,' a Red Army soldier wrote in his diary. 'The entire city and the area around it are black as if painted with soot.' Uniforms on both sides were hard to distinguish as they became impregnated with dirt and masonry dust. And on most days the smoke and dust was so thick that the sun could not be seen. The stench of bodies rotting in the ruins mixed with that of excrement and burned iron. At least 50,000 civilians (one NKVD report says 200,000) had failed to cross the Volga or been stopped, now that priority was given to the evacuation of the wounded. They huddled, starved and thirsty, in cellars of the ruined buildings as the battle went on above them, the ground shuddering from explosions.

Life was far worse for those trapped behind German lines. 'From the very first days of the occupation,' the Special Detachment of the NKVD reported later, 'the Germans started eliminating the Jews left behind in the town as well as Communists, Komsomol members and people suspected of being partisans. It was mostly German Feldgendarmerie and Ukrainian auxiliary police who were searching for Jews. Traitors from among the local population also played a significant role. To find and kill the Jews they checked apartments, basements, shelters and dug-outs. Communists and Komsomol members were searched for by the Geheime Feldpolizei, which was actively helped by traitors of the Motherland . . . There were also acts of savage rape of Soviet women by Germans.'

Many Soviet soldiers could not take the psychological strain of battle. Altogether a total of 13,000 were executed for cowardice or desertion during the Stalingrad campaign. Those arrested were forced to strip before being shot, so that their uniforms could be reused without having discouraging bullet holes in them. Soldiers referred to a prisoner receiving his 'nine grams' of lead, a final ration from the Soviet state. Those who turned a blind eye to comrades trying to desert were themselves arrested. On 8 October the Stalingrad Front reported back to Moscow that after the imposition of hard discipline 'the defeatist mood is almost eliminated, and the number of treasonous incidents is getting lower'.

Commissars were particularly disturbed by rumours that the Germans allowed Soviet deserters who crossed over to go home. A lack of political training, a senior political officer reported to Moscow, 'is exploited by German agents who carry out their work of corruption, trying to persuade unstable soldiers to desert, especially those whose families are left in the territories temporarily occupied by the Germans'. Homesick Ukrainians, often refugees from the German advance who had been put into uniform and sent straight to the front, appear to have been the most vulnerable. They had had no news on the fate of their families and homes.

The political department could have pointed to the fact that only 52 per cent of the soldiers of the 62nd Army were of Russian nationality as evidence of the all-embracing nature of the Soviet Union. And even this figure does not take into account the strong Siberian contingent. Just over a third of Chuikov's men were Ukrainian. The balance was made up with Kazakhs, Belorussians, Jews (legally defined as non-Russian), Tatars, Uzbeks and Azerbaijanis. Far too much was expected of the *levée en masse* from central Asia, who had never encountered modern military technology. 'It is hard for them to understand things,' reported a Russian lieutenant sent in to command a machine-gun platoon, 'and it is very difficult to work with them.' Most arrived untrained and had to be shown how to use a gun by their sergeants and officers.

'When we were moved to the second line because of huge losses,' a Crimean Tatar soldier recorded, 'we received reinforcements: Uzbeks and Tajiks, they were all still wearing their skull-caps, even at the front line. The Germans shouted to us in Russian through a megaphone: "Where did you get such animals from?"'

The propaganda addressed to soldiers was crude but probably effective. A picture in the Stalingrad Front newspaper showed a frightened girl with her limbs bound. 'What if your beloved girl is tied up like this by fascists?' said the caption. 'First they'll rape her insolently, then throw her under a tank. Advance, warrior. Shoot the enemy. Your duty is to prevent the violator from raping your girl.' Soviet soldiers believed passionately in the propaganda slogan: 'For the defenders of Stalingrad, there is no earth on the other side of the Volga.'

In early September, German soldiers had been told by their officers that Stalingrad would soon fall and that would mean the end of the war on the eastern front, or at least the chance of home leave. The ring around Stalingrad had been closed when the troops of the Fourth Panzer Army had linked up with Paulus's Sixth Army. Everyone knew that people at home in Germany were awaiting the triumphant news. The arrival of Rodimtsev's 13th Guards Rifle Division and the Germans' failure to take the landing stages in the centre of the city were seen as no more than temporary setbacks. 'Since yesterday,' a member of the 29th Motorized Infantry Division wrote home, 'the flag of the Third Reich flies over the city centre. The centre and the area of the station are in German hands. You cannot imagine how we received the news.' On their left flank, the Soviet attacks from the north were all driven off with heavy casualties. The 16th Panzer Division had positioned their tanks on a reverse slope and knocked out all the Soviet armoured vehicles which appeared over the top of the ridge. Victory seemed inevitable, yet doubts started to arise in some minds with the first frosts.

On the evening of 16 September, Stalin's secretary entered his office silently and laid on his desk the transcript of an intercepted German radio signal. It claimed that Stalingrad had been captured and Russia split in two. Stalin went to the window and stared out, then rang the Stavka. He ordered them to send a signal to Yeremenko and Khrushchev demanding the exact truth on the current situation. But in fact the immediate crisis had already passed. Chuikov had begun to bring further reinforcements across the river to make up for his terrible losses. Soviet artillery, massed on the east bank, was also becoming more adept at breaking up German attacks. And the 8th Air Army was starting to send up more aircraft to face the Luftwaffe, although its aircrew still lacked confidence. 'Our pilots feel that they are corpses already when they take off,' a fighter commander admitted. 'This is where the losses come from.'

Chuikov's tactics were to ignore the orders from Stalingrad Front to launch major counter-attacks. He knew he could not afford the casualties. Instead he relied on 'breakwaters', using reinforced houses as strongpoints, and anti-tank guns concealed in the ruins to fragment the German attacks. He coined the term 'the Stalingrad academy of street-fighting', to describe the night raids by fighting patrols of men armed with sub-machine guns, grenades, knives and even sharpened spades. They attacked through cellars and sewers.

Fighting day and night would take place from floor to floor in ruined building blocks, with enemy groups on different floors, firing and throwing grenades through shellholes. 'A sub-machine gun is useful in house-to-house fighting,' a soldier recorded.

'Germans would often throw grenades at us, and we would then throw grenades at them. Several times I actually caught a German grenade and threw it back, and they exploded even before they hit the ground. My section was ordered to defend one house, and in fact we were all on its roof. The Germans would get to the ground and first floor, and we fired at them.'

The resupply of ammunition became a desperate problem. 'The ammunition brought over during the night is not collected in time by representatives of the 62nd Army command,' the NKVD Special Detachment reported. 'It is unloaded on the bank and then often blown up by enemy fire during the day. The wounded are not taken out until the evening. Heavily wounded men don't get any aid. They die and their corpses are not removed. Vehicles drive over them. There are no doctors. The wounded men are helped by the local women.' Even if they survived the crossing of the Volga and reached a field hospital, their prospects were far from encouraging. Amputations were carried out hurriedly. Many were evacuated in hospital trains to Tashkent. One soldier recorded how, in his ward of fourteen soldiers from Stalingrad, just five men had 'a full set of limbs'.

The Germans, dismayed to have lost their advantages of man-oeuvre, dubbed this new form of combat *Rattenkrieg*, the war of rats. Their commanders, appalled by the intimate savagery of the fighting in which their casualties mounted at a terrifying rate, felt that they were being forced back to the tactics of the First World War. They tried to respond with storm-groups, but their soldiers did not like fighting at night. And their sentries, frightened by the idea of Siberians creeping up to seize them as 'tongues' for inter-rogation, panicked at the slightest sound and began firing. The Sixth Army's expenditure of ammunition in September alone ex-ceeded twenty-five million rounds. 'Germans are fighting without counting ammunition,' the Special Detachment reported back to Beria in Moscow. 'Field guns can fire at just one man while we begrudge a machine gun a belt of rounds.' Yet German soldiers were also writing home to complain of short rations and hunger pains. 'You can't imagine what I am experiencing here,' wrote one. 'Some dogs ran by the other day and I shot one, but the one that I shot turned out to be very thin.'

Other means were used to wear down the Germans and prevent

them getting any rest. The 588th Night Bomber Regiment specialized in flying their obsolete Po-2 biplanes low over the German lines at night and switching off their engines as they made their bombing run. The ghostly swish made a sinister noise. These outstandingly brave pilots were all young women. They were soon dubbed the 'Night Witches', first by the Germans and then by their own side.

During the day psychological pressure was exerted by sniper teams. At first, sniper activity was random and ill planned. But soon Soviet divisional commanders recognized its worth in striking fear into the enemy and bolstering the morale of their own men. 'Sniperism' was raised to a cult by political officers, and as a result one has to be fairly cautious about many of the Stakhanovite claims made about their achievements, especially when propaganda turned ace snipers almost into the equivalent of football stars. The most famous sniper in Stalingrad, Vasily Zaitsev, who was not the highest performer, was probably promoted because he belonged to Colonel Nikolai Batyuk's 284th Rifle Division of Siberians, a formation favoured by Chuikov. The army commander was jealous of the publicity given to Rodimtsev's 13th Guards Rifle Division, so its star sniper Anatoly Chekhov received less attention.

The broken terrain of the smashed city and the closeness of the front lines were ideal. Snipers could hide themselves almost anywhere. A high building offered a far greater field of fire, but escape afterwards became much more dangerous. Vasily Grossman, the correspondent soldiers trusted the most, was even allowed to accompany the nineteen-year-old Chekhov on one of his expeditions. Chekhov, a quiet introverted boy, recounted his experiences to Grossman during long interviews. He described how he selected his victims from their uniforms. Officers were a priority target, especially artillery spotters. So were soldiers fetching water when German soldiers were tortured by thirst. There are even reports that snipers were ordered to shoot down starving Russian children, bribed by German soldiers with crusts of bread to fill their water bottles from the Volga. And Soviet snipers had no qualms about shooting any Russian women seen with the Germans.

As on a fishing expedition, Chekhov would take up a carefully selected position before dawn so as to be ready for 'the morning rise'. Ever since his first kill, he went for head shots and the satisfying spurt of blood which it produced. 'I saw something black spring out from his head, he fell down . . . When I shoot, the head immediately jerks backwards, or to one side, and he drops what he was carrying and falls down . . . Never did they drink from the Volga!'

The captured diary of a German Unteroffizier with the 297th Infantry Division just to the south of Stalingrad revealed how even outside the city ruins snipers had a demoralizing effect. On 5 September, he wrote: 'The soldier who was carrying up our breakfast was shot by a sniper just as he was about to drop into our trench.' Five days later he noted: 'I have just been to the rear and I cannot express how nice it was there. One can walk upright without fear of being shot by a sniper. I washed my face for the first time in thirteen days.' On returning to the front, he wrote: 'The snipers don't give us any rest. They shoot bloody well.'

The Stakhanovite mentality was deeply ingrained in the Red Army, and officers felt compelled to inflate or even invent accounts, as a junior lieutenant explained. 'A report had to be sent in every morning and evening on the losses inflicted on the enemy and on the heroism of the men in the regiment. I had to carry these reports because I had been appointed liaison officer since our battery had no guns left . . . One morning just out of curiosity I read a paper marked "SECRET" sent by the regimental commander. It said that troops of the regiment had repulsed the enemy's attack and damaged two tanks, suppressed the fire of four batteries and killed a dozen of Hitler's soldiers and officers with artillery, rifle and machine-gun fire. And yet I knew perfectly well that the Germans had been sitting peacefully all day in their trenches and that our 75mm guns did not fire a single shell. I cannot really say that this report surprised me. By that time we were already used to following the example of the Sovinform Bureau [an official news agency].'

Red Army soldiers did not just endure fear and hunger and lice, which they referred to as 'snipers', they also suffered from a craving to smoke. Some risked severe punishment by using their identity documents to roll a cigarette if they still had some *makhorka* tobacco left. And when truly desperate, they smoked cotton wool from their padded jackets. All longed for their vodka ration of a hundred grams a day, but supply corporals stole part of it and topped up the remnants with water. Whenever soldiers had the chance, they would barter equipment or clothing with civilians for *samogonka*, or moonshine.

The bravest of the brave in Stalingrad were the young women medical orderlies, who constantly went out under heavy fire to retrieve the wounded and drag them back. Sometimes they returned fire at the Germans. Stretchers were out of the question, so the orderly either wriggled herself under the wounded soldier and crawled with him on her back, or else she dragged him on a groundsheet or cape. The wounded were then taken down to one of the landing stages for evacuation across the huge river, where they ran the gauntlet of artillery, machine guns and air attack. Often there were so many that they were left untended for many hours, sometimes even days. The medical services were overwhelmed. And in the field hospitals, which lacked blood banks, nurses and doctors offered their own in arm-to-arm transfusions. 'If they don't, soldiers will die,' Stalingrad Front reported to Moscow. Many collapsed from giving too much blood.

The critical battle for Stalingrad also saw a major shift in power within the Red Army. On 9 October, Decree No. 307 announced 'the introduction of a unified command structure in the Red Army and the elimination of the post of commissar'. Commanders who had suffered from the interference of political officers felt triumphant. It was an essential part in the renaissance of a professional officer corps. Commissars, on the other hand, were appalled to find that commanders now ignored them. The political department of Stalingrad Front deplored the 'absolutely incorrect attitude' which had emerged. Numerous examples were sent back to Moscow. One commissar reported that the 'political department is considered to be an unnecessary appendix'.

Soviet military intelligence and the NKVD were also alarmed to discover from interrogations of prisoners that a large number of their soldiers taken prisoner were now working for the Germans in various capacities. 'On some parts of the front,' the Stalingrad political department reported to Moscow, 'there have been cases of former Russians who put on Red Army uniform and penetrate our positions for the purpose of reconnaissance and seizing officer and soldier prisoners for interrogation.' But they never imagined that there were just over 30,000 of them attached to the Sixth Army alone. Only after the battle did they discover the scale from interrogations, and how the system worked.

'Russians in the German army can be divided into three categories,' a prisoner told his NKVD interrogator. 'Firstly soldiers mobilized by German troops, so-called Cossack [fighting] platoons which are attached to German divisions. Secondly *Hilfsfreiwillige* [known as 'Hiwis'] made up of local people or Russian prisoners who volunteer, or those Red Army soldiers who desert to join the Germans. This category wears full German uniform, and has ranks and badges. They eat like German soldiers and are attached to German regiments. Thirdly, there are Russian prisoners who do the dirty jobs, kitchens, stables and so on. These three categories are treated in different ways, with the best treatment naturally reserved for the volunteers.'

In October 1942, Stalin faced other problems. Chiang Kai-shek and the Kuomintang leadership in Chungking were keen to exploit Soviet weakness at this moment, when German armies threatened the Caucasian oilfields. For several years Stalin had been increasing Soviet control over the far north-western province of Sinkiang, with its mines and the important Dushanzi oilfield. With careful diplomacy, Chiang began to reassert Chinese Nationalist sovereignty over the province. He forced the Soviets to withdraw troops and hand back mining and aircraft-manufacturing enterprises which they had set up. Chiang sought American assistance, and eventually the Soviets pulled out with ill grace. Stalin could not risk alienating Roosevelt. Chiang's very clever handling of the situation prevented the Soviet Union from taking over Sinkiang, in the same way as it controlled Outer Mongolia. The Soviet withdrawal also signified a major setback for the Chinese Communists in the province. They would not return until 1949 when Mao's People's Liberation Army captured it towards the end of the civil war.

The relentless German attacks in Stalingrad were renewed with even greater vigour during October. 'A furious artillery bombardment began when we were preparing breakfast,' wrote a Soviet soldier. 'The kitchen in which we were sitting was suddenly filled with foul-smelling smoke. Plaster fell into our mess-tins with their watery millet broth. We immediately forgot about our soup. Someone outside shouted "Tanks!" His cry broke through the noise of thunder, of walls collapsing and someone's heartbreaking screams.'

Although the 62nd Army had been pushed back dangerously close to the bank of the Volga, it continued to fight a terrible battle of attrition in the ruined factories of the northern part of the city. Stalingrad Front reported that its troops showed a 'real mass heroism'. It was, however, greatly helped by the massive increase in Soviet artillery fire from across the Volga, breaking up German attacks.

During the first week of November, Stalingrad Front noted a change. 'In the last two days,' observed a report to Moscow of 6 November, 'the enemy have been changing tactics. Probably because of big losses over the last three weeks, they have stopped using big formations.' In the course of three weeks of heavy and expensive attacks, the Germans had not managed to advance more than an average of 'fifty metres a day'. The Russians identified the new German tactic of 'reconnaissance in force to probe for weak points between our regiments'. But these new 'sudden attacks' were achieving no more success than the old ones. The morale of Soviet soldiers was improving. 'I often think of the words of Nekrasov that the Russian people are able to bear everything that God is able to throw at us,' wrote one soldier. 'Here in the army one can easily imagine that there is no force on earth which can do away with our Russian strength.'

German morale, on the other hand, was suffering badly. 'It's impossible to describe what is happening here,' a German corporal wrote home. 'Everyone in Stalingrad who still possesses a head and hands, women as well as men, carries on fighting.' Another acknowledged that 'the [Soviet] dogs fight like lions'. A third even wrote home: 'the sooner I am under the ground, the less I will suffer. We often think that Russia should capitulate, but these uneducated people are too stupid to realize it.' Infested with lice, weakened by short rations and vulnerable to many ailments, of which the most prevalent was dysentery, their only comfort was to look forward to winter quarters and Christmas.

Hitler demanded a final push to seize the west bank of the Volga before the snows came. On 8 November, he boasted in a speech to the Nazi 'Old Fighters' in the Bürgerbräukeller in Munich that Stalingrad was as good as captured. 'Time is of no importance,' he claimed. Many officers in the Sixth Army listened in disbelief to his words, broadcast by Berlin radio. Rommel's Panzerarmee Afrika was in retreat and Allied forces had just landed on the North African coast. It was an example of terrible bravado which would have a disastrous effect on German fortunes, especially those of the Sixth Army. Out of pride, Hitler would not be able to countenance a strategic withdrawal.

A series of ill-considered decisions followed. Führer headquarters ordered that most of the Sixth Army's 150,000 artillery and transport horses should be sent several hundred kilometres to the rear. Huge quantities of fodder would no longer have to be sent forward, thus saving greatly on transport. This measure deprived all the unmotorized divisions of mobility, but perhaps Hitler intended to remove any possibility of retreat. His most disastrous order was to command Paulus to send almost all his panzer forces into the 'final' battle for Stalingrad, even spare tank drivers to be used as infantry. Paulus obeyed him. Rommel, if he had been in his place, almost certainly would have ignored such an instruction.

On 9 November, the day after Hitler's speech, winter arrived in Stalingrad. The temperature suddenly dropped to minus 18 degrees Centigrade, which made crossing the Volga even more dangerous. 'The ice floes collide, crumble and grind against each other,' wrote Grossman, affected by the eerie sound. Resupply and the evacuation of wounded became almost impossible. German artillery commanders, aware of the problems their enemy faced, concentrated their fire even more on the crossing points. On 11 November, battle groups from six German divisions, supported by another four pioneer battalions, began their offensive. Chuikov promptly sent in counter-attacks that night.

Chuikov in his memoirs claimed that he had no idea of what the Stavka was planning, but this is untrue. He knew, as a report to Moscow reveals, that he had to keep the maximum number of German forces fighting in the city at that time so that the Sixth Army could not strengthen its vulnerable flanks.

German commanders and staff officers had long been acutely

conscious of how weakly held their flanks were. Their left rear along the Don was held by the Romanian Third Army, and the sector to their south was defended by the Romanian Fourth Army. Neither of these formations was well armed, their men were demoralized and they lacked anti-tank guns. Hitler had dismissed all warnings, claiming that the Red Army was at its last gasp and was incapable of launching an effective offensive. He also refused to accept estimates of Soviet tank production. The output of Soviet men and women workers, in improvised and unheated factories in the Urals, had in fact reached over four times that of German industry.

Generals Zhukov and Vasilevsky had been aware of the great opportunity offered ever since 12 September, when it looked as if Stalingrad was about to fall. Chuikov had been given sufficient reinforcements to hold the city, but no more. In fact the 62nd Army had been kept as the bait in a vast trap. All through the terrifying autumn battles, the Stavka had been building up its reserves and forming new armies, especially tank formations, and deploying Katyusha rocket batteries. They had discovered how effective their new weapon was in terrifying their enemy. Soldat Waldemar Sommer of the 371st Infantry Division told his NKVD interrogator: 'If the Katyusha sings just a couple more times, all that will be left of us will be our iron buttons.'

Stalin, usually so impatient, had finally listened to his generals' arguments that they needed time. They had persuaded him that hammering away from the outside at the Sixth Army's northern flank was futile. What the Red Army needed to aim for was a huge envelopment with large tank formations from much further back, to the west along the Don and from the south of Stalingrad. Stalin was not bothered that this meant a return to the doctrine of 'deep operations' advocated by Marshal Mikhail Tukhachevsky, which had become heretical after his execution in the purges. The prospect of a massive revenge opened his mind to this bold plan which would 'shift the strategic situation in the south decisively'. The offensive was to be called Operation Uranus.

Since mid-September, Zhukov and Vasilevsky had been assembling new armies and training them with short periods on different sectors of the front. This procedure had the added advantage of confusing German intelligence, which began to expect a major offensive against Army Group Centre. Deception measures – *maskirovka* – were put in place, with assault boats openly displayed on the Don near Voronezh where no attack was planned, while troops were made to dig defensive positions conspicuously on the sectors where the offensive would take place. But German suspicions of a major offensive against the Rzhev Salient west of Moscow were in fact well founded.

Soviet military intelligence had accumulated encouraging reports on the state of the Romanian Third and Fourth Armies. Interrogation revealed a hatred among their conscripts for Marshal Antonescu, who had 'sold their Motherland to Germany'. A soldier's daily pay was no more than 'enough to buy one litre of milk'. Officers were 'very rude to soldiers and often strike them'. There had been many cases of self-inflicted wounds, despite lectures from officers that they were 'a sin against the Motherland and God'. German troops insulted them frequently, leading to fights, and Romanian soldiers had killed a German officer who shot two of their comrades. The interrogator concluded that Romanian forces were in a 'low political moral state'. NKVD interrogations of prisoners also discovered that soldiers from the Romanian army were 'raping all the women in the villages to the south-west of Stalingrad'.

On the Kalinin and Western Fronts, the Stavka was also planning Operation Mars to be launched against the German Ninth Army. The main objective was to ensure that not a single division could be 'moved from the central part of the front to the southern part'. Although Zhukov was responsible for supervising this operation as a Stavka representative, he devoted far more time to planning Uranus than Mars. Zhukov spent the first nineteen days in Moscow, just eight and a half days on the Kalinin sector of the front, and no fewer than fifty-two days on the Stalingrad axis. This alone indicates that Mars was an ancillary operation, despite its deployment of six armies.

In the view of Russian military historians, the factor which demonstrated conclusively that Mars was a diversion and not, as David Glantz has argued, a coequal operation, was the allocation of artillery ammunition. According to General of the Army M. A. Gareev of the Russian Association of the Second World

War Historians, the Uranus offensive received '2.5 to 4.5 ammunition loads [per gun] at Stalingrad compared with less than one in Operation Mars'. This striking imbalance suggests a remarkable disregard of human life on the part of the Stavka, which was prepared to send six armies into battle with insufficient artillery support to tie down Army Group Centre during the Stalingrad encirclement.

According to the spymaster General Pavel Sudoplatov, this ruthlessness was wholly cynical. He described how details of the forthcoming Rzhev Offensive were deliberately passed to the Germans. Together, the Administration for Special Tasks of the NKVD and GRU military intelligence had prepared Operation Monastery, an infiltration of the German Abwehr. Aleksandr Demyanov, the grandson of the leader of the Kuban Cossacks, had been instructed by the NKVD to allow himself to be recruited by the Abwehr. Generalmajor Reinhard Gehlen, the German intelligence chief for the eastern front, gave him the codename Max and claimed that he was his best agent and network organizer. But Demyanov's underground organization of anti-Communist sympathizers was entirely controlled by the NKVD. Max had 'defected' across the lines on skis during the chaos of the Soviet counter-attack in December 1941. Since the Germans had already identified him as a likely agent during the Nazi–Soviet pact, and his family was well known in White Russian émigré circles, Gehlen trusted him completely. Max was then parachuted behind Red Army lines in February 1942 and soon began to radio back plausible but inaccurate intelligence provided by his NKVD controllers.

In early November, preparations were well advanced for Operation Uranus around Stalingrad and the diversionary attack of Operation Mars near Rzhev. Max was now instructed to give the Germans details of Mars. 'The offensive predicted by Max on the central front near Rzhev', wrote General Sudoplatov, chief of the Administration for Special Tasks, 'was planned by Stalin and Zhukov to divert German efforts away from Stalingrad. The disinformation planted through Aleksandr was kept secret even from Marshal Zhukov, and was handed to me personally by General Fedor Fedotovich Kuznetsov of the GRU in a sealed envelope . . . Zhukov, not knowing that this disinformation game

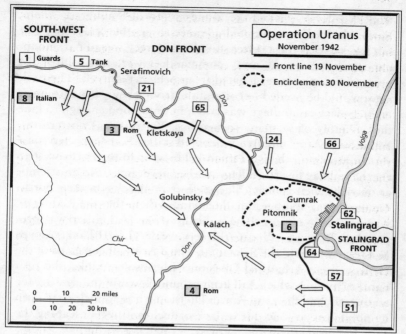

SOUTH-WEST FRONT

DON FRONT

Operation Uranus
November 1942

Front line 19 November

Encirclement 30 November

1 Guards
5 Tank
Serafimovich
21
8 Italian
65
Don
3 Rom Kletskaya
24
66
Volga
Golubinsky
Gumrak
Pitomnik
62
Kalach
6
Stalingrad
Chir
Don
STALINGRAD FRONT
64
57
4 Rom
51

0   10   20 miles
0 10 20 30 km

was being played at his expense, paid a heavy price in the loss of thousands of men under his command.'

Ilya Ehrenburg was one of the few writers to visit the fighting there. 'One part of a small wood on the outskirts of [Rzhev] had been a battlefield; the trees blasted by shells and mines looked like stakes driven in at random. The earth was criss-crossed by trenches; dugouts bulged like blisters. One shell-hole gaped into the next . . . The deep roar of guns and the furious bark of mortars were deafening, then suddenly, during a lull of two or three minutes, the chatter of machine guns would be heard . . . In the field hospitals they were giving blood-transfusions, amputating arms and legs.' The Red Army had suffered 70,374 dead and 145,300 wounded, a massive sacrificial tragedy that was kept secret for nearly sixty years.

For the great encirclement operation against the Sixth Army, Zhukov reconnoitred in person the attack sectors on the Don while Vasilevsky visited the armies south of Stalingrad. There, Vasilevsky ordered a limited advance to just beyond the line of salt lakes to provide a better start-line. Secrecy was of paramount importance. Even the army commanders were not told of the plan. Civilians were evacuated from behind the front. Their villages would be needed to conceal the troops being brought up at night. Soviet camouflage was good, but not good enough to hide the assembly of so many formations. Yet this was not critical. While Sixth Army and Army Group B staff officers expected some sort of attack on the Romanian-held sector to the north-west to cut the railway line to Stalingrad, they never imagined an attempt at outright encirclement. The ineffective attacks on their northern flank near Stalingrad had convinced them that the Red Army was incapable of launching a deadly strike. All Hitler was prepared to do was to allocate the very weak XLVIII Panzer Corps as a reserve behind the Romanian Third Army. It consisted of the 1st Romanian Armoured Division with obsolete tanks, the 14th Panzer Division which had been ground down in the fighting for Stalingrad, and the 22nd Panzer Division whose vehicles had been immobile for so long due to lack of fuel that mice, escaping the cold, hid inside them and gnawed through the wiring.

As a result of transport shortages, Operation Uranus had to be postponed until 19 November. Stalin's patience was severely taxed. With more than a million men now in position, he was terrified that the Germans would discover what was happening. From north of the Don the 5th Tank Army, the 4th Tank Corps, two cavalry corps and other rifle divisions crossed at night into the bridgeheads. South of Stalingrad, two mechanized corps, a cavalry corps and supporting formations were brought across the Volga in the dark, a perilous undertaking with the ice floes coming down the river.

During the night of 18–19 November, Soviet sappers in the Don bridgeheads had crawled forward through the snow in white camouflage uniforms to clear minefields. In the thick, freezing mist they were invisible to the Romanian sentries. At 07.30 hours, Moscow time, howitzers, artillery, mortars and Katyusha rocket regiments all opened fire simultaneously. Despite the bombardment, which made the ground tremble fifty kilometres away, the Romanian soldiers resisted far more tenaciously than

German liaison officers had expected. As soon as the tanks were thrown into the attack, steamrolling the barbed wire, the Soviet advance began, with T-34s and cavalry cantering across the snowfields. Caught in the open, German infantry divisions found themselves fighting off cavalry charges 'as if it were 1870', as one officer wrote.

Sixth Army headquarters was not unduly alarmed, and it heard that the XLVIII Panzer Corps was advancing to counter the breakthrough. But interference from Führer headquarters and changes of orders caused confusion. With 22nd Panzer Division barely able to move because most of its tanks' electrics were still unrepaired, Generalleutnant Ferdinand Heim's counter-attack collapsed in chaos. When Hitler found out, he wanted Heim shot.

By the time Paulus started to react it was far too late. His infantry divisions lacked their horses and thus their mobility. His panzer formations were still tied down in Stalingrad itself, and unable to disengage quickly because of attacks launched by General Chuikov to prevent this. When they were finally free, the panzer troops were ordered west to join Generalleutnant Karl Strecker's XI Corps to block the breakthrough far in their rear. But this meant that the southern flank, guarded by the Fourth Romanian Army, was left with just the 29th Motorized Division as a reserve.

On 20 November, General Yeremenko gave the order for the southern attack to begin. Led by two mechanized corps and a cavalry corps, the 64th, 57th and 51st Armies began to advance. The moment of revenge had come, and morale was high. Wounded soldiers refused to be evacuated to the rear. 'I'm not leaving,' said a member of the 45th Rifle Division. 'I want to attack with my comrades.' Romanian soldiers surrendered in large numbers, and many were shot out of hand.

Without air reconnaissance at this crucial moment, Sixth Army headquarters failed to apprehend the Soviet plan. This was for the two thrusts to meet up in the area of Kalach on the Don, having encircled the whole of the Sixth Army. On the morning of 21 November, Paulus and his staff in their headquarters at Golubinsky, twenty kilometres north of Kalach, had little idea of the danger. But as the day progressed, with alarming reports arriving of the progress of the Soviet spearheads, they became aware of the imminent catastrophe. There were no units available to stop the enemy, and their own headquarters was now threatened. Files were burned rapidly, and disabled reconnaissance aircraft on the landing strip destroyed. That afternoon Führer headquarters signalled Hitler's order: 'Sixth Army stand firm in spite of danger of temporary encirclement.' The fate of the largest formation in the whole Wehrmacht was about to be sealed. Kalach, with its bridge over the Don, was virtually undefended.

The commander of the Soviet 19th Tank Brigade discovered from a local woman that German tanks always approached the bridge with their lights on. He therefore put two captured panzers at the head of his column, ordered all drivers to turn on their lights, and drove straight on to the bridge at Kalach before the scratch unit of defenders and Luftwaffe anti-aircraft guncrews realized what was happening.

The next day, Sunday, 22 November, the two Soviet spearheads met up in the frozen steppe, guided towards each other by firing green flares. They embraced with bear-hugs, exchanging vodka and sausage to celebrate. For the Germans, that day happened to be *Totensonntag* – the day of remembrance for the dead. 'I don't know how it is all going to end,' Generalleutnant Eccard Freiherr von Gablenz, the commander of the 384th Infantry Division, wrote to his wife. 'This is very difficult for me because I should be trying to inspire my subordinates with an unshakeable belief in victory.'

25

Alamein and Torch

OCTOBER–NOVEMBER 1942

In October 1942, while Zhukov and Vasilevsky were preparing their great encirclement of the Sixth Army at Stalingrad, Rommel was in Germany on sick leave. He had been suffering from stress, with low blood pressure and intestinal problems. His last attempt to break through the Eighth Army in the Battle of Alam Halfa had failed. Many of his troops were also ill, as well as desperately short of food, fuel and ammunition. After all his dreams of conquering Egypt and the Middle East had turned to ashes, Rommel refused to accept personal responsibility. He went on to convince himself that Generalfeldmarschall Kesselring had deliberately held back supplies for the Panzerarmee Afrika out of jealousy.

The Panzerarmee Afrika's position was indeed serious. The Italians in the rear areas and the Luftwaffe were keeping the bulk of the supplies for themselves. German morale was very low. Thanks to Ultra intercepts, Allied submarine attacks and bombing sank even more freighters in October. Hitler's distrust of his 'anglophile allies' convinced him 'that German transports were being betrayed to the English by the Italians'. The possibility that German Enigma codes were being broken did not occur to him.

General der Panzertruppe Georg Stumme, the corps commander who had been court-martialled for the loss of the plans for Operation Blau, commanded the army in Rommel's absence, and Generalleutnant Wilhelm von Thoma took over the Afrika Korps. Hitler and the OKW did not believe that the British would attack before the next spring, and therefore there was still a chance for the Panzerarmee Afrika to break through to the Nile Delta. Rommel and Stumme were more realistic. They knew that they could do little in the face of Allied air power and the Royal Navy's attacks on their supply convoys.

Rommel was further dismayed by the complacency he

encountered in Berlin when he received his field marshal's baton. Göring dismissed Allied air power, saying: 'Americans can only make razor blades.' 'Herr Reichsmarschall,' Rommel replied, 'I wish we had such razor blades.' Hitler promised to send forty of the new Tiger tanks, together with units of Nebelwerfer multi-barrelled rocket launchers, as if these would be more than enough to make up for his shortages.

The OKW played down any suggestion that the Allies might land in north-west Africa in the immediate future. Only the Italians took the threat seriously. They made contingency plans to occupy French Tunisia, a project which the Germans opposed for fear of resistance from the Vichy French forces. In fact, Allied planning for Operation Torch was more advanced than even the Italians suspected. In early September, Eisenhower's headaches began to lessen as transatlantic disagreements were resolved. There would be simultaneous landings at Casablanca on the Atlantic coast, and at Oran and Algiers in the Mediterranean. But the supply problem, due to confusion and a shortage of shipping, became a nightmare for his chief of staff, Major General Walter Bedell Smith. Most of the troops crossing the Atlantic arrived without weapons or equipment, so amphibious training was delayed.

On the diplomatic front, both the American and British governments began to reassure Franco's regime in Spain that they had no intention of violating Spanish sovereignty, either in North Africa or on the mainland. This was necessary to counter German rumours that the Allies planned to seize the Canary Islands. Fortunately, the pragmatic General Conde Francisco de Jordana was again foreign minister after Franco had removed his pro-Nazi and over-ambitious brother-in-law, Ramón Serrano Súñer. The diminutive and elderly Jordana was determined to keep Spain out of the war, and his appointment in September was a great relief to the Allies.

Stumme, although lacking precise intelligence, remained certain that Montgomery was preparing a major offensive. He stepped up patrol activity and accelerated the laying of nearly half a million mines, in so-called 'devil's gardens' in front of the Panzer-armee Afrika's positions. Following Rommel's guidance, Stumme

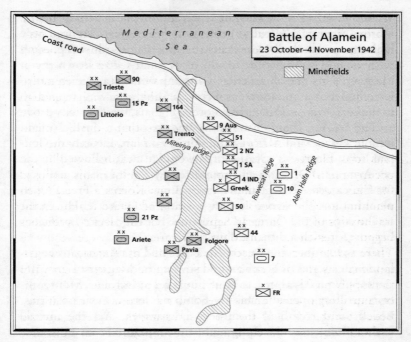

strengthened the Italian formations with German units and split the Afrika Korps, with the 15th Panzer Division behind the northern part of the front and the 21st Panzer Division in the south.

General Alexander acted as an umbrella, shielding Montgomery from Churchill's impatience. Montgomery needed time to train his new forces, especially Lieutenant General Herbert Lumsden's X Armoured Corps, which he proudly and over-optimistically called his *corps de chasse*. The newly arrived Shermans were being prepared, bringing the Eighth Army's strength up to over a thousand tanks. Lumsden, a flamboyant cavalryman who had won the Grand National, was hardly Montgomery's favourite but Alexander liked him.

Montgomery's plan, Operation Lightfoot, consisted of making his main attack in the northern sector, which was also the most heavily defended. He assumed that the Germans would not expect this. Lumsden's X Corps was to exploit the breakthrough once XXX Corps made it across the minefield south of the coast road.

With the aid of a sophisticated deception plan carried out by Major Jasper Maskelyne, a professional illusionist, Montgomery hoped to persuade the Germans that his main push was coming in the south, so that they would move their forces down there. Maskelyne installed hundreds of dummy vehicles and even a fake water pipeline in the southern sector. Radio traffic was stepped up in the area, transmitting pre-recorded signals, while trucks drove around towing chains behind the lines to stir up dust. To lend weight to this vital part of Montgomery's plan, Lieutenant General Brian Horrocks's XIII Corps would attack, followed by the 7th Armoured Division and supported by a third of his artillery. On the extreme left of the Alamein Line, Koenig's Free French would attack the strong Italian position of Qaaret el Himeimat on the edge of the Qattara Depression, but they lacked sufficient support for such a difficult objective.

On 19 October, the Desert Air Force and the Americans began to launch a series of bombing and strafing raids against Luftwaffe airfields. Four days later, at 20.40 hours on 23 October, Montgomery's artillery opened a massive bombardment of Axis positions. The ground trembled from the shockwaves, and the muzzle flashes illuminated the entire night-time horizon. From a distance it looked like sheet lightning. Allied bombers attacked the reserve positions and rear areas. General Stumme, afraid of using up his ammunition, ordered his own artillery not to respond.

Since dusk, sappers had been moving slowly forward as the moon rose, prodding the sand with bayonets and lifting mines to create corridors marked by white tape and oil lamps. At 22.00 hours, XXX Corps started to advance through them with four divisions – the 51st Highland, 9th Australian, 1st South African and 2nd New Zealand – each supported by at least one armoured regiment. The newly arrived Highlanders went in with pipes skirling and bayonets fixed, having heard that the Italian troops seemed to fear cold steel more than almost anything else. Infantry casualties were comparatively light, but, to Montgomery's irritation, the tanks of Lumsden's X Corps became mixed up in the minefields. The delays meant that they were hit hard once dawn came.

General Stumme wanted to see the situation at the front for himself, but when his vehicle came under fire the driver drove away, not realizing that Stumme had got out. Stumme died from a heart attack and his body was not found until the following day. When General von Thoma heard the news and took command, he was reluctant to launch a major counter-attack, because he did not dare use up fuel before his forces were resupplied. But on 25 October both the 15th Panzer Division in the north and 21st Panzer in the south put in successful local responses.

Montgomery's master plan was not going well. The Germans had not swallowed his feint, and no forces had been sent to the south to face the diversionary attack by XIII Corps. Meanwhile in the north, the German minefields and Axis resistance had proved much stronger than expected. Montgomery unfairly blamed the 10th Armoured Division, even accusing it of cowardice, when in fact it was being misused. Montgomery's anti-cavalry prejudice did not help him learn how best to use his armour.

On hearing of the British offensive and Stumme's death, Rommel ordered a plane to fly him to Africa via Rome. He reached his headquarters at dusk on 25 October, having heard in Rome that the fuel situation was worse than ever due to the Royal Navy and the Allied air forces.

The British attack was then helped when the Australians captured two German officers carrying detailed maps of their minefields. The Australians seized a key hill during the night, which they held against heavy counter-attacks the next day. With the build up of XXX Corps and X Corps, the pressure in the north on the Panzerarmee Afrika was becoming irresistible. Rommel then heard that the tanker on which they had been counting had also been sunk. He warned OKW that with little fuel and a lack of ammunition he would find it hard to continue the battle. By now it was clear that Montgomery was concentrating the bulk of his forces in the north, so Rommel moved the 21st Panzer Division up to help. Without the necessary fuel for his panzers to withdraw and fight a battle of movement in the open, he was now tied down to a slogging match which he could not win. Over half his panzers had been destroyed, falling victim either to the six-pounder anti-tank gun or to air attacks. The new 37mm gun on the American P-39 Airacobras proved a most effective tank-busting weapon.

Montgomery, forced to change his plan in the face of such a determined defence, prepared a new offensive while the Australians bore the brunt of the continuing counter-attacks. On 2 November, Operation Supercharge began in the early hours, with another heavy bombardment accompanied by air attacks. Montgomery sent in the 9th Armoured Brigade in a charge against dug-in anti-tank guns. He was warned that it would be suicidal, but replied that it had to be done. The attack proved another Balaklava, and the brigade was virtually wiped out. Freyberg's New Zealand Division advanced well north of Kidney Ridge, but German counter-attacks with both panzer divisions prevented a breakthrough. Containing the bridgehead, however, represented the Panzerarmee's last effort. Montgomery was finally winning the battle of attrition.

Rommel gave orders to withdraw towards Fuka, even though he knew that the unmotorized troops, mostly Italian, would be rapidly overrun. Many German troops seized Italian trucks for themselves at gunpoint, producing ugly scenes. That evening Rommel sent a message to the OKW, outlining the situation and giving reasons for his retreat. Due to a misunderstanding on the part of a staff officer, Hitler did not receive the signal until the next morning. Suspecting a conspiracy to prevent him from countermanding Rommel's retreat, Hitler became incoherent with rage, and hysterical scenes ensued at Führer headquarters. The shock of Rommel's defeat was totally unexpected because Hitler's attention had been focused on Stalingrad and the Caucasus. His belief in Rommel as a commander had made him incapable of imagining such a setback.

Shortly after midday on 3 November, he sent Rommel an order: 'In the position in which you find yourself, there can be no other thought than to stand fast, not to take even one step back, and to throw every available weapon and soldier into the battle.' He promised Luftwaffe support and supplies and finished: 'This is not the first time in history that resolute determination will prevail over the stronger battalions of the enemy. There is only one choice you can offer your troops: victory or death.'

Rommel was shaken and bewildered by the insanity of this command. Yet Hitler's self-deluding lies that enabled him to reject the reality of defeat would be repeated very soon afterwards, to General Paulus in the Don steppe west of Stalingrad. Rommel, despite all his military instincts, felt he had to obey. He issued orders to halt the withdrawal. Only the Italian divisions in the south were told to move north-westwards. This allowed Horrocks's XIII Corps to advance unopposed on 4 November. Further north, X Corps broke through, capturing the Afrika Korps headquarters and General von Thoma, who surrendered to the 10th Hussars.

Assured of Kesselring's support, Rommel ordered a general retreat. He told Hitler that it would only be to the Fuka Line, but it carried on all the way across Libya. That the remnants of the Panzerarmee got away at all was due to Montgomery's slow reactions and excessive caution. Having achieved his victory, he did not want to risk any reverse. It has been argued that his failure to trap Rommel in his retreat prompted Hitler's disastrous decision to send more troops to North Africa, all of whom would eventually be captured. But this is hardly a testimonial to Montgomery's generalship, since that was never part of any master plan.

The victory of Alamein had certainly not been won by strategic or tactical genius. Montgomery's decision to attack the strongest part of the German line was questionable, to say the least. His infantry and armoured troops had certainly fought bravely, greatly helped by his success in turning around the Eighth Army's mood. But in most respects the battle had been won by the formidable contribution of the Royal Artillery and by the Desert Air Force in its relentless destruction of the Luftwaffe, panzers and supply lines, as well as by the Royal Navy and the Allied air forces cutting the Axis lifeline in the Mediterranean.

On 7 November, when Hitler was travelling to Munich to make his speech to the Nazi Party old guard, his special train was halted in Thuringia. A message from the Wilhelmstrasse warned that an Allied landing in North Africa was imminent. He promptly gave orders that Tunisia was to be defended. But when informed that the Luftwaffe would be able to do little at such a range from its bases, he became furious with Göring. All the conflicting rumours over the past few months about Allied intentions, and his obsession with the final capture of Stalingrad, had meant that the OKW was completely unprepared for a new front. The big question was how the Vichy regime would react to an Allied invasion of its North African colonies.

Ribbentrop joined the train at Bamberg, and urged Hitler to

let him make overtures to Stalin through the Soviet ambassador in Stockholm. Hitler rejected the suggestion out of hand. The idea of negotiating at a moment of weakness was unthinkable. He continued to work on the speech which claimed that the German capture of Stalingrad was imminent, and emphasized his resolve to fight on until final victory. His pride prevented him from considering any other option. He passed over Rommel's defeat and never mentioned the Allied landings in North Africa, preferring to hark back to his prediction that the Jews would be annihilated. Yet even Goebbels recognized that they were 'standing at a turning point of the war'. Apart from fanatically loyal Nazis, most Germans now felt that victory was further away than ever, as reports on civilian morale by the Sicherheitsdienst showed only too clearly. Few shared Göring's notion that the Americans were capable of manufacturing only razor blades. The mounting Allied bombing offensive against their cities demonstrated a growing material superiority.

For Eisenhower and his planners, the reaction of Vichy France and Franco's regime in Spain had also been a key question. The politically naive Eisenhower soon found that he had entered a minefield of French politics. Roosevelt did not want to have anything to do with General de Gaulle, and he put pressure on Churchill not to tell the Frenchman what was afoot. Churchill's relationship with de Gaulle had been even more strained by French suspicions that the British coveted Syria and Lebanon, and Churchill knew that he would be furious at being kept in the dark. De Gaulle would also never accept that in order to avoid heavy fighting the Allies had to come to some arrangement with the Vichy authorities in North Africa. But Churchill had one offering in the hope of pacifying the proud general.

The Royal Navy, unable to forget that Japanese aircraft flying from Vichy airfields in Indochina had sunk the *Prince of Wales* and the *Repulse*, continued to be concerned by the French colony of Madagascar, which lay parallel to their convoy routes off the south-east African coast. Within a few weeks of the disaster off Malaya, a landing force was allocated to Operation Ironclad – the seizure of the main port Diego Suarez, at the northern tip of Madagascar. At first, both General Brooke in London and Wavell in the Far East had opposed the plan when so much else was threatened.

Then, at the beginning of March 1942, American intercepts of Japanese naval codes had revealed that Berlin was urging Tokyo to intervene in the western Indian Ocean to attack British supply ships going round southern Africa to Egypt. On 12 March, the War Cabinet finally approved Operation Ironclad.

At the beginning of May the British force, sailing from South Africa, stormed the port of Diego Suarez with marines landed at night in fine Nelsonian style. That was as far as the plan went, for it was assumed that a modus vivendi would be established with the Vichy authorities in the capital of Tananarive. But on 30 May a Japanese midget submarine torpedoed the battleship HMS *Ramillies* in the harbour of Diego Suarez. The Japanese submarine flotilla went on to sink twenty-three ships with supplies for the Eighth Army, marking the only direct assistance which the Japanese gave their German ally during the war.

A reluctant Churchill, persuaded by Field Marshal Smuts that the Japanese might establish bases in other Vichy ports on Madagascar, agreed to the conquest of the whole island. He also thought it might be a way of pacifying de Gaulle, who had wanted to take the island with Free French forces and then been furious to discover that the British planned to deal with the Vichy authorities there. Once the whole island was captured, it could be handed over to de Gaulle. This was finally achieved on 5 November, after a fruitless guerrilla campaign waged by the Vichy governor, Armand Annet. A week before Annet's surrender, Churchill had been able to enquire graciously of General de Gaulle whom he would like to appoint as governor of Madagascar. De Gaulle suspected that the Allies were planning to land in North Africa, but if he had known of all the American dealings with Vichy generals that had been going on to prepare for Operation Torch, he would probably have stormed out of the room.

Robert Murphy, who had been the American chargé d'affaires in Vichy and was now Roosevelt's emissary in French North Africa, was also convinced that de Gaulle should be kept out of the picture entirely. For most officers of the French colonial army, de Gaulle was still seen as little better than a traitor in the pay of the English. They needed to be reassured with a figurehead to their liking. General Henri Giraud was a tall and brave officer with a magnificent moustache, but not famed for his intelligence.

De Gaulle called him the 'tin soldier'. Giraud, who had been captured at the head of the French Seventh Army in 1940, had escaped from Königstein, a fortress prison in Saxony. He had made his way to Vichy where Pierre Laval, Pétain's prime minister, had wanted to hand him back to the Germans, but the Maréchal refused.

Murphy felt that Giraud could best serve Allied interests, but Giraud had his own ideas. He insisted that he should be the commander-in-chief of Operation Torch and he demanded that the Allies should land in France as well as North Africa. He also did not want the British involved, since the Royal Navy attack on the French fleet at Mers-el-Kébir had not been forgotten or forgiven. Giraud was also a close friend of General Charles Mast, a key commander of French forces in North Africa. Murphy, who had developed a network of contacts among senior officers and officials, arranged a secret meeting between General Mast and his fellow conspirators with Eisenhower's deputy, Lieutenant General Mark Clark.

On the night of 21 October, Clark had been landed near Algiers from the British submarine HMS *Seraph*, accompanied by commando bodyguards. His main task was to convince Mast that the American forces would be so overwhelming that the French should not attempt to oppose them. Clark claimed that half a million men would be landed, when the forces consisted of only 112,000. Mast warned him that, although the army and air force could be won over, the French navy would resist with determination. Other French officers provided Clark with valuable intelligence on the disposition of their troops and defences. Fear of discovery by the local gendarmerie, who had been told that smugglers had landed, led to Clark's undignified return to the submarine the following night without his trousers. Despite this minor humiliation, his dangerous mission had proved largely successful.

The submarine HMS *Seraph*, this time pretending to be American, was sent to collect Giraud from the Côte d'Azur and then convey him to Gibraltar to join Eisenhower. Axis agents and air reconnaissance reported the growing presence of shipping at Gibraltar. Fortunately for the Allies, German intelligence assumed that the vessels were intended either to reinforce Malta or to land forces in Libya to cut off Rommel's line of retreat. German U-boats in the Mediterranean were therefore ordered to concentrate off the Libyan coast, well to the east of where the invasion forces were going to land. Another Axis theory was that the Allies intended to take Dakar on the west African coast as a naval base, to help them in the Battle of the Atlantic.

Through Murphy, the Americans had received overtures from Admiral Darlan. Admiral William D. Leahy, Roosevelt's former ambassador to Vichy, saw Darlan as a dangerous opportunist. The fact that Darlan loathed Laval, who had replaced him as Pétain's deputy, was hardly a guarantee of his trustworthiness. Yet even Churchill was prepared to have dealings with this most determined anglophobe, if it might lead to the French fleet at Toulon coming over to the Allied side. Eisenhower preferred to stick with Giraud, but then Giraud, on reaching Gibraltar, again expected to be made Allied commander-in-chief. Seldom had a military operation been so complicated by politics and personal rivalries.

On 4 November, just four days before the landings, Darlan, who had been on a tour of French African colonies, flew to Algiers. He had just heard that his son, a naval lieutenant suffering from polio, had suddenly taken a turn for the worse. Darlan had no idea that Allied fleets were at sea, and when his son's condition improved he planned to fly back to Vichy. Western Task Force, containing 35,000 troops commanded by Major General George S. Patton, had already left Hampton Roads, bound for Casablanca. The other two task forces which had sailed from England were headed into the Mediterranean for Oran and Algiers. Altogether the troopships were escorted by 300 warships under the overall command of Admiral Cunningham, who was delighted to return to the Mediterranean.

On the evening of 7 November, Darlan was at dinner at the Villa des Oliviers, the residence of General Alphonse Juin, the commander-in-chief in Algiers. Juin had replaced Weygand, who was now imprisoned at Königstein in Giraud's place because Hitler feared that he would side with the Allies. They were interrupted towards the end by the chief naval officer at Algiers, who rushed in to tell them that the Allied ships were perhaps not heading for Malta after all. They might be coming to land troops at Algiers and Oran. Darlan dismissed such fears and went off to get some sleep before his flight early next morning. At midnight, Murphy heard the codeword over the French service of the BBC to confirm that the landings were going ahead. He sent the French irregulars that he and General Mast had recruited to seize key installations and headquarters.

In the early hours of 8 November, Murphy went to the Villa Oliviers and had Juin woken. He informed him of the landings. Juin was dumbstruck at first. He then said that he must first consult his senior officer Admiral Darlan, who was present in Algiers. Murphy felt that he had no alternative but to talk to Darlan. Murphy's Buick was sent to fetch him.

Darlan arrived in a fury. The short, bald, barrel-chested admiral, who constantly smoked a pipe, was soon nicknamed 'Popeye' by the Americans, who were amused by his built-up shoes. Darlan's hatred for the English had an illustrious pedigree since his great-grandfather had been killed at the Battle of Trafalgar. But he was also a practised turncoat. Just after the armistice in 1940, the veteran French politician Édouard Herriot had said of him, 'This admiral knows how to swim,' when Darlan, having promised the British total resistance, secretly joined the *capitulards*.

While Murphy was trying to calm Darlan and persuade him that resistance to the landings would be futile, a group of Mast's irregulars turned up and took Darlan and Juin prisoner. Then a squad of Gendarmerie arrived to release them and take the insurgents and Murphy prisoner. Murphy had been expecting American troops to have arrived by this time, but they had landed by mistake further down the coast.

But a far greater disaster was unfolding. The British plan to take both the ports of Algiers and Oran in a coup de main was a complete failure, involving massive casualties. This, not surprisingly, provoked considerable American anger. In the harbour, French shore batteries and naval vessels bombarded two Royal Navy destroyers flying the stars and stripes, as they attempted to bring in American landing parties, just as they had at Diego Suarez. An airborne operation with a single American parachute battalion to capture Oran's airfields also proved a fiasco. Operation Torch appeared to be falling to pieces in a grotesque farce.

Despite Roosevelt's request to keep the Free French in

ignorance, Churchill had asked General Ismay to call General Pierre Billotte, de Gaulle's chief of staff, to warn him of the invasion just before the troops began to land. But Billotte decided not to wake de Gaulle, who had gone to bed early. When de Gaulle heard the news next morning, he was incandescent with rage. 'I hope the Vichy people will throw them into the sea,' he stormed. 'You don't get France by burglary!' But by the time he had lunched with a soothing Churchill, de Gaulle had calmed down. That evening he made a broadcast fully in support of the Allied operation.

Only when American troops arrived in strength, many hours late due to the chaotic landings, did Darlan's attitude change. He asked to meet the commander of the 34th Infantry Division to discuss a ceasefire, and one was agreed for Algiers. French troops would march back to barracks without surrendering their arms.

Hitler's suspicions about the reliability of the Vichy regime as an ally flared up. Severing diplomatic relations with the United States was not enough, nor was Pierre Laval's agreement to allow Axis aircraft to use French airfields in Tunisia. On 9 November, Laval was summoned to Munich and challenged to prove his loyalty to Germany by declaring war on the Allies. This was a step too far for Laval, and also for the rest of the administration in Vichy.

Darlan, meanwhile, would not extend the ceasefire to Casablanca and Oran, where fighting still continued. He needed to know what was happening in Munich and in France. Confusion mounted with the arrival in Algiers of General Giraud, followed by General Mark Clark, who indicated that they should prepare to drop Giraud and deal with Darlan instead. Giraud fortunately accepted that Darlan was his senior and did not make a fuss. But Eisenhower, back in the humid tunnels of the Rock of Gibraltar, had only a few confusing reports on which to assess progress. Nothing had been heard from General Patton on the Casablanca landings. A keyed-up Eisenhower chain-smoked his Camel cigarettes and prayed for the best.

In Munich Hitler, accompanied by Count Ciano, Mussolini's foreign secretary, received Laval and demanded that French troops should secure ports and airfields in Tunisia for the landing of Axis troops. French resentment against Italy, after Mussolini's stab-in-the-back in June 1940, was so intense that Laval hesitated over allowing Italian forces on French territory. But he indicated that he would bow to a German ultimatum, providing Marshal Pétain could make a formal protest.

The next morning, 10 November, Darlan came to the Hôtel Saint-Georges in Algiers, which Clark had taken over as his headquarters. Clark's undiplomatic manner did not go down well with Darlan, who emphasized that he held a much more senior rank. Clark even threatened to impose Allied military government on the whole of French North Africa. Darlan kept his temper, because he had to play for time. He could not order the ceasefire which Clark so urgently wanted until Hitler ordered troops into the demilitarized zone of France, thus breaching the 1940 armistice agreement. Eisenhower, on hearing from Clark that negotiations had stalled, exploded: 'Jee-sus Christ! What I need around here is a damned good assassin.' At least Oran was secured that day by the US 1st Infantry Division at the cost of 300 casualties, but French forces were still resisting Patton's troops in Morocco even after almost all their warships had been sunk off Casablanca in a furious battle.

Early the next day, Hitler announced that German troops would occupy southern and south-eastern France in Operation Anton. He would still recognize Pétain's government, but the Marshal's reputation was now in tatters. Many of his supporters felt that he should have fled to North Africa to join the Allies. Hitler also gave orders that the Pyrenees should be occupied by German troops. Franco's government feared that Hitler might demand the passage of troops through Spain to attack Gibraltar, and a council of ministers in Madrid on 13 November ordered a partial mobilization.

With the German move into the unoccupied zone of France, Darlan was now able to argue that Pétain was a prisoner. He gave instructions that the ceasefire should extend throughout French North Africa. But Darlan did not manage to deliver the French fleet in Toulon, as Churchill had hoped. The commander there, Contre-Amiral Jean de Laborde, who resented Darlan and feared that his sailors and officers wanted to join the hated Anglo-Saxons, remained loyal to Vichy in splendid isolation. Assured by officers of the Kriegsmarine that German forces would not try to seize his ships or the port of Toulon, Laborde decided to stay put. But the arrival of SS panzer troops, and increasing dissent among his crews, forced him to make up his mind. As German forces entered the port, he gave the order to scuttle the fleet. Almost a hundred warships were sunk or blown up.

Operation Torch had cost the Allies 2,225 casualties, of whom roughly half were killed, and the French lost around 3,000. As both Patton and Clark acknowledged, the chaos of the landings had been lamentable. If they had been fighting the German army instead of badly armed French colonial troops, they would have been massacred. British officers made supercilious jokes about 'How Green is our Ally', but the disorganization and chaotic logistics made painful reading in the after-action reports. Above all it proved that General Marshall's desire to launch an early invasion of France would have led to catastrophe. Whatever the motives of Churchill and General Brooke in forcing the Americans to invade North Africa, the result was undeniably the right one. The US Army had a great deal to learn before it could take on the Wehrmacht in northern Europe or even in Tunisia.

The morale of troops is often volatile, swinging wildly between dejection and exultation. The easy victory in Morocco and Algeria prompted an unsustainable optimism. Their mood boosted by the cheap local wine, American soldiers believed that they had been blooded and were almost battle-hardened. Those who had seen the obsolete French Renault tanks brought to a halt with their new bazookas, yelled: 'Bring on the panzers!' Even Eisenhower told Roosevelt that he expected to take Tripoli by late January.

26

Southern Russia and Tunisia

NOVEMBER 1942–FEBRUARY 1943

Out on the frozen Don steppe, word of the Soviet encirclement spread rapidly in the Sixth Army. On 21 November
1942, Paulus and his chief of staff flew from their headquarters at
Golubinsky in the two remaining Fieseler Storch light aircraft to
Nizhne-Chirskaya, outside the *Kessel*. There, they held a conference the next day with General Hoth of the Fourth Panzer Army
to discuss the situation and to communicate over a secure line
with Army Group B. But Hitler, on hearing where Paulus was,
accused him of abandoning his troops and ordered him to fly back
to rejoin his staff at Gumrak, fifteen kilometres west of Stalingrad. Paulus was deeply aggrieved by this slur and Hoth had to
calm him down.

They discussed Hitler's order for the Sixth Army to stand firm
despite the threat of 'temporary encirclement'. Assuming that
Hitler would soon come to his senses, they agreed that the Sixth
Army needed urgent resupply by air of fuel and ammunition in
order to break out. But the commander of VIII Fliegerkorps
warned them that the Luftwaffe simply did not have enough
transport aircraft to supply a whole army. With his panzer formations short of fuel, and his infantry divisions deprived of their
horses, Paulus knew that the Sixth Army would have to abandon
all its artillery, to say nothing of its wounded, if it were to escape.
His chief of staff, Generalleutnant Arthur Schmidt, 'a bull-necked
man, with small eyes and thin lips', observed that 'that would be
a Napoleonic ending'. Paulus, who had studied the campaign of
1812 in great detail, was haunted by the prospect. Generalmajor
Wolfgang Pickert, the commander of the Luftwaffe 9th Flak Division, arrived during the meeting. He said that he was pulling his
division out immediately. He too knew that the Luftwaffe could
never hope to supply the Sixth Army by air.

Hitler had no intention of allowing his troops to withdraw

from Stalingrad. He had invested so much of his reputation in the capture of the city, especially his boasts during the Munich speech just two weeks before, that he could not bear to pull back. He ordered Generalfeldmarschall von Manstein to leave the northern front and form a new Army Group Don, to break through and relieve the Sixth Army. Göring, on hearing what Hitler intended, summoned his most senior transport officers. Although the Sixth Army needed 700 tons of supplies per day, Göring asked his officers whether they could manage 500. They replied that 350 tons would be the absolute maximum, and then only for a short time. Göring, hoping to curry favour with Hitler, then assured Führer headquarters that the Luftwaffe could resupply the Sixth Army. This false promise sealed the fate of Paulus and his forces. On 24 November, Hitler ordered 'Fortress Stalingrad' with its front on the Volga to hold out 'whatever the circumstances'.

Altogether the Red Army had surrounded some 290,000 men in the Stalingrad *Kessel*, a figure which included over 10,000 Romanians and more than 30,000 Russian Hiwi auxiliaries. Hitler refused to allow the news to be released in Germany. OKW communiqués deliberately falsified the true state of affairs, but rumours began to spread at home. Hitler wanted to blame anyone but himself for the Soviet triumph. A furious exchange took place with Marshal Antonescu at the Wolfsschanze in East Prussia, when Hitler tried to place responsibility for the disaster on the Romanian armies on the flanks. Antonescu pointed out angrily that the Germans had refused to provide his men with adequate anti-tank guns, and that all their warnings of an imminent attack had been disregarded. He did not know that the Sixth Army was now refusing to provide rations to his troops. German officers were saying: 'it's useless to feed Romanians because they surrender just the same'.

Sixth Army troops cut off west of the Don had managed to fall back just in time to rejoin the main body. The Stalingrad *Kessel* took on the shape of a squashed skull, with the forehead in the city and the rest defending a perimeter out in the Don steppe, measuring sixty kilometres by forty. German soldiers referred to it cynically as 'the fortress without a roof'. Rations, which had been insufficient even before the encirclement, were cut drastically. Men became exhausted digging trenches in the frozen ground. In the bare steppe, there was little wood to cover the earth bunkers. Officers attempted to stiffen soldiers' resolve with the argument: 'Even death is preferable to a Russian prison, and we must hold out to the end. The Fatherland cannot possibly forget about us.'

The Soviet encirclement took back large areas of occupied territory. The arrival of Red Army troops was greeted with tears of joy by the plundered and starved civilians, but the NKVD arrived in their wake to seize any suspected of collaboration. Don Front headquarters launched a series of attacks in the first week of December, hoping to split the *Kessel*, but their intelligence department had grossly underestimated the number of troops they had surrounded. General Rokossovsky's chief of intelligence thought that they had trapped 86,000 men, not 290,000.

Soviet officers also failed to imagine how determined the Germans were to hold on. The Führer's promise that they would be relieved was accepted as the gospel truth, especially by the younger soldiers brought up under National Socialism. 'The worst is past,' a soldier in the 376th Division wrote home with naive optimism. 'We all hope that we'll be out of the *Kessel* before Christmas . . . Once this battle of encirclement is over, then the war in Russia will be finished.' Supply officers, having cut rations to between a third and a half of the normal issue, were more realistic. The shortage of fodder meant that the few remaining horses would have to be slaughtered.

According to the calculations of the Sixth Army's chief quartermaster, a minimum of 300 flights a day would be needed, yet during the first week of the air-bridge, there was an average of fewer than thirty flights a day. In any case, a considerable proportion of the tonnage brought in was aircraft fuel for the return journey. Göring had also failed to take into account the fact that the airfields within the *Kessel* were within the range of Soviet heavy artillery, while enemy fighters and anti-aircraft batteries created a constant danger. On a single day twenty-two transport planes were lost through enemy action and crashes. And on some days the weather was so bad that hardly any aircraft got through. Richthofen kept ringing Generaloberst Hans Jeschonnek, the Luftwaffe chief of staff, to tell him that the whole plan of resupply by air was doomed. Göring could not be contacted because he had retired to the Ritz Hotel in Paris.

During this period, Stalin had the Stavka working on more ambitious plans. Following the success of Operation Uranus, he wanted to cut off the rest of Army Group Don and trap the First Panzer and the Seventeenth Armies in the Caucasus. Operation Saturn would consist of a major attack by the South-West and Voronezh Fronts, down through the Italian Eighth Army towards the lower Don where it entered the Sea of Azov. But Zhukov and Vasilevsky agreed that, since Manstein was likely to try to relieve the Sixth Army by striking north-east from Kotelnikovo at the same time, they should restrict the plan to an assault on the left rear flank of Army Group Don. It was renamed Little Saturn.

Manstein was indeed planning what they thought he was. An advance from Kotelnikovo was just about the only course left open to him. His offensive was codenamed Operation Winter Storm. Hitler simply wanted the Sixth Army to be reinforced, so that it could maintain its 'cornerstone' on the Volga ready for further operations in 1943. Manstein, however, was secretly preparing a second operation called Thunderclap to extricate the Sixth Army, and hoping that Hitler would come to his senses.

On 12 December, the remnants of General Hoth's Fourth Panzer began their attack north. He had been reinforced with the 6th Panzer Division from France and a battalion of the new Tiger tanks. Sixth Army soldiers on the southern edge of the *Kessel* heard the opening barrage a hundred kilometres away, and the word ran round: 'Der Manstein kommt.' Hitler's promise was about to be fulfilled, they told themselves. They did not know that he had no intention of letting them retreat.

Hoth's attack came earlier than Soviet commanders had expected. Vasilevsky feared for the 57th Army in its path, but Rokossovsky and Stalin refused to change their dispositions. Finally, Stalin agreed, and ordered General Rodion Malinovsky's 2nd Guards Army to be diverted. The delay was not as serious as it might have been, because a sudden thaw with torrential rain bogged down Hoth's tanks as they fought a heavy battle on the Myshkova River less than sixty kilometres from the edge of the *Kessel*. Manstein hoped that Paulus would use his own initiative and start to break out to the south, ignoring Hitler's orders. But Paulus was too obedient to the chain of command and would not have moved without a direct order from Manstein himself. In any case, his troops were too starved to march far and his panzers had insufficient fuel.

Stalin agreed to the modified Little Saturn and ordered it to start in three days. On 16 December, the 1st and 3rd Guards Armies and the 6th Army attacked the weakly held Italian front. The Italian attitude to the war against the Soviet Union was very different to the German. Italian officers were shocked by the Germans' racist attitude towards the Slavs, and when they took over from Wehrmacht units they made much greater efforts to feed the Russian prisoners employed on heavy duties. They also made friends with the local villagers who had been stripped of clothing and foodstuffs by the Germans.

The best Italian formations were the four in the Alpini Corps – the Tridentina, the Julia, the Cuneense and the Vicenza Divisions. Unlike the ordinary Italian infantry, the Alpini were used to harsh winter conditions, but even they were badly equipped. They had to make new footwear out of the tyres from destroyed Soviet vehicles. They lacked anti-tank weapons, their rifles dated from 1891, and their machine guns, having not been designed for Arctic conditions, frequently froze solid. Their vehicles, still painted in desert camouflage, also failed to work in the extreme temperatures, which sometimes fell below minus 30 degrees Centigrade. And their mules, unable to cope with the deep snow, died from exhaustion, lack of forage and cold. Many men suffered from frostbite, so like the Germans they tried to make good their deficiencies by taking the padded jackets and *valenki* felt boots from dead Red Army soldiers. Rations of minestrone and bread arrived frozen hard. Even the wine ration was solid. Italian soldiers and officers hated and despised the Fascist regime, which had sent them into this war so badly prepared.

As the Red Army divisions attacked in waves with their battlecry 'Urrah! Urrah!', many of the Italian Eighth Army formations resisted with far greater determination than expected. But, badly armed and without reserves, their defence soon crumbled in chaos. Italian troops, exhausted and weak from dysentery, retreated in long columns through the snow like refugees, with blankets wrapped around them and over their heads. The Alpini Corps stood firm, reinforcing the flank of the Hungarian Second Army on their left.

Soviet tank brigades fanned out into their rear, the broad-tracked T-34s charging forward over the freshly fallen snow. A sudden drop in temperature meant that the ground was hard again. Supply dumps and railway junctions, with goods trains, were taken with impunity. Since the 17th Panzer Division had been transferred to help Hoth's attack, the rear areas of Army Group Don contained no reserves.

The greatest danger to the Sixth Army came as the 24th Tank Corps overran the airfield near Tatsinskaya, which was the main air transport base for supplying the *Kessel*. General der Flieger Martin Fiebig ordered his Junkers 52 crews to take off for Novocherkassk as the tanks reached the edge of the airfield. They began to take off in a stream while the tanks fired at them. Some exploded in fireballs, and one tank rammed a plane as it taxied into position for take-off. Altogether 108 Ju 52s managed to get away, but the Luftwaffe lost seventy-two aircraft, almost 10 per cent of its entire transport fleet. The only other airfields capable of supplying Stalingrad lay much further away.

Little Saturn forced Manstein to rethink his entire strategy. Not only was the relief of the Sixth Army now out of the question, soon he would have to withdraw from the Caucasus. Manstein did not have the heart, or else he lacked the nerve, to tell Paulus of the truly hopeless situation which his army now faced. Some officers had a clear idea of their fate. 'We'll never see our homes again,' wrote the divisional chaplain of the 305th Infantry Division, 'we'll never get out of this mess!' Soviet intelligence officers, however, found their German prisoners still in a state of denial and confused logic at the possibility of defeat. 'We have got to believe that Germany will win the war,' said a Luftwaffe navigator from a Ju 52 shot down on the Stalingrad run, 'or what is the use of going on with it?' A soldier reflected the same obstinacy: 'If we lose the war we have nothing to hope for.' In Stalingrad, they had no idea that Germany's North African front was now being squeezed from both ends.

The main point of Operation Torch was to occupy French Tunisia before the Axis transferred troops there, but the Germans reacted with a breathtaking rapidity. On the morning of 9 November, before Algiers and Oran had been secured, the

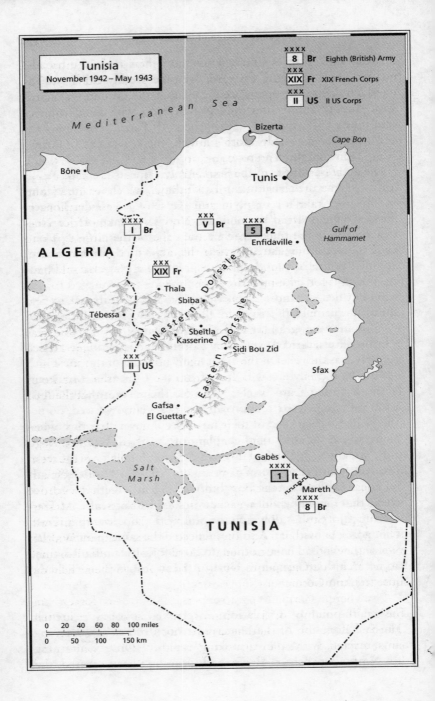

Tunisia
November 1942 – May 1943

XXXX
8 Br   Eighth (British) Army

XXX
XIX Fr   XIX French Corps

XXX
II US   II US Corps

Mediterranean Sea

Bizerta

Cape Bon

Bône •

Tunis •

XXXX
I Br

XXX
V Br

XXXX
5 Pz

Gulf of
Hammamet

Enfidaville •

ALGERIA

XXX
XIX Fr

• Thala

Sbiba •

Western Dorsale

Eastern Dorsale

Tébessa •

Sbeïtla •
Kasserine •

• Sidi Bou Zid

XXX
II US

Sfax •

Gafsa •
El Guettar •

Salt
Marsh

Gabès •

XXXX
1 It

Mareth

XXXX
8 Br

TUNISIA

0   20 40 60 80 100 miles

0   50   100   150 km

first German fighters landed. Advance parties of infantry and paratroopers followed in transport planes the next day. The local French commander, still acting on orders from Vichy, backed away from protesting at this breach of the 1940 Armistice conditions.

Hitler had no intention of allowing the Allies a base for the invasion of southern Europe, an attack which he knew would knock Italy out of the war. He intended a massive reinforcement of North Africa, even at this critical moment on the eastern front. So, despite Stalin's scepticism and the mass demonstrations in London demanding a 'Second Front Now', the North African theatre was proving rather more effective than the stillborn plan to invade France in 1942. And the airlift across the Mediterranean occupied a fleet of Junkers 52 transport planes, which could have been better used to supply the Sixth Army.

The Allied advance east towards Tunis was ill organized and almost unplanned. The skeleton British First Army, commanded by a gloomy Scot, Lieutenant General Kenneth Anderson, was bolstered by several American armoured units and some French infantry battalions. Despite the small size of his force, which amounted to less than a corps, Anderson made the mistake of splitting it into four axes of advance. He had no idea that the Axis had already deployed 25,000 men by 25 November.

The First Army's only real success came on that day when Blade Force, with the 1st Battalion of the US 1st Armored Regiment and the 17th/21st Lancers, advanced on Tunis from the west. The American Stuart tanks came across a forward Luftwaffe airfield near Djedeïda. Attacking like an SAS raid, their crews drove across the runway shooting up stationary Junkers 52s, Messerschmitts and Stukas. They destroyed more than twenty aircraft. This attack caused panic and convinced Generalleutnant Walther Nehring, who had commanded the Afrika Korps under Rommel, to pull in his defence perimeter. But the attack on the airfield did little to blunt German air superiority.

Elsewhere, German paratroopers and other forces ambushed the mainly British columns, inflicting heavy casualties. The 2nd Battalion of the Lancashire Fusiliers lost 144 men in a single attack on Medjez against a paratroop battalion, backed by 88mm guns and some panzers. To make matters worse,

American aircraft strafed their own ground troops. They began to fire back at any aeroplane which appeared, with the slogan 'If it flies – it dies.' The arrival of the 10th Panzer Division and a few of the new Tiger tanks punished Anderson's troops on 3 December, forcing them back with heavy losses. It was an unequal struggle against a much more proficient and better-armed enemy.

Eisenhower was relieved to reach Algiers, after his weeks in the damp tunnels of the Rock of Gibraltar. But instead of being able to focus on the faltering campaign in Tunisia, he became enmeshed in the problems of supply and of French politics. Eisenhower was driven to distraction by French officers and their 'morbid sense of honor'. He had hoped that the Allies had now arrived at a workable compromise, with Darlan appointed high commissioner for North Africa, and Giraud as commander-in-chief of French forces, although he still wanted supreme command over all Allied troops. On the other hand, Churchill's only reason for supporting Darlan – that he might win over the French fleet in Toulon – had now disappeared along with its scuttled ships.

Eisenhower soon received a nasty shock. Once news of the 'Darlan deal' leaked out in the United States and in Britain, moral outrage knew no bounds. The press and public opinion were appalled by the idea that the Allied supreme commander had made a Vichy quisling the leader of North Africa, especially when it became clear that anti-semitic legislation was still in place and political opponents had not been released from prison. In fact Gaullists were being treated particularly badly. Darlan did not, however, show much satisfaction in his position. He was well aware that the Americans might soon discard him as a 'squeezed lemon'.

De Gaulle wisely held his tongue in public, since this problem had been created by the Americans. Perhaps he had already perceived that Vichy officers loathed him almost as much as they loathed the British. Although he never acknowledged it, the American policy of dealing with Darlan and Giraud ahead of him would work ultimately in his favour. These two stepping stones prevented a civil war in North Africa.

The Special Operations Executive was alarmed by the deep distrust that the Darlan deal was causing not just among the Gaullists in London, but above all in Allied relations with the French resistance of the interior and even in other countries. Along with the American OSS (Office of Strategic Services), SOE had rapidly set up bases in Algiers to train the many young French volunteers for work in Tunisia. One of their recruits was called Fernand Bonnier, who had started to mix in monarchist circles and added de la Chapelle to his name in a grandiose gesture. Those dreaming of a restoration, with the Comte de Paris becoming King of France, viewed de Gaulle as a possible regent who would pave the way, if only because the general's family was known to have been monarchist.

In this murky world of conspiratorial complications, a plot to assassinate Darlan took shape. It involved Gaullists, who passed $2,000 from London via General François d'Astier de la Vigerie to finance the operation; Lieutenant Colonel Douglas Dodds-Parker of the Grenadier Guards, the senior SOE officer in Algiers; and Fernand Bonnier, who carried it out. Dodds-Parker, who had accompanied the French resistance leader Jean Moulin to his aircraft on his final return to France, trained Bonnier in pistol shooting and later claimed, inaccurately as it turned out, that his own gun had been used in the assassination. The plan was for Bonnier to be spirited away from Algiers on board the *Mutin*, a boat commanded by Gerry Holdsworth of SOE's secret flotilla for infiltrating agents in the Mediterranean. But just after ambushing and shooting Darlan in the stomach on 24 December, Bonnier was captured, court-martialled and executed with indecent haste.

Eisenhower, shaken by the event although he had earlier longed for 'a damned good assassin', summoned Dodds-Parker to Allied Force Headquarters to demand a categorical assurance that SOE was not involved. Dodds-Parker gave it to him. How far knowledge of the plot had spread in advance is hard to establish. OSS in London was certainly aware of it and approved, but it seems that neither Churchill nor Sir Charles Hambro, the head of SOE, gave any form of authorization. The despatch of the 'squeezed lemon' provoked few tears, even among those Allies who had supported him. Roosevelt cold-bloodedly remarked to one of his White House guests on New Year's Eve that Darlan was just a 'son-of-a-bitch'.

*

In the Stalingrad pocket, troops in the encircled Sixth Army kept up their spirits as Christmas approached. Although they were suffering from lice, cold and hunger, it offered an escapist alternative to pondering their fatal predicament. They knew that Manstein's Operation Winter Storm to relieve them had failed, yet many soldiers were still prey to 'Kessel fever', imagining that they could hear the artillery of the SS Panzer Army, which Hitler had promised, coming to their rescue. They could not believe that their Führer would abandon the Sixth Army. But both the OKW and Manstein realized that it would have to be sacrificed to tie down the Soviet armies surrounding it, while the German forces in the Caucasus were evacuated.

Sixth Army soldiers dreamed of celebrating Christmas 'in the German way'. They prepared small gifts to give to each other, often little carvings or secretly hoarded food, which they could ill afford. In their bunkers under the snow, an extraordinary generosity of comradeship developed in the face of adversity. On Christmas Eve, they sang 'Stille Nacht, heilige Nacht', the familiar words making many break down in tears at the thought of their families back in Germany. Yet Christian instincts did not extend to the Soviet prisoners held in two camps within the Kessel. Deprived of any food so as not to reduce German rations, the few survivors were reduced to eating the bodies of their comrades.

Reality could not be denied for long. No supply flights had arrived for two days, because of the Soviet tank attack on Tatsinskaya airfield. The Sixth Army was dying by degrees from starvation on its diet of Wasserzuppe – a few pieces of horsemeat boiled in melted snow. The army's pathologist, Dr Hans Girgensohn, who had been flown into the Kessel in mid-December, soon came to an alarming discovery after carrying out fifty autopsies. Soldiers were dying of hunger far more rapidly than they would do in other circumstances. This, he concluded, came from the interacting effect of stress, prolonged malnutrition, lack of sleep and intense cold. This interfered with the body's metabolism. Although the soldier might have consumed a few hundred calories worth of food, his digestive system absorbed probably only a fraction. The resulting weakness also reduced his ability to survive disease. Even those who were not ill were far too weak to attempt a breakout through deep snow, and in any case Paulus lacked the courage to defy Hitler's orders.

Conditions in the field hospitals were appalling beyond belief. Blood from open wounds froze even inside the tents. Limbs gangrenous from frostbite were sawn off. Pliers were used on fingers. No anaesthetic remained, and those with stomach or serious head wounds were left to die. The desperately overworked surgeons had to carry out a pitiless triage. 'The German soldier suffers and dies with uncomplaining bravery,' wrote the chaplain of the 305th Infantry Division. 'Even the amputees were composed.'

Only walking wounded were now evacuated by transport plane, because stretchers took up too much room. Feldgendarmerie armed with sub-machine guns tried to hold back the crowds of wounded and malingerers who attempted to storm each plane on the ice runways at Gumrak and Pitomnik airfields. Even a secured place on a plane was no guarantee of survival. The heavily loaded Junkers 52s and large Focke-Wulf Condors struggled to gain height before reaching the perimeter, where Soviet anti-aircraft batteries fired away at them. Soldiers watched a number crash in a fireball, knowing they were full of wounded comrades.

The new year of 1943 brought another irrational surge of hope when Hitler in his message promised that 'I and the whole German Wehrmacht will do everything in our power to relieve the defenders of Stalingrad, and that with your staunchness will come the most glorious feat in the history of German arms.' Out of respect for the suffering of the Sixth Army, Hitler banned the consumption of brandy and champagne at Führer headquarters.

The German people were still not told that the Sixth Army had been surrounded, and soldiers writing home were threatened with severe punishment if they revealed this fact. One sent home a New Year's drawing, but in the corner in tiny letters he wrote in French: 'It's twenty days since we were encircled. It's terrible to be sitting here in this trap. But they say to us, "Hold on, hold on!", but we get 200 grams of bread per day and some horsemeat soup. We have almost no salt. Lice are a torture and it is absolutely impossible to get rid of them. It is dark in the bunkers and it is minus twenty or thirty outside.' But his letter never reached home, for it was in a Feldpost sack on one of the transport planes shot down.

The Don Front intelligence department was using German Communists and deserters to sift all this intercepted mail. Another soldier wrote sarcastically: 'On the first day of the holidays, we had goose with rice for dinner, on the second day, goose with peas. We have been eating geese for a long time. Only our geese have got four legs and horseshoes.'

Stalin begrudged every delay in the mounting of Operation Ring, the coup de grâce for the Sixth Army. Rokossovsky would have forty-seven divisions supported by 300 aircraft. On 8 January, Don Front headquarters sent two emissaries under a white flag offering surrender terms to Paulus. But almost certainly on the orders of his chief of staff, Generalleutnant Schmidt, they were sent back with the document they had brought.

Two days later at dawn, Operation Ring began with a heavy artillery bombardment and the scream of Katyusha rocket batteries. Red Army officers now referred with pride to their massed guns as the 'God of War'. The main attack was directed against the 'Marinovka nose', a salient in the south-west of the *Kessel*. German soldiers, wrapped up like scarecrows, could hardly fit their swollen, frostbitten fingers round their triggers. The white landscape, with little mounds of snow marking unburied bodies, was pitted with black shellholes stained yellow at the edges by cordite. On the southern sector, the remnants of a Romanian division broke and ran, leaving a kilometre gap in the defence line. The 64th Army immediately sent in a brigade of T-34 tanks, their tracks churning through the frozen snow-crust.

German divisions in the south-west, forced to withdraw, found it impossible to establish a new defence line as the ground was too hard to dig trenches. They had so little ammunition left that soldiers waited until their Soviet attackers were at almost point-blank range. The chaplain of the 305th Division recorded the ruthless Soviet attack, 'crushing the wounded with tanks, pitiless shooting down of wounded and prisoners'.

Pitomnik airfield was a chaotic mess, with blackened, smashed aircraft and piles of frozen corpses outside the hospital tents. There was little fuel left to evacuate the remaining wounded back to field hospitals. Some were dragged on sledges, until their comrades gave up exhausted. The scenes of misery were almost beyond imagination. Dispirited and shell-shocked soldiers tried to escape back towards the ruined city in such numbers that the Feldgendarmerie found it hard to maintain discipline. Yet most men fought on, joined in many cases by Russian Hiwis, who knew full well what fate awaited them when the battle was over.

On 16 January, Pitomnik was abandoned, and the last Messerschmitts stationed there flew out on orders from Richthofen. The other smaller airfield at Gumrak was in no state to receive transport aircraft and was itself now under direct artillery fire. The Luftwaffe began to parachute supplies in, but most drifted and fell behind Soviet lines. A whole battalion of German troops from the 295th Infantry Division surrendered that day. Some battalion commanders could not face the suffering of their men any more. They limped on frost-bitten feet, their lips had cracked open, and their bearded faces had the yellow, waxen aspect of departing life. Crows circled and landed to peck out the eyes of both the dead and the dying.

The Red Army felt no pity, especially after gruesome discoveries. 'When liberating the hamlet of Novo-Maksimovsky,' Don Front NKVD reported, 'our soldiers found in two buildings with bricked-up windows and doors seventy-six Soviet prisoners, sixty of them dead from starvation, some bodies decomposed. The remaining prisoners are half alive and most of them cannot stand up because they are so starved. It turned out that these prisoners spent about two months in these buildings. The Germans were starving them to death. Sometimes they threw them pieces of rotten horseflesh and gave them salted water to drink.' The officer in charge of the camp, Dulag-205, later stated in a SMERSh interrogation that 'from the beginning of December 1942, the command of the Sixth German Army, in the person of Lieutenant General Schmidt, absolutely stopped supplying the camp with food and mass deaths from starvation started'. Soviet soldiers showed no mercy to the German wounded, especially after they came across the last few surviving Russian prisoners who had been starved in another camp at Gumrak. Tragically, their rescuers killed them unintentionally by giving them too much food.

On 22 January, Sixth Army headquarters received a signal from Hitler. 'Surrender out of the question. Troops fight on to the end. If possible, hold reduced Fortress with troops still battleworthy. Bravery and tenacity of Fortress have provided the opportunity to establish a new front and launch counter-attacks. Sixth Army has thus fulfilled its historical contribution in the greatest passage in German history.' In Stalingrad, where men had dragged themselves on all fours 'like wild animals', the conditions in cellars were even worse with perhaps as many as 40,000 wounded and sick out of those still left alive in the Sixth Army. Toes and fingers on badly frostbitten hands and feet often came away with the bandages as these were taken off. Nobody had the strength to remove the bodies of those who died. Grey lice could be seen leaving them in search of living flesh.

On 26 January, the remnants of the Sixth Army were split in two when the 21st Army reached the lines of Rodimtsev's 13th Guards Division north of the Mamaev Kurgan. Paulus himself, also suffering from dysentery, fell into a state of nervous collapse in the cellars of the Univermag department store on Red Square. Schmidt was now in charge. Several of his generals and senior officers shot themselves rather than face the humiliation of sur-render. Some men chose a 'soldier's suicide', by standing up in a trench waiting to be shot.

Hitler announced Paulus's promotion to the rank of General-feldmarschall. Paulus knew that this was a coded order to kill himself, but now that all his admiration for Hitler had evaporated, he had no intention of giving the Führer that satisfaction. On 31 January, Red Army soldiers entered the Univermag building. 'Paulus was completely unnerved,' wrote the Soviet interpreter, a Jewish lieutenant called Zakhary Rayzman. 'His lips were quiver-ing. He told General Schmidt that there was too much commotion going on, that there were too many people in the room.' Rayzman escorted 151 German officers and soldiers back to their divisional headquarters. He had to stop Red Army soldiers from trying to humiliate them on the way. 'Such is the irony of fate,' a German colonel announced, intending to be overheard. 'A Jew is seeing to it that we are not harmed.' Paulus and Schmidt were taken to the 64th Army headquarters of General Shumilov, where their surren-der was filmed. Paulus's nervous tic was still much in evidence.

Hitler heard the news of the surrender in silence. He apparently stared into his vegetable soup. But next day his anger exploded against Paulus for having failed to shoot himself. On 2 February General Strecker, commanding the few remnants of XI Corps in the ruins of northern Stalingrad, also surrendered. The Red Army discovered that they had 91,000 prisoners on their hands, far more than expected. Due mainly to lack of preparation, they received no food and no medical assistance for some time. Nearly half had died by the time spring arrived.

Soviet casualties for the whole Stalingrad campaign amounted to 1.1 million, of whom nearly half a million died. The German army and its allies had also lost over half a million men, killed and captured. In Moscow, the bells of the Kremlin rang out a victory peal. Stalin was portrayed as the great architect of this historic victory. The reputation of the Soviet Union soared around the world, bringing many recruits to Communist-led resistance movements.

In Germany, radio stations were ordered to play solemn music. Having steadfastly refused to acknowledge that the Sixth Army had been surrounded since November, Goebbels now tried to pretend that the whole of the Sixth Army had perished in a final stand: 'They died so that Germany might live.' But his attempt to create a heroic myth soon backfired. Word spread rapidly in Germany, mainly from those listening in secret to the BBC, that Moscow had announced the capture of 91,000. The shock of the defeat was overwhelming in Germany. Only Nazi fanatics still believed that the war could be won.

The OKW was disturbed by the 'great agitation caused among the German public' after the surrender of the Sixth Army at Stalingrad and issued a sharp warning to officers not to exacerbate the situation with criticism of the military or political leadership with 'so-called factual accounts' of the fighting. Attempts to infuse the armed forces with the 'National Socialist vision' increased, yet the authorities received reports that older officers from the Reichswehr 'days of apolitical soldiering' showed little interest in indoctrinating their soldiers. Committed officers and the SS complained that the Red Army was much more effective in its ideological teaching.

On 18 February, Goebbels invoked the theme 'Total War – Short War!' at a mass meeting in the Berlin Sportpalast. The atmosphere was electric. From the podium he screamed: 'Do you want Total War?' The audience leaped to its feet and bayed in the affirmative. Even an anti-Nazi journalist covering it confessed afterwards that he too had jumped to his feet in enthusiasm and only just stopped himself from bellowing 'Ja!' with the rest of the crowd. He said later to friends that if Goebbels had yelled, 'Do you all want to go to your deaths?', the crowd would have roared back their consent. The Nazi regime had trapped the whole population of the country as accomplices, willing or not, in its own crimes, and its own insanity.

27

Casablanca, Kharkov and Tunis

DECEMBER 1942–MAY 1943

During December 1942, while Anderson's First Army struggled in the rain-lashed hills of Tunisia, Montgomery's Eighth Army failed to follow up Rommel's retreating Panzerarmee with any dash. Montgomery, anxious not to harm his reputation as a guarantor of victory, did not want to get a bloody nose from the sort of sudden counter-attack in which the German army excelled. Many regiments were also content to leave 'other buggers to do the chasing', as the commanding officer of the Sherwood Rangers put it. They felt that they had done their bit, and preferred to concentrate on loot, such as Luger pistols, alcohol, cigars and chocolate taken from abandoned German vehicles.

Montgomery was perhaps right to acknowledge that the British army was still not yet ready to match the Germans in a war of movement, but his anti-cavalry prejudices entrenched his over-cautious conduct of operations. Only armoured car regiments, the 11th Hussars and the Royal Dragoons, were far enough forward to harry the retreating Germans in a consistent fashion. Even though Rommel's forces were by then reduced to around 50,000 men and less than a battalion of tanks, Montgomery's reluctance to take risks made him at one point consider leaving Tripoli as well as Tunis to Anderson's First Army. This complacency was reflected lower down. 'We had all seen the enemy so disorganized that it did not seem possible he could regroup enough to give us much trouble,' wrote the poet Keith Douglas, a lieutenant with the Sherwood Rangers. 'When we heard of the North African landings there were very few people who expected more than a few more weeks of mopping up before the African campaign ended.'

The Desert Air Force in Egypt has also been criticized for its inability to cripple Rommel's armour when it retreated over the

Halfaya Pass back into Libya. But it had been hampered by the time it took to bring up fuel and supplies to its forward airfields. Air Vice Marshal Coningham turned to the Americans for help, and Brereton's command, now designated the Ninth Air Force, began to airlift fuel to the front. Rommel, certain that the war in North Africa was lost, established a defence line at Mersa el Brega, just east of El Agheila on the Gulf of Sirte, where he had begun his desert campaign in February 1942.

On 14 January 1943, Roosevelt arrived in Casablanca, exhausted by his five-day journey from the US. He and Churchill met that evening at Anfa, and the next day the combined chiefs of staff assembled to hear Eisenhower's report on the campaign in North Africa. The Allied forces commander was distinctly nervous. He had been ill with influenza, not helped by his voracious consumption of Camel cigarettes, and suffered from very high blood pressure. The improvised attack on Tunis had been a failure. Eisenhower blamed the rain and mud, and the difficulties of working with the French rather than Anderson's refusal to concentrate his already weak forces. He also acknowledged the chaos of the supply system, which his chief of staff Bedell Smith was trying to sort out.

Eisenhower then outlined his plan for a thrust through to Sfax on the Gulf of Gabès, with a division from Major General Lloyd Fredendall's II Corps. This was shot down by General Brooke in his incisive way. The attacking force, he pointed out, would be crushed between the retreating Rommel and Generaloberst Hans-Jürgen von Arnim's so-called Fifth Panzer Army in Tunis. Brooke, stooping forward, with his hooded eyelids and gaunt, beaky-nosed face, looked like a cross between a bird of prey and a reptile, especially when he ran his tongue over his lips. Eisenhower, deeply shaken, offered to rethink the plan and retreated from the room.

The Casablanca conference was not Eisenhower's finest hour, and he confessed to Patton that he feared he might be sacked. He was also taken to task by General Marshall over the bad discipline of American troops and chaos in the rear. Patton's smartly turned-out corps at Casablanca, on the other hand, made a fine impression on everyone, as he had ensured it would.

The main task of the conference was to establish strategy. Admiral King made no bones about his belief that all the Allies' resources should be directed against Japan in the Pacific. He passionately disagreed with the policy of 'holding operations' in the Far East. And the Americans were far more interested than the British in supporting Chiang Kai-shek's Nationalists. General Brooke, however, was determined to get full agreement on finishing the war in North Africa, then invading Sicily. He despaired of Marshall's lack of strategic grasp. Marshall still clung to the idea of a cross-Channel invasion in 1943, when it was clear that the American army was still far from ready to take on the forty-four German divisions in France, and the Allies lacked the necessary shipping and landing craft. Marshall was forced to concede. Thanks to good staff preparation, the British had all the statistics at their fingertips. The Americans did not.

Brooke felt that Marshall was a brilliant organizer of American military strength, but did not know what to do with it. Once the Americans had been argued out of an invasion of France, and were uncertain what course to follow in its stead, Brooke managed to wear them down. He also had to win a battle over the British planning staff, who wanted to invade Sardinia instead of Sicily. Finally, on 18 January, Brooke, helped by Field Marshal Dill, now the British military representative in Washington, and Air Chief Marshal Sir Charles Portal, chief of the air staff, persuaded the Americans to agree to their Mediterranean strategy with Operation Husky, the invasion of Sicily. Brigadier General Albert C. Wedemeyer, a War Department planner, who deeply distrusted the British, was forced to admit afterwards that 'we came, we listened, and we were conquered'. The Casablanca conference was the high water mark of British influence.

Britons and Americans got to know each other better during the Anfa conference, but not always with admiration. Patton, in his cavalier way, considered General Alan Brooke to be 'nothing but a clerk'. Brooke's analysis of Patton was much closer to the truth. He described him as 'a dashing, courageous, wild and unbalanced leader, good for operations requiring thrust and push, but at a loss in any operation requiring skill and judgment'. The one thing on which British and Americans agreed was that General Mark Clark was interested only in General

Mark Clark. Eisenhower got on well with Admiral Cunning-ham and Air Marshal Sir Arthur Tedder, who would become his deputy later, but in American eyes 'Ike' bent too far backwards in accommodating British influence in the theatre. General Alex-ander was appointed under him to command all the ground forces. Although Patton at first rather admired Alexander, he was disgusted by what he saw as a downgrading of the US Army. It was not long before he wrote in his diary that 'Ike is more British than the British and is putty in their hands.'

But even Eisenhower did not like the idea of having to work with a British political counsellor in the form of Harold Macmil-lan. Macmillan was determined to support de Gaulle, and after Darlan's assassination there was little that either Eisenhower or Roosevelt could do to exclude him for much longer. Eisenhower also feared interference in the chain of command, given Mac-millan's close links to Churchill and his ministerial status, but Macmillan had no intention of pulling rank. He recognized that the Americans would soon wield almost total power within the alliance, so he preferred a more subtle approach. Harking back to a classical education by comparing the Americans to the Romans, he thought that the best way to deal with Britain's more powerful ally was to take on the role of 'the Greek slaves [who] ran the operations of the Emperor Claudius'.

Eisenhower was still feeling battered by the reaction to the Darlan deal by the American and British press. 'I am a cross between a one-time soldier,' he had written to a friend, 'a pseudo-statesman, a jack-legged politician and a crooked diplomat.' Having drowned himself in detail across every field, he handed over political dealings to Bedell Smith, as well as many of his other problems, a burden which did not help 'Beetle's' ulcers. But Bedell Smith, although famously acerbic with American officers, managed to get on well with the British and the French.

The one outstanding problem in North Africa, which Church-ill and Roosevelt made an effort to resolve at Casablanca, was the role of General Charles de Gaulle. Roosevelt had lost none of his distrust for de Gaulle, but at Churchill's urging Giraud and de Gaulle were brought together and made to shake hands for the cameras. The American President had blithely promised Giraud the weapons and equipment for eleven French divisions without checking whether this was possible. De Gaulle, who had initially refused the summons to Casablanca, was, however, content to leave Giraud as commander-in-chief of French forces in North Africa, providing he achieved the political leadership. For that, he needed to wait a little longer. This reversal of power should not, he knew, be too difficult. The brave 'tin soldier' was no match for the most determined of political generals.

Once the embarrassing charade of the two French generals reluctantly shaking hands had been repeated for the photographers, President Roosevelt announced that the Allies intended to achieve the unconditional surrender of Germany and Japan. Churchill then stated that Britain was in full agreement, even though he had been taken by surprise that Roosevelt had decided to make the aim public. In his view, the implications had not been fully thought through, even though he had obtained the War Cabinet's agreement in advance. Yet this declaration, which would go some way towards reassuring the suspicious Stalin, probably did not make that great a difference to the outcome of the war. Both the Nazi and the Japanese leaderships intended to fight to the very end. The other important decision designed to hasten the result was to step up the strategic bombing campaign against Germany using both Bomber Command and the US Eighth Air Force.

Stalin, as Churchill expected, was not impressed when he received a joint signal from Roosevelt and the prime minister sent from Marrakesh, reporting on the decisions reached at Casablanca. Yet the Torch landings had provoked Hitler into reinforcing Tunisia and occupying southern France. This diverted German troops much more effectively than a failed cross-Channel operation. It also forced the Luftwaffe to redeploy 400 aircraft from the eastern front, with disastrous results. By the late spring of 1943 Göring's formations had lost 40 per cent of their entire strength in the Mediterranean. But Stalin was not mollified by such details. The Anglo-American decision to delay confronting the Germans in France in a battle of attrition was what angered him. The Red Army still faced, and would continue to face, the overwhelming bulk of the German army.

On 12 January, just a few days before the Casablanca conference started, the Red Army launched Operation Spark to break the German encirclement of Leningrad south of Lake Ladoga. Zhukov, sent back by Stalin to coordinate the offensive, used the 2nd Shock Army attacking from the 'mainland', the 67th Army from the Leningrad side and three brigades of ski troops crossing the great frozen lake. The 67th Army had to cross the Neva, and the offensive was delayed until the ice on the river was thick enough to support the lighter tanks.

The offensive opened with a heavy bombardment, finishing in a storm of screaming Katyusha rockets. In temperatures of minus 25 degrees Centigrade, Soviet troops in white camouflage surged across the ice. On the south-western corner of Lake Ladoga, the Tsarist fortress of Shlisselburg was surrounded. In two days of fighting in the forests and frozen marshland, the vanguards of the two attacking armies were within ten kilometres of each other. Soviet troops even managed to recover a Tiger tank intact, an important prize for their engineers to study.

On 15 January Irina Dunaevskaya, a young interpreter, walked across the frozen Neva to visit the battlefield. She saw dead men 'under a transparent crust of ice, as if in a glass sarcophagus'. In a captured German headquarters, she found Red Army soldiers rolling cigarettes with the paper from lists recommending the award of medals. Because of their nicknames, she guessed that they were released criminals transferred from the Gulag. Outside there were 'treetops knocked off and branches on the ground, felled trees, snow that is black with soot, and bodies of soldiers, individual and in piles, mostly those of the enemy, but also ours, corpses of horses, scattered ammunition, and broken weapons – too much for a woman's eyes ... The corpse of a very young, blond German was lying on the road in a very natural pose, as if he were still alive. Three scorched corpses of German soldiers were still sitting in the front seat of their huge vehicle. Once again there were corpses of our soldiers under the ice on the highway, as if under glass, squashed into a flat sheet by the heavy vehicles that had recently driven over them ... Far away from us the landscape was of a whitish-grey colour, the pine trunks were greyish-brown. All the colours were stern, cold and lonely.'

'Your prayers', a tank driver wrote home to his mother, 'must be guarding me in the battles, as I have gone four or five times unharmed through a minefield where a lot of tanks were blown up, and a shell that exploded in the tank and killed the commander and the gunner did me no harm. One becomes here both a fatalist and an extremely superstitious person. I have become very blood-thirsty. Each killed Fritz makes me delighted.'

On 18 January, the two Soviet armies closed the gap at a cost of 34,000 casualties. The encirclement of Leningrad was broken, even if the land-bridge from the city to the 'mainland' was no more than a dozen kilometres wide. Stalin that day promoted Zhukov to marshal of the Soviet Union.

With a new railway laid across the conquered strip south of Lake Ladoga, supplies to Leningrad increased greatly. The line, however, remained within easy range of German artillery, so the Soviet command launched yet another offensive, Operation Polar Star commanded by Marshal Timoshenko. Timoshenko ordered that the town of Sinyavino had to be taken by Red Army Day on 23 February. This attempt to deepen the bridgehead opened with a heavy artillery bombardment. The ground was so boggy that the exploding shells did little more than send up geysers of mud, and many rounds never exploded at all. Red Army troops broke through the German lines and advanced through the fir and birch forest. Vasily Churkin recounted how they passed a field brothel: 'a two-storey barrack that the Germans had knocked together from rough boards. People said that 75 Russian girls from nearby villages were living there. The Germans had forced them.'

The German XXVI Army Corps timed its counter-attack with great skill. 'We saw several Tiger tanks moving towards us and firing as they moved,' Churkin wrote. 'They were followed by German infantry. As the tanks approached our soldiers started leaving the trenches and retreating. Platoon commanders were shouting at the cowards, telling them to return to their trenches, but the panic spread fast.'

One of the Wehrmacht formations to suffer heavily in Oper-ation Polar Star was the Spanish División Azul, or Blue Division, of mainly Falangist volunteers. The decision to form it had been taken in Madrid only five days after the launch of Operation Bar-barossa. The Spanish right still blamed the Soviet Union as the chief instigator of their civil war. Almost a fifth of the early volun-teers were students and it could be argued that the Blue Division was one of the most intellectually over-qualified formations ever to go to war. Commanded by General Agustín Muñoz Grandes, a regular army officer who had become a Falangist, it was constituted as the 250th Infantry Division and sent to the Novgorod front after training in Bavaria. In that region of forests and marshland, its men suffered badly from sickness and then frostbite. But Hitler was impressed by their resilience under attack, and by their contribution to the destruction of General Vlasov's 2nd Shock Army in the spring of 1942.

The Blue Division, defending a sector on the Izhora River, held on despite suffering 2,525 casualties in twenty-four hours of fighting. One of its regiments collapsed, but the line was re-established with German reinforcements. It was the division's largest and most costly battle of the whole war, and certainly contributed to the failure of the Soviet offensive.

In the south of Russia, Operation Little Saturn had forced Manstein to withdraw the First Panzer and Seventeenth Armies to the Kuban bridgehead in the north-western corner of the Caucasus, south of Rostov. Rokossovsky grumbled that the downgrading of the offensive, and the failure to advance to Rostov to cut the enemy off completely, had been a missed opportunity. But Stalin had once again suffered a rush of optimism just as he had a year before. Forgetting how quickly the German army recovered from a disaster, he wanted to liberate the eastern Ukraine in the Donbas and Kharkov operations with armies now freed by the surrender of the Sixth Army.

On 6 February Manstein met Hitler, who at first accepted responsibility for the defeat at Stalingrad, but then blamed Göring and others for the disaster. He complained bitterly about Paulus's failure to commit suicide. Yet the Japanese were even more upset by the news. In Tokyo, Shigemitsu Mamoru, the new foreign minister, and an audience of about 150 Japanese generals and senior officials, watched a film of Stalingrad made by Russian cameramen. The scenes which showed Paulus and the other captured generals shocked them deeply. 'Can this possibly be the case?' they demanded in disbelief. 'If it is true, why did Paulus not commit suicide like a real soldier?' The Japanese leadership suddenly realized that the invincible Hitler was going to lose the war after all.

Manstein was now in a better position to demand flexibility of action. Hitler wanted a dogged defence of occupied territory, but the threat of a collapse in southern Russia paradoxically gave Manstein the opportunity to achieve one of the most startling counter-attacks in the whole war.

The Red Army, having crushed the Hungarian Second Army and encircled part of the German Second Army with the Voronezh Front, on Manstein's left flank, then pushed on westward to seize what would become the Kursk Salient. 'For the last week and a half,' a soldier wrote to his wife on 10 February, 'we've been marching on land that has just been liberated from the fascists. Yesterday our armoured vehicles broke into Belgorod. A lot of booty has been taken and many prisoners of war. While on the march we constantly encounter huge groups of captured Hungarians, Romanians, Italians and Germans. If only you could see, Shurochka, what a pitiful sight this famous gang of Hitler's has become. They are wearing army boots, some in straw galoshes, summer uniforms, only a few wear greatcoats, and on top of all that they are wearing the overclothes that they've stolen, male or female. On their heads are fore and aft caps, and women's shawls are wrapped around over them. Many of them have frostbite; they are dirty, with lice. It gives one a revolting feeling to think that this riff-raff had got so far into our country. We've already marched 270 kilometres in the provinces of Voronezh and Kursk. So many villages, towns, factories and bridges have been destroyed. Civilians are going back home as the Red Army arrives there. They are so happy!'

Another part of the Voronezh Front advanced on Kharkov. On 13 February, Hitler insisted that the city should be held by Gruppenführer Paul Hausser's II SS Panzer Corps, with the *Leibstandarte Adolf Hitler* and the *Das Reich* Divisions. Hausser, on his own initiative, disobeyed orders and withdrew. At the same time, Manstein pulled back the First Panzer Army to the River Mius. The Soviet South-Western Front with four armies had thrust westwards. It was spearheaded by four tank corps (although no greater in strength than a single panzer corps) commanded by Lieutenant General M. M. Popov. The Stavka thought that a great victory was about to be achieved by exploiting the gap in the German front south of Kharkov, but their own supply lines were desperately over-extended.

On 17 February, furious that his orders were being ignored, Hitler flew to Zaporozhye for a showdown with Manstein. But Manstein had things well in hand. He moved Fourth Panzer Army headquarters to take control over the II SS Panzer Corps, now reinforced with the *Totenkopf* Division, and prepared the First Panzer Army to strike the Soviet attackers from below. Hitler felt obliged to fall in with his plans. Manstein's double counter-attacks destroyed Popov's armoured force and almost encircled the 1st Guards and the 6th Army. The troops of the 25th Tank Corps, by then out of fuel, had to abandon all their vehicles and make their way on foot back towards Soviet lines.

In the first week of March, Fourth Panzer Army advanced back on Kharkov, and Hausser eventually retook the city on 14 March after an unnecessarily costly battle. Heavy spring rains soon brought further operations to a halt. Soviet prisoners of war were put to work burying the dead. Most were so famished that they searched the bodies for scraps of food in pockets, but this was deemed to be looting the dead. Usually they were just shot, but the odd sadist would take it further. One tied three Soviet prisoners accused of theft to a gate together. 'When his victims had been secured,' wrote another soldier, 'he stuck a grenade into the pocket of one of their coats, pulled the pin, and ran for shelter. The three Russians, whose guts were blown out, screamed for mercy until the last moment.'

Hitler had his eye on the immense Kursk Salient for a summer offensive to restore German superiority on the eastern front. Yet the German army in the Soviet Union had been disastrously weakened. Apart from the loss of the Sixth Army and those of its allies, there had been heavy casualties in the withdrawal from the Caucasus, to say nothing of the fighting around Leningrad and the Red Army's Rzhev Offensive against the Ninth Army. Many vehicles had been abandoned in the retreat when they ran out of fuel, and were finished off with a grenade in the engine. Panzers were often reduced to towing several trucks filled with wounded.

The Wehrmacht's strength on the eastern front had also been reduced by the transfer of troops to Tunisia, and to France in case of an Allied invasion. Operations in the Mediterranean continued to inflict heavy losses on the Luftwaffe, as did the strategic bombing campaign against German cities and aircraft factories. And the need to protect the Reich had led to the withdrawal of fighter squadrons and anti-aircraft batteries, giving air superiority to the Soviets for the first time. By the spring of 1943, German strength stood at just over 2,700,000 men, while the Red Army mustered just under 5,800,000, with four and a half times as many tanks, and three times as many guns and heavy mortars. The Red Army also possessed greater mobility, thanks to the flow of Jeeps and trucks provided by American Lend–Lease.

A part of the increase in the Red Army's strength came with the recruitment of young women to a maximum strength of 800,000. Although many had served from early in the war, and well over 20,000 had done so in the Battle of Stalingrad alone, the greatest intake began in 1943. Their military roles now extended well beyond their previous ones of doctor, medic, nurse, telephone operator, signaller, pilot, air observer and anti-aircraft guncrew. The bravery and competence shown by women, especially during the Battle of Stalingrad, encouraged the Soviet authorities to recruit more, and there were more women serving in the Red Army than in any other regular army during the war. Although there had been a number of women snipers who became famous for their deadly skills, the main influx came with the establishment of a woman's sniper school in 1943. Women were considered to resist cold better than men and to have a steadier hand.

These intrepid young women, however, also had to cope with the attentions of male comrades and especially superiors. 'These girls evoked memories of school-leaving dances, of first love,' wrote Ilya Ehrenburg. 'Almost all those I met at the front had come straight from school. They often winced nervously: there were too many men around with hungry eyes.' A number found themselves forced to become a senior officer's 'campaign wife' – known as a 'PPZh' (short for *pokhodno-polevaya zhena*) because it sounded like PPSh, the Red Army's standard sub-machine gun.

Coercion was often crudely applied. A soldier recounted how an officer ordered a young woman in their signals platoon to accompany a fighting patrol, simply because she had refused to sleep with him. 'Many were sent back to the rear because they were pregnant,' he wrote. 'Most soldiers did not think badly of them. This was life. Every day we spent facing death at the front line, so people wanted to get some pleasures.' But very few of the men acknowledged any responsibility and took every means to avoid their tearful victims before they left. Ehrenburg's friend and colleague Vasily Grossman was appalled by the flagrant exploitation of rank to achieve sexual favours. He regarded the 'campaign wife' as the Red Army's 'great sin'. 'Yet all around them,' he added, 'thousands of girls in military uniform are working hard and with dignity.'

In the rugged hills west of Tunis, Anderson's First Army still struggled to hold on. Its performance was hindered by a confused command structure, a failure to concentrate its badly coordinated forces and fraying tempers between British, French and American officers. Allied troops were no match for the highly professional German counter-attacks, combining Stuka dive-bombers, artillery and panzers.

Both sides complained bitterly about the pouring rain and the filth and mud. 'It's unbelievable what one has to endure,' a Gefreiter wrote home, clearly unaware of how much worse conditions were on the eastern front. General von Arnim had arrived to take over the forces in Tunisia, now designated the Fifth Panzer Army. Arnim prepared defences against renewed Allied attacks and Tunisian Jews were rounded up for forced labour. The Jewish community was also ruthlessly plundered for gold and money.

Rommel's withdrawal from the Mersa el Brega Line in December 1942 and the lack of Allied success in Tunisia encouraged Montgomery to push on. But he missed every opportunity to encircle the remnants of the Panzerarmee, especially when it halted at the Buerat Line. On 23 January 1943, the Eighth Army entered Tripoli led by the 11th Hussars. But again Rommel had already pulled back to begin fortifying the Mareth Line at the base of the Bay of Gabes, so as to link up with Arnim's Fifth Panzer Army.

Accepting that the war in North Africa was lost, Rommel advocated a Dunkirk-style evacuation of his troops. His forces had neither sufficient fuel nor sufficient armament, and he despaired of making Hitler see sense. During a furious exchange at the Wolfsschanze in late November, Hitler had refused him permission to withdraw from the Mersa el Brega Line, and had even accused Rommel's troops of throwing away their weapons in the retreat from Alamein. In fact, Rommel's withdrawal, evading the Eighth Army, had been the most skilfully conducted part of his whole desert war.

Mussolini's attempts to persuade Hitler to end the war in the Soviet Union fell on the stoniest ground. The surrender at Stalingrad and the loss of Libya represented a serious blow to the Duce's morale. He sacked his son-in-law, Count Ciano, from the position of foreign minister and nursed his depression by retiring to bed in an attempt to evade reality.

General von Arnim was concerned that the American II Corps under General Lloyd Fredenhall in the south might cut through from the mountains on the road from Kasserine down to the sea at Sfax. This would separate his Fifth Panzer Army from Rommel's Panzerarmee. Arnim explained the situation to Rommel, and requested his rearmed 21st Panzer Division to dislodge the badly equipped French detachment in the Faïd Pass.

The 21st Panzer attacked on 30 January, and General Fredenhall's II Corps reacted slowly in response to the French calls for assistance. The next day, when a combat command from the US 1st Armoured Division finally put in a counter-attack on the rocky pass, the Germans were waiting for them. The line of Sherman tanks suffered attacks from Messerschmitts and well-concealed anti-tank guns. Over half the force was knocked out and the survivors extricated themselves, reversing around burning vehicles. Another American attempt to advance a few hours later also failed with heavy casualties. Fredenhall, a disastrous commander, split his forces even more despite Eisenhower's instruction to the contrary. He sent another combat command off on a wild goose chase, with conflicting orders. Its infantry support, all green troops, were bombed in their trucks by Stukas. The blooding of these inexperienced troops from the 34th Infantry Division went from bad to worse over the next few days as Fredenhall, who seldom left his headquarters far in the rear, ordered more and more attacks.

Rommel decided to remove the American threat altogether with a three-pronged offensive. On 14 February, the 10th Panzer Division attacked westwards out of the Faïd Pass, while the 21st

Panzer Division came up from the south in a pincer. Seventy American tanks were destroyed in the first day's fighting round Sidi Bou Zid. One of them was knocked out at a range of 2,700 metres by a Tiger's 88mm gun. The shell of the Sherman's 75mm could not penetrate a Tiger's frontal armour even at point-blank range. On 16 February, a panzer crewman wrote home to apologize disingenuously for not having written, but his division had been fighting the Americans over the last couple of days. 'You will have heard from yesterday's Wehrmacht announcement that we shot up more than ninety tanks.'

Next day, the Afrika Korps detachment in the south advanced on Gafsa, triggering a panic-stricken withdrawal. Near Sidi Bou Zid a Sherman battalion from the 1st Armoured was ambushed and wiped out in a futile but brave counter-attack. Blazing and burned-out American tanks littered the landscape, while Tunisian Arabs continued to till their fields. American tank crewmen staggered back with blackened faces, like dismounted troopers after the charge of the Light Brigade. Neither Fredenhall nor Anderson had any idea of what was going on at the front.

On 16 February Rommel went to Gafsa. He was cheered by the surviving inhabitants, after the retreating Americans had destroyed much of the town when blowing up their ammunition dump. He wanted his Afrika Korps troops to overtake the Americans, who were pulling back towards Tébessa where he planned to capture their major supply dump. Arnim, however, regarded the idea as too risky, and a triangular argument was conducted with Kesselring.

That night, the panzer divisions advanced on Sbeïtla. And on 17 February, while some American units fled in panic, others stood and fought well, as 21st Panzer Division acknowledged. Fredenhall sent whatever detachments he could to the Kasserine Pass, but on 20 February the collapse began. Major General E. N. Harmon witnessed the debacle. 'It was the first – and only – time I saw an American army in rout. Jeeps, trucks, wheeled vehicles of every imaginable sort streamed up the road towards us, sometimes jammed two and even three abreast. It was obvious that there was only one thing in the minds of the panic-stricken drivers – to get away from the front, to escape to some place where there was no shooting.'

Fortunately for the Allies, Rommel and Arnim were in fierce disagreement. Trying to do too many things, they split their forces to take Tébessa in the west, as well as drive north to Thala and on a parallel road to Sbiba. With mixed British and American forces blocking the routes to Thala and Sbiba, supported at the last moment by American artillery, the 10th and 21st Panzer Divisions were stopped. And eventually the Afrika Korps detachment on the road to Tébessa was also halted by American anti-tank guns and artillery. Rommel was impressed by the effectiveness of American gunnery. And as the skies cleared, Allied aircraft began to attack his withdrawing panzers. He returned to the Mareth Line on 23 February, confident that he had inflicted a blow on the Allies heavy enough to discourage further advances.

Unable to believe that the Germans had retired, the Allied troops were slow to move back to the Kasserine Pass. It was littered with burned-out tanks, crashed aircraft and corpses in all directions. When they saw Tunisians looting the dead, American soldiers opened fire with Thompson sub-machine guns, either shooting to kill or just to scare them off. Fredenhall's II Corps had lost over 6,000 men, 183 tanks, 104 half-tracks, more than 200 field guns and another 500 transport vehicles. It had been a savage baptism of fire, made worse by confused orders from above. Troops fired at their own aircraft, destroying or damaging thirty-nine of them, and Allied squadrons attacked the wrong targets. On 22 February, some B-17 Flying Fortresses bombed a British airfield instead of the Kasserine Pass.

Although Rommel was promoted to command Army Group Afrika over the head of General von Arnim, he heard too late of Kesselring's plan for another offensive further north called Operation Oxhead. This did not begin until 26 February, when it should have been coordinated with attacks around Kasserine the previous week. German losses were far greater than British, and they lost the majority of their tanks.

The Comando Supremo, which Hitler had allowed to reassert control in the interests of Axis unity, refused Rommel permission to withdraw from the Mareth Line. Well aware that Montgomery was preparing an offensive, Rommel decided to put in a spoiling attack, but Ultra intercepts provided all the warning the British needed. Montgomery rushed up artillery, anti-tank guns and tanks to the threatened sector, where they were concealed. On 6 March, the Germans advanced into a killing zone targeted by a whole corps of artillery. Rommel lost fifty-two tanks and 630 men. Kesselring and Rommel unfairly suspected the Italians of betraying the plan.

Rommel, suffering from jaundice and totally exhausted, felt that it was time to return to Germany for treatment and a rest. On 9 March, he left North Africa for the last time. The following evening he was received by Hitler at the Werwolf headquarters outside Vinnitsa in Ukraine. Hitler refused to listen to his arguments that Army Group Afrika should be withdrawn across the Mediterranean to defend Italy. He even rejected any plans to shorten the front in Tunisia. Rommel, whom he now regarded as a defeatist, was ordered to depart on a rest cure.

Patton, frustrated by the lack of action in Morocco and by the way the British seemed to be running the whole war in North Africa, had recently written: 'Personally, I wish I could get out and kill someone.' At last his prayers to see action were granted. In the second week of March, Eisenhower sent him, with Major General Omar N. Bradley as his understudy, to take over from Fredenhall. Eisenhower sacked a number of other officers and Alexander wanted to get rid of Anderson, but Montgomery would not release the one person Alexander wanted as the new commander of the First Army.

Patton wasted no time at all in getting a grip on II Corps, starting with saluting and correct dress. The corps was terrified of its new commander, and military police became known as 'Patton's Gestapo'. Patton was appalled by the numbers of soldiers evacuated because of combat fatigue. He was also frustrated to hear that his orders were not to charge through to the sea and cut off Rommel's Panzerarmee (now renamed the First Italian Army) from General von Arnim in the north. Instead, his task was simply to threaten its flank to help Montgomery. Patton suspected that Montgomery wanted all the glory, but Alexander, who had been shocked by the shambles at Kasserine, was not yet ready to trust American troops.

Patton could console himself with his promotion to the three stars of a lieutenant general. Reinterpreting his orders, he pushed his divisions forward, retaking Gafsa and advancing to the Eastern Dorsale massif which dominated the plain to the sea. When the 10th Panzer Division tried to force back Patton's 1st Infantry Division from the heights at El Guettar, it was savagely mauled and lost half its remaining tanks.

Montgomery decided to send XXX Corps in a frontal attack on the Mareth Line to fix the enemy, while outflanking him to the south-west in a long manoeuvre by Freyberg's New Zealanders, supported by tanks. But the Germans were well aware of Freyberg's long left hook, and the attack on 20 March by the 50th Division proved a disaster. Montgomery, having prematurely claimed success, was shaken. But, recovering rapidly, he sent Horrocks with X Corps round to reinforce the New Zealanders in an attack towards the coast over thirty kilometres behind the Mareth Line. At the same time he sent the 4th Indian Division on a closer flanking advance. On 26 March, the New Zealanders and Horrocks's armoured brigades surged forward together, smashing the weak German defences at the Tebaga Gap. General Giovanni Messe, commanding the First Italian Army, withdrew all his forces rapidly up the coast towards Tunis. Although a success of sorts, the Axis forces had again escaped.

The Desert Air Force harried the retreating German forces. One casualty was Oberst Claus Graf Schenk von Stauffenberg, who lost a hand and an eye to a strafing fighter. On 7 April, units of the First and Eighth Armies met up. The two organizations could hardly have been more different. The desert veterans in their battered, sand-coloured tanks and trucks showed a remarkable nonchalance, to say nothing of a disrespect for dress regulations. Their war, although harsh at times, had on the whole seen a much greater respect for the lives of prisoners and very few civilian casualties in the almost empty desert. The local tribe of Senussi had been able to avoid the worst of the desert fighting, although some of them and many of their camels had legs blown off in the minefields.

The First Army, in the mainly mountain warfare of the far eastern Atlas, had found itself in a far dirtier conflict. The shock of war when over-confident green troops, especially American units, were hit by experienced panzer and panzergrenadier units was traumatic. While there were a number of psychological casualties, a majority became rapidly brutalized as a survival mechanism. A few even became totally dehumanized, with the sadistic killing of prisoners and even the random shooting of Tunisian Arabs for fun, with potshots at those on camels, treating them like a shooting range in a fairground. British soldiers were generally better disciplined, but they too were imbued with the racist ideas of the time. Only a few made friends with the locals. French troops were no better. Ironically, these officers and soldiers from the former Vichy army wanted to take revenge on their Arab subjects who had in many cases collaborated with the Germans, largely because of their anti-Jewish policies. Yet even as the campaign edged towards its end in victory, relations between the three Allies seemed to worsen, with British arrogance provoking a rampant anglophobia among many American officers.

Eisenhower's confidence, which had been badly dented during the winter months, now returned. His army was learning from its mistakes. Planning for Operation Husky, the invasion of Sicily, was well advanced, the Axis was about to be evicted from North Africa for good, and the supply system was at last working. The British were flabbergasted by the largesse of the American industrial titan. They were also shocked by the waste, although they had few grounds for complaint since they too were beneficiaries. But when it came to the inflated size of Allied Force Headquarters, with a staff of just over 3,000 officers and men, even Eisenhower was embarrassed.

By the beginning of May, the remaining Axis forces were compressed into the northern tip of Tunisia, including Bizerta, Tunis and the Cape Bon peninsula. Although they amounted to more than a quarter of a million men, just under half were German and the majority of the Italians were not fighting troops. Short of ammunition and above all fuel, Germans knew the end was in sight, making bitter jokes about 'Tunisgrad'. Hitler's refusal to evacuate his men to defend southern Europe did little for morale. They found it unbelievable that he was still sending reinforcements in April and May, all of whom would become prisoners too.

The Junkers 52 and large Messerschmitt 323 transports were easy prey for Allied fighters, waiting in ambush in the Mediterranean skies. Over half the Luftwaffe's remaining transport fleet was destroyed in the last two months of the campaign. On

Sunday, 18 April, four American fighter squadrons and a squadron of Spitfires jumped a group of sixty-five transports escorted by twenty fighters. In what became known as the 'Palm Sunday turkey shoot', the Allied fighters shot down seventy-four aircraft. While the Red Army was grinding down the overwhelming bulk of the German army, the western Allies were starting to break the back of the Luftwaffe. Air Marshal Coningham, the commander of the Desert Air Force, was furious at how little credit Montgomery gave to the RAF's role in North Africa. The combination of the Allied air forces and the Royal Navy strangling the Axis supply line across the Mediterranean had contributed at least as much to the final victory as the ground forces.

The last phase of crushing the bridgehead did not, however, go easily. Montgomery battered away at the mountainous Enfidaville sector on the coast south of Tunis with little effect and heavy losses. The Eighth Army was behind the Americans in learning the harsh lessons of mountain warfare. Other attacks by the First Army further to the west were resisted in the fiercest fighting. The Irish Guards advanced through a cornfield in a dip to attack a German position under fire from machine guns, artillery and the new Nebelwerfer six-barrelled mortar. When a man fell hit by fire, a comrade would stick his weapon upright in the ground. 'Rifle butts appeared everywhere marking the dead, dying and wounded,' wrote a corporal. 'I stopped by one poor guardsman who was calling for water. He had shocking wounds. I could see the shattered bones of his arm and he had a gaping wound in his side.'

The survivors of the attack charged the olive grove on the rising hill ahead, forcing the Germans to flee. But in one of the trenches the corporal and another two guardsmen heard German voices in a bunker. They both threw in grenades and stepped back. Afterwards, the corporal peered into the dark interior. 'There must have been twenty Germans scattered about in there. They were all bandaged up already and those that were not dead were screaming their heads off. This place was where the retreating enemy had left their wounded. I turned away without the slightest compassion for them. They had done much worse to my dead and wounded comrades lying out there in the burning cornfields.'

Only Bradley's II Corps due west of Tunis achieved a significant advance at the beginning of May. Finally recognizing his error at Enfidaville, Montgomery persuaded Alexander that a concentrated blow was required to end this battle of attrition around the perimeter. On 6 May, Horrocks with the 7th Armoured Division, the 4th Indian Division and 201st Guards Brigade launched Operation Strike from the south-west. Following an even more concentrated barrage of artillery than at Alamein, they pushed forward towards Tunis, splitting the pocket in two, while the Americans took Bizerta on the north coast. Led once again by the 11th Hussars in their battle-worn armoured cars, British troops entered Tunis the next afternoon. By 12 May it was all over. Nearly a quarter of a million troops surrendered, including twelve generals.

Hitler persuaded himself that he had been right to keep fighting in North Africa to the very end, so as to delay an Allied invasion of southern Europe and to keep Mussolini in power. On the other hand, he had again lost forces which he would badly need in future battles.

28

Europe behind Barbed Wire

1942–1943

The invasion of the Soviet Union affected German occupation policy across almost all of Europe. In the east, the intoxicating, but also frightening, idea of dominating millions of people increased the Nazis' reliance on terror to achieve results. Despite the early hopes of some senior officers and administrators that they would win over nationalities, such as the Balts and Ukrainians, to the anti-Bolshevik crusade, Hitler was interested only in instilling fear for the sake of fear. As in the case of Poland, he felt that their countries should be wiped off the map altogether.

In spite of Hitler's disgust at the idea of Slavs in Wehrmacht uniform, altogether nearly a million Soviet citizens served alongside the German army and the SS. Most were dragooned from the starvation of prison camps as unarmed Hiwi auxiliaries in German divisions. But even some of these 'Iwans' were taken on unofficially as full-time soldiers. A commander of the 12th SS Panzer Division *Hitler Jugend* later became proud of his Russian driver and bodyguard who accompanied him everywhere.

Well over 100,000 served, with widely differing degrees of enthusiasm and effectiveness, in General Vlasov's Russian Army of Liberation, and in a 'Cossack' corps fighting partisans on Soviet territory and later in Yugoslavia and Italy. The Ukrainian police and concentration camp guards achieved a terrible reputation for cruelty. Himmler also turned to conscripting Latvians, Estonians, ethnic Caucasians and even Bosnian Muslims into Waffen-SS formations. He also formed a Ukrainian division in 1943, but it was called the SS *Galicia* Division so as not to provoke Hitler's anger. A hundred thousand Ukrainians volunteered, of whom only a third were accepted.

The treatment of civilians in the occupied territories and of prisoners of war remained appalling. By February 1942, some

60 per cent of the 3.5 million Red Army prisoners had died of starvation, exposure or disease. Convinced Nazis did not just take pride in their pitilessness. Their dehumanization of victim categories – Jews, Slavs, Asiatics and Roma – was a deliberate form of self-fulfilling prophecy: to reduce them through humiliation, suffering and starvation to the level of animals, and thus 'prove' their genetic inferiority.

The chaotic rivalry between Hitler's satraps in the east exceeded even that in Germany itself, between the Nazi Party and different organs of government. Alfred Rosenberg was appointed minister for the eastern territories, but he was thwarted at every turn. His Ostministerium was derided, partly because Rosenberg was one of the few civilian officials who wanted to involve former Soviet nationalities in the war against Bolshevism. Göring, in charge of the war economy, simply wanted to strip the occupied areas and starve their populations, while Himmler wanted to cleanse them by mass murder to prepare for German colonization. Rosenberg thus had no control over security, food supply or the economy, which meant no control at all. He even had no authority over Erich Koch, the Reichskommissar for Ukraine as well as Gauleiter of East Prussia. Koch, a brutal drunkard, referred to the local population as 'Niggers'.

Herbert Backe's Hunger Plan, which was supposed to kill off up to thirty million Soviet citizens, never went beyond the drawing board. Starvation was rife, but it was hardly organized as the Nazis planned. Military commanders evaded orders to seal off the cities to starve their populations, because the Wehrmacht needed to keep large numbers of Soviet workers alive to serve their needs. Backe's idea of feeding both the Reich and the Wehrmacht on the eastern front from local resources proved a far greater failure. Agriculture in the Ukrainian 'bread-basket' had virtually collapsed due to Soviet scorched-earth tactics, war damage, depopulation, the evacuation of tractors and partisan activity. Living off the land for the Wehrmacht meant the seizure of fodder and grain, and the indiscriminate slaughter of poultry and livestock with no thought for future supplies, let alone the survival of the civilians who produced it. The lack of rolling stock and motor transport meant that the bulk of even what food there was could not be distributed effectively.

Nazi ideas for the future constituted little more than a grotesque fantasy. The General Plan East envisaged a Germanic empire reaching to the Urals, with autobahns linking new cities, satellite towns and model villages and farms manned by armed settlers, with *Untermenschen* helots tilling the soil. Himmler dreamed of *gemütlich* German colonies, with gardens and orchards built across the former killing grounds of his SS *Einsatzgruppen*. And to provide a holiday centre the Crimea, renamed Gotengau, would become the German Riviera. The dominant problem, however, was how to find enough 're-Germanizable' people to fill the eastern landmass. Very few Danes, Dutch and Norwegians volunteered. There was even a mad idea of packing Slavs off to Brazil and bringing back German settlers in their stead from Santa Caterina province. By the time of the defeat at Stalingrad and the withdrawal from the Caucasus, it had become clear that there were not nearly enough Germans, real, recycled or drafted, to fulfil the target of 120 million and thus satisfy Hitler's and Himmler's vision.

Ethnic cleansing and transfers of population throughout central Europe had been not only cruel but also incredibly wasteful in manpower and resources at a time when the war hung in the balance. Colonists proved incapable of farming the land as well as those they replaced, and so agricultural production declined disastrously.

An over-stretched German war machine found itself desperately short of manpower, so Fritz Sauckel, working with the armaments minister Albert Speer, travelled around the occupied territories and countries rounding up five million workers for factories, mines, ironworks and farms. The Reich became pockmarked with camps for this swelling mass of slave labour. German civilians watched these foreigners fearfully out of the corner of the eye, seeing them as an enemy within. Most senior Nazis were uneasily conscious of the paradox that, although they had reduced their own 'racially undesirable' population, they were now bringing hundreds of thousands into Germany itself.

Senior Nazi officials had promised a 'Greater German economic sphere' and a European economic union which would raise standards of living, yet contradictory policies and the compulsion to exploit their subject countries achieved the opposite result. Conquered countries were forced to pay for the costs of their occupation by German forces. Many businesses profited from close collaboration with their new masters, but in almost all countries, with the exception of a semi-independent Denmark, the population as a whole became far poorer. Most western European countries were forced to hand over between a quarter and a third of all their receipts, and Germany secured a large part of each country's agricultural output to ensure that its own citizens did not go hungry. In the occupied countries, this produced a rampant black market and a vertiginous rise in inflation.

Almost from the start, Churchill had great hopes of turning European discontent under Nazi occupation into outright revolt. In May 1940, he had appointed Dr Hugh Dalton, a well-off socialist, to be minister for economic warfare and supervise the creation of the Special Operations Executive. Dalton was not popular in the Labour Party, but as an anti-appeaser he had done much in the late 1930s to move it away from its pacifist position. He had long been a great admirer of Churchill, although the prime minister did not reciprocate his feelings. He could not 'stand his booming voice and shifty eyes' and said of Sir Robert Vansittart, permanent under-secretary at the foreign office in the 1930s, 'Extraordinary fellow, Van! He actually likes Dr Dalton.'

Dalton, a fervent admirer of the Poles, recruited Colonel Colin Gubbins, who had been a liaison officer with the Polish army during its battles in 1939. Gubbins later came to command SOE. Polish resistance was an inspiration for SOE. Even after the country's surrender at the end of September 1939, Polish soldiers fought on in the Kielce district under Major Henryk Dobrzański until May 1940, while others resisted in the area of Sandomierz on the upper Vistula. A Polish section had been set up in SOE, but its role was simply to work with the Polish army's Sixth Bureau in London and provide support. No military mission was sent to occupied Poland, and as a result the Poles themselves ran everything. After the great contribution of Polish pilots in the Battle of Britain, SOE managed to persuade the RAF to convert a Whitley bomber with additional fuel tanks so that they could make the long round-trip from a base in Scotland. The first drop of Polish couriers took place on 15 February 1941. Parachute containers were also designed to drop arms and explosives to what became the Armia Krajowa, or Home Army.

Polish patriotism was perhaps romantic in some ways, but it remained astonishingly resolute through the darkest days of both Nazi and Soviet oppression. In addition to the mass and individual killings which followed the German invasion, over 30,000 Poles were sent to camps, many to the new camp of Auschwitz. Although Poland's army was crushed in September 1939, a new underground resistance movement was created very soon afterwards. At its height, the Home Army reached nearly 400,000 members. The extraordinarily resourceful Polish intelligence services, which had provided the first Enigma machine, continued to help the Allies. Later in the war, the Poles even managed to spirit away a trial V-2 rocket which had landed in their marshes, and disassemble it. A specially adapted transport C-47 Dakota was flown to Poland and brought it back for examination by Allied scientists.

Both the Home Army and the intelligence networks reported to the Polish government-in-exile in London, which Stalin recognized reluctantly in August 1941 after the Nazi invasion of the Soviet Union. The Home Army was always desperately short of weapons. At first it concentrated on releasing prisoners and sabotaging rail communications, which provided great but unacknowledged assistance to the Red Army. Armed attacks came later.

The Poles, released from Soviet labour camps to join the forces commanded by General Władysław Anders, never ceased to loathe their oppressors. And the London government-in-exile's distrust of Stalin increased when it heard he was asking the British to recognize the frontier he had agreed with Hitler following the Nazi–Soviet pact. In April 1943, a crisis developed when the Germans announced to the world that they had discovered in the forest of Katyń the mass graves of Polish officers, executed by the Soviet NKVD.

The Soviet regime had always denied that it knew anything of the whereabouts of these prisoners, and at the time even the Poles had not believed Stalin's regime capable of such a massacre. The Kremlin insisted that the discovery was a German propaganda trick, and it must have been Nazis who had killed the victims.

The Polish government-in-exile demanded an investigation by the International Red Cross, while the British were acutely embarrassed. Churchill suspected that the Soviets were capable of such an act, but he felt unable to confront Stalin, especially at a time when he had to admit once again that an invasion of France was impossible that year. Further disasters for the Poles soon followed in June. The Germans in Warsaw managed to arrest the commander and other leaders of the Home Army. But far greater tragedies for Poland lay ahead.

The summer of 1941 had seen some early attacks on German troops in the Soviet Union by Red Army soldiers cut off by the Wehrmacht's advance. However, the first uprising against Nazi rule came in Serbia following the launch of Operation Barbarossa. This took the complacent German forces of occupation by surprise. Soon after their victory in the spring, a Leutnant had boasted in a letter home: 'We soldiers are like gods here!!' The rapidity of the country's surrender that April had led them to expect little trouble, but they had not considered how many Yugoslav soldiers might have retained and hidden their weapons.

Serbia came under the overall command of Generalfeldmarschall Wilhelm List's headquarters in Greece. The three divisions of Generalleutnant Paul Bader's LVI Corps were badly trained and under equipped. Ordered to respond with reprisals, they resorted mainly to shooting Jews who had already been rounded up. But executions of villagers close to the site of an ambush played straight into the hands of the Communist partisans, whose numbers rapidly swelled with those who wanted to take revenge for the death of family members.

Generalfeldmarschall Keitel at Führer headquarters demanded savage reprisals. The ratio was raised to a hundred Serbs for every German killed, in the belief that the 'Balkan mentality' only understood violence. In September, a major punitive offensive took place reinforced by the 342nd Infantry Division. The local German commanders again decided to start by shooting Jews who had been interned. So in mid-October 1941, some 2,100 Jews and 'Gypsies' were shot in retaliation for the killing of twenty-one German soldiers by Communist partisans. It was the first mass murder of Jews away from Soviet or Polish territory.

The partisan attacks were led by Josip Broz, alias Tito, an effective Comintern organizer during the Spanish Civil War. Tito, a strong figure of brutal good looks who had revived the Yugoslav Communist Party, believed in the need for Communists everywhere to help their comrades in the Soviet Union. The internationalism of the Party managed to avoid the worst ethnic and religious fault-lines in Yugoslavia, with Catholic Croats, Orthodox Serbs and Muslim Bosnians.

The rival resistance organization of Četniks led by General Draža Mihailović was almost exclusively Serb. The bespectacled, bearded and gloomy Mihailović, who looked more like an Orthodox priest than a military man, could not hope to rival Tito's charismatic leadership. He believed in building up his force ready for the day when the Allies would land, so that he could join them and restore the kingdom to young King Peter. He had rightly foreseen that Tito was going to use the partisan war to seize total power when the Red Army arrived. Mihailović did not want to provoke reprisals, yet contrary to Communist propaganda his forces did take on the Germans at times. Other groups also calling themselves Četniks cooperated closely with the Germans and the puppet government of General Milan Nedić, a confusion which later helped the Communists to blacken Mihailović's name in the eyes of the British.

An even more murderous element in the civil war developing in Yugoslavia came from the virulently anti-Serb and anti-semitic Croat Ustaše. The Croat state of Ante Pavelić was a loyal ally of the Germans, and the Ustaše brought a reign of terror to the region. Well over half a million Yugoslavs were killed in the factional fighting between rival forces during the war.

Other German massacres followed further skirmishes, including several thousand Serb civilians shot to meet the reprisal quotas. Some German officers began to see the stupidity of their policy, which targeted only the people who had not fled and who therefore had nothing to do with the attacks on their men. After some 15,000 people had been killed, and with few Jews and 'Gypsies' left to shoot, the reprisal quotas started to dwindle, without the knowledge of Berlin.

The drastic reduction in the numbers of their imprisoned hostages began in March 1942, when a large gas van arrived

in Belgrade. Some 7,500 Jews in the camp at Semlin were asphyxiated while being driven through the Serbian capital to
a mass grave dug by a shooting range on the edge of the city.
The German ambassador was deeply embarrassed by the conspicuous way in which such measures were carried out, but on
29 May 1942 the head of the security police felt able to boast to
Berlin that 'Belgrade was the only great city of Europe that was
free of Jews.'

Warfare in Yugoslavia became increasingly cruel as the Germans
launched one offensive after another into the Bosnian mountains.
Partisan wounded taken by German troops were crushed to death
with tanks. Tito organized his forces into thousand-strong brigades, but was wise enough not to attempt conventional military
tactics. Discipline was strict, and no fraternizing was allowed between the men and the large number of young women fighting in
their ranks. By the autumn of 1942, Tito's partisans had virtual
control in their mountainous region extending across western
Bosnia and eastern Croatia, and he set up his headquarters in the
town of Bihać, after expelling the Ustaše.

Having recognized the royalist Yugoslav government-in-exile
in London, the British provided aid to Mihailović, who was its
appointed representative. Moscow did not object, since it too
formally recognized the Yugoslav government. But during 1942
Ultra intercepts and other reports indicated that Tito's forces
were attacking the Germans, while the Četniks waited. Attempts
by SOE liaison officers parachuted in to persuade the rival resistance movements to work together had little success. So as Allied
interest in the Mediterranean increased, once the Germans had
been vanquished in North Africa, the British made contact with
Tito.

The Germans, afraid of a landing in the Balkans and determined
to protect the coast and secure their mineral supplies, launched
new offensives with their own forces and Italian troops. Tito
conducted a fighting retreat into Montenegro, narrowly avoiding
encirclement on the Neretva River. With his forces largely intact,
and soon with British aid parachuted in or landed on secret airstrips, the strength of Tito's partisans grew rapidly. Mihailović,
abandoned by the Allies after failing to carry out specifically requested actions, was bound to lose the parallel civil war.

Albania, to the south, was still occupied by Italian troops. Abbas Kupi, a supporter of King Zog who had fled when Mussolini invaded the country in 1939, started resistance on a small scale in the spring of 1941. Once the Nazis invaded the Soviet Union, Albanian Communists led by Enver Hoxha began their own much more aggressive campaign in the south. As in Yugoslavia, the British decided to aid the Communists on the grounds that they were fighting harder. Little support was provided to Abbas Kupi, to the disgust of the British SOE liaison officers, and eventually Hoxha's Communists were able to eliminate their rivals.

Greece was of much greater interest to the British. Churchill was a firm supporter of King George II and was not prepared to surrender the country to the Communist EAM-ELAS guerrilla movement. Embarrassingly for the British, however, many monarchists collaborated with the Germans and Italians out of a mixture of anti-Communism and opportunism. The authoritarian rule of General Metaxas had exacerbated anti-monarchist feelings, and the small Greek Communist Party rapidly extended its influence.

The Axis looting of the country, compounded by an incompetent Italian occupation, left the Greeks to suffer a terrible famine in the winter of 1941. The ruthless Communist leader, Aris Veloukhiotis, began to assemble a partisan force in the Pindus Mountains in 1942. His main rival was General Napoleon Zervas, a jolly, bearded character who formed EDES (the Greek National Republican League), a left-of-centre, non-Communist organization. Zervas's forces were much smaller and concentrated in Epirus in the north-west. As Communist strength grew, they became isolated from the rest of Greece, while other small resistance groups, such as EKKA, were eventually taken over by the Communist-controlled EAM-ELAS.

Two British SOE officers, parachuted into Greece in the summer of 1942, made contact after many difficulties with both Zervas and ELAS. Their primary task was to organize an attack on the main railway line which brought supplies south from Germany for Rommel's Panzerarmee in North Africa. They managed to persuade Zervas and ELAS to unite in an operation to blow up the great Gorgopotamos railway bridge. While the partisans assaulted the Italian positions at each end, a demolition team flown in from Cairo attached large charges of plastic explosive to the piers which supported the bridge. It was one of the most successful sabotage missions of the war, cutting the railway line for four months.

In March 1943, German forces and the SS began rounding up 60,000 Greek Jews, mainly from the city of Salonika where their large community had existed for hundreds of years. Although they sheltered the few escapees, the Greek resistance were unable to stop the railway traffic taking them to concentration camps in Poland, where many were subjected to the most horrific medical experiments.

After the rare example of cooperation between ELAS and EDES in the Gorgopotamos operation, SOE liaison officers found themselves in a minefield of political rivalries as Greece too became embroiled in a civil war between guerrilla groups. Zervas was much easier to work with, but the British had to arm ELAS as well for Operation Animals. This was a campaign of attacks in the summer of 1943 prior to the invasion of Sicily. Combined with the deception plan Operation Mincemeat, which consisted of dropping the body of what looked like a Royal Marines officer with important despatches off the southern Spanish coast, the objective was to persuade the Germans that the Allies were about to land in Greece. Like all effective campaigns of misinformation, it played to Hitler's own idea of what his enemy's intentions were and strengthened his belief that the British plan was to invade southern Europe via the Balkans. His Austrian background made him obsessive about the region. A panzer division and other forces were consequently diverted to Greece just before the landings in Sicily.

The ELAS leadership were divided over how to deal with the British. They wanted the support and legitimacy which an alliance with the Allies would bring, but they were intensely suspicious of British motives. In August 1943 partisan delegates were flown out to attend a meeting in Cairo. The Communists, like most Greeks at the time, were opposed to the restoration of the monarchy. They argued that King George should not return to the country unless a plebiscite permitted it. The Greek government-in-exile and the British, at Churchill's insistence, refused to accept this and unfairly blamed SOE for allowing such a political stand-off to develop. The ELAS partisan representatives returned with a grim resolve to defeat their rivals, establish a provisional government and pre-empt any British attempt to reinstall the monarchy.

The resistance on Crete, however, presented few political problems. Most of the guerrilla leaders known as *kapitans* accepted British guidance and, although not monarchist, were strongly anti-Communist. Only insignificant groups in the east of the island supported EAM-ELAS.

In France the vast majority of the country, including republicans, had welcomed Pétain's armistice with relief. They had no idea that German plans at that stage were to reduce France to the level of a 'tourist country' and to take Alsace and Lorraine for the Reich, thus forcing its men to serve in the German army.

Keeping their heads down, the French carried on with their daily lives as far as was possible in the new circumstances, although this was extremely hard for the wives of the 1.5 million prisoners of war still held in Germany. The depredations of occupation, with the Germans taking a considerable proportion of French agricultural output for themselves, produced great hardship in the towns and cities, especially for those with no relations in the countryside. The average height of boys dropped by seven centimetres and of girls by eleven centimetres in the course of the war.

Small resistance groups began to publish underground newspapers towards the end of 1940, in many cases inspired by de Gaulle's broadcasts from London declaring that the fight continued. They included people from different backgrounds and parties. At this stage, few acts of overt resistance against the Germans took place. Only after the invasion of the Soviet Union were armed attacks carried out by followers of the French Communist Party. Having lost face and many members during the Nazi–Soviet pact, it now began to develop an effective underground organization.

The German military occupation since 1940 had been comparatively correct, but the move towards total war and the Communist assassinations of German officers and soldiers meant that the SS started to take control. In May 1942, Heydrich travelled to Paris to install Gruppenführer Carl-Albrecht Oberg as chief of SS and police. Hitler had treated France better than most conquered nations, for the practical reason that if it policed itself in the German interest it saved the Wehrmacht a large occupation force. Yet Pétain's hope of uniting his badly bruised country under the authority of his État Français could not be maintained for long.

Defeat had exacerbated the irreconcilable divisions in French society. Even the pre-war right split in different directions. A very small minority, shamed by the defeat, wanted to resist German domination. Fascist Germanophiles, on the other hand, despised Pétain, feeling that his cautious collaboration was insufficient. Jacques Doriot's Parti Populaire Français, Marcel Déat's Rassemblement National Populaire and Eugène Deloncle's Mouvement Social Révolutionnaire supported the idea of the Nazis' New Order in Europe in the belief that France could become a great power again alongside the Third Reich. They were even more deluded than the old marshal, since the Germans never took them seriously for a moment. They were, at best, the Nazi equivalent of Lenin's 'useful idiots'.

Infighting between the zealots of the extreme right was matched by the rivalries on the German side. Otto Abetz, the francophile ambassador in Paris, was generally derided by leading Nazis, especially Göring. The SS and the military were frequently at loggerheads, and Paris attracted a plethora of German headquarters and administrative offices, all following their own policies. The centre of occupied Paris was forested with their signposts symbolically pointing in all directions.

SS Gruppenführer Oberg was, however, extremely satisfied with the assistance he received from Vichy's police. The Third Reich lacked manpower at that stage of the war on the eastern front, and Oberg had fewer than 3,000 German police for the whole of occupied France. René Bousquet, the secretary-general of police appointed by Pierre Laval, was an energetic young administrator, not a right-wing ideologue. Like the young *technocrates* who were quietly reorganizing and strengthening Vichy's system of government, Bousquet believed strongly that the État Français should keep control of security matters if it were to have any meaning at all. And if that meant exceeding his powers when it came to rounding up foreign Jews for deportation, then he was prepared to ignore Pétain's instructions that French police should not be involved.

On 16 July 1942, a total of 9,000 Parisian police under the orders of Bousquet launched dawn raids to seize 'stateless' Jews in Paris. Some 13,000, including 4,000 children who had not been asked for by the Germans, were held in the stadium of the Vélo-drome d'Hiver and at a transit camp at Drancy on the outskirts of Paris before being sent on to death camps in the east. Further round-ups followed in the unoccupied zone in the south. Oberg was more than satisfied with Bousquet's efforts, even if Eichmann was still disappointed.

The arrival of an American army in the Mediterranean, and the clear indication that the Axis would be defeated, encour-aged a rapid growth in the resistance. The German takeover of the unoccupied zone and the assassination of Darlan at the end of 1942 also had a major effect. At the end of January 1943, the Vichy regime, in an attempt to tighten its grip, established the Milice Française, a paramilitary force led by Joseph Darnand. The Milice attracted a mixture of extreme right-wing ideologues and anti-semites, arch-reactionaries often from the impoverished provincial nobility, naive country boys attracted by the power of guns, and criminal opportunists lured by the promise of looting the houses of those whom they arrested.

The creation of the Milice reignited the latent civil war between 'les deux Frances' which had existed since the revolution of 1789. On one side were the Catholic right-wingers who loathed free-masons, the left and the Republic, which they called 'la gueuse', or 'the slut'. On the other stood republicans and anti-clericals who had voted for the Popular Front in 1936. Yet many French under the occupation defied generalization. There were even *bien pensant* left-wingers who denounced Jews, and black marketeers who saved them, not always for a price.

Operation Anton, the German occupation of southern and eastern France, also prompted many who had half-heartedly supported Pétain to change sides. The only senior officer in the 100,000-strong Army of the Armistice to oppose the German army was General Jean de Lattre de Tassigny, a flamboyant leader who was flown out by the Allies and later became the commander of the French First Army. Many other officers went into hiding and joined a new movement, the ORA, or Organisation de Résistance de l'Armée. Reluctant to support de Gaulle, they acknowledged only General Giraud at first.

Predictably the French Communist Party was deeply suspicious of such late turncoats, part of what they called 'Vichy à l'envers', or 'Vichy back to front'. Other officers and officials escaped to North Africa, where Admiral Darlan's regime was known as 'Vichy à la sauce américaine'. When François Mitterrand, a Vichy official who later became a socialist president of the Republic, arrived in Algiers, General de Gaulle regarded him with distrust, not because he had come from Vichy, but because he had arrived on a British aeroplane.

De Gaulle resented any British interference in French affairs, especially SOE's support for French resistance groups. He wanted all resistance activity to be subordinated to his own BCRA, the Bureau Central de Renseignements et d'Action, and was most put out that SOE's F Section, which was directed by Colonel Maurice Buckmaster, had developed almost a hundred independent circuits on French territory.

The foreign office had originally instructed F Section to steer clear of the Free French in London. F Section was keen to do this, partly for reasons of security – the Free French were notoriously lax and their primitive code system was an open book to the Germans – but also because it soon came to see how dangerous political rivalries in France could become. As one senior SOE officer later observed, the great advantage of SOE remaining above the fray while controlling the arms supply was its ability to reduce the threat of civil war when liberation finally came.

SOE also set up Section RF, which worked closely with the BCRA, providing weapons and aircraft, and had its offices near the Bureau's headquarters in Duke Street north of Oxford Street. The head of the BCRA was André Dewavrin, better known by his *nom de guerre* of Colonel Passy. His organization was originally split between the intelligence side and its 'action service', which dealt with armed resistance. Passy was alleged, but never proved, to have been a member of the virulently anti-Communist Cagoule, although he certainly had one or two *cagoulards* working for him. The coal cellar in the Duke Street headquarters had been converted into cells where French volunteers suspected of being Vichy spies or Communists were held and interrogated by Capitaine Roger Wybot. Word of torture and suspicious deaths emerged, to the anger and embarrassment of SOE. On 14 January 1943 the security service chief Guy Liddell wrote in his diary, 'Personally, I think it is time that Duke Street was closed down.'

De Gaulle's determination to unite the resistance under his command strengthened, even though as a lifetime career officer he had little confidence in irregulars. If the resistance in France acknowledged his primacy, then the British and especially the Americans would have to take notice. Apart from networks such as the Confrérie de Notre-Dame, run by Colonel Rémy (the *nom de guerre* of the film director Gilbert Renault), there were few which were naturally Gaullist. But groups such as Combat founded by Henri Frenay gradually acknowledged the need to work together. The Communists, on the other hand, distrusted de Gaulle, whom they presumed would turn into a right-wing military dictator.

In the autumn of 1941 Jean Moulin, who had been the youngest prefect in France in 1940, appeared in London. Moulin, a natural leader, impressed both SOE and de Gaulle, who immediately recognized him as the man to unify the resistance. On New Year's Day 1942, Moulin returned to France with de Gaulle's *ordre de mission* appointing him delegate-general. His task was to reorganize as many of the networks as possible into small cells which ran less risk of being infiltrated by agents of the Abwehr and the Sicherheitsdienst (or SD), the SS counter-intelligence service often confused with the Gestapo. The resistance was not to attempt open warfare, but to prepare for the liberation of France by Allied forces.

Moulin, who needed a military man to command what would later become the Secret Army, recruited General Charles Delestraint. Working tirelessly, Moulin won over the main networks in the unoccupied zone, Combat, Libération and Franc-Tireur (confusingly, not the same as the Communist organization Francs-Tireurs et Partisans). Despite this success, the British government was still determined not to turn F Section over to the Free French.

Ironically, American support for Darlan greatly helped de Gaulle come to an agreement with the Communists. The Communists were outraged that the Allies should have supported Darlan, who had been Vichy's prime minister when their members had been executed as hostages. In January 1943, Fernand Grenier arrived in London as the French Communist Party's delegate to the Free French. The following month, Pierre Laval, bowing to German pressure for more workers to be sent to the Reich, instituted the Service de Travail Obligatoire. This outright conscription of labour was bitterly resented in France, and prompted tens of thousands of young men to escape to the mountains and forests. Resistance groups were almost overwhelmed by the influx, and although they found it hard to feed them, let alone arm them, the Maquis, as it was called, became a mass movement.

In the spring, Moulin set up the Conseil National de la Résistance and contacted networks in northern France to persuade them to join. But in June a series of disasters began, largely due to bad security. The SD managed to penetrate one group after another. General Delestraint was arrested in the Parisian Métro, and on 21 June Jean Moulin and all the members of the Conseil National de la Résistance were surrounded in a house on the edge of Lyons. Moulin was tortured so badly by SS Hauptsturmführer Klaus Barbie that he died two weeks later, without giving anything away. The British, horrified by all the lapses in security and the spate of arrests which continued, were even more reluctant to confide in the BCRA.

The Gaullists reconstituted the council of the resistance, this time headed by Georges Bidault, an honest but uncharismatic left-of-centre Catholic. Because Bidault lacked Moulin's clarity and determination, the Communists, who had suffered very few infiltrations of their tight cell system, greatly increased their influence. The Communists, having agreed to associate with the Gaullist Secret Army, hoped to receive large quantities of weapons and money from SOE. They also sought to infiltrate the various resistance committees with their own 'submarines', who were secret Communists pretending to have nothing to do with the Party. Their vision of the liberation of France was diametrically different to the Gaullist idea. By the control of committees and the growing strength of their armed groups in the Francs-Tireurs et Partisans, they wanted to carry liberation into revolution. They did not know, however, that Stalin had other priorities and they also underestimated the political skills of the Gaullists.

De Gaulle himself, who had almost been consigned to oblivion by the Darlan deal and the Americans' promotion of General Giraud, soon turned the tables on his rival. Roosevelt had sent Jean Monnet to advise Giraud, but Monnet, although he had been against de Gaulle, now showed his realism. He worked in the background to smooth a transition of power. On 30 May 1943, de Gaulle landed at Maison Blanche airfield in Algiers, where Giraud welcomed him with a band playing the 'Marseillaise'. The British and Americans watched from the sidelines. A frenzy of disagreements and rumours of plots, even of kidnappings, soon followed. The scheming prompted General Pierre de Bénouville to observe that 'nothing was more like Vichy than Algiers'.

On 3 June, the Comité Français de Libération National was set up with de Gaulle dictating virtually every aspect of what was clearly a government-in-waiting. De Gaulle, with his remarkable foresight, had also seen the need to make overtures to Stalin, and not just in order to manage the French Communists better. He decided to send a representative to Moscow. The Free French, alone among the western Allies, had already contributed a fighter group to the eastern front. On 1 September 1942, the Groupe de Chasse Normandie had formed up at Baku in Azerbaijan, prior to operational and conversion training on the Yak-7 fighter. Having entered combat on 22 March 1943, the Normandie-Nieman Group, as it became designated, would eventually claim 273 Luftwaffe aircraft destroyed. De Gaulle calculated that good relations between the Soviet Union and France offered Stalin a wild card in the west, and would improve his own position when dealing with the Anglo-Saxons.

After the conquest of Belgium, Hitler ordered that the Flemings should receive preferential treatment. He had an idea that they might become a form of sub-German annexe to the Reich, in a future reorganization of Europe. A section of Belgian territory south of Aachen, as well as the Grand Duchy of Luxembourg, had been incorporated into the Reich.

The need for more manpower on the eastern front prompted Himmler in 1942 to increase the Waffen-SS with units from 'Germanic' countries, which included Scandinavians, the Dutch and the Flemish. In addition to the Légion Wallonie, raised by the fascist Léon Degrelle, who saw himself as a future leader of Belgium in the New Order, a Flemish Legion was also incorporated. Altogether some 40,000 Belgians from both communities served in the Waffen-SS, twice as many as the number of Frenchmen who formed the SS Charlemagne Division.

The vast majority of Belgians, however, detested this second German occupation of their country in a quarter of a century. Underground newspapers flourished, and young resisters resorted to graffiti to attack the occupation. As in other occupied countries, V signs for Allied victory appeared chalked on walls. When Rudolf Hess flew to Britain in 1941, they painted 'Heil Hess!' on walls. The German army adopted a pragmatic approach, tending to ignore such pinpricks. But when a series of strikes threatened industrial production, their severity increased.

Armed resistance would have been suicidal, so a number of well-placed Belgians, including former intelligence officers, did all that they could to spy for the Allies. An underground Armée Secrète was formed eventually with some 50,000 members, but it had to wait until liberation was imminent. There was great distrust between the Belgian government-in-exile in London and the SOE section responsible for the country. The most effective controller, who took over in mid-1943, was Hardy Amies, who later became the Queen's dress designer.

A more militant organization was the Communist-led Front de l'Indépendance which, as well as fomenting strikes, assassinated collaborators in the street. Other brave groups organized escape lines for Allied aircrew shot down during the strategic bombing campaign against Germany. The most successful was the Comet line organized by a young woman, Andrée de Jongh, who had the codename Dédée. Many Belgians also took great risks in hiding Belgian-born Jews. Jewish refugees from other countries trapped there were less fortunate. They made up the bulk of the 30,000 transported to camps.

The Netherlands, which had remained a neutral country in the First World War, suffered from the shock of occupation perhaps even more than Belgium. Although a small minority collaborated or later joined the Waffen-SS *Nederland* Division, the majority of the country became bitterly anti-German. As in Belgium, the round-up of Jews in February 1941 prompted a strike, which brought severe reprisals. One Dutch resistance group burned down the registry of births in Amsterdam to hamper the Germans' searches, but most of the 140,000 Jews in Holland were transported to death camps, including the young Anne Frank. Then, with the beginning of the war in the east, German occupation authorities instituted a much harsher regime. On 4 May 1942, the Germans shot seventy-two members of the Dutch resistance and imprisoned hundreds more.

The Sicherheitsdienst had been active in the Netherlands before the war, so when opposition grew to the forced recruitment of labour, its arrests were carefully targeted. And having obtained a list of Dutch intelligence contacts from the two SIS officers seized at Venlo in 1940, the Germans rounded them up rapidly.

The Abwehr also achieved a great success against the Dutch resistance beginning in March 1942. It called this counter-intelligence coup Operation North Pole, or the *Englandspiel*. This disaster was almost entirely due to appallingly lax practices in N Section at SOE's London headquarters. An SOE radio operator was picked up in a sweep in The Hague. The Abwehr forced him to transmit to London. He did so, assuming that, because he had left off the security check at the end of his message, London would know that he had been captured. But to his horror London assumed that he had simply forgotten it, and replied telling him to arrange a drop zone for another agent to be parachuted in.

A German reception committee was waiting for the new agent, and he was in turn forced to signal back as instructed. The chain continued, with one agent after another seized on arrival. Each was deeply shocked to find that the Germans knew everything about them, even the colour of the walls in their briefing room back in England. The Abwehr and SD, for once working harmoniously together, thus managed to capture around fifty Dutch officers and agents. Anglo-Dutch relations were severely damaged by this disaster; in fact many people in the Netherlands suspected treachery at the London end. There was no conspiracy, just a terrible combination of incompetence, complacency and ignorance of conditions in occupied Holland.

*

Denmark, surprised and overwhelmed by the Nazi invasion in 1940, opted for a form of passive resistance during the early part of its occupation. The German regime maintained a light touch and basically allowed the country to govern itself, prompting Churchill to refer unfairly to Denmark as 'Hitler's tame canary'. Highly productive Danish farmers produced up to a fifth of the Reich's needs in butter, pork and beef. Himmler especially wanted to recruit as many Danes as possible for the Waffen-SS, but most volunteers came from the German-speaking minority in the south.

In November 1942 Hitler, exasperated by King Christian's open dislike, demanded a more obedient government. The detested pro-Nazi Erik Scavenius was installed as prime minister. Scavenius made Denmark join the Anti-Comintern Pact, and called on Danes to volunteer to fight in the Soviet Union. Although Denmark's fate under the Nazi regime was among the least severe in Europe, Danes managed to save almost all the Jews in their country by smuggling them in fishing-boats across the Kattegat to southern Sweden. The Danish underground, the Dansk Frihedsrådet, provided valuable intelligence to London, especially for the RAF. It also carried out its own sabotage actions and, in 1943, set up a shadow administration.

Of all the governments-in-exile in London, the Norwegian was the strongest, both in authority and in resources. The large Norwegian merchant navy was placed at the service of the British, and represented a major contribution to the war effort in Atlantic and Arctic convoys. Norway, which demonstrated a wide degree of support for King Haakon VII, also suffered far less than other occupied countries from the threat of a potential civil war, either during the occupation or at the end of the war.

After the country's defeat, Norwegian officers began to organize an underground army, the Milorg, towards the end of 1940. By the end of the war it numbered some 40,000 members. There had been considerable frustration at the inept Allied intervention, and in the early years of the German occupation there was tension between the Norwegians and SOE, which wanted to develop an aggressive campaign.

Churchill's longing to launch raids on Norway, with two on

the Lofoten Islands in 1941, then advocating an invasion in 1942, drove his chiefs of staff to distraction, but the raids encouraged Hitler's conviction that the Allies would attack across the North Sea. The German dictator's insistence on maintaining more than 400,000 troops in Norway, to the frustration of his own generals elsewhere, tied down considerable forces for nearly five years of the war. With such a huge occupying army, it was hardly surprising that Milorg did not want to start a partisan war which would have led to massive civilian casualties.

Norway's self-styled leader, Vidkun Quisling, had led a small party of Nazi sympathizers, the Nasjonal Samling, before the war. Having proclaimed himself head of a government during the German invasion, he was promptly removed by Josef Terboven, the Reichskommissar, who despised him. In February 1942, Hitler appointed Quisling minister president, but Terboven continued to undermine Quisling's delusions of power. The Rikshird, a copy of the Nazi SA, was established and attracted 50,000 members, most of them opportunists. Other Nazi organizations, such as the Hitler Jugend, were also imitated. Perhaps inevitably with such a large army of occupation, a substantial number of Norwegian women became involved with German soldiers and just over 10,000 children were born from these liaisons.

But the bulk of the population hated their German occupiers. In April 1942, the overwhelming majority of the Lutheran clergy declared against the Quisling government, and when the Germans ordered the round-up of Jews, only 767 out of 2,200 were deported. Most of the rest were smuggled by Norwegians over the border to Sweden, which, although happy to sell Germany its rich iron ore and other materials for its war industries, started to distance itself from its Nazi trading partner once the war began to turn against Germany.

A vital target for the RAF had been the Norse Hydro plant in the district of Telemark, which produced heavy water for what was suspected to be the prototype of a German atomic bomb. But bombing from the air was ruled impracticable, so SOE was called on to organize a sabotage raid. A British commando assault in November 1942 ended in disaster, with two Horsa gliders crashing in bad weather. German troops captured the survivors of one, bound their hands with barbed wire and executed them on the spot. This was in response to Hitler's recent *Kommandobefehl*, which ordered that all members of special forces or raiding parties, whether or not in uniform, were to be shot. The Germans immediately discovered from maps on the crashed aircraft what their objective had been.

The reception committee of three Norwegian commandos had parachuted into the mountains in October. They stayed on through the terrible winter, surviving in snowed-in huts and living off wild reindeer meat. Their only source of vitamin C came from the *gørr*, the semi-digested green matter in the reindeers' stomachs. Finally on 17 February 1943, another six Norwegian commandos trained in Britain parachuted in, but landed on the wrong frozen lake in the mountains. In the end the two groups met up, and successfully laid explosives at the Vermork heavy water plant on the night of 28 February. They got in and out without a shot being fired and caused considerable damage. The Germans repaired the installations and production started again four months later. US Eighth Air Force raids failed to hit the target effectively, so the Norwegian resistance was called upon again.

When a sufficient quantity of heavy water was ready in February 1944, the Germans loaded it in railway wagons on to a ferry, unaware that two elderly members of the Norwegian resistance had slipped aboard the night before and laid charges with timers fashioned from alarm clocks. The ferry sank exactly as planned in the deepest waters of the lake. Fourteen civilians had also been killed, but the Norwegian authorities in London had agreed in advance that the target justified the risk. Although German scientists were not even close to building a nuclear bomb, the Allies could not afford to take any chances. In any case, the two Vermork actions were among the most efficient sabotage operations of the entire war.

Czechoslovakia, the first victim of German aggression, was abandoned by the British and French in 1938, and then completely occupied by the Germans the following March. But Czech students marked their independence day on 28 October 1939 with a big demonstration. The Nazis closed all universities and executed nine students as a warning. The former prime minister Edvard Beneš set up a government-in-exile in London, and Czech soldiers and pilots made their way to England. Czech pilots fought with great skill and bravery in the RAF.

The Germans dismembered the country. The Sudetenland had already been incorporated into the Reich, Slovakia became a puppet fascist state under Monsignor Jozef Tiso, and the rest of the country was named the Reich Protectorate of Bohemia and Moravia. Although the Nazi regime avoided the harshest measures at first, the SD was ready to smash any signs of disaffection, especially after June 1941 and the entry of the Soviet Union into the war on the Allied side. The Czech resistance – the UVOD or Ústředuí vedení odboje domácího – began a campaign of sabotage against fuel dumps and railways, as did Communist groups.

Hitler appointed Reinhard Heydrich to take over as protector of Bohemia and Moravia to crush the opposition. Heydrich immediately opted for a policy of terror to ensure that war production was no longer interrupted. He arrested the leading officials and had them sentenced to death. Altogether ninety-two people were shot in the first few days, and several thousand others were sent to Mauthausen concentration camp. Heydrich's longer-term plan was to Germanize the territory through massive deportation. He also started the despatch of the region's 100,000 Jews to concentration camps, where almost all perished.

In London, the Czech government-in-exile decided to assassinate Heydrich. The objective of the attack was to create such a shock effect that the German reprisals would shame the Allied governments into annulling the Munich agreement, and thus re-establish the pre-1938 borders. Two young Czech volunteers were trained by SOE and parachuted into the country at the end of 1941. On 27 May 1942, after much reconnaissance, the two-man team took up position for a roadside ambush. One tried to shoot Heydrich as his open Mercedes slowed for a sharp bend, but his sub-machine gun jammed. His companion then threw an improvised bomb. Heydrich was wounded by the blast. Although his wounds were not fatal, they were contaminated and he died from septicaemia on 4 June.

Although angry that Heydrich should have taken the risk of driving around Prague in an open car, Hitler's fury against the Czechs led to massive reprisals, with killings and deportations. The villages of Lidice and Ležáky were destroyed, with the execution of all male inhabitants over the age of sixteen. The women were sent to Ravensbrück concentration camp. Although not as extreme as some Nazi atrocities, Lidice became the symbol of German oppression throughout the western world.

29

The Battle of the Atlantic and Strategic Bombing

1942–1943

The success of the Royal Navy and the RAF in sinking supply ships for Rommel's Afrika Korps in the autumn of 1941 had prompted Hitler to order the transfer of U-boats from the Atlantic to the Mediterranean and its approaches. Admiral Dönitz objected bitterly, but to little avail. These U-boats in the Mediterranean enjoyed some conspicuous successes with the sinking in November of the carrier HMS *Ark Royal* and the battleship HMS *Barham*, but the contribution of Ultra to the Eighth Army's survival in North Africa was considerable.

The US Navy's chief of staff, Admiral Ernest King, was reluctant to impose a convoy system along America's east coast, even though the country was now at war with Germany. Admiral Dönitz ordered some of his Type IX U-boats to the area, where they were to target ships, especially oil tankers, at night against the bright lights along the coastline. Losses were so high that King, under pressure from General Marshall, was forced to introduce escorted convoys at the beginning of April. The Germans then switched their attacks to the Caribbean and the Gulf of Mexico.

In February 1942, the Kriegsmarine added a fourth rotor to their Enigma machines. Bletchley called the new system 'Shark', and struggled for months without success to break it. To make matters worse, the Germans then cracked the Admiralty code known as Naval Cipher 3, which exchanged convoy details with the Americans. Although the British suspected by August that it had been broken, the Admiralty inexplicably carried on using it for another ten months with disastrous consequences.

A total of 1,100 ships were sunk in 1942, with 173 in June alone. But at the end of October an Enigma machine with its settings was seized from a sinking submarine in the eastern Mediterranean. And by mid-December the codebreakers at Bletchley were into Shark. Convoys could once again be rerouted to avoid wolf-packs, and anti-submarine aircraft from Canada, Iceland and the United Kingdom could be guided to U-boat assembly areas. This forced the wolfpacks to concentrate in the mid-Atlantic 'black gap' which was out of range of shore-based aircraft.

To extend his U-boats' range and time at sea, Grossadmiral Dönitz, who had been promoted when he replaced Raeder as chief of the Kriegsmarine, introduced 'milch cow' submarines to refuel and rearm his wolfpacks. In December he even sent several of his U-boats into the Indian Ocean. During Operation Torch, *U-173* sank three ships of the invasion fleet off Casablanca, and the following night *U-130*, captained by Ernst Kals, sank another three.

All this time, the 'Hell Run' of the Arctic convoys continued. In the summer months the nights were so short that escorts and merchant vessels alike suffered constant air attacks from Luftwaffe bases in northern Norway. As well as U-boats, the Kriegsmarine sent out heavy destroyers from anchorages in the fjords. In winter, the superstructure of the ships became buried in ice, which had to be chipped away with axes. And the crew of any ship which sank stood little chance if they had to jump into the sea. They died of hypothermia in three minutes.

Churchill, determined to improve security for the Russia-bound convoys, had wanted to invade and hold northern Norway with Operation Jupiter. Ever since the autumn of 1941, he had been worrying his chiefs of staff with plans for a landing there. Time and again they returned with sound arguments on why it was impracticable. They lacked the shipping and the warships, and it was too far for air cover. Churchill returned to the charge again in May 1942. In July he had an idea that this would be a suitable task for the Canadian Corps on the grounds that its men were used to harsh weather. General Andrew McNaughton, its commander, estimated that he would need 'five divisions, twenty squadrons and a large fleet'. Churchill wanted to send McNaughton to Moscow to discuss the project with Stalin. It would take the firm opposition of the Canadians and the chiefs of staff before the prime minister allowed the matter to drop many months later. In Washington, General Marshall was also totally opposed to such a dispersion of effort.

On 31 December 1942, Convoy JW-51B bound for Murmansk was attacked off the North Cape by the heavy cruiser *Admiral Hipper*, the *Lützow* and six destroyers. Four of the Royal Navy escorts immediately turned towards them. Although one of their destroyers HMS *Achates* and a minesweeper were sunk, they damaged the *Hipper* and sank a German destroyer. Having chased off a superior force, the escorts, led by HMS *Onslow*, managed to shepherd the convoy to its destination.

At the Casablanca conference in January 1943, U-boat bases and shipyards were designated as priority objectives for Bomber Command. On 13 February, Lorient, one of the main bases on the French Atlantic coast, was bombed heavily. Saint-Nazaire was also attacked. But despite the huge quantity of bombs dropped, usually 1,000 tons a time, the ferro-concrete shelters were too strong. It was found to be more effective to lay large quantities of mines off the Brittany coast.

Improvements in the radar mounted on anti-submarine Liberators and Sunderlands soon began to have an effect. The Bay of Biscay became a killing ground for Coastal Command squadrons, operating from south-west England. Yet the wolfpacks in the 'black gap' continued to take a heavy toll. In March 1943, in heavy seas, the fast-moving Convoy HX-229 overtook the slower SC-122. This presented the wolfpacks with ninety merchantmen as targets, protected by only sixteen escort vessels. Dönitz had concentrated thirty-eight U-boats in the area, and during the night of 20 March they sank twenty-one ships. Only the arrival of Liberators flying from Iceland the next morning saved the surviving ships of the two convoys.

Dönitz by now had 240 operational U-boats. On 30 April, he concentrated fifty-one of them between Greenland and Newfoundland to intercept Convoy ONS-5. But, with Bletchley having broken the Shark code, five extra destroyers were despatched from St John's, and Royal Canadian Air Force Catalinas stood by. Long-range Liberators now narrowed the 'black gap', and escort vessels were being equipped with a new high-frequency direction-finding system, which could locate U-boats on the surface up to sixty-five kilometres away. Convoys included escort carriers, destroyers and corvettes armed with a new device called Hedgehog, which fired depth-charges ahead of the ship, rather than just dropping them off the stern. During the first week of May, Dönitz's U-boats intercepted the convoy. They sank thirteen ships, but the counter-attack by escorts and aircraft sank seven U-boats. This forced Dönitz to call off the rest.

During May, he was obliged to accept that his massed wolf-pack tactic was not working. A group of thirty-three U-boats tried to attack Convoy SC-130. They failed to sink a single ship and five of the submarines were lost. One of them, *U-954*, was sunk by a Liberator from Coastal Command. All the crew were killed, including Dönitz's twenty-one-year-old son, Peter. Altogether the Kriegsmarine lost thirty-three U-boats during that month. On 24 May, Dönitz ordered almost all his submarines in the North Atlantic to pull out and take up station south of the Azores. Churchill's greatest worry was now behind him. With the U-boat menace now drastically reduced, the build-up of American troops for an invasion of Europe could also begin.

Hitler had seen the U-boat campaign against Britain as a just revenge for the blockade of Germany during the First World War. In a similar way the British saw their strategic bombing campaign against Germany as vengeance for the 'Blitz' on London. There was also a large element of revenge for Nazi crimes elsewhere. But the main impetus came from British weakness, and the inability to strike back in any other way.

On 29 June 1940, just after the French defeat, Churchill had acknowledged that a naval blockade of Germany was no longer possible. 'In which case,' he added, 'the sole decisive weapon in our hands would be overwhelming air attack on Germany.' The strategic bombing offensive had already begun on 15 May, when ninety-nine bombers attacked oil installations in the Ruhr. But the first year of Bomber Command's attacks proved largely ineffective. Churchill was horrified in late September 1941 when he received the Butt Report, which estimated from photoreconnaissance that only one aircraft in five dropped their bombs within five miles of the target.

The chief of the air staff, Air Chief Marshal Portal, had recently written a paper for the prime minister, advocating a heavy bomber force of 4,000 aircraft to break German morale. Portal, a highly intelligent man, was not put off by Churchill's dismay and anger at the Butt Report. He countered with the unanswerable argument that the British army was in no position to defeat Germany. Only the RAF could hope to weaken Germany fatally for the day when Britain returned to the continent of Europe. Churchill retorted with a reminder of the RAF's exaggerated claims from before the war about the decisive effects of bombing. At that time, the picture painted of 'air destruction was so exaggerated that it depressed the statesmen responsible for the prewar policy, and played a definite part in the desertion of Czechoslovakia in August 1938'.

Churchill might well have rammed the point home that the RAF's claims had much to do with its rivalry with the army and the Royal Navy. Bombing raids against Germany in the First World War had been both wasteful and ineffective. The newborn RAF fought for its survival with preposterously exaggerated claims of the damage inflicted, especially on civilian morale. Since 1918, its justification for remaining as an independent service was based on the argument that bombing was a strategic capability. This established 'a pattern of exaggeration that ultimately would help to create a gap between RAF declaratory policy and its actual capabilities'. Churchill, however, was loath to reject the advantages offered by Bomber Command. With his deep sense of history, he was all too conscious of Britain's traditional strategy of avoiding a direct confrontation on the soil of Europe until the enemy had been severely weakened at sea and at the periphery. Above all, he was determined to avoid another First World War bloodbath.

For Churchill, the most urgent need during the nightly Luftwaffe attacks on Britain in 1940 and the spring of 1941 was to be able to reassure a disenchanted and weary public that Britain was hitting back. And at a time when the army was reeling under the disasters of Greece, Crete and Rommel's advance in North Africa, the RAF's theory of offensive air power enunciated by its first chief of the air staff, Lord Trenchard – 'to bomb them harder than they do us' – was too attractive to question. The fact that Trenchard's own bombing force in the First World War had suffered massive casualties to little avail was not mentioned. Nor was the clear implication that the strategy was aimed essentially at the civilian population 'for moral effect', just as the Luftwaffe's had been. The truth in any case was that bombing remained so inaccurate that only area targets, such as densely populated cities, could be considered.

Unlike the Luftwaffe, which had retained close tactical co-operation with the German army, the RAF had distanced itself as far as possible from the other two services in its over-extended war of independence, and it rejected the concept of close support. Inter-service suspicions intensified during the 1930s. Both the British army and the Royal Navy questioned the morality and legality of the RAF's proposed bombing strategy. The Admiralty even described the bombing of towns as 'revolting and un-English'. The RAF protested hotly that 'baby-killing' was not its aim. Yet its continuing emphasis on attacking enemy morale hardly indicated an alternative.

On the outbreak of war, Bomber Command had been a long way behind Fighter Command in its readiness to carry out its stated mission. Not only were its aircraft inadequate, but navigation, intelligence, photo-reconnaissance and target-acquisition systems had been badly neglected. Bomber Command had also failed to foresee the effectiveness of German air defence.

At the beginning of the war, RAF commanders were told that the 'intentional bombardment of civil populations as such is illegal'. This was in response to President Roosevelt's appeal to combatant nations to avoid bombing cities. Bombing missions over Germany were restricted to ineffective attacks on shipping and harbours and dropping propaganda leaflets. Even after the Luftwaffe's assaults on cities such as Warsaw, and later Rotterdam, the policy did not change until after the Luftwaffe bombed London by mistake on the night of 24 August 1940, instead of the Thames estuary ports. Churchill's order to retaliate, as already mentioned, led to the beginning of the Blitz on London and to the easing of target restrictions on the RAF. Yet, despite all of Bomber Command's claims during the inter-war years, its force of Wellingtons and Handley Page Hampdens proved incapable of defending themselves against fighters, of finding their targets even in daylight, and, even when they did, of inflicting significant damage. The humiliation for the RAF was considerable.

Churchill, fortifying himself with a wholly optimistic idea of Germany's economic vulnerability, pushed ahead with plans to increase the strength of Bomber Command. When estimating the possibility of achieving victory through bombing alone, the failure of the Luftwaffe's offensive against Britain to destroy either infrastructure or civilian morale was discounted. German oil production and aircraft factories, however, proved too small as targets for the haphazard reality of aerial bombing. So Portal, arguing that the German attacks on London in 1940 allowed Britain to 'take the gloves off', proposed reverting to the old RAF mantra of creating a 'moral effect' by bombing cities, which the service knew it could hit. Churchill agreed. And on 16 December 1940, a month after the destruction of Coventry, Bomber Command launched its first deliberate 'area raid' on Mannheim.

The increasingly desperate situation in the Battle of the Atlantic then forced Bomber Command to concentrate on U-boat pens, building yards and factories producing the Focke-Wulf Condor aircraft used against convoys. But in July 1941 the arguments within the RAF for the area bombing of cities intensified, supported passionately by Lord Trenchard. There was a mistaken conviction that German morale was much more brittle than British, and that Germans were bound to crack under a relentless night-time campaign. The Butt Report on bombing inaccuracy soon afterwards convinced even the critics that there was no option but to go for area targets.

In February 1942, Bomber Command received approval from the Cabinet to pursue an area-target strategy, and Air Chief Marshal Sir Arthur Harris took command. Harris, a great bull of a man with a bristling moustache, had no doubts that the key to victory was the destruction of German cities. This, in his view, would avoid the necessity of sending forces to the continent to take on the Wehrmacht there. As a thick-skinned outsider who had spent a tough life in Rhodesia, Harris saw little reason to compromise towards those he regarded as faint-hearted gentlemen.

Ever since the nights he had spent during the Blitz on the roof of the air ministry watching Luftwaffe bombs fall on London, Harris had longed to strike back, especially with such loads of incendiaries that they would overwhelm the enemy's fire services. The Blitz on London and other cities had killed 41,000 civilians and injured 137,000 more. Harris was therefore not prepared to take any criticism, or willingly accept other requests from generals or admirals, whom he was convinced had tried to undermine the RAF since its independence. He regarded them as 'diversionists' intent on frustrating him from carrying out his key plan.

Harris's first task was to improve the morale of his aircrew. They had suffered heavy casualties – nearly 5,000 men and 2,331 aircraft in the first two years of the war – for little effect, according to the Butt Report. In many of the earlier raids, more aircrew died than Germans on the ground.

Their lives lacked the glamour of the Spitfire squadrons in the south-east, whose pilots were fêted on their frequent trips to London. Most of the bomber bases were airfields in the flat, windswept countryside of Lincolnshire and Norfolk, sited there because they lay on the same latitude as Berlin. The aircrew lived in Nissen huts, which smelled of cigarettes and smoke from coke-fired stoves, and rain always seemed to be pattering on the roof. Apart from bacon and eggs for breakfast on returning from a mission, their food consisted of a monotonous routine of macaroni cheese, over-cooked vegetables, beetroot and Spam, and most suffered from constipation. Apart from endless cups of tea, which was rumoured to be laced with bromide to reduce their sexual urges, the only drink was watery beer in dismal pubs, to which they travelled by bicycle or bus on rainy nights. The lucky ones might be accompanied by an innocent young WAAF from the airfield. Others hoped to meet locals or Land Girls at dances.

As in Fighter Command, pilots and aircrew were mostly volunteers. A quarter of them came from countries overrun by the Nazis as well as from the Dominions: Canada, Australia, New Zealand, Rhodesia and South Africa. There were so many Canadians that they formed separate RCAF squadrons, and so later did men from other countries, such as the Poles and French. Some 8,000 Bomber Command aircrew died in training accidents, around a seventh of the total casualties.

When on 'ops', they lived with numbing cold, boredom, fear, discomfort and the perpetual noise of aero-engines. Death could come at any moment, whether from flak or a night-fighter. Luck, both good and bad, seemed to dominate all their lives, and many became obsessively superstitious, clinging to personal rituals or talismans, such as a rabbit's foot or a St Christopher medal.

Whatever the target, missions began with a similar routine – the briefing which opened with the words 'the target for tonight', radio checks, take-off, circling to assemble formation in the sky, gunners firing test bursts over the Channel, and then the atmosphere in the aircraft tensing as soon as the call came through the intercom: 'enemy coast ahead'. All aircrew looked forward to the sudden lurch upwards of the aircraft as its heavy load of bombs fell away.

It was a young man's war. Even a thirty-one-year-old pilot was nicknamed 'Grandpa'. Everyone had nicknames and there was a great sense of comradeship, but to cope with the death of friends they needed to acquire a certain cynicism or cold-bloodedness to protect themselves from the effects of survivor guilt. The sight of another aircraft on fire produced a mixture of horror and relief that it was someone else. A bomber might return so badly shot up by a night-fighter that the ground crew, on finding the mangled remains of the rear gunner in his turret, 'had to hose it out'. Waiting at dispersal, not knowing whether an 'op' was on, or delayed, or even cancelled because of bad weather over the target, created a great strain. Pilots especially were 'keyed up like a violin', even though they sometimes referred to themselves as 'a glorified bus driver'.

Bomber Command's offensive power began to increase only when heavy bombers – first Stirlings, then the four-engined Halifaxes and Lancasters – started to replace the Hampdens and Wellingtons. On the night of 3 March 1942, a total of 235 bombers were sent in the first mass attack on a target in France, the Renault factory at Boulogne-Billancourt on the edge of Paris. It was a legitimate target as it manufactured vehicles for the Wehrmacht. Marker flares were used for the first time, and because there were few anti-aircraft guns around, the bombers were able to go in below 4,000 feet to improve their accuracy. The destruction of the factory complex was great, but 367 French civilians were killed, mainly in housing blocks near by.

On 28 March, the RAF bombed the north German port of Lübeck, with a mixture of high-explosive bombs and incendiaries, as both Portal and Harris had planned. The old town was burned out. Hitler was outraged. 'Now terror will be answered with terror,' his Luftwaffe adjutant records him as saying. Hitler was so furious that he demanded 'aircraft from the eastern front to be transferred to the west', but General Jeschonnek, the Luftwaffe chief of staff, managed to persuade him that they could use their bomber formations in northern France. As the British bombing campaign stepped up, however, pressure soon grew to withdraw Luftwaffe fighter formations and heavy flak batteries from the eastern front to defend the Reich. A month after the attack on Lübeck, Bomber Command launched a series of four raids on Rostock, eighty kilometres to the east, causing even greater destruction. Goebbels described it as a 'Terrorangriff' – a 'terror attack' – and from then on Bomber Command aircrews were called 'Terrorflieger'. Harris was now openly defining success by the number of urban acres his bombers had reduced to rubble.

On the night of 30 May 1942, Harris launched his first thousand-bomber raid, against Cologne. The original target had been Hamburg with its U-boat shipyards, but bad weather forced a change of plan. Churchill, preparing a coup de théâtre, had invited Ambassador John Winant and General 'Hap' Arnold, the chief of the United States Army Air Forces, to dinner at Chequers. As his guests sat down at the dining table, the prime minister made his announcement. It was a shameless but irresistible boast in that year of humiliations. Winant sent a cable to Roosevelt saying: 'England is the place to win the war. Get planes and troops over here as soon as possible.'

The devastation was great, but still comparatively little by later standards. Some 480 people were killed. Harris, a determined propagandist for Bomber Command, had assembled almost every bomber that could fly, even trainers, to achieve his thousand-bomber figure. He too wanted to impress both the Americans and the Soviet Union. 'Vengeance Begins!' was the headline in the *Daily Express*. Yet Harris knew that he had to mislead the public and even some of his superiors, especially Churchill, who had very mixed feelings, by pretending that their targets were of a military nature, such as oil depots and communications centres. Main railway stations provided his justification for bombing the whole of a city centre. Harris, however, knew that the public was behind him. Only a few lone voices, such as George Bell, the Bishop of Chichester, spoke out.

That August, when Churchill had flown to Moscow to explain to Stalin that an invasion of northern France was out of the question, the bombing of German cities was his strongest card. He was able to argue that the Bomber Command offensive was a form of Second Front. Hitler's armaments minister Albert Speer expressed the same view. The bombing campaign was the only British action of which Stalin approved. Soviet intelligence was already passing back information from prisoner-of-war interrogations which indicated that the morale of German troops on the eastern front was being undermined by concern for their families at home, under British bombing. Stalin never lost his taste for revenge, especially since around half a million Soviet civilians are estimated to have died as a result of Luftwaffe bombing. Red Army aviation had not developed a strategic bombing arm, so he was content for the British to do the work for them.

Bomber Command aircraft were now more likely to find their target, with improvements in navigation aids using radio transponder technology to guide them to their objectives. The introduction of Pathfinder aircraft which would identify the target with flares was an innovation, at first strenuously resisted by Harris, until he was overruled by Portal and the air staff. At the same time German anti-aircraft defences had also been strengthened. In Berlin, Hitler ordered the construction of huge concrete flak towers, with batteries of heavy anti-aircraft guns on top.

Bomber Command casualties mounted relentlessly with the increasing rhythm of sorties over Germany, especially the Ruhr, which was known bitterly as 'Happy Valley'. Next of kin would receive an official notification and then a letter of condolence from the squadron or station commander. Some time later, personal effects would be returned – cufflinks, clothes, hairbrushes and shaving kit, and if the airman owned a car, then that could be collected.

'The worst thing is seeing the flak,' wrote the twenty-four-year-old Wing Commander Guy Gibson, who led 617 Squadron in the 'Dambuster' raid on the night of 16 May 1943. 'You must leave your imagination behind or it will do you harm.' Feeling the flak was of course even worse. 'A shell bursting beneath you lifts the plane about fifty feet upwards in the air,' observed the actor

Denholm Elliott, then serving as a wireless operator in a Halifax. 'You certainly find instant religion.'

The unsung casualties were those who broke down before the end of their thirty-mission tour. LMF, or Lacking in Moral Fibre, was the RAF phrase for cowardice or battle shock. For most of the war, the RAF appears to have been even more callous than the army in its treatment of psychological casualties. Altogether, 2,989 flight personnel in Bomber Command were diagnosed with combat stress. Just over a third were pilots. Most striking of all, training appears to have been an even more stressful form of flying than night bombing.

In the summer of 1942, the US Eighth Air Force began to assemble in Britain. Major General Carl A. Spaatz had arrived in May to direct all US air operations in Europe, and the Eighth's bomber force was commanded by Brigadier General Ira C. Eaker. To the astonishment of the RAF, who had tried it and suffered, the Americans announced that their bombing campaign would be by daylight.

The US Army Air Forces avoided the RAF's contentious theory of destroying enemy morale. Its leaders claimed that, with their Norden bombsight, they would carry out precision bombing on 'key nodes' of the enemy's 'industrial fabric'. But target intelligence was an inexact science, and to achieve such accuracy they would also need perfect visibility and a clearly identifiable objective which was not too strongly defended. Claims of bombing so accurate that they could 'hit a pickle-barrel' seldom matched the reality of widely scattered bombs on the ground. Pilots weaving to avoid flak upset the sensitive gyroscopes on the Norden bombsight, and to expect the bomb-aimer to remain calm as he entered all the data required was optimistic, assuming that he could see the target in the first place through all the smoke, cloud and haze. American bombing patterns were no better than those of the RAF.

Having armed their B-17s with heavy machine guns in turrets, the USAAF assumed that by flying at high altitude in tight formations it could ward off fighter attacks with interlocking fields of fire. But inexperienced gunners were more likely to hit other aircraft in their formation rather than attacking Messerschmitts.

Spaatz had not considered fighter escorts were necessary, even though as early as the mid-1920s the US Army Air Service, as it then was, had tested auxiliary droppable fuel tanks to give them the extra range. Like the British before them, they had dismissed the lessons of air warfare from the Spanish Civil War and China. All these lessons would soon become apparent once the Eighth Air Force began to fly missions over Germany.

At first, Spaatz wisely decided to restrict his inexperienced crews to comparatively easy raids over France. On 17 August, a dozen B-17 Flying Fortresses took off on their first mission led by Eaker. Spaatz had wanted to go himself, but as he was privy to Ultra this idea was quashed. The bombers' target was the marshalling yards at Rouen in northern France, which was close enough to allow them Spitfire fighter cover. There were no anti-aircraft defences, and their Spitfire escorts chased off some Messerschmitts on the return journey. The crews returned to a hero's welcome from journalists and rowdy celebrations. But Churchill and Portal were concerned about the slow build-up of American bomber strength in Britain, and by their dogged insistence on daylight bombing. The delay was largely caused by aircraft and men being diverted to the Mediterranean to assist Twelfth Air Force operations in North Africa.

With General Arnold at its head, the USAAF had expanded with astonishing speed. In the early days, it was blessed with close friendships at the top. The RAF, on the other hand, was often riven by disputes, largely caused by Harris's bloody-minded obstinacy and his detestation of the air staff, whom he regarded as even more feeble-minded than the hated army and Royal Navy. Harris openly derided the 'oilys', as he called the supporters of bombing fuel installations, and the 'panacea mongers' who demanded attacks on other specific targets. Yet American daylight precision-bombing dogma was almost equally fixed. Even the reality of European weather with impenetrable cloud would not budge USAAF commanders from convincing themselves that they were hitting the target.

During the crisis in the Battle of the Atlantic from late 1942, both Bomber Command and the Eighth Air Force concentrated on the U-boat pens on France's Atlantic coast. But the massive concrete constructions proved impenetrable to their bombs even when they scored direct hits, which was fairly rare in the terrible weather of that winter. The port towns around them, Saint-Nazaire and Lorient, on the other hand, were smashed to pieces. In retrospect, the only consolation for the Allies was that this vast diversion of concrete greatly slowed the building of Hitler's Atlantic Wall, a series of coastal defences to guard against the invasion of northern Europe.

During the Eighth's raid on the pens at Saint-Nazaire on 23 November, the Luftwaffe tried new tactics against the Fortresses. Up until then German pilots had always attacked from behind, but on this occasion, using thirty of the new Focke-Wulf 190s, they attacked head on, wing tip to wing tip. It took great nerve and skill on the part of the fighter pilot, but the Fortress's Plexiglass nose containing the bomb-aimer remained the most vulnerable spot. For the crew in the forward part of the bomber, it was terrifying.

Just like RAF aircrew, the Americans found it hard to take the waiting, and then the cancellation or aborting of missions as a result of bad weather. On only two or three days out of ten was visibility good enough to see the target. American bomber boys also had their own superstitions and rituals, whether wearing a sweater backwards, carrying good-luck coins or flying in the same plane. They hated it when they were transferred to a replacement aircraft.

The freezing winds, especially for the waist-gunners at open doors, were numbing. Some of the crew had electrically heated boots, gloves and overalls, but they seldom worked consistently. In the first year of operations, more men suffered from frostbite injuries than from combat wounds. Turret gunners, unable to leave their cramped position for several hours over enemy territory, had to urinate in their trousers. The damp patches soon froze. If a gun jammed, men would tear off their gloves to clear the obstruction, and skin from their fingers would stick hard to the frozen metal. And any man badly wounded by flak splinters or cannon fire was likely to die of hypothermia before the stricken aircraft reached base. If enemy fire knocked out the oxygen supply, men would collapse until the pilot managed to bring the aircraft back to below 20,000 feet. Although deaths resulting from anoxia came to fewer than a hundred, a majority of aircrew had suffered from it at some time or another.

In thick cloud, there were numerous mid-air collisions, and many aircraft crashed on returning to base in bad weather. But the greatest shock was to see another aircraft, just ahead or to the side, disintegrate in a giant ball of fire. Not surprisingly many of the pilots turned to whisky in the evenings to calm their nerves, hoping not to suffer the recurrent nightmares which affected more and more men. They dreamed of comrades badly mutilated, of engines on fire or of fuselages riddled by cannon fire.

As with the RAF, combat fatigue became a common experience, or, in their own words, men became 'flak-happy' or suffered the 'Focke-Wulf jitters'. Many had the 'shakes', and some suffered from fainting spells, temporary blindness or even catatonia. These were predictable reactions to the stress caused by helplessness in extreme danger. In some cases, reactions were delayed. Men would seem to have overcome terrible experiences, then go to pieces several weeks later. Few statistics on psychological breakdown are available or reliable, because commanders wanted to conceal the problem.

Colonel Curtis LeMay, who had just arrived with the 305th Bombing Group, was appalled to find that American pilots over the target would jink and weave to avoid flak and thus throw their bombing aim out entirely. In the view of the combative LeMay, who was later the model for General Jack D. Ripper in Stanley Kubrick's *Dr Strangelove*, this made the whole exercise worthless. So he ordered his pilots to fly straight and true in their bombing run. Air reconnaissance showed that on the Saint-Nazaire raid of 23 November, the 305th had doubled the usual number of direct hits. Yet even with LeMay's improvement, fewer than 3 per cent of bombs were falling within a thousand feet of the target. The USAAF's initial claims of 'pickle-barrel' bombing looked over-ambitious to say the least. LeMay then adopted a different system. He put his best navigators and bombardiers in the lead planes, took the Norden bombsight out of all the rest and told their captains to drop their load only when the leaders released theirs. But, even then, the spread of the aircraft formation meant that many bombs would fall wide of the target, however accurate the leaders might be.

The combination of German flak batteries, now firing in 'boxes', and more aggressive enemy fighter attacks reduced bombing accuracy still further. A tight formation for defence against fighters also meant a more concentrated target for flak from the ground. As a historian of the American bombing campaign put it: 'The Eighth Air Force would never find a way to bomb with maximum precision and maximum protection. This threw it into a conundrum that led irrevocably to carpet bombing, with some bombs hitting the target and the rest spilling all over the place. It was combat realities, not prewar theory, that led the Eighth inexorably in the direction of Bomber Harris's indiscriminate area attacks.'

At the Casablanca conference in January 1943, General Eaker was told by General Arnold that Roosevelt had agreed to switch the Eighth Air Force to night bombing with the RAF. Eaker tried to convince Churchill that daylight bombing was more effective. He claimed that his bombers were knocking down at least two or three German fighters for every aircraft lost, a claim that the British knew to be totally untrue. But Churchill said nothing, because Portal had persuaded him in advance not to fight the Americans on the subject of daylight bombing. The combination of the USAAF attacking by day and the RAF by night was turned into a virtuous compromise of 'round-the-clock' bombing.

The Allies agreed on a bombing directive which stated that the 'primary objective will be the progressive destruction and dislocation of the German military, industrial and economic system, and the undermining of the morale of the German people to a point where their capacity for armed resistance is fatally weakened'. Harris, of course, saw this as the seal of approval of his own strategy. And although Portal was to direct the 'Combined Bomber Offensive', the key decisions would be taken by Eaker and Harris, who could pick and choose their targets.

Even with agreement on this bombing directive, which was known as Pointblank, the Combined Bomber Offensive was anything but combined, even though Harris and Eaker got on well together and Harris had done all he could to help the Eighth Air Force get up and running. Directed partly by General Marshall to prepare for the invasion of Europe, Eaker was to focus on the destruction of the Luftwaffe, both aircraft factories on the ground and fighters in the air. Harris, on the other hand, simply intended to carry on as usual, smashing cities while just paying lip-service to the priority of attacking military targets. He delighted in showing off his large leather-bound 'blue books' to important visitors at his headquarters at High Wycombe. They were filled with charts and graphs depicting the importance of his target cities and the area destroyed. Harris's anger and resentment continued to increase with his conviction that Bomber Command was not receiving the attention and the respect that it deserved.

On 16 January 1943, just as the Battle for Stalingrad was approaching its grim and frozen end, Bomber Command carried out the first of a series of raids on Berlin. It was also the first raid to use Pathfinder aircraft dropping markers. Eleven days later, the Eighth Air Force attacked targets in Germany for the first time as they went for U-boat construction yards on the northern coasts. A month after that they returned to Wilhelmshaven, with eight journalists on board, including Walter Cronkite. Soon the film director William Wyler and the actor Clark Gable were flying with the Eighth Air Force, adding a glamour that RAF Bomber Command could never hope to match. Harris's longing for newspaper coverage was dwarfed by the public relations efforts of Spaatz and Eaker.

On 5 March, Bomber Command returned to attacking the industrial heartland of Germany, especially Essen. The raid on 12 March destroyed the panzer construction shop, which delayed production of both Tiger and Panther tanks, thus contributing to the postponement of the great Kursk Offensive. The Eighth Air Force soon followed to join what was called the Battle of the Ruhr, and the total of casualties rose to 21,000 Germans killed.

Göring, humiliated by the Luftwaffe's weakness against the Allied onslaught, withdrew more fighter groups from the eastern front for home defence. Although this was not one of the stated objectives of the Allies, the effect on the outcome of the war was perhaps far greater than the damage they were inflicting at the time. Not only did Red Army aviation begin to achieve air superiority if not supremacy in places. It also meant that Luftwaffe reconnaissance flights had to be drastically reduced. This in turn allowed the Red Army, especially in the following year, to achieve major successes in *maskirovka*, or deception operations.

Although German morale did not break as the Allies had

hoped, Goebbels and other leaders were deeply concerned. Nazi propaganda was met by sarcasm in the population. A well-known poem of the time ran:

> Lieber Tommy fliege weiter,
> Wir sind alle Ruhrarbeiter,
> Fliege weiter nach Berlin,
> Die haben alle 'ja' geschrien.

> ('Dear Tommy fly on,
> We are all Ruhr workers,
> Fly on to Berlin,
> They all screamed "yes".')

This was a reference to Goebbels's speech after Stalingrad in the Sportpalast in Berlin in February 1943 when he whipped up the audience by shouting: 'Do you want Total War?' and they all yelled back in the affirmative.

In that spring of 1943, Allied air losses rose to terrifying levels. Less than one RAF aircrew in five survived a thirty-mission tour. On 17 April the Eighth Air Force over Bremen lost fifteen bombers to German fighters. Eaker, furious at not having received the reinforcements he had been promised, warned General Arnold back in Washington that he was down to a maximum of 123 bombers for a single raid. The Eighth Air Force was simply not in a position to achieve the air supremacy required to ensure the success of a cross-Channel invasion.

Arnold was in a difficult position. Every theatre of war was demanding more bombers. But in May he sent reinforcements to Britain and a huge programme of airfield construction began in East Anglia. Fresh faces were badly needed since the Eighth Air Force had lost 188 bombers and 1,900 crewmen in its first year of operations. Eaker had finally come round to the urgent need for long-range fighter escorts. The tubby P-47 Thunderbolt had a range no further than the German border.

On 29 May, the RAF created its first firestorm in a raid on Wuppertal. After the Pathfinders had dropped their marker flares, the leading wave of bombers dropped incendiaries to get fires going before the high-explosive bombs from the next wave blasted open the buildings. The blazing buildings soon created an inferno which sucked in air from all around. Many citizens were asphyxiated by the smoke or lack of oxygen, and in a way they were the lucky ones. Tarmac melted on the streets so people's shoes stuck fast. Some ran to the river and threw themselves in to protect their bodies from the heat. After the fires had died down, charred bodies were so reduced, with all fat burned, that the burial parties could collect three blackened corpses in a washtub and seven or eight in a zinc bathtub. Some 3,400 people were killed that night. Like the Luftwaffe in 1940, the RAF had discovered that incendiaries were the vital ingredient in mass destruction. They were also lighter than conventional bombs and could be scattered en masse.

Harris still resented any interruptions to his remorseless campaign against urban targets, especially when he had to divert his bombers to attack U-boat bases. He intensified the bombing of cities, especially those which had already been hit. On 10 June 1943, the Combined Bomber Offensive – Pointblank – began officially. Two weeks later, just over a year after his first thousand-bomber raid, he sent Bomber Command back against Cologne. The incendiaries and bombs began to drop in the early hours of 29 June, the feast of St Peter and St Paul.

'All the inhabitants of the house were in the cellar,' wrote Albert Beckers. 'Over us, for some considerable time, aircraft engines made the air vibrate. We were like rabbits in a warren. I was worried about the water pipes – what would happen if they burst, would we all be drowned? The air shook with detonations. We hadn't felt the hail of incendiaries in the cellar but above us everything was ablaze. Now came the second wave, the explosives. You cannot imagine what it is like to cower in a hole when the air quakes, the eardrums burst from the blast, the light goes out, oxygen runs out and dust and mortar crumble from the ceiling. We had to make our way through the breach into the neighbouring cellar.'

The journalist Heinz Pettenberg described the panic in the cellars of the house of a friend where 300 people had sought shelter while fires began above. 'With two other men, Fischer fought like mad to save the house. During the work they often had to go down to prevent a panic among the crazed group in the cellar. Fischer's wife would blow a whistle and Fischer ran down with the pistol to control the mayhem. All inhibitions had fallen.'

'The Waidmarkt afforded a dreadful spectacle,' Beckers recounted. 'Showers of sparks filled the air. Large and small burning pieces of wood floated through the air and alighted on clothes and hair. A little boy who had become separated from his parents stood next to me and pointed out the sparks. It became unbearably hot on that square. The fire whipped up into a wind and oxygen became scarce.'

In the streets 'Children were running about looking for their parents,' wrote a sixteen-year-old schoolgirl. 'A little girl was leading her mother, who had been blinded during the night, by the hand. By a large pile of rubble I saw a priest, with gritted teeth, desperately claw at the stone, brick by brick, because an explosive bomb had buried his whole family there . . . We walked through the small, narrow alleys as though through a baking oven and the cellars gave up the smell of burning corpses.'

'Everywhere you heard the screams of the wounded, the desperate calls or knocking of those trapped underground,' wrote a fourteen-year-old girl from the BDM, the female equivalent of the Hitler Youth. 'People called out names of the missing and the streets were covered with the dead laid out for identification . . . Those who came back later stood bewildered in front of what had once been their houses. We had to collect body parts in zinc tubs. It was horrifying and nauseating . . . two weeks after the raid I was still throwing up.' Concentration camp prisoners were brought in to retrieve corpses from under collapsed buildings.

The Sicherheitsdienst reported on reactions to the raid on Cologne, and the damage done to the cathedral. While many people called out for vengeance, the Nazis were alarmed by the reaction of Catholics. 'This could all have been avoided if we hadn't started the war,' said one. 'The Lord would not have allowed something like this if right had been on our side and we were fighting for a just cause,' said another. The SD report even went on to say that some people were expressing the view that the bombing of Cologne cathedral and other German churches was somehow connected with the destruction of the synagogues in Germany, and that this was now God's punishment. After using the destruction to the full in his propaganda and devoting the newsreels to it, Goebbels suddenly had second thoughts, fearing that it might deject the population more than it angered them. The SD found that people were upset by all the propaganda emphasis on destroyed churches and ancient buildings when the authorities said nothing of the suffering of the population, of whom 4,377 had died. Thousands fled the city, and word of the horror spread.

Harris was determined to increase the pressure, even though he decided to switch his forces away from the Ruhr, which was becoming too well defended. Raids continued relentlessly, with a major offensive against Hamburg beginning on 24 July. For the first time, aluminium foil strips called 'Window' were dropped in advance to be picked up by German radar and confuse their defence systems. Bomber Command struck by night, and the Eighth Air Force attacked twice by day. Harris named it Operation Gomorrah. The tragedy for Hamburg's population was that Gauleiter Karl Kaufmann ordered that nobody could leave the city without special permission, a decision which condemned thousands to death. On the night of 27 July the RAF returned with 722 aircraft. The conditions for conflagration were ideal. It happened to be the driest and hottest month in the last ten years.

The mass of incendiaries raining down in a tighter pattern than usual on the eastern side of the city accelerated the conglomeration of individual fires into one gigantic furnace. This created a chimney or volcano of heat which shot into the sky and sucked in hurricane force winds at ground level. This fanned the roaring flames still further. At 17,000 feet, the aircrew could smell roasting flesh. On the ground, the blast of hot air tore off clothes, stripping people naked and setting their hair ablaze. Flesh was desiccated, leaving it like pemmican. As in Wuppertal, tarmac boiled and people became glued to it like insects on a flypaper. Houses would explode into a blaze in a moment. The fire service was rapidly overwhelmed. Those civilians who stayed in cellars suffocated or died from smoke inhalation or carbon-monoxide poisoning. They, according to the Hamburg authorities later, represented between 70 and 80 per cent of the 40,000 people who died. Many of the other bodies were so carbonized that they were never recovered.

Survivors fled into the countryside and further afield. The local authorities rose to the crisis most impressively, considering the scale of the disaster. News of the horror spread from mouth to mouth across the country after evacuees passed through Berlin, and then were distributed east and south. Many were in a state of nervous breakdown. There were a number of cases of grief-crazed people who had retrieved the shrunken corpses of their children to take with them in a suitcase.

The shock throughout the Reich has been described as tantamount to a civilian version of Stalingrad. Even Nazi leaders, such as Speer and Generalfeldmarschall Milch, the administrative head of the Luftwaffe, began to think that a similar pattern of bombing might quickly defeat them. Harris, unable to let go, sent in another raid on 29 July, but Bomber Command casualties were much higher, with twenty-eight aircraft lost. A new German fighter group, the Wilde Sau, or Wild Boar, had adopted fresh tactics, attacking the bombers from above, even over the target, while they were silhouetted against the flames. On 2 August another Bomber Command force set forth, only to arrive in the midst of an electrical storm. It was a costly failure, with thirty aircraft lost and little damage caused.

At the beginning of August, General Eaker, after the intensive bombing of 'Blitz Week' and the loss of ninety-seven Fortresses, stood down his bomber crews to rest them before other major missions. His force of B-24 Liberators had meanwhile flown to North Africa, from where they would attack the Ploesti oilfields in Romania. Operation Tidal Wave began on 1 August. To avoid alerting the defenders, no reconnaissance was carried out. Approaching from the Danube Valley, they carried out a low-level attack, which proved to be a bad mistake. The Germans had prepared a ring of 40mm and 20mm flak batteries, and even machine guns on every roof around. The force had maintained radio silence all the way, but the Germans were ready for them. Having broken the American codes, they knew of the raid in advance.

Flying at low level among the clouds of thick black smoke, the bomber force was ravaged by anti-aircraft fire, then they were jumped by a large force of Luftwaffe fighters stationed near by. Only thirty-three Liberators out of the 178 were in a serviceable state on return. Although they had caused great damage, the Germans drafted in huge numbers of workers, and within a few weeks the refineries were producing more oil than before the raid.

Another mission imposed from Washington was to take the Eighth Air Force deep into Germany. On 17 August, it attacked the Regensburg Messerschmitt factories with 146 bombers led by Curtis LeMay, and the ball-bearings plant at Schweinfurt with 230. LeMay's force, which took off in spite of a thick mist, flew on from Regensburg over the Alps to North Africa to confuse the Germans. But the Luftwaffe fighter defences had by then been increased to 400 strong with the withdrawals from the eastern front. LeMay's force lost fourteen bombers even before it reached Regensburg. A gunner remarked that when listening to everyone praying over the interphone, 'It sounded like a flying church.' But at least they were not pursued once they reached the Alps after dropping their bombs.

The Schweinfurt force, which had been held back until the mist cleared, approached its target several hours late. This disastrous development meant that the German fighters which had attacked LeMay's group had had time to land, refuel and rearm. Once again, because of their limited range, the Thunderbolt fighters escorting the Schweinfurt Fortresses had to turn back over Belgium, just before the German border. From then on Focke-Wulf and Messerschmitt 109 squadrons rose to the attack from all directions. It is estimated that some 300 were scrambled, far more than had attacked LeMay's aircraft. The gunners in the Flying Fortresses were soon up to their ankles in empty shell cases as they swivelled their turrets, frantically trying to follow the fighters streaking through the formation. So many aircraft were stricken and so many men were baling out, one airman observed, that it looked 'like a Parachute invasion'.

On reaching Schweinfurt, the surviving aircraft were unable to bomb accurately. The formation was in chaos, they were under constant fire with black puffs of flak exploding all around them, and the Germans had screened the target with smoke generators. In any case their 1,000-pound bombs were simply not powerful enough to cause sufficient damage, even when they hit. The Eighth Air Force lost sixty bombers destroyed, and another hundred so badly damaged that they were written off. They also lost nearly 600 aircrew.

After these losses Churchill renewed his pressure on the USAAF to switch to night-time bombing. Arnold resisted strongly, but he knew that they would still be vulnerable until long-range fighter escorts became available. The leaders of the USAAF were forced to acknowledge that the concept behind the heavily armed Fortress, to which they had clung for far too long, was deeply flawed. The bitter lesson was renewed again when the Eighth Air Force once more ventured beyond fighter cover, to attack Stuttgart. It lost forty-five Fortresses out of 338.

During the Regensburg–Schweinfurt operation, the Luftwaffe lost forty-seven fighters in the vast air battle, contributing to a total of 334 shot down in August. Even more dangerously, it was losing too many experienced pilots. Their deaths hurt Germany's defences far more than the damage inflicted by LeMay's forces on the Messerschmitt factory at Regensburg. On 18 August, after furious recriminations from Hitler for allowing the destruction of Hamburg and other attacks, the Luftwaffe chief of staff General Jeschonnek shot himself. Hitler cared nothing for Jeschonnek. Now he was even more set on developing the Vengeance weapons, the V-1 flying bomb and the V-2 rocket. His priority was to inflict greater terror on his enemies.

Bomber Command, having bombed the V-weapon research base at Peenemünde on the Baltic coast, began the Battle of Berlin. Harris was convinced that, if he could do to the Nazi capital what his aircraft had done to Hamburg, Germany would surrender by 1 April 1944. Hitler, to the despair of General Adolf Galland, the Luftwaffe fighter chief, and Generalfeldmarschall Milch, refused to increase fighter production. His faith in Göring and the Luftwaffe was severely dented. He trusted his massive concrete flak towers to defend Berlin. But although the flak barrage and the criss-cross searchlight beams were terrifying for RAF aircrew approaching the city, anti-aircraft fire accounted for a considerably smaller proportion of their losses than Luftwaffe night-fighters.

Pathfinder aircraft dropped the red and green marker flares over Berlin, which the Germans nicknamed Christmas Trees. Then Lancasters and Halifaxes carpet-bombed the city from end to end. On Harris's order, each Lancaster now carried five tons of bombs. 'The sky arches over Berlin with a blood-red eerie beauty,' Goebbels wrote in his diary after one of the biggest raids. 'I can no longer stand looking at it.' Yet Goebbels was one of the very few Nazi leaders who went out to mingle and chat with the victims of the raids.

Life was rather harder for ordinary Berliners, trying to get to work on time through rubble-blocked streets, with tram tracks torn up into fantastic shapes, and S-Bahn trains cancelled because of damage to lines. Civilians looked pale and drawn from lack of sleep, as they hurried to catch up. Those bombed out of their apartments either had to move in with friends, or hope to be re-housed by the authorities. The accommodation had usually been confiscated from Jewish families, most of whom had now been 'sent to the east'. As in most cities, they were able to replace clothes and household utensils at knock-down prices from Jewish homes. Few stopped to wonder about the fate of the former owners.

Yet a surprising number of Jews, some 5,000 to 7,000, had gone underground and were also known as 'submarines'. Some were hiding in the city, either in the homes of sympathetic anti-Nazis or in little summer houses on allotments. Those who could easily pass as Aryans had removed the yellow star from their clothes, obtained false papers and mingled with the population. All feared arrest at almost any moment, either by an SA patrol in the street or by Gestapo plain-clothes men guided by a Jewish *Greifer*, or 'catcher', who had been blackmailed into spotting and denouncing 'submarines' with the dubious promise that their own family might be saved.

At night, when the sirens wailed, the population would file into air-raid shelters, cellars or the vast caverns of the flak towers. They carried thermoses and small cardboard suitcases with sandwiches, their valuables and important documents. With wry Berliner humour, the sirens were called 'Meyer's trumpet', a reference to Göring's fatuous boast at the beginning of the war that if the RAF ever bombed Berlin, his name was Meyer. The Zoo flak tower in the Tiergarten could hold 18,000 people. The diarist Ursula von Kardorff described it as 'like a stage-set for the prison scene in *Fidelio*'. Loving couples embraced on concrete spiral staircases as if taking part in a 'travesty of a fancy-dress ball'.

In the ordinary shelters, known as *Luftschutzräume*, the air smelled rancid as the place became packed with under-washed bodies and the ubiquitous problem of halitosis. Most of the population suffered from bad teeth as a result of vitamin deficiency.

Shelters were lit with blue lights, and arrows and lettering on the walls were painted in luminous paint in case the electricity supply failed. In the cellars under buildings where most people took shelter, familes sat in rows facing each other as if in a U-Bahn carriage. As the buildings began to shake from the bombs, some practised strange rituals for survival, such as wrapping their head in a towel. But as buildings above were hit or caught fire, and smoke and dust entered the cellar, hysteria could easily grip those down below. Holes had been knocked through sidewalls, so that they could escape if necessary to the cellars of neighbouring blocks. Foreign workers, identified by a large letter painted on their backs, were forbidden to enter shelters and mix in such intimate circumstances with German women and children.

As he had promised Churchill, Harris told his men that the Battle of Berlin would be the decisive battle of the war. But his campaign of attrition, night after night, wrecked the nerves of many of his own men as well as those of Berliners. His aircrews went back time and time again grasping at Harris's mantra that it would shorten the war, and thus save many more lives in the end.

The battle went on from August 1943 until March 1944, yet 17,000 tons of high-explosive bombs and 16,000 tons of incendiaries failed to destroy the German capital. The city was far too spread out to be vulnerable to a firestorm, and its wide open spaces absorbed the bulk of the bombs. Harris had badly miscalculated, and was finally forced to back down. All his assurances to Churchill had proved empty. Bomber Command lost over a thousand aircraft, the majority to night-fighters. It had killed 9,390 civilians, but lost 2,690 of its own aircrew in the process.

Harris's attempt to break German morale had failed. Yet he still refused to admit defeat and he certainly refused to recant. He despised government attempts to whitewash the bombing campaign by claiming that the RAF was going only for military targets and that civilian deaths were unavoidable. He simply regarded industrial workers and their housing as legitimate targets in a modern militarized state. He rejected any idea that they should be 'ashamed of area bombing'.

The Americans, meanwhile, were becoming as chary and euphemistic as Harris's critics in the air ministry. Although General Arnold privately acknowledged that they were bombing 'blind' in the majority of cases and going for area targets as a result, he refused to say it publicly. After all the claims of 'pickle-barrel' bombing, American bomb patterns in the autumn of 1943 were no better than those documented in the Butt Report. 'In periods of sustained bad weather,' as an air-power historian put it, 'overall American accuracy was no better than – and often worse than – that of Bomber Command.' USAAF commanders refused to believe the evidence when it was put to them.

Hitler ordered retaliatory raids on England's historic cities – Bath, Canterbury, Exeter, Norwich and York. A press official in the Wilhelmstrasse announced that 'the Luftwaffe will go for every building which is marked with three stars in Baedeker'. The name of the famous red-bound travel guide was then attached to these attacks, which became known as the Baedeker raids. Goebbels was furious about this blunder, since he wanted the British to be tarred with the brush of destroying ancient cities.

Whether or not Harris suffered from a 'Jupiter complex', flinging down thunderbolts from heaven in retribution (an idea which the British public generally supported), his was a form of that 'total war' which Goebbels had called for in his frenzied demand from the podium of the Sportpalast in February. Harris's belief that his strategy was shortening the war to save lives was strikingly similar to the huge slogan behind Goebbels during his speech which proclaimed: 'Total War – Short War'. The inevitable question of whether waging total war from the air on German civilians was the moral equivalent of the Luftwaffe's own version is too complicated to answer satisfactorily. In statistical terms, however, the Combined Bomber Offensive turned out to be slightly less murderous in the end, if you include all the western European, central European, Balkan and Soviet citizens killed by the Luftwaffe.

30

The Pacific, China and Burma

MARCH–DECEMBER 1943

After the exhausting battles to secure Guadalcanal and eastern Papua New Guinea, the Americans knew that to eliminate the Japanese base at Rabaul would be long and difficult. The command rivalries between MacArthur and the US Navy did not make it any easier. But when Admiral William 'Bull' Halsey Jr, who had now taken over as commander-in-chief South Pacific, visited MacArthur at his headquarters in Brisbane, they got on together surprisingly well. In April 1943, it was agreed that Halsey's forces would leapfrog north-westwards from Guadalcanal along the Solomon Islands chain. At the same time MacArthur's forces would clear the Japanese from New Guinea and seize the Huon Peninsula opposite New Britain, thus combining in a pincer attack on Rabaul. Two islands to the south of New Britain, Kiriwina and Woodlark, would also be seized as air bases.

The Japanese reinforced Rabaul, New Guinea and the western Solomon Islands with 100,000 troops taken from Korea, China and other areas. Their first priority was to strengthen Lae in the Huon Peninsula with the 51st Division. On 1 March, the Japanese convoy of eight troop transports, escorted by eight destroyers, steamed into the Bismarck Sea off the western end of New Britain. It was spotted by B-17 Fortresses from the Fifth Air Force supporting MacArthur. The Fifth had been greatly improved by a new commander, General George C. Kenney. Kenney's reforms included ordering his B-25 medium-bomber crews to abandon high-level bombing, which had proved so futile against ships. Instead they were to attack at low altitude, with newly mounted forward-firing machine guns to deter anti-aircraft gunners on board, and then bounce their bombs just short of the vessel's side.

The Battle of the Bismarck Sea began with low-level attacks by Australian Beaufighters, followed by some high-level bombing which sank one transport and damaged several others. The Japanese Zeros providing air cover were fought off by recently arrived P-38 Lightnings, which proved more than a match for them. Over the next two days, the convoy struggled on across the Vitiaz Strait to New Guinea. On the third day, Kenney's crews tried out their new 'skip-bombing' technique for the first time in action. After another strafing attack by Beaufighters to knock out anti-aircraft guns, the B-25s and A-20 attack planes went in bouncing their bombs, which had delayed fuses so that they would explode inside the ship. The effect was devastating. The remaining seven transports went down along with four of the destroyers. On the grounds that the Japanese would never surrender, fast PT boats and fighter aircraft machine-gunned the lifeboats and men in the water. Some 3,000 died. With skip-bombing, the United States had found its killer solution in the war at sea, and Japan was unable to reinforce or resupply its garrisons except by submarine or night-time dashes by destroyers. In many places, Japanese troops began to starve.

Admiral Yamamoto redoubled his efforts to bolster his forces in the region. A further 200 aircraft were sent to Rabaul and the island of Bougainville in the western Solomons, doubling their strength. He flew to Rabaul to supervise operations. On 17 April, in the largest Japanese strike since Pearl Harbor, dive-bombers escorted by Zeros attacked Guadalcanal and Tulagi. And during the next few days Japanese aircraft pounded Port Moresby and Milne Bay at the easternmost point of Papua.

On 14 April, the Americans had intercepted a radio message which indicated that Yamamoto would be flying from Rabaul to Bougainville, on 18 April. Admiral Nimitz sought and received approval from Washington for an ambush. They knew the time of arrival over Bougainville. Eighteen twin-tailed P-38 Lightnings from Henderson Field on Guadalcanal were waiting. While most of the Lightnings dealt with the escort of nine Japanese Zero fighters, the other pilots went for the two bombers, one of which carried Yamamoto. Lieutenant Thomas Lanphier shot the wing off the admiral's plane and it crashed on the island. The other bomber fell into the sea. The charred body of the commander-in-chief of the Imperial Japanese Navy was later retrieved from the jungle by a squad of Japanese soldiers sent out to search for him. On 5 June,

Yamamoto's ashes received a state funeral in Tokyo.

Operation Cartwheel, the advance on Rabaul, began on 30 June. A regiment from the 41st Division under MacArthur's command landed on New Guinea near Lae. Some of the landing craft became grounded in the heavy surf, and the sound of their engines racing and grinding in an attempt to free themselves in the dark sounded like tanks landing. Japanese troops fled into the jungle and a beachhead was quickly established. The same day American forces landed on the two islands of Kiriwina and Woodlark, some 500 kilometres south of Rabaul. They were unopposed, and airfields were constructed so that P-38 Lightning squadrons were now within easy striking distance of the great Japanese base.

Also on 30 June, Admiral Halsey's ships landed 10,000 troops on New Georgia in the Solomons north-west of Guadalcanal. Already the Americans had improved their landing techniques immeasurably with many more amtracs, or amphibious tractors, and the amphibious trucks known as DUKWs. They were assured of strong air support from Guadalcanal, but the dense jungle on New Georgia was more impenetrable than the planners had imagined. Soldiers who had just arrived with the 43rd Division found the jungle exhausting and disorientating, and they rapidly became spooked by the noises at night. One regiment took three days to cover just under a mile. Having not yet learned the tricks of jungle fighting, they were easily harassed and terrified by small Japanese raiding parties from their base at Munda on the western tip of the island. Before they had even fought a battle, almost a quarter of the force collapsed from combat fatigue. Halsey had to sack commanders and bring in fresh troops, increasing the ground forces to 40,000 men.

The slowness of the advance had given the Japanese the opportunity to run in reinforcements at night, bringing their strength up to 10,000. Rear Admiral Walden Ainsworth's first attempt to intercept these nocturnal convoys was initially successful, sinking the Japanese flagship *Jintsu*. But as his ships pursued, one destroyer was sunk and three cruisers were heavily damaged by Japanese warships using their deadly Long Lance torpedoes, which were far more effective than anything in the American arsenal.

During these night battles, the fast torpedo boat *PT 109*, commanded by Lieutenant John F. Kennedy, was run down by a

Japanese destroyer. Kennedy managed to get the survivors ashore on to a nearby island. Thanks to an Australian coast-watcher, they were rescued six days later. On 6 August, another naval night ambush by six American destroyers caught on radar four Japanese destroyers loaded with troops. The US Navy warships waited until they were within range, then fired twenty-four torpedoes. Only one got away. The other three sank with 900 soldiers.

The Japanese reinforcements which did reach New Georgia were used in a triple counter-attack, one of which succeeded in surrounding the headquarters of the 43rd Division. Only a superbly targeted barrage from American artillery, dropping their shells all around the perimeter, managed to force the Japanese back.

The drive on Munda proved far harder than the Americans expected. The Japanese had constructed a network of well-concealed bunkers in the jungle. Eventually by using a combination of artillery, mortars, flamethrowers and light tanks, the bunkers were destroyed, and the airfield at Munda was taken on 5 August. The battle for New Georgia was a sobering experience, requiring a numerical superiority of four to one, to say nothing of the massive sea and air support needed to secure the island.

Halsey's staff, shaken by the time and effort required, re-examined their strategy. They decided that, instead of taking every island step by step along the Solomons, they could leapfrog heavily defended islands, then construct airfields ahead, and by using air and sea power cut off the stay-behind garrisons. As a result, the next target would not be Kolombangara, but the lightly defended island of Vella Lavella. This forced the Japanese to evacuate Kolombangara, which they had just reinforced.

The first priority on almost all newly secured islands was to build an airfield. Naval construction battalions, or CBs, who became known as 'Seabees', dynamited jungle, graded the ground with bulldozers, laid perforated steel strips called Marston mat and covered it with crushed coral. Sometimes landing just behind the first wave of marines, they could have a new landing ground ready for action in under ten days. One officer said of these incredibly tough and ingenious gangs that they 'smelled like goats, lived like dogs and worked like horses'. Their contribution to the war in the Pacific was considerable.

On New Guinea, meanwhile, MacArthur's American and Australian troops converged on the Japanese base of Lae prior to seizing the Huon Peninsula. The US 503rd Parachute Infantry Regiment dropped on the airfield of Dadzab just to the west of Lae, and the next day C-47 transports began landing the 7th Australian Division. With the 9th Australian Division coming from the east, the town was doomed and fell to the Allies in mid-September. The Huon Peninsula, however, proved a far harder task. The Japanese, determined to hold on as long as possible to protect Rabaul across the Vitiaz Strait, were not dislodged from the coast until October, and it took another two months to clear them from the mountains above.

In November Halsey's forces landed on Bougainville, the last large island before Rabaul. The mangrove swamps, jungle and mountain range represented an even more formidable obstacle than the terrain on New Georgia. In addition, the Japanese garrison of 40,000 men was supported by four airfields. Halsey began with some diversionary attacks against nearby islands, then made a landing with two divisions on the west coast at a lightly defended spot and followed on with massive air attacks against Rabaul itself, destroying more than a hundred Japanese aircraft. The fast new F4U Corsair fighter was proving its worth. The Japanese were losing most of their experienced pilots, and their Zero fighter, which had proved such a war-winner in 1941, was now obsolete. After two days of raids, the new commander-in-chief of the Combined Fleet, Admiral Koga Mineichi, ordered the withdrawal of all warships from Rabaul to Truk, their main Pacific base, 1,300 kilometres to the north.

General Hyakutake, the commander of the 17th Army on Bougainville, assumed that the landing on the west coast was another diversion and made no counter-attack. This gave the Americans the chance to establish a large and well-defended perimeter before Hyakutake realized that he had made a grave mistake.

On 15 December MacArthur's vanguard landed on the southern coast of New Britain. Eleven days later, the 1st Marine Division, refreshed after its long break in Melbourne, landed on Cape Gloucester, the south-west tip of the island. For MacArthur, this part of the island was vital since it would secure the flank of his invasion route for the Philippines.

The marines landed on a beach of black volcanic sand the day after Christmas, having been told by their commander: 'Don't squeeze that trigger until you've got meat in your sights. And when you do – spill blood – spill yaller blood.' It was the rainy season, with mud, perpetual damp, corruption, leeches, jungle rot, and patrols and skirmishes carried out in rain so dense that visibility was drastically reduced. Once the key feature of Hill 660 overlooking the airfield had been secured after heavy fighting, Cape Gloucester was under Allied control. Rabaul could now be bombed from several directions, although with the departure of the Japanese fleet it had lost its importance. But MacArthur's forces still had to finish clearing the north coast of New Guinea.

While MacArthur came closer to realizing his dream of glory in the Philippines, Nimitz started to advance north on Japan, island by island across the central Pacific. Nimitz's command included Vice Admiral Spruance's Fifth Fleet, greatly strengthened with fast fleet carriers of the Essex class deploying a hundred aircraft apiece, as well as Independence class light carriers with fifty aircraft. The powerful carrier force meant that the invasion of the Gilbert Islands, the first chain to be assaulted, could take place without relying on ground-based air cover. These atolls, which were low-lying with little more than palm trees, seemed idyllic targets in comparison to the sweltering jungles, swamps and mountains of the large southern Pacific islands. But planners underestimated the problems presented by the coral reefs which surrounded them.

On 20 November, the 2nd Marine Division assaulted the Tarawa Atoll. Three battleships, four heavy cruisers and twenty destroyers bombarded the Japanese positions and landing strip. Heavy air strikes with Dauntless dive-bombers also went in, and the marines watching the explosions were greatly encouraged. It looked as if the whole island was being blown apart. But the low Japanese bunkers, built with concrete as well as palm trunks, proved far more resistant than the American commanders had expected.

The amtracs and landing craft took much longer to reach the shore than planned. The bombardment ended, and because of communications problems on the flagship USS *Maryland* a long pause followed which allowed the Japanese time to get over their shock and reinforce the threatened sector. But the greatest error was made by Admiral Turner, the obstinate task force commander, who refused to listen to the warnings of a retired British officer who had recorded the island's tides. Supported by the Marine commander, he had told Turner that at this time of year their landing craft would lack the necessary four feet clearance.

Amtracs carrying the first wave got over the reef, but then faced a terrible concentration of fire. Blocked by a low sea wall, they became targets for Japanese infantry throwing grenades. One baseball-playing marine managed to catch five grenades in a row and throw them back, but the sixth blew off his hand. The landing craft behind were then caught on the reef and became easy targets. A chaotic shuttle service began with the surviving amtracs between the beach and the reef. Even those marines who struggled to the beach were pinned down by the heavy fire. Radios soaked in seawater failed to work, so there was no communication between beach and the ships offshore.

By nightfall some 5,000 men were ashore, but at the horrific cost of 1,500 casualties, and burned-out amtracs. Corpses were littered all over the beach while many others rolled in the surf like flotsam. During the night Japanese infantrymen crept forward into some of the destroyed amtracs, and some swam to those in the bay, to turn them into firing positions behind the marines on the beach. Machine-gunners had even manned a bombed-out Japanese freighter and fought from there.

The pattern was more or less repeated at dawn next day, when reinforcements attempted to land. But, fortunately for the marines, another battalion which had cleared the north-west shore of the island was soon reinforced with tanks. The desperate fighting finally turned as marines began clearing bunker after bunker with a combination of explosive charges, gasoline and flamethrowers which reduced the defenders to little more than charred skeletons. Some were buried alive in their bunkers when an armoured bulldozer stopped up their firing slits with sand.

The battle finished at the end of the third day with a suicidal mass charge based on the *gyokusai* ideology of 'death before dishonour' to avoid being taken prisoner. Marines cut down their attackers with savage glee.

Nearly 5,000 Japanese soldiers and Korean construction

workers died over the three days. But the cost of taking a single tiny island – with more than a thousand dead and 2,000 wounded – shook American commanders and the public at home, appalled by the photographs of dead marines. Yet the losses prompted many improvements for future operations, with the introduction of underwater demolition teams, more heavily armoured amtracs and a complete reappraisal of communications and intelligence before any other landings went ahead. The limitations of bombing and naval artillery firing high-explosive shells were also re-examined. For bunkers like those on Tarawa, they needed armour-piercing ammunition.

In the spring of 1943, Roosevelt and Marshall had consolidated their strategy for China. Preferring an air offensive, they continued to reject Stilwell's arguments that Allied land power should be developed in China to defeat the Japanese there. Their chief priority was to build up Chennault's Fourteenth Air Force on the Chinese mainland. It was to expand its role to attacks on Japanese shipping in the South China Sea, and raid Japanese supply bases to help the US Navy in the Pacific. But there was a flaw to their plan. Chennault's successes were bound to provoke a Japanese reaction, and without sufficiently strong Chinese forces to defend his airfields the Fourteenth Air Force's campaign would collapse. Chiang Kai-shek's Yunnan armies were to be reinforced for this purpose, but they received little weaponry. The bulk of the first 4,700 tons of supplies was earmarked for Chennault, and Roosevelt's promise that air transport flying over the Hump of the Himalayas would then deliver 10,000 tons a month was over-optimistic to say the least.

In May the Japanese launched their fourth offensive against Changsha in Hunan province, with an amphibious landing on the shore of Lake Tungting. Another attack from southern Hupeh suggested that this was an encirclement operation to seize an important rice growing area. B-24 Liberators from Chennault's Fourteenth Air Force raided Japanese supply bases and trains with reinforcements. The Liberators and their fighter escorts accounted for twenty Japanese aircraft, boosting the morale of the Nationalist troops on the ground.

Although Nationalist losses had been far greater than those of the Japanese, Chiang Kai-shek's forces checked the attack from Hupeh and forced the Japanese back. In Shantung province, south of Peking, a Nationalist Chinese division far behind Japanese lines found itself being attacked both by the Japanese and by Chinese Communist formations.

The Nationalist government in Chungking had broken off relations with Vichy France, while the Wang Ching-wei puppet government declared war on the United States and Britain. The Vichy regime was also forced to concede France's concessions in China to Wang Ching-wei. The large White Russian community in Shanghai, which had cooperated closely with the Japanese, had become increasingly depressed since the Soviet victory at Stalingrad. The hated regime in the Soviet Union looked stronger than ever, and the war both in the Pacific and on the eastern front was now going in a very different direction to the one they had envisaged. The idea of a Communist Shanghai was becoming a distinct possibility. The Japanese had left Mao Tse-tung's forces to the north-east relatively undisturbed, and if the Red Army arrived after the defeat of Germany, then the Chinese Communists would take power.

The diplomatic shadow dance continued. Tokyo announced that Burma was to be given independence as a member of the Greater East Asia Co-Prosperity Sphere. Its puppet government accordingly declared war on Britain and the United States. And in a further attempt to bolster its claim of waging war on colonialism, the Japanese government set up an Indian National Army, led by Subhas Chandra Bose and manned by Indian prisoners of war recruited from Japanese camps.

Stilwell's rows with Chennault had become even more acrimonious through that spring. Their quarrel had begun to hamper the war effort, to the dismay of Allied officers. Brooke described Stilwell as nothing more than 'a hopeless crank with no vision', and Chennault as 'a very gallant airman with a limited brain'. Stilwell had also made an enemy of Chiang Kai-shek by wanting to send assistance to the Chinese Communists. Chiang was furious because Mao Tse-tung's Communists refused to be part of the Nationalist order of battle. Stilwell claimed that they were fighting harder against the Japanese, which made Chiang even more angry. British intelligence, however, was certain that the Communists had made an unofficial deal with the Japanese, under which both sides restricted their operations against each other. Mao was husbanding his lightly armed forces ready for the civil war which was bound to follow the eventual defeat of the Japanese. And so, of course, was Chiang.

In May 1943, in an attempt to resolve the dispute between Stilwell and Chennault, both men were summoned to see Roosevelt just before the Trident conference in Washington. Roosevelt confirmed the priority of Chennault's air offensive from China, but also allowed Stilwell to continue with his campaign to retake northern Burma. The President had a tendency to avoid disputes between commanders by allowing both options to be pursued at the same time, as was the case with MacArthur and the US Navy following the Twin Axis strategy in the Pacific.

In July Operation Buccaneer, a major landing on the Burmese coast, was proposed to clear the Japanese from the Bay of Bengal. Chiang Kai-shek supported the plan, but remained rightly suspicious that the Allies were not prepared to commit major ground forces on the south-east Asian mainland. Not surprisingly he resented the idea that he would provide troops to win back Burma, while the Americans and British accorded his forces in China such low importance. In any case, the shortage of shipping eventually put paid to Buccaneer.

Relations with Chiang Kai-shek were not helped when in mid-August the Quadrant conference in Quebec agreed to set up South-East Asia Command, or SEAC, with Vice Admiral Lord Louis Mountbatten as supreme Allied commander. Brooke, who had a low opinion of Mountbatten's competence, observed that he would need a very clever chief of staff to carry him through. This he received in the form of Lieutenant General Sir Henry Pownall. But Mountbatten would also have as his deputy 'Vinegar Joe' Stilwell, who loathed him. Mountbatten, who was glamorous and charming and made good use of his royal connections, possessed a great talent for public relations, but he remained a vertiginously over-promoted destroyer captain.

Chiang Kai-shek was horrified to learn that his troops were thus to serve in Burma under British command. He wanted to ask for the recall of the increasingly fractious Stilwell, but then changed his mind in October on recognizing that without him he might not have any American commitment to support his forces in China. Ironically, this about-turn was supported by Mountbatten, who feared that Stilwell's recall would increase the suspicions of the American press that the British were taking over in south-east Asia. American officers were already joking that SEAC stood for 'Save England's Asian Colonies'. Stalin would have laughed if he had known the full details of the rivalries and personal antipathies which bedevilled Allied strategy.

Brooke had been even more horrified before the Quadrant conference by Churchill's suggestion that Orde Wingate, recently promoted to brigadier, should be made army commander. Back in April, Churchill had not liked the British plans for Burma, saying: 'You might as well eat a porcupine one quill at a time.' And yet typically he had now become entranced by the idea of irregular operations behind Japanese lines.

Wingate, a fundamentalist Christian and ascetic visionary whom General Slim compared to Peter the Hermit, was no charlatan. He was almost certainly a manic depressive, although his earlier attempt at suicide had, in fact, been provoked by cerebral malaria. He drove his men hard; in fact he was pitiless even towards the wounded, but he was just as hard on himself. Bearded and scruffy, wearing an old-fashioned sola topi that looked too big for him, he did not conform to the image of a senior officer of the Royal Artillery. He wandered around naked, chewed raw onions, strained his tea through his socks, and sometimes wore an alarm clock on a string round his neck. He had earned his reputation as a master of irregular warfare after organizing Jewish 'special night squads' in Palestine to counter Arab attacks, and by his leadership of Gideon Force in Ethiopia. Churchill had always welcomed unconventional ideas and it seemed that Wingate would provide a solution to the stalemate in north Burma.

In India in 1942, Wingate had suggested to Wavell that columns supported by airdrops, roaming in the Japanese rear, would be very useful for attacking enemy supply lines and communications. In February 1943, he was given his first chance to prove his theories. With the 77th Brigade split into two groups, which were sub-divided into columns, Wingate's forces crossed the River Chindwin. Each detachment had a reconnaissance group from the Burma Rifles, and carried rations, ammunition, machine guns and mortars on pack mules.

By the third week in March, most of Wingate's Chindit columns were across the Irrawaddy, but radio contact was increasingly difficult and supply drops became hard to organize as two pursuing Japanese divisions forced them to keep moving. Short of food, they began to slaughter and eat the mules, which meant that most of their heavy equipment had to be abandoned. Wingate's columns were soon in retreat, having failed to cut the Mandalay–Lashio road and losing in the process nearly a third of the 3,000 men who had started out. Discipline was exerted ruthlessly, with several floggings and even some executions. A large number of wounded and sick were left behind. Of those who returned, exhausted, fever ridden and half starved, 600 were unfit for further duties for many months.

This lengthy foray may not have been successful, but it provided a boost to morale for Slim's Fourteenth Army and for the public at home, due to highly optimistic reporting. Important lessons were learned, above all the need to clear proper dropping zones and even landing strips in the jungle. And once the Allies were in a position to provide sufficient transport and fighter support, such operations were more likely to bring rewards. Yet this first long-range penetration had a more important effect. It provoked the Japanese into preparing a major offensive for the spring of 1944, which would lead to the decisive battles of the Burma campaign.

The Battle of Kursk

APRIL–AUGUST 1943

Seldom has a major offensive been as obvious to the enemy as the Germans' Operation Citadel to cut off the Soviet salient round Kursk. Stalin's commanders estimated that the Germans could afford only one major attack, and the Kursk bulge was clearly the most vulnerable sector of their line. Zhukov and Vasilevsky managed to persuade their impatient leader that the best strategy was to prepare for this double thrust, defeat it in defence and then go over to the offensive themselves.

The German build-up in April 1943 was carefully observed by air reconnaissance flights, by partisan detachments behind the lines and by Soviet agents. The British passed on a warning based on an Ultra intercept, but heavily disguised to conceal its source. The Soviet spy John Cairncross provided far more detail. Yet uncertainty was caused in Moscow by repeated German delays. Generalfeldmarschall von Manstein wanted the operation launched in early May after the end of the spring rains, but Hitler was uncharacteristically nervous and delay followed delay.

The Führer was staking virtually all their reserves on this one giant gamble to shorten the front and regain the initiative, to reassure wavering allies after the defeat at Stalingrad and the retreat in the Caucasus. 'Victory at Kursk will be a beacon for the whole world,' Hitler proclaimed in his order of 15 April. Yet during the Allied victory in Tunisia he began to look anxiously at the map of Sicily and Italy. 'When I think of this attack,' he told Guderian, 'my stomach turns over.'

Many senior officers had their own doubts about the offensive. To compensate for its numerical inferiority, the German army had always relied on its greatest ability: to wage a *Bewegungskrieg* or war of movement. But the Kursk Offensive looked as if it might turn into a battle of attrition. As in a game of chess when you are already several pieces down, the risks multiply the moment you lose the initiative and try to attack again. The German army's queen, its armoured forces, was about to be thrown into a battle which would be more dangerous for the Wehrmacht than for the Red Army, which now enjoyed such superiority in numbers and weaponry.

OKW staff officers began to voice doubts about the thinking behind Operation Citadel, but this, perversely, now made Hitler more determined to continue. Planning for the operation took on a momentum of its own. Hitler felt unable to back down. He dismissed the air reconnaissance reports on the strength of Soviet defences, claiming they were exaggerated. Yet, despite Manstein's desire for an early attack, Citadel was still postponed numerous times to allow more tanks, such as the new Mark V Panther, to be rushed to the front after the delays caused by RAF bombing. The great offensive did not in the end begin until 5 July.

This crucial breathing space granted to the Red Army was not wasted. Its formations and some 300,000 mobilized civilians were put to work on the construction of eight lines of defence, with deep tank ditches, underground bunkers, minefields, wire entanglements and over 9,000 kilometres of trenches. Every soldier, in true Soviet style, was set a target of digging five metres of trench every night since it was too dangerous by day. In places the defences went back nearly 300 kilometres. All civilians not involved in digging and who lived within twenty-five kilometres of the front were evacuated. Reconnaissance patrols were sent out at night to seize Germans for interrogation. These snatch parties consisted of men picked for their size and strength to overpower a sentry or ration carrier. 'Each reconnaissance group was given a couple of sappers who would lead them through our mines and make a corridor for them in the German minefield.'

Most importantly, a large strategic reserve known as the Steppe Front and commanded by Colonel General I. S. Konev was assembled to the rear of the bulge. It included the 5th Guards Tank Army, five rifle armies, another three tank and mechanized corps and three cavalry corps. Altogether the Steppe Front mustered nearly 575,000 men. They were supported by the 5th Air Army. The movement and the positions of these formations were concealed as far as possible, in order to deceive the Germans about the Red Army's preparations for

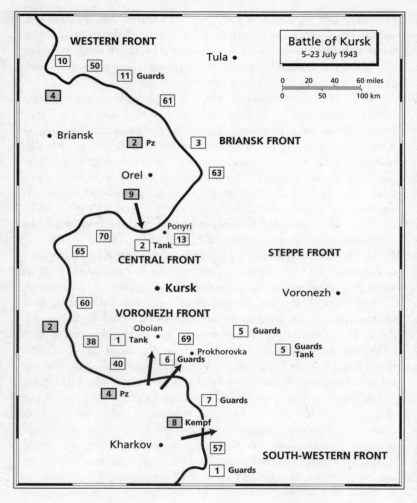

a powerful counter-stroke. Further deception measures included the massing of other forces in the south and the construction of dummy airfields to imply preparations for an offensive there.

Normally an attacking force requires a superiority of up to three to one over the defenders, but in July 1943 this was reversed. The Soviet army groups involved – Rokossovsky's Central Front, Vatutin's Voronezh Front, Malinovsky's South-Western

(*Above*) Generalissimo and Madame Chiang Kai-shek with General Stilwell
(*Below*) MacArthur, Roosevelt and Nimitz at Pearl Harbor, 26 July 1944

(*Above left*) US troops land on Bougainville, 6 April 1944
(*Left*) A Hellcat crash-landed on a carrier
(*Above*) German prisoner in Paris, 26 August 1944

(*Above*) Stretcher-bearers in the Warsaw Uprising
(*Right*) Medical services during the bombing of Berlin

(*Left*) Churchill in Athens with Archbishop Damaskinos, December 1944

(*Right*) British troops occupy Athens

(*Below*) Red Beach on Iwo Jima, February 1945

Filipina women rescued during the battle for Manila, February 1945

Front and Konev's Steppe Front – totalled over 1,900,000 men. German strength for Operation Citadel did not exceed 780,000. It represented a huge gamble.

The Germans placed their faith in panzer wedges, using companies of Tiger tanks as spearheads to batter a hole in the Soviet defence lines. The II SS Panzer Corps, which had retaken Kharkov and then Belgorod in March, was refitting. Brought up to strength mainly by Luftwaffe ground personnel, the 1st SS Panzer Division *Leibstandarte Adolf Hitler* put the new arrivals through an intensive training programme. SS Untersturmführer Michael Wittmann, who was to become the greatest panzer ace of the war, took command of his first Tiger platoon at this point. But despite the unquestioned superiority of the Tiger, the Waffen-SS panzergrenadier divisions were acutely conscious of their inferiority in equipment. The SS *Das Reich* even had to equip one of its companies with captured T-34s.

Ultra intelligence, passed by Cairncross to the Soviet Foreign Intelligence Department through his handler in London, had also identified the Luftwaffe airfields in the region. Some 2,000 aircraft were being concentrated there, the bulk of what was left on the eastern front after so many squadrons had been sent back to defend Germany from the Allied air forces. Red Army aviation regiments were thus able to launch pre-emptive strikes early in May, apparently destroying more than 500 aircraft on the ground. The Luftwaffe also suffered from a shortage of aviation fuel, which restricted its ability to support the attacking troops.

German supply problems had been growing with the ferocious partisan campaign fought far behind the Wehrmacht's lines. Certain areas, such as the forests south of Leningrad and large parts of Belorussia, were almost completely controlled by partisan forces, now directed from Moscow. The German anti-partisan sweeps grew in violence. SS Brigadeführer Oskar Dirlewanger and his group recruited from released criminals exterminated and burned whole villages. For the Germans' Kursk Offensive, Soviet partisan groups were put on standby to attack railway lines to slow supplies.

The continued postponements of the German offensive encouraged impatient commanders such as Colonel General Vatutin to argue that they should not wait. The Red Army should launch its own attack instead. Zhukov and Vasilevsky again had to calm Stalin and persuade him that they must be patient. They would destroy far more Germans for fewer losses in defence than in attack. Stalin was not in the best of moods, having heard from Churchill at the beginning of June that an Allied invasion of northern France was now pushed back until the following May.

Stalin was also bitter about the international row which had broken out over the mass murder of Polish prisoners of war, in the forest of Katyń and elsewhere. In late April the Germans, on hearing of the mass grave, summoned an international commission of doctors from allied and occupied nations to examine the evidence. The London-based Polish government-in-exile demanded a full inquiry by the International Red Cross. Stalin angrily insisted that the victims had been killed by the Germans, and that anyone who doubted this was 'aiding and abetting Hitler'. On 26 April, Moscow severed diplomatic relations with the London Polish government. The death of General Sikorski on 4 July had been the result of a tragic accident, when the cargo aboard the Liberator he was on shifted to the back of the plane on take-off. After the news from Katyń, and Sikorski's demands for a full inquiry, Poles naturally suspected sabotage.

On 15 May, Stalin, apparently in an attempt to reassure Britain and especially the United States which provided such vital assistance with Lend–Lease, announced that he had abolished the Comintern. But this gesture was also intended to divert attention from the row over the Katyń killings. In fact the Comintern, directed by Georgii Dimitrov, Dmitri Manuilsky and Palmiro Togliatti, simply continued to operate from the International Section of the Central Committee.

In the afternoon of 4 July, a hot and humid day with occasional cloudbursts, German panzergrenadier units from the *Grossdeutschland* and the 11th Panzer Division finally began their probing attacks against forward Soviet positions on the southern Belgorod sector. That night, German pioneer companies from Model's Ninth Army began to cut wire and remove mines on the northern sector. A German soldier was captured and interrogated. Information was passed to General Rokossovsky, commander-in-chief of the Central Front, that H-Hour was to be at 03.00 hours. He rapidly gave the order for a massive har-assing bombardment with guns, heavy mortars and Katyusha rocket-launchers against Model's Ninth Army. Zhukov rang Stalin to tell him that the battle had finally started.

Vatutin's forces on the southern side of the salient, who had also interrogated a German prisoner, began their pre-emptive fire against Hoth's Fourth Panzer Army soon afterwards. Both the Ninth Army and the Fourth Panzer Army felt obliged to delay their attacks by up to two hours. They even wondered whether the Soviets were about to launch their own offensive. Although the Germans suffered comparatively few casualties from this shelling, they now knew for certain that the Red Army was ready and waiting for them on their axes of advance. Combined with a heavy thunderstorm, it was hardly an encouraging start.

As dawn broke, Red Army aviation launched pre-emptive strikes against German airfields, but they were virtually bare of aircraft. The Luftwaffe had taken off even earlier and soon a mighty air battle began, to the advantage of the German pilots. With the command 'Panzer march!', the armoured spearheads moved forward at 05.00 hours. On the southern sector, Hoth's 'wedges' consisted of Tigers and huge assault guns in the van, with the Panthers and Panzer IVs on the flanks and the infantry following behind. The Panthers, which had been rushed forward from production lines in Germany, soon proved mechanically un-reliable, with many catching fire. Yet even though fewer than 200 Tigers were committed to Citadel out of a total of 2,700 tanks, they still represented a formidable battering ram.

German morale appears to have been high. 'I believe that this time the Russians are going to get a very heavy beating,' wrote a Fahnenjunker in a flak battalion. And an Unteroffizier in the 19th Panzer Division thought that the explosions and shot-down Soviet fighters would make 'a wonderful image for the newsreels, only probably nobody would want to believe it'. Officers had also been keeping up their men's morale with another encouraging thought. Stalin was getting angry with England about the lack of a Second Front. 'If something of the sort were not to happen soon,' wrote a soldier in the 36th Infantry Division, 'then he will make a peace offer to us.'

Hoth had attacked the southern sector with three prongs.

On the left the 3rd and 11th Panzer Divisions flanked the *Grossdeutschland* Panzergrenadier Division. In the middle, he deployed Obergruppenführer Paul Hausser's II SS Panzer Corps, with the *Leibstandarte Adolf Hitler*, the *Das Reich* and the *Totenkopf* Panzergrenadier Divisions. And on the right, the 6th, 19th and 7th Panzer Divisions led the III Panzer Corps. To their right rear, Army Detachment Kempf attacked south of Belgorod, attempting to cross the northern Donets River. In the north, Model's central thrust towards Ponyri consisted of two panzer corps, each one spearheaded by a Tiger battalion and vast, lumbering Elefant self-propelled guns, also known as Ferdinands.

The rolling open terrain ahead, with a few woods and farming hamlets, may have presented ideal tank country, yet the panzer crews soon found that it was hard to spot the hundreds of concealed anti-tank guns. They were attached to the forward Red Army divisions ordered to sacrifice themselves while absorbing the shock of the German armoured spearheads in a battle of attrition. Heavy artillery shells had been buried in front of many of the positions to be detonated by remote control.

Overhead, their sirens screaming, ungainly gull-winged Stukas dived on Soviet positions and dug-in T-34 tanks. The Stuka ace Hans Rudel experimented with his own invention, a 'cannon-bird', with two 37mm guns fixed beneath the wings. Other T-34s, unconvincingly disguised as haystacks, were soon dealt with. Crew members who survived the impact of the armour-piercing shells then had to scramble out through blazing straw. German soldiers were thrilled by the effect. 'Our Luftwaffe is really fantastic', a Hauptfeldwebel in the 167th Infantry Division wrote home. 'And as soon as the enemy's been hit, our panzer arm can get going at full steam.'

Soviet anti-tank guns, however, were better concealed. Experienced crews often held their fire until a panzer was barely twenty metres away. On the northern sector, just west of Ponyri, where the Tigers broke through, Vasily Grossman heard how the 45mm anti-tank 'shells hit them, but bounced off like peas. There have been cases when artillerists went insane after seeing this,' he added. Things were no better on the southern sector, he also found. 'A gun-layer fired point blank at a Tiger with a 45mm gun. The shells bounced off it. The gun-layer lost his head and threw himself at the Tiger.'

Although most of the anti-tank gun shells bounced off the heavy frontal armour of the Tigers, their tracks were vulnerable to mines. With suicidal bravery, Soviet sappers ran in with spare anti-tank mines to place them in their path. Red Army soldiers also crept up to throw grenades, satchel charges and Molotov cocktails.

Fearing a breakthrough west of Ponyri, Rokossovsky sent in anti-tank, artillery and mortar brigades. He also summoned fighters from the 16th Air Army to combat the German bombers and Messerschmitts, but they were badly mauled. German commanders were shaken to find that they had achieved no surprise at all, and that Soviet soldiers were not fleeing from their armoured onslaught. Despite heavy casualties, the German spearheads forced their way forward to a depth of almost ten kilometres on a fifteen-kilometre front. Rokossovsky prepared to counter-attack the next day, but the chaos of the vast battlefield made it hard to coordinate.

The air battle overhead was equally pitiless, with the German Sixth Air Fleet and the Soviet 16th Air Army scrambling virtually every serviceable aircraft available. Focke-Wulfs, Stukas and Messerschmitts tangled with Shturmoviks, Yaks and Lavochkins. On some occasions, desperate Soviet pilots simply rammed German aircraft.

The air battle over Hoth's Fourth Panzer Army in the south of the salient was even more intense. The Luftwaffe's Fourth Air Fleet, having just escaped the pre-emptive strike by Soviet aviation at dawn, inflicted heavy losses on its attackers. The Kursk campaign has long been portrayed, sometimes with exaggerated numbers, as the greatest tank battle in history, yet the aerial engagements were among the most intense of the whole of the Second World War.

In the south, the *Grossdeutschland* Division's advance became bogged down in a minefield made treacherously muddy by the storm of the night before. Pioneer battalions sent in to help the tanks came under heavy fire, and only a desperate charge by panzergrenadiers on foot managed to clear the Soviet defences covering the minefield. It still took many hours to extricate the tanks and clear paths through the danger zone. To dent German morale further, a brigade of the new Panther tanks brought up in support again started to suffer from mechanical breakdowns. The problem was not just limited to Panthers. 'My division is already going to the dogs,' wrote an Unteroffizier in the 4th Panzer Division. 'Half-track breakdowns very many, Panzer no fewer, also the Tigers are not the true love.' But the advance resumed.

Reshat Zevadinovich Sadredinov, a Tatar, was part of an anti-aircraft battery, with all its four guns knocked out by Stukas. The tall rye around it was on fire. The guncrews hid in earth bunkers, as the German tanks pushed on past them. When the Red Army soldiers finally emerged, they found that they were now a long way to the rear of the fighting. Sadredinov and his companions took the uniforms off dead Germans and put them on over their own. Sentries challenged them as they approached the Soviet front line. Once the Red Army soldiers found that they were Russians in German uniform, they yelled: 'Ah, you bastards, you're Vlasov men.' They were badly beaten up. Sadredinov and his companions were finally able to prove their identity when allowed to contact the chief of staff of their division.

'The Luftwaffe was bombing us,' recounted Nikifor Dmitrievich Chevola, commander of the 27th Anti-Tank Brigade brought up against the *Grossdeutschland*. 'We were there amid the fire and smoke, yet my men became wild. They kept firing, paying no attention to all this.' Messerschmitt fighters, or 'Messers' as Red Army soldiers called them, strafed the trenches from end to end. Even after being wounded several times, men seldom went back to dressing stations. 'Constant thunder, the ground was trembling, there was fire all around. We were shouting. As for radio communications, the Germans tried to trick us. They howled over the radio: "I am Nekrasov, I am Nekrasov." [Colonel I. M. Nekrasov commanded the 52nd Guards Rifle Division adjoining their sector.] I shouted back: "Bullshit! You aren't. Get lost!" They jammed our voices with howling.'

'This was face-to-face battle,' said a gun-layer called Trofim Karpovich Teplenko. 'It was like a duel, anti-tank gun against tank. Sergeant Smirnov's head and legs were torn off. We brought the head back, and also the legs, and put them all into a little ditch, and covered them over.' Dust from the black earth and cordite smoke turned their food dark grey, assuming the rations arrived. And during the odd lulls in the battle, the men found it hard to sleep in the silence. 'The quieter it is, the more tense it feels,' Lieutenant Colonel Chevola explained.

A dozen kilometres to the east, the II SS Panzer Corps, supported by a Nebelwerfer rocket-launcher brigade, had smashed into Nekrasov's 52nd Guards Rifle Division. Behind the leading tanks, flamethrower teams moved forward to clear bunkers and trenches. Theirs was an almost suicidal task, since they immediately attracted enemy fire. But if successful, their belching blast of flame left a stench of burned flesh and petroleum.

The *Leibstandarte* on the left advanced the furthest towards Prokhorovka, with *Das Reich* and *Totenkopf* pushing forward north-eastwards on their right. But even the *Leibstandarte* was brought to a halt that evening by another anti-tank brigade sent in to hold the line. Thirty kilometres to the south-east, Army Detachment Kempf, having crossed the River Donets south-east of Belgorod, managed to achieve only minor successes. Its objective of advancing to protect Hoth's right flank was clearly going to be difficult.

German panzer crews, especially the loaders, frequently suffered from heat exhaustion on that blazingly hot day. The Tigers had been adapted to take 120 of their 88mm shells instead of 90. Targets were so plentiful that the loaders, working rapidly in the boiling confines of the turret, were dropping with fatigue. On some occasions, their tanks had to be replenished two or three times during the day, and stowing the rounds inside was also tiring, even with help. A German war correspondent who had been attached to a Tiger company was almost driven mad with the noise of mush and screech in the headphones, the constant thudding of the machine guns and the heavy boom of the main armament.

Vatutin, having relied primarily on his anti-tank units during the first day of fighting, started to bring up Lieutenant General Katukov's 1st Tank Army and two guards tank corps to strengthen the second major line of defence. Although his decision to use these armoured reserves in defence, rather than in a great counter-attack, was criticized later, Vatutin was almost certainly right. A mass attack across the open would have exposed them to the Tigers whose 88mm guns could knock out the Soviet T-34s up to two kilometres away, long before they themselves were within range to take on the panzers. One of the Tiger crews managed to destroy twenty-two Soviet tanks in under an hour, an achievement which won its commander an immediate Knight's Cross.

During 6 July, while the *Grossdeutschland* Division was held up by the marshy ground and fierce resistance on the left, the *Leibstandarte* thrust further north with the *Das Reich*, breaking the second line of defence. But their flanks were exposed, and the Soviet pressure on the western side forced them away from their axis of advance to the north. This pushed them north-eastwards towards the railway junction of Prokhorovka.

On the northern sector, meanwhile, Model's Ninth Army units were suffering heavy losses. His infantry, even the panzergrenadiers, had failed to keep up with the armoured wedges. Soviet infantrymen, who had stayed hidden, ambushed the giant Elefant self-propelled guns, while sappers continued to lay mines in their path. To German dismay, even these monsters did not cause *Panzerschreck*, or tank panic, in Soviet ranks.

In the tank battle round Ponyri station on 7 July, 'everything was on fire, both vehicles and people'. Almost every house and village for miles around had been destroyed. Red Army soldiers were horrified by the badly burned tank crewmen carried past them. 'A lieutenant, wounded in the leg and with a hand torn off, was commanding the battery attacked by tanks. After the enemy attack had been halted, he shot himself because he did not want to live as a cripple.' Mutilation was the greatest fear of all Red Army soldiers. This was hardly surprising considering the way their disabled comrades were treated. Limbless veterans were callously known as 'samovars'.

Model realized that, even though his forces had managed to advance over a dozen kilometres in one sector west of Ponyri, Soviet defence lines were proving far deeper than they had imagined. Rokossovsky was also worried. His tank counter-attack, planned for dawn, had failed to come together. All he could do was to order them into hull-down positions to strengthen the line. This was just as well, for Model had decided to throw his main reserve into a desperate attempt to break through.

The intense fighting which continued in the north until the night of 8 July ground down Model's armoured spearheads. In spite of the terrible losses inflicted on the defenders, the Red Army's numerical superiority in tanks and anti-tank guns was just too great. Their Shturmovik ground-attack aircraft also began to take a heavy toll on German panzers and assault guns. Model's Ninth Army had lost around 20,000 men and 200 tanks. Once it became clear that the enemy onslaught was grinding to a halt, Rokossovsky and General Popov of the Briansk Front began to prepare their counter-attacks against the Orel Salient scheduled for 10 July. It would be called Operation Kutuzov after the great Russian commander in 1812.

On the southern side of the Kursk Salient, Vatutin's armies were in danger. The Stavka had expected the Germans' major effort on the northern flank, when in fact it had come in the south, with Hoth's Fourth Panzer Army. The German drive towards Prokhorovka led by the II SS Panzer Corps looked as if it would prevail, even against Katukov's 1st Guards Tank Army which had been pulled into the defence. On the evening of 6 July Vatutin, supported by General Vasilevsky the Stavka representative, requested Moscow to provide reinforcements urgently.

The situation was deemed so serious that Konev's Steppe Front was ordered to prepare to move forward, and Lieutenant General Pavel Rotmistrov's 5th Guards Tank Army was allocated to support Vatutin immediately. On Stalin's personal order, the 2nd Air Army would cover its 300-kilometre march during daylight, because the dust clouds thrown up by the tank columns would instantly attract the Luftwaffe.

The 5th Guards Tank Army set off in the early hours of 7 July, its advancing columns spreading some thirty kilometres wide across the steppe. 'By midday,' Rotmistrov wrote, 'the dust rose in thick clouds, settling in a solid layer on roadside bushes, grain fields, tanks and trucks. The dark red disc of the sun was hardly visible. Tanks, self-propelled guns, artillery tractors, armoured personnel carriers and trucks were advancing in an unending flow. The faces of the soldiers were dark with dust and exhaust fumes. It was intolerably hot. Soldiers were tortured by thirst and their shirts, wet with sweat, stuck to their bodies.'

The monstrous battle along the southern side of the Kursk Salient continued on 7 July, with a furious self-sacrificial defence by Soviet rifle divisions, tank brigades and anti-tank units of the 6th Guards and 1st Guards Tank Army. Hoth's forces found that, as soon as they destroyed one division, another appeared just behind to bar their way. Nobody had time to bury the bodies, which crawled with flies. Men on both sides went out of their minds from fear, stress and the inhuman din of battle. One German soldier even began dancing a can-can until pulled down by his comrades. At one point it looked as if the *Grossdeutschland* Division was about to achieve a major breakthrough towards Oboian, but then it ran into a brigade of the 6th Tank Corps, which had been moved across just in time. The SS *Leibstandarte* and *Das Reich* Divisions had managed to push up the road towards Prokhorovka on the east flank of the 6th Guards Army, but they continually had to fight off counter-attacks on their own exposed flanks.

Luftwaffe pilots accounted for large numbers of Soviet aircraft. The fighter ace Erich Hartmann shot down seven that day, and he later became the highest-scoring pilot of the whole war with 352 victories. Red Army aircrew were also achieving successes. They destroyed around a hundred fighters and bombers on the southern sector. The Luftwaffe, with its priority fixed on ground support for the troops, was unable to engage as many enemy aircraft as it wished, and a severe shortage of fuel forced it to ration the number of sorties. The Soviets began to achieve air superiority for the first time in the battle and soon they were bombing German airfields every night. Yet, despite heavy losses, one of Rudel's pilots wrote that they were in the air again before dawn. 'With an unbroken Stuka-spirit we plunged our birds on the enemy and hurled at them our destruction-laden bombs.'

On 8 July, Hausser switched the SS *Totenkopf* Division from the right flank of his panzer corps to the left, to help push their line of advance away from the direction of Prokhorovka back towards Oboian on the main road to Kursk. As the corps was redeploying, the Soviet 10th Tank Corps attacked, but in such an uncoordinated fashion that it was repulsed with heavy losses. And the Soviet 2nd Tank Corps, which was supposed to smash into the exposed flank of the SS Panzer Corps, was battered by Henschel HS-109 tank-destroying aircraft armed with 30mm cannon. Hausser's divisions (perhaps including the Luftwaffe's kills in their own tally) claimed to have destroyed 121 Soviet tanks that day.

On 9 July the II SS Panzer Corps began their attack on Vatutin's last line of defence. 'Those wearing [SS] camouflage uniforms fought extremely well,' one of the Soviet defenders in the 6th Guards Army acknowledged. He also watched as a Tiger knocked out seven T-34s, one after another. Although completely exhausted, the panzer crews kept going on Pervitin pills, which dulled a sense of danger as well as keeping them awake. Hausser was also hoping for support on his right flank, but Army Detachment Kempf was still struggling against determined resistance east of Belgorod, while its right flank was threatened by General Shumilov's 7th Guards Army.

A panzergrenadier regiment of the SS *Totenkopf* reached the River Psel. But the rest of the II SS Panzer Corps' advance had been slowed by the Soviet divisions thrown in to keep the 6th Guards Army and 1st Guards Tank Army in the battle. Late that afternoon, the German command decided to change Hausser's axis of advance again, back towards Prokhorovka. The Germans hoped that Army Detachment Kempf on the right, which had been slow to achieve a breakthrough earlier, would now advance north rapidly. But Kempf's divisions were under constant attack on both flanks.

On 10 July, the day the Allies landed in Sicily, the 1st Tank Army and the remnants of the 6th Guards Army continued, at fearful cost, to slow the attacks on the Oboian axis. This kept General Otto von Knobelsdorff's XLVIII Panzer Corps too occupied to assist Hausser's advance on Prokhorovka. The *Grossdeutschland* was utterly exhausted, yet its panzergrenadiers still managed to capture two key hills with its panzer regiment commanded by Hyazinth Graf Strachwitz, the 'Panzer-Kavallerist', who had first reached the Volga north of Stalingrad. Oboian was clearly visible through binoculars, but they sensed they would never reach it. For Strachwitz it must have been a familiar feeling. In 1914 his cavalry patrol had been in sight of Paris, until the French counter-attacked on the Marne.

Hausser's SS divisions failed to advance as rapidly on Prokhorovka as they wanted, mainly because so many regiments were caught up in battles on every side. Yet the *Leibstandarte* pushed on with part of the *Das Reich*, despite a storm of artillery fire. The SS *Totenkopf* had managed to cross the River Psel five kilometres to the left, but was held up by the desperate Soviet defence of a hill beyond, which prevented it from moving up the valley to the north-east. By now the wet ground had dried out. 'It's now very hot here,' a medic wrote home, 'and the roads are knee-deep in dust. You should see my face, it's coated with dust a millimetre thick.' For Stuka pilots, the rhythm of attack sorties never slackened. 'In five days,' a lieutenant wrote, 'I have carried out thirty combat missions, bringing my total to 285.' They were playing a decisive part in the great tank battles, he added.

On 11 July, Vatutin redeployed his defence line south-west of Prokhorovka, bringing in fresh divisions from the 5th Guards Army to block the advance of the II SS Panzer Corps. Kempf, who was under heavy pressure from Manstein to achieve a breakthrough, used his Tigers from the 503rd Heavy Panzer Abteilung and the 6th Panzer Division to overrun the defences of two Soviet rifle divisions. An Obergefreiter in the 6th Panzer wrote that it was the fifth day in which they had not been out of their tanks. 'The Russians are keeping us busy, since in the last three months they've had enough time to build a defence line the like of which we've never experienced.' The 19th Panzer Division also pushed north on the other bank of the Donets heading towards Prokhorovka.

Vatutin, well aware of this threat and closely supervised by Marshal Vasilevsky, who kept in constant contact with Stalin, told General Rotmistrov to deploy his 5th Guards Tank Army as soon as it arrived. But that evening, on a reconnaissance visit to the front with Vasilevsky, Rotmistrov saw through his binoculars that the tanks they had spied in the distance were German. The II SS Panzer Corps, in a sudden advance, had already reached the point from which Rotmistrov had intended to launch his counter-attack the next day. He drove back as fast as possible in his Lend–Lease Jeep to update the plans.

He and his staff worked through the night preparing new orders, but at 04.00 hours on 12 July Rotmistrov heard from Vatutin that the 6th Panzer Division was approaching the River Donets at Rzhavets. This meant that Army Detachment Kempf was outflanking the Soviet 69th Army and could threaten the rear of his 5th Guards Tank Army.

In fact a *Kampfgruppe* of the 6th Panzer Division had already slipped through in the dark and reached Rzhavets, using a captured T-34 to head its column. Although Red Army engineers blew the roadbridge over the Donets, in the confusion a footbridge was left intact, and the panzergrenadiers were across the river by dawn. A *Kampfgruppe* of the 19th Panzer Division raced forward to reinforce them, but the Luftwaffe was not informed of the success at Rzhavets. A formation of Heinkel 111s bombed the bridgehead, wounding Generalmajor Walther von Hünersdorff, the commander of the 6th Panzer Division, and Oberst Hermann von Oppeln-Bronikowski, the *Kampfgruppe* leader.

To meet this threat near Rzhavets, Vatutin ordered Rotmistrov during that turbulent night to divert his reserve as a blocking force. To the west of Prokhorovka, Knobelsdorff's XLVIII Panzer Corps was clearly intending to attack again towards the town of Oboian, so Vatutin ordered in a pre-emptive strike with tank brigades from the 1st Tank Army and the 22nd Guards Rifle Corps. Hoth's forces were exhausted. Having started the offensive with 916 panzers, they were by now reduced to fewer than 500. Heavy rain had also turned the thick dust to a muddy paste again, which made the going more difficult for the Germans than for the Soviets with their broad-tracked T-34s.

On 12 July, shortly after dawn, General Rotmistrov reached the 29th Tank Corps command post bunker in a hillside orchard overlooking the wheatfields below and the railway line south-east of Prokhorovka. All his rewritten orders for the counter-attack had been distributed, and the massed artillery and Katyusha regiments had redeployed during the early hours of the morning. Beyond the fields lay a forest in which part of II SS Panzer Corps was concealed. The clear sky was again covered by storm clouds, foreshadowing more heavy rain.

The battle opened with Stuka attacks. Yak and Lavochkin
fighters of the 2nd Air Army soon appeared to fight them. They
were followed by Soviet bombers, whose attack was accompanied by the deafening thunder of artillery and the heart-stopping
scream of Katyusha rocket batteries which set the wheatfields
ablaze. When the II SS Panzer Corps emerged from the edge of
the forest and advanced into the open, Rotmistrov issued the
codeword 'Stal'! Stal'! Stal'!' for his tanks to charge. They had
been concealed on the rear slope of small hills, and on the signal
of 'Steel!' moved forward at full speed. He had told them in his
orders that their only chance against the Tigers was to get in close
and overwhelm them with numbers.

Obersturmführer Rudolf von Ribbentrop, the son of the foreign minister, described the scene from the turret of his Tiger tank
in the 1st SS Panzer Regiment. 'What I saw left me speechless.
From beyond the shallow rise about 150–200 metres in front of
me appeared fifteen, then thirty, then forty tanks. Finally there
were too many to count. The T-34s were rolling towards us at
high speed, carrying mounted infantry.'

The battle resembled a medieval clash of armoured knights.
Neither artillery nor aircraft could help either side, so mixed up
were the forces. Formation and control was lost on both sides, as
tank fought tank at point-blank range. When ammunition and
fuel blew up, the turret of the tank would be sent flying. German
gunners first concentrated their fire on a command tank because it
was the only one with a radio, then they aimed for the big round
metal barrel fixed to the rear of a T-34 which carried its fuel
reserve.

'They were around us, on top of us and between us,' wrote
an Untersturmführer with 2nd Panzergrenadier Regiment. 'We
fought man to man.' All German superiority in communications,
movement and gunnery was lost in the chaos, noise and smoke.
'The atmosphere was choking,' a Soviet tank driver recorded.
'I was gasping for breath, with perspiration running in streams
down my face.' The psychological stress was immense. 'We expected to be killed at any second.' Those who were still alive and
still fighting a couple of hours later were astonished. 'Tanks even
rammed one another,' wrote a Soviet onlooker. 'The metal was
burning.' The concentrated area of the battlefield was filled with

burned-out armoured vehicles, exuding columns of black, oily smoke.

Hoth's hopes that Army Detachment Kempf would turn the flank of Rotmistrov's 5th Guards Tank Army were dashed. It had been blocked nineteen kilometres away, but only just, by Rotmistrov's reserve. The only success appeared to come on his left, when the SS *Totenkopf* looked about to break through the 5th Guards Army to the north-east of Prokhorovka. Soviet reinforcements, however, arrived in time to seal the gap. And although Knobelsdorff's XLVIII Panzer Corps fought back the pre-emptive onslaught which Vatutin had prepared, this partial success was too late to achieve a breakthrough.

When heavy rain began to fall again at dusk, both sides pulled back their forces to refuel and rearm. Medical teams evacuated the wounded and recovery teams roamed the battlefield that night, where several hundred tanks lay battered and burned. Even the ruthless Zhukov was moved by the sight when he toured the battlefield two days later.

SS prisoners were killed out of hand in the knowledge that they did not spare their captives either. And there was little respect for the fallen. 'Germans were crushed by vehicles,' recorded a young Soviet officer. 'There were piles of dead Germans with map holders and all their stuff still on them. I saw tanks drive over their bodies.'

Hoth did not know until that evening that to the north of the Kursk Salient the Red Army had just launched Operation Kutuzov to retake Orel. Model's exhausted Ninth Army and the Second Panzer Army were surprised by the size of the offensive. Once again, German intelligence had underestimated the Red Army's concentration of forces to the rear. General I. Kh. Bagramyan's 11th Guards Army attacked Model's rear, and advanced sixteen kilometres in two days. Building on this success, the 4th Tank Army, the 3rd Guards Tank Army and even Rokossovsky's exhausted 13th Army went on to the offensive.

On 13 July Hitler, greatly preoccupied by the successful Allied invasion of Sicily three days before, summoned Generalfeldmarschall von Manstein and Generalfeldmarschall von Kluge to the Wolfsschanze for a conference. Manstein had given orders to the II SS Panzer Corps and to Army Detachment Kempf to renew the attack, but Hitler announced that he needed to withdraw troops from the eastern front to defend Italy. Operation Citadel was cancelled forthwith. He suspected that the Italians were not prepared to fight for Sicily and this put Italy itself in danger of invasion.

Yet Manstein, knowing that Hoth agreed, wanted to continue the battle if only to stabilize the front. Some furious fighting still continued. Army Detachment Kempf finally linked up with Hoth's forces, but on 17 July the OKH gave orders that II SS Panzer Corps was to be pulled back from the front prior to transfer to western Europe. The invasion of Sicily, although it was not the Second Front that Stalin wanted, had still had an effect. Also that day, the Soviet South-Western and Southern Fronts launched combined attacks along the Donets and the Mius down to the Sea of Azov. This was partly a diversionary operation to attract German forces away from Kharkov, the recapture of which was the main Soviet objective.

For once Stalin's desire for a general offensive was well timed. The Germans were shaken by the number of fresh or rebuilt formations which appeared, and by the Red Army's ability to launch fresh attacks immediately after the monstrous Battle of the Kursk Salient. 'This war was never more horrific nor cruel than now,' wrote a Stuka pilot with misplaced self-pity, 'and nowhere can I see an end to it.' To make matters worse, the Soviet partisan sabotage of railway lines intensified. On 22 July, Hitler gave Model permission to prepare to withdraw from the Orel Bulge.

The implications of the victory at Kursk were so great that Stalin decided to make his one visit to the front in the whole war. On 1 August, a heavily guarded and camouflaged train took him to the headquarters of the Western Front. He then went to the Kalinin Front to the north. But since he spent no time talking with officers or soldiers, one can only assume that the purpose of the visit was to boast about it to Churchill and Roosevelt.

On 3 August, Konev's Steppe Front with other armies from the Voronezh Front was unleashed in Operation Rumyantsev, with just under a million men, more than 12,000 guns and Katyusha batteries, and nearly 2,500 tanks and self-propelled guns. Manstein had not expected such a powerful onslaught so soon. 'For the weary German infantry, it was as if their beaten enemy had risen from the grave with renewed strength.' Two days later Belgorod was retaken, and the Red Army could now focus on Kharkov.

On 5 August Soviet forces also entered Orel north of the salient to find that the Germans had just pulled out. Vasily Grossman, who remembered only too well the scenes of panic in the city in 1941, entered that afternoon. 'The smell of burning was hanging in the air,' he wrote. 'A light blue milky smoke was rising from the dwindling fires. A loudspeaker unit was playing the "Internationale" in the square . . . Red-cheeked girls, traffic controllers, were standing at all the crossroads, smartly waving their little red and green flags.'

On 18 August, Briansk was liberated. But that week, as Konev's forces advanced on Kharkov, the Germans launched a counter-attack. This time the Red Army was not caught off balance, and fought back. On 28 August, Kharkov finally fell after a bitter defence by Army Detachment Kempf, now redesignated the Eighth Army. Hitler had ordered Kharkov to be held as long as possible in an effort to reduce the demoralization of Germany's allies. The catastrophic situation in Italy had shaken him, and he feared the effect on the Romanians and Hungarians. This was ironic since Hitler's insistence on the Kursk Offensive had been to impress his allies.

The German army had received a severe battering. It had lost some 50,000 men. A number of divisions were reduced to the equivalent of a regiment or less. But the Red Army's victory had also come at an immense price. Because of Zhukov's battering-ram tactics, the Belgorod–Kharkov Offensive alone cost more than a quarter of a million casualties, an even greater figure than the 177,000 men lost in the Kursk Salient. Operation Kutuzov to retake the Orel Salient was even worse, with around 430,000 casualties. Overall, the Red Army had lost five armoured vehicles for every German panzer destroyed. Yet now the Germans had no choice but to withdraw to the line of the River Dnepr, and start to pull their remaining forces out from the bridgehead left on the Taman Peninsula. Hitler's lingering dream of securing the oilfields of the Caucasus was destroyed for ever.

The Red Army had grown immeasurably in strength and experience, but ingrained faults still remained. After the battle

Vasily Grossman visited Major General Gleb Baklanov who had taken command of the 13th Guards Rifle Division. Baklanov told him that 'the men are now fighting intelligently, without frenzy. They fight as if they are working.' But he was scornful of Red Army staff work when planning an offensive, and of the many regimental commanders who did not check on details before an attack, or lied about the position of their units. And he still felt that the cry of '"Forward! Forward!" is either the result of stupidity, or fear of one's superiors. That's why so much blood is being shed.'

There was far more resentment within the German army after the fatal loss of initiative at Kursk and Kharkov. The Nazi hierarchy became nervous and angry. Still envious of the Soviet *politruk* system, it once again demanded that army officers should take on the role of commissar. But it could do little to contain the criticism of military leadership on the eastern front and the planning of Kursk. Hitler's postponements of the operation to await the arrival of the Panthers had undoubtedly contributed to the scale of the disaster, but it is far from certain that it would have succeeded if it had been launched in May rather than July.

German commanders at the front pointed out that soldiers wanted to know the truth about the general situation, and their officers found it hard to give a straight answer. 'The 1943 warrior is a different man from the one of 1939!' wrote Generaloberst Otto Wöhler, the commander-in-chief of the Eighth Army after the fall of Kharkov. 'He has long ago realized how bitterly serious the struggle is for our nation's existence. He hates clichés and whitewashing, and wants to be given the facts, and be given them "in his own language". Anything that looks like propaganda he instinctively rejects.' Manstein, the commander-in-chief of Army Group South, fully endorsed this report.

The OKH then tried to place the blame on the Eighth Army's new chief of staff, Generalmajor Dr Hans Speidel, who was caricatured as that 'intellectual, introspective, researching Württemberger, always fond of stressing the negative and missing much that is good'. Wöhler fired back a strong rejection, and Keitel promptly forbade any further correspondence on the question. Keitel demanded that all officers should demonstrate unreserved confidence in the leadership. Anything else was tantamount to defeatism and any measure, however brutal, was justified in destroying those who tried to weaken the national will. This war would not end with a peace treaty. It was a matter of victory or annihilation. The unintelligent and pompous Keitel was for once right to be suspicious. Speidel was already becoming one of the key figures in the military resistance to Hitler and would play a major part in the July plot a year later.

32

From Sicily to Italy

On 11 May 1943, the day that American forces landed on the Aleutian Islands in the far northern Pacific, Winston Churchill and his chiefs of staff reached New York aboard the *Queen Mary*. General Sir Alan Brooke was dreading the Trident conference, due to begin in Washington, DC the next day. He suspected that the Americans were quietly going back on the 'Germany first' policy, by sending major reinforcements to the Far East. 'Their hearts are really in the Pacific,' he had written in his diary less than a month before. 'We are trying to run two wars at once which is quite impossible with limited resources of shipping.'

Brooke was also having to restrain Churchill from charging off again on another pet project, the invasion of Sumatra to deprive the Japanese of oil. The prime minister had also not given up the idea of launching Operation Jupiter to take northern Norway. Trying to contain his incontinent enthusiasms, which bore no relation to Britain's resources and above all shipping capacity and air cover, left Brooke exhausted.

In Washington, battle lines between the two allies were immediately apparent and perhaps deeper than before. Many senior American officers felt that they had been 'led up the Mediterranean garden path' by the British. General Marshall, who had been forced to concede on Operation Husky, the invasion of Sicily, was still determined that US forces should not linger in the Mediterranean. They should be brought back to Britain ready for the invasion of northern France in the late spring of 1944. If not, they should be sent to the Far East. This was probably more of a threat than a serious proposal, to force the British to commit themselves irrevocably. But it was exactly what Admiral King wanted.

Brooke argued back in his staccato style that the western Allies could not stand idly by for ten months while the Red

Army faced the bulk of the Wehrmacht alone. He was thus playing the argument for Sledgehammer back at the Americans. Either Hitler would send powerful forces into Italy at the expense of the eastern front and the Channel defences, or he would abandon most of the country, and establish a line north of the River Po in the foothills of the Alps. Besides, he continued, an invasion of the mainland across the Straits of Messina, once Sicily was taken, would bring down Mussolini and knock Italy out of the war. To regain control of the Mediterranean would shorten the route to the Far East and help save the equivalent of a million tons of shipping a year.

Where the British were either disingenuous or over-optimistic was in their assurance that the campaign in Italy would require no more than nine divisions. Churchill's idea of the 'soft underbelly of Europe', which he had first tried on Stalin, had become a mantra. He had even started to suggest an invasion of the Balkans to hold back a Soviet occupation of central Europe, an idea which provoked the deepest distrust among Americans. They saw it as another example of British politicking for the post-war period.

On 19 May, at an off-the-record meeting with just the chiefs of staff on each side, a compromise was reached. Some twenty-nine divisions would prepare in Britain for an invasion of France in the spring of 1944, and the invasion of Italy would go ahead. Marshall insisted on one proviso. After the capture of Sicily, seven divisions had to be brought back from the Mediterranean to Britain for the cross-Channel attack.

After all his forebodings, Brooke was satisfied. His plan to disperse German strength before the cross-Channel invasion had been accepted. In any case, the build-up of American forces in Britain had been far too slow to permit an invasion of France in 1943, and the Allies certainly lacked both the landing craft and the air superiority to make it a success.

Churchill and Brooke flew on to Algiers accompanied by General Marshall, in order to brief Eisenhower on the decisions made in Washington. Marshall was still opposed to the invasion of Italy and insisted that no final decision could be taken until the outcome of the Sicilian campaign was clear. Every time that Churchill tried to nobble him on strategic questions during the flight over, Marshall would head him off by innocently asking a question about a subject on which Churchill could not resist expounding at great length. But even if Marshall remained non-committal about the next stage after Sicily, Churchill and Brooke convinced Eisenhower of the advantages of an invasion of Italy, assuming Axis resistance collapsed.

Stalin, then awaiting the German onslaught on the Kursk Salient, was far more dissatisfied with the Italian project, as he made clear in a joint signal to Roosevelt and Churchill. Churchill sent back a sharp reply, yet the prime minister was entirely at fault for having told Stalin in February that they were aiming to launch the cross-Channel invasion in August, an operation which Brooke knew to be impossible. It had been a totally unnecessary deception which was bound to confirm Stalin's worst suspicions about Britain's broken promises.

The planning for Operation Husky, the invasion of Sicily, had been complicated and almost acrimonious at times. In April, Eisenhower had considered calling it off when he heard that two German divisions had been deployed on the island. Churchill had been contemptuous. 'He would have to meet a good deal more than two German divisions' when they invaded France, he pointed out. 'I trust the chiefs of staff will not accept these pusillanimous and defeatist doctrines, from whomever they come,' he minuted.

Montgomery, who had been heavily involved in the final battles for Tunis, then felt that the planners for Husky had been working at cross purposes, and thinking back to front. The problems of resupply had encouraged the idea that it would be better to make numerous landings. He rejected this approach and argued for the Eighth Army to be landed in the south-east of the island in a greater concentration, with Patton's Seventh Army to its left for mutual support. Patton suspected that Montgomery wanted to achieve the victory himself and use the Americans as little more than a flank guard.

This created a certain amount of inter-Allied friction. Patton even felt that 'Allies must fight in separate theaters or they hate each other more than the enemy.' Air Chief Marshal Tedder, the commander-in-chief of Allied air forces in the Mediterranean, shared Patton's scepticism about Montgomery. 'He is a little fellow of average ability,' he apparently said to Patton, 'who has had such a build-up that he thinks of himself as Napoleon – he is not.' Patton also thought that Alexander was afraid of Montgomery, which is why he was not firm enough with him.

Intrigues even more intense than those within Allied Force Headquarters seethed within the French colonial quarter of Algiers. Ever since the shotgun marriage of General Henri Giraud and General Charles de Gaulle, enforced by Roosevelt and Churchill at Casablanca in January, the Gaullists had been awaiting their moment. On 10 May, the third anniversary of the German invasion of France, the Conseil National de la Résistance in occupied France acknowledged de Gaulle's leadership. Neither Roosevelt nor Churchill had any idea how significant this would prove to be.

On 30 May, General de Gaulle finally arrived in Algiers at Maison Blanche airfield, having been long delayed by the American military authorities at Roosevelt's instigation. In the blinding sunlight a band played the 'Marseillaise', while British and American officers tried to stay in the background. They had good reason to try to keep out of things. The day before, Giraud had decorated Eisenhower with the medal of Grand Commander of the Legion of Honour, but de Gaulle, as Brooke found, was 'indignant that Giraud should have done this without consulting him!'

The key to power was control of the Armée d'Afrique, which was starting to be rearmed with American equipment and weapons. Inevitably, deep suspicions lingered between the traditional officers, or *moustachis*, of the former Vichy army which had been loyal to Pétain, and the *hadjis*, so-called because they had made the pilgrimage to London to join de Gaulle. The imbalance in numbers was considerable. The *moustachis* commanded 230,000 troops, while the Free French from the Middle East and Koenig's force which had so distinguished itself at Bir Hakeim had only 15,000 men. The Gaullists began poaching troops for their own formations, which caused Giraudist outrage. But de Gaulle's moral authority and superior political skills would bring him out on top.

On 10 July Husky began with pre-dawn airdrops, then 2,600 ships landed with eight divisions, as many as in Normandy

Sicily and Italy
July 1943–June 1944

Hitler Line
Gustav Line
Bernhardt Line

eleven months later. By nightfall the Allies had 80,000 men, 3,000 vehicles, 300 tanks and 900 guns ashore.

The Germans were taken by surprise. Operation Mincemeat, dropping the body supposedly of a Royal Marines officer with fake plans off the Spanish coast, together with other deception plans had misled Hitler into believing that the invasion was aimed at Sardinia and Greece. Generalfeldmarschall Kesselring still believed that Sicily or southern Italy were more likely objectives, but he was overruled. Mussolini had reinforced Sardinia, convinced that the Allies would land there after their bombing attacks on the island. There had also been strikes and unrest in Turin and Milan, which increased the Fascist regime's nervousness.

The sea had been calm when the invasion fleets set sail, but soon strong winds churned it up and the ships wallowed, provoking seasickness among the troops packed aboard. Those on a flat-bottomed LST, or Landing Ship Tank, suffered the worst, rolling and lurching in every direction. Fortunately the winds eased as they approached the coast. Montgomery's Eighth Army headed in to the south-eastern tip of the Sicilian triangle. His forces would then strike north up the coast towards Messina to cut off the Axis divisions before they could cross back to the mainland. Patton's US Seventh Army was landing to the west at three points on the southern coast, also guided in by Royal Navy submarines acting as beacons, flashing blue lights out to sea. Once ashore, no clear objectives had been set for the Seventh Army, a vagueness in planning which Patton had every intention of exploiting.

Shortly before 02.00 hours on 10 July, the order was given – 'Lower away!' – and the landing craft were winched down from davits into the water. The sea was still rough, and soon soldiers were sliding about on the vomit of the sufferers. Eventually, the assault craft were launched, and a correspondent watched the 'hordes of tiny craft, like water bugs, scooting towards the shore'. The landing was far from easy in heavy surf, and with minefields on the beaches. Often troops came ashore at the wrong place, and the confusion was at times almost as bad as during Operation Torch. Within a few hours the amphibious DUKWs went into action, bringing in supplies, fuel and even batteries of artillery.

Inland, the airborne landings in the high winds had been chaotic, with paratroopers from both the British 1st Airborne Division and the US 82nd Airborne scattered all over the place. Many suffered leg injuries. The British glider force, whose objective was a key bridge just south of Syracuse called the Ponte Grande, suffered the most. The tug pilots had little experience, and their navigation was dreadful. One glider landed in Malta and another near Mareth in southern Tunisia. Sixty gliders released too early crashed in the sea. But the thirty men who made it to the target still managed to seize the bridge, and remove the demolition charges. They were joined by another fifty men during the morning and held it against heavy attacks for most of the afternoon, until only fifteen were left unwounded. Although they were forced to surrender, the bridge was swiftly retaken by the Royal Scots Fusiliers arriving from the beach. The whole operation had cost 600 casualties, of whom almost half had drowned.

Whatever the confusion on the Allied side, the 300,000-strong Axis forces were in greater disarray. The storm at sea had convinced them that there could be no invasion that night. General Alfredo Guzzoni's Sixth Army may have been 300,000 strong in theory, but it contained just two German divisions, the 15th Panzergrenadiers and the *Hermann Göring* Panzer Division. The former had been deployed in the west of the island and was too far away to counter-attack, so Kesselring ordered the *Hermann Göring* to advance immediately on Gela, which had been captured by Rangers in Patton's central landing on the first day. The 1st Infantry Division, 'the Big Red One', had then moved inland to occupy the high ground and take the local airfield.

The attack of the *Hermann Göring* on the morning of 11 July caught the leading infantry battalions without tank support. The Shermans had not yet been landed. To the west, the Italian Livorno Division also advanced on Gela, but was soon halted by mortars firing white phosphorus, directed in person by General Patton, and naval gunfire from two offshore cruisers and four destroyers. The *Hermann Göring* to the north and north-east of the town almost reached the beaches. Their commander even informed General Guzzoni that the Americans were re-embarking. Just in time, a platoon of Shermans and some artillery were landed. The 155mm 'Long Toms' went straight into action, firing over open sights.

In a vineyard below Biazza Ridge to the east, part of the 505th Parachute Infantry Regiment under Colonel James M. Gavin came up against Tiger tanks attached to the *Hermann Göring* Division. Gavin had no doubts about the aggressiveness of his men who, before leaving Algeria, had practised their marksmanship on 'some menacing looking Arabs'. But against the Tigers they had only bazookas and a couple of 75mm pack guns.

Fortunately for the paratroopers, a naval ensign with a radio volunteered to call down naval gunfire. Gavin was understandably nervous, wondering how accurate it might be. He asked for a single ranging shot first. It was right on target. He called for a concentration. The Germans began to pull back, and then the first Sherman tanks arrived from the beach, to the cheers of the paratroopers. Together they attacked the ridge and managed to kill a Tiger crew unwisely standing outside their tank, which they captured. They looked at the bazooka strikes on the front of the Tiger, and saw that they barely dented its massive frontal armour. The *Hermann Göring* panzers had to withdraw rapidly right along the front, fired at all the time by the US Navy. Patton, who had been cheering and cursing on his troops around Gela, was well satisfied. 'God certainly watched over me today,' he wrote in his diary.

During the night, Patton's mood changed again. The 504th Parachute Infantry Regiment was due to fly in from Tunisia in the early hours and drop behind Seventh Army lines as an instant reinforcement. He wanted to cancel the operation, but found that it was too late. He suspected that his order to anti-aircraft gunners ashore and on land to hold their fire had not been disseminated properly. The guncrews could not distinguish between friend and foe, especially in the dark, and were jumpy after all the Luftwaffe attacks that day. Landing force commanders complained about the lack of Allied air cover over the beaches, but their air force colleagues remained reluctant to risk their fighters when Allied anti-aircraft gunners fired at anything that flew.

Patton's worst fears were realized. A single machine gun began firing when the C-47s appeared, and then everyone joined in, even tank gunners with their turret-mounted .50s. His men simply could not stop themselves. They continued firing at the paratroopers coming down and even after they hit the ground or the water. It was one of the worst examples of 'friendly fire' on the Allied side in the war, with twenty-three planes destroyed, thirty-seven badly damaged and over 400 casualties. Eisenhower, when he eventually found out, was furious and blamed Patton.

Patton's position, however, was eased when General Guzzoni ordered the *Hermann Göring* to move east to block the Eighth Army on the road north to Messina. The British had taken Syracuse against the lightest resistance. But over the next few days, as they advanced up the coast road towards Catania, the fighting became far harder. The Germans were in the process of reinforcing the island with the 29th Panzergrenadiers and the 1st Fallschirmjäger Division of paratroopers. General Hube's XIV Panzer Corps headquarters had been flown in to direct Wehrmacht troops. But Hube's principal objective, agreed with Guzzoni, was to fight a holding action to protect Messina and the straits, so that their forces could be withdrawn to the mainland to avoid another surrender like the one at Tunis.

On 13 July the British attempted another parachute drop, this time to capture the Primosole Bridge near Catania. Once again the aircraft were fired on by the invasion fleet as well as by Axis anti-aircraft guns, causing chaos. Out of the 1,856 men of the 1st Parachute Brigade, fewer than 300 reached the rendezvous point near the bridge. They secured it by the following morning and removed the demolition charges. Counter-attacks by the recently arrived 4th Fallschirmjäger Regiment almost drove them off, but despite losing a third of their strength, the British paratroopers just managed to hold on.

The 151st Brigade, with three battalions of the Durham Light Infantry, was coming to their relief on a forty-kilometre forced march in full kit in temperatures of 35 degrees Centigrade. On the way they were strafed by German fighters and bombed by American aircraft. The 9th Battalion of the Durhams went straight into the attack, suffering heavy losses from well-camouflaged German paratroopers firing low with their MG 42s, which the British called Spandaus. 'From the high ground where we watched the 9th Battalion make their frontal assault,' wrote a Durham, 'the sight was shocking. The River Simeto did, literally, run red with the blood of the 9th Battalion. It was all over by 09.30 hours. They had succeeded in preventing the Germans from blowing up the bridge.'

Another battalion of the Durhams managed to ford the river

later and take the Germans by surprise, but the bitter battle continued. The Durhams claimed that German snipers shot down their stretcher-bearers as they collected the wounded. As the battalion ran out of ammunition, Bren-gun carriers shuttled back and forth to replenish them. The smell of dead bodies in the heat prompted the carrier drivers to name the spot 'stink alley'. But finally the German paratroopers were forced back when the 4th Armoured Brigade arrived.

While the battle for the Primosole Bridge went on, the 51st Highland Division to the west attacked Francoforte, a typical Sicilian hilltop village above terraces of olive groves, reached only by a dirt road twisting up the steep slope in hairpin bends. To their left another part of the division managed to take Vizzini, after another short, fierce action. The Jocks of the Highland Division pushed on full of confidence. But they were soon to receive a nasty shock at Gerbini, where the Germans put up a strong defence at the adjoining airfield. The *Hermann Göring* and the Fallschirmjäger Division deployed their 88mm anti-tank guns with devastating effect. The British XIII Corps on the coastal plain was blocked, while XXX Corps had to fight from ridge to ridge. British soldiers hated fighting in the rocky hills of Sicily and began to feel nostalgic for the North African desert.

Montgomery decided to move his XXX Corps over into Patton's zone, so that it could attack around the western side of Mount Etna. Alexander agreed to this without first consulting Patton, who was understandably riled. Major General Omar Bradley, the commander of II Corps, was even angrier and told Patton that he should not allow the British to do that to him. But Patton, after Eisenhower's explosion over the airborne disaster and the lack of information he received from Seventh Army headquarters, did not want another battle with a superior officer. Bradley could hardly believe that Patton would be so docile.

Although dubbed the 'GI General' for his outward lack of pretension and homespun appearance, Bradley was ruthless and ambitious. Patton did not appreciate how much Bradley resented him. But both Bradley and Patton also faced a potential scandal. In Bradley's 45th Infantry Division, a National Guard formation which Patton had encouraged before the invasion to make itself known as 'the killer division', a sergeant and a captain massacred more than seventy unarmed prisoners. Patton's initial reaction was that the murdered soldiers should be described as snipers or as prisoners shot while attempting to escape. The military authorities decided to hush up the whole affair on the grounds that the Germans might take reprisals against Allied prisoners.

Patton managed to persuade Alexander that instead of just protecting Montgomery's left flank he should also capture the port of Agrigento on the west coast to ease his supply situation. Alexander agreed, not guessing what his real intentions were. Patton took the opportunity offered to push north-west up the coast and north over the mountains towards Palermo. With their generous supply of vehicles and self-propelled artillery, the US Army could move much more rapidly than the British, whose commanders also seemed to find fighting in the hillside vineyards and sun-baked mountains a baffling experience. The British had failed to grasp Patton's cardinal rule learned after the Kasserine debacle: always seize the highest point fast and first. Topography was everything.

On 17 July, Patton heard that Alexander and Montgomery expected the US Seventh Army to act as flank guard. Patton was no longer prepared to accept a secondary role. He flew to see Alexander in Tunis, taking with him the notoriously anglophobic General Wedemeyer, who as General Marshall's representative carried a great deal of weight. Alexander, embarrassed by the way he had pandered to Montgomery's insistence, immediately permitted Patton to continue his advance. Patton's earlier respect for Alexander had dwindled, but he now had his army group commander's permission to turn his divisions loose.

Like his soldiers, General Patton was appalled by the poverty, dirt, dungheaps and disease they encountered in Sicilian towns and villages. 'The people of this country', he wrote in his diary, 'are the most destitute and God-forgotten people I have ever seen.' Many American troops thought living conditions in Sicily worse than in North Africa. Half-starved civilians begged for food from troops and there were occasional food riots in towns, dealt with by MPs firing Thompson sub-machine guns over the heads of protesters and even at them.

Although there were places of great beauty in the hot, rocky landscape, with olive and citrus groves, the primitive existence of the population, relying on donkeys and carts for transport, seemed almost medieval. Patton remarked in a letter to his wife that 'one could buy any woman on the island for a can of beans, but there are not many purchasers'. He was clearly wrong, since the rate of venereal disease soared in both armies. One British field hospital admitted 186 cases in a single day.

On 19 July, Hitler and Mussolini met at Feltre in northern Italy. The Duce's bombast and supreme self-confidence had evaporated. Hitler now frightened him and Mussolini said nothing during a two-hour lecture on Italy's deficiencies. The Führer, perhaps fuelled by the amphetamines he was taking at the time, seemed to be vibrant with energy. The Duce, on the other hand, was a shrunken man, physically as well as psychologically. For somebody who had prided himself on his fitness and had used to love showing off his torso – a habit which Hitler considered undignified – he was now sick with stomach pains and prone to melancholia, listlessness and indecision. As Hitler was to feel later about Germans, Mussolini had decided that his countrymen were worthless and did not deserve his leadership. Yet, like Hitler, he had never visited either the front or the victims of bombing.

Mussolini's inability to confide in anybody around him had left him out of touch with reality. He pretended to be the all-knowing, all-seeing dictator, yet none of his entourage dared to tell him that he was loathed by the majority of Italians, and that they wanted to have nothing more to do with his war. The Duce's compulsion to issue streams of instructions on every subject under the sun also meant that he was, in the words of one Fascist Party secretary, 'the most disobeyed man in history'. The government was adrift and his son-in-law, Count Ciano, although not daring to oppose him openly, began to plot his downfall in the hope of taking over himself and negotiating a peace with the western Allies.

During the meeting at Feltre, news arrived that the Americans had bombed marshalling yards on the edge of Rome for the first time. Mussolini was shaken, even more so when he discovered that this had set off a panic in the city. Hitler, who feared that Mussolini's regime might be on the edge of collapse, had not only prepared a large contingent of the German army to occupy the country, he had sent tanks to the Italian Blackshirt militia to enable them to put down any attempt at an anti-Fascist coup.

On 22 July Major General Lucian K. Truscott's 3rd Division swept into the dilapidated capital of Palermo and Bradley's II Corps reached the north coast at Termini Imerese. An exultant Patton settled himself in the grandeur of the Royal Palace of Palermo, where he ate K-Rations off crested porcelain plates in the state dining room and drank champagne. The British, meanwhile, were still slogging away on both sides of Mount Etna. A regiment from the Canadian 1st Division managed to seize the town of Assoro by scaling a cliff, like General Wolfe's capture of Quebec almost two centuries before.

On 24 July, the Fascist Grand Council met in Rome. Criticism was guarded to begin with, and Mussolini failed to appreciate what was happening. In great pain, he appeared to be apathetic, almost paralysed. The meeting carried on through the night. After ten hours Count Dino Grandi, the pre-war ambassador to London, introduced a motion for a return to a constitutional monarchy and a democratic parliament. Mussolini's failure to react convinced some that he was simply looking for a way out. Grandi's motion was carried by nineteen votes to seven.

Next day Mussolini, having forgotten to shave, went to see King Vittorio Emanuele III at the Villa Savoia. He acted as if nothing untoward had happened. But when he began to speak, the diminutive King stopped him and told him that Marshal Pietro Badoglio would take over as prime minister. As the stupefied Mussolini left the royal presence, he was arrested by Carabinieri officers and taken in an ambulance to their heavily guarded barracks. A radio announcement that night brought people on to the streets cheering 'Benito e finito'. Italian Fascism collapsed in a matter of hours, disappearing like a stage-set to make way for a new production. Even the Blackshirt militia armed with German tanks did not attempt to prevent his fall. In Milan, workers stormed the prisons to release anti-Fascists.

On hearing of the coup in Rome, Hitler had wanted to drop a division of paratroopers on the city to seize both the new government and the royal family. He suspected that freemasons and the Vatican were somehow behind Mussolini's downfall. Rommel,

Jodl and Kesselring finally persuaded him against launching an attack on Rome. Hitler certainly did not trust Marshal Badoglio's promise that Italy's war would continue. German troops seized the Brenner Pass and key installations in north Italy with eight divisions. An operation codenamed Alarich had been prepared for the occupation of the whole country in the event of an Italian surrender. Hitler told his intelligence services to find out where Mussolini was being held, using any means including bribery and clairvoyants.

Patton, with his blood up, was determined to take Messina before Montgomery. He urged his men on relentlessly, even though many were succumbing to the intense heat and dehydration. Malaria, dysentery and dengue and sand-fly fevers had accounted for a high proportion of the non-combat casualties. Malaria alone would strike down 22,000 men in the two Allied armies on Sicily.

On 25 July Patton flew to Syracuse at Montgomery's request, to discuss the advance on Messina. The lack of direction from Allied headquarters made this essential. Montgomery tacitly admitted that he was blocked south of Catania, and without waiting for Alexander they began to discuss the situation over a map spread on the front of Montgomery's Humber staff car. To Patton's surprise, Montgomery agreed to American forces crossing army boundaries if that would help them get to Messina quickly. Alexander finally arrived accompanied by Bedell Smith, having been delayed by news of the momentous events in Rome. The army group commander was clearly irritated to find that his two generals had come to an agreement without him. But even though Montgomery at Syracuse had half conceded the race to the Seventh Army, Patton had every intention of winning it outright.

His men, sweat-stained and coated in dust, advanced from rocky hill to rocky hill. Like the British, they had to bring up ammunition and other supplies packed on mules. The two panzergrenadier divisions made them fight all the way, blowing bridges and planting mines and booby-traps at every opportunity. American troops were enraged by the way they booby-trapped the dead, so they sometimes took their revenge on prisoners. The countryside stank of decomposing corpses and so did the towns, smashed by Allied artillery and bombing at the cost of huge civilian casualties. Bodies were piled high amid the rubble and burned with gasoline to prevent disease.

During the first week of August, the battle for the mountain town of Troina cost the US 1st Infantry Division 500 casualties. Patton had already decided that its commander Terry Allen was exhausted, and as soon as the fighting at Troina was over he relieved both him and his second-in-command, Brigadier General Teddy Roosevelt Jr. Bradley, who loathed Allen because of his open disrespect, was deeply satisfied.

On 3 August Patton visited the 15th Evacuation Hospital. He was visibly moved surveying the wounded, but had no patience with psychological breakdown. Patton asked a soldier from the 1st Division, a young carpet-layer from Indiana suffering from battle-shock, what his problem was. 'I guess I can't take it,' the soldier replied helplessly. Patton flew into a blind rage, slapped him with his gloves and dragged him out of the tent. He booted him in the rear, shouting: 'You hear me, you gutless bastard. You're going back to the front!' A week later, Patton had another explosion when visiting the 93rd Evacuation Hospital. He even drew his pistol on the victim, threatening to shoot him for cowardice. A British reporter, who happened to be present, heard him say immediately afterwards: 'There's no such thing as shellshock. It's an invention of the Jews!'

To increase the speed of advance along the north coast, Patton persuaded the US Navy to provide enough landing craft to insert a battalion fifteen kilometres behind German lines. Both Bradley and Truscott were strongly opposed to the plan, and, as they had feared, the battalion was virtually wiped out after seizing a key hill called Monte Cipolla. Patton felt that the costly gamble was entirely justified. He had no idea that the Germans had already begun to pull their forces back across the Straits of Messina in a well-organized operation. The German retreat went into top gear on 11 August. Allied Force Headquarters had failed to put any measures into effect to block it. Tedder was instead using the B-17 Fortresses to bomb the railyards round Rome, and both the Royal Navy and the US Navy were reluctant to use large ships with all the Axis artillery positioned on the Italian coastline. Eisenhower later regretted his failure to land forces on the far side of the straits, but in the event 110,000 Axis troops were evacuated, almost without loss. To a large extent, this oversight was due to General Marshall's reluctance to commit to an all-out invasion of the mainland.

Patton was far more interested in the fact that his troops had reached Messina before Montgomery's, and he made a triumphal entry into the ruined city on the morning of 17 August. But his triumph was soon spoiled. The storm over the two hospital incidents was about to break, for Eisenhower had heard of them that same morning in Algiers from American war correspondents. Nothing was known back in the United States. President Roosevelt had even sent the volcanic Patton a message of congratulation, saying that Harry Hopkins had suggested that 'after the war I should make you Marquis of Mount Etna'.

For an officer to strike a subordinate was an offence to be tried by court martial, but Eisenhower, while furious with Patton, did not want to lose him. He managed to persuade both American and British journalists to kill the story. After agonizing over the dilemma for several days and nights, Eisenhower ordered Patton to apologize to the two soldiers as well as to the medical staff who had witnessed the incidents and publicly to the troops. Some cheered him, but the 1st Infantry Division, still resentful after the sacking of Allen and Teddy Roosevelt, heard him in silence.

The Sicilian campaign, although it permitted so many Axis troops to escape, had certainly proved its worth. Casualties were high – 12,800 from the Eighth Army and 8,800 from Patton's Seventh – but morale had been greatly bolstered and many skills sharpened, both on amphibious operations and in the fighting afterwards. The Allies now had virtual control of the Mediterranean and numerous airfields from which to attack Italy and beyond. The invasion had also prompted Mussolini's downfall and contributed to Hitler's rage, panic and depression at the Wolfsschanze. The destruction of Hamburg by the RAF had shaken Hitler more than he dared to admit, and the Red Army's offensives on the eastern front, following the Battle of Kursk, underlined how short of troops he was.

In August, Churchill, Roosevelt and their chiefs of staff assembled again, this time in Quebec for the Quadrant conference organized by the Canadian premier William Mackenzie King. A few days

before, Churchill had raised the question of the atomic-bomb project with Roosevelt. The Americans had been trying to exclude
the British from sharing in this research, known as 'Tube Alloys',
but Churchill persuaded Roosevelt that it should continue as a
joint venture.

At Quebec, the conference discussed the imminent surrender
of Italy, following secret overtures via Madrid and Lisbon from
Badoglio's emissary General Giuseppe Castellano. It was an encouraging prospect. Italian airfields could be used for bombing
Germany and the Ploesti oilfields, as General 'Hap' Arnold, the
chief of the US air force, emphasized. But British enthusiasm for
an all-out Italian campaign to advance north to the line of the
River Po was not shared by the Americans, even though Brooke
argued forcefully that it would draw German divisions away from
the Normandy front.

Roosevelt and Marshall did not want the advance to continue
beyond Rome, even if that meant leaving their forces in Italy idle.
They suspected, with some justification, that the British would
use the Italian campaign as a means to delay the invasion of
France and divert efforts towards the north-east, into the Balkans
and central Europe. Unfortunately, Churchill's gadfly approach
to strategy – he now wanted to invade Rhodes and the islands
of the Dodecanese to bring Turkey into the war – only seemed
to confirm their misgivings. Marshall remained adamant that the
seven divisions allocated for the invasion of Normandy should be
withdrawn from Italy by 1 November, as had already been agreed
at the Trident conference.

The invasion of Normandy, now called Operation Overlord,
was nevertheless fixed for May 1944. Lieutenant General Sir Frederick Morgan, the chief of staff to the (as yet unnamed) supreme
Allied commander, was already working on the initial plans.
Supported by General Arnold, he underlined the urgent need to
weaken the Luftwaffe first. Churchill had rather rashly promised
General Brooke the supreme command on three occasions. He
now faced the fact that Roosevelt would insist that an American
general should have the job, as the US would provide the majority of the troops. The Americans also believed, mistakenly, that
Brooke was against the invasion of France.

Brooke was deeply disappointed when Churchill told him

that he would not command Overlord after all, and never really got over the blow. He was even more put out when he discovered that Churchill had privately settled in return for Admiral Lord Louis Mountbatten to head SEAC, the new South-East Asia Command. The obvious candidate for Overlord appeared to be General Marshall, even though he avoided putting himself forward.

On 3 September, Churchill travelled by train from Quebec to Washington. He arrived in time for a momentous day. The dapper General Castellano, Badoglio's chief of staff, and Eisenhower's chief of staff, General Bedell Smith, had secretly signed the Italian armistice after difficult negotiations. The Germans had built up their forces in Italy to sixteen divisions, and the Italians were understandably terrified of German reprisals.

At dawn that day, British and Canadian troops landed near Reggio di Calabria. They were supported by warships and artillery fire across the Straits of Messina, but the landings were unopposed on that beautiful September morning, and the sea was calm. The British called it the 'Messina Strait Regatta'. Other landings on the toe of Italy and at the naval base of Taranto soon followed. Admiral Cunningham took a risk by sending the 1st Airborne Division into Taranto on Royal Navy cruisers. The Italian fleet sailed to Malta to surrender, but the Luftwaffe managed to sink the battleship *Roma* with one of its new rocket-propelled bombs and kill 1,300 sailors.

The whole Italian campaign would be dogged by misconceptions and wishful thinking. Because of some earlier Ultra intercepts, Allied Force Headquarters believed that in the event of an Italian surrender the Germans would pull back to the Pisa–Rimini Line in northern Italy. Hitler had since decided, however, that this would be tantamount to abandoning the Balkans behind the backs of his Croatian, Romanian and Hungarian allies. In addition the Italians, despite their earlier assurances to Bedell Smith, were not prepared to defend Rome against the Germans. A planned drop on Rome by the 82nd Airborne Division, to coincide with the main landings at Salerno, was mercifully aborted as the aircraft were taking off. The whole formation would have been wiped out if it had gone ahead.

On 8 September Hitler, having spent too much time fretting

over events in Italy, flew to Manstein's headquarters in southern Russia to discuss the crisis on the eastern front. The Red Army had broken through between Kluge's Army Group Centre and Manstein's Army Group South. When he returned to the Wolfsschanze that evening, the Führer heard that the Italian armistice had just been announced and that the first wave of General Mark Clark's US Fifth Army had landed at Salerno, fifty kilometres south-east of Naples. His mood after hearing of Badoglio's 'treachery' can be imagined, even though he had expected it. He summoned Goebbels and other Nazi leaders to a meeting the next day. 'The Führer', Goebbels wrote in his diary, 'is determined to make a *tabula rasa* in Italy.'

Operation Axis (formerly Alarich) was launched with ruthless rapidity. One of the first priorities for Generalfeldmarschall Kesselring was to seize Rome. German paratroopers marched in while the city's inhabitants were still celebrating what they imagined was the end of the war for them. The King and Marshal Badoglio escaped just in time. The sixteen German divisions disarmed Italian troops, and destroyed any who resisted. Some 650,000 were seized as prisoners of war, most of whom were later sent for forced labour. Himmler soon instructed the head of the security police in Rome, SS Obersturmführer Herbert Kappler, to round up the 8,000 Jews in the city.

While the Germans occupied Rome, they had sent forces to block off a possible Anglo-American landing in the Gulf of Salerno, which offered the obvious invasion site along that part of the Tyrrhenian coast. The recently created German Tenth Army was commanded by General Heinrich von Vietinghoff. He rapidly sent the 16th Panzer Division, the successor formation to the one destroyed at Stalingrad, to take up positions on the hills dominating the great bay. By that evening of 8 September, just after the Allied troops had celebrated news of Italy's surrender on board their invasion ships, the first German troops were already in position to welcome them when they landed in the early hours of the following day.

The unexpectedly strong resistance took the Allied troops aback. Only when minesweepers cleared a channel forward the next morning could warships come close enough inshore to identify tank concentrations and German gun batteries. Most of the things that could go wrong at Salerno did go wrong. Major General Ernest Dawley, the commander of the US VI Corps, only contributed to the confusion on land. He did not secure his left flank with the British part of the invasion force until ordered to by Clark three days later, by which time German strength had increased. The *Hermann Göring* Panzer Division and the 15th and the 29th Panzergrenadier Divisions reached the Salerno front one after another.

British and Americans alike found themselves trapped in tobacco fields or in apple and peach orchards, or back on the sand dunes, where there was little cover apart from scrub and seagrass. Under the eyes of German gunners on the high ground, casualty evacuation was difficult by day, and aid men had to do their best with sulpha powder and field dressings.

On the extreme left, only Lieutenant Colonel William Darby's Rangers had enjoyed success after they had quickly advanced inland to seize key points on the Chiunzi Pass. This snaking road led over the mountainous base of the Sorrento Peninsula to Naples. From their positions they were able to direct the heavy naval guns in the Gulf, firing on maximum elevation, to bombard German supply convoys and reinforcements coming down the coast road from Naples.

Clark, well aware that his invasion force could not hope to break out of this trap, pushed Dawley into sending the 36th Infantry Division of Texan National Guardsmen to seize a hilltop village on the morning of 13 September. The German response was savage and the Texans were badly mauled. Worse was to follow. General von Vietinghoff thought that the two Allied corps were about to re-embark, so he launched an attack with panzer units and self-propelled guns due south from Eboli. The fighting was so desperate and the German breakthrough so dangerous that Clark considered pulling out and Vietinghoff believed that the battle was as good as won.

The Eighth Army's advance north had not speeded up; its vanguard was still nearly a hundred kilometres to the south-east. Many delays were caused by bridges destroyed by the Germans in their withdrawal. Admiral Hewitt, the task force commander at Salerno, was appalled by the prospect of a re-embarkation. Early on 14 September he signalled Admiral Cunningham in Malta, who immediately despatched the battleships HMS *Warspite* and HMS *Valiant* to provide more heavy guns. Cunningham also sent three cruisers at full speed to Tripoli to fetch reinforcements. But in the meantime the situation had stabilized a little. A determined defence, with 105mm guns firing over open sights, had stopped the panzer charge, and Clark's urgent request for a regiment from the 82nd Airborne to be dropped within the bridgehead was answered.

General Alexander arrived on a destroyer on the morning of 15 September. In complete agreement with Admiral Hewitt, he cancelled any plans for evacuation. The Salerno bridgehead was soon secured by bomber support and the weight and accuracy of Allied naval gunfire. US Navy and Royal Navy warships inflicted heavy damage on the German tanks and artillery. Unfortunately, during a Luftwaffe raid at night, the *Warspite* fired its six-inch guns at one low-flying aircraft and hit the destroyer HMS *Petard* instead, causing heavy damage.

Major General James Doolittle's bombers smashed the town of Battipaglia just behind the German lines so thoroughly that General Spaatz sent the message: 'You're slipping Jimmy. There's one crabapple tree and one stable still standing.' But a new bombing doctrine was being born, which the Americans called 'Putting the city in the street'. This meant deliberately smashing a town to rubble so that enemy reinforcements and supplies could not get through. This would become a key tactic the following June in Normandy.

By this time, German intelligence had discovered Mussolini's whereabouts. After holding him first on the island of Ponza and then on La Maddalena, Marshal Badoglio had him moved secretly to a ski resort north of Rome in the Apennines, known as Gran Sasso. Hitler, horrified by this humiliation of his ally, ordered a rescue attempt. On 12 September Hauptsturmführer Otto Skorzeny, with a force of Waffen-SS special troops in eight gliders, crash-landed on the mountain. The Carabinieri guarding him did not resist. Mussolini embraced Skorzeny, saying that he knew his friend Adolf Hitler would not abandon him. He was flown out and brought to the Wolfsschanze. Hitler's Luftwaffe adjutant described him as 'a broken man'. The Germans' plan was to install him as figurehead of a so-called Repubblica Sociale Italiana, thus creating the fiction that the Axis was still in force to justify their occupation of Italy.

On 21 September Free French forces landed on the island of Corsica, which the Germans had abandoned to reinforce the mainland. At Salerno, the German withdrawal had begun three days earlier. Kesselring had told Vietinghoff to pull his army gradually back to the line of the River Volturno north of Naples. Clark finally sacked his corps commander General Dawley, and the British on the left of the beachhead attacked north to seize the base of the Sorrento Peninsula and prepare the advance up the coast to Naples. After the Coldstream Guards had taken a hill there in a night attack, the platoon commander Michael Howard described the scene. 'We stood to at dawn. In the first grey hints of light we buried the German dead. These were the first corpses I had handled: shrunken pathetic dolls lying stiff and twisted, with glazed eyes. Not one could have been over twenty, and some were little more than children. With horrible carelessness we shovelled them into their own trenches and piled on the earth.'

By 25 September the Eighth Army and Clark's Fifth Army had joined up and established a line across Italy. The American forces at Salerno had suffered some 3,500 casualties and the British 5,500. The Eighth Army advancing on the Adriatic side seized the Foggia Plain with all its airfields to be used for bombing southern Germany, Austria and the Ploesti oilfields. Clark's Fifth Army in the west pushed past Mount Vesuvius, and on 1 October the King's Dragoon Guards in their armoured cars led the way into Naples under the ubiquitous washing lines stretched across the streets. But there were no sheets hung out to dry. Naples was without water because the Germans had blown the aqueducts, in revenge for the resistance shown to their brutal occupation. They had wrecked as much of the city as they could, including ancient libraries, sewers, electricity stations, factories and above all the port. Time bombs were left in other major buildings to explode over the following weeks. Already the war in Italy was beginning to replicate the horrors of the eastern front.

The Bletchley Park intercept which indicated that Hitler planned to evacuate most of Italy was not followed by other signals revealing that Führer headquarters was changing its mind, largely under pressure from Kesselring who wanted to defend the country from south of Rome. Rommel's advice to pull back was discarded partly because Hitler feared the effect it would have on his Balkan allies, but also because the Allied invasion was floundering. Yet Hitler's determination to hold Italy, and his conviction that the British would invade the Balkans and the Aegean, meant that a total of thirty-seven German divisions would be tied down in the region while the Wehrmacht was fighting for its life on the eastern front.

Goebbels and Ribbentrop urged Hitler to initiate peace talks with Stalin, but the Führer angrily rejected such an idea. He would never negotiate from weakness. General Jodl of the OKW recognized the mad logic in which they were trapped by the Nazi mantra of 'final victory'. 'That we will win, because we must win,' he noted soon afterwards, 'means that world history has lost all sense.' Since there was now no hope of negotiating from strength, the implication was all too clear. Germany would fight on until its total destruction.

33

Ukraine and the Teheran Conference

SEPTEMBER–DECEMBER 1943

After the Red Army had recaptured Kharkov on 23 August 1943, the German army faced a crisis in the south. The defensive line along the River Mius was broken, and on 26 August Rokossovsky's Central Front smashed through on the boundary between Army Group South and Army Group Centre. On 3 September, Kluge and Manstein asked Hitler to appoint a commander-in-chief for the eastern front. Hitler refused and still insisted that the industrial area of the Donbas should be held even if a withdrawal from the Mius was now necessary. Once again Hitler promised reinforcements, but by now Manstein knew that he could not believe him. It was also the day that British troops landed on the mainland of Italy in the south.

Five days later, following a teleprinter signal from Manstein on the scale of the Soviet attack, Hitler flew to Army Group South's headquarters at Zaporozhye. Manstein's briefing was so stark that even Hitler felt obliged to authorize a retreat to the River Dnepr. This was his very last visit to the occupied territory of the Soviet Union. On his return to the Wolfsschanze at the end of that ill-fated day, he heard about the Allied landings at Salerno and the imminent capitulation of the Italian army.

After Hitler's reluctant decision, the German army had to race back to the Dnepr to avoid being cut off. The Red Army, although also weakened by the Battle of Kursk, pushed on at all speed to seize bridgeheads over the river before the Germans had a chance to establish an effective defence. This immense river was supposed to form the basis of a defended line running from Smolensk to Kiev and then on down to the Black Sea. Like most great Russian rivers running from north to south, it had an unusually high western bank which formed a natural rampart.

In their retreat across eastern Ukraine the Germans tried to carry out a ruthless scorched-earth programme, but they did not have time to destroy as much as they had intended. *Land-sers*, having stuffed their pockets and packs, almost wept as they watched their own supply dumps going up in flames. Harried by Shturmovik fighter-bombers by day, they pulled back across the Dnepr under cover of night and the early-morning autumn mists.

Stalin promised the award of Hero of the Soviet Union to the first soldier across the river. On improvised rafts made from oil barrels and planks, in small boats and even by swimming, Red Army soldiers threw themselves at the challenge. In the event, four sub-machine-gunners became Heroes of the Soviet Union, after storming the west bank on 22 September. 'There were cases', Vasily Grossman wrote in his diary, 'when soldiers transported regimental field guns on wooden gates, and crossed the Dnepr on groundsheets stuffed with hay.' Vatutin's forces seized bridgeheads north and south of Kiev in the third week of September. Soon troops were across at forty different places, but most were too small for launching further attacks inland. One group, whose boat sank, reached a peasant hut. The old woman there welcomed them: 'Children, sons, come in to my place,' she said. Having helped them warm up and dry their tattered uniforms, she gave them *samogon*, a home-brewed vodka.

In many places, Soviet casualties were heavy. A follow-up group had to deal with the corpses. 'We collected those who were killed or had drowned,' recalled a member of one squad, 'and we buried them in trenches, fifty men in each. So many soldiers had died there. The German bank was steep and well fortified while our boys were advancing from an open space.'

In an attempt to increase the bridgehead at Velikii Burin south-east of Kiev, three airborne brigades were parachuted on to the west bank of the river. But Soviet intelligence had failed to identify a German concentration in the area, of two panzer and three infantry divisions. Many of the paratroopers fell on positions occupied by the 19th Panzer Division and were massacred. The most successful bridgehead was Litezh, north of Kiev. A Red Army rifle division managed to slip across the Dnepr in a marshy area the Germans had considered impassable. Seizing the opportunity, Vatutin took a huge risk which paid off. He reinforced the bridgehead with the 5th Guards Tank Corps. Many T-34s were lost in the bogs, but enough got through by driving at full speed.

To the north, Smolensk itself was finally taken after hard fighting at the end of the month. The Rzhev Offensive, which had begun the push west on this part of the front, left complete devastation in its wake. The Australian correspondent Godfrey Blunden was taken round. 'Some peasant families of old men, women and children had returned and were camping in wigwams. In several places they had hung out their washing on lines between trees as if it were normal to have a washing day in this desecrated no-man's land. There is some lesson in human persistence in the way these people come back to their old homes, but one could not help wondering how they would survive the coming winter.' He was shaken to discover that 'a little wizened old woman' whom he met was in fact 'a girl of thirteen'.

In the south, General F. I. Tolbukhin's Southern Front cut off the Seventeenth Army in the Crimea, which had by then evacuated the Kuban bridgehead in the Caucasus. Rokossovsky's Central Front had punched a large salient due west of Kursk, and in October was approaching Gomel on the edge of Belorussia. For Stalin, and of course for Vatutin, the true prize was the Ukrainian capital of Kiev. By the end of October, Vatutin had infiltrated, night by night, Lieutenant General P. S. Rybalko's 3rd Guards Tank Army and the 38th Army into the Litezh bridgehead. Brilliant camouflage, deception operations elsewhere and a lack of Luftwaffe air reconnaissance led the Germans to overlook this particular threat. When the two armies burst out of the bridgehead they were able to encircle Kiev, which fell on 6 November, the day before the celebrations in Moscow of the anniversary of the Revolution. Stalin was exultant. Vatutin wasted no time in pushing forward other armies to seize Zhitomir and Korosten. Despite the mud of the autumn *rasputitsa*, his armies soon created a salient 150 kilometres deep and 300 kilometres wide.

As they advanced, they encountered desolation and a peasantry mute from suffering. 'Old men, when they hear Russian,' Vasily Grossman recorded, 'run to meet the troops and weep silently, unable to mutter a word. Old peasant women say: "We thought we would sing and laugh when we saw our army, but there's so much grief in our hearts, that tears are falling."' They recounted their disgust at the way German soldiers walked around naked, even in front of women and young girls, and 'their gluttony, their ability to eat twenty eggs in one go, or a kilo of honey'. Grossman met a young boy, barefoot and in rags. He asked where his father was. 'Killed,' he answered. 'And your mother?' 'She died.' 'Have you got brothers or sisters?' 'A sister. They took her to Germany.' 'Have you any relatives?' 'No, they were all burned in a partisan village.'

There were, however, Ukrainians who did not welcome the return of Soviet rule. Many had collaborated with the Germans, forming their militias or even serving as soldiers or concentration camp guards. And the Ukrainian nationalists in the UPA (Ukrainska povstanska armiia), who had turned against the Germans, were now ready to fight a guerrilla campaign against the Red Army. Their most famous victim would be General Vatutin himself, killed in an ambush.

Grossman's worst nightmares were exceeded by the reality of what he discovered. The capture of Kiev confirmed reports of the massacre at Babi Yar. The Germans had tried to conceal the crime by burning and removing bodies, but there were too many for them. After the initial massacre in September 1941, the site had continued to be used for executions of other Jews, Roma and Communists. It was estimated that by the autumn of 1943 almost 100,000 people had been killed there.

Grossman found the statistics of the great void numbing. Lacking the names of individuals, he tried to give a human face to this previously unimaginable crime. 'This was the murder of a great and ancient professional experience,' he wrote, 'passed from one generation to another in thousands of families of craftsmen and members of the intelligentsia. This was the murder of everyday traditions that grandfathers passed to their grandchildren, this was the murder of memories, of a mournful song, folk poetry, of life, happy and bitter, this was the destruction of hearths and cemeteries, this was the death of a nation which had been living side by side with Ukrainians over hundreds of years.' He recounted the fate of a much loved Jewish doctor called Feldman, who had been saved from execution in 1941 when a crowd of Ukrainian peasant women pleaded with the German commandant. 'Feldman continued to live in Brovary and treat the local peasants. He was executed in the spring of this year. Khristya Chunyak sobbed and finally burst into tears as she described to me how the old man was forced to dig his own grave. He had to die alone. There were no other Jews alive in the spring of 1943.'

Stalin, understandably proud of the Soviet Union's great military achievements that year, finally agreed to a Big Three meeting with Roosevelt and Churchill. In late November 1943, they would come together in Teheran, which like most of Iran was still occupied by Soviet and British troops, to secure the oilfields and the overland supply route to the Caucasus. Stalin had chosen the Iranian capital so that he could stay in direct touch with the Stavka.

To prepare for the Teheran conference, there would first be a meeting in October of foreign ministers in Moscow. The agenda in the Spiridonovka Palace was enormous. British concerns ranged from the Polish question to post-war international relations, the treatment of enemy states, a European Advisory Commission on Germany, trials of war criminals, and arrangements for France, Yugoslavia and Iran. Cordell Hull, the American secretary of state, emphasized Roosevelt's wish for a successor to the discredited League of Nations. This was a sensitive issue for Molotov and Litvinov, the deputy commissar for foreign affairs, following the Soviet Union's expulsion because of its invasion of Finland in 1939. Roosevelt's project of the United Nations, which would come into being at the end of the war, would have the victor nations at its core to give it greater strength.

The Soviet side insisted that the British and Americans put detailed proposals on the table which could then be dealt with at Teheran. They were giving nothing away about their own position, and insisted on only one item: 'measures to shorten the war against Germany and its allies in Europe'. That is to say, they intended to extract a precise date for the invasion of France. They also raised the question of bringing Turkey into the war on the Allied side and suggested putting pressure on neutral Sweden to allow the establishment of Allied air bases on its soil. Overall, the conference was deemed by both sides to have gone well.

The greatest success in Moscow, according to the Australian Godfrey Blunden, came in the form of a 'little wooden box with two eye pieces'. It was 'in all respects similar to peep-show boxes you used to see at a funfair, except that instead of dancing girls there was a series of startling stereoscopic pictures of bombed Germany'. This brainchild of Air Chief Marshal Harris fascinated and impressed Red Army generals in Moscow with its three-dimensional images of urban destruction.

Blunden heard all this from Harris himself when he went to see him at Bomber Command headquarters. Harris showed him the large photograph albums he had had specially bound in RAF blue leather to impress visitors. Each series of aerial photographs on the same scale was covered by a sheet of tracing paper showing the outline of the industrial and residential areas. The first in the book marked the destruction of Coventry. Harris then turned the pages one by one showing the German cities. At one point, Blunden exclaimed at the extent of the damage: 'There must be at least six Coventrys there.'

'No, you are wrong,' Harris replied with satisfaction. 'There are ten.' When they reached another town where the damage was not so widespread, Harris remarked: 'Needs another good raid and that will finish it off.'

'These photographs', Blunden wrote, 'show very graphically indeed how area bombing as first practised by Germans has developed into a weapon of immense power. The damage done to Coventry three years ago – which led Germans to coin the word "Coventrate" meaning to obliterate a city – is now almost insignificant beside this vaster damage done to German cities.'

The Americans at this time were also trying to promote Nationalist China's membership of what should become a 'Big Four' alliance. Roosevelt, knowing Chiang Kai-shek's ambitions in this direction, hoped that this would help to keep the Nationalists in the war despite their disappointment over the shortage of supplies for their armies. Chiang played the same game with the United States as he had played earlier with the Soviet Union: he used subtle threats of a separate peace with Japan to obtain more support. Although a card of deliberate weakness, Chiang's gambit still had some effect since Chinese forces were, at least in theory, tying down more than a million Japanese troops on the mainland. Yet Roosevelt was also looking towards a post-war world in which he saw China's inclusion as vital in the leadership of the United Nations. It was an idea which Churchill and his entourage certainly did not encourage. The Soviets were even more reluctant after Chiang's pressure to expel them from Sinkiang province, but an agreement in principle was reached at the Moscow conference.

Chiang had changed his position in one important way. He now wanted American support to ensure that the Soviet Union did not secure areas of northern China if it entered the war against Japan. Having done everything he could earlier to persuade Roosevelt to push Stalin into a declaration of war, Chiang now wanted to see Japan defeated without Soviet help. He feared, with justification, that Soviet involvement would boost the power and armament of the Chinese Communists.

In the fourth week of November 1943, Roosevelt and Churchill met in Cairo on their way to Teheran. At this rather improvised conference, Roosevelt had privately arranged for Chiang Kai-shek to join the proceedings at the start and not at the end, as the British had imagined. They were rather put out. 'The Generalissimo reminded me more of a cross between a pine marten and a ferret,' Brooke wrote. 'A shrewd, foxy sort of face. Evidently with no grasp of war in its large aspects, but determined to get the best of the bargains.' To the added bemusement of British generals, Madame Chiang Kai-shek, dressed in a striking black cheongsam slit to the hip, intervened frequently to correct the translator's version of what the generalissimo had said, and then proceeded to give her own interpretation of what he should have said. Stalin, still resenting the setback over Sinkiang, had refused to send a representative to the conference on the grounds that he still had a non-aggression pact with Japan.

Churchill was all too aware that his 'special relationship' with Roosevelt had been downgraded. This was partly due to his own reluctance to commit to Operation Overlord, and his yearning to strike into central Europe to pre-empt a Soviet occupation. Churchill was also out on a limb in his emotional attachment to the British Empire. Roosevelt, declaring his agreement with Chiang Kai-shek that western imperialism in Asia should come to an end with victory over Japan, promised that Indochina would not be returned to France, a proposal which would have infuriated de Gaulle if he had known of it. Throughout the conference the atmosphere was far from friendly, and at times it was openly hostile. The Americans were determined not to be led down any more 'garden paths', especially if they headed away from Normandy and towards the Balkans. The British found the Americans deaf to their arguments, and they became suspicious of how Roosevelt would play things at Teheran, when he would have Stalin to back him up on the key issues.

Roosevelt and Churchill flew on from Cairo to Teheran for their meeting with Stalin, which began on 28 November. Roosevelt, at Stalin's express request, was housed in part of the Soviet embassy, just across the road from the British embassy. Stalin went to see him dressed in his marshal's uniform, with the trousers tucked into Caucasian boots built up to make him look taller. The two statesmen set out to charm each other with a show of easy intimacy, which swayed only Roosevelt.

The President tried to curry favour with the Soviet dictator at Churchill's expense. He raised the question of colonialism. 'I am speaking about this in the absence of our comrade-in-arms Churchill, since he does not like discussing the subject. The United States and the Soviet Union are not colonial powers, and it is easier for us to discuss these matters.' According to Stalin's interpreter at this tête-à-tête Stalin was not keen on discussing such 'a delicate subject', but he agreed that 'India is Churchill's sore spot'. Yet for all the President's efforts to establish mutual confidence, Stalin could not forget his disingenuous promise to open a Second Front in 1942, simply to keep the Soviet Union in the war.

Stalin did, however, express himself strongly on the subject of France, following unrest in Lebanon where Free French troops had tried to reassert colonial power. He regarded the majority of the French as collaborators and even said that France 'must be punished for its aid to the Germans'. Stalin was no doubt still thinking of the way that the surrender of the French army in 1940 had furnished the Wehrmacht with the majority of its vehicles for the invasion of the Soviet Union a year later.

When the plenary session started late that afternoon, the main subject for debate was Operation Overlord. Stalin, with Roosevelt's tacit support, dealt with Churchill's desire for an operation in the northern Adriatic aimed at central Europe. He insisted on the primacy of Overlord, and agreed with the plan for a simultaneous invasion of southern France. He firmly rejected any other operation as a dispersal of force. Stalin greeted with amusement Churchill's attempt to claim that his plan would help the Red Army. According to the Soviet interpreter, Roosevelt winked at the Soviet leader as he broke up Herzegovina Flor cigarettes to fill his pipe. Stalin felt able to torment Churchill quietly on this issue, because he knew that the Americans were against the idea, and in any case he held all the cards when it came to determining Allied strategy. His insistence on keeping the Allies to their promise of a major invasion of France in the spring of 1944 meant that their advance through northern Europe would, as Churchill feared, leave the Balkans and central Europe under the control of the Red Army.

Watching the three leaders interact, General Brooke was deeply impressed by Stalin's handling of the discussion. The dictator remained dismissive of the campaign in Italy, probably because he was irritated that his allies had not involved the Soviet Union in the Italian surrender. This turned out to be a mistake on their part, because Stalin was able to use it later as an argument when it came to discussing the future of countries occupied by the Red Army. Stalin, very conscious of the fact that the victories at Stalingrad and Kursk had turned the Soviet Union into a superpower, had already boasted to his entourage that 'Now the fate of Europe is settled, we shall do as we like, with the Allies' consent.'

He was also well briefed on British and American thinking and reactions. Before the meeting, Stalin had summoned Beria's son Sergo and entrusted him with 'a mission that is delicate and morally reprehensible'. He wanted to know everything that the Americans and the British said in private. Their every word would be recorded by the microphones hidden in their rooms, and each morning Sergo Beria had to report to Stalin on all the conversations. The Soviet leader was amazed by the naivety of the Allies in talking so openly, when surely they must realize that they were being bugged. He wanted to know the tone of voice used as well as the content. Did they speak with conviction or without enthusiasm, and how did Roosevelt react?

Stalin was pleased when Sergo Beria reported on the genuine admiration which Roosevelt had for him and on his refusal to listen to Admiral Leahy's advice to take a firmer line. But whenever Churchill flattered Stalin during the conference, the Soviet leader retorted by reminding him of some hostile remark he had made in the past. The secret recordings also helped him exploit the differences between Churchill and Roosevelt. Apparently, when Churchill remonstrated in private with Roosevelt that he was helping Stalin to install a Communist government in Poland, Roosevelt had replied that Churchill was supporting an anti-Communist government, so what was the difference?

Poland was indeed a major issue for both Churchill and Stalin, while Roosevelt seemed concerned only with securing the American Polish vote in the next year's presidential elections. This meant appearing to be tough with Stalin until after the results of the voting were established. Considering that Roosevelt had earlier rejected any idea of changing Poland's frontiers on the basis of the Atlantic Charter, both he and Churchill now felt obliged to consider Stalin's claim to the eastern part of the country, which he had absorbed in 1939 as 'western Belorussia' and 'western Ukraine'. The rapidly approaching occupation of the region by the Red Army would make it a fait accompli. According to Stalin's plan, Poland would be compensated with German territory up to the River Oder. The President and prime minister knew that they would never be able to force the Soviets to disgorge such a prize, but the manner in which Roosevelt conceded encouraged Stalin to believe that he would have no trouble in imposing a Communist government on the Poles.

Stalin succeeded in extracting a date for the invasion of France, but when the Americans and British were forced to admit that a supreme commander had not yet been appointed, he showed his contempt for such a lack of serious planning. He agreed, however, to launch a major offensive soon after the landings and declared his intention to join the war against Japan as soon as Germany was defeated. This was exactly what Roosevelt had wanted, even though Chiang Kai-shek dreaded it. After the conference was over, Stalin considered that he had 'won the game'. In private, Churchill would have agreed with that assessment. He was utterly dejected by Roosevelt's constant siding with Stalin in the belief that he could handle him. 'Now he sees that he cannot rely on the President's support,' the prime minister's doctor Lord Moran wrote in his diary after Churchill had poured out his fears for the future. 'What matters more, he realizes that the Russians see this too.'

After the humiliating moment about Overlord at the Teheran conference, Roosevelt was determined to appoint the supreme commander when he and Allied delegates returned to Cairo. He asked Marshall to summon General Eisenhower. As soon as Eisenhower and Roosevelt were installed in the President's automobile, Roosevelt turned to him and said: 'Well, Ike, you are going to command Overlord.' Roosevelt had decided that he could not afford to lose Marshall as chief of staff because of his knowledge of all theatres, his superb talent for organization and above all for his skill in dealing with Congress. He was also seen to be the only person who could keep General MacArthur under control in the Pacific. Marshall was disappointed (although not as disappointed as Brooke had been), but loyally accepted the decision. Eisenhower's good fortune seemed to bear out Patton's private nickname for him, 'Divine Destiny', based on the initials of his two first names.

An irrational euphoria reigned among the Allied chiefs of staff in Cairo. They all seemed certain that the war would be over by March, or at the latest November, of 1944, and were prepared to place bets on it. Considering that they were over six months from launching Overlord, and that the Red Army was still several hundred kilometres from Berlin, this was over-optimistic to say the least. Churchill, on the other hand, was totally exhausted after all the bruising battles in Cairo and Teheran. He collapsed with pneumonia in Tunisia and came close to death. His recovery was aided over Christmas by a little brandy, and by the news that the Royal Navy had sunk the battle-cruiser *Scharnhorst* off northern Norway. Nearly 2,000 sailors of the Kriegsmarine perished in the freezing seas.

As Stalin had emphasized at Teheran, Vatutin's forces were facing constant counter-attacks from Manstein's Army Group South. Manstein, hoping to rework his coup at Kharkov earlier in the year, sent two panzer corps against the flanks of Vatutin's renamed 1st Ukrainian Front. He wanted to force the Soviets back to the Dnepr, retake Kiev and encircle a major Red Army formation near Korosten.

Hitler, who had aged dramatically over the last months and was suffering from stress, had entered an even deeper state of denial. He rejected any suggestion of retreat. Even his favourite, General Model, described their situation on the eastern front as 'fighting in reverse gear'. A sense of fatalism was infecting the German army. An infantry officer captured on the Leningrad front acknowledged during his interrogation: 'We are living in filth. It is hopeless.' Yet while Hitler blamed his generals and a lack of will for every reverse, he was deeply unsettled by the propaganda disseminated at the front by the Soviet organization of 'anti-fascist' German prisoners of war, Freies Deutschland. This prompted him on 22 December to establish the post of National Socialist leadership officer in all units, as a counterpart to the Soviet commissar or political officer.

Three days later Manstein, who thought that he had stabilized the front, received a very unpleasant surprise. The Red Army had brought up the 1st Tank and 3rd Guards Tank Armies near Brusilov without being spotted, and on Christmas Day they charged through towards Zhitomir and Berdichev. Shortly afterwards Konev's 2nd Ukrainian Front to the south also broke through, and soon two German corps still holding the line of the Dnepr south-east of Kiev were surrounded in the Korsun pocket. Hitler refused to allow them to retreat, and their fate was to be among the cruellest suffered by the Wehrmacht on the eastern front.

34

The Shoah by Gas

1942–1944

The scope of Heydrich's plan outlined at the Wannsee conference in January 1942 had been breathtaking. As one of his close colleagues confirmed, he possessed 'insatiable ambition, intelligence and ruthless energy'. The Final Solution was intended to encompass more than eleven million Jews, according to Adolf Eichmann's calculations. This figure included those in neutral countries, such as Turkey, Portugal and Ireland, as well as in Great Britain, Germany's undefeated enemy.

The fact that these deliberations took place within a few weeks of the Wehrmacht's setback before Moscow and the entry of the United States into the war suggests either that the Nazis' confidence in 'final victory' was unshaken or that they felt impelled to complete the 'historic task' before further setbacks rendered it impossible. The answer was probably a combination of the two. Certainly, the prospect of victory in the late summer of 1941 had contributed to the dramatic radicalization of Nazi policy. And now that world events had reached a critical point, there would be no turning back. The 'Shoah by bullets' thus advanced to the 'Shoah by gas'.

As with the Hunger Plan and the treatment of Soviet prisoners of war, the Final Solution contained a double purpose. As well as eliminating racial and ideological enemies, the other objective was to preserve food supplies for Germans. This was regarded as all the more urgent because of the huge numbers of foreign workers brought back to the Reich for labour. The Final Solution itself would consist of a parallel system of elimination through forced labour and immediate killing, both carried out by the SS *Totenkopfverbände* (Death's Head Units). The only Jews exempted for the moment would be those elderly or prominent Jews selected for the show-ghetto of Theresienstadt, those who were workers with essential skills or half-Jews and those in mixed marriages. Their fates could be decided later.

The extermination camp of Chełmno (Kulmhof) was already in operation, Bełżec soon followed and so did the complex at Auschwitz-Birkenau. At Chełmno, gas vans were used for killing Jews from towns in the region. In January 1942, some 4,400 Roma brought from Austria were also taken there and gassed. The corpses were buried in the forest by teams of selected Jews guarded by Ordnungspolizei. Chełmno would be the centre for the mass killing of the Jews still packed into the ghetto at Łódź, fifty-five kilometres to the south.

The camp at Bełżec, between Lublin and Lwów, was considered a step forward, since it had gas chambers constructed to use carbon monoxide from vehicles stationed outside. After the test killing in January of 150 Jews, the gassing of mainly Galician Jews began there in mid-March. The camp of Majdanek was built on the very edge of Lublin.

Auschwitz, or Oświęcim in its Polish version, had been a Silesian town near Kraków, with a nineteenth-century cavalry barracks from the days of the Austro-Hungarian Empire. The barracks had been taken over in 1940 as a prison camp by the SS to hold Polish prisoners. This was known as Auschwitz I. It was here that the first tests of Zyklon B – pellets of hydrogen cyanide designed to gas vermin – had been carried out in September 1941 on Soviet and Polish prisoners.

At the end of 1941 work began at nearby Birkenau, known as Auschwitz II. A pair of peasant houses were converted into improvised gas chambers, which were put to use in March 1942. Only in May did the killings start on a significant scale, but by October it became clear to the SS commandant Rudolf Höss that the facilities were totally insufficient and that mass burial was polluting the groundwater. A completely new system of gas chambers and furnaces was built during the winter.

Although Auschwitz was isolated in an area of swamp, rivers and birchwoods, the site had good access to rail communications. This was one of the reasons why the chemical conglomerate IG Farben became interested in establishing a factory there for the production of buna, or synthetic rubber. Himmler, wanting to Germanize the region, promoted the idea enthusiastically, offering labour from the concentration camp prisoners. He even went in person to brief Höss and liaise with representatives of IG Farben. Surprised by the immense size of the project and the large number of slave labourers required, Himmler told Höss that his camp would have to triple in size from its present strength of 10,000 prisoners. The SS treasury stood to gain up to 4 Reichsmark a day for each slave provided to IG Farben. In return, the SS would select violent and ruthless *kapos* from among criminal prisoners elsewhere to beat the Jewish slaves and make them work harder.

Construction of the vast Buna-Werke went ahead in the summer of 1941, while German divisions to the east appeared to be triumphing over the Soviet Union. Still short of labour, Himmler arranged to take an initial 10,000 Red Army prisoners off the Wehrmacht in October. Höss himself wrote before his execution for war crimes that they had arrived in very poor condition. 'They had been given hardly any food on the march, during halts on the way being simply turned out into the nearest fields and there told to "graze" like cattle on anything edible they could find.' Working through the depths of the winter, with little clothing and reduced in some cases to cannibalism, all of the exhausted and diseased prisoners 'died like flies', as Höss wrote. 'They were no longer human beings,' he explained. 'They had become animals, who sought only food.' Not surprisingly, they had been unable to construct more than a couple of barrack blocks, instead of the twenty-eight laid down.

The SS strategy of death through labour was even less cost-effective than in Beria's Gulag punishment camps. The Nazis' only concession to pragmatism was to build a new camp – Auschwitz III or Monowitz – adjoining the Buna-Werke, so that IG Farben's slaves did not have to waste time marching so far. Yet SS guards and *kapos* in this semi-privatized concentration camp continued to beat their labourers, as if that could force them to complete projects far beyond their means and strength.

After the war the directors of IG Farben, which partly owned the manufacturer of Zyklon B, claimed to have known nothing about the mass murder of Jews. Yet IG Farben's huge Buna-Werke complex was managed by 2,500 German employees from the Reich, who lived in the town and associated with the SS guards at

Auschwitz-Birkenau. One of them, just after he arrived, asked an SS guard about the appalling smell which spread over the whole area. The SS man replied that it was Bolshevik Jews 'going up the chimney at Birkenau'.

In May 1942, as ever increasing transports of Jews arrived at Auschwitz, the SS moved the remaining Polish political prisoners to forced labour in Germany. On 17 July, Himmler arrived to inspect the growing Auschwitz complex. As his limousine swept through the gate of Auschwitz I, the camp orchestra of Jewish musicians began to play the triumphal march from Verdi's *Aida*.

The Reichsführer-SS stepped out of the car, halted to listen to the music, and then returned Höss's salute. Together, they inspected a guard of honour of prisoners in freshly issued striped uniforms. Himmler, with his spectacles and weak chin, contemplated them in cold detachment as he passed. Höss accompanied him to the works office to show him the latest plans for new gas chambers and crematoria. Afterwards, Himmler, with his entourage, went to the railway siding to watch the unloading of a transport of Dutch Jews, as the camp orchestra played again. 'People were deceived at first by the illusion of order and music being played,' a Free French officer deported to Auschwitz later testified to the Red Army. 'But soon they smelt the dead bodies and when prisoners were separated according to their physical state, they soon guessed.'

First, the men were divided from the women and children, a splitting of families which caused much unrest, until dog-handlers and whip-wielding guards dealt with the disturbance. Himmler particularly wanted to see the selection process carried out on the 'ramp' by two SS doctors, choosing those who appeared fit for labour, and the unfit who were to be eliminated immediately. Those selected for labour were no more fortunate than those killed immediately. They too would be gassed or worked to death in the next two or three months.

Himmler followed the group selected for the gas chambers in Bunker No. 1, and watched through a small window as they died. He also looked for any effect on the SS personnel, having been so disturbed by the psychological strain imposed on the Einsatzgruppen the year before. He then observed the Jews in the work commando dispose of the bodies and told Höss that in future he should burn the corpses instead. Himmler, who shuddered at the thought of animals killed en masse in abattoirs, simply took a professional interest in the massacre of what he regarded as human vermin. 'It is not a *Weltanschauungs*-question to rid oneself of lice,' he later wrote to one of his subordinates. 'It is a matter of hygiene.' Himmler had the aseptic air of a dentist, although he revelled in neo-Gothic warrior fantasies, trying to portray the SS as an order of knights.

From Auschwitz-Birkenau, his party drove the short distance to visit the Buna-Werke at Auschwitz-Monowitz. IG Farben was responsible for the deaths of tens of thousands of forced labourers, yet the huge Buna-Werke complex never managed to produce any synthetic rubber at all. The company also financed the inhuman experiments at Auschwitz-Birkenau of Hauptsturmführer Dr Josef Mengele on children, especially identical twins, but also on adults. Apart from removing organs, sterilizing and deliberately infecting his carefully selected victims with diseases, Mengele was also testing 'prototype serums and drugs – many of which were supplied by IG Farben's Bayer pharmaceutical division'.

Mengele was not alone. Dr Helmuth Vetter, although also a member of the SS, was employed by IG Farben at Auschwitz. He carried out experiments on women. When IG Farben asked Höss for 150 women prisoners for Vetter's experiments, he demanded a fee of 200 Reichsmark per guinea pig, but IG Farben held the price down to 170 RM. Every single woman died, as the company confirmed in a letter to Höss. Vetter was thrilled with his work. 'I have the opportunity to test our new preparations,' he wrote to a colleague. 'I feel like I am in paradise.' Dangerous pharmaceutical tests were also carried out on prisoners at Mauthausen and Buchenwald concentration camps. IG Farben was particularly keen to discover an effective method of chemical castration, to be used in the occupied territories of the Soviet Union.

Himmler also strongly supported the sterilization experiments of Professor Karl Clauberg at Auschwitz. The grotesque perversion of a doctor's duties under Nazism, in which many leading German medical practitioners acquiesced, provides a chilling example of how the prospect of almost unlimited power and prestige in secret studies can distort the judgement of intelligent people. These doctors tried to justify their needlessly cruel experiments as research to help mankind at large. Significantly, in a conscious or unconscious symbiosis with the medical profession, Nazi Germany and other dictatorships of the period often adopted surgical metaphors, particularly the cutting of cancerous growths out of the body politic. And as an example of the Nazis' sick sense of humour and compulsive deception, the supplies of Zyklon B were delivered in vans marked with the Red Cross.

In spite of the oath of secrecy imposed on SS officers and men about their activities word was bound to spread, sometimes in astonishing ways. In the late summer of 1942 Obersturmführer Dr Kurt Gerstein, an SS gas expert, was so disturbed by what he had just seen on a tour of inspection that on a night express from Warsaw to Berlin he poured out everything he knew in a darkened compartment to Baron von Otter, a Swedish diplomat. Otter reported all this back to the foreign ministry in Stockholm, but the Swedish government, unwilling to provoke the Nazis, simply sat on the information. News of the death camps, however, soon began to reach the Allies through other channels, mainly the Polish Home Army.

Rudolf Höss, the commandant of Auschwitz, could hardly have been more different from the intellectual elite of the SS, mainly concentrated in the Sicherheitsdienst. Höss was a stolid, middle-aged former soldier, who had risen through the ranks of the concentration camp system without ever questioning an order. Primo Levi put him down not as 'a monster' or 'a sadist', but as 'a coarse, stupid, arrogant, long-winded scoundrel'. Höss was totally obsequious towards superiors, above all the Reichsführer-SS, whom he regarded as almost as great a god as the Führer himself. The lack of imagination shown in Höss's own account beggars belief as he upholds family values, with his own exemplary home life, while day after day destroying thousands and thousands of other families.

Verging on self-pity, he complains about the low quality of the SS personnel sent to Auschwitz and especially the *kapos* recruited from the ranks of ordinary criminal prisoners. They were known as 'greens' because of the colour of their identifying triangle. (Jews wore yellow triangles, political prisoners wore red, Spanish Republicans in Mauthausen wore dark blue, and homosexuals a pinkish mauve.) These *kapos*, in particular the women criminals in charge of a punishment detachment outside the camp at Budy, were renowned for their cruelty. 'I find it incredible that human beings could ever turn into such beasts,' wrote Höss. 'The way the "greens" knocked the French Jewesses about, tearing them to pieces, killing them with axes, and throttling them – it was simply gruesome.'

Yet for all his professed horror at the cruelty of the *kapos*, Höss still provided the male ones with a camp 'brothel'. This was in a hut where Jewish female prisoners were kept for their sadistic pleasure until they too were sent to the gas chamber. At the other end of the scale, the most privileged female prisoners were Jehovah's Witnesses, known as 'Bible-worms', who had been sent to the camps because their beliefs rejected military service in any form. SS officers used them as servants in their homes and messes. Höss had one working as a nanny looking after his small children. They were so reliable that the SS did not complain when they refused to clean or even touch their uniforms out of their pacifist principles.

The women inside the camp were kept in order by dog-handlers of the Hundestaffel. Apparently they were more frightened than male prisoners were of the snarling beasts, which handlers let off the leash from time to time for fun. It may well have been the presence of the dog-handlers which deterred women from opting for the easiest way for the male prisoners to commit suicide, which was to 'run into the wire' in the hope that the guards would shoot straight. The women were more likely to have the dogs let loose on them instead.

Women could be more complicated, Höss noted. One of the problems in the changing rooms for the gas chambers was that 'many of the women hid their babies among the piles of clothing'. So the Jewish labour detail was sent in to check. They had to throw any babies they found into the gas chamber just before the doors were slammed shut and bolted.

Höss was intrigued by the obedience shown by these Jewish prisoners, whose lives had been temporarily spared in a Faustian pact. He tried to portray them as willing accomplices. In fact, the desperate will to live overcame normal morality, a phenomenon no longer imaginable in the squalor and degradation of

Auschwitz, and even eclipsed the certain knowledge of their own imminent death. Few of them ever warned the new arrivals of what was about to happen. The Nazis, through total inhumanity, had created the conditions for that unfettered social-Darwinism in which they professed to believe.

This crushing of all social instincts and loyalties, combined with the unreal nightmare of their horrific work, was bound to have a brutalizing effect. 'They carried out all these tasks with a callous indifference,' wrote Höss, 'as though it were all part of an ordinary day's work. While they dragged the corpses about, they ate or they smoked. They did not stop eating even when engaged on the grisly job of burning corpses which had been lying for some time in mass graves.'

The most privileged male prisoners were those who worked in the warehouse called 'Kanada', the department which sorted the possessions, clothes, shoes and spectacles, and bundled up the bales of human hair. Yet they too knew that they were simply the living dead. Eventually, in the autumn of 1944, the Kanada *Sonderkommando* of Jewish prisoners attempted an armed uprising and breakout from Auschwitz-Birkenau. Four SS men died, and 455 prisoners were shot down.

As well as the extermination camps built at Chełmno, Bełżec and Auschwitz-Birkenau, other killing centres were prepared at Treblinka and Sobibór. This programme was called Aktion Reinhard in honour of the assassinated Heydrich.

Obergruppenführer Oswald Pohl of the SS Economic-Administrative Main Office (Wirtschaftsverwaltungshauptamt) took on responsibility for supervising and coordinating their activities, a difficult task with all the rival Nazi factions. Pohl, a dedicated bureaucrat, was determined to make the whole process as efficient and profitable as possible. All the victims' valuables had to be collected and accounted for, but the corruption in some of the camps dismayed and horrified Himmler. Gold from their teeth needed to be extracted before the bodies were buried or burned. Clothes, shoes, spectacles, suitcases and underwear were all collected and transported back to the Reich so that they could be reissued to the needy, usually those who had lost everything in a bombing raid. Hair fibre, harvested from victims before they entered the gas chamber, supposedly had better heat-retention properties than wool, so was woven into socks for Luftwaffe aircrew and U-boat personnel, but the bulk of it became mattress stuffing. U-boat crews on their return from the Atlantic would find a crate of watches waiting for them as a present. They soon worked out the source of this largesse.

Successful mass killing depended on the uninterrupted flow of a conveyor belt, delivering the victims naked and without fuss to the gas chamber. But on the slave-labour side of the system, Pohl would never be able to resolve the fundamental problem of the concentration camp. If you are trying to kill your labour force through ill-treatment, you cannot extract effective work from them, as was shown time and time again.

Vasily Grossman's study of Treblinka, carried out in the summer of 1944, underlined the importance of flow. Grossman was allowed to sit in with Red Army interrogators when they interviewed captured guards, Polish locals and forty survivors of the work camp Treblinka I. (Treblinka II was the adjacent extermination camp.) He immediately perceived this to be the key aspect of the Nazis' system. Never before in human history had so many people been killed by so few executioners. At Treblinka a staff of about twenty-five SS men and around a hundred Ukrainian auxiliary *Wachmänner* managed to kill some 800,000 Jews and 'Gypsies' – equivalent, as Grossman put it, to the population of 'a small European capital city' – between July 1942 and August 1943.

The most important contributions to the smooth running of the operation were secrecy and deception. 'People were told that they were being taken to Ukraine to work in agriculture.' The victims should not know their real fate until the very last moment. To ensure this, not even the guards who accompanied the trains were allowed to know the truth or enter the central area of the camp.

At Treblinka, 'the railroad dead-end siding was made to look like a passenger station ... with a ticket office, baggage room and restaurant hall. There were arrows everywhere, indicating "To Bialystok", "To Baranovichi". By the time the train arrived, there would be a band playing in the station building, and all the musicians were dressed well.' Once rumours began to circulate about Treblinka, the name of the station was changed to Ober-Maidan.

Not everyone was taken in. The sharp-eyed and the inquisitive soon spotted that something was wrong, whether personal objects abandoned on the square beyond the station, which had not been cleared properly by the work detail after the previous transport, or the high wall, or the railway track which led nowhere. The SS had learned to exploit the instinctive optimism of most people, desperate to hope that things must be better here than in the ghetto or the transit camp from which they had come. On a very few occasions, however, the intended victims guessed their fate and knocked down the guards when they opened the doors of the cattle trucks. Machine guns cut them down as they stampeded towards the forest.

Ordered to leave their luggage in the square, the crowd of three or four thousand in the new transport worried whether they would ever find it again in the confusion. In a loud voice, the SS Unteroffizier would order them to bring just their valuables, their documents and their wash things for the showers. Anxiety increased as the families were shepherded by armed guards, some grinning wolfishly, through a gate in a six-metre-high barbed-wire fence covered by machine-gun posts. Behind them in the station square, 'work Jews' from Treblinka I were already sorting through their belongings, selecting what to keep for despatch back to Germany and what to burn. They had to be careful if they surreptitiously crammed some food from a suitcase into their mouths. A Ukrainian guard would drag them off for a savage beating or shoot them.

In a second square, close to the centre of the camp, the old and sick were led off to an exit marked 'Sanatorium', where a doctor in white with a Red Cross armband awaited them. The SS Scharführer in charge then told the remainder of the crowd to separate, with women and children going to undress in the barracks to the left. This was when much wailing began, as families naturally feared a permanent separation. But, knowing this, the SS stepped up the pressure, with short, sharp commands: 'Achtung!' and 'Schneller!' Then, 'Men stay here! Women and children undress in the barracks on the left!'

Any outpouring of grief was cut off by more shouted commands, but also by an insinuation of hope that everything was normal after all. 'Women and children must take off their shoes when entering the barracks. Stockings must be put into shoes. Children's stockings into their sandals, boots and shoes. Be tidy! ... Going to the bath-house, you must have your documents, money, a towel and soap. I repeat . . .'

The women in the barracks had to remove their clothes and then submit their heads to be sheared, supposedly as a precaution against lice. Naked, they had to hand in their documents, money, jewellery and watches at a booth where another SS Unteroffizier presided. As Grossman observed, 'a naked person immediately loses the strength to resist, to struggle against his fate'. There were nevertheless a few exceptions. A young Jew from the Warsaw ghetto, connected to the resistance, managed to conceal a hand-grenade which he threw at one group of SS and Ukrainians. Another hid a knife, with which he stabbed a *Wachmann*. And a tall young woman surprised another by seizing his carbine to fight back. But she was overpowered and killed later after the most terrible tortures.

Now that the victims could have little further doubt that their death was imminent, the SS in grey uniforms and the *Wachmänner* in black began to shout more loudly and insistently to confuse them and hurry them. 'Schneller! Schneller!' They were herded into a sand-covered alley between fir trees to conceal the barbed wire behind. Ordered to raise their hands above their heads, they were forced forward with truncheons, whips and blows from sub-machine guns. The Germans called this 'The Road of No Return'.

Gratuitous sadism increased the shock effect, reducing the chance of a last-minute attempt to rebel. But the guards in question also acted from a monstrously perverted pleasure. One immensely strong SS man known as 'Zepf' would seize a child by the legs 'like a cudgel' and smash his or her head against the ground. Forced into a third square, the victims saw the temple-like façade in stone and wood which concealed the gas chambers behind. Apparently a group of naive Roma women, who still had no idea of their fate, clasped their hands in wonder as they admired the building, which prompted the SS and the Ukrainian guards to collapse in laughter.

To force their prisoners into the gas chambers, the guards unleashed their dogs. The screams as they sank their teeth into the prisoners were apparently heard for miles around. One of the captured guards told Grossman: 'They could see their death coming, and besides, it was very crowded there. They were beaten terribly, and dogs were tearing their bodies.' Silence fell only once the heavy doors of the ten gas chambers were closed. Twenty-five minutes after the gas was introduced, the doors at the back would be opened and working parties of prisoners from Treblinka I began to remove the yellow-faced bodies. Another group of Jewish prisoners would then be made to extract gold-capped teeth with pliers. They may have survived longer than the corpses they had to deal with, but they were not to be envied. 'It was a luxury to get a bullet,' one of the few survivors said to Grossman.

Packed into the gas chambers, the victims took up to twenty or even twenty-five minutes to die. The chief guard, watching through a glass peep-hole, waited until there was no more movement. The large doors at the far end from the entrance were opened and the bodies dragged out. If any showed signs of life, the SS Unteroffizier administered a rapid coup de grâce with his pistol. Then he would signal to the tooth party to get to work with their pliers, extracting gold teeth. Finally, another work party of temporarily reprieved Jews from Treblinka I would load the corpses on to carts or trolleys to take them to where steam-powered excavators had been digging another line of mass graves.

The old and the sick, meanwhile, who had been diverted into the 'Sanatorium', were finished off with a Kopfschuss or pistol shot in the back of the head. 'Work Jews' from Treblinka I dragged their bodies to pits. But, as at Auschwitz, these temporary survivors were hardly to be envied. They too were subject to an unbelievable sadism, from the shooting of prisoners to the rape of young Jewish women, who were killed afterwards. German SS guards forced the prisoners to sing a special 'Treblinka' hymn which one of them had composed. Grossman also noted details in Treblinka I of 'the one-eyed German from Odessa, Svidersky, whose nickname was "Master Hammer". He was considered the unsurpassed specialist in "cold" death, and it was he who had killed, in the course of several minutes, fifteen children aged from eight to thirteen who had been declared unfit for work.'

Early in 1943, Himmler visited Treblinka and ordered the commandant to have all the bodies dug up and burned. The ashes were to be spread far and wide. It seems that after the Stalingrad campaign the SS hierarchy were suddenly forced to contemplate the consequences if the Red Army discovered the sites of their mass murders. The putrefied corpses, up to 4,000 at a time, were spread across lengths of rail track laid over huge firepits, known as 'roasts'. There was such a backlog of corpses to deal with that the work continued for eight months.

The 800 'work Jews' forced to carry out this grisly task had their revenge. They knew that they would never be allowed to live once all the bodies were burned. On 2 August 1943, during a long heatwave, they staged an uprising led by Zelo Bloch, a Jewish lieutenant from the Czech army. Armed with little more than spades and axes, they attacked the watchtowers and guard room, killing sixteen SS and *Wachmänner*. They set fire to part of the camp and stormed the fences. In the mass breakout of about 750 men which followed, the SS brought in reinforcements and men with tracker dogs to comb the woods and marshes. Spotter aircraft flew constantly overhead. Some 550 were brought back and murdered in the camp, while others were shot on the spot when discovered. Only seventy survived until the arrival of the Red Army the following year.

But the revolt marked the end of Treblinka. The rest of the buildings, including the gas chambers and the fake railway station, were destroyed. The last ashes from the firepits were spread, and then, in a grotesque attempt to pretend that the camp had never existed, lupins were sown all over the site. But as Grossman observed, walking there, 'the earth is throwing out crushed bones, teeth, clothes, papers. It does not want to keep its secrets.'

Treblinka established a far more intense killing cycle than Auschwitz-Birkenau. Its death toll of 800,000, achieved over thirteen months, was not very far short of the million killed at Auschwitz-Birkenau over thirty-three months. While Treblinka received mainly Polish Jews, with just some from the Reich and others from Bulgaria, Auschwitz-Birkenau received its victims from all over Europe. As well as Polish Jews, they came from the Netherlands, Belgium, France, Greece, Italy, Norway, Croatia and later Hungary. Bełżec accounted for some 550,000 people, mainly Polish Jews. The camp at Sobibór, where some 200,000 died, dealt with the Jews from the region of Lublin, but also some from the Netherlands, France and Belorussia. Another 150,000 mainly Polish Jews died in Chełmno, and 50,000 Polish and French Jews in Majdanek.

On 6 October 1943, Himmler addressed Reichsleiters and Gauleiters at a conference in Posen. Grossadmiral Dönitz, Generalfeldmarschall Milch and Albert Speer (although he tried to deny it for the rest of his life) also heard his speech. For once dropping the standard euphemisms of the Final Solution – such as 'evacuated east' and 'special treatment' – Himmler was at last frank with outsiders about what they were doing. 'We faced the question: what should we do with the women and children? I decided here too to find a completely clear solution. I did not regard myself as justified in exterminating the men – that is to say to kill them or have them killed – and to allow the avengers in the shape of the children to grow up for our sons and grandsons. The difficult decision had to be taken, to have this people disappear from this earth.'

On 25 January 1944, Himmler addressed nearly 200 generals and admirals, once again in Posen. They too needed to be aware of the sacrifices which the SS had been making. The 'race struggle' carried out by his 'ideological troops', Himmler again explained, would not 'allow avengers to arise for our children'. In this total elimination of the Jews there would be no exceptions.

Himmler could have boasted to his audience how so few of his men had managed to murder so many. Through a mixture of outright deception, uncertainty and then unspeakable cruelty, the minute force of persecutors had succeeded in killing nearly three million victims, unable to believe that extermination camps could exist in Europe, supposedly the cradle of civilization.

35

Italy – The Hard Underbelly

OCTOBER 1943–MARCH 1944

The Allied invasion of mainland Italy in September 1943 had seemed a good idea at the time, with the collapse of Fascism and the promise of airfields. Yet there had been a distinct lack of clear thinking about the objectives of the campaign and how these would be achieved. Alexander, the commander of the Allied 15th Army Group in Italy, failed to coordinate the operations of General Mark Clark's Fifth Army and General Bernard Montgomery's Eighth Army. Clark was still far from happy with the slowness of Montgomery's advance to relieve him at Salerno, despite all the cheerful messages saying 'Hang on we're coming!' To make matters worse, Montgomery somehow seemed to believe that he had saved the Fifth Army at Salerno.

Allied relations were not helped by the fact that both the short, wiry Monty and the tall, gangling Clark should be so obsessed with their image. Clark, who soon increased his public relations team to fifty men, insisted that photographers should capture his most flattering profile with its truly imperial nose. Some of his officers dubbed him Marcus Aurelius Clarkus. And Monty had started to hand out signed photographs of himself as if he were a movie star.

Over them, the charming but diffident 'Alex' seemed to think that planning could be made up as they went along, an attitude which certainly suited Churchill, who wanted to keep the Italian campaign going far beyond what the Americans envisaged. Montgomery, on the other hand, did not like to do anything unless it had been carefully worked out in advance. 'There was as yet', he wrote acerbically in his diary, 'no plan known to me for developing the war in Italy, but I was quite used to that!' But, as Alexander knew from experience, Montgomery would in any case do only what he wanted to do. As his biographer remarked, Alexander played the part of 'an understanding husband in a difficult marriage'. Eisenhower also failed to get a grip on his subordinates and failed to establish any clarity in thinking about what they were trying to do in Italy.

The real problem, of course, came from the very top, and the central disagreement which had dogged Allied strategy since 1942. Roosevelt and Marshall were determined that nothing should delay Overlord. Churchill and Brooke, on the other hand, still saw the Mediterranean as the vital theatre for the time being, where the surrender of Italian troops should be exploited. In fact both men, who remained nervous of a cross-Channel invasion without air supremacy, half hoped that a run of successes in the Mediterranean might provide a good excuse to delay Overlord. The only senior American officer who agreed with them was General Spaatz, the US air force commander in the Mediterranean. Like Harris, Spaatz believed that bombing alone could win the war in three months and 'didn't think Overlord was necessary or desirable'. He wanted to continue the advance in Italy, across the River Po and even into Austria so as to get his bombers closer to Germany.

Churchill had undoubtedly been right to push for Torch and Husky against all of Marshall's opposition. Even if motivated by the wrong reasons, he had at least prevented a disastrous attempt to invade France in 1943. But he was now starting to lose all credibility with the Americans, thanks to his new obsession with retaking Rhodes and other islands in the Aegean which had been occupied by the Italians. General Marshall naturally suspected that this island-hopping in the eastern Mediterranean was part of a secret plan to invade the Balkans. Not surprisingly, he vigorously refused any American help or involvement whatsoever.

Even Brooke, who supported the Italian campaign and other operations in the region, feared that the prime minister had become completely unbalanced by what he called his 'Rhodes madness'. 'He has worked himself into a frenzy of excitement about the Rhodes attack, has magnified its importance so that he can no longer see anything else and has set his heart on capturing this one island even at the expense of endangering his relations with the President and with the Americans, and also the whole future of the Italian campaign . . . The Americans are already desperately suspicious of him, and this will make matters far worse.'

Wishful thinking that the Allies would soon be in Rome had infected American commanders as well as Churchill. Mark Clark was absolutely determined to be crowned as its conqueror, and even Eisenhower believed that the Italian capital would fall by the end of October. Alexander declared unwisely that they would be in Florence by Christmas. But there were already clear indications that the Germans would fight ruthlessly in retreat and take their revenge on Italian troops and partisans, who were actively helping the Allies.

East of Naples, in a village near Acerra, B Squadron of the 11th Hussars found the local inhabitants in the cemetery burying ten men that the Germans had put against a wall and shot. 'Just after [our] armoured cars had gone,' the regiment recorded, 'more Germans suddenly jumped over the cemetery wall and shot down the crowd with Tommy guns as they stood beside the graves.' Hitler's fury against the Italians for having changed sides had filtered right down to the ordinary German soldier.

Clark's Fifth Army, advancing north-west from Naples, faced its first major obstacle at the River Volturno, thirty kilometres further on. In the early hours of 13 October, both divisional and corps artillery opened a massive barrage across the valley. The British 56th Division had a tough time near the coast, but the main stretch of the river, although broad, was fordable, and by the following day a large bridgehead had been secured. The Volturno was only a holding position for the Germans, for Kesselring had already identified their main line of defence south of Rome. Like Hitler, he wanted to hold the Allies as far down the peninsula as possible. Rommel, who commanded the German divisions in the north and argued for a withdrawal, had been sidelined.

Both Allied armies soon discovered in the next stage of the advance that the mountainous terrain and the weather did not present the 'sunny Italy' which they had imagined from pre-war tourist posters. That autumn in Italy was like the Russian *rasputitsa* of constant rain and deep mud. Both British battledress and American olive drab were sodden for weeks at a time. Trench foot soon became a problem for those who did not put on dry socks once a day. Late autumn downpours turned the rivers to raging torrents and tracks to quagmires, and the retreating Germans had blown every bridge and mined every route. The British, although they had invented the Bailey bridge, envied the well-equipped and numerous American engineer brigades. But even the US Army was short of bridging equipment in such an abundant succession of mountain valleys.

The Germans conducted their withdrawal with defended roadblocks and mines, covered by well-camouflaged anti-tank guns. Advance to contact now meant waiting until the lead tank or armoured car hit a mine and was then knocked out by an armour-piercing round 'coming out of nowhere'. The wide-ranging manoeuvres of the desert war were far behind them. Narrow roads in narrow valleys, and well-defended hilltop villages, meant that the infantry had to take over point position. Less than thirty kilometres north of the Volturno, the advance came to a complete halt.

The Gustav or Winter Line, selected by Kesselring, ran 140 kilometres from just below Ortona on the Adriatic to the Gulf of Gaeta on the Tyrrhenian side. This was the narrowest part of the Italian boot and well chosen for defence. The Gustav Line had the natural fortress of Monte Cassino as its main strongpoint. All the unguarded optimism of the Allied commanders evaporated as Ultra confirmed that Hitler and Kesselring would mount a ferocious defence. This is the point at which Eisenhower should have insisted on a re-evaluation of the whole campaign. With the seven divisions due to be sent back to England for Overlord, the Allies no longer had the numerical superiority required for a major offensive. Churchill and Brooke seemed to think it was somehow unfair that the Americans should insist on sticking to the agreement made at the Trident conference in May.

Reconnaissance on the ground soon confirmed what the maps indicated. For Clark's Fifth Army the only path to Rome lay along Route 6, which went through the Mignano Gap, guarded by massive mountains on either side. And behind them ran the Rapido River, which in its turn was dominated by Monte Cassino.

On the left, the British X Corps faced the River Garigliano as a barrier. On 5 November, it attempted to outflank the Mignano Gap by seizing Monte Camino – only to find that this huge feature, with one false ridge after another, was well defended by the 15th Panzergrenadier Division in the first part of the Winter Line. The men of the 201st Guards Brigade, unable to break the German defence, found it impossible to dig in on what they called 'bare-arse ridge'. In freezing rain, they instead had to construct sangars, or shelters improvised with rocks. German mortar fire from above proved even more lethal than usual, with stone splinters flying in all directions. After several days, Clark had no option but to agree to pull them back off what had become known as Murder Mountain. Dead men were left propped in position, weapons pointed at the enemy, as the survivors withdrew.

Higher in the central Apennines to the north-east, the US 34th and 45th Divisions herded goats in front of them across mountain meadows to set off any mines. The uncomfortable truth was that neither the British nor the Americans had really learned the lessons of mountain warfare. In such terrain, trucks could not get near the forward positions. Food and ammunition had to be carried up the steep, zig-zag paths by mules or men. On the way back, the mule-trains would bring back the dead. The muleteers, mainly charcoal-burners hired at a daily rate, were spooked by their gruesome cargo. Wounded could only be brought out at night by stretcher-bearers, a painful journey up and down steep, slippery slopes for both the carriers and the carried.

In the afternoon of 2 December, under black skies and in the midst of yet another rainstorm, 900 guns of Fifth Army artillery opened a heavy bombardment while dripping infantrymen clambered up the slopes, the British up Monte Camino again and the Americans up La Difensa led by the 1st Special Service Force. By dawn the next day, this semi-irregular group had seized the crest and prepared for counter-attacks by the panzergrenadiers. Over the following days, the fighting for La Difensa was pitiless on both sides. The Americans, having suffered some dirty tricks, took no prisoners.

Just to their south-west, the British had finally taken Monte Camino, so the central German position astride Route 6 could now be partially outflanked. Clark sent in the 36th Division on the north-east side to break the Bernhardt Line in front of the village of San Pietro. Monte Lungo on the south-west side of the Mignano Gap had to be the first objective, because otherwise

German artillery positioned there would break up the main offensive. A brigade of Italian Alpini, keen to show their mettle against their former ally who had treated them so badly, went bravely into the assault, but they were cut to pieces by heavy machine-gun fire. Clark even tried using tanks, but they stood little chance of advancing in such rocky terrain without breaking or shedding a track. After several days of heavy losses, Monte Lungo was taken from the west, and San Pietro fell soon afterwards. The Germans simply pulled back to their next line.

Clark's soldiers presented a sorry sight by the middle of December. They were unshaven, had long, dank hair, and dark circles of exhaustion under their eyes. Their uniforms were impregnated with mud, their boots were coming to pieces, and their skin was white and wrinkled from being perpetually wet. Many suffered from trench foot. The Italian villagers from San Pietro, who had taken shelter from the fighting in caves, were also in a sorry state. They emerged to find their homes completely ruined, and their vegetable plots and vines mangled. Almost every tree on the hillsides around had been smashed by artillery fire.

On the Adriatic side of the Apennines, Montgomery's Eighth Army could have been fighting a separate war. Build-up was slow until harbours were cleared, so the Eighth Army was delayed by supply shortages, especially fuel. The bulk of shipping coming in to Bari was earmarked for the rapid development of Major General James Doolittle's Fifteenth Air Force, based on the thirteen Foggia airfields.

Montgomery recognized that the primary purpose of the Italian campaign should be to tie down as many German divisions as possible, and to use the Foggia bases to bomb the Germans in Bavaria, Austria and the Danube basin. The mountainous terrain of south central Italy favoured the Germans in defence and rendered it almost impossible for the Allies to make use of their much larger tank forces. The fighting, they found, was far more ruthless than in the desert. On the German side it had taken on what a war correspondent called an 'ordered ferocity'. The Germans shot 'every man in a platoon of Canadians who were surrounded, isolated and signalled their surrender'. And 'any civilian found in the battle area is immediately shot irrespective of whether his home is there'.

Montgomery wanted to break through to turn the flank of the Germans facing Clark's Fifth Army, but heavy autumn rains in the second week of November delayed his attempt to cross the River Sangro. The ground was so waterlogged that his tanks could not move, and cloud cover so low that his air support, still called the Desert Air Force, could not operate. The Sangro was in spate to such an extent that pontoon bridges were simply swept away. On 27 November, even though the rain had hardly let up, the 2nd New Zealand Division crossed 'and the dog-fight for possession of the high ground began in earnest'.

Montgomery summoned all the war correspondents on the Italian front to a briefing. He spoke from the steps of his caravan still in desert camouflage, concealed in an olive grove overlooking the Sangro valley. He was wearing suede desert boots, khaki corduroy trousers and a battledress tunic open at the neck with a silk scarf. He was, wrote the Australian correspondent Godfrey Blunden, 'a slight little man with a sharp nose, shrewd, calculating blue eyes overhung by greying eyebrows. He spoke in a dry precise voice with the faintest trace of a lisp.' His address, laying down his 'great principles of war', 'was interrupted only by chirrupings from a cage full of lovebirds and canaries resting against the side of the caravan'.

At the beginning of December, Montgomery ordered the Canadian 1st Division to attack along the coast towards Ortona. Twenty-five kilometres beyond lay Pescara and Route 5, which led across the Apennines to Rome. Their commander, Major General Christopher Vokes, a red-haired mountain of a man, ordered his men forward in a series of frontal attacks against the 90th Panzergrenadier Division. After an initial success, they came up against the German positions guarding a ravine running southwest of Ortona, which the Germans had planted with mines. For nine days, Vokes flung battalion after battalion into the attack, until his men called him the Butcher. Montgomery sent messages asking why progress was so slow. The Canadians found that they were facing not just panzergrenadiers, but also the 1st Fallschirmjäger Division, whom they recognized from their round paratroop helmets.

On 21 December, the Canadians finally broke through. German demolition teams blew the ancient town to pieces before their eyes, yet the paratroopers still managed to hold the ruins for another week and booby-trapped almost everything that was left. The massive Vokes collapsed in tears of rage at the losses in his division that month – 2,300, of whom 500 were dead, and numerous cases of battle fatigue that left men paralysed and speechless. Montgomery cancelled any further attacks for the time being.

Montgomery's own supply system was again in disarray. On 2 December, a heavy Luftwaffe air raid on the port of Bari had taken the Allies badly off guard. Seventeen ships were sunk, including one Liberty ship, the SS *John Harvey*, which was carrying 1,350 tons of mustard-gas bombs. Delivered in great secrecy, these bombs were to be held in reserve in case the Germans resorted to chemical warfare. The port was in chaos, with oil pipelines severed and set ablaze. Another ship with 5,000 tons of ammunition caught fire and exploded. As the *Harvey* burst apart, killing the captain and all the crew, huge surges of water were thrown up by each explosion. The mustard gas washed over all those thrown into the sea as well as many all around in the dock area. War correspondents soon found that any reference to the raid in any form was suppressed by censors.

The secrecy surrounding the mustard gas and the death of all those on the *John Harvey* meant that doctors caring for servicemen and civilians alike could not understand why so many of them, unable to open their eyes, were dying in such pain. It took two days before doctors were reasonably certain of the cause. Over a thousand Allied soldiers and sailors perished and an unknown number of Italians. The port itself was out of action until February 1944. It was one of the Luftwaffe's most devastating raids of the whole war.

Both of Alexander's armies were now condemned to a costly campaign in harsh surroundings. Southern Italy was 'not a happy place in that cold winter of 1943', an Irish Guardsman observed. Unhappiest and most destitute of all were the civilians, ready to snatch at any food scraps or pick up any cigarette butt tossed away by a soldier. Survival was a desperate business. In Naples an amateur prostitute would offer herself for 25 cents or a can of rations. In Bari on the Adriatic coast, 'five cigarettes would buy you a woman'. Uninspected brothels were marked 'Out of Bounds', but that seemed only to present the challenge of the forbidden to many soldiers. American military police, known as 'Snowdrops' from their white helmets, would take great pleasure in bursting into such establishments to check whether any military personnel were present. Venereal disease rates rose to levels far beyond those in Sicily, with more than one soldier in ten infected at any one time. Penicillin was not officially available for such non-military use until the early spring of 1944. It was only justified as a way of getting more men back into the firing line.

While the cornucopia of American industry shipped into Naples harbour stimulated an enormous black market from pilferage, ordinary Italians were close to starvation. The Germans had seized their food supplies, which were already drastically reduced through Fascist maladministration. The only edible product the occupiers had left untouched were chestnuts from mountain forests, which they considered to be nothing more than food for pigs. Italians, deprived of wheat, ground the chestnuts to make flour. One of the greatest shortages was of salt, which meant that it was impossible to slaughter and cure a pig, assuming you still had one after the Germans had passed through. German commanders and officials ignored even the pleas of Mussolini's minister for agriculture. There were virtually no men to work the fields, since the Germans had taken Italian soldiers for forced labour. Inevitably, widespread malnourishment led to children suffering from rickets. But the greatest killer, especially in Naples, was typhus. With little soap and hot water available, lice spread the disease rapidly until the Americans brought in large quantities of DDT to spray on the population.

Churchill, while convalescing in Marrakesh after Christmas from his bout of pneumonia, became impatient at the static battle lines across Italy. He returned with enthusiasm to General Mark Clark's earlier plan to outflank the German line with another amphibious landing closer to Rome. Eisenhower had been distinctly uneasy about the idea, known as Operation Shingle, but both he and Montgomery were leaving the Mediterranean for London to prepare for Overlord. Churchill had the field to himself and more or less assumed command. Clark himself was now rather less convinced of Shingle's likely success, with only two divisions allocated. If the Fifth Army failed to break through the Gustav Line, this landing force could easily find itself trapped.

The operation to land and supply two divisions required a considerable quantity of shipping – nearly ninety Landing Ships Tank (LSTs) and 160 landing craft. But most of them were due to sail for Britain in mid-January 1944 to be made ready for Overlord. Churchill, using a great deal of prestidigitation with facts and dates, managed to persuade Roosevelt that Operation Shingle would not delay things at all. Although Brooke supported the plan, he was uneasy with the idea of the prime minister playing at commander-in-chief in the Mediterranean. 'Winston, sitting in Marrakesh, is now full of beans and trying to win the war from there!' the newly promoted field marshal wrote in his diary. 'I wish to God that he would come home and get under control.'

Churchill, holding court in the Mamounia Hotel, summoned senior officers from all over the Mediterranean. He was dismissive of any doubts and refused to postpone the planned date of 22 January to allow time for rehearsals. The beaches round Anzio, a hundred kilometres behind the German lines, were selected. Most of those present backed the plan, largely because the stalemate had to be broken, but they were well aware that it represented quite a gamble. Churchill underestimated the logistical problems and the ability of the Germans to move troops to counter-attack the landing faster than the Allies could reinforce the bridgehead. Everything thus depended on the Fifth Army's ability to cross the Rapido River, seize the strongly defended town of Cassino and, hardest of all, then take the mountain fortress of Monte Cassino which loomed above it. Not only did Monte Cassino dominate the immediate vicinity, but it also provided a grandstand view of the whole area for German artillery observers.

Once again, the British X Corps would advance on the left closest to the sea. Clark had wisely placed on his right the newly arrived French Expeditionary Corps, with two divisions of tough North African troops. The *goumiers* were good mountain fighters. They travelled light, used every fold in the ground with great skill, and were ruthless to their enemies, killing silently with knife and bayonet. The main attack would again be in the centre, this time a few kilometres south of Cassino, towards the Liri Valley.

This would involve crossing the Rapido and its mine-infested banks under fire, and then attacking strong German defences on higher ground.

Clark's plan was unimaginative. Several of his divisional commanders were uneasy, but they did not voice their doubts openly. They suspected that Clark's obsession with taking Rome could cost many of their men's lives. Clark nevertheless had to mount an all-out attack to give the Anzio landings a chance of success. The 36th Division, which had been battered at Salerno, was to lead the II Corps attack against the village of Sant'Angelo overlooking the Rapido, which was defended by the 15th Panzergrenadier Division. To their south on the night of 19 January, the British 46th Division crossed the Garigliano. But they were forced back in some disorder after the Germans counter-attacked rapidly and their pioneers opened some sluice-gates upriver above the confluence with the Liri. A torrent of water roared down, scattering the assault boats.

On the night of 20 January, the 36th Division began its approach to the Rapido in a heavy river mist. Chaos ensued as many companies lost their way. German pioneers had slipped across to plant mines on the east bank, and as the would-be attackers tramped forward lugging the heavy rubber assault boats, a man would scream when his foot was blown off. Panzergrenadier mortar crews, aiming by sound, fired off a rapid sequence of rounds. Machine guns firing on fixed lines holed many of the assault boats that were launched.

Battalions that made it to the other side were forced to pull back, and next day the divisional commander was ordered to send them across again. They had more success the second time but were trapped in small bridgeheads, where they were shelled and mortared relentlessly. Eventually, the remnants of the division were pulled back, having suffered just over 2,000 casualties. It was a futile, bloody battle which led to much recrimination at the time and later. But, combined with the British attack on the left, it had convinced Kesselring that the moment of crisis was at hand. He had ordered forward his two reserve divisions near Rome, the 29th and 90th Panzergrenadier Divisions, to reinforce the line along the Garigliano and the Rapido. This meant that the Anzio–Nettuno sector was unprotected two nights later.

*

On 20 January, the British 1st Infantry Division and the US 3rd Division, supported by Commandos and Colonel Darby's three battalions of Rangers, began to embark in ports on the bay of Naples. Units marching to the ships, accompanied by bands, gave the impression of a victory parade before the battle had even started. The 1st Battalion of the Irish Guards marched to the tune of 'St Patrick's Day'. 'I was amazed to see the Italians lining the street cheering and clapping us on the way,' wrote one of them. 'I realised that many of the guardsmen had Italian girlfriends among the cheering crowd; many of these walked in step with their soldiers and gave them flowers and trinkets.' Security was so bad that most of the locals knew where the soldiers were headed.

The overall commander of VI Corps and thus of Operation Shingle was Major General John P. Lucas. He was a kindly man, who gave the impression of an elderly uncle with his white moustache and wire-rimmed spectacles, but he lacked any killer instinct. Senior officers could not resist offering encouraging advice, almost all of which proved both contradictory and inaccurate. The most disastrous came from General Clark himself. 'Don't stick your neck out, Johnny,' he told Lucas. 'I did at Salerno and got into trouble.' Clark provided no clear objectives. He suggested that he should secure the beachhead and not put his corps in danger.

To everyone's astonishment after the exuberant Italian send-off, the Germans had not the slightest inkling of the landings planned at Anzio and Nettuno. They were taken completely by surprise. In fact when the Americans and British landed in the early hours of 22 January and asked locals where the Germans were, all they received were shrugs and nods in the direction of Rome. Just a few were rounded up. They had been foraging for their units in this tranquil area, which had been a beach resort for Fascist officials from Rome.

Although the Germans had not prepared conventional military defences, they had deliberately wreaked environmental sabotage on the area. At vast expense in the 1930s, Mussolini had drained the Pontine Marshes and settled 100,000 Great War veterans to farm the reclaimed land. Mosquitoes, which had plagued the region, were virtually eliminated. After the Italian surrender, two of Himmler's scientists planned revenge on their former ally. They had the pumps turned off to flood much of the area again and destroyed the tidal gates. They then introduced the malaria-carrying breed of mosquito, which could survive in brackish water. The German authorities also confiscated stocks of quinine, so that the disease spread. The inhabitants not only found their land and homes wrecked, but more than 55,000 contracted malaria the following year. It was a clear case of biological warfare.

Unaware of the malaria threat, both Alexander and Clark visited the peaceful landing site. They seemed unconcerned by the lack of drive at senior levels, but in the forward battalions a sense of unease and dismay began to grow. 'We all had a sickening feeling of anti-climax,' wrote an Irish Guardsman. 'Each and every one of us had been keyed up for a bold advance on Rome. It might have been rough and bloody, but we would have got there. We had the element of surprise. There were no Germans. What in the name of God was stopping the Division advancing?' In British ranks there was an unfounded suspicion that they were being held back because the Yanks wanted to get to Rome first. Yet Lucas was not even pushing Major General Lucian Truscott's 3rd Division forward with any urgency, despite the need to seize the hills to the north or cut the Tenth Army's supply lines along Route 7.

The Allied landing caused panic in Rome and at Kesselring's headquarters above the Tiber Valley, especially since he had committed his two reserve divisions to the battles along the Garigliano and Rapido rivers. He was woken with the news shortly before dawn and rang Berlin. A contingency plan, Operation Richard, was put into immediate effect, bringing divisions down from northern Italy and reinforcements from elsewhere. General der Kavallerie Eberhard von Mackensen was to move his Fourteenth Army headquarters from Verona. Vietinghoff's Tenth Army headquarters was ordered to send all troops not engaged in combat back towards the Alban Hills and the Colli Laziali, which overlooked the Pontine Marshes of the coastal plain. Above all, Kesselring wanted as many batteries of guns as possible in those hills. But first he sent in his 'flying artillery', and the Luftwaffe used their 'glide bombs' against ships anchored offshore. One of them blew the Royal Navy destroyer HMS *Janus* in half. Another sank a brightly lit and clearly marked hospital ship. Mines were another hazard for the invasion fleet.

The British 1st Division on the western side of the beachhead finally began advancing rapidly on 24 January and by the next day had taken the small town of Aprilia. Truscott's 3rd Division attacked towards Cisterna, where it found itself up against the Panzer Division *Hermann Göring*. It was not long before Kesselring's gunners in the hills began an almost constant bombardment of the plain below. Lucas's refusal to hurry to seize the high ground was now shown to be disastrous. With a perverse obstinacy, he had let the huge advantage of surprise slip through his fingers. But the fault also lay with Clark and Alexander, who should have put much more pressure on him to push out his forces in the first forty-eight hours. On the other hand, it can be argued that Lucas's VI Corps with just two divisions was simply not strong enough to advance inland and protect its flanks, and that the whole operation was flawed.

By the time Clark visited the beachhead again on 28 January, the rapid German build-up had passed parity with the invading Allied force of just over 60,000 men. Even more enemy reinforcements were on their way south. The comforting idea that Allied air power would prevent them deploying had proved an illusion, while German artillery fire became heavier and heavier. An eighteen-year-old Italian woman went into labour as a group of civilians and soldiers tried to shelter from shelling in a cemetery. While her mother prayed volubly to all the saints, a Royal Army Medical Corps corporal delivered a healthy boy as if it were an everyday task.

When Darby's Rangers and Truscott's 3rd Division attacked the following night, they were repelled by German forces several times greater than expected. A renewed attack led to disaster for the Rangers, with many of them killed or captured. The Germans later paraded their prisoners gleefully in Rome for photographers and Deutsche Wochenschau newsreel cameras. Hitler, who was obsessed with the symbolic significance of capital cities, was determined not to lose that of his most prominent ally. As a result, he was giving Kesselring even more resources for the defence of Italy than he had asked for.

Allied regimental aid posts, casualty clearing stations and the evacuation hospital were all overwhelmed with stretcher cases as German shelling increased dramatically. Small German fighting patrols infiltrated the perimeter. The battle was 'a series of short sharp engagements', an Irish Guards sergeant wrote. 'There was so much cover in the culverts and deep irrigation ditches that the enemy were upon you in seconds.' With the skies heavily overcast, the Allies could no longer rely on air support. Americans and British alike had to dig in and face the fury of Mackensen's expected counter-attack, now nearly 100,000 strong with the newly arrived reinforcements.

The Anzio landings had utterly failed to undermine the Tenth Army's defence line on the Garigliano and Rapido. The great rock of Monte Cassino, crowned by its Benedictine monastery, was its strongpoint. But less than ten kilometres to the north-east the French corps of two North African divisions commanded by General Alphonse Juin had crossed the River Secco and seized Monte Belvedere inside the Gustav Line. They suffered 8,000 casualties in the harshest mountain combat. Back down the Rapido Valley, artillery duels of counter-bombardment continued relentlessly.

On 30 January the US 34th Infantry Division, having initially been forced back, managed to ford the Rapido north of Cassino. Over the next few days it fought its way from hill to hill round the back of the great mountain. But the battle for the town of Cassino and Monte Cassino itself swung back and forth, in freezing weather and flurries of snow. The 34th Division, exhausted and mangled by its courageous advance, had to be replaced soon afterwards by the 4th Indian Division.

Lieutenant General Bernard Freyberg, the New Zealand corps commander, now took over the sector. The huge and fearless Freyberg, known to British colleagues as 'a bear of very little brain', saw things in straightforward terms. He concluded that the great Benedictine monastery of Monte Cassino was impregnable as it stood. Instead of trying to spare it, as both Eisenhower and Alexander had earlier laid down, the Allies should destroy it completely. Inaccurate reports that the Germans had secretly turned it into a fortress were believed, and reports that it was filled with refugees were discounted. General Juin was strongly opposed to its destruction, so was Clark and the commander of the US II Corps. But Alexander stepped in firmly to support Freyberg. The pressure for results from Churchill in London was too great.

On 4 February, Mackensen's attack on the British salient at Anzio began, with panzergrenadiers driving a huge flock of sheep in front of them over the minefields. The 1st Battalion of the Irish Guards and the 6th Gordons took the brunt of the fighting, as Mark IV Panzers came on behind. The 1st Infantry Division was forced back, losing 1,500 men, of whom 900 were taken prisoner. Another German attack came three days later against Aprilia. Once more a breakthrough to the sea was held off only by massed artillery and the guns of Allied warships offshore.

Hitler in the Wolfsschanze, having pored over large-scale maps of the Anzio beachhead, issued detailed orders to Mackensen for a massive attack to crush it completely. He wanted a conspicuous and salutary lesson to be inflicted on the Allies to discourage them from a larger undertaking on the Channel coast later in the year. On 16 February the fighting rose to a new intensity. The 3rd Panzergrenadier Division and the 26th Panzer Division attacked Aprilia again, and the area between the US 45th Division and the recently arrived British 56th Division. Two days later, Mackensen threw in his reserves as well.

Panzergrenadiers attacked almost in Napoleonic columns down the same axis from Carroceto. Artillery observers had seen them coming and within minutes batteries of Allied field guns had ranged in to produce a devastating effect. Americans dubbed this approach road 'the Bowling Alley'. While Allied casualties had been high, Mackensen lost over 5,000 men.

Clark, under pressure from Alexander, returned to the Anzio beachhead to sack Lucas as VI Corps commander and replace him with Truscott. It was ironic that this decision came just after the battle had started to turn in the Allies' favour. Churchill's timing was also out when he made his famous remark about Anzio a week later at a meeting of the chiefs of staff in London: 'We hoped to land a wildcat that would tear out the bowels of the Boche. Instead we have stranded a vast whale with its tail flopping about in the water!'

On 29 February, Mackensen, under orders from Kesselring and Führer headquarters, sent in another major attack. Allied batteries fired 66,000 shells at these forces. Hitler was taking as close an interest in the dozen kilometres of the Anzio beachhead as in the eastern front. But he refused to recognize that his troops could not win if they lacked artillery ammunition and air cover, while the Allies grew stronger and stronger in the *Materialschlacht*, the battle of hardware. Kesselring, on the other hand, understood that a turning point in the war had been reached in Italy. The Wehrmacht could not continue to expend troops and weaponry for much longer against an enemy with such apparently inexhaustible reserves of firepower. At Anzio, three-quarters of its casualties had been caused by shellfire.

On 15 February, the full destructive potential of the Allies was unleashed on Monte Cassino. Leaflets had been showered over the ancient monastery the evening before to warn all those sheltering there to abandon the place as rapidly as possible for their own safety. But, due to confusion and suspicion, few left. The abbot refused to believe that the Allies were capable of such an act. The B-17 Flying Fortresses and waves of B-25 Mitchells and B-26 Marauders bombed the mountain top in relays while the entire artillery of the Fifth Army in the Rapido Valley added its own explosive contribution. Several hundred refugees were killed.

Freyberg's plan backfired in every possible way. He failed to launch his attack until long after the bombers had departed. Even then it was in insufficient strength and ill coordinated. The Allied bombardment gave the Germans the right and opportunity to turn the partly ruined monastery into a veritable fortress. And Allied attempts to blame the Germans, with false claims that they had occupied the monastery, were firmly contradicted by the abbot in a filmed interview with General der Panzertruppen Fridolin von Senger und Etterlin, the commander of XIV Panzer Corps.

The town of Cassino, now defended by the 1st Fallschirmjäger Division, became Freyberg's primary objective, but his decision to attack with his 2nd New Zealand Division and the 4th Indian Division was thwarted by relentless rain. He needed dry ground for the tanks, but everywhere was waterlogged. When the rain stopped on 15 March, the town was pounded by bombers and artillery. Despite the claims of Fifteenth Air Force bomber crews, it was not their finest hour in navigation and aiming. Five other towns were also hit by mistake; in fact the US aircraft managed to bomb just about every nationality on their own side – the Indian Division, Eighth Army headquarters, the newly arrived Poles and General Juin's headquarters – causing 350 Allied casualties and seventy-five civilian.

Following standard German practice when a major attack was expected, the town of Cassino had been held with only a small force. The bulk of the paratroopers had been pulled back to second- and third-line positions. The subsequent advance of Freyberg's forces was not helped by the rubble blocking the streets and huge craters. The Sherman tanks could not get through, and then, despite the encouraging weather forecast, the rains began again.

The German paratroopers defended the ruined town with deadly skill. The New Zealanders, who had their defeat on Crete to avenge, certainly did not lack courage or determination, nor did the Indian Division, especially the 9th Gurkha Rifles. But to Clark's frustration Freyberg went at his own pace, showing no tactical flair and hammering away obstinately. The battle went on for eight days, with Freyberg's corps losing twice as many men as the Germans. Isolated detachments, such as the Gurkhas who had seized hills at great cost, were called back. The whole corps was withdrawn, battered, embittered and dispirited.

At Anzio, meanwhile, the self-perpetuating nature of the war in Italy had continued with Allied forces in the beachhead perimeter increased to almost 100,000 men, thus retaining parity with the Germans. But this, the most savage of battlefronts, had now sunk into a routine behind the nightly skirmishing of fighting patrols. Soldiers planted vegetables and bought livestock off the evacuated Italian families before they left. Bored troops bet on anything from beetle-racing to baseball. American business enterprise flourished with the sale of hooch from improvised alembics. 'Bootleggers from the 133rd Infantry blended fifty pounds of fermented raisins and a dash of vanilla to make "Plastered in Paris".' British soldiers caught rats in sandbags and hurled them like satchel-charges into German trenches. Cases of self-inflicted wounds were worryingly high, mainly it seems out of anticipated fear rather than the immediacy of fear itself. Combat fatigue, as psychiatrists soon noted, was always likely to increase in surrounded beachheads and bridgeheads. It dropped dramatically only when a war of movement began.

On 23 March, while the fighting for Cassino was at its height, Italian partisans in Rome ambushed a detachment of German police as they marched through the city. An enraged Hitler ordered reprisals, ten executions for every German killed. Kappler, the SS chief in Rome, selected 335 hostages for execution the next day at the Ardeatine Caves outside the city. Kappler's hunt for Jews had been less successful, with just 1,259 rounded up and sent to Auschwitz. The majority had been hidden by Italians, including by the Catholic Church, even though the Pope had not spoken out against the persecution.

Across the Adriatic, German reprisals in Yugoslavia became more savage. Himmler had authorized the recruitment of Bosnian Muslims into the 13th SS Gebirgs Division *Handschar* to fight Tito's partisans, depicted to them as the hated Serbs. They wore a grey fez with the SS death's-head. In fact the partisans came increasingly from all the Yugoslav nationalities, while the almost exclusively Serb Četniks of General Mihailović had backed away from confrontation with the Germans after the appalling reprisals of October 1941. Tito's Communist forces, on the other hand, had no scruples about escalating the conflict, counting on German atrocities to swell their numbers. Once it became clear to the British that the Četniks were hanging back, SOE withdrew its military mission to them and increased its support to Tito's brigades. Supplies from the SOE base in Bari were flown in, and on 2 March 1944 bombing raids on targets in Yugoslavia began from the Foggia airfields.

As the Allied bombing of Germany intensified, Hitler wanted revenge and terror inflicted on Britain, but most ordinary Germans had become depressed by Nazi ranting. They wanted protection from the bombers and to hear some message of hope that the war would end. Only Party loyalists now used the 'Heil Hitler!' greeting and salute. The overthrow of Mussolini in Italy prompted wishful thoughts in many German minds, but the two regimes and their grip on power were simply poles apart. To ensure the

Nazis' continued control in Germany, Hitler appointed Heinrich Himmler, the Reichsführer-SS, minister of the interior as well. But, to the dismay of Goebbels, Hitler had cut himself off even more from the German people and still refused to visit bombed-out civilians or wounded soldiers.

Hitler had ensured, consciously or subconsciously, that all boats had been burned. There were no alternatives save victory or total destruction. And having promised the inevitability of Nazi victory, he now, quite shamelessly, could threaten the horrors of defeat, without ever admitting that anything had changed, or that he was responsible in any way for this catastrophic state of affairs. Hitler blamed recent reverses on the treacherous French in North Africa, on the even more treacherous Italians, and on reactionary generals in the Wehrmacht who lacked Nazi faith and failed to obey his orders.

During rare moments of lucidity, it seemed that Hitler could visualize how the war was going to end. He was at least consistent in his social-Darwinistic view that might was always right. After the Stalingrad disaster, he had begun to apply this notion to his own countrymen. He told Goebbels that 'if the German people turned out to be weak, they would deserve nothing else than to be extinguished by a stronger people; then one could have no sympathy for them'. He would return to this theme as the downfall of the Reich approached.

36

The Soviet Spring Offensive

JANUARY–APRIL 1944

On 4 January 1944, Generalfeldmarschall von Manstein flew to the Wolfsschanze to underline the threat facing Army Group South. The Fourth Panzer Army between Vinnitsa and Berdichev was threatened with destruction. This would leave a huge gap between his forces and Army Group Centre. The only answer was to bring troops back from the Crimea and the Dnepr bend.

Hitler refused to consider it. To abandon the Crimea risked losing the support of Romania and Bulgaria, and he could not take forces from the north as that might encourage the Finns to leave the war. He claimed that there were so many disagreements on the enemy side that the alliance would fall to pieces. It was just a question of hanging on. Manstein asked to see Hitler alone. Only General Kurt Zeitzler, the army chief of staff, remained with the two men. Hitler quite clearly sensed what was coming and did not like it.

Manstein returned to his earlier recommendation that Hitler hand over the direction of the eastern front to him. Thinking of the constant refusal of Führer headquarters to allow a retreat until it was too late, Manstein remarked that some of their problems came from the way they were commanded. 'Even I cannot get the field marshals to obey me!' Hitler replied in a cold fury. 'Do you imagine, for example, that they would obey you any more readily?' Manstein retorted that his own orders were not disobeyed. He had won the point, but Hitler abruptly ended the meeting. Manstein, too clever for his own good, had achieved nothing except to arouse Hitler's profound distrust. His days as a commander-in-chief were numbered.

In January 1944, even after losses of 4.2 million men, the German armed forces were at their greatest mobilized strength with 9.5 million in uniform. Just under 2.5 million were on the eastern front, bolstered by some 700,000 allied troops, a slightly larger figure than for Operation Barbarossa two and a half years before. But numbers were misleading. The German army was a very different organization to the one which had started the invasion. On average, it was losing the equivalent of a regiment a day, with many of the best junior officers and NCOs killed in the fighting. Notional strengths were kept up by pressganging Poles, Czechs, Alsatians and *Volksdeutsche* into the army and Waffen-SS. Between 10 and 20 per cent of a division's ration strength consisted of Hiwis and forced labourers. The other great difference was that the German army could no longer count on effective support from the Luftwaffe, the bulk of which had been withdrawn to defend the Reich from Allied bombing.

The Red Army deployed 6.4 million men almost entirely on the eastern front, and also enjoyed a massive superiority in tanks, guns and aircraft. Yet even the Soviet Union was suffering a manpower crisis after the staggering losses of the previous two years and the mass mobilization for war industries. Many rifle divisions were down to 2,000 men or fewer. The Red Army was, nevertheless, an incomparably more professional and effective organization than it had been during the disasters of 1941. The asphyxiating fear of the NKVD's dead hand had been replaced with a much greater sense of initiative and even experimentation. For the early part of 1944, Soviet priorities were clear. Force back the Germans from Leningrad, reoccupy Belorussia and liberate the rest of Ukraine.

After the successful Zhitomir–Berdichev operation carried out by Vatutin's 1st Ukrainian Front, which fought off all of Manstein's counter-attacks, Marshal Zhukov, the Stavka representative, aimed to destroy the strong German salient on the Dnepr around Korsun. On 24 January, the XI and XLII Corps, which Hitler had not allowed Manstein to withdraw, were taken by surprise and cut off by the 5th Guards Tank Army and the 6th Tank Army from Konev's 2nd Ukrainian Front. Manstein, determined to get them out after the failure of the rescue mission at Stalingrad, assembled four panzer divisions.

Zhukov's great rival, General Konev, was equally keen to destroy the four infantry divisions and the 5th SS Panzer-Division *Wiking* before help arrived. Konev, who according to Beria's son had 'wicked little eyes, a shaven head that looked like a pumpkin, and an expression full of self-conceit', was utterly ruthless. He ordered the 2nd Air Army supporting him to rain incendiaries on the wooden buildings of the towns and villages within what had become the Cherkassy pocket. This would force the under-nourished German troops out into the bitter cold.

On 17 February the encircled troops made their attempt to break out, struggling through deep snow. Konev was ready and sprang his trap. With their broad tracks, his T-34s could cope with the drifts. Their crews chased the weakened German in-fantrymen, crushing them under their tracks. Then the cavalry charged on their Cossack ponies, and with their sabres hacked off the raised arms of those trying to surrender. It is said that some 20,000 Germans died there on that day alone. Stalin was so impressed by Konev's vengeance that he promoted him to mar-shal. Vatutin might also have been promoted if he had not been ambushed by Ukrainian nationalists on 29 February and left mor-tally wounded. Zhukov took over command of his 1st Ukrainian Front and continued to attack the northern flank of Army Group South, while Malinovsky's 3rd Ukrainian Front and Tolbukhin's 4th Ukrainian Front crushed or forced back the German forces in the Dnepr bend.

Hitler had been even more reluctant to contemplate withdrawal from Leningrad. Any hope of destroying the 'cradle of Bolshevism' had long disappeared, but he feared that it would give the Finns the excuse they wanted to make peace with the Soviet Union. His soldiers could not understand why they were being held in these marshlands, especially when word spread that the Red Army had made major advances in the south.

Expecting a major attack soon, the German military authori-ties forced the civilian population in northern Russia further to the rear to prevent the Red Army from recruiting them in an ad-vance. 'Our car passed the body of a woman lying in the snow,' wrote Godfrey Blunden near Velikie Luki. 'Our driver did not stop. Such sights are common in the Russian war zone. The woman who had probably fallen out of line while being marched to Germany had been shot or had died of cold. Who will ever know who she was? She was just one of many million Russians.'

On 14 January 1944, the Leningrad, Volkhov and 2nd Baltic

Fronts began a series of attacks to break the siege entirely. Over the previous two months, the Leningrad Front had secretly been ferrying the 2nd Shock Army at night into the Oranienbaum bridgehead on the Baltic coast west of the city. Then, once the Gulf of Finland had frozen hard, another 22,000 troops, 140 tanks and 380 guns crossed the ice into the pocket.

In a dense, freezing fog, the Red Army and the Baltic Fleet opened an exceptionally heavy bombardment with 21,600 guns and 1,500 Katyusha rocket batteries. So great was the trembling from 220,000 shells fired in a hundred minutes that plaster fell from ceilings in Leningrad twenty kilometres away. 'The shells were throwing up a whole wall of earth, smoke and dust with flashes of fire inside it,' wrote a mortarman. The attack out of the Oranienbaum bridgehead was joined by one from the Pulkovo Heights on the south-west flank of the city. Generalfeldmarschall Georg Küchler, the commander-in-chief of Army Group North, had not expected such skilfully coordinated attacks. But German *Kampfgruppen* fought back with their usual professionalism. An 88mm gun hit one Soviet tank after another from a well-built pill-box. Advancing Soviet infantry could smell the scorched flesh of those inside the tanks.

They found no civilians in the villages, since they had been evacuated behind the German lines. The advance continued towards Pushkin (Tsarskoe Selo) and Peterhof. German corpses, face down in the snow, had been flattened by the tracks of the advancing T-34 tanks. Some soldiers sang as they advanced, others prayed. 'I realized that I myself was trying to remember prayers that I had been taught as a child,' an officer recorded, 'but I could not remember any.' When they reached Gatchina, they found the palace 'covered in shit'. The Germans occupying the place had not bothered to go outdoors in the cold. The British correspondent Alexander Werth, however, claimed that Red Army soldiers were furious to find that part of the palace at Gatchina had been turned into a German officers' brothel.

On the morning of 22 January, General Küchler flew to the Wolfsschanze to ask Hitler's permission to withdraw from Pushkin, a pointless exercise since the retreat was unstoppable. The next day, the last German shell fell on Leningrad. On 27 January 1944, after 880 days, the siege was truly broken. Victory salutes were fired in Leningrad, but the celebrations were overshadowed by thoughts of all who had died. The predominant feeling among most people was one of survivor guilt.

The desire for revenge among front-line troops was strong. Vasily Churkin described in his diary how, when they entered Vyritsa, they 'caught four Russian teenage boys who were wearing German uniforms. They were immediately shot, so great was the hatred of all things German. But the boys were innocent. The Germans had used them as horse drivers in the rear. They were given greatcoats and forced to wear them.'

Hitler soon sacked Küchler and replaced him with Generalfeldmarschall Model, his favourite commander in a crisis, but this failed to stop the Soviet advance which continued for over 200 kilometres. Foreign Waffen-SS formations, including the Belgian Walloon Legion commanded by Léon Degrelle, were thrown back from Narva. To the south, the central front line across Belorussia remained stable during those early months of 1944. But the German campaign against partisans in Belorussia was as savage as any fighting at the front. The German Ninth Army forced 50,000 Soviet civilians regarded as unfit for labour out into no-man's-land, a virtual death sentence.

In the western Ukraine, the German army continued to receive a battering, with no time to recover between one offensive and another. On 4 March, Zhukov's 1st Ukrainian Front smashed the German line with two tank armies and headed for the Romanian border. Another tank army crossed the Dnestr and advanced into north-eastern Romania.

Hitler had left the Wolfsschanze in East Prussia on 22 February while concrete bunkers were constructed now that his headquarters was within range of Soviet aviation. He moved to the Berghof, which also happened to be closer to his increasingly undependable Balkan allies. Early in March he decided to tackle the problem of Hungary's 'treachery', having heard of overtures made by Admiral Horthy to the western Allies. Hitler intended to take over the country, keep Horthy in protective custody and deal with the Hungarian Jews.

On 18 March, Horthy arrived at Schloss Klessheim, accompanied by senior figures in his government. He and his entourage thought that they had been summoned to discuss their request to withdraw Hungarian forces from the eastern front, to defend the Carpathian frontier from the Red Army. But Hitler simply presented Horthy with an ultimatum. Horthy, although outraged by Hitler's blunt threats, even against his own family, was left with no option. He returned by train to Budapest a virtual prisoner in the company of SS Obergruppenführer Ernst Kaltenbrunner, head of the RSHA. A puppet government was installed the next day and German forces entered the country. They were immediately followed by Eichmann's 'experts', ready to round up Hungary's 750,000 Jews and send them to Auschwitz.

On 19 March, as German troops drove into Budapest, Hitler also held a bizarre ceremony at the Berghof. He had summoned all the field marshals in the Wehrmacht to declare their loyalty to him. Their doyen, Generalfeldmarschall von Rundstedt, began by reading out a statement which they had all signed. Hitler appeared to be moved by this totally artificial performance, which left the field marshals fearing for his sanity.

Hitler and Goebbels had become increasingly unsettled by the 'anti-fascist' propaganda emanating from the League of German Officers. This group of prominent prisoners in the Soviet Union, manipulated by the NKVD, was led by General der Artillerie Walther von Seydlitz-Kurzbach and other senior officers captured at Stalingrad. Seydlitz, now virulently anti-Nazi, had proposed in September to the NKVD that he should form a 30,000-strong corps from German prisoners of war, who could be flown into Germany to overthrow Hitler. When informed of this, Beria wrongly suspected that it was an elaborate and over-ambitious attempt at a mass escape.

The ceremonial vows of loyalty from the field marshals looked even more unconvincing on 30 March when Manstein of Army Group South and Kleist of Army Group Centre were brought back to the Berghof to be relieved of their positions. Their crime was to have requested permission to withdraw their forces, to evade another encirclement.

Just over a week later, the German and Romanian forces trapped on the Crimea by the 4th Ukrainian Front were forced to pull back after a devastating attack on the Perekop Isthmus. On 10 April the German forces in Odessa had to escape by sea. And just over a month later, the last 25,000 German and Romanian troops left in Sebastopol surrendered. The Wehrmacht had now been cleared from the Black Sea coast to the Pripet Marshes on the edge of Poland. In the south, the Red Army had won back almost all Soviet territory and had entered foreign territory. In the north, the Leningrad Front had reached the Estonian border. For Stalin, the next objective was clear. If the Stavka plan to cut off the whole of Army Group Centre in Belorussia worked, it would be the greatest victory of the war, especially if timed to coincide with the Allied invasion of Normandy.

By night, RAF Lancasters continued to pound Berlin in Britain's original 'Second Front', although at a very heavy cost in bombers and aircrew. Göring did not show himself in public any more. Hitler despaired of the Luftwaffe's failure to wreak revenge on England, and yet he could not bring himself to remove his old comrade. But Air Chief Marshal Harris's plan 'to wreck Berlin from end to end' to win the war remained a figment of his obstinate imagination. The destruction caused in his Battle of Berlin was immense, but the city had failed to burn.

US air force and RAF raids built up into the crescendo of 'Big Week' in late February 1944. Long-range Mustang fighter escorts dramatically reduced American losses as their heavy bombers attacked fuel and aircraft targets at Regensburg, Fürth, Graz, Steyr, Gotha, Schweinfurt, Augsburg, Aschersleben, Bremen and Rostock. It had taken the air chiefs in Washington a long time to accept that their doctrine of unescorted daylight bombing had been flawed, but with the Mustang and its Rolls-Royce engine they finally had the machine to make it work. The new tactic also contributed massively to the necessary weakening of the Luftwaffe before Operation Overlord.

Despite the Allied bombing campaign, German aircraft production, switched in some cases to tunnel factories, increased. But the aerial battles had left the Luftwaffe with few experienced pilots. The novices, rushed through flying school because of fuel shortages, were sent straight into front-line squadrons where they provided easy pickings for Allied pilots. The Luftwaffe, just like the Imperial Japanese Navy, had failed to send their best pilots back as flying and aerial combat instructors. Instead, they had kept them on a relentless round of sorties until they were exhausted and made fatal mistakes. By the time the Allied invasion came in June, the Luftwaffe was a spent force.

37

The Pacific, China and Burma

1944

Once the islands of Tarawa and Makin had been secured in November 1943, and the lessons digested, Nimitz began planning to seize the Marshall Islands to the north. His first objective was the Kwajalein Atoll in the centre. Some of his commanders were concerned by the number of Japanese air bases in the area, but Nimitz was adamant.

The balance of power in the Pacific had by now switched decisively in favour of the US Navy. The astonishing American shipbuilding programme far exceeded even what the late Admiral Yamamoto had feared before his attack on Pearl Harbor. The United States had also shown itself capable of catching up and overtaking the Japanese in aviation technology. The Imperial Japanese Navy had begun the war with a far superior fighter, the Zero, but had failed to modernize it sufficiently. The US Navy, on the other hand, brought in new aircraft, especially the Grumman F6F Hellcat, and continually experimented with new techniques.

On 31 January 1944, Rear Admiral Marc A. Mitscher's Task Force 58, with twelve fast carriers and eight new battleships, advanced on the Marshall Islands well ahead of the invasion force. Its 650 aircraft destroyed almost every Japanese aircraft in pre-emptive strikes and the battleships shelled the airstrips. The Americans had also prepared a much longer and more intense naval bombardment, and introduced more heavily armoured amtracs. As a result, the landings on and around Kwajalein, which began on 1 February, succeeded with a much lower loss of life – just 334 men as opposed to the 1,056 who had died at Tarawa.

Encouraged by the Kwajalein operation, Admiral Nimitz decided to push straight on to take the Eniwetok Atoll, nearly 650 kilometres to the west. He again decided to use the fast carrier force to eliminate any Japanese threat from the air. In the case of Eniwetok, it would come from the great Japanese naval and air base at Truk, 1,240 kilometres further west in the Caroline Islands. Admiral Mitscher took nine carriers, and once within range they launched wave after wave of fighters and dive-bombers. In thirty-six hours, US Navy pilots destroyed 200 aircraft on the ground and, together with the surface ships, sank forty-one Japanese vessels totalling more than 200,000 tons. The Japanese Combined Fleet could never use Truk again, and Eniwetok and neighbouring islands were duly taken.

General MacArthur, the viceroy of the south-west Pacific based in Brisbane, was gradually building up his forces in order to satisfy his vow to retake the Philippines. By the end of the year he would have accumulated under his command the Sixth and Eighth Armies, the Fifth Air Force and the Seventh Fleet, which became known as 'MacArthur's Navy'.

MacArthur suspected, with justification, that although the official policy was to give his advance to the Philippines equal priority with that of Nimitz in the central Pacific, the US Navy was bound to win. Its strategy of advancing towards Japan by island group was now strongly supported by the air force chief of staff 'Hap' Arnold. Once the new B-29 Superfortress, with a bombing range of 1,500 miles, entered service, they could attack Japan directly from the Mariana Islands.

MacArthur had little choice but to continue his progress westwards along the northern coast of New Guinea, in the hope that the joint chiefs would then allocate the resources he needed to begin his reconquest of the Philippines. But MacArthur suddenly decided to seize the Admiralty Islands, 240 kilometres to the north, ahead of schedule. Air reconnaissance indicated that the Japanese airfield had been abandoned. It was an extremely risky venture, especially with a small invading force, but it paid off. The Japanese were forced to abandon their defence of Madang on the north coast of New Guinea, while American warships could now use the great natural harbour of the Admiralties and cut the Japanese supply line to New Guinea.

Freshly arrived army divisions were slow to adapt to Pacific island combat. Sentries made nervous by jungle noises at night or overreacting to deliberate Japanese scare tactics could cause chaos. Troops from the 24th Division guarding Lieutenant

General Robert Eichelberger's I Corps headquarters in Hollandia at the western end of New Guinea even began a night battle among themselves, firing machine guns and hurling grenades when no Japanese were near. Eichelberger described it as 'a disgraceful exhibition', yet fire discipline continued to be an alien concept for many US units, despite constant complaints by senior officers of 'promiscuous shooting'.

Chiang Kai-shek was painfully aware that the twin strategies of MacArthur and the US Navy were making his country even more of a backwater. He had discovered after the Teheran conference that Operation Buccaneer, the plan for landings in the Bay of Bengal, had been cancelled since the amphibious craft were needed for Overlord. China's main interest to the joint chiefs of staff in Washington was now simply to act as an unsinkable aircraft carrier within range of Japan. And even that role would be undermined once the Mariana Islands had been captured, and air bases built for the B-29 Superfortresses.

Chiang also suspected that, while the Allies were focused on the invasion of France, the Japanese would launch a major offensive against him before the United States could redeploy forces from Europe to the Far East. He warned Roosevelt of this in a signal on 1 January 1944. General Stilwell had also been concerned about a renewed Japanese attempt to destroy US air bases in China, after the Chekiang–Kiangsi offensive of the year before. But his plans to modernize more of the Chinese army had been downgraded. The Japanese were particularly provoked by the American Fourteenth Air Force's raids on the Hsinchu naval airfield on Formosa, which was followed by bombing raids against their home islands.

The Americans and the British ignored these warnings of a major Japanese retaliation, partly because the generalissimo had cried wolf before, but mainly because their intelligence analysis was deeply flawed. They considered the Imperial Japanese Army incapable of undertaking a major campaign, and even assumed that it would start to withdraw troops from China to reinforce the Philippines.

In fact Imperial General Headquarters had already approved plans for the Ichi-gō Offensive into southern China with half a million men, and for Operation U-gō, attacking from

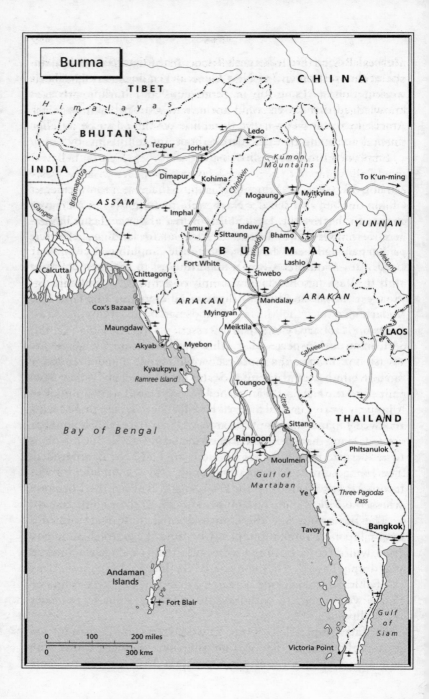

Burma

northern Burma into India with 85,000. In the first half of 1943, the operations section in Imperial General Headquarters had been working on a 'Long-Range Strategic Plan'. This tacitly acknowledged that Japan could not now win in the Pacific against American naval supremacy. Instead it would relaunch its continental war to destroy the Nationalist Chinese forces.

Emperor Hirohito wanted a great victory, which he believed would allow Japan to negotiate a favourable peace with the western powers. General Okamura Yasuji, the commander-in-chief in China, on the other hand, saw the Ichi-gō Offensive as their one chance to destroy the Nationalists before the Americans landed in force on the south-western coast of China in 1945. The two primary objectives of the Ichi-gō Offensive laid down by Imperial General Headquarters were to destroy the US airfields in China and, through 'an overland clearing operation', to link up the Japanese armies in China with those in Vietnam, Thailand and Malaya.

On 24 January, General Tōjō restricted the objective to the destruction of American airfields and the Emperor gave his assent. But the idea of securing a corridor from Manchuria down through China all the way to Indochina, Thailand and Malaya remained very much in the forefront of the general staff's thinking. American air supremacy over the South China Sea combined with attacks by US submarines threatened to sever maritime connections. A land route was therefore seen as vital.

In Burma, both sides were preparing their own offensives. Lieutenant General Mutagachi Renya, the commander of the Japanese 15th Army in Burma with 156,000 men, had become obsessed with invading India. Other senior Japanese officers, especially those with the 33rd Army in north-east Burma, were very sceptical. They wanted to attack the Chinese Nationalists across the Salween River from the west and destroy the US air base at K'un-ming.

The British tend to see the Burma campaign of 1944 as one of Chindit columns deep in the jungle, and the brave defensive battles of Imphal and Kohima under Slim's leadership turning defeat into victory. Americans, if they think of Burma at all, conjure up images of 'Vinegar Joe' Stilwell and Merrill's Marauders. For the Chinese, it was the Yunnan–north Burma campaign. Their best divisions played a major role here, when they should have been used to defend southern China against the Ichi-gō Offensive, which destroyed Nationalist power and helped the Communists to win the civil war to come.

On 9 January Indian and British troops from the Fourteenth Army, having advanced down the Arakan coast, captured Maungdaw. Once again they wanted to take the island of Akyab with its airfield, but once again they were forced to retreat when the Japanese 55th Division threatened to cut them off. Stilwell, meanwhile, was advancing into north-east Burma with the Chinese divisions in X-Force, which had been trained and equipped by the Americans in India. His plan was to seize the communications centre of Myitkyina, with its airfield. The Allies wanted to eliminate the Japanese air base there because its aircraft threatened the most direct air route to China over the Himalayan Hump. And once Myitkyina had been secured, the Ledo Road could be joined up with the Burma Road to provide a land route once more to K'un-ming and Chungking. The thrust south of the Chinese divisions in X-Force was also designed to join up with the Chinese Expeditionary Force, usually known as Y-Force, attacking from Yunnan across the Salween River into Burma.

Y-Force had just under 90,000 men, less than half its planned strength. A shortage of weapons and equipment was mainly to blame. Chennault's Fourteenth Air Force took the vast bulk of the supplies air-freighted over the Hump, and since there was a frequent shortfall in the planned deliveries of 7,000 tons a month, the Chinese divisions received little. Stilwell compared the task of rearming them to 'trying to manure a ten-acre field with sparrow shit'. Relations between Chennault and Stilwell had deteriorated even further. Chennault, in an attempt to justify his supply priority, claimed that his aircraft had sunk 40,000 tons of Japanese shipping in the summer of 1943, when the true figure was just over 3,000 tons.

Stilwell's command in the north-east had been increased by the only American combat formation on the mainland of Asia. This was the 5307th Provisional Regiment, codenamed Galahad, and dubbed 'Merrill's Marauders' by a journalist after their commander Brigadier General Frank Merrill. The combined chiefs of staff in Washington had been so impressed by Orde Wingate that they had authorized an American version of the Chindits. Loyal tribesmen from the north-eastern highlands known as the Kachin Rangers scouted for them as they did for British imperial troops.

Stilwell's forces had pushed back the experienced Japanese 18th Division in the Hukawng Valley, but failed to trap it. The Japanese retreat accelerated, however, when Wingate's Chindits landed in gliders on 5 March well to the south and cut the railway to the Japanese base and airfield at Myitkyina. Operation Thursday was the most ambitious deep-penetration offensive of the war in the Far East. It was far better prepared and supported than the Chindits' first foray behind Japanese lines.

The 16th Brigade commanded by Brigadier Bernard Fergusson would suffer a 'very tedious' march from Ledo to Indaw. It was 360 kilometres as the crow flies, but there was never a straight line over high hills and through thick jungle, where they seldom saw the sky. One stretch of fifty-five kilometres took them seven days. Tropical downpours meant that rivers and streams were swollen and the Chindits 'remained wet for weeks'. 'There were four thousand men,' Fergusson observed, 'and seven hundred animals strung out sixty-five miles from end to end, one abreast, because the paths and tracks were not wide enough.'

Two other brigades and another two battalions were flown in by glider and C-47 transports once airfields had been cleared in the jungle. This was done with light bulldozers transported in large American Waco gliders. Mules, 25-pounder field guns, Bofors anti-aircraft guns and all the other heavy equipment also came in by air. One frenzied mule had to be shot dead on the flight out in a C-47 transport, but most casualties had occurred in crash-landed gliders from the first wave. Wreckage was just pushed to the side of the airfield by a bulldozer and left there with the bodies rotting inside, because nobody had time to bury them. It was not an encouraging smell for later arrivals.

Once the airstrips were prepared, the perimeters of these jungle bases were secured with barbed wire and defensive positions ready for the inevitable Japanese counter-attacks. A brigade headquarters staff officer commented that 'it was extraordinary to be landing at night in a Dakota on a strip with a lit flare-path in enemy territory'. The Japanese attacks became suicidally methodical, because they almost always came at the same point and at the same time. Out of pride, they would continue to try again and again, however many men they lost. Machine-gun posts mowed them down on the wire time after time, and their corpses hanging there attracted swarms of flies.

Soon RAF Hurricanes were operating out of Broadway, the largest base. On 24 March an American B-25 landed there bringing Wingate. Two American war correspondents asked for a lift when he was leaving, and he took them despite the pilot's protest that the plane was overloaded. It crashed in the jungle killing all aboard.

To the north-east Galahad Force, exhausted, sick and under-nourished, struggled on in appalling conditions towards Myitkyina. Monsoon rains, leeches, lice and the usual jungle diseases, especially malaria – and even cerebral malaria – took their toll. So too did sepsis, pneumonia and meningitis. The dead were buried but jackals soon dug up their bodies. Resupplying Merrill's men by air was almost impossible in a terrain of deep valleys with impenetrable bamboo thickets and elephant grass, as well as the steep ridges in the Kumon Mountains which rose to 1,800 metres.

The Chindits were also exhausted and famished, and many fell sick, but this time providing they were close to an airstrip they could be evacuated by light aircraft along with the wounded, rather than abandoned as on the earlier foray. Those too badly hurt to be moved were finished off with 'a lethal dose of morphine' or a revolver shot so that they would not fall alive into Japanese hands.

Almost everyone was emaciated after living on K-Rations, which simply did not provide sufficient calories. The exhaustion and strain was such that there were many psychological casualties towards the end. 'You could see people going downhill,' observed the chief medical officer of the 111th Brigade. 'Some even died in their sleep. The Gurkhas were the most resilient in our brigade. The Gurkha has a very tough upbringing in Nepal, and is used to hardship and disaster.'

Stilwell had little idea of what the Chindits were up to and how much they had achieved by cutting off Myitkyina from the south and west. The liaison between Stilwell and the British was almost non-existent and led to even greater ill-feeling. The obsessively anglophobic Stilwell, in the words of one observer, seemed to be 'fighting the War of Independence all over again'.

While Stilwell's forces struggled towards Myitkyina, the decisive battles of the war in Burma were taking place to the north-west. General Mutagachi's ambitions for the 15th Army knew no bounds. He was encouraged by Subhas Chandra Bose to believe that with the so-called Indian National Army, recruited from prisoners of war in Japanese camps, the British Raj could be overthrown easily in a 'March on Delhi'. But Mutagachi severely underestimated the logistical problems which his offensive with three divisions would face.

He based his plan on first seizing the well-stocked British base at Imphal and making use of what he called 'Churchill supplies'. After defeating the Indian division at Imphal, he intended to cut the Bengal–Assam railway line which supplied Stilwell's Chinese divisions, and thus force them to retreat to their start-point of Ledo. Then he planned to destroy the airfields in Assam, which were used to support Slim's Fourteenth Army and fly supplies over the Himalayas to China.

On 8 March, three days after the Chindits had landed well to their rear, Mutagachi's 15th Army began to cross the River Chindwin. Slim told the headquarters of IV Corps to pull its divisions back to defensive positions on the Imphal Plain. Even though this withdrawal was demoralizing for his men, Slim saw that he needed to stretch the supply lines of the Japanese and shorten his own. Logistics would be the key to the battle in such terrain. Mountbatten also wasted no time. He commandeered US transport planes to fly in the 5th Indian Division as reinforcements, and sought permission from the combined chiefs of staff in Washington afterwards.

What the British command had failed to see was that a far stronger Japanese force than they had imagined was threatening Kohima eighty kilometres to the north of Imphal. This would cut off IV Corps and threaten the other supply base and airfield at Dimapur. The Japanese 31st Division had advanced rapidly from the Chindwin north towards Kohima, using mainly jungle trails. The British, not expecting them to move without motor transport, were taken by surprise. But the 50th Indian Parachute

Brigade held them up in a magnificent week-long struggle around Sangshak.

Kohima was a small hill-station, 1,500 metres up in the Naga Highlands. It had white colonial bungalows and a mission chapel with a red corrugated-iron roof, all set against a backdrop of forest and blue mountains in the distance. The deputy commissioner's bungalow on Garrison Hill boasted a clay tennis court which became no-man's-land in the deadly battle to come.

The battle fought by the 50th Parachute Brigade had given Slim just enough time to redeploy some of his reinforcements. But on 6 April, when the Japanese arrived, Kohima was defended by only the 4th Royal West Kents, a detachment of Rajputs, the locally raised Assam Rifles, a mountain battery and some sappers. Once the Japanese encircled the town and blocked the road to Dimapur, they were cut off.

The battle for Garrison Hill and the tennis court was savage. Bizarrely, the Japanese would shout 'Give up!' in English before they attacked, which provided ample warning to the defenders. The British troops fought with a new vengeance. After the way the Japanese had bayoneted wounded prisoners in the Arakan, the company commander of the West Kents said: 'They had renounced any right to be regarded as human, and we thought of them as vermin to be exterminated . . . Our backs were to the wall, and we were going to sell our lives as expensively as we could.'

This they proceeded to do with Bren guns, grenades and rifles, exacting enormous casualties. 'The sheer weight of the attacks threatened to overwhelm the battalion,' said the headquarters company commander. 'The outer part of the defences became piled with Japanese corpses.' British casualties came mainly from snipers and light artillery. Their wounded were laid end to end in trenches. Many were hit a second time by shrapnel as they lay there. Water was very short and had to be parachuted down in metal jerrycans. The Japanese, on the other hand, were running out of rice due to Mutagachi's assumption that they could easily take British supplies. Part of their desperate, even senseless bravery came from the need to capture some food.

The British 2nd Division, advancing down the road from Dimapur with the tanks of the 3rd Carabineers, began to fight through to relieve the defenders of Kohima. When they finally reached Garrison Hill, the place looked like a scene from the First World War, with smashed trees, trenches collapsed by shellfire and the stench of death. But, although the battered West Kents were relieved, the battle for Kohima continued for almost another four weeks. The monsoon was starting, however, which meant that the Japanese could expect even less from their supply lines. On 13 May they broke off the battle, and many were slaughtered as they pulled out.

Two days before, on 11 May, the Chinese divisions of Y-Force in Yunnan began to cross the Salween River to meet up with Stilwell's X-Force. The Japanese 56th Division, defending the line of the Salween, was well aware of their plans. It had already made raids across the river to push back the Chinese further into Yunnan, but increased Nationalist strength supported by a part of Chennault's Fourteenth Air Force indicated the preparation of a major offensive. This was confirmed by signals intercepts. The Japanese, having captured a Chinese codebook, were able to decipher all the radio traffic from K'un-ming and Chungking. Although the Japanese achieved a certain success in counter-attacks against troops crossing the river, Chinese forces were too strong.

On 17 May, Stilwell launched a glider assault with part of Galahad Force on Myitkyina airfield and seized it. 'This will burn the Limeys,' Stilwell gloated in his diary. But the Japanese rapidly reinforced the 300-strong garrison in the town and soon the Americans were besieged. The Japanese had stockpiled large supplies of ammunition there. Exhausted and sick, with jungle skin sores, Merrill's men began to collapse. Some suffered so badly from dysentery that they simply cut a flap in the seat of their pants to save time.

Stilwell showed little sympathy, either to his own men or to the Chindits. But with his reinforced Chinese divisions now surrounding the town, the Japanese became the besieged. And on 24 June a simultaneous attack by Chinese troops and the Chindits of Brigadier Michael Calvert's severely weakened 77th Brigade seized the key town of Mogaung to the west. Yet it would take until the beginning of August before the Japanese commander in Myitkyina committed *seppuku*, and his surviving troops slipped away into the jungle across the Irrawaddy. At last work on the Ledo Road to China could be started, and US transport aircraft were able to fly a much shorter and less dangerous route, almost doubling the tonnage of supplies delivered to China.

As the great battle round Imphal continued against Mutagachi's 15th Army, Allied regiments counter-attacked. But they, like the Americans, were astonished and appalled by the Japanese talent for excavation into hills to make bunkers. A newly arrived subaltern joining the 2nd Border Regiment was told by his platoon sergeant: 'By Christ, them little bastards can dig. They're underground before our blokes have stopped spitting on their bloody hands.'

General Slim's prediction that the monsoon would harm the Japanese supply routes far more than his own proved true. His Fourteenth Army could rely on air drops, while Mutagachi's men were starving. Lieutenant General Tanaka Noboru, who had arrived on 23 May to take over command of the 33rd Division in the south, wrote in his diary: 'Both officers and men look dreadful. They've let their hair and beards grow until they look exactly like wild men of the mountains . . . They have had almost nothing to eat – they're undernourished and pale.' By June his division had lost 70 per cent of its strength. Some of his men went for days on end with nothing to eat but wild grass and lizards. Their officers had secured what few supplies there were for themselves. In many cases, they attacked in the vain hope of finding tins of bully beef in Allied trenches.

Japanese soldiers were by no means immune from combat fatigue and psychosis, but only a small number were evacuated. Sufferers unable to take the strain any more committed suicide. Japanese soldiers had various names for paralysing fear, such as 'losing your legs' or 'samurai shakes' for uncontrolled trembling. They tended to cope with fear by adopting one of two extremes: either profound fatalism, with the acceptance that they were bound to die, or else denial, convincing themselves that they were invulnerable. On their departure for the army, most had been presented with a 'thousand-stitch' scarf by their mothers which was supposed to ward off bullets. But as Japan's defeat became more evident, fatalism became almost obligatory since field service regulations forbade any soldier to allow himself to be taken prisoner, even if badly wounded.

General Mutagachi was becoming deranged. He called for attack after attack, but his divisional commanders ignored his orders. On 3 July, the Imphal Offensive was finally called off. The Japanese retreat across the Chindwin left a trail of horror. Allied troops on their advance passed abandoned Japanese wounded, infested with maggots. In most cases they simply put them out of their misery. Mutagachi's 15th Army had lost 55,000 men. Around half of their casualties were due to starvation or disease. Both General Kawabe Masakusu, the commander-in-chief of the Burma Area Army, and Mutagachi were relieved of their commands. Allied casualties during the battles for Imphal and Kohima amounted to 17,587 killed and wounded.

In China, the Ichi-gō Offensive had begun in April. It was the largest operation that the Imperial Japanese Army had ever undertaken, with 510,000 men out of the total of 620,000 men in the China Expeditionary Army. But for once the Japanese did not have air superiority. In fact by the beginning of 1944 relative strengths had been reversed. The Nationalists had 170 aircraft and the US Fourteenth Air Force 230, while the Imperial Japanese Navy had only a hundred, the rest having been withdrawn to make up for the disastrous losses in the Pacific. Chennault believed that he had enough aircraft to defend his bases, but Imperial General Headquarters in Tokyo authorized the doubling of air strength for the forthcoming operations.

The main objective of the Ichi-gō Offensive was, as Chiang had also warned, to eliminate the airfields of the Fourteenth Air Force. The first phase, the Kogō Offensive, came from the Japanese 1st Army in the north-east, heavily reinforced from the Kwantung Army in Manchukuo. The Japanese did not attack Mao Tsetung's Communist forces based on Yenan to the west, which had done little for some time except kill collaborators. The Japanese were interested only in crushing the Nationalists.

In April, the 1st Army attacked south across the Yellow River to meet up with part of the 11th Army advancing north from round Wuchang–Hankow. This cleared the Peking–Hankow railway, establishing the first part of the corridor. The

Nationalist troops in Honan province recoiled in disorder. Officers fled, commandeering military trucks, carts and oxen to evacuate their families and all the booty they had looted from towns and in the countryside. Outraged peasants who had been robbed of their food and pathetic belongings disarmed officers and soldiers. They killed many, even burying some alive.

Their hatred for the local authorities and the army was more than understandable. A severe drought in 1942, made worse by the Nationalist food taxes in kind, and exacerbated by the cynical exploitation of local officials and landowners, had led to a terrible famine that winter and into the spring of 1943. Three million out of thirty million people in the province are thought to have died.

Chiang Kai-shek's worst fears had come to pass, and his best-equipped divisions were tied down at American insistence in the Burma–Yunnan campaign. After Chennault had taken the lion's share of the supplies, and Stilwell had allocated the rest to X-Force and Y-Force, little had been left to re-equip other Nationalist armies. Those in central and southern China lacked weapons and ammunition, and in many cases had not been paid. When Chiang had asked Roosevelt for a billion-dollar loan to keep his forces going, Washington instantly saw it as a form of blackmail to obtain money for himself, as the price of keeping Nationalist China in the war.

In January, Chiang's reluctance to commit Y-Force on the Salween front for fear of a Japanese offensive had prompted Roosevelt to threaten to cut off Lend–Lease completely. And once the Ichi-gō Offensive began, Roosevelt did not want Chennault's Fourteenth Air Force or the recently arrived 20th Bomber Command's B-29s to be used in support of Nationalist troops, even though Chennault's attacks had been a major factor in provoking the Japanese onslaught. Roosevelt, despite all his championship of the Nationalist Chinese, was cynical and dismissive of anything which did not speed the triumph of American arms in the short term. Convinced that the United Nations led by America and the Soviet Union would be able to solve everything afterwards, he had a dangerous disregard for post-war consequences.

On 1 June, once the Chinese army of 300,000 men in Honan had crumbled away, the Japanese drive south from Wuchang to Changsha began. South of Changsha and Heng-yang, the US air base at Kweilin was a key Japanese objective. Japanese intelligence knew every detail about it from their agents, working through the mass of prostitutes catering to USAAF personnel in the town. General Hsueh Yueh, the Cantonese commander whose forces had successfully defended Changsha three times already, was bitterly disappointed. His armies had seen no American supplies, yet were still expected to defend the Fourteenth Air Force. As even Theodore White, that most bitter critic of the Nationalists, wrote: 'Hsueh defended the city as he always had, with the same tactics and the same units, but his units were three years older, their weapons three years more worn, the soldiers three years hungrier than when they had last seen glory.'

Chennault did not hesitate to throw his Mustang fighters and B-25 bombers into night attacks on the Japanese columns advancing down the road from Changsha. His bases there and at Heng-yang were at risk. Flying three or four missions a day, and sustained by coffee and sandwiches, pilots of the Fourteenth Air Force certainly did what they could. The Japanese drive to push on increased when on 15 June B-29 Superfortresses flying from Chengtu in the west began a series of heavy raids on the home islands of Japan. These rapidly tailed off when they ran short of aviation fuel.

General Hsueh followed the same tactics as before at Changsha, giving in the centre, then attacking on the flanks and in the rear. But his malnourished soldiers lacked the strength to hold back the Japanese, while quarrels among commanders led to disaster. The Japanese seized Changsha and all Hsueh's artillery at minimal cost. The commander of the Chinese Fourth Army, who escaped in a convoy of military trucks taking his personal belongings and booty, was arrested on Chiang Kai-shek's order and shot. South-western China lay open and the US air base at Heng-yang fell on 26 June.

While the Japanese stepped up their offensive to destroy the American air bases on mainland China, they had no idea that their efforts were soon to become irrelevant. Admiral Spruance's Fifth Fleet was the largest in the world with 535 warships. It was heading for the Mariana Islands to turn them into airfields, from which B-29 Superfortresses could bomb Japan. With the Fifth

Fleet sailed Vice Admiral Turner's Joint Expeditionary Force with 127,000 men.

Japanese positions on Saipan, the largest and first target island, had been bombed by land-based aircraft for some time. By early June, Japanese air strength in the Marianas had been greatly reduced. But the defending force of 32,000 men was still far greater than expected. Admiral Mitscher's Task Force 58 provided a two-day bombardment with its seven battleships before the marines went in, but it was not very effective. It smashed conspicuous targets such as a cane-sugar processing plant, but failed to hit the bunkers near by.

On the morning of 15 June, the first waves of the 2nd and 4th Marine Divisions began to land on Saipan in armoured amtracs against artillery, mortar and heavy machine-gun fire. The idea was for the amtracs to storm right across the beaches, but few made it. There were too many obstacles, and they lacked sufficient armour in front against the Japanese shells. But at least the infantry avoided the heavy casualties of the past when wading in through the surf. By nightfall, a beachhead with nearly 20,000 men had been established on the twenty-two-kilometre-long island. The Japanese sent in two suicidal infantry charges, but with US destroyers firing illuminating shells overhead, the marines were able to gun them down.

That night, 2,400 kilometres to the west, the submarine USS *Flying Fish* sighted part of the Imperial Japanese Navy off the Philippines in the San Bernardino Strait. She surfaced to get off her warning signal to the Fifth Fleet. Vice Admiral Ozawa Jisaburō's First Mobile Fleet was to be reinforced with the heavy battleships *Yamato* and *Musashi*. He would have almost all the main Japanese warships afloat in the Pacific – nine carriers with 430 aircraft, five battleships, thirteen cruisers and twenty-eight destroyers – for a decisive battle. Admiral Spruance, on the other hand, had fifteen fast carriers with 891 aircraft in Mitscher's Task Force 58, and Ozawa did not know that most of the land-based Japanese aircraft in the region had been eliminated. Ozawa's greatest weakness, however, lay in his pilots' lack of experience. Few had served for as long as six months, and most had little more than two months' flying training.

Spruance sent Mitscher's task force off to intercept Ozawa's fleet 290 kilometres to the west of the Marianas, but then pulled them back towards Saipan in case the Japanese split their forces. Ozawa's search planes sighted the task force on 18 June, and early next morning he sent off a first strike of sixty-nine aircraft. They were picked up on radar by Mitscher's screen of destroyers out in front. Hellcat fighters on a raid over Guam were summoned back to their carriers, while bombers were despatched to Guam to wreck the runways, in case Ozawa's pilots tried to land there. The Americans now made use of their huge advantage in numbers. With their fifteen carriers they had enough aircraft to maintain a fighter umbrella overhead the whole time.

At 10.36 hours, a patrol of Hellcats sighted the incoming attackers and dived. They shot down forty-two out of the sixty-nine aircraft, for the loss of only one of their own. As the second wave of 128 planes came in later, the US Navy's fighter pilots shot down another seventy. Ozawa, unable to admit defeat, sent in two more waves. Altogether 240 Japanese carrier-launched aircraft were shot down as well as nearly another fifty planes from Guam. American warships suffered only a couple of minor hits, while US submarines sank two carriers, the *Shokaku* and Ozawa's flagship, the *Taiho*.

When the majority of his aircraft failed to return, Ozawa made a fatally mistaken assumption. He thought that most of them had landed on Guam and would soon return to their carriers, so he kept his fleet in the area. Admiral Mitscher obtained Spruance's agreement to go in pursuit the next day. Finally, late in the afternoon of 20 June, one of Mitscher's reconnaissance planes spotted the Japanese fleet. The enemy was at extreme range and it would soon be dark, but this was their last chance. The flat-tops turned to the wind and managed to launch 216 aircraft in twenty minutes. The Hellcats soon dealt with Ozawa's fighter screen, shooting down another sixty-five aircraft, while the dive-bombers and torpedo bombers sank the carrier *Hiyo* and two oil tankers, and caused serious damage to other warships.

Despite the threat of submarines, Mitscher ordered his ships to turn on their lights, searchlights and fire flares to guide in the returning aircraft. One pilot described the scene as 'a Hollywood premier, Chinese New Year and the Fourth of July all rolled into one'. Many planes were running out of fuel. Altogether eighty crashed on landing, or ditched into the sea – four times as many aircraft as were lost in their attack. It was a chaotic ending, but the Great Marianas Turkey Shoot, as the navy flyers liked to call it, had cost the Japanese more than 400 aircraft and three carriers. It could have been more if Spruance had not played safe by keeping Mitscher's task force so close to Saipan.

The battle for the island also became known for the way Lieutenant General Holland Smith, the corps commander from the Marines, sacked the US Army general in charge of the 27th Division, a National Guard formation. Furious at its slow, cautious and ill-coordinated attack which held up his two Marine divisions, Holland Smith was backed by Admiral Spruance. The basic problem was that the Marine Corps had a very different and direct approach to fighting.

The Japanese were nevertheless forced back to the northern point of the island, and early on 7 July the survivors launched the largest *banzai* attack of the war. More than 3,000 Japanese soldiers and sailors, charging with bayonets, swords and grenades, descended on two battalions of the 27th Division. Marines and soldiers alike could not shoot fast enough as the Japanese swept on at them. The battle ended two days later. The American invasion force suffered 14,000 killed and wounded, while the Japanese forces left 30,000 corpses on the island. Added to them were around 7,000 Japanese civilians out of 12,000, most of whom committed suicide by throwing themselves from cliffs into the sea. Appeals to them by interpreters through loudspeakers not to kill themselves were largely ignored.

After Saipan, the islands of Tinian and Guam were invaded. Tinian was taken in a clever coup de main, with two Marine regiments landing unexpectedly while a major feint was made on the other side of the island. Guam, the first US territory to be recaptured, witnessed another mass Japanese counter-attack. But this time the Japanese ran straight into a concentration of artillery batteries, which fired over open sights. The airfields on Guam were secured before the end of July, and soon engineer battalions and Seabees were extending the airfields to take the B-29 Superfortresses. The Marianas offered far better bases for the bombing of the Japanese home islands than those in mainland China. They were unthreatened by Japanese ground forces, and at the same time ordnance, spare parts and aviation fuel could arrive by sea rather than having to be flown over the Himalayas. Imperial General Headquarters in Tokyo could see clearly that the endgame had begun.

38

The Spring of Expectations

MAY–JUNE 1944

After all the delays, detailed planning for Operation Overlord had begun in earnest in January 1944. Much valuable work had already been carried out by a group headed by Lieutenant General Sir Frederick Morgan, under the acronym COSSAC, or chief of staff to the supreme Allied commander. But since they had been working without a supreme commander, key decisions had been hard to make.

Both Eisenhower, the supreme commander, and Montgomery, the commander of 21st Army Group, had the same reaction on examining COSSAC's draft invasion plans for Normandy. Three divisions were not enough, they concluded, and the Allies needed more beaches. They had to widen the invasion area to include the base of the Cotentin Peninsula. Eisenhower also insisted that he had to have full control over the Allied air forces. This signalled an interference in the bombing of Germany which neither Harris nor Spaatz, the 'bomber barons', welcomed.

Lieutenant General Bedell Smith, Eisenhower's chief of staff, had much to thrash out with Montgomery. The postponements of D-Day had as much to do with the shortage of landing craft as with British reluctance to commit to the invasion. Overlord was now an imminent reality, even if Brooke and Churchill still had their private fears. Senior British officers, who were privy to the wider picture, could not resist observing that American commitment to the 'Germany first' policy was rather hard to credit after the massive diversion of men, shipping, weaponry and equipment to the Pacific. The US Navy and MacArthur had won that battle in Washington. The Pacific theatre even managed, with General 'Hap' Arnold's connivance, to grab the new B-29 Superfortresses to attack Tokyo, while Ira Eaker's Eighth Air Force received none to bomb Germany.

The other problem which Bedell Smith tried to deal with

during Eisenhower's brief return home was the question of Operation Anvil, the invasion of southern France. Eisenhower felt that the United States had made a 'very considerable investment' in re-equipping the French army and that 'a gateway for them into France must be obtained'. But the shortage of landing craft, partly caused by Churchill's insistence on the Anzio landing, suggested that a simultaneous invasion of the south of France would weaken Overlord. Bedell Smith agreed with the British that Anvil should be dropped or at least postponed. Eisenhower was very angry at any suggestion that 'Anvil [would] have to be sacrificed'. But, despite his obstinacy on the point, he was forced to acknowledge that it might have to be pushed back.

The long-awaited invasion of France, although the common Allied goal, was bound to create tensions with the French. Neither Roosevelt nor Churchill had a clear idea of conditions in France, nor of the widespread support for de Gaulle and what was essentially a provisional government-in-waiting. The Conseil National de la Résistance acknowledged his leadership and even the French Communists were rallying. Yet Roosevelt's deep distrust of de Gaulle had not abated, and even the more sympathetic British were shaken in March by events in Algiers. Pierre Pucheu, the former Vichy minister of the interior who in 1941 had selected Communist prisoners for execution as hostages by the Germans, was on trial for his life. Pucheu had turned up in Algiers, wanting to join the anti-German struggle. He had been furnished with what appeared to be a laissez-passer from General Giraud, a piece of paper which put paid to any lingering Giraudist hopes.

The Communists and their allies in Algiers immediately demanded revenge justice. De Gaulle confirmed Pucheu's death sentence after this first trial of the Vichy regime. He felt he had little choice. The 'pitiless civil war' in France between the greatly increased Vichy Milice and the swelling resistance raised the threat of lynch-mobs taking revenge at the Liberation. Such chaos, de Gaulle feared, would give the Americans every excuse to impose the dreaded acronym AMGOT – Allied Military Government of Occupied Territory – on France.

Resistance groups were equally determined to make the liberation of France a French affair, and they were becoming more defiant as the Allied invasion approached. In the mountains of

Haute-Savoie on the Plateau des Glières above Annecy, 450 *résistants* including fifty-six Spanish Republicans fought back with doomed heroism against 2,000 Gardes Mobiles, Francs-Gardes and Milice as well as five battalions of German troops.

In Italy, General Mark Clark's determination to take Rome with his US Fifth Army before Overlord had only intensified. Yet, despite Allied air supremacy preventing German motor and rail transport from moving by day, Wehrmacht resistance in Italy under Kesselring proved far more durable than even Hitler had expected.

The bloody stalemate in the Apennines had a demoralizing effect on Allied forces. There was a high rate of self-inflicted wounds and combat fatigue. Nearly 30,000 men had deserted or were absent without leave from British units in Italy, and American divisions also suffered.

There were few cases of combat fatigue among the 56,000 men in II Polish Corps under General Władysław Anders. After the failure in March of Freyberg's New Zealanders and Indian troops to take Monte Cassino, the task was then handed to the Poles. They made it abundantly clear to British colleagues that they had no intention of taking German prisoners. The Poles were not just eager for revenge, they knew that they had to obtain a spectacular victory to help the cause of a free Poland. Stalin was openly hostile to their government-in-exile, especially after the discovery at Katyń of the Polish officers murdered by the NKVD. He was planning to set up a puppet Communist government, with the Red Army now poised once again to invade their homeland.

The renewed assault on Cassino was part of Operation Diadem, a general offensive planned by Alexander. Nearly half a million men from ten nations were involved. Clark's Fifth Army in the west on the Tyrrhenian coast, with Juin's French Corps in the mountains and the Eighth Army under Montgomery's replacement, Lieutenant General Sir Oliver Leese, were to overwhelm Kesselring's forces on the Gustav Line. Alexander called for numerous deceptions to be used. Fake bunkers were built conspicuously on attack sectors, while radio traffic and dummy landing craft gave the impression of another amphibious assault. Truscott's forces in the beachhead were greatly strengthened. Alexander's plan was for the attack on the Gustav Line to bring forward German reserves, then Truscott's corps would thrust north-east to Valmontone to cut off Vietinghoff's Tenth Army.

Clark was furious. He was not interested in trapping the Tenth Army. 'The capture of Rome is the only important objective,' he told Truscott. Clark, verging on paranoia, seemed to think that Alexander's plan was a British trick to take his Roman triumph away from him and give it to the Eighth Army instead. Alexander's assurances that the Fifth Army would be allowed to take Rome seemed only to increase Clark's suspicions. Army group orders were perfectly clear, but Clark secretly prepared to disobey them.

At 23.00 hours on 11 May, the Allied artillery – 25-pounders, 105mm howitzers, 5.5-inch medium guns and 155mm Long Toms – opened fire in a deafening roar, with blinding flashes of light all along the horizon. The Poles went straight into the attack, but found, to their dismay, that the Germans were relieving all their front-line battalions that night. The enemy force was thus almost double the estimated strength, and Polish casualties were appalling. So were those of the 8th Indian Division on their left crossing the Rapido River against the fortified village of Sant'Angelo, where the American 36th Division had suffered heavy losses at the beginning of the year. At last the engineers managed to get bridges in place and the Gurkhas, supported by tanks, cleared the village. But the British bridgehead was small and Monte Cassino still dominated the whole area.

The American II Corps close to the coast met heavy opposition across the Garigliano River. Juin's French colonial divisions in between the Americans and the British also received a murderous response. Juin decided to change tactics. He switched his axis to seize Monte Majo in a sudden attack with strong artillery support. It cost his men more than 2,000 casualties, but the Gustav Line was broken. His *goumiers* pushed on, out for blood and booty. 'Most wore sandals, wool socks, gloves with the trigger fingers snipped off, and striped djellabas; a beard, a soup-bowl helmet, and foot-long knife at the belt.' The knives were used for cutting off fingers and ears from the German dead as trophies. The *goumiers* were formidable mountain fighters. But they terrorized Italian civilians, and there were tales of brutal rapes, which their French officers tended to shrug off as the price to be paid in war.

Clark was furious with his American corps for not advancing as fast as the French and contemptuous of the Eighth Army, still held up by the 1st Fallschirmjäger Division at Monte Cassino. But Polish courage and gradual encirclement forced the paratroopers to withdraw. On 18 May, the white and red flag of Poland flew from the ruins of the great Benedictine abbey. It had cost them nearly 4,000 casualties.

The German withdrawal to the Hitler Line, ten to twenty kilometres behind the Gustav Line, did not go smoothly. Juin's troops allowed them no rest, and when the Eighth Army finally advanced into the bottleneck of the Liri Valley, it was clear that this second line of defence was at risk. Kesselring, desperate to hold it, transferred divisions from Mackensen's Fourteenth Army containing the Anzio beachhead. This was the moment for which Alexander had been waiting.

Truscott's VI Corps, secretly reinforced to seven divisions, was now stronger than Mackensen's whole army. On 22 May, Clark flew into the Anzio beachhead to try to demonstrate to the world that he, not Alexander, was in control of this operation. The next morning, Truscott's divisions attacked north-east towards Valmontone as Alexander had ordered. Casualties were heavy but the following day, finding that the Germans had pulled out, II Corps on the coast joined up with the Anzio beachhead. Clark, with a group of war correspondents and photographers in Jeeps, dashed over to have the event immortalized.

On 25 May, Truscott's 1st Armored Division was within striking distance of Valmontone, and within twenty-four hours he could have cut the Tenth Army's line of retreat. But that afternoon he received orders from Clark to switch his axis of advance to the north-west, towards Rome. Truscott and his divisional commanders were most uneasy, but Truscott loyally followed Clark, who concealed what he was up to from Alexander. Clark's obsession was so intense that one can assume that he had become slightly deranged. His later attempts to justify his actions were confused and contradictory. Clark even claimed at one point that he had warned Alexander that, if units of the Eighth Army attempted to get to Rome before him, he would order his men to open fire on them.

Clark was not merely determined that Alexander should have no credit, he was not prepared even to acknowledge Truscott's role. The Second World War saw many examples of egomania. Clark's desire to enter Rome as conqueror before Overlord was one of the most flagrant. Field Marshal Brooke once wrote in his diary: 'It is astonishing how petty and small men can be in connection with questions of command.' Alexander described Clark's behaviour as 'inexplicable', but then proceeded to explain it: 'I can only assume that the immediate lure of Rome for its publicity value persuaded him to switch the direction of his advance.'

While Alexander's forces fought the main battle of the Italian campaign, far greater events were in preparation in north-west Europe. Overlord would be the largest amphibious operation in history, with more than 5,000 ships, 8,000 aircraft and eight divisions in the first wave. There was considerable nervousness, known as 'D-Day jitters'. Senior British officers had painful memories of Dunkirk and other evacuations, to say nothing of the disastrous Dieppe raid. But the planning which went into Operation Neptune – the Channel-crossing stage of Overlord – was extraordinary in its detail. On receiving their orders, which ran to several hundred pages, the 3rd Canadian Division dubbed it 'Operation Overboard'.

The Germans were expecting an invasion, but they did not know exactly when or where it would come. The British staged an intricate series of deception plans under the general heading of Plan Fortitude. Fortitude North hinted that a 'Fourth British Army' would land in Norway, where Hitler, to the despair of his generals, had insisted on keeping more than 400,000 men. Fortitude South, using dummy tanks, aircraft and even landing ships in south-east England, persuaded the Germans that a second invasion would be unleashed on the Pas de Calais with a 1st Army Group led by General George Patton, the leader the Germans feared most.

Using double agents and captured spies, the Double Cross system set out to persuade the Germans that the landing in Normandy was just a preliminary or a feint, and that the real attack would come later south of Boulogne. German military intelligence, having greatly overestimated the forces and manpower available to the Allies, swallowed this scenario. Later when the scale of the deception became clear and anti-Nazi officers conspired to kill Hitler in July, the Gestapo began to suspect that the intelligence officers had allowed themselves to be misled, as part of a treasonous plot to lose the war.

Overlord planners had foreseen that success or failure would be decided during the dangerous days immediately after the landings. The Allied build-up of forces might not be able to match German reinforcements arriving to counter-attack the beachheads. The response to this was the idea developed in Italy, that you should seal off the combat zone by destroying all communications to the enemy's rear: bridges, railway lines, marshalling yards and key road intersections. They would isolate the Normandy invasion area by making sure that little could come across the Seine to the east and the Loire to the south. But, to conceal the invasion target area, they had to extend their attacks all the way across to Holland and even Denmark.

The bull-headed Air Marshal Harris was not impressed. He had convinced himself that, if his Lancasters continued to pound Berlin and other cities, an invasion of France would be unnecessary. He also tried to argue that his bombers could not hit precision targets such as railway lines. General Spaatz wanted to continue with his 'oil plan', attacking refineries and synthetic-oil depots and also bombing aircraft factories. But morale was not good in the Eighth Air Force. Almost ninety crews deliberately landed their aircraft in Sweden or Switzerland, where they were interned for the rest of the war. The USAAF had made great claims about its daylight bombing accuracy, when in fact it was little better than that of Bomber Command at night. Its aircraft had even bombed towns in Switzerland instead of Germany.

Eisenhower, however, decided to bring the bomber barons to heel through his deputy, Air Chief Marshal Tedder. But hatreds within the RAF ran deep, and Tedder had to get Eisenhower to pull rank, with Roosevelt's full backing. Harris and Spaatz fell into line. Churchill was appalled to discover that the planners were preparing an intensive destruction of French towns as this was the only way of blocking major road junctions.

The prospect of heavy civilian casualties and towns reduced to rubble would outrage the French. He appealed against this part of the 'Transportation Plan' to Eisenhower and then to Roosevelt, who backed the supreme commander's argument that it would save Allied lives. Churchill asked for a limit of 10,000 civilian casualties, but even this notional figure was not conceded. In the event, some 15,000 French civilians were killed and 19,000 others seriously injured in the lead-up to D-Day.

Churchill's other preoccupation was what to do with General Charles de Gaulle. British and American commanders did not want the secrets of Overlord to be passed to the French leadership in Algiers because they knew that the Germans had broken their old-fashioned codes. Eisenhower, however, insisted on taking General Pierre Koenig into his confidence. Koenig, as the commander-in-chief of all resistance groups now known as the Forces Françaises de l'Intérieur, would be sending out instructions to them just before the landings to sabotage communications and transport. And a number of French warships, air force squadrons and ground-force units were also taking part in the invasion.

Roosevelt wanted to remind his subordinates that the Allies were not liberating France to install General de Gaulle in power. Most senior American officials were depressed by the President's intransigence, and Churchill did his best to persuade him that they had to work with de Gaulle. But Roosevelt still wanted to impose a military government until elections were held, and insisted on creating an occupation currency. Banknotes were printed of such unconvincing appearance that the troops compared them to 'cigar coupons'.

Roosevelt reluctantly agreed to Churchill issuing an invitation to de Gaulle to come to London, and two York aircraft were sent to Algiers to fly him and his staff back. At first de Gaulle refused to come because Roosevelt had rejected any discussion of French civil government. Duff Cooper, Churchill's representative in Algiers, warned him that he would be playing into Roosevelt's hands if he did not go to London. On 3 June the Comité Français de Libération Nationale in Algiers officially took the name of Gouvernement Provisoire de la République Française, and de Gaulle agreed at the very last moment to accompany Cooper to England.

*

South of Rome, Mark Clark's dream was about to come true. An American infantry division had managed to slip through a gap in the Germans' last line of defence and forced its collapse. Kesselring ordered an immediate withdrawal. Hitler allowed Rome to be declared an open city and did not order its destruction. This came not out of mercy or respect for ancient monuments and art, but because his attention was focused on the Channel and the thought that he would soon be able to destroy London with his flying bombs.

In Rome on 4 June, Mark Clark summoned his subordinate commanders for a briefing on the Campidoglio, having also assembled all the war correspondents in Italy. This photo-opportunity, with an exultant Clark holding a map and pointing north towards the retreating Germans, made his corps commanders cringe with embarrassment. But the Roman triumph of Marcus Aurelius Clarkus was short-lived. Soon after dawn on 6 June, a staff officer entered his suite in the Excelsior Hotel in Rome to wake him with the news of the Allied invasion of Normandy. 'How do you like that?' was Clark's bitter reaction. 'They didn't even let us have the newspaper headlines for the fall of Rome for one day.'

Hitler eagerly awaited the invasion, convinced that it would be smashed on the Atlantic Wall. This would knock the British and Americans out of the war, and then he could concentrate all German forces against the Red Army. Generalfeldmarschall Rommel, whom he had put in charge of defending northern France, knew that the Atlantic Wall existed more in the realm of propaganda than in reality. His superior, Generalfeldmarschall Gerd von Rundstedt, regarded it simply as 'just a bit of cheap bluff'.

After his experiences of Allied air power in North Africa, Rommel knew that bringing up reinforcements and supplies would be exceedingly difficult. He had become embroiled in an argument with General der Panzertruppen Leo Freiherr Geyr von Schweppenburg, the commander of Panzer Group West, and Guderian, now the inspector-general of panzer forces. They wanted to hold back the panzer divisions in forests north of Paris, ready for a massive counter-attack that would throw the

Allies back into the sea, whether in Normandy or the Pas de Calais. But Rommel suspected that they would be decimated on their approach march by squadrons of Typhoon and P-47 Thunderbolt fighter-bombers. He wanted the tanks deployed close to the possible landing sites.

Hitler, in his desire to maintain control through his policy of divide and rule, refused to have a unified command in France. As a result there was no supreme commander with authority over the Luftwaffe and Kriegsmarine. Hitler even insisted that the bulk of the panzer divisions came directly under OKW control. They could not be moved without his express order. Rommel remained tireless in his efforts to improve the beach defences, especially in the Seventh Army's sector of Normandy, where he became increasingly convinced that the attack would come. Hitler, on the other hand, kept changing his mind, perhaps partly to be able to claim later that he had predicted correctly. The Pas de Calais, defended by the Fifteenth Army, contained more of the V-weapon launch sites, it offered a shorter journey across the Channel and was much closer to fighter bases in Kent to provide air cover.

The German counter-intelligence services were certain that the invasion was near because of resistance activity and radio traffic, but the Kriegsmarine, studying the meteorological reports, concluded that there was no question of an invasion between 5 and 7 June because of bad weather. On the night of 5 June, they even cancelled all their own patrols in the Channel. Rommel, on being informed of this forecast, decided to visit his wife in Germany for her birthday and then visit Hitler at the Berghof to persuade him to release more panzer divisions.

The state of the weather was Eisenhower's greatest worry during that first week of June. On 1 June, his chief meteorologist had suddenly warned him that the hot weather was about to end. The battleships of the bombardment force were leaving Scapa Flow that very day. Everything had been timed for the invasion to start on the morning of 5 June. Weather reports were still so bad on 4 June that Eisenhower had to order a postponement. Fresh information soon showed that the weather might ease on the night of 5 June. While storms and heavy seas continued in the Channel, Eisenhower faced a terrible dilemma. Could he trust the accuracy of this forecast? General

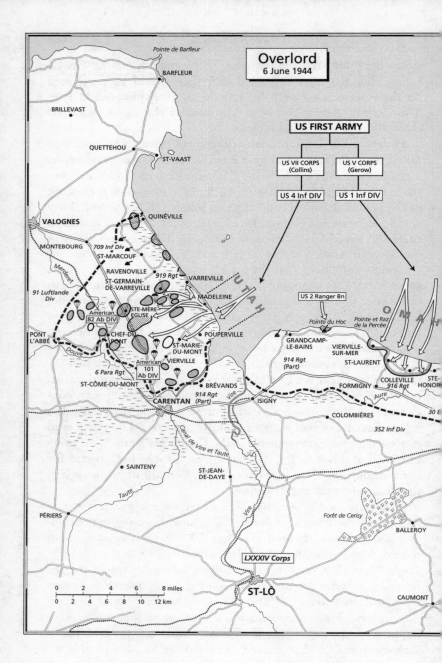

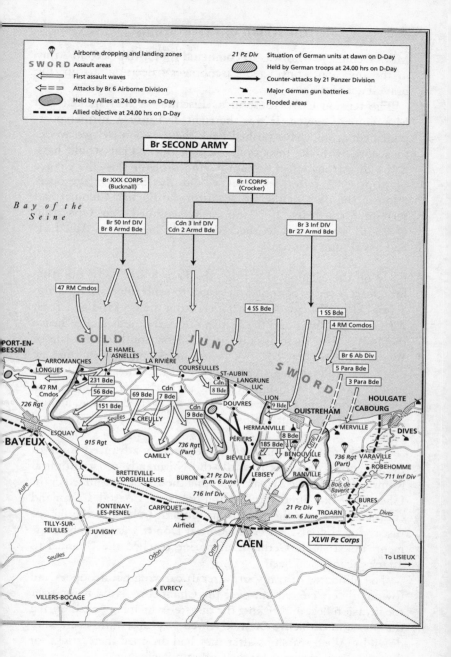

Miles Dempsey, who was to command the British Second Army in the invasion, considered Eisenhower's decision 'to go' the bravest act of the war.

The tension eased as soon as Eisenhower had spoken and Montgomery agreed. It was the right decision. A further postponement would have pushed back the invasion by two weeks to accord with the next cycle of high tides. That would have had a disastrous effect on morale and probably lost the chance of surprise. A two-week delay would also have put the operation in the path of the worst storm the English Channel had seen in forty years. It is too easily assumed that Operation Overlord was bound to succeed, simply because of Allied air and naval supremacy.

Early on the evening of 5 June, the French service of the BBC broadcast a series of coded messages to send the resistance into action. Heavily loaded paratroopers from the US 82nd and 101st Airborne Divisions and the British 6th Airborne began to heave themselves into their aircraft and gliders. South of the Isle of Wight, the invasion convoys began to assemble with ships of every size, and landing ships of every sort. Soldiers crowded the rails to gaze in astonishment at the grey, choppy Channel filled with the vessels of a dozen nationalities in every direction, including 300 warships: battleships, monitors, cruisers, destroyers and corvettes.

Out ahead, a screen of 277 minesweepers advanced south in the gathering darkness towards the Normandy coast. Admiral Ramsay feared huge casualties among these wooden-hulled craft. Liberators and Sunderland flying-boats of Coastal Command continued to scour the seas from southern Ireland to the Bay of Biscay for U-boats. To Grossadmiral Dönitz's great embarrassment, not a single German submarine reached the Channel to attack the invasion fleet.

The hundreds of transport aircraft carrying paratroopers and towing gliders curved out over the Channel to avoid flying over the invasion fleet and risking the disaster which happened during the invasion of Sicily. Even so, three C-47 Skytrains were shot down by Allied warships after they had dropped their 'sticks' of American paratroopers on the Cotentin Peninsula.

The airborne drops did not go according to plan. Heavy anti-aircraft fire as the waves of transports crossed the coast caused formations to split up. Navigation was often faulty. Only a minority reached the correct drop zones and many paratroopers had to trudge for miles to find their units. Others dropped on to German positions and were gunned down. Some fell into rivers and flooded marshes where, weighed down by all their equipment and trapped in their parachutes, they drowned. Yet the wild dispersion of drops had the unintended effect of confusing the Germans about the true targets of the operation, and this contributed to the impression that the attacks were part of a massive diversion in Normandy before the real attack came in the Pas de Calais. Only one operation, the seizure of Pegasus Bridge over the River Orue on the eastern flank, went spectacularly well. The glider pilots landed their craft in exactly the right position, and the objective was seized in a matter of minutes.

Before dawn on 6 June, almost every airfield in England began to throb with the sound of revving engines as squadrons of bombers, fighters and fighter-bombers began to take off to follow strictly marked corridors to avoid collision and clashes. Pilots and aircrew came from almost all Allied countries: Britain, America, Canada, Australia, New Zealand, South Africa, Rhodesia, Poland, France, Czechoslovakia, Belgium, Norway, the Netherlands and Denmark. Some squadrons, mainly of Halifaxes and Stirlings, had departed earlier on deception missions, dropping aluminium 'Window' and dummy paratroopers which exploded on landing.

The crews of the minesweepers and Admiral Ramsay could not believe their luck when, having accomplished their task, they turned back without a shot fired. The rough seas which had persuaded the Kriegsmarine to remain in port had proved their greatest blessing. They signalled good-luck messages to the destroyers which crept closer towards land, to take up their bombardment positions before first light. Cruisers and battleships anchored much further offshore.

The 130,000 troops crammed on the ships slept little that night. Some gambled, some tried to learn some French phrases, some thought of home, some wrote last letters, some read the Bible. Soon after 01.00 hours the troops, especially on US Navy ships, received generous breakfasts, then they began to put on their equipment which they continued to adjust out of nervousness while smoking compulsively. At around 04.00 hours troops were ordered to assemble on deck. To clamber down the scramble nets into the landing craft, which bucked and heaved alongside in the heavy swell, was a perilous undertaking, especially when so many men were overloaded with weapons and ammunition.

As soon as each landing craft was ready, its coxswain steered it away from the ship's side to join a circling queue, following the little light on the stern of the one in front. A member of the 1st Infantry Division departing from the USS *Samuel Chase* described how 'the light would disappear and then reappear as we rose and fell with the waves'. Very soon men began to regret the munificence of their breakfast and were sick over the side, into their helmets or between their feet. The decks became slippery with vomit and seawater.

As a grey glow began to penetrate the overcast sky, the battleships opened up with their 14-inch main armament. Cruisers and destroyers immediately joined in. Generalleutnant Joseph Reichert of the 711th Infantry Division, watching from the coast, noted that 'the whole horizon appeared to be a solid mass of flames'. By then there was enough dawn light for the Germans to see the size of the invasion fleet. Field telephones jangled furiously in command posts. Teleprinters chattered at Army Group B's headquarters at La Roche-Guyon on the Seine, and in Rundstedt's headquarters at Saint-Germain just outside Paris.

While the naval bombardment continued, landing craft filled with rocket launchers approached the shore, but most of their ordnance fell short in the water. The most frightening moment then came for the crews of the Duplex Drive Shermans, which began to flop off the front of landing craft into a sea which was far rougher than anything in which their tanks' swimming abilities had been tested. In many cases, the upright canvas screen around the turret collapsed under the force of the waves and a number of tank crews went down trapped inside their vehicles.

On Utah Beach at the base of the Cotentin Peninsula, the US 4th Infantry Division landed with far fewer casualties than expected, and began to move inland to relieve the paratroopers of the 82nd and 101st Airborne. The long curving beach known as Omaha, dominated by bluffs covered in seagrass, proved an even deadlier objective than the Allies had expected. Much went wrong even before soldiers of the 1st and 29th Infantry Divisions landed. The naval bombardment, although intense, had still been too short to be effective, and the bombing was a waste of time. Instead of following the line of the coast, which would have given aimers a better fix in the bad visibility, the US air commanders had insisted on coming in from the sea to avoid being shot at from the side. As they flew in over the landing craft, aircrew decided to wait a moment longer to avoid hitting their own men, so their loads dropped on to fields and villages inland. None of the beach defences, bunkers and fire points were touched. There were not even any craters on the beach in which the assaulting infantry could take cover. As a result the first wave suffered very heavy casualties, with enemy fire from machine guns and light artillery raking the landing craft as their ramps came down. Many landing craft became stuck on sandbars.

'Some boats were coming back after unloading,' wrote a member of the 1st Division, 'others were partly awash, but still struggling. Some were stuck, bottomed out, racing their motors and getting nowhere. Some were backing up short distances and trying again . . . I saw craft sideways, being upturned, and dumping troops into the water. I saw craft heavily damaged by shellfire being tossed around by the waves. I saw craft empty of troops and partly filled with water as though abandoned, awash in the surf. Men were among them struggling for the pitiful protection they gave.'

Traumatized soldiers froze at the foot of the bluffs, until officers managed to force them up with the warning that they would die on the beach unless they got inland and killed Germans. The defenders had been reinforced with a small part of the 352nd Infantry Division, but not nearly as many men as some accounts have claimed. Fortunately for the Americans, the 352nd's main reserve some 3,000 strong was first sent off on a wild-goose chase in the early hours of the morning in response to the exploding puppet paratroops, and then was wiped out by a British brigade which had advanced diagonally inland from Gold Beach. In any case, the slaughter and chaos at Omaha during the morning was enough to make General Bradley consider abandoning the beach altogether. Just in time, news came back that some groups had made it up the bluffs comparatively unscathed, and that Omaha could yet be won. A combination of a few Sherman tanks engaging the bunkers, and American and British destroyers sailing dangerously close in and firing with impressive accuracy at the German positions, also tipped the balance in the invading force's favour.

On Gold Beach, the British 50th Division wasted little time pushing inland. One brigade halted just short of Bayeux at nightfall and took the town without casualties the next morning. The Canadian 3rd Division had a much tougher time on the Juno sector, where the Germans had fortified seaside villages and created networks of tunnels. On Sword, which ran up to the small port of Ouistreham, the British 3rd Division had trouble with the unusually high tide which delayed the landing of tanks. Minefields on either side of roads and artillery fire blocking them with blazing vehicles meant that the rapid attack inland on the city of Caen was slow off the mark. And the dogged defence of a large German bunker complex made things worse. On their flank, the 6th Airborne Division had secured its allotted area between the Rivers Orne and Dives, blowing bridges to prevent a panzer counter-attack from the east.

Montgomery's plan was to seize Caen and the land beyond for airfields as rapidly as possible, but German resistance with machine guns and anti-tank guns concealed in solid Norman farmyards and hamlets proved far harder to crack than they had thought. Allied intelligence had also failed to spot that the 21st Panzer Division was already in the area of Caen. There was too a strange contradiction in Montgomery's scheme. On the one hand, he wanted to take the ancient city of Caen in the first twenty-four hours of the battle, an objective which was clearly over-optimistic. On the other, he had ordered the destruction of Caen with a massive raid by heavy bombers on 6 June, yet the rubble blocking the streets could only hinder his own troops and aid the defenders. Hardly any Germans were killed at all in the raid, while the shock and suffering of the civilian population was terrible.

Allied commanders were afraid of a great German panzer counter-attack, which contributed to their excessive caution. Luckily, Hitler's failure to take a decision until the late afternoon of 6 June to commit his tank formations played to their advantage. And while ground-force commanders had overestimated the effect of the heavy bomber missions, they underestimated the success of the fighter-bomber squadrons, roving inland to attack any German armoured columns heading for the invasion area. The 1st SS Panzer Division *Leibstandarte Adolf Hitler*, the 12th SS Panzer Division *Hitler Jugend* and, most of all, the Panzer Lehr Division received a battering from Typhoons and P-47 Thunderbolts.

The Canadian 3rd Division saw the need to seize villages and bring forward their anti-tank guns quickly to strengthen the defence. But the British 3rd Infantry Division, with certain honourable exceptions, was slow in pushing forward. The result was that the British Second Army on the eastern flank failed to take ground at the moment when it could have been seized with comparatively light casualties. Once Rommel flung Panzer Group West against the British and Canadian sectors, as General Morgan had predicted, it would be a whole month before Montgomery's forces took the city which had been their first objective. The shortage of space on the British side of the invasion area prevented the RAF from establishing forward airfields and slowed the build-up of forces. It is surprising, in the light of the failure to seize either Caen or Carpiquet airfield, that Montgomery should have signalled Eisenhower on 8 June: 'Am very satisfied with the situation.'

Bradley's First Army to the west of Caen and on the Cotentin Peninsula faced lighter opposition but much worse terrain. Field Marshal Brooke had warned of the difficulties of the Normandy *bocage*, with its small fields surrounded by very high, dense hedgerows that rose from solid banks, with sunken tracks in between. Brooke had studied the topography in 1940, but those who had never seen such unusual countryside had imagined it to be like western England, with small hedges which a Sherman tank could smash through with ease. But the first problem American forces faced was marshland and flooded areas. Paratroopers had dropped into it, with many fatal results, and much of the neck of the Cotentin Peninsula which they needed to seize was waterlogged.

After the beachhead at Omaha had been secured, Lieutenant General Leonard 'Gee' Gerow ordered his divisions to advance inland as rapidly as possible. The 1st Infantry pushed south and east to link up with the British at Port-en-Bessin on 7 June. The 29th Infantry Division, which had received such a battering, sent its reserve regiment westwards towards Isigny. Bradley hoped to link up the Omaha and Utah beachheads as rapidly as possible. But the two airborne divisions were still involved in furious fighting along the Rivers Merderet and Douve and round Sainte-Mère-Église, until the 4th Infantry Division advanced inland from Utah with tank battalions in support.

Once the Germans had been forced back from the south-east corner of the Cotentin Peninsula, the 101st Airborne managed to take the town of Carentan, largely thanks to confusion on the German side. On 13 June, the 17th SS Panzergrenadier Division *Götz von Berlichingen* mounted a counter-attack. Bradley knew of its approach from Ultra intercepts and rapidly switched part of the 2nd Armored Division across. American paratroopers south of Carentan fought a semi-guerrilla withdrawal back towards the town, until Brigadier General Maurice Rose appeared, leading his Shermans from an open half-track. The SS panzergrenadiers fled in confusion. Next day, the two invasion areas were joined up.

The Germans expected a major attack south from Carentan, but Bradley had a much higher priority: securing the Cotentin Peninsula with the port of Cherbourg at its tip. On 14 June the newly landed 9th Infantry Division and the 82nd Airborne attacked across the neck of the peninsula. Urged on by VII Corps commander Major General Lawton Collins, known as 'Lightning Joe', they reached the Atlantic coast in four days. Then, with three divisions across the peninsula, VII Corps advanced north with heavy air support and took Cherbourg on 26 June. Hitler was outraged when he heard that Generalleutnant Karl-Wilhelm von Schlieben had surrendered.

The Allies, having been so fortunate with the weather for the invasion, soon suffered badly. An enormous storm in the Channel destroyed the artificial Mulberry harbour constructed at Omaha and smashed vessels and landing craft ashore. The Americans found themselves desperately short of artillery ammunition, thus thwarting an advance southwards during the Cherbourg operation.

The British build-up of forces was also brought to a halt, just as a stalemate was developing. German resistance round Caen had intensified with the arrival of the SS *Hitler Jugend*. To make matters worse, low cloud grounded the Allied air forces. The British 50th Division with the 8th Armoured Brigade had advanced south from Bayeux, but they had come up against violent counter-attacks from the Panzer Lehr Division round Tilly-sur-Seulles and Lingèvres.

On 10 June Montgomery met Bradley at Port-en-Bessin, and with a map spread on the front of his staff car Monty explained that he did not want to hammer head-on into Caen. He intended to encircle it, with 51st Highland Division attacking from the 6th Airborne's sector east of the Orne. At the same time, 7th Armoured Division would slip down south out on his right flank into the edge of the American sector near Caumont, then swing back east towards Villers-Bocage behind the Panzer Lehr Division. It was a bold plan, and in many ways a good one, if it had been carried through promptly and with full force. In the event, it turned out to be little more than a reconnaissance in force, which was scandalously under-supported.

On 13 June the spearhead, consisting of just one regimental battle-group, reached Villers-Bocage, but without a reconnaissance screen in front. As a result the Cromwell tanks of the Sharpshooters (the 4th County of London Yeomanry) ran into a devastating ambush of Tiger tanks led by the panzer ace Michael Wittmann, of the SS 101st Heavy Panzer Battalion. This, combined with the sudden arrival of the 2nd Panzer Division on 7th Armoured Division's exposed southern flank, prompted a humiliating retreat. The French townspeople who had so joyfully welcomed the Desert Rats the day before, now found their town smashed to rubble by RAF bombers.

Montgomery had insisted on having three of his desert divisions with him in Normandy – the 7th Armoured, the 50th Northumbrian and the 51st Highland. Several of their veteran regiments were to fight well in Normandy, but the morale, and in some cases discipline, of many others was not good. They had been fighting for too long and were not prepared to take risks. A 'canny' caution slowed them down. In the case of armoured regiments, a fear of well-camouflaged German anti-tank guns was easily understandable when the 88mm could knock them out from over a mile away. And less than a third of British tanks had the excellent 17-pounder gun, which could deal with a Tiger or Panther tank at a reasonable range. After the Villers-Bocage debacle, the 7th Armoured Division's confidence was badly shaken. The 51st Highland Division's attempt to attack east of Caen also collapsed. Montgomery was so horrified by the 51st's performance that he sacked its general and considered sending the whole division back to England for retraining. It took until almost the end of the Normandy campaign before the Highland Division restored its earlier reputation.

In the US Army too combat performance varied greatly, not only between divisions but even within them. Psychological casualties could be high in green divisions, and the rate of nervous collapse among ill-trained and badly handled replacements was unnecessarily disastrous. To arrive at night in a new unit at the front without knowing anybody, and in most cases woefully under-trained, could hardly have been more demoralizing. The other soldiers shunned them, because they had arrived to replace their buddies who had just been killed and whom they were still mourning.

Any ideas that the Germans must know that the war was lost were brutally shattered by the savagely effective defence they maintained, using all the lethal tricks learned on the eastern front. Apart from the elite Allied formations, such as paratroopers or rangers, the majority of men on the Allied side were armed citizens, who just wanted to get the war over and done with. They could hardly be expected to match the fervour of those indoctrinated from early youth into the Nazi warrior mindset and now persuaded by Goebbels's propaganda that, if they failed to hold on in Normandy, their families, homes and Fatherland would be destroyed for ever.

The 12th SS *Hitler Jugend* was the most fanatical. Its officers had told their men before the battle that any SS soldier who surrendered without having suffered incapacitating wounds would be treated as a traitor. *Hitler Jugend* soldiers, if taken alive, would reject transfusions of foreign blood, preferring to die for the Führer. One could never imagine British or American prisoners of war wanting to die for King George VI, Churchill or President Roosevelt. Of course, not all German soldiers were such true believers. Many in ordinary line infantry divisions simply wanted to survive, to see their girlfriends and families again.

Once the Americans had taken Cherbourg, the battle of the *bocage* and the marshes south of the peninsula began in earnest. It was a bloody slog, with high casualties, as Bradley's divisions extending from Caumont to the Atlantic coast fought forward to reach more open country, where the American armoured divisions could be deployed in their full force.

German generals claimed, perhaps with justification, that Bradley's way of fighting with little more than single-battalion attacks, supported by a few tanks and tank destroyers, was easy for them to deal with. The commander of the 3rd Fallschirmjäger Division even boasted that it was perfect training for his green troops, many of whom had been transferred from the Luftwaffe and flight-training units simply to make up numbers. Using small combat teams with a mixture of infantry, pioneers for laying mines and booby-traps, self-propelled assault guns and well-sited anti-tank guns, German forces could inflict far more losses on the attacking Americans than they suffered themselves. Their main problem came from a shortage of ammunition and other supplies, because of Allied aircraft attacking any transport in the rear.

Bradley's objective was the capture of Saint-Lô and securing the Périers–Saint-Lô road as his start-line for the main offensive, while Montgomery again tried to encircle Caen. He did not know that Rommel and Rundstedt had asked Hitler on 17 June for permission to withdraw their forces to a more defensible line behind the River Orne and beyond the range of Allied naval guns. Hitler, on a brief visit to France to impose his will on his generals, refused to consider anything of the sort. It was this manic obstinacy and interference in command decisions which decided not just the pattern of the Normandy campaign but the fate of the whole of France.

Hitler, in his world of illusion, convinced himself that the V-1 flying bombs which he had just started to launch against London would bring Britain to its knees, and that the new jet fighters would soon destroy the Allied air forces. Rommel, who knew that this was fantasy, urged him to bring the war to an end. Hitler retorted that the Allies would not negotiate, and for once he was right. After this brief visit, Hitler returned to the Berghof. Five days later, the German army on the eastern front suffered its greatest defeat in the whole war.

Bagration and Normandy

JUNE–AUGUST 1944

While the OKH and Führer headquarters discounted the likelihood of an attack in Belorussia, apprehension grew in front-line units of Army Group Centre. On 20 June 1944, the atmosphere was heightened by the 'heat of high-summer days with distant thunder', and a crescendo of partisan attacks to their rear. Ten days before, a German intercept station had picked up a Soviet signal ordering an increase in activity behind the Fourth Army. The Germans had accordingly launched a major anti-partisan drive, Operation Kormoran. It included their notorious Kaminski Brigade, whose conspicuous cruelty against civilians seemed medieval and whose raging indiscipline was an affront to traditional German officers.

Moscow's instructions to the large partisan bands in the forests and marshes of Belorussia were specific. They were first to attack railway communications, then harass Wehrmacht forces once the offensive began. This would include seizing bridges, cutting off supply routes by cutting down forest trees and dropping them across roads, and mounting attacks to delay reinforcements from reaching the front.

At dawn on 20 June, the 25th Panzergrenadier Division was subjected to an hour's bombardment and a brief assault. Everything went quiet again. It was either a probing attack or an attempt to unsettle them. Führer headquarters did not believe that the Soviet summer offensive would be aimed at Army Group Centre. They expected an offensive north of Leningrad against the Finns, and another massive onslaught south of the Pripet Marshes into southern Poland and the Balkans.

Hitler believed that Stalin's strategy was to strike at the Axis allies – the Finns, the Hungarians, the Romanians and the Bulgarians – to force them out of the war, like the Italians. His suspicions appeared confirmed when first the Leningrad Front and then the

Karelian Front attacked. Stalin, now confident enough to choose pragmatism over revenge, did not intend to crush Finland entirely. That would divert too many forces needed elsewhere. He simply wanted to bring the Finns to heel and take back the land he had seized off them in 1940. As he had hoped, these operations in the north took Hitler's eyes off Belorussia.

The Red Army successfully employed *maskirovka* deception measures suggesting a major build-up in Ukraine, when in fact it was secretly transferring tank and other armies north. Its task was made easier by the virtual disappearance of the Luftwaffe. The Allied strategic bombing offensive, and now the invasion of Normandy, had reduced Luftwaffe support to German armies on the eastern front to a disastrous level. Soviet air supremacy prevented almost all German reconnaissance flights, so Army Group Centre headquarters in Minsk received little indication of the huge concentration of forces that was building up. Altogether the Stavka had assembled some fifteen armies, totalling 1,670,000 men, with nearly 6,000 tanks and self-propelled guns, more than 30,000 guns and heavy mortars, including Katyusha batteries. They were supported by more than 7,500 aircraft.

Army Group Centre had become a poor relation. Some sectors were so thinly manned that sentries had to remain on six-hour shifts each night. They and their officers had no idea of the furious work being carried out behind Soviet lines. Forest tracks were being widened for the large armoured vehicles, corduroy roads to take tanks were laid through marshes, pontoons were brought forward, fording points were given solid bottoms, and underwater bridges were constructed just beneath the surface of rivers.

This great redeployment of forces delayed the launch of the offensive by three days. On 22 June, the third anniversary of Operation Barbarossa, the 1st Baltic and the 3rd Belorussian Fronts carried out their reconnaissance in force. Operation Bagration itself, which Stalin himself had named after the Georgian princely hero of 1812, began in earnest the next day.

The Stavka plan was first to surround Vitebsk on the north side of Army Group Centre's bulging front, and Bobruisk on the southern side, then thrust in diagonally from both these points to surround Minsk in the middle. On the northern flank, Marshal I. Kh. Bagramyan's 1st Baltic Front and the young Colonel

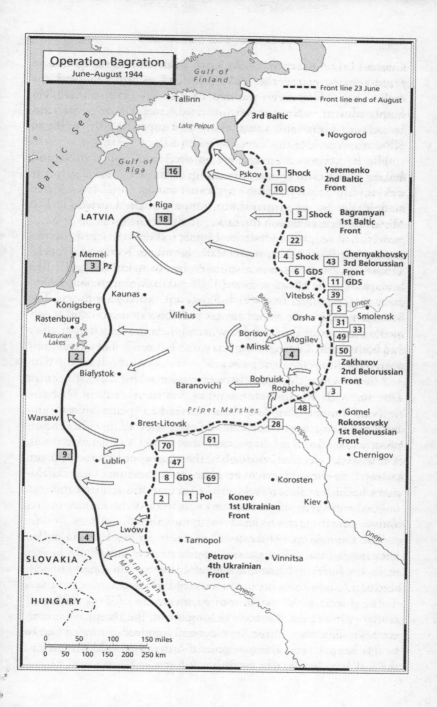

Operation Bagration
June–August 1944

- - - Front line 23 June
——— Front line end of August

Gulf of Finland

Tallinn

Baltic Sea

Lake Peipus

3rd Baltic

Novgorod

Gulf of Riga

16

Pskov

1 Shock

10 GDS

Yeremenko
2nd Baltic
Front

Riga

18

3 Shock

Bagramyan
1st Baltic
Front

LATVIA

22

4 Shock

43

Memel

3 Pz

6 GDS

Chernyakhovsky
3rd Belorussian
Front

11 GDS

39

Kaunas

Vitebsk

5

Dnepr

Königsberg

Vilnius

Orsha

31

Smolensk

Rastenburg

Borisov

Mogilev

49

33

Masurian
Lakes

Minsk

4

50

2

Zakharov
2nd Belorussian
Front

Białystok

Baranovichi

Bobruisk

Rogachev

3

Warsaw

Pripet Marshes

48

Gomel

Brest-Litovsk

28

Rokossovsky
1st Belorussian
Front

9

70

61

Pripet

Chernigov

Lublin

47

8 GDS

69

Korosten

2

1 Pol

Konev
1st Ukrainian
Front

Kiev

4

Lwów

Tarnopol

Petrov
4th Ukrainian
Front

Vinnitsa

SLOVAKIA

Carpathian Mountains

Dnepr

HUNGARY

Dnestr

| 0 | 50 | 100 | 150 miles |

| 0 | 50 | 100 | 150 | 200 | 250 km |

General I. D. Chernyakhovsky's 3rd Belorussian Front attacked rapidly to surround the Vitebsk salient before the Germans could react. They even decided to dispense with an artillery bombardment, unless it was deemed essential on a particular sector. Their tank spearheads were supported by waves of Shturmovik fighter-bombers. The Third Panzer Army was taken totally by surprise. Vitebsk lay in the middle of a vulnerable bulge, whose central part was defended by two weak Luftwaffe field divisions. The hapless corps commander had been ordered to hold Vitebsk as a fortress position, although he utterly lacked the forces to accomplish the task.

In the centre, from Orsha to Mogilev, the Tsar's headquarters in the First World War, General der Infanterie Kurt von Tippelskirch's Fourth Army was also taken by surprise. 'We really had a black day,' an Unteroffizier with the 25th Panzergrenadier Division wrote home, 'one which I will not forget in a hurry. The Russians began with their heaviest possible bombardment. It carried on for about three hours. With all their strength they tried to break through. The force was inexorable. I really had to run for it to avoid falling into their hands. Their tanks were advancing with red flags.' Only the 25th Panzergrenadiers and the 78th Sturm Division with assault guns fought back furiously east of Orsha.

The following day Tippelskirch asked for permission to pull back to the northern Dnepr, but this was rejected by Führer headquarters. With several divisions shattered and his men exhausted, Tippelskirch decided to disobey the insane orders to hold on, parroted by the subservient army group commander Generalfeldmarschall Ernst Busch in Minsk. Commanders realized that the only way to save their formations was to falsify situation reports and war diary entries to justify withdrawals.

The German 12th Infantry Division in front of Orsha pulled back just in time. When a major asked a pioneer officer why he was in such a hurry to blow a bridge after his battalion had crossed, the man handed him his binoculars and pointed across the river. Turning round, the major spotted a column of T-34 tanks, already within range. Orsha and Mogilev on the Dnepr were both cut off and taken in three days. Several hundred wounded had to be left behind. The German general ordered to hold Mogilev to the end was close to a nervous breakdown.

Behind Soviet lines, the greatest problem was presented by the huge traffic jams of military vehicles. A broken-down tank could not be circumvented easily because of the marshes and forests either side of the roads. The chaos at times was such that 'the traffic controller at a crossroads might be a full colonel', a Red Army officer later recalled. He also pointed out how fortunate the Soviet forces were that there was so little sign of the Luftwaffe, since all those vehicles stuck nose to tail would have provided an easy target.

On the southern flank, Marshal Rokossovsky's 1st Belorussian Front launched its assault with a massive preliminary bombardment which began at 04.00 hours. Explosions sent up fountains of earth. The ground was cratered and ploughed over a huge area. Trees came crashing down and German soldiers, instinctively adopting the foetal position in their bunkers, quivered as the ground vibrated as in an earthquake.

Rokossovsky's northern pincer broke through between Tippelskirch's Fourth Army and the Ninth Army responsible for the Bobruisk sector. General der Infanterie Hans Jordan, the commander of the Ninth Army, brought in his reserve, the 20th Panzer Division. But as the counter-attack began that night, 20th Panzer was ordered to pull back and move south of Bobruisk. The penetration of the other pincer led by the 1st Guards Tank Corps had proved to be far more dangerous. It threatened to encircle the town and cut off the left flank of the Ninth Army as well. Rokossovsky's surprise approach, through the edge of the Pripet Marshes, had a success similar to that of the Germans emerging from the Ardennes in 1940.

Hitler still refused to allow retreat, so on 26 June Generalfeldmarschall Busch flew to Berchtesgaden to report to him at the Berghof. He was accompanied by Jordan, whom Hitler wanted to interrogate on his use of the 20th Panzer Division. But, while they were away from their headquarters, almost all of the Ninth Army was surrounded. The next day, both Busch and Jordan were dismissed. Hitler immediately resorted to Generalfeldmarschall Model. Yet, even with this disaster and the threat to Minsk, the OKW still had no inkling of the scale of Soviet ambitions.

Model, one of the few generals able to stand up to Hitler with success, was able to make the necessary withdrawals to the line of the River Berezina in front of Minsk. Hitler had also released the 5th Panzer Division to take up position north-east of Minsk at Borisov. It arrived on 28 June, but soon found itself attacked by Shturmovik ground-attack aircraft. Reinforced with a battalion of Tiger tanks and odd SS units, the division took up position either side of the Orsha–Borisov–Minsk road. Officers and men alike had little idea of the general situation, although they had heard a rumour that the Red Army had crossed the Berezina some way to the north.

During that night, advance elements of the 5th Guards Tank Army clashed with the division's panzergrenadiers. A battalion of Panther tanks arrived to strengthen the German line, but to the north Chernyakhovsky's troops had broken through between the Third Panzer Army and the Fourth Army. A chaotic withdrawal began under constant attack from Shturmoviks and Soviet artillery fire. Terrified German transport troops drove at full speed to reach the last remaining bridge over the Berezina, cutting in on each other to get across before it was hit by the enemy. The site of Napoleon's crossing in the terrible retreat of 1812 was just to the north of Borisov.

Vitebsk was already on fire when German troops of LIII Corps pulled out in a vain attempt to break out through the encirclement to rejoin the Third Panzer Army. The stores and fuel dumps blazed, belching black smoke. Nearly 30,000 men were lost, either killed or taken prisoner. The disaster also shook the faith of many, both in the Führer and in the direction of the war. 'The Ivans broke through this morning', an Unteroffizier of the 206th Infantry Division wrote home. 'A short pause allows me to write a letter. Our orders are to disengage from the enemy. My dear ones, the situation is very desperate. I no longer believe in anybody, if it looks as it does here.'

In the south, Rokossovsky's armies had encircled almost all the Ninth Army and the town of Bobruisk, which they captured. 'When we entered Bobruisk,' wrote Vasily Grossman with the 120th Guards Rifle Division, which he had known from Stalingrad, 'some buildings in it were ablaze and others lay in ruins. To Bobruisk led the road of revenge! With difficulty, our car finds its way between scorched and distorted German tanks and self-propelled guns. Men are walking over German corpses. Corpses, hundreds and hundreds of them, pave the road, lie in the ditches, under the pines, in the green barley. In some places, vehicles have to drive over the corpses, so densely they lie upon the ground. People are busy all the time, burying them, but there are so many that this work cannot be done in a day. The day is exhaustingly hot and still, and people walk and drive pressing handkerchiefs to their noses. A cauldron of death was boiling here – a ruthless, terrible revenge over those who hadn't surrendered their arms and broken out to the west.'

Once the Germans had been beaten, civilians emerged. 'Our people whom we've liberated tell us their stories and cry (it's mostly elderly people who cry),' a young Red Army soldier wrote home. 'And young people are in such a great mood that they laugh all the time, their mouth is never shut. They laugh and talk.'

For the Germans, the retreat was disastrous. Vehicles of every sort had to be abandoned because they had run out of fuel. Even before the attack, each one had been restricted to ten to fifteen litres per day. General Spaatz's strategy of bombing oil installations was certainly helping the Red Army on the eastern front as well as the Allies in Normandy. The German wounded lucky enough to be evacuated suffered dreadfully on the back of horse-drawn carts, rattling, shaking and lurching. Many died from loss of blood before they reached the dressing stations. Because first aid had been so drastically reduced at the front with the loss of medics, a serious wound now meant almost certain death. Those that could be brought back from the front line were taken to military hospitals in Minsk, but Minsk was now the main Soviet objective.

In the forests, the remnants of German formations pushed westwards to escape. They were short of water, and many soldiers became dehydrated in the heat. All suffered from intense stress through fear of ambush by partisans or capture by the Red Army. Bombers and artillery harrying the withdrawal brought down trees, and sprayed them with wood splinters. The severity and ubiquity of the fighting was such that no fewer than seven German generals from Army Group Centre were killed in action.

Even Hitler had to abandon his compulsion to designate totally unsuitable towns as fortresses. His commanders now tried to avoid defending towns for that very reason. By the end of June, the 5th Guards Tank Army had bulldozed its way forward and begun to encircle Minsk from the north. Chaos reigned in the city as Army Group Centre's headquarters and all the German rear-area establishments rushed to escape. The badly wounded in the hospitals were abandoned to their fate. Minsk itself was captured from the south on 3 July, and the bulk of the German Fourth Army found itself trapped between the city and the Berezina.

Even a medical Obergefreiter with no access to staff maps could clearly see the bitter irony of their situation. 'The enemy', he wrote, 'has now done what we did in '41: encirclement to encirclement.' A Luftwaffe Obergefreiter observed in a letter to his wife in East Prussia that he was now only 200 kilometres away from her. 'If the Russians keep up the direction of their attack it will not be long before they are standing at your door.'

Vengeance was exacted in Minsk, especially against any former Red Army soldiers who had served as Hiwis with the Wehrmacht. Others took personal revenge after the savage repression in Belorussia which had killed a quarter of its population. 'A partisan, a small man,' wrote Grossman, 'has killed two Germans with a stake. He had pleaded with the guards of the column to give him these Germans. He had convinced himself that they were the ones who had killed his daughter Olya, and his sons, his two boys. He broke all their bones, and smashed their skulls, and while he was beating them, he was crying and shouting: "Here you are – for Olya! Here you are – for Kolya!" When they were dead, he propped the bodies up against a tree stump and continued to beat them.'

The mechanized armies of Rokossovsky and Chernyakhovsky pushed on, while rifle divisions behind crushed the trapped German forces. Soviet commanders knew by now the advantage of a headlong charge when the enemy was in full flight. The Germans should not be allowed time to recover and prepare new defence lines. The 5th Guards Tank Army headed for Vilnius, while other formations went for Baranovichi. Vilnius fell on 13 July after heavy fighting. Kaunas was their next objective. German territory in the form of East Prussia lay just beyond.

The Stavka now planned a strike up to the Gulf of Riga, to trap Army Group North in Estonia and Latvia. The army group struggled desperately to hold open a corridor to the west, while fighting back eight Soviet armies on the east. South of the Pripet Marshes on 13 July, Marshal Konev's armies of the 1st Ukrainian Front began their offensive later known as the Lwów–Sandomierz Operation. After smashing through weakly held German lines, Konev's formations advanced to encircle Lwów. Their assault on the city ten days later was helped by 3,000 men of the Polish Home Army, led by Colonel Władysław Filipkowski. But as soon as the city had been seized the NKVD, which had already secured Gestapo headquarters and its files, arrested the Home Army officers and forced the soldiers to join the Communist 1st Polish Army.

After taking Lwów Konev's 1st Ukrainian Front headed west all the way to the Vistula, yet it was the thought of Soviet formations approaching East Prussia – 'old Reich' territory – which struck most fear into German hearts. The only grounds for hope, as in Normandy, were the V-weapons, especially the V-2. 'Their effect should be many times more powerful than the V-1,' a Luftwaffe Obergefreiter wrote home, but he was not alone in fearing that the Allies would retaliate with gas. One or two even advised their families at home to buy gas-masks if necessary. Others began to fear that their own side 'might start to use gas (as a last resort)'.

Some German units were pulled back into one defensive line after another in the vain hope of halting the onrush. 'The Russians are attacking constantly,' wrote a construction company Gefreiter drafted into the infantry. 'A bombardment has been going on since 05.00 hours. They want to break through. Their ground-attack aircraft are well coordinated with their artillery fire. Impact follows impact. I am sitting in our good bunker and writing what is perhaps the last little letter.' Almost every soldier was praying privately that he would get home alive, but not really believing it.

Events were moving so rapidly, as an Obergefreiter thrown into another improvised *Kampfgruppe* observed, that 'one can no longer talk of a front'. He went on: 'I can only let you know that we are now not far from East Prussia, and perhaps then the worst will come.' In East Prussia itself, civilians observed the busy roads with mounting anxiety. A woman close to the eastern border watched 'columns of soldiers and refugees from Tilsit, which has been heavily bombed', pass her door. Soviet bombing raids forced civilians to shelter in their cellars, and they had to board up their smashed windows. Workshops and factories had virtually ceased functioning because so few women came to work. Travel over 100 kilometres was forbidden. The Gauleiter of East Prussia, Erich Koch, did not want civilians fleeing westwards, as that would be defeatist.

Konev's advance continued rapidly from Lublin, where the concentration camp of Majdanek had been discovered just to the west of it. Grossman had joined General Chuikov whose Stalingrad army, now the 8th Guards, had seized the city. Chuikov's main concern was that he might miss out on the advance to Berlin, which for him was as important as Rome had been to General Mark Clark. 'It's perfect logic and common sense,' Chuikov argued. 'Just think: *stalingradtsy* advancing on Berlin!' Grossman, disgusted with the egomania of commanders and angry that Konstantin Simonov had been sent to cover the Majdanek story instead of him, moved north towards Treblinka, which had just been discovered.

Simonov was with a large group of foreign correspondents sent to Majdanek by the Main Political Department of the Red Army to witness Nazi crimes. Stalin's position, with the slogan 'Do Not Divide the Dead', was clear. No mention was to be made of Jews as a special category when it came to suffering. The victims of Majdanek were to be described only as Soviet and Polish citizens. Hans Frank, the head of the Nazi Generalgouvernement, was horrified when details of the extermination facilities at Majdanek appeared in the foreign press. The rapidity of the Soviet advance had taken the SS by surprise, leaving them no chance to destroy the incriminating evidence. It brought home to him and others for the first time that a noose awaited them at the end of the war.

The SS had a little more time at Treblinka. On 23 July, when Konev's artillery could be heard in the distance, the commandant at Treblinka I received the order to liquidate the last survivors of the camp. Schnapps was issued to the SS and the Ukrainian *Wachmänner* before they began to execute the remaining prisoner work details. Max Levit, a carpenter from Warsaw, was the only survivor. Wounded in the first fusillade, he had been covered by other bodies. He managed to crawl into the forest from where he listened to the ragged volleys. 'Stalin will avenge us!' a group of Russian boys had cried just before they were shot.

*

Shortly before Operation Bagration crashed into his armies in the east, Hitler had transferred the II SS Panzer Corps to Normandy, with the 9th SS Panzer Division *Hohenstaufen* and the 10th SS Panzer Division *Frundsberg*. Ultra intercepts had warned the Allied leaders in Normandy that they were on their way. Eisenhower fumed with impatience, because Montgomery's next offensive against Caen after Villers-Bocage was not ready until 26 June. This was hardly Montgomery's fault since the great storm had delayed his build-up of forces for what was known as Operation Epsom. He intended once more to attack west of Caen and swing round to encircle the city.

On 25 June a diversionary attack began even further to the west, with XXX Corps renewing its battle with the Panzer Lehr Division. The 49th Division, known as the Polar Bear Division because of its insignia, managed to force the Panzer Lehr back to the villages of Tessel and Rauray, where the fighting was particularly savage. Ever since the 12th SS Panzer Division *Hitler Jugend* had begun killing prisoners, little mercy was shown on either side. Just before the attack on Tessel Wood, Sergeant Kuhlmann, a mortar platoon commander in the 1/4th King's Own Yorkshire Light Infantry, recorded the orders in his field message book. At the end is written 'NPT below rank major', which stood for 'no prisoners to be taken below the rank of major'. Others also recalled getting a 'no prisoners' order, and claim that this was why German propaganda began to call the 49th Division 'the Polar Bear Butchers'. An Ultra intercept confirmed that the Panzer Lehr suffered 'heavy losses'.

Montgomery spoke of Operation Epsom to Eisenhower as the 'show-down', while clearly having every intention of conducting the battle as cautiously as usual. The official history of the Italian campaign later observed that Montgomery 'had the unusual gift of persuasively combining very bold speech and very cautious action'. This was particularly true in Normandy.

The newly arrived VIII Corps launched the main attack with the 15th Scottish Division and the 43rd Wessex Division in front, and the 11th Armoured Division ready to exploit a breakthrough behind. The opening bombardment combined divisional and corps artillery as well as the main armament of the battleships offshore. The 15th Scottish advanced rapidly, but the 43rd Division on the left found itself having to fight off a counter-attack by the 12th SS Panzer Division. By nightfall, the Scots had reached the valley of the Odon. Although movement was slow because vehicles became dangerously congested on the narrow Norman roads, the advance continued. Next day the 2nd Argyll and Sutherland Highlanders, wisely ignoring current tactical doctrine, slipped across the Odon in small groups and captured a bridge.

On 28 June Lieutenant General Sir Richard O'Connor, who had escaped from a prison camp in Italy and now commanded VIII Corps, wanted to push far ahead with the 11th Armoured Division and seize a bridgehead over the River Orne beyond the Odon. General Sir Miles Dempsey, the commander of the British Second Army, knew from Ultra of the imminent arrival of II SS Panzer Corps, and with Montgomery at his elbow decided to play safe. He might have been rather more robust if he had known of the developments on the German side.

Hitler had just summoned Rommel to the Berghof, an extraordinary act in the middle of a battle. To compound the confusion the commander-in-chief of Seventh Army, Generaloberst Friedrich Dollmann, had just died – officially of a heart attack, but most German officers suspected suicide after the surrender of Cherbourg. Without consulting Rommel, Hitler appointed Obergruppenführer Paul Hausser, the commander of II SS Panzer Corps, to take over Seventh Army. Hausser, who had been ordered to counter-attack the British offensive with the *Hohenstaufen* and the *Frundsberg* SS Panzer Divisions, had to hand over to his deputy and hurry to his new headquarters in Le Mans.

On 29 June the 11th Armoured Division, led by its outstanding commander Major General Philip 'Pip' Roberts, managed to put its leading tanks on to Hill 112, the key feature between the Odon and the Orne. It then proceeded to fight off counter-attacks by the 1st SS Panzer Division *Leibstandarte Adolf Hitler*, part of the 21st Panzer, and the 7th Mortar Brigade with its Nebelwerfer multi-barrelled launchers, which screamed like braying donkeys. The Germans recognized the significance of the capture of Hill 112. Urgent orders were passed to Gruppenführer Wilhelm Bittrich,

Hausser's replacement, to attack on the other flank within one hour, using his SS Panzer Corps reinforced with a battle-group from the SS Panzer Division *Das Reich*. The British Second Army thus found itself under attack by seven panzer divisions, including four SS panzer divisions and part of a fifth. At that very moment, the whole of Army Group Centre in Belorussia had just three panzer divisions, and that was after being reinforced. So Ilya Ehrenburg's sarcastic remark that the Allies in Normandy were fighting the dregs of the German army could hardly have been further from the truth.

Montgomery faced the bulk of the German panzer divisions for very simple reasons, as he had been warned before the invasion. The British Second Army on the eastern side was closest to Paris. If the British and Canadians were to break through, then the German Seventh Army further west and the formations in Brittany would all be cut off.

The strength of German resistance on the British sector had forced Montgomery to reassess his ideas about seizing the flat ground south of Caen for airfields. He tried to turn a painful necessity into a virtue by claiming that he was holding down the panzer divisions to give the Americans the chance to break out further west. Neither the Americans nor the Royal Air Force, desperate for their landing strips, were convinced.

Despite his fighting words to Eisenhower, Montgomery had indicated to Major General George Erskine of the 7th Armoured Division that he was not looking for a 'show-down' after all. 'Complete change so far as we are concerned,' Erskine's intelligence officer noted in his diary just before Epsom, 'as Monty doesn't want us to make ground. Satisfied that Second Army has drawn all enemy panzer divisions, now wants Caen only on this front and Americans to press on for Brittany ports. So VIII Corps attack goes in but we have very limited objective.'

The German counter-attack during the afternoon of 29 June was aimed mainly against the 15th Scottish Division on the western side of the salient. The Scots fought well, but the real damage to the newly arrived SS Panzer Corps came from the Royal Navy. Dempsey, fearing a greater counter-attack on the south-eastern side round Hill 112, told O'Connor to pull back his tanks. Montgomery halted the offensive the next day because VIII Corps had lost more than 4,000 men. Once again the British command had failed to reinforce success rapidly. Tragically, the fighting over the next few weeks to recapture Hill 112 was to cause far more deaths than defending it would have done.

Both Rommel and General Geyr von Schweppenburg were appalled when they saw the effects of naval gunfire from thirty kilometres away on the *Hohenstaufen* and *Frundsberg*. The craters were four metres across and two metres deep. The need to persuade Hitler that they must withdraw their forces behind the River Orne became even more urgent. Geyr was shaken by the losses in this defensive battle, when he would have preferred to use his panzer divisions in a massive counter-attack. They had been drawn into the battle to act as 'corset-stiffeners' to the weak infantry divisions, and now there were not enough incoming infantry divisions to enable him to pull out his panzer formations to refit. So Montgomery, far from 'calling the tune' on the battlefield as he liked to claim, had in fact been trapped in this battle of attrition by the German army's own problems.

Geyr wrote a highly critical report of German strategy in Normandy which called for a flexible defence and the withdrawal of their forces behind the Orne. His comments on OKW interference, which clearly meant Hitler, led to his swift dismissal. He was replaced by General der Panzertruppen Hans Eberbach. The next senior casualty was Generalfeldmarschall von Rundstedt himself, who had warned Keitel that they would not be able to hold the Allies in Normandy. 'You should make an end to the whole war,' he told Keitel. Rundstedt, who had also endorsed Geyr's report, was then replaced by Generalfeldmarschall Günther von Kluge. Hitler would have liked to replace Rommel as well, but that would have created a disastrous impression both in Germany and abroad.

Kluge arrived at Rommel's headquarters, the Château de La Roche-Guyon on the Seine, and made derisive comments about the conduct of the battle so far. Rommel exploded and told him to visit the front first to see the situation for himself. Over the following days Kluge did so and was shaken by what he found. It was very different to the picture which had been painted for him at Führer headquarters, where they had claimed that Rommel was unduly pessimistic about Allied air power.

*

Slightly further west, Bradley's US First Army was bogged down in its own bloody battles in the marshes south of the Cotentin Peninsula and in the *bocage* countryside north of Saint-Lô. The constant battalion-size attacks against the German II Paratroop Corps cost many casualties. 'The Germans haven't much left,' an American divisional commander observed with wry respect, 'but they sure as hell know how to use it.'

Using lessons learned on the eastern front, the Germans managed to make up for their inferiority in numbers, artillery and above all aircraft. They dug little bunkers into the raised base of the impenetrable hedgerows, a hard and laborious task given the tangle of ancient roots, to make machine-gun nests for the first line of defence. Further back, the main line would contain enough troops for an immediate counter-attack. Behind them, usually on rising ground, an 88mm gun would be sited to knock out any Shermans supporting an infantry attack. Every position and vehicle was meticulously camouflaged, which meant that Allied fighter-bombers could do comparatively little to help. Artillery was the arm on which Bradley and his commanders relied: the French civilians, not surprisingly, felt that they did so to excess.

The Germans themselves described fighting in the *bocage* as 'a dirty bush war'. They would plant mines at the bottom of shell craters in front of their positions so that an American soldier, throwing himself in to take cover, would have his legs blown off. Alongside tracks they rigged what the Americans called castrator mines or 'bouncing Bettys', which jumped up and exploded at crotch height. Their tanks and field gunners became expert at firing tree-bursts, which meant exploding a shell in the crown of a tree to blast splinters of wood into anyone sheltering below.

American tactics tended to rely on 'marching fire' as infantry advanced, which meant constant firing at any likely enemy positions ahead. The amount of ammunition used was truly staggering as a result. The Germans needed to be more efficient. Tied to a tree, a German rifleman would wait for the infantrymen to pass, then shoot one of them in the back. This prompted the others to throw themselves flat in the open, and German mortar teams would then shell them with air-bursts as they lay there with the full length of their bodies exposed. Aid men who went to help the wounded were shot down deliberately. Quite often a single German would emerge with his hands up to surrender, and when some Americans moved forward to take him prisoner, he would throw himself sideways and hidden machine guns would shoot them down. Not surprisingly, few American soldiers took prisoners after such incidents.

Combat exhaustion was not recognized as a condition in the German army; it was treated as cowardice. Soldiers who attempted to evade fighting with self-inflicted wounds were simply shot. The American, Canadian and British armies were extraordinarily enlightened by comparison. Most of the psychoneurotic casualties had occurred as a result of the fighting in the *bocage*, and the majority of victims were replacements, thrown in ill trained and unprepared to step into the boots of battle casualties. Some 30,000 men in the US First Army were accounted psychological casualties by the end of the campaign. The surgeon-general of the US Army estimated that American front-line forces suffered a 10 per cent rate of psychiatric breakdown.

Both British and American army psychiatrists wrote after the war that they had been struck by how few cases of combat exhaustion they had found among German prisoners of war, although they had suffered far more from Allied bombing and shelling. They concluded that the Nazi regime's propaganda since 1933 had almost certainly helped prepare their soldiers psychologically. In a fairly similar fashion, one could say that the great hardships of life in the Soviet Union had toughened all those who served in the Red Army. The armies of western democracies could not be expected to withstand the same levels of hardship.

While Rommel and Kluge assumed that the main breakthrough in Normandy would come from the British–Canadian sector on the Caen front, they also imagined that an American attack would come down close to the Atlantic coast. Bradley, however, had focused on Saint-Lô as the eastern end for his forming-up area for the big attack.

After the disappointing results of Epsom Montgomery did little to confide in Eisenhower, who became increasingly exasperated by his apparent complacency. Montgomery could never admit that any of his campaigns were not going according to his 'master plan'. Yet he was aware of the resentment building both at Eisenhower's headquarters and back in London at his lack of progress. He was also acutely conscious of the country's man-power shortages. Churchill feared that, if their military strength was whittled away, Britain would have little say in the post-war settlement.

In an attempt to achieve a breakthrough without losing many more men, Montgomery was prepared to contradict a favourite dictum. In a briefing to war correspondents the previous autumn in Italy, he had stated categorically that 'heavy bombers cannot participate intimately in a land battle against the front line'. On 6 July, he proceeded to request precisely that from the RAF to help him take Caen. Eisenhower, desperate for movement, fully supported him and met Air Chief Marshal Harris the next day. Harris agreed to send 467 Lancaster and Halifax bombers that evening over the northern suburbs of Caen, defended by the 12th SS *Hitler Jugend*. But the attack suffered from target creep.

As at Omaha, the bomb-aimers delayed a moment or two before dropping to be sure of not hitting their own forward troops. The result was that the bulk of their loads dropped on the centre of the ancient Norman city. German casualties were light in comparison to those of French civilians, who were the unsung victims of the fighting in Normandy. A terrible paradox emerged from the campaign. In an attempt to reduce their own casualties, commanders from western democracies were likely to kill more civilians by their excessive use of high explosive.

The British and Canadian attack went in the following morn-ing. This delay gave the *Hitler Jugend* Division nearly twelve hours to recover, and their fearsome resistance inflicted many casualties. Then suddenly they disappeared, having received orders to pull back south of the Orne. The British and Canadians rapidly secured the north and centre of Caen. But even this very partial Allied success did not solve the Second Army's key prob-lem. It still lacked the space to build sufficient forward airfields, and to deploy the rest of the First Canadian Army waiting back in Britain.

With great reluctance, Montgomery then agreed to Dempsey's plan to use all three armoured divisions – the 7th, the 11th and the newly arrived Guards Armoured – to smash through towards Falaise from the bridgehead east of the Orne. Montgomery's doubts had more to do with his anti-cavalry prejudices against armoured formations 'swanning around'. As a profound military conservative it was not his idea of a setpiece offensive, but he could not afford more infantry casualties, and he had to do something. Complaints and jibes were not just coming from the Americans. The RAF was furious. Mutterings that Montgomery should be sacked now came from Eisenhower's deputy, Air Chief Marshal Tedder, and from Air Marshal Coningham, who had never forgiven Montgomery for hogging all the glory in North Africa and seldom mentioning his Desert Air Force.

Operation Goodwood, launched on 18 July, proved the most outstanding example of 'very bold speech and very cautious action' in Montgomery's career. He sold the possibility of a decisive breakthrough to Eisenhower so strongly that the supreme commander replied: 'I am viewing the prospects with the most tremendous optimism and enthusiasm. I would not be at all surprised to see you gaining a victory that will make some of the "old classics" look like a skirmish between patrols.' Montgomery had also given the same impression to Field Marshal Brooke back in London, but the very next day he presented Dempsey and O'Connor with a far more modest objective, which was to advance a third of the way to Falaise and see how things stood. Unfortunately, briefings to officers implied that this was going to be a bigger breakthrough than Alamein, and press correspondents were told of a 'Russian style' breakthrough which might take the Second Army forward a hundred miles. Astonished journalists pointed out that a hundred miles meant all the way to Paris.

The RAF, still desperate for its forward airfields, was again prepared to provide bombers. So at 05.30 hours on 18 July 2,600 RAF and USAAF bombers dropped 7,567 tons of bombs on a frontage of 7,000 metres. Unfortunately, Second Army intelligence had failed to detect that the lines of German defence extended back in five lines all the way to the Bourgébus Ridge, which had to be taken if the Second Army was to advance to Falaise. To make matters worse, the complicated approach march of the three armoured divisions took them over Bailey bridges across the Caen Canal and the River Orne into the restricted bridgehead beyond, where the 51st Highland Division had laid a very thick minefield. Afraid of alerting the enemy, O'Connor ordered lanes to be cleared through it only at the very last moment, instead of removing the lot. But the Germans were well aware of the impending attack. They had seen the preparations from tall factory buildings further east and from air reconnaissance. Ultra had picked up the fact that the Luftwaffe knew of the operation, yet Second Army stuck with its plan.

Troops stood on their tanks to stare in wonder and excitement at the destruction caused by the bombers, but the traffic jams which built up behind because of the narrow lanes in the minefields meant that the attack was fatally slowed. In fact the delays were so great that O'Connor halted the truck-borne infantry to allow the tanks to get through first. The 11th Armoured Division advanced quickly once they were through, but then found themselves ambushed by well-concealed anti-tank guns in stone farms and hamlets. These were objectives for their infantry to deal with, but the tanks were on their own and suffered terrible losses. The division had also lost their air liaison officer as an early casualty and so were not able to call for help from the Typhoon squadrons circling above. They then came under devastating fire from 88mm guns on Bourgébus Ridge and were counterattacked by the 1st SS Panzer Division. The 11th and the Guards Armoured Divisions between them lost more than 200 tanks that day.

General Eberbach had expected the British armoured punch to break through his over-extended forces completely, and he could hardly believe his luck. The Second Army and the Canadians managed to push forward in a number of places the next day, extending their hold south of Caen, but the Bourgébus Ridge remained entirely in German hands. Torrential rain soon began to fall. Montgomery had an excuse to call off the attack, but the damage to his reputation was done.

The Americans and the RAF were made even angrier by his premature claims and self-satisfaction afterwards, when so little had been achieved. On the other hand this very unglorious Goodwood had succeeded in confirming the belief of both Kluge and

Eberbach that the main attack in Normandy would still come up the Falaise road. As a result, when General Bradley finally launched Operation Cobra five days later, Kluge did not at first transfer any panzer divisions to face it. And on 20 July, the morning when the rains came to Normandy, a bomb went off in the Wolfsschanze near Rastenburg.

40

Berlin, Warsaw and Paris

Once the war had started, only the German army was likely to provide conspirators to overthrow Hitler and the Nazi regime. Its officers had access to him and they controlled forces which might ensure the security of a replacement regime. The tentative plans of some generals in 1938 and early in the war to remove the dictator had all collapsed through timidity or misplaced notions of obedience and honour.

Firm plans to assassinate Hitler were first suggested during the Stalingrad disaster in the winter of 1942. The discussion took place at the headquarters of Army Group Centre under Generalmajor Henning von Tresckow. The first attempt took place in March 1943 when explosives provided by Admiral Canaris were placed on Hitler's Focke-Wulf Condor. The detonator failed to work, probably due to the intense cold, and the bomb, disguised as a bottle of Cointreau, was retrieved. Two more attempts that year failed, including that of Hauptmann Axel von dem Bussche, who was ready to act as a suicide bomber at a planned inspection of new uniforms by Hitler.

Oberst Claus Graf Schenk von Stauffenberg provided a new impetus when he was posted to the headquarters of the Ersatzheer, or Replacement Army, in the Bendlerstrasse on the northern edge of the Tiergarten. The idea was to subvert Operation Valkyrie, an emergency plan which originally dated back to the eastern front in the winter of 1941. In July 1943, Generalmajor Friedrich Olbricht had begun to incorporate subtle changes to Valkyrie, so that the military resistance might use it when ready to act. This contingency plan had been created to thwart an uprising by foreign forced labourers, billeted in and around Berlin. That autumn, Henning von Tresckow and Stauffenberg added secret orders to be announced once Hitler was dead. A key element was to circumvent any involvement by the SS and retain all responsibility for internal order in the hands of the Replacement Army.

The conspirators faced many obstacles. Sympathetic officers were posted away, and it was quickly obvious that Generaloberst Friedrich Fromm, who became commander-in-chief of the Replacement Army, could not be relied on. Above all, the plotters had few illusions. They knew that they represented a tiny minority with negligible popular support. The country at large would see them as traitors and the vengeance of the Nazis against them and their families would be savage. Their ethics, often shaped by strong religious beliefs, were combined with conservative political views: several had been supporters of Hitler before Operation Barbarossa. The sort of government they wished to establish had more in common with Wilhelmine Germany than modern democracy. And the basis on which they intended to propose peace with the Allies was totally unrealistic, since they wished to maintain the eastern front against the Soviet Union and retain some occupied territories. Yet even with the odds against them, they felt a strong obligation to take a moral stand against the criminality of the regime.

A practical problem was that Stauffenberg, who had become the effective leader of the plot, was also the only one in a position to plant the bomb. He had lost an eye and a hand in Tunisia, which would be a disadvantage when arming the bomb, but as Fromm's chief of staff he was the sole member of the inner group who had access to Führer headquarters.

Several fellow officers had been recruited often on the basis that they were relations, friends or former officers from the 17th Cavalry, or the 9th Infantry Regiment at Potsdam, the successor unit of the Prussian Guards. Some had refused to join on the grounds that 'changing horses in mid-stream' was too dangerous for Germany at that stage of the war. Others referred to their oath of obedience. They were not moved by the argument that Hitler, through his criminal actions, had displaced any obligation to obey him.

On 9 July Stauffenberg's cousin Oberstleutnant Cäsar von Hofacker had visited Rommel at La Roche-Guyon. He asked Rommel how long the German armies in Normandy could hold out, and Rommel estimated a couple of weeks. This was a vital piece of information for the conspirators, who suspected that time was running out for negotiations with the Americans and British. But further details of their conversation are disputed. It is not clear whether Hofacker asked Rommel to join the conspiracy to assassinate Hitler, let alone whether Rommel agreed. But it appears that Rommel did ask Hofacker to draft a letter to General Montgomery inviting him to discuss terms.

As Stauffenberg had guessed, the most senior officers were the most unreliable. Generalfeldmarschall von Manstein and even Kluge, who had earlier allowed a resistance group under Henning von Tresckow to flourish at the headquarters of Army Group Centre, were opposed to action. But Kluge, they felt certain, would join them once Hitler was dead. In France Rommel's chief of staff, Generalleutnant Hans Speidel, was the key conspirator, and although Rommel opposed the idea of killing Hitler, they were sure that he would join after the event. But on 17 July a Spitfire strafed Rommel's staff car on his return to La Roche-Guyon from the front and effectively removed him from any participation in the plot.

Stauffenberg's plan relied far too much on the traditional chain of command, a risky dependence after the Nazis' politicization of the Wehrmacht. It was particularly dangerous in the case of the commanding officer of the *Grossdeutschland* guard battalion in Berlin, Major Otto Ernst Remer. Stauffenberg was warned that Remer was a loyal Nazi. But Generalleutnant Paul von Hase, another conspirator, who was Remer's superior, felt confident that he would follow orders. To back their coup, the conspirators counted on the panzer training unit at Krampnitz and other detachments outside Berlin. But they did not go far enough in securing the key radio stations and transmitters in and around Berlin.

Bad luck had frustrated several attempts, and an excessive perfectionism thwarted an attempt at the Wolfsschanze on 15 July. Himmler and Göring had not been present, so the conspirators in Berlin told Stauffenberg to wait for another chance. But as time was running out in Normandy, this would be their very last opportunity. Everything was set for 20 July.

Having flown from Berlin to the Wolfsschanze, Stauffenberg joined Hitler's situation conference which was held in a pinewood building. At a convenient moment, Stauffenberg slipped away to the lavatory with his briefcase to prime the two bombs. This took a long time because of his injuries, and before he had finished he was called back to the conference. After replying to the questions put to him about the Replacement Army, he pushed the briefcase with just the one bomb prepared under the heavy table where Hitler was standing. As everyone round the table bent over the maps, Stauffenberg left discreetly. He was driving away when the bomb exploded.

Stauffenberg, convinced that Hitler was dead, flew back to Berlin. Uncertainty, confusion and unexpected complications in Berlin contributed to the coup's failure. The conspirators had certainly made a number of mistakes in their planning and in its execution, but without the death of Hitler himself, who survived the blast, they had not the slightest hope of success.

Mussolini arrived at the Wolfsschanze on that afternoon of 20 July, for a visit which had been arranged long before. He was met by Hitler who, in a manically exultant mood, insisted on showing the Duce the scene of his miraculous escape. The Führer talked incessantly of his conviction that divine intervention had saved him to continue the war. Mussolini, on the other hand, was 'not altogether displeased by the bomb attack on Hitler, as it was proof that treachery was not confined to Italy'.

In his address to the nation that night Hitler compared the attempt to the stab-in-the-back of 1918. He now felt that the only reason why Germany had not defeated the Soviet Union had been because of deliberate sabotage, all along, by army officers. Parallel conspiracy theories developed over setbacks in Normandy, and these are perpetuated to this day in some German books and on neo-Nazi websites. They claim that Speidel, who was in charge of Army Group B on 6 June when Rommel was absent in Germany, deliberately interfered with the deployment of panzer divisions. Speidel is described as the centre of 'the cancer of treason in the German armed forces in the West'.

Everything which had gone wrong on 6 June is attributed to Speidel. He is accused of sending the 21st Panzer Division on a wild-goose chase down the west side of the River Orne that morning, when in fact it was the local commander who ordered it to attack the British airborne landings on that flank. He is also accused of thwarting the movement of the 12th SS Panzer Division

Hitler Jugend, the 2nd Panzer Division and the 116th Panzer Division towards the invasion area. This is said to have been part of his plot to keep the 2nd and 116th Panzer Divisions back to help the 20 July plotters to seize Paris a month and a half later.

Speidel was indeed a key member of the conspiracy, but to pretend that he had sabotaged the whole of the defence of Normandy on 6 June is completely ridiculous. After 20 July he escaped the Gestapo killing machine by a miracle, which perhaps partly explains the subsequent Nazi vituperation against him. In the 1950s he became a senior officer of the West German Bundeswehr and later a NATO commander in Europe. The Nazis and neo-Nazis see this as his pay-off for having treacherously helped the Allies in Normandy. In this all-embracing stab-in-the-back legend of the Second World War, the traitors this time were not Jews and Communists as in 1918, but aristocrats and officers of the general staff.

The Gestapo and SS, in a frenzy of righteous vengeance against the army and above all its general staff, began to round up all those involved and their relatives. With the German army in retreat on all fronts, and Hitler blaming general staff 'traitors' for his own mistakes on the eastern front, even the influence of field marshals diminished dramatically. For the Nazis, this represented a victory in itself on the home front. Their chief priority was 'not to optimize the war effort but to change the power structure within the Reich, to the detriment of the traditional elites'. Altogether, more than 5,000 suspected opponents of the regime and their relations were arrested.

As the conspirators had feared, most Germans were shocked by the attempt on Hitler's life at such a critical moment of the war. Soldiers in Normandy seem to have been either loyal or more cautious in their letters home, but some of those on the eastern front, especially in Army Group Centre, were much more outspoken about the need for change. 'The generals who carried out the assassination attempt on the Führer', wrote a Gefreiter on 26 July, 'know very well that a change of regime is necessary because the war for us Germans offers no hope. So it would be a release for the whole of Europe if the three gentlemen Hitler, Göring and Goebbels were to go. With that the conflict would be ended because mankind needs peace. Anything else is a lie . . . Our lives are not worth living as long as this firm stays in place.' Others also made remarks so critical of the regime that they would have been arrested if their letters had been checked by the censors.

On 23 July, the Nazis forced the army to adopt the 'German greeting', or Hitler salute, instead of the traditional military salute. This provoked scorn among most of those who were not committed Nazi supporters. 'With the German greeting we will win the war!' a military doctor wrote sarcastically. Opinions inevitably polarized between the true believers and those who had understood the writing on the wall. On 28 July, the OKW bulletin finally announced the evacuation of four major towns in the east, including Lublin and Brest-Litovsk. 'Certainly it looks bad,' an Unteroffizier attached to the 12th Panzer Division wrote to his wife, 'but that is no reason to lose courage. The day before yesterday, Dr Goebbels in a major speech indicated new developments (new weapons, Himmler's measures with the Replacement Army, total war commitment), which even for the strained situation in the east will have positive effects. Of that we are all convinced.'

News of Himmler's appointment to head the Replacement Army and of fresh call-ups did not impress all soldiers at the front. 'And soon they'll be calling up babies,' a gunner wrote home on 26 July. 'Here at the front you see almost nothing but snotty kids and old men.'

Some, on the other hand, did not dare face the reality of defeat. They believed only that the desperate situation should encourage them to make even greater efforts to protect their families at home. 'Dearest,' an Obergefreiter wrote home, parroting Nazi propaganda, 'do not be afraid, we will not let the Russians enter our Fatherland. Better that we should fight to the last man, because we do not tolerate this horde coming to Germany. What would they start doing to our women and children – No, that must not be. That would be a great disgrace for us, from which comes the watchword: intensified struggle until a victorious outcome!'

While the Reich was gripped by Nazi frenzy over the failed plot, the collapse on the eastern front was soon matched in the west. On 25 July General Bradley launched Operation Cobra from north of the Saint-Lô–Périers road. The first attempt the day before had been cancelled, after American bombers dropped their loads on their own forward troops. This setback turned bizarrely in the

Allies' favour. Generalfeldmarschall von Kluge believed that it must be a feint to distract him from another offensive by Montgomery down the Falaise road. Then, on the second try, a strong southerly wind blew the dust back over the American troops waiting to attack, and the bombers aimed for the dust cloud, causing yet more own casualties. Bradley still pushed on.

The offensive seemed to get off to a slow start, so Major General Collins sent in his armoured troops early. German defences collapsed. Combat commands from armoured divisions forged ahead with Shermans and infantry in half-tracks, as well as engineers with bulldozers. At last it was the Germans suffering from the vicious circle of defeat. Communications collapsed in the rapid withdrawal, commanders had no idea what was happening, vehicles ran out of fuel and soldiers received no supplies or ammunition. Their retreat was harried by strafing fighters while P-47 Thunderbolt fighter-bombers flew 'shotgun' over the armoured columns, ready to attack any attempt at ambush. When Kluge finally realized that this was the main breakthrough, he transferred the 2nd and the 116th Panzer Divisions to the west, but their arrival and counter-attacks were too late.

In London, the War Cabinet became uneasy over the effects of the V-1 attacks. On 24 July, it heard that casualties were 'thirty thousand-odd of whom four thousand odd killed'. Over the next few days ministers also discussed the threat from the V-2 rocket, which they knew would soon be ready.

On 30 July, Montgomery launched the rapidly prepared Operation Bluecoat to protect Bradley's left flank. By the next day, American armoured columns had reached Avranches and crossed the River Sélune beyond. They were out of Normandy and unopposed. The following day, 1 August, General George Patton's Third Army came into being. His orders were to seize the ports on the Brittany coast, but Patton was well aware that in the other direction the way lay open to the Seine.

While the German command on the western front begged for reinforcements, the transfer of II SS Panzer Corps to Normandy had convinced commanders on the eastern front that they were being unfairly treated. 'The effect of the major conflicts in the west and the east was reciprocal,' Jodl acknowledged under interrogation at the end of the war. 'The two-front war came into sight in all its rigour.' For many soldiers in the east, the strain was becoming too great to bear.

Nervous breakdown became a much more open subject in letters home. 'Psychologically', wrote a gunner in a heavy artillery battery, 'I am finding it increasingly hard to manage when you've just been having a good chat with a comrade and half an hour later you see him as little more than scraps of flesh as if he had never existed, or comrades who are lying badly wounded in front of you in a large pool of their own blood and beg you with pleading eyes to help them because in most cases they cannot speak any more, or pain takes away their power of speech. That is terrible . . . This war is a crushing war of nerves.'

In the last days of July, the 1st Guards Tank Army and the 13th Army managed to get forces across the Vistula south of Sandomierz and seize bridgeheads which would be joined together in spite of desperate German counter-attacks. The OKH was all too aware of the significance of Red Army footholds west of the Vistula. Another lunge would take the enemy all the way to the River Oder, some eighty kilometres from Berlin.

'We've just received our annual summer beating,' a Leutnant commanding a light anti-aircraft detachment observed cynically. 'With a surprise punch, the Russians came from Lublin towards Deblin. Apart from flak batteries and a few disintegrated units there was nothing in their way. After the bridge was blown we took up a new dug-in position on the other [western] bank of the Vistula.' He too was incredulous that the German army could have been surprised and defeated in such a way. 'We are outraged by those swine who are responsible for this crisis on the eastern front.'

Some flak batteries, on the other hand, were proud of what they had achieved in the fighting. 'Round us no fewer than 46 tanks were knocked out!' boasted an Obergefreiter from the 11th Infantry Division. 'On our own we shot down ten armoured ground attack aircraft [Shturmoviks] in five days.' The Red Army had indeed suffered grievous losses during Operation Bagration: a total of 770,888 casualties of which 180,000 were 'irrecoverable'. Army Group Centre losses may not have been so high at 399,102 killed, missing and wounded, but they were irreplaceable, and so were the guns and tanks abandoned in the retreat of over 500 kilo-metres. Overall, those three months alone accounted for a total of 589,425 Wehrmacht dead on the eastern front.

Further north on 28 July, the 2nd Tank Army attacked the *Hermann Göring* Panzer Division and the 73rd Infantry Division just forty kilometres from Warsaw. Bitter fighting followed for the approaches to the Polish capital. Red Army soldiers, kept ignorant of recent events and Stalin's treatment of Poland, were unsure what to make of the country. 'The Poles are strange,' one wrote home. 'How do they receive us? It's very hard to answer this. In the first place, they fear us very much (no less than they fear the Germans). Their ways are completely different from Rus-sian ways. It is obvious that they didn't want the Germans, but they aren't receiving us with pies either . . . Of course they are often taken aback by Russian rudeness and lack of honesty.'

Although greatly reduced, Warsaw's civilian population still stood at nearly one million people. On 27 July the German governor ordered 100,000 males to turn up next day for fortification work. The call was defied. Two days later, Jan Nowak-Jeziorański, a representative of the government-in-exile in London, arrived. He spoke to the deputy prime minister in Warsaw, Jan Stanisław Jankowski, and heard that an uprising was imminent. He warned him that the western powers would not be able to help, and asked whether the revolt could be delayed. Jankowski replied that they had little choice. The young, who had been trained and armed, were too eager to fight. They wanted to be free, and to owe that freedom to nobody.

At the same time, Jankowski felt that, if they did not issue a call for battle, the Communist People's Army would. The Com-munists in Warsaw were just 400 strong, but if they seized the town hall and raised the red flag as the Red Army entered the city, then they would claim to be the leaders of Poland. And if the Home Army did nothing, the Soviets could accuse them of collab-oration with the Germans and of holding on to their weapons to resist the Red Army. The Home Army was damned if it did and damned if it didn't.

That day Radio Moscow announced that 'the hour of action has already arrived' and called on the citizens of Warsaw to rise

up 'and join the struggle against the Germans'. Yet neither the
Soviets nor the Home Army made any attempt to contact one
another. As at Monte Cassino, the Poles were determined to
demonstrate to the world their right to live as a free nation, even
if they were doomed by their geographical position between Germany and the Soviet Union.

They knew by then that they could not count on their British
and American allies against the Soviets. The brutal realpolitik of
the Second World War had made American and British collaboration with Stalin essential, since the Red Army had broken the
back of the Wehrmacht at an appalling cost. This had been clearly
shown by their silence over the Soviet attempt to blame the Katyń
massacre on the Germans. Stalin dismissed the 400,000 members
of the Polish Home Army, the Armia Krajova, as 'bandits' and
tried to link them to the Ukrainian guerrilla force, the UPA, which
had ambushed and killed General Vatutin. He soon tried to pretend to the Allies that they had killed 200 men of the Red Army.
The truth was that any independent Polish organization was by
definition anti-Soviet in his eyes. And the 'government friendly to
the USSR' which he demanded could only be one that was totally
subservient to the Kremlin.

General Tadeusz 'Bór' Komorowski, the commander of the
Home Army, gave the order for the rising to begin, with 'W-
Hour' at 17.00 hours on 1 August. He seemed to believe that the
Red Army would be in the city almost immediately. But it would
be facile to blame him in the atmosphere of intense expectancy.
Almost all 25,000 members of the Home Army in Warsaw, a
number which doubled with volunteers and others from outside
the city, were impatient to start. They had already heard of the
NKVD persecution of their comrades in areas occupied by the
Red Army, and knew how little they could trust the Soviet leader.
They knew that 'if Stalin would use his own massacre [of the
Polish officers in 1940] as a reason to end relations with the Polish
government, how could he be expected to negotiate in good faith
about anything?'

The first priority for the Home Army was to attack German
barracks to seize weapons. This was not easy, especially in daylight, as the Germans were expecting some form of revolt. The Old
Town and the city centre rapidly fell to the Polish insurgents, but

the eastern parts on the Vistula, where most German troops were concentrated to defend Warsaw against the Red Army, remained beyond their grasp. Members of the Home Army later managed to seize the massive PAST building with its colossal neo-Norman tower, after pumping in petrol and setting it on fire. The garrison surrendered, so they took 115 German prisoners with their arms.

Members of the Home Army wore white and red armbands to identify themselves as combatants. Many soon wore captured German helmets, but with a white and red band painted round it. Polish Communists and Jews who had been in hiding since the Ghetto Uprising also joined the fight. On 5 August, the Home Army attacked the concentration camp on the site of the flattened ghetto, killed the SS guards and released the remaining 348 Jewish prisoners.

Voluntary mass mobilization was based on a planned infrastructure, with doctors and nurses running dressing stations and field hospitals. Local priests served as military chaplains. Metal-workers became armourers. They manufactured flamethrowers and their own Błyskawica sub-machine guns based on the Sten. Other cellar workshops made grenades improvised with cans and home-made explosive or, more often, the contents from unexploded German shells and bombs. Supply services were organized with former restaurants acting as field kitchens. Propaganda departments printed leaflets and the news sheets *Biuletyn Informacyjny* and *Rzeczpospolita Polska*. They also produced posters displayed around the city, urging 'One bullet – One German!' And the rising had its own radio station which continued broadcasting, despite all German efforts to destroy it, until the very end on 2 October.

Young women served as stretcher-bearers. Boys too young to fight volunteered as runners. A nine-year-old was seen to climb on to a German panzer and throw grenades inside. Both Germans and Poles froze in disbelief at the sight. 'When he jumped down,' an eyewitness recorded, 'he raced off to the gate [of a tenement building] and there burst out crying.' The courage and self-sacrifice of the young was breathtaking.

On 4 August, Stalin reluctantly agreed to meet a delegation of the Polish government-in-exile. The prime minister Stanisław Mikołajczyk did not handle the meeting well, but this almost certainly made little difference to the outcome. Stalin simply insisted that they should talk to the Soviet puppet 'Polish Committee of National Liberation'. He had already given instructions that his tame government in waiting should be moved on to Polish territory in the baggage train of the Red Army. Its members were installed in Lublin and became known in the west as the 'Lublin Poles', as opposed to the 'London Poles'.

The Lublin committee naturally accepted Stalin's border along the Molotov–Ribbentrop Line, which had roughly followed the Curzon Line, named after the British foreign secretary who had suggested it in 1919. The Lublin Poles were closely controlled by Nikolai Bulganin and Commissar of State Security Ivan Serov, the NKVD chief in 1939 who had overseen the mass deportation and killing of Poles. Bulganin and Serov were also both keeping an eye on that half-Pole Marshal Rokossovsky, commanding the 1st Belorussian Front on Polish territory. Stalin's attitude towards the Poles appears to have been that 'my enemy's enemy is still my enemy'.

Having almost washed his hands of the London Poles, Churchill was deeply stirred by the bravery of the Home Army and did his utmost to help them. On 4 August he signalled Moscow to tell Stalin that the RAF would drop weapons and supplies to the insurgents. The mainly Polish and South African bomber crews based in Italy began their dangerous missions that very day.

On 9 August, Stalin, presumably to keep up appearances, promised Mikołajczyk that the Soviet Union would help the insurgents, even though their rising had been premature. He claimed that a German counter-attack had pushed his forces back from the city. This was partly true, but, more to the point after the great advances of Operation Bagration, the Red Army lead formations were exhausted and short of fuel, and their vehicles were in desperate need of repair. In any case, Stalin soon showed that he had little intention of providing real help, nor of aiding the airlift. No Allied aircraft were to be allowed to land on Soviet-occupied territory, although one flight of American bombers was given permission to refuel. Soviet aircraft did drop some weapons to the insurgents, but without parachutes, which rendered them useless. Stalin simply wanted a couple of examples of assistance to ward off any criticism later.

The Germans brought in their most savage anti-partisan

formations, in which sadism and cruelty were glorified. They included the notorious Kaminski Brigade, part of the 15th SS Cossack Cavalry Corps, and the SS Sturmbrigade Dirlewanger, commanded by SS Brigadeführer Oskar Dirlewanger who walked around with a pet monkey on his shoulder as he directed the slaughter. This *Korpsgruppe* was commanded by SS Obergruppenführer Erich von dem Bach, one of Himmler's main supervisors for the massacre of Jews in Belorussia and the man who had told the Reichsführer-SS of the strain his killers were suffering. In Warsaw, his men appeared to enjoy their work. The wounded in Polish field hospitals were burned alive with flamethrowers. Children were massacred for fun. Home Army nurses were whipped, raped and then murdered. Himmler encouraged the idea of annihilating Warsaw and its population both physically and ideologically. He now seemed to consider the Poles to be as dangerous as the Jews. Some 30,000 non-combatants were slaughtered in the Old Town alone.

In France during the first week of August, the Canadians, the British and the 1st Polish Armoured Division fought with difficulty down the road to Falaise. Patton's Third Army had taken Rennes and charged into Brittany. On 6 August Hitler forced Generalfeldmarschall von Kluge to send his panzer divisions in a doomed counter-attack at Mortain, in the hope of advancing to Avranches on the coast to cut off Patton. Thanks to American determination and guts in the defence of Mortain, the plan proved militarily insane, and greatly accelerated the disintegration of the German army in Normandy. Hitler urged Kluge on to even greater disaster, ordering him to relaunch the attack, but by then Patton's armoured spearheads had turned east towards the Seine and were well into the German rear, threatening Kluge's supply base. The Seventh Army and the Fifth Panzer Army now risked complete encirclement in the Falaise Gap.

On 15 August, while the Falaise pocket began to shrink, Operation Anvil (now renamed Dragoon) landed 151,000 Allied troops on the Côte d'Azur between Marseilles and Nice. Most of the forces had been transferred from the Italian front. Field Marshal Alexander, unhappy to have lost seven divisions for this invasion, described Dragoon as 'strategically useless'. Like Churchill, he had his eye on the Balkans and Vienna. But the British were wrong to have opposed Dragoon. The landings in the south of France prompted a rapid German withdrawal and thus reduced the damage and suffering done to France.

The escape route from the Falaise Gap was not sealed effectively for a number of reasons, but mainly because Bradley, now commanding 12th Army Group, and Montgomery, commanding 21st Army Group, failed to liaise properly or establish priorities. Montgomery, having agreed to a 'short encirclement' at Falaise, and thinking that the First Canadian Army would get through quickly, had not concentrated sufficient forces for the purpose. He had his eye on the Seine, and diverted most of his available forces towards it. He felt that he could always achieve a 'long envelopment', trapping the Germans in front of the river. The result was that the neck of the Falaise Gap remained half open. The 1st Polish Armoured Division was left scandalously unsupported, to face the remnants of the SS panzer divisions and other formations fighting their way out of the pocket.

The other division trying to seal the exit was the 2ème Division Blindée, the French 2nd Armoured Division, commanded by General Philippe Leclerc. Leclerc had protested bitterly to his American commanders when his division was transferred from Patton's Third Army. Both Leclerc and General de Gaulle wanted their American-equipped division to enter Paris first, as Eisenhower had promised. General Gerow, the corps commander, was distinctly unsympathetic to French political concerns. He did not know, however, that the French troops had secretly been stealing gasoline at every opportunity to create a reserve to allow them to strike towards Paris without authority.

The liberation of Paris was low on Eisenhower's list of priorities. It would constitute a huge diversion of effort and supplies, at the very moment when he wanted to keep the Germans on the run all the way back to the borders of the Reich. Patton's divisions had sliced through the German rear in the sort of armoured cavalry campaign for which he had been born. When he visited the 7th Armored Division outside Chartres, he asked its commander when he was going to take the city. He replied that there were still Germans fighting in it so it might take some time. Patton cut him short. 'There are no Germans. It is now three o'clock.

I want Chartres at five or there will be a new commander.'

On 19 August, the eve of the fighting breakout from the Falaise pocket, General de Gaulle arrived from Algiers at Eisenhower's headquarters. 'We must march on Paris,' he told the supreme commander. 'There must be an organized force there for internal order.' Not surprisingly, de Gaulle was afraid that the Communists of the Francs-Tireurs et Partisans would provoke a rising and try to establish a revolutionary government. He, meanwhile, had been infiltrating his own officials into occupied Paris to create a skeleton administration and take over ministries.

The following day in Rennes, de Gaulle heard that an insurrection had started in the capital. He immediately sent General Juin with a letter to Eisenhower insisting that Leclerc's division should be sent straight there. The Paris police had gone on strike five days earlier, in protest at a German order to disarm them. General Koenig in London sent Jacques Chaban-Delmas to persuade the resistance not to rise in revolt yet. But the Communists, led by Colonel Henri Rol-Tanguy, the regional leader of the Forces Françaises de l'Intérieur (FFI), wanted to liberate Paris themselves. On 19 August, the Parisian police, armed with their pistols but dressed in civilian clothes, took over the Préfecture de la Police and hoisted the *tricolore*.

Generalleutnant Dietrich von Choltitz, the German commander of Paris, felt obliged to send in troops, and a very inconclusive engagement took place. Choltitz had been told by Hitler to defend the city to the last and destroy it, but other officers had persuaded him that this would serve no military purpose. On 20 August, a Gaullist group seized the Hôtel de Ville as the start of their strategy to take over key government buildings. The Communists, believing their own propaganda which decreed that power lay in the streets, failed to see that they would be outmanoeuvred.

Patriotic enthusiasm, with improvised *tricolores* at windows and spontaneous renditions of the 'Marseillaise', contributed to a fever of excitement. Streets were barricaded to deny freedom of movement to the Germans, Wehrmacht trucks were ambushed and isolated soldiers disarmed or killed. The Swedish consul-general negotiated a truce. Choltitz agreed to recognize the FFI as regular troops and allow them to hold on to their present buildings. In return the resistance would have to desist from attacking

German barracks and headquarters. The Communists, claiming that they had not been properly represented, denounced the deal. Chaban-Delmas managed only to persuade them to wait a day before they attacked again.

As the remnants of the German forces from Normandy began to escape across the Seine, the First Canadian and the Second British Armies were joined by the 1st Belgian Infantry Brigade, a Czech armoured brigade and the Royal Netherlands Brigade (Princess Irene's). Montgomery's 21st Army Group, with the forces of at least seven countries, was beginning to resemble Roosevelt's dream of the United Nations.

On 22 August, while the FFI responded to Rol-Tanguy's order of 'Tous aux barricades!', Eisenhower and Bradley became persuaded that they would have to go into Paris after all. Eisenhower knew that he would have to sell the decision to General Marshall and Roosevelt as a purely military one. The President would be angry if he thought that US forces were putting de Gaulle in power. De Gaulle, on the other hand, tried to ignore the fact that the United States had anything to do with the Liberation of Paris.

Bradley flew back in a Piper Cub to give Leclerc the good news that he could advance on Paris. The reaction among his soldiers was one of fierce joy. Orders from General Gerow that they were to leave the next morning were ignored, and the 2ème Division Blindée set off that night. After some hard fighting in the outer suburbs on 24 August, Leclerc sent a small column ahead into the city through backstreets. Soon after they reached the Place de l'Hôtel de Ville that night, cyclists spread the word across the city and the great bell of Notre Dame began to peal. General von Choltitz and his officers knew immediately what it signified.

Next morning, the 2ème Division Blindée and the US 4th Infantry Division entered the city to a riotous welcome, interspersed with some fighting. In reality, this was little more than a few sharp skirmishes round German-held buildings – enough for Choltitz to have pretended to resist before he signed the surrender. When he saw the document de Gaulle was deeply irritated to find that Rol-Tanguy had somehow signed above Leclerc, but the Gaullist strategy had won. With their picked men installed in the ministries, the Gouvernement Provisoire de la République Française was more or less in control. Both the Communists and Roosevelt had been presented with a fait accompli.

While Paris was saved, Warsaw was destroyed. The cheering, the *tricolore* flags, the proffered bottles and generous kisses for the liberators were a whole world away. Barbarous and gratuitous murder by the SS auxiliaries continued, as the Home Army struggled on against increasingly desperate odds. 'In fighting Warsaw', wrote a Polish poet, 'no one cries.' Poles carried on the struggle from cellars and sewers as German artillery and Stukas smashed the city around their heads. Their forces, attacking section by section, retook the Old Town. One familiar landmark after another was destroyed, especially the churches. There was no water with which to fight the fires, and the field hospitals had little to treat those with severe burns. Patients simply died in agony.

Discipline remained remarkably good among the insurgents, with little drunkenness. The Home Army had given orders that alcohol was to be destroyed. Some insurgents used what was left to wash their feet as there was little water. Life and defence depended on the parachute containers, all too many of which fell behind German lines as the area held by the Home Army shrank. Allied bombers did not come every day with their precious loads, only when the BBC's Polish service had announced their arrival by playing the old favourite 'Let's dance a mazurka again'.

The insurgents lacked armour-piercing weapons, apart from a few airdropped PIAT launchers, yet they still destroyed tanks and armoured vehicles with petrol bombs and home-made grenades. Barricades and their human defenders were crushed under tank tracks. Dust from pulverized buildings mixed indistinguishably with smoke from burning rafters. Yet others not far away suffered even more.

When the Home Army uprising began in Warsaw, the ghetto at Łódź still held 67,000 Jews. After the astonishing Soviet advance in Operation Bagration, they thought that their moment of release had finally arrived. But with the Red Army still halted on the other side of the Vistula, Himmler decided that no time should be wasted. The vast majority were sent to their death in Auschwitz.

The first request for RAF Bomber Command to attack

Auschwitz had come in January 1941 from Count Stefan Zamoyski of the Polish general staff. Portal refused, on the grounds that British bombing techniques were simply not accurate enough to destroy the railway lines. At the end of June 1944, after confirmation emerged of the gas chambers at Auschwitz, more pleas reached London and Washington to bomb the railways leading to the camps.

Auschwitz-Birkenau was by now the last major death camp operating. At that time the production-line massacre of Hungarian Jews was coming to a crescendo, with 430,000 of them killed in a few months. In August the last Jews from the Łódź ghetto were killed there, to be followed by Jews from Slovakia and then those supposedly privileged Jews from Theresienstadt. It was Himmler's last attempt at a Final Solution before the camps were evacuated and destroyed.

Harris still held to his obsession that the best course for everyone, including prisoners, was to shorten the war with his bombing strategy against Germany. He was also able to argue that in any case this was a day target and therefore a mission for the USAAF. The Americans also refused, but bizarrely, from 20 August, Allied aircraft from the Foggia air bases began to bomb the Monowitz plant of Auschwitz III because it produced methanol, and thus came under Spaatz's oil plan. The raids ended any further hope of IG Farben manufacturing buna and synthetic fuel at Auschwitz. And after Operation Bagration, the Red Army was now too close for comfort. Company employees were evacuated towards the west.

Opposite Warsaw, the Red Army hardly moved. Stalin clearly wanted the rising to fail. The more potential Polish leaders the Germans killed, the better it was for him. Finally on 2 October, after sixty-three days, General Komorowski surrendered. Bach, without Himmler's knowledge, offered the survivors the privilege of being treated as legal combatants. He hoped to recruit them in the fight against the Red Army, but none joined. Although Bach promised that there would be no more destruction in Warsaw, Himmler soon ordered the total demolition of the city with fire and explosive. Only the concentration camp on the site of the ghetto was preserved to hold the Home Army prisoners. The Poles had no illusions in either direction, trapped as they were between the

two pitiless totalitarian systems which fed off each other. Another
Home Army poet wrote: 'We await you red plague / to deliver us
from the black death.'

41

The Ichi-gō Offensive and Leyte

JULY–OCTOBER 1944

On 26 July 1944, as the Americans broke out of Normandy, as the Red Army reached the Vistula and as US Marines completed the conquest of the Mariana Islands, the cruiser USS *Baltimore* entered Pearl Harbor flying the presidential flag. A bevy of admirals in crisp white uniforms waited on the quayside.

Admiral Nimitz went on board to tell President Roosevelt that General Douglas MacArthur's plane from Brisbane had just landed. Half an hour later MacArthur, who had delayed his arrival to make a grand entrance, drove up in a large open staff car with outriders. Waving to the crowd, he too came aboard like the star of a show at a premiere.

MacArthur may have been an egomaniac obsessed with his own inflated legend. He had not concealed his disdain for the President, whom he regarded as virtually a Communist. He saw no reason why he should acknowledge the authority of General George C. Marshall, and he strongly resented the fact that Admiral Nimitz did not come under his command. Yet MacArthur now knew exactly what was necessary to defend his own power and prestige, even if it meant swallowing his pride and being agreeable to Franklin Delano Roosevelt.

MacArthur regarded this conference as politically motivated, with Roosevelt playing the part of commander-in-chief before the November elections. Fortunately, MacArthur's conquest of Papua New Guinea had gone far better than he could have hoped, and his forces were now ensconced at Hollandia on the western end. The moment had come to force through his personal mission, the reconquest of the Philippines, to which he had promised to return. 'They are waiting for me there,' was his grandiose declaration for the press. The fact that he alone among the supreme commanders and chiefs of staff advocated a complete liberation of the Philippines did not discourage him in the least. Others suspected that he had an uneasy conscience after abandoning Corregidor and Bataan, albeit on a presidential order. But the Philippines represented an important part of his life, to say nothing of his wealth after a $500,000 gift from his friend Manuel Quezon, the Filipino President.

Several of his colleagues accepted the idea of liberating Luzon, the main Philippine island, as a stepping stone to Formosa. That was linked to the idea of using China as the main bombing base against Japan. Others, most especially Admiral King, argued that Luzon should be bypassed and they should go straight for Formosa.

MacArthur, using both charm and bulldozing tactics, managed to persuade Roosevelt that they had to liberate the Philippines, if only as a matter of honour. Roosevelt, knowing that to refuse could play badly with the press and the American public in the lead-up to the presidential election in November, allowed himself to be persuaded. Some suggest that there was a private deal: the Philippines in return for MacArthur not attacking Roosevelt at home. Marshall and the air force chief 'Hap' Arnold, on the other hand, knew that MacArthur's pet project would not hasten the end of the war in the Pacific in any way. With the Marianas secured, they now had their air bases for attacking the Japanese home islands. Details recently released of the Bataan death march had provoked a wave of calls for the bombing of Japan.

In the end, after Admiral 'Bull' Halsey had carried out a series of raids on the Philippines with his Third Fleet and Mitscher's fast carriers, the joint chiefs of staff agreed at the Octagon conference in Quebec that MacArthur could go ahead. He should start with the island of Leyte in the north-west Philippines in October. All preliminary operations were cancelled, with one exception, the capture of Peleliu in the Palau Islands some 800 kilometres to the east of Leyte. An invasion of Formosa was dropped for a number of reasons, one of which was the disastrous situation on the mainland of China with the continuing Japanese Ichi-gō Offensive.

The dramatic events in Paris and Warsaw were hard to visualize for those fighting an essentially maritime war on the other side of the world, just as the palm trees, mangrove swamps and cobalt-blue Pacific were unimaginable to those locked in a death struggle on the continent of Europe.

Island fighting against Japanese soldiers who refused to surrender made American commanders consider gas warfare for clearing their bunkers and tunnels, but Roosevelt vetoed the idea. The US Navy had, on the whole, become more adept at deciding which archipelagos and atolls to bypass in its Pacific advance. Well aware of the desperate plight of Japanese troops on isolated islands, it simply left them to starve.

The blockade by American submarines was devastating. Japan had only just begun to establish a convoy system, and lacked transport ships. This was mainly because the Imperial Japanese Navy had preferred to concentrate resources on capital warships. Japanese troops abandoned by Imperial General Headquarters in Tokyo were not allowed to surrender. They were simply told to adopt 'self-sufficiency', which meant that they could expect no supplies and no relief. It has been estimated that six in every ten of the 1.74 million Japanese soldiers who died in the war succumbed to disease and starvation. Whatever the scale of their war crimes against foreign nationals, the Japanese chiefs of staff should have been condemned by their own people for crimes against their own soldiers, but this was unthinkable in such a conformist society.

Japanese soldiers took the food of the local population wherever they could, but in the country people often managed to hide theirs cleverly enough to survive. In towns and cities, however, the suffering was worse, as of course it was among their forced labourers and Allied prisoners of war. Japanese officers and soldiers resorted to cannibalism and not just of enemy corpses. Human flesh was regarded as a necessary food source, and 'hunting parties' went forth to obtain it. In New Guinea they killed, butchered and ate local people and slave labourers, as well as a number of Australian and American prisoners of war, whom they referred to as 'white pigs', as opposed to Asian 'black pigs'. They cooked and ate the fleshy parts, the brains and the livers of their victims. Although told by their commanders that they were not allowed to eat their own dead, this did not stop them. On occasions they selected a comrade, especially one who refused to join in eating human meat, or they seized a soldier from another unit. Japanese soldiers later cut off in the Philippines acknowledged that 'it was not guerrillas but our own soldiers of whom we were frightened'.

Japanese requisitions and intervention in farming had already led to famine in parts of south-east Asia, the Dutch East Indies and the Philippines. Their depredations disrupted agriculture and left little seed grain for the next season. Burma, which had been a great rice bowl for the region, was reduced to subsistence farming by the end of the war. In Indochina the Vichy French authorities, with the approval of their Japanese supervisors, fixed prices and established quotas. But then the Japanese Imperial Army would move from village to village and seize everything before the French officials arrived.

In the north of Indochina, the situation had become even more disastrous because farmers had been forced to plant jute, and with almost all the shipping seized by the Japanese they had no way of obtaining rice from the south. The consequent famine which the Tonkin peasantry suffered in 1944 and 1945 killed more than two million people. The Japanese had no intention of helping the region, mainly because of the growth in support there for the Communist Vietminh, led by Ho Chi Minh. They were aided and armed – ironically, with the perspective of later decades – by the American OSS. Roosevelt, with Stalin's agreement at the Teheran conference, had decided not to allow the French to take back their colony, but this policy died with the President himself just before the end of the war in Europe.

The Japanese regime, dominated by the military, had banked on Germany winning the war in Europe and on America lacking the stomach for a real fight. With an astounding lack of imagination, Japanese leaders thought that they could still arrange favourable peace terms in spite of American outrage over Pearl Harbor. These fatal miscalculations became compounded by the inflexibility of the Japanese military hierarchy. While Japanese commanders rejected innovation, the American forces, with intelligent and dynamic men mobilized from all walks of life, learned very quickly, both technologically and tactically. Above all, the galvanization of military industry in the United States produced an overwhelming arsenal with nearly a hundred aircraft carriers at sea by the end of 1944.

Some historians have argued that, because Japan's losses in merchant shipping were so catastrophic, its large army on the

Chinese mainland could never have been redeployed to face Allied forces elsewhere, so the question of whether or not Chiang Kai-shek's armies were holding them down was irrelevant. In fact some ground troops and much of the naval aviation were redeployed, but this school of thought still feels that all support to China was completely wasted. This argument overlooks the point that without the earlier resistance of the Chinese armies, and their persistence in staying in the war, Japanese forces elsewhere could have been much stronger.

The Japanese Ichi-gō Offensive, which had begun in April 1944, appeared to bear out the most pessimistic opinions of Nationalist fighting abilities. Even Chiang's own officers despaired. 'We got the order to retreat,' recorded a captain. 'A mass of men, horses, carts, was streaming back. It was a shambles. I suddenly saw Huang Chi-hsiang, our general, hurrying past us on a horse, wearing pyjamas and only one boot. It seemed so shockingly undignified. If generals were running away, why should ordinary soldiers stay and fight? The Japanese were sending in tanks, and we had nothing to fight tanks with.'

All the contradictions of US policy, which had tried to make maximum use of China with minimum support, had come together in a counter-productive crescendo. Having focused almost exclusively on Burma to open the road, and concentrated the rearming and training programme on the Nationalist divisions deployed there, Stilwell had achieved little for Chiang Kai-shek's armies facing the Japanese in China itself. As the Americans themselves knew only too well, these troops were too weak from malnutrition to be able to fight, even if they received the right weapons. So it was unfair to blame them for failing to defend the American air bases, especially since American bombing raids on the home islands and other targets had provoked the Japanese response in the first place. And Roosevelt did not want the B-29s diverted to help Chinese troops on the ground. The only exception came in November and December when the Superfortresses devastated Japanese supply depots in Hankow.

There were occasions when Chinese troops fought well. At Heng-yang, the surrounded Tenth Army, with good support from Chennault's fighters and bombers, held back the Japanese for more than six weeks. An American journalist described the troops attempting to relieve the Tenth Army. 'One man in three had a rifle ... There was not a single motor, not a truck anywhere in the entire column. There was not a piece of artillery. At rarest intervals pack animals bore part of the burden ... The men walked quietly, with the curious bitterness of Chinese soldiers who expect nothing but disaster ... their guns were old, their yellow and brown uniforms threadbare. Each carried two grenades tucked in his belt; about the neck of each man was a long blue stocking inflated like a roll of bologna with dry rice kernels, the only field rations. Their feet were broken and puffed above their straw sandals.' These were the pathetically ill-equipped Allied troops which Washington blamed for failing to stem the largest Japanese ground offensive of the whole war in the Far East.

The loss of Heng-yang on 8 August meant that the way was open to the other American air bases at Kweilin and Liuchow. Relations were not just strained to breaking point between Americans and the generalissimo. Chennault blamed Stilwell for having refused to listen to warnings of the Ichi-gō Offensive, while Stilwell blamed Chennault for causing it in the first place and for having taken the bulk of the supplies sent over the Hump, so that virtually none had gone to Chinese ground forces. Certainly Chennault's earlier claims that his Fourteenth Air Force could defeat a Japanese advance now looked hollow. Stilwell wanted Chennault sacked, but Marshall refused. He and General Arnold also refused Chennault's request that he should receive all the supplies sent to the B-29 Superfortress bomber command.

Roosevelt's administration and the American press, which in 1941 had idealized Chiang Kai-shek and the Nationalist regime's resistance to Japan, now turned against them with an exaggerated disgust. A failure to understand the fundamental problems along with their undoubted flaws produced another contradiction in US policy. Stilwell, the State Department and the OSS, in their exasperation with Chiang and the Nationalists, began to idealize Mao Tse-tung and the Communists.

In July, Roosevelt had told Chiang to appoint Stilwell commander-in-chief of all Chinese forces, including the Communists. The generalissimo had no intention of doing anything of the sort, especially if the Americans were thinking of arming the

Communists, but he could only play for time. A straight refusal risked losing economic and military aid. The Ichi-gō Offensive, while devastating to Nationalist armies, had greatly helped the Communists, because most of the Japanese forces involved had come from northern China and Manchuria. The Communists then profited from the Nationalists' defeats by moving forces south into areas that the Nationalists had had to abandon.

The Americans, in a doomed attempt to make both sides co-operate, demanded the right to send a fact-finding group to Mao Tse-tung's headquarters in Yenan. The 'Dixie Mission' arrived in July and was favourably impressed, as Mao intended them to be. Severely limited in what they could see and whom they could speak to freely, they had no idea of Mao's determination to destroy the Nationalists completely, nor of the savage purges, 'rooting out traitors within the [Chinese Communist Party] and enforcing Maoist ideology throughout the party ranks'. A reign of terror was established by mass rallies where suspects were de-nounced, with slogans and insults screamed at them. Confessions were extracted through physical and psychological torture and brainwashing. Mao's regime, with its obsessive use of thought control and 'self-criticism', proved even more totalitarian than Stalinism. Mao did not use a secret police. Ordinary citizens were compelled to take part in the witch-hunts, torture and murder of alleged traitors. And Mao's personality cult exceeded that of Stalin.

Communist cadres and military commanders were terrified of making a mistake. Now that the war was starting to de-velop away from purely guerrilla actions, they were afraid of being accused of contravening Maoist ideology, which had con-demned conventional warfare ever since the disastrous Battle of the Hundred Regiments. Mao remained reluctant to risk forces which he wanted to conserve for fighting the Nationalists later, even though they were growing rapidly. By the end of 1944, the Chinese Communists increased their regular formations to a strength of 900,000 while their local forces of peasant militia were around 2.5 million strong.

The situation in China became so desperate during the Ichi-gō Offensive that Chiang wanted to bring back the divisions of Y-Force on the Salween front to help stem the Japanese advance.

As this was at a critical moment in the Burma campaign, Roosevelt, Marshall and Stilwell were outraged, yet they still refused to acknowledge their responsibility for the Nationalists' desperate plight. Marshall drafted a very strong note which was tantamount to an ultimatum, instructing the generalissimo to make Stilwell commander-in-chief immediately and to reinforce the Salween front.

Stilwell read the memorandum with fierce pleasure when it arrived. He virtually barged into a meeting between the generalissimo and Major General Patrick J. Hurley, Roosevelt's new envoy. Stilwell wrote triumphantly in his diary how he 'handed this bundle of paprika to the Peanut and then sank back with a sigh. The harpoon hit the little bugger in the solar plexus and went right through him.' Hurley, on the other hand, was appalled by the tone of the communication and the loss of face it would cause. Chiang Kai-shek hid his anger. He simply said, 'I understand,' and ended the meeting.

The generalissimo later sent a message to Roosevelt through Hurley insisting on Stilwell's recall. He was perfectly prepared to accept an American general to command the Chinese forces, Chiang said, as long as it was not Stilwell. Roosevelt no longer saw China as essential in ending the war against Japan, now that Stalin had committed the Soviet Union to invade Manchuria as soon as the war with Germany ended. So he simply assessed how the row would affect his standing in the presidential November elections.

The American press had now turned against the Nationalist regime, describing it as dictatorial, incompetent, corrupt and nepotistic. Newspapers accused it of refusing to fight the Japanese and of indifference towards the Chinese people, especially during the major famine in Honan the year before. The *New York Times* claimed that support for the Nationalists made America 'acquiesce in an unenlightened cold-hearted autocratic regime'. Influential writers, such as Theodore White, vilified Chiang Kai-shek and contrasted him unfavourably with the Communists. In that era of New Deal liberalism, many State Department officials agreed.

Opinion polls in the United States during the presidential campaign showed that Roosevelt's narrow lead over Thomas Dewey was slipping rapidly. So Roosevelt, afraid of the negative effect which a Chinese Nationalist collapse might have on his campaign, decided to recall Stilwell to Washington, giving the impression that the general had done his best to enlighten Chiang Kai-shek but could do no more. The truth that the Chinese had been abandoned in the face of the Ichi-gō Offensive was completely suppressed, as were Stilwell's quarrels with Chiang, Chennault and Mountbatten.

General Marshall, who had appointed Stilwell in the first place and largely ignored his part in the disastrous state of affairs, drafted a reply to Chiang Kai-shek's demand for his recall. 'A full and open explanation of the reasons for General Stilwell's recall will have to be made,' Marshall wrote in his draft for Roosevelt to send to Chiang Kai-shek. 'The American people will be shocked and confused by this action and I regret the harm that it will inevitably do to the sympathetic attitude of the American people toward China.'

In his message to Chiang Kai-shek, Roosevelt did not in the end use Marshall's scarcely veiled threat to publicize the details behind Stilwell's recall, but he certainly made sure that the American press was briefed. In any case, Stilwell put over his version of events to correspondents in Chungking before his departure. He also made sure that sympathizers back in the States condemned Chiang as an unpleasant military dictator and accused him of not attacking the Japanese so that he could build up stocks of American weaponry to fight the Communists. The fact that Mao was deliberately husbanding his forces ready for outright civil war, and making secret deals with the Japanese, was not suspected.

Major General Albert C. Wedemeyer, who had been serving as Mountbatten's chief of staff, replaced Stilwell in October just as the Japanese renewed their offensive. The plight of the refugees mirrored that of the beaten troops. Chiang's utterly demoralized and famished armies collapsed in chaos again, allowing the Japanese to take more air bases, all of which the Americans demolished just beforehand. By now, they were used to the routine of blowing up every hut, hangar and store, then planting thousand-pound bombs in the runway to crater it beyond use.

The position was so desperate that Wedemeyer agreed to the

return of the Y-Force divisions and obtained the sudden transfer of all the air force formations supporting the Burma campaign. Yet the Japanese drive was coming to a natural end. Operation Ichi-gō had achieved its objectives, and winter was approaching. Thirteen American airfields were out of action, the Japanese had inflicted more than 300,000 casualties on the Nationalists, and their armies in China had linked up with their forces in Indochina.

The loss of all his air support was a nasty shock for General Slim, with his Fourteenth Army about to cross the great Irrawaddy. Some British officers suspected that the anglophobic General Wedemeyer was not keen on helping them anyway, now that they had played their part in helping secure the route of the Burma Road to China.

While MacArthur exulted in Roosevelt's approval for his invasion of Luzon, which represented a victory over Admiral King, preparations went ahead for the preliminary landings on Leyte. But Admiral Nimitz had refused to cancel the assault on the island of Peleliu, which had the main Japanese airfield in the Palau Islands. Commanders assumed that the capture of Peleliu would take the 1st Marine Division just three to four days.

On 15 September the amphibious assault began, with the usual bombardment from the big guns of the battleships and dive-bombers from carriers. The round bows of the Landing Ship Tanks opened, and out spilled several hundred amtracs loaded with marines. Peleliu, less than eight kilometres long and less than three wide, looked on the map like the skull of a crocodile's head with its jaws slightly open. It consisted of a hilly spine of sharp coral along the north-west shore, a flat centre on which lay the airfield, and mangrove swamps on the south-east shore. The island was ringed with coral reef which made the use of landing craft impossible. Only the amtracs could get over them.

For marines who had fought in most of the island battles, Peleliu was the worst. The heat was stifling, sometimes rising to 46 degrees Centigrade. The water in their canteens could have come from a standing kettle, but they drank it all the same. Thirst and dehydration became a major problem. The shortage of water on the island was such that old oil barrels which had

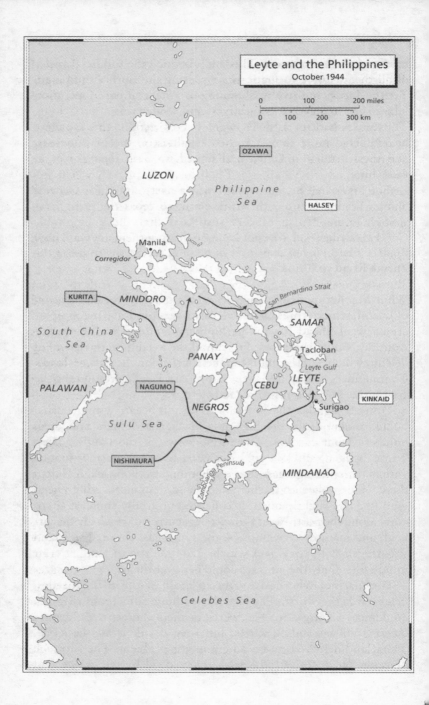

Leyte and the Philippines
October 1944

not been cleaned out were filled on board the ships in the fleet and brought ashore. Their contents tasted of rust and oil and made men feel sick, but it was all there was. Heat prostration caused many men to collapse in the first twenty-four hours.

Marines had reached the edge of the airfield, and soon afterwards they heard tanks. At first they assumed that they were American. When they realized that a dozen Japanese tanks had emerged from hiding, all hell broke loose. They had few armour-piercing weapons with them, but some Shermans and fighter-bombers soon reduced the obsolete armoured vehicles to smoking hulks.

The marines had arrived hoping that the Japanese would soon 'pull a *banzai*', which meant making a mass suicide charge as they had on other islands, since that would end things quickly. But the enemy had changed his tactic. Digging in with the solid coral was impossible. Worst of all, the sharp fragments blasted in all direction by shellbursts greatly increased their lethal effect. The only shelter was provided by bomb craters. With casualties spread all over the place, and Japanese machine guns covering the area, evacuating the wounded led to even greater losses. Eventually a young officer grabbed the reluctant driver of an amtrac, and with a pistol to his head forced him to drive around to collect the fallen.

The coral ridge on the far side of the airfield running north-east up the island was honeycombed with tunnels between natural caves in the coral. The Japanese had positioned their field guns inside with sliding steel doors. They had even installed electric fans to disperse the cordite fumes when firing. To get to grips with the defenders, the marines first had to cross the airfield and deal with blockhouses and barracks, which had been turned into a concrete fortress. In the opinion of many, Guadalcanal now seemed like a holiday outing.

On the morning of 16 September four battalions attacked in a charge across the no-man's-land of the airfield. Running forward bent low, men collapsed in a sprawl when hit. But the buildings were taken and their defenders despatched. The 1st Marine Division had suffered more than a thousand casualties since landing. Worse was to come when they began to tackle 'Bloody Nose Ridge', the name they gave to the coral spine sixty to ninety metres high. They seldom managed to get much sleep at night. During the hours of darkness Japanese soldiers would infiltrate their lines, singly or in pairs, either to stab machine-gunners or mortar-teams in their gunpits, or else to tie themselves high in trees to act as snipers when dawn came.

Clearing Bloody Nose Ridge was an arduous affair in which grenades and flamethrowers were vital tools. Its caves provided the Japanese with interlocking fields of fire, and the fighting was such that the bulk of the island was not cleared until the end of September. It was not finally secured until the end of October. By then the 1st Marine Division's casualty rate had risen to 6,526, of which 1,252 were killed. And the 81st Division, which had to be brought in as reinforcements, lost another 3,278. Yet Peleliu could have been bypassed altogether. It was one of Nimitz's rare mistakes.

Another mistake was about to be made by Admiral Halsey in the largest naval engagement of the whole war, but fortunately for the US Pacific Fleet a Japanese admiral failed to seize the opportunity offered. The Japanese had expected an assault on the Philippines and they intended, when it came, to turn it into a decisive battle.

The remaining battleships of their Combined Fleet were based close to their main source of oil in the Dutch East Indies. US submarines had sunk too many fuel tankers to allow many alternatives. Their last few carriers were kept closer to the home islands. Admiral Fukudome Shigeru on Okinawa, who had experienced a severe raid by the US Third Fleet in October, was horrified by the casualty rate of his under-trained pilots when more than 500 Japanese aircraft were shot down. He described them as 'so many eggs thrown at the stone wall of the indomitable enemy formation'. Yet the Japanese compulsion to avoid loss of face made them try to portray the disaster as a victory. They claimed two battleships and eleven carriers sunk, although the Allies had suffered only damage to two cruisers during the engagement. Emperor Hirohito called for national celebrations. The Imperial Japanese Navy also failed to tell their colleagues in the army the truth about the engagement. As a result Field Marshal Terauchi Hisaichi decided that they could after all defend the island of Leyte as well as Luzon, and he managed to persuade

Imperial General Headquarters to change their plans accordingly.

General MacArthur, certain that his moment of destiny was at hand, boarded the cruiser USS *Nashville* to join the US Sixth Army's invasion transports. They were protected by Vice Admiral Thomas C. Kinkaid's Seventh Fleet, with eighteen escort carriers and six old battleships. Predictably, the Seventh Fleet was known as 'MacArthur's Navy'. They would approach Leyte from the south. Halsey's Third Fleet, with sixteen fast carriers, six fast battleships and eighty-one cruisers and destroyers, would guard the north-eastern approaches. Altogether, the US Navy was putting to sea for the Leyte operation with 225 warships.

Neither Halsey nor Kinkaid expected the Japanese to come out to fight on this occasion. Logic seemed to dictate that the Japanese would hold back to concentrate their forces against an invasion of Luzon itself. This had indeed been the Japanese plan, but any landing in the Philippines threatened to cut Japan off from the oilfields of Java and Sumatra. Imperial General Headquarters simply could not ignore such a threat. Halsey was so relaxed that he sent one of his carrier groups back for refitting, to the vast new US Navy base in the lagoon of Ulithi Atoll in the Caroline Islands.

In the early hours of 20 October, the invasion fleet and escorts entered the straits leading to the Gulf of Leyte. The landing with four divisions began that morning and went according to plan. General MacArthur went ashore with the new President of the Philippines early in the afternoon. Having ensured that pressmen, newsreel cameras and photographers were present, MacArthur waded ashore and made his announcement: 'People of the Philippines, I have returned! By the grace of Almighty God, our forces stand again on Philippine soil.' MacArthur's almost presidential campaign over the last year had included the smuggling in of leaflets, books of matches, packs of cigarettes and propaganda buttons, all decorated with a portrait of General MacArthur, the US and Philippine flags and his slogan 'I shall return'. They had been distributed by the large resistance network on the islands, and most Filipinos knew these three words of English by the time the landings came.

The fighting on Leyte soon intensified. Once again point platoons stumbled on well-concealed machine-gun posts and foxholes, with bloody consequences. The 302nd Engineer Battalion in the form of Captain J. Carruth came to the aid of the 77th Division by advancing in an armoured bulldozer, either burying or uncovering Japanese foxholes and machine-gun nests, sometimes leaning out of the side of the cab to fire his Thompson sub-machine gun at an exposed Japanese soldier.

On 23 October, while MacArthur was being honoured at another ceremony in the provincial town of Tacloban, the invasion fleet offshore was rushing to 'General Quarters'. Two US submarines had sighted the Japanese Combined Fleet steaming in their direction.

Admiral Toyoda Soemu, the commander-in-chief of the Combined Fleet, was strong in battleships and heavy cruisers. His force had even been joined by Japan's two Yamato-class battleships, the largest in the world at 68,000 tons and armed with 18-inch guns. Since Toyoda had been left almost without aircraft and pilots after the disastrous encounters near Formosa, he decided to use his two carriers as a decoy to attract the American fleet away from Leyte. He would then attack the invasion transports and their escorts.

Toyoda's plan was, perhaps, rather too complicated for its own good. He split his forces in four. There was the decoy carrier group to the north. There were the two squadrons supposedly joining in the Surigao Straits, which eventually failed to unite because their commanders loathed each other. And finally there was the largest group, the First Striking Force commanded by Vice Admiral Kurita Takeo, with the *Yamato* and *Musashi* super-battleships. Toyoda hoped to cut through the Philippine archipelago to approach the San Bernardino Strait north of Leyte. This was the force coming from Brunei on the north coast of Borneo spotted by the two American submarines.

Having sent off their contact report, the submarines had promptly attacked with torpedoes, sinking Kurita's flagship, the heavy cruiser *Atago*, badly damaging another cruiser, the *Takao*, and sinking a third, the *Maya*. A rather discouraged Admiral Kurita, still in his midnight-blue uniform and white gloves, abandoned the *Atago* as it was settling in the water and transferred his flag to the *Yamato*.

On 24 October, an excited Admiral Halsey prepared for

Soviet troops in a burning German town

(*Above*) Civilians wait to enter a flak tower bunker in Berlin
(*Above right*) Soviet traffic controller on the road to Berlin
(*Right*) Civilians clearing rubble in Dresden, February 1945

(*Above left*) C-46 transport plane landing at Kunming
(*Below left*) Japanese kamikaze pilots pose for a memorial picture
(*Above*) Marble Gallery in the battered Reichschancellery
(*Below*) German wounded in Berlin, 2 May 1945

The Japanese
surrender on the
USS *Missouri*,
2 September 1945

Homeless civilians on Okinawa

action. He ordered Mitscher's fleet carriers to attack Kurita's force, but then radar picked up a formation of some 200 Japanese ground-based aircraft headed in their direction. Hellcat fighters took off rapidly and destroyed seventy of them. A single American pilot managed to down nine enemy aircraft in this engagement. One Japanese bomber, however, slipped through. Its bomb penetrated the flightdeck of the carrier USS *Princeton* and set her ablaze, exploding fuel and torpedoes below decks.

At 10.30 hours, the new VB-15 Curtis Helldivers and Avenger torpedo bombers attacked Admiral Kurita's large battle squadron, with the heavily armoured *Yamato* and the *Musashi*. Avengers slowed down the *Musashi* with torpedo strikes against her slightly more vulnerable bows. Further waves of American pilots, scoring seventeen direct hits with bombs and a total of nineteen hits with torpedoes, crippled the *Musashi*. A naval trumpeter played the Japanese national anthem as she began to list, and the ship's battle ensign was tied to a strong swimmer, who dived overboard. Soon the great battleship, larger than the *Bismarck*, capsized and sank taking more than a thousand of the crew down with her. The *Yamato* and two other battleships had also been damaged, slowing them down, and nine cruisers and destroyers had been sunk or severely hit.

Admiral Kurita, reluctant to tackle the San Bernardino Strait in daylight and unsure what to do next, turned his ships around. When Halsey heard of this from his pilots, who had optimistically reported greater losses than they had inflicted, he assumed that the enemy was running away. During that afternoon, Halsey had sent a signal announcing that he would separate four battleships, five cruisers and fourteen destroyers from his Third Fleet. They would constitute Task Force 34. When Admiral Kinkaid off Leyte, Admiral Nimitz in Pearl Harbor and Admiral King in Washington were informed of this move, they all approved, assuming that Task Force 34 would be left to guard the San Bernardino Strait. But at 17.30 hours a signal informed Halsey that the Japanese carrier force had at last been sighted 300 miles to the north of the strait. In his report, the pilot had unintentionally exaggerated the number of battleships in the group commanded by Vice Admiral Ozawa Jisaburō to four. Unaware that Ozawa had been sailing in a rectangle in order to be spotted, the impetuous Halsey leaped at the bait.

Kinkaid and MacArthur expected the Third Fleet to help protect the invasion. Halsey, on the other hand, wanted to act in the spirit of Nimitz's order instructing him that, if an opportunity arose for the destruction of a major portion of the enemy fleet, then that should become his primary task. Halsey also remembered the criticism directed at Admiral Raymond Spruance for not having followed up the Japanese carriers off the Marianas. So he steamed in pursuit with the whole of the Third Fleet, without leaving Task Force 34 behind to guard the San Bernardino Strait. Halsey had fallen for the decoy force, despite warnings from his own task group commanders.

As darkness fell, Admiral Kinkaid deployed the battleships of the Seventh Fleet at the top of the Surigao Strait. He knew from air reconnaissance and signals intercepts that Toyoda's other two battle squadrons would soon be upon him. He still assumed that the San Bernardino approach to Leyte was firmly guarded by Task Force 34. Five out of Kinkaid's six old battleships were resuscitated victims of the attack on Pearl Harbor. The rest of his ambush force consisted of destroyers. Out ahead, fast PT boats were called in to attack, but their torpedo runs shortly before midnight failed to strike.

The Japanese battle squadron, which consisted of four destroyers, two battleships and a cruiser, sailed right into the night-time trap. American and Australian destroyers sped past in the dark firing torpedoes. Then, in an obsolete but highly effective manoeuvre, the six old battleships formed line ahead across the strait. The radar directing their main armament ensured the accuracy of the massive broadsides. Only one Japanese destroyer escaped. All the other ships, including the battleships *Fuso* and *Yamashiro*, sank then or later. Kinkaid's group suffered just one destroyer badly damaged. The commander of the second Japanese battle squadron, who had failed to link up with his detested rival, decided that he would not risk the same fate.

Admiral Kinkaid was understandably satisfied with the night's events. But before turning in – it was now around 04.00 hours on 25 October – he asked his chief of staff if there was anything else they should think of. He replied that perhaps they should double-check with Halsey that Task Force 34 was still guarding the San Bernardino Strait to the north of Leyte. Kinkaid agreed, and a signal was sent off. Due to a backlog in decoding, Halsey did not receive the message until three hours later. He answered: 'Negative. TF34 is with me pursuing enemy carrier force.' This reply was alarming enough, but then at 07.20 hours Kinkaid received a signal from one of the small escort carriers off Leyte. They were under heavy attack. Admiral Kurita's battleships, including the *Yamato*, had come back and passed through the San Bernardino Strait unchallenged. The whole of MacArthur's invasion fleet was at risk.

Calls for help to Halsey and the Third Fleet did not produce the response expected. Far from acknowledging his error, Halsey was still determined to continue the pursuit. Mitscher's carriers had launched their aircraft in strikes against Ozawa's force, so far sinking two carriers and a destroyer. All Halsey was prepared to concede in the crisis was to recall the carrier task group on its way to replenish in the Ulithi Atoll. Even Nimitz, who avoided interfering with a subordinate commander once battle had commenced, sent a signal at 09.45 hours asking the whereabouts of Task Force 34. 'Bull' Halsey was furious, his obstinacy hardening by the hour.

Kinkaid, meanwhile, had sent some of his battleships north to help the screen of escort carriers and destroyers facing Kurita's mighty battle squadron. They were not fast enough to be of use, yet astonishingly they were not needed. With great skill and bravery, the anti-submarine pilots from the escort carriers, who had no torpedoes or bombs, made dummy attack after dummy attack to distract Kurita's battleships. At one moment, the *Yamato* turned in the wrong direction to avoid what it thought was a torpedo run and, by the time it had turned back to rejoin the other ships, found itself way behind.

All the time, US destroyers nipped in and out of a smoke-screen to fire off torpedoes. A convenient rain squall also helped. One escort carrier, the USS *Gambier Bay*, was on fire and three destroyers were lost, yet the damage to the task group was extraordinarily light in the circumstances. Suddenly, to the amazement and delighted relief of the remaining escort carriers and destroyers, they saw Kurita's ships turn away towards the north. Kurita, who still had not heard from Ozawa that Halsey was continuing to pursue him as planned, feared that he might now be caught from behind by the Third Fleet. His signallers had picked up a message in clear from Kinkaid demanding he return. By mid-morning, Kurita decided to withdraw back through the San Bernardino Strait.

Halsey, who by now had sunk all four of Ozawa's carriers, finally came to his senses. He sent his fast battleships back south, but they were too late to cut off Kurita's escape. Halsey justified his actions on the grounds of Nimitz's order to pursue the destruction of the enemy fleet, but he was still loath to admit that he had been pursuing the wrong one. The press referred to his chase as the 'Battle of Bull's Run'. Nimitz took no action against such a bold leader. The Battle of Leyte Gulf, as the Japanese themselves acknowledged, had been a decisive defeat in any case. They had lost all four carriers, the giant *Musashi* and two other battleships, nine cruisers and twelve destroyers.

On that morning of 25 October, right at the end of the battle, the Japanese unleashed a new weapon in the form of suicide air attacks by pilots from the First Air Fleet based on Luzon. They were called kamikaze, or 'divine wind', in memory of the typhoon in the thirteenth century which smashed the Emperor Kublai Khan's invasion fleet. There was an obvious advantage for the Imperial Japanese Navy. Most of its remaining pilots were incapable of aerial combat, so all these young men needed to do was aim their aircraft as a flying bomb at a ship, especially at the flightdeck of an aircraft carrier. The Americans lost an escort carrier and three others were severely damaged, but the shock effect of the kamikaze attack would prove dangerously counter-productive for Japan. The mentality it revealed undoubtedly contributed to the decision to use atomic weapons against the country less than a year later, rather than mount a conventional invasion of the home islands.

42

Unrealized Hopes

In the last days of August 1944, the collapse of the German armies in Normandy and the liberation of Paris produced a sense of euphoria in the west that the war would be over 'by Christmas'. This impression grew with the headlong advance of Allied armies towards the Rhine. On 3 September, the Guards Armoured Division entered Brussels to a welcome as ecstatic as that in liberated Paris a week earlier. Patton's Third Army was approaching Metz.

A day after Brussels, Antwerp fell to the 11th Armoured Division, which had advanced 550 kilometres in six days. On their right, the US VII Corps near Mons trapped a large force of Germans retreating from Normandy and the Pas de Calais. They killed 2,000 and took 30,000 prisoners. Among these Germans must have been the troops who, reacting to attacks by the Belgian resistance, had set fire to houses near Mons and killed sixty civilians in reprisals. Other atrocities and looting, mainly carried out by Waffen-SS units, took place elsewhere in Belgium over the next few days during the German retreat.

It then looked as if the US First Army was about to take Aachen, the first German city. Many inhabitants fled eastwards in panic. The momentum of events seemed unstoppable, and German resistance appeared on the point of collapse. The Allies did not consider that the abandoned Westwall, which they called the Siegfried Line, would prove a major obstacle. Hitler recalled Generalfeldmarschall von Rundstedt as commander-in-chief west, but it was Generalfeldmarschall Model who, in General Omar Bradley's words, 'miraculously grafted a new backbone on the German army' and stopped the panic. Göring provided six Fallschirmjäger regiments, to which were added another 10,000 Luftwaffe personnel, including ground crews and even trainee pilots whose flying courses had been stopped because of fuel shortages. They formed the basis of Generaloberst Kurt Student's First Paratroop Army deployed in southern Holland.

This was also the moment when Allied hubris collided with the shortage of fuel, which still had to be brought all the way from Cherbourg by the trucks of the 'Red Ball Express'. The whole advance depended on tonnage delivered and achieving the right priorities between fuel and ammunition. The First Canadian Army had not yet managed to retake the Channel ports, which were resolutely defended on Hitler's orders. So Antwerp was the only solution. Yet, although the British Second Army had taken the city and the port virtually undamaged, Montgomery failed to secure the land and islands along the Scheldt estuary from the North Sea. He had ignored Admiral Ramsay's warnings that mines and German coastal batteries on the islands, particularly Walcheren, would make it unnavigable and therefore render the vital port useless.

The fault also lay with Eisenhower and SHAEF (Supreme Headquarters Allied Expeditionary Forces) for not having insisted to Montgomery that he should clear the estuary before he attempted to dash on to the Rhine. The Germans had time to reinforce their garrisons on the islands. The result was that long and complex battles, including amphibious landings, were later required by the Canadians to rectify this mistake. They sustained 12,873 casualties in an operation which could have been achieved at little cost if tackled immediately after the capture of Antwerp. The Scheldt passage would not be cleared until 9 November and the first ships did not reach Antwerp until 26 November. This delay was a grave blow to the Allied build-up before winter approached.

Montgomery was still seething over Eisenhower's decision to advance on a broad front to the Rhine and into Germany. This had always been standard American doctrine, relying on overwhelming force, so Montgomery should not have been surprised. But he also believed passionately that Eisenhower was no field commander, and that he himself should have the role. Montgomery wanted his 21st Army Group and Bradley's 12th Army Group to advance together north of the Ardennes and surround the Ruhr. But Eisenhower, at their meeting of 23 August, had insisted that he wanted Patton's Third Army to link up with the US Seventh Army and the French First Army coming up from southern France.

Eisenhower, still irritated with Montgomery after his less than frank communications in Normandy, was not going to change the established plan. His only compromise was to allocate 21st Army Group a higher proportion of resources and hold back Patton's Third Army on the Moselle. Patton's reaction was predictable. 'Monty does what he pleases and Ike says "yes, sir",' he wrote in his diary. Patton was not the only one to be provoked by Montgomery's promotion to field marshal, a tribute which Churchill had approved to appease the British press when Eisenhower took over the direction of operations on 1 September. Patton went ahead and crossed the Moselle anyway, but the fortress city of Metz proved much harder than he had imagined.

Although Eisenhower had taken over field command, there was lamentably little direction, or even effective communication, during these crucial days. He had damaged his knee and was trapped back at SHAEF headquarters, which was still at Granville on the Atlantic coast of Normandy. Montgomery became exasperated at the failure to answer his signals promptly. So when Eisenhower flew to Brussels, Montgomery was in a less than tactful mood when he joined the disabled supreme commander on his aircraft beside the runway. He flourished the copies of the signals exchanged and went into a tirade about what he thought of the strategy proposed. Eisenhower waited for him to draw breath, then leaned forward, put his hand on his knee and said quietly: 'Steady, Monty! You can't speak to me like that. I'm your boss.' Montgomery, thoroughly put in his place, mumbled, 'I'm sorry, Ike.'

Montgomery was determined to be first across the Rhine, so as to open up the way for the major thrust into Germany, which he should command. This led to one of the most famous Allied disasters of the war. Bradley was amazed by Montgomery's audacious plan to leapfrog forward, with a series of airborne drops, to cross the lower Rhine at Arnhem. It struck him and others as completely out of character. 'Had the pious teetotaling Montgomery wobbled into SHAEF with a hangover,' he later wrote, 'I could not have been more astonished than I was by the daring adventure he proposed.' But Montgomery did have one justification, which

Bradley did not acknowledge. V-2 rockets had just started to fall on London, fired from northern Holland, and the War Cabinet wanted to know if anything could be done.

On 17 September Operation Market Garden began. It consisted of an airborne assault by British, American and Polish paratroop formations to capture a series of bridges over two canals, the River Maas, the Waal and then the Rhine. Warnings that SS panzer divisions had been identified in the area of Arnhem were ignored. Dogged by bad luck and bad weather, the airborne operation failed mainly because the drop zones were too far from their objectives, radio communications failed disastrously and the Germans reacted far more rapidly than expected. This was due to prompt action by the energetic Model, as well as to the fact that the 9th and 10th SS Panzer Divisions had been close to Arnhem.

Montgomery's plan had depended on the rapid advance of Horrocks's XXX Corps up a single road to relieve the paratroop forces, but German resistance at key points made it impossible to maintain the momentum. Despite truly heroic bravery by all the airborne formations, above all the American 82nd Airborne crossing the River Waal under fire in daylight, XXX Corps never managed to link up with the 1st Airborne Division. On 27 September, the paratroopers holding the Arnhem bridgehead, short of water, rations and above all ammunition, were forced to surrender. The battered remnants of the 1st Airborne Division had to be evacuated across the lower Rhine by night. The Germans took nearly 6,000 prisoners, half of whom were wounded. Total Allied losses came to nearly 15,000 men.

On the eastern front, the Red Army had extended their massive gains from Operation Bagration with another offensive further south, which had begun on 20 August. General Guderian, the new army chief of staff, appointed by Hitler in the wake of the July plot, had taken five German panzer and six infantry divisions from Army Group South Ukraine in an attempt to shore up Army Group Centre. Generaloberst Ferdinand Schörner was left with just one panzer and one panzergrenadier division to stiffen his German infantry and Romanian formations. They were stretched out from the Black Sea along the River Dnestr and east of the Carpathian Mountains.

The Stavka briefed Marshals Malinovsky and Tolbukhin. Their 2nd and 3rd Ukrainian Fronts were to drive Romania out of the war and seize the Ploesti oilfields. Romanian formations began to disintegrate and desert from the first day. The German Sixth Army, Hitler's attempt to resurrect the one lost at Stalingrad, was also surrounded and destroyed. Army Group South Ukraine lost more than 350,000 men killed or captured. Romania abandoned Germany to make terms with the Soviet Union, and Bulgaria followed suit two weeks later. The collapse came far more rapidly than either the Germans or the Soviets had expected.

For Germany, the most damaging blow was the loss of the Ploesti oilfields. In addition all their occupation forces in the Balkans, especially those in Yugoslavia and Greece, were at risk of being cut off. And with Soviet armies spilling across the Carpathian Mountains and Slovakia, Hitler's last oil supplies near Lake Balaton in Hungary lay open to the Red Army.

On 2 September, the same day as Soviet forces secured both Bucharest and the Ploesti oilfields, Finland also agreed terms with the Soviet Union as Stalin had expected. The Soviet leader was still trying to cut off Army Group North on the Baltic coast, now commanded by the conspicuously brutal Schörner, a devoted Nazi who exulted in hanging deserters and defeatists. A German counter-attack ordered by Guderian had broken the Soviet corridor to the Gulf of Riga at tremendous cost. Schörner conducted a fighting retreat through Riga with the Sixteenth and Eighteenth Armies. But a Soviet strike due west towards Memel left Army Group North completely isolated on the Kurland Peninsula.

'We are mentally and morally at the end of our strength,' wrote a soldier with a flak battery guarding the headquarters of the Sixteenth Army. 'I can only mourn the many, many comrades who have fallen without knowing what they were fighting for.' Some of Army Group North's troops were evacuated by sea, but a quarter of a million men would remain besieged there, unable to defend the Reich because Hitler refused to give up what was by now useless territory.

At this time of momentous events, Churchill, accompanied by Field Marshal Brooke, Admiral Cunningham, now chief of the naval staff, and Air Chief Marshal Portal, crossed the Atlantic in the *Queen Mary*. Another Allied conference in Quebec began on 13 September. Brooke despaired of Churchill. He considered him a sick man, since he had still not fully recovered from his pneumonia. The prime minister could not let go of distracting ideas which would only irritate the Americans. He still wanted landings in Sumatra to seize back the oilfields from the Japanese, and to capture Singapore. He had lost all interest in the Burma campaign.

Churchill also wanted landings at the head of the Adriatic on the Istrian coast to seize Trieste, and to further his pet project of getting to Vienna before the Red Army. In accordance with this dream, Churchill, like Alexander and General Mark Clark, advocated that the Italian campaign should continue way beyond the Gothic Line between Pisa and Rimini. When his chiefs of staff argued that the Italian theatre was now of secondary importance, the prime minister believed that they were secretly ganging up against him. He could not accept the idea that, even if Alexander's forces broke into the Po Valley, an advance north-east through the Ljubljana Gap in the Alps towards Vienna would be virtually impossible against a determined German defence in the mountains.

In the end, the Octagon conference in Quebec did not go nearly as badly as Brooke had feared. Surprisingly, Brooke himself swung round to support Churchill's Vienna strategy, although he was later embarrassed by this lapse of judgement. Perhaps even more surprisingly, General Marshall offered landing craft for the Istrian plan, although the Americans refused to have anything to do with a campaign in south central Europe.

Tensions arose, however, when Admiral King revealed that he did not want the Royal Navy, now under-employed in western waters, to take on a major role in the Pacific. He suspected, with justification, that Churchill was keen for it to play a conspicuous part in the Far East so that Britain could re-establish its colonial possessions. Yet King behaved so aggressively in a meeting of the combined chiefs of staff – he even called the Royal Navy a 'liability' – that he forfeited the support of General Marshall and Admiral Leahy.

On 15 September, Roosevelt and Churchill, in one of the most ill-considered decisions of the war, agreed the plan of Henry Morgenthau, the secretary of the Treasury, to split Germany up and turn it 'into a country primarily agricultural and pastoral in character'. Churchill had in fact expressed his revulsion at the plan when he first heard of it, but when the question of a $6.5 billion Lend–Lease agreement came up, he pledged his support.

Anthony Eden was firmly opposed to the Morgenthau Plan. Brooke also was horrified. He foresaw that a democratic west would need Germany as a rampart against a Soviet threat in the future. Fortunately, Roosevelt came to his senses later, although only after a savaging from the American press. But the damage was done. Goebbels had been presented with a propaganda gift to help him persuade the German people that they could expect no mercy from the western Allies, any more than from the Soviet Union. When the Allied occupation authorities later pasted up proclamations from General Eisenhower declaring, 'We come as conquerors, but not oppressors,' German civilians read them 'open-mouthed' in astonishment.

Very little was said in Quebec about relations with the Soviet Union, where Churchill was soon bound for the second Moscow conference, and astonishingly little about Poland and the Warsaw uprising, which still continued. Roosevelt and Churchill were far apart in their views on Stalin and his regime. Roosevelt was unconcerned about any post-war threat. He was sure that he could charm Stalin, and he said that in any case the Soviet Union was made up of so many different nationalities that it would fall apart once the common enemy of Germany had been defeated. Churchill, on the other hand, although wildly inconsistent in many ways, still saw the Red Army's occupation of central and southern Europe as the major threat to peace in the post-war era. Now that he realised that there was little chance of pre-empting it through an advance north-eastwards out of Italy, he attempted one of the most scandalous and inept moves in the history of realpolitik diplomacy.

On the evening of 9 October in Stalin's office in the Kremlin, the prime minister and the Soviet leader met with only interpreters present. Churchill opened the discussion by suggesting that they begin with 'the most tiresome question – Poland'. The prime minister's attempt to cosy up to the tyrant was neither subtle nor attractive. It seems that Stalin began to enjoy himself immediately, sensing what was to come. Churchill then said that the post-war eastern frontier of Poland was 'settled', even though the Polish government-in-exile had still not been consulted over the decision made behind its back at Teheran. This was because Roosevelt had not wanted his Polish voters to be upset before the presidential elections. When Prime Minister Mikołajczyk discovered this during another meeting insisted on by Churchill, he was shaken to the core by the deception. He rejected all Churchill's arguments and even threats to force him to accept the Curzon Line border in the east. He resigned not long afterwards. Stalin ignored the protests of the government-in-exile. As far as he was concerned, his puppet government of 'Lublin Poles' was now the true government. It was backed by General Zygmunt Berling's 1st Polish Army, although many of its Red Army officers felt it a farce to pretend that they were Polish. The point was that, unlike the army corps of General Anders, they were on Polish territory. Possession was nine-tenths of the law, as Stalin knew only too well. So did Churchill, but he proceeded to play a weak hand very badly indeed.

As the discussion moved on to the Balkans, Churchill produced what he called his 'naughty' document which later became known as the 'percentage agreement'. It was a list of countries with a suggested division between Soviet and western Allied influence.

Romania: Russia 90%; the others 10%.
Greece: Britain (in accord with USA) 90%; Russia 10%.
Yugoslavia: 50% 50%
Hungary: 50% 50%
Bulgaria: Russia 75%; the others 25%.

Stalin gazed at the paper for some time, then increased the Soviet proportion for Bulgaria to '90%', and with his famous blue pencil put a tick in the top left corner. He pushed it back across the table to Churchill. Churchill rather coyly suggested that it might be 'thought rather cynical if it seemed that we had disposed of these issues, so fateful to millions of people, in such an offhand manner?' Should they not burn the paper?

'No, you keep it,' Stalin replied casually. Churchill folded it and put it in his pocket.

The prime minister invited Stalin to dinner at the British

embassy, and, to the genuine surprise of Kremlin officials, he accepted. It was the first time that the Vozhd had ever visited a foreign embassy. Central Europe and the Balkans were not far from anybody's thoughts at the dinner. During one of the courses, the guests could hear the thundering artillery salute to celebrate the capture of Szeged in Hungary. In his speech after dinner, Churchill returned to the subject of Poland: 'Britain went to war to preserve Poland's freedom and independence,' he said. 'The British people have a sense of moral responsibility with regard to the Polish people and their spiritual values. It is also important that Poland is a Catholic country. We cannot allow internal developments there to complicate our relations with the Vatican.'

'And how many divisions does the Pope have?' Stalin broke in. This single, now famous, interjection demonstrated that what Stalin had, he held. The Red Army's occupation would lead automatically to the imposition of a government 'friendly to the Soviet Union'. Astonishingly Churchill, in spite of all his visceral anti-Bolshevism, still thought that the trip had been a great success and that Stalin respected and perhaps even liked him. His self-delusion could at times match that of Roosevelt.

Churchill, however, at least had obtained Stalin's agreement to intervene in Greece to save it from 'the flood of Bolshevism', as he later claimed. Lieutenant General Ronald Scobie's III Corps was put on standby to forestall any attempt by the Communist-dominated EAM-ELAS to seize power as soon as the Germans withdrew. Churchill, who was excessively well disposed towards the Greek royal family, intended to have a government in Athens which was friendly to Great Britain.

Although Field Marshal Brooke had discussed the military situation with General Aleksei Antonov of the Stavka and others, the subject of defeating the Wehrmacht had hardly come up between leaders either in Quebec or in Moscow. The Reich was under attack from both sides. To complement the Westwall, an Ostwall was ordered. In East Prussia most of the adult population, male and female, were dragooned by the Gauleiter Erich Koch and his Nazi Party officials into digging defences. The army was not consulted, and most of these earthworks were entirely useless.

On 5 October, the Red Army attacked towards Memel. It took

two days before evacuation orders were issued to the civilian population, but then they were countermanded. Koch did not like the idea of evacuating civilians and Hitler supported him, because it conveyed a defeatist message to the rest of the Reich. Panic ensued and many women and children were cut off in Memel as a result. A number drowned in the River Niemen, trying to escape the burning and looted town.

On 16 October the Stavka sent General Chernyakhovsky's 3rd Belorussian Front on an attack into East Prussia, between Ebenrode and Goldap. Guderian sent panzer reinforcements to the threatened front to push the Red Army back. In the wake of the Soviet retreat, an atrocity was discovered. A number of the women and girls in the village of Nemmersdorf had been raped and murdered and the bodies of some victims were supposedly found crucified on barn doors. Goebbels rushed in photographers. Brimming with righteous indignation, he was not going to miss the opportunity of showing the German people why they had to fight to the end. In the short term, it appears that his efforts were counter-productive. But when the real invasion of East Prussia began three months later, the terrible images published in the Nazi press resurfaced in people's minds.

Even before the events at Nemmersdorf, many women were afraid of what was to come. Despite the ignorance professed in post-war years, a large part of the civilian population had a good idea of the horrors committed on the eastern front by their own side. And as the Red Army advanced on the Reich, they imagined that its revenge would be terrible. 'You know the Russians really are coming in our direction,' wrote a young mother in September, 'so I am not going to wait, instead I will choose to kill myself and the children.'

The announcement by Himmler on 18 October of a mass militia levy to be called the Volkssturm inspired some with a determination to resist, but it was a depressing idea for most. Their armament would be pathetic – a variety of old rifles captured from different armies early in the war, and the Panzerfaust shoulder-launched anti-tank grenades. And since all available men of military age had already been called up, the Volkssturm's ranks would be filled with old men and young boys. It was soon known as the 'Eintopf' or casserole, because it consisted of 'old meat and green vegetables'. Since the government offered no uniform apart from an armband, many doubted that they would be treated as lawful combatants, especially after the Wehrmacht's attitude to partisans on the eastern front. Goebbels later organized a huge parade for the newsreel cameras in Berlin at which those called up had to make their oath of allegiance to Adolf Hitler. Veterans of the eastern front did not know whether to laugh or to cry at the spectacle.

Hitler, convinced that Patton's Third Army posed the greatest threat, ordered that the bulk of his panzer divisions should be deployed in the Saar. Commanded by Generaloberst Hasso von Manteuffel, they made up a new Fifth Panzer Army, which cannot have been an encouraging title since the two previous ones had been destroyed. Rundstedt, guessing that the Americans would concentrate first on Aachen, sent as many infantry divisions there as he could muster.

The US First Army commanded by Lieutenant General Courtney Hodges had advanced on Aachen, with a strong sense of the fact that it was at last on German territory. Just a few hundred metres across the border it seized a nineteenth-century Neo-Gothic castle in the 'Bismarckian style', with heavy iron accoutrements and massive furniture. This belonged to the nephew of Hitler's former commander-in-chief, Generalfeldmarschall von Brauchitsch. The Australian correspondent Godfrey Blunden described this first battle on German soil in the west. 'It was fought in brilliant sunshine beneath a cloudless blue sky where the Piper Cub spotting planes hovered like kites. It was fought over very beautiful landscape, across green fields with neat hedgerows, gently wooded hills and small villages with needle-spired churches.'

But now that Model had manned the Westwall, German resistance was fierce. The Allies regretted that the supply crisis of early September had halted them just short of it. A staff officer at First Army headquarters remarked: 'At that time I could have walked through it with my dog and my daughter.' Now they found field defences dug by civilian forced labour, cottages turned into pillboxes and concrete bunkers with iron doors. Sherman tanks were called up to deal with them, using armour-piercing ammunition. As soon as American infantry platoons had cleared a bunker with grenades and sometimes flamethrowers, they called in engineers who welded the doors shut with oxy-acetylene torches to prevent other German soldiers slipping back to reoccupy them.

On 12 October Hodges issued an ultimatum demanding unconditional surrender, otherwise the city of Aachen would be flattened by bombing and shelling. Refugees had told officers that between five and ten thousand civilians had refused to leave, despite Nazi Party orders. Hitler had decreed that the capital of Charlemagne and the German emperors should be defended to the last. Hodges's First Army surrounded Aachen, and now the encircling troops faced fierce German counter-attacks, a situation which produced some misleading and rather confused comparisons to Stalingrad. The German counter-attacks were smashed with relative ease by American artillery concentrations. Many of their guns were firing German shells which they had captured in France.

German defenders included a mixture of infantry, panzer-grenadiers, Luftwaffe, SS, marine infantry and Hitler Jugend volunteers. The damage to buildings was considerable, and the Rathaus or town hall was totally destroyed. With rubble and smashed glass in the streets, empty windows and trailing telephone wires, Aachen took on the 'malevolent appearance of a defeated city'. Fortunately, the American artillery and P-47 Thunderbolt fighter-bomber pilots managed to avoid the great cathedral, as they had been ordered to.

House-to-house fighting continued pitilessly during October. Starting at the top of a house, the Americans blasted their way through to the next building using a bazooka. It was too dangerous to try the street. The 30th Division suffered such a high rate of casualties that a replacement private who arrived at the start of the battle found himself a sergeant in charge of a platoon three weeks later.

Aachen was a prosperous, largely middle-class city. American soldiers began to search apartments with hefty furniture, portraits of Hindenburg and the Kaiser, Meerschaum pipes, ornamental beer steins and posed photographs of university duelling fraternities. But German soldiers booby-trapped buildings with trip wires and charges, which the Americans called 'bundling babies'. 'I don't get it,' said a GI angrily. 'They know they most likely will get killed. How come they don't give up?' GIs threw a grenade into practically every room before they entered, because German defenders concealed themselves ready to shoot back. Several of them, having just shot an American in the back, jumped up with their arms raised to surrender, as if they were playing a child's game. Not surprisingly, a number of prisoners were roughly handled.

On one occasion four German boys, the youngest of whom was eight, began firing with abandoned rifles at an American field-gun crew. A patrol went out to investigate the source of the shots. 'The American patrol leader was so incensed with the children's action that he slapped the eldest with his hand and afterward reported back that the boy stood at attention and took the slap as though he had been a soldier.'

The American military authorities managed to evacuate the German civilians from cellars and air-raid shelters as the fighting continued. They noticed that, after all the Nazi propaganda, they nervously eyed the black American truck drivers who took them off to a holding camp. Civilians were screened for Nazi Party members, but it was an almost impossible task. Most of them complained of the way they had been treated by the German troops defending the city, because they had refused to leave when told. Some were deserters who had managed to obtain civilian clothes. A Jeep outside Aachen was ambushed, and this raised fears following rumours of a Nazi guerrilla resistance codenamed Werwolf.

The US military authorities also found themselves struggling to cope with around 3,000 Polish and Russian forced labourers, including 'large blank-faced women in old ragged skirts with kerchiefs wrapped around their heads and carrying cloth bundles'. Some of the men had already started to attack and threaten German householders with knives to obtain food and sometimes loot. They had much to avenge, but MPs rounded up between seven and eight hundred offenders and kept them in a stockade. It was a small foretaste of the complications to come with an estimated eight million displaced persons in Germany.

The Nazi regime had no intention of allowing indiscipline to reign in any form. Ever since the failed July plot, which greatly increased the power of Martin Bormann, the Nazi Party secretary,

Goebbels and Himmler, Nazi ideology was increasingly imposed on the Wehrmacht. This made any subsequent attempt to remove Hitler impossible. Beyond symbols, such as replacing the military salute with the 'German greeting', the number of NSFOs or National Socialist leadership officers was increased. Soldiers and officers found behind the front without authorization to retreat were far more likely to be shot, and staff officers were searched by SS guards when entering Führer headquarters.

Increased repression also began in Soviet ranks. To make up for its huge losses, the Red Army was forcibly recruiting Ukrainians, Belorussians, Poles and men from the three Baltic states, which were once again under Soviet control. 'Lithuanians hate us even more than Poles do,' a Red Army soldier wrote home on 11 October, 'and we pay them back in the same manner.' These recently inducted soldiers were inevitably the most likely to desert. 'The Special Detachment [SMERSh] was keeping an eye on me as I was the son of a purged man,' a sergeant explained later. 'We had a lot of Asians in my unit, who often ran away, either to the rear or to the Germans. Once an entire group defected. After that we, the Russians, were told to keep an eye on the Uzbeks. I was a sergeant then, and the political officer told me: you will pay with your life if anyone in your section defects. They could easily have shot me. Once a Belorussian escaped. They caught him and returned him to the unit. The man from the Special Detachment said to him: if you are going to fight properly we will hush this affair up. But he escaped again and again was caught. He was hanged. Not shot, but hanged as a deserter. We were lined up in a forest ride. A truck appeared with a gallows mounted on it. The CheKa [NKVD] man read out the order: "To be executed for treason to the Motherland". The man was hanged, and then the CheKa man also shot him.'

Germans retreating from Belorussia after the collapse of Army Group Centre had few illusions about the fate of civilians who had been friendly to them. A medical Obergefreiter who had escaped just in time to avoid encirclement wondered: 'What will have happened to the poor people who had to stay behind, by that I mean the locals?' German soldiers knew well that the NKVD and SMERSh would arrive just behind the fighting troops to interrogate civilians to see who had collaborated.

During the Soviet advance into Romania, an officer recorded that the company had consisted almost entirely of Ukrainian peasants from the regions that had been under the 'temporary occupation' of the enemy. 'Most of them had no desire to fight and had to be forced to do this. I remember walking through the trench. Everybody was digging except for one soldier who was supposed to be digging the fire position for the Maxim. He was standing there doing nothing. I asked him what the matter was. He fell on his knees in front of me and began to whine: "Have mercy on me! I've got three kids. I want to live!" What could I say? All of us understood that an infantry soldier at the front had only two possible fates: to the hospital, or to the grave.' This officer, like most in the Red Army, was convinced that successful companies depended entirely on a core of Russian or Siberian soldiers. 'I would always select a couple of men from among the reliable Russian soldiers before an attack, and when the company got up to attack these soldiers would stay in the trench and kick out all those who were trying to hide and avoid going forward.'

Well to the rear, vengeance on a mass scale was being carried out against ethnic minorities who had welcomed the Germans in 1941 and 1942. In December 1943, Beria had deported 200,000 Crimean Tatars to Uzbekistan. Some 20,000 of these Muslims had served in German uniform so the remaining 90 per cent had to suffer, although many others had fought well in the Red Army. They had been rounded up on 18 May and given no time to prepare. Some 7,000 died on the journey and many times that number died in exile through starvation. Some 390,000 Chechens were also rounded up, and delivered to railheads in Lend–Lease Studebaker trucks intended for the Red Army. Some 78,000 of them are said to have died on the journey. Stalin had started with his own peoples before he began on his enemies and the Poles, who were allies, at least in theory.

Stalin and his generals were uneasy about the fighting qualities of the new intakes because German resistance was stiffening. In the battles for the Carpathian mountain range to defend eastern Hungary and Slovakia, the troops of Hitler's last ally surprised Soviet veterans, especially after the sudden collapse of the Romanian army. 'The Hungarians were actually a big problem for us in Transylvania,' a Red Army officer recorded. 'They fought with great courage to the last bullet and the last man. They would never surrender.'

Malinovsky, with his reinforced 2nd Ukrainian Front, tried to conduct a large encirclement in eastern Hungary. In what was called the Debrecen Operation, a bold strike which began on 6 October was thwarted by a counter-attack two weeks later with III Panzer Corps and XVII Corps. Malinovsky, on Stavka urging, launched another attack to the south near Szeged and towards Budapest, breaking through the Hungarian Third Army. But Malinovsky's considerable forces were halted short of the capital by another counter-attack with three panzer divisions and the Panzergrenadier Division *Feldherrnhalle*. It became increasingly clear that the battle for Budapest would become one of the most violent of the war.

Following the defections of Romania and Bulgaria, Admiral Horthy, the Regent of Hungary, made secret contacts with the Soviet Union. Molotov demanded that Hungary should immediately declare war on Germany. On 11 October, Horthy's representatives signed the agreement in Moscow. Four days later, Horthy informed the German envoy in Budapest and made an announcement of the armistice in a broadcast. The Germans, already informed of Horthy's moves, reacted quickly. On Hitler's orders, Otto Skorzeny, the SS commando leader who had rescued Mussolini, had already prepared to seize Horthy in his residence, the Citadel, which overlooked the Danube. The Germans would replace him with Ferenc Szálasi, the ferociously anti-semitic leader of the Nazi-inspired Arrow Cross movement.

Operation Panzerfaust, as it was called, would be overseen by Obergruppenführer von dem Bach, who had just finished his murderous task in Warsaw. Skorzeny persuaded Bach not to repeat the same heavy-handed tactics, and avoid smashing the Citadel into submission. Instead, on the morning of 15 October, just before Horthy's announcement of the armistice, Skorzeny's SS commandos managed to kidnap Horthy's son in a street ambush after a shoot-out with his bodyguards. Miklós Horthy was trussed up, flown to Vienna and transferred to Mauthausen concentration camp, which already contained such *Prominenten* as Francisco Largo Caballero, the former prime minister of the Spanish Republic.

Horthy was told bluntly that, if he persisted with his 'treason', his son would be executed. The admiral, although in a state of nervous collapse at the threat, went ahead with his broadcast. Arrow Cross stormtroopers seized the building immediately afterwards and put out a denial, insisting on Hungary's determination to fight on. Ferenc Szálasi took power later that afternoon. Horthy was given little option. He was brought back to Germany in protective custody.

Horthy had put a stop to Eichmann's deportation of Jews in the summer, by which time 437,402 had been killed, mostly at Auschwitz. But even though Himmler was halting the mass extermination programme with the approach of the Red Army, the remaining Jews were rounded up for slave labour and forced to march to Germany because of a lack of rolling stock. Tormented, beaten and clubbed to death by SS and Arrow Cross guards, many thousands died on the way. Although Szálasi stopped these death marches in November, more than 60,000 Jews remained prisoners in a tiny ghetto in Budapest. Most of his followers were now determined to embark on their own 'Final Solution to the Jewish question'. The notorious Arrow Cross activist Father Alfréd Kun, who later admitted to 500 murders, used to give the command: 'In the name of Christ – Fire!'

Arrow Cross militia, some of them aged from fourteen to sixteen years old, would seize groups of Jews from the ghetto, force them to strip to their underclothes and march them barefoot through the freezing streets to the Danube embankments of the city for execution. In many cases, their firing was so inaccurate that a number of victims managed to jump into the icy river and swim away. On one occasion a German officer halted a mass killing and sent the Jews home, but this was probably no more than a temporary reprieve.

Although some NCOs of the Hungarian Gendarmerie joined the 4,000 Arrow Cross militiamen in torturing and murdering Jews, others helped them. There were even a few members of the Arrow Cross itself who helped Jews escape, proving that one can never make sweeping generalizations. The efforts of one of them, Dr Ara Jerezian, later received full acknowledgement from Yad Vashem, the Holocaust memorial in Israel.

The greatest operation to save Jews was mounted by the Swede

Raoul Wallenberg who, despite having no more than semi-official status in Hungary, issued tens of thousands of documents stating that the bearer was under the protection of the Swedish government. Later, during the siege, the Arrow Cross invaded the Swedish embassy and murdered several of its staff in revenge for their activities. Along with the Swedes, the Swiss diplomat Carl Lutz, the Portuguese diplomat Carlos Branquinho, the International Red Cross and the papal nuncio issued their own protection papers to help other Hungarian Jews escape.

The embassies of El Salvador and Nicaragua provided several hundred certificates of citizenship, but the most extraordinary bluff emerged from the Spanish embassy. The Spanish chargé d'affaires, Angel Sanz-Briz, knew that the Szálasi regime was desperate to be recognized by his government. He encouraged its members in this illusion, while taking on the Arrow Cross even more robustly than the Swedish embassy. Sanz-Briz was forced to leave, but he handed over to a new 'chargé d'affaires', Giorgio Perlasca, who was in fact an Italian anti-Fascist. Perlasca assembled 5,000 Jews in safe houses under Spanish protection, while Franco's government in Madrid had no idea of what was being done in its name. An even braver confidence trick was carried out by Miksa Domonkos, a member of the Jewish Council, who forged safe conducts in the name of a superintendent of Gendarmerie. All these attempts to save lives took on a greater urgency as the Red Army advanced on Budapest, and the Arrow Cross became more deadly.

On 18 October, just as the First Army was securing Aachen, Eisenhower presided over a conference to discuss strategic options in Brussels at 21st Army Group headquarters. This was rather a pointed choice of location, since Montgomery had angered his American colleagues by failing to attend the previous one on 22 September at SHAEF headquarters in Versailles. He had sent in his place Lieutenant General Freddy de Guingand, his much liked chief of staff and 'genial peacemaker' as Bradley put it. This time Monty could not avoid attending.

One option was to sit out the winter, waiting until more divisions arrived from the United States and a good reserve of supplies built up, having arrived through Antwerp once it was open.

The other was to launch a major offensive in November using the resources available. Inaction in the west was unthinkable simply because of what Stalin would say about the Allies' reluctance to fight. Montgomery's renewed argument for a major push north of the Ruhr was again overruled. Eisenhower, strongly backed by Bradley, wanted a double thrust, with First and Ninth Armies on the northern side, and Patton's Third Army attacking in the Saar. Montgomery was told to swing south from Nijmegen between the Rhine and the Maas. This concentration of forces north and south of the Ardennes would leave a very weakly held sector in the middle. To cover this part of the front, Bradley brought in Major General Troy Middleton's VIII Corps, which had been finishing off in Brittany.

Aachen itself was not cleared until the end of the third week in October. On 30 October, Cologne received a virtual coup de grâce from Harris's bombers in another heavy raid. The destruction of the Reichsbahn meant that there were insufficient trains to evacuate those left in the ruins. The city then saw the only example of civilian armed resistance against the Nazis, when Communists and foreign workers seized weapons from isolated policemen. Fighting an urban guerrilla war, they attacked the police and even managed to kill the local head of the Gestapo, until a vicious retaliation wiped them out.

Allied bombing intensified. The RAF and USAAF no longer had a great deal to fear from the Luftwaffe, although Spaatz was worried that the new Me 262 jet fighters would suddenly appear and blast his bombers from the sky. Approximately 60 per cent of all the bombs dropped on Germany fell in the last nine months of the war. Hitler's armaments minister Albert Speer acknowledged that the damage to Germany's economic infrastructure 'only became insurmountable during the autumn of 1944, largely as a consequence of the systematic destruction of the transport and communications network through a relentless Allied bombing campaign that had begun in October'. And despite Harris's scepticism, Spaatz's oil plan against refineries and benzol plants was also having a marked effect on Wehrmacht operations, especially the Luftwaffe's. Only arms production held up, largely thanks to Speer's energy and talents.

In fact Harris's determination to keep bombing the Ruhr, an

area target, also succeeded in knocking out so many benzol plants there that there were none left in operation by November. The difference between the strategy of the RAF and the American Eighth Air Force was more one of presentation than effect. While the USAAF always defined its operations as precision bombing, the reality was very different. 'Marshalling yards' given as a target was really a euphemism for hitting the whole of the adjacent city. Largely because of the bad visibility during winter months, more than 70 per cent of Eighth Air Force bombs were delivered 'blind', almost exactly the same as Bomber Command. Harris simply made no bones about bombing cities, and despised anybody who was squeamish on the subject. Where he was proved totally wrong was in his repeated claims that bombing alone could end the war.

Since the dark days of 1942, Britain had invested so much in Bomber Command, financially, industrially and in sacrificed lives, to create this bludgeon that an almost unstoppable momentum had developed. It continued even though many of its attacks towards the end of the war bore little military logic, let alone moral justification. The obsessive Harris had made it a point of honour that no German city or town of any size should be left standing by the time the war ended. On 27 November, Freiburg on the edge of the Black Forest was bombed, leaving 3,000 dead and the medieval city centre destroyed. It was a communications centre behind the front and thus a legitimate target under the original Pointblank directive, but whether it shortened the war by a day, by an hour or a single minute is far from certain.

Like the concentrated use of artillery, bombing revealed a disconcerting paradox about democracies. Because of intense pressure at home, in the press and from public opinion, commanders were compelled to minimize their own losses. And so they resorted to the maximum application of high explosive, which inevitably killed more civilians. Many Germans cried to the heavens for vengeance. The V-1 had not brought Britain to its knees, the V-2 did not appear to be changing the course of the war either, so rumours were spread of a V-3. 'The prayer for our Führer and the people is also a weapon,' wrote a woman. 'The Lord God cannot abandon our Führer.'

On 8 November General Patton, refusing to wait any longer

for the weather to improve, began the Third Army's offensive in the Saar without air support. 'At 05.15, the artillery preparation woke me,' he wrote in his diary that day. 'The discharge of over 400 guns sounded like the slamming of doors in an empty house.' His XX Corps began a major assault on the fortress city of Metz. The sky cleared and the fighter-bombers went in, but torrential rain had swollen the River Moselle to unprecedented levels. Patton told Bradley how one of his engineer companies had taken two days of frustration and hard work to connect a pontoon bridge across the fast-flowing river. One of the first vehicles across, a tank destroyer, snagged on a cable which then snapped. The bridge broke loose and swung downstream. 'The whole damn company sat down in the mud', Patton related, 'and bawled like babies.'

The weather was equally bad further north for the First and Ninth Armies. The IX Tactical Air Command of Major General Elwood 'Pete' Quesada had been attacking bridges over the Rhine to prevent reinforcements getting through. On 5 November, one fighter pilot had been astonished when a whole bridge blew up and collapsed into the Rhine, after he had inadvertently hit the demolition charges laid by German pioneers in case of a breakthrough.

The terrible weather continued, with rain thirteen days in a row. On 14 November Bradley drove up through the Ardennes, which had just had its first light covering of snow. He headed for First Army headquarters in the Belgian resort of Spa, which had been the Germans' GHQ in the First World War. Now Hodges's staff sat at field desks in the casino under immense chandeliers, as V-1 flying bombs and V-2 rockets streaked across the sky overhead bound for London and for Antwerp.

In the early hours of 16 November, the meteorological report promised good weather just after Hodges had decided to attack come what may. Not long after dawn, the sun appeared for the first time in weeks. Everyone stared at it almost in disbelief. Shortly after midday, Eighth Air Force Fortresses and Liberators and Bomber Command Lancasters appeared overhead to smash a way through the Westwall. Bradley, nervous after the disaster at the start of Operation Cobra, had made sure that every precaution had been taken to prevent the bombers from hitting his troops waiting to attack. But, although there were no American casualties this time, the advancing infantry and armour soon discovered that the Germans had laid their 'devil's gardens' in breadth and in depth.

First Army was to advance from Aachen through the Hürtgen Forest to the River Roer. It needed to seize the dams south of Düren, which the Germans could use to destroy any attempt at a subsequent crossing of the Roer. Putting their faith in air and artillery bombardments to blast a way through, both Bradley and Hodges underestimated the horrors ahead. They were to be far more terrible than in the Norman *bocage*.

The Hürtgen Forest, south-east of Aachen, was a dark, sinister concentration of pine trees up to thirty metres tall on steep hillsides. Soldiers constantly lost their bearings in its frightening depths. They saw the area as an 'eerie haunting region fit for a witch's lair'. This was to be an infantry battle, yet the battalions, regiments and divisions thrown into it were not trained or prepared for what lay ahead. With ravines as well as the density of trees, it was no terrain for the tanks or tank destroyers whose support they were used to, nor did it make things easy for their artillery or fighter-bombers. For the German 275th Infantry Division, on the other hand, adept at camouflage, earth bunkers, mines and booby-traps, it was ideal ground to defend.

The heavy level of infantry losses since D-Day meant that an increasing proportion of front-line platoons consisted largely of barely trained new arrivals. Bradley was angry not just about their quality, but about how few of them the European theatre received. He discovered that General MacArthur was securing the lion's share for his Philippines campaign. It seemed that in Washington not even lip-service was paid any more to 'Germany first'. The War Department had cut back Eisenhower's allotment of 80,000 replacements a month to 67,000.

The US Army's replacement system had been brutally unimaginative – and the British army's was little better. After heavy losses, any spare rear-area personnel could suddenly find themselves in a replacement depot – known as a 'repple depple' – along with green teenagers just shipped out from the States. Great efforts had been made to improve the organization so that new arrivals were not thrown into a battle at nightfall without knowing where they were or who they were fighting with. Yet they were still woefully unprepared for what lay ahead. Only if 'repples' survived their first battle, and began to create some scar tissue around their fear, would they stand a chance of living through to the next.

German tactics were cruelly simple. They intended to exact maximum casualties. German soldiers seemed to have a diabolic genius with booby-traps of all sorts, such as Teller mines linked to tripwires, and the notorious anti-personnel Schu-mine which would blow off a foot as soon as the pressure pad was released. Every firebreak or ride had been mined, and blocked by felled trees. These barricades were booby-trapped and pre-registered by mortar and artillery batteries.

Attack after attack failed. 'Squads and platoons got lost,' went one account of the hapless 28th Division, 'mortar shells landing among assault teams carrying explosive charges set off the explosives and blew up the men; an unfailing chatter of machine guns ripped through the trees when anyone moved. One man, a replacement, sobbing hysterically, tried to dig himself a hole in the ground with his fingers. In late afternoon this battalion staggered back to the line of departure.'

To make things worse, the rain seldom stopped. Trees dripped constantly, the ground was saturated and trenches filled with water. Since no foul-weather clothing had arrived, and few remembered the lessons of trench warfare from a quarter of a century before, American soldiers suffered crippling trench-foot, or 'immersion', casualties. Large numbers were infected with dysentery. More alarmingly, and perhaps accentuated by the malevolent atmosphere of the forest, there was a dramatic rise in panic-stricken retreats, self-inflicted wounds, nervous collapse, suicides and desertion. Private Eddie Slovik from the 28th Division in the Hürtgen became the only American soldier during the war to be executed by firing squad. The Wehrmacht could not believe how soft the Allies were. In German ranks it was not just the deserter who would automatically be shot, but now, under a decree of Himmler, his family could be too.

One officer after another was relieved when he could not get his men to attack. In the 8th Division almost all the officers in one battalion were sacked, and their replacements suffered the same fate. In this terrible, bloody, muddy battle, one division after another had to be pulled out of the line. Men, suffering from physical and psychological exhaustion, emerged with unblinking dead eyes, known as the 'two-thousand-yard stare'. Altogether in the Hürtgen Forest, the Americans suffered 33,000 casualties, more than one in four of the troops involved.

Hodges has been severely criticized for his lack of imagination in attempting to fight such a disadvantageous battle in the first place, which was bound to accentuate American weaknesses and German strengths. Yet the forest was the only route to the village of Schmidt and the Roer dams, which had to be secured before the river could be crossed. Even in the more open country north of Aachen, German units defended each fortified village until it was destroyed around their heads. When an American intelligence officer asked a captured young Leutnant if he did not regret such destruction to his own country, the German simply shrugged. 'It probably won't be ours after the war,' he replied. 'Why not destroy it?' And further north still, the British Second Army swinging south from Nijmegen faced conditions in the thick woods of the Reichswald similar to those of Hodges's men in the Hürtgen. The 53rd (Welsh) Division suffered 5,000 casualties in nine days.

Allied forces well to the south were enjoying much greater success. On 19 November, General de Lattre de Tassigny's First French Army broke through the Belfort Gap and reached the upper Rhine. Three days later, on the northern sector of General Jacob L. Devers's 6th Army Group, General Wade H. Haislip's XV Corps penetrated the Saverne Gap and on 23 November General Leclerc's 2ème Division Blindée entered Strasbourg, thus fulfilling a promise he had sworn in the North African desert.

A very satisfied General de Gaulle left the next day on a long, circuitous journey to meet Stalin in Moscow. He was accompanied by his chef de cabinet Gaston Palewski, the foreign minister Georges Bidault and General Juin.

The journey took embarrassingly long because the head of government's obsolete two-engined aircraft broke down with depressing frequency. They finally arrived in Baku, where they left the aircraft and boarded a train provided by the Soviet government. They found themselves installed in the old-fashioned carriages of the Grand Duke Nicholas, the Tsarist commander-in-chief in the First World War. The journey across the snowbound steppe was so slow that de Gaulle observed drily that he hoped there would not be a revolution in their absence.

De Gaulle was keen to establish good relations with Stalin, partly in the hope that he would keep the French Communist Party under control. He would not be disappointed. Stalin did not want any sort of revolutionary adventures in France for the time being. A Communist uprising might lead Roosevelt to cut off Lend–Lease material to the Soviet Union, or, in his worst nightmare, to use it as an excuse to come to some deal with Germany. Stalin knew how distrustful Roosevelt was of the French. De Gaulle's other objective was to ensure that, with Stalin's support, France would be represented at the peace conference and not shut out by the Americans.

On arrival in Moscow, the French delegation had to endure one of Stalin's sinister banquets in the Kremlin, where he forced his marshals and ministers to run round the table to clink glasses with him. He then proposed toasts, threatening them with execution in a brutal display of hangman's humour. De Gaulle described him memorably as a 'Communist dressed up as a marshal, a dictator ensconced in his scheming, a conqueror with an air of bonhomie'. Stalin's objective during the talks was to obtain recognition of his puppet government, the Lublin Poles. He was clearly hoping to open a breach in the western alliance. De Gaulle politely and firmly stuck to his refusal. At one point, Stalin turned to Gaston Palewski and said with a malicious smirk: 'One never ceases to be Polish, Monsieur Palewski.'

Stalin was prepared to be generous, in his view, even though he despised France for its collapse in 1940 which had so upset his plans. (As a further dig at de Gaulle, he arranged for Ilya Ehrenburg to present him with a copy of his novel about the Fall of Paris.) Yet Stalin, well aware of de Gaulle's resentment towards Roosevelt, had sensed that France might be a useful wild card to cultivate in the western alliance for the future. Stalin did not trust the British and the Americans. His greatest fear was that they might rearm Germany in the future. Stalin knew that de Gaulle really wanted not just the total defeat of Germany, but its dismemberment. In this they were in agreement, although

Stalin would not support de Gaulle's claim to the Rhineland in the post-war settlement.

The visit went well, despite the fact that Bidault became very drunk at the banquet. A Franco-Soviet agreement was finally signed at four in the morning just before the French delegation's departure. A compromise formula had to be reached over Stalin's puppet government for Poland, but at least de Gaulle knew that he would not have trouble from the French Communists. Their leader, Maurice Thorez, who had reached France during his absence, had not ordered his members to the barricades or to launch more strikes. He had demanded blood, sweat, increased productivity and national unity to defeat Germany. The Communists of the resistance were dumbfounded, but next day the Party press confirmed what he had said. The Kremlin had clearly spoken. De Gaulle and his companions finally got back to France on 17 December only to face a totally unexpected crisis. German armies had broken through in the Ardennes and were thought to be heading for Paris.

43

The Ardennes and Athens

In November 1944, Major General Troy H. Middleton's troops in VIII Corps were suffering from boredom on the Ardennes front. General Bradley heard of complaints from the forest warden that 'GI's in their zest for barbecued pork were hunting wild boar in low-flying Cubs with Thompson sub-machineguns.' Grenades were also used in the trout streams to break the monotony of K-Rations.

Ever since the chaotic retreat to the Westwall in September, Hitler had longed to repeat the great triumph of 1940. Once again he counted on Allied complacency, the shock effect and the speed of exploitation to achieve his goal of retaking Antwerp. This shortened version of Manstein's *Sichelschnitt* plan would also cut off the First Canadian, the Second British Army, Lieutenant General William H. Simpson's Ninth and most of Hodges's First Army. Hitler even dreamed of another Dunkirk. His generals were appalled by such a fantasy. Guderian wanted to reinforce the eastern front before the Soviet winter offensive. But Hitler's strategy, rather like Hirohito's hopes of the Ichi-gō Offensive, was to achieve a sweeping victory to knock at least one country out of the war, and then perhaps negotiate from a position of strength.

On the afternoon of 20 November, Hitler boarded his *Sonderzug* in the siding camouflaged under the forest canopy and left the Wolfsschanze for the very last time. He had not been well and also needed an operation on his throat, which provided an excuse for abandoning the threatened East Prussian front. He had been deeply depressed, apparently aware of the disaster facing Germany. Goebbels had been trying to persuade him to broadcast to the nation because rumours were spreading that he was gravely ill, mad or even dead. Hitler steadfastly refused.

Only the prospect of revenge animated him, and his Ardennes offensive produced a fierce anticipation. Hitler, with the assistance of the OKW staff, had drafted the orders down to the last detail. Originally called Watch on the Rhine as a cover name to imply a defensive operation, its real name was Autumn Mist. The attacking armies had to reach the Meuse in forty-eight hours and take Antwerp within fourteen days. He told his commanders that this would trap the First Canadian Army and knock Canada out of the war, and that in turn would persuade the United States to consider peace.

Generalfeldmarschall von Rundstedt, who was perfectly prepared to launch a limited offensive to smash the Aachen salient, knew that the objective of Antwerp was utterly unrealistic. Even if the weather remained sufficiently bad to ground the Allied air forces, and even if they managed to seize Allied fuel dumps intact, the Germans simply lacked the strength to maintain the corridor. It was just like Hitler's obsession with the Avranches counter-attack in early August, which he had forced on Generalfeldmarschall von Kluge. A dramatic and unexpected strike was no good unless you could sustain it. Rundstedt was later deeply offended when he discovered that the Allies called it 'the Rundstedt offensive', as if it had been his plan.

On 3 November, when Jodl outlined the plan to the commanders involved, they were all dismayed: Rundstedt, the commander-in-chief west; Model, the commander-in-chief of Army Group B; Oberstgruppenführer Sepp Dietrich, the commander of the Sixth SS Panzer Army; and Generaloberst Hasso von Manteuffel, the commander of the Fifth Panzer Army. Yet when it finally came to the briefing on the eve of battle six weeks later, many of their young officers and soldiers were convinced, or managed to convince themselves, that along with the V-2s fired at England, this offensive would be the turning point for which they had waited so long.

On 28 November, while savage fighting in the rain and now sleet continued on the north German border, Eisenhower visited Montgomery at his headquarters in Belgium. Almost before the supreme commander had sat down in his map caravan, Montgomery began to hector him about their lack of success in the present battles. Hoping once again to exploit Eisenhower's apparent inability to say no to him clearly, Montgomery considered that he had obtained agreement that he should command all Allied forces north of the Ardennes. But Bradley, who had no intention of allowing part of his army group to serve under Montgomery, managed to change Eisenhower's mind again soon afterwards. On 7 December, Eisenhower, Bradley and Montgomery met in Maastricht. Montgomery heard that his reinforced northern push was no longer on the cards. Bradley clearly had to work hard to conceal his smile of satisfaction.

While Eisenhower and his army group commanders had been arguing again over whether to concentrate their next attack north or south of the Ardennes, Allied intelligence suddenly noticed that they had lost track of the Sixth SS Panzer Army. It had been located near Cologne, and the assumption was that, along with Manteuffel's Fifth Panzer Army, it was preparing a counter-attack against the US First Army as soon as it crossed the River Roer. At Maastricht, Eisenhower raised with Bradley the question of the Ardennes sector, covered only by Middleton's VIII Corps, but Bradley was unconcerned. He explained that he had left it weak so as to reinforce the offensives to the north and south. None of the generals at the Maastricht conference expected a large-scale counter-offensive. The Germans were desperately short of fuel for their panzers, and even if they did break through, where would they go? There had been intelligence rumours that they had their eye on Antwerp, but no senior officer took that seriously. Montgomery planned to return to England for Christmas.

On 15 December, Hitler and his entourage moved in his personal train to the Adlerhorst (Eagle's Nest) Führer headquarters at Ziegenberg, near Bad Nauheim. Rundstedt's headquarters were already in the adjacent Schloss. To the horror of the generals, Martin Bormann's Nazi Party Chancellery came too, and Bormann complained that the facilities were insufficient for all his typists. Nazi bureaucracy, both in Berlin and at local levels, seemed only to increase as disaster threatened, no doubt to give the impression that the Party was still in control of events. Instructions, directives and regulations cascaded forth on every subject just when the transport and therefore also the postal system were collapsing under the weight of Allied bombing.

The offensive had been delayed for over two weeks because

neither panzer nor infantry formations were ready. Hitler had wanted to assemble thirty divisions for the offensive. In the end there were twenty in the attacking force, and five in reserve. On the northern side of the main thrust Dietrich's 6th SS Panzer Army would head for Antwerp, with the Fifteenth Army protecting his right flank. The Fifth Panzer Army on the southern side would first head for Brussels, with the Seventh Army on its left flank.

The very few American senior officers who voiced their concern about a possible German offensive in the Ardennes were humoured by their colleagues. Increased German activity across the Rhine had been picked up by air reconnaissance, but this was attributed to the counter-attack which they expected once they crossed the Roer to the north. Headquarters of 12th Army Group was convinced that the Germans had been so weakened that there was no threat at all. When Middleton said to Bradley that his VIII Corps was very thin on the ground on the 135-kilometre Ardennes sector, his army group commander replied: 'Don't worry, Troy. They won't come through here.' Middleton had four infantry divisions, the 99th and 106th which were unblooded, and the 28th and 4th which were both shaken and exhausted after fighting in the Hürtgen Forest. He also had the 9th Armored Division in reserve and the 14th Cavalry Group as a reconnaissance outfit.

At 05.30 hours on 16 December, German artillery opened fire. The effect of 1,900 guns along the front firing at the same moment was profoundly disorientating. Shaken GIs struggled out of sleeping bags, grabbed their weapons and crouched at the bottom of their foxholes until the bombardment was over. But once it ended they saw an eerie light. This false dawn was in fact 'artificial moonlight', with German searchlights behind the front line bouncing their beams off the cloud. The German infantry in snow camouflage advancing through freezing mist and the tall trees of the Ardennes forest looked like ghosts. While isolated forward groups fought back bravely, the bulk of the two green US divisions on the northern side were hit by the spearheads of the two panzer armies. Communications broke down, yet the front-line companies of the untested 99th Infantry Division, supported by part of the 2nd Division, conducted a dogged fighting withdrawal against a Volksgrenadier Division

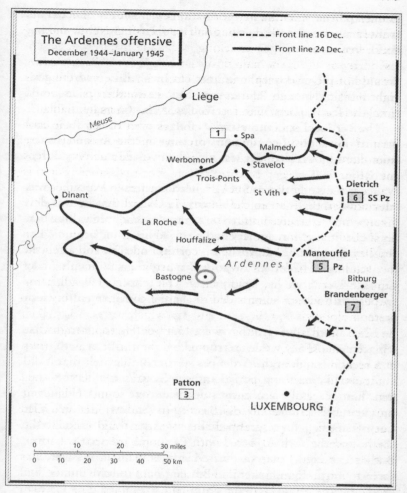

The Ardennes offensive
December 1944–January 1945

- - - - Front line 16 Dec.
――― Front line 24 Dec.

Liège

Meuse

1 • Spa
Malmedy

Werbomont •
• Stavelot
Trois-Ponts •

St Vith

Dietrich

6 SS Pz

Dinant •

La Roche •

Houffalize •

Ardennes

Manteuffel

5 Pz

Bastogne •

Bitburg •

Brandenberger

7

Patton

3

LUXEMBOURG

0   10   20   30 miles
0   10   20   30   40   50 km

and the 12th SS *Hitler Jugend* Division. But, just to the south, two regiments of the 106th Infantry Division were surrounded.

Dietrich's southern spearhead was formed by the 1st SS Panzer Regiment of his former command, the *Leibstandarte Adolf Hitler*. This regiment, reinforced with 68-ton Royal Tiger tanks, was led by Obersturmbannführer Joachim Peiper, a leader of outstanding ruthlessness. When his column was held up by a blown bridge and chaos on the narrow road, Peiper simply directed his tanks through a minefield, losing half a dozen of them but making up for lost time.

Because of the field telephone lines cut by shellfire and the general confusion, Hodges's First Army headquarters at Spa assumed from the few reports they received that the Germans had just mounted a local spoiling attack. Hodges even ordered the 2nd Infantry Division to continue its probing operation towards the Roer dams, not realizing it was already involved in a very different battle.

General Eisenhower at SHAEF headquarters in Versailles was left undisturbed to an enjoyable day. He heard that he was definitely going to receive his fifth star. It must have been galling that his subordinate Montgomery had received his at the beginning of September. Then he caught up on correspondence, and attended the wedding of his orderly who was marrying a Women's Army Corps driver from his headquarters. He expected Bradley for supper, with whom he intended to share a consignment of fresh oysters.

When Bradley arrived they went to a briefing room to discuss replacements. They were interrupted by a staff officer with news of a breakthrough in the Ardennes sector. Bradley felt that it did not sound like anything more than a spoiler to disrupt Patton's imminent attack, but Eisenhower's instincts were sound. He judged it to be more serious. He told Bradley to send Middleton's VIII Corps some help. In reserve were the 7th Armored Division to the north, and the 10th Armored with Patton in the south. Patton, as they expected, was not pleased, but both divisions were ordered to move. Eisenhower and Bradley went to have dinner, but Bradley was allergic to oysters and had scrambled eggs instead. Afterwards, they played five rubbers of bridge with a couple of SHAEF staff officers.

Bradley, starting to fear that he might have been wrong, raced back next day in his Packard staff car to his tactical headquarters in Luxembourg. He literally ran up the stairs to the war room and gazed at the huge situation map on the wall. Large red arrows showed the German advances. 'Where in the hell', he said in disbelief, 'has this son-of-a-bitch gotten all his strength?' It was still hard to get precise information. The teleprinter line to First Army headquarters at Spa had been cut. When Eisenhower's aide Harry Butcher reached 12th Army Group main headquarters at Verdun, he noted that the atmosphere there reminded him of the mood after the disaster at Kasserine.

At Third Army headquarters, on the other hand, they were spoiling for a fight. Patton had half expected a counter-offensive in the Ardennes. 'Fine,' he said. 'We should open up and let them get all the way to Paris. Then we'll saw 'em off at the base.' To the north, there was still confusion at Ninth Army headquarters on what the Germans were up to. An unusually large Luftwaffe attack on their own forces prompted suggestions that this was 'a diversion for a larger counter-offensive in First Army zone'. Staff officers were saying that 'everything depends on what troops are at von Rundstedt's disposal'. Hodges, at First Army headquarters, was either genuinely ill, as some accounts say, or had collapsed from stress. It was Hodges who had dismissed the warnings of his chief intelligence officer.

At SHAEF on 17 December, Eisenhower and his staff went through all the information available, trying to work out German intentions and how to react. They assumed that the Germans were simply trying to split the 12th and 21st Army Groups. The only reserves they had left were the 82nd and 101st Airborne Divisions, resting near Rheims after Operation Market Garden. After careful study of the map, they decided on Bastogne. Three more divisions still in England were told to prepare to move immediately. The 82nd Airborne, in the event, was diverted to Werbomont, closer to Spa.

The mistaken idea that the German offensive was heading for the French capital spread further back, with alarmist rumours. A key element in the German plan had included a parachute drop by Oberst Friedrich Freiherr von der Heydte's 6th Fallschirmjäger Regiment, to seize a bridge over the Meuse to accelerate the advance. Its approach had been disrupted mainly by anti-aircraft fire, and most of Heydte's men were scattered almost everywhere except the target drop zone. Heydte found himself with such a small force that they could only hide up near the bridge and observe events as they waited for the panzer spearheads to arrive. The widely scattered drops, however, certainly increased the confusion on the Allied side.

The Germans had also developed a deception plan. The SS commando leader Otto Skorzeny had been instructed personally by Hitler to slip through with a small force of English-speaking volunteers, dressed in American uniforms and driving captured US Army vehicles. They were to seize another bridge over the Meuse and generally cause mayhem in the rear. Skorzeny's main group, held back by the massive traffic jams, never managed to break through, but some of the small teams did. On 18 December, three of them in a Jeep were stopped at a roadblock. They did not know the password. The GIs searched them and found that they were wearing German uniforms underneath their American olive drab. But although their mission ended in failure, and subsequent execution, they managed to cause far greater chaos by telling their interrogator first that assassination teams were on their way to Versailles to kill General Eisenhower.

Eisenhower found himself confined to his quarters by submachine-gun-wielding bodyguards. Rumours spread that German squads were going after Bradley and Montgomery as well. Every soldier and officer, no matter how senior, was stopped at roadblocks by MPs and questioned on US geography, baseball and a range of other questions which only Americans were likely to know. A curfew was imposed in Paris, and SHAEF introduced a forty-eight-hour blackout on news, which fuelled speculation even more.

People became convinced that the Germans were about to retake the city. French collaborators in Fresnes Prison began taunting their warders, saying that the Germans would soon be back to set them free. The guards replied that they and the resistance would kill them all before the enemy reached the gates of Paris. Hysteria reached as far afield as Brittany, where rear-area establishments were told to prepare to evacuate. Captain M. R. D. Foot of the SAS, recovering from severe injuries in a hospital in Rennes, asked a British nurse what the commotion was about. 'We're packing up,' she told him. 'But what about the wounded who cannot be moved?' he asked. 'I am sure that the nuns next door will look after you,' she replied.

Other, more accurate stories began to spread. On 17

December, the second day of the offensive, Peiper's SS troopers from the *Leibstandarte* killed sixty-nine prisoners of war in cold blood, and then in what became known as the Malmedy massacre shot down another eighty-six in the snow. Two men escaped and reached American lines. The thirst for revenge became palpable as the account passed from mouth to mouth, and many German prisoners were shot as a result. Despite the febrile mood, there were a few indications that not everything was going the Germans' way. Some of the green troops from the 99th Infantry Division and the veterans of the 2nd Infantry Division had managed to block the 12th SS *Hitler Jugend* Division. They then withdrew in good order to the natural defensive position of the Elsenborn Ridge. Dietrich's Sixth SS Panzer Army was not making the headway expected, even though it had at least captured one minor fuel dump. Fortunately for the Allies, his forces never reached the major one near Stavelot which held four million gallons.

Weather conditions from a German point of view remained perfect, with low cloud which grounded the Allied air forces. Manteuffel's Fifth Panzer Army just to the south was doing better than Dietrich's SS Panzer Army. Having smashed through the hapless 28th Infantry Division, it was heading for Bastogne. The experienced US 4th Infantry Division on the southern flank was resisting the Seventh Army valiantly.

Eisenhower summoned a conference for 19 December at Verdun. The Ardennes crisis certainly proved to be his finest hour as supreme commander. Despite all the earlier criticism of his tendency to compromise and bend to the opinion of the last general he had spoken to, he showed good judgement and strong leadership. His message was that this presented a great opportunity to inflict maximum damage on the enemy in the open, rather than winkling him out from behind minefields and defensive positions. Their task was to prevent the German spearheads from crossing the Meuse. The enemy had to be contained until the weather changed and the Allied air forces could be let loose on him. To achieve this, they first had to strengthen the shoulders facing the breakthrough. Only then could they begin to counter-attack.

Patton, who had been well briefed by his chief intelligence officer, had already told his staff to draw up contingency plans for a major change of axis away from the Saar, to attack the southern flank of the German breakthrough. He was pleased with the idea of abandoning the 'manure-filled, waterlogged villages' of Lorraine. The German offensive reminded him of Ludendorff's great push in March 1918, the *Kaiserschlacht*. Patton appears to have been relaxed when Eisenhower turned to him at this moment of crisis. 'When can you attack?' the supreme commander asked.

'On December 22, with three divisions,' he answered. 'The 4th Armored, the 26th and the 80th.' For Patton it was an exquisite moment. All the army group and army commanders and chiefs of staff present stared in astonishment. The move required turning the bulk of his army through ninety degrees and unscrambling crossed lines of supply. 'It created quite a commotion,' Patton noted with satisfaction in his diary. But Eisenhower said that three divisions were not enough. Patton replied with his inimitable confidence that he could beat the Germans with just three, but if he waited any longer he would lose surprise. Eisenhower gave his approval.

The next morning, 20 December, Bradley was predictably put out to hear that Eisenhower had decided to give Montgomery command over both the Ninth and the First US Armies. The point was that Montgomery could be in constant contact with them, while 12th Army Group headquarters in Luxembourg was trapped south of the 'bulge', as the salient created by the German advance was now called. Eisenhower had been persuaded of this by his chief of staff Bedell Smith, partly because of the chaos in the First Army and the suspicion that Hodges might have collapsed. Bradley, who had been caught on the back foot by the offensive, feared that this development could be seen as a vote of no confidence in his performance. Above all, he hated the idea that it might encourage Montgomery in his demands to be given Allied field command. During the tense and unhappy telephone conversation, Bradley even threatened to resign. Eisenhower, despite their long friendship, was firm. 'Well, Brad, those are my orders,' he said, finishing the call.

Patton, on the other hand, was in his element, rearranging his troops, diverting tank destroyer battalions to bolster his armoured forces and preparing to attack. The 101st Airborne Division had reached Bastogne only just before Manteuffel's Fifth Panzer

Army. In fact the weak perimeter was already under small-arms fire when the trucks halted. The paratroopers trudged forward past fleeing American soldiers, whom they relieved of their ammunition. An officer of the 10th Armored Division, discovering how short they were, drove off to a supply dump and came back with a truck full of ammunition and grenades, which were thrown to the paratroopers as they marched on. As the sound of firing intensified, they began to dig shell-scrapes and foxholes in the snow-covered ground.

Like almost all the American troops in the Ardennes battles, the 101st Airborne was simply not equipped for winter warfare. Because of the supply problems over the previous three months, absolute priority had been given to fuel and ammunition. Most men were still in their summer uniforms and they suffered terribly in the freezing conditions, especially in the long nights when the temperature dropped sharply. They could not light fires, as that would immediately attract German artillery and mortar bombardment. Trench-foot cases rose alarmingly and accounted for a large proportion of the casualties. Under fire in their foxholes, standing in slushy mud by day which froze hard at night, they had little opportunity to take off their boots, and put on dry socks. There was no hope of washing and shaving. Many suffered from dysentery and, marooned in a foxhole, could only resort to using their helmet or a K-Ration box. A further horror was discovered. Boar from the forests were eating the stomachs of unburied casualties. Those who had profited from the chaotic hunting expeditions before the battle must have had queasy thoughts. Most soldiers had become indifferent to the sight of bodies, but the graves registration personnel who cleared up afterwards had no choice.

Although Patton still favoured the idea of allowing the Germans to advance further so as to destroy them better, he accepted Bradley's decision that Bastogne, a vital road hub, had to be held at all costs. The 101st Airborne was supported by two armoured combat commands, two companies of tank destroyers and an artillery battalion which was short of shells. Everything depended on the skies clearing so that C-47s could parachute ammunition and supplies into the encirclement.

Montgomery also had not been idle. As soon as he recognized

the threat to his rear, he had swung Horrocks's XXX Corps round into a blocking position on the north-west bank of the Meuse to secure the bridges. This happened to coincide perfectly with Eisenhower's plan to prepare the Meuse bridges for demolition, to prevent the Germans from seizing them.

As soon as he heard from Eisenhower that he was to take over First US Army, Montgomery left for Spa. He arrived in Hodges's headquarters, according to one of his own staff officers, 'like Christ come to clean the temple'. Hodges appears at first to have been in a state of shock, incapable of taking a decision. It transpired that he and Bradley had not been in touch for two days, proving that Eisenhower had been right to call in Monty.

What Patton called his 'chestnut pulling expedition' would be ready to start, as he had told Eisenhower, on 22 December. 'We should get well into the guts of the enemy and cut his supply lines,' he wrote to his wife. 'Destiny sent for me in a hurry when things got tight. Perhaps God saved me for this effort.'

Yet already events were turning in the Americans' favour through determination and bravery. On the northern shoulder of the breakthrough, V Corps, commanded by Eisenhower's old friend 'Gee' Gerow, was defending the Elsenborn Ridge with a mixture of infantry, tank destroyers, engineers and above all artillery. They managed to fight off the 12th SS Panzer Division *Hitler Jugend* during the night of 20 December and the following day. Altogether, some 782 German corpses were found in front of their positions.

Montgomery failed to acknowledge the extraordinary resilience and bravery of those American units holding the shoulders of the breakthrough. Instead he focused only on the mess he found at First Army and his role in clearing it up. Field Marshal Brooke was dreading how he would behave on finally receiving the command he wanted, and Montgomery confirmed his worst fears.

In a meeting with Bradley on Christmas Day, Montgomery said that things had gone wrong since Normandy because his advice had not been followed. A seething Bradley listened in silence. With his armour-plated conceit, Montgomery assumed as he had in Normandy that silence implied agreement with everything he said.

Bradley had gone to see Montgomery to persuade him to launch his counter-attack as soon as possible. But in this case Montgomery was almost certainly right to delay. Patton's rapid reaction had taken the Germans aback, but by attacking with just three divisions, instead of the six Eisenhower had wanted, he extended the Battle for Bastogne rather than ending it. Montgomery, in his deliberate way, wanted to seal the bulge, and then smash it. He would not give a date, since he needed to be sure of good weather for the Allied air forces to attack.

The weather had deteriorated even more, greatly restricting air operations. Apart from a bombing raid on Trier which included Harris's Bomber Command, little had been achieved, and this was not from lack of trying or cooperation. Coningham, the New Zealander who now commanded the RAF's Second Tactical Air Force, got on extremely well with Quesada. The skies only began to clear on 23 December. Two days later came 'a clear cold Christmas, lovely weather for killing Germans', as Patton wrote in his diary. The air forces did not waste the opportunity. P-47 Thunderbolts and RAF Typhoons established a coordinated campaign of ground attacks, while the fighters dealt with 900 Luftwaffe sorties on the first day. Allied supremacy was rapidly established. Within a week, the Luftwaffe could put up no more than 200.

Quesada's IX Tactical Air Command was greatly admired by American ground forces for its panache, but it had acquired a reputation for bad navigation and target recognition. In October when called in to attack specific positions on the Westwall in Germany, not a single aircraft found the target. One even flattened the Belgian mining village of Genk, causing eighty civilian casualties. The 30th Division was hit hard when it reached Malmedy. This was the thirteenth time since landing in Normandy that it had been attacked by its own aircraft, and GIs even started to refer to the Ninth as 'the American Luftwaffe'. This rather underlined the German army joke since Normandy that 'if it's British, we duck; if it's American everybody ducks; and if it's the Luftwaffe nobody ducks'.

On 1 January 1945, the Luftwaffe, on Göring's order, made a maximum effort, with 800 fighters from all over Germany coming in to attack Allied airfields. To achieve surprise they were to come in at tree-top level, under Allied radar cover. But the extreme secrecy precautions imposed on Operation Bodenplatte (Baseplate) meant that many pilots were insufficiently briefed and German flak units were not notified. It is estimated that nearly a hundred aircraft were shot down by their own anti-aircraft batteries. Overall the Allies lost about 150 aircraft while the Luftwaffe lost close to 300, with 214 pilots killed or taken prisoner. It was the Luftwaffe's final humiliation. Allied air power was now unchallenged.

With the encirclement of Bastogne finally broken on 27 December 1944, Montgomery came under pressure to launch his counter-attack by 3 January. But the field marshal remained obsessed with command issues. Brooke was right to be uneasy, for Monty began to lecture Eisenhower again in the same tones as he had used with Bradley. 'It looks to me', Brooke wrote in his diary, 'as if Monty, with his usual lack of tact, has been rubbing into Ike the results of not having listened to Monty's advice! Too much of "I told you so" to assist in creating the required friendly relations between them.' Once again Eisenhower failed to be tough with him, and this prompted Montgomery to write him a disastrous follow-up letter, laying down the law on strategy and insisting that he should be given command over Bradley's 12th Army Group as well.

General Marshall had also been provoked by the way the British press played Montgomery's refrain, calling for a virtually independent command. He therefore wrote to Eisenhower urging him to make no concessions. This, combined with Montgomery's letter, prompted Eisenhower to draft a signal to the combined chiefs of staff which basically said that unless Montgomery was replaced, preferably by Alexander, then he would resign. Montgomery's chief of staff, de Guingand, heard of this ultimatum. He persuaded Eisenhower to hold back for twenty-four hours and went straight to Montgomery with an apology already drafted, which asked Eisenhower to tear up his previous letter. Montgomery had been put back in his box, but only for the moment.

Eisenhower's use of Patton's Third Army created a number of side-effects further south. Devers had to take over part of

Patton's front. This would mean shifting troops from the south and withdrawing from Strasbourg to straighten the line. De Gaulle, who had not been consulted, objected angrily when he heard. The idea of giving up Strasbourg just over a month after liberating it would threaten the very stability of his government. The political implications were far more significant than Eisenhower had realized.

On 3 January, at Churchill's urging, a conference was held at Eisenhower's headquarters in Versailles with de Gaulle, Churchill and Brooke. Eisenhower conceded that Strasbourg would be held after all, and de Gaulle was so carried away that he immediately drafted a communiqué. His chef de cabinet, Gaston Palewski, took it round to the British embassy to show it first to Duff Cooper, the British ambassador. This vainglorious announcement 'suggested that de Gaulle had summoned a military conference which the Prime Minister and Eisenhower had been allowed to attend'. Duff Cooper managed to persuade Palewski to tone it down.

Bastogne might have been relieved and resupplied by air, but once the Germans had acknowledged that they could not even reach the Meuse, it became the focus for their attacks. Hitler, meanwhile, had decided to launch another offensive in Alsace codenamed North Wind. It was not much more than a diversion and achieved little.

Montgomery's counter-attack was finally launched on 3 January. The fighting was tough, and was not helped by heavy snow, but the outcome was hardly in doubt. Four days later, the battle of Montgomery's ego broke out again when he held a press conference. Churchill had given permission, because Montgomery promised him that it would improve Allied unity. It had absolutely the opposite effect. Montgomery, although paying tribute to the fighting qualities of the American soldier and emphasizing his loyalty to Eisenhower, implied that he had run the battle almost single-handedly and that there had been a massive British contribution. Churchill and Brooke were horrified, and immediately 'discussed all the evils of Monty's press interview'. Churchill made a statement to Parliament emphasizing that it had been an American battle, and that the British contribution had been minimal. But the damage to Allied relations had been done.

The Anglo-American alliance also suffered during this period due to events in south-eastern Europe, and Churchill's determination to preserve Greece from Communist rule. The collapse of German power in the region, accelerated by the advance of the Red Army into Romania and Hungary in October, brought civil war out into the open. Greece was yet another example of the Second World War merging into a latent third world war.

The terrible suffering of the occupation, with starvation and economic collapse, had led to a dramatic radicalization of a population which had been socially conservative before the war. It was this instinctive shift to the left, often without any clear ideological bent, which contributed to the widespread support for EAM-ELAS. Although Communist led, EAM was full of political contradictions reflecting many different points of view, especially when it came to ideas on socialism and liberty. Land reform and female emancipation were two of the most hotly debated questions. The only general basis of agreement was that the traditional political system, and especially the monarchy, was now irrelevant to the problems which Greece faced. Even the Communist leaders were split and uncertain whether to follow a democratic route to power or to impose it by force of arms.

Several months before Churchill's 'naughty' agreement, Stalin had sent a military mission to the Greece. It was told to warn the Greek Communist Party, the KKE, 'to face geopolitical realities and cooperate with the British'. This fact alone goes a long way to explaining why Stalin must have had to hide his amusement when he studied Churchill's 'percentage agreement' in his office in the Kremlin.

Despite Stalin's warning, anti-British emotions ran high in EAM-ELAS because of Churchill's support for King George II, who was determined to return to Greece as soon as the Germans left. British SOE officers managed early in the year to negotiate an end to the fighting between EAM-ELAS and the non-Communist EDES. Then in April 1944 EAM announced 'revolutionary elections' in an attempt to gain a sort of governmental legitimacy. The elections, needless to say, made sure that only EAM candidates could win. George Papandreou rejected approaches from EAM to act as a figurehead, for he did not want to be a figleaf for a movement manipulated from behind by the Communists. Instead he became head of the Greek government-in-exile in Cairo. Other politicians of the centre left, however, were persuaded to take part.

EAM-ELAS intensified its repression against any who disagreed with it, depicting them as traitors or enemies of the people. Many were executed. The collaborationist government in Athens, with the encouragement of the Germans, had recruited Security Battalions to attack EAM-ELAS. Its terror was answered with counter-terror. In Athens, ELAS urban guerrillas on one side and the Security Battalions and Gendarmerie on the other fought a dirty war which exploded in March. Many of the ELAS fighters rounded up were sent back to Germany for forced labour. The Security Battalions tried to rehabilitate themselves as the German departure became imminent. Prisoners were allowed to escape more frequently. Messages were also sent to Cairo to assure the Greek government-in-exile and the British that the Security Battalions would not resist the country's liberation, but would welcome it.

In early September peace feelers were extended to EAM-ELAS, which rejected them even though most people were longing for an end to the violence. Street battles resumed. German forces still in Greece dreaded being cut off by the Red Army advances to their north, and non-German troops forced into the Wehrmacht began to desert in large numbers. The withdrawal began at the beginning of October and many of the worst collaborators fled north as well to avoid being massacred by *andartes*, the Greek guerrillas. EAM-ELAS tried to impose order where it could, if only to justify its role as a government in waiting, but conditions varied enormously from place to place. On 12 October the last Germans withdrew from Athens, having removed the swastika flag which flew from the Acropolis. Exuberant crowds filled the streets as a large EAM-ELAS demonstration took place chanting 'Laokratia' – 'People's Rule'.

British troops from Lieutenant General Ronald Scobie's III Corps were greeted effusively when they arrived soon afterwards. But British policy towards Greece was conditioned partly by Churchill's monarchical sympathies, by ignorance of the occupation and the resulting political realities, and most of all by the prime minister's intention to keep Greece out of the Soviet sphere of interest. George Papandreou, who headed a government of national unity that at first included some EAM members, also appointed to his administration noted right-wingers with connections to the Security Battalions. Churchill was in no mood to compromise, especially after his agreement with Stalin. He gave Scobie, not the most politically sensitive of officers, strict directions to react strongly in the event of any attacks on British troops. On 2 December, the EAM members of the government resigned in protest at orders to disarm the *andartes*. The government was planning to form a National Guard, many of whose members would be recruited from the hated Security Battalions. At a mass demonstration called by EAM the next day in Syntagma Square, police opened fire, either out of nervousness or in response to shots fired. The left claimed that it had been a deliberate provocation to force a fight. Police stations in the city were attacked. British troops were unharmed, but Scobie sent in his troops to secure the city. ELAS gunmen opened fire. Fighting escalated and, as the situation got out of hand, RAF Beaufighters and Spitfires were sent in to strafe ELAS positions, a catastrophic misjudgement. ELAS began mass killings of 'reactionary' families in the city, and seized hostages in both Athens and Salonika.

Harold Macmillan, who was still minister resident in the Mediterranean, and Sir Rex Leeper, the British ambassador, persuaded Churchill that the King should not be allowed to return until a plebiscite had been held. With reluctance, the prime minister agreed to their suggestion of a regency by Archbishop Damaskinos. King George of the Hellenes was furious, opposing both a regency and the choice of Damaskinos. The American press began to condemn British policy in strong terms. With an often naive belief that resistance fighters against the Germans must be freedom-loving, it turned a blind eye to Tito's murderous repression in Yugoslavia and also to Stalin's violence against the Polish Home Army. American journalists proceeded to attack Churchill as an imperialist who ignored the Atlantic Charter on self-determination. Instead of the 5,000 British troops originally thought necessary to restore order in Greece, some 80,000 were allocated to disarm the *andarte* forces. Admiral King tried to veto the use of landing ships to transport more men from Italy to Greece.

Churchill also faced strong criticism in the House of Commons, but his passionate belief that only he could save Greece from Communism prompted him to fly to Athens on Christmas Eve. The city was a war zone, so he based himself aboard the cruiser HMS *Ajax* anchored off Phaleron. Archbishop Damaskinos, a tall and stately prelate in full Greek Orthodox canonicals, came aboard. Churchill, who had been very dubious about Damaskinos, was enchanted as soon as he met him. The next day Churchill, Anthony Eden, Macmillan and their party were ferried in armoured vehicles with a strong escort through the fighting to the British embassy. The building, as one historian noted, 'resembled a besieged outpost during the Indian Mutiny', where the ambassador's wife 'directed domestic operations with a courage and energy likewise worthy of a Victorian imperial drama'.

The conference to arrange a ceasefire began that afternoon in the Greek foreign office. With Damaskinos chairing the meeting, delegates from Greek factions joined them as well as American, French and Soviet representatives. Churchill buttonholed the Russian Colonel Gregori Popov and made it abundantly clear that he had enjoyed very fruitful talks with Marshal Stalin only a few weeks before. Popov had no option but to be duly impressed.

The assembly had to wait for the ELAS representatives, delayed at the entrance because of their reluctance to be relieved of their weapons. In the end the only person armed at the meeting was the prime minister, who had brought a small pistol in his pocket. Churchill shook hands with the 'three shabby desperados', as he described them afterwards. He opened the meeting with the statement that whether Greece was to be a monarchy or a republic was for Greeks alone to decide. After that, he and all the other non-Greeks rose and left the room to allow Damaskinos to proceed.

Churchill heard next day that the talks had been angry and even rowdy at times. The former dictator General Nikolaos Plastiras had at one point shouted at one of the Communist delegates: 'Sit down, butcher!' Damaskinos announced the resignation of Papandreou as prime minister and his replacement by General Plastiras, who then had to resign too when it emerged that he had offered to lead a collaborationist government during the occupation.

The fighting in Athens continued into the new year, when the *andartes* pulled out of the city, unable to prevail against the large British force. It was far from a glorious victory to install a far from liberal government. The Greek Civil War, with all its cruelties on both sides, would continue in one form or another until 1949. But Churchill's obstinate intervention at least saved the country from the fate of its northern neighbours which suffered more than four decades of Communist tyranny.

Behind the Allied lines, Belgium too underwent severe unrest. The joy of liberation in September 1944 soured through the autumn into a mood of bitterness and resentment. The government-in-exile headed by Hubert Pierlot returned to Belgium and found itself incapable of dealing with the country's problems. Half a million Belgians had been taken to Germany as forced labourers, so there was a severe shortage of manpower. Coal production was down to a tenth of the pre-war output, which meant constant cuts in the electricity supply. The rail network did not function, due partly to Allied bombing but also to sabotage undertaken by the Germans during their sudden withdrawal.

The most contentious question was the arrest and punishment of collaborators and traitors. The 90,000 members of the Belgian resistance were outraged by the inability of ministers, who had spent the war in exile, to understand the harsh realities of the occupation and their anger against those who had profited from it. Allied military authorities estimated that some 400,000 people had collaborated, yet only 60,000 were arrested. Many of them were released by the end of the year, while those who did face trial received remarkably light sentences.

Eisenhower attempted to restore calm. On 2 October he issued an order which, while paying tribute to their bravery, instructed members of the resistance to surrender their weapons. The Communist part of the resistance, the Front de l'Indépendence, was determined to challenge the government. Pierlot warned SHAEF that he had word of plans for a Communist rising, and the British rapidly armed the Belgian police. In November, British troops were deployed in Brussels to protect key buildings when the Communists organized a major demonstration, with protesters and strikers brought in from outside.

The misery of Belgian civilians was still far from over. V-1 flying bomb and V-2 rocket attacks on Liège and above all Antwerp killed and injured many. In the main areas of fighting that autumn families had fled their homes, but in December during the Ardennes offensive very few had time to escape the rapidity of the German attack.

Peiper's *Kampfgruppe* from the *Leibstandarte* did not just murder American prisoners. It wreaked revenge on the Belgians, who had been so pleased to see the SS go three months earlier. On the morning after the massacre near Malmedy, Peiper's troops entered Stavelot and shot nine civilians. But they then found that they were blocked by an American force to the north, while part of the US 30th Division blew the bridge to their rear.

Peiper's Waffen-SS troopers, having expected to charge to the Meuse, proceeded to vent their fury on families around. Over the following days, some 130 men, women and even children were shot down, in family groups and in larger massacres. Altogether around 3,000 civilians were killed in the Ardennes fighting, many of course by Allied bombardment and bombing. As well as the thirty-seven American soldiers killed in Malmedy because the Ninth Air Force had hit the wrong target, 202 civilians were killed. Those trapped in St Vith, Houffalize, Sainlez, La Roche and other towns and villages which were fought over tried to shelter in cellars, but their houses collapsed on top of them or they were burned to death by phosphorus bombs and shells. No more than twenty died in Bastogne from German shelling. Their town at least was not a target for Allied air power.

German troops looted without compunction, but Allied troops were little better. Sometimes it was justifiable, when soldiers were surrounded without rations, or when they seized blankets for warmth or sheets to act as snow camouflage. But more often it was the cynical opportunism of war. The damage to homes and communities was far worse. The town of St Vith was completely smashed and its survivors, like those of many other towns, were left with nothing.

The Ardennes Offensive constituted a major defeat for the Germans. They lost half their tanks and guns and suffered heavy casualties, with 12,652 killed, 38,600 wounded and 30,000 missing, most of whom were taken prisoner. The Americans in the battle of attrition lost 10,276 men killed, 47,493 wounded and 23,218 missing.

While the suffering of Belgian civilians was great, the majority of the Dutch fared far worse. Even those behind Allied lines were starving, as Canadian, British and American soldiers found from those begging or offering sex for food. The situation was made much worse by the flooding of arable land after dykes were destroyed as a defensive measure.

The Dutch north of the River Maas would remain under German control until the end of the war, in the grip of a famine exacerbated by their occupiers. When railwaymen went on strike to help the Allies at the time of Operation Market Garden, Arthur Seyss-Inquart, the Austrian who headed the Reichskommissariat Niederlande, stopped the import of any food as a reprisal. The population was reduced to eating tulip bulbs and any sugar beet which the Germans had not taken. Children were paralysed by rickets, and malnutrition exposed everyone to disease, especially typhoid and diphtheria. Seyss-Inquart had achieved a reputation for brutality in Poland before he arrived in Holland just after its conquest in May 1940. After Greece, Holland was the most comprehensively looted country in western Europe. Already by October 1944, it had become clear that a man-made disaster was taking place.

The Dutch government-in-exile approached Churchill with a request that Sweden be allowed to send in food, but the prime minister was firmly opposed. He believed that the Germans would simply seize it for themselves. Both Eisenhower and the British chiefs of staff felt that this risk should be taken, and during the winter the Swedes delivered 20,000 tons of food by ship to Amsterdam. This effort kept many alive who would have otherwise starved to death, but it only scratched at the surface of the problem. The British chiefs of staff, although sympathetic, were not prepared to stop mining the German coast and allow free passage through the Kiel Canal.

Queen Wilhelmina, desperate to help her starving people, lobbied Roosevelt and Churchill. She requested that, to avoid a colossal humanitarian disaster, Allied strategy should be changed, with an invasion of northern Holland instead of focusing on the Ruhr. But with large German forces which were likely to fight to the end, and which would probably flood even more of the country, it was decided that this would delay the defeat of Germany.

Finally, in April 1945, Churchill was sufficiently alarmed by reports of the radicalization of the Dutch population under Communist influence to press for all-out relief. The Germans would be warned that any attempt to stop or divert food supplies sent by ship or airdropped in northern Holland would be treated as a war crime. Roosevelt agreed, just two days before he died. But, by the time relief arrived, at least 22,000 Dutch civilians had died of starvation. The figure was probably far higher, if lack of resistance to disease is also taken into account.

That winter of snow, frost and waterlogged trenches was also terrible for Allied troops, even though they did not suffer from hunger. Exposure and trench foot accounted for almost as many casualties as enemy action. The Canadian First Army, after its very nasty time clearing the Scheldt estuary, found winter along the Maas almost as unpleasant and deadly, with the Germans defending dykes which were three to four metres high. 'For the attacking Canadians the only other approach was across the sunken fields between the dykes "flat as the local beer" as one artillery punster put it. There really was no protection at all.'

Canadian units were dangerously under-strength because Mackenzie King's government did not dare send soldiers abroad to fight against their will. The equivalent of five divisions remained in Canada guarding German prisoners of war, and little else. This of course provoked great resentment among those Canadian volunteers who shivered through that winter of mud and ice, the wettest since 1864. Sodden battledress and webbing equipment never dried out, boots simply rotted. Living conditions were unutterably squalid, as the stationary armies fouled their own nests and the countryside behind.

The morale of British troops was also low, partly out of war-weariness, cynicism and a desire not to be killed when the end was in sight. Desertion had become a major problem, with some 20,000 men absent from their units. Persuading soldiers to attack became increasingly difficult, especially when Student's First Paratroop Army fought with such professionalism and aggression. Senior officers were all too aware of their own manpower problems, which although not as acute as those in Canadian formations were still grave enough. The Americans were scornful of the British reluctance to take casualties, while the British, like the Germans, criticized the Americans for refusing to undertake any attack without a huge expenditure of shells first. But British infantry were also unwilling to advance without heavy gunfire in support. In fact all the Allies, both in the west and in the east, had developed a 'psychological dependence upon artillery and air power' the longer the war went on.

44

From the Vistula to the Oder

In the first years of the war, whether in France in 1940 or in the Soviet Union a year later, many German soldiers wrote home: 'Thank God that the war is not raging in our homeland.' By January 1945, it had become abundantly clear that the on-slaught which the Wehrmacht had inflicted on other countries was about to fall on their own. Hitler's New Year broadcast lifted few spirits. He made no mention of the Ardennes, which indicated that the great offensive had failed. And little was said of the *Wunderwaffen*, that staple of Nazi attempts to maintain hope in the face of reality. Hitler's delivery was so flat that many Germans thought that it had been pre-recorded or even faked. Deprived of reliable news, rumours of disaster increased.

Although Guderian, the army chief of staff, tried to warn Hitler of the impending explosion of the eastern front along the Vistula and into East Prussia, the Führer would not listen. He dismissed intelligence estimates of Soviet strength, which for once were quite accurate. From the Baltic to the Adriatic, the Red Army deployed 6.7 million men, more than twice the Axis forces in Operation Barbarossa.

Hitler's most immediate concern was the Budapest and Lake Balaton front. Even with the threat from the east, every situation conference at his headquarters began with Hungary. Tolbukhin's 3rd Ukrainian Front, under heavy pressure from Stalin, threw wave after wave of men against the defences south of Budapest. Stalin was determined that Churchill's proposal in October to share influence in Hungary '50–50' should be made redundant by force of arms.

A Hungarian officer described the dead Soviet soldiers mown down on a barbed-wire entanglement. One was still just alive. 'The young soldier, with his shaven head and Mongolian cheek-bones, is lying on his back. Only his mouth is moving. Both legs and lower arms are missing. The stumps are covered in a thick layer of soil, mixed with blood and leaf mould. I bend down close to him. "Budapesst . . . Budapesst," he whispers in the throes of death. In my head one thought revolves: he may be having a vision of "Budapesst" as a city of rich spoils and beautiful women. Then, surprising even myself, I pull out my pistol, load it, press it against the dying man's temple, and fire.' But despite the countless casualties they inflicted, the Germans and Hungarians knew they could not hold back the enemy flood.

Szálasi, the Arrow Cross dictator who replaced Admiral Horthy, had wanted to withdraw and declare Budapest an open city, but Hitler, who never wanted to abandon a capital city, had insisted that it be defended to the end. Szálasi's main concern, however, was not so much to save the city as to avoid being stabbed in the back by a disloyal population. The German commander, Generaloberst Hans Friessner, who shared his concerns, called in an expert on counter-subversion in the form of SS Obergruppenführer Karl Pfeffer-Wildenbruch. The Hungarian general staff were not consulted, despite all previous agreements, and they were treated in an insultingly off-hand manner.

Hitler's special envoy, Edmund Veesenmayer, insisted on the Führer's instruction that Budapest should be defended to the last brick. It did not matter, he said, if Budapest was 'destroyed ten times, so long as Vienna could thereby be defended'. Friessner, however, wanted to withdraw from Pest on the flat eastern bank of the Danube to defend Buda, with its hills and fortress high on the west bank. Hitler firmly refused. He replaced Friessner with General der Panzertruppen Hermann Balck.

Many citizens in Budapest had no idea that the city was in such danger. Radio Budapest had been playing Christmas carols for the last week as if nothing were amiss. Christmas trees were decorated with aluminium foil strips of 'Window' dropped by Allied bombers, while theatres and cinemas continued with performances as normal. On 26 December 1944, Budapest was surrounded. Forces from the 3rd Ukrainian Front had also reached beyond Lake Balaton to the south-west and to the city of Esztergom to the north-west. Altogether, 79,000 German and Hungarian troops were trapped in the twin cities of Buda on the west bank of the Danube and Pest on the east. German

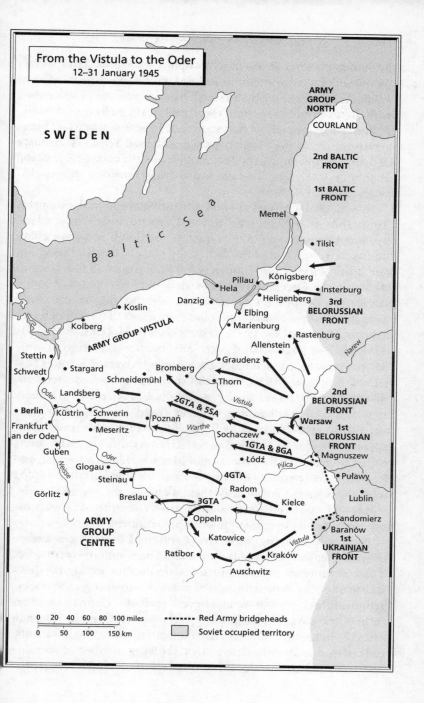

From the Vistula to the Oder
12–31 January 1945

SWEDEN

Baltic Sea

ARMY GROUP NORTH

COURLAND

2nd BALTIC FRONT

1st BALTIC FRONT

Memel

• Tilsit

• Königsberg
• Insterburg
Pillau
Hela •
Heligenberg
Danzig •

3rd BELORUSSIAN FRONT

• Elbing
• Marienburg
Koslin •
• Rastenburg

ARMY GROUP VISTULA

Allenstein
Kolberg •
Narew

Stettin •
• Stargard
• Graudenz
Bromberg •
Schneidemühl •
• Thorn

2nd BELORUSSIAN FRONT

Schwedt •
Vistula
Landsberg •
Oder
2GTA & 5SA

• **Berlin**
Küstrin •
Schwerin •
• Poznań
• Warsaw

1st BELORUSSIAN FRONT

Frankfurt an der Oder •
• Meseritz
Warthe
Sochaczew •

Guben •
1GTA & 8GA
Magnuszew

Oder
Glogau •
• Łódź
Pilica

Steinau •
4GTA
• Puławy

Görlitz •
Breslau •
Radom •
3GTA
• Kielce
• Lublin

Oppeln •
Sandomierz
Baranów •

Katowice •
Vistula
1st UKRAINIAN FRONT

ARMY GROUP CENTRE

Ratibor •
• Kraków
Auschwitz •

```
0   20  40  60  80  100 miles
0    50    100   150 km
```

- - - - - - - Red Army bridgeheads

▨ Soviet occupied territory

formations included the 8th *Florian Geyer* and 22nd *Maria Theresia* SS Cavalry Divisions, the Panzergrenadier Division *Feldherrnhalle*, the 13th Panzer Division and a lot of remnants, with even a punishment unit, the 500th Strafbataillon.

Hitler had reacted to the crisis on Christmas Day. The Hungarian oilfields offered his last source of fuel. So, to Guderian's despair, he ordered the IV SS Panzer Corps, with the *Totenkopf* and *Wiking* Divisions, to re-deploy from north of Warsaw to break the encirclement.

In Pest, chaos ensued as soon as fighting began in the suburbs. Thousands of civilians tried to break out before it was too late, and many were caught in the crossfire. For the 50,000 Jews still in Budapest, the arrival of the Red Army promised deliverance, but few would survive even though Adolf Eichmann had flown out of the city on 23 December. No provision had been made for any of the civilian population. Soon people were begging at army field kitchens. There was no water, gas or electricity. The lack of water led to a dangerous squalor as sewers became blocked.

Hungarian students and even schoolboys volunteered or were drafted into improvised units, such as the University Assault Battalion. But, apart from Panzerfaust rocket-propelled grenades, they had few weapons. Most hated the fascist Arrow Cross, many of whose members had fled, yet they could not bear to see their city fall into the hands of the Bolsheviks. At the same time, an increasing number of Hungarian regular army officers and soldiers began to defect to the Soviet side. Many were incorporated into Red Army companies, and in one case a whole battalion fought with the Soviets. To identify them as allies, they received armbands and cap-bands made out of strips from the red parachute silk taken from German ammunition containers.

Although many of the Arrow Cross had fled the city before the encirclement, 2,000 of their fanatical paramilitaries remained. These volunteers appeared to spend more time killing the Jews still in the city than fighting the enemy. Surprisingly, SS Obergruppenführer Pfeffer-Wildenbruch forbade German soldiers from participating in the killings, although other senior German officials welcomed the fact that Hungarians were taking on the task with brutal enthusiasm. An increasing number of starving Jews resorted to suicide. In the first week of January 1945, the

Arrow Cross seized a number of Jews under Swedish protection on the grounds that, since the government in Stockholm did not recognize the Szálasi regime, they did not accept the documents issued in its name. The Arrow Cross rounded up these Jews, beat them senseless and later took them in groups to the Danube Embankment for execution.

On 14 January, Father Kun took a band of Arrow Cross to the Jewish hospital in Buda. They slaughtered patients, nurses and everyone else they found there, a total of 170 people. They carried out other mass killings, including even Hungarian officers who had opposed them. Apparently, a number of Father Kun's gang raped some nuns.

On hearing of an Arrow Cross plan to attack the ghetto in Pest, Raoul Wallenberg sent a message to Generalmajor Gerhard Schmidhuber, the German commander, that he would be held responsible if he did not prevent the massacre. Schmidhuber sent Wehrmacht troops into the ghetto to forestall the Arrow Cross. A few days later, the ghetto was overrun by the Red Army.

On 30 December, after Soviet attempts to obtain a surrender were rejected, Malinovsky's offensive against Budapest began in earnest with a three-day artillery barrage and heavy bombing. In the cellars of the city, packed with civilians, condensation dripped from the ceilings and ran down the walls. Pfeffer-Wildenbruch rejected appeals for their evacuation in buses. Over the next two weeks the Soviet troops forced the German and Hungarian defenders, who were running out of ammunition, back towards the Danube through sheer force of numbers. IX SS Mountain Corps headquarters in the castle on Buda sent increasingly urgent messages demanding supplies, but parachute containers often fell outside their lines. Those bearing food were seized by starving civilians despite threats of instant execution.

Malinovsky, seeing that Pest would be occupied within a matter of days, sent the Romanian 7th Army Corps away to the northern Hungarian front. He wanted the capture of Budapest to be a uniquely Soviet victory. On 17 January, he launched his final drive to the Danube bank. Soon much of western Pest along the Danube was in flames, with heat blasting out from the buildings, searing those who escaped through the streets. Most Hungarian units were reluctant to pull back across the river to die in the defence of Buda, so more and more soldiers began to hide in the few places not ablaze in order to surrender to the Red Army. Even officers disobeyed orders.

Soviet Shturmoviks strafed the confused withdrawal across the remains of the Chain Bridge and the Erzsébet Bridge. 'The bridges remained constantly under massive fire,' an SS cavalryman recorded, 'but people were surging ahead regardless. A tangled mass of cars and trucks, peasant carts covered by tarpaulins, frightened horses, civilian refugees, wailing women, mothers with crying children and many, very many wounded were hurrying towards Buda.' Civilians still on the bridges were killed when they were blown up as the Soviet troops approached them. So was a member of the Hungarian resistance who was trying to remove the demolition charges on the Erzsébet Bridge.

By the end of December, IV SS Panzer Corps was ready to deploy on the Danube front. Its sudden attack on New Year's Day hit the 4th Guards Army and nearly broke through. Another attack to the south was launched a week later by III Panzer Corps. This was renewed on 18 January, with IV SS Panzer Corps, which had disengaged to the north of Budapest to join III Panzer Corps. German tanks experimented with infra-red sights for the first time. But again, after a striking initial success, the panzer advance was blocked when Malinovsky rapidly moved six of his own corps from the 2nd Ukrainian Front to face them.

The much smaller Buda sector, covered in snow blackened from the fires across the river, was easier to defend. Soviet attacks up its steep hills were repulsed with heavy casualties inflicted by German MG-42 machine guns concentrated at key points. Along with regular units, such as the 8th SS Cavalry and the remnants of the *Feldherrnhalle*, there were the local volunteers, such as the Vannay Battalion and the University Assault Battalion, who knew the terrain better than anyone. The Danube Embankment below Castle Hill was protected by the survivors of the 1st Hungarian Armoured Division, who did not expect the Soviets to attack across the thin ice pockmarked with shellholes. But soon harder frosts made it passable, at least for small groups of Hungarian deserters from Buda fleeing in the other direction to surrender to the Soviets in Pest.

In late January Soviet attacks increased, with flamethrowing tanks and assault squads. German and Hungarian losses mounted critically, and the wounded were packed into improvised hospitals where conditions were appalling. Some were even dumped in the corridors of command posts. A young soldier walking down one to deliver a report felt his coat seized by a hand. He looked down. 'It was a girl of about 18 to 20 with fair hair and a beautiful face. She begged me in a whisper: "Take your pistol and shoot me." I looked at her more closely and realised with horror . . . both her legs were missing.'

Even after the failure of the relief attempts, Hitler continued to forbid any talk of a breakout. Budapest still had to be defended to the end. Army Group South, like Manstein after the failure to relieve Stalingrad, knew that Budapest was doomed. Right up to 5 February, German gliders piloted by teenage volunteers of the NSFK (National Socialist Flying Corps), were crash-landing on Vérmező Meadow, delivering ammunition, fuel and some food. But it was not enough. Soviet tanks were soon crushing artillery guns which had run out of ammunition under their tracks. With all the refugees, some 300,000 people were packed into the last bastion of Castle Hill. All the cavalry horses had been eaten, and starvation was universal. So were lice, and the first outbreak of typhus caused deep alarm. On 3 February, after a plea from the papal nuncio to end the suffering, Obergruppenführer Pfeffer-Wildenbruch signalled Führer headquarters for permission to break out. It was refused again, and once more two days later.

Soviet troops, guided by Hungarian defectors or members of the resistance, began clearing some of the trapped garrisons and Castle Hill. On 11 February, white flags began to appear. In some places Hungarian troops disarmed the Germans who wanted to fight on. By the evening resistance appeared to have ceased. But Pfeffer-Wildenbruch had decided to break out in defiance of Hitler's orders. With the remnants of the 13th Panzer Division and the 8th SS Cavalry Division *Florian Geyer* in the first wave and the *Feldherrnhalle* and 22nd SS Cavalry in the second, they would try to break through that night towards the north-west with their remaining vehicles. He radioed Army Group South requesting an attack in their direction. But Red Army commanders had expected such an attempt and guessed the route they were likely to follow.

It turned into the most terrible massacre of troops and civilians. In the chaos several thousand managed to escape into the hills north of the city, but most were rounded up. Soviet troops usually shot the Germans and spared the Hungarians. Some 28,000 soldiers had taken part in the breakout from Buda. Just over 700 reached German lines.

On 12 February a deathly hush came over the city, punctuated by odd shots and bursts of fire. The writer Sándor Márai emerged to wander round Buda, and was shaken by the sights. 'Some streets must be guessed at,' he wrote in his diary. 'This was the corner house with the Flórián Café, this is the street where I once lived – no trace of the building – this pile of rubble at the corner of Statisztika Street and Margit Boulevard was a five-storey block with many flats and a café a few days ago.'

In the aftermath of the battle, Red Army soldiers shot German wounded – some were dragged out and crushed under tanks – also all members of the SS and any Hiwi auxiliaries, who were wrongly categorized as *vlasovtsy*. Anyone in German uniform who did not reply in German was also likely to be killed. Few Hungarian combatants were shot. Almost all the men, even Communists who had fought with the resistance against the Arrow Cross, were rounded up for forced labour. Prince Pál Esterházy was put to work burying dead horses in Pest.

The NKVD and SMERSh displayed full Stalinist paranoia, suspecting anyone with foreign contacts of being a spy, including Zionists. Raoul Wallenberg was arrested on 19 January along with the forensic pathologist Ferenc Orsós, who had been one of the international observers with the Germans when they dug up the Polish corpses in Katyń forest. It is assumed that Wallenberg had also seen the Katyń report, and that he was suspected of having close contacts with the British, American and other intelligence services. He was arrested by SMERSh, and executed in July 1947.

Looting took place on an epic scale, both individual and state sponsored. Art collections were seized, including the most prominent ones owned by Jews. Even neutral embassies were ransacked and their safes blasted open. Civilians in the street were stopped at gunpoint and relieved of their watches, wallets and documents.

Any surviving Jews were robbed just like gentiles. Some soldiers pulled their loot around with them in prams.

Although Soviet troops were more forgiving towards Hungarian soldiers than towards Germans, they showed no pity to Hungarian women when Malinovsky gave them a free run of the capital in celebration of the victory. 'In many places they are raping women,' a fifteen-year-old boy wrote in his diary. 'Women are being hidden everywhere.' Nurses in the improvised hospitals were raped and stabbed afterwards. Students at the university were among the first victims. According to some accounts, the most attractive women were held for up to two weeks and forced to act as prostitutes. Bishop József Grősz heard that '70 percent of women, from girls of twelve to mothers in the ninth month of pregnancy, [were] raped.' Other more reliable reports put the proportion at 10 per cent.

Hungarian Communists addressed an appeal to the Red Army, describing the 'rampant, demented hatred', which even their own comrades had suffered. 'Mothers were raped by drunken soldiers in front of their own children and husbands. Girls as young as 12 were dragged from their fathers and mothers to be violated by 10–15 soldiers and often infected with venereal diseases. After the first group, others came who followed their example . . . Several comrades lost their lives trying to protect their wives and daughters.' Even Mátyás Rákosi, the secretary-general of the Hungarian Communist Party, appealed to the Soviet authorities but without success. But not all Red Army soldiers were rapists. Some treated families, and especially children, with great kindness.

Almost every town suffered, even if not on the same scale as Budapest. In the 9th Guards Army, soldiers complained that their axis of advance offered 'no women and no booty', recorded a mortar officer, who described their men as 'incredibly brave guys, but also incredible scoundrels'. 'A solution was quickly found,' he wrote. 'In turns a quarter of the soldiers were sent to Mór where they seized houses and the women there who had failed to flee or hide. They were given one hour for that. And then the next group followed. They would use women from the ages of fourteen to fifty. They would carry out a complete pogrom in the houses, threw everything on the floor, broke it and crushed it, and looked for pocket or wrist watches. If they came across wine they of course would drink it. There had been many wine cellars in Mór, but when we entered the town they had all been emptied, the barrels smashed and the wine emptied on to the floor. It was there that we came across two soldiers who had drowned in wine.'

Feasting also took place at a more rarefied level. Field Marshal Alexander, who had flown to Belgrade for discussions with Tito, went on to Hungary to meet Marshal Tolbukhin, the commander of the 3rd Ukrainian Front. The large and elderly Tolbukhin received him with a lavish banquet, and had even provided a Red Army nurse to sleep in his room. Alexander, however, 'didn't think that was quite the thing, and she spent the night outside my door'. Just before dinner, when Alexander and Tolbukhin were alone, the old marshal examined Alexander's decorations. Among them, he spotted the Tsarist order of St Anne with crossed swords, awarded to Alexander when he had served as a liaison officer on the eastern front in the First World War. 'I have that too,' Tolbukhin sighed as he touched it, 'but I'm not allowed to wear it.'

Tolbukhin was remarkably relaxed, considering that the Sixth SS Panzer Army, transferred from the Ardennes, had just reached Hungary. It had arrived too late to help the defenders of Budapest, but Hitler still ordered it into action on 13 February 1945, in Operation Frühlingserwachen, or Spring Awakening. He had never intended to save the garrison, only to reinforce it and to defend the Hungarian oilfields near Lake Balaton. The counter-attack was a failure. When Hitler heard that Waffen-SS divisions had retreated without orders, he was so angry that he sent Himmler down to strip them of their divisional armband titles, even including the *Leibstandarte Adolf Hitler*. It was a humiliating punishment. 'This mission of his to Hungary', Guderian observed with schadenfreude, 'did not win him much affection from his Waffen-SS.'

Himmler had been one of those in the Führer's entourage who had dismissed Guderian's warnings of a massive Soviet offensive in Poland as 'an enormous bluff'. The chief of the general staff's prediction proved correct in the second week of January. Stalin pretended to the Allies that he had moved forward the date to help extricate the Americans from their problems in the Ardennes, but this was not true. The fighting there had turned decisively in the Allies' favour around Christmas. Stalin had more practical reasons. The Red Army needed the ground frozen hard for its tank formations, and Soviet meteorologists warned the Stavka that there would be 'heavy rain and wet snow' later in January. Stalin also had a more sinister reason for advancing the date. He wanted to be in complete control of Poland before the Allies met at Yalta at the beginning of February, just over three weeks later.

Along the Vistula ready to strike west were the 1st Belorussian Front now commanded by Marshal Zhukov, and the 1st Ukrainian Front commanded by Marshal Konev. Rokossovsky had been angered when he was replaced by Zhukov, but Stalin did not want Rokossovsky, a Pole, to have the glory of taking Berlin. Rokossovsky was given the 2nd Belorussian Front instead to attack East Prussia from the south while General Chernyakhovsky's 3rd Belorussian Front would invade from the eastern flank.

On 12 January Konev's massed artillery, with 300 guns per kilometre, opened a shattering bombardment. His 3rd and 4th Guards Tank Armies, with T-34s and heavy Stalin tanks, advanced out of the Sandomierz bridgehead west of the Oder, and headed for Kraków and Breslau on the Oder. Stalin had made clear to Konev that he wanted Silesia captured without heavy destruction to its industry and mines. On 13 January Chernyakhovsky launched his assault on East Prussia. Rokossovsky followed the next day, advancing from the bridgeheads north of the River Narew. Zhukov's attack also began on 14 January.

Once through the German front line, the main barrier ahead of Zhukov's forces was the River Pilica. Every commander knew that speed was essential to give the Germans no chance to recover. A colonel commanding a Guards tank brigade refused to wait for bridging equipment to come up. Guessing that the river was not deep at the spot, he simply ordered his tanks to smash the ice with gunfire and drive across the river bed, a truly terrifying experience for the drivers. On Zhukov's right, the 47th Army encircled the ruins of Warsaw while the 1st Polish Army entered the suburbs.

Hitler was beside himself with rage when the weak German garrison surrendered. He saw it as yet more evidence of treason within the general staff, and three officers were taken to Gestapo headquarters. Even Guderian had to submit to interrogations from Kaltenbrunner. Hitler returned to Berlin from

Führer headquarters at Ziegenberg to direct his armies, with predictably disastrous results. He would never allow a general to withdraw, and because of the speed of the Soviet advance and the collapse in German communications, any information on which he based his decisions was no longer accurate. By the time his orders reached the front, they were usually twenty-four hours out of date.

Hitler also interfered without informing Guderian. He decided to transfer the *Grossdeutschland* Corps from East Prussia to shore up the Vistula front, but the time it took to redeploy meant that this powerful formation was out of the battle for several vital days. To Guderian's frustration, Hitler still refused to bring out the divisions trapped on the Courland Peninsula to reinforce the Reich. The same applied to troops from the unnecessarily large German force in Norway. Worst of all, from Guderian's point of view, was Hitler's decision to transfer the Sixth SS Panzer Army to the Hungarian front.

Chernyakhovsky found that German defences on the Insterburg Line in East Prussia were much stronger than expected. So, in a clever move, he withdrew the 11th Guards Army, swung it round behind the other three armies, and sent it in on their northern flank which was less well defended. Combined with an attack by the 43rd Army across the River Niemen near Tilsit, this breakthrough caused panic in the German rear.

Rokossovsky's armies coming from the south aimed for the mouth of the Vistula to cut off East Prussia completely. On 20 January, the Stavka suddenly ordered Rokossovsky to attack towards the north-east as well, to help Chernyakhovsky. Less than two days later his 3rd Guards Cavalry Corps on the right flank entered the town of Allenstein and the following day the leading armoured troops of Colonel General Vasily Volsky's 5th Guards Tank Army bypassed Elbing and reached the shore of the Frisches Haff, the long frozen lagoon separated by a sandbar from the Baltic. East Prussia was almost completely cut off. Just to the west of the Vistula estuary lay the concentration camp of Stutthof. Camp guards, terrified by the approach of the Red Army, killed 3,000 Jewish women either by shooting or by forcing them out on to the thin ice so that they would fall through into the freezing water.

Erich Koch, the Gauleiter of East Prussia, still refused to allow the evacuation of civilians. They had heard the artillery barrages in the distance when the Soviet offensive began, but requests to leave were denied by local Nazi Party bosses. In most cases these officials slipped away, abandoning the population to its fate. Retreating German soldiers would warn farms and villages, urging everyone to get out as fast as they could. Some, especially the very old who could not face leaving their homes, decided to stay. Since almost all men had been dragooned into the Volkssturm, mothers had to harness farm-carts, perhaps aided by a French prisoner of war who had been working for them, and load it with blankets and food for themselves and their children. The 'treks' as they were called had begun across the snow-covered countryside, in temperatures as low as minus 20 degrees Centigrade.

Refugees from the capital of Königsberg thought that they had escaped safely by train, but when they reached Allenstein they were pulled from the carriages by soldiers from the 3rd Guards Cavalry, delighted to find such a source of plunder and women. Most of those attempting to flee by road were overtaken by Soviet troops. Some were simply crushed in their carts under the tracks of Soviet tanks. Others suffered an even worse fate.

Leonid Rabichev, a signals lieutenant with the 31st Army, described the scenes beyond Goldap. 'All the roads were filled with old people, women and children, large families moving slowly on carts, on vehicles or on foot towards the west. Our tank troops, infantry, artillery, signals caught up with them and cleared the way for themselves by pushing their horses and carts and belongings into the ditches on either side of the road. Then thousands of them forced the old women and children aside. Forgetting their honour and duty and forgetting about the retreating German units, they pounced on the women and girls.

'Women, mothers and their daughters, lie to the right and the left of the highway and in front of each one stands a laughing gang of men with their trousers down. Those already covered in blood and losing consciousness are dragged to the side. Children trying to help them have been shot. There is laughter and roaring and jeering, screams and moans. And the soldiers' commanders – majors and lieutenant colonels – are standing there on the highway. Some are laughing, but some are also conducting the event so that all their soldiers without exception could take part. This is not an initiation rite, and it has nothing to do with revenge against the accursed occupiers, this is just hellish diabolical group sex. This represents a complete lack of control and the brutal logic of a crowd gone mad. I was sitting in the cabin of our one-and-a-half-ton truck, shaken, while my driver Demidov was standing in one of the queues. I was thinking of Flaubert's Carthage. The colonel, who had only just been conducting proceedings, could not resist the temptation and joined one of the queues, while the major was shooting the witnesses, the children and old men who were having hysterics.'

At last the soldiers were told to finish quickly and get back on their vehicles, because another unit was blocked behind them. Later, when they overtook another refugee column, Rabichev saw similar scenes repeated. 'As far as the eye can see, there are corpses of women, old people and children, among piles of clothing and overturned carts . . . It becomes dark. We are ordered to find a place to spend the night in one of the German villages off the highway. I took my platoon to a hamlet two kilometres from the highway. In all the rooms are corpses of children, old people and women who have been raped and shot. We are so tired that we don't pay attention to them. We are so tired that we lie down among the corpses and fall asleep.'

'Russian soldiers were raping every German female from eight to eighty,' observed the Soviet war correspondent Natalya Gesse, a close friend of Sakharov. 'It was an army of rapists. Not only because they were crazed with lust, this was also a form of vengeance.'

It is far too sweeping to ascribe this pitiless behaviour simply to lust or vengeance. For a start, there were many officers and soldiers who did not take part in the rapes and were horrified by the actions of their comrades. Devoted Communists were shocked by the disorder, and the controlled nature of Soviet society made such indiscipline hard to imagine. But the extreme harshness of life at the front had created a different community, and many became surprisingly outspoken in their hatred of the collective farms and the oppression which had dominated their lives. Soldiers bitterly resented the pointless sacrifice caused by so many futile attacks as well as the demeaning treatment which they had to endure. Men were sent into no-man's-land to strip the uniforms and even underwear from dead comrades to clothe new conscripts. So, although a strong desire for revenge existed against the Germans who had violated the Motherland and killed their families, there was also a strong element of the same knock-on theory of oppression which had conditioned Japanese troops. The temptation to work off past humiliations and suffering which they had endured was overwhelming, and now it was worked off on the vulnerable women of their enemies.

Under Stalin, ideas of love and sexuality had been ruthlessly repressed in a political environment which sought to 'de-individualize the individual'. Sex education had been banned. The Soviet state's attempt to suppress the libido of its people created what one Russian writer described as a sort of 'barracks eroticism', which was far more primitive and violent than 'the most sordid foreign pornography'. And this, combined with the utterly brutalizing effect of the slaughter on the eastern front and the propaganda of indiscriminate vengeance fostered in articles and harangues by political officers, produced an explosive potential when Soviet forces invaded East Prussia.

None were more brutalized than the *shtrafniki*, the living dead of the punishment battalions. Many were hardened criminals transferred from the Gulag. (On Beria's order, those condemned for political offences were never allowed to fight.) Even their officers were influenced by the sheer ruthlessness of their lives. 'A criminal is always a criminal, in the rear or at the front,' wrote a medical officer with a *shtraf* company. 'At the front, in the role of a *shtrafnik*, their criminal nature always manifested itself. So our company was having fun. A young German woman ran up to me in Halsberg and shouted in German: "I've been raped by fourteen men!" and I walked on thinking, it's a pity that it was fourteen and not twenty-eight; it's a pity they haven't shot you German bitch . . . We, the officers in the *shtraf* company, shut our eyes to everything, we felt no pity for the Germans and we let the *shtrafniki* do whatever they wanted to the civilians.'

Looting was combined with mindless destruction. Soldiers would burn down houses and then find that they had nowhere to shelter from the cold. Rabichev described the looting of Goldap. 'The entire contents of shops were thrown out on to the sidewalks through the broken shopfronts. Thousands of pairs of shoes, plates and radio sets, all sorts of household and pharmacy goods and food were all mixed up. From apartment windows, clothes, pillows, duvets, paintings, gramophones and musical instruments were hurled on to the street. The roadways were blocked with all this stuff. Right at this moment, German artillery and mortars opened fire. Several spare German divisions hurled our demoralized troops out of the city in no time. But Front headquarters had already reported that the first German town had been captured. There was no choice. They had to recapture the place again.'

Aleksandr Solzhenitsyn, a young artillery officer in East Prussia, described scenes of looting as a 'tumultuous market', with soldiers trying on Prussian women's outsize drawers. 'Germans abandoned everything,' a Red Army soldier wrote about the sack of Gumbinnen. 'And our people, like a huge crowd of Huns, invaded the houses. Everything is on fire, down from pillows and feather-beds is flying about. Everyone starting with a soldier and ending with a colonel is pulling away loot. Beautifully furnished apartments, luxurious houses were smashed within a few hours and turned into dumps where torn curtains are covered in jam that is pouring from broken jars . . . this town has been crucified.' Three days later he wrote: 'Soldiers have turned into avid beasts. In the fields lie hundreds of shot cattle, on the roads pigs and chickens with their heads chopped off. Houses have been looted and are on fire. What cannot be taken away is being broken and destroyed. The Germans are right to be running away from us like from a plague.'

In the hunting lodge at Rominten, which had belonged to the Prussian royal family and then been taken over by Göring, Soviet infantry had smashed all the mirrors. With black paint, one of them had scrawled 'khuy', the Russian for 'prick', across a nude of Aphrodite by Rubens.

Most of the incoherent anger came from encountering a standard of living, even in farmworkers' houses, which was unimaginable in the Soviet Union. The bitter thought was almost universal: So why did they invade us and loot our country if they were so much richer? Field censorship, alarmed by the letters home which described what soldiers had discovered, passed them to the NKVD. The Soviet authorities became nervous about the widespread perception that all the propaganda about their 'workers' paradise' as opposed to the terrible conditions in capitalist countries was a lie. They were all too conscious of the way that the Decembrist revolt of 1825 had been influenced by the better way of life which Russian armies had seen in western Europe in 1814.

Zhukov's 1st Belorussian Front continued its headlong pursuit, day and night. Tank drivers frequently fell asleep from sheer exhaustion, but the exhilaration of pursuit kept them going. Retreating German troops were machine-gunned, and if they caught up with a staff car with German officers inside they simply flattened it under their tracks.

On 18 January, General Chuikov's 8th Guards Army attacked Łódź five days ahead of schedule. Members of the Home Army emerged to help in the fighting. Chuikov was not pleased when he had to take part of his Stalingrad army to tackle the fortress city of Poznań. Their street-fighting skills counted for little there. It took a month of bombardment with their heaviest artillery and assaults with satchel charges and flamethrowers before the survivors surrendered.

On the southern flank of the advance from the Vistula, Konev's troops overran Kraków. Fortunately the ancient city was abandoned without a fight. On 27 January in the middle of the afternoon, a reconnaissance patrol from the 107th Rifle Division emerged from a snowbound forest to discover the most terrible symbol in modern history.

Just over a week before, 58,000 inmates deemed capable of walking were forced westwards from Auschwitz in front of the Red Army advance. Those who were to survive this death march, an experience which was probably worse than all the horrors they had suffered so far, found themselves dumped in other concentration camps, where squalor, starvation and disease increased dramatically in the last three months of the war. Dr Mengele seized all the notes from his experiments and left for Berlin. IG Farben executives destroyed their records at Auschwitz III. The gas chambers and crematoria at Birkenau were blown up. Orders were given to liquidate the prisoners too ill to move, but for some reason the SS killed only a couple of hundred out of the 8,000 left behind. They concentrated more on attempts to destroy the evidence, but there was more than enough left, including 368,820 men's suits, 836,255 women's coats and dresses, to say nothing of seven tons of human hair.

The 60th Army immediately ordered all its medical staff to Auschwitz to care for the survivors, and Soviet officers began to question some of the inmates. Adam Kuriłowicz, the former chairman of the Polish railway workers' union, who had been sent to the camp in June 1941, recounted how the first tests of the gas chamber had been carried out on eighty Red Army soldiers and 600 Polish prisoners. A Hungarian professor told them about the 'medical experiments'. All the information was sent back to G. F. Aleksandrov, the chief of Red Army propaganda, but, apart from a small article in a Red Army newspaper, nothing was said to a wider world until the very end of the war. This was probably because the Party line insisted that the Jews did not represent a special category. Only the suffering of the Soviet people should be emphasized.

The treks increased from Silesia as well as East Prussia, and soon started in Pomerania. Nazi officials estimated that by 29 January 'around four million people from the evacuated areas' were heading for the centre of the Reich. This figure appears to have been too low, since it rose to seven million within a fortnight and to 8.35 million by 19 February. The Red Army's rampage had produced the most concentrated shift of population in history. This ethnic cleansing suited Stalin perfectly, with his plans to shift the Polish border westwards to the Oder.

Several hundred thousand civilians still remained trapped in Königsberg and on the Samland Peninsula, as well as within the encirclement of the Fourth Army at Heiligenbeil on the shore of the Frisches Haff. The Kriegsmarine made strenuous attempts to rescue as many as it could from the small port of Pillau, and evacuations began from harbours in eastern Pomerania. Soviet submarines, however, torpedoed many large ships, including the liner *Wilhelm Gustloff* which sank on the night of 30 January. Nobody knows how many were on board, but estimates of the number who died range from 5,300 to 7,400 people.

Despite the risks by sea, exhausted and hungry women with

children in their arms waited for the boats, often in vain. Rations were so short in Königsberg, less than 180 grams of bread a day, that many walked out through the snow to throw themselves on the mercy of the Red Army, but they received little pity. In the city, the execution of deserters became frenzied. The bodies of eighty German soldiers were displayed at the northern station with a placard which read: 'They were cowards, but died just the same.'

The rapidity of the advance to the Oder had bypassed thousands of German troops, who tried to make their way westwards individually or in groups. The NKVD rifle divisions in charge of rear-area security found themselves fighting pitched battles. As Konev's forces advanced on Breslau a panic-stricken flight by civilians began, with crowds storming trains while others trudged off through thick snow. Many if not most of those on foot died of cold. Some made it to safety still clinging to the frozen corpse of a baby or child. The siege of Breslau, which continued until the end of the war, was organized by the fanatical Gauleiter Karl Hanke, who ruled by terror, executing soldiers and forcing civilians including children to clear a runway under heavy Soviet fire.

Zhukov's armies had smashed through the Warthegau, the western part of Poland incorporated into the Reich. Fleeing Germans were robbed by Poles determined to avenge their own fate in 1939 and 1940. The speed of advance of the 1st and 2nd Guards Tank Armies towards the Oder was protected on their right flank by another four armies spread out across southern Pomerania. Their greatest problem was not German resistance but the difficulties of their supply services, desperately trying to keep up with them on bad winter roads and without any rail line functioning. Had it not been for the American trucks provided under Lend–Lease, the Red Army would never have made it to Berlin before the Americans.

'Our tanks have ironed, flattened out everything,' wrote one soldier. 'Their tracks crushed carts, vehicles, horses and anything else that was on the road. The slogan "Forwards, toward the West!" has been replaced by the slogan "Forwards, to Berlin!"' The town of Schwerin was sacked on the way. 'Everything is on fire,' Vasily Grossman wrote in his notebook. 'An old woman jumps from a window in a burning building.' The fires lit the whole scene as soldiers looted. He also noted the 'horror in the eyes of women and girls. Terrible things are happening to German women . . . Soviet girls who have been liberated from camps are suffering greatly too.'

A very detailed report from the 1st Ukrainian Front subsequently revealed that young women and girls taken from the Soviet Union for forced labour were also suffering from gangrape. Having longed for liberation, they were shattered to find themselves so abused by men they had thought of as comrades and brothers. 'All this', concluded General Tsygankov, 'provides fertile ground for unhealthy, negative moods to grow among liberated Soviet citizens; it causes discontent and mistrust before their return to their mother country.' But his recommendations did not mention tightening Red Army discipline. He advised instead that the political department and the Komsomol should concentrate on 'improving political and cultural work with repatriated Soviet citizens' to prevent them returning home with negative ideas about the Red Army.

There were also rare moments of pure joy. Vasily Churkin, who had advanced all the way from Leningrad and those terrible days on the ice of Lake Ladoga, was with Zhukov's 1st Belorussian Front. 'We drove closer to Berlin,' he wrote in his diary at the end of January, 'only 135 kilometres remain. The German resistance is weak. There are only our aircraft in the sky. We passed a concentration camp. The barracks where our women had been imprisoned are fenced off with several rows of barbed wire. A huge crowd of women prisoners burst free through the huge gate. They were running towards us crying and shouting. They were unable to believe that this was happening, they had known nothing until the last minute. The sight was striking. But what touched me the most was a soldier finding his own sister. How she ran to him when she recognized him. How they were hugging each other and crying in front of everybody. This was like a fairy tale.'

On 30 January, the twelfth anniversary of Nazi rule, and the day of Hitler's last broadcast to the German people, panic spread in Berlin. Zhukov's tank spearheads approached the River Oder, just over sixty kilometres from Berlin. That night, the 89th Guards Rifle Division seized a small bridgehead across the frozen river just north of Küstrin. Early the following morning, troops from the 5th Shock Army also crossed over and captured the village of Kienitz. A third bridgehead was formed south of Küstrin. The dismay in Berlin was even greater, because the propaganda ministry had tried to pretend that the fighting was still around Warsaw. Nazi prestige remained far more important to the regime than any human suffering, even that of its own people. In that one month of January 1945, Wehrmacht losses rose to 451,742 killed, roughly the equivalent of all American deaths in the whole of the Second World War.

Scratch units were formed from local Volkssturm detachments, some Caucasian volunteers (who were later arrested when they refused to fire at their own countrymen), Hitler Youth and a training battalion of teenagers destined for the Panzergrenadier Division *Feldherrnhalle* trapped in Budapest. The guard regiment of the *Grossdeutschland* Division, which had crushed the July plot the year before, was sent to the Seelow Heights in buses. This escarpment, which overlooked the flood plain of the Oder, would become the last line of defence before Berlin.

On the morning of 3 February, the US Eighth Air Force launched its heaviest raid on Berlin, killing 3,000 people. The Reichschancellery and Bormann's Party Chancellery were hit. Gestapo headquarters in the Prinz-Albrecht-Strasse and the People's Court were badly damaged. Roland Freisler, the Court's president who had screamed abuse at the July plotters, was crushed to death in its cellars.

Zhukov, meanwhile, faced the classic quandary of any successful general after a rapid advance. Should the Red Army attempt to push on to Berlin, when the enemy was in turmoil and had no defences, or should it consolidate, to allow its exhausted men to rest, resupply and service their tanks? The debate among his generals was lively, with Chuikov of the 8th Guards Army arguing fiercely that they should attack immediately. The issue was settled on 6 February by Stalin in a telephone call from Yalta in the Crimea. Before attacking Berlin, they must first join with Rokossovsky to clear 'the Baltic balcony' of Pomerania on their northern flank, where Himmler, to the despair of Guderian and other senior officers, had taken personal command of Army Group Vistula.

45

Philippines, Iwo Jima, Okinawa, Tokyo Raids

NOVEMBER 1944–JUNE 1945

Soon after General MacArthur landed so triumphantly on Leyte in October 1944, his Sixth Army faced a much harder fight than he had expected. The Japanese reinforced the island, and rapidly established air superiority. Admiral Halsey's carriers had departed and the ground was too sodden to construct airfields, after thirty-five inches of rain had fallen in the monsoon. Although the Japanese had intended to reserve their strength for the defence of Luzon, the main island of the Philippines, Imperial General Headquarters insisted that more reinforcements should be sent to the fighting on Leyte. Aircraft were also transferred from as far afield as Manchuria, but by then five American airstrips were in action and Halsey's fleet carriers had returned.

Fighting on Leyte continued well into December, partly due to excessive caution displayed by Lieutenant General Walter Krueger, who commanded the Sixth Army. The fiercest fighting was for 'Breakneck Ridge' near Carigara in the north of the island, furiously defended by Japanese troops. Krueger was, however, helped by a disastrous Japanese counter-attack against the airstrips. But by the end of December the Americans estimated that they had killed 60,000 Japanese. Ten thousand Japanese reinforcements drowned when their transports were sunk approaching the island. Some 3,500 Americans were killed and 12,000 wounded. MacArthur, never prone to modesty, proclaimed it 'perhaps the greatest defeat in the military annals of the Japanese Army'.

The insistence of Imperial General Headquarters on continuing to reinforce Leyte with troops from Luzon made the invasion of the main island, now planned for 9 January 1945, considerably easier. But first the island of Mindoro, just to the south of the main bulk of Luzon, had to be taken to create more airfields. The landings and ground operation went well, but the invasion task force suffered heavily from kamikaze attacks.

General Yamashita, the commander on Luzon who had objected in vain to the strategy of defending Leyte in strength, knew that he could not hope to defeat the forces heading in his direction. He would withdraw with 152,000 men, the bulk of his troops, to the hills of northern central Luzon. A smaller force of 30,000 would defend the air bases round Clark Field, while another 80,000 strong in the hills above Manila would be able to deprive the capital of its supplies of water.

MacArthur intended to invade the island from the Lingayan Gulf in the north-west, with a subsidiary landing to the south of the capital. This roughly followed the Japanese invasion plan of three years before. His escorting fleet during the first week of January suffered waves of kamikaze attacks, emerging low over the island. An escort carrier and a fleet destroyer were sunk while another carrier was severely damaged, as well as five cruisers, the battleships USS *California* and *New Mexico* and numerous other vessels. Many attackers were shot down by anti-aircraft fire and escort fighters, but it was impossible to deal with them all. The landing ships were let off lightly, and the invasion itself on 9 January was virtually unopposed. Filipino guerrillas had informed the American command that there were no Japanese in the area so there was no need to pummel the sector first, but Rear Admiral Jesse B. Oldendorf felt obliged to stick to his orders. Great destruction was wreaked on homes and farms causing no damage to the enemy.

While I Corps on the left soon encountered strong Japanese resistance in the hills, XIV Corps on the right pushed south over flatter country towards Manila. General Krueger suspected that MacArthur's pressure on him to advance rapidly was influenced by a desire to be back in Manila by his birthday, on 26 January. This was probably unfair. MacArthur wanted to liberate Allied prisoners held in camps and if possible seize the port of Manila before the Japanese destroyed it. A detachment of US Rangers, greatly aided by Filipino guerrillas, managed to free 486 American prisoners of war from the Bataan death march in a successful raid on a camp near Cabantuan ninety-five kilometres north of Manila. MacArthur's impatience mounted because of the slow progress, caused more by the small rivers, rice paddies and fish ponds than by Japanese resistance. MacArthur stepped in to send the 1st Cavalry Division on ahead. He wanted to rescue other Allied prisoners held in the University of Santo Tomás.

Another landing, with 40,000 men from XII Corps, took place on 29 January north of the Bataan Peninsula, but they soon came up against a very strong Japanese defence line. The other landing south of Manila by the 11th Airborne Division appeared to produce more rapid results than the advance down the plain. On 4 February they reached the Japanese defence line just south of Manila, although they did not yet know that they had been beaten to the capital the night before. A dramatic dash forward by a flying column from the 1st Cavalry on the north side, storming across a bridge after a naval lieutenant cut the burning fuse to the demolition charges, had brought them into the northern section of Manila. That evening their tanks smashed through the perimeter walls of the Santo Tomás University where 4,000 Allied civilians were interned.

The Philippines, an archipelago with some 7,000 islands, had offered ideal terrain for guerrilla resistance and the Filipinos, more than any other nation in the Far East, had begun to prepare for their liberation soon after the Japanese occupation began. Partly out of trust in the Americans, who had promised them full independence in 1946, and hatred for the arrogant and cruel Japanese, with their torture and public beheadings, guerrilla groups had formed on most of the islands. A few were led by American officers who had been cut off there in 1942. Many of the Filipino troops had hidden their arms at the time of the surrender. Once MacArthur's headquarters in Brisbane had confirmation of the size of the movement, submarines brought in more weapons, radios and medical supplies, as well as the MacArthur propaganda items.

In the large areas where Japanese troops seldom ventured, the local groups organized civic life and workshops and even issued their own currency, which was preferred to the Japanese occupation banknotes. Coast-watchers with radios passed information on Japanese shipping, which US submarines were able to use with devastating results. The main danger came from Japanese radio detection units. There was little risk of denunciation by the local population, who helped carry the bulky equipment if a Japanese army sweep approached. The Philippines produced remarkably few collaborators. Most of those in Manila, who worked for the Japanese administration, provided as much intelligence as they could to the resistance.

Japanese revenge was conspicuous after MacArthur's forces landed, especially in the fighting for the capital. Yamashita had not intended to defend Manila, and the local army commander had planned to withdraw according to his orders, but he had no control over the navy. Disregarding Yamashita, Rear Admiral Iwabachi Sanji told his men to fight on in the city. The remaining army units felt obliged to join them, making a force of some 19,000 men. As these troops withdrew to the centre, the old Spanish citadel of Intramuros and the port area, they destroyed bridges and buildings. Raging fires spread across the poorer areas, where the houses were made of wood and bamboo. In the centre, however, most of the buildings were concrete and could be turned into defensive positions.

MacArthur, who wanted to organize a victory parade, was dismayed by the battle which then developed in the city with more than 700,000 civilians trapped in the war zone. The 1st Cavalry, the 37th Infantry and the 11th Airborne Division became involved in house-to-house fighting. As with the attack on Aachen, the Americans soon recognized the need to attack each building from above and fight their way down, using grenades, submachine guns and flamethrowers. American engineers used their armoured bulldozers to clear roadblocks. The Japanese naval and army defenders, knowing that they were all going to die, massacred Filipinos and raped the women mercilessly before killing them. Despite MacArthur's refusal to use aircraft in an attempt to spare civilian lives, around 100,000 Manila citizens, more than one in eight of the population, died in the fighting which lasted until 3 March.

The most urgent priority for General Krueger's troops was to eliminate the Japanese force east of Manila, which controlled the city's water supplies. Once again the Japanese had constructed caves and tunnels in the hillsides and once again the Americans had to clear them out with phosphorus grenades and flamethrowers. They blew the entrances to the tunnels, then poured gasoline and explosives in the main opening to burn, suffocate or bury those left inside. P-38 Lightnings dropped napalm, which proved much more effective than conventional bombs. The process was greatly aided by a regiment of guerrillas who reached the main dam first in a sudden rush. The Japanese had no time to blow their demolition charges. The survivors slipped away into the hills at the end of May.

Even while the fighting continued in Manila, MacArthur launched a drive with Lieutenant General Eichelberger's Eighth Army to retake the central and southern islands of the Philippines, secure in the knowledge that the Japanese could not reinforce them. He regarded this as more urgent than finishing off Yamashita's main force in the hills of northern Luzon, since they could be bottled up and bombarded at leisure. One amphibious attack followed another, all supported by air power. Eichelberger claimed to have conducted fourteen major landings and twenty-four minor ones in just forty-four days. In many cases his troops found that Filipino guerrillas had done their work for them, dealing with the smaller garrisons.

On 28 February, the long western island of Palawan stretching between Mindoro and North Borneo was invaded. These forces discovered the charred bodies of 150 American prisoners of war, who had been doused in gasoline and set on fire by their guards in December. On 10 March they invaded Mindanao, where an American engineer, Colonel Wendell W. Fertig, led a large guerrilla force and secured a landing strip. C-47 transports touched down before the attack, bringing two companies of the 24th Infantry Division. Marine Corsair fighters then arrived to use it as a forward base. On Mindanao, the close cooperation between American infantry, guerrillas and Marine air support forced the Japanese survivors on its western Zamboanga Peninsula to take to the hills. But the operation to reduce the main eastern mass did not start until 17 April.

Once again, Fertig's guerrilla forces managed to secure an airfield and American troops advanced inland, some by a bad road, while a regiment embarked on boats and barges and escorted by sub-chasers sailed up the broad Mindanao river, taking Japanese garrisons by surprise. They knew that they were in a race against the monsoon. Slowed by the jungle and gorges, where the Japanese had destroyed almost every bridge and mined every approach, the fighting took far longer than expected. It did not end until 10 June, a month after the end of the war in Europe. General Yamashita in the northern cordilleras of Luzon resisted, prolonging the fighting to the very end. He emerged to give himself up only on 2 September 1945, the day of the official surrender.

In China, the Ichi-gō Offensive had finished in December 1944. Japanese forces had probed towards Chungking and K'un-ming, but their supply lines were vastly over-extended. Stilwell's successor, General Wedemeyer, flew in the two American-trained divisions of X-Force from northern Burma to form a defence line, but the Japanese had already begun to withdraw. The two divisions returned to Burma, and at the end of January finally joined up with Y-Force on the Salween. The remaining Japanese troops retreated into the mountains and the Burma Road was finally open again. The first convoy of trucks reached K'un-ming on 4 February.

Slim's advance meanwhile came to a temporary halt along the River Irrawaddy, after Lieutenant General Kimura Hoyotaro pulled the remnants of the Burma Area Army behind this formidable defensive barrier. Slim made a great show of mounting a major crossing with the XXXIII Corps, having secretly withdrawn his IV Corps on its flank. A dummy headquarters remained behind transmitting messages, while its divisions marched south under radio silence, then crossed the river much further down unopposed to threaten Kimura's rear. The Japanese had to withdraw rapidly, and Mandalay was captured on 20 March after a hard battle.

Slim wasted no time in pushing south along the Irrawaddy Valley towards Rangoon, in a race to reach it before the rains came. Mountbatten, meanwhile, organized Operation Dracula, an amphibious and airborne assault for early May using the British XV Corps from the Arakan. The monsoon arrived two weeks early, stopping Slim's forces sixty-five kilometres short of their objective. On 3 May, Rangoon was taken by XV Corps assisted by the Burmese Independent Army, which had changed sides to join the Allies. Kimura's forces had no alternative but to retreat into Thailand. The remnants of the Japanese 28th Army, now cut off behind Allied lines in the Arakan, attempted to break out to the east across the River Sittang. But the British knew of their plans. When the Japanese reached the river, they were ambushed and massacred by the 17th Indian Division. Only 6,000 men out of 17,000 escaped.

As far as the Japanese command was concerned, the Ichi-gō Offensive had achieved its objectives. Japanese troops had inflicted half a million casualties on the Nationalist armies and forced them to withdraw from eight provinces, with a combined population of more than 100 million people. Yet it also represented a triumph for the Communists. The Nationalists had lost not only more food-producing areas, but also a large part of their manpower reserve for conscription. However much they hated the Japanese, this must have come as a relief to the local inhabitants. As General Wedemeyer observed: 'Conscription comes to the Chinese peasant like famine and flood, only more regularly.'

After the Ichi-gō Offensive had destroyed the thirteen US airfields, two new American air bases were built at Lao-ho-k'ou (300 kilometres north-west of Hankow) and Chih-kiang (250 kilometres west of Heng-yang). In April 1945, the Japanese advanced with 60,000 men from the Twelfth Army and destroyed the airfield at Lao-ho-k'ou, but an attack by their Twentieth Army on the base at Chih-kiang was less successful. Five well-equipped Nationalist Chinese divisions, part of the modernization plan by General Wedemeyer, with another fifteen partly modernized formations, were diverted to defend Chih-kiang. On 25 April, supported by 200 aircraft, they smashed the 50,000-strong Japanese force in the last major engagement of the Sino-Japanese War. It demonstrated that with proper training and equipment, and above all food, the Nationalist divisions could take on the Japanese effectively.

Japanese forces in China and Manchuria had already been gradually reduced by transfers to the Philippines. Then Imperial General Headquarters felt obliged to divert troops from the China Expeditionary Army to defend Okinawa. The 62nd Division, which took part in the Ichi-gō Offensive, had already been transferred there to defend the city of Shuri.

Japan's other priority of joining up with its forces in Indochina had also been achieved. In January 1945, when their divisions from China crossed the border, Japanese senior officers in Indochina had been shocked by their condition. The men of the 37th Division had long hair and beards, their uniforms were in tatters and few retained any badges of rank. They were incorporated into the newly constituted 38th Army to fight in northern Tonkin against the guerrillas of Ho Chi Minh. Ho Chi Minh's men had greatly assisted the Allies with intelligence and the return of downed aircrew, as had Thai groups provided with radios and weapons parachuted in from India by SOE and the OSS.

On 12 January, Halsey's Third Fleet reached Indochinese waters to strike at two Japanese battleship-carriers, the *Hyuga* and the *Ise*, in Camranh Bay. This roving sortie in the South China Sea was Halsey's swansong before he handed over command to Admiral Spruance. The two Japanese warships had in fact left for Singapore after American submarines had sunk their tankers, but aircraft from Halsey's thirteen fleet carriers sank a light cruiser, eleven small warships, thirteen cargo ships and ten tankers, as well as the French cruiser *Lamotte-Picquet*, which had been disarmed by the Japanese. While they were in the area, the navy flyers shot up airfields round Saigon, destroying Japanese aircraft on the ground and fuel dumps.

On 9 March, the Japanese swept aside the Vichy administration of Admiral Decoux and disarmed French forces, some of whom resisted, especially in the north. Gaullist agents as well as the OSS had been working on French officers, who were already keen to change sides. Japanese forces proceeded to launch the Meigō Offensive against French colonial troops holding strongpoints, such as Liangshan fort with a garrison of 7,000 men.

The Japanese commanders in Indochina intended to send the half-million tons of stockpiled rice back to Japan and to other Japanese garrisons, but the American blockade and the shortage of shipping made this impossible. While a part of the stockpile rotted, the rest was seized in November 1945 by Chinese Nationalist troops, who had been sent to disarm Japanese forces, and they took it back to China. For many Indochinese, their experience of famine during this period was even worse than both the war of independence against the French and the Vietnam War.

*

The first information for bombing targets in Japan was provided by Thai diplomats based in Tokyo who passed it on through the Thai resistance to the OSS. By December 1944, the air bases on Guam, Tinian and Saipan were in operation. Using the great advantages which the Mariana Islands offered over the China airfields, all B-29 Superfortress operations were gradually concentrated there under the command of Major General Curtis E. LeMay. Yet bomber losses mounted, partly from fighters rising to intercept them from intervening islands, especially Iwo Jima. Imperial Japanese Navy fighter pilots at dispersal on Kyushu played bridge as they waited to be scrambled to attack Superfortresses high overhead on their way to Tokyo. Their passion for the game was a bizarre legacy from the days when the Imperial Japanese Navy wanted to ape the Royal Navy.

The American command decided to invade Iwo Jima with its airfield from which Japanese fighters operated against the bombers and the bases on the Marianas. Once seized, it could provide an emergency landing strip for stricken aircraft.

On 9 March, the same day as the Japanese removed the French administration in Indochina, LeMay's Twenty-First Bomber Command launched its first major incendiary attack on Tokyo. Just over a month before, the B-29s had made their second experiment using napalm bombs. The factory district in Kobe had been virtually burned to the ground. LeMay had been aware of the destructive potential of incendiary attacks since the devastating B-29 raid on Hankow at the beginning of the winter.

The 334 Superfortresses carpet-bombed Tokyo, sparing neither residential nor industrial zones. More than a quarter of a million buildings went up in flames spread by strong winds. Houses made of wood and paper caught fire in seconds. Altogether 83,000 people died and another 41,000 were severely injured, a far greater toll than when the second atom bomb was dropped on Nagasaki five months later.

General MacArthur opposed the area bombing of Tokyo, but American hearts had been hardened by the kamikaze campaign against US ships. LeMay, however, did not answer to MacArthur, and his only concession was to drop leaflets warning Japanese civilians to leave all towns and cities with any industry. LeMay was determined to carry on until all the major manufacturing centres of Japan were burned out. Bizarrely, the USAAF still tried to claim that these area incendiary attacks by night constituted 'precision' bombing. Coastal shipping between the home islands was also brought to a virtual halt by the dropping of mines in and around the Inland Sea.

Bomber crews in the early part of the campaign had been shaken by their losses. They started to calculate their odds on surviving a thirty-five-mission tour. One came up with the personal mantra: 'Stay Alive in '45'. But the destruction of aircraft factories and the losses of Japanese fighters, most of which had been diverted to kamikaze attacks against the US Navy, soon meant that they could roam over Japanese air space with comparatively little danger.

Iwo Jima, although only seven kilometres long, was revealed by air reconnaissance to be a tough objective. LeMay needed to reassure Admiral Spruance that it was absolutely necessary to take it for his bomber offensive against Japan. The large island of Okinawa would be invaded six weeks later.

The Japanese defenders on Iwo Jima were commanded by Lieutenant General Kuribayashi Tadamichi, a sophisticated and intelligent cavalryman. He had no illusions about the final outcome of the battle, but he had prepared his positions to prolong it for as long as possible. Once again this meant constructing cave and tunnel networks as well as bunkers which were made out of a concrete which mixed cement with volcanic shingle. Despite the small size of the island, the tunnels stretched for twenty-five kilometres. Once the small civilian population on the island had been evacuated, reinforcements arrived bringing his strength to 21,000 soldiers and marines. His men swore to kill at least ten Americans before being killed themselves.

The US air force bombed Iwo Jima from the Marianas for seventy-six days. Then, at dawn on 16 February, the Japanese saw from their bunkers and caves that the invasion fleet had arrived during the night. The naval task force of eight battleships, twelve escort carriers, nineteen cruisers and forty-four destroyers anchored offshore began to bombard the island, map square by map square. But instead of the ten days which Marine commanders had requested, Admiral Spruance reduced the softening-up operation to three days. Considering the tonnage of bombs and shells hurled at the island, damage to the defences was minimal. The only exception was when Japanese batteries opened up prematurely at some rocket-launching landing craft, which their commander assumed to be the first wave of the invasion. As soon as they revealed their positions, the battleships' heavy guns traversed on to them. But when the amphibious assault began on 19 February, most of Kuribayashi's artillery was still untouched.

The 4th and 5th Marine Divisions landed in the first wave on the south-eastern shore, and were followed by the 3rd Marine Division. The beaches of soft volcanic sand were so steep that the heavily laden marines in their camouflage helmets struggled up them with difficulty. Japanese gunfire intensified, with huge mortars of 320mm dropping their bombs on the landing area. Wounded men brought back to the beach were often killed before they could be evacuated to one of the ships. Bodies were mangled and blown apart in the most terrible way.

Part of the 5th Division swung left to attack the dormant volcano of Mount Suribachi at the southern tip. An officer had a flag ready to hoist it on the summit. The right-hand regiment of the 4th Division moved right to deal with a strongly fortified quarry. It was helped by Sherman tanks which had managed to make it up the steep sand shelving, but the pitiless fighting still lasted most of the day. One battalion 700 strong was left with no more than 150 men still able to stand.

By nightfall 30,000 marines had landed, despite the relentless shell and mortar fire. They dug in ready to fight off a counterattack, but even that was not easy in the soft volcanic ash. One marine, no doubt from a farming community, compared it to digging a hole in a barrel of wheat. But no counter-attack came. Kuribayashi had forbidden them, and especially *banzai* charges in the open. They would kill more Americans from their defensive positions.

The bombardment had at least knocked out most of the guns at the base of Mount Suribachi, but other positions were untouched, as the 28th Regiment discovered scaling the hill. 'Rock slides were tumbled down on our heads by the Japs,' recorded one marine, 'and also as a result of our own naval gunfire. Each pillbox was a separate problem, an intricately designed fortress which had to be smashed into ruins. The walls of many began with two-foot-thick concrete blocks, laced with iron rails. Then came ten to twelve feet of rocks, piled with dirt and the dirty ashes of Iwo.'

Suribachi had a garrison of 1,200 men in its tunnels and bunkers. Impervious to artillery and bazookas, the bunkers could be dealt with only at close range. Marines used pole or satchel-charges, with the cry 'Fire in the hole!', or hurled in phosphorus grenades. Flamethrowers were in constant use, but it was a terrifying task for the operator who became an urgent target for Japanese machine-gunners trying to ignite the tank on his back. The Japanese knew that to be caught in its dragon-breath was like 'a chicken being fried'. At one point, marines heard Japanese voices, and realized that the sound was coming up through a fissure in the rock. Barrels of fuel were manhandled up the mountain, then gasoline was poured in and set alight.

After three days of constant combat, a small group of the 28th made it to the summit of the volcano and raised the Stars and Stripes on a metal pole. It was a moment of great emotion. The sight was greeted with jubilation and tears of relief both below and out at sea. Ships offshore sounded their horns. The secretary of the navy, James V. Forrestal, who was observing the whole operation, turned to Major General Holland Smith and said: 'The raising of that flag on Suribachi means a Marine Corps for the next 500 years.' A larger flag was brought up and raised by six men on a long piece of scaffolding acting as a flagpole, and the photograph taken became the icon of the war in the Pacific. Suribachi had cost the lives of 800 marines, but it was not the main defensive position on the island.

Kuribayashi's headquarters were deep underground at the north end of Iwo Jima in the most complex network of tunnels and excavated caverns. There was fury when the few survivors from Suribachi appeared, having slipped through American lines. Even though they had been ordered by their dying commander to break out to take news of Suribachi's fall, they were greeted with horror and shock for having failed to fight to the last. Their officer, a navy lieutenant, was slapped, insulted as a coward and very nearly beheaded. He was already kneeling with his head bowed when the sword was pulled from Captain Inouye Samaji's hands.

By the fourth day, the marines had secured the two airfields in the centre of the island, but then, with the three divisions in line abreast, they had to advance to take the northern complex buried within the volcanic rock, a truly barren and hellish landscape. Japanese snipers concealed themselves in fissures. Machine guns were switched from cave entrance to cave entrance, and American casualties mounted. The marines were angry that they were not allowed to use poison gas against the tunnel systems. Some collapsed from combat stress, but many more displayed unbelievable bravery, continuing to fight when grievously wounded. No fewer than twenty-seven Medals of Honor were awarded for the fighting on Iwo Jima. Hardly any prisoners were taken: even the badly wounded Japanese were killed, since they usually concealed a grenade to destroy themselves and any navy corpsman who tried to help them. Some marines decapitated Japanese corpses in order to boil the head and sell the skull when they got back home.

The advance from ravine to ravine and ridge to ridge, which were given names such as 'Meatgrinder', 'Death Valley' and 'Bloody Ridge', was slow and horrific. Japanese soldiers, taking the uniforms off dead marines, slipped through American lines at night to kill and cause mayhem in the rear. On the night of 8 March, despite Kuribayashi's orders against any *banzai* charge, Captain Inouye led one when he and his force of a thousand men were surrounded near Tachiwa Point, the easternmost part of the island. They attacked a battalion of the 23rd Regiment, inflicting nearly 350 casualties in a chaotic battle, but next morning the surviving marines counted 784 Japanese bodies in and around their positions.

By 25 March when the battle for Iwo Jima ended, 6,821 marines had been killed or mortally wounded as well as another 19,217 severely wounded. Apart from fifty-four Japanese soldiers taken prisoner, two of whom committed suicide, Kuribayashi's force of 21,000 men were all dead. After Kuribayashi had received severe wounds in a final battle, his soldiers buried him deep in the caverns.

*

In the middle of March, Admiral Mitscher's Task Force 58, with sixteen fleet carriers, sailed back into Japanese waters to attack airfields on Kyushu and the main island of Honshu. This was a pre-emptive strike before the invasion of Okinawa. As well as destroying Japanese aircraft on the ground, his flyers also managed to damage the great battleship *Yamato* and four carriers. But a surprise attack by a single bomber, which was not a kamikaze, caused devastating damage to the carrier USS *Franklin*. Although given permission to abandon ship, the captain and the survivors eventually managed to bring the fires below decks under control. Mitscher's task force was about to experience far worse attacks when it took up station off Okinawa to protect the landings. There its ships would become targets for wave after wave of kamikaze aircraft.

During the last few days of March, American forces seized two groups of small islands to the west of southern Okinawa, which turned out to be more useful than they had imagined. They discovered and destroyed a base for suicide boats, prepared with charges to ram US warships. The closest islands also provided good positions for batteries of 155mm Long Toms to support the troops once ashore.

Okinawa, with a civilian population of 450,000, was the main island in the Ryuku chain. The Japanese had annexed it in 1879 and incorporated it into the home islands. The Okinawans, who had very different traditions and culture from the Japanese, did not embrace the militaristic ethos of the master race. Their conscripts were more bullied than any others in the Imperial Japanese Army.

One hundred kilometres long, Okinawa lay some 550 kilometres to the south-west of Japan and included several large towns, among them the fifteenth-century citadel of Shuri in the south. As well as rocky ridges forming a spine across the centre of the island, much of the land was intensively cultivated with canefields and rice paddies. General Ushijima Mitsuru's 32nd Army at more than 100,000 men was stronger than US intelligence had estimated, although 20,000 of them were locally raised militia, despised by Japanese soldiers who made fun of the Okinawan dialect. Ushijima had lost his best division, the 9th, which had been transferred to the Philippines on the orders of Imperial General Headquarters. However, he was unusually strong in artillery and heavy mortars.

Ushijima, from his headquarters in the citadel of Shuri, planned to defend the southern, most populated quarter of the island to the end. In the northern, hilly areas, which the Americans expected to be the main centre of resistance, he had positioned only a small force commanded by Colonel Udo Takehido. Ushijima had no intention of defending the shoreline. Like Kuribayashi on Iwo Jima, he would wait until the Americans came to him.

On 1 April, Easter Sunday, after six days of bombardment by battleships and cruisers, Admiral Turner's invasion fleet was ready to launch its amtracs and landing craft. After all the horrors of Iwo Jima, the landings proved a mixture of anticlimax and euphoric relief. The 2nd Marine Division made a feint assault on the south-eastern tip, then returned to Saipan. Only twenty-eight men were killed on the first day out of the 60,000 men from two Marine and two army divisions landed on the west coast. Facing negligible opposition, they advanced inland to secure two airfields.

The 1st and the 6th Marine Divisions advanced north-eastwards across the Ishikawa Isthmus into the main part of the island, which Ushijima had defended so lightly. After the relief of landing unopposed, they began to feel tense. 'Where the hell are the Nips?' marines kept wondering. They passed large numbers of terrified and bewildered Okinawans and directed them back to internment camps set up in the rear. The marines gave their candy and some rations to the children, who did not show fear like their parents and grandparents. The army's 7th and 96th Divisions swung south, not knowing that they were headed for Ushijima's main defence lines across the island in front of Shuri.

Only on 5 April, when the two army divisions reached the limestone hills with their natural and man-made caves, did they understand what a battle awaited them. The caves had once again been linked up with tunnel systems, and the hills were dotted with traditional Okinawan funeral vaults in stone which made excellent machine-gun nests. Ushijima's artillery batteries were positioned to the rear, with forward observation officers on the hills ready to direct their fire. His main tactic was to separate the

American infantry from their tanks, which were attacked by concealed teams who jumped out and ran up to the Shermans with Molotov cocktails and satchel-charges. Tank crews who abandoned their blazing vehicles were shot down.

While the two army divisions were shaken to find what they were up against, Admiral Turner's fleet offshore began to receive the full brunt of Japanese kamikaze attacks launched from Kyushu and Formosa. On 6 and 7 April, 355 kamikaze pilots took off. Each was accompanied by another plane flown by a more experienced pilot to escort them. Most of the kamikaze had barely completed flying training, which is why they were encouraged to volunteer. The veterans would then return to escort another wave. Although they had been ordered to target carriers, most went for the first ship they saw. As a result the destroyers spread in a semi-circle as radar-pickets suffered the worst attacks at first. With their thin armour and only a few anti-aircraft guns, they stood little chance.

Combined with the air attacks, the most conspicuous suicide mission came in the form of the giant battleship *Yamato* accompanied by a light cruiser and eight destroyers. On the orders of the commander-in-chief of the Combined Fleet, they had sailed from the Inland Sea through the straits between Kyushu and Honshu. They were to attack the American fleet off Okinawa, beach their ships and use them as fixed batteries to support General Ushijima's forces. Many senior naval officers were horrified at this waste of the *Yamato*, which had received just enough fuel for the one-way trip.

On 7 April Admiral Mitscher was warned of the *Yamato*'s approach by US submarines. He flew off his aircraft, although he knew that Admiral Spruance wanted his battleships to have the honour of sinking her. Spruance conceded the attack to the navy flyers. The Japanese suicide squadron was tailed by American reconnaissance aircraft, and they guided the Helldivers and Avenger torpedo-bombers towards it.

The first wave scored two hits with bombs and one torpedo strike. The second wave less than an hour later hit the *Yamato* with five torpedoes. Another ten bombs struck home as the great battleship slowed and began to settle in the water. The cruiser

Yahagi was also stricken. Then the *Yamato* rolled slowly over and blew up. The *Yahagi* went down too, along with four destroyers. The great sortie was one of the most futile gestures in modern warfare, costing the lives of several thousand sailors.

The second series of kamikaze attacks on the invasion fleet began on 11 April, and this time they did aim for the carriers. The USS *Enterprise* was hit by two of them, but survived with heavy damage. The *Essex* was also hit, but was not put out of action. Next day the battleship USS *Tennessee* was hit and a destroyer sunk. The destroyer's crew were machine-gunned by other fighters as they struggled in the sea. A third series of attacks began on 15 April, by which time the stress on naval crews was beginning to tell. Further attacks included one on a clearly identified hospital ship, and others on carriers including the *Bunker Hill* and the *Enterprise*.

Kamikaze attacks were also made against the Royal Navy's Pacific Fleet, which Admiral King had been so reluctant to accept in what he regarded as his theatre of war. Task Force 57, as Spruance had designated it, was bombing and bombarding airfields on the island of Sakishimagunto towards Formosa. The flight decks of British aircraft carriers consisted of three inches of armour plate. When a Zeke kamikaze smashed into the flight deck of HMS *Indefatigable* and exploded, it simply left a dent. The US Navy liaison officer aboard remarked: 'When a *kamikaze* hits a US carrier, it's six months' repair at Pearl. In a Limey carrier it's a case of "Sweepers, man your brooms."'

The US Navy paid a heavy toll. By the end of the Okinawa campaign, the suicides of 1,465 pilots sank twenty-nine ships, damaged 120, killed 3,048 sailors and wounded another 6,035.

North of Suri, the 7th Infantry Division took seven days to advance about six kilometres. The 96th needed three days to take Cactus Ridge. Afterwards, it managed to seize Kakazu Ridge beyond in a surprise attack before dawn, but it was forced back when the Japanese artillery, which had registered the ridgeline, concentrated all its fire upon it. After nine days of fighting, both divisions were blocked and had lost 2,500 men altogether.

General Simon Bolivar Buckner, the commander of the Tenth Army, at least had encouraging news from the marines advancing north. They had almost reached the northern tip of the island through the pine forests, which smelled so good after the rotting stench of jungle-fighting. Colonel Udo's force had gone to ground. The 29th Marine Regiment, encountering some well-disposed Okinawans who spoke English, discovered where Udo's base was. He had selected a peak called Yae-dake deep in the forest overlooking a river. On 14 April, the 29th and the 4th Marine Regiment attacked from opposite sides. After a two-day battle and having suffered heavy casualties, they took Yae-dake. Colonel Udo, they found, had slipped through them with some of his men to pursue the fight from elsewhere in the forest.

On 19 April, an impatient General Buckner ordered an intense bombardment of the Japanese lines and Shuri citadel, using all the artillery, navy aircraft and big guns of the fleet, in preparation for a three-division attack. The assault on the ridges right across the island failed. On 23 April, Admiral Nimitz flew to Okinawa. He was deeply worried by the losses inflicted on his ships offshore and wanted the seizure of Okinawa completed rapidly. It was suggested to Buckner that another amphibious landing should be made on the south coast by the 2nd Marine Division. Buckner firmly rejected the idea. He feared that the marines would be trapped in a beachhead and it would be difficult to supply them. Nimitz did not argue, but made it clear that the conquest of the island must be completed quickly, otherwise Buckner would be replaced.

That night the Japanese pulled back from their first line of defence, covered by a thick mist and a bombardment by their own artillery. But the next defence line on the Urasoe-Mura Escarpment, with its cliffs, was not an easy prospect. Replacements being blooded in battle often froze when they saw a Japanese soldier for the first time. Some even shouted for someone else to shoot him, forgetting to use their own weapon. The 307th Regiment of the 77th Division held off a Japanese counter-attack almost entirely with grenades. Men were 'tossing grenades as fast as they could pull the pins', a platoon leader said. To keep them supplied, a human chain behind was passing fresh crates of them forward.

At the end of the month, Buckner brought the two Marine divisions down from the north of the island. Then, on 3 May, Ushijima made his one great mistake. Persuaded by the passionate advice of his chief of staff, Lieutenant General Cho Isamu, he launched a counter-attack. Cho, an extreme militarist, responsible for the orders which led to the massacres and rapes at Nanking in 1937, advocated an attack combined with amphibious landings behind the American lines. The boatloads of soldiers were spotted by US Navy patrol boats, and a massacre ensued at sea and on the beaches. The attack by land was also a disaster. Ushijima was mortified and apologized to the one staff officer who had opposed the whole mad plan.

On 8 May, when news of Germany's surrender reached the rifle companies of the 1st Marine Division, the most usual reaction was 'So what?' It was another war on another planet, as far as they were concerned. They were exhausted and filthy, and everything around them stank. The concentration of troops on Okinawa was abnormally dense. A battalion front extended less than 550 metres. 'The sewage of course was appalling,' wrote William Manchester, a marine sergeant on Okinawa. 'You could smell the front line long before you saw it; it was one vast cesspool.'

On 10 May Buckner ordered a general offensive against the Shuri Line with five divisions. It was a terrible battle. Only a combination of conventional Sherman tanks and those converted to flamethrowers could deal with some of the cave defences. One small hill called Sugar Loaf took the marines ten days of fighting, and cost them 2,662 casualties. Even some of the toughest marines faced nervous collapse, mainly due to the accuracy of the Japanese mortar and artillery fire. Everyone suffered from thudding headaches caused by the noise of the guns and explosions. At night the Japanese would try to infiltrate their lines, so starshells or flares were fired continuously into the sky lighting up the nightmare terrain with a dead, greenish glow. Sentries needed to note the position of every corpse to their front because any Japanese soldier creeping forward during the night would freeze and lie still, feigning death.

On 21 May, just as the Americans broke through to an area where they could use their tanks, the rains came, bogging down vehicles and grounding aircraft. Everyone and everything was covered in liquid clay. For the infantry and the marines carrying ammunition, slipping and sliding in the mud, was an utterly exhausting task. Living in foxholes filled with water and with decomposing bodies all around in shellholes was even worse. Corpses in the open and partially buried were crawling with maggots.

Under the cover of the heavy rain, Ushijima's forces began to pull back to final defence positions across the southern tip of Okinawa. Ushijima knew that the Shuri Line could not hold, and with an American tank breakthrough his forces risked encirclement. He left behind a strong rearguard, but eventually a battalion of the 5th Marine Regiment occupied the citadel of Shuri. It found that it had only a Confederate flag with it, so to the embarrassment of some officers the Stars and Bars were raised until they could be replaced with the Stars and Stripes.

On 26 May the clouds parted, and aircraft from the carriers spotted vehicles moving south from Shuri. Local Okinawans, terrified by Japanese propaganda about the Americans, insisted on fleeing with the troops even though Ushijima had directed them to seek shelter in another direction. American commanders felt compelled to open fire on the column, and the cruiser USS *New Orleans* began a bombardment of the road with its eight-inch guns. Some 15,000 civilians died along with the retreating soldiers.

After the withdrawal, Ushijima's force was reduced to less than 30,000 men, but hard battles still lay ahead, even if the end was in sight. On 18 June, General Buckner himself was killed by shell splinters when watching an attack by the 2nd Marine Division. Four days later, General Ushijima and Lieutenant General Cho, by then beleaguered in their command bunker, made their preparations for ritual suicide by self-disembowelment and simultaneous beheading by their respectful aides. The body count of their soldiers came to 107,539, but many others had been buried beforehand or sealed in destroyed caves.

Marine and army formations had suffered 7,613 killed, 31,807 wounded and 26,211 'other injuries', most of which consisted of psychological breakdown. Some 42,000 Okinawan civilians are said to have died, but the true figure may have been much higher. Apart from those killed by naval gunfire, many were buried alive in caves hit by artillery fire from both sides. In any case it prompted the question of how many Japanese civilians would die in the invasion of the home islands which was already being planned. The capture of Okinawa may not have hastened the end of the war.

Its prime aim was to serve as a base for the invasion of Japan, but the suicidal nature of its defence certainly concentrated minds in Washington on the next steps to consider.

46

Yalta, Dresden, Königsberg

FEBRUARY–APRIL 1945

At the end of January 1945, while the fighting in Budapest reached its peak and Soviet armies arrived at the River Oder, the three Allied leaders were preparing to meet in Yalta to decide the fate of the post-war world. Stalin, who was afraid of flying, insisted on holding the conference at Yalta in the Crimea, where he could travel by train in his green Tsarist coach.

Roosevelt had been sworn in as president for the fourth time on 20 January. In his short inaugural address, he looked towards the peace which he would not live to see. Three days later, amid unprecedented security precautions, he embarked in secret aboard the heavy cruiser USS *Quincy*. Eleven days later the *Quincy* and her escorting warships reached Malta, where Churchill awaited him eagerly. But Roosevelt, with a smokescreen of charm and hospitality, managed to avoid discussing what they should say at Yalta. He again did not want Stalin to think that they were 'ganging up' on him. He clearly wanted a free hand without an agreed strategy. The British delegation became increasingly uneasy. Stalin knew exactly what he wanted, and he would play them off against each other. Roosevelt wanted above all to secure Soviet support for a United Nations Organization, while the top British priority was to obtain guarantees that Poland would be genuinely free and independent.

The two delegations flew overnight from Malta to the Black Sea, and landed at Saki on 3 February. Their long journey over the Crimean Mountains and along the coast took them past many areas laid waste by war. The delegations were installed in Tsarist summer palaces. Roosevelt and the Americans stayed in the Livadia Palace, where the meetings would take place.

For Stalin, the main purpose of the Yalta conference was to force acceptance of Soviet control of central Europe and the

Balkans. He was so confident of his position that he felt able to torment Churchill in a preliminary meeting, by suggesting an offensive through the Ljubljana Gap. He knew perfectly well that Churchill's pet project to pre-empt the Red Army had been consistently opposed by the Americans. And now with Soviet armies north-west of Budapest, the British were far too late. In any case, the Americans had just insisted on the transfer of more divisions from Italy to the western front. Churchill must have been deeply irked as Stalin twisted the knife with mock sincerity.

Roosevelt, still hoping to give the impression that the western Allies were not ganging up, refused to see Churchill before the real business started. This precaution was wasted since the Soviet delegation had assumed that he and Churchill in Malta had already discussed their strategy. Just before the opening session, Stalin visited Roosevelt, who immediately tried to win his trust by undermining Churchill. He spoke of their disagreements over strategy and even referred back approvingly to Stalin's toast at Teheran suggesting the massacre of 50,000 German officers, a comment which had made Churchill walk out in disgust.

Remarking that the British wanted to 'have their cake and eat it too', he brought up his complaint that the British would occupy northern Germany, which he had wanted for the United States but had failed to mention until it was much too late. He was prepared, however, to support Churchill's plea that the French should have their own area of occupation in the south-west, but even that was delivered in a disparaging way, with digs against the British and de Gaulle.

When the first session began in the ballroom of the Livadia Palace on the late afternoon of 4 February, Stalin invited Roosevelt to open the proceedings. Over the next few days, they discussed the military situation and strategy, the possible dismemberment of Germany, the occupation zones and also reparations, a subject of the greatest interest to Stalin. Churchill was horrified when Roosevelt announced that the American people would not let him keep their troops in Europe much longer. American commanders especially were keen to wash their hands of Europe and finish the war with Japan. But Churchill rightly saw it as a terrible blunder in their negotiations. Stalin was immensely encouraged. He remarked afterwards to Beria that 'the weakness of the democracies lay in the fact that the people did not delegate permanent rights such as the Soviet government possessed'.

On 6 February, Roosevelt's great dream of a United Nations Organization was the subject of long and tortuous discussions. When it came to the composition of the security council and qualifications for countries to be members of the general assembly, Stalin suspected that the Americans and British had cooked up a trap. He had not forgotten the League of Nations vote condemning the Soviet invasion of Finland in the winter of 1939.

Stalin was deft and assured. He spoke with a quiet authority and played a winning hand just as cleverly as at the conference in Teheran fourteen months before, which had created the strategy to give him dominance over half of Europe. He also had the advantage of knowing from Beria's British spies the negotiating positions of the western Allies. The other two members of the Big Three could not hope to match him. Roosevelt, looking old and frail, with his mouth hanging open most of the time, sometimes did not appear to follow what was going on. Churchill, always likely to be carried away by his own emotional rhetoric rather than focusing on hard facts, clearly did not grasp the vital aspects of certain key discussions. This was particularly true on the question of Poland, which was so close to his heart. He seems to have missed Stalin's subtle yet clear signals on the subject.

For Churchill, the key test of the Soviet Union's good intentions would be how it would treat Poland. But Stalin saw no reason to compromise. The Red Army and the NKVD were now in complete control of the whole country. 'On Poland Iosef Vissarionovich has not moved one inch,' Beria told his son Sergo in Yalta. (Sergo Beria was in charge of bugging all the rooms and even of placing directional microphones to pick up Roosevelt's conversations outside.)

Churchill had sensed he was on his own. 'The Americans are profoundly ignorant of the Polish problem,' he had told Eden and Lord Moran, his doctor. 'At Malta I mentioned to them the independence of Poland and was met with the retort: "But surely that isn't at stake."' In fact, Edward Stettinius, the secretary of state, had agreed with Eden, but Roosevelt wanted to avoid a breach with Stalin on Poland, especially if it would hinder agreement on the United Nations.

On 6 February during the discussions on Poland, Roosevelt tried to act as if he were the honest broker between the British and the Soviets. The eastern border along the Curzon Line had been more or less agreed between the Big Three, but Roosevelt, rather to Churchill's surprise, appealed to Stalin to allow the Poles to keep the city of Lwów as a generous gesture. Stalin had no intention of doing anything of the sort. It belonged to Ukraine, in his view, and, although Poles within the city were in an absolute majority, ethnic cleansing had already started. He intended to move them all to the eastern parts of Germany with which he proposed to compensate Poland. The citizens of Lwów would eventually be moved en masse to Breslau, which would become Wrocław.

Stalin was far more concerned about western proposals for a Polish coalition government based on leaders of all the major parties to supervise free elections. As far as he was concerned, there was already a provisional government in place: the Lublin Poles who had now moved to Warsaw. 'We shall allow in one or two émigrés, for decorative purposes,' he said to Beria, 'but no more.' He had recognized his own puppet government at the beginning of January, to the protests of the British and the United States. The French recognized Stalin's puppet government, despite de Gaulle's previous stance in December. The Czechs also recognized it under pressure.

Stalin became agitated during these discussions. After a recess, he suddenly stood up to speak. He admitted that the Russians had 'committed many sins against the Poles in the past', but argued that Poland was vital to Soviet security. The Soviet Union had been invaded twice through Poland in the course of the century, and for that reason alone it was necessary that Poland be 'mighty, free, and independent'. Neither Churchill nor Roosevelt could fully understand the shock of the German invasion in 1941 and Stalin's determination to establish a cordon of satellite states so that the Russians would never be surprised again. One could well argue that the origins of the Cold War lay in that traumatic experience.

Stalin's idea of 'free' and 'independent' was of course very different to a British or American definition, because he insisted that it should be 'friendly'. He rejected any involvement in its government by representatives from the government-in-exile, accusing them of stirring up trouble behind Soviet lines. He claimed that members of the Home Army had killed 212 Red Army officers and soldiers, but of course made no mention of the appalling repression carried out by the NKVD against non-Communist Poles. The Home Army, according to his argument, was therefore helping the Germans.

It became clear the following day that any compromises on Poland and the United Nations would be linked. Stalin postponed the subject of the Polish government and thrilled the Americans by agreeing to their voting system for the United Nations. He did not want the Soviet Union to find itself massively outvoted in the general assembly. He therefore got Molotov to argue again that, on the basis that the British had several votes, if one counted the Dominions as likely to side with the mother country, then at least some member states of the Union of Soviet Socialist Republics should be admitted, especially Ukraine and Belorussia.

Roosevelt was not taken in. Nobody considered them independent of Moscow in any form and it undermined the principle of one country, one vote. To his surprise and irritation, Churchill sided with Stalin. But Roosevelt then conceded the next morning, hoping to get Stalin to commit to declaring war on Japan. Stalin's own concession on the United Nations, however, had been an attempt to persuade Roosevelt to soften his line on Poland. The three-dimensional game was becoming complicated. It was made even more complicated by disagreements within the American delegation.

When the conference returned to the subject of Poland, Stalin pretended that Roosevelt's suggestion that delegates from the rival governments should be brought to Yalta was impossible to fulfil. He did not know their addresses and there would not be sufficient time. On the other hand he appeared to offer encouraging concessions by talking of the possible inclusion of non-Communist Poles in the provisional government and the holding of general elections afterwards. He rejected American suggestions of a presidential council to oversee elections. Both Molotov and Stalin were firm that the Warsaw provisional government would not be replaced, but it could be enlarged.

Churchill presented a powerful response, explaining why there would be deep distrust, if not outrage, in the west at the idea of a government which did not enjoy widespread support in Poland. Stalin replied with unmistakable warning signals to Churchill. He had honoured the agreement over Greece. He had not protested when British troops suppressed Communist partisans in Athens. And he compared the question of rear-area security in Poland to the situation in France, where he had in fact reined in the French Communist Party. In any case, he argued, de Gaulle's government was no more democratic in composition than the Communist provisional government in Warsaw.

Stalin claimed that the Soviet liberation of Poland and his provisional government had been widely welcomed. This outright lie may have been highly unconvincing, but the message was clear. Poland was his France and Greece, only more so. Greece, as he knew, was the prime minister's Achilles heel, and Stalin's arrow was well aimed. Churchill was forced to acknowledge his gratitude for Stalin's neutrality in Greek affairs. Roosevelt, afraid of losing ground on the United Nations, insisted that the Polish question should be put aside for the moment and discussed by the committee of foreign ministers.

The President agreed to Stalin's price for entering the war against Japan. In the Far East, the Soviet Union wanted the southern part of the island of Sakhalin, and the Kurile Islands which Russia had lost after the disastrous war against Japan in 1905. Roosevelt also conceded Soviet control over Mongolia, providing it was kept secret as he had not discussed it with Chiang Kai-shek. This was hardly in the spirit of the Atlantic Charter, nor was the American compromise over Poland, announced by Stettinius on 9 February.

Roosevelt did not want to put at risk agreements achieved on his two main priorities, the United Nations and Soviet entry into the war against Japan. He had given up on any hopes of forcing Stalin to accept a democratic government in Poland. All he wanted now was an agreement on a 'Provisional Government of National Unity' and 'free and unfettered elections' which could be sold to the American people when he returned home. This approach tacitly accepted the Soviets' demand that their provisional government should form the basis of the new one and by implication cast the London government-in-exile into outer darkness. Molotov, pretending to put forward insignificant changes, wanted to drop terms such as 'fully representative', and instead of permitting 'democratic parties' to qualify he wanted that changed to 'anti-fascist and non-fascist'. Since the Soviet state and the NKVD already defined the Home Army and its supporters as 'objectively fascist', this was hardly a pedantic trifle.

Roosevelt dismissed Churchill's concerns as no more than the interpretation of certain words, but the devil was indeed in the detail, as they would find later. The prime minister would not be put off. Knowing that he could not now win on the composition of the provisional government, he concentrated on the question of free elections and demanded diplomatic observers. Stalin retorted shamelessly that that would be an insult to the Poles. Roosevelt felt obliged to support Churchill, but the next morning the Americans, without warning the British, suddenly withdrew their insistence on the monitoring of the elections. Churchill and Eden were left out on a limb. All they could obtain was an agreement that ambassadors should have freedom of movement to report on events in Poland.

Admiral Leahy pointed out to Roosevelt that the words in the agreement were 'so elastic that the Russians can stretch it all the way from Yalta to Washington, without ever technically breaking it'. Roosevelt answered that he could not do anything more. Stalin was not budging on Poland, whatever anyone said. His troops and security police controlled the country. For what appeared to be the greater good of world peace, Roosevelt was not prepared to stand up to the Soviet dictator. Stalin, disturbed to observe the frail state of the accommodating President, told Beria to provide detailed information on those around him who might play an important role after his death. He wanted every detail available on Vice President Harry Truman. He feared that the succeeding administration would be much less pliable. In fact, when Roosevelt died two months later, Stalin became convinced that Roosevelt had been assassinated. According to Beria, he was furious that the NKGB First Directorate could provide no information on the matter.

One of the last issues to be tackled at Yalta was the question of the repatriation of prisoners of war. With some camps already overrun by the Red Army, the democracies wanted to bring their men home and return the large numbers of Soviet prisoners of war and those in Wehrmacht uniform. Neither the British nor the Americans had fully thought through the implications of this agreement. Soviet authorities misled their allies, by insisting that their citizens had been forced into German ranks against their will. They should be separated from German prisoners, treated well and not categorized as prisoners of war. They even accused the Allies of beating up the very prisoners whom they intended to massacre or send to the Gulag as soon as they had them back.

The British and Americans guessed that Stalin wanted revenge on all those Soviet citizens, around a million of them, who had served in Wehrmacht uniform, or had been forced through starvation to become Hiwis. However, they did not foresee that even those taken prisoner by the Germans would be considered traitors. By the time the Allies discovered the truth about the murder of returned Soviet prisoners, they preferred to remain quiet so as not to delay the return of their own prisoners of war. And finding it impossible to screen their charges effectively to identify the real war criminals, it seemed easier to send the whole lot back, by force if necessary.

Military questions which had opened the conference were among the last to be settled. The Americans wanted Eisenhower to have the right to liaise directly with the Stavka in order to be able to coordinate plans. Although a perfectly sensible plan, this soon proved less than straightforward. General Marshall and his colleagues had failed to understand that no Soviet commander dared do anything which involved contact with a foreigner without having first had permission from Stalin. Marshall had also assumed that a genuine exchange of information would be in the interests of both parties, but again he, like all Americans without direct experience of Soviet practices, failed to understand the Russians' conviction that the capitalist countries were always trying to trick them, so they must trick them first. Eisenhower was perfectly frank about his intentions and timetable – in fact far too frank and naive in Churchill's view. The Soviets, on the other hand, deliberately misled Eisenhower on both their plans and timing, when it came to the Berlin operation.

Marshall regarded the clarification of the 'bombline', the boundary between western and Soviet zones of operation, as a matter of urgency. US aircraft had already attacked Soviet troops by mistake, thinking they were German. Again he was staggered to find that General Aleksei Antonov, the chief of the general staff, could discuss nothing without first consulting Stalin.

Churchill received little thanks from de Gaulle for having persuaded both Roosevelt and Stalin to allow France to join the Allied Control Commission with its own occupation zones. The French leader was sulking at not having been invited to Yalta, and at the refusal to give France the Rhineland. His mood was not improved when Roosevelt, on his way home, invited him to Algiers to brief him on what had been decided at Yalta. A hyper-sensitive de Gaulle did not appreciate receiving an invitation from an American to visit him on French territory, so he promptly refused. Word then leaked out that Roosevelt had called him a 'prima donna', and this further inflamed the situation.

The 'spirit of Yalta', a fairy dust which settled on American and British delegates alike, persuaded them that, even if the agreements achieved were far from watertight, Stalin's overall mood of cooperation and compromise suggested that peace could be maintained in the post-war world. It would not be long before such optimistic thoughts were upset.

While on the subject of the bombline in Yalta, General Antonov had asked for attacks on communication centres behind German lines on the eastern front. This was to prevent the transfer of German troops from the western front to the east to face the Red Army. It has been argued that 'the direct outcome of that agreement was the destruction of Dresden by Allied bombing'. Yet Antonov never mentioned Dresden.

Even before the Yalta conference, Churchill was keen to impress the Soviets with the destructive power of Bomber Command, at a time when Britain's armies had been so weakened by manpower shortages. It would also remind them that the strategic bombing campaign had been the initial Second Front, as he had attempted to persuade Stalin on several occasions earlier in the war.

Harris was also keen to attack Dresden simply because it remained one of the few major cities which had not yet been flattened. The Eighth Air Force had bombed its marshalling yards in October, but it could not be included in his blue books. The fact that this baroque jewel on the Elbe was one of the great architectural and artistic treasures of Europe did not concern him for a moment. His failure to have achieved Germany's collapse with his heavy bombers, as he had claimed he would, only seemed to spur him on. On 1 February, Portal, Spaatz and Tedder agreed a new directive which placed 'Berlin, Leipzig and Dresden on the target priority list just below oil'.

Harris did not believe in the oil plan, as he made abundantly clear to Portal, the chief of the air staff, in correspondence during the winter. A directive from the combined chiefs of staff on 1 November 1944 should have forced him to concentrate first on oil targets and secondly on communications. Even though Ultra intercepts showed that Spaatz's emphasis on oil targets was proving most effective, Harris did not want to be diverted from his personal goal. 'Are we now to abandon this vast task . . . just as it nears completion?' he demanded. Harris was obliged to react to Portal's pressure, but he used the genuine problem of bad visibility in winter as an excuse to continue on his own course of bombing cities. Harris even offered his resignation in January as the dispute continued, but Portal felt that he could not sack him. Harris, even though he had been proved wrong on almost every single one of his fixed ideas, had too many supporters in the popular press and among the public at large.

For most of the RAF crews, 'Dresden was just another target, though a long, long way away.' They were told it was to disrupt the German war effort and to help the Red Army. Their briefings did not mention that one objective was to cause a flood of refugees to impede Wehrmacht traffic – a tactic for which the British had condemned the Luftwaffe in 1940.

The American bombers were to attack first on 13 February, but due to bad weather their contribution was postponed for twenty-four hours. As a result, the onslaught on Dresden began on the night of 13 February, with 796 RAF Lancasters in two waves. The first wave, dropping the usual mixture of high explosive and incendiaries, began the fires, especially in the more flammable old city. The second, larger wave could see a bright glow on the horizon when still 150 kilometres from their target. The fires were beginning to coalesce into a huge inferno, which would soon drag in hurricane-force winds at ground level like a titanic forge.

By the time the American Fortresses arrived next day, which happened to be Ash Wednesday, the smoke from the city had risen to 15,000 feet. On the ground, the conditions were as horrifying as in the other firestorm cities – Hamburg, Heilbronn, Darmstadt – with shrunken carbonized bodies, most of them killed by carbon-monoxide inhalation, molten lead pouring from roofs and the melted tar on the roads trapping people like fly-paper. Dresden's important rail links and military traffic were a legitimate target, but Harris's obsessive desire for total extinction again prevailed. Pforzheim was next ten days later. The firestorm there brought Harris's score up to sixty-three destroyed cities. The beautiful town of Würzburg, which had even less military significance, was burned to the ground in the middle of March. To the end of his days, Harris maintained that his strategy saved the lives of untold numbers of Allied soldiers.

After the destruction of Dresden questions were raised, both in Britain and the United States. There were allegations that the Allied air forces had adopted a policy of 'terror bombing'. Churchill, who had urged the attack on Dresden and other communications centres in eastern Germany, began to have cold feet about the 'fury' of the strategic bombing campaign. He sent a minute to the British chiefs of staff, stating that 'the destruction of Dresden remains a serious query against the conduct of Allied bombing'. Portal found this deeply hypocritical and demanded that he withdraw it.

Despite his disagreements with Harris, Portal was determined to defend the sacrifice of Bomber Command. Altogether 55,573 aircrew had died out of the 125,000 who served in it. The US Eighth Air Force suffered 26,000 killed, more than the whole of the US Marine Corps. Some 350 Allied aircrew are estimated to have been lynched or murdered when shot down. Estimates of the number of German civilians killed vary, but it was around half a million people. The Luftwaffe had killed many more, including an estimated half a million civilians in the Soviet Union alone, but that is still no excuse for Harris's utterly wrong-headed conviction that Bomber Command could win the war on its own simply by smashing cities.

Goebbels apparently shook with rage when he heard of Dresden's destruction. He claimed that a quarter of a million people had died, and demanded that as many Allied prisoners of war be executed as the number of civilians killed. (A commission of historians in Germany recently reduced the estimate to 'around 18,000 and definitely less than 25,000'.) The idea of shooting Allied prisoners of war appealed to Hitler. Such a tearing-up of the Geneva Convention would force his troops to fight to the end. But calmer voices, including those of Keitel, Jodl, Dönitz and Ribbentrop, talked him out of it.

The promises of a glorious future for Germany during the early war years had now been replaced by the terror propaganda of 'Kraft durch Furcht', strength through fear. Goebbels, implicitly and explicitly, evoked the consequences of defeat, with the annihilation of Germany and a Soviet conquest with rape and deportation for forced labour. 'Victory or Siberia' provided a powerful Manichaean idea. 'The misery that would follow if the war was lost would be unthinkable,' wrote a young officer. Yet although the Nazi regime was totally opposed to negotiation, it allowed, even tacitly encouraged, its population to believe in some sort of deal with the western Allies so that they would have some hope even if they had no more faith in 'final victory'. Now that the majority of the population had lost all trust in the official media, they relied on the exchange of rumours and hearsay in bomb shelters and air-raid cellars.

The most frightening stories came from refugees who had escaped from East Prussia, Pomerania and Silesia. Nearly 300,000 troops and civilians were still trapped in Königsberg and the Samland Peninsula behind it. Their only hope still lay with the Kriegsmarine. Civilians in Pomerania were soon cut off as well. Zhukov, having been told by Stalin from Yalta to deal with the 'Baltic balcony' on his northern flank, redeployed several of his armies.

On 16 February these German forces were ordered to attack

south in the area of Stargard in an operation to which staff officers gave the codename Husarenritt (Hussar Ride), but Himmler's SS insisted that it be called Sonnenwende (Solstice). More than 1,200 tanks had been allocated to the offensive, but many never reached the start-line. A sudden thaw, turning the ground into deep mud, added to a shortage of fuel and ammunition, turned Sonnenwende into a disaster. It had to be abandoned after two days.

Zhukov, having redeployed his forces, ordered the 1st and 2nd Guards Tank Armies and the 3rd Shock Army to push up east of Stettin to the coast. This followed Rokossovsky's advance west of the Vistula with four armies towards Danzig. Leading tank brigades smashed through weak defences. In towns supposedly far behind the lines, German civilians stared in stupefied horror on seeing T-34 tanks charging down their main street, smashing any obstacle under their tracks. One seaside town was captured by cavalry sweeping in. Wehrmacht units cut off by the advance tried to make their way west, trudging in groups through silent, snowbound forests. The thousand-odd men left from the French SS Charlemagne Division managed to escape in this way from Belgard.

Once again, the Nazi Party had refused to allow the civilian population to leave in good time. Hurriedly assembled treks set out through the snow in farm-carts with improvised canopies to keep out the freezing wind. The route of the German retreat was marked by 'gallows alleys', where the SS and Feldgendarmerie had hanged deserters, with cards around their necks proclaiming their guilt. Whether the refugees headed east towards Danzig and Gotenhafen (Gdynia) or west towards Stettin, the Red Army was ahead of them and they had to turn back. Landowning families knew that they would be the first to be shot when the Soviets arrived. A number decided to commit suicide first.

Danzig, soon surrounded by the Red Army, became an inferno of flames and black smoke. Its population had swollen to 1.5 million with all the refugees, while the wounded were dumped on the quayside to await evacuation. The Kriegsmarine, using any craft available, shuttled them to the port of Hela, on the peninsula to the north, where other ships would take them back to ports west of the Oder estuary or to Copenhagen. Only the heavy guns of the *Prinz Eugen* and the old battleship *Schlesien* kept the Soviet troops out of the town until 22 March. German sailors continued to rescue civilians, despite coming under fire from tanks on the shore.

The sack of Gdynia was terrible when Soviet troops broke in. Even the Soviet military authorities were shaken. 'The number of extraordinary events is growing, as well as immoral phenomena and military crimes,' the political department reported using its usual tortuous euphemisms. 'Among our troops there are disgraceful and politically harmful phenomena, when under the slogan of revenge some officers and soldiers commit outrages and looting instead of honestly and selflessly fulfilling their duty to the Motherland.' German civilians left behind in Danzig later suffered a similar fate.

Revenge was no doubt inevitable, especially as the Soviets uncovered so many traces of atrocities. Stutthof concentration camp, where 16,000 prisoners had died from typhoid in six weeks, was destroyed in an attempt to hide the evidence. German soldiers and Volkssturm had taken part in the execution of the remaining Red Army prisoners, Poles and Jews held there. But a far worse discovery was made in the Danzig Anatomical Medical Institute, where Professor Spanner and Assistant Professor Volman had since 1943 been conducting experiments on corpses from the camp at Stutthof, to turn them into leather and soap.

'The examination of the premises of the Anatomical Institute', stated the official Soviet report, 'revealed 148 human corpses which were stored for the production of soap ... The executed people whose corpses were used for making soap were of different nationalities, but mostly Poles, Russians and Uzbeks.' Spanner's work had evidently received approval at a high level, because his institute had been 'visited by the Minister of Education Rust and Minister of Health Care Konti. Gauleiter of Danzig Albert Förster visited the institute in 1944, when soap was being produced.' It is surprising that the Nazi authorities had not disposed of such grisly evidence before the arrival of the Red Army. Even more astonishing was the fact that Spanner and his associates never faced trial, because the processing of corpses was not a legal crime.

Looting became both a game and a matter of pride, especially in the punishment companies. 'The *shtrafroty* positioned next to ours', recorded a young officer, 'was commanded by a Jew, Lyovka Korsunskii, who had the manner typical of someone from Odessa. He came to visit us during a lull in a beautiful captured carriage pulled by magnificent stallions. He took a great Swiss watch off his left wrist and threw it to somebody, then he took another from his right wrist and threw it to somebody else. Watches were an object of constant desire and often served as a reward. Our soldiers who didn't speak a word of German quickly learned to say: "*Wieviel ist die Uhr?*" and the unsuspecting German civilian took out his pocket watch and the watch immediately moved to the pocket of the warrior-victor.'

East Prussia remained the main focus for revenge. 'I've only been at war for a year,' another young officer wrote home, 'so how do people feel after four years at the front? Their hearts are now like stone. If sometimes you say to them: "Soldier, you shouldn't finish off this Hans. Let him build again what he has destroyed," he would look at you from under his eyebrows and say: "They took away my wife and daughter." And he fires his gun. He is right.'

The sandbar on the Baltic along the Frisches Haff had been the only route left open for escape from East Prussia. Thousands of civilians had fled across the ice to it, although many fell through where it had been weakened by shellfire and thaw. 'When we reached the shore of the Frisches Haff,' wrote Rabichev, 'the entire beach was littered with German helmets, sub-machine guns, unused grenades, tins of food and packets of cigarettes. Along the shore stood cottages. Wounded Fritzes were lying in beds or on the floors of these cottages. They looked at us in silence. There was neither fear nor hatred in their faces, just numb indifference, although they knew that each of us had only to raise a sub-machine gun and shoot them.'

The troops in the Heiligenbeil encirclement, with their backs to the sea, had held off the Soviet forces around them thanks only to the gunnery of the pocket battleship *Admiral Scheer* and the *Lützow*. On 13 March, however, the Red Army attacked in force.

Troops in another smaller pocket at the port of Rosenberg were refused permission by Hitler to evacuate by sea. They were destroyed in an assault on 28 March. 'The port of Rosenberg was looking like a *kasha* of metal, dirt and flesh,' wrote a Red Army lieutenant to his mother. 'Corpses of Fritzes covered the ground. What was here dwarfs the events on the Minsk highway in 1944. One walks on corpses, sits down to rest on corpses, one has one's meals on corpses. For about ten kilometres there are two corpses of Fritzes on each square metre . . . PoWs are being driven in battalions, with their commanders in front. I can't understand why we bother to take them prisoners. We've got so many already, and here is another fifty thousand. They walk without any guards like sheep.'

The Samland Peninsula west of Königsberg was defended by a mixture of army and Volkssturm troops trying to protect the evacuations by sea from the port of Pillau. An officer in the 551st Volksgrenadier Division described how they were serenaded with loudspeakers, broadcasting music interspersed with messages in German urging them to lay down their arms. 'But there was no question of that, because in our mind's eye we could still see the women of Krattlau and Ännchenthal who had been raped to death, and we knew that behind us thousands of women and children had yet to make the decision to evacuate.'

In Königsberg itself, members of the Feldgendarmerie, known as 'chain-hounds' because of the metal gorgette worn round their neck, searched cellars and ruined houses for men trying to avoid service in the Volkssturm. Many civilians longed desperately for the city to surrender to end their suffering, but General Otto Lasch had the strictest instructions from Hitler to fight to the very end. Gauleiter Koch, having fled early on and evacuated his own family to safety, now returned from time to time in a Storch plane to see that his orders were fulfilled.

Königsberg had strong defences, with old forts and a moat combined with new bunkers and earthworks. At the end of March Marshal Vasilevsky, who had taken over command of the 3rd Belorussian Front after Chernyakhovsky was killed by a shell, ordered a massive assault. It was a chaotic operation, with Soviet artillery and aircraft frequently killing and wounding their own troops by mistake. The Red Army's casualties were horrific, so when its troops finally made their way into the fortress city they showed no pity, even to civilians in houses with white sheets hung from the windows in surrender. Women were soon begging their attackers to kill them. Heart-rending screams could be heard coming from ruins in all directions. Thousands of civilians and soldiers committed suicide.

General Lasch finally surrendered on 10 April, and was promptly condemned to death *in absentia* on Hitler's order. The Gestapo arrested his family under the Nazi *Sippenhaft* law of reprisal. A group of SS and police fought on in the castle, but they too were soon killed in the blazing fire, which almost certainly destroyed the precious panels of the Amber Room, looted during the siege of Leningrad and brought back to Königsberg.

There had been an estimated 120,000 civilians in Königsberg at the start of the siege. The NKVD counted 60,526 at the end. Some of the Volkssturm were shot out of hand as 'partisans' because they had no uniform. Everyone else, with many women included, was marched off for forced labour, either in the region or back in the Soviet Union. The East Prussian campaign was finally over. Rokossovsky's 2nd Belorussian Front had lost 159,490 men dead and wounded, while the 3rd Belorussian Front suffered 421,763 casualties. Yet, even with these sacrifices, the war was not yet won. The German army at bay was still a dangerous beast. It fought on, whether prompted by fear of retribution for war crimes in the Soviet Union, or fear of the Bolsheviks and slave labour in Siberia. There were growing numbers of deserters, but the threat of the 'flying courts martial' issuing summary sentences, and the SS and Feldgendarmerie hanging any they caught, certainly had an effect. As a senior Red Army officer observed: 'Morale is low, but discipline is strong.'

47

Americans on the Elbe

FEBRUARY–APRIL 1945

American commanders had always criticized Montgomery for his caution, yet Eisenhower became extremely cautious himself after the surprise attack in the Ardennes. The counter-attack against the bulge had been slow and deliberate, allowing Model to withdraw the bulk of his forces. At one stage, Eisenhower did not expect to cross the Rhine until May, believing it would be in spate until then. He greatly over-estimated the fighting power of the German armies facing him, which were in fact crippled by fuel and ammunition shortages. Speer's achievements in the mass production of armaments in 1944 had simply not been matched by the munitions industry.

'The Germans just don't seem to understand,' was a frequent complaint by American soldiers. Why did they continue to fight when the war was so obviously lost? General Patton had asked a captured German colonel the same question in November. 'It is the fear of Russia that is forcing us to use every man who can carry a weapon,' he replied. Some historians have argued that the Germans fought to the last because of the Allies' insistence on unconditional surrender, but this was not a major factor. Roosevelt and Churchill were convinced that the German people, after the delusions over their defeat in 1918, had to be forced to recognize this time that they were totally defeated. The Morgenthau Plan, on the other hand, had been a major blunder.

Rather more to the point was the knowledge of senior Nazis that they would be executed for war crimes. Hitler had no illusions. Surrender in any form was anathema to him, and his entourage knew that the war could not end as long as he still lived. Hitler's greatest fear was not execution, but of being captured and taken back to Moscow in a cage. His plan had always been to implicate the military and civilian hierarchy in the crimes of the

Nazi state, so that they could not dissociate themselves from it when there was no further hope.

At the beginning of February 1945, the US First Army began its offensive south of the Hürtgen Forest in freezing conditions. On 9 February, Hodges's troops at last took the Roer dam near Schmidt. That same day the French First Army, supported by US armoured divisions, eliminated the Colmar pocket. Bradley's offensive, led by Major General Matthew B. Ridgway's XVIII Airborne Corps, went well, thanks to the great fighting qualities of his paratroopers. But the crossing of the River Sauer, swollen by floodwaters in a sudden thaw, cost many casualties and took three days. The Westwall was breached and many more German troops on the central sectors of the front were now ready to surrender.

To Bradley's consternation, Eisenhower then halted Collins's VII Corps advancing towards Cologne. This was to allow Montgomery the priority in supplies for Operation Veritable, an attack south-east from Nijmegen through the Reichswald between the Rhine and the Maas. There the Germans fought back with every division they could scrape together, and it was a miserable battle in rain and sleet. There was no room for manoeuvre between the rivers, and the German defences in the Reichswald were manned with determination by Student's paratroopers. The ground was still sodden, with tanks casting tracks in the glutinous mud and unable to operate effectively in the woods. It gave the British a taste of what the Hürtgen had been like for the Americans. They were not helped when they reached the ancient city of Cleve. Harris's bombers had smashed the city for once with high explosive instead of incendiaries, which made it far harder to capture because the Germans fought from the ruins.

The German concentration against the British offensive did at least give Simpson's Ninth Army a better chance when it crossed the River Roer on 19 February, but the inundated flood plain on both sides made it a difficult and messy operation. German civilians could only pray that their own troops retreated before too much damage was done to their towns and villages. They also assisted the growing number of young soldiers trying to desert. On 1 March Patton's Third Army took Trier. He scented blood and rapid advances, and pushed his divisional commanders on with his coruscating language.

Once the British Second Army had reached the Rhine at Wesel on 10 March, Montgomery began preparations for his great set-piece crossing, a model of Staff College planning, with no fewer than 59,000 engineers involved. The assault would include 21st Army Group, Simpson's Ninth Army and the drop of two airborne divisions on the east bank. The paratroopers and glider-borne infantry suffered far more casualties than the amphibious attack. Americans made caustic comments about the massive build-up and the time it took.

Montgomery's thunder was stolen before he had started. On 7 March, south of Bonn, the 9th Armored Division had seized the bridge at Remagen, which was partly destroyed by demolition charges. Showing great dash, the division grabbed the opportunity and was across before the Germans could react. On hearing the news, Hitler ordered that the officers in command should be executed immediately. He sacked Rundstedt for the third time and replaced him with Kesselring. He also ordered massive reinforcements to crush the bridgehead. This stripped other sectors and Patton's Third Army, which had been clearing the Palatinate region on the west bank of the Rhine at speed, made several crossings south of Koblenz.

A report of the coup de main at Remagen was immediately passed back to Moscow by Major General I. A. Susloparov, the Red Army liaison officer at SHAEF headquarters. The next morning, Stalin ordered Zhukov to fly back to Moscow, even though he was directing his armies in Pomerania. He was driven straight to Stalin's dacha, where the Soviet leader had been recuperating from stress. The Vozhd took him out into the garden where they walked and talked. Zhukov briefed him on Pomerania and the state of the Oder bridgeheads. Stalin then spoke of the Yalta conference, and said that Roosevelt had been most friendly. Only as Zhukov was about to leave after tea did Stalin reveal the reason for his summons. 'Go to the Stavka,' he said, 'and look at the calculations on the Berlin operation with Antonov. We will meet here tomorrow at 13.00.'

Antonov and Zhukov, who both sensed the urgency of Stalin's order, worked through most of the night. They knew they had to take 'into account the action of our allies', as Zhukov acknowledged later. From the moment Stalin heard that the Americans were across the Rhine, he knew that the race for Berlin was on. It was just as well that Zhukov and Antonov worked through the night, because Stalin brought forward the meeting and came into Moscow for it, although he was still weak.

Stalin had two vital reasons for wanting to take Berlin before the Allies. 'The lair of the fascist Beast' was the key symbol of victory after all the Soviet Union had suffered, and Stalin had no intention of allowing any other flag to fly over the city. Berlin had also been the centre for Nazi Germany's atomic research, mainly at the Kaiser Wilhelm Institute for Physics in Dahlem. Through his spies, Stalin was well aware of the Manhattan Project in the United States and its progress towards creating an atomic bomb. The Soviet nuclear research programme, Operation Borodino, had received full priority, but the Russians were short of uranium, which they hoped to seize in Berlin. Soviet intelligence, although informed of every detail of the Manhattan Project, had no idea that the bulk of the uranium and most of the scientists they wanted had been evacuated from Berlin to Haigerloch in the Black Forest.

At the meeting on 9 March, Stalin approved the outline plan for the Berlin operation drawn up by Zhukov and Antonov. The Stavka worked furiously on the details. The main problem was the time needed by Rokossovsky's 2nd Belorussian Front to complete the clearance of Pomerania. It would then have to redeploy along the lower Oder up to Stettin, so that it could attack at the same time as Zhukov's 1st Belorussian Front opposite Berlin, and Konev's 1st Ukrainian Front to the south on the River Neisse.

Stalin's main fear was that the Germans would open their western front to the British and Americans, and transfer troops east to face the Red Army. His paranoia led him to suspect that the western Allies were still capable of making a secret deal with Germany. American talks in Berne with SS Obergruppenführer Karl Wolff, discussing a possible surrender in north Italy, had aroused his worst fears. On 27 March, just before the Stavka plans were finalized, a Reuters report from 21st Army Group boasted that British and American troops were meeting hardly any German resistance.

*

Anglo-American relations came under strain again at this time, because Montgomery assumed that he would be given the task of advancing to Berlin. But on 30 March Eisenhower issued his orders. 21st Army Group would head for Hamburg and Denmark. Montgomery lost Simpson's Ninth Army, which would form the northern pincer movement on the Ruhr defended by Generalfeldmarschall Model's army group, while the US First Army would encircle it from the south. Bradley's armies would then head for Leipzig and Dresden. The main thrust was to be for central and southern Germany. Eisenhower insisted that Berlin was 'not the logical nor the most desirable objective for the forces of the Western Allies'. He had seized on some speculative intelligence which suggested that Hitler would fight to the end in an 'Alpine fortress' in the south.

Montgomery was not the only one who was furious. Churchill and the British chiefs of staff were horrified by this change of direction away from Berlin, which the supreme commander had not discussed with them. Churchill had been with Eisenhower less than a week before on the banks of the Rhine to watch Montgomery's great operation at Wesel, and the supreme commander had not even hinted at his change in thinking. To make matters worse, Eisenhower had already communicated all the details to Stalin without even warning his British deputy, Air Chief Marshal Tedder. This signal, SCAF-252, became a cause of considerable friction. Eisenhower assured Stalin that he had no intention of advancing on Berlin. His main thrust would head further south.

Churchill feared that Marshall and Eisenhower were far too keen to placate Stalin when the spirit of Yalta had already turned sour. In Romania, Vyshinsky had installed a puppet government at the end of February. He ignored the protests of the Allied Control Commission that his act was a blatant contravention of the Declaration on Liberated Europe agreed at Yalta, under which governments representing all democratic parties would organize free elections. More and more reports meanwhile indicated that the NKVD in Poland was arresting and shooting members of the Home Army, accusing them of helping the Nazis. Some 91,000 Poles were arrested and deported to the Soviet Union.

On 17 March Molotov angrily refused to allow any western

representatives to enter Poland to assess the situation there, in another overt contravention of the Yalta agreement. He pretended that it was an insult to the Communist provisional government in Warsaw, which the Americans and British refused to recognize until elections had been held. Molotov knew the British and American position on forming a new Polish government. This information had come from Donald Maclean, the British spy in Washington, and perhaps also from Alger Hiss in the State Department.

In Soviet eyes the definition of 'fascist' included anyone who did not follow the orders of the Communist Party. On 28 March sixteen representatives of the Home Army and its political wing were invited for discussions by the Soviet authorities. Although given guarantees of safe-conduct, they were immediately arrested by the NKVD and taken to Moscow. They were later put on trial, and in 1946 their leader General Leopold Okulicki was murdered in prison. Churchill tried to prompt Roosevelt into a 'show-down', but the American President, although shaken by Stalin's bad faith, wanted to 'minimize the general Soviet problem as much as possible'.

British indignation was prompted mainly by Eisenhower's obstinate refusal to accept that there were political implications in his strategy. He believed that his task was to finish the war in Europe as rapidly as possible, and he did not share British concerns about Stalin and Poland. Senior British officers referred to Eisenhower's deference to Stalin as 'Have a go, Joe', a call used by prostitutes in London when soliciting American soldiers. Eisenhower may have been politically naive, but it was Churchill who demonstrated a more serious failure to grasp geo-political reality at this moment. In one sense at least, the decisions at Yalta and his own percentage agreement were irrelevant. Ever since the Teheran conference at the end of 1943 when Stalin, supported by Roosevelt, had defined Allied strategy in the west, Europe was bound to be divided in Stalin's favour. The western Allies were finding that they could liberate half of Europe only at the cost of re-enslaving the other half.

Stalin still suspected that Eisenhower's frankness about Allied intentions was a trick. On 31 March he received the American ambassador Averell Harriman and Sir Archibald Clark Kerr, his British counterpart, in the Kremlin. They discussed the overall plan which Eisenhower had described in his signal, SCAF-252, and his intention to ignore Berlin. Stalin said that it seemed a good one, but first he must consult his staff.

The very next morning, which happened to be 1 April, Marshals Zhukov and Konev were summoned to Stalin's office. 'Are you aware how the situation is shaping up?' he asked them. They were clearly not quite sure what they were supposed to say and replied cautiously.

'Read the telegram to them,' he told General S. M. Shtemenko, the Stavka chief of operations. This message claimed that Montgomery would head for Berlin, and that Patton's Third Army would turn from its drive towards Leipzig and Dresden to attack Berlin from the south. Stalin was presumably putting pressure on the two front commanders with a faked document, which bore little relation to SCAF-252.

'Well, then,' Stalin said, staring at his two marshals. 'Who is going to take Berlin: are we or are the Allies?'

'It is we who shall take Berlin,' Konev replied immediately, 'and we will take it before the Allies.' Konev was evidently keen to beat Zhukov to the prize, and Stalin, who liked to create a rivalry between his commanders, approved. He made one alteration to General Antonov's plan, by eliminating part of the boundary between the two fronts to give Konev the chance of striking for Berlin from the south. The Stavka went to work with a vengeance. The operation involved 2.5 million men, 41,600 guns and heavy mortars, 6,250 tanks and self-propelled guns and 7,500 aircraft. Everything had to be ready in just over two weeks, by 16 April.

Once the conference was over, Stalin replied to Eisenhower's message. He told him that his plan 'completely coincided' with that of the Red Army and that 'Berlin has lost its former strategic importance.' The Soviet Union would deploy only secondary forces against it, while its main effort would be made to the south to join up with American forces, probably in the second half of May. 'However, this plan may undergo certain alterations, depending on circumstances.' It was the greatest April Fool in modern history.

*

At the meeting with Harriman and Clark Kerr, Stalin had appeared 'much impressed' by the vast numbers of prisoners the Allies were rounding up in the west. Patton's Third Army alone had taken 300,000. But such figures of course fed his suspicion that the Germans were surrendering to the British and Americans, while concentrating their forces against the eastern front. Ilya Ehrenburg reflected this in an article in *Krasnaya Zvezda*. 'American tankists are enjoying excursions in the picturesque Harz mountains,' he wrote. The Germans were surrendering 'with fanatical persistence'. But the phrase which angered Averell Harriman the most was his remark that the Americans were 'conquering with cameras', implying that they were just tourists.

Even devoted followers of the Führer found their faith in 'final victory' shaken. 'In the last few days we have been rushed by events,' an army officer on the staff of an SS corps in the Black Forest wrote in his diary on 2 April. 'Düsseldorf lost, Cologne lost. The disastrous bridgehead at Remagen . . . In the south-east the Bolsheviks have reached Wiener Neustadt. Blow upon blow. We are coming to the end. Do our leaders see perhaps a possibility? Does the death of our soldiers, the destruction of our cities and villages make any sense now?' Yet he still felt that they should fight on until told otherwise.

The war correspondent Godfrey Blunden noted how Germans still made ambushes, killed some Americans and then jumped up with their arms raised shouting 'Kamerad!' and expecting to be treated well. He was struck by the contrasts in the advance. 'We have gone through small towns perfectly preserved from war and a few miles further on entered cities lying in ruins.' Almost everywhere, they were greeted by pillow slips and sheets hung out of windows as tokens of surrender. The destruction wrought by the combined bomber offensive shook all who observed the reality on the ground. Stephen Spender later wrote of Cologne: 'One passes through street after street of houses whose windows look hollow and blackened – like the open mouths of a charred corpse.' In Wuppertal, the tram lines were 'curled up like celery stalks'. 'Roads are still thronged with slave workers steadily moving westward,' Blunden recorded. 'I saw one today with a tricolore flying from the pack on his back.' He also saw released slave workers raid a brewery, then dance in the street and smash windows.

It was not long before the full horrors of the Nazi regime became apparent. On 4 April American troops entered Ohrdruf concentration camp, part of Buchenwald, to find apathetic, skeletal figures surrounded by unburied corpses. Eisenhower was so appalled that he ordered soldiers to visit the camp, and brought in war correspondents to witness the sight. Some of the guards had tried to disguise themselves, but when they were pointed out by prisoners Allied troops shot them on the spot. Other guards had already been killed by prisoners, but few had the strength. On 11 April, American soldiers came across the tunnel factory of Mittelbau-Dora. Four days later British troops entered Belsen. The stench and the sights made most of them feel physically sick. Some 30,000 prisoners were in a limbo between life and death, surrounded by more than 10,000 rotting corpses. Belsen's population had been grotesquely swollen by the survivors of death marches who had been dumped there. More than 9,000 had died in the previous two weeks and 37,000 in the previous six, from starvation and a typhus epidemic. Of those still just alive, another 14,000 died despite all the efforts of the Royal Army Medical Corps. The senior officer present ordered a strong detachment of troops to march into the adjacent town of Bergen, to bring back the whole population at bayonet point. As they were put to work moving corpses to mass graves, these German civilians all professed shock and protested their ignorance, to the angry disbelief of British officers.

The aimless movement of tens of thousands of concentration camp prisoners from one place to another continued with murderous futility. Some 57,000 women and men from Ravensbrück and Sachsenhausen were still being herded west. Altogether, between 200,000 and 350,000 prisoners are estimated to have died on the death marches. German civilians showed them little pity. Blunden heard of the Gardelegen massacre, where SS guards handed over several thousand prisoners from Mittelbau-Dora to a mixed group of Luftwaffe personnel, Hitler Jugend and local SA members. They forced the prisoners into a barn and set fire to it, then shot down any who attempted to escape. The speed of the

Allied advance in the west prompted groups of SS, often aided by Volkssturm, to carry out many other massacres of prisoners.

Allied forces also had to care for their own prisoners of war, released from camps overrun in their advance. During the month of April a quarter of a million needed to be fed and repatriated. Eisenhower requested RAF and USAAF bombers to be diverted to this task, now that their work of destruction was virtually over.

The biggest relief operation was planned for the starving Netherlands. When Reichskommissar Arthur Seyss-Inquart threatened to drown large areas, Eisenhower's SHAEF headquarters announced that he and Generaloberst Blaskowitz, the commander-in-chief in Holland, would be treated as war criminals if that happened. Then, after complicated negotiations through the Dutch resistance, the German authorities agreed not to hinder attempts to drop food supplies in the worst-affected areas, including Rotterdam and The Hague. In Operation Manna, 3,000 sorties by RAF bombers parachuted in more than 6,000 tons. For countless people close to death, it came only just in time.

After the encirclement of Generalfeldmarschall Model's Army Group B in the Ruhr during the first week of April, divisions from Simpson's Ninth Army pushed rapidly forward towards the River Elbe. Eisenhower, taken aback by the British reaction over his change of strategy, vacillated over the taking of Berlin. Simpson, in his orders, was told to exploit any opportunity for seizing a bridgehead over the Elbe and to be prepared to continue the advance on Berlin or to the north-east. First Army on his right was heading for Leipzig and Dresden, while Patton's Third Army was already in the Harz Mountains and heading for Czechoslovakia. In southern Germany, Lieutenant General Alexander M. Patch's Seventh Army and Lattre de Tassigny's First French Army were advancing through the Black Forest.

On 8 April Eisenhower visited Major General Alexander Bolling, the commander of the 84th Infantry Division, after it had taken the city of Hanover.

'Alex, where are you going next?' Eisenhower asked him.

'General, we're going to push on ahead. We have a clear go at Berlin and nothing can stop us.'

'Keep going,' Eisenhower told him and put a hand on his shoulder. 'I wish you all the luck in the world and don't let anybody stop you.' Bolling understood this as confirmation that Berlin was their objective.

On 11 April American troops reached Magdeburg along the autobahn from Hanover, and the following day crossed the Elbe south of Dessau. Over the next two days several other bridgeheads were seized across the river. Bolling's 84th Division repulsed a counter-attack by part of General Walther Wenck's lightly armed Twelfth Army. He had bridges across the Elbe ready to take the 2nd Armored Division, and during the night of 14 April its vehicles rumbled across ready to advance on Berlin. Both Simpson and Bolling guessed that opposition would be light. They were right. Almost all the SS formations were deployed facing the Red Army, which they knew was about to unleash its own assault on the capital. Most army units were now only too happy to surrender to the Americans before the Soviets arrived.

Eisenhower suddenly had another change of heart. He talked to Bradley, who thought that the capture of Berlin might cost 100,000 casualties, an estimate he later admitted to have been far too high. They both agreed that heavy casualties were an unacceptable price to pay for a prestige objective, from which they would have to withdraw anyway when the fighting finished. The European Advisory Commission had already settled the boundary of the Soviet occupation zone along the Elbe, while Berlin itself would be partitioned. Roosevelt had died of a cerebral haemorrhage on 12 April, and perhaps this also had an effect on Eisenhower's thinking.

Early on 15 April, Simpson was summoned to 12th Army Group headquarters near Wiesbaden. Bradley was waiting for him at the airfield when his aircraft touched down. Without wasting any words, Bradley told him straight off that Ninth Army was to halt on the Elbe. There was to be no advance on Berlin. 'Where in hell did you get this?' Simpson asked.

'From Ike,' Bradley replied. Simpson, feeling dazed and dejected, returned to his headquarters wondering how he was going to announce this to his officers and men, especially as it came on top of the news of Roosevelt's death.

Eisenhower had made the correct decision even if for the

wrong reason. Stalin would never have allowed the Americans to take Berlin first. As soon as Red Army aviation pilots had spotted their advance, Stalin would almost certainly have ordered Soviet aircraft to attack them. Afterwards, he would probably have claimed that it had been the fault of the Allies for trying to trick him with their assurances of advancing further to the south. Eisenhower wanted to avoid clashes with the Red Army at all costs. And strongly supported by Marshall, he rejected Churchill's argument that the Americans and British 'should shake hands with the Russians as far to the east as possible'. They knew that Churchill wanted to put pressure on Stalin in the hope of obtaining better treatment for Poland, but they both refused to be influenced by what they saw as the post-war politics of Europe.

Goebbels, on hearing of Roosevelt's death, was overjoyed. He immediately telephoned Hitler, who was sunk in gloom in the Reichschancellery bunker. 'My Führer, I congratulate you!' he said. 'Roosevelt is dead. It is written in the stars that the second half of April will be the turning point for us. This Friday 13 April, it is the turning point!' Goebbels had been trying to raise Hitler's spirits a few days before by reading to him from Carlyle's *History of Friedrich II of Prussia*, including the passage where Frederick, tempted by suicide at the lowest point of the Seven Years War, suddenly received news of the death of the Tsarina Elizabeth. 'The Miracle of the House of Brandenburg had come to pass.' The following night Allied bombers reduced much of Frederick the Great's Potsdam to rubble.

On 8 April, as their enemies closed in, Hitler and the Nazi leadership had embarked on a frenzy of killing to pre-empt any chance of another stab-in-the-back. Prominent prisoners, especially those from the July plot and others suspected of treason, were murdered. They included Admiral Canaris, Dietrich Bonhoeffer and the cabinet-maker Georg Elser, who had tried to assassinate Hitler in November 1939. 'Flying courts martial' handed out death sentences on deserters and any who retreated without orders. Soldiers were told to shoot any officer of whatever rank who told them to pull back. On 19 March Hitler, who had already made clear to close associates that he intended 'to take a whole world' with him, had issued what was known as the 'Nero Order' to destroy bridges, factories and utilities. If the German people were incapable of victory, then in his view they did not deserve to survive. Albert Speer, supported by industrialists and some generals, managed to thwart some of this destruction with the argument that it was defeatist to wreck installations that might be recaptured in a counter-attack.

Hitler began to have doubts about the enigmatic Speer and he began to suspect even his most loyal paladin, Heinrich Himmler, who was trying to 'sell' Jews to the Allies or use them as bargaining counters. The Nazi Party's authority had disintegrated as word spread of Gauleiters escaping to safety with their families, having ordered everyone else to fight to the death. The braggarts and bullies were revealed for the cowardly hypocrites they really were. The greeting of 'Heil Hitler!' and the Nazi salute were now used only by diehard fanatics, or by others made nervous in their presence. Hardly anybody believed any more in Hitler's 'empty phrases and promises', as an SS Sicherheitsdienst report warned. People were angry that the regime refused to face the reality of defeat and avoid the senseless waste of more lives. Only the most desperate believed Hitler's fantasy that a falling-out between the Allies would somehow save Germany.

The Nazi empire was now reduced to a ribbon from Norway down to northern Italy. Only isolated pockets remained outside. Guderian's demands to repatriate forces, particularly the vast garrison in Norway and the remnants of Army Group North trapped on the Courland Peninsula, had all been angrily rejected by Hitler. His defiance of military logic reduced military commanders to despair. Guderian himself had been sacked on 28 March, after a failed attempt to relieve Küstrin. The row in the Führer bunker had shaken all those who witnessed it. 'Hitler became paler and paler,' noted the chief of staff's aide, 'while Guderian became redder and redder.'

Guderian was replaced by General Hans Krebs, the officer whom Stalin had slapped on the back on the Moscow platform shortly before Operation Barbarossa. Krebs, a short, witty opportunist, had no experience of command, which suited Hitler, since he wanted nothing more than an efficient subordinate to do his bidding. General staff officers at OKH headquarters out at Zossen did not know what to think. They were already suffering from 'a mixture of nervous energy and trance', said one of them, because of the sensation of 'having to do your duty while seeing at the same time that this duty was completely pointless'.

On 9 April in Italy the 15th Army Group, now under General Mark Clark, launched an offensive beyond the Gothic Line north towards the River Po. The US Fifth Army and the British Eighth Army had become even more of an international conglomeration, with the 1st Canadian Division which had taken Rimini in September, the 8th Indian Division, the 2nd New Zealand Division, the 6th South African Armoured Division, II Polish Corps, two Italian formations, a Greek mountain brigade, Brazilian forces and the Jewish Brigade. On 21 April, the 3rd Polish Carpathian Brigade finally captured Bologna for the US Fifth Army, commanded by Lucien Truscott, while the Eighth Army took Ferrara and also reached the Po.

Churchill was hoping for a rapid advance. He was concerned that the Soviet–Yugoslav treaty, which was signed two days later, would support Tito's claims to Trieste and Istria at the head of the Adriatic. Churchill turned down Tito's requests for more aid. Since the Yugoslavs had entered the Soviet embrace, they could look instead to Moscow for assistance. He also feared that Soviet power in the region might encourage the Italian Communists, whose partisans already represented a powerful force in northern Italy.

On 11 April the Red Army reached the centre of Vienna. Even before the battle for Berlin, a race for position in post-war Europe was on. Churchill urged Eisenhower to allow Patton's Third Army to push on to Prague, but the supreme commander insisted on consulting with the Stavka. The refusal was immediate and peremptory. Churchill also became concerned about Denmark. Once across the mouth of the Oder near Stettin, Rokossovsky's 2nd Belorussian Front could make a dash across Mecklenburg.

On 14 April Hitler issued an Order of the Day to his troops on the Oder and Neisse front. Once again it threatened that anyone who did not fulfil his duty would be 'treated as a traitor to our people'. Hitler, with rambling references to the defeat of the Turks outside Vienna in 1683, claimed that 'this time the Bolshevik will experience the ancient fate of Asiatics'. (He failed to mention that the city had in fact been saved by Polish heavy cavalry.) Hitler also seemed to ignore the fact that Vienna had just fallen to the Red Army. Goebbels instead coined the slogan 'Berlin remains German and Vienna will be German again'. Historical parallels and modern propaganda no longer had any effect on the majority of Germans.

Berliners prepared for the onslaught with foreboding. Women were offered pistol-shooting practice. Members of the Volkssturm, some of whom were wearing French helmets captured in 1940, were put to work constructing barricades across streets already littered with masonry and broken glass. Trams and railway goods wagons, filled with stone and rubble, were manoeuvred into place, pavements were ripped up, and individual foxholes dug for men and boys armed with Panzerfaust launchers. Housewives laid in what supplies they could, and they boiled water to be kept in preserving jars for drinking when the taps ran dry.

Teenage members of the Reichsarbeitsdienst, a paramilitary labour service, were inducted en masse into the army. Many of them were forced to witness executions: 'To accustom you to death!' an officer told them. Mothers and girlfriends came to see them off. These recruits, escorted by NCOs, tried to keep up their spirits with gallows humour as they departed for the Oder front on the S-Bahn local rail network. 'See you in the mass grave!' was one farewell.

48

The Berlin Operation

APRIL–MAY 1945

On the night of 14 April, German troops dug in on the Seelow Heights west of the River Oder heard tank engines. Music and sinister Soviet propaganda messages blasted at full volume from loudspeakers failed to camouflage the noise as the 1st Guards Tank Army crossed the river into the bridgehead. This extended across the Oderbruch flood plain below them, where a river mist covered the sodden meadows. Altogether nine armies of Zhukov's 1st Belorussian Front were poised to attack between the Hohenzollern Canal in the north and Frankfurt an der Oder in the south.

General Chuikov's 8th Guards Army had increased the bridgehead the day before, with an attack which pushed back the 20th Panzergrenadier Division. Hitler was so angry on hearing the news that he ordered all medals to be stripped from members of the division until they won them back. Chuikov was displeased for a very different reason. He heard that on the night of 15 April Marshal Zhukov would take over his command post on the Reitwein Spur because it had the best view of the Oder flood plain and the Seelow Heights. Relations between the two commanders had deteriorated further since Chuikov's strong criticisms over the failure to push on immediately to Berlin at the beginning of February.

More than eighty kilometres to the south of Zhukov's left flank, Marshal Konev's 1st Ukrainian Front lined the Neisse with seven armies. Its political department worked up a powerful message of revenge: 'There will be no pity. They have sown the wind and now they are reaping the whirlwind.'

News of the change in the party line in Moscow the day before had not reached the front lines. Stalin had finally understood that both the rhetoric and the reality of vengeance were simply intensifying German resistance. This was also why the bulk of the German army was so keen to surrender to the Allied armies in the west. In his view, this greatly increased the risk that the Americans would take Berlin before the Red Army.

On 14 April Georgii Aleksandrov, the head of Soviet propaganda, published an important article in *Pravda*, which was almost certainly dictated by Stalin himself. This attacked Ilya Ehrenburg's calls for revenge and his description of Germany as 'only a colossal gang'. Aleksandrov's piece, entitled 'Comrade Ehrenburg Oversimplifies', said that while some German officers 'fight for the cannibal regime, others throw bombs at Hitler and his clique [the July plotters], or persuade Germans to put down their weapons [General von Seydlitz and the League of German Officers]. The Gestapo hunt for opponents of the regime, and the appeals to Germans to denounce them proved that not all Germans were the same.' He also quoted Stalin's remark: 'Hitlers come and go, but Germany and the Germans remain.' Ehrenburg was devastated to find himself being sacrificed in this way, yet most officers and soldiers took little notice of the change in policy. The propaganda image of Germans as ravening beasts had gone too deep.

The Soviet authorities, even within sight of victory, did not trust their own troops. Officers were told to name any of their 'morally and politically unstable' men who might desert to warn the enemy of the attack, so that SMERSh could arrest them. And General Serov, the NKVD chief who had supervised the repression of eastern Poland in 1939, became alarmed about the 'unhealthy moods developed among the officers and soldiers of the 1st Polish Army'. They had become excited about the rapid advance of the British and American armies in the west, having listened illegally to the BBC. They convinced themselves that General Anders's forces were approaching Berlin. 'As soon as our troops meet up with Anders's men,' an artillery commanding officer was accused of saying by a SMERSh informer, 'then you can say goodbye to the [Soviet-controlled] provisional government. The London government will take power again and Poland will once more be what it was before 1939. England and America will help Poland get rid of the Russians.' Serov's operatives arrested nearly 2,000 men just before the offensive.

German officers were even more concerned about disaffection

in their ranks. They were horrified when young soldiers shouted back at Soviet loudspeaker broadcasts that were telling them to give up, to ask whether they would be sent to Siberia if they laid down their arms. Officers in the Fourth Panzer Army facing Konev's troops on the Neisse confiscated white handkerchiefs to prevent them being used as a sign of surrender. Men caught hiding or attempting to desert were forced out into no-man's-land and ordered to dig trenches there. Many commanders resorted to desperate lies. They claimed that thousands of tanks were arriving to support them, that new miracle weapons would be used against the enemy, and even that the western Allies were joining them to fight the Bolsheviks. Junior officers were told to have no compunction about shooting any of their men who wavered, and that if all their men ran away, then they had better shoot themselves.

A Luftwaffe Oberleutnant commanding a scratch company of trainee technicians was standing in his trench next to his senior NCO. He shivered. 'Tell me,' he said turning to the Kompanietruppführer. 'Are you also cold?' 'We're not cold, Herr Oberleutnant,' he replied. 'We're afraid.'

On the eve of battle Red Army soldiers shaved and wrote letters. Sappers were already at work in the dark removing mines ahead of their advance. Chuikov had to control his temper when he saw a convoy of staff cars bringing Marshal Zhukov and his entourage, as they approached his command post on the Reitwein Spur with their headlights on.

At 05.00 hours Moscow time on 16 April, which was two hours earlier by Berlin time, Zhukov's 'god of war' opened fire, with 8,983 guns, heavy mortars and Katyusha batteries. It was the most intense barrage of the whole war, with 1,236,000 rounds fired on the first day alone. The intensity was so great that even sixty kilometres away on the eastern side of Berlin walls vibrated. Sensing that the great offensive had begun, housewives emerged from their front doors and began to talk to neighbours in subdued tones, with anxious glances towards the east. Women and girls wondered whether the Americans would reach Berlin first to save them from the Red Army.

Zhukov was pleased with his idea of using 143 searchlights to dazzle the enemy. But both the bombardment and the searchlights proved unhelpful to his men. As the infantry charged forward, shouting 'Na Berlin!', the searchlights behind silhouetted them, and the ground ahead was so churned up by craters that their progress was slow. Surprisingly, the artillery had concentrated on the first line of defence, despite the Red Army's awareness of the German tactic of withdrawing all but a small covering force when a major attack was expected.

Zhukov, who usually reconnoitred the ground carefully before an attack, had failed to do so this time. He had relied instead on air-reconnaissance photographs, but these images did not reveal what a strong defensive feature the Seelow Heights represented. At first, Chuikov's 8th Guards Army on the left and Colonel General Nikolai Berzarin's 5th Shock Army on the right advanced quite well. The 1st Guards Tank Army would then pass through them once they had secured the crest. At dawn, Shturmovik ground-attack aircraft streaked in, flying through the fountains of earth thrown up by the shelling, to strafe and bomb German defences and vehicles. Their greatest success was to hit the German Ninth Army's ammunition depot, which blew up in a massive explosion.

Traumatized German survivors from the front line ran back up the slope of the Seelow Heights, shouting 'Der Iwan kommt!' Further back, local farmers and their families also started to flee. 'Refugees hurry by like creatures of the underworld,' wrote a young soldier, 'women, children and old men surprised in their sleep, some only half-dressed. In their faces is despair and deadly fear. Crying children holding their mothers' hands look out at the world's destruction with shocked eyes.'

Zhukov in the command post on the Reitwein Spur became increasingly nervous as the morning progressed. Through his powerful binoculars he could see that the advance had slowed, if not halted. Knowing that Stalin would hand the Berlin objective to Konev if he failed to break through, he began cursing and swore at Chuikov, whose troops had still barely reached the edge of the flood plain. Zhukov threatened to strip commanders of their rank and send them to a *shtraf* company. He then suddenly decided to change his whole plan of attack.

In an attempt to speed up the advance, he would send Colonel General Katukov's 1st Guards Tank Army in ahead of the infantry. Chuikov was horrified. He could imagine the chaos. At 15.00 hours, Zhukov put through a call to Stalin in Moscow and explained the situation. 'So, you've underestimated the enemy on the Berlin axis,' the Soviet leader said. 'And I was thinking that you were already on the approaches to Berlin, yet you're still on the Seelow Heights. Things have started more successfully for Konev,' he added pointedly. Stalin did not comment on Zhukov's proposed changes to his plan.

The change of plan caused exactly the sort of confusion Chuikov had feared. There were already massive jams, with the 1st Guards Tank Army trapped behind the vehicles of the other two armies, waiting to advance. It became a nightmare for traffic controllers trying to unscramble the mess. And even when the tanks were extricated and began to push forward, they were picked off by 88mm guns sited below Neuhardenberg. In the smoke, they found themselves ambushed by German infantry with Panzerfausts and a platoon of assault guns. Things did not improve when they finally began to climb the Seelow Heights. The mud on the steep slopes, churned by shellfire, often proved too much both for the heavy Stalin tanks and for the T-34s. On the left, Katukov's leading brigade was ambushed by Tiger tanks of the SS Heavy Panzer Battalion 502. Only in the centre did they have any success where the 9th Fallschirmjäger Division collapsed. By nightfall, Zhukov's armies had still failed to seize the crest of the Seelow Heights.

In the Führer bunker under the Reichschancellery, telephone calls were constantly being made to OKH headquarters out at Zossen demanding news. But Zossen itself, which lay to the south of Berlin, was vulnerable if Marshal Konev's forces broke through.

The 1st Ukrainian Front, as Stalin had told Zhukov, was doing rather better, despite having had no bridgeheads across the Neisse. Konev's artillery and supporting aircraft kept the Germans deep in their trenches as the leading battalions rushed the river in assault boats. A wide smokescreen was also laid by the 2nd Air Army, aided by a gentle breeze in the right direction. It was impossible for the Fourth Panzer Army to identify where the attack was concentrated. Bridgeheads were established and

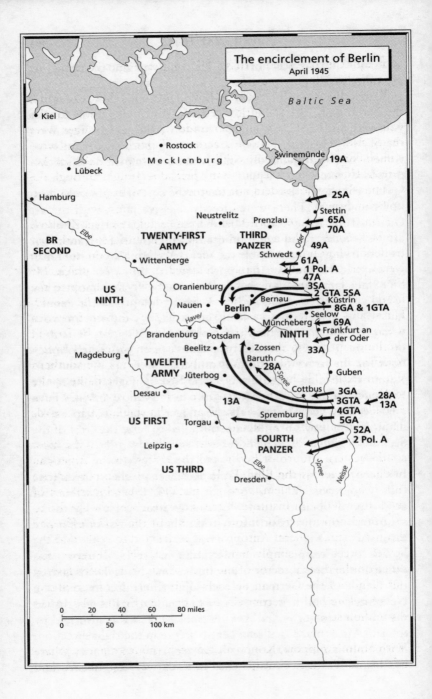

The encirclement of Berlin
April 1945

Baltic Sea

Kiel

Rostock

Lübeck

Mecklenburg

Swinemünde · 19A

Hamburg

2SA

Neustrelitz · Prenzlau

Stettin

65A

70A

TWENTY-FIRST ARMY

THIRD PANZER

49A

BR SECOND

Elbe

Wittenberge

Schwedt

61A

1 Pol. A

47A

3SA

US NINTH

Oranienburg

2 GTA 5SA

8GA & 1GTA

Nauen

Bernau

Küstrin

Havel

Berlin

Seelow

Brandenburg

Potsdam

Müncheberg

69A

NINTH

Frankfurt an der Oder

Beelitz

Zossen

33A

Magdeburg

TWELFTH ARMY

Baruth

28A

Jüterbog

Spree

Guben

Dessau

13A

Cottbus

3GA

3GTA

28A

US FIRST

Spremburg

4GTA

13A

Torgau

5GA

Leipzig

52A

2 Pol. A

FOURTH PANZER

US THIRD

Spree

Neisse

Dresden

0   20   40   60   80 miles

0   50   100 km

soon tanks were ferried across while sappers began constructing pontoon bridges.

Konev did not suffer from Zhukov's disastrous change of mind. He had already planned for the 3rd and 4th Guards Tank Armies to lead his offensive. Soon after midday, the first bridges were ready and their tanks rumbled across. While the Germans were still shaken from the bombardment and confused by the smoke-screen, Konev sent his leading tank brigades straight through the German lines with orders not to stop. The infantry would mop up behind them.

That night of 16 April was a humiliating one for Zhukov. He had to call Stalin again on the radio-telephone to admit that his troops had not yet taken the Seelow Heights. Stalin told him that it was his fault for having changed the plan of attack. He then asked Zhukov whether he was sure he would secure the heights by the next day. Zhukov assured him that he would. He argued that it was easier to destroy the German forces in the open than in Berlin itself, so time would not be lost in the long run. Stalin then warned him that he would tell Konev to divert his two tank armies northwards towards the southern side of Berlin. He hung up abruptly. Soon afterwards he spoke to Konev. 'Zhukov is not getting on very well,' he said. 'Turn Rybalko [3rd Guards Tank Army] and Lelyushenko [4th Guards Tank Army] towards Zehlendorf.'

Stalin's choice of Zehlendorf was significant. It was the most south-western suburb of Berlin and the closest to the American bridgehead across the Elbe. Perhaps it was also no coincidence that it adjoined Dahlem, with the nuclear research facilities of the Kaiser Wilhelm Institute. Three hours earlier, in response to an American request for information about the Soviet offensive against Berlin, General Antonov was instructed to reply that the Soviet forces were simply 'undertaking a large-scale reconnaissance on the central sector of the front for the purpose of finding out details of the German defences'. The April Fool continued. Never before had a 'reconnaissance' been carried out by forces 2.5 million strong.

With Stalin's support, Konev forced on his tank brigades to satisfy his ambition to beat his rival to the glorious prize. Zhukov was becoming frantic at the lack of progress. On the Seelow Heights the chaotic battle continued under clearer skies, which helped the Shturmovik fighter-bombers. The collapse of the 9th Fallschirmjäger Division, whose ranks had been filled with Luftwaffe ground personnel rather than paratroopers, eased the situation for Katukov's tank units but they still faced counter-attacks, both by the *Kurmark* Division with Panther tanks and by soldiers and Hitler Youth fighting with Panzerfausts at close range.

Conditions in German dressing stations and field hospitals were gruesome. The surgeons were completely overwhelmed by the numbers of wounded. On the Soviet side, things were little better. Soldiers wounded on the first day had still not been col-lected and cared for, as reports revealed afterwards. The numbers rose all the time as the artillery of the 5th Shock Army began shell-ing Katukov's tank brigades by mistake.

German aircraft of the Leonidas Squadron based at Jüterbog imitated the Japanese kamikaze pilots in mostly vain attempts to destroy the bridges over the Oder. This sort of suicide attack was termed a *Selbstopfereinsatz* – 'a self-sacrifice mission'. Thirty-five pilots died in this way. Their commander Generalmajor Robert Fuchs sent their names 'to the Führer on his imminent fifty-sixth birthday', assuming that it was the sort of present he would appreciate. But the insane scheme was soon halted by the advance of the 4th Guards Tank Army towards the squadron's airfield.

Konev's tank brigades raced for the River Spree south of Cottbus, in order to cross it before the Germans could organize any defence. General Rybalko, up with his lead brigade, did not want to waste time bringing up pontoon bridges. He simply or-dered the first tank straight into the Spree, which was some fifty metres wide at that point. The water came to just above the tracks, but below the driver's hatch. He drove on through, and the rest of the brigade followed in line ahead, ignoring the machine-gun bul-lets rattling against their armour. The Germans had no anti-tank guns in the area. The road to OKH headquarters in Zossen lay open.

Staff officers in Zossen had no idea of the breakthrough to the south. Their attention was still fixed on the Seelow Heights, where

Generaloberst Gotthard Heinrici had thrown in his only reserve, Obergruppenführer Felix Steiner's III SS *Germanische* Panzer Corps. This included the 11th SS Division *Nordland* manned by Danish, Norwegian, Swedish, Finnish and Estonian volunteers.

On the morning of 18 April, the fighting on the Seelow Heights reached a new intensity. Zhukov had heard from Stalin that Konev's tank armies were forging ahead to Berlin, and that if his 1st Belorussian Front did not make better progress he would tell Rokossovsky to the north to turn his 2nd Belorussian Front towards Berlin as well. This was an empty threat since Rokossovsky's forces had been so delayed that they did not cross the Oder until 20 April, but Zhukov was so desperate that he ordered attack after attack. Finally the breakthrough came later that morning. One of Katukov's tank brigades charged through along the Reichsstrasse 1, the main highway from Berlin which ran all the way to the now destroyed East Prussian capital of Königsberg. Generaloberst Theodor Busse's Ninth Army was split, and disintegration soon followed. The cost had been high. The 1st Belorussian Front had lost more than 30,000 men killed, as opposed to 12,000 German soldiers. Zhukov showed little remorse. He was interested only in the objective.

That day, Konev was troubled only by an attack launched against the 52nd Army on his southern flank by Generalfeldmarschall Schörner's forces. This was a hurried, ill-prepared operation and easily rebuffed. His two tank armies managed to advance between thirty-five and forty-five kilometres. He would have been even more encouraged if he had known of the chaos caused in Berlin as Nazi leaders interfered with those trying to organize the defence of the city.

Goebbels, the Reich defence commissar for Berlin, tried to act as a military commander. He ordered that all the Volkssturm units in the city should march out to create a new defence line. The commander of the Berlin garrison was appalled and protested. He did not know that secretly this was exactly what both Albert Speer and General Heinrici had wanted in order to avoid the destruction of the city. General Helmuth Weidling who commanded the LVI Panzer Corps was distracted by visits from Ribbentrop and Artur Axmann, the head of the Hitler Youth, who offered to send in more of his teenagers armed with

Panzerfausts. Weidling tried to persuade him to desist from 'the sacrifice of children for an already doomed cause'.

The approach of the Red Army increased the Nazi regime's murderous instincts. Another thirty political prisoners were beheaded in Plötzensee Prison that day. SS patrols in the city centre did not arrest suspected deserters, but hanged them from lamp-posts with placards round their necks announcing their cowardice. Such accusations from the SS were hypocritical to say the least. While their patrols executed army deserters and even some Hitler Youth, Heinrich Himmler and senior officers of the Waffen-SS were secretly planning to disengage their units and pull them back to Denmark.

On 19 April the Ninth Army, irretrievably split in three, reeled back. Women and girls in the area, terrified of what awaited them, begged the soldiers to take them with them. The 1st Guards Tank Army supported by Chuikov's 8th Guards Army reached Müncheberg in their advance along Reichsstrasse 1. While they headed for the eastern and south-eastern suburbs of Berlin, Zhukov's other armies began to advance around the northern edge of the city. Stalin insisted on a full encirclement to ensure that no American attempt might be made to break through, even at the eleventh hour. American troops were entering Leipzig that day and took Nuremberg after heavy fighting, but Simpson's divisions on the Elbe remained where they were as Eisenhower had ordered.

The dawn of 20 April, Hitler's birthday, followed the tradition of *Führerwetter* by providing a beautiful spring day. Allied air forces marked the day with their own greeting. Göring spent the morning supervising the evacuation of his looted paintings and other treasures from his ostentatious country house of Karinhall north of Berlin. After his possessions had been loaded on to Luftwaffe trucks, he pressed the plunger wired to the explosives planted inside. The house collapsed in a cloud of dust. He turned and walked to his car to be driven to the Reichschancellery, where along with the other Nazi leaders he would congratulate the Führer on what they all knew would be his last birthday.

Hitler looked at least two decades older than his fifty-six years. He was stooped and grey-faced and his left arm shook. That morning on the radio, Goebbels had called on all Germans to trust blindly in him. Yet it was clear to even his most devoted colleagues that the Führer was in no state to think rationally. Himmler, having drunk his leader's health in champagne at midnight according to his private custom, was secretly trying to make contact with the Americans. He believed that Eisenhower would recognize that they needed him to maintain order in Germany.

The leaders who gathered in the half-wrecked grandeur of the Reichschancellery included Grossadmiral Dönitz, Ribbentrop, Speer, Kaltenbrunner and Generalfeldmarschall Keitel. It soon became apparent that only Goebbels intended to stay with his Führer in Berlin. Dönitz, who was given supreme command in northern Germany, was leaving with Hitler's blessing. All the others were simply finding excuses to get out of Berlin before it was completely surrounded and its airfields seized by the Red Army. Hitler was disappointed in his supposedly loyal paladins, particularly Göring, who claimed that he would organize resistance in Bavaria. Several urged their Führer to leave for the south, but he refused. That day marked what became known as 'the flight of the Golden Pheasants', as senior Nazi Party members shed their brown, red and gold uniforms to escape Berlin with their families while routes to the south remained open.

In the city, housewives queued for a last issue of 'crisis rations'. They could clearly hear the sound of guns in the distance. That afternoon heavy artillery from the 3rd Shock Army opened fire on the northern suburbs of Berlin. Zhukov ordered Katukov to send tank brigades into Berlin whatever the cost. He knew that Konev's 3rd Guards Tank Army was heading for the southern edge of the city. But, unknown to Zhukov, they had run into strong forces which they had not expected. A large part of Busse's Ninth Army was escaping through the Spreewald across their path.

The German retreat from the Oder front into the city was greatly hampered by the thousands of civilians trying to flee in panic from the advancing enemy. Some decided to stay. 'The farmers stand at their garden fences at the side of the road and watch the flight with solemn faces,' wrote a young soldier. 'Their wives tearfully dispense coffee, which we gulp down greedily. We march and run, without rest or peace.' Many German soldiers indulged in looting houses on the way, and some sought oblivion in the alcohol they found. By the time they awoke, they would find themselves prisoners.

The SS *Nordland* Division in the pine forests east of the city fought some costly delaying actions, but few other formations were in any condition to put up an effective resistance. Rumours spread that American aircraft had dropped leaflets urging the Germans to hang on as they were coming to their aid, but few believed it. Squads of Feldgendarmerie and SS guarded cross-roads, not against the enemy but to seize stragglers to form into improvised detachments. Any who had thrown away their weapon, pack and helmet were arrested and shot. A police battalion was sent to Strausberg to execute those retreating without orders, but most of the policemen slipped away to hide before they got there.

On 21 April the last Allied air raid on Berlin ended early in the morning. An unnatural silence settled over the city, but a few hours later a series of explosions creating a different noise emphasized that Soviet artillery was now within range of the city centre. Hitler, who usually slept late, was woken. He emerged from his bedroom in the bunker to ask what was happening. The explanation clearly shook him. Zhukov's artillery commander, Colonel General Vasily Kazakov, had sent forward his heavy gun batteries of 152mm and 203mm howitzers. Housewives still queueing for rations were the main casualties, for few wanted to lose their place when this was clearly their last chance to stock up. The intensity of the shelling soon forced most of them back into cellars and air-raid shelters.

Although the circle round Berlin was almost closed, Stalin's paranoia still infected the NKVD's 7th Department interrogators. Any senior German officer captured was asked what he knew about plans for the Americans to join the Wehrmacht in an attempt to push Soviet forces back from Berlin. Stalin bullied Zhukov to complete the encirclement rapidly, using a totally invented threat. 'Due to the slowness of our advance,' he signalled, 'the Allies are approaching Berlin and will soon take it.' Zhukov was just as interested in blocking Konev's advance on the city. He pushed Katukov's 1st Guards Tank Army and Chuikov's 8th Guards Army further round towards the south-west.

One of Konev's tank spearheads was sighted approaching

Zossen. General Krebs was informed that his staff's defence detachment of armoured cars had been destroyed, in an unequal battle against T-34s. He telephoned the Reichschancellery, but Hitler refused to allow them to leave. Krebs and his staff officers began to wonder what Soviet prison camps would be like, but they were saved from capture only because the Soviet tanks ran out of fuel a few kilometres down the road. Another call from Berlin finally gave them permission to evacuate, and they left in a convoy of trucks.

As Berliners awaited the arrival of the Red Army, people prepared to meet their conquerors in different ways, either frivolous or tragic. In the Adlon Hotel, staff and customers listened to the sound of artillery shells. 'In the dining room,' wrote a Norwegian journalist, 'the few guests were overwhelmed by the readiness of waiters to pour the wine in a constant stream.' They did not want to leave any for the Russians. Some fathers, as they left to join their Volkssturm unit, thought only of the fate awaiting their families. 'It's all over, my child,' one told his daughter, handing her his pistol. 'Promise me that when the Russians come you will shoot yourself.' He then kissed her and left. Others killed their wife and children, then committed suicide themselves.

The city was divided into eight sectors, with the Landwehr Canal on the south and the River Spree on the north of the central district forming the last defence lines. Only Weidling's LVI Panzer Corps from the Ninth Army would bolster the garrison, bringing it up to 80,000 men. The CI Corps had withdrawn north of the city. The rest, including the XII SS Panzer Corps and the V SS Mountain Corps, were still fighting their way through Konev's forces in the forests to the south of Berlin. Konev had pushed forward the 3rd and 4th Guards Tank Armies and hurried his infantry armies forward to deal with Busse's forces. Although these German troops were a disorganized mass, with many civilian refugees mingled among them, there could be no doubt about their desperation to fight through to the Elbe to escape Soviet labour camps.

Ignorant of the situation and resorting to fantasy, Hitler gave orders that the Ninth Army should hold its positions on the Oder front. He accused the Luftwaffe of doing nothing, and threatened its chief of staff General der Flieger Karl Koller with execution. Remembering that Heinrici had a reserve, the III SS *Germanische* Corps, Hitler had a call put through to Obergruppenführer Steiner. He told him to launch a major counter-attack against the 1st Belorussian Front's northern flank. 'You will see, the Russians will suffer the greatest defeat of their history, before the gates of Berlin. It is expressly forbidden to fall back towards the west. Officers who do not comply unconditionally with this order are to be arrested and shot immediately. You, Steiner, are answerable with your head for execution of this order.' Steiner was speechless with disbelief. The *Germanische* Corps, which had been stripped of almost all its troops to strengthen the Ninth Army, had no more than a few battalions left. After recovering from the shock, Steiner rang back to remind General Krebs of the true situation, but Krebs repeated the order and said that he could not speak to the Führer who was busy.

Hitler's refusal to face reality was even more striking since he already knew that Model's army group in the Ruhr pocket had surrendered with 325,000 men. Model went off into a wood and shot himself, as a Nazi field marshal was supposed to do. In northern Germany the British 7th Armoured Division was approaching Hamburg, while the 11th Armoured Division advanced rapidly ahead towards Lübeck on the Baltic. This followed Churchill's secret instruction to Field Marshal Montgomery, three days before, to prevent the Red Army from seizing Denmark. The French First Army also entered Stuttgart, where many of its North African troops began to pillage and rape the local population.

On 22 April Himmler had a secret meeting in Lübeck with Count Folke Bernadotte of the Swedish Red Cross. He asked him to approach the Americans and British about a surrender in the west. As a token of good faith, he promised to send 7,000 women prisoners from Ravensbrück to Sweden, but since almost all of them had been marched westwards, this was hardly convincing. As soon as Churchill heard of Himmler's approach, he informed the Kremlin to avoid another row with Stalin after the aborted negotiations over Italy with SS Oberstgruppenführer Wolff.

Hitler became feverish with impatience for news of

Steiner's attack. But when he finally heard that 'Army Detachment Steiner', as he insisted on calling it, had failed to advance, a suspicion of treason within the SS began to grow. He screamed and yelled in fury during the midday situation conference, then collapsed weeping in a chair. For the first time he said openly that the war was lost. His entourage tried to convince him to leave for Bavaria, but he insisted that he would stay in Berlin and shoot himself. He was too weak to fight. Goebbels came over to calm him down, but did nothing to encourage him to depart. The propaganda minister had decided that he would stay with him to the end to create a Nazi legend for the future. Thinking in cinematic terms, just like his Führer, Goebbels considered that their deaths in the fall of Berlin would be more dramatic than in the isolation of the Berghof.

Hitler reappeared, braced by his talk with Goebbels. He seized on Jodl's suggestion that Wenck's Twelfth Army facing the Americans on the Elbe should be brought back to Berlin in a counter-attack. This was a futile plan. The Twelfth Army was far too weak, and the encirclement of Berlin was now virtually complete. Oberstleutnant Ulrich de Maizière, a general staff officer who witnessed the emotional storms in the Führer bunker that day, became convinced that Hitler's 'mental sickness consisted of a hypertrophic self-identification with the German people'. Hitler now felt that the population of Berlin should share his suicide. Magda Goebbels, who believed that a Germany without Hitler was a world not worth living in, brought her six children down into the bunker that night. Staff officers gazed in horror, sensing immediately the end in store for them.

By that evening Rybalko's 3rd Guards Tank Army had reached the Teltow Canal on the southern edge of Berlin. Heavy guns were brought up as it prepared to attack the next day. The NKVD's 7th Department, responsible for prisoner interrogation and propaganda, had leaflets dropped on the city addressed to the women of Berlin, urging them to persuade officers to surrender. It reflected the change of party line, but not the reality on the ground. 'Because the fascist clique is afraid of punishment,' it stated, 'it is hoping to prolong the war. But you women have nothing to be afraid of. No one will touch you.' Radio broadcasts repeated a similar message.

On 23 April, Generalfeldmarschall Keitel reached Wenck's headquarters. He addressed the assembled officers as if they were a Nazi Party rally, waving his field marshal's baton at them as he ordered them to advance on Berlin to save the Führer. Wenck already had a very different plan. He intended to attack eastwards, but not towards Berlin. He wanted to open a corridor to enable Busse's Ninth Army to escape from the forests to the Elbe.

General Weidling of the LVI Panzer Corps rang the Führer bunker that morning to report, now that his corps had pulled back into Berlin. General Krebs told him that he had been condemned to death for cowardice. Weidling, showing considerable courage, insisted on coming in immediately to face his accusers. He had not withdrawn his headquarters to the west of Berlin, as had been reported. Hitler was so impressed by Weidling's firm rebuttal of the charges against him that he promptly placed him in command of all of Berlin's garrison and defences. As one senior officer observed, it was a 'tragi-comedy' typical of the Nazi regime. For Weidling, this appointment was a poisoned chalice.

Weidling redeployed his forces, keeping just the 20th Panzergrenadier Division as a reserve. There was little time. That afternoon the 8th Guards Army and the 1st Guards Tank Army, working together, advanced into south-eastern Berlin. They were soon involved in vicious fighting against the SS *Nordland* on and around Tempelhof airfield, amid the wreckage of burned-out Focke-Wulf fighters. The 5th Shock Army advanced in from the east, the 3rd Shock Army entered the northern suburbs, the 47th Army tackled Spandau in the north-west with its massive brick fortress, and Konev's 3rd Guards Tank Army and the 28th Army began their assault across the Teltow Canal. All the time General Kazakov's massed artillery continued to bombard the city – it would fire 1.8 million shells by the end of the battle – while the supporting air armies roved overhead, strafing and bombing at will.

Albert Speer returned to Berlin that evening by light aircraft to see Hitler for the last time. Hitler told Speer of his intention to commit suicide with Eva Braun. A short time later Martin Bormann brought in a signal from Göring in Bavaria. Göring had heard a garbled version of events in Berlin and of Hitler's emotional outburst the day before. He proposed taking over 'total leadership of the Reich'. Bormann suggested to Hitler that this was treason, and a message was sent in reply stripping the Reichsmarschall of all his appointments and honours. Bormann sent another message to Bavaria telling the SS to put him under house arrest.

In a number of cases SS officers appeared readier to give up than army officers. On that day Fritz Hockenjos, the army officer with the SS corps which was now surrounded in the Black Forest by French troops, recorded in his diary a conversation with his commanding general. 'Do you really believe that fighting on still has a purpose?' the SS general asked him. 'Yes, as a soldier I believe it,' Hockenjos replied. 'The situation also appears hopeless to me, but so long as no order comes to cease fighting, I believe that the supreme leadership still sees a way.'

On the morning of 24 April, Konev's attack on the Teltow Canal began with heavy artillery. Zhukov had been dismayed to hear from the 1st Guards Tank Army that Rybalko's tank brigades had reached Berlin. He was even less happy when he learned that his infantry had crossed the canal that morning, and that his tanks were trundling over pontoon bridges soon after midday. But Konev too had an unpleasant moment when, after watching the crossing of the canal, he discovered that Wenck's divisions were marching east to his rear to link up with the remnants of the Ninth Army.

Many Berliners, who still had batteries for their radios, were thrilled to hear an announcement by Goebbels that Wenck's Twelfth Army was advancing on Berlin. Others feared that this would only prolong the fighting. Hitler's spirits rose again with the prospect. He gave orders that Busse's Ninth Army should join the 'Armee Wenck' in an advance on Berlin. It never occurred to him that neither Wenck nor Busse had any intention of following such an order. Dönitz also promised to fly in sailors from the northern ports to assist the defence. They would arrive by Junkers 52 transport planes landing on the East-West Axis, the avenue across the Tiergarten to the west of the Brandenburg Gate. The most surprising reinforcements to reach Berlin that night were ninety volunteers from the remnants of the French SS

Charlemagne Division, who threaded their way in trucks through Soviet forces to the north of Berlin.

Crammed in their cellars, air-raid shelters and the vast concrete flak towers, Berliners just longed for the battle to end. The air became almost unbreathable and the crush was so great that nobody could reach the lavatories or obtain water to drink. Not even a trickle emerged from taps. Water was available only from stand-pipe handpumps out on the streets, under shellfire. The smashed urban landscape was now called the 'Reichsscheiterhaufen' – the 'Reich's funeral pyre'. Yet as Soviet troops fought their way in towards the centre, cellars too became dangerous in the house-to-house fighting. Red Army soldiers sometimes threw in grenades when they encountered resistance near by.

Volkssturm, Hitler Youth and small combat groups of the Waffen-SS fought from behind barricades, from windows and on rooftops using their Panzerfausts against Soviet tanks. At first the tanks had advanced straight down the middle of the road, then they changed tactics to hug the sides, spraying likely positions with machine-gun fire. The 3rd Shock Army in the north of the city used its anti-aircraft guns against roofs, because its tanks could not elevate their main armament sufficiently. And to counter the Panzerfaust's hollow-charge explosive, tank crews strapped metal mattress springs to the front and sides of their vehicles to detonate the missile prematurely. Barricades were destroyed with heavy artillery guns, brought up and fired horizontally over open sights. Soviet casualties from their own supporting fire, or more often that of other Soviet armies, increased as they advanced towards the centre. With the smoke and clouds of dust covering the city, Shturmovik pilots found it hard to see whom they were attacking. Chuikov pushed part of his 8th Guards Army over towards the west, to block the advance of the rival 3rd Guards Tank Army. This led to many losses among his men from Konev's heavy guns and Katyusha rocket launchers.

That day, the Italian Committee for National Liberation called for an uprising against all German forces remaining in the north. The resistance attacked retreating German columns, and the next day they took control of Milan.

*

On 25 April, American troops from the 69th Infantry Division and Soviet soldiers from the 58th Guards Rifle Division met at Torgau on the Elbe. News that the Nazi Reich had been split in two was proclaimed all round the world. Stalin urged his front commanders to push troops forward to the Elbe wherever they could, although he was now finally reassured that the Americans were not making a dash for Berlin. General Serov of the NKVD brought in three frontier guard regiments to prevent German officers from sneaking out of the city. Beria's picked troops prepared to follow the 3rd Guards Tank Army into Dahlem, to secure the nuclear research facilities.

John Rabe, the German diarist who had recorded events during the Rape of Nanking, was now in Siemensstadt on the north-western edge of Berlin. The Russian soldiers 'are very amiable – so far', he noted. 'They don't bother us, even offer some of their food, but they're crazy about any kind of alcohol and are unpredictable once they've had too much.' The pattern of seizing watches and then women began. Rabe was soon writing about how neighbours committed suicide, having killed their children, and 'a seventeen year old girl was raped five times, then shot'. 'The women in a bomb shelter on Quell Weg were raped while their husbands looked on.'

In Berlin there was less violence and sadism than during the furious revenge against East Prussia. Soviet soldiers took time selecting their victims, using torches in the cellars and shelters to examine their faces first. Mothers tried to conceal daughters in attics, despite the risk of shellfire, but neighbours would sometimes give away their hiding place to divert a soldier's attention from themselves or from their own daughters. Even Jewish women were not safe. Red Army soldiers had little idea of the Nazis' racial persecution, which had been concealed by Soviet propaganda. Their reaction was simply one of 'Frau ist Frau'. The Jewish women and girls still held in the Schulstrasse transit camp in Wedding were raped after the SS guards vanished.

The two main Berlin hospitals, the Charité and the Kaiserin Auguste Viktoria, put the number of women raped at between 95,000 and 130,000. Most had suffered attacks many times. One doctor estimated that around 10,000 had died, either as a result of gang-rape or from suicide later. A number of daughters had been encouraged to kill themselves by their fathers to wipe out the 'dishonour'. Altogether on German territory some two million women and girls are thought to have been raped. East Prussia had seen by far the worst violence, as numerous reports from NKVD commanders to Beria confirm.

In Berlin even the wives and daughters of Communists, who volunteered to help in Red Army canteens and laundries, suffered the same fate. Members of the German Communist Party, the KPD, who emerged to greet their liberators, were in many cases shaken to find themselves arrested as 'spies'. The NKVD regarded their failure to help the Soviet Motherland as a betrayal. 'Why were you not with the partisans?' was the killer question, formulated beforehand in Moscow.

On 27 April the 8th Guards and the 1st Guards Tank Army broke the defence line of the Landwehr Canal, the last major obstacle before the government district. To the south of Berlin, Busse's 80,000 men were still fighting their way across the Berlin–Dresden autobahn, which several divisions of Konev's forces manned as a stop-line. They felled trees in the forests of immensely tall pines, to block the forest tracks leading to the west. But many of Busse's units, spearheaded in some cases by one of the few SS Tiger tanks which still had fuel, managed to find gaps in the Red Army cordon. All other vehicles which had not been abandoned were loaded with wounded, who screamed with pain as they were thrown about by the potholes. If any fell off they were simply crushed by the next vehicle. Hardly anybody stopped to help.

Their vanguard heading west was spotted by a Luftwaffe aircraft and the sighting communicated to the Führer bunker. Hitler could hardly believe that Busse would disobey his order. He sent off a series of signals telling him that his duty was to save Berlin, not his Ninth Army. One of them read: 'The Führer in Berlin expects that the armies will do their duty. History and the German people will despise every man who in these circumstances does not give his utmost to save the situation and the Führer.' But Hitler's orders were now disregarded by all his commanders. General Heinrici, without telling Führer headquarters, told Generaloberst Hasso von Manteuffel to withdraw in the north through Mecklenburg as Rokossovsky's 2nd Belorussian Front advanced from the lower Oder. When Keitel discovered his disobedience, he ordered Heinrici to report to the OKW's new headquarters north-west of Berlin, but Heinrici's staff officers persuaded him to save himself by disappearing until the end of the war. In Berlin itself more and more houses displayed sheets or pillowcases as a sign of surrender, despite the risk from SS patrols, who had been ordered to execute every man found in such buildings.

On 28 April American troops entered the concentration camp of Dachau, north of Munich. Around thirty of the SS guards tried to resist from watchtowers, but were soon shot down. More than 500 SS guards were killed, some by the prisoners, but most by American troops sickened by what they saw in the camp. By the side of the camp, they found cattle wagons filled with skeletal bodies. One lieutenant had 346 of the SS men machine-gunned against a wall. Of the 30,000 surviving prisoners, 2,466 were in such a bad state that they died over the following weeks, despite medical help.

Hitler's supicions of treason within the SS were confirmed when Swedish radio announced from Stockholm that Heinrich Himmler had been attempting to negotiate with the Allies. The evening before, Hitler had noticed the absence of Obergruppenführer Hermann Fegelein, who was Himmler's representative at Führer headquarters as well as being married to Eva Braun's sister. Officers were sent out in search of him. They found Fegelein drunk with his mistress in his apartment. Their bags were packed for an imminent departure. Fegelein was brought back under close arrest to the Reichschancellery. Eva Braun refused to intercede on behalf of her unfaithful brother-in-law.

Hitler was even more bitter about the defection of 'der treue Heinrich' than he had been about Göring's attempt to take the leadership. And after Steiner's failure to attack, he saw betrayal all around him. He telephoned Dönitz in Flensburg on the Baltic coast. Dönitz questioned Himmler, who denied the report. But Reuters then carried the story. Hitler, white with rage, ordered Gruppenführer Müller, the head of the Gestapo, to interrogate Fegelein. After having confessed to knowing of Himmler's approach to Count Bernadotte, Fegelein, stripped of his medals and badges of rank, was taken up to a courtyard and executed by members of the Führer's escort. Hitler claimed that Himmler's treason was the final blow. According to Speer, it was Hitler's decision to punish the Waffen-SS divisions in Hungary by stripping them of their armbands that had helped push Himmler down the path of betrayal.

Just a few hours after the execution of her sister's husband, Eva Braun married Adolf Hitler. Goebbels and Bormann were the witnesses. It was a daunting task for the bewildered registrar, who had been dragged back from a Volkssturm detachment. He had to ask both Hitler and Braun, according to Nazi law, whether they were of pure Aryan descent and free from hereditary diseases.

In the early hours of 29 April, Hitler left his bride to dictate his last will and testament. Returning to his usual deluded rant, he declared that he had never wanted war. International Jewish interests had forced it upon him. He appointed Dönitz president of the Reich in his place. Goebbels was to be Reich chancellor. Gauleiter Karl Hanke, then in Breslau managing its savage defence until he sneaked out by light aircraft, was to replace Himmler as Reichsführer-SS. When Hitler's secretary Traudl Junge had finished her dismal task, she discovered that nobody had fed the Goebbels children. She went in search of food up in the Reichschancellery, only to find a shocking orgy in progress between SS officers and young women they had tempted back with promises of food and alcohol.

Hitler's entourage were waiting anxiously for him to commit suicide. After Fegelein's execution, they could not hope to escape until he died. The sound of fighting intensified, with remnants of the *Nordland* Division and the French SS defending the southern end of the Wilhelmstrasse. The ruins of the Anhalter Bahnhof and Gestapo headquarters on the Prinz-Albrecht-Strasse had been taken by Soviet combat groups. The French SS volunteers had proved remarkably successful at stalking Soviet tanks and knocking them out with Panzerfausts. The Tiergarten now looked like a First World War battlefield, with smashed trees and shell craters.

Two divisions from the 3rd Shock Army had crossed the Spree from Moabit to seize the ministry of the interior, which they called 'Himmler's House'. At dawn on 30 April, they launched their attack on the Reichstag, which Stalin had chosen as the symbol for the capture of Berlin. The first soldier to raise the Soviet flag above it was promised the order of Hero of the Soviet Union. The Reichstag was defended by a mixture of SS, Hitler Youth and some of the sailors who had been crash-landed in the Junkers transport planes. The great danger for the attackers came from behind. The huge Zoo flak tower in the Tiergarten could fire at them as they crossed the vast expanse of the Königsplatz, where Speer had planned to build the Volkshalle, the centrepiece of the new capital, Germania.

In the Führer bunker that morning, Hitler tested one of the cyanide ampoules on his adored Alsatian bitch Blondi. Satisfied that it worked, he began to make his own preparations. He had just heard of Mussolini's death and that of his mistress Clara Petacci. Their bodies, riddled with bullets, had been strung up from the gantry of a petrol station in Milan. The details had been typed for him on one of the special typewriters with out-size script, to allow him to read without glasses. (The sheet is preserved in a Russian archive.) At around three in the afternoon, the Führer made his farewells to his entourage. The solemnity of the occasion was rather undermined by the sound of partying up in the Reichschancellery, and then by Magda Goebbels becoming hysterical at the idea of losing him.

Hitler finally retired to his sitting room with his bride, who had been cheerful during lunch although she knew exactly what was about to happen. Nobody heard the sound of the shot, but just after 15.15 hours Linge his valet entered followed by others. Hitler had fired a bullet through his head, while Eva Hitler had taken cyanide. Their bodies were wrapped in grey Wehrmacht blankets and taken up to the Reichschancellery garden, where they were set alight with petrol according to Hitler's instructions. Goebbels, Bormann and General Krebs snapped to attention and gave the Nazi salute.

That evening, while the Soviet troops fought their way into the Reichstag to hoist the flag of victory in time for the May Day celebrations in Moscow, General Weidling planned a breakout to the west with as many troops as possible. But an SS officer made his way through the shellfire to summon him to the Reichschancellery. Goebbels told Weidling the news of Hitler's death, and added that General Krebs would act as an emissary to negotiate terms with the Soviet commander.

Krebs, although supposedly a loyal apostle of total resistance, had been brushing up his Russian in the privacy of his shaving mirror each morning. As soon as a ceasefire had been arranged on the 8th Guards Army sector, he was led to its headquarters. Chuikov rang Zhukov, who immediately sent his chief of staff General Vasily Sokolovsky over. Zhukov did not want his severest critic to be able to claim that he had taken the surrender of Berlin. Zhukov then rang Stalin, insisting he be woken, to tell him that Hitler was dead. 'Now he's had it,' said Stalin. 'Pity we couldn't take him alive. Where's Hitler's corpse?' Stalin told Zhukov that no negotiations were permitted. Only unconditional surrender would be accepted. Krebs wanted a truce. He tried to argue that only the new government of Grossadmiral Dönitz could offer unconditional surrender. Sokolovsky sent Krebs back with the message that if Goebbels and Bormann did not agree to an unconditional surrender by 10.15 hours, later that morning on 1 May, they would 'Blast Berlin into ruins'. No word came, so 'a hurricane of fire' was unleashed on the city centre.

The most tenacious defenders of the government district were foreign detachments of the Waffen-SS, both Scandinavian and French. Sappers from the *Nordland* Division blew the S-Bahn tunnel under the Landwehr Canal with explosives shaped in a hollow charge. Twenty-five kilometres of S-Bahn and U-Bahn tunnels flooded. Estimates of the numbers who drowned range from just fifty right up to 15,000, but the true figure is unlikely to be much more than fifty. Many of the corpses found floating underground were already dead, because the field hospitals in the tunnels had stacked their bodies down there.

South of Berlin, some 25,000 men from the remnants of Busse's Ninth Army emerged from the forests near Beelitz, totally exhausted and weak from hunger. Several thousand civilians had escaped with them. Wenck's divisions, which had opened the corridor for them and for the Potsdam garrison to escape, had gathered every vehicle it could find to drive them to the Elbe to escape Soviet imprisonment.

That afternoon, Brigadeführer Wilhelm Mohnke, who commanded the defence of the government district, gave orders for the last Tiger tank with the SS *Nordland* to pull back. Although Goebbels still refused to consider unconditional surrender, Martin Bormann and Mohnke had already smuggled civilian clothes into the Reichschancellery ready to make a breakout that night. They expected the troops holding back the Soviet forces round the government district to fight on while they escaped. In the evening, those who wanted to get away from the Reichschancellery waited impatiently for Magda Goebbels to kill her six children with poison, and then commit suicide with her husband.

At 21.30 hours, the Hamburg radio station Deutschlandsender played funereal music before Dönitz addressed the nation to announce Hitler's death, fighting 'at the head of his troops'. Once their children were dead, Joseph and Magda Goebbels finally went up to the Reichschancellery garden. She clutched Hitler's own Nazi Party gold badge, which he had presented to her. Husband and wife crunched on cyanide capsules at the same time. One of the propaganda minister's aides then fired a bullet into each of them to make certain they were dead, sprinkled petrol on their bodies and set them on fire.

The delay meant that the escapers did not leave until eleven that night, two hours later than planned. In two groups, they followed different routes to cross the Spree on their journey north. Troops from the *Nordland* with the Tiger tank and other armoured vehicles tried to smash a way through in a charge across the Weidendammer Bridge. The Red Army, which had expected a breakout and therefore reinforced the sector, killed most of them in the chaotic night battle. Several managed to get through in the confusion, including Bormann and Artur Axmann, the Hitler Youth leader. Bormann, who became separated, appeared to have blundered into a group of Soviet soldiers and to have taken poison.

With Weidling's surrender due to come into effect at midnight, another even larger group based on the remnants of the 18th Panzergrenadier Division and the Panzer Division *Müncheberg* tried to break out to the west. A furious battle took place around the Charlottenbrücke over the River Havel to Spandau. The armoured vehicles again attempted to act as a battering ram against the troops of the Soviet 47th Army. A chaotic massacre ensued with waves of civilians and soldiers rushing the bridge, under the covering fire of self-propelled flak vehicles. It is impossible to tell how many died, but only a handful reached the Elbe. Zhukov gave orders that every body and vehicle had to be checked to see whether any of the Nazi leaders were among them, but most bodies were burned beyond recognition.

An unnatural calm descended on the blackened, smoking city on 2 May. Only distant shots from SS soldiers committing suicide and occasional bursts of Soviet sub-machine-gun fire broke the silence. In the Reichschancellery, General Krebs and Hitler's chief adjutant General Wilhelm Burgdorf had shot themselves, after consuming a large amount of brandy. Troops from the 5th Shock Army occupied the building and hung a large red banner from it, as a companion piece to the flag which had finally been raised over the Reichstag.

For civilians emerging cautiously from their cellars and air-raid shelters, the urban battlefield of corpses in the rubble-strewn streets was a shock. Burned-out Soviet tanks lay all around, knocked out at close range with Panzerfausts by the foreign SS and Hitler Youth. German women covered the faces of the dead with newspapers or pieces of cloth. Most had been little more than boys. The older men of the Volkssturm had surrendered at the first opportunity. Soviet troops carried on rounding up their prisoners, with shouts of 'Davai! Davai!' Anyone in uniform, whether soldier, policeman or fireman, was pushed into columns to be marched out of the city. Many were in tears as their wives came to see them off, and give them food and clothes. They feared that they would be sent to labour camps in Siberia.

The Berlin Operation, from 16 April to 2 May, had cost Zhukov's, Konev's and Rokossovsky's fronts a total of 352,425 casualties, of whom nearly a third were killed. The 1st Belorussian Front had suffered the worst losses because of Zhukov's desperation on the Seelow Heights.

Stalin, eager to hear every detail of Hitler's death and ensure that he was truly gone, had ordered a group from the SMERSh detachment of the 3rd Shock Army to investigate. The Reichschancellery bunker was sealed off as they went about their work. Even Marshal Zhukov was refused entry, on the excuse that sappers had not finished checking the place for mines and booby-traps. An interrogation team began to work on any prisoner who had witnessed events there, and the bodies of Joseph and Magda Goebbels were taken away for forensic examination outside Berlin. Pressure from Moscow became intense when they could not find Hitler's corpse. SMERSh operatives found it only on 5 May, buried in a shellhole along with that of Eva Braun. It was smuggled out in the greatest secrecy. No Red Army officer, including Zhukov, was allowed to know of its discovery.

49

Cities of the Dead

'I am unable to find any beautiful words,' a Soviet soldier wrote home from Berlin. 'Everyone and everything is drunk. Flags, flags, flags! Flags on Unter-den-Linden, on the Reichstag. White flags. Everyone hangs out a white flag. They are living in ruins. Berlin has been crucified.' The Soviet conquerors appeared to believe in the old Russian saying that 'Victors are not judged.'

Many Germans tried simply to survive rather than ponder on the events which had brought them to a far greater state of humiliation than the defeat of 1918. 'People were living with their fate,' a Berliner remarked. The majority of Hitler loyalists persuaded themselves that the behaviour of Soviet troops proved that they had been right to try to destroy the Soviet Union. Others started to have terrible doubts.

Fritz Hockenjos, the army staff officer with the SS corps in the Black Forest, reflected on responsibility for Germany's defeat in his diary. 'The people were not to blame for losing the war. Soldiers, workers and farmers had borne superhuman efforts and burdens and they had believed, obeyed, laboured and fought until the end. Were politicians and Party functionaries guilty, economic leaders and field marshals? Had they not told the Führer the truth and played their own game behind his back? Or was Adolf Hitler not the man he seemed to be among the people? Was it possible that perspicacity and parochialism, simplicity and ferment, loyalty and falsehood, faith and delusion lived in the same heart? Was Adolf Hitler the great, inspired leader, who could not be measured by ordinary standards, or was he an impostor, a criminal, an incompetent dilettante, a madman? Was he an instrument of God or an instrument of the devil? And the men of July '44, were they ultimately not traitors? Questions, questions. I found no answers and no peace of mind.'

Although the announcement of Hitler's death did not bring an immediate end to the fighting, it certainly accelerated the process of final collapse. On 2 May General von Vietinghoff's forces in northern Italy and southern Austria surrendered. British troops rushed to secure Trieste at the head of the Adriatic. Tito's partisans had already reached the city, but in insufficient numbers to make a difference.

The citizens in Prague, believing that Patton's Third Army was about to arrive, rose in revolt against the Germans. The Czechs were assisted by more than 20,000 men of Vlasov's ROA, who turned against their German allies, but not by the Americans as they had hoped. General Marshall had firmly rejected another of Churchill's appeals to advance to the Czech capital.

With the Red Army too far way to intervene, Generalfeldmarschall Schörner's response was almost as savage as the suppression which followed the Warsaw uprising. Changing sides did nothing to spare Vlasov and his troops from Soviet vengeance. Vlasov was denounced by one of his own officers as he attempted to escape under a blanket in the back of a car. Stalin was immediately informed of the capture of 'traitor of the Motherland General Vlasov' by Konev's 1st Ukrainian Front. He was flown to Moscow where he was later executed.

On 5 May, after negotiations with senior officers from Simpson's Ninth Army, the wounded from Busse's forces were allowed to cross the Elbe. Simpson refused to allow civilians through, because of the agreement with the Soviet Union that they should stay in their home areas. Soon unwounded soldiers, and young women camouflaged in Wehrmacht greatcoats and helmets, began to cross the half-wrecked railway bridge. US troops filtered the stream to stop civilians and to arrest members of the SS. Some of the foreigners in the SS, especially Dutch from the SS *Nederland* Division, pretended either that they were German or that they were forced labourers trying to return home. Hiwis, terrified of capture by the NKVD, also tried to escape. Once the bridgehead defended by Wenck's weak divisions came under Soviet artillery fire, the Americans pulled back to avoid casualties, and a stampede began to get to the west bank. Many soldiers and civilians seized boats or lashed together wood and fuel drums to improvise rafts. Some tried to grab the riderless horses and force them into the river to take them across. A large number of those who tried to swim for it drowned in the strong current. Others, who could not face the water or felt they had nothing left to live for, simply committed suicide.

General Bradley met Marshal Konev to provide him with a map showing the position of every American division. He received no information on Soviet dispositions in return, only an unmistakable warning that the Americans should not attempt to meddle in Czechoslovakia. In Austria the Soviets had set up a provisional government, without any consultation. No signals of friendship were emanating from Moscow. Molotov, who was in San Francisco for the founding conference of the United Nations, shocked Edward Stettinius when he stated that the sixteen Polish representatives, seized by the NKVD despite their safe-conduct passes, had been charged with the murder of 200 members of the Red Army.

On the afternoon of 4 May, Stalin had been angered to hear that Generaladmiral Hans-Georg von Friedeburg and General der Infanterie Eberhard Kinzel had come to Montgomery's headquarters on the Lüneburg Heath to surrender German forces in Holland, Denmark and north-west Germany. Montgomery sent the German delegates on to Rheims to make a full unconditional surrender at SHAEF headquarters. The procedure was unbelievably complicated. SHAEF had received no clear political instructions on the terms of the surrender and on French participation. The Germans hoped to negotiate a surrender solely with the western powers.

Not wanting to antagonize Stalin, SHAEF included in the negotiations General Susloparov, the senior Soviet liaison officer in the west. Eisenhower's chief of staff General Bedell Smith conducted the proceedings with skill. On 6 May he threatened that if General Jodl, who had arrived to lead the German delegation, did not sign a universal surrender by midnight, then Allied forces would seal the front, meaning that they would all be taken by the Red Army. The German delegation argued that they needed forty-eight hours after signing to distribute the order to surrender, because of the breakdown in communications with subsidiary headquarters. This was in fact an excuse to obtain extra time in which to bring more troops to the west. Eisenhower agreed to the delay. The 'Act of Military Surrender' was signed by Jodl and Friedeburg in the early hours of 7 May, to take effect by one minute past midnight on 9 May.

Stalin could not let the final ceremony take place in the west, so he insisted that the Germans sign another surrender in Berlin at one minute past midnight on 9 May, the moment the capitulation agreed at Rheims came into effect. Word of the great events leaked out both in the United States and in Britain. Churchill cabled Stalin to explain that, since crowds were already gathering in London to celebrate, Victory in Europe Day celebrations in Britain would take place on 8 May, as they did in the United States. Stalin retorted in displeasure that Soviet troops were still fighting. German troops were still holding out in East Prussia, the Courland Peninsula, Czechoslovakia and many other places. In Yugoslavia, German forces did not surrender for another week. Victory celebrations, Stalin wrote, could therefore not begin in the Soviet Union until 9 May.

British troops stood by to be flown across the North Sea to help the Norwegians supervise the surrender of the 400,000 German troops in the country, the largest Wehrmacht force and still completely intact. Already in the far north, a Norwegian army expedition had reoccupied Finnmark, backed by Soviet forces. Although Reichskommissar Josef Terboven had plans for turning Norway into the last bastion of the Third Reich, Dönitz recalled him to Germany and told Generaloberst Franz Böhme to take full powers. On the evening of 7 May, Böhme broadcast news of the surrender. A skeleton administration in Oslo called up some 40,000 members of the Norwegian resistance to ensure security. Terboven committed suicide soon afterwards by blowing himself up.

Just before midnight on 8 May the surrender ceremony in Berlin began in Zhukov's headquarters at Karlshorst. The Soviet marshal was flanked by Air Chief Marshal Tedder, General Spaatz and General Lattre de Tassigny. Generalfeldmarschall Keitel, Admiral von Friedeburg and Generaloberst Hans-Jürgen Stumpff of the Luftwaffe were brought in. As soon as they had signed, they were led out again. And then the party began. All over the city, gunfire broke out as Red Army officers and soldiers, who had hoarded vodka and almost any form of alcohol for the long-awaited moment, blasted off their remaining ammunition.

This victory salute killed a number of people. The women of Berlin, well aware of what the drinking would provoke, trembled with apprehension.

Stalin, afraid of Zhukov's immense popularity both in the Soviet Union and abroad, began to torment him in minor ways. He blamed him for not having found Hitler, when SMERSh had already confirmed the identity of his corpse. They had found the assistant to Hitler's dentist and made her examine the bridgework on his jaw. Zhukov did not discover that the body had been found until twenty years later. Stalin also used the deliberate mystery to suggest that Hitler had fled to Bavaria, which was occupied by the Americans. It was part of his campaign to insinuate that the Americans had a secret pact with the Nazis.

The longing for political change in the ranks of the Red Army had made the Soviet leadership very suspicious. Soldiers and officers alike had become outspoken in their criticisms of the Communist system. The Soviet authorities also feared foreign influences, after their soldiers had seen far better living conditions in Germany. SMERSh again referred to the threat of a 'Decembrist' mood, a reference to the young officers who returned from Paris after the defeat of Napoleon, recognizing that Russia remained politically primitive. 'A merciless fight is necessary against these attitudes,' the SMERSh report concluded. Arrests for 'systematic anti-Soviet talk and terroristic intentions' rose dramatically. In that year of victory, which saw little more than four months of fighting, 135,056 Red Army officers and soldiers and 273 senior officers were arrested for 'counter-revolutionary crimes'. Back in the Soviet Union, informers were at work and NKVD arrests in the early morning had become a re-established pattern.

The population of the Gulag and of forced-labour battalions swelled to its largest level. The new convicts included both civilians and an estimated three million Red Army soldiers, sentenced for having collaborated as Hiwis, or simply for having surrendered. Large numbers of others, including eleven generals, were executed after brutal interrogations at the screening centres run by SMERSh and the NKVD. Abandoned by incompetent or terrified superiors in 1941, Soviet soldiers had starved in the indescribable horrors of German camps. Now they found themselves treated as 'traitors of the Motherland' because they had failed to kill themselves. Those who survived this second round of punishment remained branded for the rest of their lives and restricted to the most menial work. Right up until 1998, well after the fall of Communism, official forms continued to demand details on any member of an applicant's family who had been a prisoner of war. The bloody revolts which took place in Gulag camps in the years after the war were almost all led by former Red Army officers and men.

The chaos which the Nazis had brought upon the entire continental landmass was demonstrated by the hundreds of thousands of displaced persons. 'On the roads of Germany today,' wrote Godfrey Blunden, 'there is the whole story of Europe, or the world for that matter.' Millions of forced labourers brought to the Reich from France, Italy, the Low Countries, central Europe, the Balkans and above all the Soviet Union began to make their way home on foot. 'An old woman traveller', Vasily Grossman noted, 'is walking away from Berlin, wearing a shawl on her head. She looks exactly as if she were going on a pilgrimage – a pilgrimage amid the expanse of Russia. She is holding an umbrella across her shoulder. A huge aluminium casserole is hung by its ear on the umbrella's handle.'

Blunden came across a group of young, half-starved American prisoners of war, with 'xylophone ribs', sunken cheeks, thin necks and 'gangling arms'. They were 'a little hysterical' from the joy of meeting fellow English-speakers. 'Some American prisoners whom I met this morning seemed to me to be the most pitiful of all I have seen. They had arrived in Europe only last December, gone immediately into the front line and had received the full brunt of the German counter-offensive in the Ardennes that month. Since their capture they had been moved almost constantly from one place to another. They told stories of comrades clubbed to death by German guards merely for breaking line to grab sugar beets from fields. They were more pitiful because they were only boys drafted from nice homes in a nice country knowing nothing about Europe, not tough like Australians, or shrewd like the French or irreducibly stubborn like the English. They just didn't know what it was all about.'

Among the displaced persons were many prisoners who had become brutalized by their treatment and longed for revenge on the Germans. Roving freely, looting and raping, they spread chaos and fear. Provost-marshals gave orders that justice was to be administered on the spot. 'Those identified as murderers and rapists were summarily shot,' a British soldier recorded. Yet German civilians who came to the occupation authorities to complain about the theft of food by forced labourers received little sympathy. Only a tiny minority had shown any compassion towards them when the Nazis had been in power.

For Churchill, in this immediate post-war period, the problem of Poland loomed above almost everything else. The prime minister's failure to attend Roosevelt's funeral had surprised and shocked people on both sides of the Atlantic. There can be little doubt that however much he vaunted their friendship later, Roosevelt's appeasement of Stalin had gravely disappointed him. Churchill was initially encouraged that Harry Truman, the new President, seemed ready to take a much more robust line with Stalin, mainly as a result of Averell Harriman's advice.

Roosevelt's abrupt announcement at Yalta that he intended to withdraw American forces from Europe as soon as possible had alarmed Churchill. Britain alone was far too weak to resist both the strength of the Red Army and the threat of local Communists profiting from a devastated Europe. He was horrified by reports of Soviet revenge and repression behind what he already called the 'iron curtain': unfortunately, a term already used by Goebbels.

Within a week of Germany's surrender, Churchill summoned his chiefs of staff. He astonished them by asking whether it might be possible to force the Red Army back in order to secure 'a square deal for Poland'. This offensive, he told them, should take place on 1 July, before the military strength of the Allies on the western front was reduced by demobilization or the transfer of formations to the Far East.

Although the contingency planning for Operation Unthinkable was conducted in great secrecy, one of Beria's moles in Whitehall passed details to Moscow. The most explosive was an instruction to Montgomery to gather up surrendered German weaponry, in case Wehrmacht units were reconstituted to take part in this mad enterprise. The Soviets, not surprisingly, felt that all their worst suspicions had been confirmed.

The planners studied the scenario in great detail, although it had to be based largely on speculation. They totally misread the reaction of British troops, thinking that they would follow such an order. That was most unlikely. The vast majority of British troops were longing to get home. And after all they had heard of the colossal Soviet sacrifice, which had spared them so many casualties, they would have greeted the suggestion of turning against their ally with incredulity and anger. The planning staff also made the unlikely assumption that the Americans would be prepared to join in.

Fortunately, the main conclusions of their report were quite clear. It was a very 'hazardous' project, and even if the Red Army were forced to withdraw after initial successes, the conflict would be long and costly. 'The idea is of course fantastic and the chances of success quite impossible,' Field Marshal Brooke wrote in his diary. 'There is no doubt that from now onwards Russia is all powerful in Europe.' 'The result of this study', he added later, 'made it clear that the best we could hope for was to drive the Russians back to about the same line the Germans had reached. And then what? Were we to remain mobilized indefinitely to hold them there?' The Second World War in Europe had begun in Europe over Poland, and the notion of a third world war following the same pattern represented a terrifying symmetry.

On 31 May, Brooke, Portal and Cunningham 'again discussed the "unthinkable war" against Russia . . . and became more convinced than ever that it is "unthinkable"'. They were unanimous when they reported back to Churchill. Truman proved equally unreceptive to the notion of pushing the Red Army back as a bargaining counter. He was not even prepared to keep American forces in those areas of Germany and Czechoslovakia which were due to be handed over to the Soviets as stipulated by the European Advisory Commission. Truman had suddenly swung back to a more accommodating approach to the Soviet Union as a result of listening to Joseph Davies, a former US ambassador in Moscow and ardent admirer of Stalin. Davies had sat through the show trials of the 1930s and seen nothing suspicious about the grotesque confessions beaten out of the accused.

The prime minister had to accept defeat, but he soon came back to the chiefs of staff and asked them to study plans for the defence of the British Isles in the event of a Soviet occupation of the Low Countries and France. By this time he was exhausted by campaigning for the general election, and became increasingly irrational. He even warned of a Gestapo under a future Labour government. Voting took place on 5 July, but because of the need to collect the ballot papers of the armed forces from all round the world, the results would not be known until three weeks later. As well as the problems of Poland, Churchill was also vexed by General de Gaulle's rash decision to send troops to Syria, where the reimposition of French colonial rule was being resisted. De Gaulle was going through a paroxysm of anglophobia and anti-Americanism at this stage, much to the distress of Georges Bidault, his foreign minister. De Gaulle still resented the failure of the Big Three to include him at Yalta, and he knew he was about to be ignored again at the forthcoming meeting in Potsdam.

Truman, on the advice of Joseph Davies, decided that only a more friendly approach to Stalin could resolve matters. Harry Hopkins, whom the Soviets trusted more than most westerners, was despatched to Moscow to arrange 'a new Yalta'. Although gravely ill, Hopkins accepted, and as a result of several meetings with Stalin at the end of May and the beginning of June, the discord over the constitution of the Polish government was settled on Stalin's terms.

The problem of Poland henceforth became the embarrassing one of quietly dropping a brave ally, unavoidably sacrificed on the altar of realpolitik. 'In a few days,' Brooke wrote in his diary on 2 July, 'we shall be recognizing the Warsaw government officially and liquidating the London one. The Polish forces then present a serious conundrum which the Foreign Office has done little to solve in spite of repeated applications for a ruling ever since May!' He wondered next day 'how the Polish forces will take it'. He had recently spoken with General Anders, before he returned to the Polish Corps in Italy. Anders made it clear to Brooke that he wanted to fight his way back to Poland if the opportunity arose.

On 5 July both the United States and Britain recognized the puppet government, which had agreed to include several non-Communist Poles. The sixteen arrested by the NKVD, however, were still to face trial on the trumped-up charge of killing 200 Red Army soldiers. And in a shameful gesture of appeasement to Stalin, the next British government decided to exclude Polish forces from the victory parade.

On 16 July, the day before the Potsdam conference began, Truman and Churchill met for the first time. Truman was cordial but guarded, after Davies had warned him that Churchill would still seek to involve him in a war with the Soviet Union. Stalin arrived in Berlin that day from Moscow in his special train. More than 19,000 NKVD troops were allocated by Beria to guard his route, and seven NKVD regiments and 900 bodyguards to provide security in Potsdam. Special security precautions were taken on the line through Poland. Stalin drove from the station with Zhukov to his accommodation in the former house of General Ludendorff. Everything had been exactingly prepared by the newly promoted Marshal Beria.

Later in the day Truman received the signal: 'Babies satisfactorily born'. The test explosion of the atomic bomb in the desert near Los Alamos had been carried out at 05.30 hours. Churchill, when told, was exultant after being forced to acknowledge that Unthinkable was out of the question. Field Marshal Brooke was 'completely shattered by the Prime Minister's outlook', and the way that he 'was completely carried away' by the discovery. In Churchill's view, 'It was now no longer necessary for the Russians to come into the Japanese war, the new explosive alone was sufficient to settle the matter.' He did not seem to grasp the fact that, after all the American requests to Stalin to enter the war against Japan, they could not now disinvite him, having promised him such rich pickings in the Far East.

Brooke then recounted what was closest to the prime minister's heart, paraphrasing his words. 'Furthermore we now had something in our hands which would redress that balance with the Russians! The secret of this explosive, and the power to use it, would completely alter the diplomatic equilibrium which was adrift since the defeat of Germany. Now we had a new value which redressed our position – (pushing his chin out and scowling) – now we could say if you insist on doing this or that, well we can just blot out Moscow, then Stalingrad, then Kiev, then Kuibyshev, Kharkov, Sebastopol etc etc.'

Churchill was certainly in a fighting mood, prompted by bitter frustration over Britain's impotence to change anything and yet at the same time encouraged by the implications of the new invention. As the conference progressed, Stalin's desire to extend Soviet power in many directions became abundantly apparent. He showed an interest in Italian colonies in Africa, and proposed that the Allies should have Franco removed. Churchill's worst fears would have been aroused if he had overheard an exchange between Averell Harriman and Stalin during one break. 'It must be very pleasant for you', Harriman said, making conversation, 'to be in Berlin now after all your country has suffered.' The Soviet leader eyed him. 'Tsar Aleksandr went all the way to Paris,' he replied.

This was not entirely a joke. Well before Churchill's fantasy of Unthinkable, a meeting of the Politburo in 1944 had decided to order the Stavka to plan for the invasion of France and Italy, as General Shtemenko later told Beria's son. The Red Army offensive was to be combined with a seizure of power by the local Communist Parties. In addition, Shtemenko explained, 'a landing in Norway was provided for, as well as the seizure of the Straits [with Denmark]. A substantial budget was allocated for the realisation of these plans. It was expected that the Americans would abandon a Europe fallen into chaos, while Britain and France would be paralysed by their colonial problems. The Soviet Union possessed 400 experienced divisions, ready to bound forward like tigers. It was calculated that the whole operation would take no more than a month . . . All these plans were aborted when Stalin learned from [Beria] that the Americans had the atom bomb and were putting it into mass production.' Stalin apparently told Beria 'that if Roosevelt had still been alive, we would have succeeded'. This, it seems, was the main reason why Stalin suspected that Roosevelt had been secretly assassinated.

Churchill received little support from Truman. The new President had been charmed and awed by the manipulative Soviet dictator, who despised him in return. The prime minister's greatest moment of intimacy with Truman came when they discussed how the President was to tell Stalin of the atomic bomb. But

Stalin had already discussed twice with Beria how he should react when given the news. On 17 July Beria had provided him with details of the successful test, obtained by his spies in the Manhattan Project. So, when Truman told Stalin about the bomb in a confidential tone, Stalin barely reacted. He summoned Molotov and Beria immediately afterwards and, 'sniggering', related the scene. 'Churchill was standing by the door, his eyes fixed on me like a searchlight, while Truman, with his hypocritical air, told me what had happened in an indifferent tone.' Their amusement was increased when the recordings from NKVD microphones revealed that, when Churchill had asked Truman how the Soviet leader had taken the news, Truman replied that 'Stalin had apparently failed to understand.'

On 26 July, the plenary session at Potsdam was suspended. The day before, Churchill had returned to London with Anthony Eden and Clement Attlee for the announcement of the general election results. Just as he departed, Churchill found himself in the strange position of being reassured by Stalin that he was bound to have beaten the socialists.

The prime minister had received warnings that things might not go his way, largely because of votes in the armed forces whose men wanted to do away with the past, both the harsh years of the 1930s and the war itself. At a dinner in London a few weeks before, when Churchill had talked about the election campaign, General Slim, back from Burma, had said to him: 'Well, prime minister, I know one thing. My army won't be voting for you.'

For most soldiers and NCOs, the military hierarchy bore too close a resemblance to the class system. An army captain, who had asked one of his sergeants how he was going to vote, received the reply: 'Socialist, sir, because I'm fed up with taking orders from ruddy officers.' When the votes were counted, it became clear that the armed forces had voted overwhelmingly for the Labour Party and for change. Churchill's greatest fault was to have shown no taste for social reform, during either the war or the campaign.

In spite of his dislike for Churchill, Stalin was genuinely shaken by the result when the news of his crushing defeat reached Potsdam. He simply could not imagine how somebody of his stature could be voted out of power. Parliamentary democracy, in his view, was clearly a dangerously unstable way of running a country. He was very conscious of the fact that, under any other regime but his own, he would have been removed from office after his catastrophic handling of the German invasion.

Clement Attlee, the new prime minister, and Ernest Bevin, who had taken over as foreign secretary from Eden, now occupied the British seats at the conference. But through no fault of their own they could exert little influence on the discussions. James F. Byrnes, the new US secretary of state, agreed to recognize the western border of Poland along the Oder–Neisse Line, and they followed suit. Stalin had achieved everything he wanted at Potsdam, even though he had been forced to cancel the invasion of western Europe out of fear of the atom bomb.

The return of prisoners of war, which had been agreed at Yalta, soon proved a terrible problem for the Allies. Both the American Counter Intelligence Corps and British Field Security had trouble identifying war criminals or even the nationalities of those they interrogated, because many from eastern Europe and the Soviet Union pretended to be German in order to stay in the west.

The greatest mixture of nationalities and ethnic groups had congregated in the province of Carinthia in south-east Austria. When units from the British V Corps reached the beautiful Drau Valley, they found tens of thousands of people camped there. There were Croats, Slovenes, Serb Četniks and most of the Cossack Corps. Those from Yugoslavia were fleeing Tito's victorious revenge in the savage civil war. The Cossacks, commanded by German officers, had played a major part in the murderous anti-partisan campaign.

Tito appeared to match Stalin in his appetite for more territory. He was hoping to seize Istria, Trieste and even part of Carinthia. Some of his partisans reached its capital, Klagenfurt, just before the British. They were terrorizing the countryside and threatening the mass of military refugees. British officers, lacking clear direction from above, found that they faced a chaotic situation, with the threat of more of Tito's forces crossing into Austria. They were then given the unpleasant task of returning Soviet citizens to the Red Army, just across the frontier to the east.

The Cossacks were notorious for the atrocities they had committed. Even Goebbels had been shaken by the reports he had received of their activities in Yugoslavia and northern Italy. But they also had women and children with them, as well as some White Russians who had been living in the west since the Bolshevik victory in 1921. The two most prominent were the Cossack ataman General Pyotr Krasnov, an officer who was perhaps as honourable as was possible in a civil war, and General Andrei Shkouro, a cruel psychopath. Since it appeared impossible to weed out the good from the bad, staff officers at V Corps headquarters ordered that they should all be handed over to the Red Army. The Cossacks knew very well what Stalin's vengeance was likely to be, and they had to be forced on to the transport by British soldiers armed with pick helms – the wooden handles of pickaxes. Although they admired the Red Army, most of the troops involved in these forced repatriations were appalled by what they had to do, and there was nearly a mutiny.

At the same time, British troops were clearly reluctant to confront Tito's increasingly aggressive forces. Nobody wanted to be killed after the war had finished. V Corps headquarters, under pressure to resolve the dangerous situation as rapidly as possible, ordered that the Yugoslavs should be forced back over their border. Again they included a mixture of those guilty of war crimes, especially the Croat Ustaše, and the less guilty. British officers and soldiers alike were horrified to have to force Četniks, the allies abandoned in favour of Tito, back over the Yugoslav border. Most appear to have been killed almost immediately. The German collapse had triggered the worst round of massacres by Tito's partisans in the civil war. In 2009, the Slovene Hidden Graves Commission identified over 600 mass graves and has estimated that they contain the bodies of more than 100,000 victims.

Vengeance and ethnic cleansing were just as brutal in northern and central Europe. For many Germans, rumours that all the country's territory to the east of the Oder – East Prussia, Silesia, Pomerania – would be handed to Poland represented the greatest fear of all. Once the fighting ended, nearly a million of the refugees made their way back to their abandoned homes, only to find that they were about to be chased out again.

As Stalin had intended, ethnic cleansing was pursued with a vengeance. Troops from the 1st and 2nd Polish Armies forced Germans from their houses to push them across the Oder. The first to go were those on pre-1944 Polish territory. Some had lived there for generations, others were the *Volksdeutsche* beneficiaries of the Nazis' own ethnic cleansing in 1940. Packed into cattle wagons, they were taken westwards and robbed of their few belongings on the way. A similar fate awaited those who had stayed behind or returned to Pomerania and Silesia, which now fell within the new Polish borders. In East Prussia, only 193,000 Germans were left out of a population of 2.2 million.

During the expulsions from Polish territory, around 200,000 Germans were held in labour camps and some 30,000 are estimated to have died. Others were among the 600,000 Germans sent for forced labour in the Soviet Union. The Czechs also expelled up to three million Germans, most from the Sudetenland. Thirty thousand were killed in the process and 5,558 committed suicide. Women with their children had to walk, some of them for hundreds of kilometres, to find shelter in Germany.

It is hard to see how such an unbelievably brutal war could have ended without brutal revenge. Mass violence, as the Polish poet Czesław Miłosz pointed out, destroyed both the idea of a common humanity and any sense of natural justice. 'Murder became ordinary during wartime,' wrote Miłosz, 'and was even regarded as legitimate if it was carried out on behalf of the resistance. Theft became ordinary too, as did falsehood and fabrication. People learned to sleep through sounds that would once have roused the whole neighborhood: the rattle of machine-gun fire, the cries of men in agony, the cursing of the policeman dragging the neighbors away.' For all of these reasons, Miłosz explained, 'the man of the East cannot take Americans [or other westerners] seriously.' Because they had not undergone such experiences, they could not seem to fathom what they meant, and could not seem to imagine how they had happened either.

'If we are American,' wrote Anne Applebaum, 'we think "the war" was something that started with Pearl Harbor in 1941 and ended with the atomic bomb in 1945. If we are British, we remember the Blitz of 1940 and the liberation of Belsen. If we are French, we remember Vichy and the Resistance. If we are Dutch we think of Anne Frank. Even if we are German we know only a part of the story.'

50

The Atomic Bombs and the
Subjugation of Japan

MAY–SEPTEMBER 1945

At the time of the German surrender in May 1945, the Japanese armies in China received orders from Tokyo to begin withdrawing to the east coast. Chiang Kai-shek's Nationalist armies were still badly battered from the Ichi-gō Offensive, and their commanders felt a deep bitterness towards the United States for having failed to heed their warnings.

Stilwell's replacement, General Albert Wedemeyer, began a programme of rearming and training thirty-nine divisions. He forced Chiang Kai-shek to concentrate his best forces in the south towards the border of Indochina. The American plan was to cut off the escape route for Japanese forces from south-east Asia. Chiang on the other hand wanted to reoccupy the agricultural regions to the north to feed his troops and the starving population in Nationalist areas, but Wedemeyer threatened to withhold all US aid if he refused. Chiang knew that the Communists had already moved south to fill the vacuum left by the Japanese retreat. Wedemeyer's intervention contributed to the Nationalists' defeat in the civil war to come, but Washington at that time assumed that Japanese resistance would carry on into 1946.

Roosevelt's representative in China, the unpredictable Patrick J. Hurley, had started negotiations between the Communists and the Nationalists in November 1944. Talks broke down the following February, largely because Chiang Kai-shek was not prepared to share power and the Communists were not prepared to subordinate their army. At this time when the Kuomintang was split between liberals and reactionaries, Chiang promised sweeping reforms in the spring, but the only changes made were those designed to satisfy the Americans. The great reformer of the past now supported the old guard, and corruption continued unabated. To complain openly risked attracting the brutal attentions of the secret police.

His capital of Chungking displayed a huge gulf between the rich minority and the impoverished majority, who suffered from spiralling inflation. American troops were conspicuous in their enjoyment of the town. 'A honky-tonk half a mile from US Army headquarters served adulterated whisky and unadulterated tarts,' wrote Theodore White. '"Jeep girls" took to riding in the open streets with American Army personnel, in full view of the scandalized citizenry.' In the countryside the forced recruitment of soldiers, with bounties paid to press-gangs, stirred the slow-burning resentment of the peasantry. Only those who could afford to pay large bribes were immune, and the grain tax discouraged farmers from selling their produce. The Communists from the headquarters in Yenan had also imposed a grain tax, and the impression given that peasant life under their rule was idyllic could hardly have been further from the truth. The opium trade, which filled Mao's war chest, had triggered a rate of inflation almost as bad as in Nationalist areas and anyone who protested or criticized Chairman Mao was treated as an enemy of the people.

Fighting between Communists and Nationalists had already begun in Honan province, and also in and around Shanghai. Despite the large concentration of Japanese forces there, Communists and Nationalists fought an underground war in the belief that control of the great port and financial capital would be crucial when the occupiers left.

Despite the imminence of their country's defeat, atrocities against the Chinese population, especially women, continued in the areas still held by a million Japanese troops. As in other areas of occupation, such as New Guinea and the Philippines, Japanese soldiers short of rations regarded the local population and prisoners as a food source. The Japanese soldier Enomoto Masayo later confessed to having raped, murdered and butchered a young Chinese woman. 'I just tried to choose those places where there was a lot of meat,' he confessed later. He then shared the meat with his comrades afterwards. He described it as 'nice and tender. I think it was tastier than pork.' Not even his commanding officer remonstrated with him when he told him the origin of their meal.

Other horrors were already known to the Allies. In 1938 the biological warfare establishment Unit 731 had been set up outside Harbin in Manchukuo, under the auspices of the Kwantung Army. This huge complex, presided over by General Ishii Shirō, eventually employed a core staff of 3,000 scientists and doctors from universities and medical schools in Japan, and a total of 20,000 personnel in the subsidiary establishments. They prepared weapons to spread black plague, typhoid, anthrax and cholera, and tested them on more than 3,000 Chinese prisoners. They also carried out anthrax, mustard-gas and frostbite experiments on their victims, whom they referred to as *maruta* or 'logs'. These human guinea pigs, around 600 a year, had been arrested by the Kempeitai in Manchuria and sent to the unit.

In 1939 during the Nomonhan fighting against Marshal Zhukov's forces, the unit had put typhoid pathogen into rivers near by, but the effect was unrecorded. In 1940 and 1941 cotton and rice husks, contaminated with black plague, were dropped from aircraft over central China. In March 1942, the Imperial Japanese Army planned to use plague-fleas against the American and Filipino defenders of the Bataan Peninsula, but the surrender took place before they were ready. And later that year typhoid, plague and cholera pathogens were sprayed in Chekiang province in retaliation for the first American bombing raid on Japan. Apparently 1,700 Japanese soldiers in the area died as well as hundreds of Chinese.

A biological warfare battalion was sent to Saipan before the American landings, but most of its members were evacuated beforehand only to be drowned when a US submarine sank their ship. There were also plans captured by marines on Kwajalein to bomb Australia and India with biological weapons, but these attacks never materialized. The Japanese also wanted to contaminate the island of Luzon in the Philippines with cholera before the American invasion, but this too was not carried out.

The Imperial Japanese Navy at its bases of Truk and Rabaul had experimented on Allied prisoners of war, mainly captured American pilots, by injecting them with the blood of malaria victims. Others were killed during experiments with different lethal injections. As late as April 1945, around a hundred

Australian prisoners of war – some sick, some healthy – were also used for experiments with unknown injections. In Manchuria, 1,485 American, Australian, British and New Zealand prisoners of war held at Mukden were used for a variety of experiments with pathogens.

Perhaps the most shocking element in the whole story of Unit 731 was MacArthur's agreement, after the Japanese surrender, to provide immunity from prosecution to all involved, including General Ishii. This deal allowed the Americans to obtain all the data they had accumulated from their experiments. Even after MacArthur had learned that Allied prisoners of war had also been killed in the tests, he ordered that all criminal investigations should cease. Soviet requests to prosecute Ishii and his staff at the Tokyo War Crimes tribunal were firmly rejected.

Only a few doctors who anaesthetized and then dissected captured American bomber crews were prosecuted, but they had nothing to do with Unit 731. Other Japanese military doctors performed vivisection on hundreds of conscious Chinese prisoners in numerous hospitals, but they were never charged. Doctors in the Japanese Medical Corps demonstrated little respect for human life, since they willingly followed orders to dispose of their own 'incapacitated soldiers, with a good chance of recovery . . . on the grounds that they are useless to the Emperor'. They also taught Japanese soldiers how to commit suicide to avoid being captured.

By the time Japanese resistance on Okinawa had ended, American commanders in the Pacific turned to re-examining the next phase, the invasion of the home islands. The kamikaze attacks and the refusal of the Japanese to surrender, combined with the knowledge of their biological warfare capability, made it a sobering task. The plan had been agreed by the joint chiefs of staff as early as 1944. It estimated that Operation Olympic to take the southern island of Kyushu in November would cost 100,000 casualties, and Operation Coronet in March 1946 to invade the main island of Honshu 250,000. Admiral King and General Arnold preferred to bomb and blockade Japan, to starve it into surrender. MacArthur and the US Army complained that that would take years and cause unnecessary suffering. It would also mean the death by starvation of most Allied prisoners of war and forced labourers.

And since the bombing of Germany had not achieved victory, the army won the navy round to the idea of an invasion.

The Imperial Japanese Army was resolved to fight to the end, partly out of an imagined fear of a Communist uprising, and partly out of *bushido* pride. Its leaders felt that they could never consent to surrender when General Tōjō's *Instructions for Servicemen* had declared: 'Do not survive in shame as a prisoner. Die, to ensure that you do not leave ignominy behind you.' Civilian politicians of the 'peace party' who wanted to negotiate would have been arrested, or even assassinated, if it had not been for the Emperor's own indecision over what to do next. The former prime minister Prince Konoe Fumimaro later pointed out that 'the army had dug themselves caves in the mountains and their idea of fighting on was to fight from every little hole or rock in the mountains'. The Japanese army also intended that civilians should die with them. A Patriotic Citizens Fighting Corps was being formed, many of whose members would be armed with nothing more than bamboo lances. Others were to have bombs strapped to them which they would detonate as they threw themselves against tanks. Even young women were pressured into volunteering to sacrifice themselves.

Japanese military leaders rejected the idea of unconditional surrender because they also believed that their conquerors intended to depose the Emperor. Although an overwhelming majority of the American public wanted exactly that, the State Department and the joint chiefs of staff had come round to the idea of retaining him as a constitutional monarch and softening the terms. The Potsdam Declaration on Japan, published on 26 July, made no mention of the Emperor to avoid a political backlash in the United States. The Japanese government had already approached the Soviet government, hoping that it would act as mediator, unaware that Stalin was redeploying his armies to the Far East to invade Manchuria.

The successful test of the first atom bomb in July appeared to offer the Americans a way of shocking the Japanese into surrender, and avoid the greater horrors of an invasion. After many studies and considerable debate, Tokyo and the ancient capital of Kyoto were rejected as targets. Hiroshima, which had not been as badly destroyed as other cities by LeMay's bombers, was chosen as the first target, and Nagasaki as a follow-up objective if the Japanese had still not indicated acceptance.

On the morning of 6 August three B-29 Superfortresses appeared over Hiroshima. Two of them carried cameras and scientific equipment to record the effect. The third, the *Enola Gay*, opened its bomb doors at 08.15 hours, and less than a minute later most of the city of Hiroshima disintegrated in a blinding light. Around 100,000 people were killed instantly, and many thousands more died later from radiation poisoning, burns and shock. President Truman's staff in Washington issued a warning to the Japanese that if they failed to surrender immediately, 'they may expect a rain of ruin from the air, the like of which has never been seen on this earth'.

Two days later, Red Army forces surged across the Manchurian frontier. Stalin did not intend to miss out on the territorial spoils he had been promised. On 9 August, when nothing had been heard from Tokyo, a second atomic bomb was dropped on Nagasaki killing 35,000 people. The Emperor was deeply moved by the terrible fate of those who had died, and requested as much information as possible. It is quite clear that without the atomic bombs he would not have mustered the quiet resolve which he showed later to end the war.

The fire-bombing of Tokyo and the decision to drop the atomic bombs were driven by the Americans' urge to 'get this business over with'. But the possibility of kamikaze resistance, perhaps even with biological weapons, threatened a far worse battle than that on Okinawa. On the basis that approximately a quarter of Okinawa's civilians had died in the fighting there, a similar scale of civilian casualties on the home islands would have exceeded many times over the numbers killed by the atomic bombs. Other considerations, most notably the temptation of demonstrating US power to a Soviet Union then ruthlessly imposing its will in central Europe, played an influential, although not decisive, part.

It is true that several civilian members of the Japanese regime were keen on negotiation, but their fundamental insistence – that Japan be allowed to keep Korea and Manchuria – could never have been acceptable to the Allies. Even this peace faction refused to accept any notion of Japanese guilt for having started the war, or international trials for crimes committed by the Imperial Army dating back to the original invasion of Chinese territory in 1931.

A few hours before the second atomic bomb fell on Nagasaki, the Supreme Council for the Direction of the War had met to consider whether it should accept the Potsdam Declaration. Representatives of Imperial General Headquarters were still firmly opposed. On the evening of 9 August just after the Nagasaki bomb had fallen, the Emperor summoned the Supreme Council's members again. He said that they should accept the terms, providing that the imperial house and its succession was preserved. This proviso was transmitted to Washington the next day. There were mixed feelings during the discussions at the White House. Some, including James Byrnes, argued that no qualifications should be allowed. Stimson, the secretary for war, argued more persuasively that only the Emperor's authority could persuade the Japanese armed forces to surrender. This would save the Americans countless further battles, and would give the Soviet armies less time to rampage across the region.

The American reply, which emphasized again that the Japanese would be allowed to choose the form of government which they desired, reached Tokyo via the Japanese embassy in Switzerland. The military leaders still refused to accept defeat. While American bombers continued their campaign, although no more atomic weapons were used on Truman's orders, the arguments continued for several days. Eventually on 14 August the Emperor stepped in and announced that he had decided that they should accept the Potsdam Declaration. Ministers and military leaders alike began to weep. He also said that he would record a broadcast to the nation, an unprecedented event.

That night army officers attempted a coup to prevent the broadcast of the Emperor's announcement. Having persuaded the 2nd Imperial Guard Regiment to join them through trickery, they entered the Imperial Palace to destroy the message recorded by the Emperor announcing the country's capitulation. The Emperor and Marquis Kido, the court chamberlain, managed to hide. The rebels found nothing, and when loyal troops arrived, Major Hatanaka Kenji, the main leader of the coup, knew that he had no alternative but suicide. Other military leaders took the same course.

At noon on 15 August Japanese radio stations broadcast the Emperor's recorded message, calling on all his forces to surrender because the war situation had evolved 'not necessarily to Japan's advantage'. Officers and soldiers listened to his words on the radio with tears streaming down their faces. Many were on their knees bowing towards the voice of the divine Mikado, whose tones they had never heard before. Some pilots set out on a final mission of *gyokusai* or 'glorious self-annihilation'. Most were intercepted and shot down by American fighters. The self-image of the Yamato race bore a number of similarities to that of the Nazi *Herrenvolk*. In an attitude reminiscent of the German army after the First World War, many Japanese soldiers continued to persuade themselves that 'Japan lost the war but we never lost a battle.'

On 30 August US forces landed at Yokohama to begin the occupation of Japan. Over the next ten days there were 1,336 cases of rape reported in Yokohama and the surrounding region of Kanagawa. Australian troops apparently also committed many rapes in the area of Hiroshima. This had been expected by the Japanese authorities. On 21 August, nine days before the arrival of Allied troops, the Japanese government had summoned a meeting of ministers to establish a Recreation and Amusement Association, to provide comfort women for their conquerors. Local officials and police chiefs were told to organize a nationwide network of military brothels staffed by existing prostitutes, but also by geishas and other young women. The intention was to reduce the incidence of rape. The first opened in a Tokyo suburb on 27 August and hundreds followed. One of the brothels was run by the mistress of General Ishii Shirō, the head of Unit 731. Some 20,000 young women were recruited, with varying degrees of coercion, by the end of the year to appease their conquerors.

The formal surrender of Japan did not take place until 2 September. General MacArthur, accompanied by Admiral Nimitz, took it at a table placed on the deck of the battleship USS *Missouri*, anchored in Tokyo Bay off Yokohama. They were watched by two emaciated figures just released from captivity: General Percival, who had conducted the British surrender at Singapore, and General Wainwright, the American commander on Corregidor.

*

Although fighting had ceased throughout the Pacific and southeast Asia on 15 August, the war had carried on in Manchuria until the day before the ceremony in Tokyo Bay. On 9 August, three Soviet fronts, with 1,669,500 men under the overall command of Marshal Vasilevsky, invaded northern China and Manchuria. A Mongolian cavalry corps on the extreme right flank crossed the Gobi Desert and the Great Khingan range of mountains. The timing and the speed of the Red Army's offensive took the Japanese by surprise. Although a million strong, their forces collapsed rapidly. Many died fighting to the end, and many committed suicide, but 674,000 were taken prisoner.

Their fate in the labour camps of Siberia and Magadan was harsh. Only half of them survived. Japanese colonist families, who had been abandoned by the army, also suffered. Mothers, carrying small children on their backs, tried to hide in the mountains. Out of 220,000 settlers, some 80,000 died. Some were killed by the Chinese, and around 67,000 starved to death or killed themselves. Only 140,000 survivors made it back to Japan. Their experience was similar in some ways to that of German colonists settled in Poland.

Red Army troops raped Japanese women at will in the former puppet kingdom of Manchukuo. A large group of women, told by Japanese officers that the war was lost, were advised to stick together. Almost a thousand packed into the hangars at the aerodrome of Beian. 'From then on it was hell,' recorded an orphaned girl called Yoshida Reiko. 'Russian soldiers came and told our leaders that they had to provide women to the Russian troops as the spoils of victory . . . Every day Russian soldiers would come in and take about ten girls. The women came back in the morning. Some women committed suicide . . . The Russian soldiers told us that if no women came out, the whole hangar would be burnt to the ground, with all of us inside. So some women – mostly single women – stood up and went. At that time I didn't understand what was happening to these women, but I clearly remember that women with children offered prayers for the women who did go out, in thanks for their sacrifice.' As well as civilians, Japanese military nurses in base hospitals suffered. The seventy-five nurses in the Sun Wu military hospital were held as a Soviet version of comfort women.

Red Army troops faced a much harder task seizing the Kurile Islands and southern Sakhalin. Woefully ill prepared for amphibious landings, they lost many men, both on the approach and on the shore. Stalin also had plans to occupy the northern home island of Hokkaido, but Truman brusquely rejected his proposal.

The Soviet invasion of Manchuria and northern China was greeted with joy by Mao Tse-tung's followers. Yet when a Red Army column advanced to Chahar, and was welcomed by guerrillas of the Eighth Route Army, the Soviet troops thought they were bandits because of their ragged clothes and primitive weapons, and disarmed them. This soon changed. Although Stalin officially recognized Chiang Kai-shek's government, Soviet forces allowed the Chinese Communists to remove the stockpiles of rifles and machine guns taken from the Japanese. Mao's forces, as Chiang Kai-shek had feared, soon became a formidably equipped army.

General Wedemeyer, under instructions from Washington to assist the Nationalists in restoring control, provided American transport aircraft to fly some of their units to cities in central and eastern China. Chiang was especially keen to re-establish his capital in Nanking. He knew that he was in a race with the Communists to seize as much territory as he could. But the Nationalists were their own worst enemies when it came to winning over the mass of the population. Their commanders were not interested in the surrounding countryside. They treated cities formerly occupied by the Japanese as conquered territory, looting whatever they wanted. And the Nationalist currency, which was reimposed, introduced uncontrollable inflation.

The Communists were far more intelligent. They knew that power lay in the countryside, for those who controlled food supplies in the coming civil war would eventually control everything. Their slightly better treatment of the peasantry enabled them to mobilize the masses in their cause, which was not difficult since support for the Nationalists had already dwindled away as the defeat of Japan approached. The young, especially students, flocked to join the Communist Party.

Chinese Communists, while they continued to hunt down 'enemies of the people', had hidden the totalitarian nature of their intended regime most skilfully from foreigners who visited their capital of Yenan. The journalist Agnes Smedley, an admiring fellow traveller and a sometime Comintern agent, became 'deeply, irrevocably convinced' that their principles 'are the principles that will guide and save China, that will give the greatest of impulses to the liberation of all subjected Asiatic nations, and bring to life a new human society. This conviction in my own mind and heart gives me the greatest peace that I have ever known.'

Smedley, Theodore White and other influential American writers could not accept for a moment that Mao might turn out to be a far worse tyrant than Chiang Kai-shek. The personality cult, the Great Leap Forward which killed more people than in the whole of the Second World War, the cruel madness of the Cultural Revolution and the seventy million victims of a regime that was in many ways worse than Stalinism proved totally beyond their imagination.

Because of the US Navy's supremacy at sea and in the air, large Japanese forces remained trapped in Canton, Hong Kong, Shanghai, Wuchang–Hankow, Peking, Tientsin and smaller towns of eastern China. The British had no intention of abandoning their claims on their colony and handing it over, as they had earlier indicated, to the Chinese Nationalists. The Americans had tried to put pressure on Churchill, but since they had promised Stalin southern Sakhalin, the Kurile Islands and parts of Manchuria, which had been Chinese territory, he saw no reason to compromise. But with American troops on mainland China, and the US Navy controlling the South China Sea, London knew that it would have to move quickly. A very unsympathetic Wedemeyer had refused permission for any SOE operations in the area. The Nationalists had infiltrated a group into Hong Kong to try to take it over when the Japanese withdrew, and the Communists' East River Column was also active in the area. Without troops on the ground, the British knew that they would never get their colony back.

At the beginning of August, it rapidly became clear that the only chance lay with the Royal Navy, and thus Operation Ethelred was born. Rear Admiral Cecil Harcourt's 11th Carrier Squadron, then in Sydney, was ordered to steam at full speed for Hong Kong on 15 August, as soon as the Japanese surrender was announced. The British Pacific Fleet was under US command, so Attlee, the new prime minister, felt compelled to seek permission from President Truman, which he did three days later. The same day, the foreign secretary Ernest Bevin sent a signal to Chiang Kai-shek explaining that since the British had been forced to surrender Hong Kong to the Japanese, he would surely understand as a soldier that honour required them to take the Japanese capitulation themselves.

Chiang was not taken in and appealed to the United States. Truman did not have the same anti-colonial fervour as Roosevelt, and he regarded Britain as a more important ally than the Chinese. General MacArthur also supported the British claim. Wedemeyer remained firmly opposed, but he had not yet redeployed his Chinese divisions. Chiang, despite Truman's rebuff, sent two of his armies into Kwangtung province, yet he was still anxious not to antagonize the British and Americans, whose help he would need in the civil war to come. The East River Column of guerrillas did move to disarm Japanese forces in Canton and the New Territories of Hong Kong, but they too were not planning to fight a British force. They simply wanted to make sure that the Nationalists did not take it.

Harcourt's squadron entered Victoria harbour on 30 August. Royal Marines and blue-jackets marched ashore in fine style, having been told to show 'face' to make up for all the prestige that Britain had lost three and a half years before. An administration in waiting, with an acting governor from the officials imprisoned there, had already made tentative steps to set up a skeleton administration. This had taken place with the consent of Japanese officers, who much preferred to surrender to the British than to Nationalist or Communist forces.

In Shanghai the underground civil war between Communists and Nationalists ceased temporarily on 19 September, when part of Admiral Kinkaid's Seventh Fleet arrived. Loaded with stores which had been stockpiled for the invasion of Japan, it was welcomed by the starving population and Allied prisoners. The war and its vocabulary had passed them by. 'What's a Jeep?' a civilian internee from Shanghai asked.

Allied prisoners of war had been the first priority for aid immediately after the Japanese surrender. In some cases, relief came quickly, while other prisoners had to wait for several weeks. A number had been massacred by guards after the surrender. In Changi Jail outside Singapore, prisoners were contemptuous when the Japanese guards suddenly began to salute them and offer water. Allied aircraft dropped supplies of food on camps already identified. Where possible medical teams were parachuted in to care for prisoners who greeted them with tears of relief, unable to believe that their misery was over. Most were walking skeletons, others so weakened by beriberi and other diseases that they could not even stand.

Of the 132,134 Allied prisoners of war who had been in Japanese hands, 35,756 died, a death rate of 27 per cent. Far greater numbers of slave labourers working for the Japanese had failed to survive as a result of the treatment that they had received. The comfort women of many nationalities who had been press-ganged by the Japanese suffered severe psychological harm for the rest of their lives. An unknown number committed suicide, feeling that they could never return home after all the humiliations heaped upon them.

Many prisoners of the Japanese had suffered a particularly gruesome and cruel fate. General MacArthur had given Australian forces the dispiriting task of clearing New Guinea and Borneo of the remaining pockets of Japanese. It became clear from all the reports collected later by US authorities and the Australian War Crimes Section that the 'widespread practice of cannibalism by Japanese soldiers in the Asia-Pacific war was something more than merely random incidents perpetrated by individuals or small groups subject to extreme conditions. The testimonies indicate that cannibalism was a systematic and organized military strategy.'

The practice of treating prisoners as 'human cattle' had not come about from a collapse of discipline. It was usually directed by officers. Apart from local people, victims of cannibalism included Papuan soldiers, Australians, Americans and Indian prisoners of war who had refused to join the Indian National Army. At the end of the war, their Japanese captors had kept the Indians alive so that they could butcher them to eat one at a time. Even the inhumanity of the Nazis' Hunger Plan in the east never descended to such levels. Because the subject was so upsetting to families of soldiers who had died in the Pacific War, the Allies suppressed all information on the subject, and cannibalism never featured as a crime at the Tokyo War Crimes Tribunal in 1946.

The war in south-east Asia and the Pacific had caused untold destruction. China was in ruins with its agriculture destroyed, and now an exhausted population faced a civil war, which would continue until 1949. More than twenty million of its citizens died. Chinese historians have recently increased that estimate towards the fifty-million mark. Anything between fifty and ninety million refugees had fled the Japanese, and now had no homes or families left to return to. These numbing scales of misery almost eclipsed those of Europe, which was also riven by political tensions.

From August 1945, ordinary Italian soldiers were sent back to Italy by the Soviet authorities. Communist groups waving red flags gathered to meet the trains bringing them home. To their outrage, they found that the released prisoners had scrawled 'abbasso il comunismo' on their wagons. Fights broke out at the station. The Communist press treated as 'Fascists' all those who criticized conditions in Soviet camps, or said that the Soviet Union was not a workers' paradise. Palmiro Togliatti, the leader of the PCI, the Italian Communist Party, had begged his Soviet masters to delay the return of Italian officers until after the elections and referendum of 2 June 1946. The first ones did not reach Italy until July.

Soviet repression continued in Poland against non-Communists. A clear indication of the NKVD's priorities was revealed by the fact that General Nikolai Selivanovsky received fifteen regiments of security troops for Poland, while Serov in Germany had only ten. Selivanovsky was ordered by Beria 'to combine the duties of representing the NKVD of the USSR [with that of] councillor at the Polish Ministry of Public Security'. Stalin's very personal definition of a 'free and independent Poland' which he had promised at Yalta was not just influenced by his hatred of the Poles. Still shaken by how close the Soviet Union had come to defeat in 1941, he wanted the Communist satellite states as a buffer. Only the sacrifice of nine million soldiers, to say nothing of eighteen million civilians, had saved him.

*

In the Second World War, the peoples who had suffered the most in Europe were those caught between the totalitarian millstones, and who 'died as a result of the *interaction* of the two systems'. Since 1933, fourteen million had died in Ukraine, Belorussia, Poland, the Baltic states and the Balkans. The vast majority of the 5.4 million Jews killed by the Nazis in Hitler's ersatz victory came from those regions.

The Second World War, with its global ramifications, was the greatest man-made disaster in history. The statistics of the dead – whether sixty or seventy million – are far beyond our comprehension. The sheer size of the numbers is dangerously numbing, as Vasily Grossman instinctively understood. In his view, the duty of survivors was to try to recognize the millions of ghosts from the mass graves as individuals, not as nameless people in caricatured categories, because that sort of dehumanization was precisely what the perpetrators had sought to achieve.

In addition to the dead, there were countless others who had been maimed, both psychologically and physically. In the Soviet Union, the limbless 'samovars' were banished from the streets. This was the fate, with its implicit loss of manhood, which every Red Army soldier had feared far more than death. The cripples were an embarrassing reminder that a purgatory existed between the heroic dead and the heroic survivors who parade with their medals on every anniversary.

Having been given the mantle of a 'good war', the Second World War has loomed over succeeding generations far more than any other conflict in history. It provokes mixed feelings because it could never live up to this image, especially when one half of Europe had to be sacrificed to the Stalinist maw to save the other half. And although it may have ended in overwhelming defeat for the Nazis and Japanese, the victory conspicuously failed to achieve world peace. First there were the latent civil wars across Europe and Asia which broke out in 1945. Then there was the Cold War with Stalin's treatment of Poland and central Europe. Mixed in with the Cold War were the anti-colonial conflicts in south-east Asia and Africa. And we can never forget that the sequence of struggle in the Middle East began with mass Jewish immigration into Palestine, following the liberation of the camps.

Some people complain that the Second World War still exerts

a dominating influence nearly seven decades after its end, as the disproportionate number of books, films and plays shows, while museums continue to spawn a remembrance industry. This phenomenon should hardly be surprising, if only because the nature of evil seems to provide an endless fascination. Moral choice is the fundamental element in human drama, because it lies at the very heart of humanity itself.

No other period in history offers so rich a source for the study of dilemmas, individual and mass tragedy, the corruption of power politics, ideological hypocrisy, the egomania of commanders, betrayal, perversity, self-sacrifice, unbelievable sadism and unpredictable compassion. In short, the Second World War defies generalization along with the categorization of humans which Grossman so passionately rejected.

There is, nevertheless, a real danger of the Second World War becoming an instant reference point, both for modern history and for all contemporary conflicts. In a crisis, journalists and politicians alike instinctively reach for parallels with the Second World War, either to dramatize the gravity of the situation, or in an attempt to sound Rooseveltian or Churchillian. To compare 9/11 to Pearl Harbor, or to liken Nasser and Saddam Hussein to Hitler, is not just to make an inaccurate historical parallel. Such comparisons are gravely misleading and risk producing the wrong strategic response. Leaders of democracies can become prisoners of their own rhetoric, just like dictators.

When we dwell on the enormity of the Second World War and its victims, we try to absorb all those statistics of national and ethnic tragedy. This makes us overlook the way the Second World War changed everyone's lives in ways impossible to predict. Very few may have shared the extraordinary experience of the young Korean Yang Kyoungjong, who was forced to serve in the Imperial Japanese Army, the Red Army and the Wehrmacht. Other stories are striking in different ways and for different reasons.

A short paragraph in a June 1945 report by the French security police, the DST, recorded that a German farmer's wife had been found in Paris having smuggled herself aboard a train bringing French deportees back from camps in Germany. It transpired that she had had an illicit affair with a French prisoner of war assigned to their farm in Germany while her husband was on the eastern front. She had fallen so much in love with this enemy of her country that she had followed him to Paris, where she was picked up by the police. That was all the detail provided.

The few lines raised so many questions. Would her difficult journey have been in vain, even if she had not been picked up by the police? Had her lover given her the wrong address because he was already married? And had he returned home, as quite a few did, to find that his wife had had a baby in his absence by a German soldier? It is, of course, a very minor tragedy in comparison to everything else which had happened further east. But it remains a poignant reminder that the consequences of decisions by leaders such as Hitler and Stalin ripped apart any certainty in the traditional fabric of existence.

ACKNOWLEDGEMENTS

This book had a very simple and unheroic genesis. I always felt a bit of a fraud when consulted as a general expert on the Second World War because I was acutely conscious of large gaps in my knowledge, especially of unfamiliar aspects. This book is partly an act of reparation, but above all it is an attempt to understand how the whole complex jigsaw fits together, with the direct and indirect effects of actions and decisions taking place in very different theatres of war.

The last twenty years have produced an astonishing wealth of excellent research and writing on this vast subject by many colleagues and friends. This book naturally owes an immense debt to their work and good judgement: Anne Applebaum, Rick Atkinson, Omer Bartov, Chris Bellamy, Patrick Bishop, Christopher Browning, Michael Burleigh, Alex Danchev, Norman Davies, Tami Davis Biddle, Carlo D'Este, Richard Evans, M. R. D. Foot, Martin Gilbert, David Glantz, Christian Goeschel, Max Hastings, William I. Hitchcock, Michael Howard, John Keegan, Ian Kershaw, John Lukacs, Ben Macintyre, Mark Mazower, Catherine Merridale, Don Miller, Richard Overy, Laurence Rees, Anna Reid, Andrew Roberts, Simon Sebag Montefiore, Ben Shephard, Timothy Snyder, Adam Tooze, Hans van de Ven, Nikolaus Wachsmann, Adam Zamoyski and Niklas Zetterling.

I am deeply grateful to my French publisher, Ronald Blunden, for the loan of the papers and despatches of his father, the Australian war correspondent Godfrey Blunden, who covered the fighting at Stalingrad and elsewhere on the eastern front, and then served as a war correspondent in Italy and during the advance into Germany. Others who have provided material, suggestions and advice include Professor Omer Bartov, Dr Philip Boobbyer, Dr Tom Buchanan, John Corsellis, Sebastian Cox of the RAF Historical Branch, Professor Tami Davis Biddle of the US Army

War College, James Holland, Ben Macintyre, Javier Marías, Michael Montgomery on the sinking of HMAS *Sydney*, Jens Anton Poulsson of the Norwegian resistance, Dr Piotr Sliwowski, head of the History Department, Warsaw Rising Museum, Professor Rana Mitter, Gilles de Margerie, Professor Hew Strachan, Noro Tamaki, Professor Martti Turtola of the National Defence University, Helsinki, Professor Hans van de Ven, Stuart Wheeler, Keith Miles and Jože Dežman for documents on the Titoist massacres in Slovenia, Stephane Grimaldi and Stephane Simmonet at the Memorial de Caen.

I am profoundly grateful to Professor Sir Michael Howard, who kindly read the whole manuscript and offered valuable criticism and advice; to Jon Halliday and Jung Chang who went through the Sino-Japanese war passages and corrected many mistakes; and to Angelica von Hase who double-checked my translations from the German. I once again owe her and Dr Lyubov Vinogradova a very great deal for all their research work for me in Germany and Russia. Needless to say, any mistakes which remain are entirely my responsibility.

I owe a great debt, as always, to my old friend and literary agent Andrew Nurnberg, and particularly to Alan Samson, the publisher of Weidenfeld & Nicolson, who encouraged the project from the very start and provided excellent advice at every step of the way; also to Bea Hemming, the editor who calmly guided everything and thus removed the stress of the whole process; and to Peter James who amply justified his reputation as the greatest copy-editor in London. Once again my wife Artemis Cooper interrupted her own work to go through the whole manuscript and improved it enormously, to my eternal gratitude, and our son Adam helped me with the bibliography and documents.

NOTES

The full and extremely extensive notes and bibliography for this book are available in the hardback edition and also on the author's website at:

www.antonybeevor.com

The sources have been omitted from the paperback to make it a more manageable and readable size.

INDEX

W&N

THE BOOKSELLER
INDUSTRY AWARDS
IMPRINT OF THE YEAR 2015

For literary discussion, author insight,
book news, exclusive content,
recipes and giveaways, visit the
Weidenfeld & Nicolson blog and
sign up for the newsletter at:

www.wnblog.co.uk

For breaking news, reviews and exclusive competitions
Follow us 🐦 @wnbooks